THE LIFE OF JESUS THE MESSIAH

E. KEITH HOWICK

WindRiver Publishing • Silverton, Idaho

The Life of Jesus the Messiah
Copyright © 2012 by E. Keith Howick

ISBN 978-1-886249-05-9
Library of Congress Control Number: 2012940614

Cover design based on an original design by Bookcraft, Inc. *Living Water* by Simon Dewey. Copyright Simon Dewey. Used with permission from Altus Fine Art (AltusFineArt.com).

WindRiver Publishing, the WindRiver mark, and the WindRiver logo are trademarks of WindRiver Publishing, Inc.

10 9 8 7 6 5 4 3 2 1
Printed in the United States of America

WindRiver Publishing
72 N WindRiver Rd
Silverton ID 83867-0446
WindRiverPublishing.com

Preface

Historically, the life of Christ has been written about many times; but in every instance, the authors chose to deal with His life historically and tried to harmonize the gospels. Beginning with the first chapter of Matthew, they attempted to match the events recorded by Matthew with those of Mark, Luke, and John—the other three Gospel writers. This was never intended by these brethren and has always led to complications because of descriptive variations of events and occasional contradictions within the Gospels themselves.

Discrepancies in scripture, however, do not discredit its authenticity; rather, just the opposite—they confirm it. Different men see things differently, even when witnessing the same event. Each narrative is unique, even considering the similarities of the Synoptics, and each writer was obviously selective. In addition, discrepancies may have occurred in translation (as is evident from reading the various Bible translations), language variance, and ancient additions and deletions before the final text was adopted. Finally, familiarity with a given event may have led the Gospel writers to eliminate some circumstances they felt were self-explanatory[1] and include others they felt enhanced the teaching or increased interest in the event. I have not attempted to reconcile these discrepancies and disagreements, nor is it necessary to do so except in limited instances where the interpretations and circumstances appear to warrant it.

I have chosen to deal with the life of Christ topically rather than historically. In addition (and where possible), I have included the customs and traditions of the Jews that existed at His time. In many instances, it was those customs and traditions that influenced how Jesus taught. The familiar events He used to teach His doctrine enhanced the understanding of His listeners since His examples and metaphors came from situations His audiences had experienced.

By presenting the life of Christ in this manner, it emphasizes the doctrine the Lord was teaching and eliminates the need to attempt reconciliation by creating theoretical or factious circumstances for which there is no supporting information. It also eliminates the need to attempt to match the various gospel records or to portray a day-by-day existence of the Lord which the gospel writers did not intend.

The Gospel writers did not write (nor did they intend to write) a biography of Jesus Christ, even though they knew His mother. Prior to the commencement of His ministry at age thirty, Matthew records only two chapters that contain early events in the Lord's life. Mark begins his record with the Lord's ministry itself, ignoring Christ's early years. Luke, generally considered the historian of the Gospel writers, records more detail of the early events that Matthew described, and includes the story of Jesus teaching in the temple at age twelve. He ends his second chapter with a single scripture that covers eighteen years of the Lord's life: "And Jesus increased in wisdom and stature, and in favour with God and man."[a] Thereafter, he only records events from the Lord's ministry. John records nothing of the birth or early life of the Savior, but opens his gospel declaring the Lord's divinity and introducing John the Baptist, the forerunner and testifier of Jesus.

The Gospels of Matthew, Mark, and Luke record the events of Christ's Galilean ministry randomly. These three Gospels are commonly called the *synoptic* Gospels because the authors used a similar approach in presenting the events of Jesus' life. (The reader will frequently encounter references to Matthew, Mark, and Luke as the Synoptics, or the synoptic Gospels.) However, not only did John often report events unrecorded in the other Gospels, he also wrote in a different style than the other three. Also, his material emphasized the Judean ministry of Jesus.

Matthew and John were Apostles—eyewitnesses to all that Jesus did during His ministry. Matthew recorded many of the events in the Lord's ministry in a straightforward, factual manner that rarely em-

a. Luke 2:52.

phasized minute detail. John recorded events that were not referenced in the other Gospels, so apparently he attempted to fill in the gaps left by the others and enhance the testimony each gave of the Messiah.

Mark appears to be the true "reporter" of the group. His style was usually shorter, but included more explicit detail than the other writers. Most scholars feel he did not witness many of the events he wrote about, presumably receiving his information from Peter.[2] Finally, Luke, the historian, was an early disciple of Jesus and thus gained much of his information firsthand; but in addition, he was a compiler of the biblical record, reporting material gleaned from other witnesses (such as Jesus teaching in the temple at twelve which he undoubtedly heard about from Mary).

The standard King James Version of the Bible is used as the scriptural basis throughout the Messiah series. The discussion of each event begins with the most detailed and relevant scriptural text quoted in its entirety. If there are cross-references to the event, they appear at the end of the quoted material. Note that when a passage of the quoted scriptural text is used in a discussion, no footnote appears (the whole source or cross-reference having been recorded at the beginning of the discussion). The name assigned to each event is derived from the material itself and is easily recognized. (Some traditional, alternative names may also appear.) Some additional cross-references may also be designated as JST or IV.[3]

The gospel writers were extremely selective in what they recorded. As noted, they did not attempt to present a historical biography of Jesus, even though a cursory reading of any one of them may leave that impression. Limited as they were with materials and replicating capabilities, they assembled their information and chose those events from the thousands they had witnessed (or were told about) to substantiate the teachings they felt supported their intent—to testify of the long-awaited and anticipated Messiah.[4]

There are five sections in this compilation, each dealing topically with events from the Savior's life as follows:

The Miracles of Jesus the Messiah

This book describes thirty-seven miracles. Thirty-three are readily recognizable; the remaining four are very unique and are often over-looked. The Savior used miracles as teaching tools—the miracles testifying of the doctrine and the doctrine teaching the necessity of the miracles.

The Parables of Jesus the Messiah

This section describes thirty-two parables.[5] And while any division or classification of a parable may be open to question (its truth having multiple applications to daily life in any age), it is evident that the gospel writers inserted them for specific teaching purposes.

The Sermons of Jesus the Messiah

This section describes thirty-five sermons from the longest sermon (the Sermon on the Mount) to those involving questions posed to the Savior by friends, inquisitors, or enemies. Sermons were Christ's most common method of teaching and studying them is like having a one-on-one conversation with the Lord.

The Mission of Jesus the Messiah

This section describes multiple events in the Lord's life, the importance of those events, and their meaning in regards to the plan of salvation (which ensures our opportunity to become joint heirs with Him in the kingdom of God).

The Second Coming of Jesus the Messiah

In this book I have attempted to gather the scriptural prophecies that reveal the signs and events that will precede the Savior's second Advent and categorize them by topic: both those that have already occurred and those that are yet to occur.

Each Book in this compilation is divided into Parts and Chapters. Each part and chapter title descriptively defines the doctrinal application of the material it contains. This classification is my own, derived from what I perceive as the doctrinal emphasis of those events in the Lord's Life.

Because of the considerable time that has elapsed since the gospel writers recorded the events of the Savior's life, it is obviously difficult to state with complete assurance the exact meaning that Jesus intended for each of His miracles, parables, sermons, actions, prophecies, and events. However, the Gospel writers selected these incidents for a specific purpose in an attempt to better illustrate the life of Christ, His doctrine, His divinity, His compassion, and the principles He taught. In determining the interpretation and significance of His teachings, careful consideration has been given to the following six areas of study:

1. Scriptures describing the event itself and the circumstances surrounding the event.

2. Other scriptural support and evidence, including prophecies and related events.

3. Historical events of the times that influenced the Lord's teaching.

4. Customs and traditions of the Jews at the time of Christ.

5. The recorded Jewish expectations of the Messiah.

6. Some of the foremost authoritative and knowledgeable writers on the life of Jesus.

The Jews during Christ's ministry did not question His ability, but they constantly questioned His claim. The events described in the gospels were recorded by men who came to know who Jesus was because they believed in Him—as opposed to those who did not want Him to be the Messiah under any circumstances. "What do we .. ?" they asked. "If we let him thus alone, all men will believe on him. . . ."[a] And so they cried, "Crucify him, Crucify him"![b]

So it is with each of us as we metaphorically walk with the disciples through the events in the Savior's life. We, like the men and women of Christ's time, can decide if we want to believe the gospel and live or disbelieve and be cast out. After Jesus healed the impotent man at the pool,[c] the Jewish leadership sought to "slay him"; but even then He gave them the same opportunity we have. "Search the scriptures," He admonished, "for in them ye think ye have eternal life: and they

a. John 11:47-48.
b. Luke 23:21.
c. John 5.

are they which testify of me."[a] Thus, it is through the scriptures that we can learn, understand, witness, and believe in the life and mission of Jesus the Messiah.

1.   Ed. 1:478.

2.   Ed. 1:478.

3.   Before publication of the 1979 edition of the Bible for The Church of Jesus Christ of Latter-day Saints, this was known as the Inspired Version. In the Church it is now generally referred to as the Joseph Smith Translation (JST). Quotations from the Inspired Version that are not found in the JST are referenced herein as IV.

a. John 5:39.   4.   Ed 1:145; 2:55.

5.   The determination of which of Jesus' teachings should be classified as parables has varied throughout the years depending on how strictly the word parable is defined. As few as twenty-seven (Siegfried Goebel, *The Parables of Jesus*, 1883, p. 3) or as many as fifty-three (A. Julicher, *Die Gleichnisreden Jesu*, 1910, p. 15) or even sixty-five (Francis L. Filas, *The Parables of Jesus*, 1959) have been so determined.

Table of Contents

The Miracles of Jesus the Messiah

Part Six: "That They May Believe That Thou Has Sent Me"

Part Seven: Faith and Miracles

Part Eight: The Message of the Miracles

The Parables of Jesus the Messiah

Part One: The Parables in Perspective

Part Two: Teaching the Gospel

Part Three: Teaching Principles and Relationships

Part Four: Teaching Accountability and Reward

Part Five: Teaching Warnings and Judgment

Part Six: Witnessing Jesus the Messiah

The Sermons of Jesus the Messiah

The Mission of Jesus the Messiah

The Second Coming of Jesus the Messiah

Alphabetical Lists

List of Sermons

Major Events in the Life of Christ

Topics Relating to the Second Coming

THE MIRACLES OF JESUS THE MESSIAH

Introduction

The standard King James Version of the Bible is used as the scriptural basis for each miracle discussed. The Gospels record the miracles, but the following important facts should be considered when studying them.

First, not every miracle that Jesus performed during His ministry is recorded by the Gospel writers. In fact, from the examination of the scriptures (Chapter 1), it is evident that the Lord performed thousands of miracles; but the gospel writers were extremely selective in those they chose to record.

Second, several miracles are exclusive to one Gospel, others appear in two or more, but only one miracle is found in all four Gospels—the feeding of the five thousand (Chapter 2). Where miracles are found in more than one Gospel, the writers do not always agree on their order, the circumstances surrounding them, or their descriptive detail. I have not attempted to reconcile these discrepancies and disagreements, nor is it necessary to do so except in limited instances where the interpretations and circumstances appear to warrant it.

Third, discrepancies in scripture do not discredit their authenticity; rather, just the opposite is true; they confirm it. Familiarity with a given miracle may have led the Gospel writers to eliminate circumstances they felt were self-explanatory.[6]

Thirty-eight specific miracles will be discussed herein. The names of the miracles are assigned on the basis of the circumstances surrounding them. Thirty-four of the miracles are readily recognized. The remaining four consist of what I have named "The Multitude of Miracles," "Passing Unseen (Before the Resurrection)," "Passing Unseen (After the Resurrection)," and the most unique and often overlooked, "Transportation by the Spirit."

The discussion of Christ's miracles is viewed topically rather than sequentially or chronologically. It is obviously difficult to state with complete assurance the exact meaning that Jesus intended for each of His miracles, actions, parables, discourses, and words. However, the Gospel writers selected these miracles from the thousands they witnessed (or otherwise learned of) in an attempt to better illustrate the principles Jesus taught, His doctrine, and the witness of His divinity. Through careful consideration of the scriptures describing the miracles, the scriptural circumstances surrounding them, other scriptural support and evidence, the historical evaluation of the times, the customs and traditions of the Jews, the recorded Jewish expectations of the Messiah, and some of the foremost authoritative and knowledgeable writers on the subject, I have attempted to determine the principal teaching of each miracle intended by the Gospel writers.

The sacred occurrences referred to as "miracles" were just that—miracles! The narrators who recorded them were great men, originally of ordinary stature, but moved upon by the Holy Spirit to write and preserve the record for all. The miracles of Jesus stand on their own in association with His teachings: the miracles testify of the authenticity of the doctrine; the doctrine teaches the necessity of the miracles. "To the believer in the divinity of Christ, the miracles are sufficiently attested; to the unbeliever they appear but as myths and fables."[7]

One particular scriptural passage is as relevant today as when Jesus uttered it. He was attempting to teach the Jewish leadership after healing the impotent man at the pool of Bethesda and He said, "Search the scriptures; for in them ye think ye have eternal life: and they are they which testify of me."[a] The miracles testify with unassailable power and authority that Jesus was, in fact, the long awaited Messiah.

a. John 5:39.

Miracles   1

Historical Expectations, the Miracles, and Jesus

The miracle is a most extraordinary thing. It appears to run counter to life's experience and facts. Yet within sacred scripture, miracle upon miracle is encountered throughout the biblical record until the miracle is seemingly a daily occurrence. Moses, for example, led the rebellious and unbelieving Israelites from day to day by miracles, and those people were held in wondering awe of God, for Israel's God was a God of miracles.

In Pharaoh's court, Aaron, at the direction of Moses, cast down his rod and it became a serpent. Pharaoh immediately called upon his magicians and they did likewise. Aaron's rod then swallowed up the rods of the magicians.[a] Thus began the great exhibition of signs and wonders to persuade Pharaoh to let enslaved Israel go.

The magicians continued to duplicate the signs and wonders that God had given Moses. They turned water to blood [b] and brought a plague of frogs[c] upon the land of Egypt. But thereafter, the magicians could not duplicate the miraculous plagues Moses brought upon the land and were forced to admit, "This is the finger of God"[d] However, the obdurate Pharaoh continued to resist through the miracles of lice, flies, cattle disease, boils, hail, locusts, and finally the deaths of the firstborn of Egypt until he succumbed to Israel's God and let the Israelites go.

This was the beginning of the miraculous events that became Israel's heritage. Miracles had occurred prior to Moses' time, of course, but Moses was the great wonder-worker. By the power of God, he

a. Exodus 7:10–12.

b. Exodus 7:19–22.

c. Exodus 8:5–7.

d. Exodus 8:19.

parted the Red Sea and delivered the Israelites from the oppressive hands of their enemies. The Lord fed them manna from heaven in the wilderness to sate their hunger, and even their "raiment waxed not old upon [them], . . . these forty years."[a] To this richness was added Elijah and Elisha, other prophets, and the traditions and writings of the Rabbis.

> From this point of view, the whole Old Testament becomes the perspective in which the figure of the Messiah stands out. And perhaps the most valuable element in Rabbinic commentary on Messianic times is that in which, as so frequently, it is explained that all the miracles and deliverances of Israel's past would be re-enacted, only in a much wider manner, in the days of the Messiah. Thus the whole past was symbolic and typical of the future—the Old Testament the glass, through which the universal blessings [of the Messianic days] were seen.[8]

All this was a prelude to the miracles of the Messiah. He came to a people whose tradition was full of miracles. Given this heritage, the Jews could believe in the miracles of Jesus; and in fact many did, even though they did not accept Him as the Messiah. Their Messiah, the one they eagerly looked forward to, was to be a second Moses—and yet greater, the greatest of the prophets.[9] They expected Him to perform miracles.[10] John confirmed this when he recorded the people's reaction: "When Christ cometh, will he do more miracles than these which this man [Jesus] hath done?"[b]

Not only was the Messiah expected to perform miracles, but the very miracles that He was to perform were anticipated. The Lord, through Moses, fed the children of Israel in the wilderness;[c] should not Christ do likewise?[11] The reaction of the people testified that they remembered and understood when He did (Chapter 2). Prophesying of the Messiah, Isaiah said: "Then the eyes of the blind shall be opened, and the ears of the deaf shall be unstopped. Then shall the lame man leap as an hart, and the tongue of the dumb sing!"[d] Should not Christ do these miracles, and even raise the dead?[e] In their exaggerated expectation, He could do no less than the greatest of His ancient prophets.

a. Deuteronomy 8:4.

b. John 7:31.

c. Exodus 16:14–17.

d. Isaiah 35:5–6.

e. 1 Kings 17; 2 Kings 4.

The people of Christ's time looked for these scriptural prophecies to be literally fulfilled. The New Testament writers understood that in Christ the prophecies had been fulfilled, and so recorded it. It is no wonder they write plainly that Christ caused the blind to see and unstopped the ears of the deaf. In giving speech to the dumb and successfully commanding the lame, the palsied, and the paralytic to take up their beds and walk, He was literally fulfilling that which was expected of the looked-for Messiah.[12]

Why then were these very happenings questioned by the Jews? The answer lies not in their disbelief in the miracles but in Jesus—so they accused Him of performing miracles through the power of the prince of devils, Beelzebub (Chapter 3). Their question was not, "Was a miracle performed?" The public occurrences of His miracles made asking this question impossible. Instead, their question was, "By what power or in what name do you perform miracles?" They did not question His ability, but His authority. They recognized His claim to the Messiahship and demanded, "Show us a sign." But they wanted more than the signs that merely fulfilled the prophecies of miracles, for Jesus more than satisfied those expectations. They desired of Him a specific sign from heaven, the Messianic sign of the Son of Man.[13] They did not look for the meek, loving, kind, and all-merciful man who had been raised in Nazareth as a carpenter whose mother, father, brothers, and sisters they knew. It was the political Messiah the Jews looked for— and still do.

The Messiah they anticipated was to rid Israel of the yoke of bondage as Moses had done, to restore their former glory and honor among nations as David had done, to come with power to rid them forever of all their enemies, and to call down God's vengeance on those who had despitefully used them. The Jews believed in miracles, even the miracles of Jesus; but they would not believe Jesus was the Messiah. They looked for and sought from Him the sign of His second coming, while the signs He gave them were of His first coming. They looked beyond the mark and missed Him.

The Purpose of Miracles

Miracles are signs. The scriptural writers at times describe them as "wonders," "powers," and "signs."[a]

a. Matthew 9:6; 24:24; Acts 14:3; Romans 15:19; Hebrews 2:4.

In the Old Testament, signs emanated from God for many reasons. For example, they verified God's word, as in the sundial of Hezekiah;[a] confirmed God's direction, as in the fleece of Gideon;[b] or confirmed God's call, as with the mantle of Elijah as it fell from him to Elisha.[c]

The miracles of Jesus in the New Testament were also signs. Each miracle that the Gospel writers recorded had its use and meaning within Jesus' ministry, generally falling into one or more of the following categories: to witness His identity as the Messiah; to witness His authority and power; to evidence and confirm His teachings; and to express His compassion.

To Witness His Identity as the Messiah

The miracles were Jesus' credentials! They were presented to the people in general and the leaders in particular as signs of His divinity. These signs substantiated Jesus' claim to the Messiahship, further revealed His character, and expanded the evidence of His divine mission. In this context, some miracles were directed specifically to the people, some to the leaders of the Jews, some toward the Law, and some to the Apostles. All this that they might prove, attest, and verify that Jesus was the Christ, the expected Messiah.

To Witness His Authority and Power

The discussion on "The Multitude of Miracles" will readily attest that both the ordinary people and the leaders of the Jews recognized that Christ held the power to perform miracles. Yet they often questioned His authority. Certain miracles required all who witnessed or heard of them to decide concerning Christ and thereby to believe or disbelieve Him—to accept or reject Him and His claim to divine authority. These miracles attested to His power over all things: the laws of nature, the elements, life, death, bodily affliction of any kind, and the world of evil spirits.

To Evidence and Confirm His Teachings

Miraculous signs brought Jesus attention early in His ministry. With every miracle, more of the curious followed and the believers looked on with awe. These miracles were intended to open the hearts of both

a. 2 Kings
20:4–11.

b. Judges
6:36–40.

c. 2 Kings
2:13–14.

those who witnessed them and those who received them. To supplement and enhance them, in every instance the miracles were either preceded or followed by instructions. Faith and belief in Christ often resulted. Although this belief was born of signs and miracles rather than a deep-seated knowledge of Jesus' divinity, it fostered faith that brought many to the Messiah. Through miracles Christ taught proper judgment, correct use of His power, testimony of the Father, and more. These miracles illustrated His sacred truths and convinced or encouraged others to rely on Him and to actively seek His blessings.

To Express His Compassion

In the Sermon on the Mount and at other times, Jesus detailed the divine relationship that was to exist among those who followed Him. "Do unto others"; "love your enemies"; "bless them that curse you"; "turn the other cheek"; "go the extra mile"; "forgive men their trespasses"; "judge not"; "freely ye have received, freely give"—Jesus exemplified these principles in His miracles as in no other recorded instances. The miracles demonstrated the compassion that He taught in His sermons and parables. They were deeds of mercy that relieved human suffering. Even when He sought privacy and seclusion so that He might rest, suffering people sought Him out and He healed them. Matthew noted that in doing this, He fulfilled Isaiah's prophecy; for He "took our infirmities, and bare our sicknesses."[a]

The Lord's teachings were evidenced and exemplified by miracles, giving richness and power to His truths. Those truths were at times obscured from the spiritually diseased, their true meaning being enmeshed in current events, in the future, and in the Messiah Himself.

Miracles are a part of the gospel. Signs both precede and follow those who believe. They benefit recipient and witness alike, both physically and spiritually, and testify to the truth and divinity of the Lord and His work.

Natural Laws, the Laws of God, and Miracles

Do miracles contradict natural laws? Are they a part of such laws? Are miracles an extension of them? Do any laws govern the working of miracles? These questions have caused speculation for centuries. Unnumbered volumes could not satisfactorily resolve the

a. Matthew 8:17; Isaiah 53:4.

divergence of opinion on this matter. But man's desire to bind God to natural laws has little or no meaning unless man's interpretation of those laws includes the existence of their author.[14] One truth seems self-evident: regardless of man's arguments or theories, some laws are outside his limited understanding and experience, and they are beyond his power to control or mimic.

Nature contains many wonderful miracles, and perhaps the miracles of Jesus do not manifest God's power any more than ordinary and often-repeated natural processes. But His miracles are a different manifestation. For example, man may plant a seed or seedling; it will grow and develop using the soil, moisture, and the sun. Each year the resulting vine uses those natural elements to produce grapes that man nurtures and processes into wine. This surely is a natural miracle, but it is quite different from drawing the best wine from pots filled with water, and doing it without so much as a command.

Some attempt to ascribe laws to the miracles, theorizing that they are the acceleration of natural processes; others assign names to unknown orders and keenly hope for the day when man can discover and duplicate the processes. But surely He who gave this earth its body of natural law can modify that law, place it in abeyance, or subject it to a higher law so that His designs and needs might be accomplished.

God speaks at all times and to all people through normal and everyday natural laws, laws that are a vast, unbroken attestation of Him. The miracle, however, is beyond the ordinary operations of natural law and reveals the very powers of God.[15]

The miracle, then, is not unnatural or in contravention of natural law at all, but is higher than natural law, at least as we know it. The natural law that we know is not lost in the miracle; it is merely suspended.

So what is a miracle? Consider the following thoughts:

Elder James E. Talmage: "We arbitrarily classify as miracles only such phenomena as are unusual, special, transitory, and wrought by an agency beyond the power of man's control . . . , the operation of a power transcending our present human understanding."[16]

Elder Bruce R. McConkie: "But in the gospel sense, miracles

are those occurrences wrought by the power of God which are wholly beyond the power of man to perform. Produced by a supernatural power, they are marvels, wonders, and signs, which cannot be duplicated by man's present powers or by any powers which he can obtain by scientific advancements. Miracles in the gospel sense are gifts of the Spirit; they take place when the Lord on His own motion manifests His powers or when man by faith prevails upon Deity to perform supernatural events.[17]

Richard C. Trench: "Miracles . . . are ultimate resources, reserved for the great needs of God's kingdom, not its everyday incidents; they are not cheap offhand expedients, which may always be appealed to, but come only into play when nothing else would have supplied their room.[18]

What is a miracle? It is a gift from God to man to fulfill a need, either temporal or spiritual, that man cannot accomplish without God's divine hand. And once received and seen, it leaves man in reverence of that God who granted the divine gift.

The Multitude of Miracles

Matthew 4:23–24　And Jesus went about all Galilee, teaching in their synagogues, and preaching the gospel of the kingdom, and healing all manner of sickness and all manner of disease among the people. And his fame went throughout all Syria: and they brought unto him all sick people that were taken with divers diseases and torments, and those which were possessed with devils, and those which were lunatick, and those that had the palsy; and he healed them.

Mark 1:32–34, 39　And at even, when the sun did set, they brought unto him all that were diseased, and them that were possessed with devils. And all the city was gathered together at the door. And he healed many that were sick of divers diseases, and cast out many devils; and suffered not the devils to speak, because they knew him. . . . And he preached in their synagogues throughout all Galilee, and cast out devils.

Mark 6:53–56　And when they had passed over, they came into the land of Gennesaret, and drew to the shore. And when they were come out of the ship, straightway they knew him, and ran through that whole region round about, and began to carry about in beds those that were sick, where they heard he was. And whithersoever he entered, into villages, or cities, or country, they laid the sick in the streets, and besought him that they might touch if it were but the border of his garment: and as many as touched him were made whole.

Matthew 15:29–30   And Jesus departed from thence, and came nigh unto the sea of Galilee; and went up into a mountain, and sat down there. And great multitudes came unto him, having with them those that were lame, blind, dumb, maimed, and many others, and cast them down at Jesus' feet; and he healed them.

Matthew 12:15–16   But when Jesus knew it, he withdrew himself from thence: and great multitudes followed him, and he healed them all; and charged them that they should not make him known.

Matthew 14:14   And Jesus went forth, and saw a great multitude, and was moved with compassion toward them, and he healed their sick.

Matthew 9:35   And Jesus went about all the cities and villages, teaching in their synagogues, and preaching the gospel of the kingdom, and healing every sickness and every disease among the people.

Matthew 19:2   And great multitudes followed him; and he healed them there.

Luke 6:17–19   And he came down with them and stood in the plain, and the company of his disciples, and a great multitude of people out of all Judea and Jerusalem, and from the sea coast of Tyre and Sidon, which came to hear him, and to be healed of their diseases; and they that were vexed with unclean spirits: and they were healed. And the whole multitude sought to touch him: and for there went virtue out of him, and healed them all.

Luke 7:19–22   And John calling unto him two of his disciples sent them to Jesus, saying, Art thou he that should come? or look we for another? When the men were come unto him, they said John Baptist hath sent us unto thee, saying, Art thou he that should come? Or look we for another? And in that same hour he cured many of their infirmities and plagues, and of evil spirits; and unto many that were blind he gave sight. Then Jesus answering said unto them, Go your way, and tell John what things ye have seen and heard; how that the blind see, the lame walk, the lepers are cleansed, the deaf hear, the dead are raised, to the poor the gospel is preached.

Mark 6:5   And he could there do no mighty work, save that he laid his hands upon a few sick folk, and healed them.

Cross-references   Matthew 8:16–17; Matthew 14:34–36; Mark 3:10; Luke 4:40–41; Luke 9:11; JST Matthew 4:22

When asked to recall the miracles of Jesus, it generally comes to mind that He healed the blind, the lame, and the sick, and raised the dead. The tendency is to limit the number of miracles to the thirty-three or thirty-four specifically identified in the Gospels. The Multitude of Miracles is often overlooked because of the lack of detail with which the Gospel writers refer to them. But within this lack of detail lies the grandeur of these miracles. The twelve examples of The Multitude of Miracles which follow verify that the ministry of Jesus was indeed a ministry of miracles.

Matthew 4:23–24. Matthew reports that Jesus was tempted in the wilderness, that John the Baptist had been cast into prison, and that Jesus had commenced His early travels preaching that the kingdom of heaven was at hand. After the call of Peter, Andrew, James, and John, Matthew records that Jesus was teaching in the synagogues of Galilee and "healing all manner of sickness and all manner of disease among the people." A very general statement, but extremely revealing of the early ministry of Jesus. Far from restricting His miracles, the Master was granting them to many. Continuing, Matthew states that Jesus' fame went throughout all Syria. Those suffering from divers diseases and torments, those possessed with devils, the mentally ill, and the palsied were brought to Him. And the scripture testifies that He healed them all.

The marvel of this experience is that unlike the purposeful miracles reported by the gospel writers, Jesus was healing hosts of people. The reaction of the people to all this seemed quite natural and honest. They came to Him wanting to be healed personally and to have the people they loved healed as well. The miracles drew attention to Jesus, and word would have been passed from person to person and village to village—a healer was among them! Pleas from the sick to be taken to Jesus must have rent the air. They had received an opportunity to gain relief from their illnesses of the moment or of a lifetime . . . and "he healed them" all. Such healings are the greatest examples of the Savior's unlimited compassion in all of scripture.

Mark 1:32–34. It was the Sabbath, and Jesus was teaching in the synagogue at Capernaum. The people there were astonished at His doctrine and recognized that He spoke with authority. It was the custom at the time to teach from the existing rabbinical writings, promulgating only doctrine that could be supported by a recognized rabbinical authority. Instead, the Lord taught using Himself as the authority, and it astounded and astonished His hearers. While in the synagogue, He further attested to His power by casting an unclean spirit out of one possessed.

From the synagogue, the Lord retired to the house where Peter's wife's mother lay sick. The Apostles entreated the Lord on her behalf and He healed her—the second miracle performed on this Sabbath day. But it was the Sabbath; the people could not travel. They could walk only two thousand paces, the maximum permitted length of a Sabbath journey under rabbinical law.[19] To carry the sick to Christ would have been forbidden. When the final blast of the trumpet signaled the end of the Sabbath and "when the sun did set," however, the people were constrained no longer, and they brought their diseased and possessed to Him from every street in Capernaum until "all the city was gathered together at the door." There was no question in their minds but that Jesus would heal them. His characteristics, not detailed to us but undoubtedly known to the people, had endeared Him to them and they came to receive of His great compassion. So far as the record shows, He did not teach or preach to them. He had done that earlier in the Synagogue. He just "healed many that were sick of divers diseases, and cast out many devils."

Mark 1:39. After the experience in Capernaum, Jesus departed to a solitary place. Peter and other disciples found Him and reported that all men sought Him. Jesus returned to His mission, preached in the synagogues throughout Galilee, and "cast out devils."

Is it any wonder that all men sought Him? The healer of body and soul, who taught with authority and not as the scribes, was giving freely of His great compassion. From these few passages it is obvious that many, many miracles were performed.

Mark 6:53–56. Prior to this experience, Mark records the miraculous feeding of the five thousand and the singular experience of Jesus walking on the water. Concluding, he notes that they landed on the shore in the land of Gennesaret. Jesus' fame had preceded Him because of the many miracles He had already performed, and the scripture reports that the people "knew him." They ran about the whole region and told everyone He was in their midst. They carried their sick to Him, for they knew He would heal them. Through every city and village and in the countryside, the word of His coming preceded Him. Wherever He went the people desired His compassion, laid their sick in the streets, and begged to merely touch the border of His garment; and as many as touched Him were made whole.

Matthew 15:29–30. After Jesus had healed the Syrophenician woman's child, He went up to a mountain, one of His favorite places for teaching, and the people came to Him. They brought the lame, the blind, the dumb, the maimed, and many others, and placed them at Jesus' feet. And He healed them. The people stayed with the Lord three days, being fed first by spiritual truths of the kingdom and then by the physical nourishment of the miraculous meal of loaves and fishes. This multitude consisted of four thousand men, plus women and children.

Matthew 12:15–16. Again it was a Sabbath day. Jesus healed a man's withered hand, after which multitudes followed Him— and He healed them all.

Matthew 14:14. Here it reports that at the feeding of the five thousand (a count that again excluded women and children), the Savior healed all the sick in the multitude.

Matthew 9:35. This scripture records that Jesus healed every sickness and every disease among the people.

Matthew 19:2. In this instance, Jesus again had multitudes follow Him and He healed them.

Luke 6:17–19. After Jesus had prayed all night he called His Apostles. He then preached in the plain, and a multitude came down to hear Him teach and to be healed of their diseases. Some of the group were vexed with unclean spirits, and He healed them. The people's emotions soared, and they sought to touch Him. Christ, the great healer, must have been touched deeply, for Luke reports that "virtue [went] out of him, and healed them all." His compassion must have been boundless.

Luke 7:19–22. While imprisoned, John the Baptist sent two of his disciples to question Jesus to ask if it was "he that should come," or if they should look for another. Jesus asked them to observe the miracles of healing He was performing and then report them to John. He then cured many people of their infirmities and plagues.

Mark 6:5. In His home town of Nazareth, Jesus could do no mighty work because of the people's unbelief, "save that he laid his hands upon a few sick folk, and healed them." There had been so many miracles that "a few sick folk" may have seemed hardly anything at all.

Jesus healed thousands. The miracles were, by sheer number, overpowering. Everywhere Jesus went He healed the sick and diseased. He did not perform just thirty or forty spectacular miracles; His was a ministry of spectacular miracles. The relatively few detailed miracles recorded in the gospels were preserved for specific purposes by inspired writers. They were selected from the thousands of miracles to instruct, confirm, and complete the teachings of Christ.[20]

Miracles serve a unique purpose. They astound and instantly generate wonder and excitement. They jolt people from the doldrums of common existence and summon them to open their eyes to a more spiritual plane. It was not evil to request a miracle, for most of the miracles recorded were requested to fill personal needs. The sin lies in the belief in the miracles, but the disbelief in Him who grants them. The miracles were Christ's signs to gather the people as a hen gathers her chicks, to teach principles and doctrines, and to show compassion. And above all, to declare with unassailable clarity that He was the Messiah.

A Remembrance of Old Testament Events

2

The Raising of the Widow's Son

Luke 7:11–17   And it came to pass the day after, that he went into a city called Nain; and many of his disciples went with him, and much people. Now when he came nigh to the gate of the city, behold, there was a dead man carried out, the only son of his mother, and she was a widow: and much people of the city was with her. And when the Lord saw her, he had compassion on her, and said unto her, Weep not. And he came and touched the bier: and they that bare him stood still. And he said, Young man, I say unto thee, Arise. And he that was dead sat up, and began to speak. And he delivered him to his mother. And there came a fear on all: and they glorified God, saying, That a great prophet is risen up among us; and, That God hath visited his people. And this rumour of him went forth throughout all Judea, and throughout all the region round about.

The Gospels record three instances of Jesus raising the dead. The first is that of the widow's son, recorded only by Luke. All three synoptic Gospels record the raising of the daughter of Jairus, discussed in Chapter 8, and John records the raising of Lazarus, discussed in Chapter 10.

Traditionally, the raising of the daughter of Jairus is discussed first, the raising of the widow's son second, and the raising of Lazarus last. Presumably, this traditional approach gives maximum emphasis to Christ's power over death, each body having been dead longer then the previous one. However, this sequence does not adequately explain the doctrinal teachings of these miracles; there is much more to be gleaned from the raisings than the Lord's obvious power over death.

From the reading of the scripture it appears that the Lord had never encountered this widow before. The woman expresses no faith in or prior knowledge of Jesus. The meeting of the Savior and the widow was not miraculous, and appears to have happened in the normal and natural course of events. In other words, at first glance there appears to be no specific reason for this miracle. Perhaps this is the reason historical evaluators have assumed it to be merely a second evidence of the Lord's power over death and an example of His compassion. But this particular event did not just happen—the woman's son was not raised from the dead by accident. This was not only an awakening of the dead young man, but also an awakening of a dead Israel to its Messiah.

Every Jewish household looked forward to the coming of the Messiah. Jewish life centered around religion, and that emphasis was taught in every home in Israel.[21] From their infancy Jewish children were taught the holy scriptures, and "it was, indeed, no idle boast that the Jews 'were from their swaddling-clothes . . . trained to recognize God as their Father, and as the Maker of the world;' that, 'having been taught the knowledge (of the laws) from earliest youth, they bore in their souls the image of the commandments;' . . . they were 'brought up in learning,' 'exercised in the laws,' 'and made acquainted with the acts of their predecessors in order to [sic] their imitation of them.'"[22]

These teachings and laws, "the acts of their predecessors," were indelibly imprinted upon every child's memory for one purpose—to prepare for the long-awaited Messiah. The whole of the Old Testament was nothing more than the perspective from which the Messiah would be measured and recognized. The great miracles of the Old Testament would have been recited in each home in anticipation of the coming Messiah, and the great deeds of the heroic prophets, Elijah and Elisha, would have been told and retold. "Thus the whole past was symbolic, and typical of the future—the Old Testament the glass, through which the universal blessings of [the Messianic] days were seen."[23] Israel expected the Messiah to perform the miracles of Israel's past.[24] Therefore, the raising of the widow's son was, in part, a fulfillment of that expectation.

Consider the following Old Testament experiences:

1 Kings 17:17–24. As the chapter begins, Elijah informs King Ahab that no rain would fall upon the earth except at Elijah's word. The Lord then commanded Elijah to hide for his safety. In his hiding place, a raven fed him morning and evening and the brook Cherith gave him water to drink. However, with no rain upon the land to replenish the waters of the brook, it soon dried up. The Lord then instructed Elijah to go to Zarephath, where he had prepared a widow to sustain the prophet.

Elijah, the widow, and her son survived for some time by eating miraculously replenished meal and oil, but the son of the widow fell sick and died. The widow became distraught and railed upon Elijah for the death of her only son. Elijah took the son to the loft and laid him on his bed. After crying to the Lord, Elijah "stretched himself upon the child three times" and again cried unto the Lord for the return of the child's spirit, whereupon "the Lord heard the voice of Elijah; and the soul of the child came into him again, and he revived." Elijah took the child down and "delivered him unto his mother," and the mother believed.

2 Kings 4:7–37. A similar experience involved Elisha (the successor to Elijah) and a Shunammite woman. The woman had often given refreshment to Elisha as he passed by her house on his travels. She recognized him to be a man of God, and she and her husband set up a room in their home so that Elisha, should he desire, might stop and rest. Elisha asked the woman what he could do to repay her for this kindness. She desired a child, but feeling she was too old to have a child, she withheld her answer. Elisha's servant answered for the woman, and told Elisha that she had no children. Elisha promised her a son in her old age, and it was so. But when the son was grown, he was suddenly taken ill and died. The body was laid upon the bed held in readiness for Elisha, whom the woman then set out to find.

When she found Elisha, she informed him of her son's death. Elisha sent a servant with his staff to lay it upon the child. This the servant did, but nothing happened. Then Elisha came and "lay upon the child, and put his mouth upon his mouth, and his eyes upon his eyes, and his hands upon his hands: and he stretched himself upon the child; and the flesh of the child waxed warm. Then he returned, and walked in the house to and fro; and went up, and stretched himself upon him: and the child sneezed seven times, and the child opened his eyes." Elisha called for the mother and told her to "take up thy son," and she fell at his feet in gratitude.

These exciting stories from the Old Testament would have been taught over and over in every Jewish household. Thus, the raising of the widow's son was a reminder to Israel.

And now to the Savior's miracle.

It was the day after Jesus had taught in Capernaum and had healed the centurion's servant. He had walked to Nain, a city in the area,[25] with many of the disciples and "much people." As the Lord approached the city gate, his entourage encountered another multitude of people in a quite different procession.

Undoubtedly the Lord, as was His custom, had been teaching and discussing the kingdom of heaven along the way with those who followed Him. Now they were approached by the most grievous of sorrows—the funeral procession for a loved one. A dead son was being carried out, "the only son of his mother, and she was a widow." The anxiety of such a tragedy (not only death, but the death of an only son) would have immediately aroused compassion in Jesus. He could envision the mother's future desolation and loneliness. The mourning of an only son was prescribed, symbolically following Old Testament restraints.[a] Paid mourners would have punctuated the real grief of the mother and would have preceded the company. The procession would have included those with flutes, cymbals, and perhaps trumpets, along with genuinely mourning friends and relatives.[26] It was in this setting that the Lord of Life met a widow suffering the pain and grief of death.

The Lord, undoubtedly moved with compassion, voiced His request to "weep not." However, the circumstance of the miracle, rather than the woman's personal sorrow and His compassion, provides the insight into the teaching invoked by the miracle. Here was a widow whose only son was dead, a circumstance similar to that involving the prophets Elijah and Elisha. Would not this similarity stir memories and arouse expectations in those who were about to witness this great miracle? Heedless of standard ceremonial observances, Jesus moved to the funeral procession and touched the bier. He had made physical contact with the dead, the greatest of all Levitical defilements; in His day, this was rabbinically equated with endless terrors.[27] Jesus then spoke. "Young man, I say unto thee, Arise. And he that was dead sat up, and began to speak. And He delivered him to his mother." The expectation was fulfilled—the widow's only son was raised from the dead and returned once again to his mother. Yet there was more, for Jesus used neither contortions nor staff, nor did He lay His hands upon the lifeless body. The young man's life was restored solely by Jesus' divine word, thereby showing Christ to be greater than the prophets of old.

No Jewish citizen, no descendant of Abraham, Isaac, and Jacob could have missed the association. The reactions of the people, first fear and then joyous praise, seem to confirm this. "They glorified God, saying, That a great prophet is risen up among us; and, That God hath visited his people." The Gospel writers later emphasized this obvious association when they recorded the Lord's question to the disciples, "Whom do men say that I the Son of man am? And they said [echoing the expressions of the people], Some say that thou art John the Baptist: some, Elias [Elijah]."[a] The connection was too clear to have been overlooked. He did not restrain those who had witnessed the miracle from telling others as He did on other occasions. Rather, He _wanted_ them to tell others. The scripture reports that "this rumour of him went forth throughout all Judea, and throughout all the region round about." The people recognized what He had done and told all who would listen.

The accounts give no further knowledge of the mother in the story or of her son. Perhaps they believed on Christ and followed Him; and perhaps, as with others, they did not follow him and only rejoiced in the miracle. But even this is not recorded. The raising of the widow's son was a visual sign to Israel that Jesus was the Messiah, and by this sign to His covenant people—a people who should have readily recognized it—Jesus declared, _I am He!_

The Feeding of the Five Thousand

John 6:1–15   After these things Jesus went over the sea of Galilee, which is the sea of Tiberias. And a great multitude followed him, because they saw his miracles which he did on them that were diseased. And Jesus went up into a mountain, and there he sat with his disciples. And the passover, a feast of the Jews, was nigh.

When Jesus then lifted up his eyes, and saw a great company come unto him, he saith unto Philip, Whence shall we buy bread, that these may eat? And this he said to prove him: for he himself knew what he would do. Philip answered him, Two hundred pennyworth of bread is not sufficient for them, that every one of them may take a little. One of his disciples, Andrew, Simon Peter's brother, saith unto him, there is a lad here, which hath five barley loaves, and two small fishes: but what are they among so many? And Jesus said, Make the men sit down. Now there was much

a. Matthew
16:13–14.

grass in the place. So the men sat down, in number about five thousand. And Jesus took the loaves; and when he had given thanks, he distributed to the disciples, and the disciples to them that were set down; and likewise of the fishes as much as they would. When they were filled, he said unto his disciples, Gather up the fragments that remain, that nothing be lost. Therefore they gathered them together, and filled twelve baskets with the fragments of the five barley loaves, which remained over and above unto them that had eaten. Then those men, when they had seen the miracle that Jesus did, said, This is of a truth that prophet that should come into the world.

When Jesus therefore perceived that they would come and take him by force, to make him a king, he departed again into a mountain himself alone.

Cross-references   Matthew 14:13–22; Mark 6:32–45; Luke 9:10–17; JST Mark 6:36; JST Luke 9:13

This is the only specific miracle reported by all four Gospel writers. John is used as the principal scriptural reference. There are only slight variances in the texts, and these variances are of no significance to the miracle's outcome or purpose. There are, however, varied circumstances reported about the events in the Lord's ministry immediately preceding the miracle. These differences can, in all probability, be attributed to the independent authorship of the Gospels. The scripture indicates that Jesus wanted solitude and seclusion from the crowds, desiring to get away privately with the Twelve. They left to find seclusion in the dry, uncultivated mountains of the Holy Land.

But privacy was not to be Christ's on this occasion, for the Gospels all agree that a multitude followed Him. John reports that at this time the feast of the Passover was nigh, which would have brought large crowds of people to and from Jerusalem. The annual event was the most important of the Jewish religious celebrations, and according to Josephus, "an innumerable multitude of people" thronged Jerusalem for this feast.[28] Josephus reports that Cestius once took a census of Jerusalem at the time of the Passover to inform Nero of the city's power. Cestius asked the high priests to number the multitude, which they did by counting the sacrifices slain at the feast (256,500). They then estimated that ten or eleven people would celebrate each sacrifice. (It was not lawful for anyone to feast singly, and some companies were known to include as many as twenty.) From this the priests reported that 2,700,200 Jews had come to the feast "pure and holy." (Those who were "unclean" could not sacrifice, nor could any foreigners, so the figure computed was below the actual total.)²⁹ Thus, for Christ to have five thousand men (plus women and children) follow Him at this time in no way stretches the imagination.

The reason why such a large multitude followed Jesus into the wilderness area is scripturally recorded. There is no doubt that by this time in the Lord's ministry, He had attracted much attention. He had performed many miracles. He had healed the sick and raised the dead, and His fame had been spread abroad. John notes that the great multitude followed Christ "because they saw his miracles which he did on them that were diseased." Matthew reports that upon seeing the multitude that had followed Him, Jesus "was moved with compassion toward them, and he healed their sick." Luke confirms this, reporting that Jesus "spake unto them of the kingdom of God, and healed them that had need of healing." Wherever Christ went, once the people heard of His presence they brought their sick and diseased to Him to have them healed. It was the same in this instance, and the Master did not disappoint them.

This was a Jewish multitude, and the miracle required that it be so. The Passover feast and the proximity to Jerusalem would itself attest to the crowd's "Jewishness." But there are also verifying circumstances within the miracle itself. One evidence surfaces when the blessing of the food in this miracle is compared with the prayer in the feeding of the four thousand.ᵃ There was but one blessing here, "in strict accordance with Jewish custom," whereas the bread and fish were blessed separately for the four thousand. Only one prayer was to be uttered for a Jewish meal; to do otherwise would have given offense to the Jews, and they would not have eaten.³⁰ But it is the multitude's reaction that finally verifies their Jewish nationality and reveals the major purpose for recording the miracle.

Mark records that Jesus, upon seeing the multitude, had compassion not only for their physical illnesses, but for their spiritual maladies as well. He referred to them as "sheep not having a shepherd: and He began to teach them many things." They had all come with enthusiasm "taking no thought, for the time at least, of what they should eat or what they should drink, only desirous to hear the word of life, only seeking the kingdom of heaven;"³¹ and no preparation had been made for their earthly needs.

a. Matthew 15:32–38; Mark 8:1–9.

The physical proceedings of the miracle are well defined by the Gospel writers. The disciples were concerned over the length of time the crowd had spent with Jesus. They requested the Lord to dismiss the people so that they might adequately provide for their own physical needs. But the Lord had other intentions. He asked Philip, although it was intended for all the Twelve, "Whence shall we buy bread, that these may eat?" John reports that Christ did this to "prove him," for "he himself knew what he would do."

The question required the Twelve to anticipate certain conclusions about Jesus. They had seen evidence of His Messiahship, but dare they conclude that He would feed the multitude in the wilderness as Jehovah had done of old? The "proving" of the multitude would come after the miracle. Would they recognize in the miracle the witness of His divinity and acknowledge His Messiahship? It was the Passover, the event that more than any other brought to remembrance Jehovah's promise to Israel that the Messiah would come. This event celebrated Israel's deliverance from bondage. Now, as then, Israel desired and needed that hoped-for deliverance and looked for Him who would provide it. Jesus again provided a witness of His divinity by stirring Israel's memory of Old Testament anticipations.

Exodus 16:1–35. After Moses delivered the children of Israel from slavery in Egypt, his problems did not end. Although the people were free, they were distraught because they were hungry. They murmured against Moses and Aaron and wished they had died in Egypt, for there they "did eat bread to the full." They considered that Moses and Aaron had taken them into the wilderness "to kill this whole assembly with hunger." Moses inquired of the Lord and was told, "I will rain bread from heaven for you." The people were instructed to gather all they needed each day, but no more. The next morning, after the dew had passed, "there lay a small round thing" on the ground, and the people said to one another, "It is manna." It tasted like wafers made with honey and it was white in appearance, like coriander seed.

Israel was to keep an "omer" full of the manna from generation to generation so that their children could "see the bread" wherewith the Lord had fed them. But as they continued to travel in the wilderness, the people tired of manna and demanded meat. The Lord, disgusted by their ungratefulness, provided quail for them by a wind from the sea, for (as the Lord declared) "even a whole month, until it come out at your nostrils."[a] Thereafter, "the children of Israel did eat manna forty years."

1 Kings 17:8–16. The prophet Elijah also provided food miraculously. When Elijah arrived at the home of the widow whom Jehovah had prepared to sustain him, he asked for a drink and for bread to eat. The widow responded that she had but a small portion of meal and oil left, and was about to prepare it for herself and her son so that they might eat it and die. Elijah told her to prepare it for him instead and to fear not, for "the barrel of meal shall not waste, neither shall the cruse of oil fail, until the day that the Lord sendeth rain upon the earth." And it was so.

2 Kings 4:39–44. Elisha miraculously provided for the people by first neutralizing a pot of inadvertently poisoned food so that all could eat. Then a servant brought to Elisha "twenty loaves of barley, and full ears of corn in the husks thereof." Elisha commanded the servant to feed the people. The servant immediately questioned Elisha's command for there were "an hundred men." Elisha again ordered the feeding, and the servant complied. The men ate, were filled, and had food left over.

This heritage roused the multitude's memory as Jesus again declared His Messiahship to them.

Philip's response to the Lord's question of how they could feed the multitude addressed the impossibility of purchasing enough food to provide for the people. "Two hundred pennyworth of bread is not sufficient for them, that every one of them may take a little," he responded. After noting a meager provision of only five barley loaves and two small fishes, Andrew asked, "But what are they among so many?" Jesus instructed the disciples to seat the multitude in companies of hundreds and fifties on the grass, presumably for order and convenience, and this was done. The Lord then blessed the food in the Jewish manner and gave it to the disciples to distribute to the people. As with the manna, the meal and the oil, and the bread and corn of Old Testament times, the food multiplied and all were fed. And, as in the case of Elisha and the bread and corn, all were filled. Indeed, enough extra was gathered to fill twelve baskets.

How did the Lord perform this miracle? Obviously He used His

a. Numbers
11:4–20.

creative power, but the actual process eludes the mortal mind. The important fact is that the miracle did occur. The people could not help but associate this miracle with those miraculous feedings of old. Jesus was recalling to the people's memory the great expectations they held for their awaited Messiah. The multitude recognized and remembered.

John records that those men who had witnessed the miracle said, "This is of a truth that prophet that should come into the world." What the disciples may not have dared recognize before the miracle, the people openly acknowledged afterward.

What occurred next is most significant. The multitude recognized in Jesus their looked-for Messiah. But what Messiah did they expect? The national conception of the Messiah involved political and material power. Moral reform and spiritual power were not expected to be the primary goals of the Messianic triumph (Chapter 1). Jesus perceived that the people were going to take Him by force "to make him a king." It was not the character of Jesus or His teachings that aroused the multitude to this reaction, but the influence of His miracle. The effect on the crowd was in keeping with the ideas of the time, but Jesus would not comply with their wishes. His was not an earthly kingdom, but a heavenly one. He was not sent to fill their material needs, but to fulfill their spiritual needs. His purpose was to save not the body but the soul. So after constraining His disciples to leave and dismissing the multitude, Jesus "departed again into a mountain himself alone."

Accounts of the miraculous feeding of the five thousand no doubt spread abroad to increase Christ's fame—as did the interpretation of the miracle. John reports[a] that later, the people sought Jesus and found Him; but Jesus recognized their intent and stated that they had come because of the bread and the miracles and not because of His teachings. They then asked for a sign—the Messianic sign. The miraculous provision of bread and fish was accepted, but it was not unique. They reminded Him that their fathers had been given bread from heaven. Jesus quickly emphasized that it was not Moses who provided the bread, but His Father. Then followed the sermon on the bread of life.[32]

The people had correctly interpreted the miracle and looked to Christ to confirm His Messiahship, but they still sought the coming of the politically all-powerful Messiah. However, a second sign had been given and by it Jesus once more declared, I am He.

a. John 6.

Summary

The Jews had received two great signs. Other miracles had been or would be publicly performed, but not with the same emphasis. In the raising of the widow's son and the feeding of the five thousand, the Gospel writers recorded Christ's open, public claim to His people that He was their expected Messiah.

The chosen people had been taught for centuries to expect the Messiah. The signs of His coming had been impressed upon the people and taught in every home. Jesus came to them, doing what they expected of Him, yet they missed Him; not because they did not make the association or recognize His claim, but because they had overshot the mark. They were so concerned about their material condition, their needed relief from Rome and other enemies, and their day-to-day activities, that they had transposed the signs of His two comings. They sought the second coming of the Messiah in all His power and glory, not His first coming, in which He would establish His spiritual kingdom, the kingdom that would, if accepted and followed, allow entry into His final kingdom.

The people gladly accepted His miracles, they rejoiced in the healing of their sick and diseased, they glorified God when He restored them to life, and they satisfied their hunger with His bread and fish; but they would not accept His spiritual offerings. They asked for a sign. He gave them two, and they rejected them both.

Recognized by Demons, Accused by His Own 3

Before discussing the following three miracles, all of which deal with possession, it would be beneficial to discuss evil spirits in general. This is a difficult subject, and without a knowledge of man's true relationship to the spirit world it would be impossible to arrive at any realistic understanding of the problems, circumstances, and purposes of possession, and the miracles of removing evil spirits from the possessed.

The Source of Evil, Wicked, and Unclean Spirits

In the beginning, before the creation of the physical earth, mankind existed as spirit children of our Heavenly Father. It was this Father who spoke to Adam and Eve in the Garden of Eden and who attested to the divinity of His Only Begotten Son, both at the baptism of Jesus and on the Mount of Transfiguration. There, in the pre-mortal existence, we were all spirits, with the exception of our heavenly parents. Our spirit beings did not have physical bodies, although they appeared much as man does now, only in spiritual tabernacles.

Many "noble and great ones"[a] were present who later, in their physical bodies, would occupy positions of authority and power on the earth. Jesus was present and was known by the name Jehovah. Michael and Gabriel were there also and some of their activities are recorded in the scriptures. All who would come to this earth were with them. So was another important figure. Isaiah called him Lucifer, a son of the morning.[b] John the Revelator referred to him as "a great red dragon."[c] He too was a spirit son of our Heavenly Father. All the spirits progressed in this pre-earthly existence under the tutelage of our

a. Abraham 3:22–23.

b. Isaiah 14:12.

c. Revelation 12:3.

Heavenly Father. At a certain point in that progression, a great council was called. All spirits who could potentially belong to this earth were present. There the Father's plan for mortality was presented.

At this council, Lucifer objected to the Father's plan. He presented an alternate one, one that opposed the Father's; and he said in his heart, "I will ascend into heaven, I will exalt my throne above the stars of God: . . . I will ascend above the heights of the clouds; I will be like the most High."[a] His plan was rejected by God, but he nevertheless convinced a large host to follow him. John tells us that this host consisted of "the third part of the stars [spirit children of God] of heaven."[b] Because of his disobedience to the plan of the Father, he failed in his "first estate" (the premortal, spiritual existence),[c] and he was punished, along with those who followed him, by being "cast . . . to the earth,"[d] never to receive a tabernacle of flesh and never to have any further opportunity to reenter the Father's kingdom. When he rebelled against God, he was cast down and "he became Satan, yea, even the devil, the father of all lies."[e] Thereafter, he and his angels had but one purpose—"to deceive and to blind men, and to lead them captive at his will, even as many as would not hearken unto [God's] voice."[f]

The scriptures record some of the devil's earthly exploits. In the Garden of Eden, he tempted Adam and Eve and persuaded them to disobey God's commandment; thus, they became separated from God.[g] He came to Moses and tempted him,[h] and he personally appeared to Jesus in an attempt to bring down the Savior of the World.[i] Men sin, which is evil. If a man knows God's laws, the evil that he commits is his own responsibility. Nevertheless, all evil emanates from one source—the devil and his angels—that third part of heaven's host that was cast down to the earth. Indeed, Jewish theologians believed in only two sources of power in the supernatural world: God, from whom emanated all good; and Satan, from whom came all evil.

What Did Possession Mean?

The Jews taught and believed that a wicked or unclean spirit could physically possess a human body.[33] Once that possession had taken place, the "demon"—as such a spirit was sometimes called—could then take control of the speech, arms, legs, and other functions of

a. Isaiah 14:13–14.

b. Revelation 12:4.

c. Abraham 3:26.

d. Revelation 12:9.

e. Moses 4:4.

f. Moses 4:4.

g. Moses 4; Genesis 3.

h. Moses 1:12–22.

i. Matthew 4:1–11; Mark 1:12–13; Luke 4:1–13.

the body, thus causing a person to do and say things that normally he or she would not. Such a person did not become a servant of Satan, subjectively and willingly doing his will; rather he was possessed by an evil spirit, and therefore lost control of his will and could not act independently from the demon.

This describes possession generally, but it is obvious from the New Testament accounts that different degrees of possession occurred, and that at times the possessed person could reassert himself and his conscious self would prevail, at least momentarily.

The recorded occurrences indicate that a possessed person was obviously in bondage, did not have control of his normal functions, did not control his bodily activities and behavior, often hurt or injured himself, was considered "unclean," caused fear in others, and had his life cruelly shattered. He endured the real presence of another will from an alien power whose influence and will was set against all righteousness. Not all scriptural instances of possession record physical abuse of the host, but enough do that the question is raised of why a demon spirit, so desirous of possessing the body of another, should be so bent on destroying or harming that same body?

No conclusive scriptural answer is given for this phenomenon. Logic could indicate that the evil spirit is so determined to enforce its will on its host that it would do so even by physical means. But the possessed person is not in a hopeless condition. His is "not . . . the deliberate giving in to Satanic will, of an utterly lost soul, but, in many instances at least, the still recoverable wreck of what might once have been a noble spirit."[34]

The Causes of Possession

The causes of possession in scripture arouse much thought. Undoubtedly sin—disobedience to God's law—plays a part in allowing a person to become possessed. But occasionally evil spirits have physically attacked righteous men as well.[35] Certainly the sins of those possessed, as recorded in scripture, were not beyond the Lord's mercy. Yet it can also be assumed that by gradual degrees one can choose wickedness so as to become virtually a captive of its author, the devil. Although not possessed, such was apparently the case with Korihor, who was stricken dumb for his arrogant rebellion and recalcitrance. His plea for restoration of speech was denied because, as the prophet Alma told him, if the curse were to be taken away, he would return to his former wickedness.[a] Presumably, those the Savior relieved of demoniac possession were not in this category. Yet they may have tampered with sin or unbelief in such kind or degree as to permit the entrance of an evil spirit into their bodies—although they were not entirely lost to desires for righteousness.

In Jewish thought, many diseases were connected with possession.[36] However, it would be unrealistic to infer (then as well as now) that those diseases referred to in the New Testament in association with possession were caused by evil. An example of this is the infirmity described as being "dumb," which included speech impediments as well as the inability to speak at all. At times this was connected with possession (as in Matthew Chapters 9 and 12), although the same infirmity, recorded by Mark in Chapter 7, is not associated with possession.

The experiences cited in the New Testament and our knowledge of Satan's purpose verify that possession is real. That sin affects possession and righteousness prevents it would be an obvious conclusion. But we cannot conclude that possession automatically means total wickedness and subservience to Satan any more than we can automatically conclude that any individual sin caused the possession.

It is evident that sin could be involved with possession, yet the sin would not have to be unforgivable or a sin that divine intervention could not overcome. The possessed soul could yet be allowed to come back into conformity with God's laws and be permitted entrance into the Lord's kingdom.

What About Possessions Today?

Considering the many experiences recorded or alluded to in the New Testament, why are there no such possessions today; or if there are, why are they not as numerous or as readily recognized?

Most Christian writers seem to agree that the problem of possession was more prevalent at the time of Christ.[37] Consider the following reasons. First, it was the time of the coming of the Son of Man in the flesh. The advocate of evil over good would logically exert a strong influence at the time when the presence of Christ was near. Also, the spiritual state of the chosen people was at a very low ebb. Apparently

a. Alma 30.

it had been over four hundred years since the last prophet of the Old Testament, and apostasy was rampant.

Second, this was the time when the mission of Christ would overcome the results of sin, i.e., death. Until the advent of Christ, death conquered all men, and in death the devil found momentary success over the power of God. In Christ all would be made alive, and in Him death had no power. Therefore, thwarting Jesus' purpose and mission was a prime objective of the devil.

Third was the belief of the Jews themselves. As already noted, they believed in only two sources of supernatural power—God and Satan.[38] Once Christ made His claim to the Messiahship, they must accept His powers as being from one or the other of these sources. Once they rejected Him, the only argument left was that the power He exercised was of the devil. With the great powers of evil so prevalent, the potential for confusing the people was even greater.

Fourth, the knowledge and technology of our civilization is considerably different from that of the Jews at Christ's time. Mental conditions, physical actions, and verbal invective—which were readily recognized as symptoms of possession at the time of Christ—are usually explained away today by our sophisticated scientific and medical knowledge.

Summary

The New Testament writings must stand for what they are and what they represent. No attempt should be made to place modern rationale upon the narrations concerning demoniacs. The scriptural examples of demoniac possession enhance our awareness of evil spirits. That awareness should lead to an increased understanding of the world of evil beyond the physical world and its potential influence upon us. The door through which these worlds connect is within each individual. It is our own negligence or willfulness that allows that door to open, allowing evil to enter and possess that which God has given.

The Demoniac in the Synagogue at Capernaum

Mark 1:21–28   And they went into Capernaum; and straightway on the sabbath day he entered into the synagogue, and taught. And they were astonished at his doctrine: for he taught them as one that had authority, and not as the scribes. And there was in their synagogue a man with an unclean spirit; and he cried out, saying,

Let us alone; what have we to do with thee, thou Jesus of Nazareth? art thou come to destroy us? I know thee who thou art, the Holy One of God. And Jesus rebuked him, saying, Hold thy peace, and come out of him. And when the unclean spirit had torn him, and cried with a loud voice, he came out of him. And they were all amazed, insomuch that they questioned among themselves, saying, What thing is this? what new doctrine is this? for with authority commandeth he even the unclean spirits, and they do obey him. And immediately his fame spread abroad throughout all the region round about Galilee.

Cross-reference   Luke 4:31–37

This miracle is the first specific New Testament recording of the confrontation between Christ and one who was possessed. Both Mark and Luke record the occurrence; however, Mark is used as the primary account. He records that Jesus was teaching in the synagogue at Capernaum on the Sabbath day and the people were "astonished at his doctrine." They were astonished because He spoke with "authority, and not as the scribes." The scribes spoke of probabilities and opinions. The people's response indicated that they recognized Christ's Messianic claims, for the Pharisees and scribes taught that only God could speak with authority.[39]

The scripture reports that there was one "with an unclean spirit" in the synagogue. Apparently his presence was known but not forbidden. The unclean spirit cried out while Jesus was teaching. Note that it was not the person in whom the spirit resided, but the evil spirit itself, speaking either through its voice, or the voice of the possessed person. He recognized Jesus and cried out, "Let us alone." There is no scriptural evidence that this was a multiple possession; therefore, the evil spirit was apparently referring to the general condition of the host of spirits that had been cast down to the earth from the presence of the Father, or for himself and the one possessed.

The spirit continued, "What have we to do with thee, thou Jesus of Nazareth? art thou come to destroy us?" His expectations were self-contained and self-fulfilling. He knew that Jesus could and would eventually destroy his kingdom. The spirit continued, "I know thee who thou art, the Holy One of God."

This spirit had been in that great council in heaven held before the world was. He had been present when the Father presented His plan and asked, "Whom shall I send?" Jesus had answered, "Here am I, send me." Lucifer had responded with like words (but evil intentions), and the Father had rejected him. Lucifer had become angry "and kept not his first estate; and, at that day, many followed after him."[a]

The demoniac who was now addressing the Savior was one of those who had rebelled and followed the devil to torment man and oppose the chosen Son of God. He knew Jesus from that great council, knew that He had been chosen to be the Son of God, and knew that His authority far exceeded that of his master, the devil; so he asked, "Art thou come to destroy us?" Jesus now rebuked the evil spirit, saying "Hold thy peace, and come out of him."

The evil spirit could not disobey. He once again agonized the possessed, and after he "had torn him, and cried with a loud voice, he came out of him." Luke indicates that he did not physically hurt his victim, but tormented the possessed for one last time before leaving; then he obeyed and left.

The people who witnessed the cleansing were amazed at what had happened. The Jews believed in possession and had procedures for cleansing those who were possessed, described at times by the word *exorcism.*[40] But with the Christ it was different. He had merely to command and the unclean spirit would depart. The people recognized this, for they said, "What new doctrine is this? for with authority commandeth he even the unclean spirits, and they do obey him." And they spread His fame abroad.

Another witness of Christ's Messiahship to the people had taken place. Jesus, by His command, evidenced His authority over evil. The people had difficulty in recognizing Jesus for who He was; only those who believed could do so. But the evil spirits had no such limitation. They knew Him from before and, unlike mortals, had not had a veil drawn over their memories of pre-earth events. They knew exactly who Jesus was and, in accordance with the order of things, they acknowledged it. But the people had to recognize Christ from good sources, not evil sources. So Jesus rebuked the evil spirit and would not allow him to speak. This was the first public confrontation between the two worlds of Jewish thought—good and evil—the two great influences that affected all of Jewish life. Jesus had been publicly recognized by the lesser of these two worlds as the Supreme Being that He was. The people knew that the demoniac was possessed. Jesus publicly commanded the evil spirit to leave; it acknowledged His authority and departed. The sought-for Messiah was directly assaulting the world of evil; it was now for the people to choose which they would follow.

One Possessed and Dumb

Matthew 9:32–33 As they went out, behold, they brought to him a dumb man possessed with a devil. And when the devil was cast out, the dumb spake: and the multitudes marvelled, saying, It was never so seen in Israel.

Matthew 12:22–23 Then was brought unto him one possessed with a devil, blind, and dumb: and he healed him, insomuch that the blind and dumb both spake and saw. And all the people were amazed, and said, Is not this the son of David?

Luke 11:14 And he was casting out a devil, and it was dumb. And it came to pass, when the devil was gone out, the dumb spake; and the people wondered.

The Beelzebub Argument

Matthew 12:24–45 But when the Pharisees heard it, they said, This fellow doth not cast out devils, but by Beelzebub the prince of the devils. And Jesus knew their thoughts, and said unto them, Every kingdom divided against itself is brought to desolation; and every city or house divided against itself shall not stand: and if Satan cast out Satan, he is divided against himself; how shall then his kingdom stand? And if I by Beelzebub cast out devils, by whom do your children cast them out? therefore they shall be your judges. But if I cast out devils by the Spirit of God, then the kingdom of God is come unto you. Or else how can one enter into a strong man's house, and spoil his goods, except he first bind the strong man? and then he will spoil his house. He that is not with me is against me; and he that gathereth not with me scattereth abroad.

Wherefore I say unto you, All manner of sin and blasphemy shall be forgiven unto men: but the blasphemy against the Holy Ghost shall not be forgiven unto men. And whosoever speaketh a word against the Son of man, it shall be forgiven him: but whosoever speaketh against the Holy Ghost, it shall not be forgiven him, neither in this world, neither in the world to come. Either make the tree good, and his fruit good; or else make the tree corrupt, and his fruit corrupt: for the tree is known by his fruit. O generation of vipers, how can ye, being evil, speak good things? for out of the abundance of the heart the mouth speaketh. A good man out of the good treasure of the heart bringeth forth good things: and an evil man out of the evil treasure bringeth forth evil things. But I say unto you, That every idle word that men shall speak, they shall give account thereof in the day of judgment. For by thy words thou shalt be justified, and by thy words thou shalt be condemned.

Then certain of the scribes and of the Pharisees answered, saying, Master, we would see a sign from thee. But he answered and said unto them, An evil and adulterous generation seeketh after a sign; and there shall no sign be given to it, but the sign of the prophet Jonas: for as Jonas was three days and three nights in the whale's belly; so shall the Son of man be three days and three nights in the heart of the earth. The men of Nineveh shall rise in judgment with this generation, and shall condemn it: because they repented at the preaching of Jonas; and, behold, a greater than Jonas is here. The queen of the south shall rise up in the judgment with this generation, and shall condemn it: for she came from the uttermost parts of the earth to hear the wisdom of Solomon; and, behold, a greater than Solomon is here. When the unclean spirit is gone out of a man, he walketh through dry places, seeking rest, and findeth none. Then he saith, I will return into my house from whence I came out; and when he is come, he findeth it empty, swept, and garnished. Then goeth he, and taketh with himself seven other spirits more wicked than himself, and they enter in and dwell there: and the last state of that man is worse than the first. Even so shall it be also unto this wicked generation.

Cross-references   Matthew 9:34; Mark 3:22–30; Luke 11:15–26; John 10:19–21; IV Matthew 12:19–23, 26, 37–39; JST Mark 3:21–25; JST Luke 11:15, 20, 27

This miracle is unique and distinctive, but not because of the miracle itself, for the two Synoptics leave out all but the barest of detail concerning it. It is specifically mentioned and identified here not for its miraculous contents but for its consequences. This miracle precipitates one of the few direct arguments of record between Jesus and the Jewish rulers.

The miracle occupies only one verse in Luke, who merely states that Jesus was "casting out a devil, and it was dumb. . . . And the people wondered." Matthew writes only four verses about it; however, these four verses need some additional explanation. As noted, two verses appear in each of two different chapters, and it would seem that these verses describe the same event, even though they were recorded at different times. Both describe the cure of a dumb demoniac. (In Chapter 12 he is also described as blind, which might be merely a condensation of the prelude of the miracle in Chapter 9).[41]

The possessed person was brought to Jesus, who healed him. The multitude marveled, as in Luke, but Matthew further records the multitude as saying, "It was never so seen in Israel." Chapter 12 enlarges the multitude's comment, and the amazed people proclaim, "Is not this the son of David?" Thus, they attribute the Messianic position to Jesus. These glimpses, although brief, extol the miracle's virtues and authenticity.

The Beelzebub Argument

The previous miracles performed by Jesus drew multitudes to Him. The people "wondered, marveled, and were astonished." But His success angered His enemies, and in an attempt to discredit Him they contrived an accusation against Jesus that became their defense to His miracles. The accusation centered on the source of His authority and power, and is referred to here as the Beelzebub argument. The scribes and Pharisees (the Jewish leadership) accused Jesus of casting out devils by the authority of the prince of devils, or Satan. The accusation was made on several occasions, but the Gospel writers selected the occasion of this miracle to record it in detail. Undoubtedly, to some degree the Beelzebub argument blunted the people's acceptance of Christ; because of their belief that all things came from either God or the devil, it gave them an alternative to believe in, and thus confused them.

The Jewish leadership did not want Jesus to be the Messiah, even though all of the signs and wonders pointed to that fact. By refusing to accept Him as the Messiah they had only one alternative—to accuse Him of performing such feats by the power of Beelzebub, the prince of devils; and accuse Him they did!

The Beelzebub argument is found in all four Gospels (although two of the writers excluded the miracle of the one possessed and dumb). The Beelzebub argument struck at the very heart of Judaism. It was the classic confrontation between Jesus establishing His claim as the Messiah and the Jewish leadership rejecting it, and doing so in such a manner that would also persuade the people to reject Him.

The Jewish leadership had undoubtedly awaited such an opportunity as Jesus' miracle for the possessed and dumb man to put this cunning argument to the people. As the people marveled and exclaimed, "Is not this the son of David?" the scribes and Pharisees raised the challenge of His authority: "This fellow doth not cast out devils, but by Beelzebub the prince of devils."

Jesus, perceiving their thoughts, defended Himself against their accusation. His answer was simple and direct: "Every kingdom [or house] divided against itself is brought to desolation; . . . and if Satan cast out Satan . . . how shall then his kingdom stand?" His logic was unassailable. He acknowledged their belief and pronounced it correct:

these powers came from only one of two sources—God or Satan. But He also reminded them that the two sources were mutually exclusive: God was always good, and Satan was always evil. He emphasized this with two examples. First, He declared that a good tree brings forth only good fruit, while an evil tree always brings forth evil fruit. Second, He declared that what is treasured in the heart comes out of the mouth: good treasure produces good things; evil treasure produces evil things. He then applied these examples directly to both the Jews' history and their current situation. They were the chosen people. Their history was full of miracles such as He had performed, and they had even seen some enacted by their own children (speaking of the children of Abraham, and not their literal children).

Jesus then reasoned that if He cast out devils by Beelzebub and they were the same "good things" that their own prophets had done, by what authority had the children of Israel cast them out? He forced them to judge themselves by their own standards. They were familiar with the concept of the Spirit of God. They claimed to be the keepers of the kingdom of God. They had taught that all good things previously done by the chosen people were done in the name of God. Therefore, they should judge His miracles and teachings by that same standard and spirit. They had seen His works and heard His claims. The people recognized in Him the very things expected of and looked for in the Messiah. Now the direct challenge, the alternative to His authority, or the devil, had been raised as the source of His power. But He had turned the argument upon its promulgators. He could not have spoken more clearly had He said, "I am your Messiah."

Jesus continued that if they made the comparisons and thus found His actions to be the same as those of their children—in that He had cast out devils by the Spirit of God—"then the kingdom of God is come unto you." In this direct confrontation with the Jewish leadership, Jesus drew His miracles and teachings into one overpowering argument. Simply put, He challenged them to test His claim by the Spirit; if they did, they would conclude that He was the Messiah.

Christ further emphasized His position by commenting on the sin against the Holy Ghost. It was a grievous sin, not to be forgiven. His chosen people were now flirting with that very sin. "He that is not with me is against me," he stated. They were either with Him, or against

Him and with the devil. Jesus had turned the Beelzebub argument upon His accusers.

The Jewish leadership understood; the scriptures make this quite plain. After Jesus concluded the argument, they offered no rebuttal. They couldn't because they believed what Jesus was teaching. Left without alternatives, they responded in the only manner they could without accepting Him. "Master, we would see a sign from thee." By this request they acknowledged that they understood His position; Jesus had completely and successfully refuted the very argument they had conceived to discredit Him. Even those who had challenged Him inwardly questioned their rejection of Him, so they asked the Lord to show them a sign. But they had seen multiple signs. They had just witnessed a miracle in which Jesus had cast out a devil. What they wanted, however, was the Messianic sign of the coming of the Son of Man. They were still looking for the wrong coming.

As a result of this blatant display of disbelief, Jesus called the whole generation wicked and adulterous for seeking after signs. In this unusually harsh condemnation, the Lord obviously included the specific sexual sin of adultery—but a much broader condemnation also applied. They had sought a particular sign (the sign of the coming of the Son of Man), and this displayed their complete lack of faith in Him as the Messiah. Their sins and disbelief had caused them to reject Him; they had changed the doctrines of the Mosaic Law and confused and "adulterated" them. Jesus could not give them the sign they sought. It was reserved for a later period. But He would give them a sign, one they knew and should have been looking for—the sign of the prophet Jonas which foreshadowed the Savior's resurrection. This sign, the final sign of His first coming, would prove to all believers that He had completed and fulfilled the mission of His first coming.

The balance of the material is self-explanatory. Jesus contrasted the current generation with those of Nineveh and the queen of the south (Sheba), declaring those generations to be better than this one. He warned them of their spiritual darkness because they would not see.

Jesus concluded His argument with an analogy, pointing out what their future would be like if they did not accept Him. The analogy was couched in the story of a man with an unclean spirit (like the one He had just evicted from the possessed dumb man). When the unclean spirit was gone out of the man, that spirit wandered, seeking rest and finding none. Similarly, Israel had been chosen from among all nations and people. Their former evils (unclean spirits) had been cast away, and great blessings had been given them. The evil spirit (the former status of Israel and its current apostasy) then returned to its "house" (the formerly possessed man) and found it clean, swept, and empty. It promptly found seven additional spirits, more evil than itself, and all entered to dwell there, leaving the man in a worse state than before. By the same token, the Jews had been chosen of God, their sins put aside, and correct principles taught to them; now Jesus was offering them the kingdom of God. All had been done to prepare them for the coming Messiah. If they rejected Him now, they would be worse off than before. Jesus then closed with this binding promise: "Even so shall it be also unto this wicked generation."

This little miracle, so often excluded or generalized, led to the most open claim to the Messiahship that Jesus had yet made in His ministry. Other claims would come and more miracles would be given, but none would be clearer or more concise. Israel was the chosen people, and the Messiah had come as promised.

The Demoniac that was Legion

Mark 5:1–20   And they came over unto the other side of the sea, into the country of the Gadarenes. And when he was come out of the ship, immediately there met him out of the tombs a man with an unclean spirit, who had his dwelling among the tombs; and no man could bind him, no, not with chains: because that he had been often bound with fetters and chains, and the chains had been plucked asunder by him, and the fetters broken in pieces: neither could any man tame him. And always, night and day, he was in the mountains, and in the tombs, crying, and cutting himself with stones. But when he saw Jesus afar off, he ran and worshipped him, and cried with a loud voice, and said, What have I to do with thee, Jesus, thou Son of the most high God? I adjure thee by God, that thou torment me not. For he said unto him, Come out of the man, thou unclean spirit. And he asked him, What is thy name? And he answered, saying, My name is Legion: for we are many. And he besought him much that he would not send them away out of the country. Now there was there nigh unto the mountains a great herd of swine feeding. And all the devils besought him, saying, Send us into the swine, that we may enter into them. And forthwith Jesus gave them leave. And the unclean spirits went out, and entered into the swine: and the herd ran violently down a steep place into the sea, (they were about two thousand;) and were choked in the sea. And they that fed the swine fled, and told it in the city, and in the country. And they went out to see what it was that was done. And they come to Jesus, and see him that was possessed with the devil, and had the legion, sitting, and clothed, and in his right mind: and they were afraid. And they that saw it told them how it befell to him that was possessed with the devil, and also concerning the swine. And they began to pray him to depart out of their coasts. And when he was come into the ship, he that had been possessed with the devil prayed him that he might be with him. Howbeit Jesus suffered him not, but saith unto him, Go home to thy friends, and tell them how great things the Lord hath done for thee, and hath had compassion on thee. And he departed, and began to publish in Decapolis how great things Jesus had done for him: and all men did marvel.

Cross-references   Matthew 8:28–34; Luke 8:26–39; IV Mark 5:11; IV Luke 8:33

All the synoptic Gospels report this miracle, but John excludes it. Mark and Luke give similar reports; Matthew condenses his account and reports two demoniacs, while the others report only one.[42]

The exact location of this miracle is difficult to determine. Mark and Luke record that it took place in the "country of the Gadarenes," Luke adding, "which is over against Galilee." Matthew notes it was in "the country of the Gergesenes." Scholarly historical writers have differed on the location because of the differences in the scriptural text.[43] Jesus may have come to the east shore of the lake to gain solitude, peace, and rest for His previous day had been very rigorous. This miracle—the last in this series of demoniac miracles—further confirms the supremacy of Jesus over the world of evil spirits.

Immediately upon Christ's arrival, and as "he was come out of the ship," He encountered the demoniac. The detailed description offered by the Synoptics seems to describe the absolute epitome of possession. They described the demoniac in such words as "exceeding fierce," "no man might pass by the way," "dwelling among the tombs," "no man could bind him, no, not with chains," "neither could any man tame him," "cutting himself with stones," "had devils a long time," and "ware no clothes." This was an experience like no other, and the Gospel writers emphasized it. This was also a very public miracle, and Jesus placed no restrictions on its being recounted; in fact, just the opposite as we shall see.

The demoniac had been possessed for some time and lived in the tombs. These tombs—described as "being either natural caves or recesses artificially hewn out of the rock, often so large as to be supported with columns, and with cells upon their sides for the reception of the dead"[44]—the Jews associated with the dwelling place of possessed persons and those who were unclean.[45]

The man lived naked, as a wild man, and the people were genuinely afraid of him. All those in the area knew of the demoniac, and no one doubted that he was possessed. He could not be controlled and had broken chains and fetters into pieces. This is the man that met Jesus as He disembarked from the ship.

The possessed man ran to Jesus and fell down and worshipped Him. The reaction was plain and simple. From the example of the unclean spirit in Capernaum, it is evident that the evil spirits immediately recognized Jesus and were drawn to Him, even though they dreaded His presence. The possessed man had no foreknowledge of Jesus or His works. The physical circumstances of his possession precluded that. He lived alone in the tombs, and the power of the demons over him was inexorable and so complete that his actions, perhaps for years, had been completely controlled by those who possessed him. The Gospel writers report that there were many evil spirits involved in this possession, and their control dominated the man's miserable existence.

The scriptural accounts next record a unique and interesting experience. Jesus and the evil spirit converse. Unlike His silencing of the evil spirit at Capernaum, where the Lord refused to allow open testimony of His divine calling by inhabitants of Satan's evil kingdom, He now permits conversation. The evil spirit openly acknowledges Him. "What have I to do with thee, Jesus, thou Son of the most high God?" he cries out. Jesus does not forbid the testimony. The accusation contained within the Beelzebub argument could never again be substantiated. The evil spirit had recognized Christ as the Son of God, even if the people themselves did not. The demon then begs the Lord, "I adjure thee by God, that thou torment me not." Another account reports it as saying, "Art thou come hither to torment us before the time?" Perhaps both remarks were made, and perhaps from different evil spirits. Again the comment goes unrebuked.

The Lord then continues the conversation. The demons will not be allowed to remain in the man. He commands them to come out of him and asks their name. This was not a stage healing. The evil spirits knew the Son of God and knew they could not stay in the body of him whom they had possessed for many years. The evil spirit responded and declared,

"My name is Legion: for we are many." There were clearly many evil spirits involved in this possession. Exactly how many is undetermined and unimportant, but they were all in control of this one unfortunate man.

Answering Christ's question with as much arrogance as he could, Luke reports that the evil spirit continued and "besought him that he would not command them to go out into the deep." Mark wrote that the plea was to "not send them away out of the country."

The Jews believed that certain countries were assigned to evil spirits and certain to good spirits. Once assigned to such a place, a spirit could not pass beyond its boundaries.[46] The "deep," or "abyss," as it is sometimes translated, was that referred to by John in Revelation as the "bottomless pit."[a] From our knowledge of the final disposition of the devil and his angels and all those who follow him in this life, this "bottomless pit" would refer to "outer darkness," the final and last place reserved for those evil spirits.[47] They knew that they must eventually be consigned to this place, but they begged Jesus not to send them there "before the time."

Now for the final episode of the conversation. Apparently, a herd of swine was grazing nearby. The evil spirits "besought him, saying, Send us into the swine." The wording differs slightly in the Gospel accounts, but the meaning is clear. They knew that their stay in the man was over, and rather than not possess *any* body, they preferred to inhabit the bodies of the swine. Jesus "gave them leave," and they pressed their influence upon the swine.

Did they physically enter the bodies of the swine? It is clear that the Gospel narrators wanted to leave that impression, for they say that the spirits "entered into the swine." However, whether the spirit bodies of the evil spirits entered and possessed the physical bodies of the swine is of no particular consequence, for the evil spirits' influence on the swine is amply attested to. In addition, the scripture testifies of the evil spirits' obsessive desire to exercise control over any body rather than none.[48]

The swine, which numbered two thousand, were not accustomed to such evil influence and ran violently to their deaths in the sea. The evil spirits were reduced to that spirit existence from whence they came, to await the final judgment and their total banishment to outer darkness.

Those who witnessed this episode did not react unusually. The reports state that they were afraid, and no wonder! These were su-

a. Revelation 9:1.

perstitious people. Jesus, whom they knew not, had been talking with a known demoniac, and then had cast the demons out of the man and allowed them to wreak their influence upon the swine, which promptly went berserk and plunged to their death in the sea. The witnesses ran to the nearby cities and told the story. Others came to see for themselves. What they saw was as astonishing to them as were the circumstances that brought it about. The demoniac was now calm, dressed, and sitting by Jesus, undoubtedly giving thanks to Him who had released him from his torment.

Fear spread through them. Witnesses rehearsed to them all that had occurred, but to them it was incomprehensible. They could not understand this event and its significance. They could not comprehend the recovered soul now at Jesus' feet and the reasons for the dead swine. They were terribly frightened and were not knowledgeable of the Messiah and His work. Thus, they reacted quite normally under the circumstances. They asked Jesus to leave.

The Lord obliged them and prepared to depart. The demoniac, so recently relieved of his torture, requested permission to go with Him to become a disciple; but Jesus said no. The purpose of the miracle demanded that he stay. The absolute relationship between Jesus and the evil spirits of that world controlled by Beelzebub, the prince of devils, had been revealed. There was no question about who was subservient to whom. The evil spirits were totally subject to the will of Christ. The Beelzebub argument had been forever destroyed.

The restored demoniac was told to remain in his land and to tell the inhabitants about the great things the Lord had done for him. He was to be an instrument in the Lord's work. First, he would testify of the great miracle; the people could not refute it, for he was well known, and his testimony would glorify the Messiah. Second, he would become a forerunner and would lay the groundwork among the inhabitants of his country for a greater reception of the Lord later on.

The man did as he was bid and departed, and "began to publish in Decapolis how great things Jesus had done for him." As a result, "all men did marvel." In the future, Christ would return to this area.[a] The people would then no longer request that He leave, but would bring their sick from the entire region and would seek His healing power, and He would openly grant it to them.

a. Mark 6:53–56.

The Result
of Verbal Claims

4

Passing Unseen (Before the Resurrection)

Luke 4:28–30   And all they in the synagogue, when they heard these things, were filled with wrath, and rose up, and thrust him out of the city, and led him unto the brow of the hill whereon their city was built, that they might cast him down headlong. But he passing through the midst of them went his way.

John 8:59   Then took they up stones to cast at him: but Jesus hid himself, and went out of the temple, going through the midst of them, and so passed by.

John 10:39   Therefore they sought again to take him: but he escaped out of their hand.

This is a unique miracle. It is not performed on anyone in particular, yet all in the vicinity are subject to it. "Passing unseen" describes incidents wherein Jesus was either not seen or not recognized, even though He was in the midst of people who knew Him. The examples of this miracle are divided into two categories: those that occurred before and those that occurred after the Resurrection (Chapter 12).

There are three separate occurrences of this miracle before the Resurrection. The setting for each of these situations is similar. Jesus delivers a sermon and the sermon leads to the conclusion that He is the Son of God, the promised Messiah. In each instance, the rulers of the Jews and others in the audience recognize His claim, become enraged, and seek to kill Him. The miracle prevents them from accomplishing their intent.

The miracles of Jesus generally taught and testified of His divine calling; however, in these particular miracles it is not through the miracle itself that this is done. Here His sermons claim the Messiah-ship, and the miracle protects Him from the crowd's angry reactions to those open claims.

A brief review of the sermons delivered prior to each unseen passing will help clarify the necessity and magnitude of the miracle. These sermons directly proclaim Jesus as the Messiah.

Luke 4:16–30. The first of these marvelous expositions takes place early in the Lord's ministry and is recorded by Luke. Jesus had returned to Nazareth, the place of His childhood. He was among the people who knew Him as Jesus the carpenter, the son of Joseph and Mary. It was a Sabbath, and He was preparing to give a personal witness of His divinity to these hometown people. He would give this witness in the acceptable and traditional manner of the Jews: in the synagogue where the scribes, Pharisees, teachers, and rabbis gathered to teach and expound their religion to the people.[49]

Jesus stood up to read, the prescribed method for teaching in the synagogue. He was passed the book of the prophet Isaiah. He turned to what in our Bible is the sixty-first chapter and read verses one and two. It was a recognized Messianic passage. Upon completing the short reading He sat down, which was the signal that He was about to preach on the text He had read.

All eyes were fastened on Him. He had performed many miracles before this time and His fame had preceded Him to Nazareth. However, His explanation of the passage was totally unexpected. He did not give a lengthy dissertation, but merely said, "This day is this scripture fulfilled in your ears." He had told them that He was the Messiah. They had heard of His wonders, His miracles, His mighty deeds, and now He openly declared that He was the Messiah they looked for. The people were stunned. Never had such a message been delivered in any synagogue in Israel. Luke's narrative describes their first response as wonder at "the gracious words."

Normally, the audience would have quickly discussed the teacher's comments among themselves and prepared to ask questions. But instead of inquiring about spiritual matters, they asked, "Is not this Joseph's son?" By this question they were rejecting the scriptural claim. They personally knew Jesus and thus reasoned that He could not be the Messiah. Jesus responded, "No prophet is accepted in his own country" and continued with two pointed and significant analogies. He first recounted Elijah's rejection by the chosen people and reminded His audience that Sidon, a gentile city, accepted and cared for him. He then referred to Naaman, a Gentile, and pointed out that there were many lepers in Israel, but only Naaman was healed.

These examples filled the listeners with wrath. They knew His meaning in both instances. He had claimed to be the Messiah, and they had rejected Him. He then compared their rejection of Him to Elijah's rejection by ancient Israel, and reminded them that Naaman's faith in God's word was more than that of the chosen people. Thus, Jesus accused them of being faithless and rejecting the chosen one of God. They rose up and "thrust him out of the city."[50] They did not care about their Sabbath law on this occasion, or any other law. They led Him to a nearby hilltop with the malicious intent of killing Him. They were going to "cast him down headlong" for what He had said. It was then that the miracle occurred. In the scripture it is almost neglected: "But he passing through the midst of them went his way." His time had not yet come. The bewilderment of the enraged crowd, though not recorded, must have been just as maddening as the circumstances that had brought them there, for He to whom this anger was directed was no longer among them.

John 8:1–59. John records both the remaining miracles in this category and the circumstances that led to them. The first is in John, Chapter 8.[51] Jesus had gone to the temple and had sat down to teach, as was the custom. The scheming scribes and Pharisees brought to Him a woman who had been taken in adultery, apparently to ensnare Him in some judgmental controversy of their law. He confounded them by requiring that "he that is without sin among you, let him first cast a stone at her." The accusers left. He dismissed the woman and admonished her to "sin no more."

But the Jewish leadership was relentless. They returned to speak more with Him. Christ testified of His relationship with His Father, and they rejected that relationship, though not misunderstanding it. "We [are] Abraham's seed" and "Abraham is our father," they cried to Him. Their response clearly indicated that they understood what Christ was saying. He had told them that God was His Father, and they had rejected it. He then perceived their thoughts and said, "But now ye seek to kill me." To their thinking He had blasphemed, and that meant death. Jesus renounced them, saying, "Ye are of your father the devil." Their intended sin of murder had condemned them.

Jesus again offered them spiritual clarity and eternal salvation. He told them that if they would yet believe, they should never see death. They responded by accusing Jesus of self-righteousness: "Art thou greater than our father Abraham, which is dead? and the prophets are dead: whom makest thou thyself?" Can there be any doubt that they understood?

Jesus continued expounding more on the relationship between Him and His Father and declared, "Your father Abraham rejoiced to see my day: and he saw it, and was glad." By these words He clearly told them that in vision Abraham had seen and foretold the Savior's time, and had rejoiced at it.

Then in irreverent arrogance they responded, "Thou art not yet fifty years old, and hast thou seen Abraham?" Recognizing their contempt, Jesus openly declared, "Verily, verily, I say unto you, Before Abraham was, I am." This was clear: there could be no mistake. Moses, the great lawgiver, had asked the Lord what to tell the children of Israel that would prove to them that he represented their God. "What is his name?" he had asked. "I AM THAT I AM," Jehovah had responded. "Thus shalt thou say unto the children of Israel, I AM hath sent me unto you."[a] That same Jehovah was now upon the earth as the Messiah. This name and title of Jehovah (the Messiah) would have been readily recognized by the rulers of Israel. Thus, the King James rendering of Christ's statement could correctly read, "Verily, verily, I say unto you, Before Abraham, was I AM."[52]

Jesus had declared His Messiahship openly to this hostile crowd. Their reaction was deliberate. "Then took they up stones to cast at him." The evil He had discerned and perceived in their hearts now came out openly. They wanted to kill Him. But again the miracle occurred: "Jesus hid himself, and went out of the temple, going through the midst of them, and so passed by." He did not hide from them and wait until they were gone. He passed unseen through their midst.

John 10:1–42. The final incident is recorded in John, Chapter 10.[53] Known generally as the Good Shepherd sermon, this is the most explicit of the confrontations between Christ and the Pharisees. The sermon is in two parts. The description of Christ as the shepherd and Israel as the sheep takes place in the first part of the sermon. Although important doctrinally and as background to the miracle, it is not this material that leads to the miracle. The miracle results from the second part of the sermon and the discussion that takes place between Jesus and the Pharisees.

Jesus was walking in the temple in the court called Solomon's porch when the Jews came to Him and asked, "How long dost thou make us to doubt? If thou be the Christ, tell us plainly." Jesus was near the end of His ministry and would soon make His triumphant entry into Jerusalem. He had been ministering to them for almost three years. He had performed multitudes of miracles and testified to them many times. He had told them that He was the Christ. They had developed every means of diluting and rejecting His claim, yet because He was the Christ, the inner agony resulting from that rejection persisted in their minds and hearts. And so they requested of Him candidly, "If thou be the Christ, tell us plainly."

The Lord's response was simple and just as pointed as the question. "I told you, and ye believed not." He continued: "The works that I do in my Father's name, they bear witness of me." Jesus repeated the analogy of the sheep and the shepherd, stating that His sheep hear His voice. He bore testimony that His Father had verified His works, and He concluded by stating, "I and my Father are one." He had again claimed the Messiahship. He had specifically been asked and had specifically answered.

The reaction was as before. "Then the Jews took up stones again to stone him." They would not have Him as their Messiah. Jesus avoided the crowd's contention with a question: "Many good works have I shewed you from my Father; for which of those works do ye stone me?" They cited blasphemy as the reason: "because that thou, being a man, makest thyself God." They understood His claim perfectly, but refused to believe. In His final attempt to win them over, He concluded, "Say ye of him, whom the Father hath sanctified, and sent into the world, Thou blasphemest; because I said, I am the Son of God? If I do not the works of my Father, believe me not. But if I do, though ye believe not me, believe the works: that ye may know, and believe, that the Father is in me, and I in him."

It was too much. Their request for a plain answer had been fulfilled; indeed, the answer could not have been more plainly stated, yet they still would not accept it. "Therefore they sought again to take him: but he escaped out of their hand," and again passed unseen.

Jesus openly declared His Messiahship to the rulers of Israel: first, as the fulfillment of prophecy; second, by the recognition of His position and name; and third, by open declaration. Although the rulers recognized all three instances, they would have no part of Him. They wanted to kill Him, but His time was not yet; therefore, He passed unseen from their midst before their murderous desires could be fulfilled.[54]

Miraculous Conclusions   5

The Impotent Man at the Pool of Bethesda

John 5:1–16   After this there was a feast of the Jews; and Jesus went up to Jerusalem. Now there is at Jerusalem by the sheep market a pool, which is called in the Hebrew tongue Bethesda, having five porches. In these lay a great multitude of impotent folk, of blind, halt, withered, waiting for the moving of the water. For an angel went down at a certain season into the pool, and troubled the water: whosoever then first after the troubling of the water stepped in was made whole of whatsoever disease he had. And a certain man was there, which had an infirmity thirty and eight years. When Jesus saw him lie, and knew that he had been now a long time in that case, he saith unto him. Wilt thou be made whole? The impotent man answered him, Sir, I have no man, when the water is troubled, to put me into the pool: but while I am coming, another steppeth down before me. Jesus saith unto him, Rise, take up thy bed, and walk. And immediately the man was made whole, and took up his bed, and walked: and on the same day was the sabbath.

The Jews therefore said unto him that was cured, It is the sabbath day: it is not lawful for thee to carry thy bed. He answered them, He that made me whole, the same said unto me, Take up thy bed, and walk. Then asked they him, What man is that which said unto thee, Take up thy bed, and walk? And he that was healed wist not who it was: for Jesus had conveyed himself away, a multitude being in that place. Afterward Jesus findeth him in the temple, and said unto him, Behold, thou art made whole: sin no more, lest a worse thing come unto thee. The man departed, and told the Jews that it was Jesus, which had made him whole. And therefore did the Jews persecute Jesus, and sought to slay him, because he had done these things on the sabbath day.

This is the first of three miracles discussed in this chapter. They were very public miracles, granted to people with well-known illnesses, and they confronted the religious leadership with the specific concept that Jesus was the Son of God.

John records that Jesus was at Jerusalem attending one of the feasts. John does not name the feast, nor is the current location of the pool known.[55]

John describes the pool as having a "great multitude of impotent folk, of blind, halt, [and] withered" around it. He was obviously describing a well-known area in Jerusalem. Not a "few" people surrounded the pool, but "a multitude." "Porches" had been constructed around three sides of the pool (undoubtedly constructed out of charity) to give some comfort to those who visited it, but the people were unattended. Israel's leaders, long ago charged with the care of such people, seemed to have ignored these poor folk. The pool and its inhabitants may well have been selected by the Lord to represent the spiritually impoverished condition of Israel. In the mysticism surrounding the water itself lies the evidence of this condition. Those who waited did so for the water to be "troubled," apparently due to some physical condition of the water, probably a warm natural spring.[56] The water moved, or was "troubled," in an irregular pattern.

Verse 4 assists in the application of the preceding verses to Israel's spiritual condition. The superstition was that "an angel went down at a certain season into the pool, and troubled the water." Such superstitions were common in that day. The Jews believed in many kinds of angels, and all that was unexplained was attributed to the supernatural.[57] The people believed that once the pool was "troubled," "whosoever then first after the troubling of the water stepped in was made whole of whatsoever disease he had." This superstition would have developed naturally from the one that attributed the water's movement to angelic interference.

Israel's leaders had ignored the folk at the pool for a long time. The temple, the very symbol of Israel's favored position before God, was nearby. But the temple, with its formalism and indifference, was no longer representative of God's mercy to Israel. And there is no doubt that the following elements of the temple's glory no longer existed:

> The Holy of Holies was quite empty, the ark of the covenant, with the cherubim, the tables of the law, the book of the covenant, Aaron's rod that budded, and the pot of manna, were no longer in the sanctuary. The fire that had descended from

heaven upon the altar was extinct. What was far more solemn, the visible presence of God in the Shechinah[58] was wanting. Nor could the will of God be ascertained through the Urim and Thummim, nor even the high-priest be anointed with the holy oil, its very composition being unknown. Yet all the more jealously did the Rabbis draw lines of fictitious sanctity, and guard them against all infringement.[59]

The attitude of the folk at the pool and the temple leaders who allowed such an attitude to exist was the true evidence that the superstition of the "troubled pool" held by the people and the religious fanaticism engendered by the temple could exist side by side, both evidence of a false belief and worship.[60]

This miracle was not a frontal attack on the law—that would come later. However it contrasted for the rulers and keepers of the law the purity and charity of the true kingdom of God with their own dead religion. Although the reason for Jesus selecting this one man is not specifically recorded, it would appear that in him and his circumstance Jesus found the symbol that most accurately mirrored Israel's condition.

The impotent man "had an infirmity thirty and eight years." This length of time prevented any question of the authenticity of the miracle, but even this could have symbolized Israel's longstanding plight. Jesus spoke to the man at the pool with comfort and consolation. Yet His question—"Wilt thou be made whole?"—may seem almost superfluous.

Waiting as he had those many years, the impotent man was undoubtedly watching the water with intensity and may not have even noticed Jesus. His answer indicated his only concern (even though his healer stood before him). "I have no man," he stated, "to put me into the pool." The man, like Israel, was so intent upon a false hope that he did not (or could not) see salvation embodied in Christ's presence. The man may have thought that here was one that would help him into the pool at its next movement. His deep despair is echoed in his further response and plea: "While I am coming, another steppeth down before me." He displayed the anguish of one who had tried many times but was unable to reach his goal. The water would move and he would attempt, in his superstition, to enter the water first. But others, less afflicted, would rush in before him, leaving him to wait for yet another movement of the pool. He did not realize that true healing was not to be found in the pool's water.

The Lord in His compassion commanded the impotent man, "Rise, take up thy bed, and walk." The man knew not who Jesus was and had no knowledge of His intentions. But he responded to the command without hesitation. The infirm immediately became firm, and he took up his bed and walked. Now Israel's rulers could respond to the question, "Wilt thou be made whole?"

Significantly, this miracle took place on the Sabbath. The Jews intercepted the man carrying his bed and questioned him. They did not rejoice in his miraculous healing, for they were more concerned with the law. The man defended his actions by stating that He who had healed him had told him to carry the bed, thus removing himself from the vengeance of the Sabbath protectors. Their concern now turned to the man who had performed this miracle. Their religious fanaticism prevented them from understanding either the healed man's previous cries for help or his current expression of praise and joy. But the man did not know who had healed him and Jesus had moved on, perhaps to avoid the confrontation between the man and the watchful Jews and to avoid the inevitable excitement of the miracle. Thus, the man could not see or identify Him.

Jesus did not allow His compassion for this man to go without proper spiritual attention. The man went to the temple, perhaps to give thanks, and Jesus found him there. The Lord told him he had been "made whole," to assure the man that his healing was complete. But He imparted a solemn warning: "Sin no more, lest a worse thing come unto thee." It appears that the man's affliction had been caused by his own actions; or perhaps his inability to get well had been hindered by his unfaithfulness. Regardless of the explanation, the man was admonished for contributing to his own sickness and was warned not to continue lest some worse affliction befall him.

At this point the man knew his benefactor. He immediately went to the Jewish leaders and told them; his reasons for doing so are not expressed. He may have felt some pressure because of the previous accusation against him by the rulers, but it would seem illogical to ascribe evil intent to his action. He had just been miraculously healed—physically and spiritually—after suffering thirty-eight years with both handicaps. In addition, he had been warned by one whose power he could not doubt that further evil would have even more serious consequences. Further, his very words seem to preclude such a conclusion. He told them "that it was Jesus, which had made him whole." Apparently he did not report that Jesus had told him to take up his bed, but only that He had healed him. Perhaps he hoped that they, too, might praise Him.

But this was not to be. After finding out that Jesus had performed this miracle, they ignored the healed man altogether. They persecuted Christ and "sought to slay him, because he had done these things on the sabbath day." The miracle produced only anger and rejection in the Jewish leadership and further emphasized their spiritual darkness. As a response to their murderous intentions, Jesus told them, "My Father worketh hitherto, and I work."[a] The Jewish rulers recognized the comparison immediately, and "sought the more to kill him, because he not only had broken the sabbath, but said also that God was His Father, making himself equal with God."[b] With the rulers before Him (brought there by the miracle), Jesus testified to His divine relationship with the Father and to His own works, including His Messiahship. His testimony was directed specifically to the rulers of Israel, pointed and self-fulfilling.

The response of the Jewish leaders only illustrated more vividly their failure to recognize the Master. The glory of the healer and His compassion was lost in the pompous observance of their perverted law. The impotent man at the pool had not recognized the Savior when He first spoke with Him any more than Israel's leaders did now.

Through this miracle, Jesus once more offered to save the soul of Israel. He could have performed sign upon sign, day after day, until the leaders either tired of signs or ultimately believed. But the signs were merely the evidence of His presence among them. To recognize Him required faith, and they lacked that faith. This impotent man's affliction mirrored Israel's. He exemplified the contrast between the kingdom of the Jews and the kingdom of God. Healing the impotent man was a significant example of Christ's compassion, but his was not a happenstance healing. It was a sign to be recognized and acknowledged.[61]

a. John 5:17.
b. John 5:18.

The One Sick of the Palsy

Mark 2:1–12   And again he entered into Capernaum, after some days; and it was noised that he was in the house. And straightway many were gathered together, insomuch that there was no room to receive them, no, not so much as about the door: and he preached the word unto them. And they come unto him, bringing one sick of the palsy, which was borne of four. And when they could not come nigh unto him for the press, they uncovered the roof where he was: and when they had broken it up, they let down the bed wherein the sick of the palsy lay. When Jesus saw their faith, he said unto the sick of the palsy, Son, thy sins be forgiven thee. But there were certain of the scribes sitting there, and reasoning in their hearts. Why doth this man thus speak blasphemies? who can forgive sins but God only? And immediately when Jesus perceived in his spirit that they so reasoned within themselves, he said unto them, Why reason ye these things in your hearts? Whether is it easier to say to the sick of the palsy, Thy sins be forgiven thee; or to say, Arise, and take up thy bed, and walk? But that ye may know that the Son of man hath power on earth to forgive sins, (he saith to the sick of the palsy,) I say unto thee, Arise, and take up thy bed, and go thy way into thine house. And immediately he arose, took up the bed, and went forth before them all; insomuch that they were all amazed, and glorified God, saying, We never saw it on this fashion.

Cross-references   Matthew 9:18; Luke 5:17–26; JST Matthew 9:2, 5; JST Mark 2:3, 7; JST Luke 5:23–24

This miracle was performed in Capernaum, a city that Christ later said would be "brought down to hell" because it had rejected the many mighty miracles that had been performed there.[a]

The circumstances of this miracle are quite different from those surrounding the healing of the impotent man by the pool. A comparison of the two is enlightening.

Impotent Man by the Pool	The One Sick of the Palsy
• Jesus seeks the man out	• The man seeks Jesus out
• Long illness	• Long illness
• No foreknowledge of Jesus	• Knows of and believes in Jesus
• Believes in the superstition that the pool can heal him	• Believes Jesus can heal him
• Man questioned by rulers	• Jesus perceives thoughts of questioning rulers
• Physical healing first	• Spiritual healing first
• Spiritual healing private	• Spiritual healing public

a. Matthew 11:23–24.

Impotent Man by the Pool	**The One Sick of the Palsy**
• Physical healing public	• Physical healing public
• Jesus claims verbally to be the Son of God	• Jesus forgives sins and thus claims to be equal with God
• Miracle leads into teaching	• Miracle confirms teaching

The miracle is recorded in all three synoptic Gospels; however, Mark will serve as the primary text.

Jesus had come to Capernaum several days before this miracle occurred, and it was "noised" about that He was there. The miracles Jesus had previously performed at Capernaum and elsewhere had by now made Him famous. On this particular day, "straightway many were gathered together." Jesus was teaching, and many of the Jewish rulers were present. Mark and Matthew refer to them as scribes, while Luke identifies them as Pharisees and doctors of the law. Many of the common people were also present, such that "there was no room to receive them, no, not so much as about the door." The house could not hold all who wanted to hear, and they spilled out into the yard so that none could gain entry. No specifics on what Jesus was teaching are given. The scripture merely states that He preached the word unto them. Undoubtedly, He would have been teaching about the kingdom of God and its requirements.[62] But regardless of His subject matter, His preaching did not conclude in an ordinary manner.

Four good-hearted people were coming to Jesus carrying on a litter or bed one that was "sick of the palsy." They had heard that Jesus was there and wanted to get their friend (whose soul was sick as well as his body) to Jesus. Upon arriving at the house, they could see that entrance through the door was impossible. Undaunted, they chose an alternative method of reaching Jesus. The house (typical of the construction at the time) would have had a staircase in the rear leading to the roof. They proceeded to climb the stairs.[63] The four bearing the palsied man knew in which area Jesus was teaching. They immediately took their burden to the roof and commenced tearing a hole in the ceiling area. The intensity of their determination is revealed as the story unfolds. One can imagine that as the four began to open a hole in the roof, Jesus would have stopped speaking. All eyes would have focused on the noise overhead, but Jesus would not have been offended at the disturbance. To the contrary, such determination could only be commended and rewarded. After uncovering the roof, the four "let down the bed wherein the sick of the palsy lay." One can visualize those immediately around Jesus helping to steady the bed as it came through the roof and was lowered to the floor. The four had accomplished their goal.

The scriptures do not record whether the man with the palsy said anything. Perhaps after entering the house in such a spectacular manner, he was, for the moment, left speechless. But Jesus did not need to have him voice his request. His determination and ingenuity showed that he wanted to be healed. Jesus recognized his faith immediately. Although it is not mentioned specifically, the man with the palsy and those that bore him obviously believed that Jesus could cure him. Even more, they believed that He *would* cure him. Why else go to such an extent to bring him to Jesus? They were rewarded for their faith: the man was cured of both his physical and his spiritual impairments.

As the cure was effected, the man's story ended and the teaching surrounding the miracle began. Jesus had recognized the man's desire and had granted it. But this was not just another miracle. He perceived the thoughts of others in attendance and determined that the healing of this man could be an object lesson for the Pharisees, scribes, and doctors of the law who were watching. He would prove to them again that He was the Son of God.

Without any word from the sick man Jesus said, "Son, thy sins be forgiven thee." The statement was delivered with authority. The words were not a request but a declaration. Immediately the learned and the rulers of the Jews thought and reasoned in their hearts that He had blasphemed. To them, Jesus had usurped the very attributes that they reserved for God alone.

Their law prescribed no form for giving absolution from sin, for God alone held that power.[64] In their minds, Jesus had made a "proclamation of His own sinlessness, and of His kingly dignity as the Messiah."[65] They did not openly acknowledge this, but they must have understood.

Jesus perceived their reasoning "in his spirit." "Why reason ye these things in your hearts?" He asked them, thus deliberately placing before them His claim. He was the Messiah, and they now had the opportunity to either accept or reject Him.

However, the rulers had long since developed ways of getting around the spiritual law in favor of their own needs, and they attempted to do so here. They did not answer at all, but remained silent. Jesus' question had been in response to their thoughts. They undoubtedly continued to reason mentally, perhaps thinking that although to forgive sins was blasphemy, to merely declare forgiveness of sins did not necessarily make it so. In their minds Jesus had sinned gravely, but He had given a "safe" declaration. He could declare the forgiveness of sins, but could not prove that they had been forgiven.

That Christ's enemies so reasoned is not recorded in the scriptures, but Jesus' response indicates its probability. He posed another question, answering again their perceived thoughts: "Is it easier to say to the sick of the palsy, Thy sins be forgiven thee; or to say, Arise, and take up thy bed, and walk?" Jesus would now confirm that He could forgive sins as He continued. "But that ye may know that the Son of man hath power on earth to forgive sins . . . I say unto thee, Arise, and take up thy bed." The sick man responded in the only way he could: "he arose, took up the bed, and went forth before them all." The bed that had been the sign of his disease was now the sign of his cure, and the proof that Jesus was the Messiah.

The Lord's procedure was deliberate. By first forgiving the palsied man's sins and then performing the miracle, He sealed His claim to Godhood. He had the power to forgive sins, for the miracle proved it. His relationship with the Father was exactly as He had represented it, He was the Son of God.

The procedure also implied a relationship between sin and bodily affliction. But all indications point to the Savior's witness to His Messiahship as being the primary purpose of this miracle. That the man wanted to be both spiritually and physically healed may be deduced from Matthew's record. Perhaps, to the man, the sins that tormented his mind were inseparably connected with the disease of his body. Whether they had actually caused the disease or whether the disease was the result of or punishment for sin is left to conjecture.

Through this miracle Jesus demonstrated His power to forgive sin, and He offered irrefutable proof that He was the Messiah. Despite this, the Jewish leaders, before whom the miracle was performed, refused to believe and chose to be blind to the obvious.

The One Born Blind

John 9:1–41   And as Jesus passed by, he saw a man which was blind from his birth. And his disciples asked him, saying, Master, who did sin, this man, or his parents, that he was born blind? Jesus answered, Neither hath this man sinned, nor his parents: but that the works of God should be made manifest in him. I must work the works of him that sent me, while it is day: the night cometh, when no man can work. As long as I am in the world, I am the light of the world. When he had thus spoken, he spat on the ground, and made clay of the spittle, and he anointed the eyes of the blind man with the clay, and said unto him, Go, wash in the pool of Siloam, (which is by interpretation, Sent.) He went his way therefore, and washed, and came seeing.

The neighbours therefore, and they which before had seen him that he was blind, said, Is not this he that sat and begged? Some said, This is he: others said, He is like him: but he said, I am he. Therefore said they unto him, How were thine eyes opened? He answered and said, A man that is called Jesus made clay, and anointed mine eyes, and said unto me, Go to the pool of Siloam, and wash: and I went and washed, and I received sight. Then said they unto him, Where is he? He said, I know not.

They brought to the Pharisees him that aforetime was blind. And it was the sabbath day when Jesus made the clay, and opened his eyes. Then again the Pharisees also asked him how he had received his sight. He said unto them, He put clay upon mine eyes, and I washed, and do see. Therefore said some of the Pharisees, This man is not of God, because he keepeth not the sabbath day. Others said, How can a man that is a sinner do such miracles? And there was a division among them. They say unto the blind man again, What sayest thou of him, that he hath opened thine eyes? He said, He is a prophet. But the Jews did not believe concerning him, that he had been blind, and received his sight, until they called the parents of him that had received his sight. And they asked them, saying, Is this your son, who ye say was born blind? how then doth he now see? His parents answered them and said, We know that this is our son, and that he was born blind: but by what means he now seeth, we know not; or who hath opened his eyes, we know not: he is of age; ask him: he shall speak for himself. These words spake his parents, because they feared the Jews: for the Jews had agreed already, that if any man did confess that he was Christ, he should be put out of the synagogue. Therefore said his parents, He is of age; ask him. Then again called they the man that was blind, and said unto him, Give God the praise: we know that this man is a sinner. He answered and said, Whether he be a sinner or no, I know not: one thing I know, that, whereas I was blind, now I see. Then said they to him again, What did he to thee? how opened he thine eyes? He answered them, I have told you already, and ye did not hear: wherefore would ye hear it again? will ye also be his disciples? Then they reviled him, and said, Thou art his disciple; but we are Moses' disciples. We know that God spake unto Moses: as for this fellow, we know not from whence he is. The man answered and said unto them, Why herein is a marvellous thing, that ye know not from whence he is, and yet he hath opened mine eyes. Now we know that God heareth not sinners: but if any man be a worshipper of God, and doeth his will, him he heareth. Since the world began was it not heard that any man opened the eyes of one that was born blind. If this man were not of God, he could do nothing. They answered and said unto him, Thou wast altogether born in sins, and dost thou teach us? And they cast him out. Jesus heard that they had cast him out; and when he had found him, he said unto him, Dost thou believe on the Son of God? He answered and said, Who is he, Lord, that I might believe on him? And Jesus said unto him, Thou hast both seen him, and it is he that talketh with thee. And he said, Lord, I believe. And he worshipped him.

And Jesus said, For judgment I am come into this world, that they which see not might see; and that they which see might be made blind. And some of the Pharisees which were with him heard these words, and said unto him, Are we blind also? Jesus said unto them, If ye were blind, ye should have no sin: but now ye say, We see; therefore your sin remaineth.

Cross-reference   JST John 9:4, 32

This is the final miracle of this series. In some respects, the miracle is a combination of the previous two. For the rulers, it encompassed all the difficulties of Jesus healing the one sick of the palsy and the explicitness of His healing the impotent man at the pool. The miracle occurred in Jerusalem after the Feast of Tabernacles. Jesus sent His brethren to the feast a day before He arrived and He went up to the feast "not openly, but as it were in secret."[a] Jesus taught in the temple during the last two days of the feast. The discourses He taught served as a prelude to this miracle and assist in its explanation.

In John, Chapters 5 and 7, Jesus teaches of His relationship with the Father; His "Light of the World" discourse is found in Chapter 8.[66] This miracle offered proof for the claims in the discourses. It would be hard to find a single, more complete miracle coupled with His discourses than this. The miracle contains the following:

1.   All the elements of Jesus' previous claims to the Messiahship.

2.   The dilemma concerning the acceptance or rejection of His claims.

a. John 7:10.

3. The foreshadowing of His future witness, specifically aimed at the Sabbath law (Chapter 6).

Although the following are secondary, the miracle also contains:

4. A reference to the sin-disease-punishment problem.

5. The first open declaration in defense of Jesus before the Jewish leadership.

Jesus had preached for several days at the feast in Jerusalem. His discourses had openly proclaimed Him as the Messiah. He may have performed other miracles during this stay in Jerusalem, but John recorded only this one.

Jesus and His disciples were walking in the city when they saw a beggar. The scripture seems to indicate that the man was well known, and he probably sat daily at this same spot. Justifiably a beggar (because he was blind), he would sit and beg daily for his living, receiving from those who passed by as was required of them to give.[67] This was a Sabbath. The man could not openly beg on this day but could only sit and receive of the kindness of others as they passed and observed his condition.

As they passed, the disciples posed the first of several interesting questions raised by this miracle. They asked Jesus, "Master, who did sin, this man, or his parents, that he was born blind?" Much speculation has arisen from this question. Although the sin-disease-punishment (including physical disabilities and handicaps) relationship has been mentioned in previous miracles, we will now consider it in greater detail.

The controversy arising from this question raises several possibilities, but at least four should be considered:

1. That the offspring himself could commit some transgression that would cause the malady to be present from birth. Obviously this would have to be committed prior to birth.

2. That a sin or sins could be committed by the parents that would cause the offspring to suffer some malady.

3. That neither of the above two situations is applicable, but that

God's divine plan is involved in some way which may or may not be known to us, and this is the cause of the malady. (Apparently this was the explanation in this case.)

4.   That normal and natural consequences of life—the result of man coming to and living upon the earth—may affect man to the extent of producing diseases, disabilities, and handicaps.

Let us discuss each of these possibilities in relation to the scriptures:

(1) That the sin of the unborn offspring caused his disease or disability. The first part of the question seems to indicate that the disciples had some knowledge of pre-earth existence; however, the extent of their knowledge is unknown. The idea that an unborn soul could have sinned may have evolved from existing Jewish teachings and customs. For example, the story of Jacob and Esau in the Old Testament was sometimes used to justify the commonly held belief that a child could commit sin before his birth.[68]

The Jews gave no accurate teachings on this matter at the time of Jesus. Therefore, the question posed by the disciples probably resulted from their incorrect teachings. However, if Jesus had already instructed them on the pre-earth life doctrine, then they may have been requesting clarification on this particular man's circumstances.

There is no question that in the premortal state each individual was capable of obeying or disobeying God's commandments. We know that one-third of the children of God rebelled and were forever punished for this; as a result of that disobedience they could have no physical bodies, and will end up with Satan in outer darkness forever (Chapter 1). This example seemingly verifies that premortal obedience or disobedience may have consequences upon each person's subsequent existence. The problem is to determine situations in which these consequences occur.

(2) The sins of the parents could cause disease or disability in the child. The following quote best explains the ancient Jewish view on this matter (the words are couched as if from the mouth of God): "The good man, if prosperous, was so as the son of a righteous man; while the unfortunate good man suffered as the son of a sinful parent. So, also, the wicked man might be prosperous, if the son of a goodly parent; but if unfortunate, it showed that his parents had been sinners."[69]

The Jews were trained to regard special suffering as necessary or consequential to special sin.[70] Through apostate deviation they determined many situations as consequential to undisclosed or known sin. For example, "up to thirteen years of age a child was considered, as it were, part of his father, and as suffering for his guilt. More than that, the thoughts of a mother might affect the moral state of her unborn offspring, and the terrible apostasy of one of the greatest rabbis had, in popular belief, been caused by the sinful delight his mother had taken when passing through an idol-grove. Lastly, certain special sins in the parents would result in specific diseases in their offspring, and one is mentioned as causing blindness in children."[71]

The question thus posed by the disciples could have been completely Jewish, based on the common view that the merits or demerits of the parent would appear in the children, so the children became the evidence whereby the parents could be judged.[72] The question would have been perfectly normal in Jesus' day, and the disciples may have suspected that the parents' sins could have caused the poor man's predicament. Like the first possibility, this too was rejected by Jesus in the case we are now considering.

Nevertheless, the fact that the actions of parents can cause physical consequences for their children is well documented, and a specific cause of a malady can upon occasion be assigned in these cases. For example, if a mother is involved in drug abuse and her child is born addicted, or if a mother is affected with venereal disease and her child is consequently born blind, the cause-effect relationship is clear. Spiritual violations of God's commandments can also cause consequences for the children, the sins of Noah's contemporaries being a case in point. While the children may suffer such consequences of parental sin, in God's plan the parents and not the children will be punished for that sin, for "men will be punished for their own sins, and not for Adam's [or anyone else's] transgression."[a]

(3) God's providence was the cause. Jesus offered another alternative to the two possibilities raised by the question of the disciples. The man had been born blind for a purpose, that through him the power of God might be made manifest to others. He had been born blind so that Jesus could heal him, thereby verifying and testifying to the Jews that He was their Messiah. But this reason was unknown to the blind

a. Article of Faith 2; 2 Nephi 4:3–6; D&C 68:25.

man prior to his healing. Clearly, only divine knowledge could correctly ascribe this reason to an individual malady.

(4) Normal and natural consequences of life. While God does not decree every malady that each individual mortal is subjected to, the overall plan of salvation (the plan accepted by God's spirit children in the council prior to the earth's creation) included the circumstances that cause these different maladies. As the Creator, God could undoubtedly issue a decree and make all disease, disability, and handicaps disappear. Mortality, however, is by its very nature imperfect and problem oriented. In the plan, sadness is the opposite of happiness; evil contrasts with good; hot opposes cold; and certainly mortality is the opposite of immortality. Mortality implies decay and ultimately death. Within mortality are accidents caused by man's actions that may result in injury. Imperfection means that in the ordinary course of events, mistakes will be made that produce unpleasant results. If all knowledge, all insight, and all reason were available to mankind, traceable patterns could be seen in the causes and results of people's actions. In each occurrence there would appear a sequence of "laws," placed by God in His plan of creation, that would trace each of these occurrences to its ultimate reason or source. This principle is basic to modern science and medicine and by its implementation, some diseases, disabilities, and handicaps have been overcome by man. Undoubtedly others will be in the future, for the potential is always there.

In the final analysis, it seems that most diseases, physical disabilities, and handicaps are the result of natural and normal consequences rather than as a punishment for sin. We may conclude this partly from Luke 13:1–5. Apparently some Galileans had been slain by Roman soldiers at the altar while sacrifices were being offered, and in telling Jesus of this tragic event, those stating it assumed it was caused by the victims' sinfulness. Jesus specifically responded to this: "Suppose ye that these Galileans were sinners above all the Galileans, because they suffered such things? I tell you, Nay." He then recounted another historical example His listeners were familiar with. "Or those eighteen, upon whom the tower in Siloam fell, and slew them, think ye that they were sinners above all men that dwelt in Jerusalem?" Again he answered, "I tell you, Nay." Frequently such life occurrences are beyond any given individual's control and occur as a natural consequence of mortality. Because they are beyond any mortal's control, it is a miracle when one of them is prevented or corrected by the power of God.

Life-limiting and disabling conditions may or may not be caused by sin, and we should not attribute them either to God's will or to the breaking of His laws; it was only the centuries-old apostasy of the Jews that caused them to think this way.

The sin-punishment question has been discussed here in detail because of the obvious questions raised by the disciples' query to Jesus and the inferences drawn from other miracles. This question, however, was not the reason for the miracle. In fact, it was nothing more than a by-product of the historical treatment that has been given this miracle. The question of imputed sin as a reason for the blindness was inconsequential, and was treated as such by Jesus. He merely stated that neither the man nor his parents had sinned. He then proceeded to the miracle itself, the benefit the man received, and more significantly, the witness of His divinity. Jesus "spat" upon the ground, made clay, and anointed the eyes of the blind man. Then He told him to go to the pool of Siloam and wash his eyes; and when he had done so, he "came seeing." The miracle was simple; the witness, more complex. This was a very public miracle, performed on the Sabbath and in a unique way.

Much has been written concerning Jesus' method of effecting this cure. He did not need the spittle or the clay. He did not need to anoint the eyes nor have the man wash in the pool. Further, the cure had nothing to do with the Jewish teaching and belief in their primitive medicinal application of saliva (especially saliva from one fasting) to aid irritation and diseases of the eye.[73] All of these procedures were superfluous to the healing. So why did He do it?

Consider two possible reasons. The first involves the blind man himself. No indication is given that he knew or had even heard of Jesus before the miracle. He apparently learned the Lord's name at some time, for when he was questioned after the restoration of his sight he knew Jesus' name and disclosed this to the Pharisees, but he did not know His whereabouts. The value of Jesus' procedure in this case was found in the increase of the blind man's faith. The physical use of the clay on his sightless eyes may have somehow strengthened his belief in Christ, but it was not the clay that cured him. After the inquisition of the man was complete and he had been excommunicated, Jesus sought him out and asked, "Dost thou believe on the Son of God?" The man, confessing he did not know who the Son of God was, asked, "Who is he, Lord, that I might believe on him?" When Jesus told him it was He, the man worshipped Him. The private benefits of this miracle were now complete for the blind man, resulting in both his physical healing and his spiritual growth.

The second possible reason for the Lord's unique method of healing exposes and illustrates the principal purpose of the miracle. Therein is contained two significant teachings, the first of which is symbolic. The blind man seemingly represented blind Israel; Jesus was the light of the world. The blind man had been given a set of instructions to follow. He followed these instructions completely, and his vision was restored. This simple relationship between the Lord's instructions and the obedience that produces the blessings brings to mind the Old Testament story of Elisha and Naaman. Naaman was told exactly what to do to be cleansed of his leprosy. At first he did not want to do it, but a servant reminded him of his desire to be clean. He then did as he had been instructed, and was healed.[a]

Jesus had told Israel's rulers exactly who He was and how they could prove His claim. The rulers recognized Jesus' claim as the Messiah and knew the procedure necessary to prove Him. All they had to do to receive a witness was follow this procedure, but they refused; that awful, willful blindness of those who will not see controlled their action.

The second teaching revolves around the Sabbath day and how it was observed by the rulers. Jesus made clay, anointed the eyes of the blind man, and instructed him to go and wash in the pool, thus deliberately breaking the Sabbath law that had been established by Israel's rulers. He had confronted the leaders with His claims earlier when He had healed the impotent man and had openly asserted His Messiahship. When He healed the man with the palsy, He placed them in a position of either accepting or rejecting Him, and they remained silent, attempting to avoid the confrontation. But in this miracle, His challenge and position was clear. He once more protested the strictness of the rabbinical observance of the law (which totally destroyed its true significance), thereby proclaiming Himself Lord of the Sabbath. They knew that He had performed the miracle. They could no longer remain silent.[74]

a. 2 Kings 5:1–14.

By breaking their Sabbath law, Jesus opened Himself to a charge that could be sustained against Him. His teachings during the previous days also led to the inevitable conclusion that He was claiming to be the Messiah. But the Jewish leadership was in a dilemma. If they pressed the Sabbath-breaking charge, they would have to admit the validity of the miracle. If they admitted the miracle, they could not portray Christ as the criminal they wanted Him to be.

Their predicament was such that even this unlearned and now healed blind man could confound them. They just could not overcome the fact that Jesus was right and they were wrong. Obviously a miracle had occurred, but they still attempted to discredit it. They first questioned the man and then his parents. They firmly established that he had been blind from birth and could now see. He who was blind called his benefactor a "prophet," but not even this status could be acknowledged by the rulers. Prophets could, under their law, set aside the Sabbath law, and they wanted Jesus to be a violator of the law. If they would not accept Him, there was only one thing left for them to do: they must discredit Him.

To the blind man, the Pharisees accused Jesus. First, they said that He was not from God because He had broken the Sabbath. Second, they declared that He was a sinner. Finally, they boasted that they were Moses' disciples and that they knew "that God spake unto Moses: as for this fellow, we know not from whence he is."

But the recently healed man would not allow this. "Why herein is a marvellous thing," he began, "that ye know not from whence he is, and yet he hath opened mine eyes. Now we know that God heareth not sinners: but if any man be a worshipper of God, and doeth his will, him he heareth. Since the world began was it not heard that any man opened the eyes of one that was born blind. If this man were not of God, he could do nothing."

At this irrefutable argument the leaders became enraged. "Dost thou teach us?" they railed at him, declaring that he was "altogether born in sins." Then they "cast him out." The right was before them; it had been placed in direct contrast with their error, yet they chose to keep the error. They could not succeed in refuting the miracle; they could not blemish the character of Jesus; they could not even refute the unlearned man. In their frustration, they excommunicated the man who had been blind. Jesus found him later in the temple and completed his spiritual healing so that he might have the opportunity to be saved. And the man "worshipped him."

Jesus continued to teach and declared that He had come into the world that "they which see not might see; and that they which see might be made blind." Some Pharisees that were with Jesus heard this and asked, "Are we blind also?" They understood the application. They were saying that they were not blind and could see. But Jesus responded, "If ye were blind, ye should have no sin: but now ye say, we see; therefore your sin remaineth."

Those that previously could not see but accepted the proffered light were heirs of salvation. But those that said they could see and would not, still remained in sin. There are none so blind as those who will not see. The light of the world had come and they had refused Him.

Summary

Through His sermons and discourses, Jesus evidenced His Messiahship to the Jews and their leaders; by healing the impotent man at the pool at Bethesda, the one sick of the palsy, and the man born blind, He irrefutably confirmed it. The three individuals healed by these miracles received great blessings, both physically and spiritually. They would not forget Jesus. But in the divine plan, even the individuals and their healings were eclipsed. These miracles were signs—signs that Jesus was the Messiah. He proclaimed it by His word and sealed the proclamation with His miraculous power. In each instance the Jewish leaders could have proclaimed Jesus their king, but they would not. Centuries of apostasy and modification of the law had corrupted their concept of the Messiah. Christ's miracles placed the rulers of Israel at odds with their expected Savior. They must either reject their error and accept Him, or reject Him and continue in darkness. The light of the world had come to shine in the darkness, but the darkness would not accept it. "We be Abraham's seed," they cried. "We are Moses' disciples"; "as for this fellow, we know not from whence he is." In His sermons the Lord had promised the Jews, "Ye shall know the truth, and the truth shall make you free." But they chose enslavement.

An Appeal to the Law 6

The three miracles discussed in this chapter center on a single theme: that of the Lord openly confronting the bastion of Jewish traditionalism, the Sabbath Law.

Jesus came to His chosen people to claim His rightful place as their Messiah, but the religion they practiced had changed significantly from that of old. Four hundred years had passed since the last of the Old Testament prophets. During the ensuing time, the rabbinical rulers had risen to power. As the Jewish religion evolved without divine prophetic instruction, its principal hold upon the people was "the Law."

There is no way to determine just when the rabbis came into existence. They had developed gradually, probably beginning around the time of Ezra and Nehemiah.[75] Ezra is described as a "ready scribe," one who "had prepared his heart to seek the law of the Lord, and to do it, and to teach in Israel statutes and judgments.[a] The Law of Moses had been altered, lost, or destroyed in the Diaspora and the destruction sustained through numerous wars. From Ezra's efforts and the efforts of others, who had similar intent but less divine instruction, developed the traditional law that governed the Jews when Jesus came.

At the time of Jesus the traditional law was divided into three sections. The first dictated scriptural investigation and contained the ordinances found in the written law. These included eternal laws delivered by Moses. Second was that which was to be observed. This was the "oral law" or the traditional teaching, and was implied in or deduced from the Law of Moses. Third was the oral teaching in the broadest sense. This was "the hedge" placed around the Law by the

Rabbis "to prevent any breach of the Law or customs, to ensure their exact observance, or to meet particular circumstances or dangers." It constituted the "sayings of the Scribes, or of the Rabbis," and traditionally was emphasized more than the written law and canonized each activity of life.[76]

The stronghold of this daily prescription was the Sabbath Law. "Nothing in Judaism had been left unfixed; every religious act, and indeed every act whatsoever, must follow intimately prescribed laws."[77] Jesus selected one particular element of the Sabbath Law to openly challenge—doing good on the Sabbath.

To heal on the Sabbath was strictly forbidden, except to save a life. The Jews had developed intricate procedures for giving medical aid on the Sabbath, and "their fine-spun casuistry had elaborate endless rules for the treatment of all maladies on the sacred day."[78] The Sabbath rules had grown into a law controlling all laws. The daily prescribed laws governing Jewish activities were reemphasized in stricter terms on the Sabbath.

An example of the complexity of Sabbath worship, specifically as it applied to health and sickness, follows:

> We have already seen, that in their view only actual danger to life warranted a breach of the Sabbath-Law. But this opened a large field for discussion. Thus, according to some, disease of the ear, according to some throat-disease, while, according to others, such a disease as angina, involved danger, and superseded the Sabbath-Law. All applications to the outside of the body were forbidden on the Sabbath. As regarded internal remedies, such substances as were used in health, but had also a remedial effect, might be taken, although here also there was a way of evading the Law. A person suffering from toothache might not gargle his mouth with vinegar, but he might use an ordinary toothbrush and dip in vinegar. The Gemara [a book of the Law] here adds, that gargling was lawful, if the substance was afterwards swallowed. It further explains, that afflictions extending from the lips, or else from the throat, inwards, may be attended to, being regarded as dangerous. Quite a number of these are enumerated, showing, that either the Rabbis were very lax in applying

their canon about mortal diseases, or else that they reckoned in their number not a few which we would not regard as such. External lesions also might be attended to, if they involved danger of life. Similarly, medical aid might be called in, if a person had swallowed a piece of glass; a splinter might be removed from the eye, and even a thorn from the body.[79]

Such was the Sabbath at the time of Christ. Concerning this, Jesus instructed His disciples:

Matthew 23:4–8 For they bind heavy burdens and grievous to be borne, and lay them on men's shoulders; but they themselves will not move them with one of their fingers. But all their works they do for to be seen of men: they make broad their phylacteries, and enlarge the borders of their garments, and love the uppermost rooms at feasts, and the chief seats in the synagogues, and greetings in the markets, and to be called of men, Rabbi, Rabbi. But be not ye called Rabbi: for one is your Master, even Christ; and all ye are brethren.

The Lord directly confronted the Law in these three miracles because it was the foundation of Judaism at His time. He, as Jehovah in the Old Testament, had declared the sacredness of the Sabbath day. But the Jews had made a mockery of it. "The sabbath was made for man, and not man for the sabbath," Jesus declared. He was "Lord also of the sabbath."[a]

This declaration concerning the Sabbath resulted from an act of His disciples on the Sabbath. The group was traveling, passing through cornfields as they went. The disciples began "to pluck the ears of corn,"[b] "and to eat,"[c] a lawful act under the Law of Moses.[d][80] Luke adds that the disciples "rubbed" the corn in their hands to separate the kernel from the husk.[e] This was considered "thrashing" and thus was unlawful on the Jewish Sabbath. When the Pharisees saw it (for they constantly watched Jesus to accuse, discredit, or destroy Him), they challenged Jesus, saying, "Behold, thy disciples do that which is not lawful to do upon the sabbath day."[f]

The inquiry, presented as a statement in Matthew and as a question in Mark and Luke, attempted to place Jesus at odds with either the Law or His disciples. The cunning of it reflects the Pharisees' continuous attempt to entrap Jesus, for in their minds He would either be forced to

a. Mark 2:27–28.

b. Mark 2:23.

c. Matthew 12:1.

d. Deuteronomy 23:25.

e. Luke 6:1.

f. Matthew 12:2.

confess that His disciples had transgressed the law or He would have to defend His disciples in their purported transgression.

But Jesus would take neither position. Instead, He justified His disciples' actions as being exempt from the Law and presented two examples to clearly vindicate them. The first example was of David and the showbread.[a] At one time, David and his men had eaten the sacred temple bread and were justified because of their extreme need.

The Lord's second example was even more relevant. The priests involved in the Levitical service did not cease from their work upon the Sabbath. Yet the Pharisees considered them blameless because the work was done in the temple. Lest His accusers resist this example with the argument that He and His disciples were not temple workers, Jesus added, "In this place is one greater than the temple."[b] Thus His disciples were blameless, as were the priests and David, for the needs of their circumstance transcended the Law.

The Jews had made the Sabbath a day of prescribed activity that men observed only in form. The people were obsessed, avoiding transgressions with justified exactness. Likewise, the rulers defined with exactness the slightest potential transgression.

Christ's instructions on the Jewish Sabbath law might well be broadened to include all of their dull, mechanical obedience to every form of the Law. All of God's Law was made for man, not man for the Law. God's Law culminated in man's salvation. Man, in return, was to live the Law out of love for the giver of the Law, not just outwardly observe the Law for the Law's sake. The Law, after all, had been given to prepare Israel for the Messiah. But it had become the end instead of the means. The Jews had turned their devotion to the Law itself, and away from its giver.

Through the following three miracles, Jesus declared the "spirit" as well as the "letter" of the Law. It was the gospel versus the Law as changed by rabbinic embellishment; Christ versus the rabbis. The gospel required a change of heart.[c] The Law required constant instruction, refinement, and arbitration on technical points. The gospel required that each action be made out of charity—the pure love of Christ. Under the Law, each act was to be in strict accordance with specific legal forms. Every detail of Jewish religious observance was prescribed and rigidly followed from the cradle to the grave.[81] In

a. 1 Samuel 21:1–6.

b. Matthew 12:6.

c. Alma 5.

the gospel, man's action was testified to and confirmed by the Holy Ghost. Under the Law, man's inaction (or disobedience) was punished by the court ostracizing him from the community. Judgment, mercy, and faith, "the weightier matters of the law," had been eliminated.[a]

"If ye continue in my word, then are ye my disciples indeed," Jesus said. "And ye shall know the truth, and the truth shall make you free."[b] The truth would free the Jews from the over-legalized Law and allow them to overcome temptations and worldliness and accept Jesus for what He was—the Messiah.

Jesus confronted the Law to provide yet another witness of His Messiahship. This witness was evidenced by each of the following three miracles: the healing of the one with a withered hand, the woman with a spirit of infirmity, and the man with the dropsy.

The One with a Withered Hand

Mark 3:1–6   And he entered again into the synagogue; and there was a man there which had a withered hand. And they watched him, whether he would heal him on the sabbath day; that they might accuse him. And he saith unto the man which had the withered hand, Stand forth. And he saith unto them, Is it lawful to do good on the sabbath days, or to do evil? to save life, or to kill? But they held their peace. And when he had looked round about on them with anger, being grieved for the hardness of their hearts, he saith unto the man, Stretch forth thine hand. And he stretched it out: and his hand was restored whole as the other. And the Pharisees went forth, and straightway took counsel with the Herodians against him, how they might destroy him.

Cross-references   Matthew 12:9–14; Luke 6:6–11

This miracle is recorded by all three of the Synoptics. A minor discrepancy between Matthew's record and that of the other two concerns the question: "Is it lawful to do good on the sabbath days, or to do evil?" Matthew records that the rulers asked the question while Mark and Luke record that Jesus did. Resolution of this minor conflict would seem possible, for Luke records that Jesus "knew their thoughts." It is therefore probable that Matthew, who usually condensed the record, merely combined the question (which was in the minds of the Pharisees and scribes and perceived by Jesus) with the actual asking of the question itself. Either way, the result and purpose of the miracle are unaffected.

Jesus' performance of this miracle intentionally revealed the shallowness of the Law. The Pharisees were "watching him" to see if He would heal the man on the Sabbath. The man's life was not in immediate danger, so such a healing would violate their law.[82] The man was seated in the congregation in the synagogue. It is not recorded whether he was brought there by the Pharisees or by happenstance.

The afflicted man did not request a healing (which also would have been contrary to the Sabbath Law).[83] Jesus called for the man to "stand forth." After perceiving the thoughts of the Pharisees and scribes, He presented a question to the learned men. "Is it lawful to do good on the sabbath days, or to do evil? to save life, or to kill?" His question presented the basis for the miracle. Judaic law dictated that even doing good must be left to other days if it violated the rules of the Sabbath. The Lord's question postulated that if you failed to do good on the Sabbath, especially when the opportunity was specifically presented to you, then you had done evil. Thus the question made doing good not only allowable, but a duty. The cunning, watchful Pharisees and scribes resorted to silence for to answer "no" would condemn them and their law. To say "yes" would approve of what they must have known was about to happen. Again Jesus had placed them in an inextricable position.

Jesus looked "about on them with anger, being grieved for the hardness of their hearts." He told the man to stretch forth his hand; when he did, it "was restored whole as the other." Nothing else is said of the man, which suggests that he was neither the culprit of a plot nor the sole end of the miracle. He was the physical means Jesus used to declare His witness against the Law. Jesus had proclaimed Himself "Lord also of the sabbath." The question and the miracle verified Him as such. Again they must accept or reject Him; there was no alternative. But their Law was now the very obstacle between them and their Messiah. They remained silent, shut their eyes against the truth, and "went forth, and straightway took counsel with the Herodians against him, how they might destroy him."

Christ had broken Jewish tradition and put the Pharisees and scribes to open shame.

The Woman with a Spirit of Infirmity
Luke 13:10–17   And he was teaching in one of the synagogues on the sabbath.

And, behold, there was a woman which had a spirit of infirmity eighteen years, and was bowed together, and could in no wise lift up herself. And when Jesus saw her, he called her to him, and said unto her, Woman, thou art loosed from thine infirmity. And he laid his hands on her: and immediately she was made straight, and glorified God. And the ruler of the synagogue answered with indignation, because that Jesus had healed on the sabbath day, and said unto the people, There are six days in which men ought to work: in them therefore come and be healed, and not on the sabbath day. The Lord then answered him, and said, Thou hypocrite, doth not each one of you on the sabbath loose his ox or his ass from the stall, and lead him away to watering? And ought not this woman, being a daughter of Abraham, whom Satan hath bound, lo, these eighteen years, be loosed from this bond on the sabbath day? And when he had said these things, all his adversaries were ashamed: and all the people rejoiced for all the glorious things that were done by him.

This miracle indicated with power and testimony Christ's position on the Sabbath day issue. He was again teaching in the synagogue on the Sabbath. A woman was present that had "a spirit of infirmity eighteen years." She was bent over and could not straighten herself. She did not request the miracle, but her presence in the synagogue might indicate her personal hope for the Lord's help. Jesus called her to Him and told her that she was loosed from her infirmity. He then laid His hands upon her to perform the miracle. Jesus seldom used this method, but perhaps He did so here to assist the faith of the woman and to instruct the disciples in the method they would later use to exercise the priesthood.[a]

That the woman needed both physical and spiritual healing is evident from the words of Jesus. She was "loosed" from her infirmity, and he said Satan had bound her "these eighteen years."

Again, the Lord would do "good" on the Sabbath. In the case of the one with the withered hand, the Lord communicated His intentions before the miracle; here, the miracle was performed and His counsel followed. After the miracle had taken place, the ruler of the synagogue upbraided the congregation. He was incensed at the "Sabbath breaking," and expressed the thoughts and conclusions of the Pharisees concerning Christ's actions on the Sabbath. "There are six days in which men ought to work," he stated. "In them therefore come and be healed, and not on the sabbath day." This comment was made as if healing was a common occurrence. What the Pharisees and scribes at the healing of the one with the withered hand would not say, this

a. James 5:14–15;
   D&C 42:44.

ruler openly and angrily put forth. Although apparently berating the congregation as a whole, it was obvious that his comments were also directed to the woman and Jesus. Although the woman (perhaps a member of his congregation)[84] had received a great blessing, he could see only an irregularity, a departure from the normal Sabbath worship. He cared not for her healing; he was cold and bound by tradition, a rabbinical pedant.

Jesus again openly confronted the Law as He denounced the ruler's empty formalism. Unusually severe, He responded, "Thou hypocrite, doth not each one of you on the sabbath loose his ox or his ass from the stall, and lead him away to watering?" This was a "daughter of Abraham," he declared, "whom Satan hath bound, lo, these eighteen years." Surely this woman of the covenant should merit as much compassion as those dumb animals.

His adversaries were "ashamed" but unconverted. The people rejoiced, but still could not apply these teachings and recognize their long-awaited Messiah.

The Man with the Dropsy

Luke 14:1–6 And it came to pass, as he went into the house of one of the chief Pharisees to eat bread on the sabbath day, that they watched him. And, behold, there was a certain man before him which had the dropsy. And Jesus answering spake unto the lawyers and Pharisees, saying, Is it lawful to heal on the sabbath day? And they held their peace. And he took him, and healed him, and let him go; and answered them, saying, Which of you shall have an ass or an ox fallen into a pit, and will not straightway pull him out on the sabbath day? And they could not answer him again to these things.

This last of these healing miracles was directed at the Jewish Law and was performed late in the ministry of Jesus. Its circumstances indicate that even at this late date, Jesus had not given up offering the kingdom to the Pharisees. It also indicated that even though He again offered them the kingdom, they had so hardened their hearts against Him that they would not see the obvious.

Jesus had been invited to the home of one of the chief Pharisees to partake of the Sabbath meal. At Jesus' time, the rabbis often used the Sabbath day for social entertainment.[85] The invitation was not abnormal, but it concealed sinister intentions. Luke reports that they "watched him," and it appears that the sole purpose of the invitation was to lure Him to do evil in their eyes.

A man with dropsy was present at the dinner. The scripture does not say whether he had been placed there specifically by the Pharisees to provoke Jesus to yet another healing on the Sabbath or whether he came on his own. These meals were partly for charitable purposes, and the poor and the sick were permitted to come in uninvited and eat.[86] The man might have heard that Jesus was in the home and went to the dinner hoping that the Master would take notice of him and grant his desire.

Jesus brought the man before Him and asked the Pharisees the same question he had asked before. "Is it lawful to heal on the sabbath day?" His purpose was still the same: he would place the kingdom of God and the Messiah in direct confrontation with the Law as the rulers dictated it. And as before, they held their peace. There could be no alternative explanations or answers. Jesus had phrased His Sabbath question in such a manner that it left no such possibility. Rabbinical schools had arisen based on disputes over the Law. But to Jesus, the Law had been meant to lead people to the kingdom of heaven, and only one answer was possible. His question, if answered with a "no," had to be answered before the guests, for the Pharisees were responsible to so instruct those present.[87] But since the answer was obviously "yes," the leaders remained silent lest they in any manner seem to approve or accept Christ. They would not reject the law they held so dear.

Jesus healed the man and "let him go." Whether the man came hoping to be healed or had been invited (not knowing the purpose of the Pharisees) did not matter. He had received the blessing and was excused.

The "chief Pharisee," "perhaps a member of the Great Sanhedrin itself," and the other "prominent and influential"[88] guests, would now be chastened by the Messiah. Jesus had been invited to dine with this group of self-aggrandizing leaders who, as was their tradition, scrambled for places at the table according to reputation and social status.[89] But He disapproved of this social custom. To aspire to the so-called honor of men was not important to Him. To assist "the poor, the maimed, the lame," [and] the "blind" *was* important, "for whosoever exalteth himself shall be abased; and he that humbleth himself shall be exalted."[a]

The teaching example was over. The Jewish leaders could no more accept Christ now than they could earlier. He had given them testimony and example, specifically applied it to the Sabbath Law, and sealed it with a miracle to prove His authority. But still, "they held their peace."

a. Luke 14:11–13.

Selection and Call   7

The First Draught of Fish

Luke 5:1–11   And it came to pass, that, as the people pressed upon him to hear the word of God, he stood by the lake of Gennesaret, and saw two ships standing by the lake: but the fishermen were gone out of them, and were washing their nets. And he entered into one of the ships, which was Simon's, and prayed him that he would thrust out a little from the land. And he sat down, and taught the people out of the ship. Now when he had left speaking, he said unto Simon, Launch out into the deep, and let down your nets for a draught. And Simon answering said unto him, Master, we have toiled all the night, and have taken nothing: nevertheless at thy word I will let down the net. And when they had this done, they inclosed a great multitude of fishes: and their net brake. And they beckoned unto their partners, which were in the other ship, that they should come and help them. And they came, and filled both the ships, so that they began to sink. When Simon Peter saw it, he fell down at Jesus' knees, saying, Depart from me; for I am a sinful man, O Lord. For he was astonished, and all that were with him, at the draught of the fishes which they had taken: and so was also James, and John, the sons of Zebedee, which were partners with Simon. And Jesus said unto Simon, Fear not; from henceforth thou shalt catch men. And when they had brought their ships to land, they forsook all, and followed him.

Cross-references   Matthew 4:18–22; Mark 1:16–20

This section of the book contains the miracles that Christ specifically directed to the Twelve Apostles. Some were performed before their call and some after. These were the men who would live and travel with the Savior throughout His ministry. They were different from those disciples that followed Him generally. They were to lead the church and testify of Him, that others might come to know and believe. The miracles were a special witness to them that Jesus was the Messiah, the promised Savior of the world.

Then, as now, a disciple was someone who elected to follow Jesus and generally believed on His word. They were devoted to Him, but they did not receive the special witness that the Apostles did. The Apostles did not volunteer for their calling. Luke reports that the Lord "continued all night in prayer to God"[a] prior to the selection of the first Twelve. Having selected and called these from His disciples in general, He ordained them to the Apostleship. He reminded them of this special calling in His last instructions to them, given just before His death. "Ye have not chosen me," he said, "but I have chosen you, and ordained you."[b] The call of Apostle is one reserved for the Melchizedek Priesthood, "comprising as a distinguishing function that of personal and special witness to the divinity of Jesus Christ as the one and only Redeemer and Savior of mankind."[90]

At the time of the miracle of the first draught of fish, four of these future, special witnesses were called to follow the Savior: Peter, his brother Andrew, James, and his brother John. Although the selection of the four is mentioned in all three of the synoptic Gospels, only Luke records the miracle.

The call to follow Jesus in His ministry was a sacred experience, and how each of these four men chose to report it may well be reflected in the accounts that have come down to us. While each of the three Synoptics recorded at least some portion of the event, John elected to remain silent about it, as he so often did when he was personally involved in close relationships with the Lord. From the detail that is recorded, it is evident that the experience was an extremely personal and impressive one, causing the deepest soul-searching and commitment.

How well these disciples had known Jesus or followed Him prior to this call is not known. It should be evident from the text and circumstance of the miracle, however, that they certainly knew of Him, and perhaps had even received personal witness of His divine mission.

Although He did not report the calling of the four, John indicates that they had had some association with Jesus before the miracle. He records that the day after the baptism of Jesus, John the Baptist and two of his disciples were standing as Jesus walked by. The Baptist, true to his mission and call, testified, "Behold the Lamb of God."[c] The two disciples followed Jesus. The Lord asked them what they were doing, and they inquired where He was staying. Invited to come and see, they stayed with the Lord that day. John identifies one of these

a. Luke 6:12.

b. John 15:16.

c. John 1:36.

two as Andrew, Peter's brother. The other has always been thought to be John himself.

As the miracle develops, Luke reports that Jesus was teaching by the Lake of Gennesaret, one of His favorite teaching places. The crowd of people "pressed upon him" to hear the word of God. Two empty fishing boats stood by the shore. The fishermen were washing their nets nearby. The ships belonged to Peter, his brother Andrew, and James and John. Jesus went aboard Peter's boat and requested that Peter "thrust out a little from the land." This gained Him some separation from the crowd, allowing the multitude to sit or stand on the shore, that all might see and hear Him as He continued to teach "the people out of the ship." When He had finished the sermon, He requested that Peter "launch out into the deep." Although Jesus had just taught of the kingdom of God from the deck of their boat, Peter and his partners were now to gain a much stronger testimony of Him.

"Let down your nets for a draught," Jesus told Peter. The partners had been fishing all night, possibly in that very area, but had caught nothing. Peter told the Lord of this and continued, "Nevertheless at thy word I will let down the net."

Obviously Peter had confidence in the Lord. Perhaps hearing Christ's sermon had instilled this unquestionable belief, but more probably it was built upon Peter's previous acquaintance with the Lord. His confidence and faith had grown; thus, despite having labored all night in vain, when instructed to do so Peter let down the nets.

This simple act symbolized the Savior's plan for these four fishermen. He would later choose them from among all His disciples to become Apostles, and at least three of them would hold a special position in His eyes, even among the Twelve. Jesus drew these four fishermen to Him just as the fishermen drew in the "multitude of fishes." They cast their nets in, and the catch was so great that the net broke. When they called to their partners, James and John, for help, they gladly came so that they, too, might participate in the catch. There were so many fish that when they took them into the ships, both were filled and began to sink. The future Apostles knew that they were in the presence of one greater than themselves.

Only Peter's reaction to the miracle is recorded. He fell at Jesus' knees saying, "Depart from me; for I am a sinful man, O Lord." Peter and his brethren were frightened at the Lord's display of power. Peter's response was not a sign of weakness or unbelief, nor did Peter desire that the Lord should actually depart from him. Peter had merely expressed his own feelings of personal unworthiness at being in the Lord's presence.

This reaction is not unusual. Moses, Isaiah, Jeremiah, Gideon, Paul, and even John the Revelator are recorded as reacting in much the same way when the Lord called them to serve Him.[a] All these great men expressed their personal unworthiness, yet in no instance was weak faith implied. So it was with Peter. He did not feel worthy to stay in the presence of the Lord, but the Lord would not leave him; he had a great work for Peter and the others to do. In His response to Simon, Christ comforted him and said, "Fear not; from henceforth thou shalt catch men." At that point they brought their ship to shore and the newly called apostles "forsook all, and followed him."

These four fishermen recognized Christ's witness to them through the miracle He performed, and they acknowledged it. The Psalmist had sung of Him: "Thou madest him to have dominion over the works of thy hands; . . . the fowl of the air, and the fish of the sea.[b] Jesus' control over these creatures had received ample witness. He had spoken only to Peter to instruct him to let down his net, yet the "fish of the sea" had gathered that they might be drawn in. In so doing, Jesus had symbolically let down the gospel net, and had brought in four men who would be special witnesses of Him. They would now be fishers of men, to draw in all who would come unto the kingdom of God. A rich man once asked Jesus how to gain eternal life. Jesus enumerated the basic commandments, to which the man openly acknowledged his compliance. The man continued his inquiry: "What lack I yet?" Jesus told him to sell all that he had, give the proceeds to the poor, and follow Him. "But when the young man heard that saying, he went away sorrowful: for he had great possessions."[c]

Not so with the four fishermen. "They forsook all, and followed him." All that had meant so much to them—their boats, their nets and gear, their livelihood, and even their families—they left behind. These things had occupied their thoughts daily, but "from that moment the four were His devoted followers. The rich gain they would have prized so highly but an hour before, had lost its charm. Called to decide there

a. Exodus 3:11; 4:10–17; Isaiah 6:5; Jeremiah 1:6; Judges 6:15; Acts 9:6; Revelation 1:17.

b. Psalms 8:6, 8.

c. Matthew 19:16–26.

and then, as a proof of their meekness for discipleship, they forsook all, and followed Him at once."[91]

Not all of the Twelve were present when this miracle occurred but they would eventually hear of it, for these humble fishermen would bear witness of it to them.

The Final Draught of Fish

John 21:1–10   After these things Jesus shewed himself again to the disciples at the sea of Tiberias; and on this wise shewed he himself. There were together Simon Peter, and Thomas called Didymus, and Nathanael of Cana in Galilee, and the sons of Zebedee, and two other of his disciples. Simon Peter saith unto them, I go a fishing. They say unto him, We also go with thee. They went forth, and entered into a ship immediately; and that night they caught nothing. But when the morning was now come, Jesus stood on the shore: but the disciples knew not that it was Jesus. Then Jesus saith unto them, Children have ye any meat? They answered him, No. And he said unto them, Cast the net on the right side of the ship, and ye shall find. They cast therefore, and now they were not able to draw it for the multitude of fishes. Therefore that disciple whom Jesus loved saith unto Peter, It is the Lord. Now when Simon Peter heard that it was the Lord, he girt his fisher's coat unto him, (for he was naked,) and did cast himself into the sea. And the other disciples came in a little ship; (for they were not far from land, but as it were two hundred cubits,) dragging the net with fishes. As soon then as they were come to land, they saw a fire of coals there, and fish laid thereon, and bread. Jesus saith unto them, Bring of the fish which ye have now caught.

This miracle mirrors that of the first draught of fish. All its elements are basically the same. However, this final draught takes place after the resurrection of the Lord, but prior to His ascension.

The first draught of fish had instituted the call to four fishermen to follow Christ. Through their testimonies it extended to the other Apostles. The final draught of fish reaffirmed that call. Christ, through this "duplicate" miracle, seemingly confirmed and verified to the Apostles four specific things:

1.   He was the Son of God, the Messiah—the resurrected Lord.

2.   The Apostles had been called to Christ's ministry, and despite their actions at His trial and death, they were acceptable before Him—except for Judas.

3.   He had "chosen" them.

4. They would again completely yield themselves and all that they had to Him and His service.

Interestingly, John did not record the first miracle at all, but he is the only gospel writer to record this one.

After His resurrection, Jesus had appeared to the Apostles at least twice prior to this appearance.[a] He had told the Apostles to go into Galilee where He would show Himself to them,[b] and they had done so. Not all of the group were present for this miracle. John records that he, Peter, James, Thomas, and Nathanael were present, plus two other "disciples" who are left unnamed. It has been assumed that the "two disciples" here referred to were also numbered among the Apostles.[92] It would appear from the scriptures that the group had been in Galilee some time, perhaps several days, and they were impatient for the Lord's impending visit. Peter finally exclaimed, "I go a fishing." The others readily agreed, and they all departed for the lake. The Apostles had just experienced several days of very unusual happenings. The Lord had been crucified and had risen from the tomb. He had appeared and taught them, and had performed many signs and wonders.[c] They would now relax the stress and tension of these days by fishing. Because they were in Galilee, they would use their own boats. In all probability, this miracle occurred in the same location as that of the first draught.

Just as with the first draught, the Apostles fished all night and caught nothing. As the morning broke, a figure appeared on the shore. It was Jesus, but the Apostles "knew not that it was Jesus" (Chapter 12). He did not want to be known to them at first. Jesus inquired, "Children, have ye any meat?" He knew that they had nothing, but He would have them remember the former miracle and the call to the work. They responded and answered no, still unaware that it was Jesus.

Jesus then told the Apostles to "cast the net on the right side of the ship," and they would find fish. The same setting now existed as in the miracle of the first draught of fish. The "unknown stranger" in that instance was the same as in this. He had been unknown to them as the Messiah then, and in a different sense was unknown as the Messiah now. Their faith and confidence in Him had been sufficient at the first

a. Luke 24:33–36; John 20:19, 26.

b. Matthew 28:10.

c. John 20:30.

miracle to "let down the net," but now they did not recognize Him as the Messiah. However, perhaps subconsciously recalling the earlier miracle, they cast the net on the right side of the boat. The Spirit was now moving upon them. "They cast therefore, and now they were not able to draw it for the multitude of fishes." When the stranger in the first draught was revealed, Peter knew and acknowledged Him. In the second draught, John said unto Peter, "It is the Lord."

The character of some of the Apostles is beautifully shown in the recording of this miracle. John, who was always reserved when it came to his relationship with Jesus, did not even record his own name. He recorded himself as one of the "sons of Zebedee" at the commencement of the miracle, and as "that disciple whom Jesus loved" when he recognized Christ.

Peter was so excited when he recognized the Lord that he grabbed his coat and "cast himself into the sea." He wanted to swim to shore and to his Master. The "multitude of fish" was no more important to him now than in the earlier miracle. The others followed in the small boat, "dragging the net with fishes." But Peter's excitement and love for the Lord overcame his normal tendencies to share in such work.

Jesus had prepared a fire, and He now asked the men to bring Him some fish. Peter returned to the net and helped drag it ashore. They then dined.

A curious comment is now recorded. As Jesus invited them to dine, none dared ask, "Who art thou?" for they knew "that it was the Lord." No one had been resurrected before; they wanted reassurance, yet in their hearts they knew. John now notes that it was the third time that the Lord had appeared to them.

After they had finished eating, Jesus instructed them and reaffirmed their call. Again the Lord addressed only Peter (as in the first draught of fish), although the charge obviously was applied to all of the Apostles. Referring to the fish, the Lord said, "Simon . . . lovest thou me more than these?" Even though differently phrased, the same question had been asked in the first draught, wherein the Lord said "Follow me."[a]

To the question Peter responded, "Yea, Lord; thou knowest that I love thee." Twice more the Lord asked and twice more Peter answered. By the time the third inquiry came, "Peter was grieved." He

a. Matthew 4:19.

undoubtedly remembered that dreadful night when he stood listening to the trials and condemnation of the Lord and three times had denied that he knew Him.

Peter answered, "Lord, thou knowest all things; thou knowest that I love thee." Gone now was the previous fear in his heart for his personal safety. He stood before his Savior, knowing that Jesus knew his feelings and the reasons for his former denial. Peter openly confessed his love for Jesus. He was forgiven.

Soon, blessed with the reception of the Holy Ghost,[a] Peter went on to become the chief Apostle, the earthly leader of Christ's church. He developed such strong faith that his reputation spread among the Saints and "they brought forth the sick into the streets, and laid them on beds and couches, that at the least the shadow of Peter passing by might overshadow some of them."[b]

As in the first draught of fish, the Lord (now the resurrected Savior) extended His call to the Apostles, and they received a personal manifestation that He was the Messiah.

a. Acts 2:2–4.

b. Acts 5:15.

8

Signs and Powers

Stilling the Tempest

Mark 4:35–41   And the same day, when the even was come, he saith unto them, Let us pass over unto the other side. And when they had sent away the multitude, they took him even as he was in the ship. And there were also with him other little ships. And there arose a great storm of wind, and the waves beat into the ship, so that it was now full. And he was in the hinder part of the ship, asleep on a pillow: and they awake him, and say unto him, Master, carest thou not that we perish? And he arose, and rebuked the wind, and said unto the sea, Peace, be still. And the wind ceased, and there was a great calm. And he said unto them, Why are ye so fearful? how is it that ye have no faith? And they feared exceedingly, and said one to another, What manner of man is this, that even the wind and the sea obey him?

Cross-references   Matthew 8:23–27; Luke 8:22–25; JST Luke 8:23

This chapter deals with four miracles directed to the Apostles to teach them more of Jesus and instruct them of His authority. As in all the miracles, the teaching specifically evidences that Jesus is the Son of God; however, these miracles also reveal His personal power and authority.

The stilling of the tempest, like walking on the water, is a miracle that might stretch one's faith in the miraculous. Over the centuries, no miracles have created more consternation for those who would explain away the miraculous than these two miracles.[93] The Apostles' reaction to each of these remarkable miracles, however, testifies to their authenticity.

The stilling of the tempest cannot be explained by any known laws, and there are no natural theories that apply. To cast it out as fabrication brings suspicion on all of the miracles, and may destroy the validity of the entire scriptural text. It must either be believed or rejected, thereby causing acceptance or rejection of Him who performed it.

All three Synoptics record the stilling of the tempest. They give divergent reports, but such divergence can be attributed to the individual impressions of the writers, especially regarding the order of events surrounding the miracle. All the writers agree upon the descriptive circumstances of the miracle itself.

Jesus, possibly after a long and arduous day, had decided to "pass over unto the other side" of the Lake of Gennesaret. Mark emphasized that no particular preparation had been made for the trip, which provides a potential explanation for some of the teachings that Jesus had just delivered. As they embarked, several members of the multitude asked if they could accompany Him. First was a scribe, to whom Jesus responded, "Foxes have holes, and the birds of the air have nests; but the Son of man hath not where to lay his head."[a] Another asked to go, but indicated that he must first bury his dead father. The Lord responded, "Let the dead bury their dead."[b]

These teachings are better understood if coupled with Christ's instructions to depart immediately without making any preparations. To follow Him meant to go at His command and to place the needs of the kingdom above personal, worldly needs. Not that one should literally have to leave immediately and force others to bury a dead father to be required to wander homeless, but that the requirements of the kingdom were more important than worldly problems. These conflicts were always to be satisfied in favor of the kingdom of God, not of the mundane cares of this life.[94]

As the ship left the shore, the Lord found refreshment from His weariness.[95] Physically exhausted, He fell asleep, and was still in the rear of the ship asleep on a pillow when the storm arose on the lake.

It was not unusual for storms to arise quickly on the Lake of Gennesaret, and "a sudden and violent squall [arose], such as these small inland seas, surrounded with mountain gorges, are notoriously exposed to."[96] But this was no ordinary storm. The wind was so great that "the waves beat into the ship, so that it was now full." These men were sailors and fishermen and had been out on the lake many times, yet this storm caused the boat to become unmanageable. The waves were

a. Matthew 8:20.

b. Matthew 8:22.

high, all but swamping the boat. Through the darkness of the clouds, the fierce wind, and the tumult and confusion of the storm, Jesus slept.

Many hundreds of years before, a similar storm had raged in the Mediterranean Sea. Jonah had been called of the Lord to go to Nineveh to cry repentance and to warn them of impending destruction should they not heed his call. Fearful for his own life, he attempted to escape the Lord. He took passage on a ship headed for Tarshish. But the "Lord sent out a great wind," and a great tempest arose so that "the ship was like to be broken." Although all the mariners on the ship were terrified and feared death, Jonah slept. Awakened by the sailors, he recognized the perilous position the ship was in and acknowledged that he was the cause. He suggested that they throw him overboard so that the storm would cease. Hesitating for only a moment, the anxious mariners gladly accepted the suggestion and obligingly threw Jonah into the sea.

The balance of Jonah's story is well known and of no importance to this miracle, but the result of casting Jonah into the sea is. The scripture reports, "they took up Jonah, and cast him forth into the sea: and the sea ceased from her raging."[a] As the Lord's requirements were fulfilled, the storm ceased.

Although both Jonah and the Lord slept through the tempest, they did so in different frames of mind. There was no peace in Jonah's heart, and the analogy ends with the calming of the tempest. But the Apostles would have known the story of Jonah from childhood and would have been taught the power of God over the elements. Now they were in like peril, and they awakened the Savior and cried, "Master, carest thou not that we perish?"

Jesus arose and rebuked the wind "and said unto the sea, Peace, be still. And the wind ceased, and there was a great calm." His power over the elements was again revealed—His Messiahship witnessed. The elements obeyed Jesus because He was their Master. As the Creator, He had brought them into being on this earth, and they obeyed His will.

When Jehovah calmed the sea in Jonah's time, even the heathen mariners recognized His power.[b] Now incarnate, Jehovah again displayed His power over the elements. This powerful authority Christ held was encompassed in the authority He endowed the Apostles with when He ordained them.[c]

a. Jonah 1:1–15.
b. Jonah 1:16.
c. John 15:16.

During the storm, the Apostles sought the Lord's help to alleviate their immediate danger, and He did not leave them helpless. But in their seeking, the Lord found a teaching moment. He mildly rebuked them saying, "Why are ye so fearful? How is it that ye have no faith?" It was not that they did not have "any" faith, for their call to the Lord for help signified that they believed He could and would assist them. Their error had been in the great fear they had displayed—as if a storm would or could destroy the Son of God.[97] They also held His priesthood authority,[a] and through it they could have calmed the storm and alleviated their fears. But they were still learning.

The Apostles' response to this miracle is interesting. They were in awe of the Lord and asked, "What manner of man is this?" They understood His power—He had demonstrated that—but they were still trying to understand the man. Perhaps, like the people of Nazareth, they still looked upon Him as a man and not as the Messiah.

This miracle also contains a symbolic teaching concerning the tempest within each soul. Isaiah said, "But the wicked are like the troubled sea, when it cannot rest, whose waters cast up mire and dirt. There is no peace, saith my God, to the wicked."[b] As the Lord calmed the troubled sea, so will the troubled soul tossed by the tempest of a sinful world find peace in the Lord, and the resulting calm will testify of His power.[98]

The Psalmist sang, "O Lord God of hosts, who is a strong Lord like unto thee? or to thy faithfulness round about thee? Thou rulest the raging of the sea: when the waves thereof arise, thou stillest them."[c] The Apostles had gained greater insight into the Messiah. They had strengthened their testimony of Him as the Son of God and had a greater understanding of the power that He had given them. But most of all, He had indelibly confirmed in their hearts that He was the Prince of Peace.

Walking on the Water

Matthew 14:24–33   But the ship was now in the midst of the sea, tossed with waves: for the wind was contrary. And in the fourth watch of the night Jesus went unto them, walking on the sea. And when the disciples saw him walking on the sea, they were troubled, saying, It is a spirit; and they cried out for fear. But straightway Jesus spake unto them, saying, Be of good cheer; it is I; be not afraid. And Peter answered him and said, Lord, if it be thou, bid me come unto thee on the water. And he said,

a. Mark 3:14.

b. Isaiah 57:20–21; Jude 1:13.

c. Psalms 89:8–9.

Come. And when Peter was come down out of the ship, he walked on the water, to go to Jesus. But when he saw the wind boisterous, he was afraid; and beginning to sink, he cried, saying, Lord, save me. And immediately Jesus stretched forth his hand, and caught him, and said unto him, O thou of little faith, wherefore didst thou doubt? And when they were come into the ship, the wind ceased. Then they that were in the ship came and worshipped him, saying, Of a truth thou art the Son of God.

Cross-references   Mark 6:47–51; John 6:16–21; JST Mark 6:50

This miracle is recorded in three of the four Gospels, but not the same three that recorded the stilling of the tempest. Luke does not record this miracle, whereas John does. The stories recounted by the three are very similar. As noted in the discussion on the stilling of the tempest, Jesus, as Jehovah, had placed on the earth the elements and the laws governing them that He was now miraculously "defying." There is no contradiction in this, for clearly the God who established the law can hold it in abeyance for His purposes.

All of the Gospel writers agree on the circumstances preceding this miracle. The feeding of the five thousand had just taken place. The events of that miracle, in which the Apostles were participants, were particularly Jewish in expectation of the Messiah (Chapter 2). The reaction of the multitude was to make Jesus their king. Perhaps the Apostles were in danger of being caught up in the emotion and the worldly desires of the multitude. At any rate, Jesus "constrained" them to "get into a ship, and to go before him unto the other side" of the lake. He "constrained" them to get on the ship and leave "while he sent the multitudes away." Jesus then went to a mountain to pray.[a] He stayed for some hours in the solitude He must have desired but seldom obtained.

Meanwhile, the Apostles had taken the ship and left for the other side of the lake. They intended to cross over and wait for Jesus as He had instructed them to do, but "the wind was contrary." As they were "toiling in rowing," Jesus, still on the land, saw them. The ship was unmanageable, and He determined to go to their aid. They had been rowing for hours but had not progressed far, even though it was now the fourth watch, or between 3:00 A.M. and 6:00 A.M.[99] Jesus approached them, walking upon the water. The Apostles saw the Lord upon the water and were frightened, just as they had been at the stilling of the tempest. This was not a public miracle intended to receive the plaudits of a stricken and astonished multitude. This was the Messiah witnessing to His chosen Twelve that He was the Son of God, and reaffirming that He had total power over heaven and earth. This was He who had gathered together the waters and called them seas, and said that it was good.[a]

Although the Lord had given authority to Moses to part the Red Sea[b] and Elijah and Elisha (by use of the mantle) to part the Jordan River,[c] neither had walked on other than dry ground. Elisha also performed an interesting miracle involving the same principle that Jesus now exercised. The story would have been known to the Apostles. Elisha had gone with others to the banks of the Jordan River to cut timber. As one of the group "was felling a beam, the axe head fell into the water." The man expressed concern to Elisha, for the axe had been "borrowed." Elisha asked where it had entered into the river, and the man showed him the place. Elisha then cut a stick and "cast it in thither; and the iron did swim." The man took up the head, and it was restored to him. This story is unique, to say the least. Elisha used the power of the priesthood to locate the axe head, bring it to the surface of the river, and cause it to move toward the man that he might reclaim it. The head of the axe was iron, and therefore could not "float" of its own accord. But the power Elisha exercised caused it to "defy" the law of gravity and become buoyant, even mobile, that it might "swim" to him who lost it.[d]

The same principle is used in this miracle. There is no natural law that can be quoted in an attempt to explain the miracle. Did Jesus' body become exempt from the law of gravity, or did the water become solid under His feet? We do not know; nor does it matter. As in the case of the iron axe head, the normal laws became inoperative and a higher power replaced them. Seeing the Savior walking toward them on the water, the Apostles were frightened and "troubled," and they "cried out for fear." They thought He was "a spirit" or a ghost. They were unprepared for what they were witnessing. But Jesus had come to help, not to cause further problems to the toiling Apostles; He immediately calmed them by saying, "Be of good cheer; it is I; be not afraid." The Apostles must have recognized Him immediately, for no further concern on their part is recorded.

He next taught the Apostles the lesson of the miracle. Once again, as in so many examples, it was Peter who desired to experiment with the words and deeds of the Savior. "Lord, if it be thou," he declared, "bid me come unto thee on the water."

In the stilling of the tempest, Jesus had rebuked the Apostles because of their lack of confidence or their feelings of fear. Now Peter desired to overcome both. Jesus' response supported this desire. "Come," He said. He encouraged Peter to walk on the water with Him.

The scene must have been electric with excitement. One can almost envision Peter as he cautiously slid over the side of the ship and started toward the Savior. "He walked on the water, to go to Jesus." But the wind became "boisterous." Although Peter had almost reached the Lord, the wind stirring the water made him afraid. It was then that he lost confidence in his ability to walk on the water. He began to sink and cried out, "Lord, save me." Jesus immediately stretched forth His hand and caught him. Then followed Jesus' teaching and mild rebuke: "O thou of little faith, wherefore didst thou doubt?" The rebuke was only for instructive purposes. In trying, even though he failed, Peter had in part succeeded. He now knew through his own experience that the power he witnessed in the Savior could be exercised by others in appropriate circumstances.[100]

A distinctive teaching on faith can also be gleaned from this miracle. Peter's attempt to walk on water was successful; only when his faith waned did his ability to exercise the power fail. Had Jesus forbidden Peter to walk on the water, it would have greatly diminished his confidence. The experience clearly demonstrated to Peter that faith itself was a principle of power, and that through it even the laws and forces of nature could be controlled. Further, that the source of this power (faith) was Jesus the Messiah.[101] As in the stilling of the tempest, the miracle of walking on water can be applied to life's general circumstances. The boisterous wind and the restless sea equate with the temptations of a tempestuous and sinful world. Peter's fear of the struggle and danger of the contrary winds and restless sea overcame his ability, and he cried out for help. The same situation exists in life. Many struggles and dangers confront our effort to "come" to the Savior. Sometimes we delay our cry for help. Sometimes it seems to go unheeded. But the example is clear. Just as Peter's fears and doubts were about to overpower his faith, the Lord extended His hand in comforting assurance so that Peter might not sink.[102] The Apostles knew that they, too, could use and exercise the power of the Lord, and they recognized more fully that the Lord was the source of that power.

Jesus entered into the ship with Peter and the wind ceased. John reports that "they willingly received him into the ship: and immediately the ship was at the land whither they went."

This miracle taught the Apostles many things. They would never again look upon the Lord as a mortal man. He had taught them from the beginning that He was the master of all. He was the Son of God, the promised Messiah, and they now acknowledged Him as such. Through Peter's experience, they learned that if their will was in complete harmony with Christ's, they could do all the miracles that He did.

The Raising of the Daughter of Jairus

Mark 5:22–24, 35–43 And, behold, there cometh one of the rulers of the synagogue, Jairus by name; and when he saw him, he fell at his feet, and besought him greatly, saying, My little daughter lieth at the point of death: I pray thee, come and lay thy hands on her, that she may be healed; and she shall live. And Jesus went with him; and much people followed him, and thronged him. . . . While he yet spake, there came from the ruler of the synagogue's house certain which said, Thy daughter is dead: why troublest thou the Master any further? As soon as Jesus heard the word that was spoken, he saith unto the ruler of the synagogue, Be not afraid, only believe. And he suffered no man to follow him, save Peter, and James, and John the brother of James. And he cometh to the house of the ruler of the synagogue, and seeth the tumult, and them that wept and wailed greatly. And when he was come in, he saith unto them, Why make ye this ado, and weep? the damsel is not dead, but sleepeth. And they laughed him to scorn. But when he had put them all out, he taketh the father and the mother of the damsel, and them that were with him, and entereth in where the damsel was lying. And he took the damsel by the hand, and said unto her, Talitha cumi; which is, being interpreted, Damsel, I say unto thee, arise. And straightway the damsel arose, and walked; for she was of the age of twelve years. And they were astonished with a great astonishment. And he charged them straitly that no man should know it; and commanded that something should be given her to eat.

Cross-references Matthew 9:18–19, 23–26; Luke 8:41–42, 49–56; IV Matthew 9:25

This is the second raising of the dead discussed in the Gospels. Luke records the raising of the widow's son[a] prior to this miracle. The raising of the daughter of Jairus is recorded by all of the Synoptics, but is unrecorded by John. However, there are some minor differences between Matthew and the other two Gospel writers. Matthew, as usual, records the bare facts. His eye is focused on the parties, the circumstances, the miracle performed, and the Lord's part in it. To Matthew, detail seems to be of minor importance. His view is directed to the teaching and to Christ's witness of His divinity. For instance, Matthew records the daughter as dead, but in the other two she is only "near" death when Jairus comes to Jesus. However, Mark and Luke both describe Jairus as a man who believes his daughter is so near death that she may die before he can return home. Perhaps to Matthew, her condition did not matter as Jairus approached Jesus, for she was dead when Jesus arrived at the house. Other divergent details of the miracle are similarly insignificant and can be ignored.

With regard to the circumstances surrounding the miracle, Mark and Luke agree; but Matthew is completely different and cannot be reconciled with the other two. It should always be remembered that none of the writers attempted to record the Master's daily activities.[103] Therefore, the placement of the miracle may not directly reflect the surrounding circumstances in any of the Gospels and need not concern us.

This miracle, perhaps more than any other, emphasized the pure love of Christ. Through it the Apostles would learn of Christ's boundless love and endless patience in bringing souls to Him. They would also gain a firsthand witness of His power over death.

The teachings of the miracle are reviewed topically.

Jesus and the Rulers of the Jews

Jairus was a ruler in the synagogue at Capernaum. He may[104] or may not[105] have been one of those who came to Jesus on behalf of the centurion (Chapter 9). Perhaps he had been present when Jesus cast out the evil spirit from one in his synagogue.[106] But whatever the reason, it is obvious that Jairus displayed faith in Christ's ability to help him, no matter how limited or fragile that faith was.

There is a much deeper significance, however. A cursory reading of the scriptures might leave the impression that none of the rulers accepted or believed in Jesus, with the possible exception of Nicodemus."[107] From this miracle, however, it would appear that several (and perhaps many) of the rulers believed in Him, not necessarily as the Messiah, but at least as one who had powers from God. By coming to Jesus, Jairus showed confidence in the fact that He could and would help him. He approached Jesus with a desperate appeal. His daughter was dying, and the pain and distress of her impending death overcame the pressure of his peers and quickened his faith. He went to Jesus for a specific reason: he wanted the Lord to heal his daughter.

The Development of Faith

A great teaching on faith is evidenced in this miracle. It comes in the way the Lord nurtured the faith of Jairus and assisted its growth. The Synoptics record that Jairus begged Jesus in all earnestness to come with him to heal his "little daughter." The Lord treated the request with great compassion. He went with him immediately, thus comforting Jairus, for he might have thought that Jesus would not come.

As Jesus traveled to Jairus's sick daughter, another miracle took place. A woman with an issue of blood (Chapter 13) touched Jesus and delayed the procession. Jairus waited patiently as the Lord took the time to extend His healing power to the woman. This, too, would have increased his belief that Jesus would and could help him. But now the event that Jairus so feared occurred: he received notice that his daughter was dead.

Regardless of his prior belief in the Lord, this news could have destroyed that hope and belief. Even the messenger expressed his hopelessness. "Thy daughter is dead," the messenger reported. "Why troublest thou the Master any further?" Luke records it more definitively: "Thy daughter is dead; trouble not the Master."

Seemingly death had conquered. But Jesus would not have Jairus's faith so easily destroyed. "Be not afraid, only believe," He told Jairus. In Luke it was recorded, "Fear not: believe only, and she shall be made whole." Although death had momentarily taken away the initial reason for his mission to the Lord, Jairus was assured that his daughter would yet be whole. His faith thus renewed and strengthened, he apparently showed no impatience or ingratitude at the Lord's delay.

When they reached the home, funeral ceremonies were already under way. Jairus made no objections when Jesus put the mourners out and declared that the girl "sleepeth." There was no doubt that she was dead, but death held no power to the Master. Quiet now, the bedchamber contained only Jairus, his wife, the Master, Peter, James, and John. Jesus took the girl by the hand and commanded her to arise. From the world of spirits He called her back, and she responded.

Astonished and overjoyed, Jairus and his wife received their daughter back once more. Their faith had been nurtured and enlarged. Their petition had been granted. No further mention of Jairus is made, and it is not known what he did thereafter—but can there be any doubt that he would have glorified God and worshipped Him who had granted such a blessing to his house?

Concerning the miracle, Jesus instructed Jairus to "tell no man what was done." But how could this instruction be complied with? Few witnessed the raising, but many knew of the death. It would be impossible to tell no one. Perhaps Jesus gave this instruction because He did not want the parents to glory in the miracle. He had carefully cultivated and developed the faith exhibited by Jairus. He did not want him to boast of the miracle and spread it abroad. He wanted Jairus to make of it a hidden treasure (as later referred to in parable form)[a][108] that once found, all may acquire. In truth, broadcasting such a miracle at this time might also have hindered the Lord's mission, for His enemies were always watching.

This was a private miracle intended for Jairus, his family, and Peter, James, and John. It had generated true faith and belief from that kernel of faith that had brought Jairus to Jesus in the first place, and augmented the faith of His apostles.

Unbelief

When Jesus arrived at the house of Jairus, the minstrels and mourners had already commenced the obsequies. Jesus spoke to them that they, too, might believe. The girl was not dead but merely "sleepeth," He said. The result was illuminating. "They laughed him to scorn, knowing that she was dead." Although minor differences exist in the phrasing between the three Synoptics, all of the writers agree on this point: the people knew the girl was dead. They had awaited the moment,

a. Matthew 13:44.

perhaps hoping that Jesus could be brought in time; but when death came, they lost all hope in Him. They mocked His words. They probably wondered how Jesus could believe differently; He had just arrived and the girl was dead! Their spirit of unbelief contrasted sharply with Jairus's belief. Jairus had been totally pliant in Jesus' hands, awaiting His will. But from the mourners, the Lord received only scorn.

Jesus "put them all out." They were no longer needed. He would not let their disbelief infect the others. Their despair at the death of the young girl was nothing compared to what they would undoubtedly feel when they found out what marvelous thing they had missed because of their unbelief.

Life in Himself

The comparisons between the raisings of the dead in the Old Testament and those that Jesus performed have already been discussed (Chapter 2) and need not be reviewed again. But the emphasis is again noted: Jesus raised the girl by the command of His voice. He did not go through the contortions of Elijah and Elisha. In Him was life; death had no power over Him. This astonished Jairus and his wife. They witnessed the sign of His divinity. He was the Son of God.

The Effect on the Apostles

This was a special teaching time for the Apostles. All of them would have followed as Jesus went to the house of Jairus. They would have observed the compassion and gentleness with which He nourished the faith Jairus needed to receive such a blessing. But He chose only Peter, James, and John to witness the actual raising. In this instance, they alone witnessed the power of the Lord unveiled. They had been privy to the miracle of the first draught of fish at the time of their call as Apostles, and they would be with Christ at His transfiguration and His final prayer to His Father. They, with several others, would witness the miracle of the final draught of fish. Through their testimony they would strengthen their brethren. That they related their experience was obvious, for John, the only eyewitness to write a Gospel, did not mention it. It was a special witness for the Apostles. Influenced by this and other miracles, John would later write: "In him was life; and the life was the light of men."[a]

a. John 1:4.

This miracle was a personal one for Jairus and his wife and brought them the opportunity for salvation. It also provided a teaching time for the Twelve, particularly Peter, James, and John, so that they might know that Jesus was the Christ, the Savior of the world, the long-awaited Messiah.

The Barren Fig Tree

Mark 11:12–14, 20–24   And on the morrow, when they were come from Bethany, he was hungry: and seeing a fig tree afar off having leaves, he came, if haply he might find any thing thereon: and when he came to it, he found nothing but leaves; for the time of figs was not yet. And Jesus answered and said unto it, No man eat fruit of thee hereafter for ever. And his disciples heard it.

And in the morning, as they passed by, they saw the fig tree dried up from the roots. And Peter calling to remembrance saith unto him, Master, behold, the fig tree which thou cursedst is withered away, and Jesus answering saith unto them, Have faith in God. For verily I say unto you, That whosoever shall say unto this mountain, Be thou removed, and be thou cast into the sea; and shall not doubt in his heart; but shall believe that those things which he saith shall come to pass; he shall have whatsoever he saith. Therefore I say unto you, What things soever ye desire, when ye pray, believe that ye receive them, and ye shall have them.

Cross-references   Matthew 21:18–22; JST Matthew 21:20

This miracle was the Lord's final, private witness of record to the Apostles prior to His resurrection. Until now, the recorded miracles of Jesus were to life and the joy of its rewards. Here it was to death, and the certainty of the judgment and eventual punishment for evil.

There are at least four major teachings involved in this miracle:

1.   Jesus is the Christ, the promised Messiah

2.   The true principle of judgment

3.   Hypocrisy and Judaism

4.   The power of faith

Again there are discrepancies between Matthew and Mark. The principal difference concerns the time it took for the fig tree to wither and die. Matthew records that the tree died immediately (or at least gives that impression). Mark records that a day intervened between the cursing and the death. Yet even in Matthew's account, the day could have intervened. Note that Matthew records, "And presently the fig tree withered away."

The Lord was staying in Bethany during the last week of His ministry, traveling each day into Jerusalem. The scripture reports that on His journey this particular morning He was hungry. He saw a fig tree some distance ahead in full leaf. At the proper harvest time this would not have been unusual. But it was not "the time of figs." However, this tree seemed to indicate that it was. The fruit of the fig tree appears prior to the leaves, and by the time the tree is in leaf, the fruit is edible.[109] Jesus approached the tree, seemingly anticipating the fruit that might satisfy His hunger; but the tree provided no food. It had shown forth the promise of much fruit, but had produced nothing.

He who could perceive men's thoughts knew that no fruit was on the tree. But one of the great lessons of the miracle was to be learned through the anticipation He expressed as He and the Apostles approached the tree.

Jesus was the master teacher. He had drawn moral teachings from every facet of life for three years. He would now use this tree and the anticipation it caused to emphasize a parabolic teaching experience that the Apostles would never forget.

Upon finding no fruit Jesus cursed the tree, commanding that "no man eat fruit of thee hereafter for ever." This was no angry response arising from personal disappointment. It was a teaching experience, vividly illustrating to the Apostles the consequences of rejecting the Lord, His teachings, and His kingdom. The next morning, Peter remembered the curse and drew Jesus' attention to the withered and dead tree. Now the teaching sequence began.

Jesus is the Christ, the Promised Messiah
There were few more effective ways to show the power Jesus held over life and death than in this example. The Apostles had been with the Lord for three years. They had witnessed almost overwhelming human sorrows relieved by His great compassion. His patience and love had restored health, corrected disabilities and deformities, and raised the dead. Now they vividly saw before them the power of His wrath and judgment, and from this example of His control over life

they would know that He gave His life voluntarily; no one could have taken it from Him.

He Taught the True Principle of Judgment

Jesus taught openly to the Pharisees that the Father had given Him all rights to judgment.[a] He had undoubtedly instructed the Apostles in private on the use and meaning of this power. The fig tree had promised fruit according to its representation. When the time to harvest arrived, no fruit was available. The Lord cursed the tree in judgment of its hypocrisy and failure, and it received its just reward. The analogy was clear. The Lord held power over all things and would execute judgment on "they that have done good, unto the resurrection of life; and they that have done evil, unto the resurrection of damnation."[b]

Hypocrisy and Judaism of His Day

The tree was a true hypocrite. It professed something it did not have. But it was cursed not because it did not have figs, but because it had falsely represented that it had them. This was Judaism's condition at the time of Christ.[110] The fig tree, as the emblem of Israel, was used many times by the rabbis in their teachings. The Jews had all of the vesture of professed religion, but they, like the tree, brought forth no fruit. The sin of Judaism was not that they were part of the chosen people and not that they had been given the only true religion; but that they had allowed it to degenerate into artificial religionism. They cried loudly to the world of the truth, yet they were mere pretenders themselves. With exactness they rigorously lived the outward law, and inwardly rejected Him who gave it. The tree displayed the letter of the law with its full leaves, but its branches bore no fruit. Therefore, its destruction was a representation to Israel of their ultimate judgment if they persisted in their present course. But the time for final judgment upon Judah was not yet. Because they rejected the Messiah, the kingdom would be taken from them for a time; yet before the end, another effort would be made to save them.[c]

Paul, using this analogy, defined the principle to the Romans. The Jews had boasted to others of their favored condition but had failed to learn themselves. They had declared themselves righteous because of the Law, healed and secure through its ritualistic observance. Believ-

a. John 5:22.

b. John 5:29.

c. 2 Nephi
25:15–18.

ing themselves to be whole and at one with God, they rejected their Messiah.[a] Consequently, they were left barren, only the leaves of their professed belief hiding the nakedness of their pretentious show.

The Power of Faith

Jesus now taught the Apostles directly of faith and authority. Once again Peter expressed his recognition of the power Jesus had exercised when he said, "Master, behold, the fig tree which thou cursedst." The Lord's answer led Peter away from the apparent vengefulness of the miracle. "Have faith in God," Jesus answered. The Apostles could command mountains to move and they would go, but they must believe. "What things soever ye desire, when ye pray, believe that ye receive them, and ye shall have them." He cautioned them not to doubt, but to believe with all their hearts and to pray earnestly. They, too, held the authority over nature, life, and death. The key to its use was faith. With it they could do all that Christ had done.

Through this personal miracle, the Apostles could see that Jesus was the Lord of all. He could bless and save or curse and destroy. They might well adapt the symbolism of the tree not only to Judaism, but also to themselves. The mercy and hope Jesus had taught them must rule their use of His authority and power.

Their ministry was yet before them. In Him, their Messiah, they saw the perfect example of what they must become.

Summary

The miracles discussed in this chapter were miracles of power, exposing the Apostles to Jesus' authority as the Son of God. He showed them He was Lord over all the earth. The elements and laws of nature were His to command and use for His purposes. He raised the dead and proved that death held no power over Him. He cursed the fig tree and taught that He held power over life and death, both here and in eternity. All these evidences were given as a personal witness to the Apostles that He was the Son of God.

Through ordination, Christ gave His power and authority to the Apostles. He instructed them in its use. They in turn, however, could only exercise this power through undoubting faith in the Lord.

a. Romans 2:17–
27; 10:3–4.

A Gospel for All People

9

The Centurion's Servant

Luke 7:1–10   Now when he had ended all his sayings in the audience of the people, he entered into Capernaum. And a certain centurion's servant, who was dear unto him, was sick, and ready to die. And when he heard of Jesus, he sent unto him the elders of the Jews, beseeching him that he would come and heal his servant. And when they came to Jesus, they besought him instantly, saying, That he was worthy for whom he should do this: for he loveth our nation, and he hath built us a synagogue. Then Jesus went with them. And when he was now not far from the house, the centurion sent friends to him, saying unto him, Lord, trouble not thyself: for I am not worthy that thou shouldest enter under my roof: wherefore neither thought I myself worthy to come unto thee: but say in a word, and my servant shall be healed. For I also am a man set under authority, having under me soldiers, and I say unto one, Go, and he goeth; and to another, Come, and he cometh; and to my servant, Do this, and he doeth it. When Jesus heard these things, he marvelled at him, and turned him about, and said unto the people that followed him, I say unto you, I have not found so great faith, no, not in Israel. And they that were sent, returning to the house, found the servant whole that had been sick.

Cross-references   Matthew 8:5–13; JST Matthew 8:9

This chapter deals with three miracles that gave evidence to the Twelve that the kingdom of God was not reserved for Israel alone. Their nationality, background, and upbringing would have been traditionally Jewish. Thus, anyone not "of the Covenant" was considered inferior. A Gentile could not be considered a fit candidate for the kingdom of God. In one of the early rabbinical lessons the Apostles might have studied, God was depicted as saying, "In the future world I shall spread for you Jews a great table, which the Gentiles will see and be ashamed."[111]

These three miracles served to overcome this doctrinal error. They have several things in common. First, they are public miracles. Second, the recipients of the miracles are those whom the Jews thought of as Gentiles—heathens. And third, the miracles are granted as a reward for faith.

The healing of the centurion's servant is recorded by Matthew and Luke. Again there are differences. Historically, it is viewed that Matthew primarily addressed himself to Jewish readers whereas Luke wrote to the Gentiles. Matthew, writing principally to the Jews, emphasized the Lord's direct dealing with the centurion and commended the centurion's faith to them. Luke, on the other hand, writing principally to the Gentiles, emphasized the involvement of the local Jewish leadership in their praise of the Gentiles. Matthew persuades his countrymen that the Gentiles are favorable to the church, while Luke invokes sympathy from the Gentiles in favor of the Jews.[112]

The miracle took place in Capernaum, a Jewish community. A Roman garrison was stationed in the city and the centurion (commander of a hundred soldiers) was attached to this garrison. The scriptures do not indicate that the centurion had any previous contact with Jesus; however, that the centurion had heard of Jesus and had confidence in Him is undeniable.

The "elders of the Jews" came to Jesus and presented the centurion's request. They praised the centurion and informed Jesus that he had been particularly good to them and was worthy of the request. The centurion apparently loved Israel and had built their local synagogue. Further, the scripture specifically notes that the servant was "dear" to the centurion. Jesus recognized the goodness of the man immediately, assented to the elders' request, and left for the home of the centurion. Some must have gone ahead to tell the centurion that Jesus was coming, but the centurion did not feel worthy to have the Lord in his house. He sent other friends to intercept the Lord and indicate that the Savior's actual presence was not necessary for his request to be granted. He believed that the Lord had only to speak the word and his servant would be healed.

His message reflected his deep respect for, and faith in, Jesus. "Trouble not thyself," he stated through the messengers, "I am not worthy that thou shouldest enter under my roof." "Say in a word," his message continued, "and my servant shall be healed."

The centurion was a soldier, and used the example of his authority and command to illustrate his request. He believed that Jesus had the power to heal and expressed his great faith in Him. He may not have received Jesus into his home, but he had certainly received Jesus into his heart. He had no doubt: "speak the word only," he said, "and my servant shall be healed."

The centurion's strong faith filled the Lord with admiration. His own chosen people had invited Him into their houses, but had rejected Him in their hearts. Yet this Gentile had recognized Him as the king He was. Jesus "marvelled" at this centurion, and turning to the crowd that was following Him He said, "I say unto you, I have not found so great faith, no, not in Israel." The miracle was granted and the servant was healed.

Luke, writing primarily to the Gentiles, ended the miracle here. Matthew, however (writing to the Jews), extended the teaching, showing that the kingdom of God was for Jew and Gentile alike, and that the Jews would be in great jeopardy if they rejected the Gentiles.

According to Matthew, Jesus continued His teaching to those around Him. He stated: "Many shall come from the east and west, and shall sit down with Abraham, and Isaac, and Jacob, in the kingdom of heaven. But the children of the kingdom shall be cast out into outer darkness." Jesus confirmed the great faith and hope of the centurion by declaring that the kingdom was not limited to members of the chosen race. This declaration would shake the very foundation upon which Judaism rested. It removed the very basis of their pride, intolerance, and self-righteous assurance. People from all the earth could enter the kingdom and be welcome. Israel's previous chosen condition was no longer an assurance that they would inherit the kingdom. The Lord was warning Israel that they were already in danger of forfeiting the promised blessings, for others were proving themselves more worthy than they.[113]

Later, Jesus would tell them, "The kingdom of God shall be taken from you, and given to a nation bringing forth the fruits thereof."[a] If the Jews would not accept Him, others would; indeed, they were anxiously awaiting the opportunity. The centurion was but the first fruits of a vast harvest outside the chosen people. The Jews' disbelief was a millstone about their necks. Their reliance on historical salvation

a. Matthew 21:43.

would deny them the very blessings they longed for. John the Baptist had warned them of this early in his ministry: "Think not to say within yourselves, We have Abraham to our father: for I say unto you, that God is able of these stones to raise up children unto Abraham."[a] But they did not learn. This plague of self-righteousness would continue until they crucified their Master, and beyond.

Paul and Barnabas later struggled with this concept. But they "waxed bold, and said, It was necessary that the word of God should first have been spoken to you [the Jews]: but seeing ye put it from you, and judge yourselves unworthy of everlasting life, lo, we turn to the Gentiles."[b] From Rome, Paul again warned the Jews of their endangered position by saying, "Be it known therefore unto you, that the salvation of God is sent unto the Gentiles, and that they will hear it."[c]

Paul gave the Romans the analogy that perhaps best explains this teaching. He used a favorite comparison of the rabbis—the tame and wild olive tree. The tame tree was Israel, the chosen people; the wild branches, the Gentiles. Some of the tame branches would be broken off, he taught, and wild branches grafted in so that they might partake "of the root and fatness of the olive tree." The "root and fatness" was Israel, not in the day of Christ, but in the day that they were chosen. The branches were the tribes; the broken branches were the Jews and all those who would reject Christ's teachings. The "wild" branches grafted in were the Gentiles. He declared that the branches were broken off because "of unbelief," and warned the Gentiles not to get high minded, "for if God spared not the natural branches, take heed lest he also spare not thee." Then he once again extended the promise to the Jews that if they would but give up their unbelief, God would graft them in again. In Paul's words:

Romans 11:17–24 And if some of the branches be broken off, and thou, being a wild olive tree, wert grafted in among them, and with them partakest of the root and fatness of the olive tree; boast not against the branches. But if thou boast, thou bearest not the root, but the root thee. Thou wilt say then, The branches were broken off, that I might be grafted in. Well; because of unbelief they were broken off, and thou standest by faith. Be not high-minded, but fear: for if God spared not the natural branches, take heed lest he also spare not thee. Behold therefore the goodness and severity of God: on them which fell, severity; but toward thee, goodness, if thou continue in his good-

a. Matthew 3:9.

b. Acts 13:46.

c. Acts 28:28.

ness: otherwise thou also shalt be cut off. And they also, if they abide not still in unbelief, shall be graffed in: for God is able to graff them in again. For if thou wert cut out of the olive tree which is wild by nature, and wert graffed contrary to nature into a good olive tree: how much more shall these, which be the natural branches, be graffed into their own olive tree?

The kingdom was for all mankind.

The Daughter of the Syrophenician Woman

Matthew 15:22–28   And, behold, a woman of Canaan came out of the same coasts, and cried unto him, saying, Have mercy on me, O Lord, thou Son of David; my daughter is grievously vexed with a devil. But he answered her not a word. And his disciples came and besought him, saying, Send her away; for she crieth after us. But he answered and said, I am not sent but unto the lost sheep of the house of Israel. Then came she and worshipped him, saying, Lord, help me. But he answered and said, It is not meet to take the children's bread, and to cast it to dogs. And she said, Truth, Lord: yet the dogs eat of the crumbs which fall from their masters' table. Then Jesus answered and said unto her, O woman, great is thy faith: be it unto thee even as thou wilt. And her daughter was made whole from that very hour.

Mark 7:24–30   And from thence he arose, and went into the borders of Tyre and Sidon, and entered into an house, and would have no man know it: but he could not be hid. For a certain woman, whose young daughter had an unclean spirit, heard of him, and came and fell at his feet: the woman was a Greek, a Syrophenician by nation; and she besought him that he would cast forth the devil out of her daughter. But Jesus said unto her, Let the children first be filled: for it is not meet to take the children's bread, and to cast it unto the dogs. And she answered and said unto him, Yes, Lord: yet the dogs under the table eat of the children's crumbs. And he said unto her, For this saying go thy way; the devil is gone out of thy daughter. And when she was come to her house, she found the devil gone out, and her daughter laid upon the bed.

Cross-reference   JST Mark 7:22–23

Both Matthew and Mark record this miracle, and both texts are needed to ascertain its full meaning.

Upon occasion, Jesus sought time alone with the Twelve. This trip to Phoenicia appears to have been one of those times, perhaps brought on by the recent execution of John the Baptist in Galilee or by the constant pressure from the people and His enemies. Apparently Jesus had previously performed miracles in Phoenicia,[a] and His fame had preceded Him.

a. Mark 3:7–10.

This miracle itself has no distinguishing features. Its significance lies in the method of its performance and the teachings derived from it because of the nationality of the woman. Both writers emphasize that the woman was a heathen. She is called a Greek and a Syrophenician by Mark, and a Canaanite by Matthew. Jehovah of old had commanded Israel to "smite [the Canaanites] and utterly destroy them."[a] Now He would extend the blessings of the kingdom to them.

When the centurion's servant was healed, it became clear that the gospel would be taken to both Jew and Gentile. This concept would now be expanded. There were no interceding Jews as was the case with the centurion. The miracle was performed on the borders of Judah, and no implications could be drawn except those that pertained to the relationship between the kingdom of God and the Gentiles. Thus the woman's race was clearly established. She was of a race cursed by God and hated and despised by the Jews. And yet the kingdom of God was offered to her.

Jesus "could not be hid" as he arrived in Phoenicia. This woman discovered His presence and went to Him. She undoubtedly had heard of His claim to the Messiahship because of how she addressed Him: "O Lord, thou Son of David"; yet perhaps to her He was but another god among her many gods, "for David had never reigned over her or her people."[114]

The woman had a daughter possessed with a devil and she wanted the Lord to cast it out. Although a heathen, she was ready to accept Jesus as Israel's Messiah—but perhaps not yet as her Messiah. But having obviously heard of Jesus' miracles, she believed that He could and would heal her daughter.

Her first plea to Jesus went unanswered, but she persisted. This was a teaching moment for the woman so that she would come to recognize who He was. It was also a teaching moment for the Apostles, that they might recognize for whom the kingdom had been established. Matthew records that the Twelve became impatient at the woman's persistence. They asked Jesus to "send her away; for she crieth after us." Possibly they were embarrassed, but more probably they still held fast to their old Jewish belief. They were the "chosen people," and He was *their* Messiah. They may still have considered the kingdom of God to be a Jewish kingdom.

a. Deuteronomy 7:2.

But the woman would not be discouraged. Jesus finally responded to her and at first seemed to confirm the expressions of the Twelve. "I am not sent but unto the lost sheep of the house of Israel," He stated. But she would not be denied. She now had His attention and would not let the moment pass. She worshiped Him and pleaded for His help. Jesus again discouraged her. "It is not meet to take the children's bread, and to cast it to dogs." Without malice or anger, she understood and accepted the relationship. The "children" were Israel, the chosen people; the "dogs" were the heathens. The children were within the kingdom, while she was yet without. But still she persisted.

Following the Lord in His analogy she continued, "Truth, Lord: yet the dogs eat of the crumbs which fall from their masters' table." Hers was a truly perceptive response. Her belief and hope in Christ had elevated her not to a perfect knowledge, but to a true belief in Him. Now she waited for His answer. The Apostles witnessing this experience observed that they had been shortsighted.

"O woman, great is thy faith," Jesus responded, and He granted the desired blessing. The Lord had initially delayed speaking to the woman that He might better teach her and the Twelve two things: first, that she would come to know with a surety Christ's identity and calling; and second, that the Lord would dispel the unacceptable Jewish traditionalism which exhibited only prejudice and error concerning the kingdom.

The simple love of a Canaanite mother had triumphed—the Messiah would offer the rewards of the kingdom of God to Jew and Gentile alike.

The Feeding of the Four Thousand

Matthew 15:29–39   And Jesus departed from thence, and came nigh unto the sea of Galilee; and went up into a mountain, and sat down there. And great multitudes came unto him, having with them those that were lame, blind, dumb, maimed, and many others, and cast them down at Jesus' feet; and he healed them: insomuch that the multitude wondered, when they saw the dumb to speak, the maimed to be whole, the lame to walk, and the blind to see: and they glorified the God of Israel.

Then Jesus called his disciples unto him, and said, I have compassion on the multitude, because they continue with me now three days, and have nothing to eat: and I will not send them away fasting, lest they faint in the way. And his disciples say unto him, Whence should we have so much bread in the wilderness, as to fill so great a multitude? And Jesus saith unto them, How many loaves have ye? And they said, Seven, and a few little fishes. And he commanded the multitude to sit down on the ground. And he took the seven loaves and the fishes, and gave thanks, and brake them, and gave to his disciples, and the disciples to the multitude. And they did all eat, and were filled: and they took up of the broken meat that was left seven baskets full. And they that did eat were four thousand men, besides women and children. And he sent away the multitude, and took ship, and came into the coasts of Magdala.

Cross-reference   Mark 8:1–9

This miracle is often compared to the feeding of the five thousand, but they do not merely duplicate each other. The uniqueness of each is emphasized by the following comparison:

Feeding of the Five Thousand	Feeding of the Four Thousand
• Five thousand men plus women and children fed	• Four thousand men plus women and children fed
• Time: extended afternoon and evening	• Time: three days
• Twelve baskets of food left over	• Seven baskets of food left over
• Audience: Jewish	• Audience: Gentile and heathen
• Time of year: spring	• Time of year: late summer, early fall
• Single blessing performed on food	• Two blessings performed on food

The substantial differences in this comparison emphasize the need for and purpose of the two similar miracles. Consider the following.

Circumstances. The feeding of the five thousand took place during an established event. Devout Jews were gathering to Jerusalem for the Passover, annually the most important religious event celebrated. As they traveled, they paused to hear Jesus, whom they recognized as an interesting teacher and a worker of miracles. The setting for the feeding of the four thousand was quite different. This multitude had come to Jesus not out of curiosity or religious zeal but as a result of His miracles, including the casting out of the evil spirit from the Syrophenician's daughter. He then performed a multitude of miracles (Chapter 1), healing the sick, lame, blind, dumb, maimed, and all manner of diseases. Included in this multitude of miracles was the healing of one deaf and dumb (Chapter 16). After Jesus had performed these miracles, the people "were beyond measure astonished, saying, He hath done all things well,[a] and the multitude stayed with Him.

Purpose. The feeding of the five thousand was given as a sign to the chosen people so that they might recognize in it the Old Testament expectation of the anticipated Messiah (Chapter 2). The multitude made this association, and tried to "take him by force, to make him a king."[b] In the feeding of the four thousand, there was no such reaction. The miracle served as a reward for faith, and further demonstrated to the Apostles that the gospel was universal and was not limited to the Jews alone. The Gentile multitude "wondered" and "glorified the God of Israel." Note that they glorified the *God of Israel.* The Jews considered Jesus to be a teacher, but the heathen accepted Him as a god (albeit they did not at first understand which god).

Jesus taught these people for three days. In that time He would have discussed many things concerning the kingdom of God and His divinity. The first fruits reaped through the centurion were now about to become a vast harvest. The Apostles witnessed firsthand what results could be obtained when the historical animosity harbored by the Jews was set aside.

An additional point of interest may be gleaned from the miracle. The Lord did not question the Twelve concerning the feeding of the four thousand as He had in the feeding of the five thousand. He merely stated that He would not have the multitude go away "fasting, lest they faint in the way."

The Apostles answered much as they had at the feeding of the five thousand: "Whence should we have so much bread in the wilderness, as to fill so great a multitude?" Had they already forgotten the previous feeding? Had they not seen the many miracles so recently performed? Why did they respond in this manner? Several possibilities arise (even though their personal feelings are left unrecorded) that might explain their reaction. Seemingly, within these reasons lies the teaching of the miracle itself.

1. The Apostles had previously been taught the use of Christ's authority, but they had evidenced little control over it and seemed to lack confidence in the authority they held.

2. They may still have been hampered by the old traditional, Jewish belief. They were dealing with Gentiles. It was allowable to feed the Jews in the feeding of the five thousand, but were these Gentiles worthy of such a miracle?

3. They may have hesitated to call for the repetition of a previous miracle. They had witnessed requests for miracles from people that had had them granted, but they had also seen people condemned for asking. They may have hesitated out of fear.[a]

4. They may have doubted whether Jesus would perform a duplicate feeding. The Apostles' reaction seemed to indicate this dilemma. As each new situation and difficulty arose, it appeared to be one that they could not solve themselves. They still had to learn to rely on the Lord.

Israel's history had been replete with miracles, but the Israelites continually lacked reliance on the Lord. This was nowhere more vividly displayed than in their exodus from Egypt. They had been spared the death of the firstborn; they were led by miracles from Egypt through the Red Sea; they had been given manna—yet in all this they complained. As they journeyed, they ran out of fresh water and became thirsty. Again they chided Moses and murmured against him.[b] They had learned nothing from the past. They were not confident in God's deliverance; they only demanded more.

The Jews of Christ's time had learned little from God's treatment of their ancient ancestors. In spite of all the miracles, past and present, the Jews still did not have faith in Jesus as the Messiah.

The Twelve had witnessed all or most of Christ's miracles. This witness would give them additional confidence and trust in the Lord and further develop their faith in Him.

The Gentiles in this miracle had followed Jesus and thirsted after righteousness. He fed them living water and the bread of life, and confirmed their acceptance before Him with this miracle. Again the Apostles witnessed that the Jews, although the chosen people, were not the only ones that would enter into the kingdom of God. Many would reject it, but none were to be excluded deliberately.

a. Matthew 12:38–39.

b. Exodus 17:1–7.

Summary

There were probably greater miracles performed by Jesus than the three discussed in this chapter, but perhaps none were more important to the future direction of the church. These miracles evidenced that all were to be given the opportunity to be accepted into the kingdom of God. Peter would yet receive a vision that would lead him to Cornelius,[a] Paul would take the gospel to the gentile nations, and James would offer a positive solution to the Apostles and other church leaders in Jerusalem when the propriety of enjoining Mosaic practices upon gentile converts was being considered.[b] However, in the miracles now under discussion, the universality of the kingdom was witnessed to the Apostles, and it would remain with them so that later incidents could be decided correctly.

Jesus was sent first to the house of Israel—that was the promise. But he was not sent *exclusively* to the house of Israel—that was the teaching. The kingdom of God was for all men: Gentile and Israelite, heathen and chosen. This instruction was preserved in these three miracles. Christ extended His compassion, mercy, and blessings to all. The Apostles needed this special instruction and witness so that they might be better prepared to serve Christ after His ascension.

a. Acts 10.

b. Acts 15.

They Ask of Him a Sign

10

The Raising of Lazarus

John 11:1–46   Now a certain man was sick, named Lazarus, of Bethany, the town of Mary and her sister Martha. (It was that Mary which anointed the Lord with ointment, and wiped his feet with her hair, whose brother Lazarus was sick.) Therefore his sisters sent unto him, saying, Lord, behold, he whom thou lovest is sick. When Jesus heard that, he said, This sickness is not unto death, but for the glory of God, that the Son of God might be glorified thereby. Now Jesus loved Martha, and her sister, and Lazarus. When he had heard therefore that he was sick, he abode two days still in the same place where he was. Then after that saith he to his disciples, Let us go into Judea again. His disciples say unto him, Master, the Jews of late sought to stone thee; and goest thou thither again? Jesus answered, Are there not twelve hours in the day? If any man walk in the day, he stumbleth not, because he seeth the light of this world. But if a man walk in the night, he stumbleth, because there is no light in him. These things said he: and after that he saith unto them, Our friend Lazarus sleepeth; but I go, that I may awake him out of sleep. Then said his disciples, Lord, if he sleep, he shall do well. Howbeit Jesus spake of his death: but they thought that he had spoken of taking of rest in sleep. Then said Jesus unto them plainly, Lazarus is dead. And I am glad for your sakes that I was not there, to the intent ye may believe; nevertheless let us go unto him. Then said Thomas, which is called Didymus, unto his fellowdisciples, Let us also go, that we may die with him. Then when Jesus came, he found that he had lain in the grave four days already. Now Bethany was nigh unto Jerusalem, about fifteen furlongs off: and many of the Jews came to Martha and Mary, to comfort them concerning their brother. Then Martha, as soon as she heard that Jesus was coming, went and met him: but Mary sat still in the house. Then said Martha unto Jesus, Lord, if thou hadst been here, my brother had not died. But I know, that even now, whatsoever thou wilt ask of God, God will give it thee. Jesus saith unto her, Thy brother shall rise again. Martha saith unto him, I know that he shall rise again in the resurrection at the last day. Jesus said unto her, I am the resurrection, and the life: he that believeth in me, though he were dead, yet shall he live: and whosoever liveth and believeth in me shall never die. Believest thou this? She saith unto him, Yea, Lord: I believe that thou art the Christ, the Son of God, which should come into the world. And when she had so said, she went her way, and called Mary her sister secretly, saying, The Master is come, and calleth for thee. As soon as she heard that, she arose quickly, and came unto him. Now Jesus was not yet come into the town, but was in that place where Martha met him. The Jews then which were with her in the house, and comforted her, when they saw Mary, that she rose up hastily and went out, followed her, saying, She goeth unto the grave to weep there. Then when Mary was come where Jesus was, and saw him, she fell down at his feet, saying unto him, Lord, if thou hadst been here, my brother had not died. When Jesus therefore saw her weeping, and the Jews also weeping which came with her, he groaned in the spirit, and was troubled, and said, Where have ye laid him? They said unto him, Lord, come and see. Jesus wept. Then said the Jews, Behold how he loved him! And some of them said, Could not this man, which opened the eyes of the blind, have caused that even this man should not have died? Jesus therefore again groaning in himself cometh to the grave. It was a cave, and a stone lay upon it. Jesus said, Take ye away the stone. Martha, the sister of him that was dead, saith unto him, Lord, by this time he stinketh: for he hath been dead four days. Jesus saith unto her, Said I not unto thee, that, if thou wouldest believe, thou shouldest see the glory of God? Then they took away the stone from the place where the dead was laid. And Jesus lifted up his eyes, and said, Father, I thank thee that thou hast heard me. And I knew that thou hearest me always: but because of the people which stand by I said it, that they may believe that thou hast sent me. And when he thus had spoken, he cried with a loud voice, Lazarus, come forth. And he that was dead came forth, bound hand and foot with grave, clothes: and his face was bound about with a napkin. Jesus saith unto them, Loose him, and let him go. Then many of the Jews which came to Mary, and had seen the things which Jesus did, believed on him. But some of them went their ways to the Pharisees, and told them what things Jesus had done.

Cross-reference   JST John 11:2, 16–17

The Parable of Lazarus and the Rich Man[115]

Luke 16:19–31   There was a certain rich man, which was clothed in purple and fine linen, and fared sumptuously every day: and there was a certain beggar named Lazarus, which was laid at his gate, full of sores, and desiring to be fed with the crumbs which fell from the rich man's table: moreover the dogs came and licked his sores. And it came to pass, that the beggar died, and was carried by the angels into Abraham's bosom: the rich man also died, and was buried; and in hell he lift up his eyes, being in torments, and seeth Abraham afar off, and Lazarus in his bosom. And he cried and said, Father Abraham, have mercy on me, and send Lazarus, that he may dip the tip of his finger in water, and cool my tongue; for I am tormented in this flame. But Abraham said, Son, remember that thou in thy lifetime receivedst thy good things, and likewise Lazarus evil things: but now he is comforted, and thou art tormented. And beside all this, between us and you there is a great gulf fixed: so that they which would pass from hence to you cannot; neither can they pass to us, that would come from thence. Then he said, I pray thee therefore, father, that thou wouldest send him to my father's house: for I have five brethren; that he may testify unto them, lest they also come into this place of torment. Abraham saith unto him, They have Moses and the prophets; let them hear them. And he said, Nay, father Abraham: but if one went unto them from the dead, they will repent. And he said unto him, If they hear not Moses and the prophets, neither will they be persuaded, though one rose from the dead.

In spite of all the Lord's miracles and teachings, the majority of the Jews did not accept Him as the Messiah. Rather, they attempted to discredit Him, and accused Him of performing His miracles by the power of the devil.

Yet the Jewish leadership recognized that Jesus claimed to be the Messiah. On four recorded occasions they sought a sign from Him to verify that claim, but they desired a very specific sign.[a] They had misinterpreted the signs and teachings of the Second Coming for those of the first; and so they looked for the sign of the coming of the Son of Man (Chapters 1, 2).

The Jews' concern about the Messianic claim centered around three specific issues.

Their Political Situation

They had been in bondage for the better part of the previous four hundred years, and they believed that the coming Messiah would grant them their freedom. They envisioned that He would take them from bondage, destroy their enemies, rain down judgment and disaster upon the wicked, and punish with death and destruction those who had oppressed Israel. This intense desire to be free from bondage had been a driving force for generations.[116]

Christ, however, offered freedom not of the body but of the soul. The intent of His first coming was to establish His spiritual kingdom. He did not promise freedom from bondage but freedom from sin. The Jews wanted an earthly king, not a spiritual one. The reaction of the multitude in the feeding of the five thousand exemplified this. They wanted to force Him to become their political king (Chapter 2). Israel's leaders were no different than the common people in this matter. They accepted Christ's signs, but refused His person. They wanted His kingdom, but on the earth, not in heaven.

a. Matthew 12:38–40; Mark 8:11; John 2:18; 6:30.

Their Earthly Positions

The scribes, Pharisees, and chief priests had developed into the religious ruling class of the people. They had done this to preserve the nation for the coming Messiah. But in so doing, they became so imbued with their own self-importance that they would not sacrifice their position to accept the Messiah. The development of the teachings and doctrines of the Rabbinical Law had, over the centuries, elevated these positions. They denounced the sinner, the publican, the heathen, and the Sabbath breaker. They extolled the teacher, the rabbi, the Law, and the Pharisee. Meanwhile, Jesus came and ate with sinners and publicans, mingled with heathens, offered the kingdom to all, and denounced the ruling class as hypocrites and "whited sepulchres."[a] To accept Him meant that they must serve instead of being served, must give rather than receive, and must proclaim rather than be proclaimed.[117]

The Things of the World

Although the rich man was symbolic in the parable of Lazarus and the rich man, he actually existed in practice. The Lord taught that there was no relationship between worldly things and the kingdom of God. Worldly things were of no importance, and acquiring them bore no relationship to attaining salvation.

Thus, for the leaders of the Jews to accept Jesus as their Messiah meant rejection of all they had thought of as being important.[118] They refused to give up all even to gain all. Rather than accept and believe, they asked for another sign.

These specific requests for Messianic verification brought comments from the Lord on the leadership's inability to believe unless they had a sign.[b] So great was their curiosity pertaining to signs that even during His trial as He was brought before Herod, Herod did not have justice on his mind; rather Herod "hoped to have seen some miracle done by him."[c]

However, the sign of the coming of the Son of Man was not to be theirs. The Master would answer their desires and give them a sign—not at their request, and not the one they wanted—but a sign. The sign would be public and irrefutable, accompanied with doctrinal teachings that would leave them without excuse. This sign was encased within

a. Matthew 23:27.

b. John 4:48.

c. Luke 23:8.

a parable and a miracle: the parable of Lazarus and the rich man, and the miracle of the raising of Lazarus.

The parable of Lazarus and the rich man compared two men. The first man was rich. He was clothed in purple (to indicate his noble heritage) and "fared sumptuously every day." He had all the things the world treasured. The second man was a poor beggar. He had to eat leftovers from the rich man's table and was full of sores. His deplorable condition was accentuated by the "dogs [that] came and licked his sores."

Eventually, the two men died. The rich man awoke in hell and was tormented. Looking up, he saw the beggar in Abraham's bosom—or paradise. The rich man cried to Abraham and asked that he might send down the beggar to dip "the tip of his finger in water" to cool the rich man's tongue, for he was "tormented" in the flames of hell. Abraham told the rich man that during his lifetime he had had his good things and the poor beggar had had evil things. But now the beggar was comforted and the rich man tormented. Furthermore, he said that a great gulf existed between them so that passage from one side to the other was not possible.

The rich man, now resigned to his fate, pleaded one more cause. He had five brothers yet alive upon the earth. He cried to Abraham to send the poor beggar down to testify to his brothers of their awful course. They were apparently living the same, senseless, error-filled life that the rich man had. Abraham reminded him, "They have Moses and the prophets; let them hear them."

"Nay, father Abraham," the rich man replied, "but if one went unto them from the dead, they will repent."

But Abraham wisely responded, "If they hear not Moses and the prophets, neither will they be persuaded, though one rose from the dead." The rich man of the parable went unnamed; however, the poor beggar's name was Lazarus.

The rich man symbolizes the Jewish nation at Christ's time, particularly its rulers. They had what they considered the "true treasure"—like the rich man—all the good things of life that they revered. Poor Lazarus, the beggar, represented the impoverished, the sinners, the heathen, the publicans, and all who were despised by the Jewish leaders.[119] However, their reversed position in the spirit world demonstrated that the things of the world have nothing to do with attaining the kingdom of God.

This example is reminiscent of the Twelve's response after a certain young rich man had left Jesus, he being unwilling to sell all that he had and give it to the poor so that he could follow the Lord.[a][120] On that occasion, the Lord said that it would be difficult for the rich to get to heaven—so difficult, in fact, that He compared it to a camel going through the eye of a needle. The Twelve's response was most interesting. Matthew reported that the "disciples . . . were exceedingly amazed, saying, Who then can be saved?"[b] At that time, they, too, perhaps felt that worldly success was related to heavenly attainment. But it was not so.

The great gulf between Lazarus and the rich man was a separation that existed at the time of the parable between paradise (the place where righteous and obedient spirits go after death to await the resurrection) and the spirit prison (where the disobedient and those who died without law go to await, perchance, some grace from God that would relieve them of their suffering). Jesus later bridged that gulf by setting in motion a missionary program while He resided momentarily in the spirit world after His death and before His resurrection.[121] That program made it possible for those in the spirit prison to hear the gospel.[122]

These seem to be the basic, doctrinal teachings of the parable of Lazarus and the rich man (summarily reviewed). In the parable, Abraham had testified that those still upon the earth had Moses and the prophets and could learn from them of the kingdom of God and the Messiah. But the rich man in the parable had wanted more; he had wanted a sign. The Pharisees, scribes, chief priests, and the people had the same resources that the rich man had—Moses and the prophets. But they also wanted a sign. The rich man wanted one sent from the dead to warn his five brothers; the Pharisees wanted a sign from Christ to satisfy their doubts. But Abraham said, "If they hear not Moses and the prophets, neither will they be persuaded, though one rose from the dead." Jesus had taught them the parable. Now he would give this "wicked and adulterous generation" a sign!

a. Matthew
19:16–26.

b. Matthew
19:25.

John is the only Gospel writer that reports the miracle of the raising of Lazarus. There is no explanation as to why the others did not, for they obviously would have known of it. On the subject of the house in Bethany, the Synoptics say very little. Perhaps it had something to do with the raising, or perhaps they were afraid of bringing persecution upon Mary, Martha, and Lazarus, for they were known disciples of Jesus. Regardless of the reason, John preserved this spectacular miracle and the reaction of the Jews in splendid detail. That it was a deliberate, public sign is evident from the miracle itself.

Mary and Martha were sisters who lived in Bethany. They were very close to Jesus and aided Him upon many occasions.[123] Lazarus, their brother, was stricken with an undisclosed illness, an illness serious enough that the two sisters sent messengers to Jesus. They did not request His return (perhaps because they knew that He could heal Lazarus by merely speaking the word). They did not even ask for a healing. But within their message their desire is evident. "Lord, behold, he whom thou lovest is sick." They knew that the Lord would know their desires, and He did.

Upon hearing the message Jesus said, "This sickness is not unto death, but for the glory of God, that the Son of God might be glorified thereby." This was to be a very special miracle. He declared its purpose before it occurred. He knew that Lazarus would die, and that He would raise him from the dead. The miracle would be for the glory of God and, coupled with the parable, a specific sign of Jesus' divinity.

John records that Jesus loved Martha, Mary, and Lazarus, a statement probably inserted because of Jesus' delay for it would become obvious after the miracle that He had allowed Lazarus to die, causing Mary and Martha to suffer the anguish of his death. But there was an exalted purpose to the miracle, and the suffering that took place was soon lost in the experience that Mary and Martha shared with their Lord.

Jesus tarried two more days before announcing His intention to return to Judea. His disciples became concerned, for they were in mortal danger in Judea. Jesus responded with a simple analogy. "Are there not twelve hours in the day?" he said. "If any man walk in the day, he stumbleth not . . . but if a man walk in the night, he stumbleth." Jesus was the light of the world. Those who did not stumble followed Him and His light. Those who were against Him and disbelieved were in darkness and could not see, even at high noon, and would stumble and fall. Those who walked in the light need not worry that they might stumble, for as long as His mission was yet unfulfilled, He would not die.

Jesus then reminded the Apostles of Lazarus, but stated that Lazarus "sleepeth." He continued that they must go and awaken him "out of sleep." The Apostles misunderstood and replied that if Lazarus was sleeping, "he shall do well," thinking that if he was sleeping, it was good for him and would aid in his recovery. But Jesus did not allow misinterpretation or misunderstanding of this miracle at any stage. "Lazarus is dead," He told them flatly. Then He again clearly stated the purpose of the miracle. "I am glad for your sakes that I was not there, to the intent ye may believe." Had He been there, or if He had but spoken the word, Lazarus would have been healed; but the spectacular witness would not have been made and the sign and teaching would have been left incomplete.

Once His resolve to go was plain to the disciples, they went with Him. Thomas, often remembered for doubting at the Lord's resurrection, displayed now a positive quality we prefer to remember him by as he boldly stepped forward and declared his loyalty and love for the Savior: "Let us also go, that we may die with him."

It took two days to return to Bethany. When they arrived, Lazarus had "lain in the grave four days already." John notes that many Jews had come to Bethany to comfort Mary and Martha. Bethany was near Jerusalem, and the family was well known. Their popularity may even have been enhanced by their association with Jesus. Fellow disciples would have given the family comfort. Disbelievers and enemies may have been there in anticipation that Jesus would come, so that they might have cause to again accuse Him. Still others may have just been acquaintances, for one of the most binding of the Jewish directives was "to obey the Rabbinical direction of accompanying the dead, so as to show honor to the departed and kindness to the survivors."[124] It was to these people that Jesus came: to Mary and Martha, grieved at the loss of their brother, and to the others—some friendly, some indifferent, and some hostile.

When Martha heard that the Lord was approaching she left to meet

Him, leaving Mary in the house. When she met Jesus she expressed her innermost feelings: "Lord, if thou hadst been here, my brother had not died." Her testimony was strong; she knew that had Christ been there, He could and would have healed her brother. Whether she knew that Jesus had deliberately delayed His return or not is not indicated, but she knew that Lazarus was dead and she sorrowed; yet her faith in the Lord was not diminished. "But I know, that even now, whatsoever thou wilt ask of God, God will give it thee," she continued. Did she dare to dream of divine intervention, but because of timidity was restrained from asking for such a blessing? She knew that Jesus had raised the dead, but was it her place to request such a miracle?

Jesus responded, "Thy brother shall rise again."

Martha willingly responded, for she had been taught the principle of resurrection. "I know that he shall rise again in the resurrection at the last day," she stated.

By her response Jesus knew that additional teaching was necessary. He stated forcefully, "I am the resurrection, and the life." He was the power that determined life and death. He would soon suffer death, but in so doing would also conquer it. But now, in advance of that day, He would witness and make clear His divinity. "Whosoever liveth and believeth in me shall never die." Continuing, He asked Martha, "Believest thou this?" She did believe, and she confessed her testimony of Him as the Savior, the Son of God. She then went quickly and told Mary "the Master is come." Mary left immediately to go to Jesus who was still outside the town.

As Mary left to greet Jesus, the Jews thought she was going to the tomb to mourn, and they followed her. But she led them to Jesus, and the public teaching and witness of His divinity began. Mary fell at Jesus' feet and, independent of Martha, repeated the same words of love and confidence to Jesus. The Lord observed these mourning people, truly humbled in the sorrow of death. John recorded that he "groaned in the spirit, and was troubled." No doubt He was affected by the deep sorrow displayed at the physical death of Lazarus. But this was the Lord—He that took upon Himself all sorrows. Isaiah had declared centuries before that the Messiah would be "a man of sorrows, and acquainted with grief. . . . Surely he hath borne our griefs, and carried our sorrows."[a] The grief of those who knew Lazarus was

a. Isaiah 53:3–4.

genuine, and so it was that Jesus "groaned in the spirit," for He took upon Himself their sorrow and suffering. He was also troubled that even those who believed in Him did not fully understand. So "Jesus wept," and asked where they had laid Lazarus. His emotion caused mixed feelings among the crowd; some assumed that it was due to His grief for Lazarus, and noted "how he loved him." Others, even on this occasion, questioned why He had allowed such a friend to die. Under this criticism Jesus again groaned. He wept not only for the genuine sorrow of His friends, but for the disbelief and mockery of His enemies.

Christ arrived at the tomb, a cave with a large stone sealing its entrance, and asked that the stone be removed. Martha's response was practical. "Lord, by this time he stinketh: for he hath been dead four days." The dead were buried immediately in the hot climate of Judea, for without modern preservation techniques the decaying process began very rapidly. She still did not understand, and Jesus remonstrated her. "Said I not unto thee, that if thou wouldest believe, thou shouldest see the glory of God?"

They then took away the stone, and Jesus lifted up His eyes and said, "Father, I thank thee that thou hast heard me. And I knew that thou hearest me always: but because of the people which stand by I said it, that they may believe that thou hast sent me." He did not pray to receive authority or power, for He already possessed it.

The crowd must have been astonished at the opening of the tomb. Christ had twice before openly declared the purpose of this miracle, and now, before the entire crowd (friends and enemies alike), He openly declared it again. They had asked for a sign many times, and He had refused them on each of those occasions. Now He would give them a sign that they could not forget, and He would tell them plainly of its source. "Lazarus, come forth," He cried with a loud voice, so that all might hear. With the napkin tied around his face, and bound hand and foot with grave clothes, Lazarus came forth!

Christ is the life; in Him is power over death; He is the resurrection. The Jews demanded a sign, and they received it. How could they doubt? John reports that many of the Jews who were there "believed on him"; but others "went their ways to the Pharisees, and told them what things Jesus had done." Regardless of their intentions in doing this, the results were evil.

The Pharisees and chief priests gathered a council. The Sanhedrin existed at the time of Christ, but not in the original form. Since Herod had effectively broken it of its real power,[125] its activity was principally confined to ecclesiastical or semi-ecclesiastical causes,[126] and it was definitely shorn of the power to pronounce capital sentences.[127] The chief priest's office was still recognized by Rome, and councils were called to discuss local policy and religious matters.[128] But this council was different. This was, in all probability, the "standing 'council of the temple,'" whose members were also called "the elders of the priests." It consisted of fourteen members, and was a judiciary body. Although it did not ordinarily "busy itself with criminal questions, [it] apparently took a leading part in the condemnation of Jesus."[129]

"What do we?" they questioned themselves. "If we let him thus alone, all men will believe on him." Then they uttered their real concern: "The Romans shall come and take away both our place and nation." They were not concerned whether Jesus was the Messiah. They were like the rich man of the parable: concerned only with the things of the world, their political existence as a nation, and their prominence among the people. Caiaphas stepped forward and unwittingly acknowledged the Messiah's mission: "It is expedient for us, that one man should die for the people, and that the whole nation perish not." In his record John recognized that Caiaphas was prophesying the Savior's death. He would indeed die for all, but not to save the nation; rather He would save the souls of all who would follow Him and live His commandments. No longer was it "if" they would kill Him, but when and how. "Then from that day forth they took counsel together for to put him to death."

The raising of Lazarus was the ultimate sign—Christ's greatest teaching! There is no question that the Jews understood both the miracle and the parable. John recorded that after the miracle, many of the Jews "consulted that they might put Lazarus also to death.[a] They obviously would not accept the teachings of Moses or the prophets. They made mockery of the Law and as prophesied in the parable, they did not believe "though one rose from the dead."

One Last Chance

11

Malchus's Ear

Luke 22:49–51   When they which were about him saw what would follow, they said unto him, Lord, shall we smite with the sword? And one of them smote the servant of the high priest, and cut off his right ear. And Jesus answered and said, Suffer ye thus far. And he touched his ear, and healed him.

Matthew 26:51   And, behold, one of them which were with Jesus stretched out his hand, and drew his sword, and struck a servant of the high priest's, and smote off his ear.

Mark 14:47   And one of them that stood by drew a sword, and smote a servant of the high priest, and cut off his ear.

John 18:10   Then Simon Peter having a sword drew it, and smote the high priest's servant, and cut off his right ear. The servant's name was Malchus.

All four Gospel writers record the circumstances that gave rise to this remarkable miracle. Only Luke records the miracle itself, and John names the participants: the Apostle Peter and Malchus, the servant of the high priest. The setting to this event is most significant. It was the final day of Jesus' life. He had prophesied of Jerusalem's coming destruction, of problems in the latter days, and of His second coming;[130] He held the last supper and instituted the sacrament;[131] He saw His betrayer dip the sop and leave with malicious intent; and He took the eleven and went to Gethsemane to atone for the sins of mankind.[132] He asked Peter, James, and John to watch and pray as He prayed to His Father, and He returned to find them asleep. His personal anguish in the Garden completed, He said to His sleeping disciples, "Sleep on now, and take your rest: behold, the hour is at hand, and the Son of man is betrayed into the hands of sinners."[a]

Jesus was in Gethsemane, across the brook Cedron, and His betrayal was near. John records that "a band of men and officers from the chief priests and Pharisees, cometh thither with lanterns and torches and weapons."[b] Luke describes the group as "a multitude." The rulers of Israel had dispatched the group with Judas at its head. Judas had agreed that for thirty pieces of silver he would take them to where Jesus was and point Him out. Judas "knew the place" where Jesus would be;[c] and so it was that he who would betray the Son of Man led them to Him.[133]

As the group approached, Jesus asked, "Whom seek ye?"[d] They responded, "Jesus of Nazareth," whereupon the Lord answered, "I am he." The group "went backward" in fear of Him. Again they asked the same question and the Lord gave the same answer and requested that the Apostles be allowed to "go their way."[e] Luke adds that when the arresting group approached the Lord, Judas "went before them, and drew near unto Jesus to kiss him." Jesus spoke directly to Judas and asked, "Betrayest thou the Son of man with a kiss?"[f] Matthew reports that Judas actually kissed the Savior; that it was the "sign" that Judas had prearranged to identify the Lord to the arresting officers.[g] Mark agrees with Matthew concerning the sign of the betrayal and with Luke about the multitude. He also attests to the fact that the arresting officials had swords and staves.[h]

In this instance, the differences between the Gospels add to what otherwise would have been a very sketchy report. By combining them, the scene can be summarized as follows:

1. The arresting group was large, but certainly not a "multitude" in the sense used to describe situations such as the feeding of the five thousand.

2. Judas was at its head.

3. A kiss had been predetermined as the sign agreed upon to single out the Lord for arrest. (A kiss was a common form of salutation in that day.)

a. Matthew 26:45.

b. John 18:3.

c. John 18:2.

d. John 18:4.

e. John 18:5–8.

f. Luke 22:47–48.

g. Matthew 26:48.

h. Mark 14:43.

4.   Some of the arresting group were armed with swords and
     staves.

Thus the scene was set for Jesus' arrest.

As the scenario developed, Peter perceived an immediate danger to
the Lord's life. One of the Apostles asked the question, "Lord, shall
we smite with the sword?" Thereupon Peter drew his sword, and with
the love he had for the Savior and the natural courage of his heart,
he struck Malchus, a servant of the high priest and one of those that
would take Jesus. The blow cut off Malchus' right ear.

Jesus immediately calmed the situation: "Put up again thy sword
into his place: for all they that take the sword shall perish with the
sword."[a] He reminded the Apostles of His power. He need only call to
His Father, and legions of angels would be at His command; but that
would defeat the purpose of His life. Jesus then restored Malchus' ear
as it was before.

This is the only healing of record where the wound was caused by
external violence. Jesus restrained the anger of the Apostles with a mild
rebuke. "Suffer ye thus far," he stated. They had come this far with
Him, and they should not consider actions that might destroy them,
their past work, and work yet to be performed. Through this act of compassion Jesus fulfilled and exemplified His own teachings: "Love your
enemies," and "do good to them that hate you."[b] No mention is made
of any reaction by the arresting officials to either the blow or the healing. In plain view of all who had witnessed the blow, before those who
would have heard the cries of pain and seen the blood, Jesus touched the
injured ear and healed it. Still the officials pursued their goal.

The Apostles quickly scattered and fled in fear of their lives. According to Matthew's account, Judas, remorsefully aware of his part in
this evil plot, killed himself.[c] All that the Lord had taught His Apostles would be given to them again—but on this night, they deserted
Him. In the future, the Apostles would establish the church in many
nations and be responsible for the conversion of many souls. They
would testify of Christ and give their lives for the work. But on this
night of betrayal, the Savior stood alone; and in one last miraculous
act of mercy and compassion He witnessed to them all that He was
the long-awaited Messiah.

a. Matthew 26:52.

b. Matthew
5:44.

c. Matthew
27:3–5.

12

It is I

Passing Unseen (After the Resurrection)

This chapter contains three more examples of the miracle of passing unseen as discussed in Chapter 4, but these miracles occurred after the Resurrection while the previous examples took place before the Resurrection. The previous use of this miracle was to extricate Jesus from the pressure of an angry mob bent on killing Him. These later miracles involve loved ones, friends, and disciples. These people knew Jesus personally, yet in each case they were unable to recognize Him until He wanted them to. Two of the miracles are recorded in John, and the third in Luke with a cross-reference to Mark.

Jesus taught the disciples of His coming resurrection, yet it seemed difficult for them to understand. "After all that Christ had taught concerning His rising from the dead on that third day, the Apostles were unable to accept the actuality of the occurrence; to their minds the resurrection was some mysterious and remote event, not a present possibility."[134] Although Jesus had raised others from death, it was to a renewal of mortality. Now the disciples must comprehend His immortality. It appears that this miracle was used to enhance the disciples' understanding so that they might better testify of His resurrection.

Mary at the Tomb

John 20:14–17   And when she had thus said, she turned herself back, and saw Jesus standing, and knew not that it was Jesus. Jesus saith unto her, Woman, why weepest thou? whom seekest thou? She, supposing him to be the gardener, saith unto him, Sir, if thou have borne him hence, tell me where thou hast laid him, and I will take him away. Jesus saith unto her, Mary. She turned herself, and saith unto him, Rabboni;

which is to say, Master. Jesus saith unto her, Touch me not; for I am not yet ascended to my Father: but go to my brethren, and say unto them, I ascend unto my Father, and your Father; and to my God, and your God.

Cross-references   Luke 24:1–10; JST Luke 24:14

After the crucifixion, the body of Jesus was hastily taken down from the cross, quickly prepared for burial, and placed in the tomb. Some disciples had intended to reopen the grave after the Sabbath to further prepare the body of the Lord with spices; yet even this act of love displayed their lack of understanding concerning the Resurrection. Had they fully understood His rising they would not have anticipated this need.

On the first day of the week, one of Christ's female disciples came to the sepulcher. Her name was Mary Magdalene. According to John she was alone, but in Luke's version others were with her. They had brought spices to further prepare the Lord's body. When they arrived at the tomb, the stone covering its entrance had been rolled away. Two angels sitting at the entrance to the tomb spoke to the women, and asked why they sought the living among the dead. They further declared that Jesus had risen and that the women should return and tell the Apostles. Mary, now alone, pondered this announcement. She was weeping and when the angels asked why, she responded, "Because they have taken away my Lord, and I know not where they have laid him."[a] She turned and saw the Lord, "and knew not that it was Jesus." They conversed briefly, but she still did not recognize Him.

Jesus then addressed her personally and called her by name. It was then that she recognized Him and responded, "Master." Apparently she moved toward Him, perhaps to embrace Him, but the Lord admonished her not to touch Him and told her to go and tell the Apostles that He had risen.[135]

On the Road to Emmaus

Luke 24:13–16, 31   And, behold, two of them went that same day to a village called Emmaus, which was from Jerusalem about threescore furlongs. And they talked together of all these things which had happened. And it came to pass, that, while they communed together and reasoned, Jesus himself drew near, and went with them. But their eyes were holden that they should not know him. . . . And their eyes were opened, and they knew him; and he vanished out of their sight.

a. John 20:13.

Cross-reference   Mark 16:12–13

Two disciples were walking to Emmaus, "about threescore furlongs" from Jerusalem. They were discussing the monumental events that had taken place concerning Jesus: undoubtedly His recent trial and crucifixion. They probably recounted the stories that surrounded the disappearance of Jesus' body, and pondered the testimony of those who said they had seen Him.

Jesus drew near and walked with them. He must have joined them in a normal manner, for nothing miraculous is recorded concerning this. "But their eyes were holden that they should not know him." Jesus talked to them, asked them questions about the subject of their conversation, and noted that they were sad. One of the two disciples was named Cleopas; the other remains unnamed, but is generally thought to be Luke.[136] Cleopas responded to the question and asked Jesus if He were "only a stranger in Jerusalem."[a] While continuing their journey, they rehearsed the events of the crucifixion to Him, and in due time they arrived at Emmaus. They asked Jesus to stop and dine with them, still not recognizing Him. Jesus agreed. He took bread, broke it, blessed it, and gave it to them; "And their eyes were opened, and they knew him; and he vanished out of their sight."

On the Shore of Galilee

John 21:4   But when the morning was now come, Jesus stood on the shore: but the disciples knew not that it was Jesus.

The last of these miracles was briefly mentioned earlier (Chapter 7) in connection with the miracle of the last draught of fish. Peter and six others had been waiting in Galilee for further instructions from the Lord. They had already seen Him after His resurrection. They decided to go fishing, and spent the night casting their nets without success. As the morning drew near, they headed toward the shore. A figure was standing on the shore, "but the disciples knew not that it was Jesus." They conversed with Him and He then provided the miracle of the final draught of fish, having them cast their nets again and receiving the sea's bounty. At that point, John recognized that it was the Lord and informed Peter. The group immediately went ashore, ate of the meal that the Lord had prepared, and received His instructions. a. Luke 24:18.

The people involved in these miracles were all disciples of the Lord. Mary had been converted and forgiven of her sins. The Apostles were with Him almost continuously for three years during His ministry. In the case of Cleopas and the unnamed disciple, their previous acquaintance with the Lord is not known, but from their discussion it is obvious that they had known Him. In these instances the Lord simply did not want His disciples to recognize Him.

He apparently used this miracle for clarification and witness. No resurrection had occurred prior to that of Jesus Christ. Consequently, His disciples, including the Apostles, must clearly understand two things: first, that He had risen; and second, exactly what His resurrection meant. He had told them several times prior to His death that He would rise again, but they had not understood. When Mary and the women told the Apostles that Jesus had risen, their "words seemed to them as idle tales, and they believed them not."[a] Peter ran to the tomb and looked in. He saw the linen clothes by themselves; the body was gone. He departed, "wondering in himself at that which was come to pass." Clearly he did not fully comprehend. The Lord would use this miracle to bring to the memory of the Apostles and the disciples precious teachings and instructions that they had previously received. He did this to strengthen their witness of Him.

Encouraged by the Lord's questions, the disciples on the road to Emmaus rehearsed the circumstances of their acquaintance with the man named Jesus. They asked Him to dine, and then Jesus broke bread and blessed it. With the performance of this familiar sacrament, they knew Him. Their eyes were opened and the Spirit bore witness; their bosoms burned, and they received a testimony of the resurrected Christ.

Mary's case is somewhat different. She was the first to see the resurrected Lord. She, too, had not fully understood the teachings concerning His coming forth. The Lord's questions invoked her innermost feelings concerning Him. When He called her by name, the personal manner became familiar to her. She recognized Him, even though she could not touch Him. She could now testify that He had risen, and she was instructed to do so.

The miracle in each case allowed Jesus' Apostles and other disciples time to recall their former associations with Him. In the future when

a. Luke 24:11.

they testified of His resurrection, they would be asked to explain how they knew it was so. Thanks to the Lord's use of this miracle, the experience was clear to them, and they would be able to testify with assurance that the Lord had been resurrected. Mary could say that she had seen Him, but more important, that He addressed her as He always had—in the same manner, with the same tone, generating the same feelings.[137] The disciples on the road to Emmaus would remember their conversation with Him and would report that He broke bread and blessed it as before.[138] The Apostles had already seen Him several times, but after finally recognizing Him at the second draught of fish, their testimony would be even more secure.

The Lord declared His resurrection in many ways to His disciples. He talked with them, walked with them, allowed them to touch Him, and permitted them to see Him with their own eyes. On one of these occasions, He declared that He was not a "spirit" as they supposed, but a resurrected body of "flesh and bones."[a] These physical, sensory experiences added strength to the witness of those who saw Him, invoking an emotional and spiritual witness that allowed them to testify that they _knew_ Jesus had been resurrected and that He was, indeed, the Messiah.

a. Luke 24:36–39.

The Source of His Power   13

The Nobleman's Son

John 4:45–54   Then when he was come into Galilee, the Galileans received him, having seen all the things that he did at Jerusalem at the feast: for they also went unto the feast. So Jesus came again into Cana of Galilee, where he made the water wine. And there was a certain nobleman, whose son was sick at Capernaum. When he heard that Jesus was come out of Judea into Galilee, he went unto him, and besought him that he would come down, and heal his son: for he was at the point of death. Then said Jesus unto him, Except ye see signs and wonders, ye will not believe. The nobleman saith unto him, Sir, come down ere my child die. Jesus saith unto him, Go thy way; thy son liveth. And the man believed the word that Jesus had spoken unto him, and he went his way. And as he was now going down, his servants met him, and told him, saying. Thy son liveth. Then inquired he of them the hour when he began to amend. And they said unto him, Yesterday at the seventh hour the fever left him. So the father knew that it was at the same hour, in the which Jesus said unto him, Thy son liveth: and himself believed, and his whole house. This is again the second miracle that Jesus did, when he was come out of Judea into Galilee.

Jesus repeatedly told the Jews that God was His Father and that His Father had given Him the authority to do God's work.[a]139 He spake "as one having authority, and not as the scribes."[b] The two miracles dealt with in this chapter emphasize this principle.

The healing of the nobleman's son is often compared to the healing of the centurion's servant, for the blessing was granted by the word of Christ while some distance from the afflicted person. However, the nuances of the miracle would seem to indicate that the nobleman was driven to Jesus by the anguish he felt at the anticipated loss of his son, and not by any inner conviction of Christ's divinity. Only John records the miracle.

a. John 5, 6, 7, 8
b. Matthew 7:29.

Jesus had been to a feast in Jerusalem prior to coming to Cana of Galilee and apparently had performed many miracles there. None are recorded, but we infer them from John's introduction to the miracle: "Then when he was come into Galilee, the Galileans received him, having seen all the things that he did at Jerusalem at the feast." This knowledge, coupled with the nobleman's pressing need, brought him to Jesus.

It has been speculated that the nobleman was one of the officers of the court of Herod Antipas.[140] Some specifically identify him as Chuza,[141] Herod's steward. They base this on Luke's statement that "Joanna the wife of Chuza Herod's steward . . . ministered unto him of [her] substance."[a]

The nobleman lived in Capernaum and his son was sick, "at the point of death." He came to Jesus and "besought" Him to heal his son; but more than this, he requested that Jesus "come down" to his home to perform the healing. He seemed to believe that Jesus, as the great rabbis of Israel, must be present to invoke the blessing upon his son, thereby adding His presence to the strength of His supplications to God. Jesus rebuked the nobleman's request, not because he asked for a miracle, but because of his lack of understanding. He responded: "Except ye see signs and wonders, ye will not believe. Except ye see me come and lay my hands on the head of your son, as ye are aware I have done to others, ye will not believe that he shall be healed. Do ye not know that it is written of me 'He sent his word, and healed them?'"[142] The nobleman appeared to have faith in Christ as a miracle worker and healer, but not as the Messiah.

The nobleman seemingly took no offense at Jesus' remark, for he persisted in his goal. He again requested Jesus to "come down" ere his son die. Jesus now taught the man, the Apostles, and others that were with Him of His authority. The distance from the sick son meant nothing—in Jesus was the life! "Go thy way; thy son liveth," Jesus commanded.

With his faith strengthened by the promise of the Lord, the nobleman went his way. Capernaum was some twenty miles away. He could readily have reached his home that evening for it was early afternoon when he spoke with Jesus, but for some reason he tarried. He spent the night either in Cana or between Cana and Capernaum, and in the

a. Luke 8:3.

morning continued the journey to his house. As he journeyed, he met his servants coming to tell him the news: his son lived! He asked them the "hour when he began to amend." They responded that the fever left him in the seventh hour on the previous day. The hours of the day were calculated from sunrise forward, so the boy would have been healed about 1:00 P.M. on the previous day.[143] The father must have noted the hour when he left Jesus, for John records that he "knew that it was at the same hour." This conversation perhaps revealed the reservation remaining in the nobleman's mind; but knowing his son had been healed again strengthened his faith.

Jesus performed two miracles on this occasion; the son's body was healed, and the father's spirit was enlightened. As the Psalmist said, "He sent his word, and healed them, and delivered them from their destructions."[a] All those involved in this miracle ultimately recognized the Savior's authority. The nobleman and his entire house were converted, and the Apostles were strengthened. To the Savior, healing the soul is more important than healing the body. The physical healing, as with all of His miracles, was secondary to spiritual growth. Such was the case with the nobleman and all his house.

The Woman with an Issue of Blood

Mark 5:25–34   And a certain woman, which had an issue of blood twelve years, and had suffered many things of many physicians, and had spent all that she had, and was nothing bettered, but rather grew worse, when she had heard of Jesus, came in the press behind, and touched his garment. For she said, If I may touch but his clothes, I shall be whole. And straightway the fountain of her blood was dried up; and she felt in her body that she was healed of that plague. And Jesus, immediately knowing in himself that virtue had gone out of him, turned him about in the press, and said, Who touched my clothes? And his disciples said unto him, Thou seest the multitude thronging thee, and sayest thou, Who touched me? And he looked round about to see her that had done this thing. But the woman fearing and trembling, knowing what was done in her, came and fell down before him, and told him all the truth. And he said unto her, Daughter, thy faith hath made thee whole; go in peace, and be whole of thy plague.

Cross-references   Matthew 9:20–22; Luke 8:43–48

This miracle teaches several doctrines, but none more pointedly than that pertaining to Christ's authority and compassion. It is re-

a. Psalms 107:20.

corded by all three Synoptics. Mark is used as the primary text, but all the Synoptics agree on the miracle's main points and the circumstances surrounding it.

The circumstances of this healing are unique, for they are contained within the framework of yet another miracle. Jairus had come to Jesus to request the healing of his sick daughter, and Jesus had agreed to go with him to his house where the sick child lay. While Jesus was on the way to Jairus's house, a woman apparently overheard the discussion between Jairus and Jesus, and she joined the crowd that thronged about Jesus as He walked toward Jairus' home. The woman was unknown to Jesus before the miracle and no record of her exists after it.

The woman had an "issue of blood," an ailment involving frequent hemorrhaging. The ailment had been with her for twelve years. She had made many efforts to cure the disease. The scripture notes that she had "suffered many things of many physicians," for this was a disease which had several prescribed cures. One Talmud treatment for the ailment reads: "Take of the gum of Alexandria the weight of a zuzee (a fractional silver coin); of alum the same; of crocus the same. Let them be braised together, and given in wine to the woman that has an issue of blood. If this does not benefit, take of Persian onions three logs (pints); boil them in wine and give her to drink, and say, 'Arise from thy flux.'"[144] Throughout the years she had undoubtedly used this and many other mystical remedies prescribed by the physicians of the day.

Alfred Edersheim states: "On one leaf of the Talmud not less than eleven different remedies are proposed, of which at most only six can possibly be regarded as astringents or tonics, while the rest are merely the outcome of superstition, to which resort is had in the absence of knowledge."[145] One of those superstitions required carrying "the ashes of an Ostrich-Egg, carried in summer in a linen, in winter in a cotton rag."[146] It is easy to see how, after trying such "remedies" for twelve long years, she had spent "all that she had, and was nothing bettered, but rather grew worse."

The woman, like Jairus, had heard of the healings that Jesus had performed and had come to Him to be healed. But unlike Jairus, who openly sought Christ out, she had conceived in her heart that if she could but touch His clothes, or the hem or "border of his garment," she would be made whole.

This hem or border was not the bottom of the skirt-like garment traditionally worn at that time, but a special border applied to the upper shirt, or shawl-like garment worn over the shoulders.[147] It was a mark of the Levitical Priesthood, commanded by God to be worn. "And the Lord spake unto Moses, saying, Speak unto the children of Israel, and bid them that they make them fringes in the borders of their garments throughout their generations, and that they put upon the fringe of the borders a ribband of blue: And it shall be unto you for a fringe, that ye may look upon it, and remember all the commandments of the Lord, and do them . . . and be holy unto your God."[a] The Jews wore this shawl to indicate to the people that they were Pharisees or scribes and that they lived the commandments and were accounted teachers of the Law. But the symbolism of the shawl had deteriorated, and Jesus rebuked what had become a meaningless practice. "But all their works they do for to be seen of men: they make broad their phylacteries, and enlarge the borders of their garments."[b] Some portions of the accustomed dress for teachers of Christ's day were absolutely necessary if they were to "publicly read or 'Targum' the scriptures or exercise any function in the Synagogue."[148] It can therefore be assumed that Jesus wore these garments. However, "we may safely assume [that He would] go about in the ordinary, . . . not in the more ostentatious, dress, worn by the Jewish teachers of Galilee."[149] The woman eventually succeeded in touching the Lord's garment, and immediately "she felt in her body that she was healed of [her] plague." Upon being healed, she attempted to shrink secretly back into the crowd.

Her faith in the Lord was great, but it was incomplete. She did not understand that her faith had drawn a tangible power from Jesus, and without it she would not have obtained the blessing. The power Christ possessed was from His Father and was not inherent in His garments or in the flesh and bone of His body. The healing power had not come from Him against His will, even though it had been drawn from Him by the woman's great faith. There was to be no misunderstanding as a result of this miracle; therefore, He did not allow the woman to escape unnoticed after she had been healed.

Jesus immediately knew "that virtue had gone out of him."[150] He turned, looked at the crowd, and asked, "Who touched my clothes?" The disciples were not aware of what had taken place. They, along with a large crowd, were anxiously following Jesus to the home of Jairus, eagerly anticipating the coming miracle involving Jairus's daughter.

Therefore, when the Lord asked who had touched Him, the disciples responded incredulously, "Thou seest the multitude thronging thee, and sayest thou, Who touched me?" But Jesus had perceived that "virtue had gone out of him." His question was not directed to His disciples but to the woman.

The woman was being called before her Lord and Savior to account for her actions. Her intentions had been pure and her faith sure. Therefore, "fearing and trembling, knowing what was done in her, [she] came and fell down before Him, and told Him all the truth." With love and compassion the Lord responded, "Daughter, thy faith hath made thee whole; go in peace, and be whole of thy plague."

Christ would not withhold a blessing from this faithful woman, but He wanted to teach her, the Apostles, and the multitude that He was the source of the healing power, and that it was extended by His will. That the woman had drawn upon it by her faith was true, but the reservoir of the power and the well from which the life-giving water had been drawn was Jesus Christ. Faith had made her cure possible, but Christ had done the healing.

Sin and Leprosy

The Law of Moses and the Levitical ordinances created a very orderly society. This orderliness separated the Jews from their neighbor nations. But the ordinances were given for reasons other than merely creating this orderly society. They created a relationship—not just among themselves, but with God. The Law was to bring the chosen people closer to God and to direct every moment of their lives toward Him.

Conversely, the Law was also evidence of their sinfulness; for through it they came to know the cause of their separation from God. Yet it provided the means whereby they could symbolically cleanse themselves from sin and regain the purity God demanded. By complying with the Law, they were schooled in the two great commandments: to love God and to love their neighbor. Loving God resulted in spiritual growth and reminded them to do all things with God in mind. Loving their neighbor involved regulation upon regulation dictating exactly how this was to be done. Thus, the Law was their schoolmaster through which they could again achieve a closeness with God that had been lost through sin.

To be cast out of this order or deprived of its regulations meant exclusion from God Himself. The greatest symbol under their Law that exemplified this condition was the disease of leprosy.[151] The Talmud said, "These four are counted as dead, the blind, the leper, the poor, and the childless."[152] Even though sin was often accounted as the reason for blindness, poverty, and childlessness, individuals with these afflictions were nonetheless accepted within the community and society. But the leper was different. He was morally dead, cursed of God; his disease was a symbol of sin and uncleanliness.[153] The leper was excluded from the camp of Israel and considered to be a loathsome member of the living dead.[a]

The consequence of sin was spiritual death, and God set leprosy aside as an example to Israel of that principle. It was the living definition of sin. It progressed slowly, eating the flesh, thriving and increasing, sustaining itself upon the body, with the inevitable conclusion—death.[154]

The results of sin were looked upon in like manner. To the Jews, God was a God of the living, not the dead. The leper was thus excluded from Jewish life in the same manner that the sinner was excluded from the presence of God.[155]

Only Israelite lepers were regulated among the chosen people. Strangers and sojourners in their land were expressly exempted from the ordinances and regulations of the Law regarding leprosy.[156] An Israelite had to cry "Unclean" as another approached, had to wear a torn garment, and had to cover his lower lip.[157] God could easily have made all sickness unclean, for illness often led to death. But He took one example, leprosy, and made it a visible sign of sin's nature. It was the sign that evil was not from nor acceptable to God and that those who were sinful could not dwell with Him. It alone was selected as a witness against sin and its results.[158] "This did not mean that the disease borne by any individual attested that he was a worse sinner than his fellows, only that the disease itself was a symbol of the ills that will befall the ungodly and rebellious."[159]

The fact that leprosy was incurable added to the reasons why it was singled out. So closely connected was the disease with sin that a man's true repentance was recognized as a precondition to having leprosy leave him.[160] The purity sought after by obedience to the Law was unattainable to the leper unless God willed it. He must literally be purified by God to be cleansed, thus giving rise to the belief that he had truly repented.[161]

A leper bore the emblems of death[b] and was literally mourned as if he were dead. Contact with a leper meant defilement, and the cleansing procedures were the same as when defiled by a dead body.[c] David purged himself of spiritual leprosy with this cleansing procedure.[d]

a. Leviticus 13:46; Numbers 5:2–4.

b. Leviticus 13:45.

c. Numbers 19:6; Leviticus 14:4–7.

d. Psalms 51:7.

God on occasion used leprosy to punish those who sinned against His divine government. When Miriam spoke against Moses, she was smitten and "became leprous, white as snow";[a] Uzziah was smitten because he did not remove the "high places" where the "people sacrificed and burnt incense";[b] and Gehazi was cursed with the disease of Naaman for his evil before the Lord.[c]

There could be no better way for the Lord of life to show that His mercy, love, and kingdom were extended to all than to heal the leper.

The Cleansing of the Leper

Mark 1:40–45   And there came a leper to him, beseeching him, and kneeling down to him, and saying unto him, If thou wilt, thou canst make me clean. And Jesus, moved with compassion, put forth his hand, and touched him, and saith unto him, I will; be thou clean. And as soon as he had spoken, immediately the leprosy departed from him, and he was cleansed. And he straitly charged him, and forthwith sent him away; and saith unto him, See thou say nothing to any man: but go thy way, shew thyself to the priest, and offer for thy cleansing those things which Moses commanded, for a testimony unto them. But he went out, and began to publish it much, and to blaze abroad the matter, insomuch that Jesus could no more openly enter into the city, but was without in desert places: and they came to him from every quarter.

Cross-references   Matthew 8:1–4; Luke 5:12–16

A man "full of leprosy" came to Jesus and requested a miracle. His belief in the Lord was explicit. He did not ask to be made clean, but stated, "If thou wilt, thou canst make me clean." Here was a simple, open confession of faith, perhaps the first such confession in the Lord's public ministry. He believed that Jesus could heal him; his question was whether Jesus *would* heal him.

The request touched the heart of Jesus, and He "was moved with compassion." He put forth His hand and touched the leper, answering, "I will; be thou clean. And as soon as he had spoken, immediately the leprosy departed from him, and he was cleansed." The Lord had extended His power and healed the leper, but the miracle's significance went much deeper.

To the Jews, the leper represented the filthiest of mankind. To touch him or be touched by him made one immediately unclean in the Levitical sense, yet Jesus simply reached out and touched him. In the touching and healing can be seen the purity and life offered by

a. Numbers
   12:1–10.

b. 2 Kings 15:4–5.

c. 2 Kings
   5:27.

the kingdom of God. Jesus did not become unclean; rather, the man became clean.

The stories of Moses and the burning bush and Peter's dream of the sheet with food upon it represent a like principle. As Moses approached the bush, God spoke unto him: "put off thy shoes from off thy feet, for the place whereon thou standest is holy ground."[a] The ground itself was not holy; God's presence made it holy.

Peter's vision occurred as he rested, waiting for dinner. In his vision a sheet, knitted "at the four corners," was let down, and all manner of meat was on it, including that which was forbidden under the Mosaic law. Peter was commanded to arise and "kill, and eat." He refused because the food was "common or unclean." The voice of God then attested to Peter, "What God hath cleansed, that call not thou common." The vision directed Peter concerning gentile membership in the kingdom of God; shortly thereafter, Cornelius and his house were admitted to the church.[b] Here it was the same. What God had cleansed could not be declared unclean.

Jesus did not need to touch the leper to heal him, but by His touch and through this miracle He declared Himself the Messiah, opened the kingdom to all, and abrogated Judaism henceforth.[162]

Two instructions were now given to the leper. First, he was to "say nothing to any man"; second, he was to show himself to the priest, thus complying with the cleansing requirements of the Mosaic Law. Judaism was in apostasy, yet the Mosaic Law was still in force. Jesus would not replace it until every "jot and tittle" had been fulfilled. Showing himself to the priest was not a requirement for Jesus' benefit, but for the leper's. He had to comply with the Law before he could reenter the Jewish community.

Christ's first instruction ("say nothing to any man") is not as easily dealt with. On at least three other occasions Jesus left the recipient of a miracle with a similar instruction.[163] No immediate reason for such an instruction is given in the scriptures, but knowing that the Lord's primary concern is for all men to attain His kingdom, consider the following.

The Effect Upon the Individual

Jesus gave this instruction upon four recorded occasions, and in each

a. Exodus 3:5.
b. Acts 10:11–20.

instance it was virtually impossible to fulfill. In this case, the leper must publicly declare his cleansing; and certainly family members, friends, and associates would know that he was now clean. All would question him concerning his healing, for they believed that a leper could only be cleansed by miraculous intervention.[164] Similarly, the two blind in the house were known to be blind (Chapter 15). They had shouted after Jesus and followed Him into the house. The miracle could not be hidden, for they went into the house blind and came out seeing. Yet they were instructed to tell no one. In the raising of the daughter of Jairus (Chapter 8), all who were there and who had come with Jesus knew that the daughter had died, yet they saw her alive again. The healing of the deaf and dumb man (Chapter 16) stood amidst a multitude of miracles. Many had been healed, and the multitude that witnessed those healings acknowledged that Jesus had "done all things well." How can such a miracle be kept a secret?

The Lord's instruction was apparently not meant to be a literal ban on all communication concerning the miracle. Rather, it cautioned the recipient on how he should speak of the miracle. Further, it focused attention on Jesus as the Messiah. Those healed were not to glory in the miracle. The Lord knew the personalities and feelings of the recipients. Perhaps if they focused on the temporal results, reveling in the miracle itself, they might jeopardize the spiritual offering of the kingdom of God.

Only Mark emphasizes the leper's reaction in this miracle. Although Luke acknowledges that the miracle increased Christ's fame, he does not attribute it to the leper. Due to the joy the leper experienced at his healing, he probably found it difficult to remain silent. Although the immediate effect is recorded by Mark, the total effect upon the leper's life thereafter is not recorded in the scriptures.

The Effect Upon the Immediate Community

In the cleansing of the leper, the effect of the miracle on the public was so overwhelming that Jesus could "no more openly enter into the city." The publicity brought great multitudes to hear Him and to be healed by Him. The emphasis of the multitude was, undoubtedly, on the temporal healing, and not on the spiritual blessing. The excitement sensationalized the Lord's healing powers rather than glorified

His mission and kingdom. The Lord undoubtedly knew what effect publicizing the miracle would have upon the community in each case where the instruction, "Tell no one," was given. His miraculous powers were not just an appeal to the feelings and emotions of those who witnessed them, but were intended to be lodged in understanding and loving hearts. His desire, as always, was that all mankind would come unto Him, repent, be baptized, and receive of His kingdom.

The Cleansing of Ten Lepers

Luke 17:12–19   And as he entered into a certain village, there met him ten men that were lepers, which stood afar off: and they lifted up their voices, and said, Jesus, Master, have mercy on us. And when he saw them, he said unto them, Go shew yourselves unto the priests. And it came to pass, that, as they went, they were cleansed. And one of them, when he saw that he was healed, turned back, and with a loud voice glorified God, and fell down on his face at his feet, giving him thanks: and he was a Samaritan. And Jesus answering said, Were there not ten cleansed? but where are the nine? There are not found that returned to give glory to God, save this stranger. And he said unto him, Arise, go thy way: thy faith hath made thee whole.

Luke records that as Jesus entered a certain village, He encountered ten lepers. One is known to be a Samaritan and the other nine have always been assumed to be Jews.[165] Lepers could mingle and associate with each other, but with no one else. They heard that Jesus was coming and called after Him, begging for His mercy. He immediately extended it and then instructed the men to "Go shew yourselves unto the priests." His instruction implied that the blessing had been granted, even though the miracle had not yet taken place. All ten believed that they would be healed, for they immediately left to comply with the Levitical Law; as they hurried to the priest, they were cleansed.

These men had the faith necessary to do as they were instructed, and the healing that took place witnessed not only their faith but the Lord's capacity as a healer. However, only one leper recognized who the healer was. As the healing took place, the Samaritan stopped and returned to Jesus, falling at the Lord's feet and giving thanks. Jesus acknowledged him and asked, "Were there not ten cleansed?" The other nine, in the joy of their temporal healing, had lost this opportunity for added spiritual growth; they were not to be found.[166] "Go thy way," Jesus stated. "Thy faith hath made thee whole." The Samaritan now received the added spiritual blessing the nine had missed. All ten had enough faith to go at His bidding and be healed; only one had enough faith to return and give thanks and glory to the healer.

This miracle is a perfect example of the universal charity that Jesus taught His disciples. The healed leper was a Samaritan—to the Jews a heathen from a hated race—yet he received the Lord's blessings, both physically and spiritually. "The occurrence must have impressed the Apostles as another evidence of acceptability and possible excellence on the part of aliens, to the disparagement of Jewish claims of superiority irrespective of merit."[167]

Finally, this incident provides a great object lesson on miracles. The miracle was simple and quick. There was no extensive test of faith or development of belief. The lepers requested the miracle and immediately received it. The ten lepers did not know that Jesus was the Messiah; they only believed that He could heal them. To the nine, once the blessing had been granted, the goal had been attained; but to the Samaritan, the healing was only the road to his goal. The healing brought joy and happiness to all the lepers, for it ended their misery. They rejoiced, and in that joy proceeded to comply with the Law and return to normal society. Nine were satisfied with a physical healing and did not see past it; the Samaritan saw past the temporal blessing and seized the opportunity for spiritual growth.

By healing the lepers Jesus extended His compassion to all, opened wide the doors of His kingdom, and abrogated Jewish exclusiveness forever.[168]

Spiritual Blindness

As with the lepers, the blind were considered "dead" by the Talmud,[169] even though they were treated with special kindness and mercy. Blindness had a special, symbolic meaning concerning the spiritual condition of Israel. It symbolized moral and spiritual decay and apostasy.[170] The Pharisees and scribes were offended at the teachings of Jesus. The Lord responded to their offense by instructing the disciples, "Let them alone: they be blind leaders of the blind. And if the blind lead the blind, both shall fall into the ditch."[a] By healing the blind, Jesus symbolically testified to the Jews that He was offering them relief from their spiritual blindness and granting them new light.

That physical blindness and spiritual sight were associated is attested to in the Old Testament where the Lord emphasized that disobedience to His commandments resulted in spiritual darkness. Moses summarized the cursings for disobedience to the Law in Deuteronomy: "If thou wilt not hearken unto the voice of the Lord thy God, to observe to do all his commandments and his statutes which I command thee this day; . . . all these curses shall come upon thee, and overtake thee."[b] A list of specific curses followed. Then Moses described Israel's disobedient condition as a people that "grope at noonday, as the blind gropeth in darkness."[c]

Isaiah used the analogy to describe the spiritual darkness of the last days. He said, "We grope for the wall like the blind, and we grope as if we had no eyes: we stumble at noonday as in the night; we are in desolate places as dead men."[d] When Job discussed his beleaguered

a. Matthew 15:14.

b. Deuteronomy 28:15.

c. Deuteronomy 28:29.

d. Isaiah 59:10.

condition with his friends and associates, he compared those without God's light to those who "grope in the dark without light, and . . . stagger like a drunken man."[a] Zephaniah described this spiritual darkness clearly. He said of the Lord's reaction to those who would neither heed nor accept His word, "And I will bring distress upon men, that they shall walk like blind men, because they have sinned against the Lord."[b]

Blindness indicated a loss of the spiritual light God had given. Thus, to be healed meant deliverance from sin and the removal of this spiritual blindness.[c] Jesus declared openly that He was "the light of the world."[d] Through Him their spiritual blindness would be taken away. The healings of the blind were the embodiment of that testimony.

The Two Blind in the House

Matthew 9:27–31   And when Jesus departed thence, two blind men followed him, crying, and saying, Thou Son of David, have mercy on us. And when he was come into the house, the blind men came to him: and Jesus saith unto them, Believe ye that I am able to do this? They said unto him, Yea, Lord. Then touched he their eyes, saying, According to your faith be it unto you. And their eyes were opened; and Jesus straitly charged them, saying, See that no man know it. But they, when they were departed, spread abroad his fame in all that country.

Cross-reference   IV Matthew 9:36

The Blind at Jericho

Luke 18:35–43   And it came to pass, that as he was come nigh unto Jericho, a certain blind man sat by the way side begging: and hearing the multitude pass by, he asked what it meant. And they told him, that Jesus of Nazareth passeth by. And he cried, saying, Jesus, thou Son of David, have mercy on me. And they which went before rebuked him, that he should hold his peace: but he cried so much the more, Thou Son of David, have mercy on me. And Jesus stood, and commanded him to be brought unto him: and when he was come near, he asked him, saying, What wilt thou that I shall do unto thee? And he said, Lord, that I may receive my sight. And Jesus said unto him, Receive thy sight: thy faith hath saved thee. And immediately he received his sight, and followed him, glorifying God: and all the people, when they saw it, gave praise unto God.

a. Job 12:25.

b. Zephaniah 1:17.

c. Isaiah 29:18; Ephesians 5:8.

d. John 8:12.

Cross-references   Matthew 20:29–34; Mark 10:46–52

Since these two miracles are very similar they will here be discussed together. Further, they will be treated topically rather than sequentially.

The Divergence Between the Synoptic Accounts

Only Matthew records both miracles. Perhaps the differences between Matthew and the other two Synoptics are caused by duplicating or superimposing facts from Matthew's Chapter 9 miracle on his Jericho miracle. The difficulties of this have been discussed before and need not be taken up again here (Chapter 3). With this interpretation, the facts of the two Matthew miracles would be coordinated in favor of the Chapter 9 miracle. This would leave the balance of the facts describing the Jericho miracle in agreement with Mark and Luke. Thus, there would be two blind men in the miracle in Chapter 9 (the two blind men in the house) and only one in the Jericho miracle (whom Mark names Bartimaeus). Jesus touched the eyes of the blind in the Chapter 9 miracle, but not in the Jericho miracle. It is not possible to determine whether Jesus performed the miracle upon entering (Luke) or exiting (Matthew and Mark) Jericho.

The Blind Men's Unique Request and Their Persistence

These were requested miracles. The blind were disadvantaged compared with the other sick people that came to Jesus requesting help. They did not have freedom of movement and had to be told when Jesus was present. Once these blind men knew Jesus was in their vicinity, they would not let the opportunity pass. They cried after Him, for that was the only way they could attract His attention. They were not ashamed of their desire. And even though Jesus seemed at first to ignore them, they would not be still. In Matthew, Chapter 9, they followed Him into a house to further petition their cause; in the Jericho miracle the multitude surrounding Jesus wanted to quiet them, but they "cried so much the more," for it was their only chance. In both circumstances it is evident that Jesus was known to them, and once the opportunity to be healed presented itself, they would not be denied. Their cry for help and their persistence demonstrated their faith in His power to restore their sight.

The Title Used to Address Jesus; i.e., the Son of David

It is unlikely that these blind men recognized Jesus as the Messiah. They probably addressed Him in this manner as a title of homage. In their cry for help was the "hope" of the Messiah, expressed in a common form of address of the time,[171] rather than a sure knowledge or belief that He was the awaited Savior.[172] Their cry did evidence, however, that they hoped and believed that He could and would heal them. They petitioned for the Lord's mercy, and when questioned concerning their desire their response was direct and to the point: they wanted their sight restored. After receiving the blessing they desired, they followed and praised the Lord. Only in the title they used to address Him is there an indication of anything other than a temporal desire for the healing of their blindness. The title itself was not denied by Jesus; He was the Son of David.

The Lord's Question

In the Lord's question and action lay a source of help to those who could not see. In terms of the men's immediate need it was redundant for Jesus to ask what the blind men wanted, for what they wanted was obvious. But the question allowed a strengthening of the faith first demonstrated by their cry for help. Jesus ignored their initial request and by so doing witnessed their determination. His next actions encouraged that persistent desire. He "stood" or stopped to talk with the man in the Jericho miracle, and He received the blind into the house in the Chapter 9 miracle. Such actions could only have increased the confidence of the blind. In the Jericho miracle, the blind man eagerly responded to His question by answering that he wanted to receive his sight; in the Chapter 9 miracle, the blind acknowledged their belief that the Lord could perform the miracle. Thus the Lord helped them obtain their desire by helping them increase their faith.

The Crowd's Reaction to the Jericho Miracle

The crowd's reaction in this miracle is interesting. The blind man heard the crowd coming and asked who was causing so much excitement. He was eagerly told that Jesus of Nazareth was passing by. The blind man immediately began shouting after Jesus to gain His attention. The people "rebuked him, that he should hold his peace." Perhaps they did not want the Master to be interrupted or disturbed. Jesus often taught as He walked, and the crowd may have been trying to hear Him. The disciples had, on a previous occasion, attempted to restrain little children from coming to the Master.[a] On another occa-

a. Mark 10:13–
14.

sion, when Jesus initially ignored the plea of the Syrophenician woman, the disciples attempted to send her away to silence her.[a] But now Jesus stopped and called for the man, and the crowd quickly changed its attitude. "Be of good comfort...; he calleth thee," they said. But the crowd remained spiritually blind. They had tried to silence the one whose sight was dead, and who was, in their minds, spiritually dead as well; but the Light of the world would have it otherwise and gave him his sight.

The Instruction to Tell No One

This material was previously discussed in detail (Chapter 15) and need not be reiterated here except to determine its importance in this particular situation. The blind men were undoubtedly well known in the area. They cried after Jesus, followed the crowd, and then went with the Lord into the house. They went in blind, but they came forth seeing.

It was virtually impossible to avoid publicizing this miracle. The Lord would have known this, but His admonition sought to direct the attention of the healed to the miracle's source rather than to their joy over its temporal effects. The Lord was revealing His Messianic identity.[173] This realization would best come to the blind men through contemplation and following the Master, not by demonstrating their newly regained sight. However, the men chose to "spread abroad his fame."[174]

These two miracles testified of Jesus as the Light of the world, and seemingly were directed at blind Israel. Isaiah had prophesied, "See ye indeed, but perceive not . . . shut their eyes; lest they see with their eyes, . . . and convert, and be healed."[b] After the parable of the sower, the Lord said of them (the Pharisees and scribes), "seeing [they] see not; . . . and their eyes they have closed."[c] The Light of the world had come so that the blind—both physically blind and spiritually blind— might see.

a. Matthew
   15:22–23.

b. Isaiah 6:9–10.

c. Matthew
   13:13, 15.

Increasing Faith Through Miracles   16

One Deaf and Dumb

Mark 7:31–37   And again, departing from the coasts of Tyre and Sidon, he came unto the sea of Galilee, through the midst of the coasts of Decapolis. And they bring unto him one that was deaf, and had an impediment in his speech; and they beseech him to put his hand upon him. And he took him aside from the multitude, and put his fingers into his ears, and he spit, and touched his tongue; and looking up to heaven, he sighed, and saith unto him, Ephphatha, that is, Be opened. And straightway his ears were opened, and the string of his tongue was loosed, and he spake plain. And he charged them that they should tell no man: but the more he charged them, so much the more a great deal they published it; and were beyond measure astonished, saying, He hath done all things well: he maketh both the deaf to hear, and the dumb to speak.

This miracle occurs while Jesus is by the coasts of Decapolis. It is given to a people classified as heathens and Gentiles,[175] people who did not have Israel's history and did not believe in or look forward to a Messiah. Only Mark records the miracle and it occurs some time between the raising of the daughter of Jairus and the feeding of the four thousand.

After the miracle involving the daughter of the Syrophenician woman, Christ's fame spread rapidly. As a result, many came to Him to be healed,[a] their faith being based on the miracles He performed. As more came, their faith increased as they witnessed the continuous healing of all the sick and disabled in the multitude. The miracle of the deaf and dumb man was one from this multitude of miracles.

A man was brought to Jesus to be healed. He was described as being deaf and dumb with an impediment of speech. The Lord "took

a. Matthew
15:29–30

him aside from the multitude" to perform the miracle. This was to be a miracle of instruction for the one deaf and dumb and the Twelve, not for the multitude in general. The Lord then performed this miracle in a most peculiar manner (perhaps the procedures He used during the healing process were peculiar to Gentile healings).[176]

First, he carefully put His fingers in the man's ears. This physical act had nothing to do with the healing process itself, but to the man it may have seemed that He was thrusting in His fingers to make way for the sound.[177] The Lord's actions were presumably a sign that He was removing the man's deafness. Jesus then spit (probably upon His fingers) and touched the man's tongue. Again it was a sign, symbolizing the healing of the man's speech impediment. Each act of the Lord "seemed a fresh incitement to his faith"[178] and was a manifestation solely for the man's benefit. He completed the healing process with a vocal command. He looked up to heaven and sighed. The sigh may have been an expression of concern for these heathen or evidence of His compassion and deep concern for their physical and spiritual problems. He spoke the word "Ephphatha," which Mark interpreted as "Be opened." The signs of healing that Jesus had given were now confirmed. The command was obeyed, and the man both heard and spoke clearly.

Jesus next admonished both the man and those who had brought him to "tell no man" about the miracle, but they could not be silent. Mark records that "the more he charged them, so much the more a great deal they published it." The man did not obey Christ's admonition, but it appears that in his disobedience additional belief in Jesus was generated. He could not contain his joy, but "published it." The reaction of the community was favorable, for they concluded that "he hath done all things well."

It appears that the more miracles the Gentiles saw, the more readily they accepted Christ's teachings. Thus they might come to understand Him as the Messiah. Later teachings could build on this foundation and increase their spiritual enlightenment. They would be taught the words of life and salvation. No doubt the man who had been deaf and dumb would also receive the Lord's teachings. His healing would have prepared him to receive and understand Christ's words, and his faith would have been expanded as a result of the Lord's miraculous power.

One Blind at Bethsaida

Mark 8:22–26   And he cometh to Bethsaida; and they bring a blind man unto him, and besought him to touch him. And he took the blind man by the hand, and led him out of the town; and when he had spit on his eyes, and put his hands upon him, he asked him if he saw ought. And he looked up, and said, I see men as trees, walking. After that he put his hands again upon his eyes, and made him look up: and he was restored, and saw every man clearly. And he sent him away to his house, saying, Neither go into the town, nor tell it to any in the town.

Cross-reference   IV Mark 8:27

Mark records that the blind man in this miracle was brought to Jesus in Bethsaida-Julias, a Gentile city filled with heathenism and Hellenism.[179] Since this miracle and the healing of the deaf and dumb man are so similar in approach and style, it seems logical to assume that this blind man was a heathen also.[180] The individuals who brought the man to Jesus petitioned Him to touch him, as did those who accompanied the deaf and dumb man. Again, as in the previous miracle, the blind man does not speak on his own behalf before the miracle begins.

This is the only recorded instance where Jesus healed someone by stages. He took the man by the hand and led him outside the town. This also was not a miracle for exhibition, but for the blind man, his companions, and the Twelve. Upon arriving at a private area, Jesus "spit on his eyes," and "put his hands upon him." This procedure was uniquely tailored to this blind man, that he might gain confidence in His healer.[181] As with those used on the deaf and dumb man, apart from the priesthood ordinance of the laying on of hands (which may or may not be what is being described) such procedures had nothing to do with the Lord's power to heal, but were performed so that the blind man could believe in the person performing the healing.[182] At this point, the Lord asked the blind man if he could see. His strange response was, "I see men as trees, walking." He could not see normally, but apparently was only partially cured. Jesus then put His hands on his eyes again and "made him look up: and he was restored, and saw every man clearly." The Lord then instructed the man to go to his house and not into the city. He was not to tell "any in the town" about his healing. This instruction was probably given to best accommodate the man's future spiritual growth and the growth of those he would come in contact with (Chapter 14). No information is given on the outcome of the instruction, but it can be assumed that the man followed the Lord's directions.

Mark gives no explanation for the gradual healing the Lord performed on this occasion. Knowing the thoughts of all men and women, the procedures Christ used were undoubtedly geared to strengthen the blind man's faith as step by step He led him through the miracle, and step by step his faith and knowledge of the Savior increased.

Summary

The Lord used His miracles for many purposes, including the teaching and nurturing of faith. The healing of the deaf and dumb man and the one blind at Bethsaida seem to have been recorded to specifically illustrate this purpose. Both miracles were requested. From the evidence available, both men were heathen, ready believers in mysticism and miracles. Yet the Lord's peculiar method of healing led them away from their heathen gods and mystical powers. Throughout the healing process, Christ strengthened their faith and led them step by step to a stronger belief in Him. They came to Him with a temporal need, requesting a temporal blessing. He adapted their cure to fit their spiritual needs, that He might lead them beyond the temporal blessing to the spiritual opportunity.

The Dumb Lunatic Child

Mark 9:14–29   And when he came to his disciples, he saw a great multitude about them, and the scribes questioning with them. And straightway all the people, when they beheld him, were greatly amazed and, running to him saluted him. And he asked the scribes, What question ye with them? And one of the multitude answered and said, Master, I have brought unto thee my son, which hath a dumb spirit; and wheresoever he taketh him, he teareth him: and he foameth, and gnasheth with his teeth, and pineth away: and I spake to thy disciples that they should cast him out; and they could not. He answereth him, and saith, O faithless generation, how long shall I be with you? how long shall I suffer you? bring him unto me. And they brought him unto him: and when he saw him, straightway the spirit tare him; and he fell on the ground, and wallowed foaming. And he asked his father, How long is it ago since this came unto him? And he said, Of a child. And ofttimes it hath cast him into the fire, and into the waters, to destroy him: but if thou canst do any thing, have compassion on us, and help us. Jesus said unto him, If thou canst believe, all things are possible to him that believeth. And straightway the father of the child cried out, and said with tears, Lord, I believe; help thou mine unbelief. When Jesus saw that the people came running together, he rebuked the foul spirit, saying unto him, Thou dumb and deaf spirit, I charge thee, come out of him, and enter no more into him. And the spirit cried, and rent him sore, and came out of him: and he was as one dead; insomuch that many said, He is dead. But Jesus took him by the hand, and lifted him up; and he arose. And when he was come into the house, his disciples asked him privately, Why could not we cast him out? And he said unto them, This kind can come forth by nothing, but by prayer and fasting.

Cross-references   Matthew 17:14–21; Luke 9:37–43; JST Mark 9:15, 20

This is one of the most public of Jesus' miracles. Each miracle has its place in the Lord's teachings, but on the subject of faith this miracle is outstanding. While it is recorded by all three Synoptics, Mark is used as the primary text.

The miracle initially benefited only one young boy, but its influence went far beyond the physical healing. Its powerful message taught the principle of faith to the multitude, to the boy's father, and especially to the Twelve. It taught the relationship between the worlds of Christ and of Satan and between belief and unbelief; and it demonstrated whether faith is precedent or antecedent to blessings. It also afforded a glimpse into Jesus' personal character.

Prior to this miracle Jesus was on the Mount of Transfiguration with Peter, James, and John.[183] These Apostles witnessed the Lord's transfiguration and heard the Father's testimony of His Son's divinity. At the conclusion of this exalting, spiritual experience, the four came down from the Mount and interrupted a dispute between the scribes and the other nine Apostles. The nine had failed to perform a miracle. A young boy had been brought to them by his father to have an evil spirit cast out. He had come in search of Jesus, but when Jesus could not be found, he presented the child to the nine and requested them to heal him. Their failure resulted in the dispute.

No detail is given of the argument, but the scribes undoubtedly relished the fact that the nine Apostles could not perform the healing. Their elation was to be short lived, however. As Jesus approached the disputing parties, He immediately removed the burden of conversation from the nine Apostles and assumed it Himself. "What question ye with them?" he asked. No response came from the scribes or the nine Apostles. The father of the afflicted boy stepped forward, described his son's illness, and disclosed that the nine could not cast out the evil spirit.

"O faithless generation," Jesus exclaimed. His words were a rebuke to them all: to the scribes for contending with the nine and lacking faith in the Son of God; to the father for his wavering faith; to the multitude for their avid interest in seeing miracles performed and their blindness in recognizing the Messiah; and to the nine Apostles because they had allowed their faith to weaken, even though they had specifically been given the power to heal and cast out devils.[a] Jesus then declared, "How long shall I be with you?" His words bemoaned the fact that He would not be with the Apostles much longer, and yet they still

a. Matthew
10:1, 8.

seemed to lack faith in Him and His authority. He questioned, "How long shall I suffer you?" The failure of the nine Apostles to cure the dumb lunatic child and the contending scribes undoubtedly aroused doubt in the minds of the multitude. Christ's arrival had caused great excitement, and the crowd was "greatly amazed" to see Him.[184] Jesus commanded that the child be brought to Him, and the eager crowd pressed close to see what would happen next.

As the child approached Jesus, the evil spirit that possessed him attacked him anew, causing him to fall to the ground and foam at the mouth. Jesus asked the father how long the boy had been ill. The father indicated that he had suffered since childhood, and he explained the history of the malady. The Lord's presence and His question produced the desired effect upon the father; the love he had for his only son subdued his doubt. He asked for the Lord's help, but the phrasing of his request evidenced lingering apprehension. He pleaded with the Lord as he asked, "If thou canst do any thing, have compassion on us, and help us." The "if" conveyed the doubt the father still held.

Although unwittingly used, the word may have recalled to Christ His encounter with Satan when the devil tempted Him. Satan's approach was cleverly couched in such a manner as to tempt Jesus to question His ability, His mission, and His relationship with the Father. "If thou be the Son of God," the devil had said as he tempted Him.[a][185]

Jesus now began teaching the father, the Apostles, and the entire multitude concerning the necessity of having faith in Him. To the father He declared, "If thou canst believe, all things are possible to him that believeth."

The man cried out to the Lord and "with tears" in his eyes said, "Lord, I believe; help thou mine unbelief." He had again mustered that same hope and belief that had originally brought him in search of Jesus. But now, and most importantly, the father recognized his limited faith and cried for help; not just help to cure his son, but help to increase his faith in the Lord.[186]

When Jesus saw that the multitude was running to see what was happening, He rebuked the evil spirit, charging it to come out and "enter no more into him." The evil spirit cried out, and "rent him sore" as it left him. The boy appeared dead, but was raised up by the Lord and given to the father.

a. Matthew 4:3, 6.

Jesus returned to the house with the Twelve, and the nine Apostles asked why they could not cast out the evil spirit. Jesus responded that "this kind can come forth by nothing, but by prayer and fasting." This was the key to the miracle for the Apostles. They had failed because of unbelief. It was the source of their weakness and of all weakness where divine intervention is concerned.[187] It was not the Lord's ability that was in question, but their own. As they watched, the Master had easily cast out the evil spirit, even though they could not. In their failure Christ prescribed a method that would help keep their faith constant and vital—prayer and fasting.

This miracle was a lesson to the Twelve on the principles of belief and unbelief. By their ordination to the Apostleship, they had been given the power to perform such healings as this one, but its use depended upon their complete faith in the Lord. All men stand in the same position and need constant assurance that divine help will be forthcoming to fortify us against unbelief.

The possession of this afflicted boy dated from childhood. Its description evidenced the powerful control the evil spirit had over him. But more than this, when they brought the boy to Jesus, the spirit violently rebelled. It "straightway" forced him to the ground, "tare him," and caused him to foam at the mouth. When Jesus commanded the spirit to leave the boy, it "cried, and rent him sore," before coming out of him. The possession was so overpowering that after leaving the boy's body, he "was as one dead."

The two kingdoms, Christ's and the devil's, had once again come together in open conflict. Jesus is the head of His kingdom, and others (such as the Twelve) have designated authority in it. The devil is the head of his kingdom, and others have authority under him.[188] Jesus described the spirit as "this kind," which might indicate that this particular evil spirit was one with authority. To the Lord of all it was but a simple task to cast him out, for the evil spirit was bound to obey Him. But the nine, with their doubts and weakened faith, could not maintain the spiritual strength that would allow them to exercise the power Jesus did, and so they failed. Yet they learned from this failure.

An interesting example in the book of Acts illustrates this principle. After explaining that Paul wrought special miracles, the scripture reports that "certain of the vagabond Jews, exorcists," attempted to cast out evil spirits. They "adjured" them in the name of "Jesus whom Paul preacheth" to come out. The spirits communicated with the Jews and answered, "Jesus I know, and Paul I know; but who are ye?" The evil spirits then attacked them, and they fled "naked and wounded." The spirits knew and recognized proper authority when it was exercised with proper faith.[a]

Several principles concerning faith are taught by this miracle:

1. Faith in Jesus is personal, and it may increase or decrease depending upon the individual and his reaction to a given circumstance.

2. The use of Jesus' divine authority and power, even when properly held, is dependent upon individual faith.

3. One procedure for increasing and renewing faith in Him is prayer and fasting.

4. When faith and belief have been replaced by doubt and disbelief, a personal renewal is necessary prior to Christ's intervention and assistance.

5. The Lord will always aid and assist those who believe in Him and rely on His divine compassion and mercy.

6. Jesus, by analogy, taught that even an amount of faith as small as the grain of mustard seed could move mountains. By this example, He emphasized that it was not the quantity of faith that was important, but the quality. All things are possible as a result of unwavering faith.

7. Perfect faith is not required to receive God's blessings. Miracles can be received by those of weak or nonexistent faith, the miracle being used as a teaching tool to build faith.[189] This tool would be used repeatedly by the Apostles.[b]

a. Acts 19:13–16.

b. Acts 1:14;
   9:9; 10:9, 30;
   13:2–3; 14:23.

Resolving Personal Problems 18

The Water to Wine

John 2:1–11   And the third day there was a marriage in Cana of Galilee; and the mother of Jesus was there: and both Jesus was called, and His disciples, to the marriage. And when they wanted wine, the mother of Jesus saith unto him, They have no wine. Jesus saith unto her, Woman, what have I to do with thee? mine hour is not yet come. His mother saith unto the servants, Whatsoever he saith unto you, do it. And there were set there six waterpots of stone, after the manner of the purifying of the Jews, containing two or three firkins apiece. Jesus saith unto them, Fill the waterpots with water. And they filled them up to the brim. And he saith unto them, Draw out now, and bear unto the governor of the feast. And they bare it. When the ruler of the feast had tasted the water that was made wine, and knew not whence it was: (but the servants which drew the water knew;) the governor of the feast called the bridegroom, and saith unto him, Every man at the beginning doth set forth good wine; and when men have well drunk, then that which is worse: but thou hast kept the good wine until now. This beginning of miracles did Jesus in Cana of Galilee, and manifested forth his glory; and his disciples believed on him.

Cross-reference   JST John 2:4; IV John 2:11

The miracles in this chapter deal with personal problems. The miracle of turning the water to wine is reported as the "beginning of miracles." It is a miracle of declaration, kindness, joy, and testimony. It was performed in Cana of Galilee at a marriage feast. Jesus and His disciples had been invited to join the festivities. Prior to the miracle, John records his call and that of Peter, Andrew, Philip, and Nathanael; therefore, it is assumed that these five were present with Jesus on this occasion. John is the only Gospel writer that reports the miracle.

Marriage was a sacred event to the Jews. It symbolized the union of God with Israel,[190] and entrance into matrimony was thought to carry with it a forgiveness of sin.[191] The sacredness of the marriage covenant had almost been elevated to the level of a sacrament,[192] and the pious even fasted before it.[193] Nothing is known about the participants in this wedding. It has been assumed that either the bride or the bridegroom was of Jesus' immediate family, perhaps a brother, sister, or nephew. This assumption is made because of the prominence of Mary, the mother of Jesus, in the order of the festivities.[194]

The Lord's participation in this event demonstrated His approval and endorsement of marriage and the propriety of social interaction.[195] His life was not to be like that of John the Baptist—a life withdrawn from the paths of other men and their social habits. Jesus was destined to be among men, to share their joys, sorrows, and social engagements, and to enter into their family life. Through His involvement, men's lives would be purified and elevated to a higher spiritual level.[196]

Jesus was the second of two witnesses who came in a manner that Israel would recognize. John the Baptist was the first, and like the great prophets of the desert (Elijah and Elisha), he exemplified the ascetic or highest form of Jewish religious life.

[John] had spent his days in penitential austerity and wilderness seclusion; had drunk no wine, had eaten no pleasant food, and had kept apart from human affairs and relationships. But a new and higher ideal of religion was now to be introduced. Jesus [the second witness to Israel] came to spiritualize the humblest duties of life, and sanctify its simplest incidents, so as to ennoble it as a whole. Henceforth, pleasures and enjoyments were not to be shunned as unholy; religion was not to thrive on the mortification of every human instinct, and the repression of every cheerful emotion. It would mix with the crowd of men, affect no singularity, take part in the innocent festivities of life, interest itself in whatever interested men at large, and yet, amidst all, remain consecrated and pure; in the world, by sympathy and active brotherhood, but not of it; human in its outward form, but heavenly in its elevation and spirit.[197]

Jesus came to Israel in the tradition of Isaiah, Jeremiah, and Eze-kiel. He was known to the Jews and participated in their customs and traditions.

As the wedding festivities progressed, need for a personal miracle developed. There was a call for additional wine but none was available. Mary came to Jesus and told Him of the problem. What she wanted of Jesus is not specifically stated, but it appears that she expected His assistance to solve her dilemma.[198] No great catastrophe would have occurred without Jesus' intervention, but mockery and scorn would have come upon the bridal couple if they had run out of wine. The Jewish traditions had become so inflexible that failure to comply with them threatened disgrace on the family for life. The marriage feast was the highest of social activities, and the tradition of the feast required abundant wine.[199]

Thus, Mary petitioned her son for help with this personal problem to avoid social disgrace. According to the King James Version, the Lord's response was, "Woman, what have I to do with thee, mine hour is not yet come." His response was not an insult to His mother,[200] and in fact, the salutation "woman" was commonly used in that day. It denoted the "queenliest and most loved."[201] However, the Lord's answer appears to contain a mild rebuke similar to that response given to Mary when He was twelve years old and was found teaching in the temple.[a] There the scripture reports that Mary did not understand His comments.[b] In the current instance, Joseph Smith added to the understanding of the event, translating the verse to read: "Woman, what wilt thou have me to do for thee? that will I do; for mine hour is not yet come." Jesus would help His mother, but He reminded her that He was more than the son of Mary—He was the Son of God. By this time Jesus had already been baptized, received the Holy Ghost, been tempted in the wilderness by the devil, and called the first of His Apostles. His ministry had officially commenced; the tender, earthly relationship with His mother would not be forgotten, but His "business," His mission from the Father, was not primarily concerned with these earthly relationships and needs.[202]

It is evident that Mary took no offense, for she immediately instructed the servants to do as he bade them. Even though her problem was personal and confined to a social situation, she had complete confidence that He would assist her.

Jesus instructed the servants to fill six nearby pots with water. John is particular to note that the water pots were there according to custom, "after the manner of the purifying of the Jews."[203] After filling the pots with water, He instructed the servants to "draw out now, and bear unto the governor of the feast." The water had been made into wine, and the bridegroom was complimented for his generosity in keeping the "good wine" for last.

The Lord's act of consideration confirmed two principles involving divine intervention in personal lives: first, that requests for divine assistance can be made to resolve specific personal problems; and second, that such assistance will be granted to those with a firm belief in the Lord's ability to help them.

The miracle of turning the water to wine was completed without fanfare or public notice. But its circumstances have given rise to several questions.

Had Christ Performed Previous Miracles?

There is no scriptural evidence or testimony that Jesus performed any miracles prior to the official commencement of His ministry. The circumstances in this miracle, however, indicate that miracles may have been performed prior to turning the water to wine. Mary's request intimated that she knew Jesus had such capabilities, whether He had demonstrated them or not.[204] Jesus brought to the feast several men He had called to the Apostleship. The call of these men (Peter, Andrew, John, Nathanael, and Philip) was treated summarily by John,[a] yet there is evidence of Christ's using His miraculous abilities. When Nathanael was called, Jesus revealed that He saw him "under the fig tree" before Philip brought him to the Lord. There is additional evidence in the other Gospels that He had used His powers prior to the wedding at Cana. The miracle of the first draught of fish (Chapter 7) took place when Jesus called Peter, Andrew, James, and John as Apostles. It would, therefore, be reasonable to assume that changing water into wine was not the literal "beginning of miracles," but the first recorded by John. If previous miracles (i.e., previous to the commencement of Christ's ministry) had been performed, it would seem likely that they were performed in the privacy of His family and were not publicly known.

a. John 1:37–49

How was the Water Changed to Wine?

Historically, there has been much speculation on this subject. Some writers have suggested that Jesus brought the wine and mixed it with the water. Others claim Mary brought it as a gift to Jesus, and He merely gave it to those at the feast.[205] Still others feel that it was a mere acceleration of the natural laws of nature.[206] Some reject the miracle altogether, because to them it was a miracle of luxury rather than one of beneficence.[207] All rational attempts at an explanation are fruitless. The Lord of heaven and earth could easily perform such a task, and speculation on the actual process is superfluous.

What was This Wine?

There has been some question raised as to whether Jesus drank fermented wine or whether the wine was nonalcoholic. The scriptures clearly use the term "wine," and no attempt is made by the writers to exclude Christ from its general use. Many different types of wine were common during Christ's time.[208] Jesus undoubtedly drank the common beverages of His day, and the Mosaic Law did not prohibit Israelites in general from drinking wine. There were some specific situations in which wine was prohibited. Aaron and his sons were prohibited from drinking wine when they entered the tabernacle.[a] An individual who took the vow of a Nazarite was prohibited from using wine[b] along with many other restrictions.[c] The mother of Samson was not a Nazarite, but she was commanded to observe the prohibitions of that order until Samson was born, for he was to be a Nazarite from birth.[d]

Matthew reports a discussion Jesus had with His Apostles concerning the prophecies of His coming among the Jews. Jesus describes both John the Baptist and Himself as the witnesses to Israel of the Messiah, and states, "John came neither eating nor drinking, and they say, He hath a devil. The Son of man came eating and drinking, and they say, Behold a man gluttonous, and a winebibber."[e] John the Baptist was raised as a Nazarite,[f] symbolizing the prophets of old in his witness of Christ. The Lord came among His people "eating and drinking" and participating in the Jews' daily activities.

Wedding celebrations could extend beyond a single day.[209] The comment of the governor of the feast that the best wine was usually served first, and "when men have well drunk, then that which is

a. Leviticus 10:9.

b. Numbers 6:1–3

c. Numbers 6:4–21.

d. Judges 13:4–5, 7.

e. Matthew 11:18–19; Luke 7:33–34.

f. Luke 1:15.

worse" was served, might lead some to speculate that at such feasts, overindulgence was tolerated. But such was not the case. The Lord would not have sanctioned such behavior, and definitely would not have augmented it by His miraculous service. The Jews knew the pros and cons of wine, and they held drunkenness in abhorrence. In Christ's household, this license would not have been allowed.[210] One of the popular parables of the time exemplified this principle. It stated:

> When Noah planted his vineyard, Satan came and asked him what he was doing? "Planting a vineyard," was the reply. "What is it for?" "Its fruits, green or dry, are sweet and pleasant: we make wine of it, which gladdens the heart." "I should like to have a hand in the planting," said Satan. "Good," replied Noah. Satan then brought a lamb, a lion, a sow, and an ape, killed them in the vineyard, and let their blood run into the roots of the vines. From this is come that a man before he has taken wine, is simple as a lamb, which knows nothing, and is dumb before its shearers; when he has drunk moderately he grows a lion, and thinks there is not his like; if he drink too much, he turns a swine, and wallows in the mire; if he drink still more, he becomes a filthy ape, falling hither and thither, and knowing nothing of what he does.[211]

Jesus would no more have participated in the excessive use of wine or in drunkenness than in any other sin whose consequence would exclude the sinner from the kingdom of God.[a]

Summary

This was not a public miracle yet it would be publicized. The report indicates that the governor did not know the water had been made into wine—only the servants did. The miracle's primary purpose was to solve a personal problem. However, as in all miracles, the Lord used it as a teaching tool. John notes that Christ "manifested forth his glory; and his disciples believed on him." He had used His miraculous power on a work of mercy for His mother, but it instilled confirmation and trust in His disciples. He unveiled His glory before them, and it increased their growing faith.

a. 1 Corinthians
6:10.

Peter's Wife's Mother

Matthew 8:14–15   And when Jesus was come into Peter's house, he saw his wife's mother laid, and sick of a fever. And he touched her hand, and the fever left her: and she arose, and ministered unto them.

Cross-references   Mark 1:29–31; Luke 4:38–39

This was the second miracle performed to resolve a personal problem. Jesus was returning after healing the demoniac in the synagogue at Capernaum. He was accompanied by Peter, Andrew, James, and John. When they arrived at Simon Peter's house, they found his mother-in-law seriously ill with a fever (frequently translated from the Greek as "burning fever").[212] Peter and the others petitioned Jesus on her behalf that He might heal her. It was a completely natural petition. In view of the fact that Jesus had just compassionately healed a complete stranger, it was only logical that He should do likewise for one that loved Him.

The Talmud prescribed a detailed cure for this precise problem. The afflicted person was told to "tie a knife wholly of iron by a braid of hair to a thorn bush, and . . . repeat on successive days Exodus 3:2–3, then verse 4, and finally verse 5, after which the bush is to be cut down, while a certain magical formula is pronounced."[213] Jesus merely took the woman by the hand and rebuked the fever with the power vested in Him. She was healed instantly and completely, and arose immediately and "ministered unto them."

All three Synoptics record this miracle, but none detail or record any reaction to it. The miracle would have increased the faith of all who witnessed it, but not even this is mentioned. It seems its only purpose was to grant the righteous desire of a loved one, and the Lord freely gave of His love and compassion to assist with this personal problem.

The Coin in the Mouth of the Fish

Matthew 17:24–27   And when they were come to Capernaum, they that received tribute money came to Peter, and said, Doth not your master pay tribute? He saith, Yes. And when he was come into the house, Jesus prevented him, saying, What thinkest thou, Simon? of whom do the kings of the earth take custom or tribute? of their own children, or of strangers? Peter saith unto him, Of strangers. Jesus saith unto him, Then are the children free. Notwithstanding, lest we should offend them, go thou to the sea, and cast an hook, and take up the fish that first cometh up; and when thou hast opened his mouth, thou shalt find a piece of money: that take, and give unto them for me and thee.

Cross-reference   IV Matthew 17:24

This last personal miracle is recorded by Matthew. It appears to have but one functional purpose—that of providing a solution to Peter's self-caused dilemma. But it is full of meaning, though it is often overlooked.

The miracle revolves around the tribute money assessed as a tax for the temple. The tax was an annual one and was assessed upon every male Israelite over the age of twenty years, including proselytes and freed slaves. It was a tax of redemption from sin assessed under the Law of Moses, and was assessed to all in the same amount, whether rich or poor.[a][214]

The collectors of this tax had the right to ask Peter, "Doth not your master pay tribute?" They also had the right to collect the fee. Priests and rabbis claimed an exemption from the tax,[215] and the phrasing of the tax collectors' question indicated that they did not know whether Jesus paid the tax or claimed the exemption.

The tax was used for the following items:

1.   To purchase beasts for the temple sacrifices.

2.   To pay copiers, bakers, judges, and others connected with the temple service.

3.   To pay the rabbis for inspecting the sacrifices.

4.   To furnish funds for building repair and water supply.

5.   To provide for numerous other items, including women who wove or washed the temple linen.[216]

The tax was due in the spring of the year, and it was now fall.[217] Although the scriptures do not mention it, it seems logical to assume that Jesus had paid this tax in other years, especially those prior to His ministry.[218] But now He had revealed Himself to be the Son of God; He who would pay a ransom for all need not pay the tax for the

a. Exodus 30:13–16; 38:25–26.

temple. It was His temple, and the offerings were made to Him. The tax collectors' question concerned the basic relationship between the Lord and the Jewish rulers.

Peter, in answering the question and in his zeal to protect the honor of his Master, pledged the payment. He then retreated to the house to converse with the Lord on the matter. Jesus, who could perceive the thoughts of all men, apparently knew his intent and before Peter could speak, He questioned him in the form of an allegorical teaching. The question was based on custom; kings assessed tribute and were paid—but by whom, their children or strangers? Peter answered that strangers paid the tributes. The Lord continued and asked if the children were not then free? The meaning was clear. The Son of God was free from the tax, but others were required to pay it. Once again it was affirmed to Peter who the Lord really was.

Jesus chose to avoid the potential conflict over this trivial matter and to support Peter. But the funds were not to come from the Apostles' treasury. Peter was to cast a hook into the lake; the first fish he caught would have lodged in its mouth sufficient money to cover the tax for both Jesus and Peter, who apparently had not paid the tax either. Jesus instructed Peter to take that money and "give unto them for me and thee."

It is not recorded what the collectors did throughout this entire sequence, but they undoubtedly waited outside while Peter went into the house to get the tribute. If that were the case, they would have seen Peter leave to go fishing. They might have watched as he threw his hook into the sea, caught the fish, and retrieved the coin from its mouth and paid the tax. It would be more than amusing to have seen their reaction.

An interesting distinction comes from the phrasing Jesus used when He agreed to pay the tax. He stated that the money should be used for "me and thee," and not "us." After His resurrection, Christ declared to Mary at the tomb that she should inform the Apostles that He was ascending "unto my Father, and your Father; and to my God, and your God."[a] He was not as other men, even with His disciples.

Jesus used Peter's dilemma to teach a spiritual lesson, and the miracle sealed the teaching. Peter had created the problem in his overzealous desire to protect the Lord's honor. The Lord knew of his a. John 20:17.

predicament even before Peter told Him about it. Jesus was constantly aware of and concerned with every activity of His Apostles, whether He was with them physically or not.[219]

The Miracle of Transportation

John 6:21   Then they willingly received him into the ship: and immediately the ship was at the land whither they went.

Cross References   Ezekiel 37:1; Ezekiel 40:1–2; Acts 6:3–6; 2 Corinthians 12:2; Revelation 17:3; Revelation 21:10; 1 Nephi 11:1; 2 Nephi 4:25; Moses 1:1; JST Matthew 4:5.

This is a very interesting miracle. However, in each of the scriptures that refer to it, it is dealt with summarily and without detail. The primary scripture used is John 6:21 which concludes the miracle of walking on the water (Chapter 8). John inserts the evidence of the miracle as if it were a common occurrence; because he also records it occurring to him in the book of Revelation, perhaps it was. The other Gospels do not record or infer the miracle.

When Jesus came into the ship after both He and Peter had walked on the water, the purpose and teaching of that miracle was over. At that point John records that they were "immediately . . . at the land whither they went." The apostles were on the lake because the Lord had "constrained" them to leave after the miracle of feeding the five thousand (Chapter 2). That miracle had raised the expectations of the multitude to such a degree that the scripture reports they would take the Lord by force "to make him a king." Rather than risk the Apostles being caught up in the multitude's reaction, Jesus sent them away. They entered a boat to cross over to the other side of the lake as instructed, but the wind was "contrary" and although they struggled to row, they had made little progress before the Lord came to them walking upon the water. After both the Lord and Peter entered the boat, the miracle occurred. They did not continue rowing or using sails to catch the wind, but were transported by the power of the Lord through the remaining distance — and were immediately at their destination.

There are other specific examples of this miracle wherein prophets have also been transported by the Spirit (frequently recorded as "in the spirit") to designated areas to receive visions from the Lord, such as recorded by Ezekiel, Paul, and again, John the Revelator.

Perhaps the most detailed example of this miracle is recorded in Acts in the New Testament. Philip, one of the seven called to assist the Apostles,[a] experienced such travel. He had completed his teaching of a eunuch and had baptized him. When he came "up out of the water, the Spirit of the Lord caught away Philip, that the eunuch saw him no more: . . . But Philip was found at Azotus," preaching.[b] Philip had traveled under the influence of the Spirit of the Lord, and the ordinary requirements of travel were not binding upon him.

Nephi, the son of Helaman, had a similar experience: "He was taken by the Spirit and conveyed away out of the midst of them. And . . . he did go forth in the Spirit, from multitude to multitude, declaring the word of God."[c] The Spirit carried Nephi away to mountaintops,[d] and Adam was baptized during such an experience.[e]

Finally, from the inspired translation of Joseph Smith, the transportation recorded in Matthew of the Lord's movements during His temptations by the devil were by the Spirit, and not by the devil as Matthew infers. In the second temptation, He was transported by the Spirit (not the devil) to the holy city of Jerusalem and set upon a pinnacle of the temple.[f]

Although such events are not described in detail, it is obvious from the scriptures that this miraculous power has been used many times to further God's work.

a. Acts 6:3–6.

b. Acts 8:39–40.

c. Helaman 10:16–17.

d. 1 Nephi 11:1; 2 Nephi 4:25.

e. Moses 6:64.

f. JST, Matthew 4:5

The Message of the Miracles

19

The miracles Jesus performed dramatically characterized His personality. They mirrored His love, His compassion, His kindness, and His personal concern for mankind. They taught and witnessed gospel principles and testified of the long-awaited Messiah.

The Gospels preserve but a glimpse of Jesus' life. To record all that He accomplished would require volumes. Through the Atonement, He took upon Himself the sins of the world; through His miracles, "he hath borne our griefs" as well.[a] The people came to Him wherever He was. They brought their sick and afflicted of every kind, and with His boundless compassion He healed them all.

The individual miracles found in the Bible were recorded for specific reasons. They taught doctrine, witnessed Christ's divinity, provided examples in the use of His authority, and evidenced His love and concern for the smallest common problems. Christ witnessed His divinity to the people and to the rulers, and He appealed to their law. The people recognized the signs of the looked-for Messiah and remembered, but for the most part they would not accept Jesus in that role. The demons from the world of evil spirits recognized and obeyed Him, but His chosen people would not. He openly claimed to be the Messiah and performed miraculous feats to seal His testimony, but He was accused of doing it by the power of Beelzebub. The people loved their law more than they loved the Lawgiver. Isaiah accurately prophesied that the people of Christ's day would say, "we did esteem him stricken, smitten of God."[b]

The Lord cast out evil spirits and caused the blind to see. He made

a. Isaiah 53:4.

b. Isaiah 53:4.

the lame to walk and cured all manner of disease, both publicly and privately. Ultimately, He raised the dead as a specific witness to His power, majesty, and teaching. He healed by His word, in stages, by touch, and from a distance.

He caused the miraculous to become commonplace among the people, and He proved that He ruled natural laws and the elements. He taught the Apostles of His great power and assisted them as they developed their faith in Him and in the authority He had given them. He forgave men's sins, both great and small. And even as they arrested Him to kill Him, He healed one more time that He alone would suffer.

Christ healed the body so that the spirit could more freely believe. He offered temporal blessings in the hope that God's children might accept eternal blessings. Some were satisfied with only a temporal healing, but others saw through the facade of the flesh and glimpsed the spiritual meaning in all He did.

The message of the miracles is no different today than it was when Jesus delivered it. Some see and yet want another sign, and some accept immediate blessings that better only their temporal existence. But His sheep hear His voice, regardless of how He calls. In New Testament times, the Lord's miracles produced hate, disbelief, anger, and rejection; they also produced faith, belief, hope, acceptance, and salvation. It is the same today with the miracles of Jesus the Messiah.

Notes

1. Ed. 1:478.
2. Ed. 1:478.
3. Before publication of the 1979 edition of the Bible for The Church of Jesus Christ of Latter-day Saints, this was known as the Inspired Version. In the Church it is now generally referred to as the Joseph Smith Translation (JST). Quotations from the Inspired Version that are not found in the JST are referenced herein as IV.
4. Ed 1:145; 2:55.
5. The determination of which of Jesus' teachings should be classified as parables has varied throughout the years depending on how strictly the word parable is defined. As few as twenty-seven (Siegfried Goebel, The Parables of Jesus, 1883, p. 3) or as many as fifty-three (A. Julicher, Die Gleichnisreden Jesu, 1910, p. 15) or even sixty-five (Francis L. Filas, The Parables of Jesus, 1959) have been so determined.
6. Farrar2:9.
7. JC p. 149.
8. Ed 1:162–63. For a detailed listing of Old Testament passages Messianically applied with reference to rabbinical works Ed 2:710–41.
9. Strauss p. 413.
10. Ed 1:162–63.
11. Ed 1:176.
12. Ed 1:162–69 for a thorough treatment of the rabbinical expectations of the Messiah.
13. Life p. 854.
14. Farrar 1:170.
15. Trench p. 13.
16. JC p. 148–49.
17. MD p. 506.
18. Trench p. 50.
19. Geikie 2:6.
20. MM 3:28; Farrar 1:168.
21. Ed 1:227.
22. Ed 1:230.
23. Ed 1:163.

24. Ed 1:162–63.
25. This is the only mention of the city of Nain in the scriptures. There has been speculation on its location, but its exact location is of no particular importance to the miracle. For detail on this material see Trench pp. 258–59; Ed 1:552–53.
26. Ed 1:554–57 for details of the funeral and burial ceremony in existence among the Jews at the time of Christ.
27. Ed 1:557.
28. Josephus, Wars, Book II, 1:3.
29. Josephus, Wars, Book VI, IX:3.
30. Ed 2:65.
31. Trench p. 289.
32. Sermons p. 104.
33. Ed 2:770–76; JC pp. 182–83.
34. Trench p. 171.
35. HC 2:503.
36. Ed 2:773–75.
37. MM 2:37; Geikie 2:4; Trench p. 162.
38. Ed 2:748–63.
39. Ed 1:478–79.
40. Farrar 1:455.
41. Ed 2:197.
42. IV Matthew 8:29 resolves this conflict, reporting only "a man."
43. It is generally agreed between the scholarly authorities that the Gospel writers were not describing an exact location but a general area. The scripture reports that after the miracle the herdsmen who witnessed it went into both city and country to report the event and the people then gathered to see the results. Historically, three cities have been identified with the general location, i.e., Gadara, Gerasa, and Gergesa. Gadara has generally been rejected because it was too far inland. Gerasa and Gergesa have both been identified with the ruins of Kersa, the location generally thought of as the site of the miracle. For further detail; Ed 1:606–07; Farrar 1:333–34 and notes; JC p. 323, note 3; Trench pp. 162–64 and notes.
44. Trench p. 179.
45. Ed 1:607–8, Trench p. 179.
46. Trench p. 184–85.
47. TG, Outer Darkness.
48. MM 2:282.
49. For detailed information on the synagogue at the time of Christ, its regulations, the conduct of those within, and the service itself, Ed 1:430–50.
50. Under rabbinical law there were two corporal punishments (considered divine punishments) that could be inflicted upon individuals for religious violations. They were known as the "forty stripes save one," and the so-called "rebel's beating." The forty stripes save one was "inflicted after a regular judicial investigation and sen-

tence, and for the breach of some negative precept or prohibition; while the . . . [rebel's beating] was, so to speak, in the hands of the people, who might administer it on the spot, and without trial, if any one were caught in supposed open defiance of some positive precept, whether of the law of Moses or of the traditions of the elders" [Ed Temple pp. 66–67]. The rebel's beating was usually to the death. Stephen was martyred in this manner (Acts 7:57–58), and it was attempted upon Paul when he brought a Gentile beyond the designated limit in the temple: "and the people ran together: and they took Paul, and drew him out of the temple: . . . and . . . they went about to kill him" (Acts 21:30–31). Another time, Paul was stoned and left for dead (Acts 14:19). The justification for this procedure supposedly came from the example of Phinehas, the son of Eleazar (Numbers 25:7–8). But the punishment inflicted upon Stephen and Paul (and attempted upon the Lord) was, in each case, contrary to all the rules of rabbinical criminal law [Ed Temple pp. 65–68].

51. Life p. 406.

52. DNTC 1:462–64.

53. Life p. 415.

54. An interesting experience in the history of The Church of Jesus Christ of Latter-day Saints involving this miracle is recorded by Joseph Smith: "Towards the latter end of August [1830], in company with John and David Whitmer, and my brother Hyrum Smith, I visited the Church at Colesville, New York. Well knowing the determined hostility of our enemies in that quarter, and also knowing that it was our duty to visit the Church, we had called upon our Heavenly Father, in mighty prayer, that He would grant us an opportunity of meeting with them, that he would blind the eyes of our enemies, so that they would not know us, and that we might on this occasion return unmolested. Our prayers were not in vain, for when within a little distance of Mr. Knight's place, we encountered a large company at work upon the public road, amongst whom were several of our most bitter enemies. They looked earnest-at [sic] us, but not knowing us, we passed on without interruption. That evening we assembled the Church, and confirmed them, partook of the Sacrament, and held a happy meeting, having much reason to rejoice in the God of our salvation, and sing hosannas to His holy name. Next morning we set out on our return home, and although our enemies had offered a reward of five dollars to anyone who would give them information of our arrival, yet did we get out of the neighborhood, without the least annoyance and arrived home in safety. Some few days afterwards, however, Newel Knight came to my place, and from him we learned that, very shortly after our departure, the mob came to know of our having been there, when they immediately collected together, and threatened the brethren, and very much an-

noyed them during all that day." (HC 1:108–9.)

55. For specific information on these materials, Trench p. 268; Geikie 2:86–87.

56. JC p. 206.

57. Geikie 2:87–88.

58. A word used by later Jews to denote the cloud of brightness that symbolized God's divine presence. It was a symbol of God's special blessing of Israel. (Exodus 24:16; 1 Kings 8:10; Isaiah 6:1–3.) The symbol was further perpetuated in some New Testament occurrences. (Matthew 17:5; Luke 2:9.)

59. Ed (Temple) pp. 61–62

60. Farrar 1:374–75.

61. Sermons p. 99.

62. MM 2:48.

63. Trench pp. 217–18; Geikie 2:21–22. The house may have been a two-story home having on the second floor a larger room designed for meetings, or it may have been a single-story house with a covered courtyard. Both were common for the day.

64. Ed 1:505.

65. Geikie 2:23.

66. Life pp. 396, 406, 455.

67. Ed 2:178.

68. Geikie 2:297–99.

69. Geikie 2:298.

70. Farrar 2:80.

71. Ed 2:178–79.

72. Ed 2:178.

73. Ed 2:180–81; MM 3:200–201.

74. MM 3:201.

75. Ed 1:94.

76. Ed 1:93–108.

77. Geikie 2:24.

78. Geikie 2:99.

79. Ed 2:59–60.

80. Ed 2:56.

81. Geikie 2:24; Ed 2:777–87.

82. Ed 2:59–60.

83. Geikie 2:99.

84. MM 3:228.

85. Geikie 2:318.

86. MM 3:230.

87. MM 3:230.

88. Geikie 2:317.

89. JC p. 449.

90. JC p. 227.

91. Geikie 1:516–17.

92. MM 4:288.

93. Strauss pp. 496–99; JC pp. 308–9.

94. MM 2:273–74.

95. MM 2:276; Ed 1:600.

96. Trench p. 154.

97. Trench p. 156.

98. MM 2:278.
99. Geikie 2:177.
100. JC p. 336.
101. JC p. 337.
102. JC p. 337.
103. Ed 2:55.
104. Trench p. 193.
105. Ed 1:619.
106. MM 2:289.
107. Nicodemus came to Jesus to ask questions of Him (John 3:1–7), but also defended Jesus before the officers of the Pharisees that would arrest Him (John 7:50–51). He also brought myrrh to anoint Christ's body after His death (John 19:39). Life p. 420.
108. Life p. 217.
109. Ed 2:374–75.
110. MM 3:346; Ed 2:375.
111. Geikie 2:105.
112. Ed 1:544.
113. MM 2:182–83; JC p. 251.
114. Ed 2:39.
115. Life p. 304.
116. Ed 1:168–79.
117. Ed 1:167, 308–35.
118. Ed 2:275–77.
119. Ed 2:276–77.
120. Life p. 438.
121. Life p. 640.
122. Jesus did not personally go to the spirit prison because those who were there could not abide His presence. But He opened the way so that others from paradise might pass over and teach the gospel to those in the prison who might then, through diligence, repentance, and the grace of God, extricate themselves from that awful condition (Life p. 642).
123. MM 3:270.
124. Ed 2:317.
125. Geikie 2:315; Ed 1:238.
126. Ed 1:128.
127. Ed 2:556.
128. Ed 2:556.
129. Ed Temple p. 100.
130. Life p. 683.
131. Life p. 591.
132. Life p. 597.
133. Life p. 601.
134. JC p. 683.
135. Life p. 644.
136. MM 4:275.
137. JC p. 681.
138. JC p. 686.
139. Life p. 396, 400, 406, 455.
140. Ed 1:424.
141. Trench p. 128.

142. MM 2:11.
143. Ed 1:428.
144. Geikie 2:157.
145. Ed 1:620.
146. Ed 1:620, note 1.
147. Ed 1:622–26.
148. Ed 1:624.
149. Ed 1:624.
150. An interesting experience is recorded in Church history involving "virtue going out" of the Prophet Joseph Smith, as follows: "Elder Jedediah M. Grant enquired of me the cause of my turning pale and losing strength last night while blessing children. I told him that I saw that Lucifer would exert his influence to destroy the children that I was blessing, and I strove with all the faith and spirit that I had to seal upon them a blessing that would secure their lives upon the earth; and so much virtue went out of me into the children, that I became weak, from which I have not yet recovered; and I referred to the case of the woman touching the hem of the garment of Jesus. . . . The virtue here referred to is the spirit of life; and a man who exercises great faith in administering to the sick, blessing little children, or confirming, is liable to become weakened." (HC 5:303.)
151. Ed 1:491–96.
152. Geikie 2:13.
153. Trench p. 230–34.
154. MM 2:45.
155. Ed 1:495.
156. Ed 1:492.
157. Trench pp. 231–32.
158. Trench p. 230.
159. MM 2:45.
160. Trench p. 233.
161. Ed 1:492.
162. Geikie 2:13.
163. The raising of the daughter of Jairus, Chapter 8; the two blind in the house, Chapter 15; and healing one who was deaf and dumb, Chapter 16.
164. Ed 1:492.
165. JC p. 471.
166. MM 3:285.
167. JC p. 471.
168. DNTC 1:537.
169. Geikie 2:13.
170. Trench p. 212.
171. Trench p. 469.
172. Ed 2:49.
173. MM 2:297.
174. MM 2:298–99.
175. Ed 2:44–45.
176. Ed 2:45.
177. Ed 2:46.
178. Ed 2:46.

179. MM 3:28–29.

180. Ed 2:47.

181. Ed 2:48.

182. MM 3:29.

183. Life p. 571.

184. Some have speculated that Jesus still shone from the experience on the Mount of Transfiguration, but it is highly unlikely that Jesus would display such evidence of that special, spiritual experience and testimony before the multitude when He had reserved it solely for the three leading Apostles and instructed them not to disclose it until after His resurrection.

185. Life p. 566.

186. MM 3:72–73.

187. MM 3:73.

188. MM 3:74.

189. The healing of the Syrophenician woman, Chapter 9; and the healing of one deaf and dumb, Chapter 16.

190. "Israel is said to have been ten times called in Scripture "bride' (six times in Canticles, three times in Isaiah, and once in Jeremiah)." Ed 1:353, note 2.

191. "The Biblical proofs adduced for attaching this benefit to a sage, a bridegroom, and a prince on entering on their new state, are certainly peculiar. In the case of a bridegroom it is based on the name of Esau's bride, Mahalath (Genesis 28:9), a name which is derived from the Rabbinic 'Machal,' to forgive." (Ed 1:353, note 1.) Edersheim's interpretation apparently comes from the fact that prior to the marriage she was called "Bashemath" (Genesis 36:3), but changed her name at the marriage and was "forgiven."

192. A sacrament was that which was to be kept sacred, an outward spiritual sign. Ed 1:352.

193. Ed 1:352.

194. Farrar 1:16263.

195. DNTC 1:136.

196. Geikie 1:450.

197. Geikie 1:450.

198. MM 1:452.

199. Farrar p. 163.

200. Of this salutation Edersheim states, "No one who either knows the use of the language, or remembers that, when commending her to John on the Cross, He used the same mode of expression, will imagine, that there was anything derogatory to her, or harsh on His part, in addressing her as 'woman' rather than 'mother.'" Ed 1:361.

201. Farrar p. 165.

202. Ed 1:361.

203. John's Gospel was written to the Jews. Obedient Jews would have such water pots in their homes. Purification was one of the main requirements of the rabbinical law. The water was used to wash or purify the hands, both before and after dinner, and was also used to purify the vessels used. Ed 1:357.

204. DNTC 1:137.

205. Ed 1:362, note 4.

206. Ed 1:363.

207. Strauss pp. 519–27.

208. "The wine was mixed with water. . . . Various vintages are mentioned: among them a red wine of Saron, and a black wine. Spiced wine was made with honey and pepper. Another mixture . . . consisted of old wine, water, and balsam; yet another was 'wine of myrrh' . . . [and] wine in which capers had been soaked. To these we should add wine spiced, either with pepper, or with absinthe; and what is described as vinegar, a cooling drink made either of grapes that had not ripened, or of the lees. Besides these, palm-wine was also in use. Also various foreign drinks . . . and Palestinian apple-cider." (Ed 2:208.) "It was customary to provide at wedding feasts a sufficiency of wine, the pure though weak product of the local vineyards, which was the ordinary table beverage of the time." (JC p. 144.) "Fruit of the vine (Matthew 26:29), a light, sweet wine (normally unfermented); eaten with bread it was one of the staple foods of the day." DNTC 1:136.

209. Ed 1:355.

210. Geikie 1:451.

211. Geikie 1:450–51.

212. Ed 1:485.

213. Ed 1:486.

214. Ed Temple pp. 70–72.

215. Farrar 2:42.

216. Geikie 2:249; Ed Temple pp. 74–75.

217. Ed 2:111–12.

218. Ed 2:113.

219. Geikie 2:250.

THE PARABLES OF JESUS THE MESSIAH

Introduction

Parables as a teaching tool were not unique to the Lord, but were uniquely used and applied by Him to proclaim the kingdom of God. He utilized every facet of daily life in His parables, revealing the depth of His understanding. Crowds thronged to hear Him, and through the skillful use of parables He used the simple incidents of life to imprint vividly on their minds His great spiritual truths.

Mark records that Jesus taught only in parables to the multitudes: "With many such parables spake he the word unto them . . . but without a parable spake he not unto them."[a] Although Mark emphasized this teaching method in the everyday ministry of Jesus, he personally recorded only four of the parables from the many he must have heard or been told about. It therefore seems obvious that the Gospel writers were very selective in the parables they chose to record.

This same procedure was followed when recording the miracles, sermons, and other events of the Lord's ministry—only a limited number of them were actually used.[1] We can therefore conclude that in their individual recordings of the Lord's ministry, the synoptic Gospel writers selected those parables they felt would best enhance and clarify the Savior's teachings.

The following should be considered when studying the parables:

First, the allegorical method of interpretation should be rejected, even though it was a common method of interpretation by early Christian writers during the early and middle ages.[2] Although some words or phrases in some of the parables may hold interpretive meaning, not every word or phrase need do so. There is no secret or hidden interpretation needed to understand the Lord's parables. He taught them because the people could understand them.

Second, in all probability Jesus used many parables multiple times, which may have produced variations and adaptations to fit the circumstances of the people being taught.

Third, it is not possible to place the parables in historical order, nor is it necessary, for it is the doctrinal teaching in the parables that is important, not their historical order.

Fourth, it is possible, and perhaps probable, that the parables have undergone changes. This may have occurred because the Gospels were recorded long after the ministry of Jesus concluded. Thus, the oral tradition or expression of His teachings as recorded by the gospel writers may have varied somewhat from the original. This may have produced some of the scriptural discrepancies in the parables, but at this late date it would be impossible to determine those potential variations; therefore, because there is no practical alternative, we must accept the recorded word as authentic.[3]

Thirty-two parables are discussed in this book.[4] Matthew recorded sixteen parables, ten of which are exclusive to his gospel. Mark, who emphasized that "without a parable spake he not unto them," recorded only four parables: one exclusively. Luke recorded twenty-one parables, fifteen exclusively. Six of the parables were recorded by more than one of the Synoptic writers; however, John did not record any of them.

This book is divided into parts and chapters. Chapter 1 considers the topic of parables in general. Chapters 2 through 11 deal with specific parables. Chapter 12 deals with the message of the parables. Each part and chapter title descriptively defines the doctrinal application of the material that portion contains. This classification is my own, derived from what I perceive as the doctrinal emphasis of the parables. Keep in mind, however, that any division or classification of a parable may be open to question, for a parable may have multiple applications to daily life in any age, and its truth may leap over any boundary that attempts to circumscribe it.

Parables greatly enhanced the Lord's teachings. Under His masterful usage they became a teaching method "so stimulating, so full of interest . . . in its unapproachable beauty and finish, [that it] stands unrivalled in the annals of human speech."[5]

The Lord's parables were heard by both the unschooled and the educated, simple folks and rulers. As the Master Teacher, He rehearsed the doctrines of the kingdom to the people of His day: doctrines that could be instantly understood or misunderstood, applied or rejected, or, as with the "seed growing secretly," await some future everyday experience to stir the memory so that the hearer could recognize and accept the teachings of Jesus the Messiah.

Parables   1

The word *parable* comes from the Greek word *parabole,* as translated from the Hebrew *mashal.* In Greek it means to put forth one thing before or beside another. But in Hebrew, from which it was originally translated, it has a wider significance as exemplified by the balanced metrical form of the poetic books and teachings of the Old Testament.[6] This method of teaching was not new; "the Parable or Mashal was a mode of instruction already familiar to Israel since the days of the Judges, and was in constant use among the Rabbis."[7] Jewish teachers used the parable as a common and well-understood method of illustration.[8]

What Is a Parable?

Perhaps to best determine the nature and characteristics of a parable we should first differentiate it from the myth, fable, proverb, and allegory—all of which are other methods of symbolistic teaching. This differentiation enhances the ultimate purpose, definition, and description of the parable.

The Myth: Myths are fictitious traditions or stories. They are usually thought of as being without symbolism of spiritual truth. However, historically this was not so. Myths were devised to account for natural phenomena and the nature of divine beings. They explained the origin of reality. This reality, the end product of the myth, was determined through the deeds and stories of supernatural beings. The myth usually dealt with forms of creation, but at times also described patterns of behavior. It implied a genuine religious experience and was not used merely as a vehicle of the truth: It was considered to be the truth itself.[9]

The Fable: The fable, in its widest sense, is an imaginative or fictitious story of any description. Construed more narrowly and in the modern sense, it would be a narrative in prose or verse conveying a moral or useful lesson; but its purpose is generally to entertain or amuse rather than to teach the listener. The characters used in fables are most often animals but inanimate objects, human beings, or gods (real or mythological) may also appear. Commonly, the fable depicts only a fantasy. The moral is always stated within the structure of the fable itself.[10]

The Proverb: Proverbs are very short, pithy statements in common use. Generally, they are preserved through spoken language and are representative of the behavior of those people who originally preserved them. They transmit tribal wisdom and rules of conduct, and refer to old customs. They commonly summarize well-known fables such as the "wolf in sheep's clothing" or "don't count your chickens before they hatch." A proverb could possibly be described as a condensed parable, an example of which might be "the blind leading the blind."[11]

The Allegory: The allegory can be described as an extended parable, but it is more detailed. It is complex and can involve many relationships. The allegory is imaginative. It is usually expressed through symbols or images of deeper meaning than the surface reveals. Its subjects are generally natural things used as symbols to refer to man, rather than man himself.[12]

Myths, fables, proverbs, and allegories may contain elements, or refer to elements, of the spiritual world, but they also involve other facets of life. The parables taught by Jesus, on the other hand, are concerned only with the doctrines of the kingdom and convey spiritual truths.[13]

As stated before, parables were in common use prior to and at the time of Jesus Christ.[14] The Jewish writers before Christ extolled parables as placing the meaning of the Law within the comprehension of the common man.[15] Since the time of Christ, however, Christianity has assigned the word *parable* to mean only those parables expressed in the New Testament and as recited by the Lord. "Others have uttered parables; but Jesus so far transcends them, that He may justly be called the creator of this mode of instruction."[16]

However, this distinction is unnecessary. It does not distract from the Lord's parables to admit the existence of earlier ones. Rather, just the opposite is true. Earlier use of parables made the Lord's parables more acceptable to those who heard them; in fact, they served to enlarge the meaning of the Lord's parables. Since the Jews were accustomed to parables, this common teaching vehicle became highly effective in pictorially carrying the truth of the kingdom of God to Christ's audiences. Scenes from ordinary life with which the listener was familiar coupled with skillful comparisons made the homeliest trifles symbols of the highest truths of the kingdom.

The parables of Jesus were not scientifically accurate; nor were their facts included or omitted according to the ignorance or knowledge of the hearers. They drew pictures—pictures of life as it was at Christ's time—adapting them to the needs and purposes of His stories. The hues, the characters, and the contrasts of the stories were drawn in by the Lord with words. As Jesus spoke, the great truths of His kingdom passed before the eyes of His audience. At their simplest, the parables of Jesus depicted the common life of the people while step by step they announced with particular clarity the "good news" of the gospel.

The Master Teacher left nothing unused. As He spoke, His listeners could envision the sower in the field scattering his seed upon the various soils, the miraculous production achieved from a forgotten seed growing secretly, or leaven as it raised in a woman's dough. They could envision the treasure disclosed to the passerby, previously hidden from the view of all; the pearl of the traveling merchant from far-off lands; the shepherd searching for the lost sheep while the flock rested calmly; and the woman diligently cleaning to retrieve the coin she had lost through negligence. The Savior's audience pictured Pharisees, the publicans, the good Samaritan, and stewardship over others' goods; the fig trees as they grew on the hillside and by the paths; and the great supper, to which every Jew looked forward as the culmination of earthly life and entry into the kingdom of God. They envisioned wedding ceremonies and feasts; beggars by the wayside; laborers awaiting hire; common mustard plants; and the draw net seen daily on the lake. Using all of these common, simple things, the Lord taught His sublime lessons.

The uniquely applied and well-known scenes of daily life portrayed in the parables with such vividness directed the understanding of Christ's audiences, compelling them to apply His stories and their significance to the doctrines of His new kingdom, to His person as the Son of God, and to His mission. It was this teaching tool that helped the Lord declare pictorially, openly, and graphically His new gospel of salvation.

The nature and characteristics of a parable now begin to unfold:

First, a parable must bear reference to well-known scenes of daily life or events. The picture painted in words by the parable must be familiar to the contemporary mind, otherwise interpretation and application would be impossible.

Second, the circumstances in a parable must be connected to known spiritual realities. This specifically guides the listener's thoughts toward the spiritual application.

Third, in their vivid portrayals, parables draw specific comparisons between abstract spiritual values and real-life situations, thus avoiding general maxims and focusing attention specifically on the heavenly doctrine.

Fourth, parables are generally not labored literary productions. (Sometimes we forget that Jesus, in all probability, composed His parables spontaneously.)

Although we are most familiar with the parables in the New Testament, the Old Testament also contains parables. The most famous of these was delivered by Samuel to David.[a] Another familiar parable is found in Isaiah.[b] But more than this, there are interesting examples of "show and tell" *living parables* throughout the Old Testament. These "parables" were individuals who lived parabolic lives, representing things higher than themselves and acting out, as it were, a parable in the eyes of the chosen people. Such was the case of Abraham casting out Hagar,[c] Jonah in the belly of the great fish,[d] and David in his hour of agony.[e] Further, Jehovah commanded Jeremiah to break the potter's vessel[f] and to wear a yoke.[g] All of these stories exemplified parabolic teachings of the Lord's great truths which passed before the eyes of His chosen people, incorporated symbolically in individual's lives.

When Jesus taught, He used the situation of the moment that best portrayed to His listeners His divine calling and the teachings of the

a. 2 Samuel 12:1–7.

b. Isaiah 5:1–7.

c. Genesis 21:1–14; Galatians 4:30

d. Jonah 1:17

e. Psalm 22.

f. Jeremiah 19:1–11

g. Jeremiah 27:2; 28:10.

kingdom of heaven. Each of His parables called for and allowed an immediate response and conclusion, yet the stories lingered on in the memory, to be recalled each time the life-experience portrayed in the parable occurred. Some of His listeners understood, accepted, and followed Him while others understood, rejected, and angrily plotted His destruction. But to many, the knowledge imparted by this form of teaching was as the parable of the seed growing secretly.[17] They may not have initially understood, accepted, or rejected; but the imagery would lie dormant until they were touched by the Spirit and the imagery so subtly yet simply taught would be brought to their remembrance. Then the meaning of what they had heard would unfold, and they would discover the truths in these simple stories.

Why Did Jesus Teach in Parables?

The Lord teaches people in a manner they're familiar with. He "giveth light unto the understanding; for he speaketh unto men according to their language, unto their understanding."[a] He allowed the Nephites "plainness" of speech, for which Jacob and others were grateful, for Jacob knew that not all people were taught in this manner.

The Nephites had the record of the Jews—from the creation up to the time Lehi left for Jerusalem—so they were familiar with Jewish teaching methods. In Jacob's opinion, the Jews were a "stiffnecked people" who "despised the words of plainness . . . and sought for things that they could not understand."[b]

The Jaredites were also taught "in plain humility . . . in [their] own language,"[c] and Joseph Smith was told that the commandments he had received were given "after the manner of their language, that they might come to understanding."[d]

Paul also taught in this manner, declaring "unto the Jews I became as a Jew, that I might gain the Jews. . . . To the weak became I as weak. . . . I am made all things to all men, that I might by all means save some."[e]

Therefore, Jesus taught the Jews in parables because it was a method they were accustomed to (Chapter 1). But after His first group of parables,[f] the Apostles seemed both surprised and disturbed, for He had undoubtedly been teaching them in plainness. They knew of the linguistic intricacies used by the Jewish leadership in their parables,

a. 2 Nephi 31:3.

b. Jacob 4:14.

c. Ether 12:39

d. D&C 1:24.

e. 1 Corinthians 9:20–23.

f. Matthew 13.

and were surprised that Jesus was teaching in a similar format. They came to Jesus after the parable of the sower and asked, "Why speakest thou unto them in parables?"[a] Jesus gave the following answer (recorded with varying degrees of completeness in all three of the synoptic Gospels):

> **Matthew 13:11–14** Because it is given unto you to know the mysteries of the kingdom of heaven, but to them it is not given. For whosoever hath, to him shall be given, and he shall have more abundance: but whosoever hath not, from him shall be taken away even that he hath. Therefore speak I to them in parables: because they seeing see not; and hearing they hear not, neither do they understand. And in them is fulfilled the prophecy of Esaias, which saith, By hearing ye shall hear, and shall not understand; and seeing ye shall see, and shall not perceive.

The Lord referred to Isaiah 6:9 in these comments which states, "And he said, Go, and tell this people, Hear ye indeed, but understand not; and see ye indeed, but perceive not."

Christ did not continually speak in parables after introducing this method of instruction.[b][18] Clearly, the rulers and His audiences generally understood the Messianic claim that He presented to them throughout His ministry—on this the scriptures are replete with examples.[19] Yet even as Jesus taught in the temple during the last week of His life, they came to Him (still seeking an accusation against Him) and asked, "How long dost thou make us to doubt? If thou be the Christ, tell us plainly."[c] Jesus had replied, "I told you, and ye believed not."[d] But when He finally made the clear declaration, "I am the Son of God,"[e] they accused Him of blasphemy and ultimately sought to destroy Him.

The very nature of the Lord's parables made them readily understandable; and as we shall see, there is evidence verifying that His listeners did, indeed, understand them. For example, Jesus taught the parable of the wicked husbandmen,[20] and Matthew reports that the Jews "perceived that he spake of them."[f] Again, at the conclusion of the parable of the marriage of the king's son,[21] the leadership understood, and Matthew reports that they "took counsel how they might entangle him in his talk."[g]

The parables took the common, everyday aspects of life and un-

a. Matthew 13:10.
b. John 7, 8, 10.
c. John 10:24.
d. John 10:25.
e. John 10:36.
f. Matthew 21:45.
g. Matthew 22:15.

mistakably associated them with the kingdom of God and its doctrines. They proclaimed spiritual truth and awakened in the hearer a consciousness of that truth. Their aim was "to show by an example of human action in natural life, how men should act in the sphere of spiritual life."[22]

Thus, the teachings of the parables were not hidden, but generally clear to the Lord's audiences. The problem was not understanding, but applying the parables. A perfect example of this occurs in the Old Testament. The prophet Nathan came before King David and told him a parable:

> **2 Samuel 12:1–7** There were two men in one city; the one rich, and the other poor. The rich man had exceeding many flocks and herds: but the poor man had nothing, save one little ewe lamb, which he had bought and nourished up: and it grew up together with him, and with his children; it did eat of his own meat, and drank of his own cup, and lay in his bosom, and was unto him as a daughter. And there came a traveller unto the rich man, and he spared to take of his own flock and of his own herd, to dress for the wayfaring man that was come unto him; but took the poor man's lamb, and dressed it for the man that was come to him. And David's anger was greatly kindled against the man; and he said to Nathan, As the Lord liveth, the man that hath done this thing shall surely die: and he shall restore the lamb fourfold, because he did this thing, and because he had no pity.
>
> And Nathan said to David, Thou art the man.

It is obvious that Nathan (through the Lord) knew of David's involvement with Bathsheba. The parable was presented so that David might recognize his transgression. He clearly understood the story, but he was hearing with the ears of the transgressor and was unwilling to apply the parable to himself. He rightly judged the man in the parable as a sinner, but the parable applied specifically to David, not some stranger, and Nathan so declared.

So it was with the parables of Jesus. He knew the transgressions and errors of the covenant people and they knew of the anticipated Messiah. He used His parables to help them recognize their doctrinal errors and sins, repent, accept Him as the Savior, and return to His Father's kingdom: if only they would apply His parables to themselves.

Still, let's specifically answer the questions: Why did the Lord teach in parables and why, when the Apostles questioned Jesus about this teaching method, was His explanation given to them in such a manner? And how, by teaching in parables, did Jesus fulfill the prophecy of Isaiah?[a] In answering these questions, consider the following: first, the intent of Isaiah's prophecy; and second, the spiritual condition of the people at Jesus' time.

First: The scripture of Isaiah is Messianic;[23] the fact that Jesus applied this scripture to Himself is ample evidence of this. But in addition, John attests to its Messianic fulfillment with regard to Christ's miracles;[b] and Paul's testimony—both to the Jews[c] and to the Romans[d]— also attests that it was Messianic. Therefore, the rejection of the light taught in the parables (as well as in other teachings) was an open rejection of the prophesied Messiah. To interpret Isaiah otherwise would distort the prophesied Messianic expectation. Jesus did not teach because He wanted to fulfill the prophecies; rather, the prophecies were fulfilled by His teaching.

Second: Israel's spiritual condition at the time of Jesus was one of darkness and apostasy. Since the parables demanded a spiritual response from the hearer, this seems to provide the key to understanding the answer that Jesus gave to His disciples when He declared, "If any man have ears to hear, let him hear."[e] He was inviting His listeners to accept His teachings and apply them in their lives. But He also warned, "Take heed what ye hear. . . . For he that hath, to him shall be given: and he that hath not, from him shall be taken even that which he hath."[f]

The responsibility of those who heard the Lord's parables was threefold: first, to recognize Jesus as the Messiah; second, to learn the doctrines of the kingdom; and third, to accept and follow both. To hear carelessly or to reject what they heard would draw down the punishments of God upon them. Thus, if the listener was willful, stolid, or indifferent, that attitude would be compounded.[24] The parables conveyed to the hearer religious truths, but his application of those truths was exactly in proportion to the hearer's faith and intelligence in spiritual matters, and willingness to obey (as it was with David in Nathan's parable). To the dull, disobedient, and unintelligent in spiritual matters, and those unwilling to acknowledge their errors, the parable was understood only as a story or rejected. Seeing, they saw not; hearing, they heard not. To those willing to receive the testimony

a. Isaiah 6:9.

b. John 12:39–41.

c. Acts 28:25–27.

d. Romans 11:7–8.

e. Mark 4:23.

f. Mark 4:24–25.

of Jesus, the parable opened the way to a revelation of the mysteries of God's kingdom and revealed the pathway to eternal salvation.

Those who refused to heed the call fulfilled Isaiah's prophecy of the Messiah. They were the wicked and the unrepentant who would not hear by the Spirit of the Lord, and the parables became nothing more than a story and a mystery to them. "Two men may hear the same words; one of them listens in indolence and indifference, the other with active mind intent on learning all that the words can possibly convey; and, having heard, the diligent man goes straightway to do the things commended to him, while the careless one neglects and forgets. The one is wise, the other foolish; one has heard to his eternal profit, the other to his everlasting condemnation."[25]

Therefore, the effect of the parables upon the hearer lay not within the parabolic method of teaching, but with the willingness and state of spiritual sensibility or insensibility with which the hearer applied it. Although the parables conveyed spiritual instruction to those who accepted Christ, they only served to further darken and dull the spiritually insensible mind.[26] The parables clearly separated the Lord's listeners. To him who had, He would give more. To him who had not, that which he had would be taken away. Parabolic teaching required the listener to recognize his sins and spiritually discern the parables' truths; then he had to apply those truths in his life.

Now the Lord's reply to the Apostles takes on new meaning. He taught the people in parables (a teaching method they were familiar with) to enlighten them and assist their understanding. If they refused to accept the doctrine being taught, recognize their sins and errors, and repent of them, the parable would become a mystery to them, having no effect on their minds and hearts. If they accepted the doctrine and applied the teachings of the parables to their lives, their minds would be expanded and they would grow spiritually. The Apostles, and others who knew of the doctrine and accepted the Messiah, undoubtedly received instruction from Jesus in "plainness," thus learning the mysteries of God's kingdom. They received light upon light while those who rejected Him and His parables grew darker and darker until finally the light was gone and they could neither hear nor see nor understand. Thus, they fulfilled the words of Isaiah—for although they saw, they "perceived not."

"The appeal [of the Lord] and [His] success caused scandal. Could this be the coming of the Kingdom of God, when all the moral safeguards laboriously built up by the teachers of the law were cast aside, and the lawless were welcomed into fellowship? To those who raised such objections Jesus appealed in parables with an ironical point. If invited guests did not come to the feast, something must be done to fill the vacant seats."[27]

Classification of Parables

A basic understanding of how the Synoptic writers treated the life of Jesus is enlightening and helpful when discussing the classification of the parables. Even with a cursory reading of the Gospels, it is obvious that the writers did not attempt a complete biography of Christ.[28] The story of the Lord's birth is given in some detail, yet in reality only limited facts are recorded. From His birth and the flight to and from Egypt, no record is given of His childhood other than His experience of teaching in the temple at age twelve.[a] The next eighteen years are vacant, except for a solitary scripture: "And Jesus increased in wisdom and stature, and in favour with God and man."[b] Thereafter, His three-year ministry is reported with less than the barest detail, except for isolated incidents selected by each Gospel writer. It can therefore be concluded that the intent of the Gospel writers was not to disclose a history of the life of Jesus. Indeed, from "their point of view, [this] would have been almost blasphemy."[29] Rather than appealing to the human-interest aspects of Christ's life, they wrote of the long-awaited Messiah and the advent of the kingdom of God.

Historically, it is generally accepted that the Gospels were directed at specific groups of people. Because Matthew and Luke record all of the parables (except one that is exclusive to Mark), the belief in the historical direction of their works has greatly influenced the classification of the parables they recorded. For instance, it is felt that Matthew wrote primarily to Jewish readers, to convince them that Jesus was the expected Messiah, while Luke apparently wrote to the Gentiles, declaring that Jesus was not just the King of the Jews but the Savior of the world.[30]

The difficulty with this historical method of examination is obvious: no exact historical order to the parables or the Gospels is possible. In

a. Luke 2:42–49.

b. Luke 2:52.

fact, the order in which the parables were recorded may or may not reflect the order in which Jesus gave them. Because so little detail is given of the life of Jesus (except in a few specific instances), only incomplete conclusions can be drawn from the order of the parables in the historical record, and it lends little to the interpretation of the parables to attempt to so order them.

In the final analysis, it is the doctrinal purpose of the parables that dictates how they are to be classified, and that is the method used in this work. Any classification of the parables may prove limiting, for they have such universality of application to all people, in all times, that they transcend any boundary applied to them. But an examination of the circumstances in which they were given (where possible), and the associated teachings of the kingdom given by the Lord (or revealed elsewhere in the scriptures), leads logically to the classifications herein.

The parables of Jesus were teaching tools. Just as the miracles and sermons of Jesus were selected by the writers to exemplify some specific purpose or teaching,[31] so, too, the Synoptic writers selected specific parables to emphasize and clarify Jesus' teachings during His ministry on the earth.

Interpreting Parables

The interpretation of the parables has probably been more troublesome during the centuries since Jesus lived than it was to those who heard them originally, resulting in teaching the application of the parable to current situations rather than recognizing its original doctrine. However, to glean the original meaning of the parables, the following six general concepts should be used when interpreting them:

First, their interpretation should not be dictated by current or modern needs. No doubt the Lord's parables may be applied to circumstances of any age, and have significance far beyond their original meaning, but we should not force on the original audiences the mores of our age.

Second, and perhaps most important, I have attempted to recover the meaning of the parables as they were originally presented. Jesus taught parables in specific situations to specific groups of people in specific discourses, and for specific reasons. Therefore, not only the phrases or elements of the parables need to be interpreted and applied, but the experiences described in them must be viewed in the context in which they were given, not allegorically.[32]

Third, each parable explained or illustrated a principle of the gospel, a teaching of the kingdom of God, or a witness to His divinity. Therefore, its interpretation must be in agreement with and couched within all the teachings of the Lord.

Fourth, generally speaking, there are no secret meanings to the stories or words in the Lord's parables. There are no layers of understanding that when finally comprehended lead to the mysteries of God available only to the privileged few.

Fifth, although the historical placement of the parables by the Gospel writers may give enlightenment and credibility to their interpretation, it is not the principal guideline.

Sixth, the interpretation of the parables must be simply and rationally applied. Any figure of speech is of service only if it is not "carried beyond the bounds of reasonable intent." If it is, it "may become meaningless or even absurd."[33]

With these general concepts of interpretation firmly in mind, I suggest the following:

1. Accept the stories in the parables as examples of real life, and form the interpretation of the parables based on those circumstances. Interpretation should be applied as much as possible to the actual setting contemplated in the Gospels and to those who existed in that setting.

2. Remember, the Lord's parables were delivered to teach and emphasize specific spiritual principles, even though they may be expanded to incorporate general principles.

3. Do not force a meaning on any specific parable, or situation within a parable. Always subordinate the incidents of the parable to the principle for which it was delivered.

4. Do not necessarily regard as parallel parables that are connected by similar imagery.

5. Keep in mind that the illustration used in a particular parable does not always have the same significance elsewhere. For

example, in various scriptures leaven signifies the principles of both good and evil.[a]

6. The factual comparisons in the parables may not be complete. The intention appears to have been to draw a well-known picture of life and quickly compare it with heavenly principles.

7. Maintain a proper balance between the various elements of the parable, thus determining the essential elements and disregarding the parabolic dressing.

8. Seek the meaning of the parables within the doctrine of the kingdom as taught by Jesus.

Again we note that parables may have significance far beyond their original setting and they may be applied to many situations. But each application should be guided by the particular events which were presented by the Savior, and the way those events apply to the kingdom of God.

Due to the limited record of the Gospel writers, not every parable will comply with each of the foregoing requirements. However, each of the parables is "like fruit, which however lovely to look upon, is yet more delectable in its inner sweetness."[34]

a. Matthew 13:33;
   16:6.

The Gospel's Inherent Strength

2

The word gospel means "good news," and Jesus offered it first to the Jews. It was His declaration that He was the long-awaited Messiah and had come to establish His kingdom.

He taught the laws and doctrines of the kingdom in many ways, but with a single purpose—to save the souls of men. Jesus dedicated His life to this purpose. He taught openly and in private, to multitudes and to individuals. He used discourses to explain His principles, miracles to witness them, and parables to add clarity and richness to His teachings and strength to His testimony.

The Sower

Matthew 13:3–9, 18–23   And he spake many things unto them in parables, saying, Behold, a sower went forth to sow: and when he sowed, some seeds fell by the way, and the fowls came and devoured them up: some fell upon stony places, where they had not much earth: and forthwith they sprung up, because they had no deepness of earth: and when the sun was up, they were scorched; and because they had no root, they withered away. And some fell among thorns; and the thorns sprung up, and choked them: but other fell into good ground, and brought forth fruit, some an hundredfold, some sixtyfold, some thirtyfold. Who hath ears to hear, let him hear. . . .

Hear ye therefore the parable of the sower. When any one heareth the word of the kingdom, and understandeth it not, then cometh the wicked one, and catcheth away that which was sown in his heart. This is he which received seed by the way side. But he that received the seed into stony places, the same is he that heareth the word, and anon with joy receiveth it; yet hath he not root in himself, but dureth for a while: for when tribulation or persecution ariseth because of the word, by and by he is offended. He also that received seed among the thorns is he that heareth the word; and the care of this world, and the deceitfulness of riches, choke the word, and he becometh unfruitful. But he that received seed into the good ground is he that heareth the word, and understandeth it; which also beareth fruit, and bringeth forth, some an hundredfold, some sixty, some thirty.

Cross-references   Mark 4:3–9, 14–20; Luke 8:5–8, 11–15

The parable of the sower is recorded in all three Synoptics, but Matthew is used as the primary text. Matthew records six additional parables in the same chapter as the sower,[35] Mark records three others (one differing from Matthew), and Luke only records the sower. All of the Synoptics note the parable of the sower as the beginning of the parabolic style of teaching by Jesus.

By this time, the Lord's ministry had reached great heights and His fame brought multitudes to hear Him.[a] But His plain and straightforward teaching had produced some bitter hostility.[b] and "many of his disciples went back, and walked no more with him."[c] His success, however, inspired the cunning Jewish leadership to concoct the Beelzebub argument in an effort to confuse the people.[36]

But on the day He gave the parable of the sower, the magnitude of the Lord's presence drew people from "every city," and as He was wont to do on other occasions, He separated Himself from the multitude, boarded a ship, and pushed a little way from shore, that He might teach the multitude as they stood on the shoreline.

With the beautiful Sea of Galilee behind Him and the fruitful fields of the countryside before Him, He taught the multitude the parable of the sower. Although all those listening to the Lord yearned for the Messiah's presence, the parable depicted to them the awful reality of the reception they and all mankind would give Him and His gospel. It reflected that reception both historically (that which had already occurred in the ministry of Jesus) and futuristically (that which would yet occur as the gospel was taken to all the world). It not only portrayed Jesus as the Sower, but indicated that all others who delivered His message of salvation would also be thought of as sowers.

The scenes the Lord described were very familiar to His audiences. They had seen the circumstances time and time again. This was real life—a situation that could not be misunderstood. As the parable unfolded, the audience could envision the sower walking up and down his field spreading the seed by hand. Or perhaps they could

a. Matthew 13:2; Mark 4:1.

b. Mark 3:6.

c. John 6:66.

see the seed in bags strapped on the sides of an animal as was also the custom. Small holes had been punctured in the bottom of the bags; from these the seeds would randomly fall as the animal was led or driven up and down the field.[37]

The seed represented the word of God—the gospel. It was sown by the sower indiscriminately. There was no limit to its quantity, and it fell on all of the ground, that all might be given equal opportunity to bring forth fruit.

This was the scene presented to the mind of the hearer as the Master told His story, but these were not the important elements of the parable. Neither the sower nor the seed emphasized the eternal principles being taught by the Master.[38] These eternal principles were being taught in the description of the soil on which the seed fell. This was the main thrust of the parable; the rest was parabolic dressing. The soil represented the hearts of men.

The "Wayside" Soil

This was the most hardened of the soils. As the story unfolded, the audience could envision the hardened path or road through the fields that had been continually trampled by the feet of travelers. They might have turned to see the fields that spread out behind them and the hardened paths or roads they had walked on in order to hear the Master.

As the sower spread the seed, some fell on this wayside soil. Unable to penetrate the hardness of the surface, the seed lay upon the ground and was easily destroyed by the birds that came and devoured it. Some of mankind could be compared to this wayside soil. Perhaps there were some in the very audiences that stood before the Lord, their hearts so worn down and bereft of the Spirit by constant sin, disbelief, or lack of faith that they would not receive His word. They had no comprehension or understanding of the teachings of the Messiah. All that Jesus spoke was meaningless to them and the spiritual significance of His words was totally deadened by their worldly thoughts, actions, and total opposition to the word of God. These were "men who have no principle of righteousness in themselves, and whose hearts are full of iniquity, and have no desire for the principles of truth, [and] do not understand the word of truth when they hear it. The devil taketh away the word of truth out of their hearts, because there is no desire for righteousness in them."[39]

These were the men and women of Christ's day (and of future days) who totally rejected Him. They would accept neither His teachings nor His miracles. Their hearts were so perverted by sin and by opposition to the Messiah that there was no possibility of change in them. Their lack of understanding and unwillingness to apply His teachings in their lives made it possible for the wicked one to "[catch] away that which was sown in [their hearts]," because "there is no desire for righteousness in them." Because of the hardness of their hearts, they rejected the gospel in its entirety and did not allow the seed to commence its growth.

The "Stony Places" Soil

This is not to be interpreted as soil mingled with stones, but rather a thin layer of soil covering a rocky surface that is deceitfully hidden beneath, out of the sight of men.[40] This soil described the majority of the people who followed Jesus—the multitudes of curiosity seekers.[a] This soil caught the seeds, and the seeds sprang up quickly. The people represented by this soil heard the word with gladness and enjoyed the sweetness of each discourse, but they had no roots. These were they with temporary faith, who ultimately gave their earthly life more importance than the riches of the Lord's kingdom.[41] They did not stubbornly reject the word, nor did they overtly conspire to destroy Jesus; they merely lacked the roots of commitment, and their faith quickly withered and died.[42] Of these the Lord said, "Yet hath he not root in himself, but dureth for a while." These were the people offended by the word during persecution or tribulation. The Lord described these souls in the Sermon on the Mount as they who had built upon the sand, and when "the rain descended, and the floods came, and the winds blew, and beat upon that house," it fell.[b][43]

The soil found in stony places, like the soil by the wayside, described those who rejected the Messiah. Because of their sins and their desire for the praise of men, their hearts were set against Him. The gospel meant less to them than the way they were living; therefore they would not change. They would not take up His cross. They would not repent. They would not believe. They could not understand, or would not understand the parable because they refused, in their disbelief and rejection of Christ, to apply the parable to themselves.

a. Luke 14:25–33.

b. Matthew 7:27.

The Lord next described the soils where the seed had a chance to grow:

The "Full Of Thorns" Soil

Here there was no lack of good soil as was the case in the first two examples, but this soil was encumbered with weeds that would crowd out the seed, or prevent the seed from growing.

The Old Testament provides an analogy that brings understanding to the interpretation of the seed growing in this type of soil. After God created the earth, He created man and placed him in the Garden of Eden wherein all things grew naturally. Adam was commanded not to partake of the forbidden fruit and was told that he would be punished for disobedience. Adam partook of the fruit and in so doing transgressed, and was brought before God to receive the results of his transgression. God expelled him from the Garden of Eden and cursed the earth for his sake stating, "Thorns also and thistles shall it bring forth to thee; and thou shalt eat the herb of the field; in the sweat of thy face shalt thou eat bread, till thou return unto the ground."[a] Adam could no longer draw upon the natural growth of the earth for his food for there would be thorns growing in its soil. But by his labor, or the sweat of his brow, he could toil and properly prepare the soil so that it might produce the food that he needed.

Such was the third soil portrayed in the parable of the sower. It would not produce because of the careless husbandman. Because he did not remove the weeds, thorns, and thistles from the ground, the Lord said of him, "the care of this world, and the deceitfulness of riches, choke the word, and he [the husbandman] becometh unfruitful." The husbandman professed spiritual life, but there was no power to his conviction. The cares of the world were more important to him than the word of God.[44] Jesus cautioned His Apostles that they must ever "take heed to [themselves]" that their hearts be not "overcharged with surfeiting, and drunkenness, and cares of this life."[b] They could not serve two masters.[c]

The "Good Ground" Soil

It is only here that fruitful growth occurs. Those exemplified by this type of soil hear the word and understand it; although they may sin

a. Genesis 3:17–19.

b. Luke 21:34.

c. Matthew 6:24.

(as do all men), they recognize their sins and without self-justification that would alter the truth, they repent of their transgressions. These have prepared their hearts to receive the word of God as represented by the seed.

An example of this type of individual is given in the New Testament in the story of Zacchaeus. He was accounted by the Pharisees and rulers of the Jews as a sinner because of his occupation—he was a tax collector. When the Lord met Zacchaeus He asked if he could dine at his home, and Zacchaeus graciously received the Lord into his house. There he told Jesus of his personal spiritual preparation. He had given to the poor one-half of his goods, and he declared that if perchance he took from any man by false accusation, he restored it to him fourfold. In this confession Jesus saw the true believer and declared, "This day is salvation come to this house."[a]

Another example that is even more cogent is that of Nathanael when he was called to follow Jesus. As Nathanael approached Jesus (never having seen the Lord before), Jesus said, "Behold an Israelite indeed, in whom is no guile!"[b] Nathanael acknowledged the salutation of the Lord, for he had properly prepared himself to receive the word. He had been totally faithful to the light that he had and was prepared to receive more when it came.

These are the four soils of the parable depicted by the Master. It was into these soils that the seed was scattered. The condition of the soil symbolically represented the condition of the heart of the hearer and the preparation he had made in his spiritual quest. Some hearts were so hard that they would not receive the gospel at all; others rejected it because of their lack of preparation to receive the word. Only the last group, representing one-fourth of the people (if the parable were to be taken literally), had prepared themselves sufficiently that when they received of the word it brought forth good fruit.

The description of the soils and the interpretation thereof was the main purpose of this parable. However, it seems to have a secondary purpose, found in the declaration by the Lord of the fruits brought forth from the good soil.[45] Even here there was a difference in the quantity of fruit brought forth. It was at that certain moment of harvest (or the judgment) when the field had to be ready, but not all the "good soil" produced the same amount of fruit—there was a variable harvest.

a. Luke 19:1–9.
b. John 1:47.

The seeds had been sown at the same time and had the same amount of time to grow; only the soils were different. The seed was abundant and spread on all the soils equally. Each received the same rain, light, and heat; but even the good soil produced varying results for as the parable pointed out, it produced some an hundredfold, some sixty, and some thirty. Although those represented by the good soil had prepared themselves sufficiently to receive of the seed and to produce fruit, they still struggled (perhaps because of their abilities) with the successful use of the seed itself.[46] Yet, as the parables of the talents and the pounds reveal in Chapter 8, the rewards would be the same.

Various applications of this parable can be made to the gospel in everyday life. But the simplicity of the parable and its common scenery were contemporary with the time, place, and circumstance in which Jesus was laboring and depicted the reaction of the people to Him and His ministry. The sower performed his job in a typical and recognizable manner, and the seed was good. Only the soils were different. The parable taught clearly where the responsibility lay with regard to the kingdom of God and the reception of the gospel. It was not with the sower and it was not in the seed; it was in the soil—the heart of man.

The Wheat and Tares

Matthew 13:24–30, 37–43   Another parable put he forth unto them, saying, The kingdom of heaven is likened unto a man which sowed good seed in his field: but while men slept, his enemy came and sowed tares among the wheat, and went his way.   But when the blade was sprung up, and brought forth fruit, then appeared the tares also. So the servants of the householder came and said unto him, Sir, didst not thou sow good seed in thy field? from whence then hath it tares? He said unto them, An enemy hath done this. The servants said unto him, Wilt thou then that we go and gather them up? But he said, Nay; lest while ye gather up the tares, ye root up also the wheat with them. Let both grow together until the harvest: and in the time of harvest I will say to the reapers, Gather ye together first the tares, and bind them in bundles to burn them: but gather the wheat into my barn.   . . .

He answered and said unto them, He that soweth the good seed is the Son of man; the field is the world; the good seed are the children of the kingdom; but the tares are the children of the wicked one; the enemy that sowed them is the devil; the harvest is the end of the world; and the reapers are the angels. As therefore the tares are gathered and burned in the fire; so shall it be in the end of this world. The Son of man shall send forth his angels, and they shall gather out of his kingdom all things

that offend, and them which do iniquity; and shall cast them into a furnace of fire:
there shall be wailing and gnashing of teeth. Then shall the righteous shine forth as
the sun in the kingdom of their Father. Who hath ears to hear, let him hear.

This parable is recorded only by Matthew and is the second of the
recorded parables that the Lord interpreted for the Apostles. It is a
realistic story garnered from the agricultural life of His day.[47] It is
told vividly and naturally, simple in its terms yet complicated in its
interpretation; and it is perhaps the most un-Jewish of the parables.[48]

The first problem in interpreting this parable arises when the Lord
opens the parable with a quick analogy, likening the kingdom of heaven
to a man who sowed good seed in his field. However, the kingdom of
heaven is not actually like the man, the seed, or the field. The Lord
used this type of introduction in several of His parables.[49] It is called
a "datival" introduction, and is part of the puzzle to be solved by the
hearer. Because the Jews had such a complete misconception of what
the kingdom of heaven would be like, Jesus attempted to teach them
the truth through examples that would be familiar to them. However,
the datival introduction required the hearer to discern the identity of
the kingdom of heaven as he progressed through the parabolic story.[50]

The Lord's interpretation to the Apostles verifies that the kingdom
of heaven was not like any part of the parable. Therefore, what is it
like? In this instance, it is like the church, even though unidentified
in the parable itself.[51] The church is the kingdom of heaven upon the
earth, and the parabolic story described what happened therein. This
description applies to the church whenever it is in existence (not just
at the time of Christ); therefore, the parable applies specifically to the
following:[52]

1. To the meridian of time when Jesus established the church, to
    the church as it flourished thereafter, and to the reasons behind
    its eventual apostasy.

2. To the establishment of the church on the Western Hemi-
    sphere, which occurred after the resurrection of Jesus and His
    visit there.[a] (Again the church flourished, but eventually was
    overcome by the evils of the world.)

3. To the restoration of the gospel and the establishment of the

Church in the latter days.[a] (Although the Church is flourishing today, evil exists within its membership along with the good. However, in this, the last dispensation, the Church will not again be overcome and taken from the earth.[b] Thus, the growth of weak or evil members of the Church, as they exist side by side with those who actively seek righteousness, will continue until the judgment, or the "end of the world.")

4. To future light and knowledge to be restored to the church by the Lord, for the parable prophetically explained that the evil sower of seed will always mimic the Lord's good work in an attempt to destroy His earthly kingdom.

Even though this parable does not directly describe the kingdom of heaven or the church, it does describe what takes place within it. The simple reference to the seed, the blade, and the fruit (whether good or evil) pertains to and represents the members of the church, or "the children of the kingdom." The sower of the good seed is the Son of Man, or Jesus Christ. The sower of the bad seed (the enemy) is the devil or Satan. This moral battle between these two great sources of good and evil takes place in the "field" (or the world).

The good and bad seed represents the members of the church. The wheat sown by the Lord, the Son of Man, is the good seed. The enemy (the devil) mimics the Lord by oversowing the same field (or the entire church) with a degenerate kind of wheat (the tares) so that he might easily confuse and deceive the mind of man.

Oversowing was a common deed of enmity in Christ's time, and was a form of malice (with little risk) that resulted in great harm. It was a form of enemy retribution, and would have been very familiar to the hearers of the parable.[53]

The two types of seed grew together and at first were indistinguishable, the one from the other. They were watered and cultivated together until the time of harvest when they brought forth fruit—then the tares were discovered.

An interesting association can be made between this parable and that of the sower. In the sower, three of the four soils were unable to produce fruit at all. Only in the last soil, the good soil, was fruit produced. If we associate the wheat and tares with the good soil (where

a. D&C 86.

b. D&C 13.

one-fourth of the seed brought forth fruit), it sheds added light on the difficulty even those in the good soil will have in their struggle to overcome evil and the temptations of the world.

The second problem of interpretation surrounds the man who sowed the good seed. The parable of the wheat and tares applies to the church whenever it is established upon the earth, so this phrase must be reconciled with the interpretation given by Jesus in His ministry (that He was the Sower) and the interpretation revealed in the latter-day restoration of the gospel identifying the Apostles as the sowers.[a]

When He interpreted the parable, Jesus told His disciples, "He that soweth the good seed is the Son of man." This interpretation is obvious, for the church was first established by Jesus in the meridian of time; therefore, the sower was the Savior Himself. But he would not always remain on the earth with the church. He therefore had to prepare the Apostles to continue the work. To do this, He gave them His authority and charged them to take His gospel to all the world.[b] Thereafter, under His authority, they in turn became sowers of the seed.

This same situation existed in the establishment of the church on the Western Hemisphere. Jesus came personally to establish His church. He taught both the people in general and His disciples in particular. When His ministry to the Nephites was complete He departed, again bestowing authority on His twelve chosen disciples and charging them to continue to spread the gospel.[c] Thus, they became sowers.

Today, after a long and complete apostasy from the truth, the Lord has again established His Church.[d] He has called, authorized, and empowered Apostles to spread the gospel throughout the world.[54] The basic organizational structure of the church has been the same in all ages. The head of the church is Jesus Christ. During His ministry He lived and walked among the children of men, and He Himself began to sow the seed as He established His church. When He completed His earthly ministry, He empowered His Apostles to continue the work. Their authority came directly from Him, as did the authority of the disciples on the Western Hemisphere and those of the latter days. Therefore, Jesus could accurately interpret the parable of the wheat and tares to His Apostles, both of His time and in the latter days, and declare that they as well as He "were the sowers of the seed."[e]

a. D&C 86:2.

b. Matthew 28:19–20.

c. 3 Nephi 11–28.

d. JS—History 1:17–74.

e. D&C 86:2.

Next, the parable openly declared that "while men slept, his enemy came and sowed tares among the wheat, and went his way." The enemy was specifically identified by the Lord as the devil, and that fact is confirmed in the latter-day application of the parable found in the Doctrine and Covenants.[a] The sowing of the tares within the Church and throughout the world represents the open hostility of Satan toward the Savior.[55] This is the moral battle within the Church between good and the evil initiated by the devil. He is a mimicker of Christ, lying in wait to carefully sow a degenerate gospel, that he might stealthily deceive the children of the Father and lead them carefully down to hell.[b][56]

The parable now reaches its conclusion and the third problem of its interpretation. The two seeds grow and the blades spring up to the point where fruit is discernible. It is at this time that the servants of the sower recognize that not all in the field is of the good seed (or of the righteous). They ask the Lord who sowed the tares, and He tells them that the enemy (or the devil) was responsible. Again the servants earnestly ask, "Wilt thou then that we go and gather them up?" The Lord quickly responds, "Nay; lest while ye gather up the tares, ye root up also the wheat with them." It was not the time to harvest the wheat or to disturb the growth of the church while it was newly established and tender.

The servants (or authorities of the church) were now confronted with two situations concerning its evil or corrupt members. First, if they stepped forward and plucked the evil growth out, they might cause harm to the good growth. Because the church was young and inexperienced, the plucking up of the tares would probably disrupt the operation of the church itself; this, in its infancy, might be a threat to its very existence. The good and evil were therefore allowed to grow and ripen together.

Herein is found an important, secondary lesson of the parable—the teaching of patience, long-suffering, and tolerance within the church by its authorities.[57] Those who choose evil over good should have sufficient time to either repent of their transgressions or mature in their iniquity, so that at the time of final judgment they can easily be discerned from the righteous.

Second, there is a caution in the Lord's answer concerning man's capability of judging his fellowman (as opposed to the judgment of

a. D&C 86:3.

b. 2 Nephi 28:21–22

the Lord). Man may judge his fellowman for purposes of preserving the integrity of the church and to effectively outline procedural repentance—thus allowing the repentant sinner the opportunity of restoring himself to the church. But those permanent judgments pertaining to our eternal existence are to be left for a later time[a] and a greater Judge.[58] Through these instructions, the church could avoid the error committed by the Jews under the Law of Moses. In their over-zealous effort to preserve and protect the purity of the Law, they had condemned their people as violators of it. Their punctilious eradication of "evil" had destroyed the very Law given to protect them. The leadership of the Lord's church was cautioned and instructed through this parable so that they might not duplicate this error.

Thus, the parable declared that the wheat and the tares should grow together "until the harvest." Then the Lord will instruct the reapers, "Gather ye together first the tares, and bind them in bundles to burn them: but gather the wheat into my barn."[b] The reapers are the Lord's angels, and they will be sent forth to gather out of His kingdom "all things that offend, and them which do iniquity." The wicked will be cast into the fiery furnace (or representatively destroyed) while the righteous will be gathered into the kingdom of God.[59] This was the reason the wheat and the tares were allowed to grow together, and why the servants were restrained from plucking out the tares when they first appeared. The books of accountability for the children of men are not balanced daily.[60] The wicked are allowed to ripen temporarily, and in the final day, the evil and the good shall stand together face to face—Christ and the anti-Christ—distinguishable in all their deeds: the one totally light and the other in total darkness.

One last note should be made concerning the title, "the Son of Man." Although this was the most common appellation the Lord ascribed to Himself, the title was not prevalent anywhere else in the scriptures. However, Daniel used the title in his vision pertaining to the Messiah,[c] so the leadership of the Jews would have recognized this title as a claim by Jesus to the Messiahship. Evidence of this recognition is recorded in the reaction of the Jewish rulers to the interrogation of Stephen and his subsequent vision. Stephen preached before the rulers with such power and force that they became enraged. During his ensuing trial, the heavens opened and Stephen said, "Behold, I see

a. D&C 86:6.

b. D&C 86:7.

c. Daniel 7:13.

the heavens opened, and the Son of man standing on the right hand of God." This declaration was more than the Jewish leadership could stand, and in their rage they "stopped their ears, and ran upon him with one accord." He was cast out of the city and stoned to death.[a]

The Mustard Seed, The Leaven, The Seed Growing Secretly

After hearing the parables of the sower and the wheat and tares, the disciples undoubtedly experienced some despair, for the sower limited the fertility of the gospel (the seed) to only one-fourth of the ground; and because of the tares, even that ground contained great obstacles that could destroy the production of the fruit and thus dampen the enthusiasm of the harvest. Therefore, the Lord gave three more short parables on this subject to help the disciples see that the power of the kingdom was far beyond that created by men or mimicked by the devil.

These three parables—the mustard seed, the leaven, and the seed growing secretly—further illustrate the disparity of belief previously discussed in connection with the sower and the wheat and tares. The perception held by the children of Israel concerning the anticipated Messiah was incorrect. The Jews expected the kingdom of God to come in great political strength that would relieve them of the bondage that had been inflicted upon them for hundreds of years.[61] In this context, these parables were very un-Jewish since they showed that the kingdom of God would not come in the manner the Jews anticipated. This further separated the true followers of Christ from those who merely *professed* belief.

The Jews' anticipated Messiah was not like Jesus. Jesus grew up in a despised province. Even from one who would be His disciple came the disdainful question, "Can there any good thing come out of Nazareth?"[b] The Jewish leadership said, "Shall Christ come out of Galilee?"[c] and "Search, and look: for out of Galilee ariseth no prophet."[d]

The Savior entered His public ministry at the age of thirty and taught for only three years in Jerusalem and its neighboring villages. His knowledge of the Law was unsurpassed, but the tradition-bound populace wondered, "How knoweth this man letters, having never learned?"[e] His converts were not generally of the leadership or the learned; rather, they were of the poor, the sinners, the Gentiles, and

a. Acts 7:54–58.

b. John 1:46.

c. John 7:41

d. John 7:52.

e. John 7:15.

the uneducated. And finally, at the conclusion of His ministry, He fell into the hands of His enemies and died a shameful death on the cross.

Although this was not the Messiah or kingdom the Jews traditionally expected, such was the commencement of the kingdom of God; and it was clearly illustrated in the parables of the mustard seed, the leaven, and the seed growing secretly.

Before discussing these parables, it might be helpful to note their similarities:

First: The use of the seed as a simile to describe the planting or growth of the gospel was a common one. It was used by the Lord many times and had been used by the rabbis before him.[62]

Second: These parables have what was previously defined as a datival introduction, wherein the Lord declares that the kingdom is like unto something, whereas the kingdom may or may not be like the initial analogy or any portion of the parable.[63]

Third: These parables contain three elements that pertain to the kingdom of God.

1.   The seed (or leaven);

2.   The capacity of the seed for growth;

3.   The harvest, or the great results of the reaping of the fruit. All of these items are supplementary and complementary to the parables of the sower and the wheat and tares, and is undoubtedly why Matthew recorded them all together, regardless of whether the Lord delivered them all at once or not.

The following paragraphs illustrate the common points of interpretation in all of these parables:

The seed or leaven. In each of the parables, the seed (or leaven) represents the small beginnings of the kingdom of God (or His church) on the earth. All the people that come to the earth will have the opportunity to accept the Lord and come into His kingdom. In the mustard seed and the leaven, this principle is applied openly. In the seed growing secretly, the application is hidden and the growth of the seed is not immediately anticipated.

The capacity of the seed. This shows the power and influence of the gospel, whether from without, as in the mustard seed, or from within, as in the leaven. It demonstrates how the secret capabilities of the seed can act upon those who might initially ignore the gospel, yet later receive it, as in the seed growing secretly. In all three parables, the seed is sustained by its own power. Paul accurately described this method of growth in the kingdom of God when he said, "I have planted, Apollos watered; but God gave the increase."[a]

The sower of the seed. Whether the sowing of the seed was done by the Son of God or His agents is immaterial, for it could be interpreted as both. Regardless of who applies, nourishes, or strengthens the seed, it is only the power of the seed itself, as drawn upon by the Spirit of the Holy Ghost, which gives the increase and produces the fruit.

The harvest. The final stages of the parables teach that the gospel will not be destroyed from within or without, nor will the devil succeed against it.

Through these parables, the Lord gave the disciples great hope that the kingdom of God would prevail and give to all men the protection they needed to return to the Father.

These three short parables, as well as those of the sower and the wheat and tares, apply directly to the kingdom of God as established by the Savior; but their simplicity and beauty can stretch forward and encompass the restoration of the gospel in the latter days. The sower and the wheat and tares deal with the *tribulation* of accepting the truth. The mustard seed, the leaven, and the seed growing secretly teach the *joy* of accepting the truth. These parables assured the Apostles of the kingdom's eventual success. From small beginnings, the gospel would grow to encompass the whole earth.

The Mustard Seed

Mark 4:30–32   And he said, Whereunto shall we liken the kingdom of God? or with what comparison shall we compare it?   It is like a grain of mustard seed, which, when it is sown in the earth, is less than all the seeds that be in the earth: but when it is sown, it groweth up, and becometh greater than all herbs, and shooteth out great branches; so that the fowls of the air may lodge under the shadow of it.

Cross-references   Matthew 13:31–32; Luke 13:18–19

The parable of the mustard seed was an exciting little story that

a. 1 Corinthians 3:6.

described what the kingdom of God would eventually be like. It was in such contrast to the Jewish expectation that it was a difficult parable for them to understand, but the implication of the parable could not have gone unnoticed.[64] They expected the Messianic kingdom to be great, both at its inception and at its conclusion. But the gospel Jesus offered was not initially impressive, and the Jews could not envision it providing for their temporal and spiritual salvation. They ritualistically observed the Law of Moses with its complicated doctrines and interpretations, and their view of acceptance before God required years of study and application of the Law before an individual could qualify for the kingdom. But Jesus readily offered the gospel to all who would come unto Him: the weak, the sinner, and the unlearned as well as the learned.

The mustard seed was used as an example because of the smallness of the seed as compared to the size of its product. It was not a tree, but a giant shrub; yet the shrub produced shade for those who passed by and provided lodging for birds that offered them protection from the elements. This type of comparison had been used by Old Testament prophets and would have been familiar to those who heard it.[a]

The immense growth inherent in the mustard seed described the destiny of the kingdom of God and undoubtedly gave the disciples great hope. They could see that the kingdom would eventually grow far beyond the limited size evidenced thus far in the ministry of Christ and the growth which they themselves would produce in their own ministry after the Lord's resurrection. Their work was only the beginning. The seed (or gospel) would sprout forth quickly under their efforts, but would eventually be trodden down by the apostasy foreshadowed in the parable of the wheat and tares. Only in the restoration of the gospel in the latter days would the parable of the mustard seed attain its fulfillment.[65] The refuge provided by the branches of the tree represented the protection the gospel gives those who will embrace its requirements. As Elder James E. Talmage stated, "So the seed of truth is vital, living, and capable of such development as to furnish spiritual food and shelter to all who come seeking."[66]

In the application of the parable to the restoration of the gospel in modern times, Joseph Smith specifically declared:

a. Ezekiel 17:23;
31:6; Daniel
4:10–22.

Now we can discover plainly that this figure is given to represent the Church as it shall come forth in the last days. Behold, the Kingdom of Heaven is likened unto it. Now, what is like unto it?

Let us take the Book of Mormon, which a man took and hid in his field, securing it by his faith, to spring up in the last days, or in due time; let us behold it coming forth out of the ground, which is indeed accounted the least of all seeds, but behold it branching forth, yea, even towering, with lofty branches, and God-like majesty, until it, like the mustard seed, becomes the greatest of all herbs. . . . Behold, then is not this the Kingdom of Heaven that is raising its head in the last days in the majesty of its God, even the Church of the Latter-day Saints, like an impenetrable, immovable rock in the midst of the mighty deep, exposed to the storms and tempests of Satan, but has, thus far, remained steadfast.[67]

The Leaven

Luke 13:20–21   And again he said, Whereunto shall I liken the kingdom of God? It is like leaven, which a woman took and hid in three measures of meal, till the whole was leavened.

Cross-reference   Matthew 13:33

This small parable is most un-Jewish, and to nonbelievers, most mysterious.[68] It is very similar to the mustard seed as both the mustard seed and the leaven symbolically possess the inherent vitality necessary for the development of the kingdom of God.[69]

The Lord used leaven in this parable as the symbol of the kingdom of God, although at other times He used it to describe evil influences infecting the kingdom.[a] Here, however, the wholesome influence of the leaven permeates dead Judaism with the vitality of the kingdom's truth. Unlike the outward growth of the mustard seed, the leaven grew from within, indicating that when heard, the gospel could pervade and transform a person's whole life.[70] The parable emphasizes the end results of the leaven rather than its rapid growth, and therefore adds to the thought initially taught in the mustard seed.

The establishment of the gospel by the Savior did not reach its ultimate destiny (of permeating the entire earth) during Christ's lifetime or the lifetime of His Apostles; the fulfillment of the parable would

a. Mark 8:15.

not come until after the restoration of the gospel. Therefore, the parable prophesied of the final triumph of the kingdom of God in the latter days. When Joseph Smith was questioned about the parable he responded, "It alluded expressly to the last days, when there should be but little faith on the earth, and it should leaven the whole world; also there shall be safety in Zion and Jerusalem, and in the remnants whom the Lord our God shall call."[71] In another setting the Prophet Joseph said, "It may be understood that the Church of the Latter-day Saints has taken its rise from a little leaven that was put into three witnesses. Behold, how much this is like the parable! It is fast leavening the lump, and will soon leaven the whole."[72]

And so this little parable, so mysterious to the Jews of Christ's day yet so simple in its application, had a far-reaching impact that would not see its final fulfillment until the angels should receive permission to go forth and separate the wheat from the tares and gather the good fruit into the kingdom.

The Seed Growing Secretly

Mark 4:26–29   And he said, So is the kingdom of God, as if a man should cast seed into the ground; And should sleep, and rise night and day, and the seed should spring and grow up, he knoweth not how. For the earth bringeth forth fruit of herself; first the blade, then the ear, after that the full corn in the ear. But when the fruit is brought forth, immediately he putteth in the sickle, because the harvest is come.

Finally, we come to the seed growing secretly, the only parable that is exclusively recorded by Mark. This parable elaborates on the inherent strength of the gospel as discussed in the mustard seed and the leaven, but adds the dimension of time between hearing the gospel and accepting it.

After the seed is sown, its growth commences "dependent on the law inherent in seed and soil," but even more dependent "on Heaven's blessing of sunshine and showers, till the moment of ripeness, when the harvest-time is come."[73]

The parable describes the vitality of the gospel in the listener, even though the listener does not immediately accept it.[74] The growth of the seed waits until an experience exists that brings to memory the teachings that the Lord had given, whether they were heard during His ministry or some later date, including after the restoration or the reading of the word. The constant growth of the seed is assured and the harvest is anticipated.[a]

The Lord used these three parables to give His Apostles encouragement after He had described the difficulties the kingdom would encounter in the parables of the sower and the wheat and tares. Peter gave the same type of encouragement to the Saints when he spoke of "Being born again, not of corruptible seed, but of incorruptible, by the word of God, which liveth and abideth for ever. For all flesh is as grass, and all the glory of man as the flower of grass. The grass withereth, and the flower thereof falleth away: But the word of the Lord endureth for ever. And this is the word which by the gospel is preached unto you."[b]

There will always be obstacles in the path of those who receive the kingdom, but if the path is followed, the harvest is assured.

a. Revelation 14:14–15.

b. 1 Peter 1:23–25.

The Gospel Once Discovered

3

Throughout His entire ministry, Jesus preached the nearness of the kingdom of God and laid claim to the Messiahship. The coming of the Messiah was looked for in all that was done in Jewish life. The Old Testament prophesied of it and the Law that governed the lives of the children of Israel prepared them for that great event. But their perception of what the Messiah would be like was incorrect. They anticipated that the Messiah would establish a political kingdom, not a spiritual one. The gospel Jesus preached was intended to save souls eternally, not the nation temporally.

It was this choice, between spiritual salvation and temporal existence, which faced the people Jesus taught. They had to decide for themselves just how important the gospel was as compared to their temporal needs and desires. Jesus clearly taught the course that would lead to eternal life. Some believed on Him and some did not.

A Candle Under a Bushel

Matthew 5:14–15 Ye are the light of the world. A city that is set on an hill cannot be hid. Neither do men light a candle, and put it under a bushel, but on a candlestick; and it giveth light unto all that are in the house.

Cross-references Mark 4:21–22; Luke 8:16–17

Most writers do not refer to these few sentences as a parable; but this little analogy, couched in general parabolic form, is an excellent introduction to the parables that describe what is required of those who have discovered the gospel. The saying is a simple one and is obvious in its interpretation. One does not light a lamp or turn on a light in order to hide it so that no one will see it. This analogy was given to the Apostles (but was applicable to all) so that those who heard the gospel would fully understand their responsibility pertaining to it. It was not to be something that they were ashamed of, nor was it to be neglected; it was to be received with gladness and expanded upon.

Some of the Jews who heard the gospel were reluctant to associate with it openly. The best example of this might be Nicodemus. He first went to Jesus by night to ask questions, that he might better understand the Lord's teachings.[a][75] Later, he timidly defended Jesus before the Sanhedrin,[b] and at the burial of Jesus, he provided certain ointments to anoint the Lord's body.[c] We do not know whether he became an open follower of the Lord.

The leaders and many of the people who initially accepted Jesus were very reluctant to openly acknowledge Him. They hid their "light" rather than acknowledge and proclaim it.

This teaching, parabolic in form, supplements the parables that were given to symbolize the importance of the gospel once discovered.

The Hidden Treasure

Matthew 13:44   Again, the kingdom of heaven is like unto treasure hid in a field; the which when a man hath found, he hideth, and for joy thereof goeth and selleth all that he hath, and buyeth that field.

This is the first of two very short parables given by the Lord as a general instruction concerning the discovery of the gospel.

The kingdom of heaven is compared to a treasure hidden in a field. The man who discovers the treasure is not looking for it, but apparently stumbles upon it. There are only two ways to discover the gospel: one is by accident, as depicted here, where the individual is not looking for or struggling in any way to acquire the kingdom of heaven; the second, referred to in the parable of the pearl of great price (following section), is represented by the individual who is diligently seeking the kingdom.

As the parable of the treasure hidden in a field progresses, it appears that in his first moments of discovery, the man fears that he might lose the treasure so recently uncovered. So he immediately hides the treasure and proceeds to acquire it by purchasing the field. The law

a. John 3:1–5.

b. John 7:50–51.

c. John 19:39.

and tradition of the time was in full accord with this procedure.[76] But this is not the point of the parable, and no emphasis should be placed here. Neither is there a question of morality involved in such a procedure. These were merely the trappings of the parabolic story and they should be disregarded as unimportant to the parable's intended spiritual lessons.

The parable next discloses that the man goes with joy to purchase the field. The Lord had declared that the treasure was the kingdom of heaven (or the gospel), and the joy the man experienced upon such a valuable discovery is quite in harmony with the intent and meaning of the parable for it was the man's discovery that precipitated his joy, that made him intent on acquiring the treasure, and that made him willing to pay the necessary price to obtain it.

The parable contains only two elements that require interpretation. The first is the discovery of the treasure and the immediate recognition of its inestimable value. This was a favorite theme in Oriental folklore,[77] and would have been readily recognized by the Lord's listeners. But it was not the ultimate purpose of the parable. The treasure, by definition, was the kingdom of heaven; therefore, its worth was far beyond the worth of all treasures (since it is the most desirable of all treasures that can be acquired).

The second element of the parable to be interpreted was the requirement of the individual to acquire the valuable treasure once it had been found.[78] The Lord taught that principle when He declared that the man "selleth all that he hath, and buyeth that field." This is the requirement for those who discover the gospel. In the things of the world, some are rich and some are poor; but the total value of their possessions does not matter for it is required of those who discover the gospel to give all in order to possess it. The parable did not put a price on the treasure. It required that all things of the world be subjugated to the gospel to assure its acquisition[79]—not that we should give up all things, but that the gospel comes first. The gospel is only obtained by the joyful self-sacrifice of all worldly things and the realization of the worthlessness of all human possessions in comparison.

Such a requirement has been vividly portrayed elsewhere in the scriptures. Jesus declared, "If any man will come after me, let him deny himself, and take up his cross, and follow me";[a] "let the dead bury their dead";[a] "No man, having put his hand to the plough, and looking back, is fit for the kingdom of God";[b] "If any man come to me, and hate not his father, and mother, and wife, and children, and brethren, and sisters, yea, and his own life also, he cannot be my disciple";[c] "sell that thou hast . . . and come and follow me."[d] And in yet another place He indicated that it was better, figuratively speaking, to cut off a hand or a foot, or pluck out an eye, than to allow the worldly to overcome the spiritual.[e] These teachings forcefully demonstrate the meaning of the parable—once discovered, the kingdom was to be placed above all else.

A most interesting example of the discovery of the gospel is recorded in the fourth chapter of John. As Jesus was journeying through Samaria, he stopped and rested at the well Jacob had given his son Joseph. A woman appeared and drew water, and Jesus requested a drink from her. The woman was startled because Jesus was a Jew and she was a Samaritan. In response to the astonishment of the woman, Jesus questioned her: "If thou knewest the gift of God, and who it is that saith to thee, Give me to drink; thou wouldest have asked of him, and he would have given thee living water."[f] But the woman misunderstood and asked the Savior to give her this "living water" so that she would not thirst. She had not yet discovered the kingdom, and thought only of the earthly requirement of the thirst of the body. Jesus continued His instruction and she, beginning to glimpse His meaning, declared that she was waiting for the Messiah to come, who would be called Christ. Jesus then openly declared to her, "I that speak unto thee am he."[g]

The woman hurriedly returned to her village and declared to all she met that the Christ had come, and the people followed her out of the city to see the wonder she spoke of. By this time the disciples had returned to Jesus, and as the people approached, he declared, "Lift up your eyes, and look on the fields; for they are white already to harvest."[h]

In their eagerness to acquire the treasure so recently found, the people requested that the Lord stay with them. As a result, He spent two additional days there. They had discovered the gospel and wanted more of its teachings that they might enjoy its fullness, and the scripture declares that "many more believed because of his own word."[i][80]

These examples only emphasize the poignant meaning of the par-

a. Matthew 8:22.

b. Luke 9:62.

c. Luke 14:26.

d. Matthew 19:21.

e. Mark 9:43–48.

f. John 4:10.

g. John 4:26.

h. John 4:35.

i. John 4:41.

able. The worth of the kingdom was obvious, but those who discovered it assumed an absolute obligation to acquire it and to set aside all worldly possessions and concerns in order to possess the previously hidden treasure.[81]

The Pearl of Great Price

Matthew 13:45–46 Again, the kingdom of heaven is like unto a merchant man, seeking goodly pearls: who, when he had found one pearl of great price, went and sold all that he had, and bought it.

With simplicity and beauty, the Lord used this parable to again point out what we should do once we have discovered the gospel. The parable of the treasure hidden in the field explained what the responsibility was for those who accidentally stumbled upon the kingdom. This parable, on the other hand, declares a similar responsibility for those who are actively seeking the kingdom of heaven and find it.

The parable begins by declaring that the kingdom of heaven is like unto a merchant man who was seeking goodly pearls. However, the kingdom of heaven in the parable is not symbolized by the merchant man, but by the pearl.[82] The merchant was a dealer in pearls, and he knew exactly what he was searching for. This situation is totally opposite that of the man who accidentally stumbled upon the hidden treasure.

The value of the pearl the merchant was looking for is assumed, but it must be kept "in mind the esteem in which pearls were held in antiquity, so that there is record of almost incredible sums offered for single pearls, when perfect."[83]

The merchant, once he saw the perfect pearl, immediately recognized its value. This is directly comparable to those devoted investigators who search diligently for the kingdom of heaven.[84] They may not immediately discover the kingdom, but they have the necessary characteristics within their makeup to continue the quest until the kingdom is found.

There is no surprise implied in this parable as there is in the treasure hidden in the field, for the merchant knows exactly what he is searching for; and once the priceless pearl is identified, the merchant knows exactly what he must do to acquire it. The price is the same as it was for the hidden treasure, and the merchant sold all that he had in order to obtain the pearl.

Once again, it is made clear that the kingdom must be acquired with all that we have, whether we are actively in search of it or stumble upon it accidentally. Once we discover the gospel, we must part with all else that would conflict or be foreign to it.[85] This does not necessarily mean that we must deprive ourselves of our earthly possessions, but it does mean that the Lord and the gospel come before the things of the world. We may be required to give up old ways, and perhaps change our minds about certain doctrines or acquired beliefs. The seeker may, as Paul declares, have to reject certain philosophies or "science falsely so called"[a] in order to acquire the pearl.

The story of Christ's encounter with the rich young man[b] exemplifies this parable's teaching. The rich man could not bring himself to sacrifice his wealth and follow the Savior. The Apostles, on the other hand, had "forsaken all." They had done what the rich man could not—they had paid the price and purchased the pearl. Because of their willingness to follow the Lord, they were promised the reward; they would be with Him in His glory and would "sit upon twelve thrones."[c]

The conclusion is simple: when we are willing to give our all for the kingdom, the kingdom will be ours.[86]

a. 1 Timothy 6:20.

b. Matthew 19:16–27.

c. Matthew 19:28.

*L*ost and Then Found 4

The gospel Jesus taught provided the way into the kingdom of God. The way was straight and narrow, and the requirements explicit. "I am the way, the truth, and the life," He said, "no man cometh unto the Father, but by me." All who heard His words had the freedom of choice to accept or reject them, but the meaning was clear: without the gospel, entrance into the kingdom was impossible.

Once the kingdom was accepted, freedom of choice continued. In the following parables, the Lord taught of those who failed to keep the requirements of the kingdom and became lost, and of the leadership's responsibility to them.

The Lost Sheep

Luke 15:1–7   Then drew near unto him all the publicans and sinners for to hear him. And the Pharisees and scribes murmured, saying, This man receiveth sinners, and eateth with them.

And he spake this parable unto them, saying, What man of you, having an hundred sheep, if he lose one of them, doth not leave the ninety and nine in the wilderness, and go after that which is lost, until he find it? And when he hath found it, he layeth it on his shoulders, rejoicing. And when he cometh home, he calleth together his friends and neighbours, saying unto them, Rejoice with me; for I have found my sheep which was lost. I say unto you, that likewise joy shall be in heaven over one sinner that repenteth, more than over ninety and nine just persons, which need no repentance.

Cross-reference   Matthew 18:12–14

The parable of the lost sheep is recorded twice in the scriptures. Its interpretation, although generally the same in both instances, was applied to two widely differing groups of people: enemies in Luke, friends in Matthew.

Luke records that Jesus was teaching a group of publicans and sinners who had come to hear Him and the Pharisees and scribes murmured, saying, "This man receiveth sinners, and eateth with them." The Lord answered the accusation by teaching a sequence of parables beginning with the lost sheep, continuing on to the lost coin, and ending with the prodigal son.

The Pharisees, scribes, and rulers of the Jews despised the publicans and sinners. In their self-righteousness, they considered themselves superior. Their self-aggrandizement had risen to such heights that they felt no need for repentance, believing that they had committed no sin; therefore, they felt the association of publicans and sinners would defile them, making them unworthy for the kingdom of God.[87]

Publicans (considered sinners) were accounted as traitors "who for the sake of filthy lucre had sided with the Romans, the oppressors of the theocracy, and now collected for a heathen treasury. No alms might be received from their money chest; their evidence was not taken in courts of justice, and they were put on the same level with heathens."[88]

The Pharisees and scribes were accounted as the keepers of the covenant, protectors of the law, possessors of the kingdom—the shepherds of Israel. Now, however, the true Shepherd of Israel stood before them. These erstwhile shepherds had long since ignored their lost sheep. While forsaking their duty, they had rejoiced in the "evil" of the publicans and sinners and were thankful that they themselves were not one of them.[89] But Ezekiel had seen their day and had issued this warning to them: "Son of man, prophesy against the shepherds of Israel, prophesy, and say unto them, Thus saith the Lord God unto the shepherds; Woe be to the shepherds of Israel that do feed themselves! should not the shepherds feed the flocks? Ye eat the fat, and ye clothe you with the wool, ye kill them that are fed: but ye feed not the flock."[a]

Zechariah further emphasized this warning when he prophesied:

Zechariah 11:16–17. For, lo, I will raise up a shepherd in the land, which shall not visit those that be cut off, neither shall seek the young one, nor heal   a. Ezekiel 34:2–3.

that that is broken, nor feed that that standeth still: but he shall eat the flesh of
the fat, and tear their claws in pieces. Woe to the idol shepherd that leaveth
the flock! the sword shall be upon his arm, and upon his right eye: his arm
shall be clean dried up, and his right eye shall be utterly darkened.

The prophesied criticism of the "shepherds" of Israel had come to
pass. Now the Pharisees and scribes were finding fault with Jesus for
doing the very thing that they should have been doing. Jesus offered
the gospel to both shepherd and sheep alike. But the shepherds, in
their self-righteous conceit, had refused association with the sheep,
whom they considered "sinners." They took offense at Jesus, for He
received lost souls graciously and lived in close association with them,
while they themselves "had neither love to hope for the recovery of
such, nor medicines to effect it."[90]

The ninety-nine sheep in this parable are described as those "just
persons, which need no repentance." Perhaps they were righteous
partakers of the gospel who did not need immediate attention. On the
other hand, perhaps the Master intended the sheep to represent the
very critics then confronting Him[91] since this parable was given in response to the murmurings of the Pharisees and scribes. They relished
the Law and their cold, self-righteous correctness within it. The Lord
may have been saying, "If you (the Pharisees and Sadducees) are 'in the
sheepfold, I have no mission for you,' for 'I am sent to look up sheep
that are lost,' those you have 'despised.'"[92]

The "one lost sheep" in the parable was representative of those
publicans and sinners who had drifted away from the Law, and were
excluded, avoided, and shunned by the very keepers of it. It was to
these errant souls that Jesus extended the glad tidings of the gospel
while reemphasizing the leadership's obligation to seek out and recover
those Israelites who had been spiritually lost. It was their duty to recover these souls, not to rejoice over their evil and ostracize them from
the religious community. The joy expressed in the parable resulted
from the recovery (through repentance) of the sheep that was lost.[93]

In Matthew's account, the circumstances that led to the use of this
parable were quite different. In Luke, the Lord was speaking to the
self-righteous rulers of the Jews who had rejected Him and become
His most bitter enemies. But in Matthew, He was speaking to His disciples—followers of the word eager for instruction. Yet the question

they asked Jesus exemplified the same attitude as that of the Pharisees and scribes in Luke. To Jesus they said, "Who is the greatest in the kingdom of heaven?"[a]

The nuances of the Law, as taught by the Pharisees and rulers of the Jews, had given rise to a desire for personal aggrandizement and a separation of classes among the Jews. Jesus did not want the errors of the old Law to creep into the new. He prefaced the answer to His disciples' question with an analogy of little children: "Whosoever therefore shall humble himself as this little child, the same is greatest in the kingdom of heaven."[b] He then continued with a discussion on offenses and the need to eliminate them as He declared, "For the Son of man is come to save that which was lost."[c] It was at this juncture that He delivered the parable of the lost sheep. He made it clear that the shepherds of the new gospel, as well as those of the old Law, were responsible to look after the Lord's sheep.

The one lost sheep underlined the value of each member of the flock in the eyes of the Father. If one was lost, it was God's will that the leadership should go after him, and his repentance would bring great joy to all.

This parable is an outstanding example of the Lord's use of parables. It applied to both enemy and friend. To the Pharisees, who believed that "there is joy before God when those who provoke Him perish from the world,"[94] it pointed out that there was greater rejoicing over a repentant sinner than over those who were adhering strictly to the Law.

This parable taught the Apostles that their ascension to leadership in the church should facilitate not only the gathering of souls into the kingdom of God, but the retention of those souls within the kingdom. For it is "not the will of your Father which is in heaven, that one of these little ones should perish."[d]

One last, important point can be drawn from this parable. The sheep that was lost had *strayed* from the flock. It is natural for sheep to wander, and as they drift farther and farther they eventually are lost from the safety of the flock and are unable to find their way back without a diligent search on the part of the shepherd. When a diligent search proves successful, however, and the sheep is found, he will be joyously returned to the flock in full fellowship and accord.

a. Matthew 18:1.

b. Matthew 18:4.

c. Matthew 18:11.

d. Matthew 18:14.

The Lost Coin

Luke 15:8–10   Either what woman having ten pieces of silver, if she lose one piece, doth not light a candle, and sweep the house, and seek diligently till she find it? And when she hath found it, she calleth her friends and her neighbours together, saying, Rejoice with me; for I have found the piece which I had lost. Likewise, I say unto you, there is joy in the presence of the angels of God over one sinner that repenteth.

The parables of the lost sheep and the lost coin appear similar on the surface, but it would be incorrect to assume that they say exactly the same thing. The Lord's teachings, initiated in the parable of the lost sheep, are expanded in the parable of the lost coin, and expanded still further in the parable of the prodigal son. In these parables, it appears that the Lord is teaching two things simultaneously and progressively: (1) the responsibility of leadership toward errant individuals within the covenant, gospel, or church, and (2) the responsibility of the wayward individual toward the covenant, gospel, or church.

A comparison of the parable of the lost sheep with that of the lost coin is helpful in defining and discussing the simultaneous and expanded teachings:

Lost Sheep	Lost Coin
• <u>Individual</u> wanders	• <u>Individual</u> negligently loses coin
• Accepted back (repentance assumed)	• Accepted back (repentance emphasized)
• Blessings restored	• Blessings restored
• Attitude: disinterested	• Attitude: negligent
• <u>Leadership</u> responsibility for loss undefined	• <u>Leadership</u> responsible for loss
• Leaves to find	• Diligent search required
• Discovers: brings back to flock	• Recovers through diligent search
• Rejoices at finding	• Rejoices at finding

In the parable of the lost sheep, the flock represents the chosen people within the covenant, gospel, or church; the shepherd represents the Jewish leadership; and the lost sheep represent errant individuals. But in the lost coin, the parabolic players become more complicated and assume dual roles as the Lord expands the teaching. The woman plays the role of the shepherd when she is the keeper of the coin, but she also portrays the errant individual who has lost the gospel. The coin also takes on two identities, representing the wayward sheep entrusted to the church when the woman represents the shepherd, and the gospel itself when the woman represents the errant individual. The parable of the lost coin was specifically directed to the Pharisees and Sadducees as the leadership of Israel, but it can be applied to any of the authorized leaders of the church in any age.[95]

While it is clear in the parable of the lost sheep that both the leadership and the individual have undefined and perhaps limited responsibility in the separation of the sheep from the flock, this is clearly not so in the lost coin. The coin was lost solely through the negligence of the woman;[96] thus, separation from the church can come through the negligence of the leadership (Jesus denounced the Jewish leadership on several occasions for this very sin[a] or the negligence of the individual.

In the parable of the lost sheep, the sinner merely strayed from the Lord in the normal course of life's events whereas in the lost coin, the sinner was lost as a result of culpability and negligence. The owner of the coin recognized immediately that something valuable had been lost and needed to be recovered. This fact is stressed in the parable, for the emphasis immediately focuses on the search for the coin.[97] The recovery of the lost sheep was simple and uncomplicated, but not so with the coin. Negligent loss requires diligent seeking.

The first thing the woman in the parable did was find a candle so that she could search past the normal daylight hours and probe into every darkened corner of her house. She meticulously swept the house, undoubtedly searching the furniture and even moving it to be certain the search would be complete. The woman's diligence in attempting to find the coin directly relates to both the effort required by the leadership to recover lost souls for the Lord, and the individual's effort, through repentance, to return to the fold.

When the woman finds the coin she rejoices, and even invites her neighbors in to share her happiness. Anyone who has been influential in changing a person's life for good can relate to these feelings. Similarly, there is joy in heaven over one recovered soul or one repentant sinner.

Through these two succinct parables (the lost sheep and the lost coin), the leadership of the church was admonished in their responsi-

a. Luke 11:37–51; Matthew 23.

bility toward lost souls, and the individual was admonished in his responsibility toward the gospel. The third parable, that of the prodigal son, will graphically depict what happens when an individual leaves the fold deliberately—as a result of choice. Although the leadership's responsibility is again elaborated upon, the main emphasis of the prodigal son shifts from the responsibility of the leaders to the responsibility of the individual.

The Prodigal Son

Luke 15:11–32 And he said, A certain man had two sons: and the younger of them said to his father, Father, give me the portion of goods that falleth to me. And he divided unto them his living. And not many days after the younger son gathered all together, and took his journey into a far country, and there wasted his substance with riotous living. And when he had spent all, there arose a mighty famine in that land; and he began to be in want. And he went and joined himself to a citizen of that country; and he sent him into his fields to feed swine. And he would fain have filled his belly with the husks that the swine did eat: and no man gave unto him. And when he came to himself, he said, How many hired servants of my father's have bread enough and to spare, and I perish with hunger! I will arise and go to my father, and will say unto him, Father, I have sinned against heaven, and before thee, and am no more worthy to be called thy son: make me as one of thy hired servants. And he arose, and came to his father. But when he was yet a great way off, his father saw him, and had compassion, and ran, and fell on his neck, and kissed him. And the son said unto him, Father, I have sinned against heaven, and in thy sight, and am no more worthy to be called thy son. But the father said to his servants, Bring forth the best robe, and put it on him; and put a ring on his hand, and shoes on his feet: and bring hither the fatted calf, and kill it; and let us eat, and be merry: for this my son was dead, and is alive again; he was lost, and is found. And they began to be merry. Now his elder son was in the field: and as he came and drew nigh to the house, he heard musick and dancing. And he called one of the servants, and asked what these things meant. And he said unto him, Thy brother is come; and thy father hath killed the fatted calf, because he hath received him safe and sound. And he was angry, and would not go in: therefore came his father out, and in treated him. And he answering said to his father, Lo, these many years do I serve thee, neither transgressed I at any time thy commandment: and yet thou never gavest me a kid, that I might make merry with my friends: but as soon as this thy son was come, which hath devoured thy living with harlots, thou hast killed for him the fatted calf. And he said unto him, Son, thou art ever with me, and all that I have is thine. It was meet that we should make merry, and be glad: for this thy brother was dead, and is alive again; and was lost, and is found.

The prodigal son is one of the most moving and enlightening parables in the Bible. It is a parable of heavenly doctrine that draws its comparisons from real-life situations. Meaning does not need to be forced upon this parable, for its setting was completely understandable to the Jews, as was its heavenly application.[98]

The parables of the lost sheep and the lost coin gave instructions to the leaders of the Jews that centered on their responsibility toward the wayward souls of the church, whether those souls had merely wandered away or were lost through negligence. However, in the prodigal son the leadership is depicted as having successfully completed its responsibility to the individual. The individual is already an heir to the Lord's blessings and is lost through deliberate choice—he willfully chooses to separate himself from the flock.

Two sons are described in this parable. The younger son impatiently asks his father for an early inheritance, desiring to use his wealth immediately. He does not want to wait until his father's death. The father consents to his request, and divides to him his portion of the inheritance. The son does not immediately leave after receiving his goods. He lingers several days in order to gather together all that he has, so that he will be adequately prepared for his journey into the world. He then leaves for a far country where he can forget both his father and God.[99]

The emphasis of the parable at this point is clear. The son deliberately chooses to separate himself from his father. The father in this case may be interpreted as representing either God or the church (the consequences being the same in either case).

The Lord had now expanded His teachings with regard to the individual's responsibility to the gospel to include all the methods of losing it. In the lost sheep the loss occurred inadvertently, the soul simply strayed away. In the lost coin, the soul was lost through culpable negligence. But in the prodigal son, the soul deliberately chose to leave the church.

An Old Testament story that has some similarities with that of the prodigal son is the story of Esau and Jacob. Esau, the twin brother of Jacob, had returned from a long hunt and was faint. He asked Jacob to feed him some of the pottage that Jacob had prepared. Jacob agreed, but first requested that Esau sell him his birthright to pay for the food. Esau decided that his hunger was such that he would die if he did not immediately receive nourishment, even though he was home, and he said, "What profit shall this birthright do to me?"[a] So, he sold Jacob his birthright for a bowl of pottage.

In like manner, the prodigal son willfully desired to exchange his inheritance for the things of the world. He spent his inheritance, never to recover it. The parable reports that he wasted his substance with "riotous living." He lost his kingdom by succumbing to the bondage of the world, his own lusts, and the tyranny of the devil.[100]

When the prodigal son first departed from the safety of the fold, the attractions and pleasures of the world undoubtedly gave him satisfaction. He probably congratulated himself on his newfound liberty and worldly enjoyment. But eventually his inheritance was dissipated, and the time came when the creature delights of his worldly passions forsook him. His desperate circumstances made him recognize the true calamity of his departure from his father (representing the church or the kingdom of God).[b]

He had spent all of his inheritance when there arose a mighty famine in the land. With no funds to provide for himself, the prodigal began to want. He hired out to a citizen of the country in which he was residing and was given the task of feeding the swine in the fields. The cup of his misery and despair was full. He did not have enough to eat, no one would help him, and he had sunk so low that he "would fain have filled his belly with the husks that the swine did eat."

The prodigal's situation was graphically described by the Savior. He made it clear in the parable that those who would not be ruled by God would find themselves serving Satan. The prodigal son had squandered his inheritance through sin and had debased himself into the depths of hell. But adversity proved to be a powerful prodder, and he suddenly recognized that even the hired servants in his father's house had bread to eat while he perished with hunger. He decided to return to his father, admit that he had sinned against him and heaven, openly avow that he was no more worthy to be his son, and request that his father let him be one of the hired servants. With this in mind, he returned to his father's house where he was undoubtedly overwhelmed to be received openly and joyously and have all his earthly needs abundantly provided for. His candid confession and his recognition of disobedience proclaimed his future state. He had rejected his home and squandered his inheritance. He knew that he could no longer be a

a. Genesis 25:32.

b. Jeremiah 2:19, 17:5–6.

son. He would have to be satisfied with what his father gave him. We cannot make inference from this parable that the repentant sinner will be given precedence over a righteous soul who has consistently lived the gospel throughout his life.[101] Clearly this is not the case.

The Lord now interjects into this parable the anger of the firstborn son who had served faithfully through the years, as was his duty. Even though he had conscientiously fulfilled his obligations to his father, he had not received any of the attention now being showered upon his errant younger brother.

At this juncture, the emphasis of the parable shifts. No longer is the returning son the center of attention; the first son now takes center stage. The younger son had lived but for today, deliberately rejecting his eternal inheritance in the kingdom to satisfy his immediate, earthly desires and passions. His inheritance had been dissipated, and he would never enjoy it again.[102] The father assured the faithful, older son that he was ever with him, and all that the father had was his. On the other hand, the prodigal would never enter into the fullness of the father's kingdom, but would indeed participate only as a servant. He would not share again in that which he had rejected.[103]

No emphasis need be laid upon the apparent dissatisfaction of the elder brother because of the celebration given at the return of the prodigal son. This information probably was only parabolic dressing intended to define the relationship between the brothers and their position in the kingdom of God.

Undoubtedly, the Lord's disciples were with Him as He taught the parables of the sheep, coin, and prodigal son; but the rest of his audience was comprised of sinners and outcasts of the Jewish people as well as the critical rulers of the Jews. In these three parables the Lord implicitly revealed to this audience what their responsibility was in the kingdom of God once they had discovered it. The contest, after all, is our individual contest of faith; only our faith in God makes us strong enough to be victorious over the things of the world.

Anciently, the children of Israel exemplified this principle when they petitioned Samuel to approach the Lord to have Him "make us a king to judge us like all the nations."[a] Samuel was displeased with their request and prayed to the Lord for direction. In His response, a. 1 Samuel 8:5.

the Lord commiserated with Samuel's displeasure but explained, "they have not rejected thee, but they have rejected me"[a]—just as the prodigal son had rejected the kingdom of God. Saul was then selected to be the first king of Israel and he determined to be the kind of king Israel wanted, but this was not what the Lord wanted. Saul did not have sufficient faith in the Lord, and his weakness made him bow to a wicked people. Saul's kingdom was not of God; therefore, it could not continue.

Even though their circumstances were different, Saul became as unfit for his kingship as Esau was for the inheritance rights of a firstborn son, or as the prodigal son was for the inheritance he received from his father. Whatever qualifications they may have originally had for the kingdom, they all rejected them to satisfy their own desires for a worldly existence. They rejected the kingdom willingly and knowingly and openly dissipated their inheritance. The blessings of the kingdom are assured only to those who remain faithful to the Lord.

The responsibility of the individual to the gospel was clearly presented to those who heard the parable of the prodigal son. The parables of the pearl of great price and the treasure hidden in the field determined that a person must readily sacrifice all he has in order to acquire the gospel. The parables of the lost sheep and the lost coin dictated that those who inadvertently or negligently found themselves separated from the gospel could rightfully return upon complete repentance. Just as plain is the reality that if the gospel is wholly accepted and then completely rejected, willfully, knowledgeably, and permanently, the rewards of the kingdom cannot be obtained, and inheritance in the Father's kingdom will be forfeit.[104]

a. 1 Samuel 8:7.

Teaching Gospel Principles   5

Implicit in all the teachings of the gospel are the principles that form its foundation. They provide the guidelines that constitute the fundamental policies of Christ's instruction. He taught these principles in everything He did. His daily activities exemplified them, His love of children emphasized them, His discourses described them, and His miracles provided visual evidence of their importance, truth, and divinity.

The principles of the gospel were the "weightier" matters of the law, and had been forgotten or ignored through the ritualistic observance of the Law of Moses. Through these principles, the Lord taught the importance of the spirit of the law as well as the letter of the law. This chapter deals with the parables that taught these important principles.

Prayer: The Importunate Widow (The Unjust Judge)

Luke 18:1–5   And he spake a parable unto them to this end, that men ought always to pray, and not to faint; saying, There was in a city a judge, which feared not God, neither regarded man: and there was a widow in that city; and she came unto him, saying, Avenge me of mine adversary. And he would not for a while: but afterward he said within himself, Though I fear not God, nor regard man; yet because this widow troubleth me, I will avenge her, lest by her continual coming she weary me.

Luke states that this parable was given to show "that men ought always to pray, and not to faint." It teaches the principle of prayer. However, it is not a parable on how to pray, but one that tells us we should pray—not out of duty, but out of necessity. The characters in the parable perfectly emphasize the principle.

The first character is the judge. The Lord emphasized His independence from all of the normal influences that affect daily activities by stating that this judge "feared not God, neither regarded man." These words would have been recognized by the Jews as describing a person of "utterly unprincipled character."[105] By this it was evident that the judge would give only those judgments that he wished to give or that would enhance his chosen position. He did not fear retribution from God for unjust judgments, and his power was so strongly consolidated that he feared no man. Although he is the main character in the parable, his position should not be compared to that of Christ or the Father.[106] He is merely parabolic dressing to emphasize the principle being taught.

The second character is the widow. She petitions the judge to avenge her of an adversary. She is also parabolic dressing and she does not correlate to any higher meaning. She is a foil to the judge. She accentuates his power and represents the most defenseless and helpless of individuals in the real-life situations of Jesus' time.[a][107] The more unjust the judge, the more helpless the widow; the more indifferent to God and man the judge is, the less apt the widow is to receive her petition from him. These comparisons help to emphasize the point of the parable.

The poor widow's first petition to the judge went unanswered, but eventually he relented and came to the conclusion that he should answer her, not because he feared God nor regarded man, but "because this widow troubleth me, . . . lest by her continual coming she weary me." It was not that her petition was just or that the judge of necessity must respond to it; he was simply tired of her perpetual nagging. Therefore, to rid himself of the widow he decided to grant her petition.

The setting in this parable emphasized the following teachings on prayer.

Persistence. It is obvious from the story that the widow persisted in her petition to the unjust judge. We are not told whether her petition was a righteous one, although it may be assumed that such was the case. From this we can conclude that our own prayers to God should be persistent in righteous purposes. It is not the intention of the parable to teach that persistence in prayer will always bring the answer we seek, only that we should pray persistently and continually to our Father in Heaven anticipating that an answer will eventually be given.[108]

There may be times when prayer is more fervent or intense than

a. Isaiah 1:23;
   Matthew 23:14.

others, but it might be argued from the parable that our prayers should not be limited to those intense times when our need of heavenly assistance is crucial and urgent. For instance, we should also be persistent in seeking long-term blessings and in giving thanks for blessings granted. Prayer of this type is a proper exercise of our faith in our Father in Heaven,[109] and it further fulfills the instructions of the Savior that we should ask if we desire to receive, we should seek if we desire to find, and we should knock if we desire to have the door opened.[a]

It would appear from the parable that if we are persistent in prayer, it will automatically lead to the reward sought. But it is more probable that the idea of persistence was taught to provoke man to recognize his constant need to rely on his Father in Heaven, "even when all around seems to forbid the hope of answer."[110]

Patience. The widow continually petitioned for redress. She was patient in those petitions, anticipating that they would eventually be granted—even though the circumstances and the power of the judge seemed to discourage the hope of such. The Lord expects us to continue in patient prayer for as long as it takes to gain the answer we need,[111] regardless of what the answer is—even though it may seem that God is deaf to our pleas and petitions.[112] In this manner, we evidence our faith to the true and living God.

An interesting miracle occurred in the Lord's ministry which emphasized these two principles of persistence and patience. This was the miracle of the healing of the Syrophenician's daughter.[113]

In this miracle, a woman (who was a heathen) petitioned the Lord to heal her daughter who was grievously vexed with a devil. But the Lord did not immediately answer her. Her petitions continued and the Apostles came to the Lord and besought Him to send her away, for she continued to cry after them and was apparently an embarrassment to them. The Lord then turned His attention to the woman and told her that He had been sent only to the lost sheep of the house of Israel. Not to be deterred, she immediately worshipped Him and continued to earnestly seek His help. The Lord turned to her and said, "It is not meet to take the children's bread, and to cast it to dogs."[b] But the woman would not be denied. She persisted and responded, "Yet the dogs eat of the crumbs which fall from their masters' table."[c] Jesus immediately recognized the great faith of the woman and granted her petition.

a. Matthew 7:8;
3 Nephi 14:8;
Moroni 7:26.

b. Matthew
15:26.

c. Matthew
15:27.

The woman in the miracle of the Syrophenician's daughter is comparable to the importunate widow. Her petition was righteous; she desired a healing for her daughter. She patiently persisted in her petition and by so doing demonstrated the great faith she had in the Lord. The disciples did not immediately recognize this, and the Lord instructed them as well as the woman as He granted her petition.

The Lord Himself concluded the parable of the importunate widow by emphasizing the principle it contained. He declared: "Hear what the unjust judge saith. And shall not God avenge his own elect, which cry day and night unto him, though he bear long with them? I tell you that he will avenge them speedily. Nevertheless when the Son of man cometh, shall he find faith on the earth?"[a] A loving God will grant the desires of those faithful souls who persistently petition Him for their righteous needs and await patiently His response.[114]

Prayer: The Friend at Midnight (The Importuned Friend)

Luke 11:5–10   And he said unto them, Which of you shall have a friend, and shall go unto him at midnight, and say unto him, Friend, lend me three loaves; for a friend of mine in his journey is come to me, and I have nothing to set before him? And he from within shall answer and say, Trouble me not: the door is now shut, and my children are with me in bed; I cannot rise and give thee. I say unto you, Though he will not rise and give him, because he is his friend, yet because of his importunity he will rise and give him as many as he needeth. And I say unto you, Ask, and it shall be given you; seek, and ye shall find; knock, and it shall be opened unto you. For every one that asketh receiveth; and he that seeketh findeth; and to him that knocketh it shall be opened.

This parable was given as a result of the disciples' request that Jesus teach them how to pray. The Lord began His instructions by giving them the Lord's Prayer as an example; then He taught them the parable of the Friend at Midnight—which again emphasizes the necessity of enduring, persistent prayer.

Unlike the importunate widow (in which the participants were antagonistic toward each other), here the participants are friends. The principle the Lord is teaching occurs within the framework of the parable rather than the conversation between the parties.

A man asks his friend to loan him three loaves of bread. How often have we gone to neighbors and friends to borrow what we lack in times of need? But the importance of the parable was not simply in the borrowing, it was in the late hour that the petition was made. The man does not go to borrow during the normal daylight hours but extends his plea at midnight, long after his friend has retired. Thus the request appears unreasonable, and the man could not be sure that his friend would help him.[115]

The request itself was not unjust. The hospitality of the Jewish social system of the time required that a friend lay food before his visitor, and that a neighbor assist in said courtesy if necessary.[116] But these normal rules of hospitality were waived in this parable because of the unreasonable hour.

The neighbor, awakened by the knocking, denied the man's request, indicating that his doors were shut and his children and family all in bed.

The man continued to plead his just cause. Finally, the friend arose and unbolted the door, not only because he was a friend, but because he was being strongly persuaded. He gave the man not just that which he requested, but all that was needed. "The Lord's lesson was, that if man, with all his selfishness and disinclination to give, will nevertheless grant what his neighbor with proper purpose asks and continues to ask in spite of objection and temporary refusal, with assured certainty will God grant what is persistently asked in faith and with righteous intent."[117]

Through this parable the Lord instructs us to "ask" in earnestness, believing that a response will be received. He expects us to "seek," not halfheartedly, but energetically and persistently, and to "knock" intently and loudly.[118]

Many things can get in the way of receiving an answer to prayer. Sometimes the Father delays granting our petitions, requiring that our asking be more fervent.[119] In this parable, the persistence of the man overcame the reluctance of his ungracious friend. How much more shall our persistence prevail with our Father in Heaven, "who loves us better than we ourselves, and who is more ready to hear than we to pray."[120]

An example from the Old Testament illustrates this righteous petitioning of the Lord.[121] The Lord stood before Abraham and declared that He would destroy Sodom and Gomorrah because of their grievous sins before Him. Abraham, knowing that his nephew Lot and Lot's family were in the city, drew near to the Lord and questioned whether He would destroy the righteous along with the wicked. His earnest persistence came in the form of bargaining. He asked the Lord if He would spare the city if He could find fifty righteous souls therein. The Lord agreed that if fifty righteous souls could be found within the city, He would spare it for their sakes. But there were not fifty members in Lot's family, so Abraham again petitioned the Lord and asked if forty-five righteous souls would suffice. Again the Lord agreed, but forty-five could not be found; so the bartering continued from forty righteous to thirty, down to twenty, and even ten. But there were not ten righteous souls to be found in all the environs of Sodom and Gomorrah, so the Lord had Lot and his family removed from the city before He destroyed it.[a]

Although there were not a sufficient number of righteous souls to convince the Lord to spare the city, this incident still exemplifies the principle taught in the parable of the friend at midnight. A petition was righteously made and persistently followed up. It would have been granted had the conditions been met.

The parable of the friend at midnight taught the disciples a simple lesson about prayer. Prayer was not to be merely repetitious; believing souls needed sincerity and perseverance to acquire answers and blessings, both for themselves and others. If they are couched in faith and trust, God will assuredly hear our petitions.[122] The Lord strongly emphasized this point to His disciples when He declared: "If a son shall ask bread of any of you that is a father, will he give him a stone? or if he ask a fish, will he for a fish give him a serpent? Or if he shall ask an egg, will he offer him a scorpion? If ye then, being evil, know how to give good gifts unto your children: how much more shall your heavenly Father give the Holy Spirit to them that ask him?"[b]

Obedience: The Two Sons

Matthew 21:28–32   But what think ye? A certain man had two sons; and he came to the first, and said, Son, go work to day in my vineyard. He answered and said, I will not: but afterward he repented, and went. And he came to the second, and said likewise. And he answered and said, I go, sir: and went not. Whether of them twain did the will of his father? They say unto him, The first. Jesus saith unto them, Verily I say unto you, That the publicans and the harlots go into the kingdom of God before you. For John came unto you in the way of righteousness, and ye believed him not:

a. Genesis 18:20–33; 19:15-25.

b. Luke 11:11-13.

but the publicans and the harlots believed him: and ye, when ye had seen it, repented not afterward, that ye might believe him.

This is one of those parables which draw their importance and meaning from the circumstances in which they are set. It is a parable of moral criticism, given during the last week of the ministry of Jesus as He taught in the temple.

Several important events had occurred just before Jesus gave this parable. He had returned to Jerusalem for the last time. On His way He had passed through Jericho, where two blind men sitting by the roadside had publicly acclaimed Him as the Son of David.[a123] Then came His triumphant entry into Jerusalem, where the multitudes likewise proclaimed Him king.[b124] After entering Jerusalem, he cleansed the temple for the second and last time.[c125] These public demonstrations greatly disturbed the Pharisees, and they came to Him seeking a public disavowal; but He would not accommodate them.[d] They had previously asked Him, "If thou be the Christ, tell us plainly."[e126] He had confirmed that He was the Messiah, and they "took up stones again to stone him."[f127]

Now, the chief priests and the elders of the people again came to Him as He was teaching in the temple and questioned His authority. They said, "By what authority doest thou these things? and who gave thee this authority?"[g]

Jesus took this last opportunity to offer the kingdom of God to the rulers of the Jews who had so openly rejected Him and fought His ministry. He bargained with them, agreeing to reveal the source of His authority if they would answer a question. "The baptism of John," He said, "whence was it? from heaven, or of men?"[h]

The obdurate rulers reasoned among themselves, noting that if they said the authority of John was from heaven, Jesus would ask them why they had not believed Him; however, if they claimed John's authority was of man, they feared the reaction of the people, for the people accepted John as a prophet. So they hedged and answered, "We cannot tell." Jesus then replied, "Neither tell I you by what authority I do these things."[i]

The parable of the two sons was directed to these disbelieving and rebellious rulers of Israel that they might have one more chance

a. Matthew 20:29–34; Mark 10:46–52; Luke 18:35–43

b. Matthew 21:1–11; Mark 11:1–10; Luke 19:29–38

c. Matthew 21:12–13; Mark 11:15–18; Luke 19:45–48.

d. Matthew 21:15–16.

e. John 10:24.

f. John 10:31.

g. Matthew 21:23.

h. Matthew 21:25.

i. Matthew 21:27.

to open their eyes, recognize their false position, and accept Jesus as the Messiah.[128] They were on the verge of rejecting Him totally, a sin of monumental proportions, and through this parable the Lord gave them the opportunity to see the seriousness of what they were doing and repent of their transgressions.

This was a simple parable. A father had two sons. He asked the first to go and work in his vineyard and the boy initially refused, but afterward repented and went to do the work his father requested. The second son was asked to do the same work. He readily responded that he would go, but he didn't.

The first son in the parable represented the publicans and harlots, those of the chosen people who had been given the Mosaic Law, but openly transgressed it. They refused the call of the Father because of their careless and reckless life of sin. However, in the parable they recognized their sin, repented of their transgressions, and went to work in the vineyard as the Father had requested. The second son represented the Pharisees and other rulers of the Jews, those who professed righteous zeal for the Law. But they refused the truth when it was offered to them.[129] Their zeal for the Law had made them self-righteous to the point that the Lord referred to them as "whited sepulchres," which outwardly appeared beautiful, but inwardly were full of dead men's bones and all uncleanliness.[a]

Jesus did not immediately declare the moral of His parable to them, but first asked them another question. "Whether of them twain [the sons in the parable] did the will of his father?" Unaccustomed to such candid questioning before the people, the Pharisees were left with only one possible answer, and they entrapped themselves by responding, "The first."[130] Now Jesus directly applied the parable to their situation. He told them that the publicans and the harlots would go into the kingdom of God before the Pharisees and the rulers of the Jews. He then referred back to the question of John's authority, which had prompted the parable in the first place. John came in the cause of righteousness, He declared, and the Pharisees and rulers believed Him not. They, the protectors of the covenant, had seen the righteousness of John's teachings, but had rejected them and would not repent. Yet the publicans, harlots, and sinners had accepted and

a. Matthew 23:27.   believed. The parable points out that sins of both commission and omission are possible. Those who repent and accept the gospel are readily accepted by God into His kingdom. Those who do not repent, yet profess obedience to the call of the Father while refusing to do the simple things required, are rejected (even though they may be holders of the covenant).[131]

As Jesus continued His teaching, the chief priests and Pharisees "perceived that he spake of them."[a] They wanted to restrain Jesus but they were afraid, for the people thought of Him as a prophet.

The lesson of this parable is clear. We must be obedient to the Lord if we are to regain His kingdom. Some may initially reject the gospel but later accept it; if they sincerely repent, they can still achieve the goal of salvation. However, those who profess obedience and acceptance of the Lord's call yet do not magnify it will surely be rejected.

Forgiveness: The Two Debtors

Luke 7:36–50 And one of the Pharisees desired him that he would eat with him. And he went into the Pharisee's house, and sat down to meat. And, behold, a woman in the city, which was a sinner, when she knew that Jesus sat at meat in the Pharisee's house, brought an alabaster box of ointment. And stood at his feet behind him weeping, and began to wash his feet with tears, and did wipe them with the hairs of her head, and kissed his feet, and anointed them with the ointment. Now when the Pharisee which had bidden him saw it, he spake within himself, saying, This man, if he were a prophet, would have known who and what manner of woman this is that toucheth him: for she is a sinner. And Jesus answering said unto him, Simon, I have somewhat to say unto thee. And he saith, Master, say on. There was a certain creditor which had two debtors: the one owed five hundred pence, and the other fifty. And when they had nothing to pay, he frankly forgave them both. Tell me therefore, which of them will love him most? Simon answered and said, I suppose that he, to whom he forgave most. And he said unto him, Thou hast rightly judged. And he turned to the woman, and said unto Simon, Seest thou this woman? I entered into thine house, thou gavest me no water for my feet: but she hath washed my feet with tears, and wiped them with the hairs of her head. Thou gavest me no kiss: but this woman since the time I came in hath not ceased to kiss my feet. My head with oil thou didst not anoint: but this woman hath anointed my feet with ointment. Wherefore I say unto thee, Her sins, which are many, are forgiven; for she loved much: but to whom little is forgiven, the same loveth little. And he said unto her, Thy sins are forgiven. And they that sat at meat with him began to say within themselves, Who is this that forgiveth sins also? And he said to the woman, Thy faith hath saved thee; go in peace.

This simple story is often overlooked as a parable. It is generally thought to be an illustration used by the Lord in His discussion with

a. Matthew 21:45.

Simon. But because of its parabolic form and spiritual application, I have classified it as one of the Lord's parables.

This is another parable that derives its meaning from its setting. Jesus had been invited to the home of a Pharisee whose name was Simon, a situation that was not uncommon in His time.[132] However, as Jesus came to the feast, the traditional observances and customs of hospitality to honor such a guest were not observed. Simon had not provided the common courtesies: no water had been prepared for the Lord to wash His feet and hands;[a] the courtesy of a kiss in peace was not extended to Him;[b] nor was oil provided for His head, as was customary at such festivities.[c] Apparently intentionally, His host had been sadly lacking in warmth and hospitality.[133]

The houses at that time were constructed to allow easy access, and it was not uncommon to have someone enter on such an occasion to listen to the discussion or for the poor to actually participate in the meal. It was, however, uncommon for a woman to do so.[134] A woman, unnamed in the scriptures, came to the feast because she knew that Jesus was in the house.

In the scriptures the woman is designated as "a sinner."[135] This classification usually meant that she had been immoral, but nowhere is that sin specifically identified. She had brought with her "an alabaster box of ointment" and stood at the feet of Jesus as He was reclining in the traditional mode of eating, His head and body leaning toward the table on a low couch or cushions and His feet away from it.[136] Simon observed the woman touch Jesus, and he demonstrated a "holier than thou" attitude when he thought to himself, "This man, if he were a prophet, would have known who and what manner of woman this is that toucheth him: for she is a sinner." The Jews believed that the mark of a great prophet, and certainly the Messiah, was the ability to discern spirits,[137] a belief grounded in scripture.[d] Simon's conclusion was that Jesus could not discern that the woman was a sinner and thus lacked one of the qualifications of a prophet. Jesus perceived his thoughts, and countered with the parable of the two debtors as an explanation of His acceptance of the woman:

There were two debtors, one with a great debt and one with a small one. They both had the same creditor, and due to their penniless condition, the creditor forgave them of their debts. The Lord asked

Simon, "Which of them will love him most?" "I suppose," Simon responded, "that he, to whom he forgave most." Jesus immediately acknowledged that this was the correct answer. Then He applied the parable to the sinful woman and Simon. Simon had offered the Savior no water, but the woman had washed the Savior's feet with her tears and wiped them with her hair. Simon had given Jesus no kiss of salutation, yet the woman had not ceased to kiss His feet. Simon had provided no oil, yet she had anointed Jesus' feet with ointment. The Lord readily forgave her sins, concluding, "For she loved much: but to whom little is forgiven, the same loveth little." Simon painfully understood the application of the parable.

Several questions raised by the parable need further discussion.

First, there has been much speculation as to who the unnamed woman in this parable was. Many feel it was either Mary, the sister of Lazarus (a speculation partially derived from the fact that she had given Jesus a similar anointing,[a] or Mary Magdalene. But there is no evidence to support either theory, and no such inference should be drawn.[138]

Even though it might seem unusual to have two such anointings reported in the scriptures, it seems clear from the record that such was the case. Consider the following:

1. Although offense was taken at both anointings, in Luke the offense was taken by Simon, the host, and was directed toward the Lord. The offense in the other Gospels was taken by Judas, and was directed toward Mary.

2. Although Simon is the name of the host in both instances, it is "perhaps the commonest of Jewish names."[139]

3. The reasons for the anointings are different. In Luke, the woman anoints Jesus because of the love she has for the Savior and the forgiveness she is seeking. According to Jesus, Mary anoints Him in token of His burial.[b]

4. The woman in Luke is reported to be a sinner. Such sinfulness was never imputed to Mary, the sister of Lazarus.

5. The two anointings are recorded in different stages of the Lord's ministry. The Luke anointing occurred early, sometime

a. Matthew 26:6–13; Mark 14:3–9; John 12:1–8.

b. JST John 12:7.

during the Lord's Galilean ministry,[140] whereas Mary's anointing occurred during the last days of Christ's ministry. Both anointings were purposefully recorded by the Gospel writers to edify the teachings surrounding them.[141]

Second: The parable of the two debtors used the analogy of a creditor to refer to God, a debtor to refer to sinners, and debts to represent sins. In the parable, the larger debtor represented the woman and the smaller debtor represented Simon. When the Lord applied the parable to Simon and the woman, He indicated that she loved much, because she had been forgiven much; but that one who had been forgiven little possessed little love for God. It seems to appear from the parable that the more sins one has, the more love one is capable of. But it is more probable that the word *sinner* as used here does not refer to the quantity of one's transgressions as much as it does to the degree of consciousness one has of his sins and his desire for forgiveness. Had Simon felt a great desire for forgiveness of his transgressions (even though they may not have been as serious or numerous as the woman's), he, too, would have felt great love for the Lord.

This great desire for forgiveness was produced by the woman's faith in Jesus, which He acknowledged when He forgave her.[a] This is exactly what Simon, the proud Pharisee, lacked. He derived little or no good from his meeting with the Christ, whereas the woman, in her brief encounter, bore away the blessings of forgiveness.

Third: There is no indication that the woman in the parable had known or been taught by Jesus prior to this occasion; however, it is evident that she was deeply repentant and contrite. On a previous occasion Jesus had taught, "Come unto me, all ye that labour and are heavy laden, and I will give you rest,"[b] and the woman's actions indicate that perhaps she had heard this teaching, either from Jesus or from others, for she seemed to come to Jesus for that specific reason.[142]

The principle of forgiveness would be taught by the Lord in other ways and at other times, but it could not have been more beautifully exemplified than by this simple parable.

Mercy: The Unmerciful Servant

Matthew 18:23–35   Therefore is the kingdom of heaven likened unto a certain king, which would take account of his servants. And when he had begun to reckon, one was brought unto him, which owed him ten thousand talents. But forasmuch as he had not to pay, his lord commanded him to be sold, and his wife, and children, and all that he had, and payment to be made. The servant therefore fell down, and worshipped him, saying, Lord, have patience with me, and I will pay thee all. Then the lord of that servant was moved with compassion, and loosed him, and forgave him the debt. But the same servant went out, and found one of his fellowservants, which owed him an hundred pence: and he laid hands on him, and took him by the throat, saying, Pay me that thou owest. And his fellow-servant fell down at his feet, and besought him, saying, Have patience with me, and I will pay thee all. And he would not: but went and cast him into prison, till he should pay the debt. So when his fellow-servants saw what was done, they were very sorry, and came and told unto their lord all that was done. Then his lord, after that he had called him, said unto him, O thou wicked servant, I forgave thee all that debt, because thou desiredst me: shouldest not thou also have had compassion on thy fellowservant, even as I had pity on thee? And his lord was wroth, and delivered him to the tormentors, till he should pay all that was due unto him. So likewise shall my heavenly Father do also unto you, if ye from your hearts forgive not every one his brother their trespasses.

It would be impossible to derive the full impact and meaning from this parable without discussing the Lord's teachings prior to it. His Apostles had come to Him asking who would be the greatest in the kingdom of heaven, and in answer to this verbal evidence of ambition, Jesus had used the example of a small child[a] to indicate that their efforts at self-aggrandizement were not acceptable in the kingdom of God.[143] He emphasized this with the parable of the lost sheep.[144] He then taught them concerning the second great commandment and their responsibility with regard to offenses from their fellowman.[b]

At the conclusion of these instructions, Peter continued to question the Lord about relationships, asking, "How oft shall my brother sin against me, and I forgive him?" Without waiting for an answer from the Lord he added, "till seven times?"[c] The question, with its self-proclaimed answer, might very well indicate how far Peter had already been influenced by the spirit of the Lord.[145] The Jewish masters required that the offender be forgiven only three times.[146] This requirement was grounded upon Jehovah's instructions to Amos.[d] Yet Peter more than doubled the legal requirement in his comment to the Lord, and he undoubtedly thought that he had caught the true spirit of the Master's teachings. But Jesus proceeded to raise Peter's limited earthly vision to the eternal heights of the kingdom of God. The ap-

a. Matthew 18:1–6.

b. Matthew 18:15–17.

c. Matthew 18:21.

d. Amos 1:3; 2:6.

parent error in Peter's question came from the implication that in forgiving, a man gave up a right that he might under certain circumstances exercise; that is, not forgiving. It seems to be the purpose of the Lord's response to "make clear that when God calls on a member of His kingdom to forgive, He does not call on him to renounce a right, but that he has now no right to exercise in the matter; asking for and accepting forgiveness, he has implicitly pledged himself to show it."[147]

Thus, the Lord responded that to forgive seven times only was not enough, but that a person should forgive "until seventy times seven."[a] The answer indicated the responsibility of the righteous to forgive, not just on occasion, but at all times.[b] At this point, the Lord gave the parable of the unmerciful servant.

The parable begins with a certain king who was determined to take account of his servants. The king represents God and the servants represent his children, or mankind.[148] One of the servants was brought before the king to give an account of his debt. Note that he was "brought" before the king rather than coming of his own accord. Although some may report of their own accord for an accounting, others must be forced to appear. "The messengers who serve the summons may be adversity, illness, the approach of death," or some other catastrophe or calamity. Whatever the messengers' disguise, "they enforce a rendering of our accounts."[149]

The servant owed an enormous debt of ten thousand talents to the king. It was a debt so large that it was obvious the servant could never repay it.[150]

In his wrath, the king commanded that the servant's wife and children and all that he had be sold in order that payment be made. This was a circumstance not unfamiliar at the time of Jesus,[151] but was parabolic dressing in the parable, pointing out man's utter hopelessness without God's forgiveness. Yet the servant pleaded his case, falling down and worshipping the king. In his prostrate position, he begged the king to have patience with him and he would repay the entire debt.

The parable portrays man as a debtor to God,[c] a mere steward over God's abundant blessings. If we misuse those blessings or disobey the commandments, we incur an enormous debt to the Lord. Justice would require retribution and punishment.[152] However, through faith, humility, and repentance, we can, so to speak, cast ourselves at the

a. Matthew 18:22.

b. D&C 64:10.

c. Mosiah
   2:23–24.

feet of the King and invoke His infinite compassion to save us from punishment. And through adherence to the laws of repentance, we can be relieved of the debt which we have incurred.

Now the second point of the parable unfolds. The servant leaves the presence of the king and finds a fellow servant who owes him a very small amount of money (when compared to the enormous debt he has so recently been forgiven). The first servant now has the opportunity to extend to his fellow servant the same mercy he has just received from the king.

When the first servant demands payment from his fellow servant, the fellow servant asks him to have patience and he will pay all. But the first servant ignores the great mercy recently extended to him by the king and taking his fellow servant by the throat, he drags him to the prison and casts him in until he can pay the debt.

His actions are totally incongruous with those of the king and are placed in the parable to emphasize the moral of the parabolic story. The actions of the unmerciful servant are reported to the king and he is again brought before him. The king reminds him of the great forgiveness and mercy that he has received, and asks him why he did not show similar compassion to his fellow servant.

The parable now draws to a conclusion. All of the previous debt that had been forgiven is now restored. Because the servant cannot pay it, he is delivered to the tormentors until he pays all that is due. But he cannot suffer enough to pay the debt, nor could he ever make amends sufficient to absolve himself from his guilt; therefore, the banishment is endless[153]—but not because of the debt, as is emphasized in the parable's conclusion.

The requirement in Peter's question of "how oft shall my brother sin against me, and I forgive him?" was not the seven times volunteered by Peter or the amplified seven times seventy expressed by the Lord. For the Lord, in explanation of the parable, stated, "So likewise shall my heavenly Father do also unto you, if ye from your hearts forgive not every one his brother their trespasses."

In the Sermon on the Mount the Lord had declared, "Blessed are the merciful: for they shall obtain mercy."[a] He now demonstrated this principle in His parable. If we are to expect mercy from our Father in Heaven, we are required to extend mercy to our fellowman; clearly we

a. Matthew 5:7.

must forgive without retribution or vengeance, and "we must forgive even if [the] offender [does] not repent and ask forgiveness."[154]

Stephen exemplified this principle. As he was being stoned for preaching the resurrected Christ, he "kneeled down, and cried with a loud voice, Lord, lay not this sin to their charge."[a] As demonstrated in the parable, the first servant came under condemnation not for defaulting on his debt, but for not showing mercy to a fellow servant after the king had extended such great mercy to him. His sin was that he remained unmerciful after having received mercy.

James taught this principle in His admonitions to the Saints when he declared, "For he shall have judgment without mercy, that hath shewed no mercy."[b] Lack of mercy for our fellowman is a sin of serious proportions.[155] By sinning anew and not extending the mercy he had so readily received, the servant in the parable fell back into the darkness out of which he had been delivered.

Paul later admonished the Colossians to put on the new (spiritual) man, "Forbearing one another, and forgiving one another, if any man have a quarrel against any: even as Christ forgave you, so also do ye."[c] And to the Ephesians he declared, "And be ye kind one to another, tenderhearted, forgiving one another, even as God for Christ's sake hath forgiven you."[d] "He who will not forgive others breaks down the bridge over which he himself must travel."[156]

Those who extend to others the divine forgiveness which they have experienced characterize the true love of Christ. On one occasion the disciples asked the Savior to teach them how to pray. He responded with what is called the Lord's Prayer, which contains the phrase, "Forgive us our debts, as we forgive our debtors."[e] Through the parable of the unmerciful servant the Lord taught His disciples this divine principle of mercy with unprecedented clarity.

Mercy is for the merciful.

a. Acts 7:60.

b. James 2:13.

c. Colossians 3:13.

d. Ephesians 4:32.

e. Matthew 6:12.

Teaching Relationships 6

As the Lord taught the gospel He gave instructions governing the relationships between man and God, man and worldly possessions, and man and his fellowman. The Law of Moses had been a preparatory law. All things contained therein looked forward to the coming of the Messiah and His kingdom and attempted to prepare the children of Israel for that great event. But now the Messiah had come, and a new law had been given. The old law was in the process of fulfillment while the new law was capable of giving man exaltation in the kingdom of God. Man's relationship to God, to the world, and to his fellowman would no longer be rigidly prescribed but was to flow from the depths of human love and understanding. The parables in this chapter teach these relationships.

Man-to-God: The Unprofitable Servants

Luke 17:7–10   But which of you, having a servant plowing or feeding cattle, will say unto him by and by, when he is come from the field, Go and sit down to meat? And will not rather say unto him, Make ready wherewith I may sup, and gird thyself, and serve me, till I have eaten and drunken; and afterward thou shalt eat and drink? Doth he thank that servant because he did the things that were commanded him? I trow not. So likewise ye, when ye shall have done all those things which are commanded you, say, We are unprofitable servants: we have done that which was our duty to do.

This parable is not uniformly treated as a parable by all writers, and perhaps could be referred to as a parabolic sermon.[157] The Lord used this parable as an analogy in His instructions to His disciples when He admonished them to be diligent and full of unselfish devotion, tolerance, and forgiveness.[158] As He concludes, His disciples make a request: "Lord, increase our faith." It was not that they did not have faith in God and in Jesus as the Messiah, they wanted enlightenment. They had heard His admonitions of godliness; now they wanted Jesus to elaborate on their relationship with their Father in Heaven. In this parable, the Lord compared the Apostles and God to a servant and his master. The parable may have reflected the incorrect religious beliefs of the day, that is, that rewards received were in direct proportion to exactness in work and obedience to the Law.[159]

In this parable the master had a servant who had worked all day. The servant did not expect, immediately upon completion of his work, to eat and rest. When he finished his normal work, he was required to do more. He must first serve the master his supper before he himself could eat. The servant was not thanked by the master, for it was his duty to do that which he was commanded to do—that was his obligation as a servant. The master had the right to demand it of him. The servant could not even demand compensation for his services.[160] The estimate of his worth was solely the responsibility of the master. The Lord was trying to teach His disciples that the quality of their faith would be gauged by their obedience and untiring service to the Master.[161]

When the servant had done all of the things that he had been commanded to do, he was yet accounted as an unprofitable servant, for he had done only that which he was required to do.[162]

King Benjamin, in his final address to the people, enumerated clearly the principle taught in this parable when he declared:

Mosiah 2:20–21   I say unto you, my brethren, that if you should render all the thanks and praise which your whole soul has power to possess, to that God who has created you, and has kept and preserved you, and has caused that ye should rejoice, and has granted that ye should live in peace one with another—I say unto you that if ye should serve him who has created you from the beginning, and is preserving you from day to day, by lending you breath, that ye may live and move and do according to your own will, and even supporting you from one moment to another—I say, if ye should serve him with all your whole souls yet ye would be unprofitable servants.

The Savior's instruction left the Apostles with a clear understanding of their relationship to Him and His Father. Their obligation as disciples and Apostles was as the servant to the master. They were expected to do their duty without concern for compensation; this was to be their simple and earnest faith. Faith was to be the seed planted and nourished until it sprouted and began to grow; it was not to have a perfect knowledge of things, but was the substance of things hoped for and the evidence of things not seen.[a]

The Apostles were to give no offense and take no offense from the Master. God was their Master, and would continually support them, granting them all that they needed in order to perform the duty which they, as servants, were obligated to perform. Still, they would be accounted as unprofitable servants, "still indebted unto him . . . and will be, forever and ever."[b] God's gifts to His people are far greater than they will ever be capable of repaying.

Man-to-Worldy Treasures: The Unjust Steward

Luke 16:1–9 And he said also unto his disciples, There was a certain rich man, which had a steward; and the same was accused unto him that he had wasted his goods. And he called him, and said unto him, How is it that I hear this of thee? give an account of thy stewardship; for thou mayest be no longer steward. Then the steward said within himself, What shall I do? for my lord taketh away from me the stewardship: I cannot dig; to beg I am ashamed. I am resolved what to do, that, when I am put out of the stewardship, they may receive me into their houses. So he called every one of his lord's debtors unto him, and said unto the first, How much owest thou unto my lord? And he said, An hundred measures of oil. And he said unto him, Take thy bill, and sit down quickly, and write fifty. Then said he to another, And how much owest thou? And he said, An hundred measures of wheat. And he said unto him, Take thy bill, and write fourscore. And the lord commended the unjust steward, because he had done wisely: for the children of this world are in their generation wiser than the children of light. And I say unto you, Make to yourselves friends of the mammon of unrighteousness; that, when ye fail, they may receive you into everlasting habitations.

All of the parables in the sixteenth chapter of Luke are recorded only by Luke. They contain a common philosophy involving the debilitating effect of the things of the world (or those things highly esteemed by man) upon the spiritual requirements of the kingdom of heaven. Luke's Gospel is heavily laden with this emphasis.[163] "The love of money had become a characteristic of [the] decaying religiousness" of the Pharisees and the rulers of the Jews, even to the extent that

a. Alma 32:21–30; Hebrews 11:1.

b. Mosiah 2:24.

the rich should use their wealth "to make friends for the future world, instead of enjoying it here."[164] This teaching would have been known to the Apostles, and it seems that they believed it to some degree. The story of the rich young ruler and Christ's instructions to him, as well as the questions the Apostles posed afterward, seem to confirm this.

The rich young ruler came to Jesus before His final entry into Jerusalem and asked, "What shall I do to inherit eternal life?"[a] It was not an unusual question,[165] and Jesus answered it by enumerating several commandments. To this the man responded that he had kept all of these commandments from his youth. Jesus accepted this answer, but desired that the young man should proceed beyond the Law of Moses. So He commanded him to sell all that he had, distribute it to the poor, and follow Him. The young man received these instructions sorrowfully, for he was very rich. Consequently, he would not comply with the Lord's request. Acknowledging the young man's problems, Jesus commented, "For it is easier for a camel to go through a needle's eye, than for a rich man to enter into the kingdom of God."[b]

The Apostles were astonished at the Lord's comment and the relationship that He had drawn between the possession of the things of the world and the attainment of spiritual position. After the Lord had concluded His instructions they asked, "Who then can be saved?"[c]

The relationship between worldly wealth and heavenly blessings— so distinctly taught in the rich ruler discourse—had been expressed earlier in the parable of the unjust steward and the instructions surrounding it. This parable dealt with man's relationship to worldly wealth, and was given to help mankind so manage "the affairs and interests and possessions of this life as not to lose hereafter their heritage of the eternal riches."[166] Now to the parable.

A rich man had a steward whom he accused of wasting his goods. The rich man called the steward before him and required him to give an account of his stewardship as well as informing him that he would no longer be his steward.

The steward, knowing that he would soon lose his stewardship, determined that he must provide for himself and for his future. He decided to do this by further dissipating the goods of the master so that those to whom he gave the boon would be indebted to him in

a. Luke 18:18.
b. Luke 18:25.
c. Luke 18:26.

the things of the world and would therefore "receive [him] into their houses." He called in first one debtor and then another and reduced the amount they owed the rich man, again unjustly dissipating the goods of the master. Then Jesus made what appears to be an unusual comment: "And the Lord commended the unjust steward, because he had done wisely: for the children of this world are in their generation wiser than the children of light."

All of the salient points of the parable support this statement as the moral of the story.[167] Unless this moral is clearly understood, confusion might easily arise as to why the Lord would commend what appears to be an unethical and dishonest activity. The steward was accused of wasting the master's goods, and apparently was guilty of this misdeed for he made no attempt to defend himself.[168] As a steward he had authority to act as he did, yet his actions were totally unrighteous.

After being caught misusing his master's goods, the steward made no attempt to repent; he only showed fear and concern over the potential poverty and ruin that would come upon him. He determined that he would continue in his works of unrighteousness in order to secure his future existence.

The commending of the unjust steward is the turning point of the parable. The Lord complimented the steward for his prudence and foresight in preserving his worldly existence.[169] In the same breath, He chastised the children of light (or the saints of God) for not being as prudent as the unjust steward in preserving their spiritual rewards.[170] He proposed that the saints imitate the steward's prudence. He declared with forthrightness and clarity that the saints of God are "in the same position as this steward who saw the eminent disaster . . . but the crisis which threatens [them], in which, indeed, [they] are already involved is incomparably more terrible."[171] The unjust steward recognized his circumstance and boldly took action to preserve himself. That he incorrectly chose the things of the world over the things of eternity is obvious, but his actions to preserve himself were commendable.

The Lord emphasized the point He was trying to make when he stated: "He that is faithful in that which is least is faithful also in much: and he that is unjust in the least is unjust also in much. If therefore ye have not been faithful in the unrighteous mammon, who will commit to your trust the true riches? And if ye have not been faithful in that which was another man's, who shall give you that which is your own? No servant can serve two masters."[a] The things of the world often create opposition to the things of God. Using wealth unwisely can cause us to forfeit eternal riches whereas wealth put to good purposes can increase our eternal rewards.

Worldly possessions are governed by one of two masters: mammon and God. With mammon, man can choose to invest his time in earthly gratifications and yield to the sensual temptations of unrighteousness. God, however, requires man to place the things of the world in proper perspective with eternal requirements, using earthly possessions in such a manner as to glorify God and lay up eternal treasures in heaven.[172]

The reaction of the Pharisees who heard the parable of the unjust steward indicates that they understood it clearly, for they "derided him."[b] Jesus immediately chastised them for being "in their generation" the children of "this world," and said, "Ye are they which justify yourselves before men; but God knoweth your hearts: for that which is highly esteemed among men is abomination in the sight of God."[c]

Thus ended one of the most unusual of the Lord's parables—the only one in which a negative statement taught the positive things of God. However, the conclusion of the parable is clear. Things of the world, highly esteemed by man, have little value to God.

To gain exaltation in the kingdom of heaven, the things of the world (the mammon of unrighteousness) must be subordinated to the things of God. Man should "emulate the unjust steward and the lovers of mammon, not in their dishonesty, cupidity, and miserly hoarding of the wealth that is at best transitory, but in their zeal, forethought, and provision for the future."[173]

The things of the world are not to become our master, but our servant.

Man-to-Your Fellowman: The Wedding Guests

Luke 14:7–11 And he put forth a parable to those which were bidden, when he marked how they chose out the chief rooms; saying unto them, When thou art bidden of any man to a wedding, sit not down in the highest room; lest a more honourable man than thou be bidden of him; and he that bade thee and him come and say to thee, Give this man place; and thou begin with shame to take the lowest room. But

a. Luke 16:10–13.

b. Luke 16:14.

c. Luke 16:15.

when thou art bidden, go and sit down in the lowest room; that when he that bade thee cometh, he may say unto thee, Friend, go up higher: then shalt thou have worship in the presence of them that sit at meat with thee. For whosoever exalteth himself shall be abased; and he that humbleth himself shall be exalted.

The setting of this parable is similar to that of the two debtors.[174] Jesus had been invited to the home of one of the chief Pharisees to partake of the Sabbath meal. The Sabbath at Jesus' time was a day used by the rabbis for social entertainment.[175] The invitation was not abnormal, but those who extended it in this case had sinister intentions. Luke reports that they "watched him,"[a] and it appears that the sole purpose of the invitation was to lure Him to do evil in their eyes. (It was at this dinner that the miracle of the man with the dropsy was performed.)[176]

As was the tradition at the time, the places at the table were assigned according to the reputation and social status of those in attendance—the most "important" guests receiving the best positions. The customs of the Pharisees had deteriorated to the point that they were totally self-aggrandizing, even in their hospitality.[177] Jesus used their customs to instruct the Pharisees in humility. "Sit not down in the highest room," He admonished them, lest you have to give up your seat and become ashamed because a more honorable man than you should come to the gathering. But "when thou art bidden, go and sit down in the lowest room" that the host may bid you to a higher position, and "then shalt thou have worship in the presence of them that sit at meat with thee." Serve your fellowmen, He taught, and wait for your recompense to be made by God "at the resurrection of the just."[b]

Christ's teachings were breathing new life into the customs and traditions of the Jews[178] as He taught them of the second great commandment: Love your fellowman.

a. Luke 14:1.

b. Luke 14:14.

The Second Great Commandment

There is no doubt that Israel clearly understood the first great commandment: "Thou shalt love the Lord thy God with all thy heart, and with all thy soul, and with all thy strength, and with all thy mind."[a] The second great commandment was like unto it: "Thou shalt love thy neighbour as thyself."[b] But this commandment lacked the emphasis and definition of the first commandment.

Whereas the Law of Moses was centered on the first commandment, the gospel of Christ recognizes that the two commandments are completely interrelated. How man loves and treats his fellowman determines how he loves his God. Jesus taught, "Inasmuch as ye have done it unto one of the least of these my brethren, ye have done it unto me," and, "Inasmuch as ye did it not to one of the least of these, ye did it not to me."[c] On these two laws rested all the law and the prophets.

The following parable, the good Samaritan, beautifully teaches the principles encompassed within the second great commandment.

The Good Samaritan

Luke 10:30–37 And Jesus answering said, A certain man went down from Jerusalem to Jericho, and fell among thieves, which stripped him of his raiment, and wounded him, and departed, leaving him half dead. And by chance there came down a certain priest that way: and when he saw him, he passed by on the other side. And likewise a Levite, when he was at the place, came and looked on him, and passed by on the other side. But a certain Samaritan, as he journeyed, came where he was: and when he saw him, he had compassion on him, and went to him, and bound up his wounds, pouring in oil and wine, and set him on his own beast, and brought him to an inn, and took care of him. And on the morrow when he departed, he took out two pence, and gave them to the host, and said unto him, Take care of him; and whatso-

a. Luke 10:27.

b. Matthew 22:39.

c. Matthew 25:40, 45.

ever thou spendest more, when I come again, I will repay thee. Which now of these three, thinkest thou, was neighbor unto him that fell among the thieves? And he said, He that shewed mercy on him. Then said Jesus unto him, Go, and do thou likewise.

A lawyer stood before Jesus and, as Luke reports, "tempted him" by posing a question. The use of the words *tempted him* might lead some to assume that the question was posed to the Savior for some evil intent. Although this may have been the case on other occasions, it was not necessarily so in this instance. Though he may have wished to test the well-known teacher, possibly even to embarrass Him, there does not appear to have been any malicious intent on the part of the lawyer[179] when he asked, "What shall I do to inherit eternal life?"[a][180]

The lawyer was, in all probability, an expert in Jewish canon law and knowing the habits of his class (that it was common to test or try great rabbis in the rabbinical writings), he asked the question so as to involve Jesus in dialectic difficulties and subtle disputations. "Indeed, this was part of Rabbinism, and led to that painful and fatal trifling with truth, when everything became [a] matter of dialectic subtlety, and nothing was really sacred."[181]

Jesus responded to the lawyer's question with a question of His own. "What is written in the law? how readest thou?"[b] The lawyer answered by reciting the first great commandment: "Love the Lord thy God with all thy heart, and with all thy soul, and with all thy strength, and with all thy mind."[c] To this he added the second great commandment, "and thy neighbour as thyself," since this was also required under the Levitical law.[d] Jesus readily acknowledged the accuracy of the response and continued, "This do, and thou shalt live."[e]

Had the discussion between the lawyer and the Lord ended with this admonition, the parable would not have been forthcoming. But the lawyer continued the discussion in an attempt to "justify himself" and asked Jesus, "Who is my neighbour?"[f] This question gives additional credence to the theory that the lawyer had engaged Jesus in conversation without malice or evil intent, and only for the purpose of displaying dialectical skills. By asking the second question, he sought to vindicate himself from the first and demonstrate to Jesus that the subject was not quite so easily settled as Jesus' answer implied.[182]

God had long since separated the people of Israel unto Himself, and

a. Luke 10:25.

b. Luke 10:26.

c. Luke 10:27;
Deuteronomy
6:5.

d. Leviticus
19:18.

e. Luke 10:28.

f. Luke 10:29.

had sought to purify them that they would be holy and sanctified before Him. As a result, the question "who is my neighbour?" frequently engaged the rabbis, and the answer was only too clear. To the Jews, their neighbor was indeed another Jew, or member of the house of Israel.[183]

The principle involved in the question "who is my neighbour?" is very similar to that posed by Peter when he asked the Lord how many times he should forgive his brother.[a] Jewish law dictated that the requirement was to forgive your brother three times. Clearly, both Peter and the lawyer asked their questions to determine the limitations of the Law and to explicitly define their responsibility under it. But the second great commandment could not be restricted in this manner. While the lawyer sought a definite limitation on who his neighbor was, the fact remained that no boundary existed.[184]

The Lord gave the parable of the good Samaritan to enlighten His questioners as well as all those who heard His voice. He was trying to show the people how far the Law had gone astray from its original purpose, for the parable portrayed not an enlargement of the Law, as understood by the chosen people of His day, but a change in it.[185] Those who would follow the Master would no longer be bound by duty but by love. And there was no limitation as to whom this love should be given: It was to be given freely to all mankind. To this extent, the parable was a rebuke to the second question proposed by the lawyer with its legal ramifications and nuances inferred from the Rabbinical Law. Once again Jesus did not directly answer the question, but instead gave the following parable.

A certain man went down from Jerusalem to Jericho and fell among thieves and was wounded and left for dead. The setting of the parable is purely local and Jewish in nature.[186] A man had been following the solitary desert road between Jerusalem and Jericho, "a district notoriously insecure,"[187] and had been attacked and injured.

A priest and then a Levite came upon the man as they traveled the same eighteen- to twenty-one-mile stretch of road. They viewed his plight, but passed by on the other side. Both should have assisted the injured traveler, but the intention of the parable was to depict how far astray the Mosaic Law had gone and how little the Jews understood the second great commandment.

Both men may have justified their actions: the priest might have assumed that the man was dead and to come in contact with the dead under Levitical Law was to become unclean. And so he passed by. However, the Levite "looked on him" and knew that he was not dead, yet he also passed by, perhaps fearing that the robbers were still in the vicinity or that the man was pretending to be injured in order to ensnare unsuspecting travelers. However they salved their consciences, the parable exemplified the selfish nature of Judaism common at the time of Jesus.

Finally, a Samaritan came upon the injured man. Jesus undoubtedly chose a Samaritan to show compassion because the race was severely hated by the Jews. To have a Samaritan be the one who stopped to help the injured man would have been completely unexpected and would have mortified and humbled the Lord's Jewish audience.[188] The Lord described, with minute detail, the compassion and love of the Samaritan as He developed the last part of the parable.

The Samaritan first cleansed the injured man's wounds with wine and then poured oil into them to soothe the pain. This was the costliest of remedies, but was highly esteemed in the East.[189] He then bound the wounds and took the injured man to an inn, cared for him throughout the balance of the day and night and as he departed, left two pence to ensure that the care would continue. Then he went the extra mile and left instructions with the innkeeper to continue treatment until the man was healed, and if it cost more than two pence, he would pay the innkeeper when he returned.

The lawyer had asked Jesus, "Who is my neighbour?" Now Jesus countered that question and said, "Which now of these three, thinkest thou, was neighbour unto him that fell among the thieves?" The Lord had changed the lawyer's question from "who is my neighbour" to *"whose neighbor am I?"*

The lawyer had asked his question from a stilted, narrow, and unloving perspective. The Lord's response alluded to a far greater principle than that in which the lawyer had been trained. The Lord's question made the lawyer aware of the great gulf that existed between his knowledge of the Law and his actions under it.[190]

To the one learned in the Law, the intent of the parable was now plain, and the lawyer saw only one possible response to the question. Although it humbled him to acknowledge it, and unable to even speak the word Samaritan, he answered, "He that shewed mercy on him." The Lord responded succinctly, "Go, and do thou likewise." The lawyer had answered his own question and had been clearly instructed in his duty. Never again could he use the technical legalities of the old Law to justify inaction and discrimination, for the Messiah had declared that it is the responsibility of everyone to become a neighbor to all by serving those who are in need.[191]

Parables That Teach Accountability and Reward   8

Responsibility was fundamental to Christ's new gospel. Under its provisions, there would be no more competition between individuals to achieve promised rewards. No longer was it vital to seek out the chief seats in the synagogue or uppermost rooms at feasts.[a] Nor was it important to receive public salutations, to be called Rabbi, or to enlarge phylacteries and the borders of garments to be seen of men.[b] The Savior's disciples were expected to excel—to be better than before—but not as compared with someone else. Competition was to be against oneself. In the future, each person would be responsible for what he had been given and what he did with it. Each possessed different talents and different abilities, but all had been given something. The Lord gave us the requirements for achieving His kingdom, and He will judge how well we fulfill them.

The Talents

Matthew 25:14–30   For the kingdom of heaven is as a man travelling into a far country, who called his own servants, and delivered unto them his goods. And unto one he gave five talents, to another two, and to another one; to every man according to his several ability; and straightway took his journey. Then he that had received the five talents went and traded with the same, and made them other five talents. And likewise he that had received two, he also gained other two. But he that had received one went and digged in the earth, and hid his lord's money. After a long time the lord of those servants cometh, and reckoneth with them. And so he that had received five talents came and brought other five talents, saying, Lord, thou deliveredst unto me five talents: behold, I have gained beside them five talents more. His lord said unto him, Well done, thou good and faithful servant: thou hast been faithful over a few things, I will make thee ruler over many things: enter thou into the joy of thy lord. He

a. Matthew 23:6.

b. Matthew 23:5; Mark 12:38.

also that had received two talents came and said, Lord, thou deliveredst unto me two talents: behold, I have gained two other talents beside them. His lord said unto him, Well done, good and faithful servant; thou hast been faithful over a few things, I will make thee ruler over many things: enter thou into the joy of thy lord. Then he which had received the one talent came and said, Lord, I knew thee that thou art an hard man, reaping where thou hast not sown, and gathering where thou hast not strawed: and I was afraid, and went and hid thy talent in the earth: lo, there thou hast that is thine. His lord answered and said unto him, Thou wicked and slothful servant, thou knewest that I reap where I sowed not, and gather where I have not strawed: thou oughtest therefore to have put my money to the exchangers, and then at my coming I should have received mine own with usury. Take therefore the talent from him, and give it unto him which hath ten talents. For unto every one that hath shall be given, and he shall have abundance: but from him that hath not shall be taken away even that which he hath. And cast ye the unprofitable servant into outer darkness: there shall be weeping and gnashing of teeth.

This parable was given to the Apostles in private during the last days Jesus served with them—just before His betrayal and crucifixion. It was first interpreted by the primitive church in the Christological sense (which applied it directly to the second coming of Christ).[192] However, it should be interpreted in conjunction with the other teachings of Jesus concerning accountability and reward.[193] It was given to arouse the Apostles and the people to a realization of the significance of their daily actions rather than make them anticipate the Second Coming and the Judgment as the only time they would be called to account.[194]

The application of the parable might be directly compared to Nephi's admonition concerning our laxity in this life when he envisaged people saying, "Eat, drink, and be merry, for tomorrow we die; and it shall be well with us"; or when he said of Satan, "Others will he pacify, and lull them away into carnal security, that they will say: All is well in Zion; yea, Zion prospereth, all is well."[a] It is necessary to recognize that not all judgments take place at the second coming of Christ or at the final judgment. Man can be called to account at any moment, as graphically depicted in the parable of the foolish rich man.[195] In addition, Amulek declared that this life was the day given to us to prepare for eternity, and warned us against procrastinating the day of our repentance until we are brought to that awful crisis. Amulek then said, "If ye have procrastinated the day of your repentance even until death, behold, ye have become subjected to the spirit of the devil, and . . . the Spirit of the Lord hath withdrawn from you."[a]

Therefore, the parable of the talents warns each person of the impending account he will be required to make and the potential reward he will be given (regardless of the time that these will take place). Although specifically given to the Apostles, this parable can be applied to all those who receive entrusted gifts from God.[196] It is not limited to spiritual gifts, but can apply to all that man has been given and that he has the power to acquire through his abilities, whether these gifts are mental or physical. Any and all of the endowments that man has been given come from God and are to be used for spiritual purposes. For it is God "who has created you from the beginning, and is preserving you from day to day, by lending you breath . . . and even supporting you from one moment to another."[b]

The main theme of the parable deals with how God-given gifts should be used. It intimates that where much is given, much is required.[c] As the Lord tells the story of the talents, certain scenes come to mind:

First Scene: The Stewardship

The Lord tells the story about a man who was going to travel into a far country. He would be gone for some time; therefore, he entrusted his goods to the care of his servants. The inference is that they were to use the goods in his behalf while he was gone, and not just hold them in safekeeping.

He gave one servant five talents; another, two; and a third, one. Each had been given according to their ability to use the talents they received. The master left, fully expecting an increase on his goods when he returned.

The parable was deliberately couched in this manner. The servant that received two talents might not have been able to successfully handle five; and the servant receiving one might not have been able to handle two. However, the parable assumed that they could all handle that which they had received.[197]

In spite of the varying number of talents entrusted to the servants, their ability to labor was equal. They were equally capable of using the talents they had received for and in behalf of the master.[198]

a. Alma 34:35.

b. Mosiah 2:21.

c. Luke 12:48; D&C 82:3.

Second Scene: The Accounting

The master was gone "a long time," but eventually he returned and reckoned with the servants to determine how they had used their talents. Those who had received five and two talents, respectively, stepped forward boldly to declare their gain for and in behalf of the master. They had been diligent in their application of the talents and although they had been entrusted with diverse amounts, they each had an increase to present to the master—each had doubled the amount left with him. To this the master gave his wholehearted congratulations. He commended the faithful servants, promising them that they would be made rulers over many things and inviting them to "enter . . . into the joy of thy lord."

Now the servant who had received but one talent stepped forward and presented his talent to the Lord. He had been afraid of the responsibility he had been given, and had been idle and unwilling to work. His excuses are indicative of his mendacious attitude, and his grumbling answer to the master even implied that his master had been unrighteous.[199] He had not used his talent at all, but had dug into the earth and hidden it.

This imagery depicts a slothful and unwise servant.[a] He had performed no labor, shown no devotion, and exemplified no faithfulness in the use of his talent. He had completely wasted his opportunity.[200] His failure to use the gift fulfilled Moroni's statement that if the day should ever come "that the power and gifts of God shall be done away among you, it shall be because of unbelief."[b]

With this imagery, the lord emphasized the complete negligence of the inept servant. The man was deceiving himself, for in his heart he attributed to the lord the slothful traits that he himself possessed.[201] He had not even performed that which was considered to be the least he could have done, for the lord pointed out that he could have placed the money with "the exchangers," so that when he returned he could have received something for the talent he had entrusted to the servant.

Final Scene: The Reward

The servants who had done well for the lord received his grace and were granted the promise of a future reward—entrance into God's kingdom. All who are diligent in the righteous use of their talents can anticipate receiving the same reward, whether their talents be of a spiritual, mental, moral, or physical nature.[202]

Then the lord turned his attention to the third servant. His talent was taken away from him. It cannot be said that this action was unfair; rather it was a natural and normal consequence of the servant's actions.

An example of just such an occurrence appears in the Old Testament. The children of Israel had been led by judges and prophets since leaving Egypt, but now they demanded that the prophet Samuel find them a king, for they refused to accept the Lord as their King.[a] They specifically requested that Samuel provide them with a king so that he might "judge us like all the nations."[b] The Lord obliged the Israelites, and Samuel called Saul to lead them.

Saul accepted the kingship, but he did not act in conformity with the requirements placed upon him by the Lord. He acted as the servant had with his talent. He did not obey with faithfulness, and in spite of his fear of the Lord, he rejected His counsel. Samuel then evoked the judgment of the Lord upon Saul, just as the master in the parable evoked his judgment upon the servant. "For thou hast rejected the word of the Lord, and the Lord hath rejected thee from being king over Israel."[c] In the parable of the talents, the Lord took from the servant the single talent with which he had been entrusted. In the example of Saul, Samuel said, "The Lord hath rent the kingdom of Israel from thee this day,"[d] and He gave the kingdom to another.

After the lord of the parable took the talent from his faithless servant, he gave it to the one who had ten talents. Although some have thought this inappropriate, it follows the natural sequence of the parable. The one who had received five talents and had labored diligently and faithfully to gain five more had demonstrated his ability to use the greater gift. So from the servant who did not perform was taken even that which he had been given, and his judgment was decided; as an "unprofitable servant," he was cast into outer darkness.

This principle is in total conformity with modern revelation. The Lord revealed to Joseph Smith:

D&C 58:26–29 It is not meet that I should command in all things; for he that is compelled in all things, the same is slothful and not a wise servant;

a. 1 Samuel 8:6–7.

b. 1 Samuel 8:5.

c. 1 Samuel 15:26.

d. 1 Samuel 15:28.

wherefore he receiveth no reward. Verily I say, men should be anxiously engaged in a good cause, and do many things of their own free will, and bring to pass much righteousness; for the power is in them, wherein they are agents unto themselves. And inasmuch as men do good they shall in nowise lose their reward. But he that doeth not anything until he is commanded, and receiveth a commandment with doubtful heart, and keepeth it with slothfulness, the same is damned.

In the parable, the talents were bestowed upon each servant in accordance with his ability to successfully use them. So, also, are we apportioned a varying number of talents. Each may not have the same number or quality of talents, but we all have at least one. We are commanded to use our talents for and in behalf of the kingdom of God. We have the agency to choose how we will use them, but if we are to achieve the kingdom, we must use them as we have been commanded by the Lord. For those who do so the promise is clear—the reward will be granted. If we do nothing, or waste the talent we have, the Lord considers us slothful and unprofitable servants, and our talents will be taken from us.[203] "Every good and faithful servant of Christ must, whatever his circumstances, personally and directly use such talent as he may have to make gain for Christ."[204]

The Pounds

Luke 19:11–27   And as they heard these things, he added and spake a parable, because he was nigh to Jerusalem, and because they thought that the kingdom of God should immediately appear. He said therefore, A certain nobleman went into a far country to receive for himself a kingdom, and to return. And he called his ten servants, and delivered them ten pounds, and said unto them, Occupy till I come. But his citizens hated him, and sent a message after him, saying, We will not have this man to reign over us. And it came to pass, that when he was returned, having received the kingdom, then he commanded these servants to be called unto him, to whom he had given the money, that he might know how much every man had gained by trading. Then came the first, saying, Lord, thy pound hath gained ten pounds. And he said unto him, Well, thou good servant: because thou hast been faithful in a very little, have thou authority over ten cities. And the second came, saying, Lord, thy pound hath gained five pounds. And he said likewise to him, Be thou also over five cities. And another came, saying, Lord, behold, here is thy pound, which I have kept laid up in a napkin: for I feared thee, because thou art an austere man: thou takest up that thou layedst not down, and reapest that thou didst not sow. And he saith unto him, Out of thine own mouth will I judge thee, thou wicked servant. Thou knewest that I was an austere man, taking up that I laid not down, and reaping that I did not sow:

wherefore then gavest not thou my money into the bank, that at my coming I might have required mine own with usury? And he said unto them that stood by, Take from him the pound, and give it to him that hath ten pounds. (And they said unto him, Lord, he hath ten pounds.) For I say unto you, That unto every one which hath shall be given; and from him that hath not, even that he hath shall be taken away from him. But those mine enemies, which would not that I should reign over them, bring hither, and slay them before me.

Although similar to the parable of the talents, the parable of the pounds cannot be assumed to be merely a duplication of it, for such is not the case. A comparison of the two quickly establishes the points of difference between them.

Pounds	Talents
• Nobleman, not commoner	• Unidentified wealthy man (indicates private citizen)
• Nobleman leaves to claim kingdom	• Man leaves, reason unknown
• Ten entrusted servants	• Three entrusted servants
• Servants given same amount <u>regardless</u> of ability	• Servants given varied amounts <u>according</u> to ability
• Citizens of the kingdom hated nobleman	• No mistrust indicated
• Example drawn from political life	• Example from social life[205]
• Accountability demanded at return	• Accountability demanded at return
• Successful servants rewarded	• Successful rewarded
• Extra gain varies according to success and ability	• Extra gain equals success and ability
• Pound taken from slothful servant	• Talent taken from slothful servant
• Enemies punished and destroyed	• No such occurrence

From these differences, additional doctrine can be gleaned pertaining to the accountability and reward expected by those upon the earth. At one time or another, we all must come to judgment where we will be held accountable for the stewardship given us while we were on the earth.

The pounds, as the talents, represent the gifts of God, or the stewardship He has given us. The distinctive feature of this parable is that each servant is given the same amount (one pound) to do the best he can in behalf of the absent nobleman. The gain is to be given to the nobleman upon his return. The injection of hatred by the citizens and their attempt to block the nobleman from receiving his kingdom is one of the more interesting facets of the parable. It perhaps reflects the recorded instance of Archelaus when he left the area of Judea for Rome. Through inheritance, he was to be endowed with a kingdom from Caesar, and the people strongly objected to that inheritance.[206]

Because this parable has a definite political involvement it must first, of necessity, be specifically applied to the Jews of Christ's day. It reflects how they viewed the Messiah and the Law under which they awaited Him—but its meaning can also be projected into modern times.

The Jewish leaders believed that their meticulous observance of the Law would assure them a place in the kingdom of heaven. The Israelite nation as a whole had developed a philosophy of selfish exclusiveness based on this belief (this policy was in direct opposition to the gospel principle that the kingdom of heaven must be spread throughout the world and encompass all mankind). The Jews anticipated a political Messiah and the immediate establishment of an earthly kingdom as indicated by the Lord's comments when He introduced the parable. Even Christ's disciples anticipated that the establishment of the final kingdom of God would not be long in coming. But that was not the case, and the parable was given to clarify that point and to firmly establish the fact that the servants (or mankind) must continually abide in faithfulness and devotion to the Lord in order to receive their reward.[207] If we become slack and negligent in the application of our gifts within the kingdom, our reward will be taken from us.

A division of goods occurred in this parable as in the parable of the talents, but the unique feature here is that each recipient received the same amount—one pound. There was no consideration of ability, but "success would imply greater ability, even as it would require more constant labour."[208] The servants attained differing degrees of success in their use of the gifts and were rewarded accordingly. Unlike the talents, which were given in consideration of the servants' abilities, the pounds multiplied according to the industry of each individual servant.

As with the parable of the talents, the story of the pounds revolves around the one servant who did nothing with the pound that he had been given. He attempted to return it unused to the nobleman, hoping still to gain his reward, and he held the same austere view of God and misapplication of the principles of the kingdom as did the servant in the parable of the talents.

He refused to do the minimum that was required of him to insure that something would be returned to the nobleman. In accordance with the requirements of the kingdom, the pound was taken from him and given to another. The parable sharply emphasized the fact that one cannot be selfishly exclusive with his gift; he must actively expand his talents if he is to acquire the kingdom of God.

The entrusted servants in this parable represented the members of the kingdom at the time of Christ. They thought that during their lifetime they would see the kingdom ushered in, and that their responsibility was only to prepare themselves for that event. They gave little credence to the requirement that they must actively use their gifts to prepare the world for the coming of the Messiah.[209] The pound was taken from the slothful servant and given to the one who had brought the greatest increase to his king—those who work the hardest receive the greatest reward.[210]

The last part of the parable talks of the citizens who rejected the nobleman and did not want him to rule over them. They were representative of the Jewish rulers of the chosen people[211] who, during the trial of Jesus, would reject the Lord. Pilate would bring the Lord before them and state, "Behold your King!"[a] Their response would be similar to that of the citizens in the parable, for they would cry, "Away with him, away with him, crucify him." Pilate would say, "Shall I crucify your King?" and the chief priests would answer, "We have no king but Caesar."[b][212]

It is obvious that this open and willful rejection of the Messiah was explicitly predicted in the parable of the pounds. The Jews would not have Jesus be their king, and they actively attempted to destroy His kingdom. Their reward was parabolically predicted, for in the parable the nobleman stated that he would destroy the wicked and rebellious citizens, and they would receive no kingdom.[213]

This parable is very straightforward. The king, or nobleman, repre-

a. John 19:14.

b. John 19:15.

sents Christ.[214] The various uses of the pounds represent the different ways man can successfully use the gifts he has been given. A reward was granted according to the degree that the servants applied their gifts. The slothful servant was punished for his refusal to work at all,[215] a warning to lazy and fearful men and women of all ages. And finally, the citizens represent those who reject the Lord and attempt to destroy his kingdom.[216]

A final application of this parable can be made both to the Jews of Christ's time and to His Apostles, who, although anxiously involved in His work, had the mistaken idea that His political kingdom would soon be established.[217] He cautioned these beloved brethren and explained to them that they would assuredly be called upon to account for their stewardship, and that their reward would be based on the application of that stewardship toward the growth and glory of the kingdom of God.

The Labourers in the Vineyard

Matthew 20:1–16 For the kingdom of heaven is like unto a man that is an householder, which went out early in the morning to hire labourers into his vineyard. And when he had agreed with the labourers for a penny a day, he sent them into his vineyard. And he went out about the third hour, and saw others standing idle in the marketplace, and said unto them; Go ye also into the vineyard, and whatsoever is right I will give you. And they went their way. Again he went out about the sixth and ninth hour, and did likewise. And about the eleventh hour he went out, and found others standing idle, and saith unto them, Why stand ye here all the day idle? They say unto him, Because no man hath hired us. He saith unto them, Go ye also into the vineyard; and whatsoever is right, that shall ye receive. So when even was come, the lord of the vineyard saith unto his steward, Call the labourers, and give them their hire, beginning from the last unto the first. And when they came that were hired about the eleventh hour, they received every man a penny. But when the first came, they supposed that they should have received more; and they likewise received every man a penny. And when they had received it, they murmured against the goodman of the house, saying, These last have wrought but one hour, and thou hast made them equal unto us, which have borne the burden and heat of the day. But he answered one of them, and said, Friend, I do thee no wrong: didst not thou agree with me for a penny? Take that thine is, and go thy way: I will give unto this last, even as unto thee. Is it not lawful for me to do what I will with mine own? Is thine eye evil, because I am good? So the last shall be first, and the first last: for many be called, but few chosen.

This is the last of the parables that teaches accountability and reward. It introduces two additional elements to the concepts covered in the talents and pounds. First, the spirit in which you perform your labors in the kingdom of God will be taken into consideration on judgment day. Second, the reward will be universal, regardless of the length of time spent laboring.

The setting of the parable is important to its interpretation. The Lord had been giving instructions to His disciples and had been asked by the rich young ruler how he could attain eternal life. As noted earlier, Jesus had instructed the ruler to sell all that he had, give it to the poor, and follow Him. But the ruler's love for his "great possessions"[a] had preempted his compliance, which led to Christ's comment concerning the difficulty of a rich man entering God's kingdom. The astounded Apostles questioned, "Who then can be saved?"[b] Jesus calmly responded that all things were possible. Then Peter, speaking for himself and presumably for all of the Twelve, asked, "Behold, we have forsaken all, and followed thee; what shall we have therefore?"[c]

Jesus acknowledged their devotion and assured them that their sacrifices and continued labor would entitle them to sit upon thrones in the kingdom of His Father. "But," He cautioned, "many that are first shall be last; and the last shall be first."[d] He then gave the parable of the labourers in the vineyard.

This parable was a direct answer to Peter's question and an example of the philosophy of the Jewish rulers of the time. They believed that they earned rewards in the kingdom of heaven through their labors on the earth, and that the greater the labor, the greater the reward. This belief overlooked some of the factors in the equation, including that of the grace of God. The Lord did not want this concept to carry over into the teachings of the gospel, and through this parable He essentially declared that "he who works in my kingdom for the sake of a reward hereafter, may do his work well, but he honours me less than others who trust in me without thinking of future gain."[218]

This parable was a warning that the spirit in which one labors for the kingdom is what gives the service its value, and the answer to Peter's question indicated that just because the Twelve had been called first to the work, they should not necessarily trust in that call to insure their reward.[219] They were not to be boastful or proud in the work they performed, nor to compete in order to assert themselves one above another.[220]

a. Matthew 19:22.

b. Matthew 19:25.

c. Matthew 19:27.

d. Matthew 19:30.

This parable, like that of the talents, is also set forth in scenes. In the first scene, a householder goes out early in the day to hire men to work in his vineyard. The householder is representative of God and the laborers might well have represented Peter and the others who had just asked what they would receive; but they also represent anyone laboring in the vineyard. The first laborers and the householder agree at the outset that their wages will be "a penny a day." And so they go into the vineyard.

As the day progressed the householder continued his solicitation for laborers, and at the third hour he hired others and told them to go into the vineyard to labor. However, this time, instead of bargaining with them for their reward, he merely stated, "Whatsoever is right I will give you," and the laborers were satisfied to trust in the goodness of the householder.

Again the householder went out in the sixth and the ninth hours and hired additional laborers. To emphasize the teaching of the parable, Jesus had the householder go out even in the eleventh hour. Still finding potential laborers, he asked why they were standing idle. They explained that they were idle because no one had hired them. The householder immediately told them to go into the vineyard and work, saying, "Whatsoever is right, that shall ye receive." The hiring of different laborers at different hours indicated the abundance of work that was available in the vineyard and the anxiety of the householder to complete the work.[221]

The laborers could have refused the opportunity to labor, but they did not. Those called first bargained for their wages, and an amount was promised and agreed upon. Those later called into the ministry did not bargain for their labors but relied upon the goodness and mercy of the householder, knowing that he was just and that they would be paid fairly.

In the second (and last) scene of the parable, the householder called for the laborers to come forth and give an account of their labor, that they might receive the reward for their hire. But instead of calling those who had been hired first, the householder called those who were hired in the eleventh hour so that they might be paid first. (This was again a direct reference to Peter's question and the Lord's answer.)

The laborers who had been hired early and had negotiated their wages watched as the householder paid all the other laborers a penny for their work, regardless of the length of time they had labored. In view of this, they felt they were entitled to more than a penny for their long hours, and keenly anticipated a greater reward from the householder. But when the master got to them, he paid them only the penny that had been agreed upon and they murmured against the master because they felt that since they had "borne the burden and heat of the day," they were entitled to additional wages.

But this was the point of the parable. The laborers of the morning claimed injustice but had received just the opposite. They were paid exactly what they had bargained for. The others received the same pay because it was all the Lord had to give. Each servant in turn, whether among those who were called first to the service or those who were called last, had the same opportunity to gain the reward. Their reward (as symbolized by the penny—and the only reward the Lord has available) was entrance into the kingdom of God and the receipt of all the Father has—even joint heirship with Jesus Christ.[a][222] Thus, once the servants had accepted the call, the work they performed up to the time of accountability was sufficient for them to enter into the kingdom of God—providing they performed their labor with all faithful diligence and devotion to God.

The complaining and the bickering of the first laborers perhaps bespoke their mental and moral unfitness.[223] The householder reminded them that it was lawful for him to do with his own that which he would, and he asked them if they were behaving evilly because he had been good. He again reiterated that the last shall be first and the first last, for many were called, but few chosen. This warning indicated that "those who seem chiefest in [the] labor, yet . . . may altogether lose the things which they have wrought; and those who seem last, may, by keeping their humility, be acknowledged first in the day of God."[224] The kingdom of heaven is God's to give, and the reckoning of man's stewardship will be determined by *how* he performs his labors as much as *whether* he performs his labors.

In the parables of the talents and the pounds, the ultimate question of accountability was whether any labor had been performed at all. Now, in addition to that consideration, accountability includes whether labor has been performed with the proper spirit. If not, per-

a. Romans 8:16–17.

haps there is a risk that the reward could be lost, for "the kingdom of heaven is not a matter of mercenary calculation or exact equivalent— there [is] no bargaining with the Heavenly Householder."[225] Therefore, the reward in the parable was a gift from God and *not a payment of debt* as a result of labor performed.[226]

It is not *when* we are called to serve the Lord that determines our reward but *how* we serve Him. Those called late in life to the service and who serve well will stand equal with, and perhaps above, those who are called early but serve poorly. A story illustrating this principle deals with Thomas after the resurrection of Jesus. Jesus had appeared to the Apostles when Thomas was not with them. They later told Thomas that the Lord had risen. Instead of readily accepting the testimony of his fellow Apostles, Thomas said that he could not believe until he had seen the Lord personally and placed his fingers in the prints of the nails and thrust his hand into His side. Eight days later the Lord again appeared to the Apostles; this time Thomas was with them. Jesus instructed Thomas to "reach hither thy finger, and behold my hands; and reach hither thy hand, and thrust it into my side: and be not faithless, but believing."[a] Thomas did as he was told and acknowledged that it was the Savior. Jesus then said, "Because thou hast seen me, thou hast believed: blessed are they that have not seen, and yet have believed."[b]

The vineyard in this parable represents the kingdom of God on earth. The laborers represent the servants of the Lord, and Jesus is the husbandman. The parable can apply to those who are outside the church and are converted late in life as well as to those who are already members of the church and are laboring diligently therein; but it can also include those who have not done the Lord's bidding and who, after repentance, accept the call and find their work graciously accepted.

The Lord has indicated that many will be called but few chosen. Modern revelation continues: "And why are they not chosen? Because their hearts are set so much upon the things of this world, and aspire to the honors of men."[c] Hence, the moral of this parable: there is no precise equation between work done and the reward received. We receive a reward through the grace of God because he has promised it, not because we have earned it.[d][227]

a. John 20:27.

b. John 20:29.

c. D&C 121:34–35.

d. Ephesians 2:4–10; Moroni 10:32–33.

Parables That Teach Warnings   9

The Lord wants everyone to live the gospel requirements and acquire His promised blessings, but He warns of potential failure. Although the Jews of Christ's time belonged to a favored race, the people of Israel, this esteemed position led them to believe that they were automatically entitled to the Lord's promised kingdom. But it was not to be so.

The things of the world can blind a person to spiritual decisions. Even when living within the parameters of the gospel's teachings, all of the Lord's children must be cautious so that their humility and meekness are not overcome.

The Foolish Rich Man

Luke 12:13–21   And one of the company said unto him, Master, speak to my brother, that he divide the inheritance with me. And he said unto him, Man, who made me a judge or a divider over you? And he said unto them, Take heed, and beware of covetousness: for a man's life consisteth not in the abundance of the things which he possesseth. And he spake a parable unto them, saying, The ground of a certain rich man brought forth plentifully: and he thought within himself, saying, What shall I do, because I have no room where to bestow my fruits? And he said, This will I do: I will pull down my barns, and build greater; and there will I bestow all my fruits and my goods. And I will say to my soul, Soul, thou hast much goods laid up for many years; take thine ease, eat, drink, and be merry. But God said unto him, Thou fool, this night thy soul shall be required of thee: then whose shall those things be, which thou hast provided? So is he that layeth up treasure for himself, and is not rich toward God.

The twelfth chapter Of Luke is a teaching unit based on the theme of godliness as contrasted with worldliness (these same concepts appear in widely divergent sections of the other Gospels).[228] Like many other parts of Luke's Gospel, this parable is set in a real-life situation that gives added insight into the Lord's character and reputation. Luke did not identify the whereabouts of Jesus on this occasion, but the Lord was teaching His Apostles and others when He was interrupted by a man in the crowd. The intruder was apparently totally disinterested in the spiritual truths that the Lord was teaching and interrupted Him with a selfish, secular question.

The man asked the Lord to intervene in an inheritance problem between himself and his brother. The Jewish law on inheritance was clearly defined, and it can be assumed that the man had no just legal claim or he would not have appealed to Jesus.[229] But the fact that he did gives insight into the stature the Lord had attained by this time in His ministry.

The Savior treated the man's question with complete forthrightness, stating that He would not act as judge between the man and his brother. He warned the man and those who had drawn close around Him about their covetous nature and having their hearts set only upon the things of the world. After this admonition, Jesus taught the parable of the foolish rich man to warn the individual about the relationship between worldly things and the things of the spirit.

The Lord began the parable by declaring that during the harvest, the ground of a certain man produced an unanticipated abundance. The man wondered what he should do with his newfound wealth. He had always been obsessed with the accumulation of worldly things and was concerned about how he should preserve his huge surplus. This reaction is characteristic of a covetous man.[230] His thoughts and actions were centered around how he could secure his personal ease and sensuous enjoyment.[231] His heart was proud, selfish, and self-indulgent, and he considered his carefully planned future as if it were a foregone conclusion.

The Lord purposely embodied in this wealthy man the selfish propensities He was warning against. The man, by his declarations, admitted that the innermost thoughts of his heart were set upon his provisions for the flesh.[232] His plans stretched no higher than to satisfy his earthly desires, and he failed in all particulars to include God in his gain.[233] He had placed the things of the world above the worship of God, and thus had broken the first great commandment. In addition, he had decided to use his abundance for his personal, selfish, and lustful desires rather than in the service of his fellowman—thus breaking the second great commandment. Although he was laying up in abundance worldly things, he was impoverished spiritually.[a][234] Then God gave the warning embodied in the parable when He said to the rich man, "Thou fool, this night thy soul shall be required of thee."

This is an interesting use of the word *fool.* The Psalmist had recorded many centuries before, "The fool hath said in his heart, There is no God,"[b] thus emphasizing the biblical meaning of the word fool as "a man who practically denies the existence of God."[235]

The emphasis of the parable thus far had been on the relationship between the laying up of spiritual versus worldly treasures and the competition between them. Now it shifted to a warning about making the wrong choice. It was not the imminent death of the individual, but his impending judgment that the Lord warned of. The man had carefully assessed his personal situation and judged his needs, but had made the wrong choice. "Whose shall those things be, which thou hast provided?" the Lord asked in the parable. All that the man had accounted so dear, all that he determined he would profit by, was now for naught. The author of Ecclesiastes had warned, "He that loveth silver shall not be satisfied with silver; nor he that loveth abundance with increase: this is also vanity."[c] The rich man had emphasized all the wrong things (self, world, riches) and had forgotten all the right ones (God, his neighbor, the poor).

The relationship was perfectly clear: "The man whose treasure is of earth leaves it all at death; he whose wealth is in heaven goes to his own, and death is but the portal to his treasury."[236] The Talmud records "that a Rabbi told his disciples, 'Repent the day before thy death;' and when his disciples asked him: 'Does a man know the day of his death?' he replied, that on that very ground he should repent to-day, lest he should die to-morrow. And so would all his days be days of repentance."[237]

Our personal pathway to the kingdom of God is one of choices, and the parable emphatically warned that we would be judged according to those selections. "How brief, yet how rich in significance, is that little parable which He told them, of the rich fool who, in his greedy,

a. Matthew
6:20–21.

b. Psalm 14:1.

c. Ecclesiastes
5:10.

God-forgetting, presumptuous selfishness, would do this and that . . . who . . . thought that 'my fruits,' and 'my goods,' and 'my barns,' and to 'eat and drink and be merry' could for many years . . . sustain what was left him of a soul, but to whom from heaven pealed as a terrible echo to his words, the heart-thrilling sentence of awful irony, 'Thou fool, this night!'"[238]

After giving the parable, Jesus finished His instructions by concluding, "For all these things do the nations of the world seek after: and your Father knoweth that ye have need of these things. But rather seek ye the kingdom of God; and all these things shall be added unto you."[a]

Paul expanded the warning when he declared to the Romans, "But put ye on the Lord Jesus Christ, and make not provision for the flesh, to fulfill the lusts thereof"[b]—a strong warning for each of God's children.

The Pharisee and the Publican

Luke 18:9–14   And he spake this parable unto certain which trusted in themselves that they were righteous, and despised others: Two men went up into the temple to pray; the one a Pharisee, and the other a publican. The Pharisee stood and prayed thus with himself, God, I thank thee, that I am not as other men are, extortioners, unjust, adulterers, or even as this publican. I fast twice in the week, I give tithes of all that I possess. And the publican, standing afar off, would not lift up so much as his eyes unto heaven, but smote upon his breast, saying, God be merciful to me a sinner. I tell you, this man went down to his house justified rather than the other: for every one that exalteth himself shall be abased; and he that humbleth himself shall be exalted.

In the parable of the rich fool, the Lord had declared His warning with regard to the individual's choices between worldliness and spirituality. Now the Lord would, in parabolic form, warn those of the covenant who "trusted in themselves that they were righteous, and despised others."

The characters in the parable are a Pharisee and a publican. Although the Lord selected these character types for use in the parable, the parable was not addressed to Pharisees and publicans exclusively.[239] It was a general warning to all those within the covenant, and is as applicable today as it was at the time Jesus gave it. The message of the parable is portrayed through the prayers of the Pharisee and the publican, but it is not the principle of prayer that is being taught. The prayers are simply the tools used by the Lord to teach the principle and warn against self-righteousness within the kingdom.[240]

a. Luke 12:30–31.
b. Romans 13:14.

The Pharisee stood as he prayed. This was one position for prayer used by the Jews and Israelites of old.[a] Sometimes, perhaps in moments of greater humility and supplication, they knelt.[b] The early moments of the Pharisee's prayer showed promise, but his thanksgiving quickly deteriorated. He offered only proud, cold thanks for his own merits while emulating the lifeless formality of the rabbis of his day. "The religion of the day was so largely mechanical, that they were in danger of mistaking the outward form for the substance."[241]

In his "righteous observance" of the Law, the Pharisee sought only self-justification in his excessive zeal and assurance that he would be separated from sinners. He thanked God that he was not as those whom he looked down upon, and he felt nothing but contempt for those in a class lower than his. Perhaps as he prayed he cast his eyes upon the publican and now, along with all others he despised, he dragged him into his prayer as one whom he held in contempt.

He declared his righteousness openly. He fasted twice a week, whereas Rabbinical Law demanded only once a year.[c242] He tithed all he possessed, rather than that which he earned annually, as the Law required.[d243] He would have God as his debtor, and confessed none of his sins or inadequacies before Him.

The Lord now placed the publican in direct contrast with the Pharisee. The publican stood afar off, not wanting to press near the holy place, even though as a Jew he had the right to be there. In reverence he smote upon his chest, a sign of his inward grief, and begged the mercy of God. He was overwhelmed by the bitter sense of his distance from God. Under the Jewish Law his calling placed him and his family in a hopeless position, yet his prayer indicated that he was in the process of repentance.[244]

After drawing this parabolic picture, the Lord quickly concluded by issuing a warning that may have completely overwhelmed His audience. The parable disclosed that the publican, rather than the Pharisee, departed to his house justified. Those who exalted themselves under the Law would be abased, and those who humbled themselves would be exalted.[245] The Pharisee departed, justified only before men, and prouder than ever of his haughty observance of a dead, cold Law. The publican went away, hated by man but justified before God.[246]

The covenant people who used the Law merely to fulfill social

a. 1 Kings 8:22;
   Matthew 6:5.

b. Daniel 6:10;
   2 Chronicles
   6:13; Psalm
   95:6.

c. Leviticus
   16:29.

d. Deuteronomy
   14:22; Leviticus
   27:30.

needs, to gain personal gratification, or to be visibly self-righteous had been warned. God would reject the self-righteous, but His mercy would be boundless to those who came to Him with a broken heart and a contrite spirit.

The Barren Fig Tree

Luke 13:6–9   He spake also this parable; A certain man had a fig tree planted in his vineyard; and he came and sought fruit thereon, and found none. Then said he unto the dresser of his vineyard, Behold, these three years I come seeking fruit on this fig tree, and find none: cut it down; why cumbereth it the ground? And he answering said unto him, Lord, let it alone this year also, till I shall dig about it, and dung it: and if it bear fruit, well: and if not, then after that thou shalt cut it down.

This is the last of the warning parables and it was directed to Israel as a nation. The essence of this parable was that the salt had lost its savor and was therefore good for nothing and should be cast out and trodden under foot of man.[a]247

Before teaching this parable, Jesus had been told of a terrible calamity that had befallen certain Galileans. Their blood had been mingled with pagan sacrifices by Pilate and Jesus, in response to this story, asked if the people thought that this made those Galileans sinners above all Galileans.[b] Then He raised the example of the eighteen upon whom the tower in Siloam had fallen.[c] He noted that these were merely calamities of life and that although sin and suffering might be generally related, it was not always possible to link individual sin to a given disaster; rather, disasters were usually the result of life's circumstances.

The focus in this parable should not be on the sins of others but on our own sins and the eternal calamity which will befall us if we do not repent. It concerns both the long-suffering and the severity of God.

As the parable began, a certain man (representing God) owned a fig tree. When he came to see how much fruit the tree had produced, none was found. Apparently this had occurred for a period of three years so the owner of the vineyard instructed his dresser to cut the tree down so that it would no longer encumber the ground. This was all done in accordance with the traditional law of the people, for "a barren tree would be of threefold disadvantage: it would yield no fruit; it would fill valuable space, which a fruit-bearer might occupy; and it

a. Matthew 5:13.

b. Luke 13:1–2.

c. Luke 13:4–5.

would needlessly deteriorate the land. Accordingly, while it was forbidden to destroy fruit-bearing trees, it would, on the grounds above stated, be [a] duty to cut down a 'barren' . . . tree."[248]

In the parable, the fig tree—long an emblem of the Jewish nation[a]— represented Israel. Man's actions and attitudes (his works) toward the kingdom of God were often compared to the production of fruit.[b] Three kinds of actions, or works, were commonly referred to: First were good works, for the tree bearing good fruit represented those who were categorized as bringing forth good works. Second were dead works, wherein people acted in conformity with the Law but in form only, and not for the glory of God. Third were evil works, wherein a corrupt tree brought forth corrupt fruit.[249]

Upon being ordered to cut the tree down, the dresser of the vineyard (representing the Savior) requested that one more year be given to determine whether the tree would bring forth fruit. He said he would "dig about it, and dung it" during that period of time, to see if the tree would produce. Such a request for the deferment of God's judgment was not uncommon.[c] Thus, additional time would be given and the punishment prescribed in the parable would be deferred in order to grant more time for repentance.[250]

The pleading by the dresser of the vineyard depicts Jesus in His role as our intercessor with the Father. But he agreed that if the tree did not bear fruit this time, it would be cut down and destroyed. The symbolism of the parable could not have been missed by those who heard it. The announcement of a judgment and then the suspension of the sentence to allow one more attempt at repentance was a process familiar to the leadership of the Jews. Noah had preached and prophesied before the Flood, and other eminent prophets appeared prior to the great catastrophes suffered by Israel. God's impatience had been graphically depicted before their eyes.

Although the Israelites had been chosen as God's elect, that election did not guarantee them the kingdom; it was merely a means to that end. If the tree bore not good fruit, it would be cut out and discarded. The time had come for Israel to determine whether it would accept God or its inevitable destruction. Although time would be granted for repentance, the destruction of the tree that would not bring forth good fruit was decreed. The warning to the chosen people had been given.[251]

a. Joel 1:7; Jacob 5.

b. Psalm 1:3; John 15:2–5; Romans 7:4.

c. 2 Peter 3:9.

Parables That Teach Judgment

Christ's gospel established the requirements for entry into the kingdom of God. It provided laws and ordinances whereby all mankind would be judged and could be saved. That the judgment would be fair was beyond doubt, for all judgment was entrusted to Jesus Christ. The standards were well-defined, and the entire population of the world would ultimately be judged by them. This chapter deals with the parables that taught of this judgment.

To the Rulers of Israel: The Wicked Husbandman

Matthew 21:33–41 Hear another parable: There was a certain householder, which planted a vineyard, and hedged it round about, and digged a winepress in it, and built a tower, and let it out to husbandmen, and went into a far country: and when the time of the fruit drew near, he sent his servants to the husbandmen, that they might receive the fruits of it. And the husbandmen took his servants, and beat one, and killed another, and stoned another. Again, he sent other servants more than the first: and they did unto them likewise. But last of all he sent unto them his son, saying, They will reverence my son. But when the husbandmen saw the son, they said among themselves, This is the heir; come, let us kill him, and let us seize on his inheritance. And they caught him, and cast him out of the vineyard, and slew him. When the lord therefore of the vineyard cometh, what will he do unto those husbandmen? They say unto him, He will miserably destroy those wicked men, and will let out his vineyard unto other husbandmen, which shall render him the fruits in their seasons.

Cross-references Mark 12:1–9; Luke 20:9–16

This is one of the few parables recorded in all three Synoptics. The three versions differ slightly due to their independent authors, but they do not disagree in any significant points. All three writers agree that Jesus was teaching the people in the presence of the Pharisees and the rulers of the Jews. These men had come to Jesus and asked Him by what authority He taught the people. He, in turn, asked them concerning the authority of John, and they refused to answer whether it was from God or from man but rather indicated they could not tell. Jesus likewise refused to declare His authority and then taught them this parable.[252]

The parable is historical in nature, in one sense describing God's relationship to the chosen people from Israel to Christ and in a larger sense describing His relationship with the entire human family from Adam to the Second Coming.[253] It is judgmental in its conclusion, and could be considered both descriptive of an existing situation and prophetic of a future one.[254] The story is told in a realistic manner that would have been recognized and understood by the rulers of the Jews, as all three Synoptics attest.

The opening words of the parable are similar to those of Isaiah in his song of the vineyard[a] wherein the house of Israel is portrayed as a vine stock or a vineyard—a common analogy in the Old Testament.[b]

The symbolism of the parable and its principal parts are as follows:

The householder: the owner of the vineyard representing God.

The vineyard: could be considered generally as the human family, but specifically as the house of Israel.

The embellishment of the vineyard (hedged about, digged around, tower provided): the covenant established between God and Israel that made Israel distinct and separate from other nations and chosen above all other people.[255]

The husbandmen: might have symbolically referred to the nation of Israel and its responsibility to the rest of mankind, but specifically referred to the spiritual overseers or ecclesiastical leaders of Israel.[256]

The far country: God departing and leaving the vineyard (or the children of men) in the hands of the religious leaders.

The servants: the prophets who came to the children of Israel in the name of God.

The son: Jesus Christ.

The fruits: the souls of men brought into the kingdom of God

a. Isaiah 5.

b. Psalm 80:8–16; Isaiah 5:1–7; 27:1–7; Jeremiah 2:21.

through instruction, repentance, and adherence to the commandments.[257]

Although the vineyard in this parable was planted by the householder, it was let out to certain husbandmen (representing the leadership of Israel). They were given charge of the vineyard as part of their commission.[a] The lord of the vineyard, or the householder, then withdrew and awaited the growth of the fruit. When the harvest season arrived, the householder sent a servant that he might collect and receive of the fruit of the vineyard. This represented the prophets who were sent by God to call the children of Israel to repentance, teach them the errors of their ways, and encourage them to return to His kingdom. Luke indicates that the servants were sent three times while Mark and Matthew add that many others were also sent. But rather than being glad, the leaders of Israel received the prophets with disdain and hatred. They beat, wounded, and shamefully mistreated them, stoning some and killing others.[258]

The patience of the householder is clearly depicted in this parabolic story. Even though the servants (or prophets) were evilly mistreated, the householder, in his goodness, continued to send others. He did this for two reasons: first, so that adequate time might be allowed to recover God's children; and second, to show that the rebellious children and wicked overseers had time after time rejected the call to repentance and by so doing would suffer the consequences of their actions.

After the rejection and abuse of the prophets had taken place, the householder sent his son, the long-awaited Messiah. Surely "they will reverence my son," he said. But instead of reverencing the son, they came out in open rebellion against him. "This is the heir," they said; "come, let us kill him, and let us seize on his inheritance." The last effort of God's divine mercy was rejected, and the vineyard became ripened in sin.

The husbandmen of the vineyard thought they could defeat the purpose of God by killing His son; but rather than defeat God's purpose, they would help to bring it about. This portion of the parable is prophetic for the death of the Savior had not yet occurred. However, the die had been cast. As He predicted, they would indeed cast out the Son of God and kill Him.

After Jesus finished telling the parable, He applied it directly to the rulers of the Jews and let them publicly judge themselves. He asked them a question: "When the lord therefore of the vineyard cometh, what will he do unto those husbandmen?" The Jewish rulers generally attempted to avoid questions put to them by the Lord and had just recently avoided the question of John's authority, but they could not avoid this question. They were standing before the people, so they answered the only way they could. "They say unto him, He will miserably destroy those wicked men, and will let out his vineyard unto other husbandmen, which shall render him the fruits in their seasons."

Luke's account tells us that, immediately recognizing the application of the parable, they exclaimed, "God forbid." They knew that the Lord was applying the parable to them; that He was predicting their rejection and ultimate destruction and the end of Israel's favored position; and that the kingdom was to be given to another nation, one that would bring forth the fruits demanded by the householder. Their wickedness and disobedience had been graphically portrayed in the parable. "They had been entrusted with a valuable institution; an elect nation furnished with good laws . . . speaking generally, they had lost sight of the end of Israel's calling. . . . They had occupied their position for their own glory . . . they had neglected the vineyard . . . thinking only of privilege and forgetting duty."[259]

To emphasize to His listeners that He was the "son" of the parable whom they had rejected, the Lord answered their exclamation with a recognizable Messianic scripture. "The stone which the builders rejected, the same is become the head of the corner."[a] It was an Old Testament quotation specifically referring to the Messianic claim.[b] By its use, Jesus openly called Himself the Son of God, the expected Messiah.

He now warned the rulers of the Jews of their impending judgment. He stated that whosoever fell upon the stone would be broken, and on whomsoever it should fall, it would grind them to powder. He went beyond the analogy of the parable and made an open declaration of His Messiahship, at the same time emphasizing the malice of the Pharisees. He told them that they could not defeat the purposes of God. He warned them that they had already stumbled at the stone and were about to be crushed by it because they had deliberately set themselves in opposition to Him, knowing who He was.[c]

a. Matthew 21:42.

b. Psalms 118:22.

c. Matthew 21:44.

There is no question that the Pharisees and the rulers of the Jews knew and understood the application of this parable. All three of the Synoptics declare that they knew that He spoke of them. Their reaction clearly indicates this, for they sought how they might lay hands on Him; they sent spies that they might take hold of His words, and they sent other Pharisees and Herodians to catch Him in His words.[a]

Their rage at Christ's candor concerning their wickedness was thwarted, for the scriptures note that they would not lay hands on Him because they feared the people, who thought Jesus was a prophet.[b] Although they had understood and perceived the meaning of other parables, they "saw now, more clearly than ever, the whole bent and drift of these parables, and longed for the hour of vengeance! . . . He had depicted the trust and responsibility of their office, and had indicated a terrible retribution for its cruel and profligate abuse."[260]

They could not claim ignorance for they had acknowledged their understanding; they could not claim mercy for they had rejected repentance; they could not claim obedience for they had stoned and killed the prophets. Their evils and disobedience had culminated in their open rebellion against God, and for it their house would be left desolate.

Two parables given by Jesus taught the covenant people of their impending judgment: the parable of the great supper and the parable of the marriage of the king's son. They deal with the same principle, but produce differing results.

To the Covenant People: The Great Supper

Luke 14:16–24   Then said he unto him, A certain man made a great supper, and bade many: and sent his servant at supper time to say to them that were bidden, Come; for all things are now ready. And they all with one consent began to make excuse. The first said unto him, I have bought a piece of ground, and I must needs go and see it: I pray thee have me excused. And another said, I have bought five yoke of oxen, and I go to prove them: I pray thee have me excused. And another said, I have married a wife, and therefore I cannot come. So that servant came, and shewed his lord these things. Then the master of the house being angry said to his servant, Go out quickly into the streets and lanes of the city, and bring in hither the poor, and the maimed, and the halt, and the blind. And the servant said, Lord, it is done as thou hast commanded, and yet there is room. And the lord said unto the servant, Go out into the highways and hedges, and compel them to come in, that my

a. Mark 12:13.

b. Matthew 21:46.

house may be filled. For I say unto you, That none of those men which were bidden shall taste of my supper.

The setting of this parable is quite important to its interpretation. During the Perean ministry, Jesus had been invited to the house of one of the chief Pharisees to eat on the Sabbath day. The scripture declares that the Jews invited Him that they might watch Him[a] (the healing of the man with the dropsy was performed on this occasion).[261] As the discussion progressed, Jesus gave the parable of the wedding guests as a reprimand to the Jews for their custom of seating people at their feasts according to social stature.[262] He upbraided them for their self-aggrandizement, and the exclusion of the poor and the afflicted. He taught them not to invite the self-indulging rich (in an attempt to climb the social ladder), but to invite the meek and lowly (those of no influence or importance). By so doing, they would receive their compensation at the resurrection of the just.[b]

Apparently, those who heard the Lord did not fully comprehend the parable of the wedding guests, or else they chose to ignore the chastisement it contained, for one of them still gloried in his anticipation of the Messiah's kingdom where the righteous would be invited to sit down at a great supper with Him.[263] The man cried aloud, "Blessed is he that shall eat bread in the kingdom of God."[c] This great feast, "by which the Messianic reign was to be ushered in was a favorite theme of jubilant exposition in both synagog and school; and exultation ran high in the rabbinical dictum that none but the children of Abraham would be among the blessed partakers."[264]

But Jesus would not allow this misunderstanding of both His miracle and His parable; He gave the Pharisees and other guests at the dinner the parable of the great supper as His final teaching of the day.

The parable of the great supper told of a certain man who invited a large number of select guests to come and partake of his sumptuous meal. The customs and traditions of the time were reflected in the story. The guests were invited and given sufficient time to respond to the invitation so that the host could adequately prepare for those who would be in attendance.[265] At the proper time, a servant was sent to tell those who had been bidden that "all things are now ready." Those who had been invited and had accepted could now properly come to

a. Luke 14:1.

b. Luke 14:13–14.

c. Luke 14:15.

the supper, but they began to give excuses, each in his turn, that they might not attend.

The invited guests represented the covenant people of Israel, and the servant sent to bid them to the meal was the Lord, their long-awaited Messiah.[266] The excuses the guests gave represented the Lord's rejection by the covenant people.

The first guest declared that he had purchased a piece of ground and must go and see it—a weak excuse at best, for he had no real desire to go to the feast and no reverence for the host. The possessions of the world had taken precedence over his desire to enter the kingdom.

The second guest had purchased five yoke of oxen and had need to prove them. Again, a meager excuse. This man placed his business endeavors above his respect for his host.

The last guest had married a wife and could not come. Thus the pleasures of social life were represented, for during his marriage celebration he would declare his own feast,[267] placing his own pleasures above his commitment to his host.

The Lord was presenting a concise analogy. Advancement to the kingdom, even for those previously called and separated out from among the people of the world in general, required giving up that which seemed to them necessary and most desirable for their immediate, personal enjoyment.[268]

The guest's activities mentioned as excuses were not in and of themselves sinful, but became so because the guests placed them above their responsibility to the kingdom of God. Paul, perhaps with this parable in mind, cautioned the people about choosing between the things of the world and the kingdom of God when he said, "This I say, brethren, the time is short: it remaineth, that both they that have wives be as though they had none; and they that weep, as though they wept not; and they that rejoice, as though they rejoiced not; and they that buy, as though they possessed not; and they that use this world, as not abusing it: for the fashion of this world passeth away."[a]

After the servant heard all of the guests' excuses, he returned to his lord and told him what they had said. The master became angry and instructed the servant to go quickly into the "streets and lanes of the city, and bring in hither the poor, and the maimed, and the halt, and the blind." The servant complied with his master's instructions, but there was yet room at the supper, and the lord instructed the servant to go out a second time into "the highways and hedges, and compel them to come in," in order that his house would be full. Note that even though these people were invited, they had to be "compelled" to come to the supper. These, it would seem, are those who truly feel unworthy to be in the presence of the Lord. Therefore, they must be persuaded to come and recognize that the benevolence and patience of the house-holder was intended for them also. This was the most deadly thrust of the parable, for it struck at the most cherished of Jewish prejudices.

The first invitation was given to the poor, the outcast, the sinners and publicans, and the hated multitudes who neglected the rabbinical rules but were still the covenant people. They gladly accepted the lord of the parable's summons. But more than that, the second invitation to those in the highways and hedges indicated that the covenant, so cherished by the Jews, would now be taken from them and given to the Gentiles and the heathens.[269] The spiritually sick and needy, those abhorred by Israel throughout their history, would now receive the kingdom of God.

This was an irrefutable warning of judgment. The covenant that had bound Israel together as they looked for the anticipated Messiah would now be taken from them and given to another.

It was the proclamation, once more, of the mighty truth which might well be too hard for those who first heard it, to understand, since it is imperfectly realized after nineteen centuries; that external rites and formal acts are of no value with God, in themselves; that He looks at the conscience alone; that neither circumcision nor sacrifices, nor legal purifications, nor rigid observance of Sabbath laws, nor fasts, but the state of the heart, determines the relation of man to God.[270]

The one who had sat at meat with Jesus and with exultation proclaimed the anticipated hope to eventually eat bread with the Messiah in the kingdom of God was wrong. Jesus said that to be invited into the kingdom was one thing and to accept the invitation was another, but even that was not enough. The chosen people had to *go to the supper* in order to eat with the king and receive their reward, and going to the supper required more than just being invited. The parable told them that they had openly rejected the invitation because of their worldly desires: the management of property, the acquisition of riches, and the pursuit of the more sensual comforts of life. All these things were incompatible with the desire to attend the Lord's supper in the kingdom of heaven.

But other invitations were extended. They were given to people who had been excluded by the Jews in their rabbinical sophistry and to those who had excluded themselves because of their sins. All these were offered the kingdom and, based on their own merits, they would enter before those who "thanked God that they were not as other men."[271]

Now Jesus concluded the parable. To those who refused the Messiah, the host declared that "none of those men which were bidden shall taste of my supper." The contemptuous guests who had initially accepted the Lord's invitation but refused to come when bidden were warned that if they continued to refuse the Messiah, others would take their place and they would not enter into the feast which they had so eagerly anticipated.

To the Covenant People: The Marriage of the King's Son

Matthew 22:1–14   And Jesus answered and spake unto them again by parables, and said, The kingdom of heaven is like unto a certain king, which made a marriage for his son, and sent forth his servants to call them that were bidden to the wedding: and they would not come. Again, he sent forth other servants, saying, Tell them which are bidden, Behold, I have prepared my dinner: my oxen and my fatlings are killed, and all things are ready: come unto the marriage. But they made light of it, and went their ways, one to his farm, another to his merchandise: and the remnant took his servants, and entreated them spitefully, and slew them. But when the king heard thereof, he was wroth: and he sent forth his armies, and destroyed those murderers, and burned up their city. Then saith he to his servants, The wedding is ready, but they which were bidden were not worthy. Go ye therefore into the highways, and as many as ye shall find, bid to the marriage. So those servants went out into the highways, and gathered together all as many as they found, both bad and good: and the wedding was furnished with guests.

And when the king came in to see the guests, he saw there a man which had not on a wedding garment: and he saith unto him, Friend, how earnest thou in hither not having a wedding garment? And he was speechless. Then said the king to the servants, Bind him hand and foot, and take him away, and cast him into outer darkness; there shall be weeping and gnashing of teeth. For many are called, but few are chosen.

The Lord gave this parable on the third day of the last week of His life. He was about to close His public ministry and give His last instructions to His Apostles. He would then be betrayed into the hands of His enemies to be crucified before His chosen people. He taught this parable in the temple at a time when the Pharisees and rulers of the Jews had openly declared their hostility and made formal determination to do away with Him by violent means.

In the parable of the great supper (a parable comparable to this one), a man had arranged for a large meal. In this parable a king would call for the celebration of the marriage of his son. Before, Christ appeared as the servant, being the last of a long line of prophets and teachers. Now He was the founder of a new kingdom, the central person of that kingdom, and the Royal Son.[a]

The imagery of this parable again involved bidding invited guests to come to a feast. Great festivals[b] and marriage celebrations[c] were favorite themes of the Jewish rabbis and teachers,[272] and both of these were used in the parable of the marriage of the king's son.

The festive portion of the marriage was traditionally given prominence by the Jews, but here that emphasis is superseded by the conduct of the invited guests. The parable was based on the belief that the Jews would be invited to dine with the Savior in the Messianic kingdom, and that this great festival would usher in the arrival of the Messiah.[d] But the kingdom was not to come suddenly, as the Jews expected, for their "invitation" had been issued many centuries before, and now the call to attend the celebration (or enter God's kingdom) was being extended.

That the Jews were God's elect people was undisputed, for this position had been emphasized by all the prophets throughout their history. They presumed themselves worthy of entering the Lord's kingdom throughout this entire time. But this parable showed that they would make themselves unworthy, for the invited guests (who represented Israel) deliberately rebelled against the authority of the king. The guests proffered feeble reasons to be excused from the banquet and through their own actions excluded themselves from the very thing they wanted.

At first, the guests merely told the servants that they would not come. But in his great patience, the lord again sent forth other servants to tell them that all was ready. He had prepared the dinner and killed

a. Psalm 72:1.

b. Isaiah 25:6; 65:13.

c. Isaiah 61:10; 62:5; Hosea 2:19.

d. Zephaniah 1:7.

the fatlings and bade them come to the marriage. But now the invited guests indicated their total contempt and rejection of the king. They made light of the call and went their ways, considering their personal possessions and affairs more important than the kingdom of God. Some of the guests went one step further and spitefully treated the servants and killed them, coming out in open rebellion against Him who had made the covenant.

Perhaps the first of these servants to "bid the guests to the wedding" and proclaim the Lord's new kingdom with its anticipated Messiah was John the Baptist. His mission was accomplished during the lifetime of the Lord, even though he met a premature end. The Lord received no mistreatment during the commencement of His ministry; but as He proceeded to claim the Messiahship, the people openly declared (through their rejection of Him) that they would no longer be the people of God. Ultimately, their leaders had Him crucified.

At this point, the king became angry and sent forth his armies to destroy the murderers and burn the guests' city. As in the great supper, the guests who had been originally invited were rejected, but now in a harsher and more permanent manner. The Lord was warning the Jews that unless they repented and accepted Him, their swift rejection could carry with it destruction and even death.

Now the king again sent out servants to the highways in order to bring others into the marriage festival. "Both bad and good" were brought in so that the wedding would be furnished with guests.[a] Again the doctrine so hateful to the Jews was declared—if they rejected the Lord, the call would go to the Gentiles.[b] And so the hall was filled with guests.

But now, the parable indicated that a second judgment would take place. As the guests were brought into the palace they were given special clothing so that they would be attired in a manner worthy of the king's son.[c] They could not just sit down at the wedding feast without proper preparation.[273]

Those who had been properly clothed (or properly taught the principles of the gospel and His kingdom) had, through repentance, "put on Christ," and adorned themselves as new, spiritual beings through their obedience to His requirements. But one man considered himself worthy to stand before God without the proper preparation, and when

a. D&C 58:11.

b. Romans 11.

c. Isaiah 61:10; Zephaniah 1:7–8; Revelation 19:7–9.

he was discovered the king asked him why he was there without the correct attire.[274] Even though the king gave him the opportunity to explain his presence and justify it, the man stood speechless before him. He knew he was not properly prepared to be in the Lord's presence, and he stood condemned.

The unqualified intruder was bound hand and foot, taken away, and cast out of the kingdom where he, along with those originally invited to the wedding, would not be able to participate in the feast (or the kingdom of God). The Lord concluded the parable by stating, "Many are called, but few are chosen." All mankind are called and eventually given the opportunity to enter the Lord's kingdom, but the chosen are those who, being properly "attired," have met all the requirements of repentance and obedience. Thus, their presence is justified before the Lord.[275]

The warning of judgment about to come upon Israel, which had been alluded to in the parable of the great supper, was now openly declared to the people and the rulers of the Jews in the parable of the marriage of the king's son. The guests had rejected the kingdom and openly showed their hatred toward the king's son (or the Messiah) by killing the servants of the king. Later scriptures support this prophesied rejection.[a]

The parable of the great supper threatened the invited guests with exclusion from the feast, but the marriage of the king's son taught them that they would be destroyed by the king for their rejection of the Son. By their open enmity toward Him, they condemned themselves. Those who had thought themselves worthy had now proven themselves unworthy. Those who thought only to exalt themselves would now be abased. The covenant they so exclusively cherished would now be offered to all mankind, that through repentance and obedience all could be properly attired and received at the wedding feast to dine with the Son.

The warnings of impending judgment upon the covenant people were now complete, and the Jews recognized their application. Consequently, at the conclusion of this parable the Pharisees "took counsel how they might entangle [Jesus] in his talk,"[b] with the intention of justifying themselves for putting Him to death.

God established His kingdom through His Son and offered it to the

a. Acts 4:3; 5:18, 40; 7:58; 8:3; 12:3; 14:5; 17:5; 19:24–31; 21:30–32; 23:2.

b. Matthew 22:15.

chosen people. He would now "call the heathen to a share in it, while the people of Israel, with their religious leaders . . . had rejected His repeated invitations [and] would no longer be the one people of God."[276]

Conclusion

Because of the similarity between these two parables (the great supper and the marriage of the king's son) there is a temptation to treat them exactly alike. Although they have reference to the same principle, there are significant and substantial differences between them.

It is interesting to make a direct comparison of the parables in order to have their similarities and differences clearly in mind.

The Great Supper	Marriage of the King's Son
• Location/time: during the Perean ministry. The Perean ministry extended from the feast of the tabernacles to the week preceding the Lord's last Passover, and was cut in half by Christ's visit to Jerusalem during the Feast of Dedication. It was a six-month ministry to Peraea. This parable took place during the last three months, after the Feast of Dedication; thus, it was sometime between December and April of the last year of the Lord's ministry.[277]	• Location/time: given by Jesus in the temple on the third day of the last week of His life.
• Giver of the feast: a man (apparently for himself).	• Giver of the feast: a king for the marriage of his son.
• Invited guests: all guests had previously been invited and had formally replied, which was a normal custom of the time.	• Invited guests: all guests had previously been invited and had formally replied.
• Servants sent to declare all things now ready.	• Servants sent to declare that the wedding would commence. Guests would not come.

The Great Supper	Marriage of the King's Son
	• Second group of servants sent: Declared all things for dinner and marriage were ready, bade guests to come.
• Excuses made: (a) bought a piece of ground and must see it; (b) bought five yoke of oxen and must prove them; (c) married a wife and cannot come.	• Excuses made: (a) made light of invitation and went their way, one to his farm, one to his merchandise; (b) remnant refused servants, treated them spitefully, killed them.
• Man was told of refusals, became angry, but made no retribution.	• King became wroth at refusals and violence; sent armies, destroyed those who murdered servants and burned their city.
• Man directed servants to bring in other guests from streets and lanes of the city: the poor, the maimed, the halt, and the blind.	• Servants instructed that invited guests were not worthy. Sent for other guests: a. as many as found on highway bade to marriage; b. bad and good invited.
• More room available at feast.	• King inspected guests, discovered man without wedding garment.
• Servants instructed to go back to highways and hedges. Compelled more guests to come.	• Uninvited intruder was questioned, but was speechless.
	• Intruder bound and cast out of the wedding.
• Declaration by man: none of those formally invited would taste of his supper.	• Declaration by king: many called but few chosen.

From the parable of the great supper, it was clear that a warning had been given to the covenant people of Israel. If they did not accept the invitation to come into the kingdom of God and accept their Messiah, they would be excluded and others brought in to replace them. In the parable of the king's son, the Lord determined that the children of the chosen people had rejected Him, and rather than merely issue a warning of impending judgment He portrayed the painful result of that judgment. Their exclusion from the supper and the kingdom of God could be final. Because they had abused and killed the servants of God, they would be utterly destroyed, their covenant would be eliminated, and others would take their places.

To the World: The Gospel Net (The Draw Net)

Matthew 13:47–50   Again, the kingdom of heaven is like unto a net, that was cast into the sea, and gathered of every kind: which, when it was full, they drew to shore, and sat down, and gathered the good into vessels, but cast the bad away. So shall it be at the end of the world: the angels shall come forth, and sever the wicked from among the just, and shall cast them into the furnace of fire: there shall be wailing and gnashing of teeth.

Because of the fisherman's net used in the comparison, this parable would have great meaning to those who heard it. The draw net was leaded at the bottom so that it would drop to the floor of the sea and scrape along the floor as the net was pulled together. Cork held the top of the net on the water's surface so that all that came within the boundaries of the net might be drawn into it.[278]

Just as the net gathered all fish that were within its reach, so, too, will the gospel gather all men. Not just good men of the earth will come within its grasp and be taught the gospel, but all men of whatever nature will be affected. However, how people react to the demands of the kingdom will cause them, through their actions and attitudes, to pass judgment upon themselves. Therefore, the gathering process is nonselective, with the separation of good and evil following at the end of the harvest.

This parable seems to indicate that inclusion within the net (or within the structure of the Lord's kingdom upon the earth) is not enough to guarantee righteousness. Eventually there will be a separation of good and evil.[279] Just as there was a Judas within the Twelve, there will be good and bad disciples gathered to the gospel as it spreads throughout mankind.

The final separation which takes place in the parable comes at the end of the world,[280] after all the children of God have been given an opportunity to come within the bounds of the net (or receive the gospel) and be taught that there must be a final payment for all sin. This teaches us that although the wicked seem to thrive here in this life, they will not be able to escape the scrutiny of the final judgment[281] which will come to all mankind.[282] The righteous will be taken home, and the wicked "cast away."

The Watching Servants

Luke 12:36–48   And ye yourselves like unto men that wait for their lord, when he will return from the wedding; that when he cometh and knocketh, they may open unto him immediately. Blessed are those servants, whom the lord when he cometh shall find watching: verily I say unto you, that he shall gird himself, and make them to sit down to meat, and will come forth and serve them. And if he shall come in the second watch, or come in the third watch, and find them so, blessed are those servants. And this know, that if the goodman of the house had known what hour the thief would come, he would have watched, and not have suffered his house to be broken through. Be ye therefore ready also: for the Son of man cometh at an hour when ye think not.

Then Peter said unto him, Lord, speakest thou this parable unto us, or even to all? And the Lord said, Who then is that faithful and wise steward, whom his lord shall make ruler over his household, to give them their portion of meat in due season? Blessed is that servant, whom his lord when he cometh shall find so doing. Of a truth I say unto you, that he will make him ruler over all that he hath. But and if that servant say in his heart, My lord delayeth his coming; and shall begin to beat the menservants and maidens, and to eat and drink, and to be drunken; the lord of that servant will come in a day when he looketh not for him, and at an hour when he is not aware, and will cut him in sunder, and will appoint him his portion with the unbelievers. And that servant, which knew his lord's will, and prepared not himself, neither did according to his will, shall be beaten with many stripes. But he that knew not, and did commit things worthy of stripes, shall be beaten with few stripes. For unto whomsoever much is given, of him shall be much required: and to whom men have committed much, of him they will ask the more.

Cross-reference   Matthew 24:43–51

The Lord's use of this illustration is not generally regarded as a parable, but Peter interpreted it as one when he questioned the Lord: "Lord, speakest thou this parable unto us, or even to all?" Although not phrased in the true style of a parable, this reference has application to all those who would be encompassed within the gospel (as described in the parable of the gospel net).

The master of the house had left to enjoy a wedding celebration and did not indicate the hour of his return. The servants of the master were left with the admonition that they should remain alert and watch for his imminent return. The journey of the master and his return received no emphasis in the parable; the emphasis falls on the faithful servant who performs his duty throughout the entire absence of the master and is totally prepared for his return.

Others, who are also within the kingdom of the master, betray his trust in them through their own self-indulgence. The Lord uses a further analogy in the parable itself when He indicates that if a householder knew when a thief or burglar would come to his home, he would be watchful and not allow his house to be broken into. Through this analogy He again admonishes those listening to wait and watch and be prepared for the Son of Man when He comes, for they know not the hour of His coming.[283]

Those servants who are faithful—who watch and perform their duty well regardless of how long the master is gone—will be rewarded. Those who are unfaithful and are not watching, thinking the master has delayed his coming, who mistreat the other servants and indulge themselves in things that prevent them from faithfully performing their duty, will be cast out by the master upon his return.

The parable gives a general warning that those who deem themselves safely within the gospel net, those entrusted with the kingdom, are not automatically granted salvation. When the master returns, He will know those who have successfully cared for His covenant.

Those who have been faithful will receive a just reward; but those who have been unfaithful in their watch will be separated from the faithful and cast out with the unbelievers.

To the Church: The Ten Virgins

Matthew 25:1–13 Then shall the kingdom of heaven be likened unto ten virgins, which took their lamps, and went forth to meet the bridegroom. And five of them were wise, and five were foolish. They that were foolish took their lamps, and took no oil with them: but the wise took oil in their vessels with their lamps. While the bridegroom tarried, they all slumbered and slept. And at midnight there was a cry made, Behold, the bridegroom cometh; go ye out to meet him. Then all those virgins arose, and trimmed their lamps. And the foolish said unto the wise, Give us of your oil; for our lamps are gone out. But the wise answered, saying, Not so; lest there be not enough for us and you: but go ye rather to them that sell, and buy for yourselves. And while they went to buy, the bridegroom came; and they that were ready went in with him to the marriage: and the door was shut. Afterward came also the other virgins, saying, Lord, Lord, open to us. But he answered and said, Verily I say unto you, I know you not. Watch therefore, for ye know neither the day nor the hour wherein the Son of man cometh.

Cross-references   Doctrine and Covenants 45:56–59; 63:54

This outstanding parable is a culmination of those parables given by the Lord concerning the judgment that would befall mankind prior to entrance into His heavenly kingdom. In the previous parables, Jesus issued warnings to the leaders of Israel and the covenant people as a whole. In the simple parables of the draw net and the watching servants, He gave a general warning to the world. Now that His kingdom had been established on the earth, Jesus also warned its members so that they might not fall into the same pit that Israel had before them. Simply belonging to His church does not ensure residence in His kingdom.[284]

This parable encompasses all of the doctrine taught in the other parables on judgment. The marriage feast and celebration is again used as the analogy, and the invited guests also play a role. The period of delay between the anticipated coming of the Lord and His actual coming is clearly defined, and emphasis is placed on the need for constant personal preparedness. The parable stresses the fact that although judgment can come at many different times during man's sojourn upon the earth, there will eventually be a final consummation of things and a final judgment. Relying upon membership within the covenant is not sufficient, for unless a person has properly prepared himself, he will still be shut out of the kingdom.

This parable was couched in a setting familiar to the Jews. It dealt with the customs and traditions of the marriage ceremony, for "on the evening of the actual marriage, the bride was led from her paternal home to that of her husband."[285] Everyone around would have been in festive array, and as the procession proceeded, they would have risen to salute and honor both the bride and groom.

The parable discloses that in this anxiously waiting group along the route of the procession there awaited ten virgins bearing lamps. "According to Jewish authorities, it was the custom in the East to carry in a bridal procession about ten such lamps . . . since, according to rubric, ten was the number required to be present at any office or ceremony, such as at the benedictions accompanying the marriage-ceremonies."[286] "Even in this number selected by the Lord, it was not accidental, for one of the rules of the law at that period of time was that wherever ten Jews were living in one place there was to be a Synagogue built for worship."[287]

Thus, ten virgins took their lamps and went forth to meet the bridegroom. The bridegroom represented the Son of God, Jesus the Messiah. The virgins represented the "good" members of the Church, those who had been brought within the covenant, who had a pure profession of faith, were guiltless of apostasy before God, and who believe in their hearts that they had the right to be there anticipating the arrival of the bridegroom.[288]

Of the ten virgins, five were classified as foolish and five as wise. All of the virgins possessed lamps and all of them had oil in their lamps. However, five of the virgins had the thoughtfulness to bring extra oil with them, whereas the other five carried no surplus. The lamps they carried indicated that they all belonged to the Church and that they had been sufficiently diligent and obedient to be classified as disciples and members of the Lord's earthly kingdom.[289]

The foolish virgins were not hypocritical, just negligent. They were not thoroughly diligent in all of their preparation, and might be compared to the rocky soil found in the parable of the four soils[290] wherein the seed sprang up and had initial growth, but as the sun grew hot it was scorched. These virgins openly manifested external profession of the gospel, but they lacked the deep commitment exemplified by the good soil.[291]

The wise virgins, on the other hand, realized that more was necessary than just external obedience to the commandments and the casual heeding of occasional good impulses. The oil, both that which was contained in the lamps and the extra oil carried by the wise virgins, represented the personal spiritual preparedness each of the virgins had acquired as she contemplated entrance into the kingdom of God.[292] The oil had been accumulated drop by drop through righteous living and obedience to the commandments.[293]

There now occurred a fateful pause as the bridegroom tarried during the celebration, and the tired virgins slumbered while they waited for him. They had done all that they deemed necessary to be received by the bridegroom, and they did not know how long it would be before he arrived. Perhaps they had heard of his coming for such a long time that the cry of his coming had become meaningless to them, and so they slept.[294]

The tarrying of the bridegroom, like the leaving of the nobleman,[295] represents the space of time allotted before the final judgment. The end of this earthly probation can occur at any moment during one's life, as was evidenced by the parable of the foolish rich man;[296] but eventually a final reckoning will take place when every soul must answer for himself.[297] Ultimately, all must face a final judgment.[298]

The virgins slept until midnight when they were awakened by the cry, "Behold, the bridegroom cometh." The late hour emphasized the unexpectedness of his coming.[299]

The ten virgins arose, trimmed their lamps, and prepared to meet the bridegroom and be admitted to the wedding feast. The wise had sufficient oil to light their way to the marriage, while the foolish discovered that their lamps had gone out and they could not properly meet the bridegroom. They had not complied with the admonition given by Amulek to the people of the Western Hemisphere when he declared: "This life is the time for men to prepare to meet God; yea, behold the day of this life is the day for men to perform their labors. . . . Therefore, I beseech of you that ye do not procrastinate the day of your repentance until the end; for after this day of life, which is given us to prepare for eternity, behold . . . then cometh the night of darkness wherein there can be no labor performed."[a]

It was not lack of perseverance that had brought the five foolish virgins to this state, but the absence of their personal preparedness. Their overt obedience to the Lord's commandments had been the same as that of the five wise virgins; however, their spiritual commitment, the motivation behind their obedience, was found lacking.

The foolish virgins now did what most of us would do in a like situation. They asked the five prepared virgins to share their oil with them. The wise virgins replied in the only way they could; they said no, "lest there be not enough for us and you," and they told the foolish virgins to go and buy more oil from those who sold it.

No unchristian like conduct can be imputed to the five wise virgins for refusing to help their foolish sisters, for that was not the intent or the purpose of the parable. Just the opposite was true. Their refusal

a. Alma 34:32–33.

to share their oil emphasized the proper source of the oil. How can one share his testimony, his willingness to pay tithing, his knowledge, temple work, or any of the other spiritual commitments which must be made in order to properly prepare for the coming of the Savior?[300]

It was already too late for the foolish virgins. They left to find more oil, but while they were gone the bridegroom came, welcomed the prepared virgins into the wedding, and closed the door. Spiritual preparedness cannot be shared at the last minute, nor can a mere request make up for previous unpreparedness. The five foolish virgins returned and knocked on the door, anticipating the mercy of the Lord to allow them entrance. But, as with the improperly clothed guest at the marriage of the king's son, the time had passed for preparation and the Lord refused them entry. Those who thought they were close to the kingdom of God missed it after all.

Tennyson exquisitely captured in poetry the thoughts of the virgins who failed in their preparation when he wrote of Guinevere and her contrition. As her remorse swept over her she requested her attentive maiden to sing, and in that moment she painfully recognized her own lack of preparedness as the maiden sang:

> Late, late, so late! and dark the night and chill! Late, late, so late!
> but we can enter still! Too late, too late, we cannot enter now.
> No light had we; for that we do repent; And learning this the bride-
> groom will relent. Too late, too late! ye cannot enter now.
> No light; so late! and dark and chill the night! O, let us in, that we
> may find the light! Too late, too late: ye cannot enter now.
> Have we not heard the bridegroom is so sweet? O, let us in tho'
> late, to kiss his feet! No, no, too late! ye cannot enter now.[301]

The reward of the wise virgins was obvious, for they were received into the presence of the bridegroom and the kingdom of heaven. It is said of them, "For they that are wise and have received the truth, and have taken the Holy Spirit for their guide, and have not been deceived . . . shall abide the day."[a]

The Lord concludes the parable with this solemn warning: "Watch therefore, for ye know neither the day nor the hour wherein the Son of man cometh." It was a warning that judgment can come on any day—

at any hour—and we are required to be ready, for "that which should have been the work of a life cannot be huddled into a moment."[302]

All of the virgins thought they were properly prepared and would be accepted by the bridegroom. Did not membership in the Church promise such reward? But at that day the delay of His coming may strain even the patience of members of the Church, for none know the hour or the day of His coming. He "cometh as a thief in the night,"[a] and those who await Him may become weary and "sleep."

The five wise virgins slept with peace of mind acquired through a constant "repentant attitude, seeking forgiveness of sins both large and small, and thus coming ever closer to God. For Church members, this is the essence of their preparation—their readiness to meet the Savior when He comes. Any other course will align them with the five foolish virgins in the Master's parable."[303]

a. 1 Thessalonians 5:2.

They Ask of Him a Sign   11

The principles, ordinances, and laws that make up the gospel have been taught throughout the ages to provide a path for the human race to follow back to God's presence. But all this knowledge would be mere rhetoric were it not for the Savior. Man fell forever from God's kingdom through sin, but through the Redeemer he has the opportunity to be saved.

The basis of the Law of Moses and of all the principles, ordinances, and teachings of the gospel, both ancient and modern, is Jesus the Messiah. To help us recognize and accept Him as the Son of God and the Savior of all mankind was the reason why the scriptures were preserved, and the parable of Lazarus and the rich man provides us with one of the most powerful witnesses ever given of His divinity.

Lazarus and the Rich Man

Luke 16:19–31   There was a certain rich man, which was clothed in purple and fine linen, and fared sumptuously every day: and there was a certain beggar named Lazarus, which was laid at his gate, full of sores, and desiring to be fed with the crumbs which fell from the rich man's table: moreover the dogs came and licked his sores. And it came to pass, that the beggar died, and was carried by the angels into Abraham's bosom: the rich man also died, and was buried; and in hell he lift up his eyes, being in torments, and seeth Abraham afar off, and Lazarus in his bosom. And he cried and said, Father Abraham, have mercy on me, and send Lazarus, that he may dip the tip of his finger in water, and cool my tongue; for I am tormented in this flame. But Abraham said, Son, remember that thou in thy lifetime receivedst thy good things, and likewise Lazarus evil things: but now he is comforted, and thou art tormented. And beside all this, between us and you there is a great gulf fixed: so that they which would pass from hence to you cannot; neither can they pass to us, that would come from thence. Then he said, I pray thee therefore, father, that thou wouldest send him to my father's house: for I have five brethren; that he may testify unto them, lest they also come into this place of torment. Abraham saith unto him, They have Moses and the prophets; let them hear them. And he said, Nay, father Abraham: but if one went unto them from the dead, they will repent. And he said unto him, If they hear not Moses and the prophets, neither will they be persuaded, though one rose from the dead.

It is obvious from the scriptures that the Jewish leadership recognized the meaning of the parables of Jesus.[304] But even though they "perceived" that He spoke of them in His parables, they refused to abandon their errors and follow Him. They earnestly looked for their Messiah, but they did not want Jesus to be Him.

This parable was given by the Lord after the parable of the unjust steward[305] wherein Christ enumerated specific instructions and admonitions pertaining to worldly things as related to the kingdom of God. The Pharisees had heard the parable and the admonitions, and "they derided him" because of them.[a] In response to their derision Jesus said, "Ye are they which justify yourselves before men; but God knoweth your hearts: for that which is highly esteemed among men is abomination in the sight of God."[b]

The Pharisees and rulers were the keepers of the Mosaic Law but they used the Law to justify their actions before men, allowed the Law to separate them from the people, and esteemed the praises of men more than the praises of God. They allowed their position and the things of the world to influence their ability to recognize the Messiah. As a result, the Messiah they anticipated was not the one who arrived. They had mistaken the signs and teachings of the Second Coming for those of the first. They were looking for the sign of the coming of the Son of Man, or the Second Coming of the Lord. The reasons for this centered around three specific situations:

The first was political in nature. The Jews had been in bondage for hundreds of years, and it was their belief that the coming Messiah would grant them freedom from this bondage.[306] He would destroy their enemies, rain down judgment and disaster upon the wicked, and punish with death and destruction those who oppressed Israel. However, Jesus offered freedom not of the body, but of the soul. The intent of His coming in the meridian of time was to establish His spiritual

a. Luke 16:14.

b. Luke 16:15.

kingdom, not His earthly one. He did not promise freedom from bondage but freedom from sin.[307]

But the Jews wanted an earthly king, not a spiritual one. This general expectation of both the leaders and the common people of Israel is confirmed by the reaction of the multitude in the miracle of the feeding of the five thousand.[308] In this miracle they wanted to force Jesus to be their king. They wanted His kingdom —but on the earth, not in heaven.

The second reason the Jews missed the Messiah involved the positions the Jewish leaders held. The scribes, Pharisees, and chief priests had developed into a religious ruling class. They had done this in an attempt to preserve the nation for the coming Messiah, but in doing so they had become so imbued with their own self-importance that they would not sacrifice their positions to accept their Savior.

The development of the teachings and doctrines of the Rabbinical Law had, over the centuries, elevated these leaders above the people they wanted to preserve. They denounced the sinner, the publican, the heathen, and the Sabbath breaker; they extolled the teacher, the rabbi, the Law, and the Pharisee. They cringed when Jesus ate with sinners and publicans, mingled with heathens, and offered the kingdom to all nations as He denounced the ruling class as hypocrites and whited sepulchers.[a] To accept Him meant that they must serve rather than be served, they must give rather than receive, and they must glorify Him rather than be glorified by others.[309]

The third reason for missing the Savior evolved naturally from the previous two. It revolved around the things of the world. In the parable of the unjust steward (delivered just before this one), the Lord taught that there was no relationship between earthly things and the kingdom of God. Earthly things were of no eternal importance, and the acquisition of them bore no relationship to the attainment of salvation.

This concept was repugnant to the Pharisees and other leaders of the Jews. To accept Jesus as their Messiah meant denying all they perceived as being important.[310] If they believed in Him, they felt they would lose their leadership positions and the worldly things that they had accumulated; moreover, as a nation they would still be in political

a. Matthew 23:27. bondage.

Still, the teachings of Jesus, His miracles, and His claims to be the Messiah stirred their consciences and led them to earnestly seek from Him a sign. On four recorded occasions they asked Him to prove that He was the Savior:

1. The leaders requested signs of Him after He had performed some of His miracles.[a]

2. Prior to His sermon on the bread of life they asked, "What sign shewest thou then, that we may see, and believe thee?"[b]

3. When the Pharisees and the Sadducees came tempting Him they specifically requested "that he would shew them a sign from heaven."[c]

4. During the healing of the nobleman's son they asked for a sign and Jesus responded, "Except ye see signs and wonders, ye will not believe."[d] The Lord received added insult during His trial when He was sent to Herod, who "hoped to have seen some miracle done by him."[e]

This attitude on the part of the Jews appears to be the reason for the parable of Lazarus and the rich man. It was a culminating parable that specifically pointed out the erroneous concepts of the Pharisees and the rulers of the Jews. It was based on their belief that worldly wealth and attainment guaranteed them the kingdom (because they were the chosen people); further, it foretold the sign they so longed to see. The parable was also given to denounce what the Law had become, to rebuke the Jews' disbelief in Him, and to witness to the world that Jesus was the Messiah.

The first part of the parable was couched in a story that was common in the folklore of Judaism.[311] The two main characters were portrayed as being at opposite ends of the economic spectrum. There was a rich man who was clothed in purple and fine linen (symbolic of his wealth and royal position) who "fared sumptuously every day," meaning that he ate in abundance and only the best.

In opposition to this grandeur and worldly attainment (so highly esteemed by the Pharisees) was the other character of the parable—

a. Matthew 12:38–40; Luke 11:16; John 2:18.

b. John 6:30.

c. Matthew 16:1.

d. John 4:48.

e. Luke 23:8.

Lazarus. Lazarus was a beggar who lay at the rich man's gate. The affluent lifestyle of the rich man contrasted sharply with Lazarus's poverty. The beggar was reduced to eating the crumbs which had fallen from the rich man's table. It was the custom of wealthy Jews to use pieces of bread dipped in water as napkins. The bread was then discarded under the table, and later gathered up to be given to beggars and the poor.[312] With this and other food scraps that came from the rich man's table, Lazarus tried to satisfy his needs. His physical condition was so deplorable that open sores covered his body, and dogs came and licked them.

Eventually both men died. The beggar was carried to Abraham's bosom, but the rich man went to hell. The Lord reversed the positions of Lazarus and the rich man to dramatize the relationship between earthly achievements and the kingdom of heaven. Lazarus was with the great patriarch Abraham, where every Jew longed to go. But the rich man, who had been so successful in acquiring material things on the earth, lifted up his eyes in hell, "being in torments."

The Lord now moved quickly to the next part of the parable. A discussion commenced between the rich man and Abraham. The rich man, realizing that his heavenly anticipations had not been fulfilled, asked Abraham to send Lazarus to comfort him and give him relief. "Send Lazarus," the rich man pleaded, "that he may dip the tip of his finger in water, and cool my tongue; for I am tormented in this flame." This was not Dante's inferno; the rich man was in torment because of the comforts he had lost as a result of his selfish and unrepentant life.

Abraham quickly explained the differences between the two men. During his earthly life, the rich man had selfishly sought and acquired all the good things he wanted. Lazarus had received none of these comforts, but we assume his life was a righteous one for he was allowed to enter into paradise at his death. His lack of accomplishment in the things of the world had not hindered his spiritual progress. The Pharisees would have thought Lazarus's earthly condition was the result of his sins and that he was being punished by God.[313] Lazarus's heavenly achievements would have surprised them, since the situation specifically contradicted their beliefs and practices.

Abraham explained to the rich man that there was a great gulf between him and Lazarus that could not be crossed. Many scholars of the past did not understand what this great gulf was.[314] Fortunately, because of the restoration of the gospel, we are not left in darkness any longer concerning this phenomenon. It was the separation that existed at the time of the parable between paradise (the place where righteous and obedient children of the Father reside after death to await the resurrection) and the spirit prison (the place where disobedient children or those who die without a knowledge of the gospel go to await, perchance, some grace or plan from God that would relieve them of their awful state). That gulf would later be bridged by Jesus as He resided for a short time in the spirit world after His death and before His resurrection.[315]

Having thus been instructed by Abraham, the rich man resigned himself to his own fate. But his conversation with Abraham continued as the Lord commenced teaching the most important doctrine of the parable. The rich man declared that he had five brothers. They were doing the same things that he had done, and he requested that Abraham send Lazarus to them that they might be told what their fate would be if they continued in their earthly ways. Abraham reminded the rich man that his brothers had "Moses and the prophets" to direct their lives.

The parable now reaches its climax. Jesus was instructing the covenant people, rich or poor, that they had had Moses and the prophets to teach them for hundreds of years. The goal of this teaching had remained the same: recognition of the long-awaited Messiah and admission into the kingdom of God. Referencing Moses and the prophets, Jesus witnessed His divinity to the people. He had fulfilled their prophesies. "Search the scriptures," he said; "for in them ye think ye have eternal life: and they are they which testify of me."[a]

But the rich man in the parable wanted more: he wanted a sign. This was the same position the Pharisees were in, and the Lord told them that they had the same resources as the rich man—Moses and the prophets. But they, too, wanted more— they also wanted a sign.

Just as the rich man in the parable pleaded for Lazarus to be sent from the dead to warn his five brothers, the Pharisees wanted a sign from Christ to satisfy both their desire for the Messiah and their

a. John 5:39.

doubts that Jesus was Him. As the parable drew to a close, Abraham informed the rich man that not even if one came from the dead would they (the brothers) change if they would not believe Moses and the prophets. This truth was vividly illustrated by the miracle of the raising of Lazarus, the brother of Mary and Martha.

The Miracle of the Raising of Lazarus[316]

John 11:1–44   Now a certain man was sick, named Lazarus, of Bethany, the town of Mary and her sister Martha. (It was that Mary which anointed the Lord with ointment, and wiped his feet with her hair, whose brother Lazarus was sick.) Therefore his sisters sent unto him, saying, Lord, behold, he whom thou lovest is sick. When Jesus heard that, he said, This sickness is not unto death, but for the glory of God, that the Son of God might be glorified thereby. Now Jesus loved Martha, and her sister, and Lazarus. When he had heard therefore that he was sick, he abode two days still in the same place where he was. Then after that saith he to his disciples, Let us go into Judaea again. His disciples say unto him, Master, the Jews of late sought to stone thee; and goest thou thither again? Jesus answered, Are there not twelve hours in the day? If any man walk in the day, he stumbleth not, because he seeth the light of this world. But if a man walk in the night, he stumbleth, because there is no light in him. These things said he: and after that he saith unto them, Our friend Lazarus sleepeth; but I go, that I may awake him out of sleep. Then said his disciples, Lord, if he sleep, he shall do well. Howbeit Jesus spake of his death: but they thought that he had spoken of taking of rest in sleep. Then said Jesus unto them plainly, Lazarus is dead. And I am glad for your sakes that I was not there, to the intent ye may believe; nevertheless let us go unto him. Then said Thomas, which is called Didymus, unto his fellowdisciples, Let us also go, that we may die with him. Then when Jesus came, he found that he had lain in the grave four days already. Now Bethany was nigh unto Jerusalem, about fifteen furlongs off: and many of the Jews came to Martha and Mary, to comfort them concerning their brother. Then Martha, as soon as she heard that Jesus was coming, went and met him: but Mary sat still in the house. Then said Martha unto Jesus, Lord, if thou hadst been here, my brother had not died. But I know, that even now, whatsoever thou wilt ask of God, God will give it thee. Jesus saith unto her, Thy brother shall rise again. Martha saith unto him, I know that he shall rise again in the resurrection at the last day. Jesus said unto her, I am the resurrection, and the life: he that believeth in me, though he were dead, yet shall he live: and whosoever liveth and believeth in me shall never die. Believest thou this? She saith unto him, Yea, Lord: I believe that thou art the Christ, the Son of God, which should come into the world. And when she had so said, she went her way, and called Mary her sister secretly, saying, The Master is come, and calleth for thee. As soon as she heard that, she arose quickly, and came unto him. Now Jesus was not yet come into the town, but was in that place where Martha met him. The Jews then which were with her in the house, and comforted her, when they saw Mary, that she rose up hastily and went out, followed her, saying, She goeth unto the grave to weep there. Then when Mary was come where Jesus was, and saw him, she fell down at his feet, saying unto him, Lord, if thou hadst been here, my brother had not died. When Jesus therefore saw her weeping, and the Jews also weeping which came with her, he groaned in the spirit, and was troubled, and said, Where have ye laid him? They said unto him, Lord, come and see. Jesus wept. Then said the Jews, Behold how he loved him!

And some of them said, Could not this man, which opened the eyes of the blind, have caused that even this man should not have died? Jesus therefore again groaning in himself cometh to the grave. It was a cave, and a stone lay upon it. Jesus said, Take ye away the stone. Martha, the sister of him that was dead, saith unto him, Lord, by this time he stinketh: for he hath been dead four days. Jesus saith unto her, Said I not unto thee, that, if thou wouldest believe, thou shouldest see the glory of God? Then they took away the stone from the place where the dead was laid. And Jesus lifted up his eyes, and said, Father, I thank thee that thou hast heard me.

And I knew that thou hearest me always: but because of the people which stand by I said it, that they may believe that thou hast sent me. And when he thus had spoken, he cried with a loud voice, Lazarus, come forth.

And he that was dead came forth, bound hand and foot with grave-clothes: and his face was bound about with a napkin. Jesus saith unto them, Loose him, and let him go.

Lazarus was the brother of Mary and Martha and they lived in Bethany. They were close friends with the Lord. When Lazarus became ill, his sisters sent a message to Jesus declaring, "Lord, behold, he whom thou lovest is sick." Jesus received the message and declared that the sickness was not unto death, but that "the Son of God might be glorified thereby." He remained two days where He was and then told His Apostles that He would go again into Judea. They cautioned Him because of the antagonism toward Him there, but Jesus was intent on going. He told them that Lazarus was asleep and He would go and awaken him.

The disciples misunderstood, thinking that the sleep would benefit Lazarus. But Jesus would not have this miracle misunderstood, and He openly declared to them, "Lazarus is dead." They then proceeded back to Bethany and found that Lazarus had been in the grave for four days.

Mary and Martha went separately to Jesus as He approached Bethany. Each voiced her concern that He had not come in time to save Lazarus, and Martha acknowledged that "even now, whatsoever thou wilt ask of God, God will give it thee." Jesus reminded her of who He was and told her that Lazarus would rise again. She acknowledged Christ's words, and agreed that Lazarus would rise in the resurrection. But she misunderstood the Lord's intentions so He openly declared to her, "I am the resurrection, and the life: he that believeth in me, though he were dead, yet shall he live." He asked if she believed this, and she again acknowledged Him as the Messiah.

Mary and Martha were not alone at this time for many of the Jews from Jerusalem and its environs were with the sisters in their hour of grief. The family was well known, and their popularity might have been enhanced by their association with Jesus. Fellow disciples would have given the family comfort, and disbelievers and enemies may have been there in anticipation of Jesus' arrival so that they could again accuse Him. Regardless of their motivation, many people would have been with Mary and Martha, for one of the most binding of the Jewish directives was "to obey the Rabbinic direction of accompanying the dead, so as to show honour to the departed and kindness to the survivors."[317]

The sequence of events that then took place is fundamental to the purpose of both the miracle and the parable. Mary and Martha and the other mourners approached Jesus and the scripture reports that Jesus groaned in the spirit and was troubled. He was undoubtedly affected by the intense sorrow displayed at the physical death of Lazarus. But this was the Savior, He who took upon Himself all sorrows. Isaiah had declared centuries before that He was "a man of sorrows, and acquainted with grief. . . . Surely he hath borne our griefs, and carried our sorrows."[a] But He was also troubled—for even those who believed in Him did not fully understand His power.

Jesus wept, and asked where they had laid Lazarus. This visual show of emotion caused mixed feelings among the crowd. Some assumed that it was due to His grief for Lazarus, and noted how He loved him. Others, with rancor in their hearts, questioned why He had allowed such a friend to die. Jesus wept not only for the genuine sorrow of His friends, but for the disbelief and mockery of His enemies.

Christ arrived at the tomb (a cave with a large stone sealing its entrance) and asked that the stone be removed. Martha's response was logical: "Lord, by this time he stinketh: for he hath been dead four days." She still did not understand what was happening, and Jesus chided her. "Said I not unto thee, that, if thou wouldest believe, thou shouldest see the glory of God?" The stone was rolled away and

Jesus lifted up His eyes and said, "Father, I thank thee that thou hast heard me. And I knew that thou hearest me always: but because of the people which stand by I said it, that they may believe that thou hast sent me."

The crowd was observing all that the Lord did, and they must have been astonished at the opening of the tomb. Christ had twice before openly declared the purpose of this miracle and now, before the entire crowd—friends and enemies alike, He openly declared it again. His enemies had asked Him for a sign many times and He had refused them on each of those occasions. But now He would give them a sign that they could not forget. "Lazarus, come forth," He cried with a loud voice so that all might hear. And Lazarus came forth!

John reports that after this miracle, many of the Jews believed on Christ—and no wonder! But there were others who "went their ways to the Pharisees, and told them what things Jesus had done." These same Pharisees had stood before Jesus as He gave them the parable that declared His divinity; but now they gathered a council, for in their minds the very root of the tree of their authority was endangered. "What do we," they said, "if we let him thus alone, all men will believe on him." Then they revealed the real reason for their concern (and fulfilled the teaching of the parable) when they said, "The Romans shall come and take away both our place and nation."

They were not concerned whether Jesus was or was not the Messiah. They were like the rich man of the parable, concerned only with the things of the world, their existence as a nation, and their personal prominence among the people. Caiaphas stepped forward and unwittingly acknowledged the Messiah's mission when he declared, "It is expedient for us, that one man should die for the people, and that the whole nation perish not."[a] Jesus would die for all, not to save the nation, but to save the souls of all those who would follow Him and live His commandments.

From that moment on Christ's fate was sealed. It was no longer a question of *if* the Jewish leaders would kill Him, but *when* and *how*. Even Lazarus was in jeopardy for John records that after the miracle, many of the Jews counseled that they might put him to death also.[b]

In the parable of Lazarus and the rich man, Abraham told the rich

a. John 11:46–50.

b. John 12:10.

man that if his five brethren would not listen to Moses and the prophets, they would not be persuaded to repent—even if one rose from the dead. The actions of the Jewish leadership after the raising of Lazarus proved that this was true. They made a mockery of the Law and, as prophesied in the parable, they did not believe "though one rose from the dead."

The Jews asked Christ to give them a sign of His Messiahship and He raised Lazarus from the dead in fulfillment of parabolic prophecy; yet they denied this perfect witness. They sought to preserve a nation, but they rejected the very Man who could ensure its deliverance.

As It Was Then, So It Is Today

12

The parables of Jesus were stories of everyday life, teaching tools that encompassed the marvelous truths of the kingdom of heaven. Although only a small portion of Christ's life is detailed in the New Testament Gospels, we know from the parables that He was familiar with every aspect of life, and He used that great knowledge to illustrate His teachings.

As the people stood before Him and listened to His discourses, they heard His verbal claim to the Messiahship. In His miracles they could see the power of His divinity. But in His parables they heard simple stories of life, stories that used everyday activities to teach eternal truths.

They could think about the gospel and their responsibility within it as they sowed in their fields or mixed leaven into their bread. They could relate to the joy of finding treasure, either sought for or inadvertently discovered. And as they tended their sheep or put their money to the exchangers, they could again remember the eternal principles He had taught.

Jesus taught the people of prayer, obedience, forgiveness, and mercy. He taught eternal relationships through the two great commandments. His people were to love and care for each other, to live in the world but not be a part of it, and to give their eternal devotion to God. Their selfish limitations were expanded and their limited vision enlarged. The exactness of the Mosaic Law had helped them determine who their neighbor was; the gospel's second great commandment required them to review in their hearts, "Whose neighbor am I?"

Through talents, pounds, and vineyards the Lord taught account-ability and reward for laboring in the kingdom; He couched warnings in the stories of the foolish rich man and the prayers of the Pharisee and the publican. All this He taught to impress upon the minds of His Father's children that the things of the world bore no relationship to the kingdom of God.

He taught the Jews of their impending judgment, and reminded them that their chosen position was in jeopardy when He said, "Of stones God could raise up children unto Abraham." He compared the rulers of Israel to the husbandmen of a vineyard, and declared that their eventual judgment would be based on how well they tended that vineyard.

Through their ceremony and celebration of marriage, He warned the covenant people that to be invited to the festivities was one thing and to accept the invitation was another, but to eat with the King of heaven required much more.

Henceforth, when fishermen who had heard His parables threw their nets into the sea, drew forth fish, and separated the good from the bad, they would be reminded of the eternal judgment they faced. The solemn warning given to the church was that mere membership, just being under the auspices of the covenant, would not guarantee en-trance into the Lord's kingdom.

Agonized by His verbal claims, His miracles, and His very presence, the Jewish leadership sought a sign from Christ to confirm His Mes-siahship. He would not show His power when they demanded it, but through the parable of Lazarus and the rich man He prophesied of the sign's coming, and finally fulfilled their incessant desire for a sign with the miracle of the raising of Lazarus.

For the most part, the chosen people understood the parables and applied them correctly. Some believed and followed the Savior, seek-ing additional guidance so that they might enter His kingdom. Others openly rejected Him, refusing to give up their social or political posi-tions and the rich things of the world. Ultimately, the Jewish leaders gathered together and discussed how they might entrap Him in His words and destroy Him.

The parables had specific meaning for the Jews of Christ's time, yet their impact has extended forward, applying not only to our day but to the future as well. Although times have changed, the stories were so simply and beautifully given that it requires little imagination to apply the principles encased within them.

The impact of the parables in our day is the same as in days of old. Some people hear the Savior's voice and accept of His knowledge and love, striving to be lifted up to the Father's kingdom. But others disbelieve and reject the Lord's principles, sometimes seeking additional ways to destroy Him. The Carpenter from Nazareth tried in many ways to teach the gospel, and His powerful message is clearly portrayed in the parables of Jesus the Messiah.

Notes

1. Life p. 5, 327.
2. See note 32.
3. Bruce p. viii.
4. The determination of which of the teachings of Jesus should be classified as parables has varied throughout the years depending on how strictly the word parable is defined. As few as twenty-seven (Siegfried Goebel, The Parables of Jesus, 1883, p. 3) or as many as fifty-three (A. Julicher, Die Gleichnisreden Jesu, 1910, p. 15) or even sixty-five (Francis L. Filas, The Parables of Jesus, 1959) have been so determined.
5. Farrar 1:325.
6. Bible Dictionary, "Parables."
7. Geikie 2:144.
8. Dodd p. 4; Ed 1:580.
9. Trench p. 4; EB, myth.
10. JC p. 298; EB, fable.
11. Trench p. 4; EB, proverb.
12. JC p. 299; Trench p. 5; EB, allegory.
13. JC p. 298.
14. JC p. 296; Ed 1:580; Barclay pp. 9–11.
15. Ed 1:581.
16. Geikie 2:145.
17. Chapter 2.
18. Life p. 323.
19. Further proof of the leadership's understanding is evidenced by the Synoptics' report that the leaders held councils against the Lord (Matthew 12:14), watched him (Luke 20:20), tried to catch Him in His words (Mark 12:13), and contrived arguments against His claim (Matthew 12:24).
20. Chapter 10.
21. Chapter 10.
22. Bruce p. 310.
23. PM p. 511.
24. Geikie 2:146.
25. JC p. 297.
26. Ed 1:584.
27. Dodd p. 161.
28. Ed 1:145.
29. Ed 2:55.
30. Ed 1:544; Trench p. 13; Bruce p. ix, 313; Filas p. 4.
31. Life p. 5, 327.
32. The church of the Middle Ages interpreted the parables allegorically; every word, person, event, and detail of the parables had a secret inner meaning. One example is Augustine's interpretation of the parable of the Good Samaritan: "A certain man went down from Jerusalem to Jericho: Adam himself is meant; Jerusalem is the heavenly city of peace, from whose blessedness Adam fell; Jericho means the moon, and signifies our mortality, because it is born, waxes, wanes, and dies. Thieves are the devil and his angels. Who stripped him, namely, of his immortality; and beat him, by persuading him to sin; and left him half-dead, because in so far as man can understand and know God, he lives, but in so far as he is wasted and oppressed by sin, he is dead; he is therefore called half-dead. The priest and Levite who saw him and passed by, signify the priesthood and ministry of the Old Testament, which could profit nothing for salvation. Samaritan means Guardian, and therefore the Lord Himself is signified by this name. The binding of the wounds is the restraint of sin. Oil is the comfort of good hope; wine the exhortation to work with fervent spirit. The beast is the flesh in which He deigned to come to us. The being set upon the beast is belief in the incarnation of Christ. The inn is the Church, where travellers returning to their heavenly country are refreshed after pilgrimage. The morrow is after the resurrection of the Lord. The two pence are either the two precepts of love, or the promise of this life and of that which is to come. The innkeeper is the Apostle (Paul). The supererogatory payment is either his counsel of celibacy, or the fact that he worked with his own hands lest he should be a burden to any of the weaker brethren when the Gospel was new, though it was lawful for him 'to live by the Gospel. (Quaestiones Evangeliorum, II. 19—slightly abridged.)" (As quoted in Dodd pp. 1–2.) Clearly erroneous, this concept was cast aside as the Reformists developed their own methods of interpretation which also led to embellishment by the teacher or translator. (Jeremias p. 89.)
33. JC p. 286.
34. Trench p. 15.
35. It is most unlikely that Jesus actually delivered seven or eight parables on this singular occasion. It is more likely that Matthew simply chose to record the seven parables together, that he might deliver them to the saints for their edification. Farrar p. 323.
36. In an effort to counter the effect of the many miracles of Jesus, the leadership of the Jews accused Him of performing them by the power of Beelzebub, the prince of devils. This argument undoubtedly had a damaging effect upon the people's belief in Christ, for it gave them an alternative to believe in. For further detail see Miracles, Chapter 3.
37. Ed 1:586–87.
38. DNTC 1:288.
39. HC 2:266.
40. Trench p. 31.

41. Buttrick p. 46.

42. Trench p. 31.

43. Life p. 330.

44. MM 2:252.

45. DNTC 1:288.

46. DNTC 1:289.

47. Dodd p. 148.

48. Ed 1:590.

49. For example: the pearl of great price, the lost coin, the sower, the ten virgins, the great supper, labourers in the vineyard.

50. Jeremias p. 101.

51. DNTC 1:296.

52. TPJS pp. 97–98; DNTC 1:296–97.

53. Trench p. 35; Ed 1:589.

54. HC 2:181–200, HC (Index) Apostles.

55. Trench p. 36.

56. MM 2:257.

57. JC p. 287.

58. MM 2:258–59.

59. TPJS p. 101.

60. MF p. 303.

61. JC p. 290.

62. Ed 1:592.

63. Jeremias p. 147.

64. Ed 1:592.

65. DNTC 1:298.

66. JC p. 291.

67. TPJS pp. 98–99.

68. Ed 1:594.

69. JC p. 291.

70. DNTC 1:299.

71. HC 5:207.

72. HC 2:270.

73. Ed 1:588.

74. DNTC 1:292.

75. Life p. 420.

76. Ed 1:595–96.

77. Jeremias p. 198.

78. JC p. 293.

79. MM 2:265.

80. Life p. 389.

81. An interesting modern application was made of this parable by Joseph Smith. He applied it to the gathering of the Church. He said, "See the Church of the Latter-day Saints, selling all that they have, and gathering themselves together unto a place that they may purchase for an inheritance, that they may be together and bear each other's afflictions in the day of calamity" (HC 2:272).

82. Chapter 2, notes 14, 15.

83. Trench p. 49.

84. MM 2:264.

85. JC p. 294.

86. Joseph Smith applied the parable to the early members of the Church as follows: "The Saints again work after this example. See men traveling to find places for Zion and her stakes or remnants, who, when they find the place for Zion, or the pearl of great price, straightway sell that they have, and buy it." (HC 2:272.)

87. Geikie 2:328.

88. Trench p. 133.

89. JC p. 454–55.

90. Trench p. 133.

91. JC p. 455.

92. HC 5:261–62.

93. MM 3:246.

94. Ed 2:256.

95. JC p. 456.

96. JC p. 456.

97. Ed 2:257.

98. When Joseph Smith was asked his opinion of the parable of the prodigal son, he stated: "The Elders of this Church have preached largely upon it, without having any rule of interpretation." He continued and asked the question, "What is the rule of interpretation? Just no interpretation at all. Understand it precisely as it reads." (HC 5:261.)

99. Trench p. 143.

100. MF p. 307.

101. JC p. 461.

102. MF p. 307.

103. Smith, p. 21.

104. DNTC 1:510–12.

105. Bruce p. 158.

106. JC p. 436.

107. Bruce p. 159.

108. JC p. 436.

109. DNTC 1:542.

110. Ed 2:285.

111. DNTC 1:542.

112. Trench p. 178.

113. Life p. 104.

114. This parable was used by the Lord to admonish the persecuted Saints in the early history of the restored church. During the Missouri period the persecutions were unusually severe, ending with the Saints' expulsion from Missouri under the extermination order of Governor Boggs (HC 3:175, 426). These Saints, called the "children of Zion" by the Lord, were likened to the "parable of the woman and the unjust judge." After quoting the parable, the Lord admonished the Saints to petition all forms of government for the deserved redress, with the comforting conclusion that if the seats of government did not heed them then the Lord would "arise and come forth out of his hiding place, and in his fury vex the nation." (D&C 101:81–94.)

115. Ed 2:240.

116. Ed JSL pp. 47–49; Ed 2:240.

117. JC p. 435.

118. Ed 2:241.

119. JC p. 435.

120. Farrar p. 453.

121. An interesting experience in the history of the Church also illustrates this need for continuous righteous petitioning. During the Missouri persecutions, Joseph Smith was commanded by the Lord to organize companies of the members to go to Missouri for the redemption of Zion. The Lord admonished Joseph and the early brethren to pray earnestly and seek diligently to obtain His will. The Lord desired five hundred men to go up to redeem Zion but recognized that man would not always do His will. He therefore admonished them to seek for three hundred, or no less than one hundred (D&C 103). By this order Zion's Camp was organized for the redemption of Zion (HC 2:61–83).

122. Geikie 2:296.

123. Life p. 147.

124. Life p. 575.

125. Life p. 377.

126. Life p. 414.

127. Life p. 48.

128. Geikie 2:384.

129. JC p. 532; Ed 2:422.

130. Geikie 2:384.

131. MF pp. 95–96.

132. Ed 1:564.

133. JC p. 261.

134. Ed 1:564.

135. Bruce pp. 238–39.

136. Ed 1:564.

137. Trench p. 104.

138. JC p. 263; Ed 1:563.

139. Ed 1:563.

140. Ed 1:561.

141. A similar recording was given of the two cleansings of the temple: one at the beginning of Christ's ministry (John 2:13–25), and one at its close (Matthew 21:12–13; Life p. 374.)

142. JC p. 262.

143. Life p. 245.

144. Chapter 4.

145. Bruce p. 401.

146. Trench p. 55.

147. Trench p. 55.

148. DNTC 1:429.

149. JC p. 394.

150. Josephus records that Archelaus received tribute from Perea, Galilee, Idumea, Judea, Samaria, and certain cities including Jerusalem: the annual sum was six hundred talents. (Antiquities, Book XVII, XI, 4) Although the sum may vary depending on the talent used to calculate it, it was not the intent of the parable to declare an exact amount due, but to convey the reality of such an enormous amount that repayment was hopeless.

151. Ed 2:293.

152. JC p. 395.

153. Ed 2:296.

154. FPM pp. 193–94.

155. MF p. 59.

156. MF p. 269.

157. Ed 2:306.

158. JC p. 469.

159. Bruce p. 170.

160. Geikie 2:339.

161. JC p. 470.

162. JC p. 470.

163. Central to Luke's theme on the uses and abuses of worldly wealth, in addition to this parable, are the parables of the prodigal son and Lazarus and the rich man. In addition, he records the discussion between Jesus and the rich young ruler (Luke 18:18–25; Matthew 19:16–29; Mark 10:17–30). Luke continues this theme connecting the parables of the unjust steward and Lazarus and the rich man with additional verses on worldly possessions (Luke 16:10–16). Although these topics are sequential in Luke Chapter 16, they are widely dispersed in Matthew. Luke 16:10 is only referred to in Matthew 25:21 in association with the reward of the parable of the talents; verses 11 and 12 have no parallel in the Gospels; verse 13 appears in Matthew 6:24. In verses 14 and 15 the Lord applied the teachings of the parable to the Pharisees; the only comparable reference is His comment in Matthew 23:14 on "devour[ing] widows' houses," a reference, it would seem, to their greediness. Verse 16 appears in Matthew 11:12–13; verse 17 in Matthew 5:18; and verse 18 in Matthew 5:32.

164. Geikie 2:333.

165. Ed 2:339; Life p. 252.

166. Farrar 2:125.

167. Ed 2:266.

168. Trench p. 154.

169. JC p. 464.

170. JC p. 463.

171. Jeremias p. 182.

172. DNTC 1:513.

173. JC p. 464.

174. Chapter 5.

175. Geikie 2:318.

176. Life p. 70.

177. Ed 2:303–4.

178. DNTC 1:500.

179. Ed 2:234; Trench p. 109. The scriptures record several examples of questions being posed to Jesus, with both good and evil intentions. Mark reports that upon one occasion, the Pharisees and Herodians specifically sent people to the Savior to "catch him in his words"

(Mark 12:13). Luke reports that after a particularly strong denunciation of the rulers of the Jews, the scribes and Pharisees again began to "urge him vehemently, and to provoke him to speak many things: lying wait for him and seeking to catch something out of his mouth, that they might accuse him" (Luke 11:53–54). Luke, in the Good Samaritan parable, does not impute the antagonism to the questioner as specifically noted in the other examples. (Matthew and Mark report a similar instance, perhaps the same as that of Luke, but without the parable (Mark 12:28–34; Matthew 22:35–40). It could therefore be concluded that the phrase tempting him could properly mean "to make trial of," or that he would "make proof of" the skill of Jesus. (Trench p. 109.) An example of this type of meaning is found in Genesis, where God "tempts" Abraham in the story of the proposed sacrifice of Isaac (Genesis 22:1). God did not "tempt" Abraham in the evil sense of the word; but put him to proof, trying his faith by the means described in the story. James, in the New Testament, supports this interpretation, assuming the successful overcoming of the trial, when he states, "Blessed is the man that endureth temptation: for when he is tried, he shall receive the crown of life" (James 1:12).

180. JC p. 430. Perhaps we should be grateful to the lawyer for the question, since it elicited such a memorable response.

181. Ed 2:234–35.

182. Barnett pp. 79–80.

183. Ed 2:237.

184. JC pp. 430–31.

185. Ed 2:239.

186. Ed 2:237.

187. Ed 2:238.

188. Jeremias p. 204; Geikie 2:295.

189. Trench p. 111.

190. Trench p. 114.

191. Ed 2:239; DNTC 1:471.

192. Jeremias p. 63.

193. The parables of the pounds and the labourers in the vineyard.

194. Life p. 262.

195. Life p. 275.

196. MF pp. 100–101.

197. Trench p. 93.

198. Ed 2:459; Bruce p. 210.

199. JC pp. 583–84; Ed 2:463.

200. Bruce p. 205.

201. JC p. 583.

202. JC pp. 582–83.

203. HC 2:24; MF pp. 100–101.

204. Ed 2:464.

205. Ed 2:466.

206. Geikie 2:366; Josephus, Antiquities XVII, IX, 1; XVII, XI, 2.

207. DNTC 1:573.

208. Ed 2:466.

209. Trench p. 186.

210. JC pp. 509–10.

211. DNTC 1:572.

212. Mission, p. 138.

213. DNTC 1:573.

214. JC p. 510.

215. JC p. 509.

216. DNTC 1:572.

217. DNTC 1:571; JC p. 508.

218. Geikie 2:357.

219. JC p. 482.

220. Ed 2:416.

221. Ed 2:417–18.

222. DNTC 1:561; Trench p. 65.

223. Ed 2:416.

224. Trench p. 63.

225. Farrar p. 504, as quoted in MM 3:307.

226. Farrar 2:164.

227. Bruce R. McConkie, A New Witness for the Articles of Faith (Salt Lake City: Deseret Book, 1985), pp. 149—51; Philippians 2:12; 2 Nephi 10:24; 25:25; 3 Nephi 27:19; Moses 1:6; TG, Grace.

228. The introduction in Luke 12:1 is unique to Luke, but the last part of verse 1 is found in Matthew 16:6, 12 and Mark 8:15. Verses 2–9 of Luke associate with Matthew 10:26–33 and verse 9 also relates to Mark 8:38, verse 10 to Matthew 12:32 and Mark 3:29, verse 12 to Matthew 10:19–20 and Mark 13:11. Verses 13–21 cover the parable discussed, which is unique to Luke. Verses 22–34 appear in Matthew as part of the Sermon on the Mount compares to Luke 6:25–30, 19–21. Verses 35–59 relate to Matthew 24:43–51; 10:34–36; 16:2–3; 5:25–26.

229. Ed 2:243.

230. Ed 2:243.

231. JC p. 439.

232. Trench p. 118.

233. JC p. 439.

234. MF p. 140.

235. Jeremias p. 165.

236. JC p. 440.

237. Ed 2:245.

238. Farrar 1:463.

239. JC p. 472.

240. JC p. 472.

241. Geikie 2:346.

242. Ed Temple p. 338.

243. Ed 1:311–13; 2:290–91.

244. Jeremias p. 143.

245. DNTC 1:543.

246. JC p. 473.

247. This was because the nation as a whole had given

itself up in anticipation of a political Messiah who would free them from their earthly problems. Geikie 2:167.

248. Ed 2:247.

249. Trench p. 123.

250. Ed 2:247.

251. DNTC 1:477.

252. Matthew records that Jesus delivered the parable of the two sons first (Chapter 5) and then gave this parable. Mark and Luke record that He taught the parable directly after the discussion on John's authority, leaving out the parable of the two sons.

253. DNTC 1:593; The Second Coming of Jesus the Messiah.

254. JC p. 535.

255. MM 3:361.

256. DNTC 1:593; JC p. 534.

257. Ed 2:423–24.

258. MM 3:361.

259. Bruce p. 453.

260. Farrar 2:223–24.

261. Life p. 77.

262. Life p. 249.

263. Ed 2:249.

264. JC p. 538.

265. JC p. 451; DNTC 1:501.

266. JC p. 452.

267. Trench p. 129.

268. Ed 2:250.

269. JC p. 452; Ed 2:251.

270. Geikie 2:323.

271. The parable of the Pharisee and publican, Chapter 9.

272. Ed 2:425–26.

273. DNTC 1:598.

274. JC p. 540.

275. This relationship is used many times in New Testament teachings (drawing upon the Old Testament for examples). All of the children of Israel that went out of Egypt were called, but not all were chosen to enter the promised land (1 Corinthians 10:1–10; Hebrews 3:7–19). Other examples might include that of the spies from the children of Israel who were originally sent into the promised land to spy it out for occupation; of them, only Caleb and Joshua were chosen to actually enter therein (Numbers 13–14). Of the twenty-two thousand assembled by Gideon to repel the army of the Midianites, God chose only three hundred to perform the task (Judges 7).

276. Geikie 2:390.

277. Ed 2:195 et seq; 248.

278. Trench p. 52.

279. MM 2:266.

280. JC p. 295.

281. MF pp. 304–5.

282. Joseph Smith summarized the parable in this manner: "For the work of this pattern, behold the seed of Joseph, spreading forth the Gospel net upon the face of the earth, gathering of every kind, that the good may be saved in vessels prepared for that purpose, and the angels will take care of the bad. So shall it be at the end of the world—the angels shall come forth and sever the wicked from among the just, and cast them into the furnace of fire, and there shall be wailing and gnashing of teeth." (HC 2:272.)

283. SC p. 198.

284. JC p. 576; MF p. 366.

285. Ed 1:354.

286. Ed 2:455.

287. Trench p. 85.

288. JC p. 579; FPM p. 253.

289. FPM p. 253–54.

290. The parable of the sower, Chapter 2.

291. JC p. 579.

292. JC p. 579.

293. FPM p. 256.

294. FPM p. 254.

295. Life p. 261.

296. Life p. 275.

297. JC p. 579.

298. SC p. 240.

299. Ed 2:457.

300. FPM p. 256.

301. Tennyson pp. 228–29.

302. Trench p. 90.

303. MF p. 366; SC p. 155.

304. Chapter 1.

305. Chapter 6.

306. Ed 1:168–79.

307. Life p. 5, 115;

308. Life p. 17.

309. Ed 1:167, 308–35.

310. Ed 2:275–77.

311. Jeremias p. 182.

312. Jeremias p. 184.

313. Jeremias p. 185.

314. This phrase (the great gulf) has perplexed interpreters and scholars of the past, leaving them to declare openly that they did not know its meaning (Trench p. 168); or that it meant God's judgment was irrevocable (Jeremias p. 186).

315. Jesus did not personally go to the prison, for those that were there could not abide His presence. But He opened the way that others from paradise might pass over and teach the gospel to those in the prison that perchance they might, through diligence, repentance, and the grace of God, extricate themselves from that awful condition (D&C 138; Life p. 640).

316. Life p. 115.

317. Ed 2:317.

THE SERMONS OF JESUS THE MESSIAH

Introduction

The sermon (or discourse) was the principal means by which Jesus taught the "good news" of His new gospel. He emphasized His teachings through the power of His miracles and exemplified them with His parables; but His predominant method of teaching remained the sermon.

When we think of the sermons of Jesus we should not envision a formally prepared speech delivered in a traditional setting; rather, Jesus extemporaneously used the circumstances in which He found Himself to deliver His messages. He did not confine Himself to particular places or fixed times. Although He addressed the people in the temple and in the synagogue, more often He was found teaching on the hillside, the lakeshore, in the streets and marketplaces, in private homes, or as He walked from place to place with the disciples, the curious, and His ever–present enemies who were constantly watching Him. He was ready to teach whenever and wherever people were ready to listen.

This Book discusses thirty–five sermons. The name of each sermon is taken from the body of the sermon or from a common historical title. While they are not discussed in historical order, at times the historical setting is very important when interpreting them. However, the classification of the sermons is my own and I used the doctrinal teachings of the discourses to determine their classification.

Because the sermons are presented doctrinally rather than historically, there is no need to reconcile discrepancies in the scriptural texts except where they are obvious. Scriptural discrepancies do not discredit the authenticity of the record since each writer was clearly selective in what he chose to record and how he chose to record it.

The discourses introduced the kingdom of God, gave gospel instructions, answered questions, and declared Jesus as the Messiah. They were given to friends, strangers, disciples, the curious, enemies, and the Apostles. Many were given as a result of controversies between Jesus and the rulers of the Jews. Jesus presented them regularly throughout His ministry, commencing with His longest, the Sermon on the Mount, and concluding with those private discussions delivered to the Apostles prior to His arrest and crucifixion. His enemies questioned His competence as a teacher; Jesus responded by questioning their competence as listeners.

Christ's miracles caused astonishment. They made His followers wonder and caused His enemies to question. His parables animated His teachings, bringing to life His new gospel through everyday events. But in His sermons, the Master Teacher declared and explained His Messianic claim and expounded the doctrines of the kingdom of God. He shaped the illustrations of His discourses into sermons that would become indelibly fixed in the memories of those who heard them and testified to all who looked for and anticipated the Messiah that He had come.

Sermons   1

The Sermons of Jesus were more like conversations than lectures. Of course, there were times when He delivered them in the formal atmosphere of the temple[a] or synagogue,[b] but often they were merely informal conversations, frequently interrupted by questions from friends and enemies. Jesus would often pass over the question and substitute a great moral lesson for the direct answer, thereby making it difficult for His audience to disassociate the question asked from the principle He wanted to teach. Thus, He stressed the value of both the sermon and the question.[1]

Discussing the sermons is not the same as discussing the parables[2] or the miracles.[3] The problems created by these different modes of instruction, however, are very similar, and centered around the basic conflict between Jesus and the synagogue throughout His entire ministry. But perhaps it went even deeper. It stemmed from Jesus' claim to be the long–awaited Messiah; but He was not the Messiah the Jews anticipated. The Jews knew they were the chosen people, knew they were living the Law God had given them, and did not believe they were in doctrinal error. Perhaps they therefore felt they had no need for a Savior.[4]

In their distorted view of the Messianic expectation, the Jews earnestly awaited the kingdom of God and the promised Messiah. But they no longer looked for the spiritual kingdom offered by Christ. The kingdom they expected was based on worldly, material things. They wanted meat and drink and wilderness–banquets—not manna. They wanted all the earthly delights, "not to speak of the fabulous Messianic

a. John 7:14.

b. Matthew 4:23.

banquet which a sensuous realism expected."[5] Jesus fulfilled the very Law the Jews used to reject Him, a Law "the Pharisees had refined . . . into a microscopic casuistry which prescribed for every isolated act."[6]

Their expectations of the Messiah had advanced beyond all logical reality:

> The fruit–trees were every day, or at least every week or two, to yield their riches, the fields their harvest; the grain was to stand like palm trees, and to be reaped and winnowed without labour. Similar blessings were to visit the vine; ordinary trees would bear like fruit trees, and every produce, of every clime, would be found in Palestine in such abundance and luxuriance as only the wildest imagination could conceive.[7]

Jesus openly published His Messianic claim and carefully taught the requirements of His new kingdom through His discourses. Many believed,[a] but His candid claims and explanations also caused many to follow Him no more.[b] To the believers He promised life eternal, but the disbelievers were told, ". . . where I am, thither ye cannot come."[c]

The Lord used parables to illustrate the principles He taught and made the miraculous commonplace in Israel. Yet because of the course of their religious experience, the Jews generally (and the leadership specifically) found it all but impossible to believe in Him. Their rejection of Jesus was not a spur–of–the–moment frenzy, but "the outcome and direct result of their whole previous religious development."[8] Through Isaiah, the Lord declared that He knew they were an "obstinate" people; therefore, He declared things before they came to pass so that when they came to pass, the people would not attribute them to their idols.[d] They had constantly resisted the Lord's prophets, believed in false prophets, and hardened their hearts. And in Jeremiah the Lord concluded, "my people love to have it so."[e] They would not believe because they "loved the praise of men more than the praise of God."[f][9]

In His teaching, Jesus used illustrations of almost every scene and object familiar to the Israelites of His day. He spoke of flowers, fields, budding trees, and the red of the lowering sky; of sunrise and sunset, wind and rain and stars, and lamps lighted in both home and

a. John 7:31.
b. John 6:66.
c. John 7:34.
d. Isaiah 48:5.
e. Jeremiah 5:31.
f. John 12:43.

temple. He used many examples of food, comparing the word of God to bread, salt, eggs, wine, water, fish, corn, and oil—things used in the Jews' everyday meals, banquets, ceremonies, and sacrifices. He was obviously familiar with the simple things of life and used them to teach the Jews about the kingdom of heaven. He participated in life's joys and sympathized with its sorrows. Although He was rejected time and time again and accused of all types of evil, He continued to teach the gospel and offer it to all who would listen to His words.

The Lord declined all outward honor and flattery. He walked among all types of men, from the despised Samaritan and the outcast leper to the rulers of the synagogues and the temple. He dined with both rabbi and publican, and He gave His precious time to heathen and chosen alike. His life was destined to influence all men's lives, yet in His ministry He was rejected by those who looked for Him in all they did, those whom He sought to save.

From our limited record of Christ's life, it is evident that His sermons were His most common method of teaching.[10] He used the spoken word, coupled with illustrations from life, to persuade the conscience and influence the will of those who heard Him. Christ's miracles are very exciting, and His parables are alive with comparisons and interpretive possibilities. But the discourses are like a one–on–one conversation with the Lord Himself.

The Sermon on the Mount
Matthew 5, 6, and 7

Cross–references   See Appendix: Topical Index to the Sermon on the Mount

There are four recordings of the Sermon on the Mount. Matthew is the source used in this chapter. Luke records the subjects of the sermon in various chapters, but not as a complete text.[11] In addition to these Bible references, the Book of Mormon records that the Lord delivered a slightly expanded version of the same discourse to the Nephites when He appeared on the Western Hemisphere after His resurrection. However, the most extensive and comprehensive version of the discourse is found in the Joseph Smith Translation of the Bible.[12] Although some of the changes made by Joseph (the first prophet of this dispensation) were insignificant, a careful reading indicates that almost every verse was touched by his inspired mind.

As recorded by Matthew, the Sermon on the Mount appears to be out of historical sequence. It would seem that a group of miracles and events which Matthew later recorded actually preceded the Sermon, and that one important event, the call and ordination of the Twelve Apostles (not recorded at all by Matthew but referred to in Chapter 10), definitely occurred before to its delivery.[13]

Jesus' fame had already spread prior to this discourse for He had performed many miracles and had taught throughout all Galilee, "teaching in their synagogues, and preaching the gospel of the kingdom."[a] Undoubtedly it was from these people, gathered from the densely populated shores of Galilee and from the environs of Jerusalem, Tyre, Sidon, and other parts of Decapolis, that the multitude had gathered to hear the Lord.

Luke verifies that the Savior called His Apostles before He gave this discourse. He also records that prior to this sermon, Jesus went "out into a mountain to pray, and continued all night in prayer to God."[b] After concluding His prayer, Jesus called His disciples to Him and from them He selected twelve men whom He called as His Apostles.[c] After enumerating the names of the Twelve, Luke records that Jesus "came down and stood in the plain," and there (in the company of additional disciples, the Twelve, and "a great multitude of people") He delivered the discourse known as the Sermon on the Mount.

Luke adds that once the Lord had chosen the Twelve and had returned to the multitude, He healed their diseases.[d] The Spirit abounded in their presence and they "sought to touch him: for there went virtue out of him, and healed them all."[e] It was probably the supernatural power of the Lord that brought the multitude together in the first place, and He rewarded them with His miracles. Then He delivered the longest of His recorded discourses.[14]

Matthew indicates that this discourse was delivered on a mount whereas Luke reports that its setting was on a plain. We can imagine that the sequence of events occurred as follows: The evening before the delivery of the sermon, Jesus went up to the mountain by Himself and petitioned His Father in Heaven concerning the call of the Twelve Apostles. As the morning dawned He joined His waiting disciples, who had undoubtedly tarried as they anticipated His return. After choosing the Twelve, He descended further down the mount into a natural amphitheater where the multitude patiently awaited Him.[15]

Although the Lord had delivered previous discourses, Matthew uses the Sermon on the Mount as the commencement of Christ's ministry. Consequently, the sermon may be one of the most accurately recorded events in the ministry of Jesus, and perhaps He used it to officially inaugurate His new kingdom among the Jews. Before them now stood the Messiah, whom the children of Israel had long awaited. But the Messiah the Jews had looked for and the kingdom of God they had anticipated were not embodied in the discourse Jesus taught that day.[16]

a. Matthew 4:23–24.

b. Luke 6:12.

c. Luke 6:13.

d. Luke 6:17.

e. Luke 6:19.

The Old Testament Jehovah instituted the Mosaic Law from the desolation of Mount Sinai with thunder and lightning while the Israelites stood in wondering awe. The Law was given as a teaching tool and as a schoolmaster to prepare those waiting for the Messiah to recognize Him and believe in Him when He came. Now, in contrast to Sinai, the incarnate Jehovah stood on the green hillside slopes above the beautiful Sea of Galilee and inaugurated His kingdom for His chosen people. He did not abrogate the old Law;[17] the Law and teachings of the Old Testament had been but a precursor of things to come.

Jesus warned the Israelites that He came not to abolish the Law but to obey and fulfill it. The threats and the fear of God demanded by the old Law required obedience through explicit rules of conduct, but not the strict letter of the law taught by the rabbis. While obedience to God's commandments is required, the new gospel would emphasize mercy (the love of God) and understanding (the reason for obedience). This was not the strict Levitical adherence to the letter of the Law, "but was rather a surrender of the heart and will."[18]

The Lord's sermon contrasted His new gospel with the apostasy of the Levitical Jewishness of His day.[19] Under the Pharisees and the scribes, the chosen people were constantly striving and laboring toward the goal of entrance into God's kingdom. They accomplished this by obeying a Law which described in minute detail the duties of their mortal life.[20] But the new law went much further, requiring a far greater spiritual commitment.[21]

The Sermon on the Mount portrays man's righteous relationship to God, to sin, to temptation, and to salvation.[22] It describes the entrance into a new life. Paul would later describe it as putting "off concerning the former conversation the old man, which is corrupt according to the deceitful lusts; and be renewed in the spirit of your mind; and that ye put on the new man, which after God is created in righteousness and true holiness."[a]

The Sermon

The kingdom of heaven was the basic text of the Sermon on the Mount. Through this sermon the Lord taught the means for reaching the kingdom and defined the glories of its citizens.[23] The sermon clearly exemplified that Christ came to found a kingdom and not a

a. Ephesians
4:22–24.

school. Its concepts contrasted sharply with the prevailing law, and detailed how counterfeit the old Law was in its moral and religious aspects. The new law emphasized sincerity of action as opposed to merely the profession of duty,[24] and Jesus was the perfect example of this concept. The sermon contained no mention of rabbis or of the requirement of circumcision (the sign of the old Law), and it confirmed that the evidence of the new law was righteousness and love.[25]

> The teaching of [the Jewish] Scribes was narrow, dogmatic, material; it was cold in manner, frivolous in matter, second–hand . . . with no freshness . . . no force, no fire; servile to all authority, opposed to all independence; at once erudite and foolish, at once contemptuous and mean; never passing a hair's breadth beyond the carefully–watched boundary line of commentary and precedent . . . elevating mere memory above genius, and repetition above originality; concerned only about Priests and Pharisees, in Temple and synagogue, or school, or Sanhedrin, and mostly occupied with things infinitely little. It was not indeed wholly devoid of moral significance, nor is it impossible to find here and there, among the debris of it, a noble thought; but it was occupied a thousandfold more with Levitical minutiae about mint, and anise, and cummin, and the length of fringes, and the breadth of phylacteries, and the washing of cups and platters, and the particular quarter of a second when new moons and Sabbath–days began. But this teaching of Jesus [the Sermon on the Mount] was wholly different in its character, and as much grander as the temple of the morning sky under which it was uttered was grander than stifling synagogue or crowded school.[26]

Jesus approached the multitude, sat upon the ground (a customary method of teaching at that time), and "opened his mouth" to speak.[27] From that time forward His followers would never return to the lifelessness of rabbinism.

The Beatitudes

The teachings of this discourse applied not only to the Twelve but also to anyone who wished to be a true disciple of Christ. This seems to be confirmed by the additions Joseph Smith was inspired to make in his introduction to the discourse:

IV Matthew 5:3–4   Blessed are they who shall believe on me; and again, more blessed are they who shall believe on your words, when ye shall testify that ye have seen me and that I am. Yea, blessed are they who shall believe on your words, and come down into the depth of humility, and be baptized in my name; for they shall be visited with fire and the Holy Ghost, and shall receive a remission of their sins.

Following this introduction, the Lord commenced His discourse with what has become known as the "Beatitudes." Through the Beatitudes He openly contrasted His new kingdom with that of the old[28] and described the felicity of the kingdom independent of the outward conditions of temporal happiness. The individual Beatitudes enumerate and define blessed conditions of mankind. They each contain a recompense plus a reward for the suffering they describe; yet they are presented in a simple and unambiguous manner.[29]

Matthew 5:3   Blessed are the poor in spirit: for theirs is the kingdom of heaven.

These are the rightful heirs of the kingdom of heaven,[30] those who overcome evil and are determined to live God's commandments regardless of life's circumstances. They do not automatically gain the kingdom just because they are poor, however, as Joseph Smith's inspired version of the scriptures clarifies. Even poor Saints must accept Jesus by obeying His laws, teachings, and ordinances before they can be heirs in the kingdom of heaven.[a][31]

Matthew 5:4   Blessed are they that mourn: for they shall be comforted.

Even though grief and sorrow are expressed in this life, mourning in and of itself does not bring comfort. Comfort is received through the assurance Christ has given us that we will once again be able to associate with our loved ones in the eternities. As Paul said, "If in this life only we have hope in Christ, we are of all men most miserable."[b] Assurance of divine comfort in this life comes from faithfully living the principles and ordinances of the gospel. Then the promise of the

a. IV Matthew 5:5;
   3 Nephi 12:3.

b. 1 Corinthians
   15:19.

Comforter, the Holy Ghost, will intercede for those that mourn, "and God shall wipe away all tears from their eyes."[a]

Matthew 5:5   Blessed are the meek: for they shall inherit the earth.

The meek are those who are righteous and live the celestial law.[32] They are willing to suffer injury rather than jeopardize their souls in contention.[33] They are promised that they will inherit the earth[b] and obtain mercy from the Lord.[c]

Matthew 5:6   Blessed are they which hunger and thirst after righteousness: for they shall be filled.

Again, Joseph Smith's inspired translation adds a significant conclusion to this promise. It states that those who hunger and thirst after righteousness shall be filled "with the Holy Ghost."[d] This assumes that the individual is hungering and thirsting after the righteousness of the kingdom of God. If so, the Lord promises that the Holy Ghost will fill them with the Spirit in rich abundance[34]—a significant addition to compliment those who mourn.

Matthew 5:7   Blessed are the merciful: for they shall obtain mercy.

This is a specific promise; however, later in His ministry the Lord elaborated on this principle by giving the parable of the unmerciful servant [35] which taught that if we expect God to show mercy toward us, we are required to show mercy toward our fellowman.

Matthew 5:8   Blessed are the pure in heart: for they shall see God.

The pure in heart are those who have forsaken their sins and have come to an understanding of, and received a testimony of, the divinity of Christ. Having lived His commandments, they will ultimately be admitted into the presence of God.[e][36]

Matthew 5:9   Blessed are the peacemakers: for they shall be called the children of God.

There is no doubt that there is great merit in saving yourself and

a. Revelation 7:17.

b. D&C 88:17.

c. D&C 97:2.

d. IV Matthew 5:8.

e. D&C 93:1.

your fellowman from worldly strife, and certainly those who accomplish this feat can be numbered among the children of God.[37] But there is a greater peace that can be obtained through the gospel, for the very work of righteousness is peace "and the effect of righteousness quietness and assurance for ever."[a] Isaiah further points out that there is no true peace for the wicked.[b] Paul declared that "the peace of God, which passeth all understanding, shall keep your hearts and minds through Christ Jesus."[c]

Before His crucifixion Jesus said to the Twelve, "Peace I leave with you, my peace I give unto you: not as the world giveth, give I unto you. Let not your heart be troubled, neither let it be afraid."[d] Having overcome the world, Jesus again declared to His Apostles that in this world they would have tribulation, and "in me ye might have peace."[e] The gospel of Jesus Christ is a gospel of peace, the inner peace that comes from knowing the way to eternal life and knowing you are valiantly involved in obtaining it. This peace can come to anyone in their search for, and adherence to, the requirements of the kingdom of God.

Matthew 5:10 Blessed are they which are persecuted for righteousness' sake: for theirs is the kingdom of heaven.

Matthew states that the persecuted are blessed when they are persecuted for righteousness' sake; but again, Joseph Smith declared that they are blessed for being persecuted for "my [the Lord's] name's sake."[f] It appears that this is the fate the faithful will inherit: having forsaken the world and having come unto Christ, they are to suffer oppression.[38] Paul confirmed this teaching in his second letter to Timothy when he declared, "Yea, and all that will live godly in Christ Jesus shall suffer persecution."[g] The Lord emphasized this point in His sermon, seemingly anticipating the suffering that would be associated with true discipleship. He knew that true disciples would be reviled and falsely accused of evil, but He told them to rejoice and be exceedingly glad, "for so persecuted they the prophets which were before you."

The Beatitudes promised great blessings, but they held no attraction for the insincere and worldly. They portrayed the kingdom in a manner that would repel all but the earnest and devoted searchers of the truth: the chaff was being fanned from the wheat. The discourse compelled

a. Isaiah 32:17.

b. Isaiah 48:22.

c. Philippians 4:7.

d. John 14:27.

e. John 16:33.

f. IV Matthew 5:12.

g. 2 Timothy 3:12.

the true believer to distinguish between the earthly realization of blessings and the blessings to be realized beyond the grave—between mere earthly pleasure and eternal happiness.[39]

Luke follows his rendition of the Beatitudes with a series of "woes," woes that will befall those who accept earthly conciliation over eternal rewards. His woes provide an explicit contrast between the old Law and the new.[40]

Luke 6:24 But woe unto you that are rich! for ye have received your consolation.

The first woe was a warning to the rich, who not only made the acquisition of worldly wealth their primary goal but believed wealth came as a result of their righteousness. If they counted their reward in earthly possessions, the Lord stated that they had received their "consolation."

Luke 6:25 Woe unto you that are full! for ye shall hunger.

To those who felt that their riches and/or the Law of Moses filled their needs (causing them to look no further), Jesus said they would "hunger" because of their rejection of the gospel. His comment was reminiscent of the prophecy of Amos wherein he declared, "the days come, saith the Lord God, that I will send a famine in the land, not a famine of bread, nor a thirst for water, but of hearing the words of the Lord."[a]

Luke 6:25 continued Woe unto you that laugh now! for ye shall mourn and weep.

To those who felt secure in their own righteousness under the Law of Moses and laughed or scoffed at those who they considered sinners or at Christ's message, He warned of impending mourning and weeping. In the Book of Mormon, Nephi warned that there would be many who would say, "Eat, drink, and be merry, for tomorrow we die; and it shall be well with us." And others will Satan "pacify, and lull them away into carnal security, that they will say: All is well in Zion; yea, Zion prospereth, all is well—and thus the devil cheateth their souls, and leadeth them away carefully down to hell."[b]

a. Amos 8:11.

b. 2 Nephi 28:7, 21.

Luke 6:26 Woe unto you, when all men shall speak well of you! for so did their fathers to the false prophets.

Last, Luke recorded Christ's warning to all those who sought only the praise of their fellowmen and basked in their deceiving flattery. To these the Lord declared, "for so did their fathers to the false prophets," thereby denoting their eventual destruction.

The Beatitudes and woes concluded the Lord's introductory phase of the sermon and opened the gates of the kingdom to all who would enter. They condemned the corrupt religious teachers of His day, not only because the teachers had contaminated and changed the Law, but because their subtle casuistry and immoral additions to it had led men astray along their evil paths. Jesus strenuously opposed the idea "that strict observance of the traditions and commands of their schools in itself satisfied the requirements of God. . . . The 'hedge' round the Law had proved one of thorns, for Rabbis and people alike."[41] This was the old Israel which, because of the rabbis, had sunk to a painful observance of only the letter of the Law. The new Israel would not be characterized by the thunderings of Sinai. The Lord's disciples were not to look for a Messiah of great political strength who would take the yoke from their necks, take vengeance upon their enemies, and reign in earthly splendor. Rather, they were to await a sweeter manna than the wilderness had known and eagerly anticipate the riches of poverty, the royalty of meekness, the greatness of sorrow and persecution, and all the attributes of godliness embodied in patience, humility, gentleness, and a pure love of their fellowman.

The Disciples Admonished

Having completed His introduction to the kingdom of God, Jesus turned specifically to the Apostles and with the multitude listening in, instructed them in their responsibilities in the ministry. Only the Apostles had been specifically called to serve, yet additional disciples, after developing a testimony of the gospel and the Lord's kingdom, would assume other duties as they were added to the ministry.

The next four verses of the sermon draw a series of quick comparisons. The responsibility to which the comparisons relate is implicit, yet they emphasize the fact that all disciples of Jesus must extend the Lord's teachings to those who have not yet heard them.[42]

Matthew 5:13 Ye are the salt of the earth: but if the salt have lost his savour, wherewith shall it be salted? it is thenceforth good for nothing, but to be cast out, and to be trodden under foot of men.

Jesus first compared the disciples to salt, the great preservative cleanser of His day—they were to be the "salt" of the earth. To the Jews, salt specifically symbolized fidelity and hospitality: it was an evidence of their covenant with the Lord and it was used in every meat offering under the Law.[a] The salt had to be pure; no additives or mixtures of any kind were allowed. Any object which adulterated the salt caused it to lose its savor or cleansing power.

The disciples would lose their savor if they became fainthearted or slothful or if they broke the commandments. Such an occurrence would cause the disciples to become adulterated and, if unrepentant, to lose their worth to the kingdom of God. They would thenceforth be "good for nothing but to be cast out and trodden under foot of men."

Matthew 5:14–15 Ye are the light of the world. A city that is set on an hill cannot be hid. Neither do men light a candle, and put it under a bushel, but on a candlestick; and it giveth light unto all that are in the house.

Jesus described His disciples as the "light of the world." He expected them to be perfect examples of righteousness[43] and by their words, as well as their teachings, to declare the gospel to all people.[44] The Lord enumerated two examples to emphasize this point: a city on a hill that could not be hidden, and the light of a candle that should not be hidden under a bushel.

The Lord concluded these two instructions by admonishing, "Let your light so shine before men, that they may see your good works, and glorify your Father which is in heaven."[b] Perhaps with this in mind, Paul admonished the Philippian Saints that "those things, which ye have both learned, and received, and heard, and seen in me, do."[c]

The Law of Moses Compared

Matthew 5:17–20 Think not that I am come to destroy the law, or the prophets: I am not come to destroy, but to fulfil. For verily I say unto you, Till heaven and earth pass, one jot or one tittle shall in no wise pass from the law, till all be fulfilled. Whosoever therefore shall break one of these least commandments, and shall teach men so, he shall be called the least in the kingdom of heaven: but whosoever shall do and

a. Leviticus 2:13; Numbers 18:19; 2 Chronicles 13:5.

b. Matthew 5:16.

c. Philippians 4:9.

teach them, the same shall be called great in the kingdom of heaven. For I say unto you, That except your righteousness shall exceed the righteousness of the scribes and Pharisees, ye shall in no case enter into the kingdom of heaven.

Jesus emphasized the continuity between the Law of Moses and the new gospel He was promulgating by declaring He had not come to destroy the Law but to fulfill it. Although no destruction of the old Law would occur, the new gospel eliminated the mundane parts of the Law that the Jews so meticulously adhered to. The Messiah's gospel did not cast away the sacred truths of the Law, but rather enlarged upon them and clarified them. The Law of Moses had been a schoolmaster: its rites and ceremonies had provided the simple people of previous ages with the material symbols they needed to cling to.[45] It was, as it were, the childhood stage of a religion that Jesus would now bring to maturity.

Paul used a like comparison when writing to the Corinthian Saints. He chided them for not progressing and for still needing to be fed with "milk, and not with meat."[a] He stated, "When I was a child, I spake as a child, I understood as a child, I thought as a child: but when I became a man, I put away childish things."[b]

The Law had been a sacred, moral command from Sinai—an apparatus to teach God's requirements to the children of Israel. The ancient prophets had drawn pure and exalted concepts from it, often anticipating the teachings of Christ yet to come. But the Law had been given for only one purpose, which Paul clearly stated to the Galatians: "Wherefore the law was our schoolmaster to bring us unto Christ."[c] Jesus had respect for the Law of Moses for He was not only the giver of the Law, but the fulfillment of it. He condemned its corruption by the religious leaders and teachers of His day, and warned the disciples that their "righteousness [should] exceed the righteousness of the . . . Pharisees." The Lord now decisively demonstrated the superiority of the gospel over the Law of Moses. He proceeded to contrast the two laws—at the same time criticizing the Pharisaic abuses implemented by tradition and literalism. He did not enumerate every facet of the Law, yet step by step in the examples He used He went from the outward observance (indicated by the traditions of the elders) to the higher concepts taught by the gospel.

a. 1 Corinthians 3:2.

b. 1 Corinthians 13:11.

c. Galatians 3:24.

Matthew 5:21–26   Ye have heard that it was said by them of old time, Thou shalt not kill; and whosoever shall kill shall be in danger of the judgment: but I say unto you, That whosoever is angry with his brother without a cause shall be in danger of the judgment: and whosoever shall say to his brother, Raca, shall be in danger of the council: but whosoever shall say, Thou fool, shall be in danger of hell fire. Therefore if thou bring thy gift to the altar, and there rememberest that thy brother hath ought against thee; leave there thy gift before the altar, and go thy way; first be reconciled to thy brother, and then come and offer thy gift. Agree with thine adversary quickly, whiles thou art in the way with him; lest at any time the adversary deliver thee to the judge, and the judge deliver thee to the officer, and thou be cast into prison. Verily I say unto thee, Thou shalt by no means come out thence, till thou hast paid the uttermost farthing.

Murder

The sin of murder was condemned under both the Law of Moses and the gospel, but according to the traditions of the elders, the guilty person was not only in danger of the judgment of God but also, in some cases, the Sanhedrin. The subtle change in this penalty caused the Jews to fear the Sanhedrin's punishment more than God's.[46] Thus, the literalism of the Law had narrowed the concept of the crime for which a man could be punished.

The gospel, on the other hand, not only condemned the act of murder itself, but also the intent or passion that led to the act.[47] Thus, even feelings of anger with one's fellowman were unacceptable. Not only was the hand that struck the blow censured, but also the heart that hated and precipitated the blow.

There was no approval for unholy and contemptuous feelings or for any language that conveyed improper sentiments toward another person. Matthew leaves the impression that only anger expressed "without a cause" was sinful; however, Joseph Smith omitted these words, leading to the conclusion that in no instance is one justified in showing anger toward another.[48]

The Lord emphasized this principle by giving an example that the Jews would have readily understood. Part of their daily lives—indeed their very existence—involved the procedure of presenting gifts at the altar of God; but the new law permitted no one to present a gift to God if he was at odds with any one of his fellowmen; if he did so, he would be under the influence of the adversary.

Adultery

Matthew 5:27–30   Ye have heard that it was said by them of old time, Thou shalt not commit adultery: but I say unto you, That whosoever looketh on a woman to lust after her hath committed adultery with her already in his heart. And if thy right eye offend thee, pluck it out, and cast it from thee: for it is profitable for thee that one of thy members should perish, and not that thy whole body should be cast into hell. And if thy right hand offend thee, cut it off, and cast it from thee: for it is profitable for thee that one of thy members should perish, and not that thy whole body should be cast into hell.

Adultery was the second example the Lord used to compare the old Law with the new. As with murder, both laws prohibited it; but now the spirit of the law would extend to the conception of the act rather than just the act itself—so much so that it was better to be blind than to look lustfully upon another, or to be maimed than to abuse the law of chastity. Thus, an unclean glance was a virtual commission of the transgression, one which required the offender to mortify himself symbolically rather than allow guilty thoughts to imperil his soul. In this specific manner, the Lord instructed the chosen people and those who would be His disciples that sin originated in the heart (or mind), and that no self–restraint was too great an effort when spiritual salvation was endangered.

Divorce

Matthew 5:31–32   It hath been said, Whosoever shall put away his wife, let him give her a writing of divorcement: but I say unto you, That whosoever shall put away his wife, saving for the cause of fornication, causeth her to commit adultery: and whosoever shall marry her that is divorced committeth adultery.

Because of the liberal divorce laws the Pharisees practiced, the Lord unsparingly condemned them. The Pharisaic law of divorce was so shamefully loose that "if any one see a woman handsomer than his wife, he may dismiss his wife and marry that woman."[49] Other reasons for divorce included a woman's going out in public without having shrouded her face with a veil, and a husband's general displeasure with his wife's behavior. Some maintained that if the wife had cooked the food badly, or over–salted or over–roasted it, or even if the wife became grievously ill, it was grounds for divorce.[50]

Divorce had become so scandalous among the Jews that "even to their heathen neighbours . . . the Rabbis were fain to boast of it as a privilege granted to Israel, but not to other nations!"[51] The Lord swept aside these frivolous and sinful reasonings and declared that only for the sin of infidelity could one justify divorce.

Jesus later reiterated this same principle, as recorded in Matthew 19:9, and even His disciples, recognizing how strictly He applied this law, questioned the Savior concerning it. Jesus acknowledged the difficulty that this law imposed but emphasized that it was possible to comply with it.

Although the Church today recognizes civil divorce and cancellation of temple sealings, it strenuously teaches the sanctity of the marriage covenant and stresses that neither marriage nor divorce should be entered into lightly.

Oaths

Matthew 5:33–37   Again, ye have heard that it hath been said by them of old time, Thou shalt not forswear thyself, but shalt perform unto the Lord thine oaths: but I say unto you, Swear not at all; neither by heaven; for it is God's throne: nor by the earth; for it is his footstool: neither by Jerusalem; for it is the city of the great King. Neither shalt thou swear by thy head, because thou canst not make one hair white or black. But let your communication be, Yea, yea; Nay, nay: for whatsoever is more than these cometh of evil.

The Jews indulged themselves in the taking of endless oaths by which they conducted not only business relationships, but also family affairs. They swore by the sun and the temple, Jerusalem, the prophets, and their own heads. The taking of oaths had reached such a refined state that under certain conditions even perjury was sanctioned.[52] But now the Lord cautioned them in all their communications, advocating moderation in speech and forbidding the use of profanity and oaths.[53] He pointed out that the simple truth was sufficient and an oath could neither enhance nor detract from it.[54]

Retaliation

Matthew 5:38–48   Ye have heard that it hath been said, An eye for an eye, and a tooth for a tooth: but I say unto you, That ye resist not evil: but whosoever shall smite thee on thy right cheek, turn to him the other also. And if any man will sue thee at the law, and take away thy coat, let him have thy cloak also. And whosoever shall compel thee to go a mile, go with him twain. Give to him that asketh thee, and from him that would borrow of thee turn not thou away.

Ye have heard that it hath been said, Thou shalt love thy neighbour, and hate thine enemy. But I say unto you, Love your enemies, bless them that curse you, do good to them that hate you, and pray for them which despitefully use you, and persecute you; that ye may be the children of your Father which is in heaven: for he maketh his sun to rise on the evil and on the good, and sendeth rain on the just and on the unjust. For if ye love them which love you, what reward have ye? do not even the publicans the same? And if ye salute your brethren only, what do ye more than others? do not even the publicans so? Be ye therefore perfect, even as your Father which is in heaven is perfect.

The Lord now turned His attention to the vengeful part of the Law of Moses wherein so much emphasis had been placed upon the doctrine of "an eye for an eye" that the second great commandment had been practically eliminated. The enjoyment of life and the desire for unbroken prosperity caused the Jews to interpret God's tolerance of their vengeful ancestors to mean that they themselves were justified in seeking, by any means, an abundance of worldly comforts and continuous success in all their undertakings so as to be triumphant and victorious over their enemies.[55] But under the higher law, Jesus made it clear that there were no grounds for this self–righteous justification for retaliation, thus placing the second great commandment in its proper position.

The gospel would now require its disciples to suffer persecution without resistance rather than do evil to any man (although they still had the right to self–protection).[56] Love was now to replace fear and the true disciple was to avoid contention.[57] Patience and meekness were to replace retaliation—righteousness would conquer sin. The Lord followed this command with examples: if a person smites us on the cheek, we should turn to him the other also; if a person sues us at the law and takes our coat, we should give our cloak also.[58] If someone compels us to go a mile, we should go two.[59] The Lord then concluded with the requirement that we should give to him that borrows and not turn him away.

After receiving these examples, the disciples could no longer hate their enemies and feel justified. The Lord admonished them to love their enemies, bless those who cursed them, do good to those who hated them, and pray for those who despitefully used and persecuted them. By so doing, the disciples would become children of the Father.

It is true that in Moses' time retaliation was acceptable before God under certain circumstances, but the Pharisees and Sadducees had corrupted the Law and had made hasty retaliation the rule of the day. Individual rights superseded the rights of others, and deliberate revenge was the usual practice rather than compassion. The Jews had forgotten the law of "love thy neighbor,"[a] and taught that it was a duty to hate the heathen and the Samaritan. Eventually, the Pharisees hated the publicans, and the rabbis hated the priests, and the Pharisees and Sadducees hated the common people because they did not know the Law.[60] So pervasive was this doctrine of retaliation that it invaded their personal lives—to the extent that each could have his own private enemies and could hate and injure them with total justification of the Law. This doctrine sharply divided the nation into classes, and excluded all other people as heathens.[61]

The Lord swept away this abrogation of the second great commandment by stating: "For if ye love them which love you, what reward have ye?" The Old Testament often commended kindness and mercy,[b] and it also sanctioned revenge and triumph over the fall of an enemy;[c] but the Lord introduced a new era by teaching the concept of universal love without distinction of any kind. He would later elaborate on this principle in the parable of the Good Samaritan where He taught that we should be a neighbor to all who are in need of help.[62]

The Lord concluded this portion of His discourse with a sweeping commandment: "Be ye therefore perfect, even as your Father which is in heaven is perfect." Jesus was commanding all men to be perfect in doing God's will while on the earth, just as He had required Abraham to be perfect when He inaugurated His covenant with him.[d] True, some elements of perfection (for example, the resurrection and glorification of the body) would be left until a later time, but in this life the Lord's chosen people were to obey all the commandments. Jesus had outlined the way to perfection, and He expected the disciples to follow it.

Citizenship Requirements for Christ's New Kingdom

At this point in His discourse, Christ's comparisons of the old and the new law strongly criticized the Pharisaic traditions of His day; and His subsequent teachings would carry this criticism much deeper into the ancient Jewish law. In the following four examples, He specifically

a. Leviticus 19:18.

b. Exodus 23:4, 5; Psalm 7:5; Proverbs 24:17; 25:21; Job 31:29–30.

c. Psalms 7:6, 54:7.

d. Genesis 17:1.

outlined the requirements of citizenship in His "new" kingdom and taught the disciples that the spiritual reasoning for obedience to the Law was more important than the mere temporal observance of it.[63]

Almsgiving

Matthew 6:1–4   Take heed that ye do not your alms before men, to be seen of them: otherwise ye have no reward of your Father which is in heaven. Therefore when thou doest thine alms, do not sound a trumpet before thee, as the hypocrites do in the synagogues and in the streets, that they may have glory of men. Verily I say unto you, They have their reward. But when thou doest alms, let not thy left hand know what thy right hand doeth: that thine alms may be in secret: and thy Father which seeth in secret himself shall reward thee openly.

In this section, Jesus first noted what almsgiving had become, then He explained what it should be. Alms (or acts of charity toward one's fellowman) were not to be given in order to receive the praises of men; therefore, giving was not automatically meritorious before God. He denounced ostentatious and hypocritical displays of "charity" concluding that if alms were given in this manner, the giver had already received his reward.[64] The test in almsgiving was not the amount given (the amount was inconsequential in spiritual terms), but the degree of sincerity which prompted the almsgiver. Alms should be given in secret with no thought of reward.

Prayer

Matthew 6:5–13   And when thou prayest, thou shalt not be as the hypocrites are: for they love to pray standing in the synagogues and in the corners of the streets, that they may be seen of men. Verily I say unto you, They have their reward. But thou, when thou prayest, enter into thy closet, and when thou hast shut thy door, pray to thy Father which is in secret; and thy Father which seeth in secret shall reward thee openly. But when ye pray, use not vain repetitions, as the heathen do: for they think that they shall be heard for their much speaking. Be not ye therefore like unto them: for your Father knoweth what things ye have need of, before ye ask him. After this manner therefore pray ye: Our Father which art in heaven, Hallowed be thy name. Thy kingdom come. Thy will be done in earth, as it is in heaven. Give us this day our daily bread. And forgive us our debts, as we forgive our debtors. And lead us not into temptation, but deliver us from evil: For thine is the kingdom, and the power, and the glory, for ever. Amen.

Jesus next moved to the topic of prayer. The practice of daily prayer had become formal and mechanical in Judah at Christ's time. The Jews had specifically defined both the hours for praying and the manner in which one prayed. In many instances the Jews used memorized prayers. Many prayed in the streets clothed in their broad phylacteries, while others prayed in the synagogues, making merit out of the duration of their prayers.[65] For Jesus' disciples such hypocritical prayers—often wordy and filled with illustrations and repetitions—were forbidden. If the heart is found wanting, prayer is a mere form and a worthless parade.[66]

In this discourse, Jesus provided a pattern of prayer for His disciples and the world which has come to be known as the Lord's Prayer. Through it He instructed us how to pray and what to pray for. We commence our prayers by addressing the Father, thus subjecting our will to His.

The Lord recognizes our need for daily sustenance, so He instructed us to pray for it—as Amulek put it, to pray over our flocks and our fields and all things that we require for our livelihood upon the earth.[a]

Jesus next directed attention to our need for God's mercy. Joseph Smith again expressed that need more clearly than does the same passage in the King James Version. His translation states, "And forgive us our trespasses, as we forgive those who trespass against us."[b] In this statement, Jesus defined two relationships pertaining to sin (trespasses): first, our relationship with our Father in Heaven (wherein He requires us to completely rely upon Him to gain forgiveness of our transgressions); and second, our relationship with our fellowman (defined later in the Lord's parable of the unmerciful servant).[67] The Lord clearly taught us in His sample prayer that our being forgiven was dependent upon the forgiveness we extended to our fellowman.

In Matthew it states that we should not be led into temptation, but Joseph Smith clarified this even further by stating, "and suffer us not to be led into temptation,"[c] again emphasizing our reliance upon the Father to deliver us from all evil (for God would never lead us into temptation). Paul taught this reliance when he declared, "There hath no temptation taken you but such as is common to man: but God is faithful, who will not suffer you to be tempted above that ye are able; but will with the temptation also make a way to escape, that ye may be able to bear it."[d] That way to escape, at least as applied to the example before us, is prayer.

a. Alma 34:20–25.

b. IV Matthew 6:13.

c. IV Matthew 6:14.

d. 1 Corinthians 10:13.

The Lord closed His sample prayer by glorifying the Father forever. We in turn are admonished to do all things in the name of Jesus Christ,[a] and thus we close our prayers in that manner. Then the Lord again reiterated the importance of forgiving our fellowmen their trespasses if we expect God to forgive us: "For if ye forgive men their trespasses, your heavenly Father will also forgive you: But if ye forgive not men their trespasses, neither will your Father forgive your trespasses."[b]

Although the Lord provided a form and a model to teach us how we can express our thoughts to our Father in Heaven, the teaching emphasis was not on the form but on the underlying purpose of prayer. We should not use prayer as a means for acquiring the praise of other men. The Lord gave it to us as a method of opening our hearts to God and receiving wisdom and help from Him. Again, Christ stressed the spirit rather than the outward observance of the Law.

Fasting

Matthew 6:16–18   Moreover when ye fast, be not, as the hypocrites, of a sad countenance: for they disfigure their faces, that they may appear unto men to fast. Verily I say unto you, They have their reward. But thou, when thou fastest, anoint thine head, and wash thy face; that thou appear not unto men to fast, but unto thy Father which is in secret: and thy Father, which seeth in secret, shall reward thee openly.

Moses commanded the people to fast only on the Day of Atonement,[c68] but the Pharisees had added many other days. "When fasting, they strewed their heads with ashes, and neither washed nor anointed themselves nor trimmed their beards, but put on wretched clothing, and showed themselves in all the outward signs of mourning and sadness used for the dead."[69] In this manner, they sought the applause and recognition of others and also the credit or gain they supposed would come to them as a result of their outward showing of godliness; but all such pretense was unnecessary and pretentious to Jesus.

Fasting, as the Lord taught, was not to be a public virtue but a private self-denial—anything else was hypocrisy.

a. Moses 5:8.

b. Matthew
   6:14–15.

c. Leviticus
   16:29.

Worldly Wealth and Needs

Matthew 6:19–34   Lay not up for yourselves treasures upon earth, where moth and rust doth corrupt, and where thieves break through and steal: but lay up for yourselves treasures in heaven, where neither moth nor rust doth corrupt, and where thieves do not break through nor steal: for where your treasure is, there will your heart be also. The light of the body is the eye: if therefore thine eye be single, thy whole body shall be full of light. But if thine eye be evil, thy whole body shall be full of darkness. If therefore the light that is in thee be darkness, how great is that darkness!

No man can serve two masters: for either he will hate the one, and love the other; or else he will hold to the one, and despise the other. Ye cannot serve God and mammon. Therefore I say unto you, Take no thought for your life, what ye shall eat, or what ye shall drink; nor yet for your body, what ye shall put on. Is not the life more than meat, and the body than raiment? Behold the fowls of the air: for they sow not, neither do they reap, nor gather into barns; yet your heavenly Father feedeth them. Are ye not much better than they? Which of you by taking thought can add one cubit unto his stature? And why take ye thought for raiment? Consider the lilies of the field, how they grow; they toil not, neither do they spin: and yet I say unto you, That even Solomon in all his glory was not arrayed like one of these. Wherefore, if God so clothe the grass of the field, which to day is, and to morrow is cast into the oven, shall he not much more clothe you, O ye of little faith? Therefore take no thought, saying, What shall we eat? or, What shall we drink? or, Wherewithal shall we be clothed? (For after all these things do the Gentiles seek:) for your heavenly Father knoweth that ye have need of all these things. But seek ye first the kingdom of God, and his righteousness; and all these things shall be added unto you. Take therefore no thought for the morrow: for the morrow shall take thought for the things of itself. Sufficient unto the day is the evil thereof.

Although Jesus had already contrasted the riches of the world with spiritual wealth, He concluded this portion of His discourse by emphasizing the transitory nature of worldly wealth when compared with the riches of eternity.[70] He stated that we cannot serve two masters at the same time, and that where our desires are, there will our true treasure be. The things of the world must be subservient to the things of heaven.

Jesus declared that God knows our needs. He illustrated this by citing examples of the fowls of the heaven and the lilies of the field, proclaiming that all of Solomon's glory was not comparable to these. The Lord stated that man should take no thought for the needs of this earth life; the disciples responded by murmuring among themselves as this was a very difficult law for them to obey. They tried to excuse their disobedience of it because they sincerely felt they needed worldly things.[a] Jesus acknowledged this need, but stated that His Father in Heaven already knew the things they required. It is not that we should disregard the need to provide for ourselves in this life, but that we should not put these concerns before the things of God.

a. JST Matthew 6:36.

Joseph Smith added, "Wherefore, seek not the things of this world but seek ye first to build up the kingdom of God, and to establish his righteousness, and all these things shall be added unto you."[a]

As the Lord's sermon drew to a close, He again gave the disciples and the multitude a list of instructions and warnings regarding their duty toward their fellowman. He began with instructions on how to judge.

Judgment

Matthew 7:1–5 Judge not, that ye be not judged. For with what judgment ye judge, ye shall be judged: and with what measure ye mete, it shall be measured to you again. And why beholdest thou the mote that is in thy brother's eye, but considerest not the beam that is in thine own eye? Or how wilt thou say to thy brother, Let me pull out the mote out of thine eye; and, behold, a beam is in thine own eye? Thou hypocrite, first cast out the beam out of thine own eye; and then shalt thou see clearly to cast out the mote out of thy brother's eye.

This subject is recorded in verses 1 through 9 of Joseph Smith's inspired translation of Matthew 7, and it differs significantly from the same passage in the King James Version. The latter records that we should not judge lest we be judged, while the Joseph Smith version declares that we should not judge "unrighteously," but "judge righteous judgment." With this in mind, the example of the mote and beam that Jesus gave takes on more meaning, for He gave it as a warning for us to take note of our own spiritual condition when we feel inclined to judge others.[b]

After giving this example, Jesus specifically instructed the disciples to admonish the Jewish leadership (the Pharisees, priests, Levites, and scribes) that "they teach in their synagogues, but do not observe the law, nor the commandments; and all have gone out of the way, and are under sin."[c] Jesus specifically instructed the disciples to call these leaders to repentance, declaring that the kingdom of heaven had come unto them.

This counsel is also applicable in our day. Judgment often takes place—and the Lord's admonition remains in effect. We should judge cautiously, for the Lord highly disapproved of prejudiced or unsupported judgments. If we apply this counsel to the Lord's admonitions on charity and mercy, we can conclude that if we make errors of judg-

a. IV Matthew 6:38.

b. IV Matthew 7:1–9.

c. IV Matthew 7:6.

ment, we should make them on the side of mercy. The Lord clearly warned the disciples (and all who heard His voice) that their own house must be in order before they could judge the house of another.

What to Teach

Matthew 7:6–8   Give not that which is holy unto the dogs, neither cast ye your pearls before swine, lest they trample them under their feet, and turn again and rend you. Ask, and it shall be given you; seek, and ye shall find; knock, and it shall be opened unto you: for every one that asketh receiveth; and he that seeketh findeth; and to him that knocketh it shall be opened.

After discussing how His disciples should call the chosen people to repentance (particularly their leadership), the Lord informed them which doctrines of the kingdom they should teach. He did not outline a specific program of instruction, but He did warn them not to teach the "mysteries" of the kingdom. The Apostles were yet young in the ministry and the Lord cautioned them that "the world [could not] receive that which [they themselves were] not able to bear." If they taught these "mysteries," it would be like casting pearls before swine, which would only cause problems for the new kingdom. If they taught doctrines without understanding, the Lord warned them that those they were teaching would "turn again and rend [them]." Jesus wanted those who heard His doctrine to verify its truthfulness by asking God. By so doing, He promised them they would discover that the kingdom of God had, in fact, already come to them.

Acceptance of the Kingdom

Matthew 7:9–14   Or what man is there of you, whom if his son ask bread, will he give him a stone? Or if he ask a fish, will he give him a serpent? If ye then, being evil, know how to give good gifts unto your children, how much more shall your Father which is in heaven give good things to them that ask him? Therefore all things whatsoever ye would that men should do to you, do ye even so to them: for this is the law and the prophets. Enter ye in at the strait gate: for wide is the gate, and broad is the way, that leadeth to destruction, and many there be which go in thereat: because strait is the gate, and narrow is the way, which leadeth unto life, and few there be that find it.

The disciples asked Christ to help them prepare to answer the questions they expected to receive from the Jewish leadership as they went forth to teach them His doctrine. "They will say unto us," the disciples explained, "We ourselves are righteous, and need not that any man should teach us. . . . We have the law for our salvation, and that is sufficient for us."[a] Jesus taught His disciples to handle comments like this by citing various examples, such as:

> **IV Matthew 7:17–19**   What man among you, having a son, and he shall be standing out, and shall say, Father, open thy house that I may come in and sup with thee, will not say, Come in, my son; for mine is thine, and thine is mine? Or what man is there among you, who, if his son ask bread, will give him a stone? Or if he ask a fish, will he give him a serpent?

The Lord was pointing out that the Jews knew how to be good to one another when there was a need. Accordingly, He queried if their Father in Heaven would not fulfill their spiritual needs as they fulfilled the earthly requests of their children.

The Savior concluded this part of His sermon with the admonition known as the Golden Rule wherein He commanded all men to treat one another as they would be treated. The Father wants all of His children to enter the gate that leads to His kingdom. The way is narrow and strait and requires belief and repentance; whereas the wide, broad way (which is easier and requires no repentance or belief) leads only to destruction.

False Prophets

Matthew 7:15–23   Beware of false prophets, which come to you in sheep's clothing, but inwardly they are ravening wolves. Ye shall know them by their fruits. Do men gather grapes of thorns, or figs of thistles? Even so every good tree bringeth forth good fruit; but a corrupt tree bringeth forth evil fruit. A good tree cannot bring forth evil fruit, neither can a corrupt tree bring forth good fruit. Every tree that bringeth not forth good fruit is hewn down, and cast into the fire. Wherefore by their fruits ye shall know them.

Not every one that saith unto me, Lord, Lord, shall enter into the kingdom of heaven; but he that doeth the will of my Father which is in heaven. Many will say to me in that day, Lord, Lord, have we not prophesied in thy name? and in thy name have cast out devils? and in thy name done many wonderful works? And then will I profess unto them, I never knew you: depart from me, ye that work iniquity.

Jesus warned that there would be both false and true prophets (or disciples) preaching the word of God, and from His instructions it ap-

a. IV Matthew
7:14–15.

pears that it will always be so.[71] Both the false and the good prophets will be known by their works. Many will profess knowledge of the Lord and His kingdom and will claim they are serving Him. But on judgment day, only good works will be accepted; those who performed bad (or evil) works, even in the name of Christ, will be cast out.

The teachings of this discourse indicate that to be a true disciple one must accept the gospel (as taught by the Savior), repent of his iniquities, be baptized, receive the Holy Ghost, and, by keeping every standard of the church, righteously endure to the end.[72]

Conclusion

Matthew 7:24–29 Therefore whosoever heareth these sayings of mine, and doeth them, I will liken him unto a wise man, which built his house upon a rock: and the rain descended, and the floods came, and the winds blew, and beat upon that house; and it fell not: for it was founded upon a rock. And every one that heareth these sayings of mine, and doeth them not, shall be likened unto a foolish man, which built his house upon the sand: and the rain descended, and the floods came, and the winds blew, and beat upon that house; and it fell: and great was the fall of it. And it came to pass, when Jesus had ended these sayings, the people were astonished at his doctrine: for he taught them as one having authority, and not as the scribes.

The Lord ended His sermon by giving a general admonition to those who had heard or would hear His instructions. He stated in simple terms that those who built their house upon a rock were those who heard and lived the gospel. They could withstand the fiery darts of the adversary (or the trials of life that would come upon them). However, he who heard Christ's words and did not do them was like the foolish man who built his house upon the sand, and when adversity and temptation came, the house (the man) was destroyed.

The scripture now records that the people were astonished at Christ's doctrine, for He taught them as one having authority and not as the scribes. But this should not be surprising since His teachings were clear and concise, even though the Jews considered Him to be unlearned and untrained. His coherent teachings dispelled the cobwebbery of Phariseeism and brought an end to the verbal trifling and sophistries of the Jews.

His admonitions and teachings dealt with faith, hope, and charity: they were concerned with the destiny of the soul. There were no definitions, no explanations, no meticulous scholastic systems or philosophical theorizing, and no mazes of difficult and dubious decisions. His precepts touched the human heart and appealed to the consciousness of the spirit. He spoke as no other man had spoken. With solemn warning He indicated that life was a struggle between worldly attractions and spiritual values.

Although He taught in concepts totally familiar to the people of His time, His kingdom was in complete contrast to contemporary Jewish thought. He taught with perfect understanding when He expounded that the spirit must match the action of the Law. Whether the Jews recognized it or not, the kingdom of God had come unto them from one having authority.

New Leadership 3

It had been approximately a year since Jesus was baptized and had entered His public ministry,[73] and His miracles and teachings had already made Him famous in the immediate environs of Jerusalem and Galilee. Even in these early stages of His ministry, it was quite clear that those of the ruling class (the rabbis, teachers, Pharisees, scribes, and all the learned Jews of His day) deemed themselves better than Jesus and the disciples that followed Him. Pride did not allow them to become His disciples; therefore, they excluded themselves from the opportunity of leadership in the Lord's new kingdom. New wine would not be placed into old bottles, nor new cloth into old garments.[a]

The "educated" men of Christ's day, prejudiced and perverted in their adaptation and interpretation of the Law of Moses, would not change; so the Lord could not look to these authorities for leadership in His new kingdom.[74] But the time had come for Him to select His Apostles: His ministry would be short, and He needed to train some of His disciples in the doctrine He was restoring. These prospective leaders needed the opportunity to teach and become fellow laborers in the work of salvation so that upon Christ's death, they could continue in the promulgation of the church upon the earth.

Some of those whom Christ would select as His Apostles had been occasional companions in His early ministry, particularly on festive occasions. Some were with Him at the marriage in Cana,[b] some at His first Passover in Jerusalem when He visited the scene of John the Baptist's ministry,[c] and some stayed with Him on His journey through Samaria.[d] But as to the exact time and place of their selection, no accurate information is available.[75]

a. Matthew 9:16–17.

b. John 2:2.

c. John 2:13; 3:22–23.

d. John 4:1–27.

The Call of the Twelve

Luke records that before selecting the Twelve Apostles, the Lord spent the entire night in seclusion and prayer.[a] When dawn came, having received the counsel of His Father in Heaven, He called His disciples to Him. From those who had been with Him through the early stages of His ministry He chose twelve and, as Luke specifically states, He named them Apostles.[b] It was also at this time that He undoubtedly ordained them (as He later reminded them).[c]

These men would now serve with Him continually (much like apprentices) to learn their duty from both His public discourses and the private intimacy of His fellowship. In this way, they would each gain a testimony of Him and learn what they must do and what they must teach to be witnesses and ambassadors of the Lord Jesus Christ. The training of the Twelve became a prominent part of Christ's ministry.[76] Although these men were not of the learned and authoritative class of Christ's day, they had been disciples prior to their call. They believed in Him and perhaps to some degree recognized His divine calling as the long–awaited Messiah. It is doubtful, however, that they fully understood the significance of the Savior's work at this early stage.[77] "It is evident by the later remarks of many of them, and by the instructions and rebuke they called forth from the Master, that the common Jewish expectation of a Messiah who would reign in splendor as an earthly sovereign after He had subdued all other nations, had a place even in the hearts of these chosen ones."[78]

All of Christ's Apostles came from common stock, were utterly devoid of social consequence, and might generally be classified as illiterate;[79] not because they had no education, but because of their lack of training in the rabbinical schools of the day. But to Jesus they were His little ones, His children, His servants, and His friends.[d]

The word *apostle* comes from the Greek *Apostolos,* which means "one who is sent." In selecting twelve to be sent to magnify His kingdom before the world, Christ fell back upon the rustic, simple, sincere, and energetic men of Galilee (with the exception of Judas Iscariot, the one Judean). They all needed to learn, but they were receptive souls, imbued with humility and eagerness to serve. Jesus was content with them and devoutly thanked His Father in Heaven for giving them to Him.

The names of the Twelve Apostles appear in four different places

a. Luke 6:12.

b. Luke 6:13.

c. John 15:16.

d. Matthew 10:42; John 13:16; 21:5.

in the New Testament. Each of the three Synoptics name them and the book of Acts enumerates them again[a] (excluding Judas Iscariot who had committed suicide)[b] at the ascension of Jesus. There are differences in these accounts, and it is not possible to discern an exact order pertaining to the seniority of the Twelve in the Quorum. It is interesting to note, however, that they always appear in groups of four:

Peter, James, John, and Andrew. Peter is always listed as the first and chief Apostle in the Quorum of the Twelve. In Matthew and Luke, Andrew is listed second; in Mark and Acts, James and John take the second and third positions, and Andrew is fourth.

Although the Quorum of the First Presidency of the church may not have been established as such in the early New Testament days (i.e., as a quorum separate from that of the Twelve Apostles), it is apparent that Peter acted as the President of the church and that James and John stood in the positions of first and second counselor, respectively.[80]

The Gospel writers undoubtedly mention Andrew in this first group of four for two reasons: (1) he was the brother of Peter, and (2) he learned of the Lord before Peter and later introduced Peter to the Savior.

Philip, Bartholomew, Thomas, and Matthew. Philip is always listed at the beginning of this group. After him, the order varies: Mark and Luke list the order enumerated above while Matthew and Acts give differing orders.

It is interesting to note that Bartholomew, Thomas, and Matthew are identified with second names in the scriptural text: Bartholomew is also known as Nathanael, Matthew has the second name of Levi, and Thomas is also known as Didymus (signifying a twin).

James, Thaddaeus, Simon, and Judas Iscariot. In this group James, the son of Alpheus (also known in scriptural history as James II or James the Less), always heads the list, and Judas Iscariot always ends it. Thaddaeus is also known as Lebbaeus and Judas (not Iscariot); and Simon is also known as Zelotes or the Canaanite.

The first group of Apostles is the best known, the second group is next, and the last group is the least known (except for Judas Iscariot). Peter always comes at the head of the Quorum and Judas Iscariot is always at the end.

The prophets of the New World saw these twelve Apostles in a

a. Acts 1:13.
b. Matthew 27:5.

vision of the coming of the Messiah in the flesh. Father Lehi "saw twelve others following [Jesus], and their brightness did exceed that of the stars in the firmament."[a] Nephi also saw "twelve others following him. And it came to pass that they were carried away in the Spirit from before my face, and I saw them not."[b]

There is no question that the number twelve was significant and not just a random number selected by the Savior. It symbolically represented the twelve tribes of Israel.[81] Little detail is available on the lives of the Lord's Twelve Apostles, but one can assume that all of them (with the exception of Judas Iscariot) served the Lord faithfully. Without attempting to create a personality for each of these men that does not exist, note the following information:

Peter. Although Peter is the common name by which we know the Lord's senior Apostle, his given name was Simon.[c] Apparently (because of character traits known by the Lord) Jesus changed his name to Peter, or Cephas in Aramaic.[d] He was the son of Jonah or Jonas and is the first–named Apostle in all three of the Synoptics.

Peter was married[e] and was a fisherman by trade. He was a partner with James, John, and his brother Andrew. They owned their own boats and employed others to help them in the business.[f] His early home was in Bethsaida on the west shore of Galilee.[g] At some time during the Lord's ministry, however, he moved to Capernaum.[h]

That Peter was prosperous materially seems evident, for when he mentioned the breadth of the sacrifice he had made to follow the Lord, the Lord did not dispute nor deny his claim.[182] He was not an ignorant man, but he was unlettered and untrained in the rabbinical schools of his day.[83] Although Peter did not write a Gospel, many believe that Mark received his information from Peter.[84]

Peter was one of the three Apostles present with the Lord on the Mount of Transfiguration,[j] at the raising of the daughter of Jairus,[k] and in the Garden of Gethsemane.[l] He spoke for both himself and the Twelve[m] when he confessed Jesus as the long–awaited Messiah.

Peter was impulsive and initially lacked firmness, but even from the beginning he was more than willing to give up his whole soul for the Master. He was usually the first to speak and the first to experiment upon the words of the Lord.[85] Peter boldly taught the gospel after the resurrection of Jesus, and the "reward" for his endeavors was

a. 1 Nephi 1:10.

b. 1 Nephi 11:29.

c. 2 Peter 1:1.

d. John 1:42, Matthew 16:18.

e. Matthew 8:14.

f. Mark 1:16–20; Luke 5:10.

g. John 1:44.

h. Matthew 8:14; Mark 1:29; Luke 4:38.

i. Mark 10:28; Luke 18:28.

j. Matthew 17:1.

k. Mark 5:37.

l. Matthew 26:37.

m. Matthew 16:13–19.

imprisonment.[a] From his own writings we learn that Peter labored in Babylon,[b] which is more likely a name Peter used to refer to Rome than the city on the Euphrates. Peter's greatness is affirmed in the book of Acts where it tells of some Saints who thought so highly of him that they "brought forth the sick into the streets, and laid them on beds and couches, that at the least the shadow of Peter passing by might overshadow some of them."[c]

Although we do not know the exact time or method of his death, the scriptures appear to prophesy how he would die. The Lord knew of his death[d] and Peter foresaw it, also.[e] It is generally believed that he was crucified, perhaps in Rome along with Paul during the persecutions by the Emperor Nero sometime between A.D. 64 and 68. Tradition has it that even at his death Peter felt unworthy to die in the same manner that the Lord had suffered; so his captors, adhering to his request, crucified him upside down.[86]

As a resurrected being, Peter appeared (along with James and John) to the Prophet Joseph Smith to restore the Melchizedek Priesthood to the earth in the dispensation of the fulness of times.[f]

James. This James, the brother of John and the son of Zebedee, is sometimes referred to as James I to distinguish him from the other James in the Quorum. He, his father, and his brother John were fishermen by trade, and were in business with Peter and Andrew. The Lord gave him, along with John, the name Boanerges, which means "sons of thunder."[g] These men probably received this name because of their desire to call down fire from heaven upon certain Samaritan villages that had rejected the Lord.[h]

Through his mother's petition, James aspired (along with John) to the highest honors of the kingdom—namely, to sit by the Lord's side in heaven,[i] and along with John and Peter, he witnessed certain singular events in the life of Christ (e.g., the Master's raising of the daughter of Jairus[j] and the transfiguration of Jesus).[k] He was near Jesus in the Garden of Gethsemane during the last moments of the Lord's life before His arrest and trial,[l] and with Peter and John he restored the Melchizedek Priesthood to the earth in 1829.

James was the first apostolic martyr after the death of Jesus. He was beheaded by Herod Agrippa I near the time of the Passover, approximately A.D. 44.[m][87]

a. Acts 12:1–19.

b. 1 Peter 5:13.

c. Acts 5:15.

d. John 21:18–19.

e. 2 Peter 1:14.

f. D&C 27:12.

g. Mark 3:17.

h. Luke 9:54.

i. Mark 10:35–41; Matthew 20:21.

j. Mark 5:37; Luke 8:51.

k. Matthew 17:1–2; Luke 9:28–29.

l. Matthew 26:36–37.

m. Acts 12:1–2.

John. John was the brother of James and one of the sons of Ze-bedee. He was a fisherman and was in business with his father, his brother James, and Peter and Andrew. Along with James and Peter, he also witnessed the singular events in Christ's life noted under "James" above. Like James, he aspired to the highest honors of the kingdom through the petition of his mother. The scriptures denote John as "the disciple whom Jesus loved,"[a] indicating that he had a close, personal relationship with the Lord.

It appears that John was originally a disciple of John the Baptist;[b][88] but when the Baptist testified of the divinity of the Savior, John left him to follow the Messiah.

His "hot zeal" earned him (and his brother) the name *sons of thunder.* This zeal came from his intense loyalty toward Jesus.

John was perhaps the most thoughtful of the disciples. He alone of the Twelve stood at the foot of the cross and, at the request of Jesus, took charge of His mother's earthly needs.[c] We read that at the Last Supper he leaned upon Jesus' bosom,[d] and at the miracle of the second draught of fish,[89] it was John who first recognized the Savior on the shore of Galilee after His resurrection.[e]

Paul refers to his meeting with John in Jerusalem,[f] but he is only mentioned occasionally in Acts.[g] John himself tells of his banishment to Patmos because of his zeal for teaching the gospel.[h]

John, together with James and Peter, participated in restoring the Melchizedek Priesthood to the Prophet Joseph Smith;[i] but unlike his two brethren, John was not a resurrected being. On the shores of Galilee he had received a special blessing from the Lord; the Savior charged him to minister to the children of the earth and blessed him that he would remain on earth until the Lord's Second Coming.[j]

John's unique and intimate Gospel emphasizes the Savior's Judean ministry whereas the Synoptics stress His journeys in Galilee and Perea. John treats the life of Christ in a singular fashion, noting many events in the Savior's ministry that are not recorded by any of the other Gospel writers.

In addition to his Gospel, John wrote the book of Revelation—his vision from the Lord while exiled on the isle of Patmos. He also wrote First, Second, and Third John as general epistles to the church.

Andrew. Andrew was the brother of Peter and the son of Jonah. He

a. John 13:23;
19:26; 20:2.

b. John 1:35–42.

c. John 19:25–27.

d. John 13:23,
25.

e. John 21:7.

f. Galatians
2:9.

g. Acts 3:1, 11;
4:13; 8:14.

h. Revelation
1:9.

i. D&C 27:12.

j. John 21:21–
23; D&C 7.

is mentioned less frequently than Peter, James, or John. He also followed John the Baptist initially, but after receiving a testimony of the divinity of Jesus, he testified to his brother, Peter, that the Messiah had come.[a] He shared in Peter's call to the ministry[b] and was involved in one of the private interviews Jesus had with Peter, James, and John.[c] John mentions Andrew in conjunction with the miracle of feeding the five thousand,[d] and we also read that Philip asked Andrew, on behalf of some Greek converts to Judaism, to arrange a private interview with Jesus.[e]

During the last discourse the Lord delivered, Andrew asked a question concerning the end of the world.[f] While there are no other authentic records of his life or death,[90] tradition has it that Andrew was widely traveled and spread the Gospel among the Scythians in what is modern–day Russia. Tradition states he was put to death upon a cross in Achaia.[91]

Philip. John 1:43–45 notes that Jesus was the one who found Philip, and Philip may have been the first to receive the call from the Savior to follow Him.[92] Philip's original home was in Bethsaida. He was mentioned in the feeding of the five thousand,[g] and it was Philip to whom some Greek converts to Judaism applied for a personal interview with Jesus.[h] The Savior reproved him mildly for asking to see the Father,[i] and he was present with the eleven Apostles at Jesus' ascension. Nothing else is recorded of his ministry.

Tradition has it that he was a chariot driver by profession[93] and that he was an earnest inquirer after the truth—being thoroughly acquainted with the scriptures and the Messianic promise.[94]

Philip is credited with seeking out Nathanael (Bartholomew) to inform him that the Messiah had come, and it is reported that he died in Hierapolis.[95]

Bartholomew/Nathanael. The name *Bartholomew* means "son of Tolmai,"[96] but he was called Bartholomew only at his ordination and at the Ascension. In John's Gospel, he is referred to as Nathanael, the one in whom Jesus found "no guile."[j] Because of this comment by the Lord, it is evident that he was a man of great moral strength. When Philip told him about the Lord, his comment was, "Can there any good thing come out of Nazareth?"[k] He was undoubtedly referring to the fact that generally the leaders of the Jews and the Judeans of his

a. John 1:35–42.

b. Matthew 4:18–19.

c. Mark 13:3.

d. John 6:8.

e. John 12:20–22.

f. Mark 13:3–4; Matthew 24.

g. John 6:5–7.

h. John 12:20–22.

i. John 14:8–9.

j. John 1:45–51.

k. John 1:46.

day despised the Galileans (including himself), considering them to be poor and ignorant. In response to his question Philip merely told Nathanael to "come and see."[a]

The reason for assuming that Bartholomew and Nathanael are the same person is that each of the three synoptic Gospels refers to Bartholomew as an Apostle, but not Nathanael; whereas the book of John names Nathanael twice as an Apostle, and makes no such reference to Bartholomew at all. In addition, the Synoptics record Bartholomew and Philip together, while in John's writings Nathanael and Philip appear together—thus the assumption that the two names describe the same man.[97]

There is no other authentic scriptural record of this Apostle's work. He is traditionally thought to have been a shepherd or a gardener.[98]

Thomas/Didymus. Didymus is the Greek equivalent of the Hebrew name for Thomas, which means "a twin."[99] From the references we have of him, it is apparent that he was a warmhearted but melancholy individual who was ready to die for the Lord but slow to believe in His resurrection.

Thomas was ready to risk his life for the Lord when Jesus returned to Jerusalem at the request of Lazarus's sisters;[b] however, as much as we would like to remember him for this loyalty and bravery, his name is usually associated with doubting—"doubting Thomas." Prone to taking somber views of things, he questioned the Lord on the eve of His crucifixion: "Lord, we know not whither thou goest; and how can we know the way?"[c] Apparently he did not know "the way," and could not believe that any of the others did either. His statement was somewhat like an apology for his ignorance; however, Jesus' response was compassionate and sympathetic: "I am the way, the truth, and the life: no man cometh unto the Father, but by me."[d]

After His resurrection, the Savior appeared to the Apostles in the upper room and Thomas was not there. The scriptures give no reason for his absence. When they met together again, the other ten Apostles testified of Christ's resurrection, but Thomas was not satisfied with their testimony. It was not that he was unwilling to believe but that he could not believe. When Jesus again appeared to the Apostles, Thomas was with them. Jesus requested that the doubting Apostle touch Him

a. John 1:46.
b. John 11:16.
c. John 14:5.
d. John 14:6.

so that he might believe. Thomas's doubt being satisfied, he joyfully exclaimed, "My Lord and my God."

The Lord drew an important lesson from Thomas's practical attitude when He said, "Thomas, because thou hast seen me, thou hast believed: blessed are they that have not seen, and yet have believed."[a]

Tradition has it that Thomas was killed by being run through with a lance in Persia or India.[100]

Matthew/Levi. Matthew is the son of Alpheus and one of the seven original Apostles to receive a preliminary call before his ordination to the Quorum of the Twelve. He is the author of the first Gospel in the New Testament. His second name would indicate that he was of the priestly lineage of the tribe of Levi.[101]

When Matthew received his call he gave a feast in honor of the Lord. The Pharisees publicly criticized Jesus for this.[b] The criticism came as a result of Matthew's occupation: he was a publican (or tax collector). His home was in Capernaum and he undoubtedly knew of Jesus before his call because of the many mighty works that Jesus had performed in that area.

The call of Matthew to the Twelve was probably a disconcerting event in the public view of Jesus' ministry because of Matthew's hated profession. His call would have been an additional aggravation to the Jewish leaders, but it also exemplified the Lord's total disregard of worldly opinions and His high regard for spiritual preparedness.[102]

The scriptures make no mention of Matthew's ministry; however, other secular writers indicate that his was one of the most active ministries of all the Apostles after the death of Jesus.[103]

James (James II). There appear to be three individuals named James associated with Jesus in the New Testament. The first is James I, the son of Zebedee and the brother of John. All references to this James seem to be explicit and easily identified. The second is James II, the son of Alpheus Clopas.[104] The third James is the Lord's brother.[c]

Tradition has James II being younger and smaller than James, the brother of John, and it is believed that he died by being thrown down from the temple and stoned (his head being beaten with a fuller's club).[105]

Judas/Lebbaeus/Thaddaeus. This Apostle is commonly referred to as the "three-named Apostle," for obvious reasons. Matthew refers

a. John 20:29.

b. Matthew 9:9–13; Mark 2:13–17; Luke 5:27–32.

c. Matthew 13:55; Mark 6:3; Galatians 1:19.

to him as Lebbaeus and Thaddaeus, Mark as Thaddaeus, and Luke as "Judas, the brother of James." The only other scriptural reference to this Apostle is in John where he asked the Lord a question during His last discourses to the Twelve before His crucifixion.[a] John specifically notes that the question was by Judas, "not Iscariot." No other information is available on this Apostle.

Simon Zelotes. This is another call to the Twelve that indicates Christ's total disregard for public opinion. The name of "Zelotes"[b] identifies Simon with a rebellious political group led by Judas the Zealot in the days of taxation.[c] The group was in existence twenty years before Christ's ministry began. Matthew and Mark also designate Simon as a Canaanite, but this had no reference to lineage or geographical origin. "Canaanite" is the Syro–Chaldaic equivalent of the Greek, which in English means "Zelotes."[106]

The people who belonged to this political group had an enormous zeal for the maintenance of the Mosaic ritual.[107] They were a political party of malcontents who believed in the physical restoration of the Messianic kingdom and Jewish national supremacy.[108] They used swords and daggers, while Jesus taught with the omnipotent weapon of truth.

What caused Simon Zelotes to leave the camp of Judas the Zealot in favor of Jesus is not known. He would have had to make a radical change in his political and spiritual feelings before he could have become one of the Lord's Apostles. There is no mention of him apart from his association with the Twelve, and he is as obscure as Peter is celebrated. He and Matthew were disciples of extremes. Simon had been a tax–hater and Matthew a tax–gatherer. Simon would have been extremely patriotic and would have chafed under the yoke of Rome, longing only for emancipation; Matthew would have been described as a most unpatriotic Jew who had degraded himself by becoming a servant to an alien ruler.

Judas Iscariot. All of the Apostles were from the province of Galilee except Judas Iscariot. He was the only Judean among the Twelve. His father's name was Simon,[d] and it is believed that the family was from the town of Kerioth in the southern borders of Judah.[109] If these facts are accurate, Judas may have become a disciple of Jesus on one of the Lord's early visits to Jordan.[e]

a. John 14:22.
b. Acts 1:13;
   Luke 6:15.
c. Acts 5:37.
d. John 6:71;
   13:26.
e. John 3:22.

Judas was the treasurer for Jesus and the Twelve, both receiving and disbursing their common funds. John records that he was unprincipled and dishonest in this trust.[a] Although he apparently embezzled from the funds, he had undoubtedly been entrusted with the job because he was capable of doing it. One should not assume that he had been selected as treasurer merely to provide the Savior with a traitor.

Perhaps Judas was initially drawn to Jesus because he believed in Him as "the Jewish Messiah" and anticipated that He would triumph as such.[110] Yet at times he had a turning of the soul, which is exemplified in his complaints (such as that concerning the waste of the rich oil Mary used to anoint the feet of Jesus before His crucifixion).[b] The small rebuff the Lord issued at that time seemed to only further canker his soul. When the Lord corrected the other Apostles in this manner, the result was positive; but with Judas it was different. It appears that he felt Jesus could see through him and that the Lord did not think well of his spirit and his evil habits.

Although he was avaricious and covetous, it seems that his betrayal of the Lord for thirty pieces of silver involved more than a mere bargaining for money; that his deep alienation from Christ had turned love to hate, and that he was being consumed with vindictive passions. The manner of the betrayal indicated not just a covetous man, but one that was malicious and vengeful. Not only did he betray the location of Jesus for a price, he personally conducted the band that would arrest the Savior and singled Him out with an affectionate salutation.[c] John indicates that Satan had taken hold of Judas.[d] Finally, having bound himself to the devil and having betrayed the Savior of the world, Judas took his own life and was ultimately classified as a son of perdition.[e][111]

What a melancholy end was that of Judas to an auspicious beginning! Chosen to be a companion of the Son of Man, and an eye and ear witness of His work, once engaged in preaching the gospel and casting out devils; now possessed of the devil himself, driven on by him to damnable deeds, and finally employed by a righteous Providence to take vengeance on his own crime. In view of this history, how shallow the theory that resolves all moral differences between men into the effect of circumstances! Who was ever better circumstanced for becoming good than

a. John 12:6.

b. John 12:1–7.

c. Matthew 26:49.

d. John 13:2, 27.

e. Matthew 27:5; Acts 1:18; John 17:12.

Judas? Yet the very influences which ought to have fostered goodness served only to provoke into activity latent evil.[112]

A Charge to the Twelve

Matthew 10:1–42   And when he had called unto him his twelve disciples, he gave them power against unclean spirits, to cast them out, and to heal all manner of sickness and all manner of disease. Now the names of the twelve apostles are these; The first, Simon, who is called Peter, and Andrew his brother; James the son of Zebedee, and John his brother; Philip, and Bartholomew; Thomas, and Matthew the publican; James the son of Alphaeus, and Lebbaeus, whose surname was Thaddaeus; Simon the Canaanite, and Judas Iscariot, who also betrayed him. These twelve Jesus sent forth, and commanded them, saying, Go not into the way of the Gentiles, and into any city of the Samaritans enter ye not: but go rather to the lost sheep of the house of Israel. And as ye go, preach, saying, The kingdom of heaven is at hand. Heal the sick, cleanse the lepers, raise the dead, cast out devils: freely ye have received, freely give. Provide neither gold, nor silver, nor brass in your purses, nor scrip for your journey, neither two coats, neither shoes, nor yet staves: for the workman is worthy of his meat. And into whatsoever city or town ye shall enter, inquire who in it is worthy; and there abide till ye go thence. And when ye come into an house, salute it. And if the house be worthy, let your peace come upon it: but if it be not worthy, let your peace return to you. And whosoever shall not receive you, nor hear your words, when ye depart out of that house or city, shake off the dust of your feet. Verily I say unto you, It shall be more tolerable for the land of Sodom and Gomorrah in the day of judgment, than for that city.

Behold, I send you forth as sheep in the midst of wolves: be ye therefore wise as serpents, and harmless as doves. But beware of men: for they will deliver you up to the councils, and they will scourge you in their synagogues; and ye shall be brought before governors and kings for my sake, for a testimony against them and the Gentiles. But when they deliver you up, take no thought how or what ye shall speak: for it shall be given you in that same hour what ye shall speak. For it is not ye that speak, but the Spirit of your Father which speaketh in you. And the brother shall deliver up the brother to death, and the father the child: and the children shall rise up against their parents, and cause them to be put to death. And ye shall be hated of all men for my name's sake: but he that endureth to the end shall be saved. But when they persecute you in this city, flee ye into another: for verily I say unto you, Ye shall not have gone over the cities of Israel, till the Son of man be come. The disciple is not above his master, nor the servant above his lord. It is enough for the disciple that he be as his master, and the servant as his lord. If they have called the master of the house Beelzebub, how much more shall they call them of his household? Fear them not therefore: for there is nothing covered, that shall not be revealed; and hid, that shall not be known. What I tell you in darkness, that speak ye in light: and what ye hear in the ear, that preach ye upon the housetops. And fear not them which kill the body, but are not able to kill the soul: but rather fear him which is able to destroy both soul and body in hell. Are not two sparrows sold for a farthing? and one of them shall not fall on the ground without your Father. But the very hairs of your head are all numbered. Fear ye not therefore, ye are of more value than many sparrows. Whosoever therefore shall confess me before men, him will I confess also before my Father which is in heaven. But whosoever shall deny me before men, him will I also deny before my Father which is in heaven. Think not that I am come to send peace on earth: I came not to send peace, but a sword. For I am come to set a man at variance against his father, and daughter against her mother, and the daughter in law against her mother in law. And a man's foes shall be they of his own household. He that loveth father or mother more than me is not worthy of me: and he that loveth son or daughter more than me is not worthy of me. And he that taketh not his cross, and followeth after me, is not worthy of me. He that findeth his life shall lose it: and he that loseth his life for my sake shall find it.

He that receiveth you receiveth me, and he that receiveth me receiveth him that sent me. He that receiveth a prophet in the name of a prophet shall receive a prophet's reward; and he that receiveth a righteous man in the name of a righteous man shall receive a righteous man's reward. And whosoever shall give to drink unto one of these little ones a cup of cold water only in the name of a disciple, verily I say unto you, he shall in no wise lose his reward.

Cross–references   Mark 3:13–19; Mark 6:7–13; Luke 6:12–16; Luke 9:1–6; Luke 12:1–12, 22–35

Having been chosen and ordained, the Twelve were now ready to become active proselyting agents in the new kingdom that Christ had established, and He prepared to send them forth to proselyte in the towns and villages of Galilee. It was to be their first mission without the Lord, and it would be a great learning experience for them. Jesus gave a discourse on this occasion that covered the following topics:

Sphere of the Work

At a future time, Jesus would command the Twelve to go into all the world.[a] But for the present, they were instructed to go only to Israel, the Lord's "lost sheep." He further restricted them to their native province of Galilee. He specifically forbade them to go to the Gentiles and the Samaritans, as "their hearts were too narrow, their prejudices too strong: there was too much of the Jew, too little of the Christian, in their character."[113]

The duration of their mission is unknown, but it is unlikely that it was for any extensive period of time.[114]

a. Matthew 28:19.

Nature of the Work

The Savior specifically instructed the Apostles that they should preach repentance unto the people and teach them that the kingdom of God was at hand. Perhaps He restricted them so narrowly because they had such limited knowledge at the time. The Lord had given them the priesthood so they might perform miracles, and they were instructed to freely use this gift on their missions.

The Lord specifically instructed them to be cautious of men. He knew the ways of the Jews were such that the Apostles would have nothing to look forward to but persecution. They would be testified against, dragged before the Jewish councils, and scourged in their synagogues. The work they were to embark upon and the gospel they were to preach would bring peace to the individual, but would divide brother against brother, father against child, and children against parents. Yet in His instructions, Jesus clearly indicated that they could win over the hearts of men through their unselfish devotion and the truth that they would teach.[115]

Personal Needs and Comforts

It is clear from the Lord's instructions that the Apostles were to carry neither purse nor scrip.[116] They were not to indulge in empty courtesies, but were to pay strict attention to their mission by teaching those who would receive them and casting the dust from their feet on the household or town that would not.[117] He intended them to sacrifice all their personal desires to follow Him, even though He offered no earthly reward. Their basic equipment was simple: they were to go in essentially the clothing they had on and they were not to take extra coats, shoes, or staves to assist them in their travels. (These instructions also implied that the length of their mission would be short.) He told them, "Are not five sparrows sold for two farthings, and not one of them is forgotten before God?" Obviously the Apostles were more important than sparrows. He also comforted them by explaining that even the hairs on their heads were numbered to the Father.

Perhaps the Lord required this austerity to emphasize the fact that there could be no diversions from the mission upon which they were embarking. They had no prospects except privation, persecution, and possible martyrdom; but He told them to walk in faith, relying upon God, and He promised them that the very words which they should speak would be given to them in the hour that they were needed. They were to be fearless, yet not foolhardy; wise as serpents, but harmless as doves.[118]

It is evident that the Lord intended His Apostles to eventually abandon their formal callings and vocations and even forsake family ties for the gospel, if necessary. Through His instructions, they would learn to curb their reactions to persecution and suppress even justified resentment in order to completely mold their lives to His service. They could look for a reward in heaven, but they would not find one on this earth; in this world they would be "hated of all men, for my [Christ's] name's sake." Yet even with this bleak prospect presented to them, the Apostles knew that their only fear lay in him who could destroy their souls; but the Lord assured them that His eye would be continually upon them.

Results

It would appear that Jesus chose the Twelve to go on a mission at this particular time because of the great success He had already enjoyed in His own ministry. They must have gone forth with enthusiasm for they returned with joy, noting that many multitudes had followed them. Their success was obviously considerable, but it may have been related more to their miracles than to their message. The Savior returned to Capernaum to receive the Twelve from their missions at about the same time that the news reached Him of the death of John the Baptist.[119] Perhaps John's death is why the Lord cautioned the Apostles at that time not to be overly elated with their success, but their missions must have brought great joy to the Savior.

Although the Twelve were young in their callings and would yet stay with Jesus throughout His ministry and receive much instruction from Him, it was time for them to "take up their cross." They had to be willing to do whatever was necessary to promulgate the gospel and build the kingdom of God upon the earth. Whether they completely understood what "taking up their cross" meant at this time is not indicated, but the analogy would certainly have both impressed and terrified them.[120] As a result of this command, they would "shoulder any grievous burdens placed upon their shoulders because of the cause of righteousness."[121]

The Seventy

Luke 10:1–24   After these things the Lord appointed other seventy also, and sent them two and two before his face into every city and place, whither he himself would come. Therefore said he unto them, The harvest truly is great, but the labourers are few: pray ye therefore the Lord of the harvest, that he would send forth labourers into his harvest. Go your ways: behold, I send you forth as lambs among wolves. Carry neither purse, nor scrip, nor shoes: and salute no man by the way. And into whatsoever house ye enter, first say, Peace be to this house. And if the son of peace be there, your peace shall rest upon it: if not, it shall turn to you again. And in the same house remain, eating and drinking such things as they give: for the labourer is worthy of his hire. Go not from house to house. And into whatsoever city ye enter, and they receive you, eat such things as are set before you: and heal the sick that are therein, and say unto them, The kingdom of God is come nigh unto you. But into whatsoever city ye enter, and they receive you not, go your ways out into the streets of the same, and say, Even the very dust of your city, which cleaveth on us, we do wipe off against you: notwithstanding be ye sure of this, that the kingdom of God is come nigh unto you. But I say unto you, that it shall be more tolerable in that day for Sodom, than for that city. Woe unto thee, Chorazin! woe unto thee, Bethsaida! for if the mighty works had been done in Tyre and Sidon, which have been done in you, they had a great while ago repented, sitting in sackcloth and ashes. But it shall be more tolerable for Tyre and Sidon at the judgment, than for you. And thou, Capernaum, which art exalted to heaven, shalt be thrust down to hell. He that heareth you heareth me; and he that despiseth you despiseth me; and he that despiseth me despiseth him that sent me.

And the seventy returned again with joy, saying, Lord, even the devils are subject unto us through thy name. And he said unto them, I beheld Satan as lightning fall from heaven. Behold, I give unto you power to tread on serpents and scorpions, and over all the power of the enemy: and nothing shall by any means hurt you. Notwithstanding in this rejoice not, that the spirits are subject unto you; but rather rejoice, because your names are written in heaven.

In that hour Jesus rejoiced in spirit, and said, I thank thee, O Father, Lord of heaven and earth, that thou hast hid these things from the wise and prudent, and hast revealed them unto babes: even so, Father; for so it seemed good in thy sight. All things are delivered to me of my Father: and no man knoweth who the Son is, but the Father; and who the Father is, but the Son, and he to whom the Son will reveal him.

And he turned him unto his disciples, and said privately, Blessed are the eyes which see the things that ye see: for I tell you, that many prophets and kings have desired to see those things which ye see, and have not seen them; and to hear those things which ye hear, and have not heard them.

Luke is the only Gospel writer to record anything about the mission of the seventy. He begins his record by stating that the Lord appointed "other seventy also." There is no other record of the call of the seventy into the mission field.[122]

Just as the number twelve signified the twelve tribes of Israel, so, too, the number seventy had significance in the call of these special witnesses to the Lord's divinity. For example:

1. When the children of Israel were in the wilderness they refused (as a body) to enter into the presence of the Lord. Moses selected seventy "of the elders of Israel" along with Aaron, Nadab, and Abihu, and took them to see the God Jehovah so that they could be special witnesses to the Israelites.[a]

2. Seventy elders of the children of Israel were to assist Moses in judging the people,[b] and the Lord empowered them with special prophetic gifts so that they could receive the mysteries of their judgment through revelation.[c]

3. The Jewish Sanhedrin (the religious authority of the time) was made up of seventy of the elders of Israel. (There were, in fact, seventy–two or three members in the Sanhedrin. The two additional members were the president and vice–president. The third would have been the "master in Israel," whether he was counted separately or as part of the seventy.)

4. The scriptural record that Israel used at the time of Christ was known by the title LXX, or seventy.[123]

5. The number seventy was also significant of the priesthood calling of the seventy (missionary work) throughout the kingdom of God upon the earth, and the Jewish leaders could not fail to recognize this. Israel also used this number to represent the world's Gentile nations; for this reason, seventy oxen were sacrificed each year during the Feast of Tabernacles.[124]

Whereas Jesus had specifically restrained the Twelve from going to the gentile nations and to the Samaritans, He placed no such limitation upon the seventy. The time had come for the gospel to be spread throughout the world. Jewish exclusiveness in hearing the gospel, as set forth in Christ's instructions to the Twelve, was forever surrendered in His instructions to the seventy.

Like John the Baptist, the seventy heralded the coming of Jesus and

a. Exodus 24:1–11.

b. Numbers 11:16

c. Numbers 11:17.

prepared the way before Him; but unlike John, they served at the end of the Lord's mission, not at the beginning. Many of the instructions the Lord gave the seventy were similar to those He had given to the Twelve, but He also gave the seventy the following directives:

"Salute no man by the way." In other words, do not take time to visit with old acquaintances, for doing so would take precious time away from their work and the Lord had much to accomplish in the short span of His ministry.

If the head of a house saluted them, they were to pause, eat, drink, and abide in that house without seeking better accommodations.

Jesus also pronounced "woes" upon various cities that had rejected His mighty works: the severity of the "woe" seemed to be in direct proportion to the amount of mighty works rejected.

The seventy returned to Jesus after completing their missions and they were filled with joy. They noted that even the devils were subject to them through the name of Jesus Christ. The Lord also had great joy and hailed the success of the seventy as the downfall of the kingdom of Satan (perhaps referring to the specific defeat of Satan by Michael and the heavenly hosts rather than the general defeat that would occur at the end of the world).[125]

Just as the call of the seventy (and their mission) in the new Testament was a significant event in the ministry of the Savior, so, too, the call of the first seventy in the latter days was a significant event in the development of The Church of Jesus Christ of Latter–day Saints.

The first specific instructions pertaining to the call of seventy in the latter days occurred on February 8, 1835. Joseph Smith had called Brigham Young and Joseph Young to his home in Kirtland, Ohio. After referring to the call of the Twelve Apostles, he noted to Joseph Young that the Lord had made him "president of the seventies." Later that month, the Prophet established and ordained both the First and Second Quorums of the Seventy of the latter days.[126]

From the limited record in Luke's Gospel and the establishment of the seventy in the latter days, it is apparent that those who fill this calling are truly special witnesses to the divinity of Jesus Christ.

They are required to be special witnesses of the Lord Jesus Christ. It is expected of this body of men that they will have burning in their souls the testimony of Jesus Christ, which is the spirit of prophecy; that they will be full of light and of the knowledge of the truth; that they will be enthusiastic in their calling, and in the cause of Zion, and that they will be ready at any moment, when required, to go out into the world, or anywhere throughout the Church and bear testimony of the truth, preach the gospel of Jesus Christ, and set examples for the world of purity, honesty, uprightness, and integrity to the truth.[127]

Cleansing the Temple   4

The First Cleansing

John 2:13–25   And the Jews' pass–over was at hand, and Jesus went up to Jerusalem, and found in the temple those that sold oxen and sheep and doves, and the changers of money sitting: and when he had made a scourge of small cords, he drove them all out of the temple, and the sheep, and the oxen; and poured out the changers' money, and overthrew the tables; and said unto them that sold doves, Take these things hence; make not my Father's house an house of merchandise. And his disciples remembered that it was written, The zeal of thine house hath eaten me up.

Then answered the Jews and said unto him, What sign shewest thou unto us, seeing that thou doest these things? Jesus answered and said unto them, Destroy this temple, and in three days I will raise it up. Then said the Jews, Forty and six years was this temple in building, and wilt thou rear it up in three days? But he spake of the temple of his body. When therefore he was risen from the dead, his disciples remembered that he had said this unto them; and they believed the scripture, and the word which Jesus had said.

Now when he was in Jerusalem at the passover, in the feast day, many believed in his name, when they saw the miracles which he did. But Jesus did not commit himself unto them, because he knew all men, and needed not that any should testify of man: for he knew what was in man.

John records the first cleansing of the temple by the Savior. It occurred after the marriage at Cana and after Jesus had returned to Capernaum, a city which had become known as His own.[a]

The Passover was near and in compliance with the Law, Jesus went up to Jerusalem. The synoptic Gospels do not record this visit for their interest was primarily with the Savior's Galilean and Perean ministries. At the time of the Passover feast, the temple tax was due from "all Jews and proselytes— women, slaves, and minors ex-

a. John 2:12;
   Matthew 4:13;
   9:1.

cepted."[128] The Passover was the greatest of all Jewish festivals and a time when the law required every male Israelite to present himself at the temple.

Josephus reports that Cestus once took a census of Jerusalem at the time of the Passover to inform Nero of the city's power. Cestus required the priests to number the multitude which they did by counting the sacrifices slain at the feast. They counted 256,500 sheep and estimated that ten or eleven people would celebrate each sacrifice (it was not lawful for anyone to feast singly, and some companies were known to include as many as twenty people). The priests reported to Cestus that 2,700,200 Jews had come to the feast pure and holy. Those who were "unclean" could not sacrifice, nor could any foreigner, so the estimated figure was probably below the actual total.[129] It is no wonder with such an enormous congregation being required to sacrifice and pay the temple tax that the area of the temple had become heavily trafficked.

From the fifteenth to the twenty–fifth of Adar (corresponding to our months of February and March), it was the custom for the priests of the temple to set up stalls in the country towns surrounding Jerusalem to exchange the traditional currency the Judeans carried for the Galilean shekel the travelers would need to pay the temple tax while attending the Passover. After this period passed, however, the country stalls were closed and the money changers would sit within the precincts of the temple itself.[130] In addition to the exchange of funds (for which there was a charge), there was also a lively business in the selling of sacrificial animals. If an individual brought his own offering for the sacrifice, it had to be inspected (pursuant to the rabbinical law of the day), and there was also a charge for that inspection. A complicated "market" in the temple handled all business matters connected with the Passover.[131] Consequently, the greatest of the Jewish religious ceremonies had become a huge yearly fair in Jerusalem. There were booths at which poorer women bought doves to use in their ritual of purification, potters sold dishes for the Passover meal, and other vendors would cry their wares, selling such things as wine, oil, and salt.

To make matters worse, the normal traffic pattern through the city now cut through the temple courtyard instead of going around the temple as it had in the past.[132] Also, Josephus records that Annas, the ruling high priest at the time of Christ's ministry, was a great hoarder of money. He and his sons were full of greed and corruption, and had become exceedingly rich by violently spoiling the common priests of their official revenues and keeping the funds for themselves.[133]

Once we recognize what Jerusalem was like at the time of Christ, it is easy to understand why the Lord would call the temple "a den of robbers." Quoting Psalm 69:9 as fulfillment of prophecy, and making Himself a whip of small cords,[134] He drove the sacrificial beasts through the gates of the temple into the streets of the city and ordered those who sold the caged doves to take them away. The money changers fared much worse as Jesus overturned their tables (scattering their spiritually desecrating coins on the floor) and expelled them from the premises.[135] Acting as Israel's refiner and purifier[a] the Lord inaugurated His mission and claimed His Messiahship by declaring that the Jews had desecrated His Father's house.

The common people did not object to Jesus clearing the temple because they did not approve of the business practices being carried on there;[136] and although the Jewish leadership was angry, they did not challenge what Jesus had done for they knew that He was right! Rather than laying hands upon Him or reproving Him, they came to Him and asked for a sign. This request, which was, in essence, a challenge to Christ's authority, essentially determined the manner in which they would carry on their contest with Him throughout His mission. The sign they sought was the Messianic sign, or the sign of the Second Coming of Christ.[137] Jesus answered them by declaring the sign of His first coming (or the Resurrection) and told them that if they destroyed "this temple" He would raise it again in three days. The incredulous Jews declared that it had taken forty–six years to raise the temple, and it was not yet complete. How could Jesus claim to be able to "rear it up" in only three days? But Jesus was speaking of the resurrection of His body, and although the Jews pretended to misunderstand Him, they later proved their comprehension. At His trial they testified of this claim,[b] accusing Him of blasphemy; they taunted Him with the claim as He hung upon the cross;[c] and finally, they used it as an excuse to secure the tomb where His body lay.[d]

In reality, it would appear that the Jews' own sense of guilt prevented them from interfering with the Master's cleansing of the temple,

a. Malachi 3:1–3.

b. Mark 14:58.

c. Mark 15:29–30.

d. Matthew 27:63.

for they stood before Him "self–convicted of corruption, avarice, and of personal responsibility for the temple's defilement."[138]

The Second Cleansing

Mark 11:15–19   And they came to Jerusalem: and Jesus went into the temple, and began to cast out them that sold and bought in the temple, and overthrew the tables of the moneychangers, and the seats of them that sold doves; and would not suffer that any man should carry any vessel through the temple. And he taught, saying unto them, Is it not written, My house shall be called of all nations the house of prayer? but ye have made it a den of thieves. And the scribes and chief priests heard it, and sought how they might destroy him: for they feared him, because all the people was [sic] astonished at his doctrine. And when even was come, he went out of the city.

Cross–references   Matthew 21:12–16; Luke 19:45–48

The first cleansing was a warning to the Jews; the second cleansing was their symbolic judgment. The first cleansing occurred at the commencement of the Savior's ministry; the final cleansing took place four days before His crucifixion. The first time He cleansed His "Father's house"; but at the end of His ministry, He had triumphantly entered Jerusalem declaring His Messiahship, and so it was also *His* house that He cleansed.[139] Although the first cleansing caused anger and motivated the Jewish leaders to ask Jesus for a sign, the final cleansing produced a desire to destroy Him.

According to Mark, Jesus began the day of the second cleansing with the miracle of the fig tree,[140] which emphasized the symbolic judgment that would come upon the children of Israel[a] Although the first cleansing had cleared the temple of its several abuses, in time all the abuses were restored.[141] The degrading confusion of . . . . . . the lowing of oxen, the bleating of sheep, the cries of the money–changers, and the noisy market chaffering of buyers and sellers of doves or other accessories to a ceremonial worship, filled the air with discordant sounds of the outside world, which had no right in these sacred precincts. The scene roused the same deep indignation in Jesus, as when He formally rose in His grand protest against it. He had now, in His triumphal entry, formally proclaimed His Kingdom, and would, forthwith, vindicate its rights, by once more restoring the Temple to its becoming purity; for while it stood, it should be holy.[142]

a. Mark 11:12–14.

The two episodes of Christ clearing the temple contradict our traditional view of the Savior. We normally think of Him as being gentle and unassertive.

Gentle He was, and patient under affliction, merciful and long–suffering in dealing with contrite sinners, yet stern and inflexible in the presence of hypocrisy, and unsparing in His denunciation of persistent evil–doers. His mood was adapted to the conditions to which He addressed Himself; tender words of encouragement or burning expletives of righteous indignation issued with equal fluency from His lips. His nature was no poetic conception of cherubic sweetness ever present, but that of a Man, with the emotions and passions essential to manhood and manliness. He, who often wept with compassion, at other times evinced in word and action the righteous anger of a God. But of all His passions, however gently they rippled or strongly surged, He was ever master. Contrast the gentle Jesus moved to hospitable service by the needs of a festive party in Cana, with the indignant Christ plying His whip, and amidst commotion and turmoil of His own making, driving cattle and men before Him as an unclean herd.[143]

The Test for Those Who Followed

5

Disciples Indeed

Mark 9:33–50   And he came to Capernaum: and being in the house he asked them, What was it that ye disputed among yourselves by the way? But they held their peace: for by the way they had disputed among themselves, who should be the greatest. And he sat down, and called the twelve, and saith unto them, If any man desire to be first, the same shall be last of all, and servant of all. And he took a child, and set him in the midst of them: and when he had taken him in his arms, he said unto them, Whosoever shall receive one of such children in my name, receiveth me: and whosoever shall receive me, receiveth not me, but him that sent me.

And John answered him, saying, Master, we saw one casting out devils in thy name, and he followeth not us: and we forbad him, because he followeth not us. But Jesus said, Forbid him not: for there is no man which shall do a miracle in my name, that can lightly speak evil of me. For he that is not against us is on our part. For whosoever shall give you a cup of water to drink in my name, because ye belong to Christ, verily I say unto you, he shall not lose his reward. And whosoever shall offend one of these little ones that believe in me, it is better for him that a millstone were hanged about his neck, and he were cast into the sea. And if thy hand offend thee, cut it off: it is better for thee to enter into life maimed, than having two hands to go into hell, into the fire that never shall be quenched: where their worm dieth not, and the fire is not quenched. And if thy foot offend thee, cut it off: it is better for thee to enter halt into life, than having two feet to be cast into hell, into the fire that never shall be quenched: where their worm dieth not, and the fire is not quenched. And if thine eye offend thee, pluck it out: it is better for thee to enter into the kingdom of God with one eye, than having two eyes to be cast into hell fire: where their worm dieth not, and the fire is not quenched. For every one shall be salted with fire, and every sacrifice shall be salted with salt. Salt is good: but if the salt have lost his saltness, wherewith will ye season it? Have salt in yourselves, and have peace one with another.

Cross-references   Matthew 18:1–11; Luke 9:46–50

This discourse has essentially the same historical introduction in all of the synoptic Gospels—there are only minor differences. Mark is used here as the primary source, but all three Synoptics are needed to acquire a complete text.

The Transfiguration of Christ[a][144] and the casting out of an evil spirit from a young boy[145] occurred just prior to this sermon. After these events, Jesus left the area and proceeded on His way to Capernaum (apparently in secret so that the multitudes would not follow Him). While they were traveling, the Apostles began disputing which of them would be the greatest in the kingdom of heaven. Jesus took no part in their discussion, but noticed that they were contending one with another.

Throughout the early ministry of Jesus, it appeared that He had favored some of the Apostles above the others. Special honors had come to Peter and he had participated in some of the Lord's conversations and miracles more often than the other Apostles; in addition, there was obviously a strong friendship between the Lord and the Apostle John.[146] These situations may have caused some of the brethren to feel that the favored Apostles would receive more in Christ's kingdom than they would.

It was during this journey that Jesus told the Apostles of His impending death and resurrection.[b] Apparently they did not really understand what was going to happen to Him, and still felt that He would eventually found a great political kingdom and restore the nation of Israel to its previous greatness.[147] They obviously thought that they would be worthy of high positions in that kingdom. Lacking understanding of the Lord's mission and thinking only of their personal ambitions, they "surrendered themselves to the selfish contemplation of their prospective stations."[148] Nothing seems to have changed them from their "invincible belief that He would soon proclaim Himself as the Messiah in the Jewish sense, and found a great political kingdom."[149]

Jesus did not enter into their conversation—or perhaps He was not close enough to participate since the Apostles were trailing behind Him at this point. Finally, perceiving the thought in their hearts, He asked them, "What was it that ye disputed among yourselves by the way?" But as Mark records, the Apostles "held their peace." Then,

a. Matthew 17.

b. Matthew 17:22–23; Mark 9:31–32.

taking a small child in His arms for emphasis, Jesus proceeded to teach them the requirements for entrance into the kingdom of God.

First, He explained that to qualify for the kingdom of heaven one must become as a little child—not that one has to become childish, but that true greatness is exemplified by some childlike character traits. A child knows nothing of the distinctions of rank so coveted by humanity. Children are unpretentious and humble. As the inspired version of the Bible reads: "Whosoever shall humble himself like one of these children, and receiveth me, ye shall receive in my name."[a]

To be great in the kingdom of God—to even gain the kingdom at all—it is necessary to be humble, for "what children are unconsciously, that Jesus requires His disciples to be voluntarily and deliberately."[150] The Lord's Apostles had confused the nuances of the Mosaic Law (as taught by the Pharisees and rulers of the Jews) with the Lord's message. Jesus emphasized that moral fitness alone would secure entrance into the kingdom. Entrance would not be based on earthly claims, whether they were of legal decree, national privilege (as taught by the Pharisees), or (as in the case of the Twelve) a sacred calling. All of these qualifications would be worthless without the humble, moral fitness personified in the young child upon Christ's knee.

Second, the Lord declared that the Apostles should receive little children not only in the literal sense, but in the sense that children represent the weak, insignificant, and helpless qualities in all mankind. The Lord warned His Apostles (and through them all of us) that they should not offend His children with worldly ambitions—even the ambitious spirit that the Twelve had been evidencing.

As yet, the refining powers of the gospel had not yet operated in the lives of the Apostles: they still had to be converted, "changed from their carnal and fallen state to a state of righteousness, becoming again pure and spotless as they were in their infancy. Such is the state of those who become heirs of salvation."[151]

The Lord then described the punishment for offending His children, a punishment which the Twelve should have been familiar with for the Romans had actually used it on some of the leaders of a previous Judean insurrection in Galilee. (The Romans had hung large millstones around the necks of the Jewish rebels and thrown them into the sea of Galilee.)[152] Take special note that the Lord did not say there would be no offenses against the children of His kingdom; He was well aware of the nature of man. But He stated strongly, "Woe to that man by whom the offence cometh! . . . It were better for him that a millstone were hanged about his neck, and that he were drowned in the depth of the sea." The Lord elaborated this point by stating that it was better to have a member of the body cut off than to have that member cause the eternal loss of the soul. Mark adds that even offending members of the kingdom would have to be cut off to ensure that the kingdom was incorruptible.

In Mark's report of this discourse he gives special emphasis to the use of salt. This would have conveyed special meaning to the Apostles. They knew the importance of salt in the proper worship of Jehovah under the Law of Moses. Every sacrifice for the altar had to be salted[a] for it symbolized the incorruptibility of the sacrifice. Thus, the Lord compared an errant soul to salt that had lost its savor, saying that if he would not repent, he would be cut off.[b][153]

At this point in the discourse, John interrupted and asked a question about someone the Apostles had observed casting out devils in the name of the Lord—even though he was not one of Jesus' disciples. Jesus responded with an interesting comment. He said, "For he that is not against us is on our part," and he told the brethren that they should not curtail the man's activities. Perhaps the man had witnessed the goodness of the Lord and the results of His many miracles and was simply imitating that goodness, not really understanding the Messiah or His kingdom. Yet, assuredly, he would have to come to that understanding in order to acquire salvation. No further information is given in the scriptures as to who the man was or anything about him.

John's question being resolved, the Lord moved to the third and last point of His discourse. He concluded that if anyone despised or injured one of His little ones (His disciples), they were totally out of harmony with the mind of heaven.

Suddenly, the Apostles realized that the distinctions of knowledge, merit, and worth—so heavily emphasized by the Jews of their day— were not enough. They needed a simpler and more unconscious form of humility. Submission to the commandments and requirements the Lord was teaching them would merit the kingdom. No one who desired Christ's love could deliberately offend or heartlessly condemn

a. Leviticus 2:13.
b. D&C 64:12–13.

a brother—however insignificant he seemed to be. To acquire the kingdom of God, emphasis must not only be placed on the first great commandment, but on the second great commandment as well.

This was the point that Jesus wished to impress upon His disciples. He wanted them to understand that self–interest was inconsistent with the dictates of the kingdom. They must exercise the charity that He was exemplifying to them. They must be simple and earnest in their faith and have absolute trust in Him.

To the Twelve

Matthew 20:17–28   And Jesus going up to Jerusalem took the twelve disciples apart in the way, and said unto them, Behold, we go up to Jerusalem; and the Son of man shall be betrayed unto the chief priests and unto the scribes, and they shall condemn him to death, and shall deliver him to the Gentiles to mock, and to scourge, and to crucify him: and the third day he shall rise again.

Then came to him the mother of Zebedee's children with her sons, worshipping him, and desiring a certain thing of him. And he said unto her, What wilt thou? She saith unto him, Grant that these my two sons may sit, the one on thy right hand, and the other on the left, in thy kingdom. But Jesus answered and said, Ye know not what ye ask. Are ye able to drink of the cup that I shall drink of, and to be baptized with the baptism that I am baptized with? They say unto him, We are able. And he saith unto them, Ye shall drink indeed of my cup, and be baptized with the baptism that I am baptized with: but to sit on my right hand, and on my left, is not mine to give, but it shall be given to them for whom it is prepared of my Father. And when the ten heard it, they were moved with indignation against the two brethren. But Jesus called them unto him, and said, Ye know that the princes of the Gentiles exercise dominion over them, and they that are great exercise authority upon them. But it shall not be so among you: but whosoever will be great among you, let him be your minister; and whosoever will be chief among you, let him be your servant: even as the Son of man came not to be ministered unto, but to minister, and to give his life a ransom for many.

Cross–references   Mark 10:32–45; Luke 18:31–34; 22:24–27

This discourse occurred as Jesus and His Apostles were traveling to Jerusalem for the last time. The Apostles did not immediately understand the instructions the Lord gave in this discourse, but Matthew ultimately perceived them to have been a prediction of those terrible days when the betrayal, trial, and crucifixion of Christ took place, and he recorded them from that perspective.[154]

According to Matthew's writings, the rich young ruler's question preceded this discourse. During the ensuing interview the Lord told the young ruler to sell all that he had and follow Him, concluding that it was very difficult for a rich man to enter the kingdom of heaven.[a] This conclusion had amazed the Lord's disciples, and it motivated Peter to ask what the Apostles would receive since they had forsaken all to follow Jesus. The Lord acknowledged that they had given up all and promised them that eventually they would sit upon thrones of glory and judge the twelve tribes of Israel[b] Perhaps the moment of elation this promise elicited caused the Apostles to be "completely possessed by romantic expectations, their heads giddy with the sparkling wine of vain hope; and as they drew nigh the holy city their firm conviction was, 'that the kingdom of God should immediately appear.'"[155] The Lord dampened their spirits by warning them for the third time of His impending death and resurrection[156]—yet they still failed to comprehend.[157]

This continuous misunderstanding by the Twelve might be explained by their continued reluctance to accept the truth after having been taught the advent of a glorious, politically powerful Messiah in their youth: they undoubtedly found it difficult to accept the fact that they were following the Savior to the cross and to the grave.[158]

While the Lord's warning was still fresh in the Apostles' minds, Salome, the mother of James and John (and Mary's sister), petitioned Jesus for a favor. The request itself was evidence that none of the Lord's disciples understood the things which He had been teaching them concerning His coming death and resurrection.[c][159] Salome's request was ambitious: she wanted her sons to sit "one on thy right hand, and the other on thy left, in thy glory."

With the prediction of the death and resurrection of the Savior still fresh in their memories, the timing of this request seems to be incredible; yet the Lord received the petition with unbelievable patience and tenderness, as if it had come merely as a result of the love of a mother for her devoted sons. He answered them without rebuke by asking James and John if they were willing to "drink of the cup that I shall drink of," to which these zealous followers readily agreed. But this honor was not His to give as a result of mere favoritism.

When the ten heard what James and John were aspiring to, they were "moved with indignation against the two brethren." At this point

a. Matthew
19:16–24.

b. Matthew 19:28.

c. Luke 18:34.

in the Lord's ministry, it would appear that at least some of the Twelve were harboring feelings of self–importance and sought to elevate themselves one above another.

These twelve, special men, who should have been closely united in the last solemn hours before the Lord's crucifixion, had been distracted from His teachings by thoughts of aggrandizement and future glory. The Lord called them together and calmly taught them that only their service would ensure their greatness in His kingdom. He used the example of the gentile kings and how they "lorded it over" their subjects, noting how differently His power should be acquired and used. He told them, "Whosoever will be great among you, let him be your minister;" and "Whosoever will be chief among you, let him be your servant." He concluded by stating that He would give His life as a ransom for others; that He had come not to be ministered to but to minister; and that those who would be great among them in His service must emulate His greatness—"not greatness through service, but the greatness of service; and, whosoever would be chief or rather 'first' among [you], let it be in service."[160]

The Testimony of Twelve

Matthew 16:13–28 When Jesus came into the coasts of Caesarea Philippi, he asked his disciples, saying, Whom do men say that I the Son of man am? And they said, "Some say that thou art John the Baptist: some, Elias; and others, Jeremias, or one of the prophets. He saith unto them, But whom say ye that I am? And Simon Peter answered and said, Thou art the Christ, the Son of the living God. And Jesus answered and said unto him, Blessed art thou, Simon Barjona: for flesh and blood hath not revealed it unto thee, but my Father which is in heaven. And I say also unto thee, That thou art Peter, and upon this rock I will build my church; and the gates of hell shall not prevail against it. And I will give unto thee the keys of the kingdom of heaven: and whatsoever thou shalt bind on earth shall be bound in heaven: and whatsoever thou shalt loose on earth shall be loosed in heaven. Then charged he his disciples that they should tell no man that he was Jesus the Christ.

From that time forth began Jesus to shew unto his disciples, how that he must go unto Jerusalem, and suffer many things of the elders and chief priests and scribes, and be killed, and be raised again the third day. Then Peter took him, and began to rebuke him, saying, Be it far from thee, Lord: this shall not be unto thee. But he turned, and said unto Peter, Get thee behind me, Satan: thou art an offence unto me: for thou savourest not the things that be of God, but those that be of men.

Then said Jesus unto his disciples, If any man will come after me, let him deny himself, and take up his cross, and follow me. For whosoever will save his life shall lose it: and whosoever will lose his life for my sake shall find it. For what is a man profited, if he shall gain the whole world, and lose his own soul? or what shall a man give in exchange for his soul? For the Son of man shall come in the glory of his Father with his angels; and then he shall reward every man according to his works. Verily I say unto you, There be some standing here, which shall not taste of death, till they see the Son of man coming in his kingdom.

Cross–references   Mark 8:27–38; 9:1; Luke 9:18–27

Jesus was alone with the Twelve on the coast of Caesarea Philippi, and for perhaps the first time in a long while He had the opportunity to confidentially instruct them. He had recently delivered a memorable discourse at Capernaum, where He clearly claimed to be the "bread of life," the Son of God. This had led to the defection of many of His disciples[a] and had obviously raised questions in the minds of the Twelve, for Jesus had asked them, "Will ye also go away?"[b] The Pharisees and Sadducees had asked the Lord some difficult questions, and perhaps His answers had disappointed the Twelve, for He would not openly confront nor publicly challenge the Jewish leaders.[161] With these experiences fresh in the Apostles' minds, they silently set sail with their Lord across the Sea of Galilee.

With the many miracles and teachings Jesus had thus far produced in His ministry, it was obvious that He had become the talk of all Israel; but He had "neither by word nor deed . . . measured up to the popular and traditional standard of the expected Deliverer and King of Israel"[162]—even though they had seen Him in the context of the prophets of old.

In their private setting Jesus asked the Twelve, "Whom do men say that I the Son of man am?" They responded that some thought He was Elijah, some Jeremiah, and others John the Baptist. Their answer did not mean that the Jews thought Christ was literally the incarnate Elijah, Jeremiah, or John the Baptist (the Jews did not believe in the transmigration of souls),[163] but rather that He was continuing the work of these prophets by preparing the way for the Messiah yet to come. Although the Jews differed on the purpose of Christ's mission, they did not regard Him as an ordinary man. They recognized that He had a mission from heaven—but they would not accept Him as the Messiah.[164]

a. John 6:41–66.
b. John 6:67.

Next, Christ asked His Apostles, "But whom say ye that I am?" Peter boldly stepped forward and undoubtedly spoke for all of the Twelve when he replied, "Thou art the Christ, the Son of the living God."

None of the three Synoptics agree on the exact words Peter used in this response. Mark reported that Peter said, "Thou art the Christ," and Luke reported his answer to be "the Christ of God," but the meaning is the same. It is another testament of the independence of the gospel writers. The Twelve understood at that point that Jesus was the bread of life, the Son of God, the long–awaited Messiah and Savior of the world. Their belief was based upon a confirmation from the Spirit as given from the Father, and the Savior so confirmed it.

The Lord then congratulated Peter for having received the revelation necessary to confirm his belief and promised him the keys of the kingdom of heaven. The keys which the Savior promised Peter were those of the right of presidency and the sealing power.[165] The "rock" upon which the church would be built was not Peter (even though he was to act as the first President of the church), but was that means by which Peter and all others after him would receive the knowledge from God that Jesus was the Christ. It was upon the rock of revelation that the Lord would build His church, and against which the gates of hell would not prevail.[166]

From this time forth the Lord instructed the Twelve more clearly and with greater detail concerning His coming death and resurrection. Prior to this time He had borne witness of these coming events, but the witness had been couched in riddles, the meaning of which would only become clear after the Crucifixion had taken place. He had spoken of His body as a temple which, after being destroyed, would rise again in three days.[a] Another time He spoke of lifting the Son of Man up like Moses had raised the brazen serpent in the wilderness.[b] On yet another occasion He spoke of the separation of the bridegroom from the children of the bride chamber,[c] and of giving His flesh for the world.[d] He said that a sign would be given, the sign of the prophet Jonas:[e] but now it was necessary that the Twelve, having confessed Him as the Messiah, prepare themselves for the coming events. The Lord specifically taught them what was going to happen to Him, and He charged them that they should not openly testify to others that they knew He was the Messiah. Perhaps this charge by the

a. John 2:19.
b. John 3:14.
c. Matthew 9:15.
d. John 6:53.
e. Matthew 16:4.

Lord—a charge similar to that given to Peter, James, and John after their experience on the Mount of Transfiguration[a]—was a contributing reason why Peter denied knowing Jesus when he was challenged by the people watching the Lord's trial.[b] Undoubtedly, if the Twelve had testified of the Lord prior to His crucifixion, they may have been crucified also, and there would have been no one in authority left to carry on the Savior's work. The ministry of the Messiah in the midst of His chosen people had to continue to its inevitable end at Jerusalem.

When Peter finally realized what was going to happen to Jesus, he became greatly alarmed. He took the Lord aside and began to "rebuke" him. Jesus' response was stern, and He associated Peter with the very devil himself; for what Peter had said, undoubtedly out of love for the Lord, was in essence what the devil had said to tempt Jesus in the wilderness after He had been fasting for thirty days. Peter was essentially saying, "If thou be the Son of God, why must you suffer such a scandalous death?" Thus, Peter's ill–conceived attempt to counsel the Lord was, in fact, an effort "to tempt the Lord."[167] The Lord's response, "Get thee behind me, Satan," was a total rebuke of Peter's intentions.

The Lord used this chastisement of Peter to teach the Twelve Apostles some general principles concerning God's kingdom and true discipleship. The disciples could either choose to save their mortal lives and lose the Lord's kingdom, or lose their mortal lives through self–denial and persecution while saving their souls in heaven.[168] When the Son of Man comes again in His glory, eternal gains and eternal losses will be judged according to the deeds men have performed in His service, not according to the material successes they achieved in this life.

Jesus concluded this discourse with a reference to the blessing He would bestow on John the Beloved, for John would never taste of death. He would live to minister to people in the flesh until Christ should come again.

a. Matthew 17:9.

b. Matthew
 26:69–75.

"I Know That Messias Cometh"　　　　6

"I Know That Messias Cometh"

John 4:1–42　　When therefore the Lord knew how the Pharisees had heard that Jesus made and baptized more disciples than John, (though Jesus himself baptized not, but his disciples,) He left Judaea, and departed again into Galilee. And he must needs go through Samaria. Then cometh he to a city of Samaria, which is called Sychar, near to the parcel of ground that Jacob gave to his son Joseph. Now Jacob's well was there. Jesus therefore, being wearied with his journey, sat thus on the well: and it was about the sixth hour. There cometh a woman of Samaria to draw water: Jesus saith unto her, Give me to drink. (For his disciples were gone away unto the city to buy meat.) Then saith the woman of Samaria unto him, How is it that thou, being a Jew, askest drink of me, which am a woman of Samaria? for the Jews have no dealings with the Samaritans. Jesus answered and said unto her, If thou knewest the gift of God, and who it is that saith to thee, Give me to drink; thou wouldest have asked of him, and he would have given thee living water. The woman saith unto him, Sir, thou hast nothing to draw with, and the well is deep: from whence then hast thou that living water? Art thou greater than our father Jacob, which gave us the well, and drank thereof himself, and his children, and his cattle? Jesus answered and said unto her, Whosoever drinketh of this water shall thirst again: but whosoever drinketh of the water that I shall give him shall never thirst; but the water that I shall give him shall be in him a well of water springing up into everlasting life. The woman saith unto him, Sir, give me this water, that I thirst not, neither come hither to draw. Jesus saith unto her, Go, call thy husband, and come hither. The woman answered and said, I have no husband. Jesus said unto her, Thou hast well said, I have no husband: for thou hast had five husbands; and he whom thou now hast is not thy husband: in that saidst thou truly. The woman saith unto him, Sir, I perceive that thou art a prophet. Our fathers worshipped in this mountain; and ye say, that in Jerusalem is the place where men ought to worship. Jesus saith unto her, Woman, believe me, the hour cometh, when ye shall neither in this mountain, nor yet at Jerusalem, worship the Father. Ye worship ye know not what: we know what we worship: for salvation is of the Jews. But the hour cometh, and now is, when the true worshippers shall worship the Father in spirit and in truth: for the Father seeketh such to worship him. God is a Spirit: and they that worship him must worship him in spirit and in truth. The woman saith unto him, I know that Messias cometh, which is called Christ: when he is come, he will tell us all things. Jesus saith unto her, I that speak unto thee am he.

And upon this came his disciples, and marvelled that he talked with the woman: yet no man said, What seekest thou? or, Why talkest thou with her? The woman then left her waterpot, and went her way into the city, and saith to the men, Come, see a man, which told me all things that ever I did: is not this the Christ? Then they went out of the city, and came unto him.

In the mean while his disciples prayed him, saying, Master, eat. But he said unto them, I have meat to eat that ye know not of. Therefore said the disciples one to another, Hath any man brought him ought to eat? Jesus saith unto them, My meat is to do the will of him that sent me, and to finish his work. Say not ye, There are yet four months, and then cometh harvest? behold, I say unto you, Lift up your eyes, and look on the fields; for they are white already to harvest. And he that reapeth receiveth wages, and gathereth fruit unto life eternal: that both he that soweth and he that reapeth may rejoice together. And herein is that saying true, One soweth, and another reapeth. I sent you to reap that whereon ye bestowed no labour: other men laboured, and ye are entered into their labours.

And many of the Samaritans of that city believed on him for the saying of the woman, which testified, He told me all that ever I did. So when the Samaritans were come unto him, they besought him that he would tarry with them: and he abode there two days. And many more believed because of his own word; and said unto the woman, Now we believe, not because of thy saying: for we have heard him ourselves, and know that this is indeed the Christ, the Saviour of the world.

This chapter deals with the first of Christ's discourses which are formal declarations of His Messiahship. All of these discourses are found in the Gospel of John.[169] Whereas the synoptic Gospels are set primarily in Galilee and Perea, Jerusalem and Judea are the setting for John's Gospel. The accurate descriptions emanating from the pages of his work belong to a writer who was born and had lived among the people and places that he was writing about. It is evident that he grew up with an expectation of the Messiah, and that he personally experienced the life and ministry of Jesus.[170]

Prior to this discourse, Jesus had gone to Jerusalem to attend the Passover and inaugurate His formal ministry. He had amazed the multitudes at the Passover feast by performing many miracles.[a] As His fame increased, the Pharisees began paying greater attention to Him (as they did with John the Baptist before Him). Their antagonism

a. John 2:23.

toward Jesus and John indicated that they had been keeping a careful watch over the Lord's new religious movement.[171]

John the Baptist had been very popular among the Jewish people, and the scriptures note that the movement of Jesus had caught on with even greater enthusiasm. Jesus baptized, though "not so many as his disciples,"[a] and it is not unreasonable to assume that He administered all of the ordinances of the gospel as an example to the newly called Twelve.[172]

Turning from Jerusalem after the Passover feast, Jesus undertook His first, long missionary journey through Samaria. The Judeans would normally have detoured through Perea in order to avoid the hostile and ignorant Samaritans, but the Galileans would not have done so as they traveled home toward their capital.[173]

After a hot and dusty walk that took most of the day, Jesus arrived at the well of Jacob. He was tired from His long journey, and He rested in the shade of the well while He sent His disciples to Sychar for food and provisions.[174]

While He was resting, a woman approached with a water jar on her head and a long cord for lowering the jar down into the well.[175] As she drew near, Jesus asked her for a drink of the water to quench His thirst. The woman was obviously astonished, for she immediately recognized Him as a Jew. Such recognition would not have been difficult, for undoubtedly His language differed from hers and His attire would have included the blue fringes required by the Levitical Law for those who taught in the synagogues.[176] She asked Jesus why He would make such a request, "for the Jews have no dealings with the Samaritans." The Jews reserved the very name, Samaritan, as a term for reproach, and used it to describe those who were of a foreign race.[177]

After the ten tribes had been deported to Assyria, heathen transplants from various parts of the Assyrian Empire colonized Samaria.[b] (A scattering of the ten tribes still remained, and perhaps other settlers from Judea.) The Old Testament notes that the lions in the land came and terrorized these colonists and slew some of them, and it further attributes the ferocity of the lions toward the colonists to the fact that they knew not the God of Israel.[c] Therefore, they sent for some of the exiled priests from the tribes of Israel and added the worship of Jehovah to their worship of idols.[d] Ultimately, the foreigners be-

a. IV John 4:3.

b. 2 Kings 17:24.

c. 2 Kings 17:26.

d. 2 Kings 17:27.

came more rigidly attached to the Law of Moses than the Jews.[178] The animosity between the new inhabitants of Samaria and the Jews grew more intense at the time of Ezra and Nehemiah because the Jews would not let the Samaritans participate in the reconstruction of the temple.[a]

The Samaritans built a temple of their own on Mount Gerizim, but by Jesus' time it had been destroyed. They still claimed, however, that Mount Gerizim in Samaria was more holy than Mount Moriah in Judea. They claimed Abraham and Jacob had worshipped on Mount Gerizim, and had built altars there for the blessing of the people.[b] Traditionally, they believed that Abraham had offered his son Isaac upon the mount and that he had met Melchizedek there returning from his wars.[179]

The Samaritans accused the Jews of "adding" to the word of God because the Jews believed in all the prophets since Moses while the Samaritans vehemently denied their authenticity. They believed that only the Pentateuch was inspired and that no prophets had been called since Moses. Also, they steadfastly looked forward to the coming of an anticipated Messiah.[c][180] As a result of their beliefs, "the Samaritan conception of the mission of the expected Messiah was somewhat better founded than was that of the Jews, for the Samaritans gave greater prominence to the spiritual kingdom the Messiah would establish, and were less exclusive in their views as to whom the Messianic blessings would be extended."[181]

The Samaritans favored Herod because the Jews hated him; they would kindle small fires upon the hills in an attempt to confuse the Jewish reckoning of the new moon and to throw the Jewish feasts into disorder; and they also defiled the temple at Jerusalem by strewing human bones in it at the Passover.[182]

The Jewish hatred for the Samaritans was no less intense. A Jew could not eat food touched by a Samaritan; the Samaritans could not be proselyted, nor would they be resurrected; no friendships could be kindled with them, no bargains between them were valid; testimony from a Samaritan could not be used in a Jewish court; and if a Samaritan entered into a Jewish household, he brought the curse of God upon that home.[183] In spite of all these hatreds and animosities, unavoidable interaction did exist between the races (the Jews inventing casuistry upon casuistry to allow such).[184]

a. Ezra 4:1–3.

b. Deuteronomy
    11:29; 27:12.

c. Deuteronomy
    18:18.

None of these strifes and prejudices mattered to Jesus, and there is perhaps no greater example in all of the New Testament than this discourse to indicate that Jesus taught the kingdom of God wherever there was spiritual darkness. It is possible that one reason why John included this discourse in his Gospel was to testify to the fact that Jesus was attempting to abolish the deep–seated enmities that exist between people.[185]

Jesus' meeting with the woman at the well occurred naturally, as did His request for a drink. He was hot and thirsty and the water in the well was cool. The woman had undoubtedly come to the well in the course of her normal daily routine and, like the parable of the hidden treasure,[186] "stumbled" upon the gospel.

When, during the course of their conversation, Jesus told her that He could provide her with "living water," she did not understand,[187] and she responded logically by stating that He had nothing to draw water with. Perhaps she partially understood His meaning, however, because she asked Jesus if He was greater than father Jacob who had dug the well. To this Jesus responded, "Whosoever drinketh of this water shall thirst again [referring to the well water], but whosoever drinketh of the water that I shall give him shall never thirst." But again the woman missed the spiritual analogy and thought only of how nice it would be to receive relief from the tedious chore of drawing her water from a well.

Apparently having exhausted this line of conversation, and perhaps to further awaken a sleeping conscience of the religious instruction He was attempting to give her, the Lord abruptly changed the subject and asked the woman to call her husband: but she had no husband and so stated. The Lord acknowledged her honest answer and declared unto her that she had in fact had five husbands and was now living with a man that was not her husband. No indication is given in the scriptural text of the status of these prior husbands, but the woman was astounded that Jesus knew these things about her and at once recognized that someone greater than an ordinary man was before her. She declared, "Sir, I perceive that thou art a prophet."[188]

Then the woman quickly turned the subject away from her personal problems and sins by asking the Lord whether it was the Samaritans or the Jews who were worshipping correctly. Jesus replied that neither worshipped correctly. He acknowledged that anciently the Jewish religion had been accurate and hers had been wrong, but now neither was right. He explained that future worship would be directed toward Him, through the Spirit, and only He and His church would dispense the truth.

With this instruction, the woman's spiritual awareness expanded and she could envision the kingdom of the Messiah. She spoke eagerly of her anticipation for that kingdom. Her anxious yearning for the Messiah must have cheered the Savior's heart and for the first time, to a humble Samaritan woman, He openly disclosed, "I that speak unto thee am he."[189]

With this knowledge burning in her soul, the woman abandoned her waterpot and hurried into the city to testify that she had seen the Messiah. The actual sequence of events in this discourse is blurred in the scriptural narrative, but John reports that at about this time the disciples returned from purchasing some meat. John notes that they were astonished when they saw Jesus in conversation with the Samaritan woman, not just because she was a Samaritan, but because relationships between the sexes were severely restricted in the Jewish culture. Women were considered inferior to men to the extent that the Talmud recorded, "No one is to speak with a woman, even if she be his wife, in the public street."[190] The Apostles did not voice their astonishment, but requested that Jesus eat the provisions they had procured. But Jesus was preoccupied—all thoughts of hunger had left His mind. He stated, "I have meat to eat that ye know not of." He could envision the results of His ministry to these people, and was undoubtedly saddened at the apparent lack of understanding on the part of His disciples. Anticipating their thoughts, He told them to not think of the harvest (yet four months away) but to "lift up your eyes and look on the fields; for they are white already to harvest."[191] The woman at the well had perceived what the disciples could not yet comprehend, for what had been rejected in Judea would now produce a spiritual harvest in Samaria.

The Samaritans flocked to see Jesus as a result of the woman's testimony.[192] They asked Him to tarry with them, which He did for two days. During that time He reaped the first of His great spiritual harvests, and many Samaritan men and women gained a personal testimony of Him as the Messiah.

The scriptures do not give a detailed account of what occurred during the ensuing two–day period, but from previous activity, we can assume that Jesus preached the gospel and healed and comforted those who came to see Him. The kingdom of God was not to be based upon tribal privilege or the narrow designation of nationality,[193] for Jesus was proclaiming that all people are equal in God's eyes and can be acceptable to Him.

The Messiah They Looked For

7

"The Father Hath Sent Me"

John 5:17–47   But Jesus answered them, My Father worketh hitherto, and I work. Therefore the Jews sought the more to kill him, because he not only had broken the sabbath, but said also that God was his Father, making himself equal with God. Then answered Jesus and said unto them, Verily, verily, I say unto you, The Son can do nothing of himself, but what he seeth the Father do: for what things soever he doeth, these also doeth the Son likewise. For the Father loveth the Son, and sheweth him all things that himself doeth: and he will shew him greater works than these, that ye may marvel. For as the Father raiseth up the dead, and quickeneth them; even so the Son quickeneth whom he will. For the Father judgeth no man, but hath committed all judgment unto the Son: that all men should honour the Son, even as they honour the Father. He that honoureth not the Son honoureth not the Father which hath sent him. Verily, verily, I say unto you, He that heareth my word, and believeth on him that sent me, hath everlasting life, and shall not come into condemnation; but is passed from death unto life. Verily, verily, I say unto you, The hour is coming, and now is, when the dead shall hear the voice of the Son of God: and they that hear shall live. For as the Father hath life in himself; so hath he given to the Son to have life in himself; and hath given him authority to execute judgment also, because he is the Son of man. Marvel not at this: for the hour is coming, in the which all that are in the graves shall hear his voice, and shall come forth; they that have done good, unto the resurrection of life; and they that have done evil, unto the resurrection of damnation. I can of mine own self do nothing: as I hear, I judge: and my judgment is just; because I seek not mine own will, but the will of the Father which hath sent me. If I bear witness of myself, my witness is not true.

There is another that beareth witness of me; and I know that the witness which he witnesseth of me is true. Ye sent unto John, and he bare witness unto the truth. But I received not testimony from man: but these things I say, that ye might be saved. He was a burning and a shining light: and ye were willing for a season to rejoice in his light.

But I have greater witness than that of John: for the works which the Father hath given me to finish, the same works that I do, bear witness of me, that the Father hath sent me. And the Father himself, which hath sent me, hath borne witness of me. Ye have neither heard his voice at any time, nor seen his shape. And ye have not his word abiding in you: for whom he hath sent, him ye believe not.

Search the scriptures; for in them ye think ye have eternal life: and they are they which testify of me. And ye will not come to me, that ye might have life. I receive not honour from men. But I know you, that ye have not the love of God in you. I am come in my Father's name, and ye receive me not: if another shall come in his own name, him ye will receive. How can ye believe, which receive honour one of another, and seek not the honour that cometh from God only? Do not think that I will accuse you to the Father: there is one that accuseth you, even Moses, in whom ye trust. For had ye believed Moses, ye would have believed me: for he wrote of me. But if ye believe not his writings, how shall ye believe my words?

This discourse constitutes a direct confrontation between Jesus and the rulers of the Jews, and is one of the few times that such a confrontation occurs. It appears from the scriptural rendering and the circumstances immediately prior to the discourse that Jesus may have anticipated making this declaration of His Messiahship before the Jewish rulers. He had previously made a public declaration of His divinity to the Samaritan woman at the well, and He had undoubtedly testified of His mission and Messiahship throughout the rest of His Galilean ministry.

At the conclusion of His mission, Jesus returned to Jerusalem to attend a feast. John does not name the feast, although some have determined that it was the Feast of Purim.[194] Upon His arrival in the city, Jesus went to the pool of Bethesda and healed an impotent man who had been ill for thirty–eight years.[a][195] The healing was performed on the Sabbath day, which allowed the Jews to bring the specific charge of Sabbath breaking against Jesus. At the time of this healing the impotent man did not know that his benefactor was the Lord, but he later learned His name and reported it to the Jewish leadership. They proceeded to ignore the miraculous healing that had taken place and "sought to slay him [Jesus] because he had done these things on the sabbath day."[b] In response to their murderous intentions, Jesus delivered the following discourse.

The discourse can be divided into three sections:

1.   Christ's relationship to the Father.

a. John 5:2–9.

b. John 5:16.

2.　　Christ's function as the judge of all men.

3.　　Christ's personal witness of His own divinity.

Christ's Relationship to the Father

After the miracle at Bethesda and the subsequent confrontation with the Jewish leaders, Jesus was charged with Sabbath breaking. He responded to this charge by stating, "My Father worketh hitherto, and I work." The Jews hallowed the Sabbath above all other days of the week. They exercised extraordinary strictness in their observance of its laws. They had developed a vast array of prohibitions and injunctions for the Sabbath, defining everything from the amount of food that one could carry to the number of letters one could write. There were special kinds of knots that one had to use that day, and if perchance a man were unfortunate enough to be buried by a cave–in on the Sabbath, rescuers could dig for him, but if they found him dead they had to leave the body in the hole until the next day—they could only remove him if he was alive.[196]

Healing on the Sabbath was strictly forbidden,[a] but when the leaders of the Jews accused Jesus of Sabbath breaking they were ill–prepared for His defense. The Jews understood the implication of His comment and sought to kill Him all the more because He had claimed that God was His Father. Jesus had declared Himself to be the Messiah and in the eyes of the Jewish leadership, He had blasphemed. He had declared that His Father had always done the work of salvation on the Sabbath day, and therefore He (being the Son) could also do such work. Through this statement Jesus taught that there was a greater work to be performed than that of the Sabbath.[197] Undoubtedly shocked by Christ's claim, the Jewish leaders listened to the rest of His sermon.

Jesus first declared that even in a personal sense, God was His Father.[198] He then declared that He did nothing of Himself, but only that which He had seen the Father do. Because the Father loved Him, He had been shown all things that the Father had done.[199] The Lord concluded this section of the sermon by openly disclosing that His Father would raise up the dead, a power that had also been given to the Son. This is the "most comprehensive sermon in scripture on the

a. Luke 13:14.

vital subject of the relationship between the Eternal Father and His Son, Jesus Christ."[200]

Christ's Function as the Judge of All Men

After announcing His divine commission, Jesus explained the authority that had been granted to Him by the Father.[201] He boldly proclaimed that the Father had given all judgment into the hands of the Son, and that if men honored the Son they would honor the Father: but that if they honored not the Son, they would not honor the Father. By this statement Jesus again declared His equality with God. To emphasize this point, He stated that those who heard His words and believed on them would have everlasting life while those who did not would be condemned. He continued by announcing that the dead would soon hear His voice and that He had inherited from the Father the power of immortality, stating that He had "life in himself."

Then the Lord returned to the topic of the resurrection, stating that all that were in the grave would hear His voice and be resurrected: those who were good to the resurrection of life, and those who were evil to the resurrection of damnation.[a] Having unquestionably affirmed the universality of the resurrection, the Lord again testified that He was doing the will of His Father.

Christ's Personal Witness of His Own Divinity

The Lord next provided six witnesses of His divinity for the angry and astonished Jewish rulers.

First, he bore His own testimony of His calling; but without other witnesses, the Law of Moses disallowed such evidence, and Jesus acknowledged that. The Lord declared that the second witness was John the Baptist, and He noted how they had received John's testimony at first, but eventually rejected it. The third witness of His divinity was His own works, which He declared to be an even greater witness than John the Baptist. The fourth witness was God the Father. He stated that the Father had borne witness of Him (to the condemnation of the leadership before Him, for they had neither heard the Father nor had His word abide in them). He proclaimed the fifth witness of His divinity by admonishing the scholars and learned men who stood before Him to search the scriptures, for "they are they which testify of   a. D&C 76:17.

me." The sixth and last witness of His divinity was the Jews' revered prophet, Moses. "For," he said, "had ye believed Moses, ye would have believed me: for he wrote of me."

The Lord was very plain in pointing out the problems the Jewish leaders were having in accepting Him. He told them that their main ambition was to receive honors from one another and from their fellowman. They could believe in false Messiahs more easily than they would believe in Him who had come in the Father's name. They did not believe in Him because they were not of His spirit.[202] He testified to them that He did not have to accuse them before the Father for "there is one that accuseth you, even Moses, in whom ye trust."

By this time, the angry Jewish leaders were completely committed to taking the Lord's life; but in the confusion that followed His discourse, He departed from Jerusalem. This was a turning point in the life of Christ. Until this discourse He had enjoyed at least a measure of tolerance and perhaps even acceptance in Jerusalem, but it was no longer safe for Him there. Even in Galilee His determined enemies would watch and follow Him.

The Bread of Life

John 6:22–71   The day following, when the people which stood on the other side of the sea saw that there was none other boat there, save that one whereinto his disciples were entered, and that Jesus went not with his disciples into the boat, but that his disciples were gone away alone; (howbeit there came other boats from Tiberias nigh unto the place where they did eat bread, after that the Lord had given thanks:) when the people therefore saw that Jesus was not there, neither his disciples, they also took shipping, and came to Capernaum, seeking for Jesus. And when they had found him on the other side of the sea, they said unto him, Rabbi, when earnest thou hither? Jesus answered them and said, Verily, verily, I say unto you, Ye seek me, not because ye saw the miracles, but because ye did eat of the loaves, and were filled. Labour not for the meat which perisheth, but for that meat which endureth unto everlasting life, which the Son of man shall give unto you: for him hath God the Father sealed. Then said they unto him, What shall we do, that we might work the works of God? Jesus answered and said unto them, This is the work of God, that ye believe on him whom he hath sent. They said therefore unto him, What sign shewest thou then, that we may see, and believe thee? what dost thou work? Our fathers did eat manna in the desert; as it is written, He gave them bread from heaven to eat. Then Jesus said unto them, Verily, verily, I say unto you, Moses gave you not that bread from heaven; but my Father giveth you the true bread from heaven. For the bread of God is he which cometh down from heaven, and giveth life unto the world. Then said they unto him, Lord, evermore give us this bread. And Jesus said unto them, I am the bread of life: he that cometh to me shall never hunger; and he that believeth on me shall never thirst. But I said unto you, That ye also have seen me, and believe not. All that the Father giveth me shall come to me; and him that cometh to me I will in no wise cast out. For I came down from heaven, not to do mine own will, but the will of him that sent me. And this is the Father's will which hath sent me, that of all which he hath given me I should lose nothing, but should raise it up again at the last day. And this is the will of him that sent me, that every one which seeth the Son, and believeth on him, may have everlasting life: and I will raise him up at the last day. The Jews then murmured at him, because he said, I am the bread which came down from heaven. And they said, Is not this Jesus, the son of Joseph, whose father and mother we know? how is it then that he saith, I came down from heaven? Jesus therefore answered and said unto them, Murmur not among yourselves. No man can come to me, except the Father which hath sent me draw him: and I will raise him up at the last day. It is written in the prophets, And they shall be all taught of God. Every man therefore that hath heard, and hath learned of the Father, cometh unto me. Not that any man hath seen the Father, save he which is of God, he hath seen the Father. Verily, verily, I say unto you, He that believeth on me hath everlasting life. I am that bread of life. Your fathers did eat manna in the wilderness, and are dead. This is the bread which cometh down from heaven, that a man may eat thereof, and not die. I am the living bread which came down from heaven: if any man eat of this bread, he shall live for ever: and the bread that I will give is my flesh, which I will give for the life of the world. The Jews therefore strove among themselves, saying, How can this man give us his flesh to eat? Then Jesus said unto them, Verily, verily, I say unto you, Except ye eat the flesh of the Son of man, and drink his blood, ye have no life in you. Whoso eateth my flesh, and drinketh my blood, hath eternal life; and I will raise him up at the last day. For my flesh is meat indeed, and my blood is drink indeed. He that eateth my flesh, and drinketh my blood, dwelleth in me, and I in him. As the living Father hath sent me, and I live by the Father: so he that eateth me, even he shall live by me. This is that bread which came down from heaven: not as your fathers did eat manna, and are dead: he that eateth of this bread shall live for ever. These things said he in the synagogue, as he taught in Capernaum. Many therefore of his disciples, when they had heard this, said, This is an hard saying; who can hear it? When Jesus knew in himself that his disciples murmured at it, he said unto them, Doth this offend you? What and if ye shall see the Son of man ascend up where he was before? It is the spirit that quickeneth; the flesh profiteth nothing: the words that I speak unto you, they are spirit, and they are life. But there are some of you that believe not. For Jesus knew from the beginning who they were that believed not, and who should betray him. And he said, Therefore said I unto you, that no man can come unto me, except it were given unto him of my Father.

From that time many of his disciples went back, and walked no more with him. Then said Jesus unto the twelve, Will ye also go away? Then Simon Peter answered him, Lord, to whom shall we go? thou hast the words of eternal life. And we believe and are sure that thou art that Christ, the Son of the living God. Jesus answered them, Have not I chosen you twelve, and one of you is a devil? He spake of Judas Iscariot the son of Simon: for he it was that should betray him, being one of the twelve.

After the miracle of feeding the five thousand had taken place, Jesus sent the multitude away and went into the hills to pray. The multitude had recognized Christ's witness of His divinity and wanted to force Him to be their political king,[203] but this was not the Lord's way. His reaction to the crowd's demands undoubtedly weakened the effect of the miracle, for "henceforth there was continuous misunderstanding, doubt, and defection among former adherents, [which gave way] to opposition and hatred unto death."[204]

From His hillside retreat, Jesus could see that the Apostles (who had sailed for Capernaum) were having trouble in a storm. He joined them, much to their astonishment, by walking on the water.[205] The Apostles "willingly received Him into the ship: and immediately the ship was at the land whither they went."[a206] The next morning when the people saw that Jesus and His disciples were gone, they also booked passage for Capernaum on ships that had sailed in during the night from Tiberias.[207]

Jesus was on His way to the synagogue in Capernaum to teach when the multitude finally caught up with Him.[208] They were joined by crowds from Capernaum, for excitement must have run high as the news of the Lord's arrival spread throughout the area. The multitude from the night before asked Him how He had come to Capernaum. They had seen the Apostles leave in the only boat, and they knew that the Savior was not with them. He did not answer their question, and declared that they sought Him not because of the miracle but because of the food they had freely received. Jesus attempted to take them beyond their desire for material goods when He said, "Labour not for the meat which perisheth, but for that meat which endureth unto everlasting life, which the Son of man shall give unto you." He was trying to feed their spirits, not their bodies. He declared (using a well–known Jewish expression)[209] that the Son "hath God the Father sealed," and by saying this He proclaimed Himself to be the Messiah and conveyed "to His hearers that for the real meat, which would endure to eternal life—for the better Messianic banquet—they must

a. John 6:21.

come to Him, because God had impressed upon Him His own seal of truth, and so authenticated His Teaching and Mission."[210]

Then the people asked, "What shall we do, that we might work the works of God?" For centuries they and their ancestors before them had painstakingly lived the Mosaic Law, and they were willing to add to those requirements, if necessary, to gain the kingdom of God. But it was not the Law that Jesus was referring to. He was trying to teach the multitude that the work of God was to "believe on him whom he [God] hath sent." Now the people clearly understood that He had announced Himself as the Messiah, so they asked for a "sign" that they might "believe" in Him.

The previous day the multitude had participated in a great sign, but they wanted an even greater one. The food that they had eaten had constituted but a single meal and the miracle was now a day old.[211] They reminded the Savior that although He had given them one meal to eat, Moses had fed their forefathers manna in the wilderness for years. Jesus quickly corrected their misinterpretation of that great miracle in the desert and reminded them that Moses had not given them the bread from heaven, but that His Father had given it. Again He declared Himself to be the "bread of God" which had come down from heaven to give life unto the world.

The people continued to respond with their temporal expectation of the Messiah by asking the Lord to "evermore give us this bread." Like the woman by the well who initially sought only to sate her continual thirst, they primarily only sought to satisfy their continual hunger; however, they still craved more wonders and signs.[212] They wanted Jesus to justify His Messianic claim by giving them the sign that would be associated with His second coming. They did not want a "spiritual" kingdom.

What they waited for, was a Kingdom of God—not in righteousness, joy, and peace in the Holy Ghost, but in meat and drink—a kingdom with miraculous wilderness–banquets to Israel, and coarse miraculous triumphs over the Gentiles. Not to speak of the fabulous Messianic banquet which a sensuous realism expected, or of the achievements for which it looked, every figure in which prophets had clothed the brightness of those days was first literalized, and then exaggerated, till the most glorious poetic descriptions became the most repulsive incongruous caricatures of spiritual Messianic expectancy. The fruit–trees were every day, or at least every week or two, to yield their riches, the fields their harvest; the grain was to stand like palm trees, and to be reaped and winnowed without labour. Similar blessings were to visit the vine; ordinary trees would bear like fruit trees, and every produce, of every clime, would be found in Palestine in such abundance and luxuriance as only the wildest imagination could conceive.[213]

These were the desires the multitude expressed when they said to the Savior, "Give us this bread." Jesus would not tolerate their erroneous thoughts, so He specifically declared, "I am the bread of life." They had to look to Him and believe, if they were to never hunger or thirst again. There were no requirements that they could add to their Law and no additional "works" that they should perform to gain the kingdom. He shattered their vision of temporal ease and explained to them that the Father had sent Him to save them spiritually. He stated that He only did the will of the Father and those who followed Him and believed would be "raised up" (a reference to the resurrection).

Then the Jews murmured at Christ. They recognized His metaphor of the bread sent by the Father, but they knew of His earthly father and mother. How could He be the Savior sent from heaven? Jesus answered them by again declaring Himself as the one sent from the Father; He witnessed to them that the prophets had so taught them of His divine heritage,[a] and He again told them that He was the bread of life. He emphasized the point by returning to the example of the manna eaten in the wilderness. He declared that those who had eaten this manna were now dead, but "I am the living bread which came down from heaven: if any man eat of this bread, he shall live forever: and the bread that I will give is my flesh, which I will give for the life of the world." Christ gave His life so that all mankind could live again. When we "eat of his flesh" we accept Him as the Savior and live our lives in obedience to His commandments. But the literal–minded Jews immediately questioned how any man could eat of Jesus' flesh. Jesus responded by insisting that "except ye eat the flesh of the

Son of man, and drink his blood, ye have no life in you." By accepting the Lord and living the commandments of His gospel, it was possible for them to cleanse their souls and come to a spiritual oneness with the Father.

The allusion to food and drink was commonly used metaphorically in the schools and synagogues of Christ's time.[214] Jesus often used these metaphors in His sermons, and while we may not always understand the significance of His examples, the Jews would have.[215] "Their failure to comprehend the symbolism of Christ's doctrine was an act of will, not the natural consequence of innocent ignorance."[216] To eat of His flesh and drink of His blood meant to keep His commandments and believe and accept Him as the literal Son of God and Savior of the world.[217] Christ was instructing the Jews how they could make Him an "abiding part" of their spirits, even as the food they ate was assimilated into the tissues of their bodies.[218] The Lord was making an open declaration to the Jews that they must unconditionally accept Him as the Savior by being obedient to the laws and ordinances of His gospel. But the Jews' preconceived notions of the Messiah, their dreams of political glory, and their desire for a luxurious, carefree lifestyle were in severe conflict with Christ's discourse, and it caused a turbulent discussion among them. Some contended for the literal interpretation of His words while others espoused the metaphorical.[219] But the mere fact that they continued to strive for the meaning of Christ's message indicates that at least to some degree, they *did* understand the Savior when He declared that He was the Son of God.

This was the Savior's last discourse at Capernaum, and it proved to be an extraordinary test of faith.[220] Some of the Lord's disciples finally recognized that He would never be the great political leader they were looking for. Their national glory would not be restored through Him, and He would not usher in the times of luxury and idleness they had been eagerly anticipating.[221] Those gathered in the synagogue to hear Him had trouble accepting His doctrine. As they murmured among themselves, Jesus perceived their thoughts and asked them point-blank, "Doth this offend you?" He then openly declared that He would again ascend to "where he was before," and reiterated that it was "the spirit that quickeneth; the flesh profiteth nothing: the words that I speak unto you, they are spirit, and they are life."

The Lord's popularity had grown and flourished from the time John the Baptist had begun preaching, but since John's fateful murder it had faded, and now the people had to decide whether He was indeed the Messiah. They had seen His works and His works seemed to prove His Messiahship, in spite of the arguments against them.[222] But even though they wanted to make Him their earthly king, He would not become such. Instead, He attacked their traditionalism,[223] and His death would eventually become the "stumblingblock" of the nation.[a]

Jesus spoke only of self–sacrifice and inward purity while the Jews expected great glory and material wealth.[224] "This was not the Messiah Whom the many—nay, Whom almost any—would own."[225] And so there was a parting of the ways, and many of Christ's disciples "walked no more with him." They began to see clearly what Jesus stood for, and they did not like it. Apparently, even the Twelve were concerned by this sermon and Jesus asked them, "Will ye also go away?" Perhaps they were not able to totally comprehend the Lord's doctrine, but none of them deserted Him.[226] It must have been deeply rewarding to the Savior when Peter stepped forward and said, "Lord, to whom will we go? thou hast the words of eternal life." Yet Jesus sadly declared that one of them was a devil (speaking of Judas Iscariot).

Like a great fan, the discourse on the bread of life separated the true believers from the non–believers: and like the grain tossed on the thrashing room floor, the winnowing breeze blew away the chaff, leaving only the good wheat behind.

The Light of the World

John 8:1–59   Jesus went unto the mount of Olives. And early in the morning he came again into the temple, and all the people came unto him; and he sat down, and taught them. And the scribes and Pharisees brought unto him a woman taken in adultery; and when they had set her in the midst, they say unto him, Master, this woman was taken in adultery, in the very act. Now Moses in the law commanded us, that such should be stoned: but what sayest thou? This they said, tempting him, that they might have to accuse him. But Jesus stooped down, and with his finger wrote on the ground, as though he heard them not. So when they continued asking him, he lifted up himself, and said unto them, He that is without sin among you, let him first cast a stone at her. And again he stooped down, and wrote on the ground. And they which heard it, being convicted by their own conscience, went out one by one, beginning at the eldest, even unto the last: and Jesus was left alone, and the woman standing in the midst. When Jesus had lifted up himself, and saw none but the

a. 1 Corinthians 1:23.

woman, he said unto her, Woman, where are those thine accusers? hath no man condemned thee? She said, No man, Lord. And Jesus said unto her, Neither do I condemn thee: go, and sin no more.

Then spake Jesus again unto them, saying, I am the light of the world: he that followeth me shall not walk in darkness, but shall have the light of life. The Pharisees therefore said unto him, Thou bearest record of thyself; thy record is not true. Jesus answered and said unto them, Though I bear record of myself, yet my record is true: for I know whence I came, and whither I go; but ye cannot tell whence I come, and whither I go. Ye judge after the flesh; I judge no man. And yet if I judge, my judgment is true: for I am not alone, but I and the Father that sent me. It is also written in your law, that the testimony of two men is true. I am one that bear witness of myself, and the Father that sent me beareth witness of me. Then said they unto him, Where is thy Father? Jesus answered, Ye neither know me, nor my Father: if ye had known me, ye should have known my Father also. These words spake Jesus in the treasury, as he taught in the temple: and no man laid hands on him; for his hour was not yet come. Then said Jesus again unto them, I go my way, and ye shall seek me, and shall die in your sins: whither I go, ye cannot come. Then said the Jews, Will he kill himself? because he saith, Whither I go, ye cannot come. And he said unto them, Ye are from beneath; I am from above: ye are of this world; I am not of this world. I said therefore unto you, that ye shall die in your sins: for if ye believe not that I am he, ye shall die in your sins. Then said they unto him, Who art thou? And Jesus saith unto them, Even the same that I said unto you from the beginning. I have many things to say and to judge of you: but he that sent me is true; and I speak to the world those things which I have heard of him. They understood not that he spake to them of the Father. Then said Jesus unto them, When ye have lifted up the Son of man, then shall ye know that I am he, and that I do nothing of myself; but as my Father hath taught me, I speak these things. And he that sent me is with me: the Father hath not left me alone; for I do always those things that please him. As he spake these words, many believed on him. Then said Jesus to those Jews which believed on him, If ye continue in my word, then are ye my disciples indeed; and ye shall know the truth, and the truth shall make you free.

They answered him, We be Abraham's seed, and were never in bondage to any man: how sayest thou, Ye shall be made free? Jesus answered them, Verily, verily, I say unto you, Whosoever committeth sin is the servant of sin. And the servant abideth not in the house for ever: but the Son abideth ever. If the Son therefore shall make you free, ye shall be free indeed. I know that ye are Abraham's seed; but ye seek to kill me, because my word hath no place in you. I speak that which I have seen with my Father: and ye do that which ye have seen with your father. They answered and said unto him, Abraham is our father. Jesus saith unto them, If ye were Abraham's children, ye would do the works of Abraham. But now ye seek to kill me, a man that hath told you the truth, which I have heard of God: this did not Abraham. Ye do the deeds of your father. Then said they to him, We be not born of fornication; we have one Father, even God. Jesus said unto them, If God were your Father, ye would love me: for I proceeded forth and came from God; neither came I of myself, but he sent me. Why do ye not understand my speech? even because ye cannot hear my word. Ye are of your father the devil, and the lusts of your father ye will do. He was a murderer from the beginning, and abode not in the truth, because there is no truth in him. When he speaketh a lie, he speaketh of his own: for he is a liar, and the father of it. And because I tell you the truth, ye believe me not. Which of you convinceth me of sin? And if I say the truth, why do ye not believe me? He that is of God heareth God's words: ye therefore hear them not, because ye are not of God. Then answered the Jews, and said unto him, Say we not well that thou art a Samaritan, and hast a devil? Jesus answered, I have not a devil; but I honour my Father, and ye do dishonour me. And I seek not mine own glory: there is one that seeketh and judgeth. Verily, verily, I say unto you, If a man keep my saying, he shall never see death. Then said the Jews unto him, Now we know that thou hast a devil. Abraham is dead, and the prophets; and thou sayest, If a man keep my saying, he shall never taste of death. Art thou greater than our father Abraham, which is dead? and the prophets are dead: whom makest thou thyself? Jesus answered, If I honour myself, my honour is nothing: it is my Father that honoureth me; of whom ye say, that he is your God: yet ye have not known him; but I know him: and if I should say, I know him not, I shall be a liar like unto you: but I know him, and keep his saying. Your father Abraham rejoiced to see my day: and he saw it, and was glad. Then said the Jews unto him, Thou art not yet fifty years old, and hast thou seen Abraham? Jesus said unto them, Verily, verily, I say unto you, Before Abraham was, I am. Then took they up stones to cast at him: but Jesus hid himself, and went out of the temple, going through the midst of them, and so passed by.

This discourse took place at the Feast of Tabernacles, one of the three annual festivals wherein every male Israelite was to present himself (if possible) before the Lord in the temple at Jerusalem.[227] It was held on the fifteenth day of the seventh month (called Tishri, corresponding to September or the beginning of October), and began five days after the day of Atonement wherein the sins of Israel were to be removed and its covenant with God restored. The feast celebrated the completion of the harvest and the abundance Jehovah had given His chosen people, and it was to be kept by a sanctified nation.[228] The joyful feast also commemorated Israel's hope for the conversion of the heathen, and directed the Jews' thoughts forward to the coming of the Messiah.[229]

Traditionally the people lived in outdoor "booths" while they attended this feast, in remembrance of Israel's wanderings in the wilderness.[a] The booths were erected throughout Jerusalem, and residents and visitors alike lived in them during the feast. It was a re-

a. Leviticus
23:42–43.

quirement of all who came to the feast that they spend the first night in the city. After that, they could sleep elsewhere as long it was within a Sabbath day's journey of the temple.[230] Jesus did not participate in this custom, for the scripture notes that He came to the feast late.[a] Presumably, He stayed with friends on the Mount of Olives, or perhaps with Mary, Martha, and Lazarus at their home in Bethany.

This feast was rich in tradition and symbolism. During the first night of the feast, four great candelabra were filled with oil and lighted. They burned throughout each night of the celebration, providing light for the courts of the temple and illuminating "every court in Jerusalem."[231] The light from the candelabra represented the light of Jehovah, and the Midrash[232] specifically referred to Jehovah as the "Enlightener." The Midrash further recorded the words, "the light dwelleth with him,"[233] applying them specifically to the Messiah. The symbolic meaning of this portion of the celebration was in the "express Messianic expectation of the Rabbis."[234] Jesus constantly used the circumstances of life to enhance the understanding of those who heard Him, and in this sermon He used an analogy that the Pharisees in particular and the people in general could not misunderstand. He came to the temple early, before dawn had broken. The four giant candelabra were still glowing in the inner courts of the temple, piercing the darkness of night, when the sun rimmed the crest of the Mount of Olives. It may have been at this point that Jesus announced His Messiahship to those around Him (including the proud Pharisees and rulers of the Jews) by declaring, "I am the light of the world." It was the Lord's intention to teach those who accompanied Him that morning, so He proceeded on to the area in the temple that custom had designated for that purpose.[235] This great discourse on the light of the world is found in the eighth chapter of John, and it falls into three definite sections:

Section One: John 8:1–11

The Pharisees brought a woman to Jesus and accused her of adultery—taken in the very act![236] Under Jewish law they could stone her (and her consort) to death for this crime. They asked Jesus what He would do to punish the woman. They were "tempting" Him, hoping He would say something they could use to accuse Him before their courts. The Law of Moses was clear in these circumstances; therefore,

a. John 7:10, 14.

it was obvious that the Pharisees were trying to trap Christ before the people.[237]

Only the woman "taken in adultery" was brought before the Savior. Her consort was conspicuously absent. This would seem to indicate how deliberately devious the Pharisees were being for the Law specifically required that the man be punished along with the woman if they were found guilty of adultery.[a] In any case, the matter involved no legal complications since the punishment decreed by the Law of Moses had long since lapsed.[238] Jesus stooped down and wrote on the ground with His finger as if He had not heard the Pharisees. They continued to ask Him, so He stood up and responded simply, "He that is without sin among you, let him first cast a stone at her." Then He again stooped down and wrote upon the ground. His answer totally disarmed His antagonists. His appeal to their consciences placed the burden of sin upon their shoulders, and finding themselves convicted they slowly went out "one by one, beginning at the eldest, even unto the last." After a moment's pause, Jesus looked up and found Himself alone with the woman. He asked her where her accusers were. She said no man had stayed to condemn her. The Lord then answered compassionately, "Neither do I condemn thee: go, and sin no more."

Section Two: John 8:12–32

The narrative of the second part of this discourse begins while Jesus was in the treasury, or the "court of the women," where thirteen silver, trumpet–shaped receptacles had been placed to receive charitable contributions.[239] Jesus began by declaring, "I am the light of the world: he that followeth me shall not walk in darkness, but shall have the light of life." As previously noted, the Lord used an analogy in His Messianic claim which would not have gone unnoticed by the Pharisees.[b][240] His declaration was reminiscent of the aged prophet Simeon who, when he saw the babe Jesus brought into the temple, declared, "A light to lighten the Gentiles, and the glory of thy people Israel."[c]

This Messianic declaration was too much for the Pharisees and they immediately challenged Jesus. But they did not address themselves to the question of His Messiahship; rather, they accused Him of self–aggrandizement (a crime under their Law) and questioned the legality of His statement since He had no witness to corroborate it (their Law

a. Leviticus 20:10.

b. Isaiah 49:6;
   60:1–3.

c. Luke 2:32.

required that acceptable evidence be presented by two or more witnesses; Deuteronomy 17:6). The Lord was appealing to the spiritual nature of His audience, but the Pharisees rejected that appeal and reverted to their temporal concept of the anticipated Messiah. The Pharisees were relying on the technicalities of the Law when they demanded more evidence than the Lord's own testimony. They knew full well that such a request would require the Savior to perform the Messianic sign to prove His Messiahship.[241] Their request for this sign was simply another form of the temptation presented by Satan to Jesus when he challenged, "If thou art the Christ . . . ." They were obviously judging the Lord "as one suspected, and charged with guilt."[242]

Jesus was very candid in His reply to the Pharisees. He acknowledged the technicality they had raised under the Law, but clarified two points concerning it. First, although He had testified of Himself, He was qualified to do so because He knew the facts of His origin and what His mission was, and He declared that the Pharisees did not. The Jewish leaders only judged pertaining to the flesh and He would judge no man in that manner, for He judged by the Spirit which was after the manner of His Father. He declared that the second of His witnesses was His Father, who also testified of Him. By saying this, Jesus overcame the requirements of the rabbinical law, for under that law the testimony of an accused was rejected only if it was not supported by a witness—if another testified in behalf of the accused, the accused could then also testify for Himself.[243]

Jesus was correct in His interpretation of their law and the inquiring Pharisees recognized it, so they asked Him a second question: "Where is thy Father?" Once again their thoughts were literal and not spiritual. Although they recognized the Lord's claim to the Messiahship, they continued to question the physical and not the spiritual nature of that claim: Jesus immediately silenced them by declaring that they did not know Him or the Father, for had they known either of them, they would have accepted Him. This exchange obviously made the Pharisees angry, but the scripture states, "No man laid hands on him; for his hour was not yet come."

The text seems to indicate that Jesus now left the treasury area and perhaps moved to one of the "porches" of the temple where His conversation could be extended to more than the Pharisees. He told

His listeners in a second declaration of His Messiahship that He would soon leave them and because of their sins, where He went they could not come. He was referring to the spiritual nature of His kingdom, but the Pharisees again took His comments in a literal sense and asked if He would kill Himself. In their blind hypocrisy they felt that this was the only way He could separate Himself from them in death, for they believed that suicide warranted the darkest reaches of the grave.[244]

Jesus responded to their deliberate ignorance by plainly stating that He was from above (from heaven), and they were of "this world." They would be separated from Him because they would die in their sins, and this because they would not repent and believe in Him. In exasperation the unrighteous Pharisees asked, "Who art thou?" Jesus patiently responded, "Even the same that I said unto you from the beginning."

The apparent, feigned misunderstanding on the part of the Pharisees precipitated the Lord's third declaration of His Messiahship in this section of the discourse. He turned to His antagonists and declared, "When ye have lifted up the Son of man, then shall ye know that I am he, and that I do nothing of myself; but as my Father hath taught me, I speak these things." Only when they had killed Him would they recognize that He spoke the truth, and that He was only doing the will of His Father in Heaven. John reports that "many believed on him" because of this open declaration and His defense under the Law. Jesus told the Jews that believed, "If ye continue in my word, then are ye my disciples indeed; and ye shall know the truth, and the truth shall make you free."

Section Three: John 8:33–59

It is clear from the Lord's comments that the Jewish leadership was planning His death. He tried to turn them from their evil purpose by claiming His rightful station and affording them the opportunity of accepting Him—but they would not. They longed for a temporal, powerful Messiah, not what they considered an ineffectual, spiritual one. To recognize Jesus as the Messiah meant that they had to acknowledge God as His Father, and that would give Jesus a moral kinship with God that they did not have. The Jews did not believe that as a result of the Fall all men had become corrupted (because of sin); therefore, they did not have a need for a spiritual Savior.[245] Their apostasy from the truth had led them to misunderstand the Fall, Moses, and the prophets; therefore, it was difficult for them to now accept what Jesus was claiming. Before they would accept Him as the Messiah, they wanted a direct confirmation from God: some great, temporal sign they could not miss. They kept ignoring the spiritual application of the Lord's words and reverting back to their temporal beliefs.

Jesus told the Jews that He would make them free, but they felt that as Israelites they were already "free." It was an excommunicable offense to call any Israelite a slave.[246] With great pride they challenged Jesus' authority, declaring that they were "Abraham's seed." Jesus ignored their pomposity and stated flatly, "Whosoever commiteth a sin is the servant of sin." Then He added, "If the Son . . . shall make you free, ye shall be free indeed." Jesus was talking about freedom from sin through repentance, but the obdurate leaders were still applying His words to their temporal condition. Jesus acknowledged that they descended from Abraham, but waved aside the claim that they would inherit the kingdom as a result of that lineage. Then He openly confronted them with seeking to kill Him, and He alienated Himself from them even further by declaring that He only did that which He had "seen with [His] Father," and they were doing that which they had seen with their "father."

Again the Jews boastfully claimed Abraham as their father, to which Jesus boldly replied, "If ye were Abraham's children, ye would do the works of Abraham." He again reminded them that they sought to kill Him, a deed not dictated by Abraham, but by their real "father." The indignant Jews recognized the association Jesus was making and declared that they had but one Father, "even God."

The anger of the Jewish leaders must have been increasing. But the Lord continued by declaring that if God was their Father they would love Him [Jesus], for He proceeded forth from God Himself. The Lord then asked them a simple question, perhaps expressing impatience with the Pharisees when He exclaimed, "Why do ye not understand my speech?" Without waiting for their answer the Lord candidly continued, "Ye are of your father the devil, and the lusts of your father ye will do." The angry Jews retorted with an insult: "Thou art a Samaritan, and hast a devil." They knew what the Lord meant, but rejected His appraisal of their sinful nature, which in their meticulous adherence to the Law they would never have even considered.[247]

Jesus was trying to teach the Jews that although they were literal descendants of Abraham, they could not simply inherit salvation. By their disobedience they had become adopted sons of the devil.[248] The Lord's argument was unimpeachable, so they accused Him of having a devil and being a Samaritan; they were calling Him a heretic, a prince of demons, Satan, literally a "child of the devil."[249] Jesus quickly put aside this ridiculous charge by stating, "I have not a devil; but I honour my Father, and ye do dishonour me." Again He offered them eternal life, stating that if they would but keep His sayings they should "never see death." He would not be distracted from His discourse, but they again rejected the spiritual application of His words and declared that Abraham and the prophets were dead, and asked whether He therefore was greater than their father, Abraham. Again they asked Him, "Whom makest thou thyself?"

The sermon now comes to a conclusion. Jesus halted the continual wrangling that had been taking place by leaving the Jews with one more open declaration of His Messiahship, forcing them to apply His discourse to their own condition by claiming Father Abraham had "rejoiced to see [His] day." The Jews were incredulous, and said, "Thou art not yet fifty years old, and hast thou seen Abraham?" Their dull, spiritual condition continued to lead them to literal interpretations, but in great strength Jesus quietly stated, "Before Abraham was, I am."

The Lord could not have stated His position more clearly. The Jewish leaders did not misunderstand His words, but chose to wilfully misinterpret them.[250] Jesus had symbolically used the sacred title of Jehovah (the Messiah) in His own behalf. Moses, the great lawgiver, had asked the Lord what he could tell the children of Israel that would prove that he (Moses) represented God. "What is [thy] name?" Moses had asked. "I AM THAT I AM," Jehovah had responded.[a] John's rendering of the Lord's statement could correctly read, "Verily, verily, I say unto you, Before Abraham, was I AM."[251] He had declared Himself the God of Abraham.

This divine declaration blinded the Pharisees with rage. They rushed to pick up stones that they might cast them at Jesus and kill Him, but "his hour was not yet come." The scriptures state that he "hid" himself, "and went out of the temple, going through the midst of them, and so passed by."[252]

The Good Shepherd

John 10:1–42   Verily, verily, I say unto you, He that entereth not by the door into the sheepfold, but climbeth up some other way, the same is a thief and a robber. But he that entereth in by the door is the shepherd of the sheep. To him the porter openeth; and the sheep hear his voice: and he calleth his own sheep by name, and leadeth them out. And when he putteth forth his own sheep, he goeth before them, and the sheep follow him: for they know his voice.   And a stranger will they not follow, but will flee from him: for they know not the voice of strangers. This parable spake Jesus unto them: but they understood not what things they were which he spake unto them. Then said Jesus unto them again, Verily, verily, I say unto you, I am the door of the sheep. All that ever came before me are thieves and robbers: but the sheep did not hear them. I am the door: by me if any man enter in, he shall be saved, and shall go in and out, and find pasture. The thief cometh not, but for to steal, and to kill, and to destroy: I am come that they might have life, and that they might have it more abundantly. I am the good shepherd: the good shepherd giveth his life for the sheep. But he that is an hireling, and not the shepherd, whose own the sheep are not, seeth the wolf coming, and leaveth the sheep, and fleeth: and the wolf catcheth them, and scattereth the sheep. The hireling fleeth, because he is an hireling, and careth not for the sheep. I am the good shepherd, and know my sheep, and am known of mine. As the Father knoweth me, even so know I the Father: and I lay down my life for the sheep. And other sheep I have, which are not of this fold: them also I must bring, and they shall hear my voice; and there shall be one fold, and one shepherd. Therefore doth my Father love me, because I lay down my life, that I might take it again. No man taketh it from me, but I lay it down of myself. I have power to lay it down, and I have power to take it again. This commandment have I received of my Father.

There was a division therefore again among the Jews for these sayings. And many of them said, He hath a devil, and is mad; why hear ye him? Others said, These are not the words of him that hath a devil. Can a devil open the eyes of the blind?

And it was at Jerusalem the feast of the dedication, and it was winter. And Jesus walked in the temple in Solomon's porch. Then came the Jews round about him, and said unto him, How long dost thou make us to doubt? If thou be the Christ, tell us plainly. Jesus answered them, I told you, and ye believed not: the works that I do in my Father's name, they bear witness of me. But ye believe not, because ye are not of my sheep, as I said unto you. My sheep hear my voice, and I know them, and they follow me: and I give unto them eternal life; and they shall never perish, neither shall any man pluck them out of my hand. My Father, which gave them me, is greater than all; and no man is able to pluck them out of my Father's hand. I and my Father are one. Then the Jews took up stones again to stone him. Jesus answered them, Many good works have I shewed you from my Father; for which of those works do ye stone me? The Jews answered him, saying, For a good work we stone thee not; but for blasphemy; and because that thou, being a man, makest thyself God. Jesus answered them, Is it not written in your law, I said, Ye are gods? If he called them gods, unto whom the word of God came, and the scripture cannot be broken; say ye of him, whom the Father hath sanctified, and sent into the world, Thou blasphemest;

because I said, I am the Son of God? If I do not the works of my Father, believe me not. But if I do, though ye believe not me, believe the works: that ye may know, and believe, that the Father is in me, and I in him. Therefore they sought again to take him: but he escaped out of their hand, and went away again beyond Jordan into the place where John at first baptized; and there he abode. And many resorted unto him, and said, John did no miracle: but all things that John spake of this man were true. And many believed on him there.

The good shepherd discourse actually consists of two discourses delivered on two separate occasions. The Savior gave the first (verses 1–21) while He was at the Feast of Tabernacles (where He also delivered the previous discourse, "the light of the world," and the discourse on "how knoweth this man letters?"). The second (verses 22–42) was delivered at the Feast of Dedication.[253]

Although delivered at two different times and with two months between them, John undoubtedly placed them in the same chapter because Jesus declared His Messiahship by giving the same allegory to the same people in both discourses. These two discussions comprise the last public sermon Jesus gave in His ministry. The allegory of a shepherd appears often in the scriptures and is one the rabbis of Christ's day also used frequently. This familiar comparison would have undoubtedly caused the Jewish leadership to remember the warnings of the Old Testament prophets against false and evil shepherds.[a] One could say that the Lord was fulfilling the prophecy of Ezekiel when He delivered His sermon of the good shepherd.[b]

In this discourse, Jesus first refers to Himself as the door to the sheepfold and then as the shepherd—a shepherd who first watches over the sheep and later gives His life for them. The true shepherds of Israel entered into the sheepfold by the door, whereas thieves and robbers attempted entry by some other way.

The Lord appeared to be describing the Pharisees and Sadducees of His day who had attained religious leadership over the flock but who had not done so in accordance with God's requirements. Further, they refused to recognize the correct way to enter the sheepfold. Their voice was that of a stranger, not of the shepherd. True, they looked forward to the coming of the Messiah and believed that the Old Testament prophesied of His advent, but they refused to accept Jesus as that Messiah. They not only rejected Him, they also sought to kill Him.

a. Jeremiah 23:1–4; 25:32–38; Isaiah 56:10–12; Ezekiel 34; Zechariah 11.

b. Ezekiel 34:23.

These would–be "shepherds" had entered the flock through the wrong door, and by their rejection of the Lord had shown themselves to be false shepherds indeed. "Never has been written or spoken a stronger arraignment of false pastors, unauthorized teachers, self–seeking hirelings who teach for self and divine for dollars, deceivers who pose as shepherds yet avoid the door and climb over 'some other way,' prophets in the devil's employ, who to achieve their master's purpose, hesitate not to robe themselves in the garments of assumed sanctity, and appear in sheep's clothing, while inwardly they are ravening wolves."[254]

Having chastised the false shepherds of Israel, the Lord again declared His Messiahship, describing Himself as the good shepherd who would give His life for His sheep while contrasting Himself with the hireling shepherds who would leave the sheep to scatter at the first sign of danger. He prophesied His untimely death and His resurrection from the grave by declaring that He would provide salvation and care for the sheep.[255]

Although Jesus considered the Jews of His time as His sheep, He noted that He also had other sheep which were not of the Jewish fold. These sheep must also hear His voice, for there was but one fold and one shepherd. The other sheep Jesus spoke of were the remaining tribes of the House of Israel.

Some of these "other" sheep included those who, under Jehovah's personal direction, had migrated from Jerusalem to inhabit the Western Hemisphere. These sheep had also been told of the Savior's coming, and were anxiously awaiting that great event which would occur after His resurrection.[a] But these were not the only sheep Jesus was referring to, for He would also visit the ten lost tribes of Israel.[b]

The Jews' reaction to this doctrine differed and there was a "division among them." Some chose not to believe the Lord and, resorting to their familiar ploy, declared that He had a devil or was mad. But Jesus had opened the eyes of a blind man[256] the previous day, and this caused some to wonder and question whether a devil could open the eyes of the blind. Thus ended the part of the discourse delivered at the Feast of Tabernacles.

John states that when Jesus gave His discourse at the Feast of Dedication, He entered the temple and went to Solomon's porch. His

a. Helaman
14:2–5, 20–21;
3 Nephi 11–28.

b. 3 Nephi 21:26.

appearance caused many of the leaders of the Jews to literally crowd around Him and bar His way. They immediately began to question Him, and Jesus again took up the theme of the good shepherd. This is evidence that the Jews had recognized Christ's previous claim to the Messiahship, and hemming Him in with an undoubtedly hostile spirit they demanded, "How long dost thou make us to doubt? If thou be the Christ, tell us plainly!"

Jesus had been forced to leave the Feast of Tabernacles and even Judea because of the hostility of the Jewish leadership. The question now presented to Him was couched in that same hostile spirit.[257] It demanded a simple yes or no answer, but Jesus would not reply in this manner. He did not claim to be the political Messiah the people were looking for—an earthly conqueror who would save their bodies rather than their souls.[258]

The answer the Lord gave them was probably more than the Jewish leadership bargained for. He declared, "I told you, and ye believed not: the works that I do in my Father's name, they bear witness of me." Then Jesus returned to the allegory of the sheep by declaring, "Ye believe not, because ye are not of my sheep." He concluded His testimony by promising the true sheep eternal life because His Father had given Him the power to do so. Then He abruptly ended with the statement, "I and my Father are one."

The rage of the Jews was instantaneous! They had asked for a direct answer and Jesus had given it. It is obvious that they found no ambiguity in His words for the scripture states that they immediately took up stones to stone Him. Jesus forestalled their attack by asking them for which of His good works they would stone Him? They tersely stated, "For a good work we stone thee not; but for blasphemy; and because that thou, being a man, makest thyself God." Can there be any doubt of their understanding?

With the leadership's attention focused on Him, Jesus refuted the charge of blasphemy by citing the example of Israel's judges being awarded the title of "god," and "sons of the highest," because as God's representatives they had wielded His authority.[a] In this instance they were called gods because they did the very acts of God. Christ concluded that if these men were called gods because they did the work of God, why was it blasphemy for Him, who had been sancti-

a. Psalm 82:6.

fied and sent into the world by that same Deity, to say He was the Son of God? He testified that He did the Father's works and challenged them to compare His claim to His works. If the works were not of the Father, they were justified in not believing Him; but if His works were of the Father, then they would know that "the Father is in me, and I in Him." The result of the Lord's claim was predictable for the Jewish leaders again sought to capture Him; but He "escaped out of their hand"[259] and traveled over beyond Jordan to the place where John had first baptized. This was the Lord's last visit to the Holy City before His crucifixion. The people had become so hostile toward Him that it was again necessary for Him to leave both Jerusalem and Judea.

The scriptures do not indicate how long Jesus stayed in Perea, but His rejection by the Jewish leaders in the Holy City was at least momentarily salved by the success He enjoyed in this area of John's ministry. The scriptures state that many followed Him, "and many believed on him there."

Principles   8

Baptism

John 3:1–21   There was a man of the Pharisees, named Nicodemus, a ruler of the Jews: the same came to Jesus by night, and said unto him, Rabbi, we know that thou art a teacher come from God: for no man can do these miracles that thou doest, except God be with him. Jesus answered and said unto him, Verily, verily, I say unto thee, Except a man be born again, he cannot see the kingdom of God. Nicodemus saith unto him, How can a man be born when he is old? can he enter the second time into his mother's womb, and be born? Jesus answered, Verily, verily, I say unto thee, Except a man be born of water and of the Spirit, he cannot enter into the kingdom of God. That which is born of the flesh is flesh; and that which is born of the Spirit is spirit. Marvel not that I said unto thee, Ye must be born again. The wind bloweth where it listeth, and thou hearest the sound thereof, but canst not tell whence it cometh, and whither it goeth: so is every one that is born of the Spirit. Nicodemus answered and said unto him, How can these things be? Jesus answered and said unto him, Art thou a master of Israel, and knowest not these things? Verily, verily, I say unto thee, We speak that we do know, and testify that we have seen; and ye receive not our witness. If I have told you earthly things, and ye believe not, how shall ye believe, if I tell you of heavenly things? And no man hath ascended up to heaven, but he that came down from heaven, even the Son of man which is in heaven.

And as Moses lifted up the serpent in the wilderness, even so must the Son of man be lifted up: That whosoever believeth in him should not perish, but have eternal life.

For God so loved the world, that he gave his only begotten Son, that whosoever believeth in him should not perish, but have everlasting life. For God sent not his Son into the world to condemn the world; but that the world through him might be saved.

He that believeth on him is not condemned: but he that believeth not is condemned already, because he hath not believed in the name of the only begotten Son of God. And this is the condemnation, that light is come into the world, and men loved darkness rather than light, because their deeds were evil. For every one that doeth evil hateth the light, neither cometh to the light, lest his deeds should be reproved. But he that doeth truth cometh to the light, that his deeds may be made manifest, that they are wrought in God.

Cross–reference   JST John 3:18

It was time for the Feast of the Passover, and Jesus had come to Jerusalem to attend His first Passover since the commencement of His public ministry.[260] At the beginning of this celebration, Jesus had forcefully expelled the money changers and other traffickers from the temple. The Jews did nothing to stop the Lord's evictions, but they asked Him for a sign of His authority to exercise such control over their customs and traditions. Jesus would not give them a public sign, but He performed many miracles among the people, which produced initial belief in Him as the Savior.[a]

A man named Nicodemus lived in Jerusalem at this time. He was a leader of the Jews and a member of the Sanhedrin. There may have been multiple rulers and leaders who initially believed in Christ, but the scriptures identify only Nicodemus. They generally portray the Pharisees and other Jewish leaders as being opposed to Christ, "but it [would] be strange indeed if there [were] to be found among them no exceptions to the general characteristics; strange if honesty, candour, and sensibility, [were] utterly dead among them all. Even among rulers, scribes, Pharisees, and wealthy members of the Sanhedrin, Christ found believers and followers."[261]

We hear of Nicodemus only in the Gospel of John. In addition to his nocturnal meeting with Jesus, John records Nicodemus's limited defense of the Savior before the Sanhedrin[b] and his consideration for the Lord's body at the time of His burial.[c] It would seem evident that Nicodemus had an "honest desire to befriend and acknowledge One whom he knew to be a Prophet, even if he did not at once recognize in Him the promised Messiah."[262]

John's brief record indicates that Nicodemus was a Pharisee by training and a wealthy member of the Sanhedrin. It is evident that he was sincere with the Lord, although his limited faith in Him was apparently based on miracles.[263] He was cautious by nature and timid of character,[264] and he did not have the strength to make the sacrifices necessary to openly align himself with the Lord.

Jesus identified Nicodemus as a "master of Israel," which suggests he may have been one of the three leading officers in the Sanhedrin. The Sanhedrin consisted of seventy educated and intellectual

a. John 2:23.
b. John 7:50.
c. John 19:39.

Jewish leaders plus a president, vice–president, and "the 'Master' or wise man" (sometimes one of the seventy).[265] The discussion between Jesus and Nicodemus reads like an outline, enumerating only the important subjects and high points and leaving obvious gaps in the conversation.[266]

The scripture reports that Nicodemus came to Jesus by night, thus veiling his initial conversation with the Lord in secrecy. In his salutation to the Lord he said, "Rabbi, we know that thou art a teacher come from God: for no man can do these miracles that thou doest, except God be with him." Nicodemus's use of the word *we* might indicate that he came as a representative of the Sanhedrin. The miracles that Jesus had performed would qualify Him for such a salutation because the Jews believed in miracles, and they would not have accepted a teacher of a new faith without that teacher first evidencing the miraculous.[267]

Jesus may not have been particularly impressed that one of the Jewish rulers was so addressing Him, but "we can scarcely realize the difficulties which [Nicodemus] had to overcome. It must have been a mighty power of conviction, to break down prejudice so far as to lead this old Sanhedrist to acknowledge a Galilean, untrained in the Schools, as a Teacher come from God, and to repair to Him for direction on, perhaps, the most delicate and important point in Jewish theology."[268]

In response to Nicodemus's salutation and declaration (and perhaps also to an unrecorded question) Jesus declared, "Except a man be born again, he cannot see the kingdom of God," thus defining the universal requirement for entrance into the kingdom of heaven. Nicodemus, skilled in the subtle expositions of the Law and totally familiar with the scriptures, incredulously responded with a statement that showed a total lack of understanding of his own religion: "How can a man be born when he is old? can he enter the second time into his mother's womb, and be born?" Jesus ignored Nicodemus's literal interpretation of this spiritual teaching and with greater detail reiterated the fundamental requirements for entry into the kingdom of God. He again declared that all men (Jew or Gentile) must be "born again," first of water, and then of the Spirit. They had to be reborn through baptism by immersion and spiritually regenerated (by the Holy Ghost) through repentance before they could enter the kingdom of God.[269]

This undoubtedly threw Nicodemus's thoughts into a state of confusion because it put his basic beliefs in question. The Jews considered every act a man or woman performed to be either good or evil. The Jewish concept of "an eye for an eye" applied both in life and after death. When the Lord said that a man had to be born again to enter the kingdom of heaven, He was graphically explaining to Nicodemus that, although the outward observance of legal acts would be taken into account, the motive for those acts would also be considered. Nicodemus had come to Jesus "trusting implicitly to his being a Jew, as a Divine title to citizenship in the new theocracy, and thinking only of formal acts by which he might show his devotion, and increase his claim to the favour of God, here and hereafter."[270] But now he was confronted with the realization that "neither [his] national descent, nor the uttermost exactness of [his] Pharisaic observance . . . availed at all as such, to secure entrance into the kingdom of God."[271]

These teachings were strange to Nicodemus. They were beyond the scope of his Jewish background, and he exclaimed, "How can these things be?" Using the wind as an example, Jesus explained that the physical senses and intellectual learning could not give a man an understanding of the things of God. True, the physical senses could detect the wind, but they could not determine where it came from. Likewise, the physical senses could not detect spiritual confirmation of gospel principles from God.

By now Nicodemus had twice admitted his lack of understanding, causing Jesus to question his ability as the "Master of Israel." He pointedly asked Nicodemus why it was that he knew not these things. If he could not understand these simple, earthly requirements, how could he expect to know of heavenly things? This was undoubtedly a humbling and humiliating experience for Nicodemus. Jesus continued with His discourse by bearing Him a personal testimony that He was the Messiah, the Son of man come down from heaven; and just as Moses lifted up a brazen serpent in the wilderness to save Israel from poisonous snakes,[a] so, too, would the Son of God be lifted up to provide eternal life for all who would believe on Him. The Father had sent the Son not to condemn the world, but to save it. Nicodemus must have recognized this common representation of the Messianic expectation.

Jesus continued to elaborate on the principles necessary to attain exaltation, stating that all these things had previously been taught "by the mouth of the holy prophets; for they testified of me."[a] The Lord did not have to condemn the people of the world; they would condemn themselves.

Light had come into the world, but men loved darkness more than light because their "deeds were evil." Nicodemus could see that the principle of judgment (taught as a present reality) would eventually be consummated before the Savior at the judgment day. Those who heard the testimony of Jesus had to decide whether or not He was the Messiah; some believed, but many did not.

In closing this discourse, Jesus enumerated the reasons why men rejected the light that had come to them. He said that "every one that doeth evil hateth the light, neither cometh to the light, lest his deeds should be reproved. But he that doeth truth goeth to the light that his deeds may be made manifest, that they are wrought in God."

This sermon is striking evidence that even in the early days of His ministry, Jesus was using plain, straightforward language to testify that He was the long–awaited Messiah.[272]

On Marriage and Divorce

Matthew 19:1–15   And it came to pass, that when Jesus had finished these sayings, he departed from Galilee, and came into the coasts of Judea beyond Jordan; and great multitudes followed him; and he healed them there.

The Pharisees also came unto him, tempting him, and saying unto him, Is it lawful for a man to put away his wife for every cause? And he answered and said unto them, Have ye not read, that he which made them at the beginning made them male and female, and said, For this cause shall a man leave father and mother, and shall cleave to his wife: and they twain shall be one flesh? Wherefore they are no more twain, but one flesh. What therefore God hath joined together, let not man put asunder. They say unto him, Why did Moses then command to give a writing of divorcement, and to put her away? He saith unto them, Moses because of the hardness of your hearts suffered you to put away your wives: but from the beginning it was not so. And I say unto you, Whosoever shall put away his wife, except it be for fornication, and shall marry another, committeth adultery: and whoso marrieth her which is put away doth commit adultery.

His disciples say unto him, If the case of the man be so with his wife, it is not good to marry. But he said unto them, All men cannot receive this saying, save they to whom it is given. For there are some eunuchs, which were so born from their mother's womb: and there are some eunuchs, which were made eunuchs of men: and there be eunuchs, which have made themselves eunuchs for the kingdom of heaven's sake. He that is able to receive it, let him receive it.

Then were there brought unto him little children, that he should put his hands on them, and pray: and the disciples rebuked them. But Jesus said, Suffer little children, and forbid them not, to come unto me: for of such is the kingdom of heaven. And he laid his hands on them, and departed thence.

Cross–reference Mark 10:1–16

This discourse takes place during Jesus' last Perean mission, before He journeyed to Jerusalem to be crucified. All three of the Synoptic writers agree on the setting; however, Luke omits the discourse and includes the miracle of the healing of ten lepers[273] (perhaps filling in gaps he felt were in Matthew and Mark). All three writers note that multitudes followed Jesus and they testify that He healed those in need. They undoubtedly made their selections from those occurrences in the ministry of Jesus which they felt were "most important or novel, or else best accorded with the plans of their respective narratives."[274]

It seems that whenever the ministry of Jesus became at all public, the Pharisees and rulers of the Jews were there, lying in wait to entrap Him in His speech.[275] On this occasion, the Pharisees came to deliberately provoke Jesus that they might accuse Him.[276] Jesus had met them before in this same part of the country under similar circumstances,[a] and had answered their taunts and objections by charging them with breaking the spirit of the Law because of their views on the subject of divorce.[b] The indefatigable Pharisees again took up that topic right where they had previously left off. They "tempted him" by asking the question, "Is it lawful for a man to put away his wife for every cause?" Their question required Christ to give an exposition on the Jewish law in regard to the practice of divorce, one of the most debated questions of the day.[277] The two major schools of Pharisaic Law were in contention on this point: the school of Hillel contended that a man had a literal right to divorce his wife for any cause while the school of Shammai contended that the marriage bonds could only be broken for offenses against chastity. Although the Jews protected their women in general and discouraged divorce, it was still a very common occurrence.[278] There are two recorded instances where a rabbi desired to be married for only a single day, and then divorced.[279] Grounds for divorce had become extremely liberal, ranging from the sin of adultery to any cause which the man might assign. For instance, if a man ceased

a. Luke 16:14.

b. Luke 16:17–18.

to love his wife, if he liked another woman better, or if his wife had spoiled his dinner, he could divorce her.[280]

The Jews undoubtedly asked Jesus this question because they assumed that they could easily sway Him from the Mosaic doctrine and the teachings of the rabbis. They felt this was one of the most difficult questions they could ask because (1) the Old Testament was so ambiguous in explaining the institution of divorce, (2) there was strong opposition between the doctrine of the two rabbinical schools, (3) the customs and traditions throughout Israel varied radically, and (4) the Lord's answer might produce strong political implications. Jesus was in Herod's domain, the same Herod who had previously put John the Baptist to death for crying out against the illegal marriage of Herod Antipas with Herodias, Herod's brother's wife. It therefore seemed to the Pharisees that this was the perfect question whereby they could ensnare Jesus.

The Lord avoided the various cavils of the Law and the schools of His day by appealing to a higher authority—His Father. He indicated that God had made man in the beginning and had commanded him that he should leave his father and mother and "cleave to his wife" and "be one flesh." He concluded that what God had joined together, no man could put asunder.

Without directly stating it, Jesus condemned both of the Jewish schools of thought. He stated emphatically that man could not undo at his pleasure what God had joined together, thus indicating that divorce was an invention of man.[281]

The Pharisees responded to Jesus with a second question. They asked Him, "Why did Moses then command to give a writing of divorcement," if God commanded otherwise? Jesus wasted no time in answering their question. "He saith unto them, Moses, because of the hardness of your hearts, suffered you to put away your wives: but from the beginning it was not so." In other words, Moses had permitted divorce for the protection of the wife, but this was not the original law. Originally God had declared that only for the sin of adultery could a marriage be dissolved. The Mosaic Law had become permissive because of the general unrighteousness of the people.[282]

The Lord now concluded that when the higher law was faithfully lived, no divorce was justified except in the case of unchastity. If a man put away his wife for any other reason, it was a breach of the Law; and if the man remarried, he committed adultery (as did the man who married the divorced woman). Even the Jewish Law in practice during Christ's time dictated that an adulteress could not marry the man with whom she had committed adultery.[283]

This interpretation of the Law must have startled the Pharisees and convicted them in their consciences.[284] It is recorded that the Lord's answer definitely caused His disciples some consternation, and they concluded that it was better not to marry because of the potential sin involved; but the Lord disapproved of their solution—except in special cases and for different reasons.[285]

Although Jesus did not condone their view of celibacy, He did enumerate two instances where it would be natural if an individual did not marry, and a third instance where men had selected to forego marriage for the kingdom's sake. He did not necessarily consider any of these conditions to be generally better than marriage—only different. While the disciples' premise may have been wrong, their conclusion was correct—but only in exceptional cases.[286]

The principle concerning divorce, as taught by the Lord, is the same today as it was when He gave it to the Pharisees. "The Lord may allow divorces in one day among a certain people and deny them in another day among a more enlightened populace."[287] Divorce is not a part of the eternal gospel plan, regardless of the type of marriage, but the Lord does permit divorce in some circumstances and for various legitimate reasons (depending on the spiritual stability of the people involved).[288] "Under the most perfect conditions there would be no divorce permitted except where sex sin is involved. In this day divorce is permitted in accordance with civil statutes, and the divorced persons are permitted by the Church to marry again without the stain of immorality which under a higher system would attend such a course."[289]

The Lord's answer silenced the Pharisees and established for His new kingdom the law regarding family life. He changed the position of women from that of slave or toy to the status of equal rights within the family, a position they justly deserved.

Although the Lord had concluded His sermon at this point, the event that followed it augmented the principle He was teaching. Several mothers who had listened to His discussion with the Pharisees brought their little children to Jesus for a blessing.[290] In apparent disregard for the instruction they had received in a prior, similar experience, the disciples attempted to prevent the children from being brought to Jesus. Perhaps they thought that these circumstances were beneath the dignity of a great rabbi;[291] but as if to emphasize the importance of family life, the Lord again chastened the disciples and allowed the children to come unto Him. He reminded the disciples that to enter the kingdom of God they must be as a little child—not in size or intellect, but in humility, receptiveness, meekness, and teachability.

The Widow's Mite

Mark 12:41–44 And Jesus sat over against the treasury, and beheld how the people cast money into the treasury: and many that were rich cast in much. And there came a certain poor widow, and she threw in two mites, which make a farthing. And he called unto him his disciples, and saith unto them, Verily I say unto you, That this poor widow hath cast more in, than all they which have cast into the treasury: for all they did cast in of their abundance; but she of her want did cast in all that she had, even all her living.

Cross–reference Luke 21:1–4

On one occasion, Jesus was sitting by the treasury watching the people make contributions. It was the Lord's last visit to the temple before His crucifixion. Earlier in the day He had fielded questions from several Jewish leaders, finally denouncing them for their unbelief.

The treasury was located in the court of the women and occupied a very large area, one capable of accommodating as high as fifteen thousand charitable souls at one time. Along the colonnades of the court were thirteen trumpet–shaped containers. Each bore inscriptions and markings denoting the reason for the contributions it contained. One was used to receive the gifts of those who were behind in their contributions. The gifts in others were used to pay for certain sacrifices or to provide incense, wood, and other items used in the temple services.[292]

Jesus had probably stopped at the court to rest after His tedious discussion with the Pharisees. As He sat, He observed the people who were depositing their gifts in the trumpets. Some gave ostentatiously and others gave meagerly, but they were all cheerfully performing a happy duty.[293]

Josephus notes that the wealth of the temple treasury was considerable,[294] and one could easily observe that many of the rich contributed liberally; but it was apparent to the Lord that they cast in only of their excess abundance. Then a poor widow came and contributed two mites—all that she had. It was not lawful under the Jewish law for her to contribute less than two mites, and this was "all her living"; but she cast it into the treasury as her humble offering to God. Obviously, the widow's contribution was a mere trifle compared with the rich offerings Jesus had observed, but He was deeply impressed with her sacrifice. He called His disciples to Him and said, "Verily I say unto you, That this poor widow hath cast more in than all they which have cast into the treasury." He stressed the fact that the attitude of the giver was greater than the gift itself.[295]

The widow exemplified the essence of charity and self–denial. Her gift was more acceptable to the Lord because of her great sacrifice and devotion.[296] She did not know that the eyes of the Master were upon her, but she truly touched His heart.

> He spake not to her words of encouragement, for she walked by faith; He offered not promise of return, for her reward was in heaven. She knew not that any had seen it— for the knowledge of eyes turned on her, even His, would have flushed with shame the pure cheek of her love; and any word, conscious notice, or promise would have marred and turned aside the rising incense of her sacrifice . . . this deed of self–denying sacrifice [was of] far more, [value] than the great gifts of [the wealthy's] 'super-fluity' . . . And though He spake not to her, yet the sunshine of His words must have fallen into the dark desolateness of her heart; and, though perhaps she knew not why, it must have been a happy day, a day of rich feast in the heart, that when she gave up "her whole living" unto God.[297]

Paul later expanded the principle Jesus was teaching when he declared to the Corinthians: "For if there be first a willing mind, it is accepted according to that he hath, and not according to that he hath not."[a]

a. 2 Corinthians 8:12.

Your Fellowman

Matthew 25:31–46   When the Son of man shall come in his glory, and all the holy angels with him, then shall he sit upon the throne of his glory: and before him shall be gathered all nations: and he shall separate them one from another, as a shepherd divideth his sheep from the goats: and he shall set the sheep on his right hand, but the goats on the left. Then shall the King say unto them on his right hand, Come, ye blessed of my Father, inherit the kingdom prepared for you from the foundation of the world: for I was an hungred, and ye gave me meat: I was thirsty, and ye gave me drink: I was a stranger, and ye took me in: naked, and ye clothed me: I was sick, and ye visited me: I was in prison, and ye came unto me. Then shall the righteous answer him, saying, Lord, when saw we thee an hungred, and fed thee? or thirsty, and gave thee drink? When saw we thee a stranger, and took thee in? or naked, and clothed thee? Or when saw we thee sick, or in prison, and came unto thee? And the King shall answer and say unto them, Verily I say unto you, Inasmuch as ye have done it unto one of the least of these my brethren, ye have done it unto me. Then shall he say also unto them on the left hand, Depart from me, ye cursed, into everlasting fire, prepared for the devil and his angels: for I was an hungred, and ye gave me no meat: I was thirsty, and ye gave me no drink: I was a stranger, and ye took me not in: naked, and ye clothed me not: sick, and in prison, and ye visited me not. Then shall they also answer him, saying, Lord, when saw we thee an hungred, or athirst, or a stranger, or naked, or sick, or in prison, and did not minister unto thee? Then shall he answer them, saying, Verily I say unto you, Inasmuch as ye did it not to one of the least of these, ye did it not to me. And these shall go away into everlasting punishment: but the righteous into life eternal.

After Jesus had completed His final conversations with the Pharisees and the leaders of the Jews in the temple (just prior to His betrayal and crucifixion), He left the temple area with His Apostles and crossed over to the Mount of Olives. There the Apostles asked questions about the prophecies the Lord had made concerning His second coming, and He responded with the Second Coming discourse recorded in Matthew, Chapter 24 (Chapter 10). After He had completed that discourse and given some general instructions to His disciples, the Lord proceeded to give the parable of the ten virgins[298] and the parable of the talents.[299]

In these instructions, Jesus generally alluded to the judgments that would come upon mankind because of their failure to truly love the Lord and accept Him as the Messiah. His conversation briefly touched on the first great commandment, but then He quickly moved away from that subject and instructed the Twelve on the judgment that would result from either keeping or breaking the second great commandment: i.e., to love their fellowman.

The Lord told His disciples that this judgment would occur at the time of His second coming, and then He told them how this would occur. The separation would be as simple as a shepherd dividing his "sheep from the goats." Likewise, the Lord's final judgment would also separate the sheep (the righteous) from the goats (the unrighteous). Those who were righteous and obedient He would place on His right hand, and those who were unrighteous and disobedient He would place on His left. This instruction was intended for those who called themselves disciples (or members of the church).[300] Although the Jews believed to some degree in the principles of eternal righteousness and eternal punishment, their instructions in this area were limited.[301]

We should take literally the Lord's teachings in this discourse because in the latter days He admonished the inhabitants of the earth that the day would eventually come when every man would receive "recompense . . . according to his work, and measure . . . according to the measure which he has measured to his fellowman."[a] Jesus taught His disciples by example who they should serve and what the results of their service would be. After using the example of the sheep and the goats to represent righteous and unrighteous souls, He elaborated by telling the righteous, "For I was an hungred, and ye gave me meat: I was thirsty, and ye gave me drink: I was a stranger, and ye took me in: naked, and ye clothed me: I was sick, and ye visited me: I was in prison, and ye came unto me."

The disciples were puzzled. They asked the Lord when they had fed Him or given Him drink. "When saw we thee a stranger, and took thee in? or naked, and clothed thee? Or when saw we thee sick, or in prison, and came unto thee?" The Lord replied "Inasmuch as ye have done it unto one of the least of these my brethren, ye have done it unto me." There were also those disciples who had been judged and found wanting in their service. They did not understand the Lord's analogy either, and questioned Jesus as to when they had failed to provide Him with food, drink, or other necessities. Again the Lord responded that because they had not done it unto their fellowman, they had not done it unto Him. King Benjamin admonished those who were listening to his final address that they would learn wisdom if they understood "that when ye are in the service of your fellow beings ye are only in the service of your God."[b][302]

a. D&C 1:10.

b. Mosiah 2:17,

According to the second great commandment, we will be judged according to how we treat (or perform services for) our fellowman, and the Lord specifically stated that those who were judged in this manner would be judged as if they had performed their acts of charity for Him. Our individual responsibility under the second great commandment is often referred to in scriptures.[a] The test of true discipleship throughout the ages has always been the same. We are commanded to "remember in all things the poor and the needy, the sick and the afflicted, for he that doeth not these things, the same is not my disciple."[b]

At the conclusion of this discourse, the Lord determined that those who observed the second great commandment would gain eternal life—a reward of inestimable value—whereas those who did not obey the second great commandment would be cast into the "unfathomable doom" of "everlasting punishment."[303]

The Jewish leaders of Christ's day had misunderstood this concept. They taught that perfect righteousness was necessary before an individual could be sealed up to eternal life, and perfect wickedness was required if a person was to be sealed to "Gehenna" or hell; those in intermediate categories had an undefined fate based on Old Testament teachings.[c][304]

Since the restoration of the gospel this concept has been more clearly explained. The Doctrine and Covenants states that "endless torment" and "eternal damnation" are definitions for God's punishment, because "Endless" is one of God's names.[d] The punishment that those on the left hand of God therefore anticipate (because of their disobedience to the second great commandment) is not endless punishment (i.e., punishment that will have no end) but punishment that is determined by God. The faithful (those on the right hand of God) will receive an inheritance based upon their charitable service toward their fellowman.

The Apostles understood what the Lord was teaching. Paul later evidenced this when he admonished the Saints in Galatia to "bear . . . one another's burdens, and so fulfill the law of Christ."[e] Paul continued to instruct the Saints in several matters, but concluded, "Let us not be weary in well doing: for in due season we shall reap, if we faint not. As we have therefore opportunity, let us do good unto all men."[f]

a. Mosiah 4:11–19, 26; D&C 56:14–16; D&C 104:11–18.

b. D&C 52:40.

c. Zechariah 13:9; Daniel 12:2.

d. D&C 19:6–12.

e. Galatians 6:2.

f. Galatians 6:9–10.

Questions

9

Question One

"Why eateth your Master with publicans and sinners?"

Matthew 9:9–13   And as Jesus passed forth from thence, he saw a man, named Matthew, sitting at the receipt of custom: and he saith unto him, Follow me. And he arose, and followed him. And it came to pass, as Jesus sat at meat in the house, behold, many publicans and sinners came and sat down with him and his disciples. And when the Pharisees saw it, they said unto his disciples, Why eateth your Master with publicans and sinners? But when Jesus heard that, he said unto them, They that be whole need not a physician, but they that are sick. But go ye and learn what that meaneth, I will have mercy, and not sacrifice: for I am not come to call the righteous, but sinners to repentance.

Cross–references   Mark 2:13–17; Luke 5:27–32; JST Matthew 9:18–21

It is obvious upon reading the Gospels that the Pharisees, scribes, and rulers of the Jews often came to Jesus or the disciples asking questions concerning the Lord's character, His actions, or His doctrine. While some of these questions were sincere, most were of a demeaning or critical nature as these wicked men attempted to find fault with Jesus. When the Pharisees saw Jesus at Matthew's dinner and noticed the type of guests that were there, they asked the Lord's disciples, "Why eateth your Master with publicans and sinners?" They were criticizing Jesus in an attempt to cause Him public embarrassment.[305]

Matthew was holding the dinner to celebrate his call to follow Jesus. Although the scriptures would lead us to believe that Matthew and the Lord had not previously known each other, it is quite apparent that Matthew had previously (and perhaps frequently) heard Jesus teach and may have witnessed His miracles[306] since Matthew's home was in Capernaum, the city where Jesus lived in the early part of His ministry.

It is significant that Jesus would select Matthew, a publican, to be one of His disciples and one of the chosen Twelve (Chapter 2). Matthew's selection graphically portrayed the Lord's total disregard for the mores of His time since the Jews considered publicans to be vile, corrupt, and evil. They had a bad reputation among the Pharisees because of their greed and exactitude.[307] They were generally thought of as "publicans and sinners," a name indiscriminately given to usurers, gamblers, thieves, shepherds, and sellers of fruit harvested on the Sabbath.[308] They were socially classified in the lower levels of the masses by the Pharisees and were considered hopelessly lost because of their "uncleanness." "It was unlawful to come into their company, even with the holy design of inducing them to read the Law, and it was defilement to take food from them, or, indeed, from any stranger, or even to touch a knife belonging to them. [They were] 'unclean' from mere ignorance, or from their callings, or from carelessness, [and] were an 'abomination,' 'vermin,' 'unclean beasts,' and 'twice accursed.'"[309] This condemnation extended not only to the individuals who held the position of publican, but also to their families. But Jesus was indifferent to such prejudice.

The rabbis had not yet formed an opinion about Jesus, but His participation in the evening's social activities with Matthew and his friends would have been highly irregular to them. Nothing would have been more abhorrent in their minds than to eat with publicans.[310]

Jesus overheard the question posed to His disciples and without allowing them to respond He quickly addressed these self–righteous "protectors of the law" by stating, "They that be whole need not a physician, but they that are sick." He admonished the Pharisees to "go . . . and learn what that meaneth." He spoke not of bodily illness, but of spiritual needs, for the Pharisees were as needy in that sense as the publicans He was eating with. While the Pharisees' question spoke of sinners and sins, Jesus' answer spoke of repentance and forgiveness. On this point rabbinism stood "self–confessedly silent and powerless as regarded the forgiveness of sins, so it had emphatically no word of welcome or help for the sinner."[311] This was the basic difference between a call to the kingdom of God and the requirements of the Pharisaic law. While the Pharisees considered themselves very religious, they were also full of pride, prejudice, and hatred—characteristics far worse than eating with "sinners."

Jesus continued His response by quoting from the Old Testament and stating that He would have mercy, not sacrifice.[a] As if to mimic the irony and sarcasm[312] of the Pharisee's question, He then proceeded to declare that He came "not to call the righteous, but sinners to repentance." The Pharisees' question intimated that they considered themselves whole and without sin; therefore, Jesus should go to those who would acknowledge their illness. The Pharisees had cleverly phrased their question in a way that denounced a whole category of sinners, but Jesus answered by quoting their own Law, which required that they heal the sick and call sinners to repentance.[313] Jesus left the Pharisees to make their own application of the answer He had given them. In God's eyes, all men have an equal opportunity to enter His kingdom.

Question Two

"Why do we and the Pharisees fast oft, but thy disciples fast not?"

Matthew 9:14–17   Then came to him the disciples of John, saying, Why do we and the Pharisees fast oft, but thy disciples fast not? And Jesus said unto them, Can the children of the bridechamber mourn, as long as the bridegroom is with them? but the days will come, when the bridegroom shall be taken from them, and then shall they fast. No man putteth a piece of new cloth unto an old garment, for that which is put in to fill it up taketh from the garment, and the rent is made worse. Neither do men put new wine into old bottles: else the bottles break, and the wine runneth out, and the bottles perish: but they put new wine into new bottles, and both are preserved.

Cross–references   Mark 2:18–22; Luke 5:33–39

Immediately after Jesus had answered the question, "Why eateth your Master with publicans and sinners?" the Pharisees presented another question to Him through the disciples of John the Baptist.[314] John was in prison at the time, and his disciples may have been confused; although John testified of the Savior as the anticipated Messiah, Jesus clearly disregarded the sacred Mosaic Law and its meticulous observance.

a. Hosea 6:6.

John had come as did the prophets of old, and his eccentric style of living may have justified his disciples' (and some of the Pharisees') punctilious observance of the Law. Their question implied that John had taught his disciples to fast and pray (seemingly in a manner similar to that observed by the Pharisees). The Law of Moses prescribed only one official fast day, the Day of Atonement,[a][315] but the rabbis had added many public and private fasts. The public fasts generally commemorated the calamities of Israel's past,[316] but the question posed to the Savior was centered around the private fast days wherein the Pharisees aimed at the highest degree of merit obtainable under the observance of their Law. They held prescribed fasts a minimum of twice a week on the second and fifth days (Monday and Thursday). They selected these days of the week because they thought that Moses had gone up on Mount Sinai for the second set of tablets on a Thursday and had returned on a Monday.[317]

The Pharisees, however, had enlarged the fast even beyond this. They celebrated it for many special occasions, believing that fasting would give them lucky dreams and the interpretations thereof, or that it would allow them to receive revelation, avert evil, or procure some good.[318] They reasoned this way because of their concept of hostility between body and spirit. They believed that the spirit could be exalted only by suppressing the body.

John's disciples' question also assumed that Jesus had not taught His disciples to pray, while John's disciples and the Pharisees prayed continually. (The topic of prayer is mentioned only in the Joseph Smith Translation of Matthew.) Nevertheless, the prayers they used were merely mechanical repetitions contrived to fit the hedge of the Law. They were tediously long and terribly depressing, with many superstitions assigned to the words. Their prayers were governed with minute rules not only to ensure the correctness of their content but also to fix the very hours they prayed.[319] At this time in His ministry, however, Jesus had given His disciples no formal rules for prayer or fasting, and in responding to the question He ignored the topic of prayer and dealt only with fasting.

Jesus did not blame John's disciples for asking this question, but He defended Himself and His followers by asking another question: "Can the children of the bridechamber mourn, as long as the bridegroom is with them?" The Lord was justified in His position. "But the days will come," He added, "when the bridegroom shall be taken from them, and then shall they fast."

Jesus had come to liberate the Jews from the yoke of the Mosaic ordinances and the bondage that had been placed upon them by the traditions of their fathers. His answer clearly implied an abrogation of the rabbinical rules and numerous traditions of that Law.[320] His answer also proclaimed that He was the Messiah who had come to declare a new law, not merely reform the old one.[321] His new kingdom would not be established by patching up the old robe of Judaism. The gospel that Jesus taught was a new garment—a new revelation and an everlasting covenant—because the rents of the old ceremonial law which Christ ignored could not be patched. Nor could the new "wine" of His kingdom be confined in the old "bottles" of Judaism.

Although Jesus (as Jehovah) had given the old Law, He avoided an open condemnation of it at this time. He treated it with indifference. Had the children of Israel been righteously observing the old Law the way the Lord gave it to them in the Old Testament, they would have accepted Him in the meridian of time.[322]

Question Three
"Who is my mother?"

Matthew 12:46–50   While he yet talked to the people, behold, his mother and his brethren stood without, desiring to speak with him. Then one said unto him, Behold, thy mother and thy brethren stand without, desiring to speak with thee. But he answered and said unto him that told him, Who is my mother? and who are my brethren? And he stretched forth his hand toward his disciples, and said, Behold my mother and my brethren! For whosoever shall do the will of my Father which is in heaven, the same is my brother, and sister, and mother.

Cross–references   Mark 3:31–35; Luke 8:19–21; JST Matthew 12:44

Unlike the previous questions, this time Jesus posed a question. "Who is my mother?" He asked. He directed it to those who were listening to Him as He sat teaching. It was apparently a request by His mother (and other members of His family) to speak with Him that invoked this query. Their interruption came shortly after the Lord had responded to the Beelzebub argument[323] and could be attributed to the Pharisaic opposition "which either filled [the] relatives of Jesus with fear for His safety, or made them sincerely concerned about His proceedings."[324] The scriptures indicate that at times the Lord's family did not truly understand or accept Him as the Messiah. Perhaps they were even somewhat jealous of Him; but for whatever reason, their belief in Him did not develop until after His resurrection.[325]

The Jews held a deep reverence for parents and family members, but the Lord's response to His family's request to speak with Him indicated that He was concerned with higher spiritual relationships, not the earthly ones that may have prompted His family's concern. He would not deviate from His mission, and He would not allow family ties to interfere with His work in any way. He did not condemn His mother or His family and He meant no disrespect by His response. He treated it like He had the incident that had occurred when He was twelve years old and was found teaching in the temple. When His parents asked Him at that time why He had not told them what He was doing, He informed them that He was "about his Father's business."

Jesus asked His question to emphasize the principles of the gospel He had been discussing and to testify of His divinity.[326] He explained that all disciples would become His brothers and sisters if they did the will of the Father. Through their obedience they would experience a new birth into His "family" and become joint heirs with Him in heaven.

The Lord's work took precedence over the claims of His family and all other temporal things. This early teaching would take on greater importance to the Twelve when the Lord later explained that He expected a like devotion from them.[a]

Question Four

"What good thing shall I do, that I may have eternal life?"

Matthew 19:16–30 And, behold, one came and said unto him, Good Master, what good thing shall I do, that I may have eternal life? And he said unto him, Why callest thou me good? there is none good but one, that is, God: but if thou wilt enter into life, keep the commandments. He saith unto him, Which? Jesus said, Thou shalt do no murder, Thou shalt not commit adultery, Thou shalt not steal, Thou shalt not bear false witness,

Honour thy father and thy mother: and, Thou shalt love thy neighbour as thyself. The young man saith unto him, All these things have I kept from my youth up: what lack I yet? Jesus said unto him, If thou wilt be perfect, go and sell that thou hast, and give to the poor, and thou shalt have treasure in heaven: and come and follow me. But when the young man heard that saying, he went away sorrowful: for he had great possessions. Then said Jesus unto his disciples, Verily I say unto you, That a rich man shall hardly enter into the kingdom of heaven. And again I say unto you, It is easier for a camel to go through the eye of a needle, than for a rich man to enter into the kingdom of God. When his disciples heard it, they were exceedingly amazed, saying, Who then can be saved? But Jesus beheld them, and said unto them, With men this is impossible; but with God all things are possible.

Then answered Peter and said unto him, Behold, we have forsaken all, and followed thee; what shall we have therefore? And Jesus said unto them, Verily I say unto you, That ye which have followed me, in the regeneration when the Son of man shall sit in the throne of his glory, ye also shall sit upon twelve thrones, judging the twelve tribes of Israel. And every one that hath forsaken houses, or brethren, or sisters, or father, or mother, or wife, or children, or lands, for my name's sake, shall receive an hundredfold, and shall inherit everlasting life. But many that are first shall be last; and the last shall be first.

Cross-references   Mark 10:17–31; Luke 18:18–30

As Jesus traveled toward Jerusalem on one of His journeys, a young man came to Him and addressing Him as "Good Master" asked, "What good thing shall I do that I should have eternal life?" It was not an unusual question. It was repeatedly put to the rabbis of the day and frequently occurred in Jewish writings.[327]

As is usual among the Gospel writers, Matthew reports the words of the young man; Mark adds the graphic touches, noting that the young man ran to Jesus and kneeled before Him; and Luke, concerned with detail, adds that the young man was a ruler. It was not common in Israel to be called "Good master,"[328] so the salutation addressed to Jesus was a unique one. It appears to have been a polite compliment, which undoubtedly is why the Lord rejected the salutation, emphasizing the distinction concerning the word good.[329]

After commenting on the salutation, the Lord responded to the question by instructing the young man that to enter into eternal life he must keep all the commandments. This answer was too general for the rich young ruler, because he apparently sought some specific "good work" or "task" that he might accomplish in order to enhance his ability to gain the kingdom. So he pressed Jesus for a specific task and asked, "Which?" desiring the Lord to enumerate some specific commandment that he might perform. Jesus enumerated several of the commandments and ended His instructions with, "Love thy neighbor as thyself." With apparent sincerity, the young man affirmed that he had accomplished all of these commandments from his youth; yet he obviously felt there was something missing, so he asked, "What lack I yet?"

The Lord did not question the young man's keeping of the outward requirements of the letter of the Law; but now, discerning what the young man needed, He tailored His answer to fit that need—that the young ruler might, in fact, attain the kingdom of heaven. Jesus instructed Him to sell all that he had, give it to the poor, and follow Him.

This was not a blanket instruction intended for all disciples;[330] rather, it was suited specifically to the young ruler standing before Jesus. The Lord undoubtedly directed the instruction to him because he had perceived that the young man needed it. His worldly possessions were standing in the way of his progress. This stern admonition was in conformity with several other admonitions which the Lord had given to those who would follow Him. To one man he declared, "Let the dead bury the dead"; to another He explained "that when the hand had been placed to the plough they must not look back"; and to yet another He commanded that they should "hate father and mother" to be worthy of Him. Beneath these requests lay the requirement that the Lord's disciples must make a total self–sacrifice for the new kingdom if the kingdom was to be successfully established upon the earth.

But this requirement was too stringent for the young ruler and only disclosed his weakness. He could not choose spiritual rewards over his earthly possessions. He was humbled before the Lord and, recognizing the great sacrifice necessary to attain the kingdom of heaven, allowed the world to get the best of him. Thereafter he retreated into scriptural obscurity.

Using this example, Jesus continued to teach the disciples, declaring to them that it was very difficult for rich men to enter the kingdom of heaven. He declared, in fact, that it was easier for a camel to go through the eye of a needle than for a rich man to get into heaven. This saying amazed the disciples exceedingly for they (along with the young ruler) believed that it was necessary to acquire material things in this life in order to attain spiritual blessings in the kingdom of heaven. This was a doctrine the Jews had developed over the years from the last instructions Moses had given to the children of Israel.[a][331]

a. Deuteronomy 28:1–14.

The stunned Apostles then turned to the Lord and asked, "Who then can be saved?" Jesus calmly responded, "With men this is impossible; but with God all things are possible." Peter now said to the Lord, "Behold, we have forsaken all, and followed thee: what shall we have therefore?" It is evident that Peter (and perhaps all the Twelve) felt that since he had done what the rich young ruler could not do (give up all to follow Jesus), he might be eligible for a reward in the kingdom of heaven, and he therefore asked the Lord what he might receive as a result of his sacrifice.

Jesus acknowledged the devotion of Peter and the Twelve and assured them that their sacrifice and continued labor would entitle them to sit upon thrones in the kingdom of His Father where they would judge the twelve tribes of Israel. Lest any of His Apostles should become proud and neglect the work required to enter His kingdom, Jesus cautioned them and said, "Many that are first shall be last; and the last shall be first."

Question Five

"Are there few that be saved?"

Luke 13:22–35 And he went through the cities and villages, teaching, and journeying toward Jerusalem. Then said one unto him, Lord, are there few that be saved? And he said unto them,

Strive to enter in at the strait gate: for many, I say unto you, will seek to enter in, and shall not be able. When once the master of the house is risen up, and hath shut to the door, and ye begin to stand without, and to knock at the door, saying, Lord, Lord, open unto us; and he shall answer and say unto you, I know you not whence ye are: then shall ye begin to say, We have eaten and drunk in thy presence, and thou hast taught in our streets. But he shall say, I tell you, I know you not whence ye are; depart from me, all ye workers of iniquity. There shall be weeping and gnashing of teeth, when ye shall see Abraham, and Isaac, and Jacob, and all the prophets, in the kingdom of God, and you yourselves thrust out. And they shall come from the east, and from the west, and from the north, and from the south, and shall sit down in the kingdom of God. And, behold, there are last which shall be first, and there are first which shall be last.

The same day there came certain of the Pharisees, saying unto him, Get thee out, and depart hence: for Herod will kill thee. And he said unto them, Go ye, and tell that fox, Behold, I cast out devils, and I do cures to day and to morrow, and the third day I shall be perfected. Nevertheless I must walk to day, and to morrow, and the day following: for it cannot be that a prophet perish out of Jerusalem. O Jerusalem, Jerusalem, which killest the prophets, and stonest them that are sent unto thee; how often would I have gathered thy children together, as a hen doth gather her brood under her wings, and ye would not! Behold, your house is left unto you desolate: and verily I say unto you, Ye shall not see me, until the time come when ye shall say, Blessed is he that cometh in the name of the Lord.

Jesus was on His last journey toward Jerusalem when someone came to Him and asked, "Are there few that be saved?" Although it is not known who asked the question, it would seem likely that the person was a representative of the Pharisees.[332] Perhaps the question came as a result of the Jewish teaching which emphasized that every Israelite was entitled to a portion in the kingdom of heaven since they believed that although God had made the world for many people to live in, He had created the hereafter for only a chosen few.[333]

The Lord did not declare that many would be saved; rather, He declared that many who strive for the kingdom would not make it because the way was narrow and once they had been shut out of the kingdom they were out of it for good, even if they pleaded for entrance. The Lord was essentially rescinding the privileges that the Israelites had been claiming. He taught them that it was their spiritual accomplishments that would qualify them for entry into His kingdom. To emphasize this, He noted that they would eventually see their own patriarchs and prophets (Abraham, Isaac, and Jacob) in the kingdom while they themselves would be outside its bounds. They must press on to gain entry into the kingdom while the door was yet open to let them in, lest it be closed and they be forever barred.

Claims based on lineage would not admit the Israelites into the kingdom of God. Earthly acquisitions would not save them. Procrastination in obeying the commandments would endanger their souls because belief in the Savior was the key that would allow them (and all men) to enter into the kingdom of heaven.[334] Jesus concluded with the warning that many whom they considered to be automatically outside the bounds of the kingdom would enter therein, while they would be "thrust out."

Sometime later that same day, the Pharisees came to Jesus and warned Him to leave the area of Perea because Herod sought to kill Him. Whether the warning was a ruse[335] or based on legitimate concerns[336] is unknown, but the danger was real enough. But Jesus would not hasten His work, regardless of threats. He chided Herod to the Pharisees and called him a "fox." He told the Pharisees to tell Herod that today He did cures and He would again do them on the morrow, but on the third day He would be perfected—thus predicting His imminent death at Jerusalem. He lamented over Jerusalem and cried, "O Jerusalem, Jerusalem, which killeth the prophets and stonest them that are sent unto thee." The Savior would not be killed by Herod. Herod ruled in Perea, and prophets perished in Jerusalem.

Jerusalem was the religious capital of the world and was like no other place. It was the Holy City and the city of the Savior's temple. It was the home of the prophets and the center of Christ's personal ministry. Yet it was a city of depravity—a spiritual Sodom and Egypt[a] where it was foreseen that the Son of God would be crucified.[b] After declaring the city's future desolate state, the Lord concluded this teaching sequence by prophesying of Jerusalem's glory in the latter days, in a time when the word of the Lord would again go forth out of that holy city.[c]

a. Revelation 11:8.

b. 2 Nephi 10:3.

c. Isaiah 2:3.

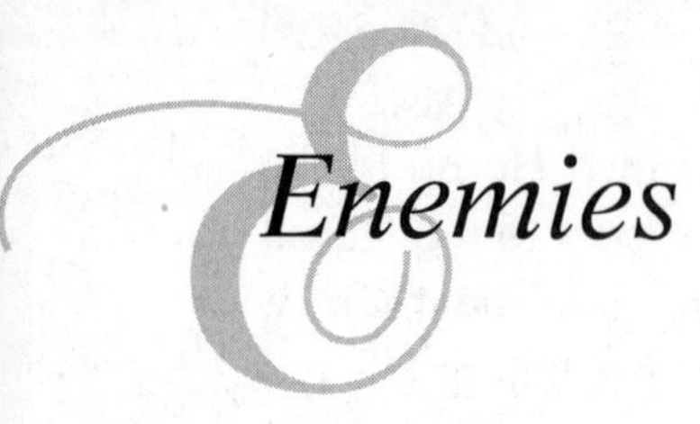

Enemies

10

"What Went Ye Out for to See?"

Matthew 11:1–30   And it came to pass, when Jesus had made an end of commanding his twelve disciples, he departed thence to teach and to preach in their cities. Now when John had heard in the prison the works of Christ, he sent two of his disciples, and said unto him, Art thou he that should come, or do we look for another? Jesus answered and said unto them, Go and shew John again those things which ye do hear and see: the blind receive their sight, and the lame walk, the lepers are cleansed, and the deaf hear, the dead are raised up, and the poor have the gospel preached to them. And blessed is he, whosoever shall not be offended in me.

And as they departed, Jesus began to say unto the multitudes concerning John, What went ye out into the wilderness to see? A reed shaken with the wind? But what went ye out for to see? A man clothed in soft raiment? behold, they that wear soft clothing are in kings' houses. But what went ye out for to see? A prophet? yea, I say unto you, and more than a prophet. For this is he, of whom it is written, Behold, I send my messenger before thy face, which shall prepare thy way before thee. Verily I say unto you, Among them that are born of women there hath not risen a greater than John the Baptist: notwithstanding he that is least in the kingdom of heaven is greater than he. And from the days of John the Baptist until now the kingdom of heaven suffereth violence, and the violent take it by force. For all the prophets and the law prophesied until John. And if ye will receive it, this is Elias, which was for to come. He that hath ears to hear, let him hear.

But whereunto shall I liken this generation? It is like unto children sitting in the markets, and calling unto their fellows, and saying, We have piped unto you, and ye have not danced; we have mourned unto you, and ye have not lamented. For John came neither eating nor drinking, and they say, He hath a devil. The son of man came eating and drinking, and they say, Behold a man gluttonous, and a winebibber, a friend of publicans and sinners. But wisdom is justified of her children.

Then began he to upbraid the cities wherein most of his mighty works were done, because they repented not. Woe unto thee, Chorazin! woe unto thee, Bethsaida! for if the mighty works, which were done in you, had been done in Tyre and Sidon, they would have repented long ago in sackcloth and ashes. But I say unto you, It shall be more tolerable for Tyre and Sidon at the day of judgment, than for you. And thou, Capernaum, which art exalted unto heaven, shalt be brought down to hell: for if the mighty works, which have been done in thee, had been done in Sodom, it would have remained until this day. But I say unto you, That it shall be more tolerable for the land of Sodom in the day of judgment, than for thee.

At that time Jesus answered and said, I thank thee, O Father, Lord of heaven and earth, because thou hast hid these things from the wise and prudent, and hast revealed them unto babes. Even so, Father: for so it seemed good in thy sight. All things are delivered unto me of my Father: and no man knoweth the Son, but the Father; neither knoweth any man the Father, save the Son, and he to whomsoever the Son will reveal him.

Come unto me, all ye that labour and are heavy laden, and I will give you rest. Take my yoke upon you, and learn of me; for I am meek and lowly in heart: and ye shall find rest unto your souls. For my yoke is easy, and my burden is light.

Cross–reference   Luke 7:18–35

John the Baptist, as the forerunner to Christ's ministry, had borne witness of Him as the Messiah—but now he was in prison, having been put there by Herod. While languishing in captivity, he undoubtedly heard of the commencement of the Savior's ministry and perhaps of the many miracles Jesus had performed. It was from this setting that John sent two of his disciples to Jesus to ask Him an interesting question: "Art thou he that should come, or do we look for another?"

Jesus responded by inviting them to listen to the things that He would say and to watch the things that He would do. After hearing the Savior's teachings and witnessing the miracles that He performed in their presence, they then returned to John and told him all that they had seen and heard. We cannot infer that John was uncertain or doubtful in his testimony of Jesus as the Messiah[337] since the record states that when John was first imprisoned, Jesus "sent angels, and . . . they came and ministered unto [John]."[a] But John may have become despondent in his prison environment, feeling that there was appreciably nothing left for him to do; and in his loneliness (a feeling not unlike that of Elijah and Moses in the Old Testament), he sent these disciples to the Messiah. Perhaps John hoped that his disciples might believe on Christ as they apparently still followed him who was but the forerunner of Jesus. But Jesus was the true leader of the kingdom, and the long–awaited Messiah.[338]

a. IV Matthew 4:11.

After John's disciples had gone, the Lord turned His attention to the multitude and proceeded with His sermon. He first bore testimony of John, praising him in the highest terms as one whom no wind of doctrine could shake. Jesus declared boldly that although John was not wearing the soft raiment of the day, he was most assuredly a prophet— even "more than a prophet"— because this man who had come in the likeness and manner of the great prophets of old was the forerunner of the kingdom of God which the prophet Malachi had foretold.[a] He was the "Elias, which was for to come."

John represented the last and greatest of the prophets of the old dispensation. He was chosen to usher in the new dispensation, and Christ now declared him to be the greatest of all the prophets that had been born of women. But so far as we know, John had performed no miracles, and the approximate length of his ministry at the time of Christ's baptism was only six months. From that time until his arrest, his ministry decreased as the Savior's increased.[339] How then was he the greatest of prophets? First, the Lord entrusted him to prepare the way before His face and declare His divinity to all men. Second, it was his privilege to lead the Son of God into the waters of baptism and witness the Holy Ghost descend upon Him. Third, during John's short ministry he "was the only legal administrator in the affairs of the kingdom . . . on the earth . . . holding the keys of power."[340] Then the Lord continued and declared, "He that is least in the kingdom of heaven [referring to Himself] is greater than he."[341]

The Jews admitted that all of the Law and the prophets looked forward to the coming of the Messiah, but the expectancy (as prophesied in the scriptures and the Law) and the reality (as anticipated by the Jews) differed sharply, and the Lord confirmed that in this discourse.[342]

The Jews anticipated the coming Messiah to be a national hero–king who would stand at the head of a great revolt and deliver them from the bondage of Rome, destroying the heathen and establishing the Jewish theocracy as it was in the days of old.[343] The spiritual and moral slavery under which they had long been bound would not allow them to accept the Lord's spiritual kingdom. Such a kingdom could not deliver them from temporal bondage. The herald of the new kingdom and the actual Messiah that followed that herald did not satisfy their

a. Malachi 3:1.   unrealistic expectations. Jesus portrayed them as "children sitting in the markets, and calling unto their fellows," declaring, "We have piped unto you, and you have not danced." Although they knew the Law and lived for the coming Messiah, they expected one who would fit the tunes they played.

John the Baptist (the first witness) had come "neither eating nor drinking," but living the austere life of the prophets of old; yet they rejected him and said, "He hath a devil." Jesus (the second witness) had come living in the normal fashion of the day, and they had accused Him of being a "winebibber [and] a friend of publicans and sinners." They justified their rejection of John because he called them sinners when they thought themselves righteous; they rejected Jesus because He did not meet the qualifications of their traditions. So the Lord declared, "Wisdom is justified of her children."

Jesus next upbraided the cities and communities that had rejected Him, even though He had given them a mighty witness of His divinity. Of Chorazin we know nothing; and of Bethsaida we know only that He healed a blind man there,[a] and the sick in general, and fed the five thousand in the immediate vicinity.[b] But the people of those cities must have witnessed mighty works since the Lord declared that if the same works had been done in Tyre and Sidon, they would have put on sackcloth and ashes and quickly repented. He condemned Capernaum, stating that it would be "brought down to hell" because it had rejected the mighty works He performed there.[344] In the day of judgment, it would be more tolerable for Sodom than for Capernaum.

Following His condemnation of these wicked cities, Jesus thanked His Father for those who had believed, even though they had not come from the learned and ruling classes.

Closing the discourse, the Lord openly taught the multitude that the Father would reveal the Son and the Son would reveal the Father to those who would believe. He then freely invited the covenant people to cast off the heavy burdens, rituals, and traditions of men that the rulers of Israel had laid upon them—men who should have recognized Him. He taught them that by accepting Him, their burden would become light, their yoke would be easy, and they would find rest for their souls.

He did not speak as a prophet but as the expected Messiah, and He called upon all who would listen to repent, forsake the world, and

a. Mark 8:22–26.

b. Mark 6:30–46; Luke 9:10–17.

come unto Him—with the promise that if they did, their souls would enter into the rest of the Lord.[a] To those who love God, His commandments are easy and His burden light.[345]

Discipleship Prevented

Luke 14:25–35   And there went great multitudes with him: and he turned, and said unto them, If any man come to me, and hate not his father, and mother, and wife, and children, and brethren, and sisters, yea, and his own life also, he cannot be my disciple. And whosoever doth not bear his cross, and come after me, cannot be my disciple. For which of you, intending to build a tower, sitteth not down first, and counteth the cost, whether he have sufficient to finish it? Lest haply, after he hath laid the foundation, and is not able to finish it, all that behold it begin to mock him. Saying, This man began to build, and was not able to finish. Or what king, going to make war against another king, sitteth not down first, and consulteth whether he be able with ten thousand to meet him that cometh against him with twenty thousand? Or else, while the other is yet a great way off, he sendeth an ambassage, and desireth conditions of peace. So likewise, whosoever he be of you that forsaketh not all that he hath, he cannot be my disciple.

Salt is good: but if the salt have lost his savour, wherewith shall it be seasoned? It is neither fit for the land, nor yet for the dunghill, but men cast it out. He that hath ears to hear, let him hear.

The Synoptic writers record many times that wherever Jesus went during His ministry, great multitudes followed Him. At the time this discourse was given, a multitude was again with Him, and He stopped to instruct them. The Lord was being assailed from all sides by His enemies, and the leaders of the Jews constantly accused Him of evil to discredit Him.

In this discourse, Jesus taught His disciples the things that would prevent them from entering His kingdom unless they were totally sincere in their belief. He did not want transitory enthusiasts—those who followed Him had to be genuine disciples. He outlined the sacrifice and devotion demanded of those who would be in His service, emphasizing that their duty to God would take precedence over all temporal commitments.

A true disciple of the Lord could not expect earthly love or acceptance but rather alienation and opposition. He therefore must be prepared to abandon (if necessary) every earthly tie. In essence the Lord warned, "Those who are not able and determined to keep the commandments are better off outside the Church."[346]

a. D&C 84:17–25.

A follower could not be a disciple unless he could "hate" all family ties. This did not imply actual hatred;[347] it was a warning that the gospel took precedence over all family or personal obligations. The Lord did not promise earthly rewards for such sacrifice; He used the analogy of "bearing his cross" to describe the reception that the disciples would receive.

A disciple must also be willing to bear the Lord's shame and give up his own life for the kingdom. To emphasize this point the Lord used two examples: first was that the builder of a tower should count his costs before beginning construction in order to ensure the tower's completion. The Lord was illustrating that a person deciding whether or not to be a disciple had to consider more than the present. He must take the cost of total commitment into account. Second, the Lord told of a king who was planning a war. Common sense dictated to the king that he must compare his forces with those of the enemy as it was better to safely withdraw from the battle in humiliation or sue for peace than to suffer a costly defeat. He who would be a disciple must "deliberately [count] the cost, and, in view of the coming trial, ask himself whether he had, indeed, sufficient inward strength . . . to conquer."[348]

The Lord brought this discourse to a swift conclusion by declaring, "Whosoever he be of you that forsaketh not all that he hath, he cannot be my disciple." One of the multitude contended, "We have Moses and the prophets, and whosoever shall live by them, shall he not have life?"[a] Jesus countered, "Ye know not Moses, neither the prophets; for if ye had known them, ye would have believed on me . . . for to this intent they were written."

Obviously, the inquirer believed that through the Law and its demands he could attain the kingdom of heaven, for he and his ancestors before him had for centuries looked for salvation through conformity with the laws and ordinances revealed by Moses and the prophets. He therefore questioned why he should follow the teachings of Jesus. But the eternal life that the inquirer sought did not come from Moses and the prophets, and the Lord so taught. Jesus finally concluded, "For I am sent that ye might have life."[b]

Jesus then used a common proverb of His day[349] when He declared that if good salt ever lost its savour, it would thereafter be good for nothing and would be cast out. He concluded by warning, "He that hath ears to hear, let him hear."

In this discourse, the Lord outlined the requirements for an aspiring disciple, emphasizing absolute self–sacrifice for His cause. In the early history of The Church of Jesus Christ of Latter–day Saints, Joseph Smith described this self–sacrifice:

> Let us here observe, that a religion that does not require the sacrifice of all things never has power sufficient to produce the faith necessary unto life and salvation; for, from the first existence of man, the faith necessary unto the enjoyment of life and salvation never could be obtained without the sacrifice of all earthly things. It was through this sacrifice, and this only, that God has ordained that men should enjoy eternal life; and it is through the medium of the sacrifice of all earthly things that men do actually know that they are doing the things that are well pleasing in the sight of God. When a man has offered in sacrifice all that he has for the truth's sake, not even withholding his life, and believing before God that he has been called to make this sacrifice because he seeks to do his will, he does know, most assuredly, that God does and will accept his sacrifice and offering, and that he has not, nor will not seek his face in vain. Under these circumstances, then, he can obtain the faith necessary for him to lay hold on eternal life.
>
> It is in vain for persons to fancy to themselves that they are heirs with those, or can be heirs with them, who have offered their all in sacrifice, and by this means obtain faith in God and favor with him so as to obtain eternal life, unless they, in like manner, offer unto him the same sacrifice, and through that offering obtain the knowledge that they are accepted of him. . . .
>
> Those, then, who make the sacrifice, will have the testimony that their course is pleasing in the sight of God; and those who have this testimony will have faith to lay hold on eternal life. . . . But those who do not make the sacrifice cannot enjoy this faith, because men are dependent upon this sacrifice in order to obtain this faith; . . .

All the saints of whom we have account, in all the revelations of God which are extant, obtained the knowledge which they had of their acceptance in his sight through the sacrifice which they offered unto him . . . and were enabled . . . [to] contend against the wiles of the adversary, overcome the world, and obtain the end of their faith, even the salvation of their souls.[350]

"The Blind Lead the Blind"

Matthew 15:1–20   Then came to Jesus scribes and Pharisees, which were of Jerusalem, saying, Why do thy disciples transgress the tradition of the elders? for they wash not their hands when they eat bread. But he answered and said unto them, Why do ye also transgress the commandment of God by your tradition? For God commanded, saying. Honour thy father and mother: and, He that curseth father or mother, let him die the death. But ye say, Whosoever shall say to his father or his mother, It is a gift, by whatsoever thou mightest be profited by me; and honour not his father or his mother, he shall be free. Thus have ye made the commandment of God of none effect by your tradition. Ye hypocrites, well did Esaias prophesy of you, saying, This people draweth nigh unto me with their mouth, and honoureth me with their lips; but their heart is far from me. But in vain they do worship me, teaching for doctrines the commandments of men.

And he called the multitude, and said unto them, Hear, and understand: not that which goeth into the mouth defileth a man; but that which cometh out of the mouth, this defileth a man. Then came his disciples, and said unto him, Knowest thou that the Pharisees were offended, after they heard this saying? But he answered and said, Every plant, which my heavenly Father hath not planted, shall be rooted up. Let them alone: they be blind leaders of the blind. And if the blind lead the blind, both shall fall into the ditch. Then answered Peter and said unto him, Declare unto us this parable. And Jesus said, Are ye also yet without understanding? Do not ye yet understand, that whatsoever entereth in at the mouth goeth into the belly, and is cast out into the drought? But those things which proceed out of the mouth come forth from the heart; and they defile the man. For out of the heart proceed evil thoughts, murders, adulteries, fornications, thefts, false witness, blasphemies: these are the things which defile a man: but to eat with unwashen hands defileth not a man.

Cross–reference   Mark 7:1–23

The enemies of Jesus recognized in the Savior a deadly threat to their traditions and position; and almost from the beginning of His ministry they followed Him, spied on Him, and attempted to entrap Him in His words.[a] From the scriptural text it would appear that the Lord had performed the miracle of the feeding of the five thousand the day before this discourse took place.[351] This miracle caused His enemies to make what they considered a serious charge against Him.[352]

a. Luke 14:1; 6:7; 20:20.

They asked Jesus, "Why do thy disciples transgress the tradition of the elders? for they wash not their hands when they eat bread." At first glance this appears to be a trifling accusation, but to the leadership who presented it, it was a crime as great as eating the flesh of swine.[353]

In all, the leadership of the Jews made three great charges against Christ: first, they accused Him of performing His great miracles by the power of Beelzebub,[a][354] "whose special representative—almost incarnation—they declared Jesus to be."[355] Second, they charged that He was not of God because He was a sinner—it was therefore their duty to unmask Him to avoid deceiving the people.[b][356] They did this by instituting charges, such as the one in this discourse, to prove that Jesus sanctioned breaches in the traditional Law "which, according to their fundamental principles, involved heavier guilt than sins against the revealed Law of Moses."[357] Third, they charged Him with blasphemy for stating that He was equal to God.[c]

The Jews considered eating with "common hands" a sin of extreme gravity, for eating "with unwashen hands was as if it had been filth."[358] Jesus treated their traditional ceremonialism with indifference and had no sympathy for a system that ignored conscience but found the essence of religion in the slavery of outward form. He immediately responded to the Pharisees' charge, but as usual did not answer it. Instead, He took the offensive by accusing His antagonists of transgressing the commandments because of their traditions. He told them that they considered the washing of pots and cups and many other similar things greater than honoring their father and mother.

Their traditions dictated that by merely speaking the word corban (meaning "a gift") they could avoid the requirement of caring for the earthly needs of their parents. So strict was the observance of this tradition that the person saying corban could "prevent the person so addressed from ever deriving any benefit from that which belonged to him. And so stringent was the ordinance that . . . it [was] expressly stated that such a vow was binding, even if what was vowed involved a breach of the Law."[359]

The Lord then quoted Isaiah and indicated that the Pharisees standing before Him had fulfilled the prophecy because their lips honored the God of their fathers, but their religion was the doctrine of men. He continued to upbraid the Pharisees by saying, "Full well is it written of you, by the prophets whom ye have rejected. They testified these things of a truth, and their blood shall be upon you."[a]

There was no salvation in the punctilious observance of their Law, even though their worship was directed toward a true God. Their worship, based upon false principles, was in vain.[360] Christ abrogated the rabbinical regulations and offerings, declaring that mercy was better than sacrifice.[b] He stated, "Not that which goeth into the mouth defileth a man; but that which cometh out of the mouth, this defileth a man." No amount of soap and water can cleanse a man's thoughts for "those things which proceed out of the mouth come forth from the heart; and they defile the man." For the first time Jesus openly denounced the Jewish leaders, accusing them of concerning themselves with the obedience of things instituted by men and neglecting that which God had established.

Jesus made it painfully clear to the Jews that their traditionalism was totally incompatible with the scriptures, and through its use they had made void the word of God.

The Savior's response bitterly offended the Pharisees and His disciples noted this to Him. But Jesus only warned them of the fate awaiting those who reject the Father for their own doctrines. "Let them alone," he declared. "They be blind leaders of the blind. And if the blind lead the blind, both shall fall into the ditch."

This must have been a harsh attitude for the disciples to comprehend. Jesus was talking to the "elite" of Israel, and His audacity alarmed them. Peter ventured to ask the Lord to explain His comment. Jesus quickly responded with a mild rebuke and stated, "Are ye also without understanding?" Then the Lord again declared that the food going into a man could not defile him, but that which came out of his mouth and proceeded from his heart could. Jesus then cited several evils and sins as examples.

The Lord made it very clear that all things were clean to those who were spiritually cleansed. This teaching was in direct opposition to the Pharisaic belief that external purification was the key to acceptance by God. Jesus made no attempt to reconcile Himself with His antagonists. It was because of their obstinacy that they refused to understand,[361] and their willful tenacity made it easy for them to reject Jesus as the Messiah.

a. IV Mark 7:10–11.

b. Matthew 9:13; 12:7.

"Beware of the Leaven of the Pharisees"

Matthew 16:5–12   And when his disciples were come to the other side, they had forgotten to take bread.

Then Jesus said unto them, Take heed and beware of the leaven of the Pharisees and of the Sadducees. And they reasoned among themselves, saying, It is because we have taken no bread. Which when Jesus perceived, he said unto them, O ye of little faith, why reason ye among yourselves, because ye have brought no bread? Do ye not yet understand, neither remember the five loaves of the five thousand, and how many baskets ye took up? Neither the seven loaves of the four thousand, and how many baskets ye took up? How is it that ye do not understand that I spake it not to you concerning bread, that ye should beware of the leaven of the Pharisees and of the Sadducees? Then understood they how that he bade them not beware of the leaven of bread, but of the doctrine of the Pharisees and of the Sadducees.

Cross–reference   Mark 8:14–21

Matthew records that after the feeding of the four thousand, certain Pharisees and Sadducees came tempting Jesus, requesting a sign. They seemed to have a consuming desire to see the Lord perform miracles, and they were constantly asking Him to show them the Messianic sign.[362]

The Jews constantly sought signs in connection with their religious ceremonies—signs that would guide them in their temporal choices or decisions and help them gain the things they wanted. One of these signs was connected with the conclusion of the Feast of Tabernacles. They would watch what direction the smoke from the evening sacrifice traveled and would then use that occurrence to discern what the weather would be for the coming year. If the smoke turned northward, they believed there would be much rain and that the poor would rejoice. If the smoke turned southward, they believed the rich would rejoice, the poor would mourn, and there would be little rain. If the smoke turned eastward, everyone would rejoice together; and if it turned westward, all would mourn together.[363]

The Jews again failed in their attempt to involve Jesus in a dispute and His abrupt response left them discomforted before the multitude. He then left with the Twelve by boat to pass over to the other side of the Sea of Galilee in an effort to rid Himself of the sign–seekers and perhaps gain a moment of solitude. Matthew notes that when they reached the other shore, the disciples had forgotten to take any bread with them. Jesus turned to them and said, "Take heed and beware of the leaven of the Pharisees and of the Sadducees." But the Apostles did not understand; they thought Jesus was referring to the fact that they had no food. It appears from the scriptures that the Apostles were constantly having trouble interpreting the metaphors Jesus used. For example, when Jesus talked to them of "meat" in the discourse with the woman at the well, they thought He was referring to the food they were seeking; later, when Jesus said that Lazarus was "sleeping," they thought Lazarus was resting when in fact he was dead.

Jesus quickly perceived their misunderstanding and told them they had little faith, reminding them of the two great miracles He had performed: first the feeding of the five thousand and, most recently, the feeding of the four thousand.

Many of the Lord's discourses were of this type—short in duration and tied to a particular doctrine—but often the analogies or metaphors He used confused His listeners, and at times even the Twelve did not comprehend His meaning. This may have indicated to Jesus that the Twelve were not yet spiritually mature.[364] Their lack of faith made it difficult for them to discern the meaning of the Lord's instructions and so He reproved them. Then He made His instructions clear to them.

It was not the leaven in the food He was referring to, but the doctrine of the Pharisees and the Sadducees. The Lord was warning the Apostles to beware of the Jewish leaders' teachings, their slander, and their misleading information. It was their false doctrine that the Lord wanted the Apostles to shun so that they would not become tainted by the opposition.[365]

"How Knoweth This Man Letters?"

John 7:1–53 After these things Jesus walked in Galilee: for he would not walk in Jewry, because the Jews sought to kill him. Now the Jews' feast of tabernacles was at hand. His brethren therefore said unto him, Depart hence, and go into Judaea, that thy disciples also may see the works that thou doest. For there is no man that doeth any thing in secret, and he himself seeketh to be known openly. If thou do these things, shew thyself to the world. For neither did his brethren believe in him. Then Jesus said unto them, My time is not yet come: but your time is alway ready. The world cannot hate you; but me it hateth, because I testify of it, that the works thereof are evil. Go ye up unto this feast: I go not up yet unto this feast; for my time is not yet full come. When he had said these words unto them, he abode still in Galilee.

But when his brethren were gone up, then went he also up unto the feast, not openly, but as it were in secret. Then the Jews sought him at the feast, and said, Where is he? And there was much murmuring among the people concerning him: for some said, He is a good man: others said, Nay; but he deceiveth the people. Howbeit no man spake openly of him for fear of the Jews.

Now about the midst of the feast Jesus went up into the temple, and taught. And the Jews marvelled, saying, How knoweth this man letters, having never learned? Jesus answered them, and said, My doctrine is not mine, but his that sent me. If any man will do his will, he shall know of the doctrine, whether it be of God, or whether I speak of myself. He that speaketh of himself seeketh his own glory: but he that seeketh his glory that sent him, the same is true, and no unrighteousness is in him. Did not Moses give you the law, and yet none of you keepeth the law? Why go ye about to kill me? The people answered and said, Thou hast a devil: who goeth about to kill thee? Jesus answered and said unto them, I have done one work, and ye all marvel. Moses therefore gave unto you circumcision; (not because it is of Moses, but of the fathers;) and ye on the sabbath day circumcise a man. If a man on the sabbath day receive circumcision, that the law of Moses should not be broken; are ye angry at me, because I have made a man every whit whole on the sabbath day? Judge not according to the appearance, but judge righteous judgment. Then said some of them of Jerusalem, is not this he, whom they seek to kill? But, lo, he speaketh boldly, and they say nothing unto him. Do the rulers know indeed that this is the very Christ? Howbeit we know this man whence he is: but when Christ cometh, no man knoweth whence he is. Then cried Jesus in the temple as he taught, saying, Ye both know me, and ye know whence I am: and I am not come of myself, but he that sent me is true, whom ye know not. But I know him: for I am from him, and he hath sent me. Then they sought to take him: but no man laid hands on him, because his hour was not yet come. And many of the people believed on him, and said, When Christ cometh, will he do more miracles than these which this man hath done?

The Pharisees heard that the people murmured such things concerning him; and the Pharisees and the chief priests sent officers to take him. Then said Jesus unto them, Yet a little while am I with you, and then I go unto him that sent me. Ye shall seek me, and shall not find me: and where I am, thither ye cannot come. Then said the Jews among themselves, Whither will he go, that we shall not find him? will he go unto the dispersed among the Gentiles, and teach the Gentiles? What manner of saying is this that he said, Ye shall seek me, and shall not find me: and where I am, thither ye cannot come? In the last day, that great day of the feast, Jesus stood and cried, saying, If any man thirst, let him come unto me, and drink. He that believeth on me, as the scripture hath said, out of his belly shall flow rivers of living water. (But this spake he of the Spirit, which they that believe on him should receive: for the Holy Ghost was not yet given; because that Jesus was not yet glorified.)

Many of the people therefore, when they heard this saying, said, Of a truth this is the Prophet. Others said, This is the Christ. But some said, Shall Christ come out of Galilee? Hath not the scripture said, That Christ cometh of the seed of David, and out of the town of Bethlehem, where David was? So there was a division among the people because of him. And some of them would have taken him; but no man laid hands on him.

Then came the officers to the chief priests and Pharisees; and they said unto them, Why have ye not brought him? The officers answered, Never man spake like this man. Then answered them the Pharisees, Are ye also deceived? Have any of the rulers or of the Pharisees believed on him? But this people who knoweth not the law are cursed. Nicodemus saith unto them, (he that came to Jesus by night, being one of them,) Doth our law judge any man, before it hear him, and know what he doeth? They answered and said unto him, Art thou also of Galilee? Search, and look; for out of Galilee ariseth no prophet. And every man went unto his own house.

Jesus had not been in Jerusalem for six months and the Feast of Tabernacles was drawing nigh.[366] At this time in the Savior's ministry Judea was no longer open to Him; but He still had to present His claim to the Messiahship in the temple in the Holy City of David.

Jerusalem was the main headquarters of the Jewish priests and rabbis and also the headquarters of the institution Jesus had come to supersede. Even though the scripture reports that after a certain point He had not previously walked in Jewry because the Jews sought to kill Him, the steadily deepening hostility could not keep Him from declaring His Messiahship to the leaders of the "chosen people."

The Feast of Tabernacles was the third of the great annual festivals held each year in Israel. At these three feasts every male of the covenant people was to appear before the Lord. The Feast of Tabernacles fell during the seventh Jewish month on the fifteenth day (which corresponds to the latter part of September or the beginning of October).[367] It was the most joyful of all the festival seasons, and it was held at the time of year when the people were naturally full of thankfulness. The crops had been stored and fruit gathered in. The thanksgiving of harvest and the Feast of Tabernacles "reminded Israel, on the one hand, of their dwelling in booths in the wilderness, while, on the other hand, it pointed to the final harvest when Israel's mission should be completed, and all nations gathered unto the Lord."[368] This joyful feast followed five days after the Day of Atonement wherein the sins of Israel were removed and their "chosen" covenant with God restored.

The Lord's "brethren" urged Him to go up to the feast in Jerusalem and show His mighty miracles. The "brethren" spoken of here were members of Christ's own family, the other children of Mary and Joseph, who apparently had not yet openly declared their belief in Him even though they were asking Him to show His signs.[369] They chided Jesus for not going openly to the feast[370] and wondered why He would not go and perform His miracles. They apparently felt like most of the Israelites who clung to the traditions that the anticipated Messiah would restore Israel to its former, national glory. They obviously did not understand the Lord, and they perhaps wondered why He stayed in Galilee if He wanted to establish His Messianic kingdom since they knew such a kingdom would have to be established in Jerusalem.[371]

But Jesus would not attend the feast in this manner, nor would He display His powers for their pleasure; so He told them to go to the feast without Him as His "time was not yet come." After His brethren had gone, Jesus waited two more days; then He departed secretly for the feast with His chosen Twelve, traveling through Samaria toward Jerusalem. The normal hospitality afforded strangers was denied Him on this trip, as the Samaritans again showed their open hostility toward the Israelites.[372]

Three groups of people attended the Feast of Tabernacles: first, the ever–present Pharisees and leaders of the Jews; second, a multitude of pilgrims (this particular feast was predominately designated for foreign pilgrims coming from great distances in order to make their temple contributions);[373] and third, those who lived in the Holy City.

All who attended the feast anticipated that Jesus would be there, and the scripture notes that they were looking for Him but could not find Him. There was general disagreement among the populace concerning Christ. They did not talk openly of Him for fear of the Jewish leadership, but curiosity ran high. Some indicated He was a good man while others rejected Him. The murmuring and whispering of the crowd, as recorded in John, is different from that recorded elsewhere in the scriptures, and John appears to have felt that the people wanted to do the right thing but were unsure what it was.

In the middle of the feast Jesus suddenly appeared in the temple and began teaching. His brethren had gone to the feast to prove themselves faithful to the Law, that they might "keep" the feast, but Jesus had gone to witness His Messiahship.

The subject of His discourse in the temple is not recorded but the reaction to it is. The people listened in astonishment. The leaders of the Jews "knew what common unlettered Galilean tradesmen were,"[374] and they were astounded at the teachings of Jesus. In their ongoing attempt to create doubt and suspicion in the Lord's teachings, they asked the question, "How knoweth this man letters, having never learned?"

To the Jews there was only one kind of learning—theology, and only one road to it—the schools of the rabbis.[375] In those schools each student learned theology from a great teacher, but Jesus had attended none of them.[376] The question the leaders posed challenged the Lord's competence as a teacher, but the answer He gave disputed their competence as hearers. He told them that the doctrine He taught was not His, but His Father's who had sent Him; they had only to do the will of the Father to know the validity of the doctrine. Jesus had bypassed the normal schools of learning (which the Jews felt could be traced from one great teacher to another on back to Moses, and thus to God Himself). The Savior had received His education directly from God: He was God's messenger to the Jews.

As the discussion continued, Jesus asked, "Did not Moses give you the law, and yet none of you keepeth the law?" The Jews were breaking the Law because they sought to kill Him. The people responded by stating incredulously, "Thou hast a devil: who goeth about to kill thee?" Perhaps the murderous intentions of the leaders were not known to the common people. Jesus declared that the reason for their evil intentions against Him was His work on the Sabbath. He specifically referred to the healing of the impotent man[377] as the reason they sought to put Him to death. They felt He was desecrating their Sabbath. Jesus defended His work by stating that they allowed the requirement of circumcision to supersede the Sabbath Law; therefore, why should they be angry at Him for making a man whole on the Sabbath day. He demanded that they "judge not according to the appearance, but judge righteous judgment." This defense immediately generated belief in some of the Jews at the festival, and some acknowledged that although this was the man the leadership sought to kill, he spoke to them boldly and the leaders did nothing. They questioned whether this was the "very Christ." The crowd began to wonder if He really was the long–awaited Messiah.

The Jewish leadership quickly attempted to curtail this belief by asking another question, this time concerning the Messiah's origin. They knew where Jesus had been raised and it was "evident that Jesus was thought of as a native of Nazareth, and that the circumstances of His birth were not of public knowledge."[378] At the time of Christ there were two divergent beliefs associated with the coming forth of the anticipated Messiah. Some believed that the Savior would be born in Bethlehem, and they based their view on the Old Testament.[a] A second group taught that the Messiah would come from an unknown source: His origin would be a mystery.[379]

Jesus now dropped all pretenses and clearly declared what His mission was and from whom He had been sent: "I am not come of myself, but he that sent me is true, whom ye know not. But I know him: for I am from him, and he hath sent me." After this powerful declaration the Jews immediately "sought to take him," but they could not for "his hour was not yet come."

Jesus undoubtedly spent many additional hours teaching in Jerusalem, but John only records fragments of His sermons.[380] Many began to believe on Him but the Pharisees could not tolerate His success, so they sent temple officers to again try to arrest Him. Jesus ignored them and closed this portion of His discourse by reiterating that He would go to His Father, "and where I am," He said, "thither ye cannot come." The leaders misunderstood this prophecy of His death and resurrection, and questioned whether or not it meant that He would go to the Gentiles.

On the last day of the Feast of Tabernacles Jesus again declared His Messiahship before all those attending the celebration. The significance of the feast helps us to understand what the Lord meant when He declared, "If any man thirst, let him come unto me and drink." On each day of the feast a priest went down to the pool of Siloam (where Jesus had healed the impotent man) and drew water into a golden pitcher. He then proceeded to the temple sacrifice area, . . . so timing it, that he returned just as his brethren carried up the pieces of the sacrifice to lay them on the altar. As he entered by the "Watergate," which obtained its name from this ceremony, he was received by a threefold blast from the priests' trumpets.

> [On the seventh day of the feast] . . . they made the circuit of the altar seven times . . . after the priest had returned from Siloam with his golden pitcher, and for the last time poured its

contents to the base of the altar; after the "Hallel" had been sung to the sound of the flute, . . . [and] just when the interest of the people had been raised to its highest pitch . . . [as] the mass of worshippers . . . were waving towards the altar quite a forest of leafy branches . . . a voice was raised which resounded through the Temple, startled the multitude, and carried fear and hatred to the hearts of the leaders.[381]

Jesus stood and cried aloud saying, "If any man thirst, let him come unto me, and drink. He that believeth on me . . . out of his belly shall flow rivers of living water."

The words the priests and the people were speaking at that point of the temple ceremony referred to the Holy Spirit, and the symbolism of the Savior's cry would have been clearly understood.[382] Jesus interpreted and fulfilled the words they spoke, thereby asserting His claim to the Messiahship.[a][383]

Some believed, some continued to question, and the division among the people remained. The Pharisees questioned the officers they had sent to arrest Jesus, asking why they had not brought Him to them. But even the officers acknowledged that they could not resist the Lord, for He spoke not as other men. The Pharisees sitting in council strongly condemned Jesus, but Nicodemus raised a legal question: "Doth our law judge any man, before it hear him, and know what he doeth?" This precipitated a response by his fellow Pharisees. They questioned the origin of Jesus again, and without thinking, they angrily declared, "Search, and look: for out of Galilee ariseth no prophet." They ignored their legal procedures[b] and apparently also overlooked the fact that at least Jonah had come from Galilee, and perhaps also Nahum, Hosea, and Elijah.[384] It was the third time that they had raised the subject of Jesus' Galilean origin, and even though He did not hail from Galilee (they apparently being ignorant of His actual birthplace), it was evidence of the enormous effect the words of Jesus had upon them.

The festival was over; the discourse had ended. The Lord's claim to the Messiahship had been asserted and rejected "and every man went unto his own house."

a. Isaiah 44:3; 55:1; 58:11.

b. Exodus 23:1; Deuteronomy 1:16; Deuteronomy 19:15.

The Last Controversies

Matthew 22:15–46   Then went the Pharisees, and took counsel how they might entangle him in his talk. And they sent out unto him their disciples with the Herodians, saying, Master, we know that thou art true, and teachest the way of God in truth, neither carest thou for any man: for thou regardest not the person of men. Tell us therefore, What thinkest thou? Is it lawful to give tribute unto Caesar, or not? But Jesus perceived their wickedness, and said, Why tempt ye me, ye hypocrites? Shew me the tribute money. And they brought unto him a penny. And he saith unto them, Whose is this image and superscription? They say unto him, Caesar's. Then saith he unto them, Render therefore unto Caesar the things which are Caesar's; and unto God the things that are God's. When they had heard these words, they marvelled, and left him, and went their way.

The same day came to him the Sadducees, which say that there is no resurrection, and asked him, saying, Master, Moses said, If a man die, having no children, his brother shall marry his wife, and raise up seed unto his brother. Now there were with us seven brethren: and the first, when he had married a wife, deceased, and, having no issue, left his wife unto his brother: likewise the second also, and the third, unto the seventh. And last of all the woman died also. Therefore in the resurrection whose wife shall she be of the seven? for they all had her. Jesus answered and said unto them, Ye do err, not knowing the scriptures, nor the power of God. For in the resurrection they neither marry, nor are given in marriage, but are as the angels of God in heaven. But as touching the resurrection of the dead, have ye not read that which was spoken unto you by God, saying, I am the God of Abraham, and the God of Isaac, and the God of Jacob? God is not the God of the dead, but of the living. And when the multitude heard this, they were astonished at his doctrine.

But when the Pharisees had heard that he had put the Sadducees to silence, they were gathered together. Then one of them, which was a lawyer, asked him a question, tempting him, and saying, Master, which is the great commandment in the law? Jesus said unto him, Thou shalt love the Lord thy God with all thy heart, and with all thy soul, and with all thy mind. This is the first and great commandment. And the second is like unto it, Thou shalt love thy neighbour as thyself. On these two commandments hang all the law and the prophets.

While the Pharisees were gathered together, Jesus asked them, saying, What think ye of Christ? whose son is he? They say unto him, The Son of David. He saith unto them, How then doth David in spirit call him Lord, saying, The Lord said unto my Lord, Sit thou on my right hand, till I make thine enemies thy footstool? If David then call him Lord, how is he his son? And no man was able to answer him a word, neither durst any man from that day forth ask him any more questions.

Cross–references   Mark 12:13–34; Luke 20:21–43

Controversy Number One: The Tribute Money

Throughout the Lord's ministry, the Jewish leadership tried unsuccessfully to entrap Him in His speech and notwithstanding their failures, they persisted in counseling with others how they "might entangle him in his talk." This attempt to entrap Jesus was unique in that the Pharisees solicited the assistance of the Herodians (men who would have otherwise been their foes)[385] in developing their plot to ruin their "common enemy."

This was the second time that the Pharisees and the Herodians had united in an attempt to ensnare Jesus[a] and to this end, on the last day of the Lord's public ministry, they devised a question that they felt would lead to His downfall. It involved the relationship between religion and state. These two parties—one watching for the smallest technical infringement of the Mosaic Law and the other constantly on guard for the slightest excuse to accuse Jesus of disloyalty to the secular powers—proceeded to send a young group of zealous disciples from the Pharisees to speak to Him. They flattered the Lord by addressing Him as "Master" and proceeded to ply Him with praise, stating that they knew He was a teacher from God, that He spoke the truth, and that He regarded not the opinions of men. They were apparently unknown to Jesus, and as yet they had not publicly evidenced personal antagonism toward Him.[386] Their approach was truthful in every word, but "as uttered by those fulsome dissemblers and in their nefarious intent, it was egregiously false."[387]

The approach had been conceived to avoid the Savior's suspicions, to perhaps appeal to His "fearlessness and singleness of moral purpose, to induce Him to commit Himself without reserve."[388] So these hand— a. Mark 3:6.

picked, young scholars asked Jesus the question, "Is it lawful to give tribute unto Caesar, or not?" The snare lay in the political obligation involved. To answer incorrectly would compromise Jesus before the Roman procurator.

Their question appeared to place Jesus in an uncompromising position which would force Him to answer no. Yet if He answered no, the Herodians would accuse Him of sedition and claim He championed rebellion. Israel was already divided on the issue of tribute. They felt that if they gave their allegiance to Caesar it would mean that they were being disobedient to Jehovah.[389] But it would have pleased the Pharisees if Jesus had answered yes, as they could then accuse Him before the populace (since the Messiah–King that Israel anticipated would never have submitted to the hated tax the tribute represented).[390] The Pharisees were certain that the cunning question they had devised would present a threat to Jesus, no matter which way He answered.

The Lord did not evidence much patience when He replied to the Jewish leaders, "Why tempt ye me, ye hypocrites?" He then asked, "Shew me the tribute money." The Lord had no intention of being trapped by the wicked Pharisees. The Roman coinage that the Jews paid tribute with had already circulated throughout Jerusalem and Galilee. They recognized the de facto government of Rome in that they had partaken of its benefits; so in practice they had already resolved their question.[391]

Taking the coin, Jesus asked His inquisitors, "Whose is the image and superscription?" "Caesar's," they quickly responded. Without hesitation Jesus replied, "Render therefore unto Caesar the things which are Caesar's; and unto God the things that are God's."

The Lord's answer established the relationship between the spiritual and the secular responsibilities of the members of His kingdom.[392] He was not opposing civil authority; He was simply stating that political and religious spheres could exist side–by–side and yet be distinct. His answer was neither treasonable nor a violation of the Law of Moses. Politics and religion do not have to involve nor exclude each other: they exist in different domains. The Lord's kingdom was not of this world. Those who were concerned with temporal things could demand the things of the world; but God required spiritual devotion.[a]

a. D&C 58:21–22; 98:4–10; Romans 13:1–7; 1 Timothy 2:1–3; Titus 3:1; 1 Peter 2:13–17; Articles of Faith 1:12.

The Lord's answer startled His inquisitors. He was correct in every particular, so they "marvelled and left him and went their way."

Controversy Number Two: A Question on the Resurrection

As soon as the controversy over tribute was put to rest, the Sadducees came to Jesus with a question. (The scriptures record only one other conflict between Jesus and the Sadducees.)[a] The Sadducees were a group of clergymen drawn from all classes of the people. They were "rich, dignified . . . affected at first only to despise the Galilean, who, like so many before Him, had stirred up commotion for the time among His rude compatriots. Even now, in Jerusalem, they were disposed to look at Him and His adherents with a lofty contempt, and to laugh the foolish rabble who listened to Him out of their fanatical dreams. His claims were, in their opinion, more silly than dangerous, and they would, therefore, bring the whole matter into contempt, by making it ridiculous."[393]

The Sadducees had carefully thought out their question. Even though they considered Jesus a fanatic, it appears that they were attempting to make Him an object of ridicule.[394] Their presentation was one of icy politeness and philosophic calm, couched in a stale piece of casuistry already settled in their law.[395] Their question concerned the fate of a woman in the resurrection who had been married to her husband and (because of intervening deaths) to each of his six brothers. This question had already been resolved for the Jews, since the writings of the Talmud indicated that a wife in this situation would have the first husband.[396] But the question was an interesting one in that the Sadducees denied the existence of the resurrection (the very basis of the question), maintaining "that it is as vain to hope that a cloud which has vanished will appear again, as that the grave will give back its dead."[397]

Jesus responded to this interrogation in a manner He had used many times before. He quickly passed over the guise of the query pertaining to marriage and declared, "in the resurrection they neither marry, nor are given in marriage." Jesus knew that these questions had to be settled before the resurrection by those holding the proper priesthood authority.[398] Next, Jesus resolved the portion of the question involving the resurrection. He told the Sadducees that they were in error

a. Matthew 16:1.

when they maintained that there was no resurrection, and that they did not know the scriptures or the power of God. He did not argue the scriptures with them but declared the very existence of God, using as examples their dead forefathers: Abraham, Isaac, and Jacob. He then testified of the reality and existence of the resurrection, stating that God was "not the God of the dead, but of the living." Jesus made it very clear to the Sadducees that their doctrine on the resurrection[399] was false, and He put them "to silence." Again the multitude was astonished at His doctrine.

Controversy Number Three: "What Think Ye of Christ?"

By this time Jesus had a question of His own to ask, but before He could present it a lawyer came "tempting him" and asked Him which was the greatest commandment. As Matthew puts it, the lawyer's question was actually more of an introduction to Christ's question to the Pharisees and the Sadducees than an attempt to entrap Him. Jesus responded quickly to the lawyer, stating that to love God was the first great commandment, and the second was like unto it, "to love thy neighbour as thyself."

The lawyer was apparently trying to make one point of the law weightier than another, but the Lord pointed out that the commandments of God were beyond the theocratic abstraction of the letter of the Law, and that the second commandment was "like unto it" because to love God was to love your fellowman. "On these two commandments hang all the law and the prophets," He explained. The things the prophets teach and the commandments we are expected to live all encourage us to love God and our fellowman, and treat them accordingly.

Jesus then took the initiative and asked the Pharisees, "What think ye of Christ? whose son is he?" They quickly responded, "The Son of David," perhaps thinking that Jesus was entering into one of their dialectic discussions. But the Lord then asked them, "How then doth David in spirit call him Lord," or in other words, how could the Messiah be David's son?

It was a question that testified of the Lord's divinity[a] and He asked it to deliberately force the Pharisees to compare the Messianic prophecies with their own false concept of the coming Messiah.[400] The question was a favorite theme in Judaism, the lineage of the Messiah being a most familiar subject in their theology.[401] Jesus had now raised the issue of His own divinity by showing them that the Messiah was David's son through mortal lineage, but that as the Son of God, He was exalted far above David. No man dared answer the Lord, so they remained silent; nor did they ask Him any more questions from that day on.

The Final Plea

John 12:20–50   And there were certain Greeks among them that came up to worship at the feast: the same came therefore to Philip, which was of Bethsaida of Galilee, and desired him, saying, Sir, we would see Jesus. Philip cometh and telleth Andrew: and again Andrew and Philip tell Jesus.

And Jesus answered them, saying, The hour is come, that the Son of man should be glorified. Verily, verily, I say unto you, Except a corn of wheat fall into the ground and die, it abideth alone: but if it die, it bringeth forth much fruit. He that loveth his life shall lose it; and he that hateth his life in this world shall keep it unto life eternal. If any man serve me, let him follow me; and where I am, there shall also my servant be: if any man serve me, him will my Father honour. Now is my soul troubled; and what shall I say? Father, save me from this hour: but for this cause came I unto this hour. Father, glorify thy name. Then came there a voice from heaven, saying, I have both glorified it, and will glorify it again. The people therefore, that stood by, and heard it, said that it thundered: others said, An angel spake to him. Jesus answered and said, This voice came not because of me, but for your sakes. Now is the judgment of this world: now shall the prince of this world be cast out. And I, if I be lifted up from the earth, will draw all men unto me. This he said, signifying what death he should die. The people answered him, We have heard out of the law that Christ abideth for ever: and how sayest thou, The Son of man must be lifted up? who is this Son of man? Then Jesus said unto them, Yet a little while is the light with you. Walk while ye have the light, lest darkness come upon you: for he that walketh in darkness knoweth not whither he goeth. While ye have light, believe in the light, that ye may be the children of light. These things spake Jesus, and departed, and did hide himself from them.

But though he had done so many miracles before them, yet they believed not on him: that the saying of Esaias the prophet might be fulfilled, which he spake, Lord, who hath believed our report? and to whom hath the arm of the Lord been revealed? Therefore they could not believe, because that Esaias said again, He hath blinded their eyes, and hardened their heart; that they should not see with their eyes, nor understand with their heart, and be converted, and I should heal them. These things said Esaias, when he saw his glory, and spake of him.

Nevertheless among the chief rulers also many believed on him; but because of the Pharisees they did not confess him, lest they should be put out of the synagogue: for they loved the praise of men more than the praise of God.

Jesus cried and said, He that believeth on me, believeth not on me, but on him that sent me. And he that seeth me seeth him that sent me. I am come a light into the world, that whosoever believeth on me should not abide in darkness. And if any man hear my words, and believe not, I judge him not: for I came not to judge the world, but to save the world. He that rejecteth me, and receiveth not my words, hath one that judgeth him: the word that I have spoken, the same shall judge him in the last day. For I have not spoken of myself; but the Father which sent me, he gave me a commandment, what I should say, and what I should speak. And I know that his commandment is life everlasting: whatsoever I speak therefore, even as the Father said unto me, so I speak.

This is the final public discourse given by the Savior before His crucifixion. The narrative is brief and written in a style reminiscent of topic headings, summaries, or outlines rather than a continuous report. No surrounding circumstances are given for this discourse other than that it occurred after Jesus' final entry into Jerusalem, and it appears that it was written as John's conclusion to the Lord's public ministry.

The discourse seems to stem from a request made by certain Greek proselytes for a personal meeting with Christ. Their request was directed to Philip; but he, for whatever reason, decided not to make the request to Jesus alone and solicited the assistance of Andrew, another member of the Twelve. Together they introduced the Greek proselytes to the Savior.

The Greeks may have requested the audience because they were impressed with Jesus' actions at the feast, or perhaps His fame had previously reached their nation,[402] but no reasons are given for the requested interview. John's clipped method of recording this discourse makes it appear that Jesus is ignoring the Greeks altogether as He never refers to them in His comments.[403]

John reports the discourse as if Jesus had been answering questions, but no questions are indicated. The Lord began by declaring openly for the first time that "the hour is come that the Son of man should be glorified" (previously He had always stated that His hour had not yet come). This opening statement to the Greeks anticipated the establishment of the gospel in its future triumphs among the heathen nations since the gospel would eventually go to all men.[404] The Lord had previously spoken of His coming death and apparently they asked Him why He would die.[405] Jesus answered with an analogy, saying that a grain of wheat must die before it could produce "much" fruit. He was obviously alluding to the fact that He, too, must die for His work if it was to bear fruit (the fruit of His labor as death to Him was not a tragedy but a triumph). John appears to have again left out some of the Lord's comments for in the very next verse Jesus applied this analogy to His disciples and followers; requiring them also to yield their lives completely to the kingdom, emphasizing the necessity of their faithfulness to Him, and citing the blessings attached to such action.

The Lord then seemed to be caught in a moment of introspection as He reflected on the ignominious circumstances of His death. "Now is my soul troubled," He lamented, "and what shall I say? Father, save me from this hour." But knowing that such was not the plan of His Father, He reconciled His mind to the inevitable by stating, "But for this cause came I unto this hour." No one else in all of creation could have saved mankind from sin. Jesus turned to His Father and prayed, "Father, glorify thy name." Then a voice came from heaven, saying, "I have both glorified it, and will glorify it again." These circumstances were real, the actual voice of God was heard from the heavens.[406] But the people who stood by failed to understand or recognize it—some thinking an angel had spoken to the Lord and others perceiving His voice as thunder. Had they been spiritually in tune with the Savior and believed in Him as the Messiah, they would have undoubtedly recognized the Father's voice.

Jesus (who heard His Father's words while those around Him heard only sounds) testified of the Father and declared the voice had come "not because of me, but for your sakes." The Lord had openly declared to them that the Father had spoken from heaven that they might believe, yet they persisted in doubting. Jesus continued by testifying, "Now is the judgment of this world," and He concluded by stating that Lucifer, "the prince of this world," would be cast out. Through the atonement and the resurrection, Jesus would overcome the power of the devil.[407]

John abruptly moves to another point of the Lord's discourse as Jesus again testified of His impending death and His ascension to His rightful place in heaven, where He would "draw all men" to Him. But the people listening (apparently others were there besides the Greeks) still failed to understand the Lord's mission, and they resorted to their historical expectations of the Messiah, declaring that the Savior would not die, but live forever. With this in mind, they wanted to know why the Son of Man had to be lifted up; and then, as if to compound their misunderstanding, they asked, "Who is this Son of man?" But the time for theological discussions was over. Jesus would not enter into the controversy which their comments raised. He did, however, answer their question, declaring that while the light (meaning Himself) was with them, they should walk in the light so as not to be overcome by the darkness that would surround them when He was gone.

John himself now enters the discussion, breaking off the comments of the Savior to reiterate the continuous theme he has maintained throughout his Gospel—the unbelief of the Jews. He comments that even though Jesus had performed many miracles for the Jews, "yet they believed not on him." This, he concluded, fulfilled the prophecy of Esaias who, upon seeing the ministry of Jesus and His rejection in a vision, declared that no one would believe His report, even though "the arm of the Lord" had been revealed.[a] John continued by quoting Isaiah and noting that those who had observed the powerful ministry of the Savior had blinded their eyes and hardened their hearts so that they would not be converted and healed.[b] To emphasize the Jews' lack of commitment (even though they still looked for the Messiah), John notes that many of the rulers believed on Christ, but would not confess Him for fear of being put out of the synagogue, "For they loved the praise of men more than the praise of God."

John's comments are a summation of all the reasons why the Jews rejected Christ. That rejection was not an isolated act . . . . . . but the outcome and direct result of their whole previous religious development. In face of the clearest evidence, they did not believe, because they could not believe. The long course of their resistance to the prophetic message, and their perversion of it, was itself a hardening of their hearts, although at the same time a God–decreed sentence on their resistance. Because they would not believe through this their mental obscuration, which came upon them in Divine judgment, although in the natural course of their self–chosen religious development—therefore, despite all evidence, they did not believe, when He came and did such miracles before them . . . [because they] . . . loved the glory of men more than the glory of God.[408]

a. Isaiah 53:1.

b. Isaiah 6:8–11.

After his short soliloquy, John returned to the Lord's discourse and recorded the Savior's last great appeal to the multitude surrounding Him. He challenged them to have faith, declaring, "He that believeth on me, believeth not on me, but on him that sent me." In other words, if you believe in Jesus Christ, you believe in God. The Lord then reiterated the purpose of His mission, declaring that He had come to save the world and not to judge it. He clarified this by stating, "He that rejecteth me, and receiveth not my words, hath one that judgeth him: the word [the gospel] that I have spoken." He pointed out that He spoke not of Himself but was fulfilling the mission His Father had given Him, and that the commandment, if heeded, would provide life everlasting. With this final plea, He ended His discourse.

"Farewell, I Will Come Again"   12

Christ's Farewell

Matthew 23:1–39   Then spake Jesus to the multitude, and to his disciples, saying, The scribes and the Pharisees sit in Moses' seat: all therefore whatsoever they bid you observe, that observe and do; but do not ye after their works: for they say, and do not. For they bind heavy burdens and grievous to be borne, and lay them on men's shoulders; but they themselves will not move them with one of their fingers. But all their works they do for to be seen of men: they make broad their phylacteries, and enlarge the borders of their garments, and love the uppermost rooms at feasts, and the chief seats in the synagogues, and greetings in the markets, and to be called of men, Rabbi, Rabbi. But be not ye called Rabbi: for one is your Master, even Christ; and all ye are brethren. And call no man your father upon the earth: for one is your Father, which is in heaven. Neither be ye called masters: for one is your Master, even Christ. But he that is greatest among you shall be your servant. And whosoever shall exalt himself shall be abased; and he that shall humble himself shall be exalted.

But woe unto you, scribes and Pharisees, hypocrites! for ye shut up the kingdom of heaven against men: for ye neither go in yourselves, neither suffer ye them that are entering to go in. Woe unto you, scribes and Pharisees, hypocrites! for ye devour widows' houses, and for a pretence make long prayer: therefore ye shall receive the greater damnation. Woe unto you, scribes and Pharisees, hypocrites! for ye compass sea and land to make one proselyte, and when he is made, ye make him twofold more the child of hell than yourselves. woe unto you, ye blind guides, which say, Whosoever shall swear by the temple, it is nothing; but whosoever shall swear by the gold of the temple, he is a debtor! Ye fools and blind: for whether is greater, the gold, or the temple that sanctifieth the gold? And, Whosoever shall swear by the altar, it is nothing; but whosoever sweareth by the gift that is upon it, he is guilty. Ye fools and blind: for whether is greater, the gift, or the altar that sanctifieth the gift? Whoso therefore shall swear by the altar, sweareth by it, and by all things thereon. And whoso shall swear by the temple, sweareth by it, and by him that dwelleth therein. And he that shall swear by heaven, sweareth by the throne of God, and by him that sitteth thereon. Woe unto you, scribes and Pharisees, hypocrites! for ye pay tithe of mint and anise and cummin, and have omitted the weightier matters of the law, judgment, mercy, and faith: these ought ye to have done, and not to leave the other undone. Ye blind guides, which strain at a gnat, and swallow a camel. Woe unto you, scribes and Pharisees, hypocrites! for ye make clean the outside of the cup and of the platter, but within they are full of extortion and excess. Thou blind Pharisee, cleanse first that which is within the cup and platter, that the outside of them may be clean also. Woe unto you, scribes and Pharisees, hypocrites! for ye are like unto whited sepulchres, which indeed appear beautiful outward, but are within full of dead men's bones, and of all uncleanness. Even so ye also outwardly appear righteous unto men, but within ye are full of hypocrisy and iniquity. Woe unto you, scribes and Pharisees, hypocrites! because ye build the tombs of the prophets, and garnish the sepulchres of the righteous, and say, If we had been in the days of our fathers, we would not have been partakers with them in the blood of the prophets. Wherefore ye be witnesses unto yourselves, that ye are the children of them which killed the prophets. Fill ye up then the measure of your fathers. Ye serpents, ye generation of vipers, how can ye escape the damnation of hell?

Wherefore, behold, I send unto you prophets, and wise men, and scribes: and some of them ye shall kill and crucify; and some of them shall ye scourge in your synagogues, and persecute them from city to city: that upon you may come all the righteous blood shed upon the earth, from the blood of righteous Abel unto the blood of Zacharias son of Barachias, whom ye slew between the temple and the altar. Verily I say unto you, All these things shall come upon this generation. O Jerusalem, Jerusalem, thou that killest the prophets, and stonest them which are sent unto thee, how often would I have gathered thy children together, even as a hen gathereth her chickens under her wings, and ye would not! Behold, your house is left unto you desolate. For I say unto you, ye shall not see me henceforth, till ye shall say, Blessed is he that cometh in the name of the Lord.

Cross-references   IV Matthew 23:35; Mark 12:38–40; Luke 11:37–54; Luke 18:9–14; Luke 20:45–47

The Lord delivered this discourse in the temple during the last week of His ministry, just after His enemies presented the questions to Him discussed in the previous chapter. This discourse clarifies explicitly the teachings the Lord gave earlier in His ministry. In it He delivers His farewell to the temple authorities, the leaders of Israel, and the chosen people.

The sermon is rare in that it is formulated in a completely logical manner, enumerating successive points of warning and reasoning with examples to substantiate both. The Savior closes it with an expression of the deepest compassion concerning not only His people but also the Holy City and what the Holy City represents.

Although the Lord gave this discourse in the presence of a multitude, He directed it to His disciples.[409] It concerned the leadership of Israel but could be applied to religious leadership in any age.[410]

Jesus began by announcing that the scribes and Pharisees sat in Moses' seat, recognizing that in that position they in fact exercised at least a portion of Moses' authority.[411] The Lord was not seeking the positions of these men, nor was He encouraging immediate disobedience to their authority. Quite to the contrary, He acknowledged them as the authorized leaders in Israel; but He warned the people of their duplicity and directed the disciples not to emulate them. He instructed the multitude to follow the leadership's instructions, but He specifically warned them not to imitate their works.

Jesus described their evil works by declaring that they were outwardly punctilious in their observance of the Law while privately eschewing the spirit of it. "Rabbinism had practically superseded the law in the substitution of multitudinous rules and exactions, with conditional penalties; the day was filled with traditional observances by which even the trivial affairs were encumbered; yet from bearing these and other grievous burdens, hypocritical officials could find excuse for personal exemption."[412]

While acknowledging the legitimacy of the Jewish leaders' authority, the Lord instructed His audience not to imitate their false teachings and insincerity because the leaders were oppressive and ostentatious. They loved prominence and titles, and they were filled with avarice and pride. The Lord used specific examples to prove the truth of His accusations. First, He said that the Pharisees bound heavy burdens upon the people that they themselves would not attempt to move with even "one of their fingers." Second, they made broad their phylacteries and enlarged the borders of their garments so as to be seen of men.[a] Third, they loved "the uppermost rooms at feasts, and the chief seats in the synagogues . . . and to be called of men, Rabbi, Rabbi."

The Lord next made two specific charges against Israel's leadership and warned the disciples (and all future leaders of Israel) not to be guilty of these things. First, they lacked spiritual integrity and love for the people. Second, their obedience was merely for show, for "Rabbinism [had] placed the ordinances of tradition above those of the Law,"[413] and the burdens of their demands had become intolerable. The Lord cautioned His disciples, "Be not ye called rabbi: for one is your Master, even Christ . . . and call no man your father upon the earth: for one is your Father, which is in heaven." Jesus continued by explaining what their relationship with one another should be: "He that is greatest among you shall be your servant. And whosoever shall exalt himself shall be abased; and he that shall humble himself shall be exalted."

This strong denunciation of the leaders of Israel "rolled over their guilty heads with crush on crush of moral anger . . . [and] condemnation."[414] The spirituality of the Law of Moses had been destroyed by the Pharisees. They had reduced it to intellectualism, and the Lord warned the leadership of their errors and sins in eight specific instances, each introduced with the word woe.

The First Woe: Preventing Salvation. Because of their rigorous requirements and hypocritical piety, Israel's leadership had restricted entrance into the kingdom of heaven to those who possessed the knowledge they (the leaders) dictated. They had determined that anyone without this Pharisaic knowledge was ignorant; therefore, it was impossible for them to attain God's kingdom. They rejected the anticipated Messiah who stood before them, and while they themselves would not enter His kingdom, they also worked hard at preventing others from entering—a most grievous sin.

The Second Woe: Covetousness and Hypocrisy. The Lord had once before noted the ineffectiveness of the prayers of the Jewish leadership,[415] but now He specified that their prayers were hypocritical and only contained a pretense of righteousness. The Pharisees devoted more and more time to prayer until some boasted that they were praying nine hours out of every day,[416] and their personal avarice had increased to the point that they would "devour widows' houses" in an attempt to satisfy their greed.

The Third Woe: Proselyting. Although the Jews sought converts to satisfy the requirements of their Law, they seemed to denounce proselyting per se. In their pride and exclusiveness, they laid strict rules upon converts as a test of their sincerity (even though they spoke of them with the same contempt they reserved for the plague of leprosy).[417] In their compulsion to convert the world to an apostate form of Judaism, they condemned themselves; and due to the added restrictions they placed on their converts, they made the convert "twofold more the child of hell than [themselves]."

The Fourth Woe: Oaths of Moral Blindness. The Lord condemned the arbitrariness of their oaths. Jewish traditions dictated that it meant nothing to swear an oath by the temple, but if the oath were sworn by the gold of the temple, a man was bound. With contempt for such distinctions based on worldliness, the Lord declared, "Whether is greater, the gold, or the temple that sanctifieth the gold?" The Jews valued the temple by its gold and riches rather than by its spiritual worth. Their oaths and vows had diminished the sanctity of the temple itself.

The Lord used a second example wherein He stated they believed that if their oaths were sworn by the altar of the temple, they had no value; but if they were sworn by the gift upon the altar, the oath was valid. Again the Lord asked, "Whether is greater, the gift, or the altar that sanctifieth the gift?" The Lord called them "fools and blind" for there was no distinction between the altar and the gifts upon it—or the temple and Him who dwelled within it. An oath sworn upon heaven was an oath sworn upon God, since God sits upon the throne of heaven. Their distinctions were folly and emphasized their moral blindness.[418]

The Fifth Woe: Omitting Weightier Matters of the Law. In this denunciation, the Lord used one of the laws of the church[419] to show how they had reduced a correct principle of the gospel to unrighteousness, and in the punctilious observance of that principle they had justified their elimination of the second great commandment. They had reduced the law of tithing (which Moses had commanded) to a complicated, detailed burden, since they tithed anise and mint and sometimes even the leaves and stocks of plants.[420] While they strained out the gnat from their goblet that their drink might remain pure, they hypothetically swallowed a camel in their hearts. Expending their religious zeal on mere trifles left them no time for the weightier matters of the Law. Tithing (as Moses prescribed it) should have been paid; but justice, mercy, and faith were things that should not have been left undone.

The Sixth Woe: Purification. Purification was an important issue with the Pharisees. Jesus chose this issue to dramatize their absurdity in applying this principle.[a][421] In this discourse, the Lord accused them

a. Mark 7:4.

of being outwardly punctilious about their cleanliness while inside they were full of "extortion and excess." Outwardly they extolled their personal righteousness before the people, but their hearts were full of iniquity and sin. He exhorted them to first cleanse that which was within to ensure "that the outside of them may be clean also."

The Seventh Woe: Hypocrisy. The Jews made a great effort to keep their burial places clean, simulating the sanctity of the temple.[422] To emphasize His scathing denunciation of their ridiculous facade of righteousness, the Lord compared the leaders of Israel to these "whited sepulchres." They appeared "pure to the eye, but with death and corruption within";[423] outwardly clean and beautiful, but within full of uncleanliness and dead men's bones. They were hiding their hypocrisy and iniquity under a cloak of self–righteousness.

The Eighth Woe: The Rejection of Prophets. In this last woe the Lord expanded His comparison of whited sepulchres and plastered graves, noting that the Pharisees also built and garnished great tombs for the ancient prophets. They did this to extol their own righteousness, and they proudly boasted that if they had lived during the time of those ancient prophets, they would not have killed them. In this allegation (wherein they condemned their forefathers for murdering the prophets), they reflected the same obdurate spirit that their fathers had possessed. They loudly proclaimed that they would not have killed the previous prophets, even though their full intent was to take the life of their Savior.

It was the Messiah who stood before these Jewish leaders, and it was the Messiah who had sent the prophets they so revered. By rejecting Him (the living fulfillment of ancient prophecy), it was as if they had rejected all of the early prophets also.[424] The Lord confirmed this when He stated that the blood of all the prophets, from Abel to Zacharias (the father of John the Baptist[425] whom they slew in the temple near the altar), was upon their heads because they failed to accept the Lord's message.

Finally, Jesus condemned these leaders of the Jews to the same judgment that would befall those who had actually killed the ancient prophets—because they were knowledgeably killing the Son of God.[426]

In his "woes," the Lord contrasted His moral purity and humility with the sophistries and hypocrisy of the rabbis. The Jews had filled up their lives with petty details, and the Lord "abhorred all cant and insincerity, and all trading with religion; all striving after mere outward success . . . [and although exceptions existed], insincerity and immorality in the teachings of a religion can only multiply and perpetrate themselves in their disciples."[427]

The Jewish leaders had proved that Jesus was right by their rejection of Him. He demanded moral and religious reform, but they were wedded to falsehood and immorality and would rather kill Him than let Him lead them back to the Father.

At the conclusion of this discourse the Lord uttered a sad lamentation: "O Jerusalem, Jerusalem, thou that killest the prophets, and stonest them which are sent unto thee, how often would I have gathered thy children together, even as a hen gathereth her chickens under her wings, and ye would not! Behold, your house is left unto you desolate."

The Lord no longer claimed the great temple in Jerusalem as "His" temple; He had withdrawn His approval of that great edifice.[428] The House of the Lord was returned to the possession of evil men. He would leave Israel and its recalcitrant leaders for a time, but would look forward to the day when He could again return.

Judaism had chosen its own way.

"When Shall These Things Be?"

Matthew 24:1–42 And Jesus went out, and departed from the temple: and his disciples came to him for to shew him the buildings of the temple. And Jesus said unto them, See ye not all these things? verily I say unto you, There shall not be left here one stone upon another, that shall not be thrown down.

And as he sat upon the mount of Olives, the disciples came unto him privately, saying, Tell us, when shall these things be? and what shall be the sign of thy coming, and of the end of the world? And Jesus answered and said unto them, Take heed that no man deceive you. For many shall come in my name, saying, I am Christ; and shall deceive many. And ye shall hear of wars and rumours of wars: see that ye be not troubled: for all these things must come to pass, but the end is not yet. For nation shall rise against nation, and kingdom against kingdom: and there shall be famines, and pestilences, and earthquakes, in divers places. All these are the beginning of sorrows. Then shall they deliver you up to be afflicted, and shall kill you: and ye shall be hated of all nations for my name's sake. And then shall many be offended, and shall betray one another, and shall hate one another. And many false prophets shall rise, and shall deceive many. And because iniquity shall abound, the love of many shall wax cold. But he that shall endure unto the end, the same shall be saved. And this gospel of the kingdom shall be preached in all the world for a witness unto all nations; and then shall the end come. When ye therefore shall see the abomination of desolation, spoken of by Daniel the prophet, stand in the holy place, (whoso readeth, let him understand:) then let them which be in Judaea flee into the mountains: let him which is on the housetop not come down to take any thing out of his house: neither let him which is in the field return back to take his clothes. And woe unto them that are with child, and to them that give suck in those days! But pray ye that your flight be not in the winter, neither on the sabbath day: for then shall be great tribulation, such as was not since the beginning of the world to this time, no, nor ever shall be. And except those days should be shortened, there should no flesh be saved: but for the elect's sake those days shall be shortened. Then if any man shall say unto you, Lo, here is Christ, or there; believe it not. For there shall arise false Christs, and false prophets, and shall shew great signs and wonders; insomuch that, if it were possible, they shall deceive the very elect. Behold, I have told you before. Wherefore if they shall say unto you, Behold, he is in the desert; go not forth: behold, he is in the secret chambers; believe it not.   For as the lightning cometh out of the east, and shineth even unto the west; so shall also the coming of the Son of man be. For wheresoever the carcase is, there will the eagles be gathered together.

Immediately after the tribulation of those days shall the sun be darkened, and the moon shall not give her light, and the stars shall fall from heaven, and the powers of the heavens shall be shaken: and then shall appear the sign of the Son of man in heaven: and then shall all the tribes of the earth mourn, and they shall see the Son of man coming in the clouds of heaven with power and great glory. And he shall send his angels with a great sound of a trumpet, and they shall gather together his elect from the four winds, from one end of heaven to the other. Now learn a parable of the fig tree; When his branch is yet tender, and putteth forth leaves, ye know that summer is nigh: so likewise ye, when ye shall see all these things, know that it is near, even at the doors. Verily I say unto you, This generation shall not pass, till all these things be fulfilled. Heaven and earth shall pass away, but my words shall not pass away.

But of that day and hour knoweth no man, no, not the angels of heaven, but my Father only. But as the days of Noe were, so shall also the coming of the Son of man be. For as in the days that were before the flood they were eating and drinking, marrying and giving in marriage, until the day that Noe entered into the ark, and knew not until the flood came, and took them all away; so shall also the coming of the Son of man be. Then shall two be in the field; the one shall be taken, and the other left. Two women shall be grinding at the mill; the one shall be taken, and the other left.

Watch therefore: for ye know not what hour your Lord doth come.

Cross-references   Pearl of Great Price Joseph Smith—Matthew 1IV Matthew 24:1–46; Mark 13:1–37; Luke 17:20–37, 21:5–38; D&C 45:15–21

After Jesus had completed His last public denunciation of Jerusalem and His terrible prediction of the judgment that would come upon the temple (including its eventual destruction), the little party of disciples, with Jesus at their head, left the sanctuary and headed out of the city. They crossed the Kidron Brook on the trail that led up to the Mount of Olives. It was in the late afternoon, and it may have been that as they traveled, a turn in the road exposed the "sacred building . . . once more in full view."[429] The sight would have been magnificent as the sun shone brightly on the marble cloisters, terraced courts, and golden spikes of the temple.[430] It may have been here that the Lord paused to sit down and rest; and the view of the temple, coupled with the Lord's recent comments concerning its destruction, may have moved His disciples to sadly ask, "Tell us, when shall these things be? and what shall be the sign of thy coming, and of the end of the world?"

Their questions were not questions of doubt, but of inquiry concerning the future of Jerusalem, the temple, Israel, and the world at large. The conclusions Jesus had drawn in His discourse concerning the imminent destruction of the Jews, Jerusalem, and the temple might have seemed inexplicable to the Apostles, or perhaps their minds were still harboring some of the Jewish beliefs concerning the coming of the Messiah.[431] They may not have been able to imagine in their hearts that the Holy City and its temple would perish before the Lord's second coming and the end of the world.[432] It was Jesus' habit to pass over such questions and substitute a moral lesson for a direct reply. Therefore, while their questions dealt with time, the Lord's response dealt with events.

His comments involved predictions and warnings of events that would occur both in the immediate future, during the lifetime of the Apostles, and in the far–distant future; and He spoke of the end of the world, which perhaps did not mean the world's literal end but the end of the prevailing social conditions among the people of the earth.[433]

The Lord began by warning the Apostles not to be deceived by other men since He had foretold that false Christs would come in His name and deceive many. The prophecies uttered by false prophets could not save them from destruction in the end.[434] Such instances were hinted at or implied in several New Testament recordings,[a] and Josephus records that many such seducers came prior to the destruction of Jerusalem.[435] The woes which were to come upon Jerusalem were not a prelude to His second coming; therefore, the Apostles were to be on their guard.

The Lord next warned them of wars and rumors of wars. Nation would rise against nation, and there would be pestilence, famines, and earthquakes in diverse places; but all these were but the beginning of sorrows—another warning to the Apostles that they should not be misled by coming events. The second coming of the Savior would not take place during their lifetime. False Messiahs and violent disturbances in their political world would lead to the destruction of Jerusalem, the temple, and Israel as a nation.[436] These same signs would also occur prior to the Second Coming.

Between the destruction of Jerusalem and the Second Coming there was to be a period of unspecified duration when Satan would be allowed to deceive the world.[437] False prophets would arise and, because iniquity would abound, "the love of many [would] wax cold." When these tribulations should descend upon the Saints, many would lose their belief and fall away into apostasy.[438]

The Lord referred to the prophecy of Daniel regarding the desolation and abominations of Jerusalem, which "comprised the forcible cessation of temple rites, and the desecration of Israel's shrine by pagan conquerors,"[439] and He warned His followers to flee that destruction. Nothing should detain them—not possessions, employment, children, the weather, nor even the Sabbath day. He warned them that the tribulation would be so great prior to Jerusalem's destruction that if they hesitated to flee when they had the opportunity, they would surely be entrapped and perhaps destroyed. (The destruction the Lord spoke of referred not necessarily to the physical body but possibly to the spiritual soul.)[440]

Jesus now moved beyond the immediate prophecies concerning the destruction of Jerusalem and the temple to speak of those things that would occur after the establishment of the church in the meridian of time.[441] He warned the Apostles again of false Christs and false prophets who would come and through their great signs and wonders would, "if possible," deceive even the "very elect." Although some individuals in isolated instances might actually claim to be the Christ coming to save the church, the Lord was more likely referring to false doctrines or false claims that would be made in His name. He warned that "So profound and learned will be their doctrines, so great and marvelous their works—within some instances false miracles being done by them through the power of the Devil—that the very elect will almost be deceived."[442] Jesus was warning the Apostles and future members of the church to be constantly on guard lest they be deceived and led into secret chambers after false teachings.

After He had given these warnings to His Apostles, the Lord quickly moved to the general signs of His second coming. He reiterated the warning that the Saints should be aware of these signs since the world would view the events of those times as normal occurrences; but the Saints would know that His coming was nigh, and at His actual appearance—after the sun and moon had been darkened and the stars had fallen from heaven— they would be prepared for the great, universal sign that the Lord had designated to tell the world of His advent.[443]

Jesus prophesied that prior to this great event, the gospel would be restored to the earth. This restoration would occur after a long period of priestcraft and apostasy.[444] After the restoration there would be a gathering of the elect, and the times of the Gentiles would be fulfilled.[445] To emphasize the gathering, the Lord gave a short analogy in the parable of the fig tree. This parable also indicated to His disciples that His second coming would not be immediate or during their lifetime. Jesus told the Apostles that no man knew the time, day, or hour except His Father.

The fig tree analogy applied to both the immediate events He had predicted and the future events He prophesied. The uncertainty of the exact date of the Lord's future prophecies eliminated any potential calculations pertaining to when the Second Advent would occur.[446] This uncertainty would make men careless. Jesus therefore warned the Apostles (as well as all future Saints) to take heed lest they, like the people before the flood, give way to pleasures and indulgences or be so engrossed in the anxieties of life that they were unprepared for His return. This analogy was a particularly good one since before the flood the people were "drinking, marrying, and giving in marriage." They neither anticipated nor dreaded a catastrophe, yet the flood came and took them all away. In like manner, the righteous should not be so engrossed in their daily temporal activities as to be unable to discern the signs of His second advent.[447] When the Lord comes He will come quickly; two will be standing together and only one taken—prepared to enter the Lord's presence through membership in the Church and obedience to God's commandments.[448] But the one left in the "field" will be destroyed. Again the Lord cautioned, "Watch therefore: for ye know not what hour your Lord doth come."

The Lord noted that during the last stages of the earth's existence (prior to His second coming), the ties of companionship normally existing between people would be broken[449] and the salvation of many would be in danger because of personal unrighteousness. He cautioned the Saints to be constantly watchful of the world, to remain faithful in the work of the gospel, and to protect themselves lest enemies of the work come upon them. The Lord then concluded this discourse with the parable of the watching servants.[450]

The Apostles had asked when all of these things would occur, but the Lord would not give them exact times; however, He did indicate what signs would precede the events He had spoken of. Whether those signs would be displayed at the destruction of Jerusalem or duplicated prior to His second coming did not matter. The discourse contained all that was necessary to warn and teach His disciples (and all future disciples) to be constantly watchful and prepared. However, whatever the age one lives in, when death approaches, it seems as though the great and dreadful day of the Lord is imminent.[451]

"In My Father's House"

John 14:1–31   Let not your heart be troubled: ye believe in God, believe also in me. In my Father's house are many mansions: if it were not so, I would have told you. I go to prepare a place for you. And if I go and prepare a place for you, I will come again, and receive you unto myself; that where I am, there ye may be also. And whither I go ye know, and the way ye know. Thomas saith unto him, Lord, we know not whither thou goest; and how can we know the way? Jesus saith unto him, I am the way, the truth, and the life: no man cometh unto the Father, but by me. If ye had known me, ye should have known my Father also: and from henceforth ye know him, and have seen him. Philip saith unto him, Lord, shew us the Father, and it sufficeth us. Jesus saith unto him, Have I been so long time with you, and yet hast thou not known me, Philip? he that hath seen me hath seen the Father; and how sayest thou then, Shew us the Father? Believest thou not that I am in the Father, and the Father in me? the words that I speak unto you I speak not of myself: but the Father that dwelleth in me, he doeth the works. Believe me that I am in the Father, and the Father in me: or else believe me for the very works' sake. Verily, verily, I say unto you, he that believeth on me, the works that I do shall he do also; and greater works than these shall he do; because I go unto my Father. And whatsoever ye shall ask in my name, that will I do, that the Father may be glorified in the Son. If ye shall ask any thing in my name, I will do it.

If ye love me, keep my commandments. And I will pray the Father, and he shall give you another Comforter, that he may abide with you for ever; even the Spirit of truth; whom the world cannot receive, because it seeth him not, neither knoweth him: but ye know him; for he dwelleth with you, and shall be in you. I will not leave you comfortless: I will come to you. Yet a little while, and the world seeth me no more; but ye see me: because I live, ye shall live also. At that day ye shall know that I am in my Father, and ye in me, and I in you. He that hath my commandments, and keepeth them, he it is that loveth me: and he that loveth me shall be loved of my Father, and I will love him, and will manifest myself to him. Judas saith unto him, not Iscariot, Lord, how is it that thou wilt manifest thyself unto us, and not unto the world? Jesus answered and said unto him, If a man love me, he will keep my words: and my Father will love him, and we will come unto him, and make our abode with him. He that loveth me not keepeth not my sayings: and the word which ye hear is not mine, but the Father's which sent me. These things have I spoken unto you, being yet present with you. But the Comforter, which is the Holy Ghost, whom the Father will send in my name, he shall teach you all things, and bring all things to your remembrance, whatsoever I have said unto you. Peace I leave with you, my peace I give unto you: not as the world giveth, give I unto you. Let not your heart be troubled, neither let it be afraid. Ye have heard how I said unto you, I go away, and come again unto you. If ye loved me, ye would rejoice, because I said, I go unto the Father: for my Father is greater than I. And now I have told you before it come to pass, that, when it is come to pass, ye might believe. Hereafter I will not talk much with you: for the prince of this world cometh, and hath nothing in me. But that the world may know that I love the Father; and as the Father gave me commandment, even so I do. Arise, let us go hence.

It was time for the Passover, and the inhabitants of Jerusalem would have been prepared for a joyous celebration; but it was a somber little band that surrounded Jesus on the night of His last supper. The Twelve were undoubtedly remorseful at the thought of their Lord's impending sacrifice and ashamed of the unknown traitor in their midst. Jesus, as if perceiving the sorrow in their hearts, bade them to be of good cheer: He could look beyond their present troubles and even beyond those that would soon come upon them. He gave them encouragement and hope when He said, "Ye believe in God, believe also in me."

This is an interesting discourse. The Lord clearly wanted to instruct the Apostles on this last evening, but they kept interrupting Him with questions. Each time He would answer their questions and then return to His instructions.

John 13:38 records the Lord's prophecy that before the cock crowed at dawn, Peter would deny Him three times. The first four verses of this sermon may have been given in response to that comment, and the Lord may have wanted to reassure the Apostles that their troubles would not endure long because He promised them that in His Father's house were "many mansions" and He was going there to prepare a place for them.[452]

Jesus was giving the Apostles a glimpse of what they had to look forward to. He undoubtedly hoped that throughout His ministry they had learned these basic truths and knew both the direction He must take and the way that they must follow. But Thomas interrupted Him and asked a simple question that demonstrated once more their lack of understanding:[453] "Lord, we know not whither thou goest; and how can we know the way?"

Jesus did not reprimand Thomas but again declared His Messiahship:[454] "I am the way, the truth, and the life: no man cometh unto the Father, but by me." He thus explained to Thomas (and to the others) that there was more to life than physical existence, and that to attain the Father's kingdom they would have to follow His teachings and commandments. Then, reiterating His relationship to the Father, Jesus stated, "If ye had known me, ye should have known my Father also."

Philip was still not convinced. "Lord," he said, "shew us the Father, and it sufficeth us." To this Jesus replied, "Have I been so long time with you, and yet hast thou not known me, Philip?" The Lord again explained that anyone who had seen Him had seen the Father. They were alike in doctrine, purpose, and appearance. Mildly rebuking Philip, Jesus asked Him why he wanted to see the Father, in spite of what He, the Savior, had taught him. Jesus again reminded the Twelve of the relationship that existed between Himself and the Father and told them that they must believe on Him to understand that relationship. He testified that He had not come to do His own works nor to speak of His own words, but to do the will of the Father. Jesus admonished the Twelve that if they could not believe His allegations, they should remember the evidence He had given them through His ministry. He concluded with the promise that, "He that believeth on me, the works that I do shall he do also." He limited, however, the great power He was leaving them by making it commensurate with their faith and belief in Him.

At this point the Lord returned to His discourse and, for the first time, instructed the Apostles to pray in His name.[455] He promised them that if they would do so, He would grant their righteous petition so that the Father might be glorified in the Son. His next instruction began with an admonition to the Apostles. Merely professing love for the Lord was not enough— it was their actions that would evidence their keeping of His commandments. The Lord promised the Apostles that if they kept the commandments, He would give them "another Comforter" which the world could not receive and did not know but who would come and dwell with them; and so as to not leave them comfortless, He promised that He would return again. Joseph Smith commented on this passage of scripture:

> There are two Comforters spoken of. One is the Holy Ghost, the same as given on the day of Pentecost, and that all Saints receive after faith, repentance, and baptism. This first Comforter or Holy Ghost has no other effect than pure intelligence. It is more powerful in expanding the mind, enlightening the understanding, and storing the intellect with present knowledge, of a man who is of the literal seed of Abraham, than one that is a Gentile, though it may not have half as much visible effect upon the body; for as the Holy Ghost falls upon of the literal seed of Abraham, it is calm and serene; and his whole soul and body are only exercised by the pure spirit of intelligence; while the effect of the Holy Ghost upon a Gentile, is to purge out the old blood, and make him actually of the seed of Abraham. That man that has none of the blood of Abraham (naturally) must have a new creation by the Holy Ghost. In such a case, there may be more of a powerful effect upon the body, and visible to the eye, than upon an Israelite, while the Israelite at first might be far before the Gentile in pure intelligence.
>
> The other Comforter spoken of is a subject of great interest, and perhaps understood by few of this generation. After a person has faith in Christ, repents of his sins, and is baptized for the remission of his sins and receives the Holy Ghost, (by the laying on of hands), which is the first Comforter, then let him continue to humble himself before God, hungering and thirsting after righteousness, and living by every word of God, and the Lord will soon say unto him, Son, thou shalt be exalted. When the Lord has thoroughly proved him, and finds that the man is determined to serve Him at all hazards, then the man will find his calling and his election made sure, then it will be his privilege to receive the other Comforter, which the Lord hath promised the Saints, as is recorded in the testimony of St. John, in the 14th chapter, from the 12th to the 27th verses. . . .
>
> Now what is this other Comforter? It is no more nor less

than the Lord Jesus Christ Himself; and this is the sum and substance of the whole matter; that when any man obtains this last Comforter, he will have the personage of Jesus Christ to attend him, or appear unto him from time to time, and even He will manifest the Father unto him, and they will take up their abode with him, and the visions of the heavens will be opened unto him, and the Lord will teach him face to face, and he may have a perfect knowledge of the mysteries of the Kingdom of God; and this is the state and place the ancient Saints arrived at when they had such glorious visions—Isaiah, Ezekiel, John upon the Isle of Patmos, St. Paul in the three heavens, and all the Saints who held communion with the general assembly and Church of the Firstborn.[456]

It would appear at this point in the discourse that the Lord was about to conclude. He declared that the world would see Him no more, but that through His death He and others would live forever. He testified to the Apostles that "at that day" (referring to the resurrection) they would know that He was in the Father, "and ye in me, and I in you."

Jesus again admonished the Apostles to keep the commandments. He explained that He who kept them evidenced his love toward Him, and then said, "He that loveth me shall be loved of my Father." But again the Lord was interrupted by a third member of the Twelve who asked a question which indicated that they still lacked understanding.[457] Judas (not Iscariot) said, "Lord, how is it that thou wilt manifest thyself unto us, and not unto the world?" Jesus responded with a simple explanation: "If a man love me, he will keep my words: and my Father will love him, and we will come unto him, and make our abode with him." Those—and only those—who truly love the Lord and keep all His commandments will receive the companionship and a testimony of Jesus and His Father.

The Lord returned to the place in His sermon where He had been interrupted and extended to the Twelve the promise of the Holy Ghost (the First Comforter). He told them that the Comforter "whom the Father will send in my name . . . shall teach you all things, and bring all things to your remembrance, whatsoever I have said unto you." No longer would the visible presence of the God of Israel abide with His people, but the Holy Ghost would manifest His word to their spirit as a result of their faith and obedience.

The Lord concluded this discourse with a powerful but comforting passage: "Peace I leave with you, my peace I give unto you: not as the world giveth, give I unto you." Jesus was the "Prince of Peace." He left His disciples with knowledge of the gospel and the assurance that He would rise from the grave and give all men the gift of resurrection. "Let not your heart be troubled," he declared, "neither let it be afraid." Through the Atonement and the corresponding law of repentance He had made it possible for mankind to renew themselves and dwell eternally with Him in His Father's presence!

Finally, he warned His beloved Apostles of the coming of the "prince of this world"—or Satan. Even though the devil would temporarily conquer and Jesus would suffer death, through His death He would permanently defeat the source of all evil, provide resurrection for all men and women, and give the gift of eternal life to those who qualified to receive it. The Lord closed this discourse with His testimony: "I love the Father; and as the Father gave me commandment, even so I do." A righteous people cannot ignore this great example. To love the Lord is to serve Him and keep His commandments.

"I Am the True Vine"

John 15:1–27   I am the true vine, and my Father is the husbandman. Every branch in me that beareth not fruit he taketh away: and every branch that beareth fruit, he purgeth it, that it may bring forth more fruit. Now ye are clean through the word which I have spoken unto you. Abide in me, and I in you. As the branch cannot bear fruit of itself, except it abide in the vine; no more can ye, except ye abide in me. I am the vine, ye are the branches: He that abideth in me, and I in him, the same bringeth forth much fruit: for without me ye can do nothing. If a man abide not in me, he is cast forth as a branch, and is withered; and men gather them, and cast them into the fire, and they are burned. If ye abide in me, and my words abide in you, ye shall ask what ye will, and it shall be done unto you. Herein is my Father glorified, that ye bear much fruit; so shall ye be my disciples. As the Father hath loved me, so have I loved you: continue ye in my love. If ye keep my commandments, ye shall abide in my love; even as I have kept my Father's commandments, and abide in his love. These things have I spoken unto you, that my joy might remain in you, and that your joy might be full. This is my commandment, That ye love one another, as I have loved you. Greater love hath no man than this, that a man lay down his life for his friends. Ye are my friends, if ye do whatsoever I command you. Henceforth I call you not servants; for the servant knoweth not what his lord doeth: but I have called you friends; for all things that I have heard of my Father I have made known unto you. Ye have not chosen me, but I have chosen you, and ordained you, that ye should go and bring forth fruit, and that your fruit should remain: that whatsoever ye shall ask of the Father in my name, he may give it to you. These things I command you, that ye love one another. If the world hate you, ye know that it hated me before it hated you. If ye were of the world, the world would love his own: but because ye are not of the world, but I have chosen you out of the world, therefore the world hateth you. Remember the word that I said unto you, The servant is not greater than his lord. If they have persecuted me, they will also persecute you; if they have kept my saying, they will keep yours also. But all these things will they do unto you for my name's sake, because they know not him that sent me. If I had not come and spoken unto them, they had not had sin: but now they have no cloke for their sin. He that hateth me hateth my Father also. If I had not done among them the works which none other man did, they had not had sin: but now have they both seen and hated both me and my Father. But this cometh to pass, that the word might be fulfilled that is written in their law, They hated me without a cause. But when the Comforter is come, whom I will send unto you from the Father, even the Spirit of truth, which proceedeth from the Father, he shall testify of me: and ye also shall bear witness, because ye have been with me from the beginning.

Cross–reference   John 13:32–35

Jesus closed the discourse recorded in John 14 by declaring to the Apostles, "Arise, let us go hence." As He was preparing to leave the upper room, He may have paused to deliver this discourse or He may have delivered it while they walked; in either event, the discourse commenced with an allegory about a vine. The Lord used it to illustrate the relationship between the Father, the Apostles, and Himself and according to Elder James E. Talmage, "A grander analogy is not to be found in the world's literature."[458]

The object of this discourse was to encourage the Apostles in their future work. The Lord described the nature of their work, the honor they would receive from the Father, and the hardships and joys they would experience. He taught them that they would have to take His place and preach the gospel of the kingdom to all the world. He had already told them in His previous discourse that if they loved Him they would keep His commandments. He now reiterated that statement, noting that those who do not believe on Him and keep His commandments will be as the branch that "beareth not fruit," which will be purged from the tree. The Apostles were clean because they believed on the words Jesus taught them; yet He cautioned them that they would not continue to bear fruit unless they would abide in Him, for the alternatives (according to the discourse) were to bring forth "much fruit" or to be cast out. The emphasis of this discourse was on obedience in keeping the Lord's commandments. If the Apostles did this, they would abide in the Savior's love.

Next, the Lord taught the relationship between the disciples and their fellowman, commanding them to "love one another, as I have loved you. Greater love hath no man than this," the Lord explained, "that a man lay down his life for his friends." Jesus elaborated on this concept by stating, "Ye are my friends, if ye do whatsoever I command you." Perhaps few will ever be called upon to literally give their lives for someone else, but we can "give our lives" to the Lord through obedience to His commandments. We become His "friend" when we devote a lifetime of service to Him. Jesus said that the Apostles were His friends rather than His servants. Throughout His ministry they had only been apprentices but now, as Apostles of His church and witnesses of His kingdom, they were His partners in the work and He would fortify them against the suffering they would endure.

The Lord reminded His disciples that they did not choose Him but rather He had chosen them and ordained them to the great work upon which they were embarking. Through their devotion to Him they had separated themselves from the world, and the world would hate and persecute them for it. Then the Lord comforted them. "Remember," He said, "the servant is not greater than his lord. If they have persecuted me, they will also persecute you." Antagonism toward faithful Saints has always been a characteristic of the true church.[a]459

Jesus had testified of His divinity to the Jews—His chosen people— and they rejected and hated Him without cause. It is possible that some might not have totally understood His words but by observing His works, "which none other man did," they should have believed; instead, they ascribed His miracles to Beelzebub and rejected Him all the more.[460] In this they committed a grievous sin,[461] and they will be left without excuse at the judgment day.[462] The Lord told His Apostles that this fulfilled the Old Testament prophecy which stated that "they [would] hate [the Savior] without a cause."[b]

Jesus closed this discourse by again testifying that the Comforter

a. 2 Timothy 3:12.

b. Psalms 35:19; 69:4.

(the Holy Ghost) would be sent to the Apostles to bear testimony of Him. Then, referring to their future mission, He charged the Apostles saying, "And ye also shall bear witness, because ye have been with me from the beginning."

"Do Ye Now Believe?"

John 16:1–33   These things have I spoken unto you, that ye should not be offended. They shall put you out of the synagogues: yea, the time cometh, that whosoever killeth you will think that he doeth God service. And these things will they do unto you, because they have not known the Father, nor me. But these things have I told you, that when the time shall come, ye may remember that I told you of them. And these things I said not unto you at the beginning, because I was with you. But now I go my way to him that sent me; and none of you asketh me, Whither goest thou? But because I have said these things unto you, sorrow hath filled your heart. Nevertheless I tell you the truth; It is expedient for you that I go away: for if I go not away, the Comforter will not come unto you; but if I depart, I will send him unto you. And when he is come, he will reprove the world of sin, and of righteousness, and of judgment: of sin, because they believe not on me; of righteousness, because I go to my Father, and ye see me no more; of judgment, because the prince of this world is judged. I have yet many things to say unto you, but ye cannot bear them now. Howbeit when he, the Spirit of truth, is come, he will guide you into all truth: for he shall not speak of himself; but whatsoever he shall hear, that shall he speak: and he will shew you things to come. He shall glorify me: for he shall receive of mine, and shall shew it unto you. All things that the Father hath are mine: therefore said I, that he shall take of mine, and shall shew it unto you. A little while, and ye shall not see me: and again, a little while, and ye shall see me, because I go to the Father. Then said some of his disciples among themselves, What is this that he saith unto us, A little while, and ye shall not see me: and again, a little while, and ye shall see me: and, Because I go to the Father? They said therefore, What is this that he saith, A little while? we cannot tell what he saith. Now Jesus knew that they were desirous to ask him, and said unto them, Do ye inquire among yourselves of that I said, A little while, and ye shall not see me: and again, a little while, and ye shall see me? Verily, verily, I say unto you, That ye shall weep and lament, but the world shall rejoice: and ye shall be sorrowful, but your sorrow shall be turned into joy. A woman when she is in travail hath sorrow, because her hour is come: but as soon as she is delivered of the child, she remembereth no more the anguish, for joy that a man is born into the world. And ye now therefore have sorrow: but I will see you again, and your heart shall rejoice, and your joy no man taketh from you. And in that day ye shall ask me nothing. Verily, verily, I say unto you, Whatsoever ye shall ask the Father in my name, he will give it to you. Hitherto have ye asked nothing in my name: ask, and ye shall receive, that your joy may be full. These things have I spoken unto you in proverbs: but the time cometh, when I shall no more speak unto you in proverbs, but I shall shew you plainly of the Father. At that day ye shall ask in my name: and I say not unto you, that I will pray the Father for you: for the Father himself loveth you, because ye have loved me, and have believed that I came out from God. I came forth from the Father, and am come into the world: again, I leave the world, and go to the Father. His disciples said unto him, Lo, now speakest thou plainly, and speakest no proverb. Now are we sure that thou knowest all things, and needest not that any man should ask thee: by this we believe that thou earnest forth from God. Jesus answered them, Do ye now believe? Behold, the hour cometh, yea, is now come, that ye shall be scattered, every man to his own, and shall leave me alone: and yet I am not alone, because the Father is with me. These things I have spoken unto you, that in me ye might have peace. In the world ye shall have tribulation: but be of good cheer; I have overcome the world.

Jesus opened this discourse with a warning to His disciples. He told them that persecutions would come to them as they taught the gospel and testified of Him. He told them that their Jewish colleagues would reject them and He predicted their deaths, specifying that those who killed them would think they had done God a religious service when in reality their cruelty would be merely a result of their ignorance of the Messiah and His Father.

Jesus spoke these things so that the disciples would not stumble, be offended, or have cause to doubt when they were assailed by these future events.[463] He realized that it might be difficult for them to continue to believe their cause was just when their success waned and it seemed most of the power lay with the adversary. "But these things have I told you," Jesus explained, "that when the time shall come, ye may remember that I told you of them." The Lord was still attempting to help the Apostles better understand His death and resurrection. They had not understood before and had felt sorrow and confusion concerning these things. Jesus chided them not only for their lack of understanding but also for not asking more questions about His departure when they failed to comprehend it.[464]

Jesus continued His discourse to the Twelve by augmenting His instructions on the coming of the Holy Ghost, noting that as long as He was with them there was no need for the Holy Ghost and the Holy Ghost would therefore not come; but upon His departure, the Holy Ghost would be with them.[465] The Lord then instructed the Apostles on the mission of the Holy Ghost, indicating that this great Spirit would "reprove the world of sin and of righteousness and of judgment." He then explained further: "Of sin, because they believe not on me; of righteousness, because I go to my Father, and ye see me no more; of judgment, because the prince of this world is judged." The people did not believe in Jesus, but He fulfilled all righteousness by completing His mission and being resurrected. Because He completed His mission, the devil would be judged and totally overcome. Recognizing His Apostles' present limitations, the Lord explained that He had many more things to tell them but that they would not be able to understand those things at that time;[466] but when the Holy Ghost came to them He would both clarify and reveal all things unto them,[a] thus glorifying both the Savior and His Father.

The Lord concluded this portion of His discourse by again testifying of His impending death and resurrection and indicating that in "a little while" the Apostles would not see Him; but He said that in "a little while" they would see Him once more, after He had gone to the Father. Just as before, when the Lord spoke of His coming death and resurrection in metaphors, the Apostles did not understand. Among themselves they asked, "What is this that he saith unto us?" Apparently the Lord could not hear their discussion, but He could perceive their thoughts and "knew that they were desirous to ask him concerning these things." He asked them why they were having difficulty with His teachings and to help them better understand, He defined the first "little while" to be the time that they would lament over His death (an event that would cause the world to rejoice); the second "little while" would be the time He would have with them after He was resurrected (when their sorrows would "be turned into joy").[467] Then the Lord gave the example of a woman experiencing sorrow during the birth process who, when delivered of the child, remembered the pain and anguish no more "for joy that a man is born into the world."

The Lord told the Apostles that after He had departed from them, they should pray to the Father in His name for answers to their questions. He explained that although He had spoken to them in proverbs, in the future he would speak plainly of the Father. And, as if to keep His promise (and perhaps as a reward for their faith and love), He did speak clearly and plainly to them: "I came forth from the Father, and am come into the world: again, I leave the world, and go to the Father."

Because the Lord had perceived their thoughts without their asking, the disciples received renewed conviction from this simple declaration. "Lo, now speakest thou plainly, and speakest no proverb," they rejoiced. "Now are we sure that thou knowest all things, and needest not that any man should ask thee: by this we believe that thou camest forth from God." To this Jesus responded, "Do ye now believe?" He then prophesied that the hour would soon come when they would be scattered, "every man to his own," and He would be left alone to face His painful trial and death. Yet He would not be alone, for His Father would be with Him.[468]

In closing, the Lord strengthened the Apostles in their resolve, noting that He had spoken the things of His discourse that they might have peace: "In the world ye shall have tribulation: but be of good cheer; I have overcome the world."

The Great Prayer

John 17:1–26 These words spake Jesus, and lifted up his eyes to heaven, and said, Father, the hour is come; glorify thy Son, that thy Son also may glorify thee: as thou hast given him power over all flesh, that he should give eternal life to as many as thou hast given him. And this is life eternal, that they might know thee the only true God, and Jesus Christ, whom thou hast sent. I have glorified thee on the earth: I have finished the work which thou gavest me to do. And now, O Father, glorify thou me with thine own self with the glory which I had with thee before the world was. I have manifested thy name unto the men which thou gavest me out of the world: thine they were, and thou gavest them me; and they have kept thy word. Now they have known that all things whatsoever thou hast given me are of thee. For I have given unto them the words which thou gavest me; and they have received them, and have known surely that I came out from thee, and they have believed that thou didst send me. I pray for them: I pray not for the world, but for them which thou hast given me; for they are thine. And all mine are thine, and thine are mine; and I am glorified in them. And now I am no more in the world, but these are in the world, and I come to thee. Holy Father, keep through thine own name those whom thou hast given me, that they may be one, as we are. While I was with them in the world, I kept them in thy name: those that thou gavest me I have kept, and none of them is lost, but the son of perdition; that the scripture might be fulfilled. And now come I to thee; and these things I speak in the world, that they might have my joy fulfilled in themselves. I have given them thy word; and the world hath hated them, because they are not of the world, even as I am not of the world. I pray not that thou shouldest take them out of the world, but that thou shouldest keep them from the evil. They are not of the world, even as I am not of the world. Sanctify them through thy truth: thy word is truth. As thou hast sent me into the world, even so have I also sent them into the world. And for their sakes I sanctify myself, that they also might be sanctified through the truth. Neither pray I for these alone, but for them also which shall believe on me through their word; that they all may be one; as thou, Father, art in me, and I in thee, that they also may be one in us: that the world may believe that thou hast sent me. And the glory which thou gavest me I have given them; that they may be one, even as we are one: I in them, and thou in me, that they may be made perfect in one; and that the world may know that thou hast sent me, and hast loved them, as thou hast loved me. Father, I will that they also, whom thou hast given me, be with me where I am; that they may behold my glory, which thou hast given me: for thou lovedst me before the foundation of the world. O righteous Father, the world hath not known thee: but I have known thee, and these have known that thou hast sent me. And I have declared unto them thy name, and will declare it: that the love wherewith thou hast loved me may be in them, and I in them.

Jesus gave this discourse in the form of a prayer to His Father in Heaven. He gave it in preparation for His agony and the sacrifice He would make for all mankind. It marked the end of His earthly ministry and focused on the upcoming missionary efforts of the Twelve. He spoke as if His mission were totally complete, even though the betrayal and crucifixion still lay before Him. Since He had a perfect comprehension of the eternal plan of salvation, He prayed that His Father in Heaven would glorify Him in accordance with that plan. He prayed that knowledge of the plan would bring eternal life to as many as would believe on Him, and then declared, "This is life eternal, that they might know thee the only true God, and Jesus Christ, whom thou hast sent."

The promise of this great passage is clear. If, through study and prayer, we come to know Jesus and follow His teachings, we will receive life eternal: the same life that the Eternal Father has, the same kind, type, and quality of life as God enjoys.[a469]

In the first part of this discourse the Savior prayed about Himself. He then included the welfare of His beloved Apostles in His communication with God. The Father had given the Apostles to His Son "out of the world"; the Son had manifested His Father's name to them and they had kept the Father's word. They received the words of the Savior as if they had come directly from the Father. They gained a fervent testimony that Christ had come from the Father, and they believed implicitly that the Father had sent Him.

He continued His prayer, interceding for the Apostles and pleading with the Father to bless them because of the love that He had for them.[470] While He was in the world He could protect them; but He was leaving to return to the Father, so He pleaded not only for their

a. D&C 132:19–
22; 29:43–44;
14:7.

safety but also that they might be as Christ and the Father—"one" in all things. The Apostles had finally gained a "knowledge" testimony of His Messiahship, and they were now prepared to testify of His divinity to the entire world. They would no longer be "of the world" just as Christ was not "of the world," and they would need the protection of the Father to shield them from the evils of men. Only eleven of the Apostles were with the Savior during these last moments before His trial and crucifixion, and He noted in His prayer that He had kept them all except the one who had betrayed Him and whom the Savior now classified as "the son of perdition."

As He concluded this section of His prayer, the Savior expressed the desire that the Father would sanctify the Apostles and allow them to share in the Father's glory. Although this prayer was an intercession with the Father in behalf of the Apostles, it was also a prophecy of the great work which they would do. Their accomplishments are testified to in the Acts of the Apostles and in the other books of the New Testament.

> The contrast between the dejected, faint–hearted, material-izing Galilaean fishermen and peasants of the Gospels, and the heroic, spiritual confessors of Pentecost and after–times, is, itself, a miracle, great beyond all others. The illumination of soul, the grandeur of conception, the loftiness of aim, are a transformation from a lower to an indefinitely higher mental and moral condition, as complete as the change from early twilight to noon, and find their only solution in the admission that they must have received the miraculous spiritual enlightenment from above which Jesus had promised to send them.[471]

The third part of the Savior's prayer concerned all mankind. "Neither pray I for these alone," He said (referring to the Apostles), "but for them also which shall believe on me through their word." These Saints were also to be one as the Apostles were commanded to be one and as Christ and the Father are one. All this was to be accomplished so that the world would believe that the Father had sent Jesus Christ to be the Savior of mankind. Although the Lord interceded for and in behalf of mankind in general, the intercession for individuals was based on their belief: man could only be reconciled with God if he had faith in the Father and the Son and repented of his sins.[472] This was the work the Apostles were called to do, because as the Father had sent the Son, so the Son would now send His Apostles—in the same manner and on the same mission.

The Lord now concluded His prayer to His Heavenly Father with an expressed wish that the Apostles (and all those who would believe on Him) would be with Him in the Father's kingdom and "behold [His] glory" which the Father had given Him. The world did not know the Father and it did not recognize the Son, but the Twelve now recognized Him as the Messiah; so the Savior declared the Father unto them, and would declare Him again. He closed by praying that the great love that existed between the Father and the Son would continue to be with the Apostles and, through them, with all the Saints who would believe.

Lest We Also Look Beyond the Mark   14

Jesus used His sermons and discourses to instruct His disciples concerning the kingdom of God. He was the Word made flesh; He was with the Father in the beginning when the world was made; He accepted the great plan of salvation presented by the Father and declared, "Here am I; send me."[a]

He was the God of Abraham, Isaac, and Jacob, and He guided Moses, the great Lawgiver, to prepare the chosen people for the kingdom of God. But they changed the Law and broke the covenant[b] and thus lost the promise.

The religious leaders of ancient Israel placed a hedge around the Law to explain and protect it and contrived infinite minutia to direct the lives of the people, proclaiming that they did it to prepare them for the coming Messiah. They thought the Messiah would save them from their temporal problems, and they assumed He would restore Israel to the glory it had once known. They were concerned with their earthly positions—wealth and all material things—rather than their spiritual needs. They rigidly observed the requirements of the Law only to reject the Lawgiver; yet in His discourses, Jesus proclaimed their freedom—not on the earth, but from the evils of the earth.

The Savior taught in parables during His ministry—stories of everyday life that encompassed the marvelous truths of the kingdom of heaven, allowing everyone the opportunity to understand and continuously remember the teachings of the kingdom. Through His parables He illustrated His great spiritual teachings. He demonstrated His consummate power with miracle upon miracle, thereby proclaiming His Messiahship and promulgating His doctrine.

a. Isaiah 6:8.

b. Isaiah 24:5.

But it was in His discourses that He verbally announced His claim to the Messiahship and the establishment of His new kingdom. He would not put new wine in old bottles, nor would He use the pedantic leadership of His day. They could not see beyond their offices to find their own salvation, and in so doing they blocked the way for others. Instead, in all but one instance He called His Apostles from the simple Galileans and ordained them to be leaders in the kingdom of God. They worked with Him from day to day, observing all that He did and listening intently to His sermons. Before His mission ended, they had learned His ways and recognized Him as the Savior.

He declared His gospel in the Sermon on the Mount, which opened the way for individuals to know God and love Him with all their heart, might, mind, and strength. He presented to the people and rulers alike a doctrine that conflicted in almost every way with the religion of their Jewish society. To a lowly Samaritan woman by a well, He declared Himself to be "living water," and the ensuing discourse produced a harvest of great proportions. He used the ceremonies of the Jewish feasts and celebrations to declare Himself the "bread of life," the "light of the world," and the "good shepherd"— yet they sought only to stone Him. He taught Nicodemus, a "Master" of Israel, about baptism (both by water and by the Spirit), and He explained the change that must come upon each individual if he or she is to follow the true path.

He watched as the poor widow cast in her mite and declared her contribution greater than all the wealthy donations that had been given "in their abundance." He taught that the sanctity of the marriage vow was God–given rather than given by man. He was questioned by Pharisees, scribes, Sadducees, and lawyers, all of whom attempted to entrap Him in His words and deeds. He proclaimed John the Baptist as John had proclaimed Him. He praised John's work and condemned those who had rejected him. He accused the Jewish leadership of being blind and warned His disciples of their leaven. He knew the Law because He was the "giver" of the Law, yet they questioned Him and asked, "How knoweth this man letters?"

In their contempt, the Pharisees brought a woman before Him taken in the sin of adultery and asked Him to judge her. In reply, He proclaimed their Law to be accurate for He had given it; then He required him "who was without sin" to be the first to cast a stone at her. But they were all ashamed, being smitten by their own guilt, and they left the woman alone with Him. Though He could not forgive her without proven repentance, in great compassion He would neither punish nor condemn her, but warned her to go and "sin no more."

When the Lord's public ministry drew to a close, He lamented over Jerusalem and the holy temple (which He had called His house and His Father's house); yet He ultimately reassigned it to the Jews because of their disbelief. His final instructions to the Twelve included the forecast of His death and the prophecy of their future suffering. But He also promised them rewards beyond their wildest dreams if they endured. He left them the Holy Ghost to assure them of His love and to bring to their minds the great teachings He had given them. He taught them of His Father and promised them they would return to His presence if they would but believe. As he completed His mission, He prayed as no other man has ever prayed before and requested the Father to shower forth the blessings of heaven upon all those who would believe.

The Jews wanted an earthly king, but Jesus was a heavenly King. They wanted to be able to work their way back into the kingdom, but they refused to do the things the Lord required of them. They wanted to enjoy all earthly pleasures without limitations. They wanted to have all of the blessings the scriptures promised them, but they would only rely on their ancient covenant to acquire them. Even though they recognized the Lord's claims, they continually demanded signs of His divinity. They did not believe because they *would* not believe.

The discourses apply to modern Saints as readily as they do the ancients. The teachings are the same and they excite the same controversies. There are still some who believe but many who do not. The Lord's message is continuous—one eternal round—and the discourses, as with the parables and the miracles, contain all that is needed to come to a sure knowledge of the Father and the Son.

The Savior taught a message that was woven into the fabric of everyday life. He promised help with daily problems and future rewards for righteous living. He spoke of love of God and love of our fellowman. We can change His commandments or put hedges around them; we can limit our compliance and reject not only the law, but also the Lawgiver; or we can learn, accept, believe, and evidence our love for God through our obedience to His will. By following one of these paths, we either accept or reject the sermons and discourses of Jesus the Messiah.

Topical Index to the Sermon on the Mount

Subject	Matthew	Luke	3 Nephi	JST
Setting	5:1–2	6:12–19	12:1–2	5:1–4
Poor in spirit	5:3	6:20	12:3	5:5
They that mourn	5:4	6:21	12:4	5:6
The meek	5:5		12:5	5:7
Hunger and thirst	5:6	6:21	12:6	5:8
Merciful	5:7		12:7	5:9
Pure in heart	5:8		12:8	5:10
Peacemakers	5:9		12:9	5:11
Persecuted	5:10	6:22–23	12:10	5:12
Revile you	5:11–12		12:11–12	5:13–14
Salt of earth	5:13	14:34–35	12:13	5:15
Light of world	5:14–15	8:16; 11:33	12:14–15	5:16–17
Let light shine	5:16		12:16	5:18
Law fulfilled	5:17–20	16:17	12:17–20; 12:46–47	5:19–22
Anger	5:21–26	12:58–59	12:21–26	5:23–28
Adultery/lust	5:27–30		12:27–30	5:29–34
Divorce	5:31–32	16:18	12:31–32	5:35–36
Oath/Honesty	5:33–37		12:33–37	5:37–39
Eye/eye; cheek	5:38–42		12:38–42	5:40–44
Love enemies	5:43–47	6:27–36	12:43–45	5:45–49
Be perfect	5:48		12:48	5:50
Alms	6:1–4		13:1–4	6:1–4
Prayer	6:5–15	11:2–4	13:5–15	6:5–16
Fasting	6:16–18		13:16–18	6:17–18
Treasure	6:19–34	11:34–36; 12:22–34; 16:9–13	13:19–34	6:18–39
Judgment	7:1–5	6:37–38; 6:41–42	14:1–5	7:1–8
Holy as pearls	7:6		14:6	7:9–11
Ask/seek	7:7–12	11:9–13	14:7–14	7:12–21
Narrow way	7:13–14	13:22–24	14:13–14	7:22–23
False prophets	7:15–20	6:43–44	14:15–20	7:24–29
Do Father's will	7:21–23	6:46; 13:25–30	14:21–23	7:30–33
Rock/sand	7:24–27	6:47–49	14:24–27	7:34–35
Taught/authority	7:28–29			7:36–37

Notes

1. Farrar 2:257.
2. Life p. 184.
3. Life p. 5.
4. Ed 2:167.
5. Ed 2:28.
6. Geikie 2:195.
7. Ed 2:28.
8. Ed 2:393.
9. Ed 2:394.
10. Geikie 2:38.
11. The references refer primarily to Luke, Chapter 6; however, various elements of the doctrine are taught in the discourses recorded randomly throughout Luke.
12. Before publication of the 1979 edition of the Bible for The Church of Jesus Christ of Latter-day Saints, this was known as the Inspired Version. In the Church it is now generally referred to as the Joseph Smith Translation (JST). Quotations from the Inspired Version that are not found in the JST are referenced herein as IV.
13. DNTC 1:212, 214; MM 2:116; Geikie 2:48; Farrar 1:25–28.
14. Some have questioned whether the Sermon on the Mount was delivered all at once or merely so recorded by Matthew. That it was likely one continuous discourse is suggested by the fact that the Lord also delivered it to the Nephites on the Western Hemisphere in one uninterrupted sequence. (3 Nephi 12, 13, and 14.)
15. Geikie 2:48–49; Farrar 1:250. For detail on the composition of the multitude Ed 1:526.
16. Life p. 5; Farrar 1:261.
17. Farrar 1:260.
18. Farrar 1:260.
19. Ed 1:527–28.
20. Ed 1:527–28.
21. JC p. 232.
22. Ed 1:527.
23. JC p. 232.
24. JC p. 246.
25. Geikie 2:58.
26. Farrar 1:265–67.
27. Geikie 2:49.
28. Geikie 2:55.
29. JC p. 231.
30. JC p. 231.
31. DNTC 1:215.
32. DNTC 1:215.
33. JC p. 231.
34. JC p. 231.
35. Life p. 233.
36. JC p. 231.
37. JC p. 231.
38. DNTC 1:216.
39. JC p. 231.
40. Geikie 2:56.
41. Geikie 2:61.
42. DNTC 1:218.
43. DNTC 1:218.
44. JC p. 233.
45. Geikie 2:59.
46. Geikie 2:63.
47. DNTC 1:222.
48. DNTC 1:222.
49. Geikie 2:64.
50. Geikie 2:65.
51. Geikie 2:65.
52. Geikie 2:65–66.
53. JC p. 235.
54. DNTC 1:227.
55. Geikie 2:66.
56. JC p. 235.
57. DNTC 1:228.
58. Joseph Smith modified the automatic extension to the cloak, as indicated by Matthew, stating that if the man sues again, then we should give him the cloak also (IV Matthew 5:42).
59. Again, Joseph Smith modified the automatic extension, commanding that if then compelled to go twain, we should go the twain (IV Matthew 5:43).
60. Geikie 2:72.
61. Geikie 2:73.
62. Life p. 256.
63. Ed 1:530.
64. JC p. 237.
65. Geikie 2:76.
66. JC p. 238.
67. Life p. 233.
68. Ed Temple p. 338.
69. Geikie 2:77.
70. JC p. 242.
71. DNTC 1:251.
72. DNTC 1:254.

73. MM 2:99.

74. Geikie 2:43.

75. Although divergent opinions abound as to when the call of the Twelve occurred, it would appear that it took place between two early visits of Jesus to Jerusalem. Jesus went up to Jerusalem to the "unknown feast" (John 5:1). This feast was either the Passover (MM 2:64–65) or the Feast of Purim (Ed Temple p. 332; for his further considerations Ed 2:768). Because this feast is not named, the speculated length of Jesus' ministry varies from two and one–half to three and one–half years. These calculations involve John 4:35. If Jesus communicated with the woman at the well in December, the feast would be the Feast of Purim. The Feast of Purim (or Esther) was held between the thirteenth and the fifteenth day of the Jewish month Adar (the twelfth month), which approximately corresponds to the first of March on our present calendar (Ed Temple pp. 331–32; 207). There is no doubt that in John 6:4 Jesus went up to the Passover celebration held at the time of the spring equinox in the Jewish month Nisan, which is the first month of the Jewish calendar year and equivalent to our end of March or beginning of April (Ed Temple p. 205).

76. It is significant to note that from time to time people came to Jesus and volunteered to go with Him. In most of these incidents Jesus did not accept their offer (Matthew 8:19–22). He chose to specifically select and ordain those He wanted to have with Him in His ministry (John 15:16).

77. JC p. 226.

78. JC p. 226.

79. Bruce p. 37.

80. MM 2:104–5.

81. MM 2:102.

82. JC p. 218.

83. JC p. 218.

84. Smith p. 504.

85. Life p. 88.

86. JC p. 219.

87. Smith p. 277.

88. JC p. 220.

89. Life p. 80.

90. JC p. 221.

91. Geikie 2:46.

92. JC p. 221.

93. Geikie2:47.

94. Bruce p. 6.

95. Smith p. 510.

96. JC p. 222.

97. JC p. 222.

98. Geikie 2:47.

99. JC p. 223.

100. Smith p. 693.

101. JC p. 223.

102. Bruce p. 19.

103. JC p. 223.

104. If James II, the Apostle, is the son of Alpheus Clopas (Matthew 27:56; Mark 15:40; John 19:25), and this Alpheus is the same as the one mentioned in Acts 1:13, it would make Judas, Simon, and James brothers. It is believed that Alpheus Clopas was the brother of Joseph, Mary's husband. (Smith p. 277.)

105. Smith p. 277.

106. JC p. 225.

107. JC p. 225.

108. Josephus, Wars, IV: 3, 9; Ed 1:522.

109. JC p. 225.

110. Ed 2:473.

111. JC p. 226.

112. Bruce p. 377.

113. Bruce p. 101.

114. Geikie 2:172.

115. Geikie 2:171.

116. A purse was a girdle in which money was carried; a scrip was a small bag or wallet wherein provisions were carried. (DNTC 1:326.)

117. JC p. 329.

118. Generally speaking, the serpent used in this example was an emblem of curing power, similar to that which Moses used in the wilderness when the poisonous serpents attacked the children of Israel (Numbers 21:8). The dove was symbolic of the purity of their hearts.

119. Geikie 2:173.

120. JC p. 330.

121. DNTC 1:336.

122. Perhaps the reference by Luke to "other seventy" would indicate that the first quorum of seventy had been organized. DNTC 1:433.

123. Ed 1:26.

124. Ed Temple p. 277.

125. JC p. 427.

126. Pamphlet: "History of the Organization of the Seventies" by Joseph Young, Sr., Salt Lake City, Utah, 1878.

127. Joseph F. Smith, Conference Report, 1904, p. 3.

128. Ed 1:367. The tax was in the amount of one–half shekel and had to be paid in the temple money or ordinary Galilean shekels. It could not be paid in the money common in Palestine at that day. Many coins of different countries were used in Palestine at Christ's time, including Palestinian silver, copper coin, Persian Tyrian, Syrian, Egyptian, Grecian, and Roman. (Ed 1:36–68.)

129. Josephus, Wars, VI, IX:3.

130. Ed 1:368.

131. Ed 1:369–70.

132. Geikie 1:471.

133. Josephus, Antiquities, XX, IX:2–4.

134. JC p. 155.

135. Geikie 1:472.

136. Ed 1:374.

137. Life p. 5, 17.

138. JC p. 155.

139. JC p. 528.

140. Life p. 88. Matthew records the miracle of the fig tree after the cleansing of the temple (Matthew 21:18–22).

141. MM 3:348.

142. Geikie 2:378.

143. JC p. 158.

144. Life p. 571.

145. Life p. 156.

146. Geikie 2:246–47.

147. Geikie 2:247.

148. JC p. 386.

149. Geikie 2:247.

150. Bruce p. 202.

151. MM 3:82.

152. Ed 2:120.

153. DNTC 1:419.

154. Ed 2:345.

155. Bruce p. 282.

156. Previous declarations: First, Matthew 16:21; Mark 8:31. Second, Matthew 17:22–23; Mark 9:31.

157. JC p. 502.

158. JC p. 503.

159. Matthew reports that it was the mother of James and John who petitioned the Lord whereas Mark reports that James and John petitioned the Lord directly. These were the same Apostles who had, at a former time, requested that fire be called down from heaven to consume their adversaries (Luke 9:54). John had wished to forbid the one who cast out devils with whom he was not familiar (Mark 9:38).

160. Ed 2:347.

161. Ed 2:78.

162. JC p. 361.

163. Ed 2:79.

164. Ed 2:79.

165. MD pp. 411–13.

166. TPJS p. 274.

167. JC p. 364.

168. JC p. 365.

169. The Gospel of John is unique, and differs considerably from the treatment of the Savior's life by the synoptic Gospels; i.e., Matthew, Mark, and Luke. Generally speaking, Matthew reads like a brief summary of the life of Christ even in the more detailed reports of His discourses, miracles, and parables. Mark, the shortest of the Gospels, appears to be a succession of rapid sketches of the life of Jesus while Luke treats the life of Jesus with deeper historical purpose. Luke, however, outlines the story rather than telling it in detail (Ed 1:394). All three of the Synoptics treat the life of Jesus in a historical set-ting. John alone does not profess to give a narrative of the life of Christ, but rather selects incidents from His life which characteristically describe Jesus in His ministry and His claim to the Messiahship (Ed 1:394).

170. New Testament Commentary for English Readers, edited by Charles John Ellicott, p. 374.

171. Geikie 1:489; Ed 1:390.

172. DNTC 1:148.

173. Josephus, Antiquities XX: 6, 1.

174. Although the scripture indicates that all of the Apostles went into the small city, leaving Jesus alone, it is highly unlikely that He was left on the road without accompaniment. In all probability, John, who recorded the detail of the story, remained behind to keep Him company. (Ed 1:406.)

175. Geikie 1:494.

176. Ed 1:409, including notes 2 and 3.

177. Ed 1:395.

178. Geikie 1:495.

179. Smith p. 212–13; Geikie 1:499.

180. Morris p. 266.

181. JC p. 173.

182. Josephus, Antiquities, XVIII: 2, 2. For a detailed discussion on the traditions, religion, derivation, and history of the Samaritans, Ed 1:390–403.

183. Geikie 1:497.

184. Geikie 1:497.

185. Bruce p. 247.

186. Life p. 216.

187. JC p. 174.

188. A similar occurrence had taken place when the Lord called Nathanael to the ministry—there Nathanael declared Jesus to be the King of Israel (John 1:48–49).

189. The Inspired Version states: "I who speak unto thee am the Messias" (IV John 4:28).

190. Geikie 1:503.

191. Pertaining to the time of year of this occurrence and whether the comment of Christ in verse 35 pertains to the current time of year or whether the four months spoken of were parabolic in nature, Ed 1:419–20; Appendix XV.

192. Farrar 1:214.

193. Geikie 1:502.

194. For specific information on these materials Trench p. 243; Geikie 2:86–87; Ed Temple p. 331–33.

195. Life p. 51.

196. Geikie 2:91.

197. MM 2:70.

198. DNTC 1:191.

199. MM 2:71.

200. JC p. 208.

201. JC p. 209.

202. MM 2:76.

203. Life p. 17.

204. Ed 2:25.

205. Life p. 91.

206. Life p. 170

207. Geikie 2:179.

208. The synagogue had worship days during the week (Monday and Thursday) other than the normal Sabbath worship. It may have been on one of these days that the sermon took place. (Geikie 2:179).

209. Ed 2:29.

210. Ed 2:29.

211. JC p. 339.

212. Geikie 2:181.

213. Ed 2:28.

214. Geikie 2:184.

215. JC pp. 342, 347 note 10.

216. JC p. 342.

217. DNTC 1:358.

218. JC p. 342.

219. Geikie 2:184–85.

220. JC p. 343.

221. Bruce p. 146.

222. Life p. 28.

223. Ed 2:36.

224. Geikie 2:186.

225. Ed 2:36.

226. JC p. 344.

227. Ed Temple p. 270.

228. For detailed information on the Feast of Tabernacles, Ed Temple pp. 268–87.

229. Ed 2:165.

230. Geikie 2:279.

231. Ed Temple p. 285; Ed 2:166.

232. The ancient Jewish explanatory commentary on the Old Testament.

233. As quoted in Ed 2:166.

234. Ed 2:165.

235. It is significant to note that in John, Chapter 7, the crowds in the temple are mentioned eight times, whereas they are not mentioned at all in Chapter 8. For this reason, Edersheim determines that the "light of the world" discourse was given on the last day of the feast, or perhaps even the day after, commonly known as the Octave of the feast, after most of the crowds, common in the normal feast days, had dissipated. If this interpretation of John were adopted, it would indicate that Jesus gave the "light of the world" discourse principally before His adversaries and not the people in general.

236. Edersheim rejects this segment of the scripture as spurious. For his detail on the matter see Ed 2:163 note 1. Although some reject the story of the adulterous woman, it would appear to be authentic for the following reasons: First Joseph Smith in his inspired translation of the Bible left the story intact and did not reject it, thus indicating that the story belonged in the sacred text. Second, Elder James E. Talmage also indicated the authenticity of the story.

237. Farrar 2:65.

238. JC p. 405.

239. Ed 2:165.

240. DNTC 1:452.

241. Ed 2:168.

242. Ed 2:169.

243. Ed 2:169.

244. Farrar 2:75.

245. Ed 2:167.

246. Geikie 2:286.

247. Ed 2:173.

248. DNTC 1:461.

249. Ed 2:175.

250. Ed 2:176.

251. DNTC 1:462–64.

252. Life p. 45.

253. The Feast of Dedication was first instituted by Judas Maccabees in the year 164 B.C. to celebrate the rededication of the temple. (Ed Temple p. 334.)

254. JC pp. 417–18.

255. JC p. 418.

256. Life p. 51.

257. Ed 2:229.

258. JC p. 488.

259. Life p. 45.

260. Ed 1:366–67; MM 1:469.

261. Farrar 1:196.

262. Farrar 1:196–97.

263. JC p. 159.

264. Ed 1:381.

265. Geikie 1:481.

266. Ed 1:382.

267. Life P. 5, 17.

268. Ed 1:381.|

269. JC p. 160.

270. Geikie 1:479.

271. Geikie 1:479.

272. MM 1:478.

273. Life p. 140.

274. Ed 2:328.

275. Farrar 2:227–28.

276. JC p. 473.

277. Geikie 2:347.

278. Ed 2:332.

279. Ed 2:332 note 5.

280. For detail on the grounds for divorce practiced by the Jews at the time of Christ, Ed 2:332–34; Geikie 2:347.

281. JC p. 474.

282. JC p. 474.

283. Ed 2:335.

284. JC p. 475.

285. JC p. 475.

286. JC p. 475.

287. MM 3:293.

288. DNTC 1:547.

289. DNTC 1:547.

290. This appears to be a duplication of a previous similar experience (Matthew 18:3).

291. Ed 2:336.

292. Ed 2:387.

293. Ed 2:387.

294. Josephus, Antiquities, XIV: 7, 1 and 2.

295. DNTC 1:628.

296. JC p. 561.

297. Ed 2:389.

298. Life p. 282.

299. Life p. 261.

300. DNTC 1:691.

301. Ed 2:792–94.

302. Topical Guide: Service.

303. JC p. 585.

304. Ed 2:792.

305. JC p. 194.

306. Ed 1:514.

307. Geikie 2:27.

308. Geikie 2:30.

309. Geikie 2:32.

310. Geikie 2:31.

311. Ed 1:508.

312. DNTC 1:182.

313. Ed 1:520.

314. If the question posed by the disciples of John the Baptist, as recorded in Matthew 9:14, is viewed in this manner, then there is no conflict between the Matthew verse and the events as recorded in Mark 2:18 and Luke 5:33 (JC p. 195.)

315. Ed Temple p. 338.

316. For example, a fast commemorated the destruction of Jerusalem by the Chaldeans, and others were connected with the incidents of the siege, the troubles of the first period of captivity, or the day which commemorated the translation of the scriptures. (Geikie 2:35.)

317. Ed 1:662.

318. Geikie 2:35.

319. Geikie 2:35.

320. JC p. 196.

321. DNTC 1:186.

322. The Joseph Smith Translation adds to the Matthew text a third question posed by the Pharisees. They asked Jesus why He did not accept their baptism as they claimed to be keeping the whole law. Jesus declared to them that they did not keep the Law because if they had kept it they would have received Him, and He stated, "For I am he who gave the law." This insertion (JST Matthew 9:18–21) comes before the old cloth/old wineskins anal-

ogy, but only in the Matthew text; it does not appear in either Mark or Luke.

323. Life p. 28.

324. Ed 1:576.

325. DNTC 1:280.

326. MM 2:226.

327. Ed 2:339.

328. Ed 2:339.

329. JC p. 476.

330. DNTC 1:556.

331. Geikie 2:355.

332. Ed 2:298.

333. Geikie 2:342.

334. JC p. 445.

335. Ed 2:301.

336. JC p. 446.

337. DNTC 1:261.

338. The Lord's comment that they return and testify to John of His miracles and words could possibly indicate that John did not have a full comprehension of what the spiritual kingdom of God comprised. (JC p. 256.)

339. MM 1:382.

340. TPJS pp. 275–76.

341. TPJS p. 276.

342. Ed 1:670.

343. Geikie 2:110.

344. We know that Jesus taught extensively in Capernaum and worked many miracles there, even making it His own community. (Matthew 9:1; Mark 9:33; Matthew 8:5–17; Mark 2:1–12.)

345. DNTC 1:469.

346. DNTC 1:504.

347. Ed 2:305; DNTC 1:503.

348. Ed 2:305.

349. Ed 2:305.

350. This quotation is taken from "Lecture Sixth," Lectures on Faith. The Lectures on Faith, first known as Lectures on Theology, were given to the early elders of the Church at the School of the Prophets in Kirtland, Ohio (HC 2:175–76). Joseph was active in the preparation of these lectures on theology during this period of time (HC 2:180). The lectures were later published in the first editions of the Doctrine and Covenants under the title, Lectures on Faith, and although the same were noted as "judiciously written and compiled," there was a marked difference between the Lectures on Faith and the revelations given in the first editions of the Doctrine and Covenants. The Lectures on Faith were later dropped from the Doctrine and Covenants. (HC Index under Faith, Lectures on.) For a complete text of the Lectures on Faith, including a historical sketch see JAW. The quotation inserted is taken from this text, pages 143–44 and footnote.

351. Ed 2:7.

352. Ed 2:8.

353. Geikie 2:191.

354. Life p. 28.

355. Ed 2:8.

356. Life p. 51.

357. Ed 2:8.

358. Ed 2:10. For detail of the ritualistic requirements of washing and the sins associated with lack of observance, Geikie 2:191–92.

359. Ed 2:21.

360. DNTC 1:368.

361. JC pp. 353–54.

362. Life p. 115.

363. Geikie 2:216.

364. MM 3:27.

365. MM 3:28.

366. Only John records this appearance of Jesus at Jerusalem. From this period of the ministry until its end John records three appearances of Jesus in the Holy City. The first (the one now under discussion) at the Feast of Tabernacles; the second, at the Feast of Dedication (John 10); and the third was His final entry before the Crucifixion (which all the Evangelists agree upon). Luke, during this same period of the Lord's ministry, also records three journeys to Jerusalem (but does not record the events of the visits), and it would follow that the three journeys to Jerusalem described by Luke fit into the three appearances at Jerusalem described by John. Luke describes what took place in Christ's ministry before and after the appearance, while John describes only what took place at Jerusalem. (Ed 2:127.)

367. Ed Temple p. 270.

368. Ed Temple p. 269.

369. MM 3:111.

370. DNTC 1:438.

371. Geikie 2:263.

372. This denial of hospitality produced the story of James and John's requesting that lightning be called down from heaven to destroy some Samaritan villages, resulting in their nicknames, "sons of thunder" (Luke 9:54; Mark 3:17). Apparently they, too, had not come to the total understanding and comprehension that the kingdom of God would not be expanded by violence. By their attitude they also displayed their Jewish training, believing that everyone other than Israel was their enemy. Jesus rebuked their foolishness and passed on to another village.

373. Ed 2:148.

374. Ed 2:151.

375. Ed 2:151.

376. DNTC 1:441.

377. Life p. 51.

378. JC p. 404.

379. DNTC 1:444; Ed 2:154.

380. MM 3:128.

381. Ed Temple pp. 278–81.

382. Ed 2:160.

383. Ed 2:160; DNTC 1:445.

384. DNTC 1:449; Geikie 2:278.

385. Geikie 2:392.

386. JC p. 544.

387. JC p. 545.

388. Ed 2:385.

389. Ed 2:385.

390. JC p. 545.

391. Ed 2:385.

392. Geikie 2:395.

393. Geikie 2:397.

394. Ed 2:397.

395. Farrar 2:235; DNTC 1:605.

396. Farrar 2:235.

397. Geikie 2:398.

398. JC p. 548.

399. For detail on the Sadducean belief concerning the resurrection, Ed 2:397–99.

400. DNTC 1:612.

401. Ed 2:405.

402. JC p. 518.

403. Proselytes to the Jewish faith from Greece were pledged to the seven commandments of Noah. (1) The avoidance of murder; (2) the avoidance of bloodshed; (3) the commitment not to rob; (4) the rejection of idolatry; (5) the worship of Jehovah; (6) the obedience to Jewish courts in matters of religion; (7) to eat no freshly killed or still–bleeding flesh. In addition to these covenants, they submitted to the law of circumcision; however, they could not pass beyond the court of the Gentiles in the temple. (Geikie 2:409.)

404. MM 3:411.

405. JC p. 518.

406. JC p. 520.

407. JC p. 520.

408. Ed 2:393–94.

409. Farrar 2:244.

410. DNTC 1:615.

411. TPJS pp. 272–73, 318–19.

412. JC p. 553.

413. Ed 2:407.

414. Farrar 2:244.

415. Life p. 275.

416. Geikie 2:403.

417. Ed 2:411.

418. Ed 2:412; JC p. 556; MM 3:396.

419. DNTC 1:619.

420. Ed 2:412.

421. DNTC 1:620.

422. Farrar 2:246.

423. Geikie 2:407.

424. TPJS pp. 221–23; DNTC 1:623.

425. TPJS p. 261.

426. MM 3:405.
427. Geikie 2:406–7.
428. MM 3:408.
429. Ed 2:431.
430. Josephus, Antiquities, XV: 11, 3.
431. Geikie, 2:416.
432. Geikie 2:416.
433. DNTC 1:640.
434. Ed 2:446.
435. Josephus, Wars, II: 13, 4, 5; Antiquities, XX: 5, 1; 8, 10. For information on the Jewish belief of the anticipated Messiah, Ed 2:434–35.
436. Life p. 689.
437. JC p. 572.
438. Life p. 696.
439. JC p. 571.
440. DNTC 1:644–45.
441. DNTC 1:647.
442. DNTC 1:647.
443. TPJS pp. 286–87; SC p. 211.
444. Life p. 664.
445. Life p. 709.
446. JC p. 574.
447. Life p. 774.
448. DNTC 1:668–70.
449. JC p. 575.
450. Life p. 282.
451. MM 3:462.
452. TPJS p. 366.
453. Geikie 2:451; JC p. 602.
454. JC p. 602.
455. JC pp. 602–3; also p. 30 herein.
456. TPJS pp. 149–51.
457. DNTC 1:739.
458. JC p. 604.
459. DNTC 1:751.
460. Miracles, Chapter 3.
461. Ed 2:523.
462. JC p. 606.
463. JC p. 607.
464. DNTC 1:753.
465. DNTC 1:753.
466. DNTC 1:754.
467. JC p. 608.
468. JC pp. 608–9.
469. DNTC 1:761.
470. JC p. 610.
471. Geikie 2:470.
472. DNTC 1:764.

THE MISSION OF JESUS THE MESSIAH

Introduction

Jesus taught and established His claim to the Messiahship with miracles, parables, and sermons, but His ultimate purpose for coming to this earth was His mission.

The mission of Jesus the Messiah is revealed in a series of events which took place during His earthly life. These events, beginning with His birth and ending with His resurrection and ascension, are recorded by the Gospel writers to substantiate their testimony of His divinity. In addition, several other events occurred during His mission that the Gospel writers alluded to but did not describe in detail. These events include His work in the premortal existence "Before the World Was" and His work in "Old Testament times" when He was known as Jehovah (Chapter 1); events that occurred between His death and resurrection "In the World of Spirits" (Chapter 8); and His visit to the Western Hemisphere's "Other Sheep" as well as "The Restoration" of the gospel in the latter days and his "Second Coming" in the Millennium (Chapter 10). These events—along with those described by Matthew, Mark, Luke, and John—comprise His mission.

Discussing the mission of Jesus is not like discussing the miracles, the parables, or the sermons. Those subjects had a predetermined boundary, each with a beginning and an end. The events of the Lord's mission were also described by the Gospel writers with a beginning and an end, but they have limitless consequences. These events range from the very beginning of the plan of salvation (as presented by the Father in the premortal spirit world) to the culmination of all things — the final judgment and beyond.

The main text for my discussion of the Lord's mission is the New Testament. No other known record describes the earthly life of the Lord in detail. However, it was not the intent of the Gospel writers to record a biography of Jesus. They did not describe His life, but His ministry. They did not testify of His life, but of His divinity. As they did with the miracles, the parables, and the sermons, the authors of the New Testament testified of Christ's mission and bore witness that He was the Messiah, the Son of God.[1]

Each author recorded the events of Christ's mission in a different manner, a fact that testifies of the Gospels' independent authorship. However, Matthew, Mark, and Luke (commonly referred to as the synoptic Gospels, or the Synoptics) do deal with the life of Christ in a similar manner; that is, they record many of the events of the mission in common dealing primarily with the Lord's Galilean ministry. John, however, deals primarily with the Lord's Judean ministry and although he records some events in common with the Synoptics, he also records many others not mentioned by them. In addition to the Gospels, the Book of Mormon describes and testifies of many of these events and serves as another testament of Jesus Christ. In fact, in three specific instances (the Crucifixion, the Resurrection, and the Lord's visit to His "other sheep"), the Book of Mormon provides an extraordinary witness and testimony of the Savior's mission.

The classification and organization of the events in the Lord's mission are discussed in chronological order, beginning with the pre-earth mission of Jesus, culminating at His death and resurrection, and concluding with the Restoration[2] and the Millennial advent.[3] The scriptural story of each event is included in the text, but it is the doctrinal teaching that is emphasized and discussed. Also included are related teachings and examples that the Lord used throughout His ministry, testimony and writings of Old Testament prophets, and the scriptural and historical insight that other knowledgeable writers have given on the circumstances of His mission.

The body of the book is divided into four parts and eleven chapters. Chapters 1–10 deal with the events of Jesus' mission; Chapter 11 deals with the general message and importance of His mission.

In discussing the trials of Jesus, I have combined the four Gospels (eliminating duplications) to provide a "scriptural story" of those events (Chapter 7). This makes possible a very complete description of the trials.

The Lord's mission is an integral part of the plan of salvation, the plan that was presented by the Father in the pre-earth existence and that is our purpose for being. Each event in Christ's mission testifies of Him as the Messiah, not only for those who lived at Christ's time but for those who would follow.

The miracles of Jesus caused astonishment and wonder. His parables animated His teachings and simplified their understanding. His sermons gave gospel instruction and expounded the doctrines of the kingdom of God. They were all used to teach, to testify, and to proclaim Jesus as the Son of God. But it was the events of His mission that bore the greatest witness of Christ as the long-awaited Messiah.

In the Beginning   1

Before the World Was—The Plan

John 1:1–5   In the beginning was the Word, and the Word was with God, and the Word was God. The same was in the beginning with God. All things were made by Him; and without Him was not any thing made that was made. In Him was life; and the life was the light of men. And the light shineth in darkness; and the darkness comprehended it not.

John begins his gospel with the declaration, "In the beginning was the Word, and the Word was with God, and the Word was God." The beginning spoken of by John was the time and place in which all God's spirit children dwelt prior to this earth. This time is referred to as the preexistence, or our pre-earth or premortal life, and is a place where as spirits, "we were in all respects as we are now save only that we were not housed in mortal bodies."[4] The "Word" spoken of was none other than Jesus Christ,[5] who was the firstborn spirit son of the living God, our Father in Heaven.

Paul declared with fervor to the Hebrews that we "had fathers of our flesh which corrected us, and we gave them reverence: shall we not much rather be in subjection unto the Father of spirits, and live?"[a] Therefore, God the Eternal Father, "whom we designate by the exalted name-title 'Elohim,' is the literal parent of our Lord and Savior Jesus Christ, and of [all] the spirits of the human race."[6] In this premortal state, the entire human race existed as spirit beings in the presence of our Father in Heaven who, at some previous time, had passed through a mortal life of His own, including death and resurrection.[7]

Our birth order in premortality is unknown to us and unimportant,

a. Hebrews 12:9.

but Christ is designated as the firstborn of the Father. Undoubtedly all God's spirit children came into being as conscious identities in their own appointed order[8] and, during the period of their spirit existence, developed an infinite variety and degree of talents.[9]

Our object as spirits was to become like the Father,[10] and for this purpose He ordained and established certain laws for our advancement and progress.[11] We, through our obedience, move along the path designated by our Father in Heaven toward His ultimate goal, for He has declared that His work and glory is "to bring to pass the immortality and eternal life of man."[a]

In the spirit existence, as in this mortal life, some were more intelligent than others and had varying degrees of ability and power.[12] Regardless of ability or intelligence, however, each spirit possessed his or her own agency—a power given to each individual by the Father.[13] The eternal law of free agency was the birthright of every individual spirit child of our Father in Heaven. Agency gave them the ability to act for themselves.[14]

Of our existence in this premortal state we know very little, and although certain specifics are revealed, even these are limited. Where such revelation is given it would appear that its main purpose is to shed light upon the premortal Godhood of Jesus Christ.[15]

John the Revelator beheld in open vision limited scenes from this premortal life. From His description, we know that not all of our premortal existence was happiness and peace for he saw and described great contention, even a "war" in heaven.[b]

Apparently this heavenly conflict followed a great council held by the spirits and the Father prior to the creation of this earth. In this council, our Father in Heaven presented His plan for the continued progression of His spirit children. For the most part the plan was received with joy and jubilation;[c] however, there stood one in the council who was described by Isaiah as the son of the morning[d] and who, desiring self-aggrandizement,[16] wanted the glory of the Eternal Father for himself.[e] He not only objected to the Father's plan, he presented a modification that would result in his own exaltation while destroying the agency of man. At this time Jesus Christ, who had glory with our Father in Heaven before the world was,[f] stepped forward and offered Himself in conformity with the Father's plan, declaring "Father, thy will

a. Moses 1:39.

b. Revelation 12:7–9.

c. Job 38:4–7.

d. Isaiah 14:12–15.

e. Moses 4:1–4; Abraham 3:27–28.

f. John 17:5.

be done, and the glory be thine forever."[a] Satan's plan was rejected and Jesus was chosen and ordained "to sacrifice Himself, through labor, humiliation and suffering even unto death."[17] His sacrifice made it possible for man to be redeemed from the effects of sin and to receive exaltation through righteous achievement and the grace of God.

In the verses quoted, the beginning of the written History of Jesus the Christ commenced.[18] Because Satan rebelled and would not accept the Father's plan, he was cast out. His banishment and fall was graphically recorded by the Old Testament prophet Isaiah, who witnessed this event in a vision from the Lord.[b][19] Of this event, Moses recorded the Lord's words: "He became Satan, yea, even the devil, the father of all lies, to deceive and to blind men, and to lead them captive at his will, even as many as would not hearken unto my voice."[c]

Jesus assisted in casting Satan out[d] and under the direction of the Father and in accordance with the plan accepted by the council, He created this earth and all things thereon. "The Father operated in the work of creation through the Son, who thus became the executive through whom the will, commandment, or word of the Father was put into effect. . . . The part taken by Jesus Christ in the creation, a part so prominent as to justify our calling Him the Creator, is set forth in many scriptures."[20]

Speaking of Jesus, Paul declared with boldness and clarity, "For by him were all things created, that are in heaven, and that are in earth, visible and invisible, whether they be thrones, or dominions, or principalities, or powers: all things were created by him, and for him: and he is before all things, and by him all things consist."[e]

Although man's premortal existence and the important role Jesus Christ played in it were but dimly perceived by the multitudes who lived during Old Testament times,[21] the holy prophets of that time undoubtedly knew the truth of the Son's premortal glory and mission.[f] The evidence presented in the Holy Scriptures (which includes the Savior's prayer in Gethsemane to His Father: "Glorify thou me with thine own self with the glory which I had with thee before the world was"[g]) confirms that the man known as Jesus of Nazareth existed with the Father prior to His birth in the flesh and that while in that premortal state, He was called and ordained by the Father (and accepted by us all) as the Savior and Redeemer of the world.

a. Moses 4:2.

b. Isaiah 14:12–15.

c. Moses 4:4.

d. Moses 4:3.

e. Colossians 1:16–17.

f. Isaiah 6:8; Psalm 25:14; Amos 3:7.

g. John 17:5

Old Testament Times—Jehovah

The eighth article of faith begins, "We believe the Bible to be the word of God as far as it is translated correctly." Although some have used that expression to suggest limiting the use of the Bible, there is no question that "The Church of Jesus Christ of Latter-day Saints accepts the Holy Bible as the foremost of her standard works, first among the books which have been proclaimed as her written guides in faith and doctrine."[22]

Scholars agree that the Bible is a collection of books written by many different authors and that, in many instances, the writing of those books was separated widely in time. Further, there is no question that the Jews at the time of the Lord's earthly mission were in possession of most, if not all, of the Old Testament scriptures and considered them to be authoritative. In addition, because Jesus and the Apostles quoted from these records frequently and designated them as scripture,[a] they presumably were authentic in the form then current.

The first five books of the Bible were known among the Jews as the Torah and were designated as the written Law. They are also referred to as the Pentateuch, and their authorship is (and always has been) ascribed to Moses.[b] The Jews also had the writings of the other prophets, the poetic books, and other historical books.

When Moses ended his prophetic ministry on the earth, he commanded the priests and the Levites to preserve the scrolls containing the Law which had been given to them by the Lord in the ark of the covenant.[c] The ancient Israelites managed to maintain this record in one form or another throughout the early history of their independent empires and captivity. It appears, however, that the written books of the Law had been lost or discarded prior to the reign of Josiah, circa 640 B.C. Hilkiah, a priest in the temple during Josiah's reign, found a "book of the law" and had it read before the king.[d] In the sixth century B.C., Cyrus, king of Persia, allowed the Jews in his kingdom to return to Jerusalem and rebuild the temple according to the law of God.[e] Ezra returned to Jerusalem after the completion of the temple and has been given the credit for compiling the books of the Old Testament in existence at his time.[23]

From Ezra until Christ the Law remained essentially intact and was only added to by prophets who lived during that time. In addition, many

a. John 5:39.

b. Ezra 6:18; 7:6; Nehemiah 8:1; John 7:19.

c. Deuteronomy 31:9.

d. 2 Chronicles 34:14.

e. Ezra 1:1–6; 7:1–7.

other books (considered less authoritative) were available to the Jews at the time of Jesus.[24] It is from the teachings found in all of these works—the Law, the prophets, the poetic books, and the historical works—that the chosen people acquired their anticipation of the coming forth of the Messiah. They may have disagreed among themselves as to the time and manner of His appearance, but there is no question that the certainty of the Messiah's coming was well established in the hopes and beliefs of the Jews of Christ's day.[25] Indeed, it might be said that the Old Testament and the history of the chosen people in its entirety were "symbolic, and typical of the future—the Old Testament the glass, through which the universal blessings of [the Messianic] days were seen."[26]

Because of the fall of Adam death came into the world, and man by himself was incapable of overcoming it. The plan of salvation, voted upon and accepted by the Father's righteous children in the great council in heaven, decreed that a future Redeemer would overcome death and make it possible for man to return to the Father's presence. In their fallen state, Adam and Eve had been driven from the Garden of Eden and were unable to enjoy the Father's continuous personal association. Sometime after leaving the Garden of Eden, Adam was instructed to offer sacrifices to the Lord. On one of those sacrificial occasions an angel of the Lord came to him inquiring, "Why dost thou offer sacrifices unto the Lord?" Adam responded, "I know not, save the Lord commanded me." His answer indicated that he had not yet been fully instructed concerning the purpose of sacrifice, so the angel proceeded to clearly outline the purpose of the sacrificial commandment by declaring: "This thing is a similitude of the sacrifice of the Only Begotten of the Father, which is full of grace and truth. Wherefore, thou shalt do all that thou doest in the name of the Son, and thou shalt repent and call upon God in the name of the Son forever more."[a]

Sacrifice, as a prototype of the death of the future Messiah, was thus practiced not only from the time of Moses (as commanded by the Law) but also from the beginning of human history.[27] The Bible does not specifically designate the origin of sacrifice as prefiguring the atoning death of Jesus Christ,[28] but significant examples of this are found in the biblical stories of Cain and Abel;[b] Noah's sacrifice after the Flood;[c] the story of Abraham and Isaac;[d] and the story of Jacob, the father of the house of Israel.[e]

a. Moses 5:6–9.

b. Genesis 4:3–4.

c. Genesis 8:20.

d. Genesis 22:2, 13.

e. Genesis 31:54; 46:1.

The "significance of the divinely established requirement [of sacrifice] was explained in its fullness to the patriarch of the race [Adam]."[29] Its origin is based on specific revelation.[a] Further, the prophets of the Old Testament understood the doctrines surrounding the coming forth of the Messiah. Job rejoiced at Christ's anticipated coming[b] and the Psalms are replete with anticipation of His advent.[30] His coming was further attested to by Enoch (the father of Methuselah)[c] and by the covenant of Abraham (which promised that through father Abraham's seed, all nations of the earth would be blessed).[d] Furthermore, the blessing given to Judah by His father, Israel, presaged the birth line of the Savior.[e]

Isaiah foretold the Messiah's virgin birth[f] and sang His praise as if it had already occurred.[g] He declared the Savior's lineage as a branch from Jesse;[h] glorified Him as the foundation stone of Zion,[i] the Shepherd of the house of Israel,[j] and the Light of the world;[k] prophesied of John as His forerunner;[l] and praised the Lord Jehovah as the leader and commander of both Jew and Gentile.[m] Finally, in one sublime chapter he envisioned the Messiah of Israel in His ministry and portrayed His atonement and death.[n]

Other prophets of the Old Testament also received revelation and enlightenment pertaining to the Messiah's advent. Jeremiah knew, and through revelation was assured of Christ's safe advent.[o] Ezekiel prophesied of Him[p] as did Hosea[q] and Micah[r] Zechariah saw Christ's triumphant entry into Jerusalem,[s] noted that His own people would "pierce" their Savior,[t] observed the Jews suffering centuries of trials and tribulations as they waited for their Messiah, and then heard them question the Savior concerning His wounds when He did finally appear.[u]

Moses, the great Lawgiver of Israel, prophesied of Christ and of the condemnation He would receive from those who would not accept Him.[v] From the great exodus forward, every paschal lamb slain at every Passover looked forward to Jesus as the Lamb of God.[31] Paul affirmed this conclusion to the Corinthians when he said, "For even Christ our passover is sacrificed for us."[w] All of these great visions and prophecies from the Old Testament were given by the Lord Jehovah to His ancient prophets.

When Moses spoke with the God of Abraham, Isaac, and Jacob

a. Moses 5:5–8.

b. Job 19:25–27.

c. Moses 6:21, 52.

d. Genesis 12:3; 18:18; 22:18; 26:4; 28:14.

e. Genesis 49:10.

f. Isaiah 7:14.

g. Isaiah 9:6–7.

h. Isaiah 11:1, 10.

i. Isaiah 28:16.

j. Isaiah 40:9–11.

k. Isaiah 42:6.

l. Isaiah 40:3.

m. Isaiah 55:4.

n. Isaiah 53.

o. Jeremiah 23:5–6; 33:14–16.

p. Ezekiel 34:23; 37:24–25.

q. Hosea 11:1.

r. Micah 5:2.

s. Zechariah 9:9.

t. Zechariah 12:10.

u. Zechariah 13:6.

v. Deuteronomy 18:15–19.

w. 1 Corinthians 5:7.

on the holy mount, he asked the Lord to declare His name so that he might properly identify God for the children of Israel. In response God said, "I AM THAT I AM," and He said, "Thus shalt thou say unto the children of Israel, I AM hath sent me unto you."[a] During His earthly ministry Jesus used this name as His own, declaring to the unbelieving Jews, "Before Abraham was, I am,"[b][32] thus attesting to His divinity and revealing His identity to them. He was the same God that had communicated with Adam after the Garden of Eden and with all of the prophets: Abraham, Isaac, Jacob, Moses, Isaiah, Jeremiah, Zechariah, and others—a fact that Paul also attested to when (speaking of those who lived during the time of Moses) he declared to the Corinthians that they "drank of that spiritual Rock that followed them: and that Rock was Christ."[c]

The Jewish leadership of Christ's day understood His claim. They knew that He was claiming to be the great Jehovah, God of the Old Testament, and in their anger and disgust they took "up stones to cast at Him."[d]

It is the unqualified conviction of The Church of Jesus Christ of Latter-day Saints that Jehovah, God of the Old Testament, is and was Jesus Christ. "He was chosen and ordained to be the Savior of the unborn race of mortals, and Redeemer of a world then in its formative stages of development." He was "the God at whose instance the prophets of the ages have spoken, the God of all nations, and He who shall yet reign on earth as King of kings and Lord of lords," even Jesus the Messiah.[33]

a. Exodus 3:14.

b. John 8:58.

c. 1 Corinthians 10:4.

d. John 8:59.

"And the Word Was Made Flesh"

2

Galilee

In the days of King David, Galilee consisted of a circle of twenty cities in the circuit from Kedesh to Naphtali. Hiram, the king of Tyre, had made a peaceful alliance with David and had supplied him with artisans and timber for the palace and the temple at Jerusalem. Because of his services, Solomon, David's son, gave Hiram these twenty cities. But Hiram did not like the cities and called them "Cabul,"[a] which meant "disgusting."[34] Perhaps this designation and the fact that the area readily associated itself geographically with a mixed population and with heathens destined the people of Galilee to be despised by their fellow Israelites, particularly the Judeans.

The Galileans were looked upon with contempt not only for their association with heathens but for their less educated dialect and their lack of culture.[35] "The people of Galilee were especially blamed for neglecting the study of their language, charged with errors of grammar, and especially with absurd malpronunciation [sic], sometimes leading to ridiculous mistakes."[36]

Three caravan trade routes passed through Palestine at the time of Christ, one of them through Nazareth where He made His early home. While Galilee was not the home of Rabbinism, its inhabitants were "of generous spirits, of warm, impulsive hearts, of intense nationalism, of simple manners, and of earnest piety."[37]

Anciently, Galilee contained the possessions of the tribes of Issachar, Zebulun, Naphtali, and Asher; but at the time of Christ it stretched beyond those boundaries and bordered Tyre and Syria to the

a. 1 Kings 9:11–13.

north and Samaria to the south. Mount Carmel formed the western boundary, and the Jordan River and the Lake of Gennesaret the eastern.[38] It was a rich, fertile area and well cultivated.[39] Although this was perhaps exaggerated, it was reputed to be thickly populated, with as many as 240 towns and villages with not less than fifteen thousand inhabitants in each of them.[40]

Galilee was a gathering place or "priest-centre" for temple service[41]—a place of rich plains, luxuriant vegetation, fountains and rivers, and richly wooded hills.[42] Although the inhabitants were generally looked down upon and were not participants of the rabbinic schools of Judea, they remained a thoroughly Jewish people.

Nestled in the mountains of lower Galilee and surrounded by fifteen hilltops that almost formed an amphitheater was the hamlet of Nazareth.[43] This community marked the northern boundary of ancient Zebulun and just beyond it stretched the seemingly unbounded expanse of the Plain of Esdraelon, the site of numerous battles in ancient Israel. It was a provincial village in a despised province of a conquered land, and in this obscure setting the long-awaited Messiah of the world made His home from the time of His return from Egypt until He entered His public ministry.

What Messiah Did the Jews Expect?

The Talmud states, "All the prophets prophesied only of the days of the Messiah," and "The world was created only for the Messiah."[44] Generally speaking, the whole of the Old Testament had become the perspective from which the Messianic expectation was envisioned.

It does not appear from the Gospel narratives that the leaders of the Jews took particular exception to Christ's fulfillment of individual prophecies relating to His claim to the Messiahship, but their general perception of the Messiah completely differed from what Jesus actually represented.[45] Therein lay the seeds for the Jews' rejection of Him. Their anticipated Messiah was to perform "all the miracles and deliverances of Israel's past . . . only in a much wider manner." Thus, the Old Testament was "the glass, through which the universal blessings of the latter days [the days of the Messiah] were seen."[46]

Israel was intensely interested in the restoration of its former glory, and the Messiah was the "grand instrument" they anticipated that would make it possible for them to attain that goal. He was to be Israel's "exultation, rather than . . . the salvation of the world."[47] This purely political Messianic expectation was scarcely referred to by Jesus, and He deliberately separated Himself from the popular Messianic beliefs and ideas of His time.[48]

It was to a people drunk with the vision of outward felicity and political greatness that Jesus came, and while some—such as Zacharias, Elisabeth, Mary, Anna, Simeon, and John the Baptist —heeded the coming of the Messiah's kingdom in its spiritual purity, the general belief was that He would come to restore the "splendour of the Jewish throne."[49] He would be a great prince who would found a great kingdom, a human hero who would lead Israel to victory and subdue all nations. Some even taught that "He would not know that He was the Messiah till Elias came . . . and anointed Him."[50]

The universal kingdom of the anticipated Messiah would be an earthly paradise where "all the trees [would] bear continually. A single grape [would] load a wagon or a ship, and when it [was] brought to the house they [would] draw wine from it as from a cask. . . . The country round [would] be full of pearls and precious stones, so that Jews from all parts may come and take of them as they like."[51]

The Jews attached great mystery to the Messiah's birth and superhuman character traits to His mission.[52] Is it any wonder that the rabbinic tradition found no place for Jesus as the Messiah? Jesus so completely separated Himself from all of these ideas that there "was in such a Messiah [as Jesus] absolutely nothing—past, present, or possible; intellectually, religiously, or even nationally —to attract, but all to repel."[53] For the Messiah to be born to a virgin of Galilee who was betrothed to a humble carpenter would have been a caricature of the Jewish Messianic expectation, both unimaginable and unacceptable to the majority of the Jews of His day.

The details of Christ's birth, as described in Matthew and Luke, were contrary to the traditional and historical Jewish Messianic expectations, nor would their belief and interpretation of the Old Testament have corresponded to His simple advent.[54] Isaiah, the great prophet of old, had foreseen Israel's decay for century after century so marked with turmoil and change that he could only describe the humble citizen of Nazareth, the heir to the throne of Israel, as a "root out of a dry ground."[a]

a. Isaiah 53:2.

Joseph and Mary

Luke 1:26–35   And in the sixth month the angel Gabriel was sent from God unto a city of Galilee, named Nazareth, to a virgin espoused to a man whose name was Joseph, of the house of David; and the virgin's name was Mary. And the angel came in unto her, and said, Hail, thou that art highly favoured, the Lord is with thee: blessed art thou among women. And when she saw him, she was troubled at his saying, and cast in her mind what manner of salutation this should be. And the angel said unto her, Fear not, Mary: for thou hast found favour with God. And, behold, thou shalt conceive in thy womb, and bring forth a son, and shalt call his name JESUS. He shall be great, and shall be called the Son of the Highest: and the Lord God shall give unto Him the throne of his father David: and he shall reign over the house of Jacob for ever; and of his kingdom there shall be no end. Then said Mary unto the angel, How shall this be, seeing I know not a man? And the angel answered and said unto her, The Holy Ghost shall come upon thee, and the power of the Highest shall overshadow thee: therefore also that holy thing which shall be born of thee shall be called the Son of God.

Cross-references   Luke 1:36–80; Luke 2:1–20; Matthew 1:18–25; Helaman 14:2; 3 Nephi 1:9, 12–21

Three months had passed since the angel Gabriel visited Zacharias in the temple and told him of the forthcoming birth of John, the forerunner of the Messiah (Chapter 3). While he and Elisabeth rejoiced at their home in the south, a hundred miles to the north in the village of Nazareth lived a just man (and a strict observer of the Law) named Joseph.[55]

Joseph was betrothed to a young Jewish maiden (perhaps only fifteen years of age)[56] named Mary. He was a carpenter by trade, and both he and Mary were poor[57] even though they were descendants of the royal house of David.[58]

Christ has two genealogies recorded in the New Testament: one in Matthew and one in Luke. There are some discrepancies between the two. Whether the genealogies are considered those of Joseph and Mary[59] or whether they are both considered that of Joseph (which is the most accepted view),[60] it is still evident that both of their lines descended from the royal house. It is generally thought that Matthew's account is that of Joseph's royal lineage and that Luke's genealogy is his pedigree. Further, it is generally accepted that Joseph and Mary were cousins, one a descendant of Jacob and the other of Heli (brothers in the royal lineage).[61]

Jesus readily accepted the title "Son of David" denoting His royal lineage,[a] a fact which Paul later confirmed several times.[b] Further, of all the accusations laid against Jesus by His enemies, no mention or insinuation is given that He was not of the royal line.[62] The genealogies of the Jews were assiduously cared for,[63] and the Lord's enemies would have quickly made such an accusation if they could.

From the limited information we have about Joseph, it is evident that he was the rightful heir to the throne of Israel. Therefore, because he and Mary were cousins, both descending from King David, Jesus was by birth the King of the Jews.

In those days, a betrothal was considered as binding as marriage. Once the betrothal was sealed with the customary prayer (and perhaps the statutory cup of wine tasted first by Joseph and then by Mary), the relationship was considered sacred, "as if they had already been wedded."[64] "The betrothal was formally made, with rejoicing, in the house of the bride, under a tent or slight canopy raised for the purpose. It was called 'making sacred,' as the bride, thenceforth, was sacred to her husband, in the strictest sense."[65] To make the betrothal legal, Joseph would have given His "betrothed a piece of money, or the worth of it, before witnesses."[66] The betrothal could be sealed either by solemn word of mouth or in a formal writing.[67] "Though betrothal was virtually marriage, and could only be broken off by a formal 'bill of divorcement,' the betrothed did not at once go to her husband's house . . . an interval elapsed before the final ceremony; [which] might be so many weeks, or months, or even a whole year."[68] There were two ways to annul a betrothal, both of which were akin to divorce. The first was by public trial and judgment, and the second was by a private agreement which was written and signed in the presence of witnesses.[69]

This was the condition of the relationship between Joseph and Mary, the unwed wife and virgin mother to be, when the angel Gabriel appeared. The time of day of the angelic visit is not given in the scriptures. However, as a devout Jewess knowing the Law, Mary would have been dutiful to her daily prayers: which occurred at the morning offering, at the noon hour, and at the evening sacrifice. Perhaps it was at one of these times that the angel Gabriel made his appearance.[70]

We can assume that Mary was personally worthy of his visit because of the salutation the angel gave her. The anticipated Messiah was not

a. Matthew 9:27; 15:22; 21:9; 20:30–31; Luke 18:38–39.

b. Romans 1:3; 2 Timothy 2:8; Acts 2:29–30; 13:22–23; Psalm 132:11; Luke 1:32.

an abstract belief, it was considered a matter of certain fact;[71] and Mary certainly would have known that some Jewish maiden of the royal line was yet to become the mother of Christ.[72] Her apparent bewilderment and surprise was not because Israel's great hope, the coming of the long-awaited Messiah, would now be fulfilled, but that it would be fulfilled through her. The angel greeted Mary with a well-known salutation[73] and revealed the great blessing that had been given her.

There was no hesitation in her response to the angel—her question merely voiced concern for her unwed status. "How shall this be, seeing I know not a man?" she asked. The angel answered by announcing the birth of the coming Savior. That birth would not be contrary to natural law but it would also involve a higher law, for the Father of the Savior of the world would be Elohim,[74] thus giving Christ the combined powers of Godhood and mortality.[75] The promise given by the Father to Adam and Eve (that through the seed of the woman Satan's head would be crushed) was about to be fulfilled.[a] The promised Savior, the Redeemer who could overcome Satan's power, was about to be born into mortality.

Mary was troubled. Her understanding of the significance of the event was as yet unclear. She "like all her nation [would have] thought of the Messiah as a Jewish king who should restore the long-lost glories of her race, and make Israel triumphant over all the heathen."[76] This belief would have been contradicted by the reality of His birth, for He was to be born as all mortals have been born—a mere babe that would grow from childhood to adulthood.[77] "It is apparent that the great truth as to the personality and mission of her divine Son had not yet unfolded itself in its fulness to her mind. The whole course of events, from the salutation of Gabriel to the reverent testimony of the shepherds concerning the announcing angel and the heavenly hosts, was largely a mystery to that stainless mother and wife."[78] The "almost universal belief was that He (the Messiah) was to be simply a man, who would receive miraculous endowments, on His formal consecration as Messiah."[79]

Mary's confusion apparently continued even as her divine Son was recognizing His mission, for she was obviously perplexed at His answer when she rebuked Him at the age of twelve for staying behind at the temple following a visit to Jerusalem.[b] When He became an adult she

a. Genesis 3:15.

b. Luke
   2:48–50.

evidently misunderstood how His personal powers were to be used, for He mildly rebuked her when she implied that He should change water into wine.[a] She and His immediate family apparently continued to misunderstand His mission[b] and maintained the traditional view of the anticipated Messiah well into His ministry.[c] Her realization of His position and power seemed to grow slowly through the years, just as it did for His disciples,[d] This may have been due to the fact that the "preoccupation of the mind by fixed opinions, leads to a wrong reading of any evidence. We unconsciously distort facts, or invent them, to support our favourite theories, and see everything through their medium."[80] The evidence of the scriptures would indicate that Mary never seemed "to have fully understood her Son; at every new evidence of His uniqueness she marvelled and pondered anew."[81]

Mary had been told by the angel that her firstborn son was the Son of God, yet it would apparently be many years before she would even partially realize the importance of these words. Even the mother of the Savior of all mankind had to be led step by step to a final comprehension of His majesty just as she, as his mother, had to lead Him step by step to maturity.[82]

To Elisabeth and Bethlehem

Luke 1:36–56   And, behold, thy cousin Elisabeth, she hath also conceived a son in her old age: and this is the sixth month with her, who was called barren. For with God nothing shall be impossible. And Mary said, Behold the handmaid of the Lord; be it unto me according to thy word. And the angel departed from her. And Mary arose in those days, and went into the hill country with haste, into a city of Juda; and entered into the house of Zacharias, and saluted Elisabeth. And it came to pass, that, when Elisabeth heard the salutation of Mary, the babe leaped in her womb; and Elisabeth was filled with the Holy Ghost: and she spake out with a loud voice, and said, Blessed art thou among women, and blessed is the fruit of thy womb. And whence is this to me, that the mother of my Lord should come to me? For, lo, as soon as the voice of thy salutation sounded in mine ears, the babe leaped in my womb for joy. And blessed is she that believed: for there shall be a performance of those things which were told her from the Lord. And Mary said, My soul doth magnify the Lord, And my spirit hath rejoiced in God my Saviour. For he hath regarded the low estate of his handmaiden: for, behold, from henceforth all generations shall call me blessed. For he that is mighty hath done to me great things; and holy is his name. And his mercy is on them that fear him from generation to generation. He hath shewed strength with his arm; he hath scattered the proud in the imagination of their hearts. He hath put down the mighty from their seats, and exalted them of low degree. He hath filled the

a. John 2:3–4.

b. Mark 3:21, 31–32.

c. John 7:1–8.

d. Luke 24:13–25.

hungry with good things; and the rich he hath sent empty away. He hath holpen his servant Israel, in remembrance of his mercy; as he spake to our fathers, to Abraham, and to his seed for ever. And Mary abode with her about three months, and returned to her own house.

The angel Gabriel told Mary that her cousin Elisabeth had also been blessed by the Lord and had conceived a son in her old age.[83] With haste, Mary departed to visit Elisabeth to share in the joy extended to her formerly barren cousin and to tell her of the blessing she herself had received from God. The angel had informed Mary that Elisabeth was in her sixth month of pregnancy. Undoubtedly, Elisabeth would have learned from Zacharias about the future calling of her yet unborn son and the near advent of the Messiah. However, it is equally apparent that she did not know (nor did Zacharias) when the Messiah would arrive or of whom He would be born.[84]

The Holy Ghost had moved upon Mary to prepare her for Gabriel's visit and for the conception of the Son of God, and He would now move upon Elisabeth and the yet unborn John to testify to them of that miraculous occurrence. Such activity by the Holy Ghost among the Jews was quite familiar in Israel at the time,[85] so Mary made haste to join her cousin Elisabeth.

In all probability, Mary had told no one of the miraculous occurrence that had taken place,[86] and through her visit to Elisabeth both women would gain further understanding and testimony of the anticipated Messiah and His forerunner. The scriptures testify that upon Mary's arrival, both Elisabeth and her yet unborn son were filled with the Holy Ghost. The child leapt within her womb as a sign and testimony of the coming Messiah. This also was an experience not strange to the Jewish expectancy.[87] Elisabeth's salutation to Mary was prophetic, for she recognized that Mary was the chosen mother of the Messiah and that she, Elisabeth, carried the child that would be His forerunner, a man whom the Christ would acclaim with the words, "Among those that are born of women there is not a greater prophet than John the Baptist."[a]

Mary's response was poetic and "the rhythmical expression into which she falls was only what might have been expected from one imbued, as all Jewish minds were, with the style and imagery of the Old Testament."[88] After Elisabeth had praised Mary and her yet unborn

a. Luke 7:28.

son, Mary sang a song of praise to God in response to the salutation given her. This song was much like the songs women in Old Testament days had sung in times of joy: for example, Miriam at the crossing of the Red Sea,[a] Deborah when she saved Israel from Sisera,[b] and Hannah when she took the boy Samuel to Eli.[c] The poem was undoubtedly spontaneous and echoes the prophets and saints she had become familiar with through the imagery and language of the Old Testament. It testifies that she was well trained in the knowledge of the scriptures and gives a further indication of the spirit with which her sacred child would be trained.[89]

Mary stayed with Elisabeth until it was almost time for John to be born, then she returned to her home in Nazareth. When Joseph learned of her condition he pondered how best he could dissolve the betrothal; and rather than humiliate Mary with a public trial, which was one option, he "was minded to put her away privily."[d]

Joseph's actions on this matter support the scriptural description of him as a just man. But before he could carry out his intent, an angel appeared to him in a dream and testified of the divine parentage of Mary's child. To the Jews of that day, "a good dream was . . . regarded as [a] mark of God's favour."[90] Consequently, Joseph was well disposed to receive the message that came in that manner. With the testimony of God's divine Son confirmed, Joseph married Mary immediately so that no shame would come upon her.

Perhaps it was the intention of Joseph and Mary to remain in Nazareth after their marriage, but just as the circumstances surrounding the conception of the Messiah were beyond their control so, too, were the circumstances that would make Bethlehem Christ's birthplace.[91]

Augustus, ruler of the Roman Empire, ordered an enrollment or census of all the Empire's provinces so that he might "know the number of soldiers he could levy in each, and the amount of taxes due to the treasury."[92] In all probability this census took years to complete, and in Judea it was undoubtedly left to Herod (as it would have been to all the rulers of the individual provinces) to determine exactly how to accomplish the count.[93] Because of this, in the Roman province of Judea the citizens did not enroll their names at the town of their residence as the Romans did, but pursuant to Jewish custom they filed their registration in the ancestral home of their ancient or family

a. Exodus 15:20–21.

b. Judges 5.

c. 1 Samuel 2:1–10.

d. Matthew 1:19.

tribes.[94] Joseph and Mary were of the lineage of David; therefore, they had to leave the mountains of Zebulun and travel some eighty miles along crisscrossed roads and paths that ran through many towns and cities and across the Plain of Esdraelon before they reached the city of David—Bethlehem.

The journey could have taken up to a week, but no details of the trip are given in the scriptures. When they arrived in Bethlehem, they had to search for shelter because the town was excessively crowded with those who had also come to register. The inns were full and the only available space was a cattle stable.[95] Such a place was not necessarily degrading, but in all probability was "half kitchen and half stable, which was simply one of the countless natural hollows or caves in the hill-side, against which the house had been built."[96] The hospitality of such a place was offered willingly as a religious merit with the rabbinical promise of paradise as its reward.[97]

Thus, the lovely Mary, lodged on hay and straw in a limestone grotto only a few miles from the splendor of Herod's palace (but far from her home and amidst strangers, in circumstances devoid of all earthly comfort and splendor) gave birth to the Lord Jesus Christ.

The hope of Israel had come! The promise of God, made unto the fathers, had been fulfilled! It was the event that all of Israel had earnestly sought for in their prayers and had painstakingly integrated into almost every event and activity in their lives.[98] The Sacred Child was born a Jew, His true paternity known to few, for He was regarded as the son of Joseph of Nazareth.[a] The narrative of His birth and the events surrounding it are so simple and lacking in detail that it is apparent the Gospel writers had no intention of providing a biography of Jesus Christ; their sole purpose was to witness His divinity and generate belief in Him.

The Testimony of Shepherds

Luke 2:8–20   And there were in the same country shepherds abiding in the field, keeping watch over their flock by night. And, lo, the angel of the Lord came upon them, and the glory of the Lord shone round about them: and they were sore afraid. And the angel said unto them, Fear not: for, behold, I bring you good tidings of great joy, which shall be to all people. For unto you is born this day in the city of David a Saviour, which is Christ the Lord. And this shall be a sign unto you; Ye shall find the babe wrapped in swaddling clothes, lying in a manger. And suddenly

a. Luke 4:22;
   Matthew 13:55;
   Mark 6:3.

there was with the angel a multitude of the heavenly host praising God, and saying, Glory to God in the highest, and on earth peace, good will toward men. And it
came to pass, as the angels were gone away from them into heaven, the shepherds
said one to another, Let us now go even unto Bethlehem, and see this thing which is
come to pass, which the Lord hath made known unto us. And they came with haste,
and found Mary, and Joseph, and the babe lying in a manger. And when they had
seen it, they made known abroad the saying which was told them concerning this
child. And all they that heard it wondered at those things which were told them by
the shepherds. But Mary kept all these things, and pondered them in her heart. And
the shepherds returned, glorifying and praising God for all the things that they had
heard and seen, as it was told unto them.

Immediately after recounting the birth of the Savior, Luke tells
us of the divine witness received by the shepherds. Bethlehem was
an agrarian area[99] so it was not uncommon to find shepherds on the
hillsides tending their flocks. The biblical record gives no indication
of the time of year in which Jesus was born. Some have pictured it
during the chilly nights of winter;[100] others think it occurred in the
early spring.[101] The flocks tended by the shepherds were probably not
those of the common people but were more likely temple flocks. The
temple shepherds would have been in the fields year round to provide
sheep for the many temple ceremonies.[102]

Although His birth was practically unnoticed by mortals, the
heavens openly rejoiced at the Savior's advent. On the slopes and
heights of the hills surrounding Bethlehem, the shepherds heard and
saw the heavenly hosts celebrate that birth with hallelujah praises
and song. The shepherds had neither asked for nor anticipated these
signs—but they were blessed to receive them. And when they were
told to go and see the newborn child for themselves, they went in
haste, their hearts in tune to receive this great blessing.[103] They confirmed the angels' testimony when they witnessed the babe lying in a
manger; thereafter, they spread abroad all that they had both seen and
heard.[a] They undoubtedly told those in the inn and the residents of
the countryside; they also possibly told it to those who worked in the
temple area when they delivered their flocks for the sacrifices. Perhaps
their message was instrumental in preparing the minds of Simeon and
Anna for the witness they, too, would bear.[104]

a. Luke 2:17.

Another Testament of His Birth

Five years before the birth of Christ occurred on the Eastern Hemisphere, another people an ocean away in a choice land were being testified to by Samuel the Lamanite about the coming birth of Him who would provide their means of salvation. These people were also of the house of Israel and through six hundred years of varying degrees of righteousness and wickedness they, too, had been looking forward to the Savior's advent. Now, five years before Christ's birth, the Nephite people in the Americas were in a state of wickedness, and Samuel was prophesying and warning them about what was to come. He stood upon a wall and testified to them of their exceeding wickedness and the need for repentance. He gave them a sign of the coming Messiah. He told them that five years hence there would be a day, a night, and a day without darkness, and this miracle would occur at the time of Christ's birth.[a]

As the time approached, the wickedness of the people increased and the prophet Nephi longed for the day when the sign would occur. The wicked also began to keep track of the time, but for a different reason—they threatened that if the sign did not take place by a certain day they would put to death all the members of the church who believed.[b]

Nephi prayed fervently that the time might be made known and the Saints' lives spared. While he was praying, a voice from heaven declared that that night the sign would be given and the next day the Savior of the world would be born.[c] As the sun set and the day ended, darkness did not creep in—the land remained light as if it were noonday. This strange phenomenon continued all through the nocturnal hours until the sun again rose. As morning dawned, the Nephites and the Lamanites knew that the Redeemer, the Light of the World, had come; the testimony had been given to the Western Hemisphere as promised.[d]

In Compliance with the Law

Luke 2:21–24   And when eight days were accomplished for the circumcising of the child, His name was called JESUS, which was so named of the angel before he was conceived in the womb. And when the days of her purification according to the law of Moses were accomplished, they brought Him to Jerusalem, to present Him to the Lord; (as it is written in the law of the Lord, Every male that openeth the womb shall be called holy to the Lord;) and to offer a sacrifice according to that which is said in the law of the Lord, A pair of turtledoves, or two young pigeons.

a. Helaman 14:2–5.

b. 3 Nephi 1:5–9.

c. 3 Nephi 1:11–13.

d. 3 Nephi 1:15–19.

Although we do not know how long Joseph and Mary remained in Bethlehem, as devout Jews they would have at least stayed long enough to comply with the requirements of the Levitical Law.

The first of these requirements (the ceremonial ritual of circumcision) was complied with eight days after the birth of the Savior. It was at this ceremony that He received the given name of Jesus. Jesus is the English translation or modification of the Hebrew name Joshua, which means "salvation is Jehovah."[105] The name represented His office and in Hebrew literally meant "the Messiah" (in Greek, "the Christ").[106] It was not necessary to attend the temple for a circumcision ceremony because any rabbi could perform it; however, being so close to the temple, Joseph and Mary probably took the babe there for the ceremony.[107]

Through the act of circumcision and the ceremony surrounding it, the infant Jesus was acknowledged as an Israelite. This represented "voluntary subjection to the conditions of the Law, and acceptance of the obligations, but also of the privileges, of the Covenant between God and Abraham and his seed."[108]

This circumcision ceremony is the first of only four events in Jesus' infancy that we are told about in the scriptures. The second and third events may have occurred at the same time. The Savior was the firstborn son of Mary, and in accordance with the second requirement of the Law,[a] He had to be "redeemed" from His required service in the temple. The earliest this redemption could have taken place was thirty-one days after His birth, but it may have been that Mary waited until her purification time was completed before fulfilling the redemption requirement.

In order for a firstborn son to be redeemed from temple service, neither the father nor the mother could be of Levitical descent, and the child must be free from any and all bodily blemishes that would have disqualified Him for normal priesthood service.[109] It also required a payment of five temple shekels (less if the family was poor)[110] in compliance with the Law of Moses.[b] Again, temple attendance was not required for this since any priest could have performed the redemption ceremony.

The third event that took place was Mary's purification.[c] The Law required that forty-one days must elapse after the birth of a son before purification could take place. (The period was eighty-one days after

a. Numbers 18:16.

b. Exodus 13:13; 34:20; Numbers 18:15–16.

c. Leviticus 12:4.

the birth of a daughter.)[111] The purification ceremony could be delayed until later—on any of the feast days—for the mother was not required to attend the temple. But Mary, a devout Jewess, attended the temple for her purification and took her son with her to be redeemed.[112]

The service was considered a statutory sacrifice, and the legal purification was performed in the court of the women soon after the morning incense had been offered.[113] The sacrifice consisted of presenting two offerings to the Lord. Normally, this consisted of a yearling lamb as the burnt offering and a young pigeon or turtledove as the sin offering, both of which were required by the Law.[a] Although Joseph was a carpenter by trade, the offerings presented by Mary were those that the poor could offer in substitution for the more costly offerings. Mary's offerings consisted of two turtledoves or two young pigeons, which again the Law allowed.[b]

The offerings probably were purchased in the yard areas around the temple courts. To ensure that the public did not notice whether the offerings were the normal animals or the less expensive ones, the purchase money was deposited in the appropriate trumpet-shaped chest in the treasury (where the thirteen chests stood for contributions in the Court of the Women).[114] The priests then made the sacrifices, not knowing who the sacrifices belonged to and thus ensuring anonymity and sparing possible embarrassment to the person offering the sacrifice.

Once the ceremony commenced (but before the offering was completed), the participants for purification were found in the court of the women praying to God for their recovery. "After a time, a priest came with some of the blood [of the offering], and, having sprinkled them with it, pronounced them clean, and thus the rite ended."[115] Mary was now Levitically clean and could partake of sacred offerings.[116]

Simeon and Anna

Luke 2:25–38   And, behold, there was a man in Jerusalem, whose name was Simeon; and the same man was just and devout, waiting for the consolation of Israel: and the Holy Ghost was upon him. And it was revealed unto him by the Holy Ghost, that he should not see death, before he had seen the Lord's Christ. And he came by the Spirit into the temple: and when the parents brought in the child Jesus, to do for him after the custom of the law, then took he him up in his arms, and blessed God, and said, Lord, now lettest thou thy servant depart in peace, according to thy word: for mine eyes have seen thy salvation, which thou hast prepared before the face of all

a. Leviticus 12:1–8; Numbers 18:16.

b. Leviticus 12:6–8.

people; a light to lighten the Gentiles, and the glory of thy people Israel. And Joseph and his mother marvelled at those things which were spoken of him. And Simeon blessed them, and said unto Mary his mother, Behold, this child is set for the fall and rising again of many in Israel; and for a sign which shall be spoken against; (yea, a sword shall pierce through thy own soul also,) that the thoughts of many hearts may be revealed. And there was one Anna, a prophetess, the daughter of Phanuel, of the tribe of Aser: she was of a great age, and had lived with an husband seven years from her virginity; and she was a widow of about fourscore and four years, which departed not from the temple, but served God with fastings and prayers night and day. And she coming in that instant gave thanks likewise unto the Lord, and spake of him to all them that looked for redemption in Jerusalem.

The fourth event described in Jesus' infancy also took place during Mary's purification and her babe's redemption. Simeon, who had been prompted by the Spirit to come to the temple, met Joseph and Mary there.[a] The New Testament records no prior History for Simeon. We know only that he was an old and devout man who had been promised by the Spirit that he would not die until he had seen the Savior of the world. His heart's longing was now fulfilled, and he recognized in the baby Jesus the long-awaited Messiah. Taking the child in his arms, he broke into song and prophesied.

He first praised God and gave thanks for the fulfillment of his promised blessing. He praised Christ as "a light to lighten the Gentiles, and the glory of thy people Israel,"[b] which indicated that he had a correct understanding of the Messiah's future mission and did not totally subscribe to the contemporary Judaic belief.[117] His appearance and actions filled Joseph and Mary with wonder and they marveled at his words. Simeon next blessed Mary and Joseph, then he continued to prophesy that Jesus was the stone, the foundation, and the cornerstone upon which all would fall or rise up.[c][118] He closed his astonishing interruption of their temple visit with the promise that the Savior's mission would cause deep sorrow in Mary's heart.

Luke (who undoubtedly received his information from Mary)[119] records that upon completion of Simeon's praise, a woman named Anna appeared, a prophetess of the tribe of Asher. She had been a widow for many years. Because her tribal genealogy had been preserved (even though her tribe was numbered among those that were lost), she apparently came from a family of some distinction.[120]

a. Luke 2:25–27.

b. Luke 2:32.

c. Isaiah 8:14.

It seems probable that Anna, like Simeon, had been promised that she would see and recognize the "redemption" of Israel. The scriptures note that she had spent many long years in the temple fasting, praying, and awaiting that redemption. Mary and Joseph may have marveled at Anna's testimony as they had Simeon's, but the scriptures are silent on their reaction. Their wonder concerning their child only emphasized the fact that they did not yet understand "the magnitude and glory of his mortal ministry and the greatness of the work he would do among men"—although such would "dawn upon them gradually."[121]

With the conclusion of the stories of Simeon and Anna, Luke's description of Christ's infancy ends.

The Magi and Herod the Great

Matthew 2:1–23   Now when Jesus was born in Bethlehem of Judaea in the days of Herod the king, behold, there came wise men from the east to Jerusalem, saying, Where is he that is born King of the Jews? for we have seen his star in the east, and are come to worship him. When Herod the king had heard these things, he was troubled, and all Jerusalem with him. And when he had gathered all the chief priests and scribes of the people together, he demanded of them where Christ should be born. And they said unto him, In Bethlehem of Judaea: for thus it is written by the prophet, and thou Bethlehem, in the land of Juda, art not the least among the princes of Juda: for out of thee shall come a Governor, that shall rule my people Israel. Then Herod, when he had privily called the wise men, enquired of them diligently what time the star appeared. And he sent them to Bethlehem, and said, Go and search diligently for the young child; and when ye have found him, bring me word again, that I may come and worship him also. When they had heard the king, they departed; and, lo, the star, which they saw in the east, went before them, till it came and stood over where the young child was. When they saw the star, they rejoiced with exceeding great joy.

And when they were come into the house, they saw the young child with Mary his mother, and fell down, and worshipped him: and when they had opened their treasures, they presented unto him gifts; gold, and frankincense, and myrrh. And being warned of God in a dream that they should not return to Herod, they departed into their own country another way. And when they were departed, behold, the angel of the Lord appeareth to Joseph in a dream, saying, Arise, and take the young child and his mother, and flee into Egypt, and be thou there until I bring thee word: for Herod will seek the young child to destroy him. When he arose, he took the young child and his mother by night, and departed into Egypt: and was there until the death of Herod: that it might be fulfilled which was spoken of the Lord by the prophet, saying, Out of Egypt have I called my son.

Then Herod, when he saw that he was mocked of the wise men, was exceeding wroth, and sent forth, and slew all the children that were in Bethlehem, and in all the coasts thereof, from two years old and under, according to the time which he had diligently enquired of the wise men. Then was fulfilled that which was spoken by Jeremy the prophet, saying, In Rama was there a voice heard, lamentation, and weeping, and great mourning, Rachel weeping for her children, and would not be comforted, because they are not.

But when Herod was dead, behold, an angel of the Lord appeareth in a dream to Joseph in Egypt, saying, Arise, and take the young child and his mother, and go into the land of Israel: for they are dead which sought the young child's life. And he arose, and took the young child and his mother, and came into the land of Israel. But when he heard that Archelaus did reign in Judaea in the room of his father Herod, he was afraid to go thither: notwithstanding, being warned of God in a dream, he turned aside into the parts of Galilee: and he came and dwelt in a city called Nazareth: that it might be fulfilled which was spoken by the prophets, he shall be called a Nazarene.

While Luke recorded Israel's homage to the Messiah through his description of the early events in Jesus' life, Matthew recorded the homage of the Gentiles through the visit of the magi. As in Luke, Matthew records no specific time concerning the visit of the magi (or wise men), but by the time of their visit, Joseph and Mary undoubtedly were no longer living in the cattle stable and had probably moved into a home in Bethlehem.[122]

The descriptive word _magi_ (identified in the King James Version of the Bible as "wise men") was a common word at the time the Savior was born and had been used in the Septuagint and later by Josephus both in an evil and in a good sense.[123]

In its evil sense it denoted persons who practiced magical arts, whereas the good sense generally referred to the eastern priest-sages (especially Chaldean) who were revered as having deep knowledge and understanding (even though their knowledge was tinged with superstition).[124] _Magi_ may also have referred to a sect of Median and Persian scholars[125] or to pretended astrologers or soothsayers.

The exact number of magi described in the New Testament story cannot be ascertained, but is generally thought of as being three from the number of gifts presented to the Christ child.

The magi began their journey to visit the newborn king because they saw a new star in the heavens. A star had also been prophesied in the Western Hemisphere,[a] and the sign appeared at some time after the "night without darkness" that also occurred at the Savior's birth[b] Likewise, there is no evidence in the New Testament as to when the star

a. Helaman 14:5.

b. 3 Nephi 1:21.

first appeared in the heavens, only that upon their arrival in Jerusalem the magi asked Herod, "Where is he that is born King of the Jews? for we have seen his star in the east, and are come to worship him."[a] How long it took them to reach Jerusalem from their unknown origin in the east is not known, but they had witnessed the new star in the heavens and had regarded that star as a token of the birth of the Messiah who would be the King of the Jews.[126]

They may have begun their journey prior to the Savior's advent so that they could arrive shortly after His birth. However, the star may have appeared at the same time as the Savior's birth which would have resulted in a later arrival.[127] Whichever the case, upon their arrival in Jerusalem they immediately went to Herod's palace to gain information about the holy babe.[128] In their simplicity, they sought information from the leader of the very nation that they believed the new king was destined to rule. Although Herod was king in Israel and sat upon the throne of David, he was not of the David's lineage. He was a descendant of Ishmael through Esau and an Idumaean by birth.[129]

Herod received the magi courteously even though the information they presented to him must have filled him with suspicion and apprehension, for the new king presented a danger to his throne.[130] The magi's inquiry was made known throughout Jerusalem and the scriptures report that the people were "troubled"— perhaps concerning the report of the newborn king, but more likely from their fear of Herod's reaction to the threat to his throne.[131]

Herod responded to the magi's questions with his usual cunning when he called a council of the priests and scribes. He did not inform them that their anticipated Messiah had already been born, but merely inquired of them where the birthplace would be.

At the time of Herod, it was the general opinion that Bethlehem would be the Messiah's birthplace;[b][132] so Herod directed the magi to that city. He asked them to return and tell him if they found the babe so that he might also pay homage to the newborn king. Finally, he inquired when the magi had first seen the new star.[c]

After they departed from Herod, the star again appeared and the magi rejoiced at seeing it for apparently they had not seen it for some time.[133] Certainly they did not need the star to direct them to Bethlehem, so it would seem that the star appeared as a testimony

a. Matthew 2:2;
   Numbers
   24:17.

b. Micah 5:2.

c. Matthew 2:7.

to them that Bethlehem was indeed the birthplace of the king they sought.[134] The star seemed to move before them until "it stood over where the young child was—that is, of course, over Bethlehem, not over any special house in it."[135]

Once in Bethlehem, they discovered the location of the infant king; but no information is given as to how this was accomplished. The scriptures give no detail concerning the magi's visit to the Savior except to note that they paid homage by worshipping Him and giving Him the gifts of gold, frankincense, and myrrh.[136]

Herod had requested that the magi return and tell him of the location of the new king of the Jews. But because his intentions were evil, the magi were warned in a dream not to return to Herod and left instead for their own country. They had come out of scriptural obscurity for their brief visit, and they returned to it after the visit was completed.

When Herod realized that the magi had departed without returning to him, he became "exceedingly wroth." Their arrival and their story of the newborn king gave Herod a fresh cause for jealousy and fear. He wanted to kill the child as he had killed others who were a threat to His throne, for Herod's rule had continuously been one of revolting cruelty and unbridled oppression.[137]

With the departure of the magi, Herod had no means of identifying the infant child or of learning His exact date of birth; but he was determined to slay this pretender to the throne. Left to his own cunning and based upon his conversation with the wise men, Herod approximated when Jesus must have been born (perhaps taking into account the customary time for the weaning of a child, normally done at two years of age).[138] To ensure the death of the newborn king, the ruthless tyrant gave the order to indiscriminately slaughter all male infants in Bethlehem and its immediate neighborhood under the age of two.

No detail on the means of carrying out the order is given and perhaps twenty children at most were killed,[139] but the action was in accord with Herod's general character and fulfilled the pain and suffering prophesied by Jeremiah in the Old Testament;[a] Although Herod died within a few days of the slaughtering of the infants,[140] his descendants to the third generation continued to persecute Christ and shed the blood of His witnesses.[141] Within a hundred years from his death, there were no descendants of Herod the Great left.[142]

a. Jeremiah 31:15.

To prevent the slaughter of the infant Savior, Joseph had been warned in a dream to take Jesus and Mary and flee into Egypt. How long they spent in Egypt is unknown; it is only noted that they did not return until after Herod's death.

When they returned to the land of Israel, they intended to stop and make their home in Bethlehem; but again Joseph was warned in a dream that Herod's evil son, Archelaus, ruled in Judea, so he turned aside and returned to Galilee and Nazareth. There, in remote obscurity and sheltered by apparent insignificance, the Savior of the world spent His childhood.

After the return from Egypt and up to the time the Savior was twelve years of age, the scriptures are devoid of any detail concerning His life except for one verse: "And the child grew, and waxed strong in spirit, filled with wisdom: and the grace of God was upon him."[a]

Childhood

As little as there is recorded of the infancy of Jesus, there is nothing recorded of His childhood. From infancy to twelve years of age we have only the one verse just cited. At twelve, we have the incident of His teaching in the temple which we shall review momentarily; but from that incident until the Savior's entry into His ministry, the scriptures only state that He "increased in wisdom and stature, and in favour with God and man."[b]

The silence of the Gospel writers "teaches us once more, and most impressively, that the Gospels furnish a history of the Saviour, not a biography of Jesus of Nazareth."[143] The almost unbroken silence of the scriptures increases rather than gratifies our curiosity, for it furnishes us with no details of His life or incidence of His adventures. Yet it is evident from what we do know that He was subject to the normal and natural development of all humans.[144] He was born as all humans are born—a helpless child subject to the veil of forgetfulness that is common to us all, His infancy and boyhood undoubtedly contained experiences common to other children as He grew from grace to grace; however, He was exceptional in that He was not held back by the burden of sin.[145]

Jesus was undoubtedly raised like the other children in His community. "From the first days of [their] existence, a religious atmosphere

a. Luke 2:40.
b. Luke 2:52.

surrounded the child of Jewish parents."[146] According to Jewish tradition a child was first educated by the mother, but the primary responsibility for education was the father's, as directed by the Law.[a] In a spiritual and obedient Jewish family, no opportunity was lost to teach religious duty, whether in the morning or evening, at the meal table, at home, or abroad. Every opportunity was taken for "instilling reverence for God's Law into the minds of the family, and of teaching them its express words throughout, till they knew them by heart."[147]

Starting from the fifth or sixth year, children were sent to school where "roughly classifying the subjects of study up to ten years of age, the Bible exclusively should be the text-book; from ten to fifteen, the Mishnah, or traditional law; after that age, the student should enter on those theological discussions which occupied time and attention in the higher Academies of the Rabbis."[148] Christ's early childhood was probably quiet, simple, and uneventful. His life in Nazareth was undoubtedly occupied with home and duties[149] and His obscurity similar to that of Moses in the wilderness of Midian,[b] David tending His father's sheep,[c] Elijah before His showing to Israel,[d] and Jeremiah in His home in Anathoth.[e] The obscurity of His divinity in His early years was later testified to, the scriptures noting that the people of Nazareth felt He was one of them for they knew His mother, sisters, and brethren.[f] As a child He would have attended the synagogue, for no Israelite would have thought of neglecting those services. There "He came in contact with the religious life of His Race, in its manifold aspects."[150] Paul and Isaiah described the anonymity of the Savior by stating that He "made himself of no reputation, and took upon him the form of a servant."[g] While it is evident that the young Jesus was well taught in Jewish society and fully trained in the skills of carpentry, it must be remembered that He was the giver of the Law He studied and was Jehovah incarnate. As he advanced from grace to grace, His understanding of His mission and power came directly from His Father.

In the Temple at Twelve

Luke 2:41–51　　Now His parents went to Jerusalem every year at the feast of the passover. And when he was twelve years old, they went up to Jerusalem after the custom of the feast. And when they had fulfilled the days, as they returned, the child Jesus tarried behind in Jerusalem; and Joseph and His mother knew not of it. But they, supposing Him to have been in the company, went a day's journey; and they

a. Deuteronomy 6:7; 11:19; 49:10; Psalm 78:5–6.

b. Exodus 2:15.

c. 1 Samuel 16:11.

d. 1 Kings 17:1

e. Jeremiah 1:1.

f. Matthew 13:55–56.

g. Philippians 2:7; Isaiah 53:2.

sought him among their kinsfolk and acquaintance. And when they found him not, they turned back again to Jerusalem, seeking him. And it came to pass, that after three days they found him in the temple, sitting in the midst of the doctors, both hearing them, and asking them questions. And all that heard him were astonished at his understanding and answers. And when they saw him, they were amazed: and his mother said unto him, Son, why hast thou thus dealt with us? behold, thy father and I have sought thee sorrowing. And he said unto them, How is it that ye sought me? wist ye not that I must be about my Father's business? And they understood not the saying which he spake unto them. And he went down with them, and came to Nazareth, and was subject unto them: but his mother kept all these sayings in her heart.

The scriptural silence on the Savior's early life is briefly broken by the occasion when, at the age of twelve, the Lord of the temple visited the temple of the Lord. It may not have been His first childhood visit to the temple, but it is the only visit of record during those years, and it occurred as a result of the legal requirements of the Law of Moses. Although thirteen was the legal age when the Law of Moses became binding upon Jewish youth, it was usually anticipated by one or two years.[151]

Thirteen was an important age in Judaism. A young man then commenced learning a trade and he could no longer be sold as a slave. It was believed that at this age he began to acquire the Spirit. He began wearing a phylactery and was considered a "son of the Law"—or an adult.[152]

The reason for His visit to Jerusalem was the Feast of the Passover. The scriptures note that Christ's earthly parents had gone up every year to this feast as required by the Mosaic Law, but apparently they had not previously taken Jesus. The scriptures offer no detail of the family's activities during the feast days but after the celebration concluded, Joseph and Mary left for Nazareth. Jesus, however, "tarried behind in Jerusalem."

Joseph and Mary thought He was among the company of kin-folk they were traveling with and did not notice that He was missing until they had traveled a day's journey. Upon discovering His absence, they returned to the holy city and searched for Him for three days. They finally found Him in the temple discussing the doctrines of the Law with the learned. Where the young boy stayed during this three day period is unknown.

It was not unusual for a boy of His age to be questioned and to answer questions in the manner described in the scriptures.[153] There is no record of the questions asked Him or the answers He gave or of His questions to the doctors of the Law and their answers. All we know is that all who heard Him were amazed at His understanding and comprehension of the Law.

Undoubtedly distraught, Mary asked Jesus why He had stayed in the city without telling them , "Thy father and I have sought thee sorrowing," she lamented. But Joseph was not the boy's father and it would seem that he and Mary were momentarily unmindful of the miracle of Christ's birth.[154] Perhaps they neither understood nor comprehended the greatness of His mission, and "at times . . . seemingly lost sight of [His] exalted personality."[155] Jesus quickly reminded Mary who He was. "How is it that ye sought me?" He responded. "Wist ye not that I must be about my Father's business?" Even at this tender age, Jesus clearly knew who He was.

Jesus had been officially brought to the temple by Joseph and Mary and for the first time, in accordance with Jewish tradition, had had the opportunity to teach and to question. He had been completely engrossed in His conversation with the doctors of the Law, and seemingly unconcerned about His earthly parents' whereabouts. While others did not recognize who He was and while Joseph and Mary seemed not to have understood the importance of the moment, *He knew.* Yet because He was twelve and still a child, He submitted to the authority of His earthly parents and returned to His home in Nazareth.[156]

The Forerunner   3

The Messiah, whom John the Baptist proclaimed, declared his greatness among prophets.[a] John was baptized while yet in his youth and ordained while only eight days of age. His mission was threefold:

1.   To overthrow the kingdom of the Jews.

2.   To make straight the way of the Lord.

3.   To prepare [the people] for the coming of the Lord.[b]

He was not to be called Zacharias after his father, as was the custom of the day; rather, his name would be John. He became known throughout history as John the Baptist, the forerunner of the Savior of the world.

The Announcement and Birth
Luke 1:5–25, 57–79   There was in the days of Herod, the king of Judaea, a certain priest named Zacharias, of the course of Abia: and his wife was of the daughters of Aaron, and her name was Elisabeth. And they were both righteous before God, walking in all the commandments and ordinances of the Lord blameless. And they had no child, because that Elisabeth was barren, and they both were now well stricken in years. And it came to pass, that while he executed the priest's office before God in the order of his course, according to the custom of the priest's office, his lot was to burn incense when he went into the temple of the Lord. And the whole multitude of the people were praying without at the time of incense. And there appeared unto him an angel of the Lord standing on the right side of the altar of incense. And when Zacharias saw him, he was troubled, and fear fell upon him. But the angel said unto him, Fear not, Zacharias: for thy prayer is heard; and thy wife Elisabeth shall

a. Matthew 11:11.

b. D&C 84:28.

bear thee a son, and thou shalt call his name John. And thou shalt have joy and gladness; and many shall rejoice at his birth. For he shall be great in the sight of the Lord, and shall drink neither wine nor strong drink; and he shall be filled with the Holy Ghost, even from his mother's womb. And many of the children of Israel shall he turn to the Lord their God. And he shall go before him in the spirit and power of Elias, to turn the hearts of the fathers to the children, and the disobedient to the wisdom of the just; to make ready a people prepared for the Lord. And Zacharias said unto the angel, Whereby shall I know this? for I am an old man, and my wife well stricken in years. And the angel answering said unto him, I am Gabriel, that stand in the presence of God; and am sent to speak unto thee, and to shew thee these glad tidings. And, behold, thou shalt be dumb, and not able to speak, until the day that these things shall be performed, because thou believest not my words, which shall be fulfilled in their season. And the people waited for Zacharias, and marvelled that he tarried so long in the temple. And when he came out, he could not speak unto them: and they perceived that he had seen a vision in the temple: for he beckoned unto them, and remained speechless. And it came to pass, that, as soon as the days of his ministration were accomplished, he departed to his own house. And after those days his wife Elisabeth conceived, and hid herself five months, saying, Thus hath the Lord dealt with me in the days wherein he looked on me, to take away my reproach among men. . . .

Now Elisabeth's full time came that she should be delivered; and she brought forth a son. And her neighbours and her cousins heard how the Lord had shewed great mercy upon her; and they rejoiced with her. And it came to pass, that on the eighth day they came to circumcise the child; and they called him Zacharias, after the name of his father. And his mother answered and said, Not so; but he shall be called John. And they said unto her, There is none of thy kindred that is called by this name. And they made signs to his father, how he would have him called. And he asked for a writing table, and wrote, saying, his name is John. And they marvelled all. And his mouth was opened immediately, and his tongue loosed, and he spake, and praised God. And fear came on all that dwelt round about them: and all these sayings were noised abroad throughout all the hill country of Judaea. And all they that heard them laid them up in their hearts, saying, What manner of child shall this be! And the hand of the Lord was with him. And his father Zacharias was filled with the Holy Ghost, and prophesied, saying, Blessed be the Lord God of Israel; for he hath visited and redeemed his people, and hath raised up an horn of salvation for us in the house of his servant David; as he spake by the mouth of his holy prophets, which have been since the world began: that we should be saved from our enemies, and from the hand of all that hate us; to perform the mercy promised to our fathers, and to remember his holy covenant; the oath which he sware to our father Abraham, that he would grant unto us, that we being delivered out of the hand of our enemies might serve him without fear, in holiness and righteousness before him, all the days of our life. And thou, child, shalt be called the prophet of the highest: for thou shalt go before the face of the Lord to prepare his ways; to give knowledge of salvation unto his people by the remission of their sins, through the tender mercy of our God;

whereby the dayspring from on high hath visited us, to give light to them that sit in darkness and in the shadow of death, to guide our feet into the way of peace.

Cross-references   Luke 1:36, 41–42; Matthew 17:10–13; Mark 9:11–13

Zacharias was an officiating priest in the temple of the Lord in Jerusalem, "of the course of Abia." Originally, King David had divided the temple service of the priesthood into "twenty-four courses,"[a] each to serve two one-week periods during the year. The original courses were made up of the descendants of Aaron and the males of the tribe of Levi. However, after the Babylonian captivity only three, or at the most four, of the original courses had returned to the land of promise. Although the original arrangement and names of the courses had been preserved, the membership of the twenty-four courses was now made up by lot from those who had returned to Palestine.[157]

Luke tells us that both Zacharias and His wife Elisabeth were well stricken in years. In accordance with Jewish tradition, this would have placed them in excess of sixty years of age.[158] They lived in a small, unknown town in the hill country of Judea south of Jerusalem. Twice each year for one week, Zacharias would leave his home and come to Jerusalem to perform his priestly duties in the temple.

The scriptures note that Zacharias was a priest and that Elisabeth, his wife, was a daughter of Aaron and therefore the daughter of a priest.[159] Luke specifically mentions that Zacharias and Elisabeth were childless and from the angel's comment, we can conclude that they had prayed for many years to receive the blessing of children. But they were now well stricken in years, and the time had long since passed when the anticipation of a child was on their minds and in their prayers. Yet they are specifically identified as righteous individuals: Luke undoubtedly notes this because of the Jewish tradition that to be childless was a punishment of God.

Generally speaking, the religion of Rabbinism during this time was narrow-minded, bigoted, without spirituality, and mainly concerned with self-aggrandizement.[160] The quiet home where Zacharias and Elisabeth lived was obviously quite different, for they certainly represented "all that was beautiful in the religion of the time."[161]

While ministering during his weekly assignment, Zacharias had

a. 1 Chronicles
24:1–19.

been chosen by lot to offer the incense in the temple service.[162] The incense "symbolized Israel's accepted prayers" by God.[163] This privilege usually fell upon a ministering priest only once in his lifetime.[164]

As the worship service of the day progressed, the time came for Zacharias to enter the holy place and stand alone with the golden censer in the glow of the seven-branched candlestick before the veil of the holy of holies.[165] While Zacharias moved to the place that the Jews felt approached "the immediate Presence of God,"[166] the multitude attending the service within the temple courts stood praying, awaiting the time of the incense.[167] Suddenly an angel of the Lord appeared on the right side of the altar of incense before Zacharias. There was no traditional report of such a vision occurring previously to an ordinary priest. The scriptures note that Zacharias was troubled and fearful.

Normally, a signal would have been given to notify Zacharias that he should spread the incense upon the altar, entreating the Lord in praise and prayer in behalf of the children of Israel. After spreading the incense, he would have bowed down in worship, then reverently withdrawn. Perhaps the angel appeared before he spread the incense, causing Zacharias to pause in the ceremony. The angel immediately called him by name and announced that his wife, long since barren, would give birth to a son, and that his name should be called John. The blessing many times prayed for (and perhaps long considered impossible) would now be granted to this righteous couple.

The circumstances surrounding the blessing were not unprecedented. Sarah had given birth to a promised child in her later years when both she and Abraham, her husband, felt that their childbearing years were over.[a] Further, Hannah bore Samuel and Manoah's wife bore Samson after years of barrenness.[b]

Zacharias, startled, questioned the angel and asked for a sign that would confirm the angel's promise. The angel, announcing himself as Gabriel, told Zacharias that he would be "dumb" from that time forward, unable to speak because of his doubt.[168] The promised son was to be a special son—full of the Holy Ghost and coming in the spirit and power of Elias to prepare the way before the long-awaited Messiah. The child was to "drink neither wine nor strong drink": he would live the life of a Nazarite as Samson and Samuel of old had done.

The angel's appearance and his startling message overwhelmed the

a. Genesis 17:17–19; 18:12, 15; JST, Genesis 17:23.

b. 1 Samuel 1:1–20; Judges 13:1–24.

aged Zacharias, and he tarried long beyond the time when he should have finished the ceremony. The people attending the service waited for him and marveled that he was so long in the temple.

Zacharias emerged from the holy place and took his position at the top of the steps leading from the porch to the Court of the Priests. Here he should have completed his priestly duties in the service by pronouncing the "benediction that preceded the daily meat-offering and the chant of the Psalms of praise, accompanied with joyous sound of music, as the drink-offering was poured out."[169] But he could not speak, and while his muteness was a penalty for doubt,[170] by his silence the people knew that a vision had occurred in the temple. No further detail is given. The scriptures merely state that Zacharias finished his ministry in the temple and returned to his wife, and she conceived and bore a son.

Elisabeth hid herself during the first five months of her pregnancy. During the sixth month, the angel Gabriel appeared to Mary and told her that she had been chosen to be the mother of the Savior of the world. He also told her that Elisabeth had "conceived a son in her old age." After Gabriel departed, Mary left her home in Nazareth and went to visit her cousin Elisabeth and upon her arrival, the unborn John joyfully acknowledged the presence of his Savior when he "leaped" in Elisabeth's womb. Mary remained with Elisabeth until her cousin's delivery drew near, then she returned to her home in Nazareth.

As John's birth approached, the neighbors and family of both Elisabeth and Zacharias rejoiced with her because of the mercy that the Lord had shown her. Eight days after his birth, the child was taken for circumcision and naming, as Jewish law required. Those performing the ceremony wanted to call the newborn son Zacharias after his father. Elisabeth said no, indicating that the child was to be called John, even though no one in her family was known by that name. Zacharias still could not speak. Those performing the ceremony made signs to him to confirm how the child should be named. Asking for a writing table he wrote, "His name is John." At this moment the penalty for his doubt was lifted and his mouth was opened. His final words nine months earlier had been words of doubt and fear; now he spoke words of praise to God for granting him such favor.

The births of John and Jesus were both miraculous, and both were announced by the same heavenly messenger. While Gabriel's visit to Mary and the dream of Joseph were known to but few, the visitation of Gabriel to Zacharias and the ensuing birth of John were noised about all the hill country of Judea. Presumably, the people—from the lowliest peasant up to the mighty Herod— pondered the meaning of the birth of such a child.

With John's birth, the silence of Zacharias was broken and, being filled with the Holy Ghost, he prophesied of his miraculous son's mission. The God of Israel had truly visited his people and had raised up a prophet to prepare the way of the Lord by giving knowledge to his people and spreading light where there had long been darkness.

Nothing is known of John's childhood; however, we must assume that when Herod sent forth his edict to destroy the young children in an attempt to kill the Messiah, John (being only six months older than Jesus) fell under the same condemnation.

Zacharias must have been warned of the coming destruction just as Joseph was, for he "caused [John's] mother to take him into the [desert], where he was raised on locusts and wild honey." Unlike the birth of Jesus, John's birth was public knowledge and the officials questioned Zacharias as to John's whereabouts. But Zacharias "refused to disclose his hiding place, and being the officiating high priest at the Temple that year, [he] was slain by Herod's order, between the porch and the altar."[171]

What occurred during John's long years of seclusion in the desert is unknown and no mention is made in scripture whether Elisabeth, already stricken in years when he was born, lived to rear him to adulthood. The scriptures simply state, "And the child grew, and waxed strong in spirit, and was in the deserts till the day of his shewing unto Israel."[a]

A Voice in the Wilderness

Matthew 3:1–12   In those days came John the Baptist, preaching in the wilderness of Judaea, and saying, Repent ye: for the kingdom of heaven is at hand. For this is he that was spoken of by the prophet Esaias, saying, The voice of one crying in the wilderness, Prepare ye the way of the Lord, make his paths straight. And the same John had his raiment of camel's hair, and a leathern girdle about his loins; and his meat was locusts and wild honey. Then went out to him Jerusalem, and all Judaea, and all the region round about Jordan, and were baptized of him in Jordan, confessing their sins. a. Luke 1:80.

But when he saw many of the Pharisees and Sadducees come to his baptism, he said unto them, O generation of vipers, who hath warned you to flee from the wrath to come? Bring forth therefore fruits meet for repentance: and think not to say within yourselves, We have Abraham to our father: for I say unto you, that God is able of these stones to raise up children unto Abraham. And now also the axe is laid unto the root of the trees: therefore every tree which bringeth not forth good fruit is hewn down, and cast into the fire. I indeed baptize you with water unto repentance: but he that cometh after me is mightier than I, whose shoes I am not worthy to bear: he shall baptize you with the Holy Ghost, and with fire: whose fan is in his hand, and he will throughly purge his floor, and gather his wheat into the garner; but he will burn up the chaff with unquenchable fire.

John 1:6–13, 15, 19–28	There was a man sent from God, whose name was John. The same came for a witness, to bear witness of the Light, that all men through him might believe. He was not that Light, but was sent to bear witness of that Light. That was the true Light, which lighteth every man that cometh into the world. He was in the world, and the world was made by him, and the world knew him not. He came unto his own, and his own received him not. But as many as received him, to them gave he power to become the sons of God, even to them that believe on his name: which were born, not of blood, nor of the will of the flesh, nor of the will of man, but of God. . . .

John bare witness of him, and cried, saying, This was he of whom I spake, He that cometh after me is preferred before me: for he was before me. . . .

And this is the record of John, when the Jews sent priests and Levites from Jerusalem to ask him, Who art thou? And he confessed, and denied not; but confessed, I am not the Christ. And they asked him, What then? Art thou Elias? And he saith, I am not. Art thou that prophet? And he answered, No. Then said they unto him, Who art thou? that we may give an answer to them that sent us. What sayest thou of thyself? He said, I am the voice of one crying in the wilderness, Make straight the way of the Lord, as said the prophet Esaias. And they which were sent were of the Pharisees. And they asked him, and said unto him, Why baptizest thou then, if thou be not that Christ, nor Elias, neither that prophet? John answered them, saying, I baptize with water: but there standeth one among you, whom ye know not; He it is, who coming after me is preferred before me, whose shoe's latchet I am not worthy to unloose. These things were done in Bethabara beyond Jordan, where John was baptizing.

Cross-references	Mark 1:1–8; Luke 3:1–20

When his time came, John—a student of heavenly teachers[172] like Moses and Elijah before him[a] and the herald of the long-awaited Messiah—began his ministry.

He came from the wilderness: his hair long, his beard heavy, his body clothed in a raiment of camel's hair with a leather girdle about his loins. He was like the prophets of old, a reminder of times past.[a] His appearance was reminiscent of Elijah the Tishbite, "whom all expected to reappear before the Messiah."[173] He fulfilled Isaiah's prophecy, for he was the "voice of him that crieth in the wilderness [saying], Prepare ye the way of the Lord, make straight in the desert a highway for our God."[b]

As the forerunner, he acted as a hinge between the two testaments. He was the last prophet of the Mosaic Law, "the only legal administrator in the affairs of the kingdom,"[174] and heir of all past ages—transcending all that had gone before while making way for that which was yet to come.

He extolled the Law of Moses yet was a severe critic of what it had become. He spoke nothing of the rabbis or Levitical rites and sacrifices but demanded a moral conscience from the Jews.[175] He used the ax at the root of the tree[c] and bore witness against all the evils of his time.

John the Baptist, unlike Jesus, was the prophet of anticipation;[176] the returning Elijah who would "bring back the lost Urim and Thummim, restore the tribes of Israel, turn the hearts of the fathers to the children, reprove the times, and appease the wrath of God."[177] John stirred such deep memories within the multitude and the leadership that they could ignore neither him nor his message.

John's rite of baptism was administered to the truly penitent. Just as Jacob and Moses had attempted to purify all Israel to receive God's presence,[d] those accepting John's baptism sought purification from sins committed under the old Law.

Baptism itself was not new. Under the Law of Moses it symbolically removed the moral defilement that caused Levitical uncleanliness. New proselytes were also baptized as they accepted the Law of Moses.[178] But John's baptism differed substantially from that of his predecessors. *His baptism initiated a turning from the past in anticipation of the future, the coming Christ, and a newness of life.* Yet John was merely the harbinger for the Savior who would come and baptize with fire.

John's emphasis on repentance fit into the accepted teachings of his day for the Jewish rulers taught: "if Israel repented but one day, the Son of David would immediately come."[179] But while John's demands were

a. 2 Kings 1:8.

b. Isaiah 40:3.

c. Matthew 3:10.

d. Genesis 35:2; Exodus 19:10, 14.

full of "promise to the repentant soul, [they were] scathingly denunciatory to the hypocrite and the hardened sinner."[180] He denounced the Pharisees and Sadducees as transgressors of the spirit of the Law, and accused them of dishonoring the prophets.[181] They reveled in the belief that because they were the children of Abraham they were automatically saved in God's kingdom.[182] John chastised them for their belief, requiring them to bring forth fruits meet for repentance and stating that God could "of these stones raise up children unto Abraham." Yet they anticipated, perhaps yearned for, the very one John testified was to come. In their ignorance they sent emissaries to John to ask if he was the Christ. "No," was the swift reply. "What then? Art thou Elias?" "No." John the Baptist was the forerunner, come to "make straight the way of the Lord" in the spirit and power of Elias.[183]

John preached the fundamental principles of the gospel of Jesus Christ: faith as a revitalized belief in God; repentance as contrition for past offenses; and baptism as the symbolistic rite of the fulfillment and completion of these doctrines. His teachings were familiar to both the Jewish leadership and the multitude for they had been read and studied for centuries in the synagogues and in the scriptures.[184] Although his sermons frequently opposed the popular practices of his time,[185] the scriptures report that all Jerusalem went out to see him.

John came in the Jewish mode of prophets to raise his nation from spiritual death and direct it towards the Messiah.[186] He professed no visions or revelations: he performed no miracles. In all that he did he acknowledged the status of his mission, taking neither power nor glory unto himself. "His was not a call to armed resistance, but to repentance. . . the hope which he held out was not of earthly possessions, but of purity." He was "unbendingly firm . . . deep [with] settled conviction; not ambitious nor self-seeking . . . discarding all claim but that of lowliest service, and pointing away from himself to him Who was to come, and Whom as yet he did not even know. . . . For himself he sought nothing . . . he had only one absorbing thought: The Kingdom was at hand, the King was coming—let them prepare!"[187]

The Baptism of Jesus and the Sign of the Dove

Matthew 3:13–17   Then cometh Jesus from Galilee to Jordan unto John, to be baptized of him. But John forbad him, saying, I have need to be baptized of thee, and comest thou to me? And Jesus answering said unto him, Suffer it to be so now: for thus it becometh us to fulfil all righteousness. Then he suffered him. And Jesus, when he was baptized, went up straightway out of the water: and, lo, the heavens were opened unto him, and he saw the Spirit of God descending like a dove, and lighting upon him: and lo a voice from heaven, saying, This is my beloved Son, in whom I am well pleased.

John 1:29–34   The next day John seeth Jesus coming unto him, and saith, Behold the Lamb of God, which taketh away the sin of the world. This is he of whom I said, After me cometh a man which is preferred before me: for he was before me. And I knew him not: but that he should be made manifest to Israel, therefore am I come baptizing with water. And John bare record, saying, I saw the Spirit descending from heaven like a dove, and it abode upon him. And I knew him not: but he that sent me to baptize with water, the same said unto me, Upon whom thou shalt see the Spirit descending, and remaining on him, the same is he which baptizeth with the Holy Ghost. And I saw, and bare record that this is the Son of God.

While John was baptizing in the River Jordan at Bethabara, he baptized the Savior.[188] Although Jesus and John were cousins,[189] there is no evidence of any personal contact between them prior to this meeting.[190] However, as soon as John saw the Lord he recognized a sinless man (undoubtedly through the Spirit) and proclaimed his own need to be baptized by Jesus. John's call was to repentance and his baptism was a sign of that repentance, but before him stood one for whom he considered baptism unnecessary.[191] However, baptism was required of the Lord just as it is of all mankind, and Jesus responded to John's protest by stating that His baptism was necessary "to fulfil all righteousness."

Jesus' baptism was not a sign of repentance but a simple act of submission and obedience because baptism is "an indispensable ordinance established in righteousness and required of all mankind as an essential condition for membership in the kingdom of God."[192]

John obviously knew before he entered his ministry that he would baptize the Messiah for he had been given a sign whereby he would recognize Him. At the conclusion of the Lord's baptism a "sign" of new life occurred, similar to that previously given to Noah by Jehovah.[a] This was the sign of the dove.

The sign of the dove was the "foreappointed means by which the Messiah should be made known to [John],"[193] and it "was instituted be-

a. Genesis 8:10-12.

fore the creation of the world [as] a witness for the Holy Ghost. . . . [It was] given to John to signify the truth of the deed."[194] At the conclusion of this sacred experience, the voice of the Father was heard testifying to the divinity of His Son. The Messiah was now known to John, and henceforth he would testify that the one he had prepared for had indeed arrived and all should look to Him for salvation.

After John had baptized Jesus and borne witness of the coming of the Bridegroom (the sign of the dove having been given and the Father's testimony pronounced), John's calling was basically fulfilled. His public greatness would now wane as the Lord increased in power and authority.[a]

Disciples

John 1:35–37   Again the next day after John stood, and two of his disciples; and looking upon Jesus as he walked, he saith, Behold the Lamb of God! And the two disciples heard him speak, and they followed Jesus.

John 3:23–36   And John also was baptizing in Aenon near to Salim, because there was much water there: and they came, and were baptized. For John was not yet cast into prison.

Then there arose a question between some of John's disciples and the Jews about purifying. And they came unto John, and said unto him, Rabbi, he that was with thee beyond Jordan, to whom thou barest witness, behold, the same baptizeth, and all men come to him. John answered and said, A man can receive nothing, except it be given him from heaven. Ye yourselves bear me witness, that I said, I am not the Christ, but that I am sent before him. He that hath the bride is the bridegroom: but the friend of the bridegroom, which standeth and heareth him, rejoiceth greatly because of the bridegroom's voice: this my joy therefore is fulfilled. He must increase, but I must decrease. He that cometh from above is above all: he that is of the earth is earthly, and speaketh of the earth: he that cometh from heaven is above all. And what he hath seen and heard, that he testifieth; and no man receiveth his testimony. He that hath received his testimony hath set to his seal that God is true. For he whom God hath sent speaketh the words of God: for God giveth not the Spirit by measure unto him. The Father loveth the Son, and hath given all things into his hand. He that believeth on the Son hath everlasting life: and he that believeth not the Son shall not see life; but the wrath of God abideth on him.

John's preaching initially drew many disciples to him, including Andrew and John the Beloved and perhaps Peter, Philip, and Nathanael—all of whom would later become Apostles of the Lord.[195] His sermons

a. John 3:25–30.

prepared his disciples for belief in Jesus Christ, but it was obviously his intention that his disciples should leave him and move on to the Savior. It does not appear, however, that any of John's disciples were formally introduced to the Savior; rather, those that followed him introduced themselves, relying upon John's testimony concerning Jesus.[196]

After the Lord began His mission John briefly continued his ministry, and many of his disciples stayed with him. Some even became jealous of Jesus' rise and their master's decline.[197] It may have seemed to them that Jesus had snatched away the fruits of John's ministry. In spite of this, John continued to testify of Jesus' rise and of his own decline; however, some of his disciples remained uncertain of their master's proclamation that Jesus was the Christ. The multitudes that had followed John now followed the Lord, and some of John's remaining disciples (perhaps with some animosity) told him of the Lord's success. John's reply reflected his constant acceptance of his own mission as compared with the Messiah's. He again bore witness that Jesus was the Christ and the only one whom they should be following.

On yet another occasion, John's disciples (assisted by the Pharisees who undoubtedly harbored evil intent) apparently became entangled in a potential controversy with the Lord concerning fasting and prayer. It appears that while John and his disciples fasted often, Jesus' disciples did not. Jesus did not dispute this conflict but treated the question as one which required enlightenment rather than argument. Rather than censure John's disciples for fasting, he defended His own followers for not fasting.[198]

Imprisonment and Death

Matthew 14:1–12   At that time Herod the tetrarch heard of the fame of Jesus, and said unto his servants, This is John the Baptist; he is risen from the dead; and therefore mighty works do shew forth themselves in him.

For Herod had laid hold on John, and bound him, and put him in prison for Herodias' sake, his brother Philip's wife. For John said unto him, It is not lawful for thee to have her. And when he would have put him to death, he feared the multitude, because they counted him as a prophet. But when Herod's birthday was kept, the daughter of Herodias danced before them, and pleased Herod. Whereupon he promised with an oath to give her whatsoever she would ask. And she, being before instructed of her mother, said, Give me here John Baptist's head in a charger. And the king was sorry: nevertheless for the oath's sake, and them which sat with him at meat, he commanded it to be given her. And he sent, and beheaded John in the prison. And his head was brought in a charger, and given to the damsel: and she brought it to her mother. And his disciples came, and took up the body, and buried it, and went and told Jesus.

Cross-references   Matthew 11:1–6; Mark 6:14–29

While John was preaching in the territory of Herod Antipas, Herodias convinced Herod to arrest him for "she had a quarrel against him."[199] Herodias was living with Herod Antipas as his wife, even though she had previously married Herod's brother and had not been legally divorced from him—a circumstance which John denounced.

After John was seized by Herod, Jesus withdrew into Galilee[a] and John commenced his long incarceration in the prison at Machaerus. While the slow months of imprisonment passed, Herod frequently "heard him,"[200] for Herod found him to be a holy man and listened to him gladly.[201] Although Herod seemed fearful of John, clearly his motives for John's imprisonment were political. These political motives could be classified into three general categories: (1) John had a great influence over the people, and Herod feared that this influence might lead to a revolt within the kingdom. (2) The Jewish leadership did not like Herod's marriage to Herodias, and he feared that this dislike, coupled with the denunciations from John, might also lead to rebellion. (3) The Pharisees were constantly watching both John and Jesus, and the inference could be made "that [the] Pharisaic intrigue had a very large share in giving effect to Herod's fear of the Baptist and of his reproofs."[202]

Alfred Edersheim gives us a vivid description of the prison or "keep" into which Herod cast John:

> The foundations of the walls all around, to the height of a yard or two above the ground, are still standing. As we clamber over them to examine the interior, we notice how small this keep is: exactly 100 yards in diameter. There is scarcely any remains of it left. A well of great depth, and a deep cemented cistern with the vaulting of the roof still complete, and—of most terrible interest to us—two dungeons, one of them deep down, its sides scarcely broken in, 'with small holes still visible in the masonry

a. Matthew 4:12.

where staples of wood and iron had once been fixed'! As we look down into its hot darkness, we shudder in realizing that this terrible keep had for nigh ten months been the prison of that son of the free 'wilderness,' the bold herald of the coming Kingdom, the humble, earnest, self-denying John the Baptist.[203]

Is it any wonder that as a result of his loneliness and suffering after months of imprisonment, John should send his disciples to the Lord seemingly to ask, "Am I right, or in error?"[204] It would be an injustice to John to say that he doubted the Savior of the world whom he had baptized, but it would appear that he may not have understood fully the Messiah's mission[205] and needed assurance that the "Mighty One" of Israel had not forgotten him.[206] The Lord's response to John's disciples seems to indicate that this was the case. The Lord asked John's disciples to watch as he performed extensive acts of compassion and mercy, and then to return and tell John what they had seen.[207] After they left, Jesus testified to John's greatness, stating that no greater prophet had been born of woman. It is probably at this time that he sent angels to visit the imprisoned Baptist.[a]

Why did Jesus express Himself as He did about John's greatness as a prophet? The Prophet Joseph Smith explained:

The question arose from the saying of Jesus—"Among those that are born of women there is not a greater prophet than John the Baptist; but he that is least in the kingdom of God is greater than he." How is it that John was considered one of the greatest prophets? His miracles could not have constituted his greatness.

First. He was entrusted with the divine mission of preparing the way before the face of the Lord. Whoever had such a trust committed to him before or since? No man.

Secondly. He was entrusted with the important mission, and it was required at his hands, to baptize the Son of Man.

Whoever had the honor of doing that? Whoever had so great a privilege and glory? Whoever led the Son of God into the waters of baptism, and had the privilege of beholding the Holy Ghost descend in the form of a dove, or rather in the sign of a dove, in witness of that administration? . . .

a. JST, Matthew 4:11.

Thirdly. John, at that time, was the only legal administrator in the affairs of the kingdom there was then on the earth, and holding the keys of power. The Jews had to obey his instructions or be damned, by their own law; and Christ Himself fulfilled all righteousness in becoming obedient to the law which he had given to Moses on the mount, and thereby magnified it and made it honorable, instead of destroying it. The son of Zacharias wrested the keys, the kingdom, the power, the glory from the Jews, by the holy anointing and decree of heaven, and these three reasons constitute him the greatest prophet born of a woman.[208]

The end was near for John. Early in the spring, before the Passover, Herod Antipas (the successor to Herod the Great) ordered a feast to celebrate his birthday. As the banquet progressed, the music and shouts of revelry must have filtered into the citadel, echoing into the deep dungeon where John was imprisoned.

The merriment reached great heights of excitement until as a conclusion to the festivities, a "sensuous stimulus of dubious dances" was presented to the lords, military authorities, and political leaders of Galilee. The dancer was Salome,[209] "the fair young daughter of the king's wife, the very descendant of the Asmonean priest-princesses!" She danced her best in that exhibition, pleasing Herod and all those who sat with him. Among the ensuing plaudits, the king swore in the hearing of the whole company that he would reward her with whatever she wanted, "even to the half of His kingdom," which was a symbolic rhetoric of promise rather than an actual reward. According to Mark's account, the maiden retired from the banquet hall to consult with her mother about what gift to ask for. "[Could] there be doubt or hesitation in the mind of Herodias? If there was one object she had at heart, which these ten months she had in vain sought to attain, it was the death of John the Baptist."[210]

John had incessantly condemned her for her adulterous marriage to Herod, and so the boon was conceived and Herodias's daughter made haste to the king and said, "I will that thou give me by and by in a charger the head of John the Baptist!" All in the room must have been shocked at this sadistic request. The scriptures note that "the king was exceeding sorry," but he had sworn to reward the maiden, and although he was being "unfaithful to his God, to his conscience, [and] to truth and righteousness . . . he would yet be faithful to his half-drunken oath, and appear honorable and true before such companions!" Straightway he gave the order. Salome withdrew as the guardsmen left the banquet hall. No time for preparation was given, nor was it needed, for a few moments later the "gory head of the Baptist [was] brought to the maiden in a charger, and she [gave] the ghastly dish to her mother."[211] John the Baptist was dead.

But he was dead only as defined in mortality, and even then only for a few short years while he awaited his glorious resurrection. He would be heard from centuries later when he appeared in all his power on the banks of the Susquehanna River to bestow the priesthood upon two humble servants who had been called to overthrow a different kingdom. He restored that same priesthood which he had held with these glorious words: "Upon you my fellow servants, in the name of Messiah I confer the Priesthood of Aaron, which holds the keys of the ministering of angels, and of the gospel of repentance, and of baptism by immersion for the remission of sins; and this shall never be taken again from the earth, until the sons of Levi do offer again an offering unto the Lord in righteousness."[a]

To Fulfill All Righteousness

4

Baptism

Matthew 3:13–17   Then cometh Jesus from Galilee to Jordan unto John, to be baptized of him. But John forbad him, saying, I have need to be baptized of thee, and comest thou to me? And Jesus answering said unto him, Suffer it to be so now: for thus it becometh us to fulfil all righteousness. Then he suffered him. And Jesus, when he was baptized, went up straightway out of the water: and, lo, the heavens were opened unto him, and he saw the Spirit of God descending like a dove, and lighting upon him: and lo a voice from heaven, saying, This is my beloved Son, in whom I am well pleased.

Cross-references   Mark 1:7–11; Luke 3:21–23; John 1:32–34; 2 Nephi 31:5–12

In the words of Elder James E. Talmage, baptism has always been and remains "an indispensable ordinance established in righteousness and required of all mankind as an essential condition for membership in the Kingdom of God."[212] President Lorenzo Snow testified, "There is but one way in which men can receive salvation, exaltation and glory, and that is through the order of baptism and the ordinances connected therewith . . . that is the order that God has established."[213]

Baptism was required from the beginning. Adam was baptized[a] and Jesus began His public ministry by being baptized "to fulfil all righteousness."

Baptism was recognized and commonly practiced among the Jews at Christ's time,[214] but Jesus specifically sought out John the Baptist to perform His baptism.

John preached the necessity of repentance before baptism in order

a. Moses 6:64–65; 1 Corinthians 10:1–4.

to receive forgiveness for sin, but the Lord needed neither repentance nor forgiveness. The scriptures make it clear, however, that the Son of God did need the ordinance of baptism. Even the sinless Messiah could not regain the kingdom of the Father without it.

Nephi of old witnessed the baptism of the Savior in vision.[a] While teaching of this vision to emphasize the absolute necessity of baptism for all men, he was questioned about the need for the perfect Son to be baptized. Understanding the perfection of the Lamb of God before the Father and the fact that He had no need for repentance, Nephi then taught five basic reasons for the Savior's baptism (which also apply to all men):

1. To show "unto the children of men that, according to the flesh he humbleth Himself before the Father."

2. To witness "unto the Father that he would be obedient unto Him in keeping His commandments."

3. To show that baptism was necessary prior to receiving the Holy Ghost, which, after the Lord's baptism, descended upon Him just as it had upon Adam.[b][215]

4. To show "unto the children of men the straightness of the path, and the narrowness of the gate, by which they should enter."

5. To invite all of the children of men to "follow thou me."

Nephi continued this instruction to his brethren by exclaiming, "O then, how much more need have we, being unholy, to be baptized, yea, even by water!"[c]

The scriptures are void of detail concerning the eighteen years between the Savior's appearance at age twelve in the temple and the time of His baptism,[d] but the time eventually arrived when He left His protected life in Nazareth and entered the mission for which He had been born—to "be about His Father's business."

When John took the Savior into the waters of the Jordan, he closed the door on Israel's dead past and initiated its future; in a similar sense, the Savior's past life was finished and the new era of His minis-

a. 1 Nephi 11:27.

b. Moses 6:65.

c. 2 Nephi 31:5–12.

d. Luke 2:52.

try opened before Him. The miraculous occurrences that transpired immediately thereafter testify that the Father accepted the Son's obedience, for immediately upon His coming forth out of the waters of baptism the Holy Ghost descended upon Him as witnessed by the sign of the dove.[216] The descent of the Holy Ghost upon Him had been foreseen by Nephi and Isaiah.[a] Thus, the prophecies of the Old Testament concerning the commencement of the Lord's ministry were fulfilled.

The baptism of fire by the Holy Ghost was the foreappointed sign by which the Messiah would be made known and from henceforth, "John knew His Redeemer."[217] In addition to this sign (and as if to ratify the mission of the forerunner), the Father opened the heavens and spoke, testifying of His Son's divinity and initiating the commencement of His public ministry.

Authority and Baptism

For the Savior's baptism to be accepted and recognized in the sight of God, it had to be performed by one holding the proper authority. John had been ordained and given that authority when he was eight days old.[b] Paul taught this principle of proper authority when he was instructing certain disciples in Ephesus. Upon questioning them, he discovered that although they had been baptized by "someone," it had been done without the proper authority; he then rebaptized them all.[c] In the Book of Mormon King Limhi and many of His people desired baptism, but it was postponed because "there was none in the land that had authority from God."[d]

As Joseph Smith was translating the Book of Mormon, he came upon passages concerning the necessity of baptism. Not yet understanding the sacred doctrine, he and Oliver Cowdery, his scribe, went to the Lord in prayer for clarification and the following occurred:

> A messenger from heaven descended in a cloud of light, and having laid His hands upon us, he ordained us saying:
>
> "Upon you my fellow servants, in the name of Messiah, I confer the Priesthood of Aaron, which holds the keys of the ministering of angels, and of the gospel of repentance, and of baptism by immersion for the remission of sins." . . .
>
> The messenger who visited us on this occasion and conferred

a. 1 Nephi 11:27;
   Isaiah 11:2.

b. D&C 84:28.

c. Acts 19:1–6.

d. Mosiah
   21:33.

this Priesthood upon us, said that his name was John, the same that is called John the Baptist in the New Testament.[a]

Having received the proper authority and having conferred it upon each other as they were instructed, Joseph and Oliver then baptized each other in the Susquehanna River.

The Covenant

Nephi indicated that in the baptismal covenant, each person "witnesseth unto the Father that [he will] be obedient unto Him in keeping His commandments."[b]

Paul, writing to the Romans, declared, "Know ye not, that so many of us as were baptized into Jesus Christ were baptized into his death? Therefore we are buried with him by baptism into death."[c] In baptism, we symbolically bury our former life and existence and agree to come forth out of the water in the likeness of Christ (as if out of the grave) and to "walk in newness of life." Paul continued: "Like as Christ was raised up from the dead by the glory of the Father, even so we also should walk in newness of life. For if we have been planted together in the likeness of his death, we shall be also in the likeness of his resurrection: Knowing this, that our old man is crucified with him, that the body of sin might be destroyed, that henceforth we should not serve sin." Concluding the metaphor, Paul declared, "Let not sin therefore reign in your mortal body."[d]

The "old man" is our past—our sinful nature, the actual commission of sin, the breaking of the Lord's commandments. Paul's similitude of death is the dying of sin. Thus, we should serve sin no longer; rather, in the likeness of the resurrection of Christ, we are to be alive (acceptable) unto God.

In explaining the baptismal covenant, Paul used this metaphorical teaching in almost all of his epistles.[218] His was a consistent theme of putting off the old ways of the past, rejecting sinful habits, and setting a new course dedicated to righteousness and an absolute struggle for obedience.

The Lord confirmed Paul's teachings in a revelation to Joseph Smith when He explained that "after they are received by baptism . . . the members shall manifest before the Church, and also before the elders,

a. Joseph Smith—History 1:68–69, 72.

b. 2 Nephi 31:7.

c. Romans 6:3–4.

d. Romans 6:4–12.

by a godly walk and conversation, that they are worthy of [baptism], that there may be works and faith agreeable to the holy scriptures—walking in holiness before the Lord."[a] This is the covenant we make at baptism.

Baptism for the Remission of Sins

The fourth article of faith declares: "We believe that the first principles and ordinances of the Gospel are: first, Faith in the Lord Jesus Christ; second, Repentance; *third, Baptism by immersion for the remission of sins;* fourth, Laying on of hands for the gift of the Holy Ghost" (italics added). The ordinance of baptism does not of itself wash away sin, nor does the *water* remove sin, for if a person enters the waters of baptism filthy and unrepentant he will come out of the water filthy still. How then is baptism performed for the remission of sins?

The scriptures note that John the Baptist "came into all the country about Jordan, preaching the baptism of *repentance* for the remission of sins."[b] It is repentance that makes possible the remission of sin through the atonement of Jesus Christ. Baptism establishes a covenant between the individual and God and is the symbol of remission. Moroni explains it this way: "And the first fruits of repentance is baptism; and baptism cometh by faith unto the fulfilling the commandments; and the fulfilling of the commandments bringeth remission of sins."[c]

Baptism is the sign by which we declare to God our sincere repentance, that we have completely forsaken sin, and that we will henceforth obey all His commandments. Further, it is the sign of God's covenant with us that, providing our repentance is complete, our sins will be remitted.

Temptations

Matthew 4:1–11   Then was Jesus led up of the Spirit into the wilderness to be tempted of the devil. And when he had fasted forty days and forty nights, he was afterward an hungred. And when the tempter came to him, he said, If thou be the Son of God, command that these stones be made bread. But he answered and said, It is written, Man shall not live by bread alone, but by every word that proceedeth out of the mouth of God. Then the devil taketh him up into the holy city, and setteth him on a pinnacle of the temple, and saith unto him, If thou be the Son of God, cast thyself down: for it is written, He shall give his angels charge concerning thee: and in their hands they shall bear thee up, lest at any time thou dash thy foot against a stone. Jesus said unto him, It is written again, Thou shalt not tempt the Lord thy

a. D&C 20:68–69.

b. Luke 3:3; italics added.

c. Moroni 8:25.

God. Again, the devil taketh him up into an exceeding high mountain, and sheweth him all the kingdoms of the world, and the glory of them; and saith unto him, All these things will I give thee, if thou wilt fall down and worship me. Then saith Jesus unto him, Get thee hence, Satan: for it is written, Thou shalt worship the Lord thy God, and him only shalt thou serve. Then the devil leaveth him, and, behold, angels came and ministered unto him.

Cross-references   Mark 1:12–13; Luke 4:1–13

There are some variances in the scriptural histories which relate the events of Christ's temptations. In fact, the Gospel of John begins its historical treatment of Jesus' life after the temptations have occurred. Mark speaks of them in general, agreeing with the narratives of Matthew and Luke that Jesus was led by the Spirit into the wilderness and was with the wild beasts.

Matthew and Luke report the first temptation the same, but invert the order of the final two temptations. In Matthew we note that "angels came and ministered unto Jesus" at the conclusion of the temptations, and Luke concludes with the tempter departing from Jesus "for a season." The Gospel of Matthew will be followed in this discussion.

After His baptism, Jesus was led into the wilderness where He would receive the devil's assaults. For a period of forty days, He fasted and prayed. His formal ministry had begun, and He chose to fast at this time so that His mortal body might be made more completely subject to His spirit.[219]

Such a lengthy fast had occurred previously in Israel's History. Both Moses and Elijah had fasted for forty-day periods.[a] Moses had fasted in the presence of God and was given His commandments so that the children of Israel might obey the Law. After his forty-day fast, it was evident that the Israelites had not even obeyed the simple instructions he had given them. So with indignation he cast down and broke the tablets of the Law. Elijah also attempted to convince the children of Israel to obey the Law and tried to restore God's covenant to them, but he had no greater success than Moses. Like Jesus, the patriarchs and other Israelite leaders had been tried and proven through Satan's assaults.[220] (It is interesting to note that one of the questions presented to Jesus was why His disciples did not fast.)[221]

The three specific temptations that the Lord endured are generally reported as being the culmination of His forty-day fast. Luke's narrative seems to indicate that Jesus was tempted during the entire forty-day period, but the Joseph Smith Translation clarifies this as being otherwise.[a] Further, as the scriptures note, the devil departed from Christ for a season; but He would return to tempt Him at other times and in other ways as opportunity presented itself.[222] Echoes of the three temptations occur throughout the Lord's ministry: His brothers suggested He show Himself to the leadership of Israel at Jerusalem;[b] there was a popular attempt to make Him a political king after the feeding of the five thousand in the wilderness;[223] and Pilate tempted Him with the question, "Art thou a king then?"[c]

Thus, at the conclusion of Christ's forty-day wilderness fast, and at a time when He felt the greatest physical weariness and weakness from hunger, Lucifer initiated the three specific temptations recorded in the New Testament. The Master of all that was good would now be confronted by the master of all that was evil; and as the great "son of the morning" and deceiver of mankind stood before Him and delivered his temptations, the total experience resolved itself into "one question of absolute submission to the will of God, which is the sum and substance of all obedience."[224]

The Temptations of Jesus

The First Temptation: The scriptures report that Jesus was "an hungered." In this weakened state, Satan came with all his subtlety and cunning saying, "If thou be the Son of God, command that these stones be made bread."

The reaction of the flesh to such a long fast would typically have been predictable, for the Lord's body hungered for nourishment. He was physically weak, "and this was the tempter's moment. The whole period had been one of moral and spiritual tension . . . [and now was] . . . the hour of extreme danger . . . the moment in which [many men have] fallen a victim to insidious allurement or bold assault. It was at such a moment that the great battle of our Lord against the powers of evil was fought and won."[225]

The temptation was disguised within the need of the moment, and the father of all lies presumptuously thought he had cradled within the

a. JST, Luke 4:2.

b. John 7:3–5.

c. John 18:37.

guise of food the temptation that would destroy a God. Perhaps Satan thought that Christ, like Esau, would trade away His birthright for food.[a] Was not this Jehovah, He who had provided Hagar with water so that she could save herself and her son from death?[b] Even Israel, while being led out of captivity, had struggled with mass hunger and was fed manna in the wilderness by God.[c] And had not Elijah been shown food by an angel at the time of his need?[d] So the tempter stood before the Messiah (who would later feed five thousand and more on one occasion and four thousand-plus on another), and tempted the God of creation to yield and create food for Himself.

This temptation was not one of mere food, however, for the devil had asked the Savior to do much more than use His supernatural power to gratify His physical need. He had cunningly taunted, "*If* thou be the Son of God . . ." (italics added). Doubt was the temptation, not food. Satan was asking the Lord to doubt His divine relationship with the Father. He who was born of no earthly father, no natural man, who was eternally endowed with Godhood from birth—the Only Begotten of the Father in the flesh—was now being asked to doubt that relationship. Both the Lord and the devil had a perfect understanding of the point in question, and both knew that to yield to doubt was to fail.

With a sharp retort the Lord answered: "It is written, man shall not live by bread alone, but by every word that proceedeth out of the mouth of God." The need for physical self-preservation was great, but the Lord's answer dictated that all appetites should be kept within the bounds set by the divine standard. God's word would prevail, not Christ's temporal needs, even though He possessed unlimited power. Only forty days previously the Father had testified of the divinity of His Son, and Jesus easily overcame the first temptation by absolute trust in the Father and submission to His will.

The Second Temptation: In the second temptation, the Lord was transported by the Spirit to the holy city of Jerusalem and set upon a pinnacle of the temple.[e] The devil, persistent in his purpose to destroy the Son of God, tempted Him there. The Lord had used scripture to close the previous temptation and the devil now used scripture to open the second one. Again the insidious "if" prefaced His comments, but in the design of this temptation the devil quoted a Messianic prophecy that had to be fulfilled: "He [God] shall give his angels charge concern-

a. Genesis 25:33.

b. Genesis 21:15–19.

c. Exodus 16:15.

d. 1 Kings 19:4–8.

e. JST, Matthew 4:5.

ing thee; and in their hands they shall bear thee up, lest at any time thou dash thy foot against a stone." The evil one was subtly asking the Lord to question the very trust in the Father He had used to overcome the first temptation by wantonly throwing Himself into a predicament that would test the Father's promise.

In his first temptation, food was the guise with which the devil tried to make the Lord doubt His relationship with His Father. In this second temptation, Satan was appealing to the human side of Christ's nature—tempting Him to tempt His Father—for it was not the destruction of the body but the destruction of the Savior's soul that the devil wanted. In response to all this the Savior, as before, unveiled the subtlety of the temptation and simply stated, "It is written again, Thou shalt not tempt the Lord thy God."

The Third Temptation: The setting for the final temptation was a high mountaintop, from whence was projected in vision all of the world's riches with its kingdoms and glory. Casting aside all subtlety, the tempter exhibited His own weakness before the Master of good by promising Him the kingdoms of the world on the condition that "Thou wilt fall down and worship me." To Him who had created the earth and all therein, the offer must have seemed ludicrous; but it was personal aggrandizement that the evil one sought, and perhaps on a truly logical basis, for "in its present state, all this world '[had been] delivered' unto him, and he exercised the power of giving it to whom he would."[226]

In this temptation the devil sought to entice the Savior to be the earthly king that the chosen people had yearned for in their Messianic expectations (Chapter 2). If He had succumbed, He might have become a satanic messiah over a temporary empire. But the Lord of lords and King of kings had to be about His Father's business, so Satan's greatest temptation became "to Christ His coarsest temptation."[227] "Get thee hence, Satan," the Lord responded, "for it is written, Thou shalt worship the Lord thy God, and him only shalt thou serve."

That the Lord had the capacity and the ability to sin (had He willed to do so) is beyond question, for otherwise He would have been denied His free agency. He had undoubtedly been tried from His youth, but He had triumphed in all things and had consistently resisted temptation.[228]

Jesus met the dark prince of this world and defeated Him, and although He would yet be tempted (for evil cannot be overcome in a single encounter),[229] the devil departed from Him "for a season." Through His response to these temptations, the Lord showed the way to the kingdom of God. Only in absolute obedience and submission to the will of the Father can victory be assured.

Jesus Himself must have related these temptations to the Apostles so that they might learn that He, too, had been tempted to rebel against God's will. But He had resisted temptation because of His commitment to fulfill all righteousness.

The Transfiguration

Matthew 17:1–8   And after six days Jesus taketh Peter, James, and John his brother, and bringeth them up into an high mountain apart, and was transfigured before them: and his face did shine as the sun, and his raiment was white as the light. And, behold, there appeared unto them Moses and Elias talking with him. Then answered Peter, and said unto Jesus, Lord, it is good for us to be here: if thou wilt, let us make here three tabernacles; one for thee, and one for Moses, and one for Elias. While he yet spake, behold, a bright cloud overshadowed them: and behold a voice out of the cloud, which said, This is my beloved Son, in whom I am well pleased; hear ye him. And when the disciples heard it, they fell on their face, and were sore afraid. And Jesus came and touched them, and said, Arise, and be not afraid. And when they had lifted up their eyes, they saw no man, save Jesus only.

Cross-references   Mark 9:2–9; Luke 9:28–36; 2 Peter 1:16–18

The Apostles had been with the Lord for approximately two years at the time of His transfiguration. He had been training them for their ministry and teaching them the doctrines of the new kingdom. He had also revealed to them evidences of His divine sonship so that they might recognize Him as the true Messiah and eliminate their stubborn prejudices regarding the anticipated Messiah which had been ingrained in them from their youth.

Approximately one week prior to the Transfiguration, Jesus asked the Apostles who people thought He was. Peter responded that some said He was John the Baptist and others that He was the prophet Elias. Jesus then pointedly asked the Apostles who *they* thought He was, and Peter, responding both for himself and for the Twelve, declared that Jesus was the Christ, the very Messiah.[a][230] Evidently the Apostles had reached the high point of their faith by this time.

a. Matthew
16:13-19.

Jesus praised them for their testimony and acknowledged that their understanding had come from heaven, that they had received a witness from God through the Spirit. Thereupon He immediately began to teach them concerning His impending death and why it was necessary. But Peter protested such an ignominious end for the Messiah. Jesus reproved Peter for his lack of understanding, saying, "Get thee behind me, Satan."[a]

The realization that Jesus would enter His kingdom by suffering shame and death was a shock to all of the Twelve, and it contradicted their ingrained preconceptions of the Messiah. They lacked understanding of the Lord's spiritual mission and they became discouraged.[231] From the high point of Peter's testimony, the spirit of the Twelve seemed to wane until the Ascension, for they had continuously exhibited an unwillingness to acknowledge His impending death and they were ill prepared to share in His sufferings—or even believe in His resurrection.[232] "The proclamation that He was the Divine Messiah had not been met by promises of the near glory of the Messianic kingdom, but by announcements of certain, public rejection and seeming terrible defeat. Such possibilities had never seriously entered into [the Apostles'] thoughts of the Messiah."[233]

Six or eight days passed after this conversation[234] but nothing is said of what transpired during that interval. At the end of the week, the Savior sought seclusion for the Transfiguration on a high mountain,[235] taking with Him His three chief Apostles—Peter, James, and John. They would have climbed for some time, maybe not to the actual summit, but at least onto the cool heights where on a calm, summer evening, they could pray and be instructed without interruption. Jesus wanted to complete the preparations for the remainder of His ministry and crucifixion. Knowing that they would soon possess the keys of the kingdom, He took these three Apostles with Him so that He might strengthen them and fortify their testimony of Him and His mission.

Whether from the day's lengthy activities or from the fatigue experienced from their climb, it appears that the Apostles were tired. After finishing their nightly devotions, they wrapped themselves in their abbas and lay down on the hillside to sleep.[236] How long they slept is not noted, but according to Luke it appears that they slept long enough that they did not witness the beginning of the Transfiguration, for they were suddenly awakened by a great brilliance.

The Master was transfigured before them, and there appeared two other figures with Him—Moses and "Elias" (the New Testament [Greek] form of Elijah).[237] The scriptures do not indicate how Peter, James, and John knew that it was Moses and Elijah with Jesus, but perhaps in their spiritually enlightened state and because of the splendor of the Transfiguration in which they were participating, the Spirit quickened their understanding. Moses and Elijah, those two great prophets from the past who had founded and defended the Mosaic Law, had come to perform a mission that would supersede and fulfill the old law and make way for the gospel—the new law.

The Apostles were astounded by the three transfigured beings before them and they listened intently as the holy men spoke of the upcoming death of the Messiah. One reason why Jesus had brought Peter, James, and John with Him was that they might gain further understanding of His impending death. The experience would give them the necessary spiritual strength to bear the sight of His future humiliation, but at the same time would allow them to witness the glory that He would eventually possess. These three great Apostles would soon lead the Lord's church, and they needed to be strengthened and prepared for the powerful authority that the Savior would bestow upon them.

Moses and Elijah had been allowed to retain a translated body so that they could confer the keys of the kingdom upon Peter, James, and John.[238] Moses conferred the keys of the gathering of Israel and Elijah the keys of the sealing power. All other authority they would need was given to them by the Savior.[239] Peter later referred to the Transfiguration in his second epistle,[a] and John alluded to it in his Gospel[b] and in the opening of his first epistle to the church.[c]

The splendor of the vision they witnessed and the Transfiguration of Christ before them left the Apostles awed, confused, and bewildered.[240] The scriptures note that they were "sore afraid," but in spite of their fear Peter stated, "Lord, it is good for us to be here." In fact, as Moses and Elijah departed, he suggested that three tabernacles be built to commemorate the experience. But the magnitude of the Transfiguration was not over as a bright cloud appeared over the mount

a. 2 Peter 1:16–19.
b. John 1:14
c. 1 John 1:1–2.

and enshrouded the Apostles and the Lord. The voice of the Father emanated from within the cloud proclaiming Christ as His Son and testifying to His divinity. At the conclusion of this divine testimony, the cloud dissipated and Jesus and His Apostles were left alone on the mountainside.

Even though the Apostles had been told about the Lord's impending death and resurrection, they still seemed unable to comprehend it; moreover, they apparently still had no clear concept of resurrection.[241] However, the Transfiguration would have been a time of encouragement for the Savior and the appearance of Moses and Elijah would have undoubtedly strengthened Him, just as the ministering of angels had done after His forty-day fast with its culminating temptations.[242]

No lengthy discussion is recorded in the scriptures between the Apostles and the Savior concerning the Transfiguration. Only the Savior's admonition is recorded: that they tell no man concerning it until after His ascension.

During the Transfiguration Jesus had comforted the Apostles because they were afraid; now, when they had an opportunity to question the Lord, their questions concerned the teachings of the Jewish leadership which indicated that Elias must "first come." The three Apostles had just seen Elias, and Jesus informed them that the Elias spoken of by the Jewish leadership was, in fact, John the Baptist, who had come in the "spirit and power" of Elias to prepare the way before the Messiah (Chapter 3). Thus, the conflict in their minds between their traditional Jewish teachings and those of the Savior concerning Elias and the mission of John the Baptist was resolved.

The Transfiguration was clearly a divine attestation that Jesus was the Messiah and that His coming would fulfill the Law and supersede the Prophets.[243] The experience was a witness to Peter, James, and John that the Law of Moses and the teachings of the prophets were only preparatory to the new dispensation in which the gospel of Jesus Christ would be ushered in. From the spiritual heights of the Mount of Transfiguration, the Savior would now follow His mission into the valley of humiliation and death.

Sacred Times   5

Entrance into Jerusalem

Luke 19:28–44   And when he had thus spoken, he went before, ascending up to Jerusalem. And it came to pass, when he was come nigh to Bethphage and Bethany, at the mount called the mount of Olives, he sent two of his disciples, saying, Go ye into the village over against you; in the which at your entering ye shall find a colt tied, whereon yet never man sat: loose him, and bring him hither. And if any man ask you, Why do ye loose him? thus shall ye say unto him, Because the Lord hath need of him. And they that were sent went their way, and found even as he had said unto them. And as they were loosing the colt, the owners thereof said unto them, Why loose ye the colt? And they said. The Lord hath need of him. And they brought him to Jesus: and they cast their garments upon the colt, and they set Jesus thereon. And as he went, they spread their clothes in the way. And when he was come nigh, even now at the descent of the mount of Olives, the whole multitude of the disciples began to rejoice and praise God with a loud voice for all the mighty works that they had seen; saying, Blessed be the King that cometh in the name of the Lord: peace in heaven, and glory in the highest. And some of the Pharisees from among the multitude said unto him, Master, rebuke thy disciples. And he answered and said unto them, I tell you that, if these should hold their peace, the stones would immediately cry out.

And when he was come near, he beheld the city, and wept over it, saying, If thou hadst known, even thou, at least in this thy day, the things which belong unto thy peace! but now they are hid from thine eyes. For the days shall come upon thee, that thine enemies shall cast a trench about thee, and compass thee round, and keep thee in on every side, and shall lay thee even with the ground, and thy children within thee; and they shall not leave in thee one stone upon another; because thou knewest not the time of thy visitation.

Cross-references   Matthew 21:1–11; Mark 11:1–11; John 12:12–20

The city of Jerusalem at Christ's time was a splendor to behold! It had been established as Israel's seat of government by King David and raised to its early greatness by Solomon, David's son. He had made it the center of Israel's kingdom. However, if Solomon's subjects had seen the city in Christ's time they scarcely would have recognized it. Solomon had developed and expanded Jerusalem, but Herod had truly magnified it, making it a place of beauty and splendor beyond anything before seen in the East.

The city was surrounded by a protective wall, but even within the city additional walls divided the distinctively different city areas. These inner walls had been raised during various historical periods and had originally been built for either protection or segregation.[244]

Herod's Jerusalem was divided into two major areas—the lower city and the upper city. The lower city formed the business quarter and comprised markets, bazaars, streets of trades, and guilds.[245] The upper city contained the palaces. The palace of the Maccabees was there and adjacent to it was the Xystos—a large enclosure surrounded with colonnades to provide a place for popular assemblies. There was also the palace of Annas (the patriarch of the family of high priests) and the palace of the ruling high priest, Caiaphas, whose palace also housed the council chamber for the Sanhedrin and the public archives. Finally, there was the stately, magnificent palace of Herod the Great.[246]

Separated from both the business district and the palaces by its own walls and gates was the temple. Solomon built the first temple in Jerusalem, but it was comparatively small, perhaps the size of an ordinary church.[247] Herod later produced a structure of grandeur that was over forty-six years in the making.[248] It was so magnificent that the saying went abroad, "He that has not seen the Temple of Herod, has never known what beauty is."[249]

Herod's temple was a structure of unparalleled size and splendor, its four outer walls (each approximately a thousand feet long) enclosing the sacred area.[250] It was constructed of glistening white marble, with gold overlay on many of the buildings, columns, and roofs.[251] It had been built by over ten thousand workmen, who were supervised in all phases of its construction by one thousand temple priests.[252]

During Christ's time, Jerusalem's permanent population would have ranged between 200,000 and 250,000 people (although this number would have swelled enormously during any of the Jewish festivals).[253] Christ's final entrance into Jerusalem took place during the Passover Feast, and it was at a Passover Feast that Cestus took a census of Jerusalem in order to inform Nero of the city's power. To establish this census, Cestus required the priests to number the multitudes attending the Passover Feast. They did this by counting the sacrifices offered in the temple during the Passover. They counted 256,500 sacrificial sheep and estimated that 10 or 11 people would celebrate each sacrifice (it was not lawful for anyone to eat the feast singly, and some companies were known to have included as many as 20 people). The priests reported to Cestus that 2,700,200 Jews had come to the feast pure and holy. Because those considered "unclean" and visiting foreigners could not offer sacrifices, the estimated figure was probably below the actual total.[254]

From this enormous congregation, Jesus had drawn a company of five thousand men (plus women and children) into the wilderness to feed and teach.[255] One can easily understand, then, how quickly a large multitude would have gathered when Jesus made His final entrance into the city.

Jesus had declared His Messiahship many times throughout His ministry by means of miracles, parables, and sermons,[256] but He had never publicly established His claim in Jerusalem. In fact, on His previous visit to that city (during the Feast of Tabernacles), Jesus had traveled "as it were in secret"[a]—even though His family and some of His disciples had urged Him to go there and openly proclaim His Messiahship to the rulers.[b][257]

The Lord knew that the culmination of His ministry was drawing near and He no longer wanted to conceal His identity. The time had come for Him to enter Jerusalem and give the leadership, the residents, and the celebrants the chance to openly accept or reject Him.[258] Consequently, He entered the Holy City as the King of kings—not as Israel's political king, but as the universal Prince of Peace.

The Gospel writers place Christ's disciples in varying locations for the entrance, depending upon each writer's viewpoint.[259] For instance, Matthew and Mark do not record the events of the entrance in chronological order,[260] and from John's record it would appear that he was one of the two disciples sent by Jesus to retrieve the colt, for he records Christ's entrance from the perspective of the group which went forth

a. John 7:10.

b. John 7:2–5.

from Jerusalem to meet the Savior as he approached the city. Luke and the other Synoptics record the event from the perspective of the group traveling with the Savior from Bethany.

Bethany was located on the eastern slope of Mount Olivet, approximately two miles from Jerusalem.[261] There were three roads leading from Bethany to Jerusalem, and although we do not know which route the Savior took, He probably traveled the main trade road from Jericho because it would more easily accommodate the large number of disciples that were with Him.[262]

A short time before this, the Lord had publicly raised Lazarus from the dead in Bethany—a spectacle so astonishing that the chief priests and Pharisees had gathered in a special council to decide what should be done with Jesus. Their conclusion was that if they did nothing, "all men [would] believe on him";[a] so after deliberation, they decided that they must put Him to death. Jesus then left Bethany and went into the country of Ephraim to avoid these ill-intentioned rulers until the time of the Passover.

As the Passover approached, the excitement concerning the Lord again increased as the people anticipated His return to Jerusalem. They "sought for Jesus" and questioned whether He would come to the feast.[b] Six days before the Passover, Jesus returned to Bethany and went to the home of Mary, Martha, and Lazarus.[c][263] News of His arrival spread throughout Jerusalem, and many came to see Him.[d]

On the day of His entrance (presumably at about midday or early afternoon),[264] the Lord left Bethany for Jerusalem accompanied by many of His friends and disciples. Other disciples probably joined Him along the way, and undoubtedly some rushed ahead to spread the word of His coming. The Lord's entourage would also have included those who had come to see Lazarus as well as the curious festival celebrants who had been lodged outside the city and were now eager to take part in the day's celebration.[265]

As the group traveled they approached Bethphage, apparently a suburb of Jerusalem.[266] At this point, the Lord dispatched two disciples (generally thought to have been Peter and John)[267] to procure a colt for Him to ride upon as He entered Jerusalem. They were instructed to go into the village "over against you" (presumably Bethphage) to find the colt. If they were questioned by the colt's owner as to why they

a. John 11:48.

b. John 11:56.

c. John 12:1–2.

d. John 12:9.

were taking it, they were to say that "the Lord hath need of him," and all would be well. The two Apostles did as they were instructed and soon returned leading the unbroken colt by the bridle. They were accompanied by disciples and curiosity seekers and followed by more.[268]

What the Lord did during the time it took to get the colt is not mentioned, but John's narration bears witness that many came from Jerusalem to meet the Savior. It is evident that word of His approach had reached the city and had been spread throughout the temple area[269] because many people cut palm branches and went forth to meet Him shouting praises to the "King of Israel."

It should be noted that this crowd also included some of the jealous Pharisees and other of the Lord's antagonists who had watched His every move and were now bent on His destruction.[a] Perhaps the group also included the lame whom He had cured, the dumb that now sang His praises, and the blind to whom He had given sight—all crowding forward that they might gaze upon their benefactor.[270] Doubtless, both groups were made up primarily of disciples and curious pilgrims who had come to the Passover festival, for "the overwhelming majority of the citizens of Jerusalem were bitterly and determinately hostile to Christ."[271]

The Lord's entourage and the celebrating multitude from Jerusalem eventually merged. Jesus was placed upon the donkey's colt, and His triumphant procession into the holy city began.

The chosen people had been conditioned to expect this public Messianic occurrence,[272] and Jesus had deliberately chosen the unridden[273] colt of a donkey as His mount because it represented His kingship over the chosen people.[b274] Historically, Abraham had ridden a lowly donkey when he went to the holy mountain to sacrifice Isaac;[c] Moses, a chosen prophet of God, had led His wife into Egypt on such an animal;[d] King Ahasuerus had honored Mordecai by bringing Him triumphantly into Shushan on His own horse;[e] and King David had declared Solomon his successor by placing him on his own mule to ride through Jerusalem.[f] Because of Historical significance and prophetic expectation, every believing Jew would have anticipated the Messiah's procession[275] and "no act could [have been] more perfectly in keeping with the conception of a king of Israel, and no words could [have expressed] more plainly that that King proclaimed Himself the

a. Luke 19:39;
John 12:19.

b. Zechariah
9:9.

c. Genesis
22:1–14.

d. Exodus 4:20.

e. Esther 6:8,
11.

f. 1 Kings
1:33.

Messiah."[276] The joy of the multitude spontaneously erupted and the people cried, "Hosanna to the Son of David," and "Blessed be the King that cometh in the name of the Lord."

This salutation did not mean that all in the multitude knew that Jesus was the Messiah — their cries were partly based upon chants that the multitudes always recited on solemn festival days.[a] Further, this was the traditional greeting used by the residents of Jerusalem to welcome festive pilgrims.[277] But on this day, the acclamations were accepted by Christ as the fulfillment of prophecy because they honored Him as their King and their Messiah. As the people rejoiced over the Savior's ride into the city, they not only shouted praises and acclamations but also removed some of their garments and cut down palm branches and other foliage to lay along His path, making a carpet for the passing King.[278] The Pharisees' reaction was predictable—they instantly requested that the Savior quiet the crowd. But Jesus explained to the Pharisees that on this day, if the crowd were quieted the very stones would cry out proclaiming Him King.

As the multitude descended from the Mount of Olives with the city of Jerusalem in full view, Jesus paused, wept, and sadly uttered prophesies concerning the city and its residents. Generally speaking, the rulers and the inhabitants of Jerusalem had rejected the Savior and His claim to the Messiahship. Even now they objected to Him, and that objection would shortly lead to His crucifixion. This, in turn, would lead to the destruction of Jerusalem and the beautiful temple that lay before them, and the Lord prophesied that the enemies of the Jews would lay siege to the city on "every side." Many would die, and the stones of the city walls that had offered them such protection and security would be leveled until all was destroyed—not one stone would be left upon another. Although no one understood His prophecy at the time, less than forty short years later it was fulfilled.

Those in the multitude and even those in the city who hated the Lord and sought His destruction still craved salvation. They yearned for the Messiah that Christ claimed to be; but He refused to be their political savior. In spite of this conflict, His entrance publicly established His claim to the Messiahship—not as Israel perceived the Messiah, but as the Messiah had been prophetically proclaimed.[b][279] So great was the cry heralding the Savior as the Son of David that the

a. Psalm 118:25–28.

b. Isaiah 62:11; Zechariah 9:9.

Pharisees complained in disgust that if He were left alone, all the world would go after Him.[a][280]

The Lord's entry into Jerusalem occurred four days before the official Passover celebration began,[281] and the joyous shouts acclaiming Him king were based on the same hymn that would be sung on the day when the paschal lamb was slain in the temple for consumption on the feast day.[282] Christ had not informed His disciples or the Twelve about the significance of His entrance into Jerusalem on this particular day, and none of them seemed to really understand what was taking place.[283] Without this understanding, they undoubtedly "walked in the procession almost as in a dream, or as dazzled by a brilliant light all around—as if impelled by a necessity, and carried from event to event, which came upon them in a succession of but partially understood surprises."[284] Only the Savior knew that He was offering Himself as the paschal lamb for the sins of all mankind.

Even while the people shouted hosannas and acclaimed Christ as their king, they did not fully understand what this acclamation entailed. They enthusiastically accepted Jesus as the prophet of Nazareth from Galilee,[285] but He had not fulfilled their expectations as a powerful, political leader. The Pharisees and the rulers, however, clearly understood His claim,[286] and they watched for an opportunity to secure His destruction.

The Last Supper, Part One: The Passover Feast

Matthew 26:17–25   Now the first day of the feast of unleavened bread the disciples came to Jesus, saying unto him, Where wilt thou that we prepare for thee to eat the passover? And he said, Go into the city to such a man, and say unto him, The Master saith, My time is at hand; I will keep the passover at thy house with my disciples. And the disciples did as Jesus had appointed them; and they made ready the passover. Now when the even was come, he sat down with the twelve. And as they did eat, he said, Verily I say unto you, that one of you shall betray me. And they were exceeding sorrowful, and began every one of them to say unto him, Lord, is it I? And he answered and said, He that dippeth his hand with me in the dish, the same shall betray me. The Son of man goeth as it is written of him: but woe unto that man by whom the Son of man is betrayed! it had been good for that man if he had not been born.   Then Judas, which betrayed him, answered and said, Master, is it I? He said unto him, Thou hast said.

Cross-references   Mark 14:12–21; Luke 22:7–16, 21–38

a. John 12:19.

The Lord's triumphant entry into Jerusalem produced enormous excitement throughout the holy city and among the Passover celebrants; but as the days progressed and the feast of the Passover drew nigh, Jesus did nothing to further His claim in the people's eyes. All that they had heard from Him were His discourses in the temple.[287] They undoubtedly still anticipated the powerful advent of the long-awaited Messianic kingdom, but by now it was evident that Jesus was not the one they had looked for.[288] His Messianic claims at this time and throughout His ministry had not gone unnoticed, however. From the very moment Jesus entered Jerusalem, the Jewish leadership took counsel on how they might subtly take Him and kill Him.[a] Their deliberations were cautious for they knew that many looked upon Jesus as a prophet, so they determined that they would not take Him on the feast day for fear of a public uproar.[b] In the midst of their dilemma, an unknown ally appeared: Judas Iscariot sought them out and with diabolical avarice, "Satan's serf"[289] bargained with them over the price of the Messiah's betrayal. The bargain was completed and the covenant made: they would give him thirty pieces of silver, the price of a common slave, for the betrayal of the Savior of the world.

This may have been the only Passover that Jesus celebrated as the "head" of the company rather than as a guest.[290] At the first Passover, after beginning His public ministry, He had not yet called the Twelve Apostles, so if He attended the celebration at Jerusalem He would not have served at the head of the table.[291] During the second Passover He was not in Jerusalem, so He did not celebrate the feast there that year.[c] But on this, the third and final Passover of His mission, He gathered His group around the paschal lamb—as did all of Israel in commemoration of the past, in celebration of the present, and in keen anticipation of the future.

The scriptures report that "the day of unleavened bread came when the passover offering must be killed," so the Lord sent Peter and John to prepare the Passover feast. To properly prepare for the meal they had to acquire a male lamb, one year of age and without blemish. At "about two [2:00 p.m.], the blast of horns announced that the priests and Levites in the Temple were ready, and the gates in the inner courts were opened that all might bring their lambs for examination,

a. Matthew 26:4.

b. Matthew 26:5.

c. Matthew 15:21.

and might satisfy the priests as to the number intending to consume each."[292] Peter and John would have lined up with the other men inside the temple courts, their lamb draped across their shoulders. The knife used to slay the lamb would have been stuck in its wool or tied to its horn. When the time to slaughter the lambs approached, the gates of the temple would have been shut.

At about 2:30 p.m., the lamb for the evening offering was killed, and about one hour later this ceremony was completed when parts of the lamb were laid upon the altar. Then three blasts of the trumpets sounded and the Levites performed choral singing, signaling the time for the slaughter of the Passover lambs brought by the celebrants for the Passover meal .[293] This took place between the Jews' two evenings: the first evening was defined as the interval after the sun commenced its decline, and the second evening occurred at the hour when the sun started to disappear, or about 6:00 p.m.[294] During the ceremony, the priests held large silver bowls and golden vessels of curious shape to catch the blood of the lambs as they were slaughtered by the heads of the families. The priests passed the blood-filled containers behind them to other priests until they reached the foot of the altar where the blood was poured out. The lambs were skinned and dressed in the temple with the tail, fat, kidneys, and liver set apart for use at the altar. The rest of the animal was wrapped in the skin and taken by the celebrants to be placed on pomegranate wood and roasted in an underground oven in preparation for the Passover meal.[295]

The feast began immediately after the sun had officially set and the stars appeared. This event was also proclaimed by trumpet blasts from the temple on what was designated as the beginning of the fifteenth of Nisan.[296]

The Lord gave curious instructions to some of His disciples for preparing the room where He and the Apostles would celebrate the Passover. He told them to go into the city where they would meet a man bearing a pitcher of water and follow Him, for he was the goodman of the house they would use. They were to tell Him that the Master would celebrate the Passover with His disciples in His guestchamber, and that when they had carried out these instructions, they would know that all would be furnished—and it was so.

When evening approached and the hour of the supper arrived, the Lord took His Twelve Apostles and went to the prepared guest-chamber to celebrate the ending of the old Covenant and the beginning of the new.[297] As they commenced the last meal that the Lord would eat with them in His mortal state, a contention arose among the Twelve.

Earlier in Jesus' ministry, the Apostles had contended one with another as to who would be the greatest in His heavenly realm.[a] James and John had even requested (through their mother) that they be granted the first and second positions in the Lord's kingdom.[b] Due to their lack of understanding concerning the Messiah and His mission, they longed for and sought after the honors and glories bestowed by the world.[298] The Lord once again instructed them—even on this last night before His crucifixion—using as an analogy the earthly glories and kingdoms they desired. Rather than being like the gentile kings (exercising unrighteous authority over those whom they ruled), He exhorted them to serve others. Using Himself as the example, He indicated that although He was the Master of the feast, He was still sitting among them as "he that serveth."

This conflict had probably arisen over the seating arrangements at the feast table. Jewish custom places the greatest or most respected man at the head of the table, graduating down to the least important man at the foot of the table.[299] The Lord rebuked His disciples for their contention, but He would not have this evening spoiled either by their argument or by His rebuke; therefore, He continued His instructions on a positive note, acknowledging that they had indeed remained with Him during His temptations and trials and promising them a place in His Father's kingdom where they would "sit on thrones judging the twelve tribes of Israel."

The Passover table was undoubtedly set low to the ground, suspended on very short legs or braces or perhaps hanging from the ceiling, suspended above the ground to preserve it from any possible Levitical defilement.[300] The table was oblong, with cushions on the floor surrounding it on three sides while leaving an open end extending beyond the cushions for serving purposes. The guests reclined on the cushions rather than sitting on them, "lying on the left side and leaning on the left hand, the feet stretching back towards the ground, and each guest occupying a separate divan or pillow."[301] While differences

a. Mark 9:33–34.
b. Matthew
20:20–28.

are recorded as to the placement, description, and seating customs of the Passover table,[302] the table would probably have looked like the accompanying diagram.

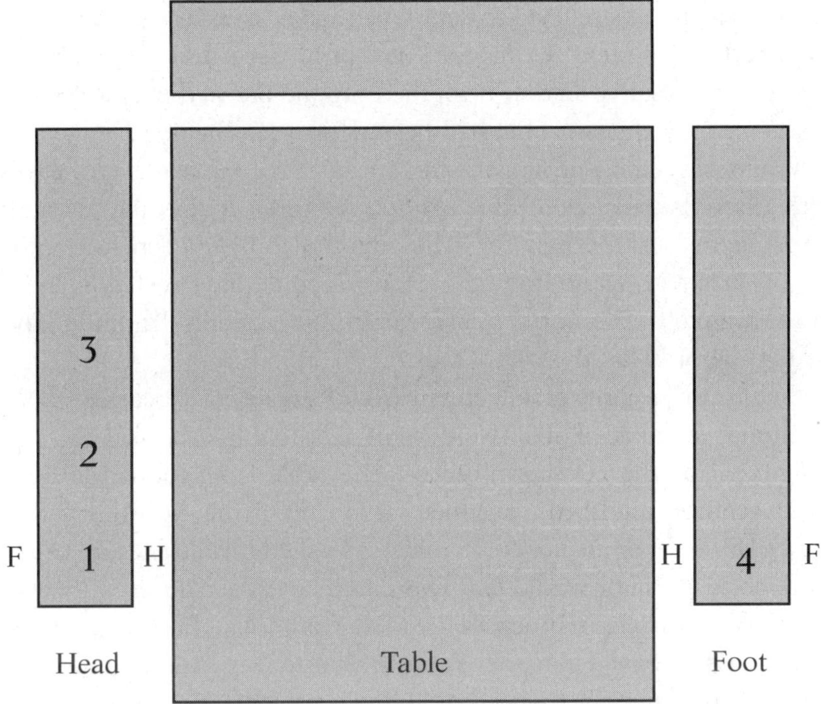

Jesus, as the host of the feast, probably occupied the traditional center place of the first three cushions. This would have been the second pillow or cushion from the end, indicated by the number 2 on the diagram. As He reclined, supporting His head with His left hand, His head would have been at "H," close to the table, His feet extending beyond the cushion in the direction of "F," away from the table. Each person around the table was in a similar position.

The chief place (reserved for the chief guest of the feast) is indicated by the number 3 in the diagram, and it appears that Judas claimed that place.[303] The seat identified as number 1 in the diagram would have been occupied by John the Beloved. This would explain why, when Christ whispered to John the sign by which the traitor could be recognized, that none of the other disciples heard it. In addition, if

Judas occupied seat number 3 at the table, it would have been perfectly normal (in fact required) for Christ to hand him the first sop. Therefore, the other disciples would have paid no special attention when Christ handed the sop to Judas. This seating arrangement would also explain why no one seemed to hear when Judas asked the question, "Is it I?" perhaps to see if the Savior knew of his treachery. When he received an affirmative answer from the Lord, no one at the table seemed to know or understand what had passed between them.[304]

While this seating arrangement is speculative, it explains how easily other circumstances described in the scriptures could take place. If John was on cushion number 1 he would also have been resting on His left arm and, while leaning backward, could have rested his head on the bosom of the Lord.[a] If he was in this position, he could have asked the Lord who the traitor was.

Finally, this seating arrangement would suggest the location of one additional member of the Twelve. Peter probably occupied the seat designated by the number 4, across the table from John. Matthew 26:21 records the Lord's prophecy that one of the Apostles would betray Him. Peter beckoned to John and asked him to inquire of the Lord who the traitor would be. This could have been done easily with Peter sitting immediately across the table from John. Further, it would have been the logical place for Peter to sit after the contention among the disciples concerning who should be the greatest in the Lord's kingdom. Peter, in his normal fashion and in an attempt to debase himself after the Lord's rebuke, would have naturally taken the last place at the table. The rest of the Twelve would have been seated around the table at their convenience.[305]

The Passover meal would have consisted of at least three courses: first, the Passover lamb, which represented God's "passing over" the houses of the children of Israel in Egypt that had been sprinkled with lamb's blood, thus sparing their firstborn from the angel of death; second, unleavened bread, which represented the haste with which the children of Israel had left Egypt; and third, bitter herbs, which represented the bitter lives led while the children of Israel were in bondage.[306]

As the formal Passover ceremony commenced, the Lord blessed the first cup of wine (as was the custom of the feast). He then revealed to

a. John 13:23.

the Apostles that this would be the last time He would eat with them until they had entered His heavenly kingdom. After blessing the cup of wine, He passed it among the Twelve so that each might drink. Jesus then arose from the table, removed His dinner garment, girded Himself with a towel, and proceeded to wash the Apostles' feet.

The Last Supper, Part Two: The Washing of the Feet

John 13:1–10   Now before the feast of the passover, when Jesus knew that his hour was come that he should depart out of this world unto the Father, having loved his own which were in the world, he loved them unto the end. And supper being ended, the devil having now put into the heart of Judas Iscariot, Simon's son, to betray him; Jesus knowing that the Father had given all things into his hands, and that he was come from God, and went to God; He riseth from supper, and laid aside his garments; and took a towel, and girded himself. After that he poureth water into a bason, and began to wash the disciples' feet, and to wipe them with the towel wherewith he was girded. Then cometh he to Simon Peter: and Peter saith unto him, Lord, dost thou wash my feet? Jesus answered and said unto him, What I do thou knowest not now; but thou shalt know hereafter. Peter saith unto him, Thou shalt never wash my feet. Jesus answered him, If I wash thee not, thou hast no part with me. Simon Peter saith unto him, Lord, not my feet only, but also my hands and my head. Jesus saith to him, He that is washed needeth not save to wash his feet, but is clean every whit: and ye are clean, but not all.

Of the four Gospel writers, only John records the washing of feet. The Lord likely celebrated the Passover in the traditional manner, for it was indeed the last supper of the old Covenant which Jehovah (the God of the Old Testament, incarnate in Jesus Christ) had made with the children of Israel as they left Egypt. As the old Covenant was passing away, the ordinances of the new covenant were being instituted, and the first of these ordinances was the washing of feet.[307] Jesus introduced it during the Passover supper at the time of the first symbolic hand washing (which was a part of the ritual from the old Covenant). "Now this was the custom of the Jews under their law; wherefore, Jesus did this that the law might be fulfilled."[a]

The ceremonial hand washing was performed twice during the paschal supper, first by the head of the company alone. He stood while the others reclined at the dinner table, thereby ritualistically distinguishing Himself from all others at the supper.[308] During the second hand washing, all members of the company stood and participated, which would

a. IV John 13:10.

have made the foot washing unnecessarily cumbersome. Therefore, while we do not know exactly when the washing of feet took place, it would have most easily been performed at the time of the first hand washing while the Twelve were still reclining on their cushions. Thus, the Lord would have arisen from the table after the first cup of wine had passed the lips of all present and "during supper," removed His outer dinner garment and girded Himself with a towel.[309]

Throughout His ministry, the ceremonial washings as the Jews performed them had meant nothing to the Lord. Indeed, He had been criticized for not complying with them.[a] Jesus considered the Jews' ceremonies as nothing more than outward observances, availing nothing to those who were not inwardly clean, and unnecessary to those whose hearts and lives had already been purified. He perhaps performed them now to mark the ceremonial end of the old Law.

Christ probably began by pouring water into a large copper bowl or basin that was always provided by the householder at such a meal.[310] He washed His hands in accordance with the Law and moved first to Peter, coming to him "not after the others, but after the place where the basin and water for the purification had stood."[311] It was only natural that the Lord should begin with Peter, for not only was he the chief Apostle, he was probably occupying the end position at the table opposite from where the Lord had been reclining (as previously described). Further, Peter's objection to the Lord washing his feet would hold more meaning if he were first to receive the service.

Peter's reaction was typical of his personality. He behaved similarly when he was called to follow the Savior after the miracle of the first draught of fish.[312] After his call he had fallen down at Jesus' feet and said, "Depart from me; for I am a sinful man, O Lord."[b] Much later in Christ's ministry when Jesus informed the Apostles that He would die at Jerusalem, Peter again began to rebuke Him saying, "Be it far from thee, Lord: this shall not be unto thee."[c] It was therefore natural that Peter object to his feet being washed by the Savior, for he considered it to be a slave's task and the lowest act of personal service.[313] The Lord's response to Peter's statement indicates that Peter did not understand the meaning of the ordinance, and in his ignorance he stubbornly maintained, "Thou shalt never wash my feet."

The Lord did not remonstrate with Peter as he had when Peter had

a. Matthew
   15:1–14; Mark
   7:1–23.

b. Luke 5:8.

c. Matthew 16:22.

rebuked Him for forecasting His future death, but He indicated to His chief Apostle that if He did not wash his feet, Peter could have no part with Him. Peter's great character and strong love for the Lord was again manifest when he immediately cried, "Lord, not my feet only, but also my hands and my head." But that was unnecessary, and the Lord indicated that washing the feet was all that was required.

This brief discussion between the Lord and Peter revealed the first reason for instituting the washing of the feet. The ordinance was necessary so that *the Apostles might have "a part" with Jesus;* to share His great work of salvation upon the earth, they must be willing to submit to Him, the Master of all. The ordinance carried with it a deep symbolic meaning regarding the service required of those who would minister in His kingdom. The Lord acknowledged that the Apostles had called Him Master and He accepted that title, but He emphasized that as He had washed their feet, so they, too, should wash one another's feet. His example was one of service: as He had served, so they should serve. The servant was not greater than the Lord, nor was the one sent greater than the Master who sent him.

The second reason for the ordinance concerned *humility, pride, and selfish ambition.* By accepting the Lord's call, the Apostles had taken up the cross and entered into His ministry; which meant that they would work as He had worked, serve as He had served, and love as He had loved. The washing of feet had been more than a service for personal comfort or an object lesson in humility,[314] the Apostles were being told that the ordinance symbolized both their desire to emulate the Savior and their willingness to rid themselves of pride and selfish ambition.[315]

Finally, the third reason for the washing of feet was expressed in the Lord's comment that by this ordinance the Apostles became "clean every whit." To this extent, the washing of feet was related to the washing of hands. If the Apostles were not inwardly clean prior to the washing, they would not be clean after it. The ordinance would have no meaning to those who had not properly and spiritually prepared for it. But those who were clean both in heart and spirit would be cleansed from the blood and sins of a wicked generation.[a316]

However, not all were clean among the Twelve and the Lord emphasized that, for Judas had also participated in the ordinance. The

a. D&C 88:74–75, 137–141.

ordinance of the washing of feet is an eternal ordinance with eternal import.[317] In the latter days, it was restored with the same significance as when instituted by the Savior at His last supper.[a][318] On 12 November 1835, after the first latter-day Apostles had been called and ordained, Joseph Smith addressed them concerning the washing of feet, instructing them that the house of the Lord then being built in Kirtland must be prepared and a solemn assembly called so that the ordinance could be attended to.[319] On 29 and 30 March 1836, all of the leading brethren of the Church (including the First Presidency, the Council of the Twelve, Bishoprics, and presidents of quorums) participated in the ordinance [320]

When He had finished washing the Apostles' feet, the Lord set aside the towel and the washing bowl, put on His dinner garment, and returned to the table to continue the paschal meal. He resumed His discussion with the Apostles by prophesying that one of the Twelve would yet betray Him, a statement that deeply saddened the disciples. They hesitantly began questioning, "Is it I?" "Is it I?" Peter asked John to inquire of the Lord concerning the betrayer's identity, and the Lord stated that it would be he to whom the first sop was given. It may seem odd that the disciples did not therefore recognize the betrayer when the sop was handed to Judas, but it need only be remembered that Judas, seated as the chief guest of the feast, was the first to receive the sop in any instance, and that after this, each of those at the table would in turn receive a sop. (The "sop" was a portion of a thin, flexible bread-cake dipped in the common dish,[321] and Jesus would have given one to each paschal participant in accord with the established ritual.)

As Jesus prepared the first sop, Judas, perhaps fearing that he might be discovered by the others, asked, "Is it I?" While the others had asked the question in anguish of heart, Judas asked with subtlety so that he might not betray himself. However, by uttering this question his mask of treachery was torn away and the Lord responded, "That thou doest, do quickly."

Even now the others did not fully understand, for they undoubtedly did not hear what had taken place and they were confused. But the devil had entered into Judas and he hastened to leave the feast while the others thought that he had gone on some errand on instruction from the Lord.[322]

a. D&C 88:137–141.

After the traitor left, the atmosphere seemed to clear and the Lord appeared to be more relaxed and at ease. He spoke as though His mission was fulfilled, and He declared that the Son of Man was glorified and the Father was glorified in Him. He continued to instruct the disciples, informing them that He would be with them only a short time longer: after He was gone they would seek after Him, but they could not go where He was going.

Then Jesus again declared His new commandment: they should love one another as He had loved them, and by this all men would know that they were His disciples. Peter again showed His lack of understanding and preparedness for the approaching events[323] when he asked the Lord where He would go. The Lord responded that Peter could not go with Him immediately, but that he would follow later. Again Peter protested that he would lay down His life for the Lord, whereupon the Lord cautioned Him, "Simon, Simon, behold, Satan hath desired to have you."

The Lord then strengthened Peter by declaring that He had prayed that Peter's faith would not fail. He then concluded by stating that when Peter was finally converted, he should strengthen his brethren. But Peter would not relent. He again protested, stating that he was ready to go with the Lord both to prison and to death. Finally the Lord prophesied to Peter that the "cock shall not crow this day, before that thou shalt thrice deny that thou knowest me."[a324]

The paschal meal continued, and during its normal course Jesus undoubtedly instituted the second ordinance of the new covenant—the sacrament.

The Last Supper, Part Three: The Sacrament

Matthew 26:26–29 And as they were eating, Jesus took bread, and blessed it, and brake it, and gave it to the disciples, and said, Take, eat; this is my body. And he took the cup, and gave thanks, and gave it to them, saying, Drink ye all of it; for this is my blood of the new testament, which is shed for many for the remission of sins. But I say unto you, I will not drink henceforth of this fruit of the vine, until that day when I drink it new with you in my Father's kingdom.

Cross-references Mark 14:22–25; Luke 22:17–20; JST, Matthew 26:22–25; 3 Nephi 9:17, 19–20; 3 Nephi 18:5–11; 3 Nephi 20:8; Moroni 4, 5; D&C 20:75–79; D&C 27:2–4

a. Luke 22:34.

Only the Synoptics record the institution of the sacrament. Although there are some discrepancies between the Synoptic writings, they are insignificant since they each attest to the significance of the sacrament and its institution as the emblem of the new covenant.

The Passover celebration commemorated the blessings Jehovah gave to the children of Israel as they escaped from bondage in Egypt. Included in the celebration was the slaying of the paschal lamb, an act which looked forward to the anticipated Messiah. This represented part of the ancient sacrifice practiced by Adam in anticipation of the future Atonement and sacrifice of the Son of God.[a325]

From the Exodus forward, the children of Israel had celebrated the Passover in the similitude of Christ's sacrifice. "All of the sacrificial similitudes of all ages combined to bear testimony of the infinite and eternal atoning sacrifice—the sacrifice of the Lamb of God who taketh away the sins of the world."[326]

Now Christ's eternal sacrifice was about to take place, and the paschal lambs that had been slain in the temple symbolically testified for the last time of that great and eternal sacrifice that would shortly come to pass. When Christ gave His life for mankind, animal sacrifice authorized by the Lord as it was practiced from Adam to the time of Christ, ceased. At the Last Supper, the Lord instituted a new ordinance to replace it. The new ordinance was called the sacrament.

The Passover meal offered the perfect situation for instituting the sacrament. The similitude of the Passover celebration and that of the sacrament was the same. Whereas the ceremonial sacrifice of animals looked forward to the great eternal sacrifice, the shedding of blood and the atonement of Christ for all mankind, the sacrament looked to the past in remembrance of that glorious event. Both ordinances focus on that moment in time when the Son of God fulfilled His earthly mission and provided through the Atonement, the Crucifixion, and the Resurrection (1) salvation for all mankind and (2) exaltation for those who would obey His words. The blood of the Passover lamb redeemed God's chosen people from the angel of death as it passed over Egypt; so, too, the blood of the Son of God will ransom all mankind from the angel of death (sin) and thus open the way for entering God's kingdom.

After Christ washed the Apostle's feet, the supper continued. The company no doubt ate bitter herbs in remembrance of the children of

a. Moses 5:5–8.

Israel's sojourn in Egypt. Whether the Lord participated in every portion of the ceremonial observance is unknown, but it is unlikely that He did, for the Jewish leaders had changed and expanded much of the ceremony over the passing centuries.[327] However, they certainly ate all the unleavened bread and the lamb, for the feast required it. At this point, the ceremony called for the blessing and drinking of the third cup of wine, and in all probability it was now that the Lord instituted the ordinance of the sacrament.[328] John does not record the ordinance of the sacrament and the Synoptics do not record the washing of feet. However, they all seem to agree on the general progression of the meal. While it seems evident that Judas participated in the washing of feet, there is disagreement as to whether he participated in the sacrament. John indicates that Judas left before the sacrament was instituted. Matthew and Mark would agree with this order, although it could be inferred from Luke that Judas remained during the majority of the meal and partook of the sacrament before leaving the table.[a]

Some have indicated that Judas partook of the sacrament in order that he might have one last opportunity to abandon his evil purpose, or finally conclude his condemnation;[329] others have indicated that Judas left the meal prior to its institution.[330] While this argument has persisted, no definite answer to the question can be determined from the scriptural record.

Just as with the washing of feet, the ceremony of the Passover feast provided the Lord with the opportunity of instituting a new ordinance without unduly disrupting the supper itself. He took bread, "blessed it, and brake it, and gave it to the disciples," with the instructions that they should eat, for, he said, "This is my body." Similarly, he took the cup, "gave thanks, and gave it to them," instructing them to drink, for, he said, "This is my blood of the New Testament, which is shed for many for the remission of sins."

The scriptures note that the Lord blessed both the bread and the wine, but the specific words of the blessings are not recorded. Although the Passover celebration contained certain ritual blessings for the bread and the wine,[331] the Lord probably would not have used them;[332] however, where the New Testament does not record specific instructions regarding the sacrament, the Book of Mormon does. It explains that after Christ's resurrection, He visited the Nephites and instituted the sacrament.[a] In this connection, the Lord no doubt gave the same instructions to the Apostles of the ancient church as He did to the Nephites and to the latter-day prophet of the Restoration.[333] These instructions would have included the sacrament prayers containing the similitudes of the bread to Christ's body and the wine to His blood, and the teaching that by worthily partaking of the sacrament, we come into fellowship with Him and spiritually feed on the remembrance of His mission.[b]

The Lord used wine for the sacrament both at the Last Supper and on the Western Hemisphere. However, in the Restoration the Lord revealed that water could be substituted for wine[c] as we do today.

We take the sacrament for the following purposes:

1. *To remember the body and blood of Christ.* The ordinance looks back on the Atonement, the Crucifixion, and the Resurrection. Like sacrifice, the Passover celebration had looked forward to those same events. Through our remembrance, we acknowledge that Jesus is the resurrection and the life, and no one can be saved but by Him.[d]

2. *To take upon us the name of Christ.* We covenant with and witness before our Father in Heaven that we will take upon us the name of Christ. By doing this we accept Christ's teachings and place them in our lives as guiding principles. Earlier in His ministry, Jesus alluded to this when He delivered a discourse at Capernaum on "the bread of life."[334] In that discourse, He used the common metaphors of food and drink[335] to teach the Jews that they must "eat of His flesh" and "drink of His blood" to become part of Him. The literal-minded Jews questioned how anyone could eat of His flesh and drink of His blood, but the Lord was using the example metaphorically, not literally. He meant that they must make His teachings and their belief in Him part of them and that they should exemplify that belief in everything they did, just as bread and wine were assimilated into their body tissues and literally became an abiding part of the body. When we partake of the sacrament worthily, we accept Christ as our Lord and King; we evidence

a. 3 Nephi
   18:3–11.

b. 3 Nephi
   18:3–11; Mo-
   roni 4, 5; D&C
   20:75–79.

c. D&C 27:2–4.

d. John 14:6.

this by living His commandments and acknowledging Him as the literal Son of God, our personal Savior.

3.   *To always remember Him.* We should direct our constant attention to the Savior's atonement. In celebrating the final feast of the Passover, the Lord fulfilled the old law and initiated the new. "Sacrifice stopped and sacrament started."[336] Sacrifice and the Passover pointed the ancients *toward* the coming atonement; the sacrament replaced these venerable ordinances and pointed the attention of His Saints (after His death) *back* to the great atoning sacrifice which He had wrought.[337]

4.   *To keep the Lord's commandments.* We specifically covenant to keep the Lord's commandments when we partake of the sacrament. The Lord put it simply: "If ye love me, keep my commandments."[a] To keep His commandments is to "live by every word that proceedeth forth from the mouth of God."[b]

5.   *To receive God's blessings.* Providing we have partaken of the sacrament worthily and continue to live righteously, God has promised us that He will grant us His Spirit to be with us so that "in due course [all] shall inherit eternal life."[338]

The church grew rapidly after Christ's resurrection and the Apostles undoubtedly instructed the new converts in proper sacrament observance. The Savior had instituted a simple rite. However, over the years various incorrect doctrines developed concerning the sacrament—until its restoration in modern times. Perhaps these errors were due to theological zeal or heated fancy, but in any event, they would have startled and shocked the original Saints.

Evidence of this problem was apparent early in the church. The Saints at Corinth had made a mockery of the sacrament by reducing it to a gluttonous feast replete with drunkenness. Paul, in correcting this wrongdoing, declared harshly, "For there must be also heresies among you. . . . When ye came together therefore into one place, this is not to eat the Lord's supper. For in eating every one taketh before other his own supper: and one is hungry, and another is drunken. What? have ye not houses to eat and to drink in? or despise ye the church of

a. John 14:15.
b. D&C 84:44.

God, and shame them that have not? What shall I say to you? shall I praise you in this? I praise you not."[a] Paul warned the Saints not to make a mockery of this ordinance nor participate in it unworthily, concluding that if a man did so, he would eat and drink "damnation to Himself. . . . For this cause many are weak and sickly among you, and many sleep [die]."[b]

The sacrament is a simple ordinance, but it is of singular importance in the lives of worthy Saints. If we partake of it unworthily, we jeopardize our salvation; but if we partake worthily, we open the door to eternal life by accepting Christ and His teachings into our lives.

When the Savior had finished administering the sacrament to the Apostles, He continued His teachings to strengthen their faith. The fateful advent of His arrest and trial would soon scatter them abroad, so He reminded them of the success of their first mission. They had gone without purse or scrip and yet lacked nothing, and the Apostles acknowledged this. But now the Lord told them to be prepared, to take purse and scrip, for now they would be subject to the harsh circumstances of the world. The sword, He said as an example, would better describe their future proselytizing problems: if they did not have a sword they should sell their garments and buy one. It was another metaphor used to describe the difficult times they would face as they taught all nations. He knew that He and His followers would be "reckoned among the transgressors" in the world's eyes. The Apostles again failed to grasp the Lord's meaning and declared they had but two swords in their possession. Without continuing His explanation Jesus closed the conversation by simply stating, "It is enough."[c]

The Passover supper was finished—the old Covenant had passed away.

a. 1 Corinthians 11:19–22.

b. 1 Corinthians 11:27–30.

c. Luke 22:38.

In the Valley of the Shadow of Death 6

The Atonement

Matthew 26:31–45   Then saith Jesus unto them, All ye shall be offended because of me this night: for it is written, I will smite the shepherd, and the sheep of the flock shall be scattered abroad. But after I am risen again, I will go before you into Galilee. Peter answered and said unto him, Though all men shall be offended because of thee, yet will I never be offended. Jesus said unto him, Verily I say unto thee, That this night, before the cock crow, thou shalt deny me thrice. Peter said unto him, Though I should die with thee, yet will I not deny thee. Likewise also said all the disciples.

Then cometh Jesus with them unto a place called Gethsemane, and saith unto the disciples, Sit ye here, while I go and pray yonder. And he took with him Peter and the two sons of Zebedee, and began to be sorrowful and very heavy. Then saith he unto them, My soul is exceeding sorrowful, even unto death: tarry ye here, and watch with me. And he went a little further, and fell on his face, and prayed, saying, O my Father, if it be possible, let this cup pass from me: nevertheless not as I will, but as thou wilt. And he cometh unto the disciples, and findeth them asleep, and saith unto Peter, What, could ye not watch with me one hour? Watch and pray, that ye enter not into temptation: the spirit indeed is willing, but the flesh is weak. He went away again the second time, and prayed, saying, O my Father, if this cup may not pass away from me, except I drink it, thy will be done. And he came and found them asleep again: for their eyes were heavy. And he left them, and went away again, and prayed the third time, saying the same words. Then cometh he to his disciples, and saith unto them, Sleep on now, and take your rest: behold, the hour is at hand, and the Son of man is betrayed into the hands of sinners.

Cross-references   Mark 14:27–41; Luke 22:40–46; JST, Mark 14:36

At the conclusion of the Passover supper, Jesus and the eleven

Apostles prepared to leave Jerusalem to go to the Mount of Olives. The temple gates on this festive night were thrown open at midnight,[339] and the streets were not deserted. As they passed the houses, bright lamps may have illuminated the night, indicating that the celebration of the paschal lamb was still taking place.

The group passed out of the city through the gate north of the temple and descended into the Valley of Kidron. They crossed over to the other side of the valley and entered the garden known as Gethsemane. The word *Gethsemane* means "oil press,"[340] and was derived from the fact that there was an olive grove growing there.[341] As they walked toward the garden, the Lord stated that all of them would be "offended . . . this night" because of Him, and that the "sheep of the flock" would be scattered abroad. Matthew reports that Peter protested, but the Lord prophesied that Peter would deny knowing Him "thrice" before the cock crowed. Again he protested, stating that he would die before denying the Savior, as did all the disciples.

Leaving eight of the Apostles at Gethsemane's entrance, the Lord took Peter, James, and John with Him into the garden. As they progressed deeper into the garden, Jesus became heavy with sorrow. Then the Lord asked these three Apostles to tarry and watch with Him. He went on ahead, "fell on His face," and prayed to His Father in Heaven. John records some of this personal conversation between the Son and the Father,[a][342] and the Synoptics record the agony of the occasion when even the Savior of the world prayed, "If it be possible, let this cup pass from me: nevertheless not as I will, but as thou wilt."

As the Lord continued in prayer, He took upon Himself the burden of the fall of Adam and all the subsequent sins of mankind; in so doing, He prepared the way by which all again could return into the Father's presence. Meanwhile, the Apostles became weary and fell asleep (just as they had done on the Mount of Transfiguration).[b] About an hour later the Lord returned to them. He roused them from their slumber and admonished Peter, "Could ye not watch with me one hour?" Again He earnestly requested them to watch and pray lest they enter into temptation, then He returned to His prayers. The Apostles apparently watched for a time, heeding the caution from the Lord, for a limited amount of the Lord's second prayer is recorded. Matthew records that

a. John 17.

b. Luke 9:32.

the Lord, fully recognizing His mission, commented that the cup *could not* pass from Him—the Father's will would be done.

Luke's gospel records the Lord's agony in detail. He writes that an angel appeared to Jesus to strengthen Him, causing Him to pray even more earnestly. The pain of suffering for the sins of mankind was so great that "His sweat was as great drops of blood falling down to the ground." The prayers continued, but again the Apostles became "heavy" and fell asleep. When the Lord returned and found them asleep once more, He again roused them. He immediately returned to pray for the third time, "saying the same words." When He had completed His prayers, the Lord returned and found the Apostles asleep for the third time. He did not immediately awaken them but allowed them to sleep on, for the hour was at hand when the Son of God would be betrayed into the hands of His enemies. (Perhaps at least one Apostle was awake from time to time or [apart from the possibility of later revelation] there would be no record of Jesus' prayers, but they all must have been asleep when the Lord returned to them.) It is impossible for the finite mind to understand or comprehend the unbearable physical and spiritual agony that the Son of God experienced in the Garden; but in spite of His anguish, He remained faithful to His Father and to His calling.

At the commencement of His mission, the Lord had contended with the devil three times at the end of His fast in the wilderness; now, as His earthly mission was ending, He overcame all that Satan had done or would ever do.[343] There is no question that the pain and suffering of the crucifixion was part of Christ's atonement, but "the triumph and grandeur of the atonement took place primarily in Gethsemane."[344]

Just how the Savior of the world took upon Himself the sins of mankind to intercede for the faithful is unknown, but that this was the Messiah's ultimate purpose in His earthly ministry is attested to by all of the prophets. Jesus had come to earth to assume the total burden of man's sin and shame, to overcome the Apostasy and the Fall, and to taste of "the bitter cup which sin had poisoned."[345] Failure would have allowed Satan to succeed. Death, both physical and spiritual, separated mankind from the Father, and only through an infinite sacrifice by one such as the Son of God could the Fall be overcome and man reunited with His Father in Heaven.

Amulek bore testimony of the great atoning sacrifice of the Lord in these words:

> **Alma 34:8–12**   I do know that Christ shall come among the children of men, to take upon him the transgressions of his people, and that he shall atone for the sins of the world; for the Lord God hath spoken it. For it is expedient that an atonement should be made; for according to the great plan of the Eternal God there must be an atonement made, or else all mankind must unavoidably perish; yea, all are hardened; yea, all are fallen and are lost, and must perish except it be through the atonement which it is expedient should be made. For it is expedient that there should be a great and last sacrifice; yea, not a sacrifice of man, neither of beast, neither of any manner of fowl; for it shall not be a human sacrifice; but it must be an infinite and eternal sacrifice. Now there is not any man that can sacrifice his own blood which will atone for the sins of another. . . . Therefore there can be nothing which is short of an infinite atonement which will suffice for the sins of the world.

Through the Atonement, the fall of Adam was overcome and victory over death secured.[a] The ransom had been paid and the Lord's mastery over Satan was finally complete. Adam had introduced spiritual and temporal death into the world, but the "second Adam"[b] had provided the opportunity for eternal life.

With the Fall overcome, man was now fully responsible for his own sins. Christ's suffering made operable the law whereby each individual could lay claim to the blessings of the Atonement—the law of repentance. Without repentance, God's justice applies to every sin and man is forever banned from His presence. However, repentance and God's mercy satisfy the demands of justice, making it possible for the eternal plan of redemption to automatically apply,[c] Although the Atonement is difficult to comprehend, its application is not. Again, simply stated, the Atonement made operative the law of repentance.

While the Lord prayed intensely in Gethsemane and the Apostles slept, Judas consummated his sinful plot with the chief priests. The Savior returned for the last time to His slumbering Apostles and, perhaps as He sat and watched, His ears might have caught the noise of treading footsteps and the ill-suppressed tumult of the advancing crowd. The traitor knew of the quiet garden, for he had been there often.[d] Soon the red glare of torches could be seen, and Jesus awakened His sleeping brethren. As Judas, the authorities, and the rest of

a. 1 Corinthians 15:22; Romans 5:12–18.

b. 1 Corinthians 15:45–47.

c. Alma 34:15–16; 2 Peter 3:9.

d. John 18:2.

the crowd approached, the Lord sadly spoke His last free words to His confused Apostles: "He is at hand that doth betray me."[a]

Never once did the Lord waver from the Father's will. Jesus alone could take upon Himself the burden of the sins of mankind, and He alone could suffer the torture and spiritual agony of soul that caused Him to "bleed from every pore." No ordinary man could have suffered so.

In March 1830, the resurrected and glorified Savior revealed the following about the agonizing atoning experience he undertook for all mankind:

> **D&C 19:16–19** For behold, I, God, have suffered these things for all, that they might not suffer if they would repent; but if they would not repent they must suffer even as I; which suffering caused myself, even God, the greatest of all, to tremble because of pain, and to bleed at every pore, and to suffer both body and spirit—and would that I might not drink the bitter cup, and shrink—Nevertheless, glory be to the Father, and I partook and finished my preparations unto the children.

The Betrayal

Matthew 26:14–16, 21–25, 46–56 Then one of the twelve, called Judas Iscariot, went unto the chief priests, and said unto them, What will ye give me, and I will deliver him unto you? And they covenanted with him for thirty pieces of silver. And from that time he sought opportunity to betray him. . . .

And as they did eat [the Passover supper], he [Christ] said, Verily I say unto you, that one of you shall betray me. And they were exceeding sorrowful, and began every one of them to say unto him, Lord, is it I? And he answered and said, He that dippeth his hand with me in the dish, the same shall betray me. The Son of man goeth as it is written of him: but woe unto that man by whom the Son of man is betrayed! it had been good for that man if he had not been born. Then Judas, which betrayed him, answered and said, Master, is it I? He said unto him, Thou hast said. . . .

[At the conclusion of the Passover supper, the Lord retired to the Garden of Gethsemane on the Mount of Olives to pray. After He had finished praying, He said to His Apostles:]

Rise, let us be going: behold, he is at hand that doth betray me.

And while he yet spake, lo, Judas, one of the twelve, came, and with him a great multitude with swords and staves, from the chief priests and elders of the people. Now he that betrayed him gave them a sign, saying, Whomsoever I shall kiss, that same is he: hold him fast. And forthwith he came to Jesus, and said, Hail, master; and kissed him. And Jesus said unto him, Friend, wherefore art thou come? Then came they, a. Matthew 26:46.

and laid hands on Jesus, and took him. And, behold, one of them which were with Jesus stretched out his hand, and drew his sword, and struck a servant of the high priest's, and smote off his ear. Then said Jesus unto him, Put up again thy sword into his place: for all they that take the sword shall perish with the sword. Thinkest thou that I cannot now pray to my Father, and he shall presently give me more than twelve legions of angels? But how then shall the scriptures be fulfilled, that thus it must be? In that same hour said Jesus to the multitudes, Are ye come out as against a thief with swords and staves for to take me? I sat daily with you teaching in the temple, and ye laid no hold on me. But all this was done, that the scriptures of the prophets might be fulfilled. Then all the disciples forsook him, and fled.

Matthew 27:3–10 Then Judas, which had betrayed Him, when he saw that he was condemned, repented himself, and brought again the thirty pieces of silver to the chief priests and elders, saying, I have sinned in that I have betrayed the innocent blood. And they said, What is that to us? see thou to that. And he cast down the pieces of silver in the temple, and departed, and went and hanged himself. And the chief priests took the silver pieces, and said, It is not lawful for to put them into the treasury, because it is the price of blood. And they took counsel, and bought with them the potter's field, to bury strangers in. Wherefore that field was called, The field of blood, unto this day. Then was fulfilled that which was spoken by Jeremy the prophet, saying, And they took the thirty pieces of silver, the price of him that was valued, whom they of the children of Israel did value; and gave them for the potter's field, as the Lord appointed me.

Cross-references Mark 14:10–11, 18–21, 42–50; Luke 22:1–6, 21–23, 47–53; John 13:18–31; John 18:1–11

The Son of the Living God was betrayed by Judas Iscariot, a member of the Quorum of the Twelve Apostles who had been with Christ from the earliest times of His ministry[346] and who had participated in all of the experiences the Twelve had had during the Lord's mission (other than those specific times when only Peter, James, and John had been allowed to participate).

Jesus forewarned the Apostles early in His ministry that one of them would betray Him. After the feeding of the five thousand, He returned to Capernaum and delivered the sermon on the bread of life.[347] This sermon was difficult for many of His followers to comprehend, so they murmured and said, "This is an hard saying; who can hear it?"[a] After Jesus questioned their murmuring, "from that time many of his disciples went back, and walked no more with him."[b] No doubt many of the disciples were disenchanted because Jesus was not the politically powerful Messiah their Jewish traditions anticipated.

a. John 6:60.
b. John 6:66.

It seems that some of the Twelve may also have expressed reservation, for the Lord asked them, "Will ye also go away?"[a] Peter then stepped forth and as spokesman for the Twelve said, "Lord, to whom shall we go? thou hast the words of eternal life."[b] He confessed his belief in Christ, acknowledging that Jesus was the Son of God.

In response, the Lord told His Apostles that although He had chosen them, one of them was a devil.[c] John, writing this account after the death of Jesus and with the benefit of hindsight, records, "He spake of Judas Iscariot, the son of Simon: for he it was that should betray him, being one of the Twelve."[d]

Clearly, the Lord knew long before the occurrence took place that He would be betrayed. However, it is unclear whether any of the Twelve were particularly concerned about this prophecy at that time. Even though both the Savior and the ancient prophets[e] had prophesied the betrayal, it came about through seemingly normal means, in keeping with the social, political, and religious atmosphere of the day wherein Satan was allowed to deceive the chosen people and their leadership.[348]

Throughout Christ's early ministry, the rulers of the Jews followed and taunted Him and constantly questioned Him.[349] At times when people heard His claim to the Messiahship, they took Him out and attempted to stone Him[f] or to throw Him from a hilltop.[g] By the close of His ministry, the mind-set of the leadership was such that when Mary and Martha informed the Savior of Lazarus's illness and he decided to return to Jerusalem that he might "awake him out of sleep,"[h] the disciples voiced great concern, noting that "the Jews of late sought to stone thee; and goest thou thither again?"[i] They were so concerned that Thomas boldly stepped forth and told his fellow disciples, "Let us also go, that we may die with him."[j]

Jesus returned to Jerusalem and performed the spectacular miracle of raising Lazarus from the dead,[350] which was immediately reported to the Jewish leadership. That leadership then gathered together to decide what to do with the Savior. They noted that He had performed many miracles and that if He were left alone, "all men [would] believe on him."[k] Their concern was self-centered—they did not care whether Jesus was the Messiah or not. If Jesus was allowed to continue, they rationalized, the Romans would "come and take away both our place and nation."[l]

a. John 6:67.

b. John 6:68.

c. John 6:70.

d. John 6:71.

e. Zechariah 11:12.

f. John 8:59; 10:31, 39.

g. Luke 4:28–29.

h. John 11:11.

i. John 11:8.

j. John 11:16.

k. John 11:48.

l. John 11:48.

From "that day forth they took counsel together for to put Him to death";[a] in addition, they spied on Jesus and let it be known that "if any man knew where he were, he should shew it, that they might take him."[b] Through the natural animosity which the rulers of the Jews had towards the Lord, and because He had failed their political expectations of the Messiah (besides the fact that they did not want to give up their worldly possessions and positions), they would not accept Him. In their zealous concern for self-preservation and national independence, they determined that they would take the life of the very one who had come to preserve them: they only sought the most acceptable method by which they could accomplish their task.

Two days before the Feast of the Passover, the chief priests, the scribes, and the elders gathered together at the palace of Caiaphas, the high priest, to consult with one another on how they might take Jesus "by subtilty, and kill him."[c] Their concern was not for Christ's guilt or innocence or even for justice under the Jewish law, but that they might not arrest Him on the feast day "lest there be an uproar among the people."[d] At this point, Judas appeared on the scene. He was an ally which they could not have hoped for, for to attempt to subvert one of the Lord's own Apostles was undoubtedly a plot beyond their wildest dreams. Nonetheless, Judas Iscariot, a divinely called and ordained Apostle, "went unto the chief priests."

Judas was reportedly from the town of Kerioth, the only Judean among the Twelve Apostles. He served as treasurer for the Twelve, both receiving and disbursing their common funds.[351] John (again with the benefit of hindsight) notes that from the very beginning, Judas was unprincipled and dishonest in this trust .[e] His basic concern was with worldly things as exemplified in his complaint regarding what he felt was the waste of expensive oil that Mary used to anoint Jesus' feet before His crucifixion.[f] As he met with the chief priests prior to the Lord's arrest, his avarice was openly displayed when he furtively asked, "What will ye give me, and I will deliver him [Christ] unto you?"

Selfishness, greed, and dishonesty had turned his love for the Savior into hate and envy, and in satanic determination he avowedly "sold his soul to another master whose disciple and follower he thus became."[352]

The Sanhedrists with which Judas met were only too glad to receive him, for Judas solved their problem of how they might destroy the Sav-

a. John 11:53.

b. John 11:57.

c. Matthew 26:4.

d. Matthew 26:5.

e. John 12:6.

f. John 12:1–7.

ior. Although they did indeed covenant "with him for thirty pieces of silver," they "treated Judas not as an honoured associate, but as a common informer, and a contemptible traitor."[353] With the bargain struck, Zechariah's prophecy was fulfilled,[a] and the temple money (which had been given for the purchase of sacrifices) would now be used to purchase the Savior—He was "bought at the legal price of a slave."[b354]

Judas rejoined the Lord and the Twelve and as noted previously, participated in those events which led up to the Passover supper. He was there when the Savior commenced the Passover celebration, received the washing of the feet, and disappeared into the night after the Lord handed him the sop that identified him as His betrayer.

While Judas and the wicked Jewish leaders organized the arresting band, the Lord concluded the Passover supper and retired to the Garden of Gethsemane. After He had concluded His prayers to His Father in Heaven, He returned to Peter, James, and John where, for the third time, He found them asleep. He did not wake them immediately, for He knew they would need their rest to strengthen them against the coming events.

Exactly how much time elapsed between the Savior's return to the sleeping Apostles and when the group came to arrest Him is unknown, but when he heard the host approaching, He awakened Peter, James, and John stating, "Rise, let us be going."[c] He probably took the three Apostles and returned to the Garden's entrance where He had left the remaining eight. (John described the group that came to arrest Christ as a "band of men and officers from the chief priests and Pharisees, [that] cometh thither with lanterns and torches and weapons."[d] Luke described the group as a "multitude.")

John points out that Judas knew the place where Jesus would be,[e] but it may have been that the arresting party had first gone to the upper room where the Last Supper had taken place and, not finding Jesus there, had proceeded on to the Garden of Gethsemane.[355] The group included some of the Jewish leadership and undoubtedly some of those who had been in the treacherous meetings between Judas and the chief priests. Perhaps others had also gathered as the group went from the upper room to the garden, and certainly some of the Roman guard in Jerusalem would have been present.[356] Although the arresting group was large, it was not a multitude in the sense used to describe such

a. Zechariah 11:12.

b. Exodus 21:32.

c. Matthew 26:46.

d. John 18:3.

e. John 18:2.

gatherings as the feeding of the five thousand. It would probably be more accurate to accept John's description: a "band" of men, of whatever number.

As the band approached with Judas at its head, Jesus "went out" to meet them. Judas hailed the Master and saluted Him with a kiss,[a] which was the designated sign by which he would identify the Savior and betray Him into the hands of the arresting party. Jesus turned to him and asked poignantly, "Judas, betrayest thou the Son of man with a kiss?"[b] It appears that Jesus then walked past Judas and went toward the arresting officers asking, "Whom seek ye?" The response was, "Jesus of Nazareth," and Jesus immediately answered, "I am he." As Jesus acknowledged who He was, the front lines of the arresting party fell back, and the action caused some of the crowd to stumble and fall. Again the Lord asked, "Whom seek ye?" And they replied the second time, "Jesus of Nazareth." The Lord answered, "I have told you that I am he: if therefore ye seek me, let these [the Apostles] go their way."[c] It was probably at this point (or just prior to the second request) that Peter drew his sword and struck off the ear of Malchus, the servant of the high priest. The Lord immediately rebuked the action and there, in the midst of His enemies, performed His last public miracle by healing the wounded ear.[357] After this, the eleven terrified Apostles forsook the Lord and fled. Their flight was undoubtedly precipitated by their relatively untried condition;[358] but with the Lord's comment to Peter that He had legions of angels at His command but would not use them, perhaps the Apostles finally recognized that He would not call upon His supernatural powers to intervene—even for Himself—so they fled.

After the miracle of Malchus's ear (which apparently went unnoticed by the malicious crowd bent only on the Savior's arrest and destruction), the band laid hands on Jesus and bound Him.

The Lord immediately protested His rights under the Jewish law, indicating that they had come out by night to take Him. He further exclaimed, "[I] sat daily with you teaching in the temple, and ye laid no hold on me"; but the hour of His enemies had come and the powers of darkness were succeeding. With the Lord safely in their custody, the crowd took Him before Annas, the father-in-law of the high priest.[†359]

a. Matthew 26:50.

b. Luke 22:48.

c. John 18:8.

† The scriptures record one additional event in the arrest of the Savior. A young man had remained behind

Judas' betrayal precipitated the Savior's trial, crucifixion, and death. Christ was fulfilling all that the Father expected of Him which would serve to exemplify the teachings of His entire ministry and would culminate in His glorious resurrection. After He had risen from the tomb, He would return to the glory that He had had with His Father.

The betrayal would also result in Judas Iscariot's death, but for him the rewards would be diametrically opposite. Having received the thirty pieces of silver, he "repented Himself" and attempted to return the money to the chief priests and elders because he had sinned by betraying innocent blood. This was not repentance in the scriptural sense, "but a change of mind and feeling came over him."[360] Judas had left his old Master, and now his new master (Satan) had abandoned him. But the leaders had no more compassion or respect for Judas in his attempt to return the tainted silver than they had had when they covenanted with him to betray Jesus in the first place. "What is that to us?" they taunted. Judas, in utter despair over the great sin that he had committed, cast the thirty pieces of silver into the temple and went and hanged himself.[361]

---

to watch the proceedings after the Apostles had scattered. The young man is unnamed but is believed to be Mark, author of the second Gospel. As the servants of the high priest noticed him they attempted to lay hold on him, and as he struggled loose from their grasp, the linen garment that he had wrapped around his body was torn from him and he fled naked into the night.

The Trials

After Jesus was arrested, He was bound (presumably by Roman soldiers) and led from the Garden of Gethsemane. The authorities had designed the Lord's capture to occur when He was relatively alone, thus creating as little disturbance as possible among the Passover celebrants.

Their objective was quite clear: proceed with the trials as rapidly as possible, find Jesus guilty, and turn Him over to the Romans for execution. They could thus (1) present Jesus before the people at Jerusalem as one already accused and judged, and (2) submit Him to the Roman authorities in such a state that they would execute Him immediately.[362]

Because the Gospels do not agree on exactly what transpired between the Savior's arrest and His crucifixion, the story must be pieced together using all four.[363]

Between the time of Christ's last supper (approximately 10:00 p.m. on Thursday) and that of His crucifixion and death (3:00 p.m. the next day), events transpired very rapidly. The trials themselves were concluded by about 9:00 a.m. Friday morning. The format followed from the scriptures shows Christ being taken first to Annas (even though no record of that interview is available)[364] and then on to three hearings before the Jewish leadership who were empowered to judge. The first hearing is a private interview before Caiaphas; the second a public hearing before Caiaphas and the Sanhedrists; and the third, another hearing before Caiaphas and the Sanhedrists held early in the morning—thus providing two trials as required under Jewish law. The Lord was then taken to Pilate. Pilate sent Him for an interview with Herod, but Herod soon returned Him to Pilate—who then condemned and crucified Him.

The Trials and the Authorities

The scriptural record that follows is an amalgamation of the four Gospels, followed by additional references.

John 18:12–14,24   Then the band and the captain and officers of the Jews took Jesus, and bound him, and led him away to Annas first; for he was father in law to Caiaphas, which was the high priest that same year. Now Caiaphas was he, which gave counsel to the Jews, that it was expedient that one man should die for the people. . . . Now Annas had sent him bound unto Caiaphas the high priest.

Luke 22:54   Then took they him, and led him, and brought him into the high priest's house. And Peter followed afar off.

John 18:19–23   The high priest then asked Jesus of his disciples, and of his doctrine. Jesus answered him, I spake openly to the world; I ever taught in the synagogue, and in the temple, whither the Jews always resort; and in secret have I said nothing. Why askest thou me? ask them which heard me, what I have said unto them: behold, they know what I said. And when he had thus spoken, one of the officers which stood by struck Jesus with the palm of his hand, saying, Answerest thou the high priest so? Jesus answered him, If I have spoken evil, bear witness of the evil: but if well, why smitest thou me?

Matthew 26:59   Now the chief priests, and elders, and all the council, sought false witness against Jesus, to put him to death;

Mark 14:56   For many bare false witness against him, but their witness agreed not together.

Matthew 26:60   . . . Yea, though many false witnesses came, yet found they none. At the last came two false witnesses,

Mark 14:57–59   . . . saying, We heard him say, I will destroy this temple that is made with hands, and within three days I will build another made without hands. But neither so did their witness agree together.

Matthew 26:62–63   And the high priest arose, and said unto him, Answerest thou nothing? what is it which these witness against thee? But Jesus held his peace. And the high priest answered and said unto him, I adjure thee by the living God, that thou tell us whether thou be the Christ, the Son of God.

Mark 14:62 And Jesus said, I am: and ye shall see the Son of man sitting on the right hand of power, and coming in the clouds of heaven.

Matthew 26:65 Then the high priest rent his clothes, saying, He hath spoken blasphemy; what further need have we of witnesses?

Mark 14:64 Ye have heard the blasphemy: what think ye? And they all condemned him to be guilty of death.

Luke 22:63 And the men that held Jesus mocked him, and smote him.

Mark 14:65 And some began to spit on him, and to cover his face . . .

Luke 22:64–71 And when they had blindfolded him, they struck him on the face, and asked him, saying, Prophesy, who is it that smote thee? And many other things blasphemously spake they against him. And as soon as it was day, the elders of the people and the chief priests and the scribes came together, and led him into their council, saying, Art thou the Christ? tell us. And he said unto them, If I tell you, ye will not believe: and if I also ask you, ye will not answer me, nor let me go. Hereafter shall the Son of man sit on the right hand of the power of God. Then said they all, Art thou then the Son of God? And he said unto them, Ye say that I am. And they said, What need we any further witness? for we ourselves have heard of his own mouth.

Luke 23:1 And the whole multitude of them arose, and led him unto Pilate.

John 18:28–32 Then led they Jesus from Caiaphas unto the hall of judgment: and it was early; and they themselves went not into the judgment hall, lest they should be defiled; but that they might eat the passover. Pilate then went out unto them, and said, What accusation bring ye against this man? They answered and said unto him, If he were not a malefactor, we would not have delivered him up unto thee. Then said Pilate unto them, Take ye him, and judge him according to your law. The Jews therefore said unto him, It is not lawful for us to put any man to death: that the saying of Jesus might be fulfilled, which he spake, signifying what death he should die.

Luke 23:2 And they began to accuse him, saying, We found this fellow perverting the nation, and forbidding to give tribute to Caesar, saying that he himself is Christ a King.

John 18:33–38 Then Pilate entered into the judgment hall again, and called Jesus, and said unto him, Art thou the King of the Jews? Jesus answered him, Sayest thou this thing of thyself, or did others tell it thee of me? Pilate answered, Am I a Jew? Thine own nation and the chief priests have delivered thee unto me: what hast thou done? Jesus answered, My kingdom is not of this world: if my kingdom were of this world, then would my servants fight, that I should not be delivered to the Jews: but now is my kingdom not from hence. Pilate therefore said unto him, Art thou a king then? Jesus answered, Thou sayest that I am a king. To this end was I born, and for this cause came I into the world, that I should bear witness unto the truth. Every one that is of the truth heareth my voice. Pilate saith unto him, What is truth? And when he had said this, he went out again unto the Jews, and saith unto them, I find in him no fault at all.

Luke 23:5–16   And they were the more fierce, saying, He stirreth up the people, teaching throughout all Jewry, beginning from Galilee to this place. When Pilate heard of Galilee, he asked whether the man were a Galilaean. And as soon as he knew that he belonged unto Herod's jurisdiction, he sent him to Herod, who himself also was at Jerusalem at that time. And when Herod saw Jesus, he was exceeding glad: for he was desirous to see him of a long season, because he had heard many things of him; and he hoped to have seen some miracle done by him. Then he questioned with him in many words; but he answered him nothing. And the chief priests and scribes stood and vehemently accused him. And Herod with his men of war set him at nought, and mocked him, and arrayed him in a gorgeous robe, and sent him again to Pilate. And the same day Pilate and Herod were made friends together: for before they were at enmity between themselves. And Pilate, when he had called together the chief priests and the rulers and the people, said unto them, Ye have brought this man unto me, as one that perverteth the people: and, behold, I, having examined him before you, have found no fault in this man touching those things whereof ye accuse him: no, nor yet Herod: for I sent you to him; and, lo, nothing worthy of death is done unto him. I will therefore chastise him, and release him.

John 19:7–9   The Jews answered him, We have a law, and by our law he ought to die, because he made himself the Son of God. When Pilate therefore heard that saying, he was the more afraid; and went again into the judgment hall, and saith unto Jesus, Whence art thou? But Jesus gave him no answer.

Matthew 27:13–14   Then said Pilate unto him, Hearest thou not how many things they witness against thee? And he answered him to never a word; insomuch that the governor marvelled greatly.

John 19:10–13   Then saith Pilate unto him, Speakest thou not unto me? knowest thou not that I have power to crucify thee, and have power to release thee? Jesus answered, Thou couldest have no power at all against me, except it were given thee from above: therefore he that delivered me unto thee hath the greater sin. And from thenceforth Pilate sought to release him: but the Jews cried out, saying, If thou let this man go, thou art not Caesar's friend: whosoever maketh himself a king speaketh against Caesar. When Pilate therefore heard that saying, he brought Jesus forth, and sat down in the judgment seat in a place that is called the Pavement, but in the Hebrew, Gabbatha.

Matthew 27:19   When he was set down on the judgment seat, his wife sent unto him, saying, Have thou nothing to do with that just man: for I have suffered many things this day in a dream because of him.

Matthew 27:15–16   Now at that feast the governor was wont to release unto the people a prisoner, whom they would. And they had then a notable prisoner, called Barabbas.

Mark 15:7   . . . which lay bound with them that had made insurrection with him, who had committed murder in the insurrection.

Luke 23:19.   (Who for a certain sedition made in the city, and for murder, was cast into prison.)

Matthew 27:17–18   Therefore when they were gathered together, Pilate said unto them, Whom will ye that I release unto you? Barabbas, or Jesus which is called Christ? For he knew that for envy they had delivered him.

John 18:39   But ye have a custom, that I should release unto you one at the passover: will ye therefore that I release unto you the King of the Jews?

Matthew 27:20–21   But the chief priests and elders persuaded the multitude that they should ask Barabbas, and destroy Jesus. The governor answered and said unto them, Whether of the twain will ye that I release unto you? They said, Barabbas.

Mark 15:12   And Pilate answered and said again unto them, What will ye then that I shall do unto him whom ye call the King of the Jews?

Matthew 27:22–25   Pilate saith unto them, What shall I do then with Jesus which is called Christ? They all say unto him, Let him be crucified. And the governor said, Why, what evil hath he done? But they cried out the more, saying, Let him be crucified. When Pilate saw that he could prevail nothing, but that rather a tumult was made, he took water, and washed his hands before the multitude, saying, I am innocent of the blood of this just person: see ye to it. Then answered all the people, and said, his blood be on us, and on our children.

Mark 15:15   And so Pilate, willing to content the people, released Barabbas unto them, and delivered Jesus . . . .

Luke 23:25   And he released unto them him that for sedition and murder was cast into prison, whom they had desired; but he delivered Jesus to their will.

Mark 15:16   And the soldiers led him away into the hall, called Praetorium; and they call together the whole band.

John 19:1–3   Then Pilate therefore took Jesus, and scourged him. And the soldiers platted a crown of thorns, and put it on his head, and they put on him a purple robe, and said, Hail, King of the Jews! and they smote him with their hands.

Mark 15:19–22   And they smote him on the head with a reed, and did spit upon him, and bowing their knees worshipped him.   And when they had mocked him, they took off the purple from him, and put his own clothes on him, and led him out . . . . Pilate therefore, willing to release Jesus, spake again to them. But they cried, saying, Crucify him, crucify him. And he said unto them the third time, Why, what evil hath he done? I have found no cause of death in him: I will therefore chastise him, and let him go.

John 19:14–16   And it was the preparation of the passover, and about the sixth hour: and he saith unto the Jews, Behold your King! But they cried out, Away with him, away with him, crucify him. Pilate saith unto them, Shall I crucify your King? The chief priests answered, We have no king but Caesar. Then delivered he him therefore unto them to be crucified. And they took Jesus, and led him away.

Luke 23:24   And Pilate gave sentence that it should be as they required.

Cross-references   Matthew 26:57–68, Matthew 27:1–2, 11–31; Mark 14:53–65; Mark 15:1–20; Luke 22:54, 63–71; Luke 23:1–25; John 18:12–15, 28–40; John 19:1–15

Christ's trials were conducted by two separate groups of authorities. The first two trials were conducted by His own people—the rulers of the Jews who had looked forward to His coming. Ironically, He was tried and condemned by them for claiming to be what He was—the Messiah.

The third trial was conducted under the authority of Rome and consisted of a sequence of hearings before Pilate and also the "interview of silence" before Herod. Herod was the tetrarch appointed by Rome to rule the province of Galilee, from which Jesus came. His attempted interview was much like the one held before Caiaphas, and he did not try the Savior nor condemn Him.

Pilate was the ruler of the Roman Empire in Judea. He was a heathen, concerned only with the protection of the Empire and of his own position. He came to his position of authority shortly before the ministry of John the Baptist[365] and was therefore the principal Roman authority during Jesus' entire ministry.

The records indicate that Jesus was taken from place to place during the night of His trials, an easy thing to do since all the principal participants in His trials either lived in Jerusalem or took up residence there during the Passover festival.

From the Garden of Gethsemane, Christ was first taken to the palace of Annas, which was located between the upper city and the Tyropoeon valley. The Tyropoeon, known as the "valley of the cheese mongers," connected the eastern and western hills of the city.[366] The scriptures record that a Roman guard[367] accompanied Christ from the Garden of Gethsemane to the palace of Annas;[368] but at this point He seems to have been turned over to the temple guard, for the Gospels do not mention the Romans again until the crucifixion. Christ was next taken to Caiaphas in the palace of the high priest, which was located on the northeastern corner of Mount Zion.[369] This is undoubtedly the place where the Sanhedrists assembled to try the Lord.[370] The palace was on the slope of the mount and had a lower story positioned beneath the principal living apartments which had a porch in front (wherein Peter walked): the porch was described as being "beneath in the palace."[371]

After the trials were finished at the palace of Caiaphas, the crowd took the bound and brutalized Savior and wound their way up the upper city's narrow streets to Pilate in the palace of Herod.[372] Pilate did not usually reside in Jerusalem, but he always came there during this particular feast so that he could be on hand to control any potential uprisings. There were two living quarters available to him in Jerusalem: the first was in the Fortress of Antonia, and the second was in the palace of Herod the Great. It is unlikely that he chose the fortress because it also contained the rough barracks where the Roman soldiers were stationed. He probably stayed in Herod's magnificent palace, which was located at the northwestern angle of the upper city.[373] The residence of the Roman governor, wherever he was staying, was always called the Praetorium.

Because Pilate, a Roman heathen, was living in Herod's palace, the Jews would not enter for fear of Levitical uncleanness during the Passover celebration.[374] During the discussions there, Pilate discovered that Jesus was a Galilean. For some reason, perhaps to relieve himself of the obligation of judging the Savior, Pilate sent Him on to King Herod (son of Herod the Great and current ruler of Galilee and Perea). Herod always came to the Feast of the Passover, and while there he occupied the palace of the Maccabees (which was close to that of Caiaphas). After the "interview of silence" before Herod, Christ was once again marched back through the same streets to the palace of Herod the Great to be judged by Pilate, where he was first condemned and then marched to the outer gates of the city—thence to Golgotha.

The Law

As already discussed, the Jewish leaders had one goal — to condemn Christ in such a manner that the Romans would execute Him immediately.[375] The Jews were forced to enlist the aid of the Romans because the Sanhedrin did not have the authority to enforce the death sentence[376] (even though they would later illegally do so in the case of Stephen[a]). Although they levied various capital charges against the Lord, the Sanhedrists were unable to convict Him until He Himself provided them with the evidence they needed to condemn Him under Jewish law. This evidence was derived from a question the high priest asked Jesus: "Art thou then the Son of God?" And the Lord replied that He was. The answer tore at the very foundations of contemporary Judaism, and the high priest immediately rent his clothes, suspended all of the feigned compliance with rules of Jewish law, and called for a vote of condemnation from the Sanhedrists.

While the charge of blasphemy was a capital offense in Judaism, Roman law did not consider it as such. The Jewish leadership had to cleverly manipulate the evidence so that the charge became that of a capital offense to Rome—*treason.*

a. Acts 6–7.

Although the Sanhedrists outwardly complied with many of their legal requirements, they blatantly ignored established legal proceedings in order to obtain their desired goal. Haste was the rule![377] Their laws demanded justice, but their actions displayed ruthless revenge.

The Jewish system of justice at the time contained the following legal requirements, each of which was violated during the Savior's trials:

1. It was unlawful for the Sanhedrin to sit at night to consider any capital charge, nor could they consider the same on the Sabbath, any feast day, or the eve of any feast day.[378]

2. A defendant was regarded as innocent until proven guilty.

3. No one could be tried or condemned in absentia.

4. Their high, moral law demanded that in all capital offense trials, they should remember the value of human life.

5. Accusers were to appear in person and were to be warned against bearing false witness. (During Jesus' trial, the Sanhedrists and the chief priest actively sought false witnesses.)

6. The accused was not to be left undefended, and the person or group defending the accused was to work diligently for the acquittal.

7. Any and all evidence that was favorable to the defendant was to be freely admitted before the trying body.

8. No member of the court would vote for condemnation once he had spoken in favor of acquittal.

9. When the trying body voted, the youngest members voted first so that they would not be influenced by their elders.

10. In a capital charge, the vote in favor of death had to be by a majority of at least two.

11. If a guilty vote was decided upon, it had to be officially taken the day following the trial.

12. No criminal trial could be carried on throughout the night.

13. No judgment recommending death could be rendered without the Sanhedrin fasting the entire day before the sentence was given.

14. No one could be executed on the same day their sentence was pronounced.[379]

15. The Law and tradition demanded that a second full hearing and trial be given when capital punishment was imposed.[380]

16. All capital charge trials must be held in the official courtroom of the Sanhedrin.[381]

17. A unanimous vote of guilty was not enforceable.

Although the Lord was personally interviewed by both Caiaphas and Annas, these were not official trials. Undoubtedly, the interviews were held (1) to see how vigorously the Lord would defend the charges brought against Him, (2) to allow time for enough Sanhedrists to be gathered at the palace of the high priest that the facade of an actual trial could be presented, and (3) to see if any of the Lord's disciples would defend Him.

Once the Jewish leadership had been assembled, the Lord would have been placed before them in a standing position—directly in front of the high priest. The Sanhedrists would have been seated both to the left and to the right of the high priest in a semicircle with a scribe at the end of each side of the semicircle to record the sentence. The accused would have been guarded by bailiffs or temple guards while a small number of court assistants would have stood directly behind the Sanhedrists to call witnesses and carry out the court's decisions.[382]

Jesus' arrest, interviews, and trials were in violation of Jewish law at the time. Any semblance of legality was trampled under the feet of the Jewish rulers in their rush to be rid of the Savior. (An excellent work on the trials of Jesus from a legal standpoint was done by Walter M. Chandler in 1925. For details, the reader is referred to that work and the citations therein.)[383]

To say that the trials of Jesus were not in accordance with Jewish law is an understatement. But it should be clearly understood that such was not the purpose of the high priest and the Sanhedrists—to try the Lord in the ordinary way and to give Him a fair trial would have ensured His acquittal. Instead, they presented a facade of a trial to justify their actions before the people—particularly those attending the Passover feast—and to specifically impress the Roman leader Pilate so that they could enlist the Roman judicial system (which they needed to carry out the sentence of death), for they had no power to enforce their wrongful verdict. The outcome of their mock trial was predetermined; throughout the Lord's ministry they had wanted to kill Him—and it became their avowed intention after He raised Lazarus from the dead.[a]

Neither the chief judge nor the Sanhedrists could bring charges against an accused; they could only adjudicate the charges.[384] The person who initiated the charge acted as the prosecuting witness (they would also have been the executioner in the case of the death penalty); no record of any kind of an "official" prosecutor is found in Israel's history.[385] When Christ was arraigned, however, no individual came forth to formally charge Him. All of the charges were made by the high priest, and false witnesses were brought forward in an attempt to accuse Him. But they failed miserably.

They could not charge Him with deliberately breaking the Sabbath, for it would raise the question of His miracles which had been unquestionably documented. They could not charge Him with secret doctrinal teachings, for He had taught openly in both the synagogues and the temple. They could not bring charges against Him because of the actions of His disciples, for He had successfully refuted their accusations concerning the Twelve.[b] Finally, knowing that He had claimed on many occasions to be the long-awaited Messiah, the high priest asked the Lord if He was, indeed, the Son of God, to which Jesus simply answered yes. Then, rather than determining whether He was the Son of God under any system of justice, they reached the foregone conclusion that He was not and that He had blasphemed: their justification for His condemnation thus came from His own mouth.

A second mock trial was held for the sole purpose of again seeming to comply with correct legal procedure, for Jewish law demanded that two trials be held when capital punishment had been imposed. This

a. John 11:53.
b. Mark 2:23–28.

time the Sanhedrists wanted only to determine whether the Lord had, in fact, claimed the Messiahship. Again He affirmed His divine Sonship, and again the Sanhedrists unanimously condemned Him. Then they sent Him to Pilate.

Throughout Israel's History, the Jews had been meticulously just in their legal procedure. They had developed a justice system which protected the rights of the accused, and they prided themselves on their fairness —but on this night, for this Man, there was no justice.

The Jewish Trials and Peter's Denials

Matthew 26:69–75   Now Peter sat without in the palace: and a damsel came unto him, saying, Thou also wast with Jesus of Galilee. But he denied before them all, saying, I know not what thou sayest. And when he was gone out into the porch, another maid saw him, and said unto them that were there, This fellow was also with Jesus of Nazareth. And again he denied with an oath, I do not know the man. And after a while came unto him they that stood by, and said to Peter, Surely thou also art one of them; for thy speech bewrayeth thee. Then began he to curse and to answer, saying, I know not the man. And immediately the cock crew. And Peter remembered the word of Jesus, which said unto him, Before the cock crow, thou shalt deny me thrice. And he went out, and wept bitterly.

Cross-references   Mark 14:66–72; Luke 22:55–62; John 18:16–27

After Jesus' arrest late on Thursday evening, perhaps between 11:00 p.m. and midnight, He was taken to the palace of Annas, the father-in-law of Caiaphas, the high priest. How long Annas interrogated Christ is not known. By the time Peter and John caught up with the Savior the interview with Annas was over, and the temple guard was probably in the process of leading Jesus to Caiaphas for trial. The two Apostles followed the Lord and His captors. John was known to the high priest and went unimpeded into the palace, but Peter could not gain access and John had to return to the door to assist his entrance. John apparently went on into the inner rooms to observe the trial while Peter was required to stay in the outer courtyard or porch area where a fire had been built to warm the guards while they waited.

Caiaphas held a personal interview with Jesus prior to the commencement of the first trial. Perhaps this interview was held to allow time for the Sanhedrists to assemble, or perhaps Caiaphas was interested in determining the strength of the Lord's defense. The old charges that had been levied against the Lord during His ministry were not pursued. "His violations of the Sabbath, as they called them, were all connected with miracles, and brought them, therefore, upon dangerous ground. His rejection of oral tradition involved a question that had the Sadducees and the Pharisees entrenched in an ongoing feud. His authoritative cleansing of the Temple might be regarded with favour both by the Rabbis and the people."[386] Therefore, the first charges brought by Caiaphas concerned the Lord's disciples and His doctrine.

Caiaphas's intent, as already mentioned, was to convict Jesus on a charge punishable by death, not only under Jewish law, but under the Roman law as well. The charges concerning the Lord's disciples and His doctrine were aimed at (1) unorthodox teaching which might be construed as heresy and therefore punishable by death under Jewish law, and (2) secret seditions which were punishable by death under Roman law.[387]

The Lord passed over the question concerning His disciples (perhaps to relieve them of any involvement in His arrest and trial) and defended the charge concerning His doctrine by declaring, "I spake openly to the world; I ever taught in the synagogue, and in the temple," the normal teaching forums for the Jews. He did not need to defend His teachings—they were not heretical or apostate—so He suggested that the high priest "ask them which heard me, what I have said unto them: behold they know what I said." The answer offended one of the officers watching Jesus, and he struck the Lord with the palm of His hand stating, "Answerest thou the high priest so?" But Jesus was right, and the high priest and the officer were wrong. The Lord responded, "If I have spoken evil, bear witness of the evil: but if well, why smitest thou me?" It was another reminder to His persecutors of His rights under Jewish law.

No further information is recorded of the conversation between Caiaphas and Jesus and there is no indication of how long the Lord was questioned prior to the arrival of the Sanhedrists for the first of the officially required "trials." Perhaps another hour or more elapsed before the formal trials began. However, it would seem probable that Peter's first denial took place during this lull.

When Peter first boldly entered the courtyard of Caiaphas' palace, he was venturing into the lair of His Lord's most bitter enemies. He sat down by a fire to warm Himself on the chilly April night, even though he was in the midst of the servants and the guards of the very men who would sit in judgment upon the Savior. A maid who was employed as the door-portress moved to the fire and fixed her attention on Peter. She apparently recognized him from some prior meeting, and accused him of being with Jesus in Galilee. The Gospels disagree as to what exactly she said. John records that she accused Peter of being a disciple, while the other writers only state that she accused Him of "being with Jesus." In the Garden of Gethsemane, Peter's fear for his safety had apparently overcome the love he held for his Master, and he had fled into the night with the other ten Apostles. Now, he was again caught off guard. Fear swelled within him as he denied knowing the Savior. For the moment his denial was accepted, and he left the fire for the safety of the porch where he could be alone.

While Peter waited, the Sanhedrists began arriving for the Lord's first formal trial. Perhaps less than half of the official body[388] had assembled when the trial began. They had sent for false witnesses to fortify the charges that had been levied by Caiaphas, but time was short and their preparation was inadequate; thus, the witnesses could not agree on their testimonies. Relentlessly, the court contin-ued to feign legality by calling other false witnesses in an attempt to convict the Lord, but they could not find any who could support the charges. Finally, two witnesses came forth to falsely testify against Jesus concerning His prophecy on the destruction of the temple. The Lord had spoken symbolically of His body and its resurrection when He had talked of the temple being destroyed and raised up again, but in an effort to create a charge that would stand up under Jewish and Roman law, the judges perverted His meaning so that it appeared that He was threatening to destroy the temple building itself—but even then the witnesses' testimonies did not agree.

The Lord had conversed with Caiaphas before the trials started, but while false testimony was being borne against Him Jesus remained silent, refusing to dignify His enemies' collusion with a reply. Finally, the high priest stood and asked the Lord why He had not answered the charges of the witnesses. The Lord again remained silent. In desperation the high priest commanded Jesus "by the living God" to speak. Obviously, the question in point did not concern any of the charges previously levied against Him, nor did it concern the false testimony being presented. Throughout His ministry the Lord had laid claim to the Messiahship; during the good shepherd discourse He had been asked plainly to tell them if He was the Christ, and they had rejected His answer.[a] Now, as he stood before the elders, the chief priests, and the members of the Sanhedrin, Caiaphas again asked, "Tell us whether thou be the Christ, the Son of God."

The Lord broke His silence and in quiet majesty said, "I am: and ye shall see the Son of man sitting on the right hand of power, and coming in the clouds of heaven." This was too much for Caiaphas: he did that which was forbidden under Jewish law and rent his clothes,[b] condemned Jesus for blasphemy, rejected all the witnesses, and called for the Savior's death. The Sanhedrists followed suit, and all pronounced the sentence of death upon Christ. The first trial was over.

During this time Peter had been on the porch in the courtyard, undoubtedly listening intently to the proceedings of the trial. He was cold, perhaps not just from the night air but also chilled by the reality of his Lord's condemnation. Some time had passed, perhaps as much as two hours or so, and he moved from the security of the porch area back toward the fire's warmth. His movement was again noticed by the door-portress, and as he drew near to the fire he was accosted and accused a second time of being one of Jesus' followers. Again he denied the accusation, but this time did so with an oath as if to emphasize his "innocence" and protect himself from further confrontation.

The Lord was condemned to death for blasphemy, a heinous crime against the God of Israel. As if the sentence of death was not enough, some in the hall verbally and physically vented their anger and hatred upon the Savior, for they now considered Him to be a false prophet.[389] They mocked Him and spat upon Him and after blindfolding Him, struck Him on the face, blasphemously taunting Him to "Prophesy," exclaiming, ". . . who is it that smote thee?" How long the Lord was treated in this inhuman manner is unknown, but His sentencing and the derision could have extended throughout another hour of that fateful morning.

Finally, the Savior was brought before the Sanhedrists for His second "trial." This trial no doubt took place in the same hall as the first, the only change being that additional leaders had probably arrived to help sit in judgment. Meanwhile, Peter's activities were reaching a climax in the courtyard.

Nothing is recorded of the conversations that may have been taking place among the excited servants and guards as they stood around the fire and observed the progress of the trial and the vehement punishment Christ was receiving. Peter undoubtedly took part in their conversation because one individual stated, "Surely thou also art one of them; for thy speech bewrayeth [reveals] thee." Perhaps the Lord's initial punishment was over and a pause took place in the proceedings. In any case, Peter was again accused of being one of the Lord's disciples. It appears that despite Peter's previous denials and oaths, he was still a suspect to the highly stimulated crowd milling about the courtyard. At last one of them, a kinsman of Malchus whose ear Peter had struck, charged him. Not only did the man accuse Peter of being a disciple, he also claimed that Peter had been with Jesus in the Garden at the time of Christ's arrest and as if to prove his accusation, the man claimed that Peter's Galilean dialect proved it.

Others joined in the damaging charges and Peter was once again faced with the fear of detection and perhaps physical harm. He began to "curse and to swear, saying, I know not this man of whom ye speak." At that fateful moment the cock crew, and the Lord, standing in the upper hall where He could observe what was taking place, turned and looked down upon Peter. Peter's gaze met his Lord's and the memory of the Lord's prophecy overcame him. Leaving the palace in the depths of humility and despair, he "wept bitterly."

Let no one accuse Peter of denying that Jesus was the Christ—he claimed only to not know this man of whom they spoke. His denials were precipitated out of fear, fear compounded by the dreadful actions taking place to the very Christ he had associated with and loved for three long years. Peter was the first man to proclaim Christ as the Messiah; he had walked upon the water to Him, had indignantly affirmed that he would rather die than deny Him, and had courageously drawn His sword in the Lord's defense. Peter's "so-called denial of His Lord . . . was rather a failure to stand up and testify of the divine Sonship" when the opportunity presented itself among His enemies and not a "denial of any divinity resident in the Son of Man."[390]

The Lord's second trial before the Sanhedrists probably began somewhere between 5:00 a.m. and 6:00 a.m. Friday. No longer was an attempt made to feign legalities. The sole question before the court at this point concerned Christ's claim to the Messiahship. "Art thou the Christ?" they asked again, and the Lord's response reflected the blind attitude of the Jewish leaders and others of the chosen people: "If I tell you, ye will not believe," He said, nor would they have responded to His questions if He were to attempt to verify His claim. Again He testified of His divinity, His answer affirming their question, but the court persisted and again asked, "Art thou then the Son of God?" The Lord again responded, "Ye say that I am." The trial was over; they had no need for further witnesses for they had "heard of His own mouth." He who was the Son of God had affirmed that relationship. Bound and condemned, the Savior of the world was next led to the heathen court of Pontius Pilate.

The Roman Trial

At around 7:00 a.m. the Lord was taken to Pilate. This was the day of the Passover, and the same Jewish leaders who had thirsted "for innocent blood" throughout the night would not enter Pilate's heathen hall for fear of the "mere proximity of leaven."[391] Pilate had probably been told of the coming delegation, for he was waiting for them in the judgment hall. However, since they would not enter his palace because of the feast, he came out to them. He had undoubtedly heard of Jesus and the potential problems that His ministry had created, but he also recognized that the Savior was being delivered to him by some very envious Jewish rulers.[a][392] Pilate asked the Jews what Christ was accused of, and his question seemed to frustrate them. In their frenzied hatred of the Lord, they had apparently not anticipated that they would have to provide justification for the death sentence they had levied against Him. Their response to Pilate was not convincing: "If he were not a malefactor, we would not have delivered him up unto thee." Pilate, however, told them to take care of the judgment themselves (perhaps in spite since he felt great animosity for the Jews). But they could not put Christ to death!

The Jewish leaders were confronted with the fact that they must change the charge against Jesus from blasphemy to treason—from a religious violation to a civil one—so again they falsely accused Him. Jesus had perverted the nation, had forbidden the giving of tribute to Caesar, and had made Himself a king, they claimed. Pilate listened to the charges and then asked Jesus, "Art thou the King of the Jews?" "Thou sayest it," was the Lord's immediate response.

Perhaps irritated that the matter had not been easily resolved, Pilate entered the judgment hall and had Jesus brought before him. Again he put the question to Him, "Art thou the King of the Jews?" Jesus answered the question with a question, for He wanted to know the background of this Roman's query. "Sayest thou this thing of thyself," He asked, "or did others tell it thee of me?" Pilate's answer showed his lack of understanding of the Messianic mission and his distaste for the Israelites. "Am I a Jew?" he contemptuously responded.

The Lord then answered Pilate's first question, matching His answer to the Roman's understanding by testifying that His kingdom was not of the world, for if it were His servants would have fought for Him at the time of His arrest. Pilate persisted, "Art thou a king then?" "To this end was I born," the Lord responded. His answer would only have meaning to those who understood the truth of who He really was, and He explained that those who sought that truth would receive it. Pilate was not interested in the religious beliefs of the Jews, however, so he ended the conversation with the dialectic, "What is truth?" Having determined that Jesus was no threat to Him or Rome, he returned to the waiting crowd and pronounced that he had found no fault in the Lord worthy of Roman justice: thus, he acquitted Christ of the Roman charges.

The Jewish rulers would not, could not, allow this to be their answer. They continued to accuse Christ, and as they argued before Pilate, blasphemy turned into civil unrest and finally became treason, "beginning from Galilee to this place." Pilate suddenly recognized a potential escape from his problems with these unwieldy subjects: if the man was from Galilee He "belonged unto Herod's jurisdiction,'," so he sent Him to King Herod, who was also in Jerusalem for the feast.

Herod was residing in the old palace of the Asmoneans near Pilate in the palace of Herod the Great,[393] and when word spread of Pilate's actions, the crowd (swollen with visitors and citizens alike) swarmed[394] through the streets of the upper city to follow Jesus, bound and heavily guarded, to Herod's abode.[395] Herod had been warned that Christ was coming and was exceedingly glad to see Him "because he had heard many things of him; and he hoped to have seen some miracle done by him." Herod questioned Jesus at length, but the Lord maintained silence before him. The "interview of silence" was brief, leaving Herod's desires unsatisfied, and the chief priests and scribes soon started vehemently accusing Jesus again. Perhaps to ingratiate himself to these religious rulers who hated him, Herod commanded his men of war to mock the Lord, and after they had finished ridiculing Him they clothed Him in a "gorgeous robe" and returned Him to Pilate.

Pilate was told of Herod's "interview of silence" and determined that Herod had also found no guilt in Christ. Pilate called the Jewish rulers together and informed them that neither he nor Herod had found fault with Jesus; therefore, he would merely chastise and release Him. This was Christ's second acquittal under Roman law.

Frustrated at their inability to successfully negotiate the charge of treason, the Jewish rulers now testified that the Lord must die because He had "made Himself the Son of God." Pilate was superstitious, and this claim made him "afraid." Again he entered the judgment hall and brought Jesus before him. He questioned the Lord concerning His origin, but the Savior did not answer. Pilate reiterated the charges and the accusations that had been brought against Jesus by His own people, but still the Lord did not respond, causing Pilate to marvel. Finally, Pilate threatened the Lord, emphasizing his power to release or crucify Him. To this the Lord responded, but not, perhaps, as Pilate had expected: He testified that Pilate could harm Him only if that power "were given thee from above," and then the Lord uttered a judgment before Pilate, indicating that the greater sin for the results of this day would be on His accusers, not on His executioner. Pilate's fears increased; perhaps he *was* less guilty than the Jewish rulers, for at this point he was anxious to spare the Savior's life.[396]

Pilate again presented the Lord to the chief priests and the rulers and advised leniency, but they shouted, "Away with this man." By now they had devised a scheme that would force Pilate to give in to their demands. "If thou let this man go, thou art not Caesar's friend," they cried. This statement put Pilate's political position in jeopardy. He could see that the Jews were not going to yield, so he returned to the judgment seat and again had Jesus brought before him. At this point a strange occurrence took place that would have only fueled the fires of Pilate's superstition. His wife sent him a message: she had had a dream concerning Jesus and, although nothing is recorded of the context of the dream, it had obviously upset her. She warned her husband to beware of the sentence he pronounced, for Jesus, she wrote, was a "just man."

Pilate found himself in an untenable situation. Obviously Christ had done nothing worthy of death and his superstitious nature made him fear the consequences of his wife's dream; on the other hand, if his Jewish subjects rioted he would incur the wrath of Rome. To rid himself of his problems he fell back on an old Roman custom: Rome always released a prisoner at the feast of the Passover to show its "benevolence" to the people of Palestine. He selected for this purpose one Barabbas, a notable prisoner that had been convicted of treason, murder, and insurrection. He had him brought forth and stood him next to Jesus so that the people could choose the man they wanted released. Pilate probably felt that the people would choose to release Jesus rather than have a recognized murderer back in their midst, and he was surprised when the Jews shouted for the release of Barabbas and continued to demand the crucifixion of Christ.

Recognizing that the situation was beyond his control, Pilate appeared before the multitude and washed his hands, symbolically ridding himself of the blood of the "just person" they were so eager to destroy. "All the people" recognized the meaning of the gesture from their traditions[a] and readily accepted the guilt for the death of their Messiah, screaming, "His blood be on us, and on our children."

"It was fitting that *they,* who had preferred an abject Sadducee to their True Priest, and an incestuous Idumaean to their Lord and King, should deliberately prefer a murderer to their Messiah."[397]

An astonished Pilate remonstrated, "What will ye then that I shall do unto him whom ye call the King of the Jews?" "Crucify him!" was the violent response. In dismay Pilate cried out, "Why, what evil hath he done?" But the cries grew louder and more vehement, "Let him be crucified." Pilate, a weak man who was fearful of another

a. Deuteronomy 21:1–9; Psalms 26:6; 73:13.

riot, yielded to their demands:[398] he released Barabbas and sentenced Jesus to death.

Yet one more cruelty would be inflicted upon the Lord prior to His crucifixion: Pilate released Him to his soldiers who took Him into the Praetorium and "scourged him." Scourging was inflicted by striking the condemned person with a whip "loaded with lead, or armed with spikes and bones, which lacerated back, and chest, and face, till the victim sometimes fell down before the judge a bleeding mass of torn flesh."[399] The soldiers also beat the Savior with their hands and with reeds, and they spat upon Him and forced a crown of plaited thorns upon His head. After placing a purple robe on His bleeding back and shoulders, they mocked Him and hailed Him as the "king" of the Jews and, in blasphemous irreverence, they bowed before Him. Finally, they replaced the regal robe with His own clothing and took Him back to Pilate, who once more appealed to the mercy of the raging multitude. He was yet willing to release Christ, but the multitude would have none of it and they screamed over and over, "Crucify him, crucify him." They were in a frenzy, and the only thing that would sate their fury was the blood of their Messiah!

In the face of their anger Pilate still pleaded for Christ, testifying that Jesus had done no evil and that He should only be chastised and then released. He again presented the Lord to them crying, "Behold your King." But the rulers and the multitude were past all reason and shouted, "Away with him, crucify him." "Shall I crucify your King?" Pilate asked again. "We have no king but Caesar," was the instant response. Pilate had no other recourse: he gave the order, and the Savior of the world—the Messiah that the chosen people had anticipated in all that they did and the King for whom they had waited for centuries —was led away to be crucified.

The Crucifixion

Matthew 27:32–66　　And as they came out, they found a man of Cyrene, Simon by name: him they compelled to bear his cross.

And when they were come unto a place called Golgotha, that is to say, a place of a skull, they gave him vinegar to drink mingled with gall: and when he had tasted thereof, he would not drink. And they crucified him, and parted his garments, casting lots: that it might be fulfilled which was spoken by the prophet, They parted my garments among them, and upon my vesture did they cast lots. And sitting down they watched him there; and set up over his head his accusation written, This IS JESUS THE KING OF THE JEWS. Then were there two thieves crucified with him, one on the right hand, and another on the left.

And they that passed by reviled him, wagging their heads, And saying, thou that destroyest the temple, and buildest it in three days, save thyself. If thou be the Son of God, come down from the cross. Likewise also the chief priests mocking him, with the scribes and elders, said, He saved others; himself he cannot save. If he be the King of Israel, let him now come down from the cross, and we will believe him. He trusted in God; let him deliver him now, if he will have him: for he said, I am the Son of God. The thieves also, which were crucified with him, cast the same in his teeth. Now from the sixth hour there was darkness over all the land unto the ninth hour. And about the ninth hour Jesus cried with a loud voice, saying, Eli, Eli, lama sabachthani? that is to say, My God, my God, why hast thou forsaken me? Some of them that stood there, when they heard that, said, This man calleth for Elias. And straightway one of them ran, and took a sponge, and filled it with vinegar, and put it on a reed, and gave him to drink. The rest said, Let be, let us see whether Elias will come to save him.

Jesus, when he had cried again with a loud voice, yielded up the ghost. And, behold, the veil of the temple was rent in twain from the top to the bottom; and the earth did quake, and the rocks rent; and the graves were opened; and many bodies of the saints which slept arose, and came out of the graves after his resurrection, and went into the holy city, and appeared unto many. Now when the centurion, and they that were with him, watching Jesus, saw the earthquake, and those things that were done, they feared greatly, saying, Truly this was the Son of God. And many women were there beholding afar off, which followed Jesus from Galilee, ministering unto him: among which was Mary Magdalene, and Mary the mother of James and Joses, and the mother of Zebedee's children. When the even was come, there came a rich man of Arimathaea, named Joseph, who also himself was Jesus' disciple: he went to Pilate, and begged the body of Jesus. Then Pilate commanded the body to be delivered. And when Joseph had taken the body, he wrapped it in a clean linen cloth, and laid it in his own new tomb, which he had hewn out in the rock: and he rolled a great stone to the door of the sepulchre, and departed. And there was Mary Magdalene, and the other Mary, sitting over against the sepulchre.

Now the next day, that followed the day of the preparation, the chief priests and Pharisees came together unto Pilate, saying, Sir, we remember that that deceiver said, while he was yet alive, After three days I will rise again. Command therefore that the sepulchre be made sure until the third day, lest his disciples come by night, and steal him away, and say unto the people, He is risen from the dead: so the last error shall be worse than the first. Pilate said unto them, Ye have a watch: go your way, make it as sure as ye can. So they went, and made the sepulchre sure, sealing the stone, and setting a watch.

Cross-references   Mark 15:20–47; Luke 23:26–56; John 19:16–42

The Gospel writers differ considerably on the facts and circumstances surrounding Jesus' crucifixion, and it seems apparent that John is the only one who was an eyewitness to the occurrence; however, a close reading of John's Gospel indicates that he was present during only portions of the crucifixion, performing certain errands which took him away from the cross from time to time.[400] The other Gospel writers seem to have acquired their information about the crucifixion from interviews with other eyewitnesses.[401]

After Pilate sentenced the Lord to death, the Roman soldiers savagely scourged Him. Had custom been followed, two days would have elapsed between the sentencing and the execution;[402] but it is apparent that after the scourging they immediately took the Lord to be crucified (at approximately nine on Friday morning). The interviews, trials, beatings, and conveyance between palaces had taken up the entire night.

It was the Roman practice to routinely assign four soldiers to each condemned prisoner and his cross. Their job was to escort the convict through the streets to the place of execution and to sit as sentries at the crucifixion until the prisoner's death. The Romans first used crucifixion on a cross in Palestine after Caesar's death, but it was not a Jewish mode of execution. Jewish executions were usually performed by strangulation, beheading, burning, or stoning.[403]

The cross was a simple structure made of roughhewn wood.[404] Three types of crosses were commonly used: one was in the shape of the capital letter X and became known as the Saint Andrew's cross; the second was in the form of the capital letter T (the victim was attached to the horizontal part of the cross while the cross lay upon the ground, then it was lifted up and dropped into a hole which held it in an upright position); the third cross, and probably the one used for the crucifixion of Jesus, was known as the Latin cross, because the horizontal bar was attached below the top of the vertical bar. (Christ's "title" was attached to His cross above His head. This information helps to identify the type of cross used in His crucifixion.)[405]

Crucifixion was a cruel method of death, each phase being designed to inflict the maximum amount of pain and suffering on the individual as well as fear in the people observing it. Even the scourging done prior to the actual crucifixion at times caused the condemned's premature death.[406] If still alive, the prisoner was then tied to the transverse bar of his cross and required to carry it through the city streets to the place of his execution; however, there is no evidence to indicate whether or not the Savior was tied to His cross during this agonizing journey.

The destination of this gruesome procession for the Messiah was Golgotha, or Calvary, interpreted as the "place of a skull," or "skull." It was located near the city but outside its gates. Its exact location is not currently known (although it was probably well known at the time of Christ's death for it was undoubtedly a recognized place of execution). It was not a hill, nor is it described as such in the scriptures—it is merely called "a place."[407] Although much has been written concerning its location, "in all probability, the actual spot lies buried and obliterated under the mountainous rubbish-heaps of the ten-times-taken city."[408]

The prisoners that were to be crucified would normally have been led down the longest possible route through the city in order to punish them further and to terrorize the spectators; but on this occasion, with the Jewish Sabbath rapidly approaching, a shorter course may have been taken with the procession exiting Jerusalem through the north (Damascus) Gate.[409]

The preceding night had taxed the Savior's strength; He had not slept or partaken of any nourishment. He was further weakened by the cruel beatings and scourging as well as the overwhelming physical, spiritual, and emotional drain of suffering in the Garden of Gethsemane prior to His arrest. All of this had weakened Him to the point that He could not physically support the crossbar's weight as He moved through the streets of Jerusalem.[410]

The guards had previously shown Jesus no mercy and there is no reason to assume that they would do so now; but His weakness undoubtedly slowed the procession, so one Simon, a Cyrenian, was pressed into service and forced to carry Christ's crossbar to Golgotha.[†411]

If custom had been followed, Christ would have been strapped to His crossbar and perhaps it was at this moment, while the bar was removed from His shoulders and tied upon Simon's, that the episode concerning a warning to the women of Israel took place. In the crowd that was following the procession were some women who were loudly wailing and lamenting over Jesus. In all probability their laments were not for the fate of the Son of God, but were in pity and sympathy for His tortured appearance and obvious suffering.[412] Christ had triumphantly entered Jerusalem just a few days before and had paused during His entry to weep for the holy city and its daughters:[a] now they were weeping for Him. Jesus turned to the lamenting women and spoke to them, telling them not to weep for Him, but for themselves and for their children—another warning of the devastating destruction and the great sorrow that would soon befall the Jews in Jerusalem. Christ told them that the days were coming when they would wish they had never had children and would beg the mountains to fall on them so their sufferings might be relieved. He referred to Himself as a "green tree," for as the true Messiah He had brought the living gospel to them (although they had rejected His message). If the green tree was

---

† Simon was probably not a disciple, but it is assumed that he and His family later became followers of the Messiah (Mark 15:21; Romans 16:13).

allowed to suffer so severely, what great sufferings would come upon them (the dry tree) when the destructions took place!

When they reached Golgotha the final, excruciatingly painful episode of punishment began:[413]

> First, the upright wood was planted in the ground. It was not high, and probably the Feet of the Sufferer were not above one or two feet from the ground. Thus could the communication described in the Gospels take place between Him and others; thus, also might His Sacred Lips be moistened with the sponge attached to the short stalk of hyssop. Next, the transverse wood . . . was placed on the ground, and the Sufferer laid on it, when His Arms were extended, drawn up, and bound to it. Then . . . a strong, sharp nail was driven, first into the Right, then into the Left Hand. . . . Next, the Sufferer was drawn up by means of ropes, perhaps ladders; the transverse either bound or nailed to the upright, and a rest or support for the Body . . . fastened on it. Lastly, the Feet were extended, and either one nail hammered into each, or a large piece of iron through the two. . . . And so might the crucified hang for hours, even days, in the unutterable anguish of suffering, till consciousness at last failed.[414]

After nailing the condemned to the crossbar and affixing that bar to the upright, it was customary to also tie or rope his arms and legs to the cross for added support; however, there is no scriptural evidence on whether this was done to Christ. We do know that just prior to the Lord being cruelly nailed upon the cross, His outer garments and His sandals were removed from His body and divided between the four soldiers who attended Him. Then His inner garment or cloak was removed, but it was of such fine quality (woven without seam) that the soldiers cast lots for it rather than destroy it—thus fulfilling one of the Old Testament prophesies concerning the Savior's death.[a]

Vinegar or wine was offered to the Savior prior to His cross being raised to an upright position. The custom was a Jewish one, perhaps initiated to placate their traditions concerning the suffering of the body.[415] The wine contained gall or myrrh, which was an opiate[416]

a. Psalm 22:18.

given to relieve some of the physical pain. Jesus tasted it, recognized what it contained, and refused to drink, apparently so that His faculties would not be dulled. The sign identifying His charges was then fastened on the cross above His head. These signs (or "titles") normally hung around the condemned prisoners' necks as they carried their crosses through the streets, or at times the guards carried them in advance of the prisoners. Although the Gospels make it appear that the Jewish leadership complained of Christ's sign after it had been placed upon His cross, it is unlikely that they would have waited until then to say something about it. In all probability they learned of the epitaph before Jesus began carrying His cross through Jerusalem, and probably complained to Pilate at the time.[417] The title read JESUS OF NAZARETH THE KING OF THE JEWS and was written in Hebrew, Greek, and Latin. The Jewish leadership wanted it to state that Jesus claimed to be the king of the Jews, for they feared that the title might influence some of the visitors at the feast. Pilate, who had perhaps devised the sign in an effort to antagonize these rulers who had precipitated the crucifixion, refused to change the sign, stating, "What I have written, I have written."

After the Lord's cross had been thrust upright, He uttered the words, "Father, forgive them; for they know not what they do."[a] This was not forgiveness for all those involved in His crucifixion; rather, it related solely to the soldiers who were carrying out their orders in completing the crucifixion.[b][418] Even in His agony, the Savior granted mercy to the unwitting instruments of their Lord's death.

Death by crucifixion is slow. While Christ hung in agony hour after hour, the soldiers taunted Him and mocked Him with toasts of wine while they waited for Him to die—not because they believed or disbelieved in Him as the Son of God but because He represented the conquered Jews whom they despised.[419] They were joined in their vile mockery by the same Jewish leaders who had contrived and confirmed the Savior's death. Ironically, their taunts summarized Christ's mission in life: "Ah, thou that destroyest the temple, and buildest it in three days," they mocked—yet it was Jesus who had taught them the relationship between Israel, the temple, and their God. "He saved others; let him save himself, if he be Christ, the chosen of God," they said—yet only through Christ could eternal salvation be obtained. "If thou be the Son of God," they jeered, as Satan had done when he challenged Jesus in the wilderness.[a] Finally, "If he be the King of Israel, let him now come down from the cross, and we will believe him" (as if by some mighty miracle their evil could miraculously be changed to good). But Christ knew that they would not repent, "though one rose from the dead."[b]

The authors of the Gospels related these mocking comments with different emphasis: Matthew and Mark emphasized the Jews' doubt and their use of blasphemy; Luke described the reasons for their mockery; and John reads like an eyewitness account of their actions.[420]

While the Savior was fasting in the wilderness, the devil had challenged His Messiahship, cunningly disguising His temptations in an attempt to create doubt in the Savior's mind regarding His trust in the Father. Now, influenced by that same king of evil, both the heathen Romans and the Jewish leaders would again challenge that trust. Nevertheless, their jeers, which were intended to make Christ think that God had forsaken Him, went unheeded and He gave them no response.

Two thieves had been sentenced to be crucified with Jesus, perhaps to emphasize the power of Rome over their hostile Jewish subjects and to strike terror into the crowd attending the Passover feast.[421] Both thieves had initially participated with the multitude in mocking the Savior, but eventually one of them had second thoughts and, perhaps moved by the Spirit, spoke of the Savior's innocence. Without knowing whether or not Christ was the Messiah, he requested the Lord's intercession in His kingdom. The request elicited Christ's second comment during His crucifixion: "Verily I say unto thee, To day shalt thou be with me in paradise"[c][422]—not that the thief would reside in the Father's celestial kingdom, but that immediately after his death he would in general terms be in the same place in which the Savior would be: "in the world of spirits."

John's detailed account of the crucifixion stops at this point and resumes after the Savior had been on the cross for about two hours. It would appear that due to the haste with which the Savior had been tried and taken to be crucified, many of His immediate loved ones and close disciples had not been told what was happening. Undoubt-

a. Matthew 4:3.
b. Luke 16:31.
c. Luke 23:43.

edly, John had followed the procession from Pilate's judgment hall to Golgotha and, after witnessing the Savior being affixed to the cross, had gone to alert the Lord's family and some of the disciples. He soon returned with Mary, the mother of Jesus; her sister; Mary, the wife of Clopas; and Mary Magdalene—all of whom his gospel records as being present at the crucifixion. How long they remained there is unknown.[423]

When the Savior looked down and saw His mother near the cross, He uttered His third statement: "Woman, behold thy son! Then saith he to the disciple [John], Behold thy mother!"[a] The statement implied that John would now be responsible for Mary's care, and he immediately took her to his home, away from the pain and sorrow of the crucifixion. Again John's account lacks detail until he returns.[424] While John was away, the remaining women and other disciples that had gathered moved away from the cross and watched the remainder of the crucifixion proceedings from a distance. The Lord had almost completed His earthly mission, yet while He hung from the cross He prayed for those who had ignorantly participated in His death, gave comfort to the penitent, and provided for those closest to Him.

It was the "sixth hour," or about noon, and Jesus had been suffering for about three hours. The records testify that the sun darkened, and it remained dark and ominous until the "ninth hour."[425] The source of the darkness is not explained and there is no historical evidence of an eclipse; however, the darkness dramatized the depths to which men had sunk, a divine manifestation of the gloom which shrouded the earth over the death of its creator.[426] The long, three-hour period of agony that the Lord experienced while He hung upon the cross in darkness concluded the atonement He had begun in the Garden of Gethsemane. He was now giving His life for all mankind, literally dying for the sins of the world. The King of kings was fulfilling His mission and was not unworthy of His kingdom, but the Jewish "kingdom," by its very words and deeds, was unworthy of its King.

The end was near by the time the Lord uttered His fourth declaration from the cross, crying in a loud voice, "My God, my God, why hast thou forsaken me?"[b] It was the climax of His suffering, for the Father had to withdraw to allow the Son to complete His mis-

a. John 19:26–27.

b. Matthew 27:46.

sion.[427] How fitting it is that even in this He was misunderstood: the Jews thought that He had cried for Elias to assist Him, and again the crowd jeered.

Almost immediately the Lord uttered His fifth statement, crying, "I thirst."[a] One of the soldiers approached to give Him some vinegar on a sponge fastened to the end of a hyssop, some of the "rough wine" that they had been drinking as the vigil wore on, but others in the multitude shouted to withhold the refreshment to see if Elias would, in fact, come and save Him. Ignoring the crowd, the soldier offered the vinegar to the Savior; He accepted it, fulfilling the prophecy given by the Psalmist centuries before: "They gave me also gall for my meat; and in my thirst they gave me vinegar to drink."[b]

By now the Savior had been on the cross for more than six hours. He had endured all things and had faithfully completed His mission. In recognition of His victory won, He uttered His sixth comment, proclaiming: "It is finished."[c]

The seventh comment—and the final words of the dying Savior—came quickly: "Father," He announced, "into thy hands I commend my spirit."[d] The Lord of Hosts was dead! One of the Roman guards, apparently impressed by the Savior's demeanor throughout His torture and crucifixion, commented, "Truly this was the Son of God."

With the end of the Messiah's mortal life the veil of the temple, which shrouded the holy of holies from the holy place, was rent in twain from top to bottom, exposing the holy of holies. The veil was an enormous structure. It has been reported that to manipulate it required three hundred priests.[428] It was sixty feet high and thirty feet wide, approximately as thick as the palm of a hand, and made of seventy-two separate squares sewn together. Only once a year was the officiating priest allowed to part the veil and enter the holy of holies—the place where God dwelt, where He had shown Himself to the children of Israel, and (although now empty) where the tokens of His goodness to them had been kept for many years.[429] God's hand had rent the veil as a sign to the chosen people that He had deserted both them and the temple.[430] A great earthquake shook the ground and the rocks were rent as the earth itself mourned the loss of its God.

a. John 19:28.

b. Psalm 69:21.

c. John 19:30.

d. Luke 23:46.

Evening was approaching and Jewish law required that the bodies of the condemned not be left hanging upon the cross overnight.[a] Crucifixion was a dilatory method of death that "lasted not only for hours, but days;"[431] however, without thought for the ignoble death of the Savior, the chief priests petitioned Pilate to shorten the suffering of the two thieves so that their execution could be completed before the Sabbath began.

As the Passover (or the first Paschal day) ended, the Sabbath began: this particular Sabbath was also considered a "high day" because it was the "second Paschal Day, which was regarded as in every respect equally sacred with the first" day, or the Passover itself.[432] Roman law required that malefactors remain on the cross for several days after their deaths, but the Romans had granted the Jews an exception to this requirement[433] so that their Sabbath would not be violated. The extreme cruelty of the Roman conquerors was sharply manifest when the soldiers took large clubs or hammers and struck the knees of the two thieves, breaking their legs before they completed the execution by running them through with a lance. When they came to Jesus, they found He had already died; therefore, again in fulfillment of prophesy,[b] the Lord's bones were not broken. To make sure He was dead, however, the soldiers pierced His side with a lance,[c] completing the Old Testament prophecies concerning His death. John's narrative is very specific, indicating that both blood and water gushed forth from the Savior's open wound; further, he bore testimony that he personally witnessed the event. John later used the symbolism of blood and water to teach that salvation comes through Christ's atonement and that we are born again through Him: born of the water through baptism, born of the Spirit by His confirming witness, and then cleansed of our sins by the blood of Christ.[d]

The Sabbath was rapidly approaching as the Savior died, so a wealthy member of the Sanhedrin, Joseph of Arimathaea (who had not consented to the proceedings but was secretly a disciple of the Savior), went to Pilate to ask for Jesus' body. Pilate was surprised that the Savior had died so quickly and questioned the soldiers to confirm the death. After he was sure the Savior was dead, he agreed to give the body to Joseph. The body was quickly wrapped in a linen cloth and taken to Joseph's tomb, which had recently been hewn out

a. Deuteronomy
   21:22–23.

b. Psalm 34:20;
   Exodus 12:46;
   Numbers 9:12.

c. Zechariah
   12:10; 13:6.

d. 1 John 5:1–8.

of the rock and in which no body had ever rested. The entrance to the tomb opened into a nine-foot square court area, where a bier had been placed for the body to rest on.[434] At this point Nicodemus (another member of the Sanhedrin) appeared, carrying ointment to help prepare the body for burial. The linen cloth that Christ had been carefully wrapped in at Golgotha was now taken from His body and stripped into pieces. With the application of the ointments, each of the Savior's limbs and His body were wrapped in the Jewish manner of burial.[435] No other disciples assisted, but several women stood outside the tomb and watched as their Master was laid to rest. After the body had been hastily prepared, the two Sanhedrists left the tomb and rolled a large stone over its entrance.

Even though the Sabbath had commenced, the Savior's avowed enemies were not content with His death and burial. Remembering that Jesus had prophesied He would rise again the third day, they went to Pilate and requested that the tomb be sealed and guarded, using the excuse that some of His disciples might come and steal the body and then falsely claim that the Resurrection had taken place. They were granted the watch and even though night had fallen, they apparently returned to the tomb to seal the stone covering the entrance, thus violating their Law and defiling their Sabbath.

Jesus Christ's death sealed the fate of all those who had precipitated it. For thirty pieces of silver, Judas had bartered away the crown and the throne the Savior had promised him. The Jewish leadership was relieved of a bitter enemy when Christ was crucified, and in the process they ensured the destruction of their temple, their city, their place, and their nation. The Roman conquerors had unwittingly participated in this tragedy and in ignorance had fulfilled the prophecies of the ancients concerning Christ's death.

The Satanic influence that had been so pervasively evident throughout Christ's arrest, trial, and crucifixion had only served to further doom its author. The victory Lucifer had temporarily won with Adam he had forever lost in Christ, for the culmination of the Savior's mortal ministry had taken place and He had won the victory over death. In accordance with the plan of salvation and with approval from a loving Father, Jesus the Messiah was dead.

In the World of Spirits

John 5:25–29   Verily, verily, I say unto you, The hour is coming, and now is, when the dead shall hear the voice of the Son of God: and they that hear shall live. For as the Father hath life in himself; so hath he given to the Son to have life in himself; and hath given him authority to execute judgment also, because he is the Son of man. Marvel not at this: for the hour is coming, in the which all that are in the graves shall hear his voice, and shall come forth; they that have done good, unto the resurrection of life; and they that have done evil, unto the resurrection of damnation.

Doctrine and Covenants 138:12, 18–20, 27–37   And there were gathered together in one place an innumerable company of the spirits of the just, who had been faithful in the testimony of Jesus while they lived in mortality; . . .

While this vast multitude waited and conversed, rejoicing in the hour of their deliverance from the chains of death, the Son of God appeared, declaring liberty to the captives who had been faithful; and there he preached to them the everlasting gospel, the doctrine of the resurrection and the redemption of mankind from the fall, and from individual sins on conditions of repentance. But unto the wicked he did not go, and among the ungodly and the unrepentant who had defiled themselves while in the flesh, his voice was not raised; . . .

But his ministry among those who were dead was limited to the brief time intervening between the crucifixion and his resurrection; and I wondered at the words of Peter—wherein he said that the Son of God preached unto the spirits in prison, who sometime were disobedient, when once the long-suffering of God waited in the days of Noah—and how it was possible for him to preach to those spirits and perform the necessary labor among them in so short a time. And as I wondered, my eyes were opened, and my understanding quickened, and I perceived that the Lord went not in person among the wicked and the disobedient who had rejected the truth, to teach them; but behold, from among the righteous, he organized his forces and appointed messengers, clothed with power and authority, and commissioned them to go forth and carry the light of the gospel to them that were in darkness, even to all the spirits of men; and thus was the gospel preached to the dead. And the chosen messengers went forth to declare the acceptable day of the Lord and proclaim liberty to the captives who were bound, even unto all who would repent of their sins and receive the gospel. Thus was the gospel preached to those who had died in their sins, without a knowledge of the truth, or in transgression, having rejected the prophets. These were taught faith in God, repentance from sin, vicarious baptism for the remission of sins, the gift of the Holy Ghost by the laying on of hands, and all other principles of the gospel that were necessary for them to know in order to qualify themselves that they might be judged according to men in the flesh, but live according to God in the spirit. And so it was made known among the dead, both small and great, the unrighteous as well as the faithful, that redemption had been wrought through the sacrifice of the Son of God upon the cross. Thus was it made known that our Redeemer spent his time during his sojourn in the world of spirits, instructing and preparing the faithful spirits of the prophets who had testified of him in the flesh; that they might carry the message of redemption unto all the dead, unto whom he could not go personally, because of their rebellion and transgression, that they through the ministration of his servants might also hear his words.

Cross-references   Isaiah 42:7; Isaiah 61:1; 1 Peter 3:18–20; 1 Peter 4:5–6; 1 Corinthians 15:29

Christ's spirit passed out of His body and into the world of spirits at His death. All men who had died prior to Christ's death (both righteous and unrighteous) were currently residing in a place known as the spirit world, and now that His mortal ministry upon the earth had ended, His ministry to those already in the spirit world commenced.

That Jesus was aware of His future mission to the spirit world is evidenced by a discussion which took place early in His mission with the rulers of the Jews, just after the healing of the impotent man by the pool of Bethesda. He first declared to them His relationship with the Father, then He informed them that the hour would come "when the dead shall hear the voice of the Son of God. . . . For . . . all that are in the graves shall hear His voice."[436]

His mission in the spirit world was twofold: (1) To proclaim the glad tidings of the resurrection, which ensured redemption from the bondage of death, and (2) To establish His ministry to the dead and thus provide them with the opportunity of salvation from the effects of individual sin.[437]

There are two main divisions in the spirit world. The first is called *paradise:* this is where the righteous and repentant in mortality reside between their physical death and resurrection. The second division is generally known as the *spirit prison:* this is reserved for the wicked, those who were without knowledge of the plan of salvation, and those who refused repentance when it was offered to them while in mortality.[438]

The inhabitants of paradise eagerly awaited their Lord's entry into the spirit world, for it signaled His victory over death. President Joseph F. Smith saw in vision the multitude of spirits who awaited the Savior's arrival and rejoiced at being in His presence.

Isaiah foresaw the Savior's mission to the inhabitants of the spirit prison and testified that He would "bring out the prisoners from the prison . . . to proclaim liberty to the captives, and the opening of the prison to them that are bound." Peter was also aware of this ministry, and he declared that Jesus (by the spirit) "went and preached unto the spirits in prison; which sometime were disobedient, when once the longsuffering of God awaited in the days of Noah."

Those in the spirit prison had to receive the gospel so that they "might be judged according to men in the flesh, but live according to God in the spirit." Those who heard the gospel of salvation in the spirit could then reject or accept the saving ordinances vicariously performed for them by others in mortality. To accept the ordinances, they must develop faith in the Lord Jesus Christ, accept His atonement and sacrifice, repent of their transgressions, and obey God's word.[439] This doctrine of vicarious ordinances, while not explicitly taught in the New Testament, was obliquely referred to by Paul who, while arguing for the reality of the resurrection, cited the early church's practice of baptizing living Saints for the dead. "Else what shall they do which are baptized for the dead," Paul questioned, "if the dead rise not at all? why are they then baptized for the dead?"

The righteous in the spirit world were anxious to see the Savior because they had looked upon the absence from their bodies as bondage, and they rejoiced at the opportunity for freedom. The Lord preached liberty to these spirits by declaring the everlasting gospel, which included the doctrines of the Atonement and the Resurrection. This provided them with redemption from the fall of Adam and forgiveness from individual sin on condition of repentance. However, Christ did not personally go to the wicked, for they could not abide His presence. Yet these, also, would be offered salvation through missionary work.

While in the spirit, the Lord organized messengers "from among the righteous" who would use His commission and authority to preach the gospel "to the captives who were bound, even unto all who would repent of their sins and receive the gospel." These spirits fell into two categories: the first consisted of those who had died in their sins without knowledge of the truth; the second consisted of those who had not only died in their sins, but had also rejected the truth while in mortality. Both groups would now be taught the saving principles of the gospel: repentance from sin, faith in the Lord, vicarious baptism for the remission of sin, and the gift of the Holy Ghost by the vicarious laying on of hands as well as any and all other principles of the gospel necessary to qualify them to be "judged according to men in the flesh, but live according to God in the spirit."

Just as the mission of Jesus Christ extended past mortality and into the spirit world, it is reasonable to assume that *all* who labor in His ministry while in mortality will be prepared to carry the message of redemption (after they leave mortality themselves) to those who reside in the spirit prison.[440]

In addition to establishing a missionary program in the spirit world, the Lord (while yet in the spirit) raised His voice to the other sheep He had spoken of in His good shepherd discourse.[441] At His death, a mist of darkness had shrouded the Western Hemisphere as a sign to the people that He had finished His mission on earth. Now the Savior spoke to those people out of that darkness to prepare them for His coming in a resurrected form.[a442]

Jesus Christ's mortal ministry lasted three years. His ministry to the spirit world lasted only three days, yet it is evident that His accomplishments in the world of spirits were far-reaching. During this short period of time, however, he made salvation available to all mankind, as God's plan provided.[443]

"He Is Risen"

The Resurrection

John 20:1–31   The first day of the week cometh Mary Magdalene early, when it was yet dark, unto the sepulchre, and seeth the stone taken away from the sepulchre. Then she runneth, and cometh to Simon Peter, and to the other disciple, whom Jesus loved, and saith unto them, They have taken away the Lord out of the sepulchre, and we know not where they have laid him. Peter therefore went forth, and that other disciple, and came to the sepulchre. So they ran both together: and the other disciple did outrun Peter, and came first to the sepulchre. And he stooping down, and looking in, saw the linen clothes lying; yet went he not in. Then cometh Simon Peter following him, and went into the sepulchre, and seeth the linen clothes lie, and the napkin, that was about his head, not lying with the linen clothes, but wrapped together in a place by itself. Then went in also that other disciple, which came first to the sepulchre, and he saw, and believed. For as yet they knew not the scripture, that he must rise again from the dead. Then the disciples went away again unto their own home.

But Mary stood without at the sepulchre weeping: and as she wept, she stooped down, and looked into the sepulchre, and seeth two angels in white sitting, the one at the head, and the other at the feet, where the body of Jesus had lain. And they say unto her, Woman, why weepest thou? She saith unto them, Because they have taken away my Lord, and I know not where they have laid him. And when she had thus said, she turned herself back, and saw Jesus standing, and knew not that it was Jesus. Jesus saith unto her, Woman, why weepest thou? whom seekest thou? She, supposing him to be the gardener, saith unto him, Sir, if thou have borne him hence, tell me where thou hast laid him, and I will take him away. Jesus saith unto her, Mary. She turned herself, and saith unto him, Rabboni; which is to say, Master. Jesus saith unto her, Touch me not; for I am not yet ascended to my Father: but go to my brethren, and say unto them, I ascend unto my Father, and your Father; and to my God, and your God. Mary Magdalene came and told the disciples that she had seen the Lord, and that he had spoken these things unto her.

Then the same day at evening, being the first day of the week, when the doors were shut where the disciples were assembled for fear of the Jews, came Jesus and stood in the midst, and saith unto them, Peace be unto you. And when he had so said, he shewed unto them his hands and his side. Then were the disciples glad, when they saw the Lord. Then said Jesus to them again, Peace be unto you: as my Father hath sent me, even so send I you. And when he had said this, he breathed on them, and saith unto them, Receive ye the Holy Ghost: whose soever sins ye remit, they are remitted unto them; and whose soever sins ye retain, they are retained.

But Thomas, one of the twelve, called Didymus, was not with them when Jesus came. The other disciples therefore said unto him, We have seen the Lord. But he said unto them, Except I shall see in his hands the print of the nails, and put my finger into the print of the nails, and thrust my hand into his side, I will not believe.

And after eight days again his disciples were within, and Thomas with them: then came Jesus, the doors being shut, and stood in the midst, and said, Peace be unto you. Then saith he to Thomas, Reach hither thy finger, and behold my hands; and reach hither thy hand, and thrust it into my side: and be not faithless, but believing. And Thomas answered and said unto him, My Lord and my God. Jesus saith unto him, Thomas, because thou hast seen me, thou hast believed: blessed are they that have not seen, and yet have believed.

And many other signs truly did Jesus in the presence of his disciples, which are not written in this book: but these are written, that ye might believe that Jesus is the Christ, the Son of God; and that believing ye might have life through his name.

John 21:1–25   After these things Jesus shewed himself again to the disciples at the sea of Tiberias; and on this wise shewed he himself. There were together Simon Peter, and Thomas called Didymus, and Nathanael of Cana in Galilee, and the sons of Zebedee, and two other of his disciples. Simon Peter saith unto them, I go a fishing. They say unto him, We also go with thee. They went forth, and entered into a ship immediately; and that night they caught nothing. But when the morning was now come, Jesus stood on the shore: but the disciples knew not that it was Jesus. Then Jesus saith unto them, Children, have ye any meat? They answered Him, No. And he said unto them, Cast the net on the right side of the ship, and ye shall find. They cast therefore, and now they were not able to draw it for the multitude of fishes. Therefore that disciple whom Jesus loved saith unto Peter, It is the Lord. Now when Simon Peter heard that it was the Lord, he girt his fisher's coat unto him, (for he was naked,) and did cast himself into the sea. And the other disciples came in a little ship; (for they were not far from land, but as it were two hundred cubits,) dragging the net with fishes. As soon then as they were come to land, they saw a fire of coals there, and fish laid thereon, and bread. Jesus saith unto them, Bring of the fish which ye have now caught. Simon Peter went up, and drew the net to land full of great fishes, an hundred and fifty and three: and for all there were so many, yet was not the net broken. Jesus saith unto them, Come and dine. And none of the disciples durst ask him, Who art thou? knowing that it was the Lord. Jesus then cometh, and taketh bread, and giveth them, and fish likewise. This is now the third time that Jesus shewed himself to his disciples, after that he was risen from the dead.

So when they had dined, Jesus saith to Simon Peter, Simon, son of Jonas, lovest thou me more than these? He saith unto him, Yea, Lord; thou knowest that I love thee. He saith unto him, Feed my lambs. He saith to him again the second time, Simon, son of Jonas, lovest thou me? He saith unto him, Yea, Lord; thou knowest that I love thee. He saith unto him, Feed my sheep. He saith unto him the third time, Simon, son of Jonas, lovest thou me? Peter was grieved because he said unto him the third time, Lovest thou me? And he said unto him, Lord, thou knowest all things; thou knowest that I love thee. Jesus saith unto him, Feed my sheep. Verily, verily, I say unto thee, When thou wast young, thou girdedst thyself, and walkedst whither thou wouldest: but when thou shalt be old, thou shalt stretch forth thy hands, and another shall gird thee, and carry thee whither thou wouldest not. This spake he, signifying by what death he should glorify God. And when he had spoken this, he saith unto him, Follow me. Then Peter, turning about, seeth the disciple whom Jesus loved following; which also leaned on his breast at supper, and said, Lord, which is he that betrayeth thee? Peter seeing him saith to Jesus, Lord, and what shall this man do? Jesus saith unto him, If I will that he tarry till I come, what is that to thee? follow thou me. Then went this saying abroad among the brethren, that that disciple should not die: yet Jesus said not unto him, He shall not die; but, If I will that he tarry till I come, what is that to thee? This is the disciple which testifieth of these things, and wrote these things: and we know that his testimony is true. And there are also many other things which Jesus did, the which, if they should be written every one, I suppose that even the world itself could not contain the books that should be written. Amen.

Cross-references   Matthew 28; Mark 16; Luke 24; 1 Corinthians 15:4–8; Acts 1:1–12; Acts 17:32

John's account of the Crucifixion and the Resurrection is enhanced by the fact that he was an eyewitness while the Synoptics seem to merely supplement his narrative.[444] All the Gospel writers tend to condense their histories of those events, but the Synoptics do so more than John—perhaps due to their lack of information. The Gospel writers were not concerned about creating an exact history of the period between the first Easter morning and the ascension some forty days later; they *were* concerned, however, about furnishing exact evidence of the Resurrection itself.

Matthew describes the impressions of both the Lord's enemies and His disciples on the morning of the Resurrection. He also describes the Lord's appearance on the shores of Galilee (where the miracle of the second draught of fish occurred)[445] and on the mount (where Jesus again commissioned the Apostles). Mark's record is extremely brief, summarizing the events from the viewpoint of the immediate family. Luke, the historian, details the facts of the resurrection day but then jumps immediately to the Ascension. John describes episodes that occurred during the entire forty-day period, both in Jerusalem and in Galilee (though not in close detail), and testifies yet again that Jesus is the Christ, the Son of the living God.[446]

It is difficult to determine exactly what went through the minds of the Lord's disciples and Apostles after His death and burial, but certain scriptural evidences indicate that although they knew He was dead, they did not expect Him to rise again. For example:

1. Nicodemus, one of the two Sanhedrists who saw to Jesus' burial, brought burial spices to prepare the Lord's body.

2. Some women who were disciples of Christ prepared and laid up spices during the Sabbath with the intent of returning to the tomb to properly prepare the Lord's body for burial. This suggests that they did not think the Lord's mortal body would rise from corruption to incorruption.

3. When the women saw the empty tomb, they supposed that the body of Jesus had been taken away by His enemies.

4. Although the Apostles had been told several times by the Savior that He would rise again, they disbelieved the first testimonies of the women, thinking them "as idle tales." John wrote that "as yet they knew not the scripture, that he must rise again from the dead."

In contrast to these doubts by the Lord's followers, the scriptures report that His avowed enemies, the Sanhedrists, seemed to understand some of the potential of the Lord's predictions about His resurrection (whether or not they believed in the doctrine of the resurrection), so they took precautions against the body being stolen so that they could avoid the claim of resurrection by His disciples.

Many Jews believed in the earthly kingdom that their anticipated Messiah would establish at His coming but did not believe in the resurrection. Their expectation was not that the Messiah would come as a glorified, resurrected being but that He would come in great power (as He will for His second coming) and thus establish His eternal kingdom upon the earth.[447]

The religious zealots at the time were among Christ's worst enemies, for they carried the letter of the Law out to its bitter end. They perceived Jesus as being in mortal conflict with their Law because He taught the spirit of the law rather than the letter. The zealots were triumphant after the Lord's crucifixion, for the apparent uncertainty of the disciples and the Apostles alike indicated that "nothing could have seemed more abjectly weak, more pitifully hopeless, more absolutely doomed to scorn, and extinction, and despair, than the Church which He had founded."[448] The eleven Apostles and the disciples in general were overwhelmed by the events that had taken place, and it is obvious that they did not have a clear understanding of the resurrection; yet without exception the scriptures testify that their thoughts (and even the thoughts of His enemies) were filled with and centered on Jesus Christ.

The disciples were filled with deep grief over the loss of their Master and the apparent triumph of His enemies; but this was not unexpected, for the Lord had foretold these circumstances on many occasions. In addition (especially since the Transfiguration), He had referred to His resurrection frequently.[449] But the Apostles' conception of the doctrine of resurrection was clouded because of their Jewish traditions,[450] and their understanding had not yet caught up with their devotion.

Resurrection as taught by the Lord was quite foreign to the Jewish beliefs of His day.[451] However, it appears that the Lord never intended to give His disciples a complete understanding of the resurrection during His mortal ministry. Once the Savior's resurrection had taken place, the reality of the event itself would be the best teacher and would clarify His teachings and the scriptures to their understanding. The physical evidence of the Resurrection (that is, the holes in His hands and the wound in His side) was undeniable proof that the Lord had risen from the grave, and without this evidence He may not have been believed. But given that personal experience with Christ's resurrection, they were able to truthfully testify of its reality.

Those who taught the resurrection after the fact were willing to be physically and mentally abused, tortured, and even put to death for their beliefs. A basic premise of the Apostles' instruction was resurrection from the dead. Paul emphasized this when he said to the Corinthian Saints, "And if Christ be not risen, then is our preaching vain, and your faith is also vain. Yea, and we are found false witnesses of God; . . . [and] ye are yet in your sins."[a]

The "hands-on" experience the Apostles and disciples enjoyed provided them with a firm conviction of the Resurrection. Those who objected and disbelieved seemed to do so because resurrection required them to believe in the miraculous. It is fitting that the life of the Lord Jesus Christ closed with a miracle as great as the one with which it began. A dead Christ would have only been a great teacher, a wonder worker, and a prophet; but a risen Christ "could be the Saviour, the Life, and the Life-Giver—and as such preached to all men."[452]

Jesus died around 3:00 p.m. on Friday, and the evening sunset marked the close of the day, the _first day_ in the tomb. During this time, the priests in the temple (so near to Golgotha) were sacrificially offering the blood of bulls and goats for the sins of Israel, completely unconscious that blood had been shed that day in a far greater sacrifice upon the cross.

While the Lord's body lay in the tomb on Saturday, the _second day,_ the last Sabbath of the old Covenant was zealously observed by the multitude of worshipers who had participated in the Feast of the Passover. During the early morning hours of Sunday, the _third day,_ some who dearly loved Him and mourned Him were busy gathering and preparing the spices needed to properly prepare His body for burial, for their oblations performed on the day of His crucifixion had been extremely hurried so that the Sabbath could be observed.

Apparently, two groups of women were preparing to go to the tomb, planning to meet there to anoint Christ's body with the spices they had prepared. Among them were Mary Magdalene; Mary, the mother of Joses; Joanna, the wife of Chuza; Salome, the mother of James and John; and several others. Undoubtedly, these were some of the same women who had participated in the vigil at Christ's crucifixion and had watched from afar as Joseph of Arimathaea and Nicodemus placed the Lord's body in the tomb and rolled a stone over its entrance. The women conversed as they traveled toward the tomb, wondering how they would remove the stone when they arrived. Apparently they were unaware that the tomb had been sealed and placed under guard; but when they reached their destination, not only were the guards gone but also the stone had been rolled away.

Matthew gives an intensely interesting account of what occurred during the early morning hours on Sunday: "And, behold, there was a great earthquake: for the angel of the Lord descended from heaven, and came and rolled back the stone from the door, and sat upon it. His countenance was like lightening, and his raiment white as snow."[a] The seal on the stone had been broken, and the guards who had been placed to watch the tomb had been terrified by the angel and had fled to report the miraculous occurrences to the chief priests. Mary Magdalene was apparently ahead of the other women as they approached the tomb and when she saw the angel and determined that the Savior's body was no longer there, she quickly ran to inform Peter and John.

While Mary Magdalene was gone, the other women arrived at the tomb, saw that the stone had been rolled away, and entered the sepulchre. Within the sepulchre they saw an angel, "a young man sitting on the right side, clothed in a long white garment,"[b] and they were frightened. But the heavenly messenger calmed their fears and told them that Jesus was no longer there—He had risen as He had prophesied. The angel instructed the trembling women to go to the disciples and inform them that Christ would meet them in Galilee, and they immediately left the tomb to fulfill the angel's instructions.

Meanwhile, Mary Magdalene had reached Peter and John and told them of the angel and the empty tomb. The two Apostles immediately left for the sepulchre. They ran the last portion of the distance (John declaring that he outran Peter), but they arrived after the other women had gone. John stopped apprehensively at the entrance of the tomb, but Peter rushed past John and immediately entered. He did not see an angel, but he did observe the wrappings that had covered the Lord's body and the napkin which had covered His face. John entered the tomb next and was led to believe that the Lord had risen from the grave, "for as yet they knew not the scripture, that the Lord must rise again from the dead." Both disciples left the tomb perplexed by the Savior's disappearance and returned to their residence.

Mary Magdalene had attempted to follow Peter and John when they ran to the tomb, but she arrived after they had departed. She stood outside the sepulchre weeping, for she loved the Lord and was concerned about the fate of His sacred body. She stooped to again look into the tomb and saw two angels in white apparel, one sitting at the head and one sitting at the foot of where Christ's body had lain. Their question was simple, "Woman, why weepest thou?" Mary seemed momentarily unable to respond, but then in her grief she said, "Because they have taken away my Lord, and I know not where they have laid him."

Mary then became conscious of another presence close to her and turning, she saw a man she thought to be the gardener. This man asked, "Woman, why weepest thou? Whom seekest thou?" It was the resurrected Lord, appearing for the first time since His resurrection; but Mary, still "supposing him to be the gardener" and overwhelmed with the loss of the Lord's remains, "saith unto him, Sir, if thou have borne him hence, tell me where thou hast laid him, and I will take him away."[453]

Jesus softly spoke her name, "Mary." She immediately recognized her Savior and moved toward Him, saying, "Rabboni; which is to say, Master." But the close familiarity of former days was no longer possible, and the Savior declared: "Touch me not; for I am not yet ascended to my Father. But go to my brethren, and say unto them, I ascend unto my Father, and your Father; and to my God, and your God." She immediately left to give His sacred message to the Apostles.

The other women arrived after Mary had left the tomb and also saw the angels. They, too, received instructions to tell the disciples all they had seen and heard. They were traveling to fulfill this commandment when the Lord appeared to them, greeting them with the familiar, "All hail." Immediately recognizing their Lord and Savior, they reverently knelt before Him, held Him by the feet, "and worshipped him."[454] The Lord instructed them to tell the brethren to go into Galilee, and they would see Him there; however, when the Apostles heard the testimony of Mary Magdalene and the other women, they felt that their words were "idle tales" and they believed them not.

During this time, the guards who had watched Christ's tomb had gone to the chief priests to report all that had occurred. The chief priests disbelieved their report—just as they had disbelieved all of the mighty witnesses that Jesus had given them throughout His ministry—but to be safe, they bribed the guards to spread the rumor that they had fallen asleep, and that while they were asleep Jesus' disciples had stolen His body so as to be able to claim that the resurrection had taken place. Because the guards feared Pilate's punishment if he learned they had slept on their watch, the chief priests told them they would intercede on their behalf and absolve them of any guilt.

The news of Christ's resurrection no doubt spread rapidly among His disciples, but the reality of the Resurrection seemed too difficult for them to comprehend. The disciples knew that the Savior had died, but they were slow to understand that His death was but a prelude to His resurrection; as a result, the disciples appeared to have lost all hope and their visions of the Messiah's earthly kingdom were dashed.[455]

According to Luke, it was probably early in the afternoon on Sunday when two of the disciples left Jerusalem for Emmaus. One of the two disciples was named Cleopas; the other remains unnamed, but it is traditionally thought that it was Luke himself. As they traveled, they discussed that eventful day and were bewildered and confused by it all.[456] Somewhere along their route a stranger joined them in their travels. The scripture states that their eyes "were holden" in order that they might not recognize the Lord. He asked them about their discussion and wondered why they were sad. Cleopas asked whether He was a stranger to Jerusalem and did not know what had taken place there. He then rehearsed all that had transpired during the fateful days from Friday to Sunday morning. He explained that Jesus had been well known, even considered to be a prophet by the people, and that the chief priests had condemned Him to death and crucified Him. He expressed the disciples' belief concerning Jesus, "that it had been he which should have redeemed Israel," and they indicated that it had been three days since His death.

He continued telling the "stranger" that certain women had gone to the sepulchre early that very morning and had been astonished when they could not find the Savior's body. The women had reported this to the disciples and the Apostles, testifying that they had seen a vision of angels who had announced that Jesus was alive. Evidently Cleopas and his companion had spoken to Peter and John, for Cleopas noted that certain of the Apostles had gone to the sepulchre to verify what the women had seen and that the body was, in fact, gone—but Peter and John had not seen the angels.

The Savior listened quietly and then, without identifying Himself, He reproved Cleopas and Luke, noting that they had been slow of heart to believe what the prophets had spoken. He began to recite evidence that Christ should have suffered all of these things in order to enter His glory and He enumerated the scriptures as evidence, beginning with the writings of Moses and continuing through all of the prophets. As they approached Emmaus, the stranger indicated that He planned to keep traveling, but the two disciples "constrained him" (having felt of the Spirit without recognizing the Lord), and asked Him to sup with them and abide with them throughout the evening. The Lord agreed, and as dinner commenced, He "took bread and blessed it, and brake and gave to them." With the performance of this familiar event, their eyes were opened and they knew their Savior. But then He "vanished out of their sight."[457] At this point, the disciples acknowledged how their hearts had burned within them while the "stranger" had been opening the scriptures to their understanding, and in their excitement they arose from their dinner and returned to Jerusalem that same night.

It is apparent that sometime during that same afternoon the Lord appeared to Peter, for Paul later testifies to the Corinthians of that appearance.[a] Undoubtedly, this personal witness to the senior Apostle was for His instruction and edification so that he could strengthen others in their conviction of the Resurrection.

When Cleopas and Luke reached Jerusalem, they found the Apostles and other disciples gathered together in an upper room for their evening meal. The scriptures note that they had shut both the outer and the inner doors to the house "for fear of the Jews."

They may have been apprehensive because they were Christ's disciples and still suspect, or perhaps they thought the stories of the empty tomb might have reached the authorities, who would again incite the hatred of the Sanhedrists. In any case, they took special precautions to prevent detection. By this time they knew that Christ had risen, but they still did not understand the resurrection itself. While they were thus assembled, Christ suddenly appeared to them and they were terrified because they thought that they were seeing a "spirit" or ghost.

The Savior allayed their fears and misunderstanding by commanding them to not only look at His hands and feet, but also touch Him so

a. 1 Corinthians 15:5.

that they would know that He was not a spirit, for spirits did not have bodies of flesh and bones as they could see He had. As if to emphasize His reality, the Lord took a piece of their broiled fish and some honeycomb and ate before them. Then, as He had with the two disciples on the road to Emmaus, He expounded the scriptures to them and opened the eyes of their understanding so they could comprehend why He had to suffer in order that He might rise again.

The Apostles were instructed to carry on the work that Christ had begun, preaching repentance and remission of sins in His name to all nations. He authorized them to do this work just as the Father had authorized Him, and He gave them the Holy Ghost to sustain them in their calling. He told them that they had the power to either remit or retain sins; in addition to this power, He bestowed the keys of the priesthood upon them so that they could preserve the integrity of the church and provide for its administrative needs. Thomas was absent when the Lord made this appearance to the Apostles, and when he was told of the marvelous occurrence he refused to believe unless he personally could witness the corporeality of the Lord.

Apparently a quiet week passed wherein the Messiah did not appear. But on the first day of the following week, the Apostles again gathered in a closed room and the Savior appeared in their midst. This time Thomas was present, and when he had seen the Lord's hands and felt His side, his doubts fled and he eagerly accepted the resurrection by acknowledging his Lord and Savior. Jesus again taught the Apostles concerning the resurrection, but now He led them away from the physical evidence and directed them to the higher element of faith—blessing those who believed and understood the reality of the resurrected Savior without having to see Him. John concluded this account of the Savior's appearance with his personal testimony:[458] "But these [things] are written, that ye might believe that Jesus is the Christ, the Son of God; and that believing ye might have life through his name."[a]

A short time later, the Apostles left Jerusalem for Galilee to await the Lord's promised visit. They undoubtedly testified to other disciples of the resurrection; however, some doubted, even though some apparently accompanied the Apostles as they traveled to Galilee. Perhaps it was during this trip that the Lord appeared on a mountain[b] to the group of "five hundred at once" that Paul mentions in Corinthians.[c]

a. John 20:31.

b. Matthew 28:16.

c. 1 Corinthians 15:6.

The brethren soon arrived in Galilee. While they were waiting for the Savior, Peter and six of the Apostles decided to go fishing. That night they fished on the lake but caught nothing. With the approach of dawn they saw a man standing on the beach. He asked them if they had caught any fish, and their response was negative. He then directed them to cast their net on the right side of the boat; as soon as they complied, their net was filled to overflowing. John then recognized the stranger and whispered to Peter that it was the Lord. Peter, eager to get to his Master, drew his fisher's coat around him and cast himself into the sea. The ship was still approximately 350 feet from shore, so the others followed in a small boat, dragging the heavy net of fish with them.[459]

The Savior had built a fire and had the morning meal ready and waiting for the Apostles. He instructed them to bring in the load of fish they had caught, and Peter returned to the shore to help his fellow Apostles pull the overburdened net onto the beach. Jesus then bade the Apostles eat the meal He had prepared, but some of them were still apprehensive. Though they knew He was the Lord, they did not dare ask Him to confirm it.

After they had finished dining, Jesus summoned Peter to Him and asked, "Lovest thou me more than these?" Peter understood what the Lord was asking him, for the Lord had told Peter that he would deny Him thrice before the cock crowed. Peter had confidently asserted that he would not deny the Lord but would follow Him even to death. However, he had denied the Lord, and those denials were "uncancelled before the other disciples, nay, before Peter himself."[460] Peter knew that he needed the Savior's forgiveness, and he responded with great humility when he said, "Yea, Lord; thou knowest that I love thee." The Lord simply responded, "Feed my lambs."

Again the Lord looked upon Peter and said, "Lovest thou me?" Peter responded as before, to which the Lord replied, "Feed my sheep." A third time the Savior looked upon his chief Apostle and said, "Lovest thou me?" Undoubtedly Peter recognized the parallel between the Lord's three-times-asked question and his thrice-given denial and was grieved. In anguish Peter cried, "Lord, thou knowest all things; thou knowest that I love thee," and this time Jesus authoritatively commanded, "Feed my sheep." Peter's repentance was accepted and the Savior forgave him. The Lord acknowledged his chief Apostle's strength and the great work which he would do in furthering the kingdom, but He prophesied that eventually Peter would give his life for the gospel—martyred in the same manner that the Lord had been.

Jesus then directed His chief Apostle to "Follow me," apparently inviting Peter to move away from the other Apostles where they could talk privately. The Lord walked away from the group and Peter followed Him, as did John, "the disciple whom Jesus loved." Peter, noticing that John was following, inquired with brotherly interest what the Lord expected of John. The Lord responded that he would not die but would tarry until the Messiah came again, a blessing which is attested to in modern revelation.[a] Although Paul mentions that the Lord also appeared to James,[b] this was the third and last recorded time that He appeared to the Apostles as a whole until the Ascension. However, John testifies that the Lord did "many other things," and that if they were written, "the world itself could not contain the books."

The Ascension

Whether on the shores of Galilee or at Jerusalem, the Lord had renewed the apostolic commission to all of His Apostles. Now, as the time of Jesus' ascension approached, they gathered on the slopes of the Mount of Olives "which is from Jerusalem a sabbath day's journey."[c] The Lord blessed His special witnesses with the promises the Father had given Him and declared that with His resurrection, the Father had given Him "all power . . . in heaven and in earth." The Apostles again asked the Savior when the kingdom would be restored to Israel, but the question went unanswered, for the promises the Lord gave and the powers He bestowed were spiritual, not worldly.[d] The Apostles were instructed to tarry in Jerusalem until they were endowed with power from heaven—the fulfillment of which came on the day of Pentecost when the Holy Ghost was manifested to them.[e] When that had been accomplished (and only then), they were to go forth to all nations, teaching the commandments, witnessing Christ's resurrection, and baptizing in the name of the Father, the Son, and the Holy Ghost.

The Savior lifted up His hands and blessed them, promising that He would be with them always. He then miraculously ascended and a cloud received Him out of their sight. Suddenly, two angels stood

a. D&C 7.

b. 1 Corinthians
   15:7.

c. Acts 1:12.

d. Acts 1:6–8.

e. Acts 2:2–3.

beside the Apostles and asked, "Ye men of Galilee, why stand ye gazing up into heaven? this same Jesus, which is taken up from you into heaven, shall so come in like manner as ye have seen him go into heaven."

The Apostles returned to Jerusalem "with great joy"—and no wonder! The Lord had risen, they were witnesses of it, and His work of salvation would continue both on earth and in heaven until the end of time.

Establishing the Kingdom   10

Other Sheep

John 10:16   And other sheep I have, which are not of this fold: them also I must bring, and they shall hear my voice; and there shall be one fold, and one shepherd.

3 Nephi 15:21–24   And verily I say unto you, that ye are they of whom I said: Other sheep I have which are not of this fold; them also I must bring, and they shall hear my voice; and there shall be one fold, and one shepherd. And they understood me not, for they supposed it had been the Gentiles; for they understood not that the Gentiles should be converted through their preaching. And they understood me not that I said they shall hear my voice; and they understood me not that the Gentiles should not at any time hear my voice—that I should not manifest myself unto them save it were by the Holy Ghost. But behold, ye have both heard my voice, and seen me; and ye are my sheep, and ye are numbered among those whom the Father hath given me.

3 Nephi 16:1   And verily, verily, I say unto you that I have other sheep, which are not of this land, neither of the land of Jerusalem, neither in any parts of that land round about whither I have been to minister.

Cross-references   3 Nephi 1, 7–10, 16–28; Helaman 14

The Book of Mormon records that six hundred years before His birth as Jesus Christ, Jehovah, the God of the Old Testament, appeared to a prophet then living in the vicinity of Jerusalem. Lehi was commanded by the Lord to take his family and leave Jerusalem for a "promised land" before the destruction of Jerusalem prophesied by Jeremiah took place. Lehi obediently left the city with his family and the family of Ishmael and traveled in the wilderness for approximately eight years. They then built a ship, crossed the oceans, and arrived on the Western Hemisphere (the "promised land") after a period of "many days."[a]

These people soon divided into two main groups, generally known as the Nephites and the Lamanites. The people maintained this division throughout the centuries prior to Christ's birth, and for the most part, continual animosity existed between them.

Approximately five years prior to the birth of the Savior in Jerusalem, a righteous Lamanite prophet named Samuel was sent to the Nephites (who had become more wicked than the Lamanites at that time) to call them to repentance in preparation for the advent of their Savior—but they became angry and would not listen to him. To convince his hearers that the Savior would soon be born, Samuel gave them a very specific sign. He prophesied that on the night before the Lord's birth, there would be no darkness; that is, there would be a day, a night, and a day wherein no darkness would occur. In addition, a new star would appear in the heavens. By these signs they would know that all that had been prophesied concerning the birth of the Messiah was true.

During the time of Christ's mortal probation on the Eastern Hemisphere, Book of Mormon prophets on the Western Hemisphere were declaring His truths so that their people might also know of the Savior. The ministry of these prophets "mirrored" the events in Christ's ministry in order to testify of Him. The people of the Western Hemisphere knew of the people in Jerusalem because they had come from there, but the people in Jerusalem knew nothing of their fellow tribesmen in the West.

John records two discourses the Savior delivered during His last visits to Jerusalem.[b] They have become known as the "good shepherd discourse." The first portion of this discourse[c] was delivered while the Savior was at the Feast of Tabernacles; two months later, while He was at the Feast of Dedication, He delivered the remaining portion.[d] The Lord declared His Messiahship in these sermons, using the allegory of the good shepherd.[461] The allegory was a familiar one in His day and was frequently used by the rabbis. In the allegory, Jesus referred to the people in Jerusalem as His sheep, but He declared He also had *other* sheep which were not of the Jewish fold. These other sheep were to hear His voice as well, for there was but one fold and one shepherd. The "other sheep" included (1) those who, under Jehovah's direction, had migrated from Jerusalem to the Western Hemisphere, and (2) the lost ten tribes of Israel.[a] The Jews did not understand the reference; they thought of the "other sheep" as the Gentiles whom the chosen people were obligated to provide the means of salvation. But Jesus had declared that He had been specifically sent to the house of Israel, not to the Gentiles (who would have the gospel preached to them by His Apostles after His death).

The "other sheep" of the Western Hemisphere could not receive Christ in His mortal form, for that was reserved for the Jews in Palestine. However, in His place they would receive great signs and wonders that would reveal to them His birth, His ministry, and His death. But such was the prevailing wickedness that as the prophesied time of Christ's birth approached, the wicked declared a "special day" upon which they would put to death the Lord's followers if the sign did not occur.

As this designated day drew near, the prophet Nephi fervently prayed to God that he might know of the time when the sign would be given. The Lord responded by telling him that upon that very night the sign would be given, and the next day He would be born.

When the sun fell below the horizon that evening, no darkness fell upon the land and all through the night it was as light "as though it was midday."[b] When morning came, the sun rose again. Thus came a day, a night, and a day without darkness. Also a new star appeared in the firmament. These events confirmed the prophecy and testified to the people on the Western Hemisphere that the Son of God—"the light of the world"—had been born in the East.

The sign was significant and had not been chosen by accident. At a celebration known as the Feast of Tabernacles held during His ministry, the Savior would use those very words to declare His divinity. At this feast, four giant candelabra in the temple were lighted and burned throughout the night, providing light for the courts of the temple and illuminating "every court in Jerusalem."[462] The light from the candelabra represented the light of Jehovah, and the symbolic meaning of this part of the celebration was found in the "express Messianic expectation of the Rabbis."[463]

a. 3 Nephi 21:26.

b. 3 Nephi 1:19.

Jesus based one of His greatest discourses on this celebration—*The Light of the World* sermon. He explained its symbolism by declaring to the rulers and to the people gathered in the temple at Jerusalem, "I am the light of the world."[a] He was *indeed* the light of the world, and while He declared it with such rich symbolism to the people in Judea, He also declared it to the people on the Western Hemisphere with an even greater sign —by literally lighting the sky the night He was born—for the "light of the world" had come.

But the Lord's sheep on the Western Hemisphere quickly forgot the sign of His birth, and as He grew into youth and early manhood in the East, the people of the West again became wicked and disbelieving. As the time for Christ's ministry approached, another prophet named Nephi (the son of Nephi) was raised up. He would administer in Christ's stead to the children of Lehi.

The Book of Mormon reports that Nephi was called by angels and that power was given to Him to not only know of His Savior, but to know about the Savior's personal ministry as it was taking place in the East. He, in turn, was called to teach repentance to the people on the Western Hemisphere and to testify of the divinity of Christ. During his ministry, angels administered to him daily. As the Christ performed mighty miracles in the East, Nephi mirrored His work by performing mighty miracles in the West—casting out devils; healing the sick; and raising his brother, Timothy, from the dead. Just as the Lord was being rejected on the Eastern Hemisphere, Nephi, a special witness for Christ, was being rejected on the Western Hemisphere. The reaction of the Jews to the Lord's miracles was one of anger and disbelief, and Nephi elicited the same response from his people.[b]

Just as Samuel the Lamanite had prophesied of the birth of Christ, so, too, had he prophesied of His death, testifying of the great darkness and destruction that would come upon the Western Hemisphere at that time.

The Bible testifies that while Jesus hung upon the cross from the sixth to the ninth hours, the sun was darkened as the earth prepared for the "light of the world" to be extinguished from mortality. In the West, a similar phenomenon commenced. For the space of three hours (which correlated with the sixth to the ninth hours in Jeru-

a. John 8:12.

b. 3 Nephi 7.

salem) a storm arose, "such an one as never had been known in all the land." The tempest was enormous: "there was terrible thunder, insomuch that it did shake the whole earth as if it was about to divide asunder. And there were exceedingly sharp lightnings, such as never had been known in all the land."[a] Cities caught fire and sank into the sea and some were buried by the earth. Great whirlwinds occurred which carried people off to unknown consequences, and highways that had been traveled for hundreds of years were broken up. Rocks were rent, and the whole face of the earth was drastically changed.

At the conclusion of this three-hour period, Christ gave up the ghost and died. Immediately, the veil of the temple in Jerusalem was rent in twain and the earth quaked. In the West, a thick darkness came upon all the face of the land, darkness so dense that the people could not see; no means of light could be lit and no fire could be kindled.[b]

This intense darkness continued while the body of Jesus lay in the tomb. The survivors mourned, wept, and lamented that as a people they had not repented of their wickedness while there was still time. Then out of the darkness came a voice: "Wo, wo, wo unto this people; wo unto the inhabitants of the whole earth except they shall repent; for the devil laugheth, and his angels rejoice, because of the slain of the fair sons and daughters of my people." It was the spirit of Jesus Christ speaking, and he explained that he had caused so great a destruction upon their land because of the wickedness of the people. He wanted "to hide their wickedness and abominations from before [His] face."[c]

He declared to them, "O all ye that are spared because ye were more righteous than they, will ye not now return unto me, and repent of your sins, and be converted, that I may heal you?"[d] He instructed them that there should be no more sacrifices or burnt offerings, because (as the scriptures had foretold) the Law of Moses had been fulfilled in Him. They should offer instead a broken heart and a contrite spirit. When the Lord concluded His message there was silence for many hours; then His voice was heard again, calling the people to repentance and painfully reminding them that they had had the opportunity to repent many times before, but had passed it by.

Slowly, the three days passed. At last, when Christ was resurrected, the darkness in the West dispersed—the light of the world had come

a. 3 Nephi 8:5–7.

b. 3 Nephi 8:22.

c. 3 Nephi 9:2, 7.

d. 3 Nephi 9:13.

out of the tomb. The resurrected Lord administered to His Apostles and disciples for forty days in the East. During that time the people in the West marveled at the great destruction in their land and started to reestablish order in their lives. When His work with the Apostles on the Eastern Hemisphere was finished, the Savior ascended into heaven. But He would soon descend again, this time to visit His other sheep on the Western Hemisphere.[464]

"And now it came to pass that there [was] a great multitude gathered together, of the people of Nephi, round the temple which was in the land Bountiful."[a] While they were conversing, they heard a voice "as if it came out of heaven; and they cast their eyes round about, for they understood not the voice which they heard."[b] A second time the soft voice was heard, but they still could not understand it. Finally, the third time they understood. The voice said: "Behold my Beloved Son, in whom I am well pleased, in whom I have glorified my name—hear ye him."[c] As the people looked toward the sky, they saw a Man in a white robe descending out of heaven. He declared unto them, "Behold, I am Jesus Christ, whom the prophets testified shall come into the world."[d] The Lord had come to His "other sheep."

The Lord established the same doctrines and practices in the West that He had in the East. He instructed the people in gospel principles and informed them that the Mosaic Law was fulfilled. He taught them the ordinances of baptism, established the sacrament, and preached the Sermon on the Mount. He selected twelve disciples, gave them power in the priesthood, and charged them with the responsibility of promulgating the gospel. He resolved the contentions of the people and established the name by which His church should be called. He declared that He still had "other sheep" whom He must visit in order to complete His mission to the covenant people (the twelve tribes of Israel), and finally, He promised the twelve disciples that if they were faithful, He would grant them their heart's desire. Nine of the disciples immediately stepped forward and requested that upon their deaths they be transmitted directly into the Lord's kingdom. The last three remained silent, and whether the Lord had taught them of John's request in the East or not, He knew what they wanted—to be able to remain on the earth and work to bring souls unto Christ until

a. 3 Nephi 11:1.

b. 3 Nephi 11:3.

c. 3 Nephi 11:7.

d. 3 Nephi 11:10.

the Lord's second coming. Their wish was granted, and then the Lord ascended into heaven.

The Messiah who testified and witnessed to the chosen people on the Eastern Hemisphere also testified and witnessed to the chosen people on the Western Hemisphere. There were no differences in the teachings He presented nor should there have been, for Christ's ministry is given for the salvation of all God's children. That a record of both civilizations was kept by the Lord's prophets and preserved for our use is a blessing that cannot be overstated, for in all things, both the Bible and the Book of Mormon serve as witnesses of the divinity of Jesus Christ.

The Restoration: In the Fulness of Times

Joseph Smith—History 1:10–17   In the midst of this war of words and tumult of opinions, I often said to myself: What is to be done? Who of all these parties are right; or, are they all wrong together? If any one of them be right, which is it, and how shall I know it? While I was laboring under the extreme difficulties caused by the contests of these parties of religionists, I was one day reading the Epistle of James, first chapter and fifth verse, which reads: "If any of you lack wisdom, let him ask of God, that giveth to all men liberally, and upbraideth not; and it shall be given him." Never did any passage of scripture come with more power to the heart of man than this did at this time to mine. It seemed to enter with great force into every feeling of my heart. I reflected on it again and again, knowing that if any person needed wisdom from God, I did; for how to act I did not know, and unless I could get more wisdom than I then had, I would never know; for the teachers of religion of the different sects understood the same passages of scripture so differently as to destroy all confidence in settling the question by an appeal to the Bible. At length I came to the conclusion that I must either remain in darkness and confusion, or else I must do as James directs, that is, ask of God. I at length came to the determination to "ask of God," concluding that if he gave wisdom to them that lacked wisdom, and would give liberally, and not upbraid, I might venture. So, in accordance with this, my determination to ask of God, I retired to the woods to make the attempt. It was on the morning of a beautiful, clear day, early in the spring of eighteen hundred and twenty. It was the first time in my life that I had made such an attempt, for amidst all my anxieties I had never as yet made the attempt to pray vocally.

After I had retired to the place where I had previously designed to go, having looked around me, and finding myself alone, I kneeled down and began to offer up the desires of my heart to God. I had scarcely done so, when immediately I was seized upon by some power which entirely overcame me, and had such an astonishing influence over me as to bind my tongue so that I could not speak. Thick darkness gathered around me, and it seemed to me for a time as if I were doomed to sudden destruction. But, exerting all my powers to call upon God to deliver me out of the power of this enemy which had seized upon me, and at the very moment when I was ready to sink into despair and abandon myself to destruction—not to an imaginary ruin, but to the power of some actual being from the unseen world, who had such marvelous power as I had never before felt in any being—just at this moment of great alarm, I saw a pillar of light exactly over my head, above the brightness of the sun, which descended gradually until it fell upon me.

It no sooner appeared than I found myself delivered from the enemy which held me bound. When the light rested upon me I saw two Personages, whose brightness and glory defy all description, standing above me in the air. One of them spake unto me, calling me by name and said, pointing to the other—This is My Beloved Son. Hear Him!

Cross-references   Daniel 2; 2 Thessalonians 2:1–3; Ephesians 1:9–10

Almost as fast as people were converted to the church after the resurrection of Jesus, some of them began to fall away. Paul foresaw this problem and cautioned the Thessalonians saying: "Now we beseech you, brethren, by the coming of our Lord Jesus Christ, and by our gathering together unto him, that ye be not soon shaken in mind, or be troubled, neither by spirit, nor by word, nor by letter as from us, as that the day of Christ is at hand. Let no man deceive you by any means: for that day shall not come, except there come a falling away first, and that man of sin be revealed, the son of perdition."[a]

Paul knew that the apostasy, the falling away, would be long-lived and so complete that it would eventually require a restoration of the gospel. Peter also understood the falling away and the eventual need for a restoration. In one of his early discourses (given in the temple shortly after the ascension of Christ), he taught both followers and rulers alike saying: "Repent ye therefore, and be converted, that your sins may be blotted out, when the times of refreshing shall come from the presence of the Lord; and he shall send Jesus Christ, which before was preached unto you: whom the heaven must receive until the times of restitution of all things, which God hath spoken by the mouth of all his holy prophets since the world began."[b]

Jesus had preached openly to the Jews, yet they had rejected and crucified Him. After His resurrection and His forty-day ministry to the Apostles on the Eastern Hemisphere, He ascended into heaven and would not come again to establish His kingdom upon the earth

a. 2 Thessalonians 2:1–3.

b. Acts 3:19–21.

until after the time of restitution (or restoration) of all that had previously been prophesied by the holy prophets from the beginning of time. Daniel saw this in the interpretation to Nebuchadnezzar's dream and indicated that *this* kingdom of God would be established in the latter days.[a] Paul also knew this when he explained, "having made known unto us the mystery of his will, according to his good pleasure which he hath purposed in himself: that in the dispensation of the fulness of times he might gather together in one all things in Christ, both which are in heaven, and which are on earth; even in him."[b]

As the Apostles were martyred one by one for the great cause they had embraced, the long night of apostasy began. The Dark Ages crept upon the earth and locked away men's minds and visions for centuries. Through this, Lucifer, the man of sin, was revealed. Although mankind continued to be bound with the forces of evil for centuries, during the Renaissance and the Reformation the Western world moved away from the darkness and into the light. As the Spirit of God moved upon men and upon nations, they were prepared for the dispensation of the fullness of times and the restoration of all things. America was founded, and in this cradle of liberty, the Lord raised up certain men who established a Constitution based upon principles which would allow the gospel of Jesus Christ to once more find a place in the hearts of mankind.[c]

The door to the fullness of times was opened to Joseph Smith in the spring of 1820 when, in the fifteenth year of his life, he went into a small grove of trees in upstate New York and knelt in prayer. God appeared in His majesty and attested to the divinity of His Son, and the "light of the world" once more shed forth His truths that man might be saved. The silence of centuries was broken, and "the current human conception of Deity as an incorporeal essence of something possessing neither definite shape nor tangible substance was" revealed as totally devoid of truth.[465] As the First Vision burst forth upon the Prophet Joseph, "he knew that the Father and the Son were individual Personages, each distinct from the other,"[466] and that their oneness, as it had been incomprehensibly formulated in the creeds of the Dark Ages, was actually a oneness "of perfection in purpose, plan, and action, as the scriptures declare it to be."[467] The Restoration had begun, and it will not cease until the second coming of the Lord Jesus Christ.

a. Daniel
   2:31–45.

b. Ephesians
   1:9–10.

c. D&C
   101:76–80.

On September 21, 1823, three years after he received the vision of the Father and the Son, Joseph was again praying when a heavenly being (who announced himself as Moroni) stood before him in the air. Moroni disclosed to Joseph the location of a sacred book of scripture which would be *another witness for Christ.* The Book of Mormon records were eventually recovered, translated, and finally published in 1830.

The authority to administer the gospel ordinances was next restored by those who had first held that authority when Christ was upon the earth. John the Baptist appeared and restored the Aaronic Priesthood on May 15, 1829.[a] Soon after that, Peter, James, and John appeared and restored the Melchizedek Priesthood and the authority of the holy apostleship.[b] The Church of Jesus Christ of Latter-day Saints was officially organized on April 6, 1830,[c][468] and the temple of the Restoration was constructed in Kirtland, Ohio, and dedicated on March 27, 1836.[d]

The authority and power of past dispensational leaders was restored shortly after the dedication of the Kirtland Temple when the great prophets of old appeared to Joseph Smith and Oliver Cowdery.[e] Moses appeared to restore the keys of the gathering of Israel; the prophet Elias appeared to restore the gospel and the covenant of Abraham; and Elijah appeared to restore the sealing power so that all things could be bound on earth and in heaven. The prophesies of Joel concerning the second coming of Christ were soon to be fulfilled,[f] and the marvelous work spoken of by Isaiah (which would be an ensign to the nations) had been established.[g] Gabriel, Enoch, Adam, and many other prophets from the beginning of time up to the dispensation of the fullness of times also appeared.[h]

The priesthood having been restored, the call of Apostle was again given and the first Twelve Apostles of the last and final dispensation were called and ordained as special witnesses of the Lord Jesus Christ. The Lord's saving ordinances (all encompassed in what we call the gospel of Jesus Christ today) were once again available to all mankind so that they might be reunited with their Father in Heaven:

> And because it is the power of God that saves men, it includes both what the Lord does for us and what we must do for ourselves to be saved. On His part it is the atonement; on our part it is obedience to all that is given us of God. Thus the gospel

a. D&C 13.

b. D&C 27:12–13; 128:20.

c. D&C 20:1.

d. D&C 109.

e. D&C 110.

f. Joel 2:28–31; Joseph Smith — History 1:41.

g. Isaiah 5:26; 11:12; 29:13–14.

h. D&C 128:21.

includes every truth, every principle, every law—all that men must believe and know. Thus it includes every ordinance, every rite, every performance—all that men must do to please their Maker. Thus it includes every priesthood, every key, every power—all that men must receive to have their acts bound on earth and sealed eternally in heaven.[469]

The promises to the fathers and the reestablishment of the Savior's ministry have all been fulfilled in the Restoration.

The Second Coming of Jesus the Messiah — The Millennial Ministry

As previously discussed, the last event in the mortal ministry of Jesus Christ was His ascension into heaven from the Eastern Hemisphere. As this took place, two angels stood by and exclaimed to the Apostles, "This same Jesus, which is taken up from you into heaven, shall so come in like manner as ye have seen him go into heaven."[a] From this point in time, many began looking forward to the second coming of Jesus Christ in the flesh—in power and great glory—"to execute judgment upon the earth and to inaugurate a reign of righteousness" during the millennium.[470] The exact time of this event has never been disclosed, but the certainty of His coming is without question. It was foreseen by many Old Testament prophets, and it was looked forward to and prophesied of by prophets of both the New Testament times and the latter days.[471] Although the Lord has not given the exact date of His coming, He has given certain signs that if recognized will alert the righteous to this great event.

The fulfillment of prophecy concerning the Second Coming commenced in 1820 with Joseph Smith's vision of God the Eternal Father and His Son Jesus Christ. The sequence of visions which followed culminated in the restoration of the gospel and the opening of the dispensation of the fullness of times.[472]

The Jews rejected the Messiah, and because of the universal apostasy which followed that rejection and the death of the Apostles, the children of Israel (the seed of Abraham, who had been chosen to spread the gospel of salvation to all the earth) were scattered throughout the earth. One of the great signs of the Second Coming is the gathering of those lost and scattered children.

The responsibility for gathering the righteous from the world falls to the tribe of Ephraim (as the presiding tribe in Israel).[473] The descendants of Ephraim trace their lineage through Joseph, one of the original twelve tribes. Ephraim's call is similar to that of the Twelve Apostles who, at the end of Christ's mortal ministry, were commissioned to take the gospel to all the world. With the restoration of the gospel and the establishment of the Church, it is now Ephraim's responsibility to disseminate the gospel's saving ordinances throughout the earth so that all may have the opportunity to receive these ordinances and be admitted into the Father's kingdom. This is the general gathering of the righteous from among the Gentiles and the lost and scattered descendants of the Israelites.[a]

"Ephraim shall assemble in Zion on the Western continent, and Judah shall be again established in the east; and the cities of Zion and Jerusalem shall be the capitals of the world empire, over which the Messiah shall reign in undisputed authority."[474]

One of the visits made by the Savior during His preparation for the Second Coming will be to the people of Judah, one of the original Twelve Tribes of Israel. The Mount of Olives shall "cleave in twain,"[b] and therein He will gather the tribe of Judah and testify and witness to its people, in an indisputable manner, that He is their long-awaited Messiah.[c475]

Finally, to complete the gathering, "the Lost [ten] Tribes shall be brought forth from the place where God has hidden them through the centuries and receive their long-deferred blessings at the hands of Ephraim."[†476]

Another general sign of the Second Coming is the great wickedness which shall be upon the face of the earth prior to the Lord's advent. Indeed, the conditions of the latter days will be comparable to the days of Noah when evil was so powerful that God destroyed all but eight souls.[477] To cleanse the earth of this wickedness in preparation for the millennial ministry of the Savior, great destructions will come upon its inhabitants so that the more wicked (those who cannot abide His coming) will be destroyed.[478]

---

† The return of the ten tribes will probably not take place until after the Lord's second coming. (D&C 133:25–35; Isaiah 35:8–10.)

a. Isaiah 11:11; 43:3–12; Hosea 1:10–11; 3 Nephi 21.

b. D&C 45:48.

c. Zechariah 12:10; Zechariah 13:1–6; D&C 45:51–52.

Before His coming, hail and fire will rain upon the earth,[a479] the sea will be smitten and the earth's waters polluted,[b480] the plagues that John the Revelator saw will be sent forth upon the earth, and man will be tormented with noisome and grievous sores.[c481] The sea will become like the "blood of a dead man," and "every living soul" will die therein.[d] The sun will also be affected so that it "[scorches] men with fire" and with great heat,[e482] and a great darkness will occur that overcomes the minds of mankind because of their wicked ways.[f483]

Rivers will dry up and false prophets will come forth working the works of Satan, performing miracles so that they can deceive their fellowman.[g484] Eventually, two great prophets will be raised up in Jerusalem to preach of the coming Messiah, and their ministry will occur while the devil makes war against the city with his great army.[h] The power of these prophets will be like that of Elijah and Nephi of old, and for three and one-half years they will preach with a warning voice, crying repentance unto the people of Judah. Finally, the armies of evil shall overcome the holy city and kill the two prophets. Their bodies will be left in the streets for three and one-half days after which they will be caught up and received by the Messiah as He descends from heaven to appear to the tribe of Judah.[i485]

While all of these calamities culminate, general conditions throughout the world will become chaotic and the third general sign of the Lord's coming will take place. Turbulence and affliction will be the norm, and a way of life contrary to that decreed by God will be pervasive throughout the children of men. Great signs and wonders will occur: fire and vapors of smoke will appear;[j] a great hailstorm will destroy the crops of the earth;[k486] flies will take hold of the earth's inhabitants;[l487] the beasts and fowls will eat men's flesh;[m] the sun will be darkened and the moon will appear as blood;[n] the stars will fall from heaven;[o488] and the rainbow will cease to appear.[489] A mighty earthquake (above all earthquakes) shall shake the earth, and the land that was split in the days of Noah and Peleg[p] will be reunited in paradisiacal glory.[q] As the devastations cease, a great conference will take place at Adam-ondi-Ahman[490] in preparation for the Savior's immediate coming.

Finally, the sign of the Son of Man will appear, which no man

a. Ezekiel 38:22; Revelation 8:7.

b. Revelation 8:10–11; 11:4.

c. Revelation 16:2.

d. Revelation 16:3.

e. Revelation 16:8.

f. Revelation 16:10.

g. Revelation 16:12–14.

h. Revelation 9:16.

i. Revelation 11.

j. Joel 2:30–31.

k. D&C 29:16.

l. D&C 29:18.

m. D&C 29:20.

n. D&C 29:14; Isaiah 13:9–11.

o. D&C 29:14; 88:87.

p. Genesis 10:25.

q. Revelation 16:18–20; D&C 133:24.

knoweth until it is seen,[a][491] and the Lord will come and reign upon earth for a thousand years. The government will be that of a "perfect theocracy, with Jesus Christ as Lord and King."[492]

At the beginning of the Millennium, Satan will be bound and cast into the "bottomless pit"; his influence (and that of his evil emissaries) will not be felt upon the earth while the Messiah reigns.[b]

When Christ comes in clouds of great glory,[c] those who have been resurrected and reunited with their God will come with Him, as will the New Jerusalem, or the righteous city of Enoch.[d] The righteous dead who have not been resurrected will have their graves opened and will also be caught up to meet Him, along with those righteous men and women who are yet alive upon the earth. But the wicked shall remain in the grave until the Millennium is over.[493]

The millennial ministry of Christ will continue for a thousand years, and during that time men in the flesh will mingle with immortal beings.[494] Those who are righteous will grow to maturity and in some manner be changed to immortality "in the twinkling of an eye"[e] while those who do not merit such an instant transition will pass into the grave and await a future resurrection. The earth will be restored to the condition it enjoyed in the Garden of Eden,[495] and the enmity between man and beast will cease.[f]

When the thousand years of the Millennium are over, Satan will be loosed from his imprisonment. He and his dark angels will again be active during the ensuing "little season," the length of which has not been revealed.[496] This "little season" will be the final testing ground of man's integrity to God. A great gathering of the forces of evil and the forces of good will take place during this time, and the final combat between the Savior of the world and the leader of darkness will take place. But the outcome of this conflict has been prophesied, and "the vanquishment of Satan and his hosts shall be complete."[497]

Ultimately, every man and woman who has ever lived upon the earth will be resurrected. The righteous will dwell with Christ and His Father in the kingdom of God forever[g] while those who are unworthy of that kingdom will be sent to the place prepared for them by the Father. The earth will be consumed as if by fire and will pass away before it is finally restored to its celestial glory.[h] The plan of salvation will

a. D&C 88:93;
   Matthew 24:26;
   Isaiah 40:5;
   Zechariah
   14:5–9.

b. Revelation
   20:1–3.

c. Daniel 7:13.

d. Moses 7:63–65;
   Ether 13:3–4;
   Revelation
   21:2.

e. D&C
   63:50–51.

f. D&C
   101:26.

g. D&C
   76:51–65.

h. Revelation
   20:11–15; D&C
   29:23; D&C
   43:32.

be fulfilled with the final judgment of mankind and Jesus Christ, our Savior and King, will finally receive His reward—He will present His kingdom to the Father, and "then shall he be crowned with the crown of his glory, to sit on the throne of his power to reign forever and ever."[a]

a. D&C 76:108.

Placing Christ in Our Lives

Jesus Christ fulfilled His mission in all things, yet He learned obedience from the things He suffered. He was the great Jehovah, God of the Old Testament. He was with the Father from the beginning. He, along with others, met in a great council in heaven[498] and under the direction of the Father, assisted in the plan of salvation. He was the firstborn of the Father in the spirit and the Only Begotten of the Father in the flesh. He was chosen from the beginning to be the Savior of the world and the Redeemer of mankind. He sacrificed His life to overcome death—which came into the world as a result of the fall of Adam—and to give the free gift of resurrection to all. He fulfilled His part in the plan by which, through repentance and obedience, all mankind can return with Him to the kingdom of His Father.

Under the direction of the Father He created the heavens and the earth while He was yet in the spirit. He and the Father created all things that live and grow upon the earth, including man. He was with the Father in the Garden of Eden when the Father visited Adam and Eve; and when Adam fell, He witnessed the Father's punishment of our first parents and understood that from thenceforth until the end of the world, all things were to be done in the Son's name. He was Jesus Christ, the Son of God, the Messiah.

Christ was born under humble circumstances, but the heavens rejoiced at His coming. Signs were given, testimonies of angels were heard, and kings came from afar to adore Him. From the very beginning Lucifer feared the Savior's mission and attempted to destroy Him. Through the evil one's influence, Herod the Great killed helpless infants in an attempt to also kill Him.

The Gospel writers bore witness that the Old Testament prophets had foretold of His birth, and they were meticulous to note His conformity with the Mosaic Law—for He was a Jew, born under the Covenant. But of His childhood they said nothing, recording only that "the child grew, and waxed strong in spirit, filled with wisdom: and the grace of God was upon him."[a] The silence is broken when Luke tells the story of Jesus teaching in the temple at twelve years of age, but nothing is known of His teen years and His early manhood. The writers testify only that "Jesus increased in wisdom and stature, and in favour with God and man."[b] Their record was not intended to be a record of Jesus Christ the man but of Jesus Christ the Savior. The recorded details of His life increase at the point when the Lord came of age and began His ministry. The gospel writers commenced His ministry with His baptism and John the Baptist's witness of His divinity. His trials with the devil (which must have been related by Jesus Himself) were recorded to show that He, too, had to conquer temptation. The authors of the Gospels proclaimed His Messiahship by recording miracle upon miracle, repeatedly demonstrating His consummate power and compassion; they recorded His parables—stories of everyday life that encompassed the truths of the kingdom of heaven—to illustrate His teachings; and they transcribed His discourses to evidence His Messiahship and to celebrate the establishment of His new kingdom upon the earth.

Jesus took Peter, James, and John upon the mount and was transfigured before them. It was here that these Apostles received the keys of the kingdom from prophets of old; but more important, they witnessed the *glory* of the Son and heard the personal *testimony* of the Father regarding His divinity.

At the close of His mission, He rode into Jerusalem as the King of kings and Lord of lords. He used *little miracles* to provide for the *little* necessities of His entrance: acquisition of the colt upon which he would ride and the procurement of a room for the Last Supper. He celebrated the end of the old Mosaic Law and the beginning of the new gospel of salvation by eating the Passover Feast, and it was at this feast

a. Luke 2:40.

b. Luke 4:52.

that He introduced the ordinance of the washing of feet and taught an impetuous Peter the importance of service. The betrayer was foretold during the feast, and when Judas left to conclude his nefarious affairs, the Lord introduced the sacrament—an ordinance that would replace sacrifice. The Savior's crucifixion fulfilled the need for sacrifice because His death was the "ultimate sacrifice" for mankind. Sacrifice looked forward to His mission and the sacrament looked back to His atonement, His trials, His condemnation, His crucifixion, and His resurrection.

After the Passover Feast, Jesus took the eleven remaining Apostles into the Garden of Gethsemane. He left eight of them near the entrance and took Peter, James, and John further into the Garden where they could watch while He prayed and be a witness to His suffering. But the three Apostles were fatigued, and although their spirits were willing, their flesh was weak. They slept, while the God of Heaven and Earth suffered and took upon Himself the sins of all mankind—an obligation so painful that it caused Him to "bleed at every pore."

Soon thereafter Christ was arrested, shamed, and tried before both the Jewish Sanhedrists and the heathen Roman conqueror. "Art thou the Christ?" they asked. "I am," He responded, and they condemned Him for being what He was. He was beaten, spat upon, scourged, and mocked as the Jewish "King."

Finally, the Lord was presented to His people—the very people who for centuries had looked for the Messiah in all they did. "Which of these two should be loosed as a boon to you on this your feast day," Pilate asked, in effect, "Jesus, your King, or Barabbas, the robber and murderer?" "Barabbas," they cried. And Jesus? "Crucify him," they shouted. The order was given. Christ was scourged and a crown of plaited thorns was forced upon His bleeding brow before He was paraded through the city streets and crucified.

Between His death and Resurrection, the Savior opened the doors of the spirit prison so that the gospel could be taught to those who had died without law, and He alerted His "other sheep" on the Western Hemisphere of His imminent coming. On a Sunday morning, He became the first fruit of the resurrection by breaking the bands of death and overcoming the fall of Adam—thus dooming the forces of evil forever.

For forty days after Jesus rose from the grave, He taught His Apostles and disciples so they could witness the reality of the resurrection. Then the Messiah ascended into heaven, only to descend soon after to appear to His disciples on the Western Hemisphere so that they, too, could witness Him. But even with the personal testimony of hundreds and thousands of souls to witness His divinity, the gospel fell away and His teachings were changed. Jesus had brought a message that was not only woven into the fabric of everyday life, but was eternal; yet they changed the commandments, refused to obey the "word," changed the ordinances, and rejected not only the law, but the Lawgiver.

After centuries of darkness, the Savior reinstituted His mission by opening the last dispensation of time. The gospel was restored so that all men and women might have the opportunity to accept Him and make Him a part of their lives. The time will come when He will again descend from the heavens, but this will be a descent with power wherein He will destroy the wicked and rule and reign a thousand years with the righteous.

Jesus Christ is the power of salvation—salvation is the purpose of life. Mankind can no more hinder the eventual course of the plan of salvation than rise from the dead without it. Yet it is in accepting Christ, in making Him an integral part of our lives in everything we do, that we acquire the power to overcome death—both physical and spiritual. Through the Lord we can again be with the Father, for Jesus Christ is the only name under heaven whereby man can be saved—and the salvation of mankind is the mission of Jesus the Messiah.

Notes

1. Ed 1:145; 2:55.
2. Life p. 664.
3. Life p. 668
4. MM 1:21.
5. JC p. 10.
6. A Doctrinal Declaration by the First Presidency and the Council of the Twelve Apostles of The Church of Jesus Christ of Latter-day Saints, Salt Lake City, Utah, 30 June 1916. As quoted in AF pp. 465–66.
7. JC p. 39, D&C 130:22; TPJS p. 345.
8. MM 1:21.
9. MM 1:23.
10. TPJS pp. 346–47.
11. TPJS p. 354.
12. JC p. 14, nl.
13. JC p. 17.
14. JC p. 17.
15. JC Chapter 4.
16. JC p. 7.
17. JC p. 18.
18. JC p. 9.
19. JC pp. 6–7, D&C 29:36–38; D&C 76:23–27.
20. JC p. 33. Hebrews 1:1–2; 1 Corinthians 8:6; Colossians 1:16–17; John 1:1–3. For additional references concerning Christ as the creator of this world see: Moses 2:26–27; Helaman 14:12; Mosiah 3:8; Mosiah 4:2; Alma 11:39; 3 Nephi 9:15; D&C 14:9; D&C 29:30–31; D&C 45:1; D&C 76:24.
21. JC p. 9.
22. A of F p. 236.
23. Ed BHOT 7:178–84; JC p. 240; Ezra.
24. A of F p. 245.
25. JC p. 42.
26. Ed 1:163.
27. JC p. 45.
28. JC p. 53, nl.
29. JC p. 54, nl.
30. Psalms 2:7; 22:1, 16, 18; 69:21; 89:8–9; 110:4; 118:22.
31. JC p. 45.
32. Sermons pp. 122–23.
33. JC. p. 4.
34. Farrar 1:53.
35. Smith p. 434.
36. Ed 1:225.
37. Ed 1:225.
38. Ed 1:224, n2.
39. Ed 1:146.
40. Ed 1:224.
41. Ed 1:147.
42. Geikie 1:21.
43. Ed 1:145.
44. As quoted in Ed 1:163.
45. Ed 1:160.
46. Ed 1:163.
47. Ed 1:164.
48. Ed 1:164.
49. Geikie 1:75.
50. Geikie 1:76.
51. Geikie 1:77.
52. Ed 1:178.
53. Ed 1:145.
54. Ed 1:209.
55. JC p. 84.
56. MM 1:322.
57. Ed 1:149.
58. Farrar 1:6; Ed 1:149.
59. Ed 1:148–49.
60. Ed 1:149; JC p. 89, n5.
61. JC p. 86; MM 1:316; Ed 1:149.
62. JC p. 87.
63. JC p. 87.
64. Ed 1:150.
65. Geikie l:99.
66. Geikie 1:99.
67. Ed 1:149.
68. Geikie 1:99.
69. JC p. 84.
70. Geikie 1:100; MM 1:317–18.
71. Ed 1:151.
72. JC p. 80.
73. Ed 1:150.
74. JC p. 81.
75. JC p. 81.
76. Geikie 1:101.
77. Ed 1:191–93.
78. JC pp. 94–95.
79. Geikie 1:101.
80. Geikie 1:102.
81. JC p. 116.
82. JC p. 97.

83. JC p. 82.
84. Ed 1:152.
85. Ed 1:152.
86. JC p. 82.
87. Ed 1:152.
88. Geikie 1:103.
89. Geikie 1:104.
90. Ed 1:155.
91. Geikie 1:108.
92. Geikie 1:108.
93. Geikie 1:109.
94. Ed 1:182–83; JC pp. 91–92.
95. Ed 1:185.
96. Geikie 1:114.
97. Geikie 1:113.
98. Ed 1:180.
99. JC p. 93.
100. Ed 1:187; Geikie 1:114; MM 1:349–50.
101. JC p. 93.
102. Ed 1:186–87.
103. JC p. 94.
104. Ed 1:189.
105. Farrar 1:20.
106. Farrar 1:20.
107. Geikie 1:119.
108. Ed 1:193.
109. Ed 1:194.
110. Geikie 1:123.
111. Ed 1:194.
112. Ed 1:194.
113. Geikie 1:120.
114. Ed 1:196.
115. Geikie 1:122.
116. Ed 1:197.
117. Ed 1:199.
118. Ed 1:199.
119. Ed 1:202.
120. Ed 1:200.
121. MM 1:356.
122. Ed 1:207; MM 1:357.
123. Ed 1:203.
124. Ed 1:203.
125. Farrar 1:26.
126. Ed 1:204.
127. Ed 1:204–14.
128. Ed 1:204.
129. Farrar 1:25.
130. Ed 1:204.
131. Ed 1:205.
132. Ed 1:206.
133. JC p. 99; Ed 1:207.
134. Ed 1:207.
135. Ed 1:213–14.
136. Ed 1:214.
137. JC p. 98.
138. Farrar 1:40.
139. Ed 1:214.
140. Farrar 1:47.
141. John the Baptist was beheaded by Herod Antipas (Matthew 14:10); the Apostle James was beheaded by Herod Agrippa I (Acts 12:2).
142. Farrar 1:49.
143. Ed 1:221.
144. JC p. 111.
145. JC pp. 111–12.
146. Ed 1:227.
147. Geikie 1:161.
148. Ed 1:232.
149. Farrar 1:61.
150. Geikie 1:187.
151. Ed 1:235.
152. Farrar 1:68.
153. JC p. 114.
154. MM 1:379.
155. JC p. 115.
156. JC p. 116.
157. Ed 1:135.
158. Ed 1:135, n4.
159. Ed 1:135.
160. Ed 1:136.
161. Ed 1:136.
162. Ed Temple p. 157.
163. Ed 1:134.
164. Ed 1:134.
165. Ed 1:137.
166. Ed 1:138.
167. Ed Temple p. 156.
168. JC p. 78.
169. Ed 1:140.
170. JC p. 78.
171. TPJS p. 261.
172. JC p. 122.
173. Geikie 1:372.
174. TPJS p. 276.
175. Geikie 1:373.
176. Ed 1:265.
177. Geikie 2:372.
178. Ed 1:273.
179. Ed 2:272.
180. JC p. 122.
181. JC p. 122.
182. Ed 1:271.
183. TPJS pp. 335–37.
184. Ed 1:269–74.
185. JC p. 124.
186. Geikie 1:386.
187. Ed 1:277.
188. Ed 1:278.

189. JC p. 125.
190. Ed 1:278.
191. JC p. 125.
192. JC p. 126.
193. JC p. 126.
194. TPJS p. 275.
195. Bruce p. 1.
196. Bruce p. 4.
197. Ed 1:391–92.
198. Life p. 435.
199. JC p. 255.
200. Ed 1:666.
201. JC p. 253.
202. Ed 1:658.
203. Ed 1:660.
204. Ed 1:667.
205. JC p. 254.
206. JC p. 255; Life p. 444.
207. Life p. 449.
208. TPJS pp. 275–76.
209. Ed 1:672–74; Smith p. 581; Bible Dictionary: Herodias.
210. Ed 1:672.
211. Ed 1:674.
212. JC p. 126.
213. Deseret Weekly News 54:482, 13 March 1897.
214. Ed 2:745–46.
215. In these two unique baptismal circumstances, no one was available to perform the ordinance for the gift of the Holy Ghost; therefore, the Holy Ghost "descended" upon them to complete the requirement of baptism both by water and by fire.
216. TPJS pp. 275–76; MM 1:404, n4.
217. JC p. 126.
218. 2 Corinthians 5:17; Galatians 6:15; Ephesians 4:22–24; Colossians 3:9–10.
219. JC p. 128.
220. Ed 1:292.
221. Life p. 435.
222. JC p. 133.
223. Life p. 17.
224. Ed 1:302.
225. Farrar 1:122.
226. Ed 1:305.
227. Ed 1:306.
228. JC p. 135.
229. JC p. 133.
230. Life p. 385–8.
231. Geikie 2:235.
232. Ed 2:91.
233. Ed 2:91–92.
234. MM 3:55.
235. Ed 2:92.
236. Geikie 2:236.
237. Bible Dictionary: Elias; TPJS p. 158.
238. JFS 2:110–11; D&C 110:11–16; D&C 133:54–55.
239. MM 3:57–58.
240. JC p. 371.
241. JC pp. 371–72.
242. JC p. 373.
243. JC pp. 373–74.
244. Ed 1:112–13.
245. Ed 1:112.
246. Ed 1:112; 2:548.
247. Ed 1:114.
248. Ed 1:114.
249. Ed 1:120.
250. Ed Tern p. 38.
251. Ed 1:243; 2:431.
252. Ed 1:120.
253. Ed 1:116.
254. Josephus, Wars, Book vi, ix:3.
255. Life p. 21.
256. Review the Miracles, Parables, and Sermons.
257. Life p. 396.
258. Geikie 2:371.
259. Ed 2:364.
260. Ed 2:364.
261. Bible Dictionary: Bethany.
262. Farrar 2:196.
263. JC p. 510; Farrar 2:195.
264. Ed 2:365.
265. Farrar 2:195.
266. The exact location of Bethphage is unknown. Some believe it to have been a part or suburb of Jerusalem while others generalize it as a description of a district near the city. (Ed 2:364.)
267. Farrar 2:196.
268. Ed 2:365–66.
269. Ed 2:365.
270. Geikie 2:374.
271. Ed 2:371.
272. Geikie 2:372.
273. That the colt was unridden was evidence of its consecration to Jehovah, as was required of certain sacrificial animals in the Law of Moses (Numbers 19:2; Deuteronomy 21:3).
274. Ed 2:364–65; JC p. 516.
275. Geikie 2:372.
276. Geikie 2:372.
277. Ed 2:368.
278. JC p. 514.
279. Ed 2:370.
280. Geikie 2:376.
281. JC p. 514.
282. Ed 2:488.
283. Geikie 2:376.

284. Ed 2:367.

285. Ed 2:373.

286. Ed 2:372.

287. Life p. 462, 472.

288. Geikie 2:429.

289. JC p. 592.

290. Ed 2:490.

291. Ed 2:491.

292. Geikie 2:436.

293. Geikie 2:436.

294. Ed 2:490.

295. Geikie 2:436.

296. Geikie 2:437.

297. Ed 2:491.

298. Geikie 2:439.

299. Ed 2:492.

300. Ed 2:493.

301. Ed 2:493.

302. Ed 2:493–95; Geikie 2:438–39; Farrar 2:278–79.

303. Ed 2:493; MM 4:31–32.

304. Ed 2:494.

305. Ed 2:495.

306. Ed Tern p. 237.

307. MM 4:36.

308. Ed 2:497.

309. Ed 2:498–99.

310. Farrar 2:281.

311. Ed 2:499, nl; MM 4:37.

312. Miracles p. 99.

313. Geikie 2:440; MM 4:38.

314. JC p. 595.

315. Geikie 2:440.

316. MM 4:38.

317. MM 4:40.

318. The ordinance of the washing of feet was restored 27 December 1832 so that the Saints could be cleansed "from the blood of this wicked generation" (D&C 88:74–75). The Prophet Joseph Smith was commanded to institute the ordinance of the washing of feet at the commencement of the School of the Prophets. When the school began on 23 January 1833, Joseph Smith washed the feet of the members of the school, and "by the power of the Holy Ghost I pronounced them all clean from the blood of this generation" (HC 1:322–24; 2:287).

319. HC 2:308–9

320. HC 2:426–31.

321. Farrar 2:287.

322. Geikie 2:442.

323. Ed 2:509.

324. Throughout the Passover supper, Jesus noted (identifying Judas and Peter individually, but including all of the Apostles in general) that certain prophecies would be fulfilled. It should be understood that the individuals involved had not been called to specifically fulfill those prophecies, but that the events which would precipitate the fulfillment were about to occur, and the fulfillment would take place because of the natural choices and selections made by those parties participating in the events. Although the scriptural statement concerning these prophecies is "that the scripture might be fulfilled," it did not mean "in order that" or "for the purpose of" the scripture being fulfilled. All things took place in the normal course of events, and each individual (including Peter and Judas) acted upon his free agency and chose to do what he did. John records these events as happening during the Pascal meal, while the Synoptics record them as taking place after the dinner as the group traveled to Gethsemane (Chapter 7).

325. DNTC 1:718.

326. MM 4:50.

327. JC p. 594; Ed 2:504–5.

328. DNTC 1:720–21.

329. JC p. 619, n2

330. Ed 2:508; DNTC 1:716

331. Ed 2:509–11.

332. MM 4:54.

333. DNTC 1:723.

334. Life p. 400; Geikie 2:184.

335. Geikie 2:184.

336. DNTC 1:719.

337. MM 4:52, 62.

338. DNTC 1:724.

339. Ed 2:533.

340. Ed 2:533.

341. Farrar 2:307.

342. Life p. 495.

343. JC pp. 613–14.

344. DNTC 1:774; JC p. 614.

345. Farrar 2:314.

346. Life p. 364.

347. Life p. 400.

348. MM 4:12.

349. Life p. 433.

350. Life p. 116.

351. Life p. 364.

352. MM 4:18.

353. Ed 2:476.

354. Ed 2:477.

355. JC p. 615.

356. Ed 2:542.

357. Life p. 126.

358. JC p. 616.

359. Ed 2:545.

360. Ed 2:573.

361. Of the four Gospels, only Matthew records the end of Judas Iscariot; however, at the commencement of the book of Acts Luke notes, speaking of Judas, "this man

purchased a field with the reward of iniquity; and falling headlong, he burst asunder in the midst, and all his bowels gushed out" (Acts 1:18). Assuming Matthew's rendition to be correct, factually it might have been that as the hanging body of Judas was being cut down, it dislodged and fell, thus satisfying Luke's statement (JST, Matthew 27:6). For another thought on the matter see Ed 2:575.

362. Geikie 2:483.

363. Farrar 2:327.

364. There are differences of opinion concerning the appearance of Christ before Annas. Some authors (Farrar 2:326; DNTC 1:782) have decided that the first public hearing of Jesus took place before Annas, with the successive two Jewish trials before Caiaphas and the Sanhedrin—then on to Pilate. Others (Ed 2:546; JC pp. 621–22) have concluded that only a private interview took place before Annas, that no record was made of it, and that the three recorded interviews before the Jews took place before Caiaphas and the Sanhedrists before the Lord was presented to Pilate. It is left up to the reader to study the scriptural text and other available writings and determine his own conclusion.

365. Ed 1:262.

366. Ed 1:112; 2:548.

367. Ed 2:541–42, 547.

368. Ed 2:546–47.

369. Ed Tern p. 34.

370. Ed 2:565.

371. Ed Tem p. 34.

372. Ed 2:566.

373. Ed 2:566.

374. Ed 2:566.

375. Geikie 2:489.

376. MM 4:155.

377. JC p. 623.

378. JC p. 623.

379. Geikie 2:487.

380. Geikie 2:499.

381. JC p. 622.

382. Geikie 2:486.

383. WMC 1:219–309.

384. Ed 1:309.

385. WMC 1:248–49.

386. Farrar 2:354.

387. Farrar 2:354–55.

388. Farrar 2:354.

389. Geikie 2:495.

390. MM 4:162.

391. JC p. 632.

392. Geikie 3:503.

393. Geikie 2:508.

394. Geikie 2:502.

395. Geikie 2:509.

396. Farrar 2:360; JC p. 640.

397. Farrar 2:377.

398. Geikie 2:514.

399. Ed 2:579.

400. Ed 2:601.

401. Ed 2:592.

402. Ed 2:582.

403. Ed 2:584.

404. Farrar 2:393.

405. Ed 2:584–85.

406. DNTC 1:807.

407. Farrar 2:398.

408. Farrar 2:398.

409. Ed 2:585.

410. Farrar 2:394.

411. DNTC 1:814.

412. Ed 2:586.

413. JC p. 667, n4.

414. Ed 2:589.

415. Ed 2:589.

416. Farrar 2:400.

417. Ed 2:591.

418. MM 4:211–12.

419. Ed 2:594.

420. Ed 2:595.

421. Farrar 2:393.

422. TPJS p. 309.

423. The women mentioned at the cross by the various gospel writers are Mary, the mother of Jesus; her sister, Salome, who was the mother of James and John; Mary Magdalene; and Mary, wife of Clopas (or Cleophas), described as the mother of James and Joses. "Thus Salome, the wife of Zebedee and St. John's mother, was the sister of the Virgin, and the beloved disciple the cousin (on the mother's side) of Jesus, and the nephew of the Virgin. . . . Nor was Mary the wife of Clopas unconnected with Jesus. What we have every reason to regard as a trustworthy account describes Clopas as the brother of Joseph, the husband of the Virgin. Thus, not only Salome as the sister of the Virgin, but Mary also as the wife of Clopas, would, in a certain sense, have been His aunt, and her sons His cousins. And so we notice among the twelve Apostles five cousins of the Lord: the two sons of Salome and Zebedee, and the three sons of Alphaeus or Clopas and Mary: James, Judas surnamed Lebbaeus and Thaddaeus, and Simon surnamed Zelotes or Cananaean." (Ed 2:602–3.)

424. Ed 2:603.

425. John's record indicates a later time, but this suggests that error has crept into it (DNTC 1:827).

426. DNTC 1:828.

427. JC p. 661.

428. Ed 2:611.

429. Ed Tem pp. 61–62.

430. DNTC 1:830.

431. Ed 2:613.

432. Ed 2:613.

433. Ed 2:61; JC p. 667 n4.

434. Ed 2:617.

435. Ed 2:618.

436. JC pp. 673–74; John 5:25–29

437. JC p. 671.

438. JC p. 671; MM 2:242.

439. JC p. 675; AF 7:18–33; James E. Talmage, The House of the Lord, pp. 63–93.

440. JC pp. 675–76.

441. Life p. 415.

442. MM 4:245.

443. It should be remembered that there are certain individuals that are not forgiven in this world or in the world to come. The fate of these individuals, known as the sons of perdition, is known only to God and to those who receive this judgment (D&C 76:43–46).

444. Ed 2:621.

445. Life p. 84.

446. Ed 2:622.

447. Ed 2:623.

448. Farrar 2:425.

449. See Matthew 16:21; 17:23; 20:19; Mark 9:31; 10:34; Luke 9:22; 13:32; 18:33.

450. Ed 2:624.

451. Ed 2:624.

452. Ed 2:629.

453. Life p. 129.

454. Concerning the comment of the Lord to Mary Magdalene wherein he stated, "for I am not yet ascended to my Father," James E. Talmage said: "If the second clause was spoken in explanation of the first, we have to infer that no human hand was to be permitted to touch the Lord's resurrected and immortalized body until He had presented Himself to the Father. It appears reasonable and probable that between Mary's impulsive attempt to touch the Lord, and the action of the other women who held Him by the feet as they bowed in worshipful reverence, Christ did ascend to the Father, and that later He returned to the earth to continue His ministry in the resurrected state." (JC p. 682.)

455. Geikie 2:555.

456. Ed 2:637.

457. Life p. 130.

458. It appears that John had intended to end his Gospel with Chapter 20 but later added Chapter 21 to include the appearance of the Savior on the shores of Galilee. (Ed. 2:647.)

459. Life p. 131.

460. Ed 2:649.

461. Life p. 415.

462. Ed Tem p. 285; Ed 2:166.

463. Ed 2:165.

464. JC p. 721.

465. JC p. 763.

466. JC p. 763.

467. JC p. 764.

468. HC 1:75–78.

469. Mill M p. 98.

470. JC p. 780; Life p. 683.

471. Acts 3:20–21; 1 Corinthians 4:5; 1 Corinthians 11:26; Philippians 3:20; 1 Thessalonians 1:10; 1 Thessalonians 2:19; 1 Thessalonians 3:13; 1 Thessalonians 4:15–18; 2 Thessalonians 2:1, 8; 1 Timothy 6:14–15; Titus 2:13; James 5:7–8; 1 Peter 1:5–7; 1 Peter 4:13; 1 John 2:28; 1 John 3:2; Jude 1:14; 3 Nephi 26:3–4; 3 Nephi 28:7–8; 3 Nephi 29:2; D&C 29:9–11; D&C 33:17–18; D&C 34:4–8; D&C 45:37–44; Matthew 24.

472. Life p. 710.

473. Life p. 730.

474. JC p. 786; Life p. 828.

475. Life p. 718.

476. JC p. 786; Life p. 272.

477. Joseph Smith—Matthew 1:37–43; Moses 5:13; 6:15; 2 Thessalonians 2:9–12; 1 Timothy 4:1–2; Moses 7:60–61; 8:22–30; 2 Peter 3:5–7; Life p. 774.

478. Life p. 786.

479. Life p. 789, 812.

480. Life p. 789, 798.

481. Life p. 797.

482. Life p. 791, 800, 824.

483. Life p. 799.

484. Life p. 754.

485. Life p. 718.

486. Life p. 812.

487. Life p. 807.

488. Life p. 825.

489. TPJS pp. 305, 340–41; Life p. 825.

490. Life p. 826.

491. TPJS pp. 280, 286–87; Life p. 854.

492. JC p. 790.

493. JC p. 790; Life p. 879.

494. JC p. 790.

495. Articles of Faith 1:10; AF p. 375; Life p. 802.

496. Life p. 874.

497. JC p. 792; Life p. 874.

498. HC 6:308, 473–79.

THE SECOND COMING OF JESUS THE MESSIAH

Introduction

Isaiah 40:5 And the glory of the Lord shall be revealed, and all flesh shall see it together: for the mouth of the Lord hath spoken it.

The scriptures prophesy of two major events: the Savior's First Coming to the house of Israel and His Second Coming to the world. All the prophecies of His First Coming were fulfilled in His birth, ministry, Atonement, death on the cross, and resurrection from the tomb. Just as those prophecies were fulfilled, so will the prophecies of His Second Coming be fulfilled. His First Coming is scriptural fact; His Second Coming is an anticipated reality.

The Lord's first coming was to the very people who were specifically and eagerly looking for Him—yet they missed Him! Why? Because they were unprepared. Their writings contained numerous prophecies of His Advent and they knew of the great miracles He was expected to perform;[1] but when He came, He fulfilled the prophecies and performed the miracles and they still rejected Him. They wanted a *different* Messiah than the one their prophets had foretold.[2]

What they waited for, was a Kingdom of God—not in righteousness, joy, and peace . . . but in meat and drink—a kingdom with miraculous wilderness-banquets to Israel, and coarse miraculous triumphs over the Gentiles. . . . The fruit-trees were every day, or at least every week or two, to yield their riches, the fields their harvest; the grain was to stand like palm trees, and to be reaped and winnowed without labour. Similar blessings were to visit the vine; ordinary trees would bear like fruit trees, and every produce, of every clime, would be found in Palestine in such abundance and luxuriance as only the wildest imagination could conceive.[3]

The Jews during Christ's ministry did not question His ability, just His claim to the messiahship. "Show us a sign," they repeatedly demanded, even though they had seen many miraculous signs. But they wanted a specific sign: the *Messianic sign of the Son of Man,* a sign that would not be given until the Lord's Second Coming—and then not just to Israel, but to the world.

We look for the same sign today. But if we are unprepared like the Jews of old, we may also look beyond the mark and miss Him. "Pray always," the Lord cautions, "that you enter not into temptation, that you may abide the day of [My] coming, whether in life or in death."[a] His warning is clear; yet daily life seems to dull even the vigilant. The Lord warned that our time would be as it was in the days of Noah, "marrying and giving in marriage,"—just doing the normal, everyday things of life. And just as the antediluvians did not anticipate the Flood, the scripture's clear inference is that latter-day humankind will either not be looking for the Lord's Second Coming, or will be looking for the wrong things. Thus, they will be unprepared when He comes. At times we do not attribute the great events of His coming to God's authorship; at other times, we attribute everything to Him. Either conclusion will mask our ability to recognize the signs of His great Advent.

Jesus Himself prophesied that when He comes again, "two [will] be in the field; the one shall be taken, and the other left. Two women shall be grinding at the mill; the one shall be taken, and the other left. Watch therefore," He cautions, "for ye know not what hour your Lord doth come."[b] To "watch" in this scriptural sense means to be spiritually prepared—to recognize and welcome the signs of the Second Coming.

Prophecies of the Lord's Second Coming are scattered throughout the scriptures: some are clear and easy to understand, others are couched in poetry or parabolic stories, and many are disguised within symbolic representations that make them difficult to identify. All,

a. D&C 61:39.

b. Matthew 24:40–42.

however, were recorded by prophets eagerly looking forward to the end of the world, when all sin would cease and the Messiah would reign in peace and love.

The Second Coming of Jesus the Messiah is divided into five parts and sixteen chapters. The signs of the Second Coming are grouped into logical and descriptive categories and are presented both topically and chronologically. In any work describing prophecy (both fulfilled and unfulfilled), considerable interpretation is required. The interpretation, classification, and organization of the prophetic utterances reviewed in this book are my own.

This text also contains material dealing with the Millennium, judgment, resurrection, the "little season," and the battles of Gog and Magog. While these topics do not deal specifically with the Second Coming (except for the first battle of Gog and Magog, called Armageddon), they must be discussed in order to complete the Lord's involvement in His Father's plan of salvation.

The signs of the Second Coming began shortly after the Lord's resurrection. The Lord prophesied of these momentous events and described them in words used as the title of Chapter 1: "All These Are the Beginning of Sorrows."[a] Thereafter, other signs of His future Advent occurred intermittently throughout the centuries, continuing through "The Great Apostasy" and "The Times of the Gentiles," Chapters 2 and 3. These signs culminated in the restoration of the gospel—which inaugurated the signs given for the latter days.

The initial signs of the latter days are dealt with in the chapters titled "The Restoration," "Judah," and "The Gathering." Part 3, titled "Babylon," deals specifically with such subjects as the devil's powerful influence over the people of the world throughout history, his evil latter-day kingdom, and his kingdom's final destruction. The cities of Enoch, Jerusalem, and Zion, and the roles they play in the signs of the Second Coming, are discussed in the chapter titled "The Three Cities." Multiple signs, symbolically envisioned by John in the book of Revelation (some general and some specific), are dealt with throughout the text. The "great and dreadful day of the Lord" and the tribulations associated with the devastations that will occur prior to that day are discussed in Parts 4 and 5. The *time* of the Savior's coming will be

a. Matthew 24:8.

examined and His actual Advent discussed; however, the exact *date* of His coming remains unknown.

Although this text deals almost exclusively with scriptural prophecies of the Second Coming, some quotations from other knowledgeable sources are used when it was determined that they added historical perspicacity. "It is hoped that this work will give the reader insight into the signs, events, and scriptures that deal with the Lord's Advent. "Its main purpose is to glorify and magnify the Savior and bring the signs of his Second Coming to our awareness so that we will be prepared to meet our God.

The fault of almost every generation in their eager anticipation of the Lord's Advent is that they try to force a current or historical event to fit a prophesied one. "This is understandable, since it is often difficult to recognize a sign as it unfolds. "But recognizing each and every sign when it occurs is not as important as being personally prepared to meet the Savior when he comes—"whether in life or in death."[a] Isaiah emphasized this message when he pled with Israel, "O house of Jacob, come ye, and let us walk in the light of the Lord."[b]

The signs of the Lord's coming were given to help us anticipate, understand, and recognize what will occur—now and in the future. They warn us to be prepared. They will help keep the righteous righteous and leave the wicked without excuse. May we be vigilant and watch for the signs of Christ's coming, for as the Lord warns in Luke, "when ye see these things come to pass, know ye that the kingdom of God is nigh at hand,"[c] even at the door, heralding the second Advent of Jesus the Messiah!

a. D&C 50:5

b. Isaiah 2:5

c. Luke 21:31.

"All These Are the Beginning of Sorrows"

1

Joseph Smith – Matthew 1:18   For then, in those days, shall be great tribulation on the Jews, and upon the inhabitants of Jerusalem, such as was not before sent upon Israel, of God, since the beginning of their kingdom until this time.

The First Signs of the Second Coming: A.D. 33 to A.D. 70

The Lord's final public discourse was delivered in Jerusalem during the last week of His mortal ministry. It was a scathing denunciation of both the leaders and the people of Judah,[a][4] and He made it clear that He no longer claimed the great temple of Herod as His temple. He had withdrawn His approval of that magnificent edifice.[5]

At the completion of this powerful discourse, a little party of disciples, with Jesus at their head, left the temple sanctuary and headed out of the city. When they were on the Mount of Olives, perhaps at a point when they could oversee the city and the magnificent temple, the Savior turned to the Apostles and made a stunning prophecy: the temple, the very symbol of Israel as the chosen people, would be destroyed! In fact, its destruction would be so complete that not one stone would be left standing upon another.[b] The Apostles were astonished: "Tell us, when shall these things be?" they asked, "and what shall be the sign of thy coming, and of the end of the world?"[c]

Instead of answering these questions directly, the Lord substituted a moral lesson (as was His habit). "Take heed," He cautioned, "that no man deceive you."[d] He then prophesied of disturbing events that would occur before His Second Coming—both in the immediate future (during the lifetime of the Apostles) and in the latter days.

◇◇◇◇◇◇◇◇◇◇◇◇◇◇◇◇◇◇◇

a. Matthew 23.

b. Matthew 24:2.

c. Matthew 24:3.

d. Matthew 24:4.

Almost every prophet that lived prior to the time of Jesus had prophesied of the Savior's First Coming so that each ensuing generation would anticipate it. They had also prophesied of His Second Coming, and the Lord, while yet in the flesh, further described some of the signs of His future Advent. The first of these signs would begin soon after His ascension (between the years of A.D. 33 and A.D. 70) so that every generation thereafter would anticipate His Second Coming just as prior generations had looked for His First. The Lord's prophecies were like those of other prophets: some were specific while others were general; some were personal while some were given to all Israel; some were intended to build faith and belief while others were meant as a warning. The Lord forewarned mankind that all of these prophecies and intense warnings of devastation and destruction would not mark the end—they were merely "the beginning of sorrows."[a]

The Savior's initial prophecies can be divided into six categories:

1. Prophecies Regarding the Apostles

Prior to His ascension, the Lord charged His Apostles to preach the gospel to the people of every nation, "baptizing them in the name of the Father, and of the Son, and of the Holy Ghost."[b] He had previously warned these brethren that although their preaching would bring much individual joy and salvation, they would be scourged from synagogue to synagogue by the Jewish councils and would be delivered "up to be afflicted," killed, and "hated of all nations" for His name's sake.[c] The Savior further prophesied that "whosoever killeth you will think that he doeth God service."[d] Just as the Jewish leaders had persecuted Him, so too would they persecute the Apostles.[e]

But the Apostles anticipated that the Lord would return in the immediate future and reign over His earthly kingdom—a conclusion that is unquestionably due to the tone of the Lord's instructions in Matthew. It was not to be so, however, as will be seen from the many signs and warnings that Jesus gave to teach them that His coming was far in the future.[f]

2. False Christs and False Prophets

Jesus warned the Apostles that many false prophets and false Christs would arise after His death, and He cautioned them not to be

a. Matthew 24:8.

b. Matthew 28:19.

c. Matthew 24:9.

d. John 16:2.

e. John 15:20.

f. Matthew 24:6.

deceived.[a] Israel had been led astray by such charlatans in the past; Jeremiah recounted such defection during his lifetime as one of the sins that caused the captivity of Israel. The false prophets had preached that Israel's sins and iniquitous ways were justified, and the wayward people had believed them.[b]

The Savior prophesied that this situation would repeat itself, as later proven in several New Testament scriptures.[6] And the Jewish historian Josephus recorded that several of these seducers came before the destruction of Jerusalem.[7] But the Lord, through Jeremiah, declared: "I have not sent these [false] prophets, yet they ran: I have not spoken to them, yet they prophesied."[c]

False Messiahs appeared before and after Christ. "Scores of rabbis, holy men, warriors, scholars and scribes stepped forth to claim they were the fulfillment" of the Messianic prophesies. Perhaps the most famous of these men was Simon Bar Kochba. He led the last revolt of organized Judaism against Rome between A.D. 132–135. He was declared to be the Messiah by Akiva, "the greatest rabbi of the era."[8] The people of the Western Hemisphere had a similar problem.[d]

3. Wars, Famines, and Pestilence

Between A.D. 33 and A.D. 70, Israel was involved in multiple wars with Rome.[9] Nation did rise up against nation,[10] and famines, pestilence, and earthquakes have always been with us. However, the claims of false Messiahs, as well as violent political disturbances, would soon lead to the destruction of Jerusalem, Herod's amazing temple, and Israel as a nation.

4. Prophecies Regarding Jerusalem

Christ prophesied that the mighty city of Jerusalem would be destroyed. He wept over its fate.[e] "O Jerusalem, Jerusalem . . . how often would I have gathered thy children together, even as a hen gathereth her chickens under her wings, and ye would not! Behold, [as a result] your house is left unto you desolate."[f]

The Savior warned the Jews that their enemies would "cast a trench about [them], and compass [them] round, and keep [them] in on every side."[g] They and their children would be killed and the temple would not have one stone left on another after the conflict.[h] This dev-

a. Matthew 24:4–5, 11, 24.

b. Jeremiah 28.

c. Jeremiah 23:21.

d. Words of Mormon 1:15.

e. Luke 19:41.

f. Matthew 23:37–38.

g. Luke 19:43.

h. Luke 19.

astation would be in the lifetime of some of the Apostles. The Jews rebelled against Rome: Titus, a Roman general, laid siege to the city for seven months, keeping it "in on every side" until he finally conquered it.[11] The siege produced unbearable famine and overwhelming destruction. Josephus, an eyewitness inside Jerusalem during the siege, recorded that the relentless famine caused one woman to kill her own child, cook it, eat half herself, and offer the other half to some defending soldiers. They were appalled, refused the offer, and left her to her own destruction.[12] The Lord warned the Apostles and all who would listen to them to flee to the mountains for protection when they saw these things coming, for this great tribulation would be a fulfillment of the prophet Daniel's "abomination of desolation."[a] The Israelites would be destroyed as a nation and dispersed out of God's sight because of their rejection of Him and their abominable sins, and the results would be the desolation of both Jerusalem and the kingdom of Judah.

5. *Prophecies Regarding the Temple and Daily Sacrifice*

Here the Lord was very specific. Herod's temple would be totally destroyed. The heathen army would desecrate it and sack its contents, and the once holy edifice would not have one stone left standing upon another. This magnificent structure—requiring more than forty years to build and of which it was said, "He that has not seen the Temple of Herod, has never known what beauty is"[13]— would simply cease to exist.[b][14]

The temple was the center of Judaism—the heart of the Law of Moses—and no ceremonies or sacrifices could be performed without it. Daniel foresaw the end of the daily sacrifice (the functional symbol of Israel's God and her anticipated Messiah) when he wrote, "And in the midst of the week he [the conquering prince of Rome] shall cause the sacrifice and the oblation to cease, and for the overspreading of abominations he shall make it desolate."[c]

With the cessation of sacrifice came the end of all "oblations" (the religious symbols of Jewish worship). Israel had rejected her Messiah—He for whom they looked in all they did. Christ had fulfilled the law and it was no longer the correct method of worshiping God. Judah had rejected the Lord's covenant (anciently made with

Abraham and renewed with Israel) by rejecting the God who gave it. It had given them a promised land and had made them custodians of the priesthood, with the responsibility to be "perfect"[a] and help fulfill the Father's purpose of bringing "to pass the immortality and eternal life of man"[b] by taking the gospel, the plan of salvation, to all the world. But now, until the time of the Second Coming, Judah (the successor to the lost tribe of Levi) would not have the priesthood of God as her authority to act. There would be no promised land for Judah until prophecy regarding the latter days began to be fulfilled, and they would not have the blessing of taking salvation to the world. Yet they would remain the chosen people, for God would not break His covenant even though Israel had rejected Him. And because of this rejection, Israel would receive the prophesied results—they would be scattered among all nations.[c]

6. *The Scattering of Israel*

Solomon was the last king of united Israel. He was a great king, but had worshiped false gods. The Lord was angry with him and sent the prophet Ahijah to pronounce judgment upon his kingdom. Ten tribes of Israel would be taken from Solomon (and his successors) and given to Jeroboam, an Ephraimite.[d] These tribes formed the Kingdom of Israel, or the Northern Kingdom. They were: Reuben, Simeon, Levi (the majority of Levi lived in the Northern Kingdom), Dan, Naphtali, Gad, Asher, Issachar, Zebulun, and Joseph (Ephraim and Manasseh).

Solomon, who was near death when the kingdom was divided, was left with the single tribe of Judah.[e] The tribe of Benjamin, which was originally aligned with the ten tribes, soon shifted its allegiance to Solomon because of its close proximity to Jerusalem. There were also individual members of the other tribes (including Ephraim and Manasseh) living in Jerusalem at the time of the division.[f][15]

The scattering of Israel began circa 721 B.C. with the destruction of the ten tribes. These tribes were conquered by Assyria, taken into captivity, and lost. The remnants of the lost tribes living in the kingdom of Judah eventually became known as Jews. It was from these remnants that Lehi (a Manassite)[g] and Ishmael (an Ephraimite)[16] were called by the Lord and led to the Western Hemisphere. The next major scattering occurred around 570 B.C. when the Babylonians finally

a. Genesis 17:1.

b. Moses 1:39.

c. Amos 9:8–9.

d. 1 Kings 11:31.

e. 1 Kings 11:36.

f. 1 Kings 12:17, 21–23.

g. Alma 10:3.

conquered the Kingdom of Judah and destroyed Jerusalem. From these two general scatterings of Israel, two tribes remain identifiable: Judah and Joseph (Ephraim and Manasseh). The other ten tribes—Reuben, Simeon, Levi, Dan, Naphtali, Gad, Asher, Issachar, Zebulun, and Benjamin—remain lost.

Moses foresaw the scattering of Israel and prophesied: "And the Lord shall scatter you among the nations, and ye shall be left few in number among the heathen, whither the Lord shall lead you."[a] The final scattering of Israel took place in A.D. 70 when the Roman general Titus conquered and destroyed Jerusalem. Jeremiah and Ezekiel described the first destruction of Jerusalem and scattering of Judah, but their words also have double reference to the scattering that occurred after Titus's successful campaign. Jeremiah recorded that the Lord would "scatter [Judah] . . . among the heathen, whom neither they nor their fathers have known."[b] Ezekiel elaborated:

> **Ezekiel 12:14–16**   And I [the Lord] will scatter toward every wind all that are about him [the tribe of Judah and any of the rest of Israel that are with it] to help him, and all his bands; and I will draw out the sword after them. And they shall know that I am the Lord, when I shall scatter them among the nations, and disperse them in the countries. But I will leave a few men of them from the sword, from the famine, and from the pestilence; that they may declare all their abominations among the heathen whither they come; and they shall know that I am the Lord.

And Nephi prophesied that the people of Judah would be "scourged by all people . . . wander in the flesh . . . become a hiss and a by-word, and be hated among all nations,"[c] because they had crucified the God of Israel.

In the book of Zechariah, the Lord described righteous Israel as the "apple of his eye,"[d] but her subsequent wickedness provoked the Lord, and in the book of 1 Nephi He compared her to "an olive-tree, whose branches [would] be broken off and scattered upon all the face of the earth."[e]

The remnants of the tribe of Joseph on the Western Hemisphere was never scattered further than that because its existence was unknown to the tribe of Judah and the Gentiles. Nevertheless, in time, these people also fell into total apostasy. The righteous among them were

a. Deuteronomy 4:27.

b. Jeremiah 9:16.

c. 1 Nephi 19:13–14.

d. Zechariah 2:8.

e. 1 Nephi 10:12.

destroyed and the wicked remnant completely rejected the covenant of Abraham. The priesthood was withdrawn from them, along with their right to a promised land.

With the scattering of Israel complete, the first prophesied signs of the Second Coming (between A.D. 33 and A.D. 70) were fulfilled. Jerusalem was no longer the center of God's law, for with remarkable clarity the prophet Zechariah prophesied: "Behold, I will make Jerusalem a cup of trembling unto all the people round about . . . and in that day [the latter days] will I make Jerusalem a burdensome stone for all people."[a] Jerusalem today is one of the most volatile spots in the world, and thus it will remain until the Lord's Second Coming.

a. Zechariah 12:2–3.

The Great Apostasy 2

Ephesians 4:11–12   And he gave some, apostles; and some, prophets . . . For the perfecting of the saints, for the work of the ministry, for the edifying of the body of Christ.

A.D. 70 to A.D. 325

"Go ye therefore, and teach all nations, baptizing them in the name of the Father, and of the Son, and of the Holy Ghost: Teaching them to observe all things whatsoever I have commanded you: and, lo, I am with you alway, even unto the end of the world. Amen."[a] With this commission to His Apostles given prior to His ascension, Christ called for the establishment of His church upon the earth. Bolstered by their witness of the Lord's resurrection, the Apostles enthusiastically began their ministry by preaching salvation "at Jerusalem."[b] Because Jesus had declared that He had been sent to "the lost sheep of the house of Israel" and not to the world at large,[c][17] the Apostles primarily taught the Jews in their synagogues and in their public places[18]—and their initial labors were rewarded by about three thousand souls being added to the church.[d]

"For a time the Church remained completely Jewish, a sect within Israel of those who believed in the resurrection of Jesus and regarded Him as the promised Messiah who was about to come again to definitively establish the reign of God."[19] But with the conversion of Cornelius, a Gentile,[e] Peter recognized that the gospel was to be expanded far beyond those of Judah's linage. And when Paul was aggressively

a. Matthew 28:19–
   20; Mark
   16:15–16.

b. Luke 24:47.

c. Matthew
   15:24.

d. Acts 2:41.

e. Acts 10.

rejected by the Jews in Corinth, he "shook his raiment, and said unto them, Your blood be upon your own heads; I am clean: from henceforth I will go unto the Gentiles."[a]

The early church spread rapidly, but with growth came dissension, disagreement, and division. The Apostles knew from the Lord's teachings that His Advent would not be soon, and they prophesied that the fledgling church would not survive until He came again. Peter was the first to make this prophecy as he and John spoke to the Jews in the temple at Jerusalem. He chastised them for rejecting Christ and called them to repentance, declaring that although Jesus had preached to them in the flesh, He had now been received into heaven "until the times of *restitution* of all things."[b] But to have a "restitution of all things" requires that a falling away must take place first.

The anticipation of Christ's immediate return grew as the gospel spread throughout the people. Without dampening the spirit generated by the desire to again receive the Lord, Paul wrote to the Thessalonians and with firm resolve instructed them concerning Christ's Second Coming. "Be not soon shaken in mind . . ." he cautioned, "for that day shall not come, except there come a falling away first, and that man of sin [the devil] be revealed."[c] Paul was making it clear to the Thessalonians that the day of Christ's coming was *not* near: they should not be deceived by "any means" on this point. The Second Coming would not take place until after the devil had caused an apostasy from the truth. He continued to explain that this was a time when Satan, with all his delusions, would show great "power and signs and lying wonders"[d] and would deceive those who did not love the truth.[e]

The falling away started early in the Apostles' ministry. Dissension over doctrine and procedure began almost as rapidly as new converts accepted the gospel. As Gentile converts were brought into the Church, the requirements of the Law of Moses and the practice of circumcision became problems. The Jews *knew* they were the chosen people; therefore, they believed that the covenants extended under the Law of Moses could not be given to the Gentiles unless the Gentiles also accepted that Law. But Paul saw the gospel as a liberation from the Law, and so argued.[f]

This was not the only problem, however. Some converts falsely claimed to be Apostles, and they presented a threat to the authority of

a. Acts 18:6.

b. Acts 3:21; emphasis added.

c. 2 Thessalonians 2:2–3.

d. 2 Thessalonians 2:9.

e. 2 Thessalonians 2:10–11.

f. Acts 13:38–39; Galatians 2:16, 21; 5:1; Philippians 3:8–9.

the church.[a] Some Jews thought they had authority over the Christian converts because of their leadership in the Jewish synagogue, but they were condemned by John the Revelator as being of the "synagogue of Satan."[b] Some even claimed that the eagerly anticipated resurrection of the righteous had already occurred.[c] Moreover, the purpose of the sacrament (remembrance of the atonement of Christ) was soon distorted.[d]

The last problem that precipitated the Apostasy was the disappearance of the Apostles. The prophesied persecution of the Twelve began to take its toll early: first with James, who was beheaded by Herod Agrippa I,[e] and then with the rest of the Apostles as they were pursued, persecuted, captured, and killed. The need for the continued presence of the Apostles is best exemplified by Paul, who, after years of absence while preaching the gospel, returned to Jerusalem and met with his fellow brethren to make sure that his teachings were still correct.[f]

As the Apostles proselyted throughout the world, they called local authorities to oversee the newly formed branches of the church. Since they were able to return to these local branches less and less often before their deaths, it was left to the local leaders to maintain the activity of the members and the doctrinal integrity of the gospel. By circa A.D. 101, all of the Apostles had either been killed or, in the case of John, taken by the Lord. With no central authority to govern the branches, they were now left to their own devices.

By the middle of the second century, a bishop had been established over each of the surviving church branches;[20] by the end of the second century, without apostolic authority to guide them, the churches had progressed through what has been described as the "development approach" (a system of authority based on the system's developing creed; its hierarchy of bishop, priest, and deacon; and the scriptures).[21] They had rejected the necessity of apostolic authority on the argument that if they (meaning the Apostles) were in charge, why had they disappeared?[22] The bishops rationalized that since they had initially been appointed by the Apostles, they "stood in legitimate succession in a line reaching back to the Apostles themselves"[23] (as well as being the protectors of the oral traditions and a developing canon of scripture).

Without central authority, the doctrinal divisions which the Apostles had rectified during their ministry continued to escalate in the

a. Revelation 2:2.

b. Revelation 2:9.

c. 2 Timothy 2:18.

d. 1 Corinthians 11:19–22.

e. Acts 12:2.

f. Galatians 2:2.

fledgling church until even the position of Christ's relationship with the Father was challenged.[24] This internal, spiritual conflagration became extensive; but the church had an even greater disruptive influence being generated from without. Rome was the center of the civilized world and had powerful legions to enforce its authority. Although the early Christians had experienced short periods of relative peace, almost from the time of the Apostles until the reign of Constantine, Rome persecuted them relentlessly. But change came with Constantine's conversion to Christianity.

One of several stories about Constantine's conversion states that he received a vision of Christ and was told in the vision to ornament his soldiers' shields with the Savior's monogram–the Greek letters *chi* and *rho*. He obliged and then won the battle that made him emperor of all Rome. Another version of his conversion stated that both he and his entire army saw a luminous cross appear in the afternoon sky bearing the message, "in this conquer."[25] According to this account, the vision inspired him to adopt Christ and have a symbolic cross painted on the shields of his troops. In reality, Constantine used both the Christian and the pagan religions to solidify his political power, and he did not personally adopt Christianity until his final illness in A.D. 337.[26] Nonetheless, he made Christianity the state religion after his purported conversion and had a powerful influence on the Christian church. His influence and assistance in resolving doctrinal conflicts within the church completed the apostasy from the truth.

Constantine's determination to unify Christianity resulted in the calling of the Council of Nicaea[27] where on May 20, A.D. 325, approximately 220 bishops met to resolve their doctrinal differences, regulate authority, and develop a religious creed. The council of Nicaea and the councils that followed after Constantine's death culminated in the Constantinople Council of A.D. 381. Prior to the meeting of these ecumenical councils, however, political factions had elevated the authority of the churches of Rome, Antioch, and Alexandria over that of the other churches. The fourth Canon of the Council of Nicaea declared that these three churches were now the supreme ruling entities of the Christian church. Rome soon became the most prominent among these three because it was (1) the capital of the empire; (2) the possessor of great wealth (and had assisted many of the other churches financially); and (3) reputed historically to be the last place Peter and Paul had taught—as well as the place of their martyrdom and burial.[28]

This centralization of authority in Rome eventually developed into the supreme papal authority of Western Christendom. "These powerful papal monarchs . . . controlled a vast ecclesiastical machinery that regulated in minute detail the moral and social behavior of medieval men—kings and princes as well as peasants and townspeople."[29]

After the Constantinople Council of A.D. 381, the remains of the original church vanished and the remaining church "erected a durable structure of authority, a framework of steel that has enabled it to meet every conceivable crisis."[30] The controversies over the relationship of God, the Son of God, and the Holy Ghost were resolved into what has become know as the Nicene Creed.[31] This creed was eventually formalized and adopted into what became known as the Creed of Constantinople.[32]

Paul had prophesied to Timothy that the time would come when "sound doctrine" would not be endured and the truth would be turned into "fables."[a] By A.D. 381, that time had arrived. Christianity did not succeed in destroying paganism, it simply adopted it![33] Thus, the falling away prophesied by Paul was complete, but the premise upon which the "development approach" of church authority was based was erroneous. The early church had been organized with Apostles because they were called and ordained by the Lord and given a specific witness of His divinity and resurrection. They were commissioned to bear witness of these truths throughout the world. Therefore, the true church must be founded on an apostolic ministry that has received a personal witness of the divinity of Jesus Christ and a commission to share this witness with the world.[b]

That the apostolic call was not to be restricted to the original Twelve was attested to when Matthias was chosen to fill the vacancy in the twelve created by the death of Judas Iscariot.[c] Also, the personal witness that Paul received of Christ's divinity and resurrection as he traveled to Damascus prepared him for his apostleship. This same commission has been given in the latter days to the Apostles of the Restoration, thus maintaining the structure of the original Christ-established gospel.[34]

a. 2 Timothy
   4:3–4.

b. 1 Corinthi-
   ans 15:5–8;
   Ephesians
   2:20.

c. Acts 1:23–26.

Early in the fourth century, the apostasy of Christianity on the Eastern Hemisphere was progressing toward its apex while the apostasy of the tribes of Joseph on the Western Hemisphere was not far behind. After the Savior appeared to the Western Hemisphere following His resurrection (all of the wicked having been killed during the destruction that occurred when He was crucified[a]), the church enjoyed two hundred years of peace and righteousness. But by the time those with a personal witness of the Savior had died (with the exception of the three special witnesses), the seeds of apostasy had begun to grow again.

The Saints on the Western Hemisphere did not have the fundamental problems faced by church members in the East—there were no Gentiles with pagan ways to spread their influence. Instead, sins connected with worldliness opened a chasm that eventually led to rejection of the gospel, apostasy from the truth, and the total destruction of the righteous. The Book of Mormon testifies that there began to be "pride . . . the wearing of costly apparel . . . [and a desire for] the fine things of the world." The people "began to be divided into classes; and they began to build up churches unto themselves to get gain, and began to deny the true church of Christ."[b] They "wilfully [rebelled] against the gospel of Christ,"[c] and became "exceeding wicked."[d] After this, it would only take about a hundred years until the people of the Western Hemisphere would be in total apostasy.

The Old Testament prophet Isaiah foresaw the total apostasy of all the tribes of Israel.[e] He declared that this apostasy would occur because the people had "transgressed the laws, changed the ordinance, [and] broken the everlasting covenant."[f] Thus, the "famine" spoken of by Amos occurred to all Israel, and by adoption, to the Gentiles as well: "not a famine of bread, nor a thirst for water, but of hearing the words of the Lord."[g] Amos prophesied that the people of Israel would "wander from sea to sea, and from the north even to the east, they shall run to and fro to seek the word of the Lord, and shall not find it."[h] The devil's fight for dominion over the people of the earth, as prophesied by John the Revelator, had begun anew;[i] and the prophecy of Isaiah, which stated that the people would want their seers and prophets to "prophesy not unto [them] right things, [but] speak . . . smooth things, [and] prophesy deceits," was being fulfilled.[j]

a. 3 Nephi 8.

b. 4 Nephi 1:24, 26.

c. 4 Nephi 1:38.

d. 4 Nephi 1:45.

e. Isaiah 5:3–19.

f. Isaiah 24:5.

g. Amos 8:11.

h. Amos 8:12.

i. Revelation 12:12–17.

j. Isaiah 30:10; emphasis added.

The Times of the Gentiles 3

Daniel 12:6–7   How long shall it be to the end of these wonders? It shall be for a time, times, and an half; and when he shall have accomplished to scatter the power of the holy people, all these things shall be finished.

Luke 21:24   Jerusalem shall be trodden down of the Gentiles, until the times of the Gentiles be fulfilled.

A.D. 325 to A.D. 1820

The next sign of the Second Coming was the prophesied "times of the Gentiles." The times of the Gentiles began circa A.D. 325 as a result of the complete apostasy from the gospel and withdrawal from the covenant of Abraham by the house of Israel and the original church.

Before we discuss these times in detail, however, it would be helpful to first understand exactly what the covenant of Abraham was—and is yet today—since it is the basis of the plan of salvation. It defines God's relationship to man and man's relationship to God, and it contains the requirements for individual and personal salvation.

The Covenant of Abraham[†]

When Abraham was 99 years old, God made a covenant with him.[a] It was an everlasting covenant which the Lord promised He would never revoke nor break. This irrevocable covenant consisted of three parts: *part one* is absolute and unconditional, but *part two* and *part three*,

---

a. Genesis 17:1.   † The covenant of Abraham is occasionally referred to as the everlasting covenant.

though absolute, are conditionally available based on the righteousness or unrighteousness of God's chosen people. If His people sin and become unworthy they will remain the chosen people, but the right to the blessings of the covenant will be withdrawn until the Lord restores them again.

> *Part One:* Abraham was promised he would have seed, and his seed would forever be designated as the Lord's *chosen people.* God chose them, and He will never reject them.

> *Part Two:* The chosen people will be blessed with a *promised land.* For Abraham, the promised land was Canaan,[a] and Canaan remained the promised land for the generations of Isaac and Jacob (Israel). When Moses led the children of Israel out of Egypt, they returned to this promised land and divided it among the twelve tribes. After the ten tribes were lost, Judah (the Southern Kingdom) retained the general area of Canaan, including Jerusalem. This area later became generally known as Palestine. When the tribe of Joseph (Ephraim and Manasseh) was later scattered, a remnant of the tribe was led out of Jerusalem and given the Western Hemisphere as its promised land.[b]

> *Part Three:* The chosen people will be given the *priesthood.*[c] This priesthood was originally given to Adam by God. That priesthood lineage then descended from Adam to Abraham,[d] and through Abraham it became part of the Abrahamic covenant. All of the blessings of the gospel of salvation, "even of life eternal" come through the priesthood.[e] Without the priesthood, eternal life (i.e., living in the presence of God) cannot be realized. It is the authority from God to perform all of the ordinances required to reenter His presence.

These three parts comprise the irrevocable covenant that God made with Abraham. All Abraham had to do to receive the blessings of this covenant was to accept it and comply with its conditions. His acceptance (and the acceptance of all those who would follow the covenant in the future) bestows two responsibilities:

a. Genesis 17:8.

b. 1 Nephi 2:20; 3 Nephi 20:13–14.

c. Abraham 1:4; 2:11.

d. Abraham 1:3; D&C 84:6–16.

e. Abraham 2:11.

1. The recipient must walk uprightly before God and be "perfect."[a] God clearly stated His intentions regarding what was expected from His chosen people: "And we [the Creators] will prove them herewith, to see if they will do all things whatsoever the Lord their God shall command them."[b] In other words, "walk before me, and be thou perfect."[c] This same requirement was reiterated by the Savior when He gave the Sermon on the Mount during His ministry.[d] Perfection is achieved by (a) learning the gospel requirements, (b) living them to the best of our ability, and (c) repenting of sins when we recognize we have committed them.

2. The recipient must offer the gospel of salvation to the world.[e] Those under the covenant are required to "testify and warn the people." This is required because the gospel—the plan of salvation—is the plan that must be followed if mankind is to regain God's presence. Once the covenant has been accepted, "it becometh every man who has been warned to warn his neighbor."[f] *Warn,* in this instance, means *present to:* giving others the opportunity to hear and learn of the gospel requirements. In other words, missionary work. The Lord's chosen people have the opportunity to take the gospel to "all nations, kindreds, tongues, and people"[g] with the result that "he that believeth and is baptized shall be saved; but he that believeth not shall be damned,"[h] "left without excuse," and their sins will then be "upon their own heads."[i]

From Abraham, the covenant passed first to Isaac[j] and then to Jacob, whose name was changed to Israel by the Lord.[k] Thereafter, it went to the twelve sons of Jacob, collectively known as the twelve tribes (or house) of Israel.[135] However, *anyone* can become one of God's "chosen" people and share in the blessings of the covenant of Abraham if he or she is willing to accept the gospel.[m] Acceptance of the gospel—evidenced by baptism, confirmation, and obedience to God's commandments—automatically makes an individual part of Israel's lineage.[n] But Israel (and those who had been adopted into Israel by membership in the original church) apostatized from the gospel of

a. Genesis 17:1.

b. Abraham 3:25.

c. Genesis 17:1.

d. Matthew 5:48.

e. Abraham 2:11; Matthew 28:19–20.

f. D&C 88:81.

g. D&C 42:58.

h. Mark 16:16.

i. D&C 88:82.

j. Genesis 17:21.

k. Genesis 32:28.

l. Exodus 6:7–8; Deuteronomy 4:20.

m. 2 Nephi 30:1–2.

n. Romans 8:14–17; Galatians 4:4–7.

the New Testament when they "transgressed the laws, changed the ordinance, [and broke] the everlasting covenant."[a] As a result, the blessings of the Abrahamic covenant were withdrawn from them and the times of the Gentiles began.

An intellectual and spiritual darkness settled upon the earth's inhabitants as the times of the Gentiles were ushered in. The light of the gospel was gone, and when the Roman Empire finally fell, the "torch of learning in the West flickered and nearly died out."[36] Lay education was rare, and "intellectual life—of the most rudimentary kind indeed—was practically confined to the monasteries."[37]

The Holy Roman Empire rose from the ashes of Rome like the mythical phoenix. It soon became powerful enough to control and regulate all within its sphere of influence—from kings to paupers.[38] It controlled spirituality by threat of excommunication (expulsion from God's kingdom to endless torment) and by controlling the availability of the scriptures, including the canonization or authorization of texts. In addition, it alone was allowed to interpret the scriptures.

These times of intellectual and spiritual darkness were prophesied by both Isaiah and Micah. Isaiah warned, "Woe unto them that call evil good, and good evil; that put darkness for light, and light for darkness; that put bitter for sweet, and sweet for bitter!"[b] For "darkness shall cover the earth, and gross darkness the people."[c] Isaiah's contemporary, Micah, similarly prophesied, "Therefore night shall be unto you, that ye shall not have a vision; and it shall be dark unto you, that ye shall not divine; and the sun shall go down over the prophets, and the day shall be dark over them."[d]

Just as God's prophets foretold of this time of vast darkness, so also did they prophesy of the light that would eventually return: "And the Gentiles shall come to thy light, and kings to the brightness of thy rising."[e] Bringing people out of the dark ages, however, was no easy task. They had gone so far astray that in A.D. 1343 the "cult of indulgences" was officially sanctioned. This "cult" maintained that the virtues of Jesus and the early saints "had left a treasury of merits" that others could draw upon to obtain a "remission of the temporal punishment due to their sins." Access to these merits was given by "church indulgence . . . often a donation of money."[39]

With the rise of universities and the expansion of knowledge in the

a. Isaiah 24:5.

b. Isaiah 5:20.

c. Isaiah 60:2.

d. Micah 3:6.

e. Isaiah 60:3.

11th century, light slowly started invading the Dark Ages. Spiritual enlightenment also increased following Martin Luther's revolt against the authority of the Holy Roman Empire in the 16th century. John Calvin, usually referred to as the "architect of Protestantism," further energized Luther's revolt. His biblical commentaries formulated the doctrine from which would spring the Protestant churches; while most non-Lutheran churches of the time were Calvinists, they eventually split into a host of separate churches.[40]

Protestantism loosened the grip of the Dark Ages in two ways: (1) it caused the universal church to release its grasp on the people as a whole, and (2) it laid the groundwork for the struggle for freedom of religion that made the restoration of the gospel possible. On the other hand, these reformations offered people alternative faiths to believe in, which made the work of Luther, Calvin, and other reformers a mixed blessing when the gospel was finally restored.

A like situation existed at the time of Christ. When the Lord and His Apostles implemented the gospel, for many it simply became another alternative to existing beliefs. In an effort to dissuade the people from believing in Jesus, the Jewish leadership claimed that His teachings were from the devil (a contention known as the Beelzebub Argument).[41]

As time went by, Protestantism became further divided in its doctrinal beliefs, resulting in the proliferation of Protestant churches and thus providing even more alternatives to the Lord's gospel. Nonetheless, with the rise of Protestantism came the Age of Enlightenment. Mankind began looking for new frontiers to conquer. Many ancient prophecies were fulfilled as men began to venture into the unknown. Columbus discovered the New World;[a] the Puritans and others seeking religious freedom began to migrate;[b] and a new and powerful nation—the United States of America—was born of war to ensure religious freedom for its citizens.[c] All of these events would in time help make the restoration of the gospel possible. The Lord prophetically warned the Gentiles, however, that even though they had discovered and populated the Americas, if they did not repent of their evil ways He would "come out in justice against [them]."[d]

The migration from Europe to the Western Hemisphere also fulfilled a prophecy that the Lord gave to the Nephites. He told them that

a. 1 Nephi 13:12.

b. 1 Nephi 13:13,16.

c. 1 Nephi 13:17–19.

d. Mormon 5:24.

the Gentiles would eventually scatter the Lamanite remnants on the Western Hemisphere and that the Gentiles would then "be a scourge unto the people of [that] land."[a]

Many prophets have described what the times of the Gentiles after the Dark Ages would be like. Nephi tells us that "in the days of the Gentiles" on the Western Hemisphere, and on all other lands, the people will be "drunken with iniquity and all manner of abominations."[b] Isaiah describes the spiritual state of the people as "drunken, but not with wine; they stagger, but not with strong drink. For the Lord hath poured out upon [them] the spirit of deep sleep, and hath closed [their] eyes."[c] And Nephi, referencing the words of Isaiah, continues: "Ye have rejected the prophets; and your rulers, and the seers hath he covered because of your iniquity" (declaring in his prophetic words, that because of their apostasy, the Lord had withdrawn His prophets from them).[d]

The people in this apostate era participated continually in the "good times" sin as described by Isaiah: "And behold joy and gladness, slaying oxen, killing sheep, eating flesh, and drinking wine: let us eat and drink; for tomorrow we shall die."[e] Jeremiah expands this theme by declaring: "And they [the false prophets and teachers during the times of the Gentiles] [will] say unto every one that walketh after the imagination of his own heart, No evil shall come upon you."[f]

Nephi provides the following detailed description of the apostasy and of the "good times" sin:

2 Nephi 28:7–15 Yea, and there shall be many which shall say: Eat, drink, and be merry, for tomorrow we die; and it shall be well with us. And there shall also be many which shall say: Eat, drink, and be merry; nevertheless, fear God—he will justify in committing a little sin; yea, lie a little, take the advantage of one because of his words, dig a pit for thy neighbor; there is no harm in this; and do all these things, for tomorrow we die; and if it so be that we are guilty, God will beat us with a few stripes, and at last we shall be saved in the kingdom of God. Yea, and there shall be many which shall teach after this manner, false and vain and foolish doctrines, and shall be puffed up in their hearts, and shall seek deep to hide their counsels from the Lord; and their works shall be in the dark. And the blood of the saints shall cry from the ground against them. Yea, they have all gone out of the way; they have become corrupted. Because of pride, and because of false teachers, and false doctrine, their churches have become corrupted, and

a. 3 Nephi 20:28.

b. 2 Nephi 27:1.

c. Isaiah 29:9–10.

d. 2 Nephi 27:5.

e. Isaiah 22:13.

f. Jeremiah 23:17.

their churches are lifted up; because of pride they are puffed up. They rob the poor because of their fine sanctuaries; they rob the poor because of their fine clothing; and they persecute the meek and the poor in heart, because in their pride they are puffed up. They wear stiff necks and high heads; yea, and because of pride, and wickedness, and abominations, and whoredoms, they have all gone astray save it be a few, who are the humble followers of Christ; nevertheless, they are led, that in many instances they do err because they are taught by the precepts of men. O the wise, and the learned, and the rich, that are puffed up in the pride of their hearts, and all those who preach false doctrines, and all those who commit whoredoms, and pervert the right way of the Lord, wo, wo, wo be unto them, saith the Lord God Almighty, for they shall be thrust down to hell!

Although the Gentiles would be "a scourge" to the descendants of Joseph on the Western Hemisphere,[a] and Jerusalem on the Eastern Hemisphere would be "trodden down,"[b] the promises the Lord made through His prophets indicate that these abominable conditions would not continue forever. Paul gave the following instructions to the Roman Gentiles who had accepted the gospel: "For I would not, brethren, that ye should be ignorant of this mystery [of why the Gentiles should be allowed into the covenant], lest ye should be wise in your own conceits [think yourselves better than Israel]; that blindness in part is happened to Israel, until the fulness of the Gentiles be come in."[c] The Lord rejected and scattered Israel, including those Gentiles on the Eastern Hemisphere that had come into the covenant through baptism, until the fulness of the Gentiles was complete.

Concerning the end of the "times of the Gentiles," the Lord declared through Isaiah that He would "proceed to do a marvellous work among this people [the Gentiles], even a marvellous work and a wonder."[d] This marvelous work would commence with a vision and with the restoration of a book that would provide a second witness to the divinity of Jesus Christ. Isaiah acknowledged that the "words of a book" would come forth; Nephi elaborated on this when he said that the book would contain the revelations of God "from the beginning of the world to the ending thereof"— revelations that would turn the things of the Gentiles upside down.[e] The restoration of this work was to consummate only after the "light" burst forth "among them that sit in darkness." That light is "the fulness" of the Lord's gospel,[f] and in

a. 3 Nephi 20:28.

b. Luke 21:24.

c. Romans 11:25.

d. Isaiah 29:14; 2 Nephi 27:26.

e. Isaiah 29; 2 Nephi 27:6–35.

f. D&C 45:28.

the generation that it was restored, *"the times of the Gentiles [were] fulfilled."*[a]

The times of the Gentiles began because of the apostasy of the Lord's people; they rejected the gospel and the covenant of Abraham. The times of the Gentiles ended and the sign fulfilled with the restoration of the gospel (which commenced in 1820) and the restoration of the covenant of Abraham. The Lord's chosen people again had access to the priesthood,[b] the promised lands of Judah and Joseph (Jerusalem and Zion) became available to them for their habitation, and the light of the gospel was back upon the earth.

a. D&C 45:30; emphasis added.

b. D&C 13, 107.

The Restoration   4

Ephesians 1:10   That in the dispensation of the fulness of times he might gather together in one all things in Christ, both which are in heaven, and which are on earth; even in him.

Fifteen hundred years passed between the time the early church apostatized from the truth and the time the gospel was restored. The Savior had ascended into heaven, His Apostles (with the exception of John) were all dead, and apostasy had totally destroyed His church on both the Eastern and the Western Hemispheres. As the "times of the Gentiles" drew to a close, however, the fore-appointed time of the restoration arrived.[a] It was time for the covenant of Abraham to be reestablished and the dispensation of the fulness of times, a time "made up of all the dispensations that ever [had] been given since the world began," to be ushered in.[42]

The restoration of the gospel was foreseen by the Old Testament prophet Daniel circa 600 B.C. He received this vision in Babylon while he was a captive of King Nebuchadnezzar. The circumstances were as follows: Nebuchadnezzar had had a distressing dream and "his spirit was troubled" to know what the dream meant—even though he could not remember what it had been about![b] When the king's wise men could not recall and interpret the dream for him, he sent out a decree ordering all of them to be slain. Since Daniel and his fellows were prophets and visionary men, they also fell under the king's decree. But Daniel had not heard about the king's problem so when he was told that his life was in jeopardy, he went to Arioch, the captain of Nebuchadnezzar's guard, to find out why the decree had been is-

a. D&C 45:24–30.
b. Daniel 2:1–9.

sued. Arioch told him about the king's dream and the inability of his wise men to recall it. Daniel then went to Nebuchadnezzar and told him that, given a little time, he could tell him what his dream was and what it meant. The king granted his petition and Daniel returned to his house.

That night, the Lord revealed the secret of Nebuchadnezzar's dream to Daniel in a vision. The next day he went back to Arioch and said, "Destroy not the wise men of Babylon: [but] bring me in before the king, and I will shew unto [him] the interpretation" of his dream.[a] Daniel was again admitted to the king's presence where he proceeded to recount and interpret Nebuchadnezzar's dream: "Thou, O king, [saw] a great image [of a man] . . . whose brightness was excellent, [and it] stood before thee; and the form thereof was terrible. This image's head was of fine gold, his breast and his arms of silver, his belly and his thighs of brass, his legs of iron, his feet part of iron and part of clay."[b]

The man-image that Nebuchadnezzar saw represented the kingdoms of the earth. The head of gold depicted Babylon, the greatest of all the kingdoms.[c] The rest of the image is commonly assumed to comprise the empires of Persia-Medes (breast and arms of silver), Greece (belly and thighs of brass), and Rome (legs of iron). Eventually, the Roman Empire would break into ten kingdoms described as the "feet and toes" of the man-image: ten kingdoms that would be partly strong yet partly broken—a mixture of iron and "miry clay."[d] These kingdoms (and the nations that descended from them during the Dark Ages) are historically described as the Holy Roman Empire, an empire that was held together by a religious power (the "seed of men")[43] based in Rome which had derived its strength from the political prowess of the old "iron" empire.[e] But the dream revealed that the nations of iron and clay would not "cleave" one to another. Eventually, the religious yoke that bound them together would be broken, and they would become individual, secular nations.

Daniel's interpretation continued: "Thou sawest . . . that a stone was cut out without hands, which smote the image upon his feet that were of iron and clay, and brake them to pieces. Then was the iron, the clay, the brass, the silver, and the gold, broken to pieces together, and became like the chaff of the summer threshingfloors; and the wind car-

a. Daniel 2:24.

b. Daniel 2:31–33.

c. Daniel 2:38.

d. Daniel 2:41.

e. Daniel 2:43.

ried them away, that no place was found for them: and the stone that smote the image became a great mountain, and filled the whole earth."[a]

The small stone "cut out without hands" represents God's kingdom, a kingdom that will never be destroyed.[b] And when it smites the image and breaks all of the kingdoms of the man-image apart—becoming a "great mountain" that fills "the whole earth—it is interpreted to mean that God's kingdom will eventually supersede or infiltrate all national boundaries; that through the restoration of the gospel, God's power will grow until it will eventually consume or be taught in all the kingdoms of the world.[c] Thus, long before Paul prophesied that the Second Coming would not occur until after a falling away,[d] and before Peter prophesied that all things would be restored after the apostasy,[e] Daniel envisioned the restoration and the establishment of God's work in the latter days.

In symbolic vision, John the Revelator actually saw the restoration of the gospel take place. He saw the devil successfully overcome the church that Christ and His Apostles had established while they were upon the earth. Then, following the passage of a long period of time,[f] he saw "another angel fly in the midst of heaven, having the everlasting gospel to preach unto them that dwell on the earth," and he saw the gospel taken "to every nation, and kindred, and tongue, and people."[g]

The prophets of the Western Hemisphere recorded a much clearer vision of the great events presaging the Second Coming. Nephi saw the establishment of America upon the Western Hemisphere and the scattering of the seed of Lehi (Native Americans) by Gentile settlers.[h] After that, he saw the Lord "proceed to do a marvelous work among the Gentiles," even the restoration of the gospel.[i] A descendant of Nephi, also named Nephi, recorded the Savior's words as He visited the descendants of Lehi following His resurrection. The Lord spoke of the future gathering of Israel (His chosen people) and then said, "I give unto you a sign, that ye may know the time when these things shall be about to take place."[j] That sign was the coming forth of the Book of Mormon, signaling the beginning of the restoration of the gospel. The Lord declared that the sign (the Book of Mormon) would "be made known unto the Gentiles,"[k] so that they, and the seed of Lehi might "know that the work of the Father hath already commenced unto the fulfilling of the covenant which he hath made unto the people who are of the house of Israel."[l]

a. Daniel
   2:34–35.

b. Daniel 2:44.

c. Daniel 2.

d. 2 Thessalonians
   2:1–3.

e. Acts
   3:19–21.

f. Revelation
   12:5–6

g. Revelation
   14:6.

h. 1 Nephi
   22:7.

i. 1 Nephi
   22:8.

j. 3 Nephi
   21:1.

k. 3 Nephi
   21:2.

l. 3 Nephi
   21:2, 7; 1–9.

One might say that the work of the restoration began in 1805 when a boy by the name of Joseph Smith was born—a boy raised up to fulfill the prophecies of the restoration given by the Book of Mormon prophet Lehi almost twenty-four hundred years earlier. Prior to his death, Lehi gave a blessing to his youngest son, who was also named Joseph. In this blessing, Lehi cited the brass plates and indicated that Joseph of Egypt had prophesied that God would raise up a seer in the last days and that he would be of his (Joseph of Egypt's) tribal lineage. This seer was compared to Moses[44] in that he would "bring forth [God's] word unto the seed of [Joseph of Egypt's] loins." His name would be called Joseph (after both his own father and after Joseph of Egypt), and he would bring to "pass much restoration unto the house of Israel, and unto the seed of [Lehi's] brethren."[a]

Joseph Smith's first vision took place in 1820. In this astounding revelation he was privileged to see God the Father and His Son, Jesus Christ. While the first vision revealed many truths which are not the purview of this discussion, it is important to note that this vision called Joseph to do the work of the Lord, ended the times of the Gentiles, commenced the restoration of the gospel, and opened the dispensation of the fulness of times.[b]

Joseph's second vision occurred on September 21, 1823. The angel Moroni, whom John the Revelator had seen in his great vision,[c] appeared to Joseph to commence the restoration of all things. Under the direction of the Lord, Moroni gave Joseph the instructions and teachings that would lead to the discovery and translation of the Book of Mormon. With the restoration of the Book of Mormon, the gospel was thereafter restored in its fullness.[d][45] The Lord later confirmed that the gospel had been restored by an heavenly angel,[e] and that it would serve as an ensign for all the nations of the earth.[f]

The Bible is the first witness of the Savior's divinity, but many plain and precious things have been lost from its pages through centuries of retranslation and interpretation. Still, it is Judah's record, preserved as a witness to the Gentiles of the chronicle of God's chosen people, and it includes the covenants and blessings He originally gave the children of Israel.[g] The Book of Mormon corrects many of the false doctrines that have arisen from incorrect interpretations or misunderstood verses found in the Bible,[h] and it confirms the truths found therein.[i] It also

a. 2 Nephi 3.

b. Joseph Smith–History 1.

c. Revelation 14:6.

d. Joseph Smith–History 1:30–54.

e. D&C 133:36–37.

f. Isaiah 5:26; 11:12.

g. 1 Nephi 13:20–29.

h. 2 Nephi 3:12.

i. 1 Nephi 13:34–41.

contains the history of part of the remnant of Ephraim and Manasseh (commonly known as the Nephites and the Lamanites). However, the Bible and the Book of Mormon together provide a *complete* witness of the divinity of the Lord Jesus Christ in the sense that out of the mouth of two or more witnesses shall the truth of all things be established.[a]

Initially, the Book of Mormon was not warmly received by most communities in mid-nineteenth century America. The unusual way it was discovered and translated caused a considerable amount of controversy, controversy that was foretold by the prophecies contained within its pages. For example, when people first heard about the Book of Mormon, their frequent response was that they had already received the "word of God" and that they had received "enough."[b] Some would cry, "A Bible! A Bible! We have got a Bible, and there cannot be any more Bible."[c] The Book of Mormon itself confounded these arguments by testifying that although the Bible was indeed a divine witness from the Jews, God had "more nations than one" capable of producing a sacred record.[d]

The Book of Mormon is not a figment of someone's imagination. Isaiah saw it coming forth out of the "dust . . . of them which have slumbered," a book that would be delivered to "him that is not learned." He further stated that a "sealed" portion of the book would be delivered in a day when "wickedness and abominations" would abound, but that the "sealed" portion would "be kept" from the wicked.[e]

Moroni echoed Isaiah's simile when he described the book as coming forth "out of the dust,"[f] and other Book of Mormon prophets recorded that the book would rest until it should come forth, "even as it were out of the ground," in the latter days.[g] But as the Lord promised Enos and Mormon, the book *would come forth*—to the Lamanites, the Gentiles, the Jews, and all the house of Israel "in his own due time."[h]

None of these ancient prophets knew exactly *when* the Book of Mormon would be restored. Moroni described the day of its restoration as one when the people would believe that "miracles [had] been] done away."[i] He said that the "blood of saints [would] cry unto the Lord, because of secret combinations and the works of darkness."[j] There would be "wars," "rumors of wars," "earthquakes," "tempests," "fires," "vapors of smoke in foreign lands," "great pol-

a. Deuteronomy 17:6; D&C 6:28.

b. 2 Nephi 28:29.

c. 2 Nephi 29:3.

d. 2 Nephi 29:1–7.

e. Isaiah 29:4–12; JST, Isaiah 29:11–20; IV, Isaiah 29:4–13; 2 Nephi 27:6–29.

f. Moroni 10:27.

g. 2 Nephi 26:15–16.

h. Enos 1:13–16; Mormon 5:12–15.

i. Mormon 8:26.

j. Mormon 8:27.

lutions upon the face of the earth," "murders," "robbing," "lying," "deceivings," and "whoredoms," and "all manner of abominations," and there would be churches established to get gain and forgive sins for money.[a] Of that time Moroni said, "There shall be many who will say, Do this, or do that, and it mattereth not, for the Lord will uphold such at the last day."[b] He further prophesied, "The power of God shall be denied, and churches [shall] become defiled and be lifted up in the pride of their hearts; yea . . . leaders of churches and teachers shall rise in the pride of their hearts, even to the envying of them who belong to their churches."[c]

Nevertheless, Moroni knew that regardless of when the book came forth, it would come forth because of its "great worth," and with an "eye single to [God's] glory."[d] Nephi supported this when he recorded Jesus' statement that the book would come in accordance with "the time and the will of the Father,"[e] and that it would evidence the fact that the Father had commenced His work on the earth for the last time.[f]

The restoration of the Book of Mormon heralded the beginning of many extraordinary events:

1. The Savior's ancient church was "called forth out of the wilderness"[g] and restored as an organized entity on April 6, 1830, in Fayette, New York.[46] John the Revelator had seen the church driven into the wilderness by Satan because of the "tares" the devil had sown among the wheat,[h47] but it would now function in the latter days "for the restoration of his people."[i]

2. The covenant of Abraham (so long withheld from the children of men) was reestablished, and the chosen people were again recognized by God.[j] With the restoration of the covenant came the restoration of its blessings and requirements:

    a. *The Promised Land:* Latter-day revelations established Zion as the promised land on the Western Hemisphere for all of Israel that would accept it.[k] Jerusalem on the Eastern Hemisphere would once more be inhabited by Judah until the Second Coming of Christ.[l]

a. Mormon 8:29–31.

b. Mormon 8:31.

c. Mormon 8:28.

d. Mormon 8:14–15.

e. 3 Nephi 23:4.

f. 3 Nephi 21.

g. Revelation 12:6; D&C 33:5.

h. Matthew 13:24–30, 37–43; D&C 86:1–7.

i. D&C 84:2.

j. Jeremiah 31:31–33; Hosea 2:18–23; D&C 52:2; D&C 86:9; D&C 110:12.

k. D&C 38:18–20; 48:5; 52:5, 42; 57:1–3.

l. Chapter 5.

b.   *The Priesthood:* The Aaronic Priesthood was restored by John the Baptist on May 15, 1829, and the Melchizedek Priesthood was restored by Peter, James, and John sometime before the end of June 1829.[a] The priesthood is an integral part of the gospel. Without it, no missionary work can be done and none of the saving ordinances can be performed. When the priesthood was restored, the Lord made it clear that it would continue uninterrupted until the time of His Second Coming—and beyond.[b]

c.   *The Gospel:* This is the "little stone" that Daniel saw in his vision. It will eventually roll forth and fill the whole earth.[c] This work heralds the gathering of the covenant people[d] and will overcome error and apostasy.[e] The gospel, with all of its saving principles and ordinances, will "be preached in all the world, for a witness" of the divinity of Jesus Christ,[f] and it will invite all that desire righteousness to share in the covenant of Abraham.[g] Finally, the gospel will specifically testify of Jesus Christ to the people of Judah so they might recognize their errors and eliminate their false gods.[h]

3.   Crucial keys from prior dispensations were gathered into this, the last dispensation (the dispensation of the fullness of times), in a vision received by Joseph Smith in the Kirtland Temple on April 3, 1836. In that vision:

a.   Moses returned to restore the keys for the gathering of Israel.

b.   Elias reinstated the covenant of Abraham.

c.   Elijah appeared to restore the sealing power, which will "turn the hearts of the fathers to the children, and the heart of the children to their fathers, lest [the Lord] come and smite the earth with a curse."[i][48]

The sealing power of Elijah gives man the ability to use God's power to perform the ordinances of salvation that are required to return to His kingdom. Without this sealing

---

a. D&C 13; Joseph Smith–History 1:72.

b. D&C 13.

c. Daniel 2; D&C 65:2; D&C 133:37–74.

d. Isaiah 18.

e. Isaiah 29:13–14.

f. Joseph Smith–Matthew 1:31,

g. Isaiah 55.

h. Zechariah 13:1–5.

i. D&C 110:15; Malachi 4:5–6.

power, the plan of salvation would become ineffective and no one would be able to return to God's kingdom.

With the covenant of Abraham once more upon the earth, it becomes the responsibility of those who share in the covenant to take the gospel of salvation to all the world—to teach the Gentiles, to gather Israel, and to restore Judah.

5

Judah

Isaiah 48:4–5   Because I knew that thou art obstinate, and thy neck is an iron sinew, and thy brow brass; I have even from the beginning declared it to thee; before it came to pass I shewed it thee: lest thou shouldest say, Mine idol hath done them, and my graven image, and my molten image, hath commanded them.

Matthew 23:37   O Jerusalem, Jerusalem, thou that killest the prophets, and stonest them which are sent unto thee, how often would I have gathered thy children together, even as a hen gathereth her chickens under her wings, and ye would not!

The "abomination of desolation" is a double-reference prophecy given by the Old Testament prophet Daniel.[a] It was later reiterated by the Lord in the New Testament.[b] It was fulfilled for the first time in A.D. 70 when the Romans conquered Jerusalem and scattered Judah, and it will be fulfilled for the second time after Judah has been gathered just prior to the Second Coming. The dispersion of Judah started much earlier than A.D. 70, however. It began when the Southern Kingdom was taken into captivity by Babylon circa 600 B.C.[c] A remnant of Judah's people returned to Jerusalem circa 530 B.C., but approximately 600 years later the Roman conquest completed her destruction and initiated her long diaspora. The diaspora of Judah (along with the rest of Israel) continued throughout the dark ages of apostasy and did not come to an end until early in the nineteenth century when the "times of the Gentiles" concluded with the restoration of the gospel (including the covenant of Abraham) to Joseph Smith as the restoration progressed.

a. Daniel 9:27.

b. Matthew 24:15.

c. Ezekiel 12:11–16.

Signs of the Second Coming Pertaining to Judah That Have Been Fulfilled

Once the Lord had reestablished His church in the latter days as an ensign to the world, it was time to "assemble the outcasts of Israel, and gather together the dispersed of Judah from the four corners of the earth."[a] In a vision granted to Joseph Smith in 1823, the angel Moroni quoted this same scripture and declared that it was about to be fulfilled, meaning that the gathering of both Israel and Judah would now begin.[b] Moses, who had gathered Israel from Egypt and led them to the promised land of Canaan centuries before, restored the keys of the gathering of Israel to Joseph Smith in the Kirtland Temple on April 3, 1836.[c] A few years later, Joseph dispatched Orson Hyde (a man of Jewish descent and one of the first latter-day Apostles) to Palestine to specifically dedicate that land for the gathering of the tribe of Judah. On October 24, 1841, Elder Hyde delivered the following in his dedicatory prayer as he stood on the Mount of Olives in Jerusalem:

> Now, O Lord! Thy servant has been obedient to the heavenly vision which Thou gavest him in his native land; and under the shadow of Thine outstretched arm, he has safely arrived in this place to dedicate and consecrate this land unto Thee, for the gathering together of Judah's scattered remnants, according to the predictions of the holy Prophets—for the building up of Jerusalem again after it has been trodden down by the Gentiles so long, and for rearing a Temple in honor of Thy name. . . .
>
> Grant, therefore, O Lord, in the name of Thy well-beloved Son, Jesus Christ, to remove the barrenness and sterility of this land, and let springs of living water break forth to water its thirsty soil. Let the vine and olive produce in their strength, and the fig-tree bloom and flourish. Let the land become abundantly fruitful when possessed by its rightful heirs; let it again flow with plenty to feed the returning prodigals who come home with a spirit of grace and supplication.[49]

Elder Hyde's prayer thus initiated the long-predicted gathering of the tribe of Judah.

The spirit of gathering is interesting in that it moves on those to be

a. Isaiah 11:12.

b. Joseph Smith–History 1:40.

c. D&C 110:11.

gathered without direction from any earthly source. In one of Elder Hyde's reports, he stated that "the idea of the Jews being restored to Palestine is gaining ground in Europe almost every day . . . the great wheel is unquestionably in motion, and the word of the Almighty has declared that it shall roll."[50]

Perhaps even more interesting than Elder Hyde's comment is the report Golda Meir made in her autobiography regarding the spirit of gathering:

> A great deal has already been written—and much more will certainly be written in the future—about the Zionist movement, and most people by now have at least some notion of what the word 'Zionism' means and that it has to do with the return of the Jewish people to the land of their forefathers—the Land of Israel, as it is called in Hebrew. But perhaps even today not everyone realizes that *this remarkable movement sprang up spontaneously, and more or less simultaneously, in various parts of Europe toward the end of the nineteenth century.* It was like a drama that was being enacted in different ways on different stages in different languages but that dealt with the same theme everywhere: that the so-called Jewish problem (of course, it was really a Christian problem) was basically the result of Jewish homelessness and that it could not, and would not, be solved unless and until the Jews had a land of their own again. Obviously, this land could only be Zion, the land from which the Jews had been exiled 2,000 years before but which had remained the spiritual center of Jewry throughout the centuries and which, when I was a little girl in Pinsk and up to the end of World War I, was a desolate and neglected province of the Ottoman Empire called Palestine.[51]

Although Golda Meir probably did not fully understand the origins of the movement she described, and had undoubtedly never heard of Orson Hyde, her description of the results of Elder Hyde's prayer and the movement of the spirit of gathering on the descendants of Judah could not have been more eloquent.

Isaiah foresaw this gathering and the process by which it would occur. He declared in beautiful prose that the Lord was the means by which salvation would be extended to both the Gentiles and to Israel.[a] He further prophesied of the gathering's commencement, declaring that the covenant of Abraham would be made available to the Gentiles and to Israel and that those so long in captivity would "go forth" and be free: they would be gathered "from far," "from the north and from the west," from the "land of Sinim," (whereabouts specifically unknown but assumed to be the most distant lands of the earth) from wherever they had been scattered. Isaiah exulted in the Lord's promise: "Sing, O heavens; and be joyful, O earth; and break forth into singing, O mountains: for the Lord hath comforted his people, and will have mercy upon his afflicted."[b]

Isaiah's prophecy notes that Israel complained bitterly during her long period of dispersion, claiming that the Lord had forgotten His chosen people. But, as the scripture states, "can a woman forget her sucking child, that she should not have compassion on the son of her womb?" "Yea," the Savior said, "they may forget [their Lord], yet will I not forget [Israel]."[c]

Isaiah continues to describe the gathering process by declaring that the gathering will be so great that the land will be "too narrow by reason of the inhabitants"— too small to contain those who want to gather to the Holy Land.[d] Under the Lord's direction the Spirit will move upon all, even kings and queens, to assist in the gathering process: "even the captives of the mighty shall be taken away, and the prey of the terrible" delivered from oppression, for the Savior declared, "I will contend with him that contendeth with thee, and I will save thy children."[e] "I will feed them that oppress thee with their own flesh; and they shall be drunken with their own blood, as with sweet wine: and all flesh shall know that I the Lord am thy Saviour and thy Redeemer, the mighty One of Jacob."[f]

The prophesied assistance from kings and queens had at least a partial fulfillment with the _Balfour Declaration._ The _Balfour Declaration,_ named for Arthur James Balfour, Britain's foreign secretary under King George V, was published on November 2, 1917. Couched in the form of a letter from Lord Balfour to Lord Rothschild, the British government committed itself to "the establishment in Palestine of a National Home for the Jewish People." The British government

a. Isaiah 49:4–6.

b. Isaiah 49:7–13.

c. Isaiah 49:14–16.

d. Isaiah 49:17–20.

e. Isaiah 49:22–25.

f. Isaiah 49:26.

declared that it would use "its best endeavors to facilitate the achievement of this objective."[52] Although progress was delayed by the First and Second World Wars, on November 29, 1947, the United Nations finally voted for the partition of Palestine and the end of the British Mandate. Thirty-three nations voted in favor, 10 abstained, and 13 were against the partition.[53] May 14, 1948, was the day the United Nations established as the deadline for the termination of the British Mandate in Palestine. On this day, the Jewish National Council assembled and resolved that "by virtue of our natural and historic right and of the resolution of the General Assembly of the United Nations, [we] do hereby proclaim the establishment of a Jewish state in the Land of Israel—the State of Israel."[54]

The creation of the State of Israel fulfilled Isaiah's prophecy concerning the restoration of Judah. Nephi cited this prophecy from Isaiah 40:9 and stated that "after they were restored they should no more be confounded, neither should they be scattered again."[a] The establishment of Israel was also a fulfillment of the 1841 prayer of Elder Hyde and the words that Zechariah uttered 500 years before Christ: "And the Lord shall inherit Judah his portion in the holy land, and shall choose Jerusalem again."[b][55]

However, Zechariah's prophecy was not completely fulfilled with the establishment of the State of Israel in 1948. The city of Jerusalem was divided between the Jews and the Palestinians at the time the State was created, and continued to be divided until the Six Day War of 1967 when Israel captured the old city.[56] At the conclusion of the Six Day War, the Holy City was once again under the control of Judah. After stating that the Lord would reestablish Judah in the holy land and "choose Jerusalem again," Zechariah continued his prophecy: "In that day will I make the governors of Judah like an hearth of fire among the wood, and like a torch of fire in a sheaf; and they shall devour all the people round about, on the right hand and on the left: and Jerusalem shall be inhabited again in her own place, even in Jerusalem."[c] This same prophecy was also made by Isaiah;[d] by the Lord;[e] and by Orson Hyde.[57]

The balance of Isaiah's prophecy regarding the "captives of the mighty" being taken away and the "prey of the terrible" being delivered from captivity may have had its fulfillment in many individual stories

a. 1 Nephi 15:20.

b. Zechariah 2:12.

c. Zechariah 2:12; 12:6.

d. Isaiah 62:5–12.

e. 3 Nephi 20:29, 33–34.

of miraculous deliverances, but it also appears to have been fulfilled in at least two major instances. The condition of the Jews under Hitler's Third Reich fits Isaiah's description of Judah as the "prey" of the mighty; and while millions of Jews were killed in the Holocaust, there were many survivors from countries all over Europe who finally made their way back to Israel. Another example was the USSR, one of the last modern strongholds of Jewish captivity. When the Russian empire disintegrated, many Jewish citizens were free to return to the Holy Land. Both of these dictatorial regimes seem to fit into Isaiah's prophetic description wherein he foresaw that the Lord would cause those who oppress Judah to "feed" upon their own flesh and become drunken with their own "blood"— a poetic description of their self-destructive activities and policies.[a]

When Elder Hyde gave his dedicatory prayer in Jerusalem, he blessed Palestine that it would rise from the "desolate and neglected" state Golda Meir described[58] to a highly productive state. This, too, was in fulfillment of ancient prophecy. Ezekiel described the dispersion and restoration of Judah and declared that in the latter days, "the desolate land shall be tilled . . . And [the people] shall say, This land that was desolate is become like the garden of Eden; and the waste and desolate and ruined cities are become fenced, and are inhabited."[b] Amos, also speaking of the latter days, declared that Israel would "build the waste cities, and inhabit them," and "plant vineyards, and drink the wine thereof," and "also make gardens, and eat the fruit of them." He prophesied that the Lord would "plant them upon their land." "No more" would they be "pulled up" out of the land the Lord had given them.[c] One need only look at modern-day Israel to see the literal fulfillment of these prophesies. Through their ingenuity and hard work, Israel has tilled and planted to make the desolate land blossom and become as the Garden of Eden.

Another of Isaiah's prophecies was fulfilled while Israel was in its birth pangs. He foresaw Judah receiving "sons from far [away]" bringing "silver" and "gold" during her restoration.[d] Wilford Woodruff made a similar prophecy when he said, "They [Judah] will go and rebuild Jerusalem and their temple. They will take their gold and silver from the nations and will gather to the Holy Land."[59] In literal fulfillment of these gathering prophecies, Golda Meir was sent to the United

a. Isaiah 49:26.

b. Ezekiel 36:34–35.

c. Amos 9:14–15; Isaiah 29:17; 35:1–2.

d. Isaiah 60:9.

States in January of 1948 on a nationwide speaking engagement; she returned to Israel with $50,000,000 to be used in building the nation's defenses.[60] Many nations (principally the United States) have given foreign aid to Israel since that time, and many Jewish individuals and groups from around the world have made private contributions to the building up of the Holy Land.

Today, with the land of their inheritance restored, the Jews once again have a "promised land"—a place to call home.

Future Signs to Judah

Although the establishment of Israel and the gathering of the tribe of Judah have produced a strong nation, many great signs pertaining to the Jews have yet to occur before the Lord comes again.

Spiritual Enlightenment: The Lord will "pardon" the sins of the tribe of Judah.[a] After suffering through centuries of the diaspora, they will yet be sanctified by their God[b] and will again become a "delightsome people," meaning righteous or acceptable before the Lord.[c] The truths of the Book of Mormon will be taught to them and to all the "remnant of the house of Israel," and will serve as a witness to them that their long-awaited Messiah came in the meridian of time and will come again in the latter days.[d]

Zechariah prophesied that as the people of Judah again begin to believe in God as their deliverer and in Jesus as their Savior, their centuries of spiritual darkness will be replaced by the light of truth. He declared that "in those days it shall come to pass, that ten men shall take hold out of all languages of the nations, even shall take hold of the skirt of him that is a Jew, saying, We will go with you: for we have heard that God is with you."[e] There are great spiritual blessings yet in store for Judah as her people begin to believe in the God who has restored and gathered them. In time, they will come to recognize Him as their Messiah.[61]

The Temple and the Daily Sacrifice: The first temple in Jerusalem was built by Solomon approximately 3,000 years ago. It was destroyed when Babylon captured Judah circa 600–560 B.C. A second temple was built by the returning Babylonian exiles and was later greatly enlarged and refurbished by Herod the Great. It was destroyed by Rome in A.D. 70. A third temple is yet to be built in Jerusalem. It will be

a. Isaiah 40:1–2.

b. Hosea 1:7;
   D&C 109:64;
   133:35.

c. 2 Nephi 30:7.

d. 3 Nephi
   29:8; Mormon
   5:12–15.

e. Zechariah
   8:23.

built upon the same temple mount as the temples of antiquity. Many prophets have seen this temple in visions from the Lord. Ezekiel described its size and layout.[a] Isaiah described its beauty: "The glory of Lebanon shall come unto thee, the fir tree, the pine tree, and the box together, to beautify the place of my sanctuary; and I will make the place of my feet glorious."[b] Zechariah was told that the Lord's house would again be built in Jerusalem,[c] and he saw in vision the day when "the foundation of the house of the Lord of Hosts was laid."[d] He also saw those who would build and occupy it.[e] Finally, the prophet Wilford Woodruff was also shown by the Lord that the temple in Jerusalem would be built in the latter days.[62]

Once the temple in Israel is completed, sacrifice will again be offered by the sons of Levi "unto the Lord in righteousness."[f][63]

Wars and the Fall of Jerusalem: It is possible that the construction (or attempted construction) of the temple in Jerusalem and the offering of sacrifice therein may be the catalyst that will bring the fulfillment of other prophecies to Judah. Prior to the Second Coming, Jerusalem will again be engulfed by her enemies. The Holy City will be encircled by what John described as an army of 200,000,000 men.[g] This may be literal, but more likely it is symbolically describing an army of enormous size that will rise up against Israel in the last days.[64] Nonetheless, after a siege that will last for three and one-half years and following the great battle of Armageddon, the ancient city of Jerusalem will fall to her enemies.[h]

In verses twelve through sixteen of the 16th chapter of Revelation, John symbolically described how the devil will exercise his power and influence in the latter days so that nations will rise up to destroy Jerusalem (the symbol of God). This period of destruction will occur at the culmination of the devil's power on the earth just prior to the Second Coming, and it is described by John as the great "plague" of the "sixth angel."

Two Prophets to Judah

Revelation 11:1–12 And there was given me a reed like unto a rod: and the angel stood, saying, Rise, and measure the temple of God, and the altar, and them that worship therein. But the court which is without the temple leave out, and measure it not; for it is given unto the Gentiles: and the holy city shall they tread under foot forty and two months. And I will give power unto my two witnesses, and they shall prophesy

a. Ezekiel 40.

b. Isaiah 60:13.

c. Zechariah 1:16.

d. Zechariah 8:9.

e. Zechariah 6:13–15; 8:7–9.

f. D&C 13:1.

g. Revelation 9:16.

h. Joel 3:1–8; Revelation 11:2.

a thousand two hundred and threescore days, clothed in sackcloth. These are the two olive trees, and the two candlesticks standing before the God of the earth. And if any man will hurt them, fire proceedeth out of their mouth, and devoureth their enemies: and if any man will hurt them, he must in this manner be killed. These have power to shut heaven, that it rain not in the days of their prophecy: and have power over waters to turn them to blood, and to smite the earth with all plagues, as often as they will. And when they shall have finished their testimony, the beast that ascendeth out of the bottomless pit shall make war against them, and shall overcome them, and kill them. And their dead bodies shall lie in the street of the great city, which spiritually is called Sodom and Egypt, where also our Lord was crucified. And they of the people and kindreds and tongues and nations shall see their dead bodies three days and an half, and shall not suffer their dead bodies to be put in graves. And they that dwell upon the earth shall rejoice over them, and make merry, and shall send gifts one to another; because these two prophets tormented them that dwelt on the earth. And after three days and an half the Spirit of life from God entered into them, and they stood upon their feet; and great fear fell upon them which saw them. And they heard a great voice from heaven saying unto them, Come up hither. And they ascended up to heaven in a cloud; and their enemies beheld them.

Sometime during the last great battles that will occur near Jerusalem prior to the Second Coming, two prophets will be raised up to Judah. Their arrival will be a specific sign of the Lord's imminent Advent. Some have speculated that they will be Apostles of The Church of Jesus Christ of Latter-day Saints;[65] others feel that they will either be Apostles or members of the First Presidency.[66] There is also the possibility that they will come from Judah herself, raised up independent of the Church as prophets to that branch of God's chosen people.

God has often raised up multiple prophets to different parts of Israel. In the eighth century B.C., He raised up Amos and Hosea to the Northern Kingdom of Israel, and Micah and Isaiah to the Southern Kingdom of Judah.[67] There is no record that these prophets knew of or communicated with each other. Lehi was raised up during the time of Jeremiah to warn Jerusalem of God's pending judgments. Later, he and his followers were led to the Western Hemisphere while Jeremiah remained on the Eastern Hemisphere to prophesy to Judah. During His ministry, Christ described Lehi's descendants as "other sheep" who were not of the tribe of Judah. After His resurrection, the Apostles on the Eastern Hemisphere established the Lord's church and preached His gospel while His disciples on the Western Hemisphere did the same thing. Although the disciples of the Western Hemisphere knew of Judah in the East, Judah knew nothing of the descendants of Lehi in the West.[a]

God clearly states that He will bring forth His word to "the children of men, yea, even upon all the nations of the earth."[b] "I shall speak unto the Jews and they shall write it; and I shall also speak unto the Nephites and they shall write it; and I shall also speak unto the other [lost] tribes of the house of Israel, which I have led away, and they shall write it . . . the Jews shall have the words of the Nephites, and the Nephites shall have the words of the Jews; and the Nephites and the Jews shall have the words of the lost tribes of Israel; and the lost tribes of Israel shall have the words of the Nephites and the Jews."[c] Nephi confirms in these scriptures that the Lord speaks to His chosen people and can obviously raise up prophets from any of them.

The two unique prophets who will preach to Judah in the last days were seen in vision by John the Revelator,[d] Isaiah,[e] and Zechariah.[f] The scriptures state that they will prophesy to Judah and the Gentiles with great power for three and one-half years prior to the Lord's coming while the last terrible siege of Jerusalem rages around them.[g][68] God will protect them from harm during this period.[h] He will give them the power to shut the heavens "that it rain not," and they will have "power over waters" to pollute them, and "to smite the earth with all plagues, as often as they will."[i] Finally, when the Second Coming draws nigh, they will be killed by the conquering armies entering Jerusalem. Their bodies will lie in the streets for three and one-half days[j] while the enemies of Israel throughout the world rejoice at their deaths and revel in their victory over the Jews.[k]

But their revelry will be short lived, for at the end of the three and one-half days, "the Spirit of life from God" will enter into the two prophets and they will stand "upon their feet," which will cause "great fear" to fall upon Judah's adversaries. The two prophets will then hear "a great voice from heaven saying unto them, Come up hither." And they will ascend "up to heaven in a cloud," and their enemies will watch them disappear.[l] It is at this time that the Savior will deliver Judah from her enemies and lead her to victory[69] in a campaign so devastating that Ezekiel metaphorically declares that the implements of war taken from the enemy will provide fuel for the fires of Judah's people for the next seven years.[m]

a. 3 Nephi 16:4.

b. 2 Nephi 29:7.

c. 2 Nephi 29:12–13.

d. Revelation 11.

e. Isaiah 51:18–20.

f. Zechariah 4:11–14.

g. Revelation 11:2–3.

h. Revelation 11:5.

i. Revelation 11:6.

j. Revelation 11:9.

k. Revelation 11:10.

l. Revelation 11:11–12.

m. Ezekiel 39:8–10.

Another David to lead Judah in the latter days: Orson Hyde petitioned the Lord in his dedicatory prayer to "constitute [Judah's] people a distinct nation and government, with David Thy servant, even a descendant from the loins of ancient David to be their king."[70] While some scriptures indicate that this great leader will be like David of old (raised up to assist in Israel's final delivery), and other scriptures seem to anticipate a strong political leader whose name will be David,[a] it would be more logical to interpret these references as symbolically referring to Christ, who is a descendant of David and who is the true King of the Jews.

Isaiah described this great deliverer as coming forth from the "stem of Jesse . . . out of his roots."[b] The "stem of Jesse" is Jesus Christ,[c] the same deity who gave the vision in Revelation to John the Revelator and who stated therein that He was "the root and the offspring of David."[d] The Savior will stand as the ensign for the Gentiles and the gathering of Judah[e] and will defend "the inhabitants of Jerusalem"[f] when the children of Israel turn again and seek the Lord their God. Jacob's original blessing on Judah foreshadowed this interpretation. The Torah states: "The scepter shall not depart from Judah, nor the ruler's staff from between his feet; So that tribute shall come to him" (emphasis added). Then, in defining the word tribute, The Torah states that it means "literally, 'until he comes to Shiloh,' or 'until Shiloh comes'. . . . One Jewish tradition, taking Jacob's blessing to be a prophecy for the end of time . . . interpreted 'Shiloh' to mean the Messiah, a new David who would come out of the house of Judah."[71] It thus seems clear from the scriptures that the "other David" will be the same individual whom David acknowledged as his King;[g] the leader who entered Jerusalem at the conclusion of His ministry as its King;[h] and the deity who declared to Isaiah, "I am the Lord, your Holy One, the creator of Israel, your King."[i][72]

Earthquakes and the Mount of Olives: After the two unique prophets seen by John the Revelator ascend into heaven (as described in Chapter 11 of Revelation), a great and devastating earthquake will occur which John symbolically states will destroy a tenth part of the city of Jerusalem and will kill seven thousand men—not to mention women and children.[j][73] There will be "voices, and thunders, and lightnings; and there was a great earthquake, such as was not since men

a. Ezekiel 34:23–24; Jeremiah 30:9.

b. Isaiah 11:1.

c. D&C 113:1–2.

d. Revelation 5:5; 22:16.

e. Isaiah 11:10; D&C 113:6.

f. Zechariah 12:8.

g. Psalm 44:4.

h. Zechariah 9:9; John 12:14–15.

i. Isaiah 43:15.

j. Revelation 11:13.

were upon the earth."[a] The Mount of Olives will cleave in two from east to west, "and there shall be a very great valley [formed]; and half of the mountain shall remove toward the north, and half of it toward the south."[b]

The Lord appears to Judah: Terrified by the enormous earthquake, many of the Jews will run into the newly formed "valley of the mountains" where the Lord will appear to them.[c] He will bear the wounds of His crucifixion on Him, and one will say, "What are these wounds in thine hands?" He will answer, "Those with which I was wounded in the house of my friends."[d] Then will the Jews recognize their Messiah, and weep and lament and worship Him[e]— and the Savior will deliver Judah and rule thereafter in Jerusalem.[74]

As the Lord ushers in His reign, Jerusalem will become the "mountain of the Lord's house"[f] and will become one of two great earthly capitals from which He will reign for a thousand years.[75]

The Promised Land: When the Second Coming occurs, the land of Jerusalem (the promised land) will revert back to its "own place"—perhaps physically as well as spiritually.[g] The land will be restored to the twelve tribes of Israel[h] for their inheritance,[i] Israel's former enemies will be overcome, the animosity between Judah and Ephraim eliminated, and the way provided for the other tribes to join them.[j] Jerusalem and Zion will be established together;[k] "for out of Zion shall go forth the law, and the word of the Lord [shall go forth] from Jerusalem."[l]

a. Revelation 16:18.

b. Zechariah 14:4.

c. Zechariah 14:5; Revelation 1:7.

d. Zechariah 13:6; 12:10; John 19:37.

e. D&C 45:52–53.

f. Isaiah 2:2–3; Psalm 122:1–9; D&C 133:13

g. D&C 133:24.

h. Ezekiel 45:4–8.

i. 3 Nephi 20:29.

j. Isaiah 11:13–15.

k. Isaiah 2:2–3; 3 Nephi 20:34–46; Ether 13:4–11.

l. Isaiah 2:3.

The Gathering

6

Ezekiel 37:21   Thus saith the Lord God; Behold, I will take the children of Israel from among the heathen, whither they be gone, and will gather them on every side, and bring them into their own land.

Jacob, whose name was changed to Israel by the Lord, had twelve sons: Reuben, Simeon, Levi, Judah, Zebulun, Issachar, Dan, Gad, Asher, Naphtali, Joseph, and Benjamin. These twelve sons became known as the house of Israel, the twelve tribes of Israel, or just Israel. God chose these tribes to be His people. He declared to Moses, "Ye shall be a peculiar treasure unto me above all people."[a][76] Isaiah confirmed this unique selection when he declared, "Thus saith the Lord that created thee, O Jacob, and he that formed thee, O Israel . . . I am the Lord, your Holy One, the creator of Israel."[b]

Israel was a united nation for the most part until the death of Solomon. After his death, the nation was divided and became known as the Northern Kingdom and the Southern Kingdom. The Northern Kingdom was also called the Kingdom of Israel. It was inhabited by the tribes of Reuben, Simeon, Zebulun, Issachar, Dan, Gad, Asher, Naphtali, and large parts of Benjamin, Joseph, and Levi. This kingdom was conquered by Assyria circa 721 B.C. The tribes living therein, having been rejected by the Lord due to their wickedness, were carried off by the Assyrians and became lost.[c] They have since been described as the *lost ten tribes* or *the lost tribes of Israel.*[d]

After the destruction of the Northern Kingdom, the Southern Kingdom eventually became known as Israel. It was also known as the

a. Exodus 19:5; in The Torah translation the same verse reads: "You shall be My treasured possession among all the peoples."

b. Isaiah 43:1, 15.

c. 2 Kings 17:6; 18:11–12.

d. 2 Nephi 29:13; 3 Nephi 17:4; 21:26.

Kingdom of Judah because Judah was the only whole tribe to inhabit it (although parts of the tribes of Benjamin, Levi, Joseph, and individual members of other tribes also resided there). Because of the predominance of the tribe of Judah, those of the populace who belonged to other tribes also became known politically as Jews. An example of this is the prophet Lehi. He records that he was a descendant of Joseph,[a] yet his son Nephi records that the remnants of his seed were Jews.[b] A second example is found in the book of Esther. Mordecai, who raised Esther, was introduced in the text as "a certain Jew," yet he was of the tribe of Benjamin.[c] Eventually (and especially today), the terms *Jews* and *Israel* have become synonymous. This amalgamation of terminology is the predominant reason for the apostate belief that the doctrine of the gathering concerns only the Jews. The Jews themselves have adopted this amalgamation of their name to the extent that they project it not only forward but also backward, at least as far as the Exodus, where one commentary on *The Torah* states that the purpose of the Passover Seder is to "[rehearse] the Exodus and the birth of the Jewish people."[77] In this quotation they clearly use the term *Jewish* rather than *Israelite.*

As the Lord told Nephi, however, "Know ye not that there are more nations than one?"[d] Twelve tribes were scattered, and twelve tribes must be gathered.

No church can claim to be God's true church without teaching the doctrine of the gathering correctly and claiming that God is the source of its authority to gather the people. The gathering is one of the greatest signs the people of the earth will receive to confirm the fact that the Savior's ancient gospel has been restored and that His Second Coming is at hand. It is also one of the doctrines that creates the most confusion in the Christian and Jewish worlds. While the gathering is defined as the physical accumulation of the people of Israel to their promised lands, it also denotes the gathering of all the people of the world—Jew and Gentile—to the Lord and His gospel.[e]

In the strict sense, a Gentile is someone who has descended from Japheth, the oldest[f] son of Noah.[g] However, the term *Gentile* is used in multiple ways throughout the scriptures to describe (1) those nations into which Israel was scattered, (2) the heathen, (3) the unrighteous,

a. 1 Nephi 5:14.

b. 2 Nephi 30:4.

c. Esther 2:5.

d. 2 Nephi 29:7.

e. Isaiah 49:6.

f. Moses 8:12; IV Genesis 7:85.

g. Genesis 10:1–5.

(4) those not of Israel, and (5) non-Jews.[78] For the purpose of gathering the people of the earth to the gospel, the term *Gentile* would include all of the above as well as those who are neither Israelite nor Gentile: i.e., those of the seed of Abraham who are descendants of Ishmael and Abraham's other children, and those who descended from Noah's son Ham. Even though these races are not classified as Gentiles in other situations and are not specifically referred to in the gathering scriptures, Isaiah 49:6 makes it clear that the Lord's gospel is to be offered to *all* the people of the earth. Therefore, this general gathering of the repentant to the gospel is inclusive of all peoples.[a]

The story of the scattering and gathering of Israel (including all who repent and come into the kingdom of God) is told by Zenos in his familiar allegory of the vineyard. The allegory compares Israel and the Gentiles to trees and branches in a vineyard. The vineyard represents the world, God the Father is the master of the vineyard, Jesus is the servant, and the others are the Savior's prophets, missionaries or representatives.[b] Israel is likened to a tame olive tree planted in the vineyard. The olive tree flourishes for a time, but eventually the master sees that it is beginning to decay, so he prunes and digs around it (allegorically calling Israel to repentance). After the pruning, the vineyard begins to bring forth tender new branches. These branches represent the Moses period where through repentance and recommitment, Israel returns to the covenant[c] and (after the generation of unbelievers die in the wilderness) is led into the promised land.[d] But in the allegory, the main top of the tree begins to perish,[e] so the master of the vineyard instructs the servant to "pluck the branches from a wild olive-tree" and replace the "main branches which are beginning to wither away."[f] The wild branches represent the Gentiles who were either conquered by or assimilated into the tribes of Israel while Israel occupied the promised land.[g]

The servant continues to work in the vineyard and eventually transplants many of the "natural branches of the tree" into the "nethermost" part of the vineyard (the lost ten tribes).[h] He then continues to prune (via the Babylonian conquest and captivity) the better parts of the vineyard where the "wild branches" have been grafted in until the tree (Judah) again produces good fruit, "like unto the natural fruit."[i] When

a. 2 Nephi
    30:1–2.

b. See Jacob 5.

c. Jacob 5:4–6.

d. Jacob 5:7–9.

e. Jacob 5:6.

f. Jacob 5:7.

g. Jacob 5:10.

h. Jacob 5:11–15;
    Nehemiah 1:9.

i. Jacob 5:16–18.

he goes to view the natural branches that he hid in the nethermost part of the vineyard (the ten tribes), he finds that they, too, have produced "much fruit."[a]

Then the master of the vineyard directs the servant to "look hither and behold the last [tree]." The master had planted this tree in a "good spot of ground" and nourished it for a long time. But only part of the tree brought forth "tame fruit" while the rest of the tree brought forth "wild fruit," even though he had nourished this tree the same as the others. This tree allegorically represents the branch of Joseph (the Nephites and the Lamanites), which was led from Jerusalem and transplanted into the best part of the vineyard (the Western Hemisphere) at the time of Jeremiah. The branches that are "part tame" represent the Nephites, and those that are "part wild" depict the Lamanites. The master wants the servant to "pluck off the branches" that have not produced good fruit and "cast them into the fire." But the servant petitions the master to have patience and "nourish" the tree a little longer.[b] The master agrees to do this, and for a time he and the servant continue to nourish *all* the trees in the vineyard.

A long time passes.[c] The master and the servant again go to labor in the vineyard. They find that the tame olive tree into which they grafted the wild branches (representing Judah after her return from Babylon up to the time of Christ) has produced much wild fruit, none of it good. The allegory then makes specific mention of the "natural branches" that were planted in the best part of the vineyard (the Nephites and the Lamanites who replaced the Jaredites, an earlier planting by the Lord).[d] The "natural branches" have also produced wild fruit and have totally overcome that part of the tree "which brought forth good fruit, even that the branch had withered away and died" (the destruction of the Nephites by the Lamanites).[e] All the trees in the vineyard have become corrupt (from the time of the Savior's earthly ministry until the Apostasy) and are producing only wild fruit. They have all overcome their roots (the covenant of Abraham).[f] And although with much work the vineyard will again produce good fruit for a short period of time (after the Lord's resurrection), eventually all parts of the vineyard will become corrupt (go into total apostasy).[g]

It grieves the master to lose his trees. "Who is it," he asks, "that

a. Jacob 5:19–22.

b. Jacob 5:25–28.

c. Jacob 5:29.

d. Jacob 5:38–51.

e. Jacob 5:40–43.

f. Jacob 5:38–39.

g. Jacob 5:38–51.

has corrupted my vineyard?"[a] And the servant explains that it is the loftiness of the vineyard (the self-righteousness of the leaders and the people) which has overcome the strong, righteous roots of the trees.[b]

The master again wants to destroy the vineyard, but the servant convinces him to withdraw the wild branches and restore the natural branches back to the tame olive tree (preparing the people for the restoration of the gospel and the gathering of the righteous).[c] The master agrees, and new servants are called to labor in the vineyard. The master gives them the covenant and instructs them to clean out the wild branches and again bring back the natural branches to the tame tree (the gathering of Israel). He then causes them to prune the vineyard for the last time.[d] (Laborers will be called to spread the gospel in the latter-days, and the fruits of their labors [the righteous] will be gathered to God in preparation for the Lord's Second Coming).[e]

After the Lord's final Advent, a "long time" will be spent "gathering the good fruit from his vineyard" (gleaning the righteous from the world during the millennial period). But eventually, the vineyard will again be infested with evil, and the master will cause both the good fruit and the bad fruit to be gathered: the good He will preserve unto Himself, and the bad He will "cast away into its own place in preparation for the final judgment. "And then," the Lord concludes, "cometh the [little] season and the end; and my vineyard [the world] will I cause to be burned with fire."[f]

Five distinct groups of people must be gathered in preparation for the Second Coming of the Lord: Judah, the ten lost tribes, the Lamanites (Manasseh), Ephraim, and the Gentiles (which would include the Arabs and those of African descent).

Judah

Judah is to be gathered to Jerusalem, a scriptural synonym for the promised land which is now encompassed within the State of Israel.[g]

The Ten Lost Tribes

Since the ten tribes are *lost,* any reference to their location is speculative. And while individual members of any given tribe may be located and brought within the gospel covenant, the unit of Israel known as the

a. Jacob 5:46–47, 49.
b. Jacob 5:48.
c. Jacob 5:51–60.
d. Jacob 5:61–69.
e. Jacob 5:70–74.
f. Jacob 5:75–77; Matthew 13:24–30; D&C 101:44–62.
g. Chapter 5.

lost tribes will not be *found* until the Second Coming. The following information is all we know about them:

1. Joseph Smith stated that John the Revelator was preaching among them.[79]

2. They are described as being located in the "north" countries. We know from the Doctrine and Covenants and the book of Jeremiah, however, that the Lord remembers them.[a]

3. The Savior went to the lost tribes after His resurrection and ministered to them.[b]

4. In the last days, the "work of the Father" will commence among them (albeit, this work will be independent of the Church because these tribes are lost).[c]

5. Their scriptural records will eventually be available to the other tribes.[d]

6. They will be gathered out from the wicked at the destruction of the devil's kingdom.[e]

7. They will be gathered from the north country[80] to join the other tribes of Israel (Judah and Joseph).[f]

8. At their return, a great highway will be cast up (probably not an actual highway but the symbolical means by which the Lord will gather them).[g]

9. Their former enemies "will become a prey unto them."[h]

10. They will eventually receive all of the blessings of the covenant of Abraham in Zion: the gospel will be preached to them, and they will receive their glory.[i]

11. They will bring their treasures to the tribe of Ephraim in Zion, "And there shall they fall down and be crowned with glory, even in Zion, by the hands of the servants of the Lord, even the children of Ephraim."[j]

12. Songs of everlasting joy will be sung at their return.[k][81]

a. Jeremiah 16:14–15; D&C 110:11; D&C 133:26.

b. 3 Nephi 17:4.

c. 3 Nephi 21:26.

d. 2 Nephi 29:13.

e. Isaiah 13:5, 14–22.

f. Jeremiah 3:18; Zechariah 2:6; Articles of Faith 1:10.

g. Isaiah 11:16; Isiah 35:8–10; D&C 133:27.

h. D&C 133:28.

i. Isaiah 35:8–10; 3 Nephi 21:26; D&C 133:28.

j. D&C 133:32; Isaiah 60:8–12.

k. D&C 133:33.

The Lamanites

Even though the Lamanites are described in the allegory of the vine-yard as an unrighteous and wild branch of the tame olive tree, the Book of Mormon promises that they will be preserved and their days prolonged until the time that they are gathered[a] and grafted back into the olive tree as a natural branch.[b] The desire to gather the Lamanites to the restored gospel of Jesus Christ commenced soon after the organization of the Church in April of 1830. During a conference of the Church on September 26, 1830, several brethren expressed the desire to serve a mission to the Lamanites. Joseph inquired of the Lord concerning this and what is now section 32 of the Doctrine and Covenants was received in response. The Lord's revelation in this section commenced missionary work among the Lamanites.

One purpose of the Book of Mormon is to convince the Lamanites of the truthfulness of the gospel.[c] In addition, through this book they will come to realize that they are of the house of Israel[d] and that it was prophesied that the gospel would be taken to them.[e]

Because of this opportunity, many Lamanites will be called to repentance, will receive the Bible and the Book of Mormon, will accept Christ, and will once again come under the covenant of Abraham.[f] Once they accept these blessings, their civilization will flourish in the wilderness and "blossom as the rose."[g][82]

Ephraim

The Lord's ancient prophets prophesied that almost immediately after the restoration of the gospel, missionaries would be sent forth to declare its glad tidings.[h] They would be sent to the nations of the world and the isles of the sea to gather Israel home.[i][83] They would gather a scattered Ephraim[j] and all Israel from the four quarters of the earth.[k]

Just as the spirit of gathering moved on the tribe of Judah after Orson Hyde's dedicatory prayer,[l] so also did it move on those who heard the gospel of salvation preached in Great Britain during the early years of the Church (even though Joseph Smith instructed those leaving for the British mission *not* to teach the gathering until the gospel had been established there and the Spirit clearly manifested otherwise).[84] However, the keys of the gathering had been restored,[m] and the gathering spirit moved upon mankind regardless of whether the missionaries taught it or not.

a. Helaman 15:11–16.

b. 1 Nephi 15:16.

c. Mormon 5:12–15.

d. 2 Nephi 30:3–6.

e. 1 Nephi 15:14; Alma 9:16–17; 3 Nephi 20–21.

f. Mormon 7:1–10.

g. D&C 49:24; 3 Nephi 5:21–26.

h. Isaiah 18; Jeremiah 16:14–16.

i. D&C 133:7–8.

j. Zechariah 10:6–12.

k. Matthew 24:31; 1 Nephi 22:25; D&C 133:7.

l. Chapter 5.

m. D&C 110:11.

No sooner were the people baptized than they were seized with a desire to gather with the main body of the Church. "I find it is difficult to keep anything from the Saints," writes Elder Taylor in his journal of this period, "for the Spirit of God reveals it to them. . . . Some time ago Sister Mitchell dreamed that she, her husband and a number of others were on board a vessel, and that there were other vessels, loaded with Saints, going somewhere. She felt very happy and was rejoicing in the Lord." Another sister, Elder Taylor informs us, had a similar dream, and was informed that all the Saints were going. Neither of these sisters nor any of the Saints at that time, knew anything about the principle of gathering, yet all were anxious to leave their homes, their kindred and the associations of a lifetime, to join the main body of the Church in a distant land, the members of which were total strangers to them. The same spirit has rested upon the people in every nation where the Gospel has been received. There has been little need of preaching the gathering, the people as a rule have had to be restrained rather than encouraged inthe matter of gathering to Zion and her stakes.[85]

The Spirit had spoken clearly and the gathering from the British Mission moved forward rapidly.

In compliance with the covenant of Abraham, the Lord commanded that the converts of The Church of Jesus Christ of Latter-day Saints be gathered to a promised land.[a] In preparation for fulfilling this commandment, the Lord told the Saints in the East to assemble in Ohio. This was the first commandment to gather in this dispensation.[b] From there, the Saints were to go westward until the Lord revealed where the city of the New Jerusalem would be located.[c] The Lord then moved rapidly to reveal the exact location of Zion, for "the Spirit of the Lord Jesus Christ is a gathering spirit."[86]

In March of 1831 He commanded:

D&C 45:64–66 Wherefore I, the Lord, have said, gather ye out from the eastern lands, assemble ye yourselves together ye elders of my church; go ye forth into the western countries, call upon the inhabitants to repent, and inasmuch as they do repent, build up churches unto me. And with one heart

a. D&C 29:7–8; September 1830.

b. D&C 37:3.

c. D&C 42:9; February 9, 1831.

and with one mind, gather up your riches that ye may purchase an inheritance
which shall hereafter be appointed unto you. And it shall be called the New
Jerusalem, a land of peace, a city of refuge, a place of safety for the saints
of the Most High God.

In June 1831, the Lord told Joseph Smith and Sidney Rigdon to
leave their houses and go to the land of Missouri.[a] They were instructed to hold a conference on "the land, which I will consecrate
unto my people, which are a remnant of Jacob, and those who are
heirs according to the covenant."[b] However, the land which was declared to be the land of their inheritance was then in the hands of their
"enemies."[c] Finally, on July 20, 1831, Joseph recounted that the "very
spot upon which He [the Lord] designed to commence the work of the
gathering, and the up building of an 'holy city,' which shall be called
Zion,"[87] was revealed to be in Missouri:

> **D&C 57:1–3** Hearken, O ye elders of my church, saith the Lord your God,
> who have assembled yourselves together, according to my commandments,
> in this land, which is the land of Missouri, which is the land which I have ap-
> pointed and consecrated for the gathering of the saints. Wherefore, this is the
> land of promise, and the place for the city of Zion. And thus saith the Lord
> your God, if you will receive wisdom here is wisdom. Behold, the place which
> is now called Independence is the center place; and a spot for the temple is
> lying westward, upon a lot which is not far from the courthouse.

The sacred location of the city of Zion "spoken of by David, in the
one hundred and second Psalm, [would] be built upon the land of
America,"[88] where the "ransomed of the Lord" could "return and come
to Zion with songs and everlasting joy upon their heads."[d]

Although Zion was *not* redeemed at that time because of the transgressions of the early Saints,[e] it will yet be redeemed in the Lord's due
time.[f]

Missionaries are now sent to gather Ephraim (along with the remnants of the other tribes of Israel) from among the wicked in "all the
lands whither [the Lord has] driven them"[g] so that they may receive the
word of God and come to the ensign (gospel) that God has established
in the latter-days.[h] Obstacles will be removed to allow the gathering to
take place, for as the Lord said in Ezekiel, "I will bring you out from
the people, and will gather you out of the countries wherein ye are scat-

a. D&C 52:3.

b. D&C 52:2.

c. D&C 52:42.

d. Isaiah 35:10.

e. D&C 105:9.

f. D&C 136:18.

g. Jeremiah
16:14–16;
Isaiah 18.

h. Isaiah
11:11; Dan-
iel 2.

tered, with a mighty hand, and with a stretched out arm, and with fury poured out . . . I will cause you to pass under the rod [of judgment], and I will bring you into the bond of the covenant."[a]

Until the Lord redeems Zion and gathers the Saints for His return to the New Jerusalem, converts are to be gathered where "the Lord shall locate a stake of Zion."[b] These stakes are to be appointed in "regions round about" as "they shall be manifested" unto the Lord's servants and will be created as "curtains or the strength" of Zion.[c]

The Gentiles (Including the Arabs and Those of African Descent)
There are nowhere near the number of scriptural references concerning the gathering of the Gentiles (and none specifically relating to the Arabs and those of African descent) as there are concerning the gathering of Israel, but there is a sufficient number to make two things clear:

1. The Gentiles (see definition page 731) will have the gospel declared unto them and will have the opportunity to gather and become heirs according to the covenant.

2. Once they repent and become heirs according to the covenant, they are included in all of the general gathering scriptures.

The title page of the Book of Mormon states that the message of the book (the gospel) is brought forth not only for the remnants of the house of Israel, but also for the "convincing of the Jew and Gentile that Jesus is the Christ." During His visit to the Western Hemisphere, the Lord stated that there were many "not of this land" who had not yet heard His voice, and He declared that His words would "be manifested unto the Gentiles."[d] He prophesied that in the latter days the truth would "come unto the Gentiles,"[e] but many would reject it.[f] He reaffirmed this teaching in Doctrine and Covenants 18:26, stating that the gospel would be declared both to the Gentiles and to the Jews, and that missionaries would be prepared to extend the gospel to them—"as many as will believe."[g] Finally, Paul wrote to the Romans describing the Gentiles as a "wild olive tree" that when grafted in among the branches of the good olive tree, could partake of the "root and fatness of the [natural] tree"[h] and become heirs to the covenant of Abraham.

a. Ezekiel 20:34, 37.

b. D&C 109:39; 136:10.

c. D&C 101:21; 115:18.

d. 3 Nephi 16:1–4.

e. 3 Nephi 16:7.

f. 3 Nephi 16:10.

g. D&C 90:8.

h. Romans 11:16–26.

The sign of the gathering, both the specific gathering and the general gathering, has been preached by almost all of God's prophets from earliest times. Enoch rejoiced in the knowledge of Zion (the New Jerusalem) and those who would gather to it[a] and Moses, after prophesying of the diaspora, declared:

> **Deuteronomy 4:29–31 (emphasis added)**   But if from thence thou shalt seek the Lord thy God, thou shalt find him, if thou seek him with all thy heart and with all thy soul. When thou art in tribulation, and all these things are come upon thee, *even in the latter days,* if thou turn to the Lord thy God, and shalt be obedient unto his voice; (for the Lord thy God is a merciful God;) he will not forsake thee, neither destroy thee, nor forget the covenant of thy fathers which he sware unto them.

Isaiah spoke of the gathering in many chapters of his book,[89] Jeremiah spoke of it in five of his chapters,[90] and Ezekiel in five of his.[91] It is also mentioned in Hosea,[b] Amos,[c] Micah,[92] Zephaniah, Zechariah, and Joel.[93] Book of Mormon prophets also spoke of it,[94] and once the restoration was complete, the Lord spoke of it repeatedly in the Doctrine and Covenants.[95]

John the Revelator was given a vision of a "little book" which symbolically represented the gathering. The Lord commanded John to eat the little book, but although it was sweet to his taste, it was bitter in his belly.[d] The book was bitter to John when he saw those who would not repent and come unto Christ. It was sweet when he saw the culmination of the gathering and the reuniting of the great cities of Jerusalem, Enoch, and the New Jerusalem at the Lord's Second Coming.[e]

The sign of the gathering is ongoing. It commenced with the restoration of the gospel and will accelerate as the Lord's Advent becomes imminent. It is recorded that angels will assist men in the final gathering,[f] and it will not be completed until all the righteous have been gathered into the Savior's kingdom.

> **Jeremiah 23:7–8 (see also16:14–16)**   Therefore, behold, the days come, saith the Lord, that they shall no more say, The Lord liveth, which brought up the children of Israel out of the land of Egypt; but, The Lord liveth, which brought up and which led the seed of the house of Israel out of the north country, and from all countries whither I had driven them; and they shall dwell in their own land."

a. Moses 7:62.

b. Hosea 1:10–11.

c. Amos 9:11–15.

d. Revelation 10:9–10; D&C 77:14.

e. Revelation 21.

f. Joseph Smith–Matthew 1:37.

The Devil and His Kingdom

7

---

2 Corinthians 11:14–15   And no marvel; for Satan himself is transformed into an angel of light. Therefore it is no great thing if his ministers also be transformed as the ministers of righteousness.

Who Is the Devil?

Satan, Lucifer, Beelzebub, leviathan, son of the morning, prince of this world, the serpent, prince of the power of the air, the beast, the great red dragon—all these titles are names of the devil, the source of all evil. He is described in the book of Moroni as an entity that "persuadeth no man to do good, no, not one."[a] Who is the devil? He is the antithesis of Jesus Christ!

John the Revelator refers to the devil's kingdom as "Babylon" or the "great and abominable church" as he defines the consummate power of the evil one's empire: "Babylon" because of the great biblical city that was the center of the devil's ancient power and sorceries; the "great and abominable church" because Satan's latter-day organization, while it may not be an actual church, is the antithesis of Christ's church upon the earth. John tells us that written on the crown of the woman who symbolically represents the city of Babylon is the phrase, "the mother of harlots and abominations of the earth."[b] All her evils are "the midst of wickedness [the center of all evil things], which is spiritual Babylon."[c]

The Devil's Past

In the beginning, Lucifer was with God the Father in the preexis-

a. Moroni 7:17.

b. Revelation 17:5.

c. D&C 133:14.

tence. He was a choice son of our Heavenly Father. Before he was cast down to the earth for disobedience, he was known as the "son of the morning."[a] But evil was found in this once noble spirit because he rejected the Father and sought to exalt his "throne above the stars of God."[b]

While citing God's condemnation of the prince of Tyrus, Ezekiel gives us a double-reference description of the devil. Ezekiel makes it clear that while there may have been an actual prince of Tyrus, it is really Lucifer that is being described. And while Ezekiel portrays him as "full of wisdom" and "perfect in beauty," God condemns him:

> **Ezekiel 28:13–19; Isaiah 14:12–16**   Thou hast been in Eden the garden of God . . . thou wast upon the holy mountain of god . . . Thou wast perfect in thy ways from the day that thou wast created, till iniquity was found in thee. By the multitude of thy merchandise they have filled the midst of thee with violence, and thou hast sinned . . . Thine heart was lifted up because of thy beauty, thou hast corrupted thy wisdom by reason of thy brightness: I will cast thee to the ground, I will lay thee before kings . . . I will bring thee to ashes upon the earth in the sight of all them that behold thee. All they that know thee among the people shall be astonished at thee: thou shalt be a terror, and never shalt thou be any more.

Isaiah concurs with Ezekiel's lament: "How art thou fallen from heaven, O Lucifer, son of the morning! how art thou cut down to the ground."[c]

Jesus was also with the Father in the preexistence, as were all of the Father's children who would come to this earth. As spirits we did not have physical bodies. We assume that our spirits appeared much as they do now, except they resided as spiritual tabernacles; however, all of the Father's spirit children were designated to come to this earth and acquire a physical body under the plan of salvation. Among these spirits were "noble and great ones"[d] who would eventually occupy positions of authority and power on the earth in their temporal manifestations.

At a certain point in our progression in the preexistence, the Father called a great council. He presented His plan for mortality—the plan of salvation. But Lucifer objected and presented a plan of his

a. Isaiah 14:12.

b. Isaiah 14:13.

c. Isaiah 14:12.

d. Abraham 3:22–23.

own. In his heart he wanted to have God's glory: "I will ascend into heaven . . ." he declared. "I will ascend above the heights of the clouds; I will be like the most High."[a]

God rejected Satan's plan, but the evil one's power and influence were so great that while yet in the presence of the Father, he convinced "the third part of the stars of heaven" (the spirit children of God) to rebel and follow him in his fight against the plan of salvation.[b] Because of his rebellion and disobedience, Satan failed his "first estate" (the premortal existence[c]) and he, as well as those who followed him, were punished by being cast out of the Father's presence: "cast . . . into the earth,"[d] never to receive a tabernacle of flesh. The "son of the morning" became "Satan, yea, even the devil, the father of all lies,"[e] forever exiled from the Father's presence, for where God is, the devil and his angels can never come.[f] Thereafter, Lucifer had but one purpose: "to deceive and to blind men, and to lead them captive at his will, even as many as would not hearken unto [God's] voice."[g]

Several of Satan's exploits on the earth are described in the scriptures.[96] He has always had the power to tempt men and women and lead them spiritually captive—*if* they subject themselves to him. John the Revelator saw Satan's past and future activities in a vision and described him as "a great red dragon,"[h] the source of all evil and all evil power. And, as the "star" that fell from heaven to earth, he held the "key" to the "bottomless pit."[i] When he opened that pit, a black smoke (representing evil in all its forms) issued forth and darkened the "sun and the air" (the light of the gospel being overcome by the devil's evil; i.e., the great apostasy).[j] Out of the smoke came "locusts upon the earth"—wicked men who were given evil power, "as the scorpions of the earth," which allowed them to inflict harm on, and control, humanity. They could not "hurt" the earth. They could not cause famines and earthly catastrophes or seal the heavens from rain as Elijah and Nephi, the Lord's true prophets, had done, nor could they kill people. But just as Job was tormented by the devil, these wicked men were also able to afflict mankind (described as the sting of the scorpion) for a symbolic "five months" (an indeterminate period of time). They were allowed to do this because the men and women they tormented had succumbed to their evil power. As a result of their torment, people "[sought] death" but could not find it.[k]

a. Isaiah 14:13–14.

b. Revelation 12:4; 12:3–9.

c. Abraham 3:26.

d. Revelation 12:9.

e. Moses 4:4.

f. D&C 29:29.

g. Moses 4:4.

h. Revelation 12:3.

i. Revelation 9:1.

j. Revelation 9:2.

k. Revelation 9:3–10.

John attempts to describe the strange, symbolic locusts of torment he is seeing by comparing them to things he knows. But the limits on his vocabulary make it difficult for us to identify them. Finally, he defines the source of evil as a king (the devil) who rules the wicked of mankind. He is not a king in the literal sense, however; this is a symbolical representation of his reign over the evil in the hearts of mankind.[a]

The Devil's Presence in the Latter Days

After John had envisioned the great power of the devil throughout the millennia prior to Christ and up through time to the Dark Ages, his vision expanded to show him Satan's extraordinary powers in the latter days—particularly just prior to the Lord's Second Coming. The devil's initial major offensive against righteousness in the last days began with the first vision received by Joseph Smith, the prophet of the Restoration. As Joseph began to pray for spiritual enlightenment, he was "seized upon" by the devil's power, a power which entirely overcame him and bound his tongue so that he "could not speak." "Thick darkness" closed around him, and he felt he was "doomed to sudden destruction."[97] Praying silently with all his strength, he was finally released from Satan's grasp and thereafter enjoyed the brilliant presence of both the Father and the Son.[b]

Lucifer has expressed his power in many ways. In the latter days he has possessed some men[98] and attacked others.[99] It is recorded in the *History of the Church* that he fought against the first Lamanite mission.[100] He was the principal cause of the Missouri persecutions,[101] an achievement which earned him the dubious title of "father" of the Missouri mobs.[102] He has deceived some individuals with revelations supposedly given through "magic" stones.[103] He influenced Sister Sally Crandall, an early member of the Church in the Hulet Branch, to think that she could "know and see men's hearts." Because of this "gift," Sally Crandall and Sylvester Hulet, the head of the Hulet Branch, would not receive even the teachings of Joseph Smith himself unless his teachings agreed with the gifts these branch members felt they possessed.[104] The Hulet Branch also believed that they "received the word of the Lord by the gift of tongues," but the Church brethren of the time determined that the devil had deceived them, "as the gift of tongues is so often made use of by Satan to deceive the Saints."[105] The devil also created secret combinations, as in days of old, to attack the Church from within.[106] "In open vision by daylight," Brother W. W. Phelps "saw the destroyer in his most horrible power, ride upon the face of the waters."[107] The *History of the Church* also tells us that an enraged devil will become the cause of much destruction and war in the latter days.[108]

Lucifer has the ability to deceive and mislead mankind by appearing as "an angel of light."[109] He was even the cause of a division in Joseph Smith's own family, and the instigator of a "division among the Twelve, also among the Seventy, and bickering and jealousies between the Elders and the official members of the Church." But Joseph was determined to "amicably dispose of and settle all family difficulties," as well as the conflicts between the Brethren. He knew that the cloud would burst and that "Satan's kingdom" would eventually be "laid in ruins."[110] Finally, Joseph said, "there are signs in heaven, earth and hell . . . The devil knows many signs, but [he] does not know the sign of the Son of Man, or Jesus."[111]

While Satan may or may not have known all the requirements and revelations surrounding the restoration of the gospel, he has always been a great anticipator of the restoration of some of the gospel's principal doctrines. Prior to the restoration of the doctrine of consecration and stewardship, he inspired a counterfeit united order to be developed in Kirtland called "common stock."[112] On another occasion, he designed a counterfeit polygamy scheme which was practiced by John C. Bennett in Nauvoo. Dr. Bennett "seduced an innocent female by his lying, and subjected her character to public disgrace . . . But his depraved heart would not suffer him to stop [there]. Not being contented with having disgraced one female, he made an attempt upon others; and . . . overcame them also, evidently not caring whose character was ruined, so that his wicked, lustful appetites might be gratified." Not only did he indulge in these practices himself, he convinced others to do the same, falsely claiming that the prophet and other authorities of the Church had sanctioned his practices. When his evil ways were discovered he attempted suicide, but he was unsuccessful. He later lost his membership in the Church and supposedly affiliated himself with some Missourians who were plotting destruction against members of the Church.[113]

Joseph rarely taught on the subject of Satan, but he did admonish the members to be aware of the devil's flattering deception of self-righteousness when he declared, "We are full of selfishness; the devil flatters us that we are very righteous, when we are feeding on the faults of others."[114] Joseph denounced self-justification for transgression, stating that if "Satan [was] generally blamed for the evils which we did . . . [and] was the cause of all our wickedness, men could not be condemned. The devil could not compel mankind to do evil; all was voluntary. God *would* not exert any compulsory means, and the devil *could* not [emphasis added]."[115]

The devil can also ensconce his power in a church or a religion. Paul, after enumerating a litany of Satan's evils among the people of the earth, describes the devil's influence among the religions of the latter days: religions that have "a form of godliness, but [deny] the power thereof." The members of these religions are "ever learning," he states, yet "never able to come to the knowledge of the truth." He writes Timothy and warns him (as he warns us all) to "turn away" from such religions.[a] Nephi declared, "Behold there are save two churches only; the one is the church of the Lamb of God, and the other is the church of the devil."[b] In another chapter, Nephi describes Satan's church as the "great and abominable church" and states that the devil is "the founder of it."[c] The "abominable church" that Nephi speaks of is not any *particular* church, but is inclusive of all religions or any other organizations that are opposed to the "church of the Lamb of God." These "forms of godliness" symbolically describe Satan's deceptive counterfeit doctrines of salvation which cause men to "ever learn," but never "come to the knowledge of the truth."

John the Revelator was describing the devil's power and the enormity of his success through deception when he symbolically referred to Satan's "church" as the "great whore that sitteth upon many waters . . . the mother of . . . abominations."[d] This power caused John to wonder "with great admiration."[e]

Satan's deceptions can take many forms besides churches or religions. Paul warns the Colossians that men will also be spoiled "through philosophy and vain deceit, after the tradition of men, after the rudiments of the world,"[f] and through "profane and vain babblings, and oppositions of science falsely so called."[g]

a. 2 Timothy 3:1–7.

b. 1 Nephi 14:10.

c. 1 Nephi 13:6.

d. Revelation 17:1, 5.

e. Revelation 17:6.

f. Colossians 2:8.

g. 1 Timothy 6:20.

The Devil's Future

Revelation 13:1–10   And I stood upon the sand of the sea, and saw a beast rise up out of the sea, having seven heads and ten horns, and upon his horns ten crowns, and upon his heads the name of blasphemy. And the beast which I saw was like unto a leopard, and his feet were as the feet of a bear, and his mouth as the mouth of a lion: and the dragon gave him his power, and his seat, and great authority. And I saw one of his heads as it were wounded to death; and his deadly wound was healed: and all the world wondered after the beast. And they worshipped the dragon which gave power unto the beast: and they worshipped the beast, saying, Who is like unto the beast? who is able to make war with him? And there was given unto him a mouth speaking great things and blasphemies; and power was given unto him to continue forty and two months. And he opened his mouth in blasphemy against God, to blaspheme his name, and his tabernacle, and them that dwell in heaven. And it was given unto him to make war with the saints, and to overcome them: and power was given him over all kindreds, and tongues, and nations. And all that dwell upon the earth shall worship him, whose names are not written in the book of life of the Lamb slain from the foundation of the world. If any man have an ear, let him hear. He that leadeth into captivity shall go into captivity: he that killeth with the sword must be killed with the sword. Here is the patience and the faith of the saints.

John the Revelator saw many elements of the devil's kingdom as they would appear in the days prior to the Second Coming, and he depicted these elements symbolically in the book of Revelation. These symbols are linked with many things—elements of the gospel, historical visions, revelations given by the Lord, miracles, even the existence of the Savior Himself—and they are infused with descriptions of Satan's false doctrines through imitation, substitution, and counterfeiting in his attempt to deceive the hearts of men. Other prophets—such as Daniel, Zechariah, Isaiah, and Ezekiel—also saw adaptations or portions of John's vision, and their descriptions help us to understand the words of Revelation.[116]

The following are definitions and explanations of the principal symbols found in John's vision of the devil's latter-day kingdom:

The Dragon: The term *dragon* always refers to the devil; however, he may also be referred to by one of his other names or by other symbols. Normally, it is not difficult to determine whether these names or symbols are referring to Satan, even when they are used to describe other elements of the vision.

The Beast: This is the beast of Revelation 13:1. It appears out of the sea and has seven heads and ten horns. It represents the symbolic Antichrist leader of the devil's kingdom.

Another Beast: This beast comes out of the earth. It has two horns like a lamb and speaks like a dragon. It is the symbolic false prophet of the Antichrist beast.

The Woman: There are two women in John's vision. The woman in Chapter 12 of Revelation represents Christ's Church.[a] The woman in Chapter 17 of Revelation represents the devil's kingdom

The Great and Abominable Church: This phrase is used to symbolically refer to the devil's latter-day kingdom, in whatever form it takes.

The waters: The waters represent people: individuals, multitudes, kings, nations, tongues, or any other general term that would designate mankind.

Time: When this term is used (as well as other symbols or terms that relate to time), it may or may not have any relevance to *actual time.* Like the term "months" in Revelation 9:5, it might represent an *undefined* period of time. An undefined short period may be designated as "hours" by John, while a longer period may be represented by "days," or a large number of "hours." Usually the sequence of the verses identifies the general time period intended. There are, however, a few specific references to time which may be literal that are identified later in the chapter.

War: John may actually be depicting a literal war when he uses this term, but it can also be used to represent other methods of destroying Christ-oriented belief.

The Lamb: "The Lamb" always refers to Jesus Christ.

Worship: This is not the type of *worship* normally associated with religion. In the context of John's vision, the term is generally symbolic. It means belonging to, in adherence with, or in agreement with the devil's kingdom.

a. IV Revelation
12:7.

Mark: There are two marks referred to in Revelation. One mark is described as a "seal" placed by God on the forehead of the righteous. The other mark is the "mark of the beast." It is represented by the number 666 and is described as being located on the right hand and the forehead. Both of these marks symbolically represent those who have had their calling and election made sure—either with God or with the devil. They are not actual marks on the body.

Buy and Sell: These terms are used to represent economic power or the material goods of the world.

Locusts: "Locusts" represent wicked men.

Scorpion's Sting: This is a symbol of torment, destruction, discomfort, or restriction.

Mystery Babylon: This phrase represents the use of sorcery and other religious or mystical deceptions which were used in the Babylonian Kingdom. It can also represent anything used by the devil to deceive mankind.

The Great Whore: This phrase refers to the devil's kingdom in whatever form it takes. Satan's kingdom is also referred to as "the woman," "the great and abominable church," and "the great city."

The Bottomless Pit, or Perdition: These phrases refer to God's final punishment of the devil and his followers.

The Great City: This phrase refers to the devil's earthly kingdom in the latter days. His kingdom is also referred to as "the woman," "the great and abominable church," and "the great whore."

Merchandise: This term depicts the things of the earth and represents worldly wealth and power in whatever forms they may take.

All of the above symbols and terms will be used in the following discussion of John's vision.

The Antichrist Beast

Paul introduced the latter-day Antichrist to the Thessalonians when he told them about the apostasy that would take place before the Lord's Second Coming. He told them that the "man of sin . . . the son of perdition" would be revealed to the world. He would oppose the Lord and exalt himself "above all that is called God, or that is worshipped." He would make himself a substitute for God by sitting "in the temple of God, showing himself that he is God." Further, Paul stated that the Antichrist would come with Satan's power and be able to create "signs and lying wonders" to deceive mankind.[a]

John saw this same Antichrist in his vision, and while his vision is symbolic, it is more informative and graphic than Paul's statement to the Thessalonians. His vision of the Antichrist beast began while he "stood upon the sand of the sea." As he gazed out from the shore he saw a beast rise up out of the water. The beast was unlike anything John had ever seen. It had seven heads and ten horns: upon each horn was a crown, and written upon each of the seven heads was the word *blasphemy*.[b]

The description of the beast lends insight into John's problem. He is seeing things in his vision that are symbolic—things representative of other *objects, people, events,* and *information*— and he does not have the words to adequately describe them. Therefore, he draws analogies to the things with which he is familiar—and this is a key to understanding the vision! John compares the symbolic images he sees to the things he knows and for which he has a vocabulary, but due to the strange complexity of the images, his descriptions do not accurately depict what he is seeing. The beast rising out of the sea is a perfect example of this problem.

John continues to describe his vision: the beast he sees is also like a leopard, except that its feet are more like those of a bear and its mouth like that of a lion. (Joseph Smith inserted the following sentence just before John's description of the beast: "And I saw another sign, in the likeness of the kingdoms of the earth.")[c]

When the prophet Daniel saw this vision he described four great beasts: the first was like a lion with eagle's wings, the second like a bear, another like a leopard with four heads, and a fourth with iron teeth and ten horns.[d] Remember, however, that it is not the image but the information that the image is conveying that is important.

a. 2 Thessalonians 2:3–11.

b. Revelation 13:1.

c. JST Revelation 13:1.

d. Daniel 7.

Thus, we see that both John and Daniel are viewing the history of nations, the influence of the devil upon them, and both the rise of and the diversity of the devil's kingdom in the latter days. And while it is interesting to attempt to envision in the mind's eye what the beast actually looks like, its appearance is unimportant. We may *wrest* the scriptures to say that the beast is cunning like a leopard, powerful like a bear, and supreme or exalted like the king of beasts (the lion), but it is inconsequential to the information conveyed in the vision.

After describing the beast, John rapidly moves to the substance of the vision. "The dragon gave [the beast] his power, and his seat, and great authority."[a] The dragon is Satan, the source of power for the historical, worldly kingdoms of the earth portrayed in the vision, and the one who gives the beast (the Antichrist) his seat (position) and his authority (power) to rule in the devil's latter-day kingdom.

As the vision progresses, John observes that one of the seven heads of the beast receives a deadly wound—a death wound! But the beast is miraculously healed, and the world wonders and worships the dragon who gave the beast power saying, "Who is like unto him, and who is able to make war with him." This element of the vision has long caused mankind to look for a leader who would receive a terrible head wound and then miraculously recover, but John's vision is symbolic; therefore, this probably does not represent the unprecedented healing of an actual man. Certainly the beast with seven heads does not! What it probably means is that whatever form the devil's kingdom takes in the latter days, it will initially have a severe problem that will threaten its survival. But it will survive.

And the world will wonder "after the beast," meaning that people will be astonished or amazed that the entity survived its injury. Thereafter, they will worship the dragon which gave "power unto the beast," the literal interpretation of which would be that the *whole world* worshipped the devil—which, of course, is symbolic. The use of the term *worship* in this instance means *adherence.* Therefore, the world adheres to, follows, is influenced by, or belongs to whatever form the devil's kingdom will take in the latter days, and perhaps the world will even be deceived into thinking that it was the miraculous intervention by God that saved the entity from destruction.

It is possible that the devil's kingdom may be an organization, a. Revelation 13:2.

a cartel, a board of directors, a company, or even a system like the Internet. The statements of the people who are so astonished by the seemingly miraculous recovery of the entity in John's vision (i.e., "Who is like unto the beast? who is able to make war with him?") are merely window dressing. They are used to describe the tremendous success of Satan's organization and serve as examples of the powerful influence the devil's kingdom will have over people in the latter days.

In the visions of both John and Daniel, the beast is given a mouth and the ability to speak "great things."[a] And what "great things" will it speak? "Blasphemy against God . . . his name . . . his tabernacle, and them that dwell in heaven."[b] Although this verse may be literal, in view of the success Satan's kingdom will enjoy in the latter days (after its miraculous recovery from near destruction), the "blasphemy against God" is probably a symbolic representation of the beast's power of communication to convince mankind of its own greatness and accomplishments, thus taking the place of God in their praise and adoration.

John's vision further relates that "power was given unto [the beast] to continue [speaking] forty and two months."[c] This means that Satan's kingdom will enjoy the pinnacle of its great latter-day success for a period of time equal to that specified in Revelation 11, wherein it states that God's two prophets will prophesy to Jerusalem for a period of three and one-half years.[d] Both the Lord's prophets and the Antichrist beast will have an equivalent period of time in which to function during the apex of their existence: forty-two months, or three and one-half years. While most references to time in John's vision are symbolic and difficult to define, this period seems to have two possible meanings: one, that God's prophets and the Antichrist will each literally function for a period of three and one-half years; or two, that their work coincides in length of time, but that period of time, though lengthy, is undefined.

John's vision now gets specific about the activities of the Antichrist beast. He will make war against the saints by attacking their beliefs and their credibility. He will make them appear offensive to the world, and he will exclude them from his organization, whatever it is. During this period his power and dominion will expand, for John declares that he will have power over all "kindreds, and tongues, and nations."[e] Taken literally, this would mean a world dictator: but again,

a. Daniel 7:8.

b. Revelation 13:5–6.

c. Revelation 13:5.

d. Chapter 5; Revelation 11:3.

e. Revelation 13:7.

the words are symbolic and describe the effects of the beast's influence, not the influence of a single individual. It is therefore apparent that the influence of the devil's kingdom in the latter days will have such an enormous effect on mankind that almost everyone in the world will either succumb to or be affected by its evil authority. This is what John means when he says, "All that dwell upon the earth [in the latter days] shall worship him [the beast],"[a] except those who are true believers, whose names are written in the Lamb's book of life, and who will be warred against or excluded from the beast's organization.

Revelation 13:1–10 teaches us five specific things concerning the devil and his kingdom:

1. The devil has exerted great influence over all the kingdoms of the world throughout history.

2. The devil will firmly establish his kingdom in the latter days, regardless of the organizational form it takes.

3. The devil will be the source of the power and authority held by the Antichrist beast.

4. Satan will use anyone who will submit to him to accomplish his ends.

5. The majority of the world's people will follow, adhere to, be influenced by, or belong to whatever organization it is that the devil establishes in the latter days.

John concludes this initial description of the Antichrist beast with a familiar scripture: "If any man have an ear, let him hear,"[b] a phrase he used in almost identical form as he closed his admonitions to each of the seven churches in Chapters 2 and 3 of Revelation. This phrase means the same in all instances: John has given us the information and it is up to us (through the Spirit) to understand it.

Finally, John issues a warning: "He that leadeth into captivity shall go into captivity: he that killeth with the sword must be killed with the sword. Here is the patience and the faith of the saints."[c] The Saints must be patient in tribulation, for they will be subject to the inversion of the Golden Rule if they are not: i.e., people will get what they give!

a. Revelation 13:8.

b. Revelation 13:9.

c. Revelation 13:10.

8

The Devil and His Kingdom– Continued

The Second Beast

Revelation 13:11–18 And I beheld another beast coming up out of the earth; and he had two horns like a lamb, and he spake as a dragon. And he exerciseth all the power of the first beast before him, and causeth the earth and them which dwell therein to worship the first beast, whose deadly wound was healed. And he doeth great wonders, so that he maketh fire come down from heaven on the earth in the sight of men, and deceiveth them that dwell on the earth by the means of those miracles which he had power to do in the sight of the beast; saying to them that dwell on the earth, that they should make an image to the beast, which had the wound by a sword, and did live. And he had power to give life unto the image of the beast, that the image of the beast should both speak, and cause that as many as would not worship the image of the beast should be killed. And he causeth all, both small and great, rich and poor, free and bond, to receive a mark in their right hand, or in their foreheads: and that no man might buy or sell, save he that had the mark, or the name of the beast, or the number of his name. Here is wisdom. Let him that hath understanding count the number of the beast: for it is the number of a man; and his number is Six hundred threescore and six.

"And I beheld another beast coming up out of the earth; and he had two horns like a lamb, and he spake as a dragon. And he exerciseth all the power of the first beast [the Antichrist] before him, and [he] causeth the earth and them which dwell therein to worship the first beast, whose deadly wound was healed."[a] This second beast (be it man

a. Revelation 13:11–12.

or entity) is the symbolic false prophet of the Antichrist beast, and an important figure in John's vision since he serves as a vanguard in the devil's kingdom. The fact that he has horns like a lamb and speaks like a dragon conjures up visions of a wolf in sheep's clothing, an individual or an organization that appears benign, but is in fact terribly dangerous. John specifically notes that this beast exercises "all the power of the first beast." This would indicate that the purpose of this beast is the same as that of the Antichrist—to deceive the people of the earth and lead them captive into sin and away from righteousness.

John's vision reveals that the beast will attempt to accomplish this goal in several ways:

Worship of the Beast

The Antichrist beast "causes" people to *worship* (belong to or be influenced by) him, and economic greed is the influence that the devil uses to entice people to participate in his organization in the latter days.

The Wonders of the False Prophet

The second beast is apparently capable of doing "great wonders," even making "fire come down from heaven." If this were a literal description of his powers, he would be capable of duplicating the power Moses exercised before Pharaoh,[a] of matching the destructive judgment God pronounced upon Sodom and Gomorrah,[b] or even using the power Elijah exercised when he called down fire from heaven to consume the sacrifice at the challenge of the wicked priests of Baal.[c] But because John's vision is symbolic, the description of the second beast's power is probably not literal. John could be symbolically representing the fact that the *influence* of the false prophet may, to the astonishment of mankind, produce an effect *equivalent* to that produced by Moses and the Lord in the examples cited. The scriptures further state that the second beast will deceive mankind by "the means" (or the way) he does his miracles. The conclusion that can be drawn from John's writing is that the false prophet is capable of accomplishing something so extraordinary that it is perceived by mankind to be miraculous. Moreover, since he has the power to perform his miracles "in the sight of the [first] beast," it seems obvious that his activities have the sanction not only of the Antichrist, but of the devil as well. Through his mi-

a. Exodus 9:23.

b. Genesis 19:24.

c. 1 Kings 18:38.

raculous deceptions he will be able to convince people that the "devil's kingdom" is the source of their blessings, thus substituting Satan and his organization for the Father and His kingdom.

Again, the "wound that was healed" is mentioned in these verses to emphasize the miraculous power of the evil Antichrist beast and his prophet. It would appear that Satan's organization makes such a miraculous recovery, and becomes so successful after nearly being destroyed, that with the help of the second beast, it is able to convince mankind to join its organization by deceiving them as to its real intent.

The Image of the Beast

John next sees the second beast direct "them that dwell on the earth" to make an image (or statue) of the Antichrist beast.[a] This is probably not the statue of a man (such as King Darius had created of himself and imposed upon his subjects and the prophet Daniel); more likely it is like the image Nebuchadnezzar saw in his dream. That image represented, among other things, the greatness of Nebuchadnezzar's kingdom. In like manner, the "image to the beast" that the false prophet causes to be constructed symbolically represents the greatness of the Antichrist's evil kingdom. This is not difficult to imagine since images of organizations and individuals are all around us today. Successful people often create an emblem or logo that expresses their purpose or accomplishments, for in the words of a once popular television advertisement, "Image is everything!" Thus, in John's vision the false prophet beast creates an image of the devil's organization that will be known and marveled at worldwide.

The Image Comes to Life

The organization represented by the image of the beast assumes a life of its own through its influence. It wields great power. People will belong to it, they will adhere to its requirements, they will desire its association, and they will relish the rewards it provides. By these means it is brought to *life,* or has a *presence* of its own.

The Image Speaks

The second beast gives the power of speech to the image of the Antichrist. This is not a statue talking: more likely this is an entity or organization communicating with its adherents through directives, bulletins, or e-mails for example. In this manner it disseminates and implements the requirements and policies instituted by Satan's organization. Regardless of the method used to spread this information, however, the *speech* will deceive, captivate, and confuse men and women so thoroughly that they will "call evil good, and good evil."[a]

Paul calls this method of speaking the "working of Satan with all power and signs and lying wonders."[b] He states that it is designed "with all deceivableness of unrighteousness"[c] so that those who are deluded by it might be "damned . . . believe not the truth, [and take] pleasure in unrighteousness."[d] Men and women may be sufficiently beguiled that they will consider themselves "wise in their own eyes, and prudent in their own sight!"[e] They may degenerate to the point that they will "justify the wicked for *reward,* and take away the righteousness of the righteous from him!"[f]

Regardless of the method Satan uses to achieve his goal, his objective will remain the same: he wants to exalt himself "above all that is called God, or that is worshipped."[g] By putting his evil "beasts" in control of all temporal blessings, he will strive to make himself a substitute for God. By deceiving and conquering the hearts and souls of mankind with worldly wealth, he will attempt to steal the "glory" of God: His children.

Nephi graphically describes the magnitude of these efforts in the last days: "For behold, at that day shall [Satan] rage in the hearts of the children of men, and stir them up to anger against that which is good. And others will he pacify, and lull them away into carnal security . . . and thus [he] cheateth their souls, and leadeth them away carefully down to hell."[h]

Worship or Be Killed

The false prophet causes all those who will not "worship the image of the beast" to be "killed." Remember, *worship* in this sense means everyone must belong to, be influenced by, or participate in whatever entity the Antichrist beast has established in order to gain the perceived blessings that membership in his organization might entail. Therefore, the word *killed* is also considered symbolic. If an actor tries out for a part in a play but does not get the part, his chances to be in the play are

a. Isaiah 5:20.

b. 2 Thessalonians 2:9.

c. 2 Thessalonians 2:10.

d. 2 Thessalonians 2:12.

e. Isaiah 2:21.

f. Isaiah 2:23; emphasis added.

g. 2 Thessalonians 2:4.

h. 2 Nephi 28:20–21.

dead. In this sense, if the righteous of the earth will not join the beast's organization or are ostracized from it, their opportunity to share in its rewards and compensations have been "killed." Although this process may cause the righteous some temporal hardships, the scriptures indicate that they will triumph in the end by inheriting God's kingdom.

The Mark of the Beast

The beast will identify those who join his organization by giving them a mark on "their right hand, or in [their] forehead." Some may feel that the beast is forcing his adherents to accept this mark, but judging from the way the word *causeth* is used in John's vision, that is not the case. The word *causeth* seems to be used when a reward is implied for those who have done all that Satan's forces require of them. This mark duplicates the seal that the Lord will place in the foreheads of the righteous. According to John, those who bear the Lord's seal cannot be harmed by the evil servants of the devil.[a]

It is not coincidental that the seal of God and the mark of the devil symbolically represent similar conclusions. The recipient of either mark knows that he or she has qualified or been sealed to the kingdom of the grantor. The symbolism makes each mark a reward of the grantor, God or the devil; however, in reality both marks are received from God—one a reward for obedience and the other a punishment for evil.

The "mark of the beast" is symbolically represented in the book of Revelation as "the number of a man." That number is 666. This does not represent a *man* in the singular sense, however, nor is it the name of a man converted to its numerical equivalent. It means that those who are members of the devil's kingdom (or organization) in the latter days will have something required of them that will cause them to become specifically identified with it in some way. In this manner the devil will know his own. This identification will not literally be engraved upon the forehead or the right hand of those who belong to his kingdom, but his disciples will acknowledge those who represent the Antichrist and his false prophet and will be given exclusive membership in his organization.

This process of *marking* a people is another example of the devil mimicking the gospel. From the very beginning, God has symbolically or literally *marked* His people. In Exodus and Deuteronomy, the dedication of the first born son (symbolized with a mark "upon [his] hand, and for a memorial between [his] eyes") commemorated the deliverance of Israel from Egypt.[a] This mark was given so that the Israelites would remember the covenant and the laws God had given them. For centuries, many Jewish men have taken this to literally mean the "wearing of the law," and consequently they wear two sets of *tefillin* (phylacteries worn on forehead and sideburns) to this day.[117]

The prophet Ezekiel records that God marked the righteous and destroyed those without the mark for idolatry: "And the Lord said . . . Go through the midst of the city, through the midst of Jerusalem, and set a mark upon the foreheads of the men that sigh and that cry for all the abominations that be done in the midst thereof . . . let not your eye spare, neither have ye pity" for those who are guilty of idolatry and who do not have the mark, "but come not near any man upon whom . . . the mark [is placed]."[b]

Finally, those living in the latter days who adhere to the gospel are baptized as a sign that they believe. When John states that the Lord *marks* His covenant people, he is referring to baptism into the Savior's church. Baptism is the *mark* or *sign* of the covenant. However, John's reference to the devil's mark does not specifically identify what that mark is. It could be referring to a loyalty oath, a membership card, or any other means which would identify those who voluntarily belong to Satan's latter-day kingdom.

The fact that both the devil's followers and the Lord's chosen people will receive symbolical marks in their foreheads could signify that in each instance the recipient understands his or her commitment and is willing to accept the requirements of the one they choose to follow. The mark in the hand may symbolize their willingness to perform the requisite tasks that pertain to their kingdom of choice. John's vision does not reveal how the devil's mark will be realized, but in all probability it will come into being during the normal course of events.

The Devil's Kingdom is Economic

Revelation 13:17 clearly identifies economics as the source of power that the devil will use against the righteous in the last days. He will make the wealth of the world appear more desirable than eternal life,

a. Exodus 13:9; Deuteronomy 6:8.

b. Ezekiel 9:4–6.

which is the wealth of God.[a] Those who belong to his organization will need the mark of identification signifying membership in his kingdom if they are to manipulate and multiply their wealth, for without the "mark of the beast," men and women will not be able to "buy or sell" their goods (whatever they may be). We are told in the scriptures that his organization (often referred to as "the great and abominable church") will exercise such great power over the hearts and minds of men in the latter days that if possible, even the very elect may be deceived into joining it.[b]

The Woman

Revelation 17　And there came one of the seven angels which had the seven vials, and talked with me, saying unto me, Come hither; I will shew unto thee the judgment of the great whore that sitteth upon many waters: with whom the kings of the earth have committed fornication, and the inhabitants of the earth have been made drunk with the wine of her fornication. So he carried me away in the spirit into the wilderness: and I saw a woman sit upon a scarlet coloured beast, full of names of blasphemy, having seven heads and ten horns. And the woman was arrayed in purple and scarlet colour, and decked with gold and precious stones and pearls, having a golden cup in her hand full of abominations and filthiness of her fornication: and upon her forehead was a name written, MYSTERY, BABYLON THE GREAT, THE MOTHER OF HARLOTS AND ABOMINATIONS OF THE EARTH. And I saw the woman drunken with the blood of the saints, and with the blood of the martyrs of Jesus: and when I saw her, I wondered with great admiration. And the angel said unto me, Wherefore didst thou marvel? I will tell thee the mystery of the woman, and of the beast that carrieth her, which hath the seven heads and ten horns. The beast that thou sawest was, and is not; and shall ascend out of the bottomless pit, and go into perdition: and they that dwell on the earth shall wonder, whose names were not written in the book of life from the foundation of the world, when they behold the beast that was, and is not, and yet is. And here is the mind which hath wisdom. The seven heads are seven mountains, on which the woman sitteth. And there are seven kings: five are fallen, and one is, and the other is not yet come; and when he cometh, he must continue a short space. And the beast that was, and is not, even he is the eighth, and is of the seven, and goeth into perdition. And the ten horns which thou sawest are ten kings, which have received no kingdom as yet; but receive power as kings one hour with the beast. These have one mind, and shall give their power and strength unto the beast. These shall make war with the Lamb, and the Lamb shall overcome them: for he is Lord of lords, and King of kings: and they that are with him are called, and chosen, and faithful. And he saith unto me, The waters which thou sawest, where the whore sitteth, are peoples, and multitudes, and nations, and tongues. And the ten horns which thou sawest upon the beast, these shall hate the whore, and shall make her desolate and naked, and shall eat her flesh, and burn her with fire. For God

a. D&C 6:7.

b. Joseph
　Smith–Matthew
　1:22.

hath put in their hearts to fulfil his will, and to agree, and give their kingdom unto the beast, until the words of God shall be fulfilled. And the woman which thou sawest is that great city, which reigneth over the kings of the earth.

The last major participant in John's vision of Satan's latter-day kingdom is a woman. The scriptures also describe her as the "dragon" or the "great and abdominal church," terms that put her on an equal footing with the evil beasts of the devil. Her persona parallels that of the woman who represents the Lord's church described in Revelation 12:1—another example from John's vision of the devil imitating elements of the gospel.

This woman, symbolically described as "the great whore," is representative of absolute evil in all its forms.[a] Her ability to deceive and control mankind is described as "fornication." Through her powerful economic hold over the nations of the earth, she has caused whole civilizations to become "drunk with the wine of her fornication" (in essence causing them to worship a false god—the greatest of all sins), for she has successfully caused the pursuit of earthly wealth and power to be substituted for the desire to know God and to obey His commandments.

John is next carried away into the wilderness where he sees this evil woman sitting on the great beast with seven heads and ten horns. This scene interlocks all of the prior elements John has seen in his vision: the Antichrist beast, the false prophet beast, the devil's influence on the nations (historically and in the latter days), and the means by which Satan's control is exercised: i.e., worldly wealth and power. However, the beasts and the evil woman are all representative of the devil's kingdom with a common goal—to cause the downfall of mankind.

John vividly describes the woman's exotic economic wealth: she wears garments of purple and scarlet "decked with gold and precious stones and pearls," and she holds "a golden cup in her hand."[b] She is most exquisite and powerful and full of lustful promise. Through her cunning she has deceived nations into willingly giving her their economic power and sovereignty. She has caused mankind to disregard both the first and second great commandments, to completely adulterate the truths of the gospel, and to negate their covenant with God.[c] Her "golden cup" is a symbol of her tremendous success, over-

a. Revelation 17:1.

b. Revelation 17:4.

c. Revelation 17:12–13.

flowing with "abominations and filthiness." She is given a title: "Mystery Babylon the Great, the Mother of Harlots, and Abominations of the Earth."[a] These names make it clear that the devil's latter-day kingdom—regardless of the wealth it bestows on its adherents—is the epitome of all evil.

Using the negative attributes of selfishness and greed, mankind has historically been deceived into believing that Satan is their god and king; through the avarice of this woman, the devil and his beasts will continue to deceive men and nations and subject them to Satan's power and authority.

Mystery Babylon

Mystery Babylon was an occult religion based on astronomy that was practiced in Nebuchadnezzar's kingdom. When Nebuchadnezzar had his famous dream, his first reaction was to call all the "magicians . . . astrologers . . . sorcerers, and . . . Chaldeans"[b] in Babylon and charge them to help him (1) recall the dream (for he had forgotten it), and (2) interpret it. The Israelites also learned the wicked and idolatrous ways of this mystical religion while they were under Babylonian captivity, and were actively worshiping its false gods when King Josiah commanded them to "put down the idolatrous priests . . . [who burned] incense in the high places . . . unto Baal, to the sun, and to the moon, and to the planets, and to all of the host of heaven."[c]

The occult Mystery Babylon religion was initially assimilated by the Babylonians from the Chaldeans and was subsequently passed down through all the kingdoms envisioned in Nebuchadnezzar's dream to Rome. Rome was still actively practicing it during John's time, along with the worship of various ancient gods by several associations of priests. ("The most influential of the priestly colleges was that of the nine augurs who studied the intent or will of the gods." Their "art went back through Etruria to Chaldea and beyond.")[118]

"Divination and augury were assiduously practiced and widely trusted" in Rome during John's time. "Astrology . . . magic and sorcery, witchcraft and superstition, charms and incantations, 'portents' and the interpretation of dreams were deeply woven into the tissue of Roman life."[119] John therefore called the evil woman in his vision Mystery Babylon because he saw that she represented all of the evils of

a. Revelation 17:5.

b. Daniel 2:2.

c. 2 Kings 23:5.

false worship, not only in Rome but in all previous and future earthly kingdoms. His conclusion is supported by Isaiah who saw Satan's evil kingdom in a vision and described it as the "virgin daughter of Babylon."[a]

The Mother of Harlots

As noted previously, John's vision describes the evil woman in his vision as the symbolic "Mother of Harlots and Abominations of the Earth." The scriptures often couch the Lord's association with Israel in the guise of a marriage alliance, with the Savior as the husband or bridegroom and His chosen people as the wife or bride (symbolically implying a family relationship).[120] John uses this same type of symbolism to describe the devil's evil kingdom as it imitates the concept of a family relationship when he calls the evil woman "the mother of harlots." By this he is saying that the devil's evil kingdom both supports and sustains its adherents as a mother does her family.

The Destruction of the Righteous

John saw the evil woman of his vision "drunken with the blood of the saints" and "of the martyrs of Jesus."[b] He was witnessing the "destruction" of the righteous by the devil and his advocates. The vision does not specify exactly *how* the righteous are destroyed, but from the descriptions of Satan's kingdom and power, there can be at least three ways:

1. Physical destruction: destruction of the body through war, persecution, or torture resulting from unrighteous or unholy relationships between men and nations.

2. Economic destruction: since the devil's kingdom is based on mankind's desire for earthly wealth and power, the righteous in the latter days could be destroyed by their exclusion from the devil's economic organization. Both historically and in modern times, many good people have died from want of the basic necessities when unrighteous regimes have withheld food and money to satisfy their own greed.

3. Spiritual destruction: this is the devil's major emphasis and

ultimate goal. Destruction of spiritual commitment can come in many forms. People can be destroyed spiritually when they substitute the things of the earth for God. A testimony left without nourishment, use of the Lord's name in vain, negligence of the scriptures, disobedience to God's commandments, sins of commission or omission, or trivializing the doctrine of the gospel are all applauded by Lucifer and can all lead to spiritual destruction. Some of the most effective weapons he uses to bring about the spiritual fall of mankind are discouragement, fear of public opinion, laziness, uncontrolled sexual desires, greed, selfishness, disobedience of civil law, feelings of inadequacy, lack of natural affection, self-pity, and unrighteous pride.

John's vision has revealed a series of unbelievably astonishing things at this point, and they cause him to sit back and marvel at the enormous power the devil and his servants possess and the obvious success they enjoy. The angel directing John's vision is surprised by John's reaction and asks him, "Wherefore didst thou marvel?" He then reveals to John the interpretation of the vision of the evil woman and the "beast that carrieth her."[a]

The beast (which John now alludes to as the devil in Revelation 17) came from the "bottomless pit" and would eventually go to "perdition," along with all those who were not named in the Lamb's "book of life."[b] The angel then used an interesting phrase to describe the existence of the beast. He said the beast "was, and is not, and yet is."[c] John has just been shown the historical development of the devil starting with his preexistent state, going through his involvement with the temporal kingdoms of the earth, and ending with the prophecies regarding his latter-day kingdom as he struggles to defeat the Savior. Therefore, the word *was* in Revelation 17:8 would probably refer to Satan's existence in heaven where, as the intelligent "son of the morning," he had participated in the pre-earth councils. The phrase "is not" implies the fact that while he has great powers to tempt men and women during their mortal probation, his status "is not" as great as it was in heaven during the premortal period. That he "yet is" appears to signify that he will yet be as powerful as John's vision portrays.

a. Revelation 17:7.

b. Revelation 17:8.

c. Revelation 17:8.

The angel then explained to John that the seven heads of the beast were seven mountains where the woman (representing the devil's kingdom) will sit. Rome has commonly been assumed to be the locality represented by the seven mountains because it is ringed by seven hills, but that seems to be too obvious since it does not match the criteria of the other symbolic representations used in John's vision: i.e., none of them have been literal. In addition, there are multiple cities around the globe that claim to sit on or are established on seven hills including Edinburgh, Scotland; Moscow, Russia; Seattle, Washington; and Jerusalem. The same literal misconception has arisen in regards to Isaiah's statement regarding the Lord's kingdom being established in the "tops of the mountains" in the latter days.[a] Isaiah is not describing a physical place where the Lord's kingdom has its headquarters. Rather, he is saying that *the Lord's kingdom will be raised up and exalted in the latter days.* In like manner, John's vision is portraying the devil's imitation of such a kingdom. His evil woman is to be elevated on the tops of seven hills, indicating that *Satan's domain will also be raised up and made powerful among all the nations as the Second Coming approaches*

The angel describes the development of the devil's kingdom through the ages by relating it to seven kings. Five of these kings have existed and fallen at some time in the past; one is in power during John's day (referring to Rome), and "the other is not yet come."[b] The nations that have "not yet come" are depicted in the interpretation of Nebuchadnezzar's dream as the toes of iron and clay[c] and the 10 horns of the beast with 7 heads in John's vision. These are the nations which evolve after the breakup of the Holy Roman Empire. According to John's vision, these kingdoms continued for a "short time" until the establishment of Satan's powerful latter-day kingdom. The "short time" is the period of the great Apostasy. It is also the time spent by the righteous woman (the church) in the wilderness. John symbolically defines this period as "1260 days," which the inspired mind of Joseph Smith interpreted as years.[d]

Finally, the angel defines an eighth kingdom which is the culmination of all that John has seen. This kingdom represents the Antichrist beast, the false prophet beast, and the woman—the mother of harlots. Next, his vision identifies the source of all their evil and decep-

a. Isaiah 2:2–3.

b. Revelation 17:10.

c. Daniel 2:42–43.

d. IV Revelation 12:5.

tion—Lucifer—who is identified in this part of the vision as simply "the beast." This eighth kingdom is representative of Lucifer's evil kingdom, which is a derivative of all the kingdoms portrayed in Nebuchadnezzar's vision. From this information we gain the following insight: first, the devil has always been involved in the kingdoms of the earth when those kingdoms based their governance on worldly wealth and power; and second, the ten horns in Revelation 17:12 represent ten kingdoms (depicted by the ten toes of Nebuchadnezzar's vision) which would have "one hour" with the beast: their wicked reigns, though powerful, would be short lived.[a]

What is the intention of the devil's kingdom? To make war against the gospel and the Lamb of God—perhaps not an open war at first (that will come later), but a war of counterfeit "blessings" based on worldly wealth. Participants in this war will adhere to the belief that if they have sufficient wealth and earthly possessions, they are blessed and therefore righteous (even if they are actually unrighteous). Consequently, they feel that the *source* of their success (which John clearly defines as being the "beast" for the wicked) must, by logical deduction, be righteous also. The Book of Mormon clearly describes cycles wherein people prosper when they are righteous. The devil is obviously able to imitate this process, however, by helping the wicked prosper also.[b]

Prior to the Babylonian captivity, the Lord (through the prophet Jeremiah) condemned the kingdom of Judah for its multitude of sins. The people were committing almost every sin conceivable; but one which the Lord noted with particular anger was the substitution of things of the world for Him. "They are waxen fat," the Lord declared. "They judge not . . . the cause of the fatherless, yet they prosper; and the right of the needy do they not judge."[c] It wasn't just the people who were guilty of this sin. The Lord further noted through Jeremiah: "The prophets prophesy falsely, and the priests bear rule by their means; and my people love to have it so."[d] The wealth of both the people and their leadership had deadened their sense of obligation to care for the needs of their fellowman, and it appears that they even paid their spiritual leaders to tell them that their actions were justified: "from the least of them even to the greatest . . . every one [was] given to covetousness; and from the prophet even unto the priest every one [dealt] falsely."[e] But the Lord would not allow them to think that

a. Daniel 7.

b. Chapter 16.

c. Jeremiah 5:28.

d. Jeremiah 5:31.

e. Jeremiah 6:13.

their wealth measured their righteousness. "Shall I not visit for these things? saith the Lord: and shall not my soul be avenged on such a nation as this?"[a] The people's lust for worldly wealth had overcome their desire to do good, and the Lord pronounced their judgment in definitive terms: "I will cast you out of my sight, as I have cast out all your brethren." Then He gave Jeremiah this unprecedented instruction: "Therefore pray not thou for this people . . . for I will not hear thee."[b]

In the latter days, the Lord declared that many are "called, but few are chosen. And why are they not chosen? Because their hearts are set so much upon the things of this world."[c] From this it is easy to understand what the Lord meant when He warned that even the righteous according to the covenant would hardly escape. Thinking that wealth equates to righteousness is a common deception that is easily believed by the unwary.

In Revelation 17:15, the angel explains to John that the waters whereon the "whore sitteth" represent "peoples, and multitudes, and nations, and tongues." He is describing the tremendous success of the devil's kingdom in the latter days. The effects of the devil's promises on the unwary are succinctly described by Nephi:

> **2 Nephi 28:8, 9, 20–22** Eat, drink, and be merry; nevertheless, fear God— he will justify in committing a little sin; yea, lie a little, take the advantage of one because of his words, dig a pit for thy neighbor; there is no harm in this . . . if it so be that we are guilty, God will beat us with a few stripes, and at last we shall be saved in the kingdom of God. . . . [Many] shall teach after this manner, false and vain and foolish doctrines. . . . At that day shall he rage in the hearts of the children of men, and stir them up to anger against that which is good. And others will he pacify, and lull them away into carnal security, that they will say: All is well in Zion; yea, Zion prospereth, all is well—and thus the devil cheateth their souls, and leadeth them away carefully down to hell. And behold, others he flattereth away, and telleth them there is no hell; and he saith unto them: I am no devil, for there is none—and thus he whispereth in their ears, until he grasps them with his awful chains, from whence there is no deliverance.

The angel further describes the evil woman in Revelation 17 as "that great city, which reigneth over the kings of the earth."[d] John was again speaking symbolically. The symbol of a great city reigning

a. Jeremiah 5:9.

b. Jeremiah 7:15–16.

c. D&C 121:34–35.

d. Revelation 17:18.

over the earth had at least three direct meanings in the vision: (1) it represented the great evil city Babylon as it ruled over its provinces, (2) it represented Rome's rule at John's time, and (3) it represented Rome's future symbolic rule over the nations of the Holy Roman Empire through the consecration and crowning of its kings. In this case, the metaphor also describes an evil entity which rules over, controls, or influences most of the world's economies just prior to the Second Coming. The "great city" is a power (not an actual city) which describes the center or headquarters of Satan's evil kingdom in the latter days. It is this central entity, under the control of the devil (working through the Antichrist and his prophet), which will enslave all but the Lord's chosen people before the Savior comes again.[a]

As great as the devil's kingdom (with its unlimited control over people and nations) will be in the latter days, John begins to see discontentment among its adherents as the Second Coming approaches. The devil's kingdom will become a "city of confusion."[b] The angel tells John that the ten horns (which represent nations) begin to "hate the whore." They make her "desolate and naked," they "eat her flesh," and they "burn her with fire."[c] It is not that the people will ultimately tire of the devil's evil dominion but that they will rebel against the forces that bind and control their economy, their wealth, and their personal freedom.

In the following scriptures, John portrays their greed as they attempt to take control of Satan's organization.

The End of the Devil's Kingdom

Revelation 18   And after these things I saw another angel come down from heaven, having great power; and the earth was lightened with his glory. And he cried mightily with a strong voice, saying, Babylon the great is fallen, is fallen, and is become the habitation of devils, and the hold of every foul spirit, and a cage of every unclean and hateful bird. For all nations have drunk of the wine of the wrath of her fornication, and the kings of the earth have committed fornication with her, and the merchants of the earth are waxed rich through the abundance of her delicacies. And I heard another voice from heaven, saying, Come out of her, my people, that ye be not partakers of her sins, and that ye receive not of her plagues. For her sins have reached unto heaven, and God hath remembered her iniquities. Reward her even as she rewarded you, and double unto her double according to her works: in the cup which she hath filled fill to her double. How much she hath glorified herself, and lived deliciously, so much torment and sorrow give her: for she saith in her heart, I sit a queen, and

a. Daniel 7.

b. Isaiah 24:10.

c. Revelation 17:16.

am no widow, and shall see no sorrow. Therefore shall her plagues come in one day, death, and mourning, and famine; and she shall be utterly burned with fire: for strong is the Lord God who judgeth her. And the kings of the earth, who have committed fornication and lived deliciously with her, shall bewail her, and lament for her, when they shall see the smoke of her burning, standing afar off for the fear of her torment, saying, Alas, alas, that great city Babylon, that mighty city! for in one hour is thy judgment come. And the merchants of the earth shall weep and mourn over her; for no man buyeth their merchandise any more: the merchandise of gold, and silver, and precious stones, and of pearls, and fine linen, and purple, and silk, and scarlet, and all thyine wood, and all manner vessels of ivory, and all manner vessels of most precious wood, and of brass, and iron, and marble, and cinnamon, and odours, and ointments, and frankincense, and wine, and oil, and fine flour, and wheat, and beasts, and sheep, and horses, and chariots, and slaves, and souls of men. And the fruits that thy soul lusted after are departed from thee, and all things which were dainty and goodly are departed from thee, and thou shalt find them no more at all. The merchants of these things, which were made rich by her, shall stand afar off for the fear of her torment, weeping and wailing, and saying, Alas, alas, that great city, that was clothed in fine linen, and purple, and scarlet, and decked with gold, and precious stones, and pearls! For in one hour so great riches is come to nought. And every shipmaster, and all the company in ships, and sailors, and as many as trade by sea, stood afar off, And cried when they saw the smoke of her burning, saying, What city is like unto this great city! And they cast dust on their heads, and cried, weeping and wailing, saying, Alas, alas, that great city, wherein were made rich all that had ships in the sea by reason of her costliness! for in one hour is she made desolate. Rejoice over her, thou heaven, and ye holy apostles and prophets; for God hath avenged you on her. And a mighty angel took up a stone like a great millstone, and cast it into the sea, saying, Thus with violence shall that great city Babylon be thrown down, and shall be found no more at all. And the voice of harpers, and musicians, and of pipers, and trumpeters, shall be heard no more at all in thee; and no craftsman, of whatsoever craft he be, shall be found any more in thee; and the sound of a millstone shall be heard no more at all in thee; and the light of a candle shall shine no more at all in thee; and the voice of the bridegroom and of the bride shall be heard no more at all in thee: for thy merchants were the great men of the earth; for by thy sorceries were all nations deceived. And in her was found the blood of prophets, and of saints, and of all that were slain upon the earth.

God "hath put [it] in [the] hearts [of the wicked] to fulfil his will, and to agree, and give their kingdom unto the beast, until the words of God shall be fulfilled."[a] This scripture is saying that because of the eternal principle of free agency inherent in the plan of salvation, God allows mankind to choose good or evil. The wicked obviously make the wrong choice, but the Lord promised them agency and He has

a. Revelation 17:17.

fulfilled His promise by letting them choose. At the Second Coming, the time of their probation will be over and He will pour out His wrath upon them without measure.[a][121] There will be no acquittal from their wickedness;[b] they will be cast out, not redeemed;[c] they will receive no mercy.[d] At that time, the devil's evil deceptions will be revealed[e] and the Lord will conqueror "leviathan . . . that crooked serpent,"[f] for the Lord will be angry with the wicked[g][122] and He will chasten them.

John tells us that the devil's corrupt dominion is responsible for all evil[h] and that it will eventually "drink of the wine of the wrath" of its own "fornication."[i] Its wicked followers will suffer from a plague of "noisome and grievous sore[s]."[j] They will be gathered as tares to be burned[k] and "cast down by devouring fire."[l][123] The Antichrist beast, the false prophet beast, and all men and women who bear the beast's "mark" will reap what they have sown,[m] and their final state will be hell,[n] the bottomless pit,[o] where they will become "perdition."[p] In spite of its initial and overwhelming success in the latter days, the devil's kingdom will ultimately suffer a violent destruction because, "There is no peace, saith my God, to the wicked."[q]

The scriptures tell us that all nations, kings, and merchants will wax rich with the abundant "delicacies" made available under the devil's reign. He has been and will be (through the influence and power of his economic kingdom) in control, and his evil influence will affect both people and governments as he works to realize his goals. Up until the Second Coming the righteous will be allowed to reside among his denizens, but as the Savior prepares to destroy the devil's kingdom, He will call for the righteous to "come out" from Satan's domain so they will not become "partakers of her sins" and receive of her "plagues" of destruction.[r]

God knows what Satan's sins are, and He will mete out to him double the punishment for the equivalent reward Satan gives mankind. The Lord will do this because the devil's kingdom "hath glorified herself, and lived deliciously."[s] She has lusted after all sins and concluded that she could not be stopped. God has judged her, and her death is assured. The "kings of the earth" (representing all nations, entities, and others who pursue the devil's kingdom) will lament her downfall because they love sin more than God.[t] They will see the "smoke of her burning,"[u] which means they will understand the full-

a. D&C 1:9.

b. Nahum 1:3.

c. Mosiah 16:2.

d. Mosiah 3:24–27.

e. Isaiah 29:20.

f. Isaiah 27:1.

g. D&C 63:32.

h. Revelation 18:24.

i. Revelation 14:8.

j. Revelation 16:2.

k. D&C 88:94; Matthew 13:38; D&C 101:65–66.

l. D&C 29:21.

m. Revelation 14:9–11.

n. 1 Nephi 15:32–36.

o. Revelation 20:1–3.

p. D&C 76:25–38, 43–49.

q. Isaiah 57:3–13, 20–21.

r. Revelation 18:4.

s. Revelation 18:7.

t. Revelation 18:9–10.

u. Revelation 18:9.

ness of her evil and destruction. They will "weep and mourn over her," not because they are repentant, but because "no man buyeth their merchandise any more: gold, and silver, and precious stones . . . pearls, and fine linen . . . purple, and silk . . . scarlet . . . thyine wood . . . ivory . . . brass . . . marble . . . cinnamon . . . odours . . . ointments, and frankincense . . . wine . . . oil . . . fine flour, and wheat . . .beasts, and sheep, and horses and chariots, and slaves," and even the "souls of men."[a] They have allowed the precious things of worldly value to become the "fruits" of their souls. But, the angel declared, all "fruits that thy soul lusted after are departed from thee, and all things which were dainty and goodly are departed from thee, and thou shalt find them no more at all."[b] Those who succumbed to the devil's kingdom and were made rich by her will cry, "Alas, alas, that great city [Babylon, Satan's kingdom]. . . in one hour is she made desolate."[c] And John sees this final destruction of Babylon in his vision when "another angel" comes to him and cries, "Babylon the great is fallen, is fallen, and is become the habitation of devils, and the hold of every foul spirit."[d]

In the end, all that are evil shall perish and shall be consumed by the wrath of God.[e][124] Those who were deceived by Lucifer shall mourn while the heavens rejoice at the destruction of wickedness. Babylon will be "found no more at all."[f] There will no longer be a need for worldly wealth,[g] and the devil's ability to deceive through mimicry will cease. The righteous will finally overcome the "beast"[h] because of their faith according to the covenant, and they will be led by the "Lamb" of God, the "Lord of lords," the "King of kings," as He goes forth into His Millennial reign.[i]

a. Revelation 18:11–13.

b. Revelation 18:14.

c. Revelation 18:16–19.

d. Revelation 18:2.

e. 1 Nephi 22:15–18.

f. Revelation 18:20–21.

g. Revelation 18:22.

h. Revelation 15:2.

i. Revelation 17:14.

Signs: Both General and Specific   9

Doctrine and Covenants 45:40   And they shall see signs and wonders, for they shall be shown forth in the heavens above, and in the earth beneath.

"The time will come when [mankind] will not endure sound doctrine; but after their own lusts shall they heap to themselves teachers, having itching ears; and they shall turn away their ears from the truth, and [the truth] shall be turned unto fables."[a] In this message to Timothy, Paul was speaking not only of the great Apostasy and the many doctrines and teachings that would evolve from it prior to the Second Coming, but also of the great flood of false teachings that would occur after the restoration of the gospel in the latter days.

While the Savior was on the earth, He warned His Apostles to "take heed that no man deceive you."[b] He gave them this warning in answer to their questions concerning His Second Coming and the destruction of Jerusalem; but as was the practice of many of His prophets before Him, His comment referenced not only the time of His Apostles but also the time of those who would live after the restoration in the latter days. This latter period was to be a time like no other, a time when the joys of the good life with its pursuit of worldly wealth would destroy men's faith on a wholesale basis. Paul warned all mankind of this pitfall when he told Timothy that "the love of money is the root of all evil."[c] He was cautioning us against coveting worldly wealth lest we "fall into temptation and a snare, and into many foolish and hurtful lusts" which would eventually drown us "in destruction and perdition."[d]

a. 2 Timothy 4:3–4.

b. Matthew 24:4.

c. 1 Timothy 6:10.

d. 1 Timothy 6:9.

We have already discussed many signs of the Second Coming—signs that have already been fulfilled, and some that are yet to be fulfilled. However, there are many more prophesied signs, both *general* and *specific,* that are being and will be fulfilled before the Lord's Advent. Each of these categories presents it own problems of recognition. General signs like wars, rumors of wars, and earthquakes have occurred in many different generations. These general signs occur regularly so that men and women will remain aware of the Lord's prophecies concerning His Second Coming and be encouraged to prepare for it. Furthermore, to compound the difficulty of recognizing general signs, the Lord often made His warnings of them general as well.

Specific signs on the other hand let us know with a surety that the Lord's promises will all be fulfilled. Through His Apostles, the Lord has given us the following admonition: "Now learn a parable of the fig tree; when his branch is yet tender, and putteth forth leaves, ye know that summer is nigh: so likewise ye, when ye shall see all these things, [shall] know that [the Second Coming] is near, even at the doors."[a]

At times the scriptures seem to explode with signs of the Savior's coming as verse after verse recounts an indiscriminate intermingling of both general and specific signs. For example, the Lord did this in a latter-day revelation wherein He referenced the symbol of the fig tree used in Matthew and then noted that through its tender leaves and early shoots, mankind would know that His coming was near. He tells us that in that day people will see "signs and wonders" in the heavens and in the "earth beneath."[b] Then He opens the floodgates and allows the signs to rush out. There will be "blood, and fire, and vapors of smoke . . . before the day of the Lord shall come . . . The sun shall be darkened, and the moon [shall] be turned into blood, and the stars fall from heaven. And the remnant shall be gathered" into one place where they will see the Savior come "in the clouds of heaven, clothed with power and great glory; with all the holy angels; and he that watches not for [Him] shall be cut off."[c] Further, "the saints that have slept shall come forth to meet" Him in a "cloud."[d] "Then shall the arm of the Lord fall upon the nations." He will "set his foot" upon the Mount of Olives and "it shall cleave in twain, and the earth shall tremble, and reel to and fro, and the heavens also shall shake." In that

a. Matthew 24:32–33; Mark 13:28–29; Luke 21:29–31.

b. D&C 45:40.

c. D&C 45:41–44.

d. D&C 45:45.

day "the Lord shall utter his voice, and all the ends of the earth shall hear it; and the nations of the earth shall mourn, and they that have laughed shall see their folly . . . Calamity shall cover the mocker, and the scorner shall be consumed; and they that have watched for iniquity shall be hewn down and cast into the fire." And then the Jews will look at the Savior and say, "What are these wounds in thine hands and in thy feet?"[a] And the Lord will explain to them that He received those wounds "in the house of [His] friends." He will then erase all doubt of His messiahship by declaring, "I am he who was lifted up. I am Jesus that was crucified. I am the Son of God."[b] Finally, in that day "Satan shall be bound," and during the Millennium he "shall have no place in the hearts of the children of men."[c]

With such a litany of signs (and these are but a few), it can easily be concluded that the fig tree has begun to bud. It is now up to each of us to recognize the fulfillment of these specific signs and to accept the ongoing general signs as a reminder that God's hand and the devil's presence are constantly with us. *Spiritual vigilance is the key to preparedness.*

The following are four general signs that we should constantly monitor:

As in the Days of Noah

The Lord tells us in the gospel of Matthew that prior to the Second Coming, men and women will behave as they did in the days of Noah. They will be "eating and drinking, marrying and giving in marriage,"[d] and participating in the normal everyday aspects of life. Luke's record supports this, using the people of Sodom and Gomorrah during the days of Lot as his example. Like Sodom and Gomorrah, the people of the latter days will be eating and drinking, buying and selling, and planting and harvesting. Life will go apace. And tragically, most of them will not recognize or heed the warnings and signs given to them so that they can prepare themselves for the Lord's coming.[e]

The cities of Sodom and Gomorrah were consumed when fire rained down on them from heaven. Of all their inhabitants, only four souls survived the conflagration, and one of those fell because of disobedience. In Noah's time, the flood came and destroyed all but

a. D&C 45:47–51.
b. D&C 45:52.
c. D&C 45:55.
d. Matthew 24:38.
e. Luke 17:28–29.

eight of God's children—the rest were too wicked to be saved. "Who then [of mankind] is a faithful and wise servant," the Lord asks, and not like the evil servant who said in his heart, "My lord delayeth his coming."[a] As a result of the lord's delay in this teaching, the servant began to "smite his fellow servants, and to eat and drink with the drunken," not recognizing that his Lord would come "in a day when he looketh not for him, and in an hour that he [was] not aware of, and [would] cut him asunder." This is exactly what is prophesied to happen at the Second Coming. If men and women ignore the prophesied warnings and signs the Lord has given them, there will be "weeping" and wailing and "gnashing of teeth" when He appears.[b]

The fact that the period of time between the restoration and the Second Coming will be as it was "in the days of Noah" is a very general sign of the Lord's Advent, so much so that it is easy to understand why signs of this type are a problem. Life goes on, and we continue to do all of the things that are required for survival as well as the things that we enjoy. Nonetheless, we can draw one specific thing from this general sign: just as the flood in Noah's time was a worldwide cataclysmic event, so also will the general signs of the Second Coming affect most of mankind—and some will have a devastating effect on the entire earth.

The Good-Times Sin

The days of Noah were times of indescribable evil—so much so that God was willing to destroy almost all the life on earth and begin again. This period has been used as an example of evil so extreme that it resulted in the Lord pronouncing a catastrophic judgment against the people. (This example is also used as a warning to the people of the latter days regarding their status before God.)

The Bible does not describe the sins of Noah's people other than in general terms, but a modern commentary on *The Torah* sheds light on what the people were doing: "The earth [had become] corrupt before God; the earth was filled with lawlessness."[c] This lawlessness is interpreted as lawlessness toward God, which "is the manifestation of a social disease" practiced by the antediluvians, and not its cause. "The Midrash speculates that it was *unbounded affluence* that caused men to become depraved, that wealth afforded them the leisure to discover

a. Matthew 24:45, 48.

b. Matthew 24:49–51.

c. The Torah: Genesis 6:11.

new thrills and to commit sexual aberrations."[125] This, along with the excesses that wealth allowed in all facets of their lives, caused the people to develop an "overbearing attitude toward God."[126] The Lord uses this example in scripture and it completely fits John's prophecies with regards to the devil's use of economics and worldly wealth in the latter days. Thus, the times of Noah, in connection with John's prophecy, illustrate what the good-times sin is: it is a materialistic society eating, drinking, and making merry—to the exclusion of God and spiritual enlightenment.[a]

Prior to their Babylonian captivity, Israel had this same problem. Isaiah describes the Israelites as a people who overindulged in their pursuits of "joy and gladness." They were "slaying oxen, and killing sheep, eating flesh, and drinking wine," saying "let us eat and drink; for to morrow we shall die."[b] As a result of their wicked state of mind, the Lord called for them to weep and mourn, to bald their heads, and to gird themselves with sackcloth as acts of repentance so that He could save their children from future destruction—but Israel would not![c] The Lord's reaction to Israel's obduracy was swift: "Surely this iniquity shall not be purged from you till ye die."[d]

This pleasure-oriented existence to the exclusion of righteousness was also at the base of Sodom and Gomorrah's destruction, and while "they were accustomed to some form or forms of sexual deviation . . . Jewish tradition stresses social rather than sexual aberrations as the reason for the cities' destruction."[127] In his condemnation of the sins of the kingdom of Judah and the city of Jerusalem (sin was the cause of the Babylonian captivity), Ezekiel compares the people of these cities to those of Sodom and Gomorrah, and he chastens Judah for "pride, fulness of bread, and abundance of idleness . . . [to the extent that she did not] strengthen the hand of the poor and needy."[e] A commentary on *The Torah* expresses the thought that "affluence without social concern is self-destructive; it hardens the conscience against repentance; [and] it engenders cruelty and excess." The Midrash says Sodom and Gomorrah deserved punishment, "both for their immorality and for their uncharitableness. For whoever grudges assistance to the poor does not deserve to exist in this world, and he also forfeits the life of the world-to-come."[128]

In the New Testament, the Lord depicts perfectly the good-times

a. Chapter 8.

b. Isaiah
   22:13.

c. Isaiah
   22:12.

d. Isaiah
   22:14.

e. Ezekiel 16:49.

sin of the people of Noah, Sodom and Gomorrah, and Judah (prior to its Babylonian captivity) through the parable of the foolish rich man:

> **Luke 12:16–20** And he spake a parable unto them, saying, The ground of a certain rich man brought forth plentifully: and he thought within himself, saying, What shall I do, because I have no room where to bestow my fruits? And he said, This will I do: I will pull down my barns, and build greater; and there will I bestow all my fruits and my goods. And I will say to my soul, Soul, thou hast much goods laid up for many years; take thine ease, eat, drink, and be merry. But God said unto him, Thou fool, this night thy soul shall be required of thee: then whose shall those things be, which thou hast provided?

This parable points out the relationship between the things of the world and the things of the Spirit. The rich man's ground brought forth an unanticipated abundance of goods, and he wondered what he should do with his newfound wealth. He was not interested in sharing his abundance or even in giving thanks for it; he was only interested in how he could preserve it for himself. He was a selfishly proud, self-indulgent man who placed his personal ease and sensuous enjoyment far above any spiritual values. The Lord purposefully type-cast the foolish rich man in this manner so that His audience would recognize the good-times sin that had been inherent in the destruction of Sodom and Gomorrah and the people of Noah, and so that readers of the scriptures in subsequent ages would become aware of the same problems in their time. His parable makes clear the propensities each of us fight against when spiritual values are challenged with temporal desires. The things of the world can make people blind to the things of the Spirit. The foolish rich man only thought to satisfy his physical appetites. He gave no thought to God's commandments and placed worldly desires above the worship of God. By doing so, he broke the first great commandment, and he broke the second great commandment by placing his personal desires above the welfare of his neighbors. He had emphasized all the wrong things in his life: worldly power, riches, self-indulgence; and he had forgotten all the right things: God, his neighbor, the poor. His spiritual impoverishment far outweighed his temporal wealth.[a] As a result, God left him (and us) with this stark warning: "Thou fool, this night thy soul shall be required of thee: then whose shall those things be, which thou hast

a. Matthew 6:20–21.

provided?"[a129] The foolish rich man had made the wrong choice! He had laid up treasure for his earthly pleasure, but he was impoverished toward God and his fellow man. The message is clear: the only things we can take with us when we die are the things of the Spirit—all else is left behind.

The preacher in Ecclesiastes was warning mankind about the good-times sin long before Christ taught the parable of the foolish rich man in Luke. He wrote: "He that loveth silver shall not be satisfied with silver; nor he that loveth abundance with increase: this is also vanity."[b] The teachings of the preacher and the parable of the foolish rich man show us how easy it is for the devil to control the hearts and minds of men. The rich man of the parable thought only of his *fruits*, his *goods*, and his *barn* so that he could "eat, drink and be merry."

In the Book of Mormon, Nephi also described the good-times sin:

> **2 Nephi 28:8**   And there shall also be many which shall say: Eat, drink, and be merry; nevertheless, fear God—he will justify in committing a little sin; yea, lie a little, take the advantage of one because of his words, dig a pit for thy neighbor; there is no harm in this; and do all these things, for tomorrow we die; and if it so be that we are guilty, God will beat us with a few stripes, and at last we shall be saved in the kingdom of God.

Wrong! Nephi aptly described this rationale as "false and vain and foolish doctrines."[c] Luke warned mankind of the good-times sin by saying:

> **Luke 21:34–36**   And take heed to yourselves, lest at any time your hearts be overcharged with surfeiting, and drunkenness, and cares of this life, and so that day come upon you unawares. For as a snare shall it come on all them that dwell on the face of the whole earth. Watch ye therefore, and pray always, that ye may be accounted worthy to escape all these things that shall come to pass, and to stand before the Son of man.

All of this teaches us a great principle: God keeps calling and warning, but our *things* keep getting in the way. He made it clear that we "cannot serve God and mammon."[d]

Although the good-times sin has occurred throughout the millennia, it is also a general sign of the Lord's Second Coming in the latter days: if we become so involved in the things of the world that we miss the

a. Luke 12:20.

b. Ecclesiastes 5:10.

c. 2 Nephi 28:9.

d. Matthew 6:24.

signs of the Lord's prophesied Advent, we will be unprepared for Him when He comes. By allowing our hearts to become set on the things of the world, and by justifying the use and aggrandizement of them, the things of God will cease to exist in our hearts. Paul warned the Romans, "Put ye on the Lord Jesus Christ, and make not provision for the flesh, to fulfill the lusts thereof"[a]—a strong warning against the good-times sin. For as the Lord declared, "Where your treasure is, there will your heart be also."[b]

The Effect of Signs on Mankind

Whether we watch for them or not, the signs of the Second Coming will occur! And when they occur, they will confuse and confound mankind by violently disrupting people's lifestyle. Their magnitude will be so great that "men's hearts shall fail them" as a result.[c] This does not mean that everyone will literally die of a heart attack: the Lord is explaining to us in a graphic manner that the signs announcing His Advent will be so powerful and disruptive that many will be terrified. At that time "all things" will "be in commotion," and "a desolating sickness shall cover the land."[d] The Lord has decreed that wars will come "upon the face of the earth, and the wicked shall slay the wicked, and fear shall come upon every man; and the saints also shall hardly escape."[e] Luke tells us that the very "powers of heaven shall be shaken."[f] The Doctrine and Covenants is even more graphic: "The sun shall be darkened, and the moon shall be turned into blood, and the stars shall fall from heaven . . . [and] there shall be a great hailstorm sent forth to destroy the crops of the earth."[g] These will not be normal occurrences, and all mankind will be subject to their fury.

With such devastating events occurring, all men and women will fear for their possessions, their loved ones, and their lives. One unfortunate result of these phenomena is that "the love of men shall wax cold."[h] Men and women will become selfish and will withhold assistance from those in need "because their hearts are corrupted." As a result, "the things which they are willing to bring upon others, and love to have others suffer, may come upon themselves to the very uttermost; that they may be disappointed also, and their hopes [of salvation] may be cut off."[i] Mankind's fear throughout this period of destruction will cause some to say that God isn't ever going to come,[j]

a. Romans 13:14.

b. Matthew 6:21.

c. D&C 45:26.

d. D&C 88:91; 45:31.

e. D&C 63:33–34.

f. Luke 21:26.

g. D&C 29:14, 16.

h. D&C 45:27.

i. D&C 121:13–14.

j. D&C 45:26.

while others may contend that there is no God at all and that the terrors they are experiencing are of their own making. "Iniquity shall abound" during this period, and only those who are not overcome by the world will be saved.[a]

Enoch saw this period of great tribulation and prophesied that mankind would look "forth with fear for the judgments of the Almighty God, which should come upon the wicked."[b] John the Revelator described this fear in vivid terms: "And the kings of the earth, and the great men, and the rich men, and the chief captains, and the mighty men, and every bondman, and every free man [shall hide] themselves in the dens and in the rocks of the mountains; and [they will say] to the mountains and [to the] rocks, Fall on us, and hide us from the face of him that sitteth on the throne, and [hide us] from the wrath of the Lamb."[c] In the Gospel of Mark, the Lord warns us that brother will betray brother causing his death, and fathers will betray their sons. Even children will "rise up against their parents, and shall cause them to be put to death."[d]

Zechariah graphically describes those who are found fighting against Jerusalem at the Second Coming: "Their flesh shall consume away while they stand upon their feet, and their eyes shall consume away in their holes, and their tongue shall consume away in their mouth."[e] The Lord broadened Zechariah's prophecy to include all the wicked on the earth who would not repent: "Their tongues shall be stayed that they shall not utter against me; and their flesh shall fall from off their bones, and their eyes from their sockets."[f] He stated that He would send flies upon the earth to "take hold of the inhabitants thereof . . . [to] eat their flesh," and he would "cause maggots to come in upon them."[g] He further asserted that these deplorable conditions would cause the "beasts of the forest and the fowls of the air [to come and] devour them up."[h][130]

Before the Second Coming of the Messiah there will be a great division between the righteous and the unrighteous inhabitants of the earth.[i] The wicked will fear and tremble at this time, but Nephi tells us that the righteous need not fear, for they will not be confounded by anything that occurs during this period.[j] Jeremiah, the writer of Lamentations, gives us the reason for this: "The Lord is good unto them that wait for him, to the soul that seeketh him. It is good that a man

a. Joseph Smith–
Matthew 1:30.

b. Moses 7:66.

c. Revelation
6:15–16.

d. Mark 13:12.

e. Zechariah
14:12.

f. D&C 29:19.

g. D&C 29:18.

h. D&C 29:20.

i. 2 Nephi
30:10–11.

j. 1 Nephi
22:22.

should both hope and quietly wait for the salvation of the Lord."[a] In other words, the righteous will not necessarily be spared the devastation of the Second Coming, but they will be prepared for it, and their preparation will ensure them a place in the Father's kingdom.

The Lord warns us that by the time of His Advent, the whole of His vineyard will be "corrupted every whit;" there will be "none which doeth good save it be a few; and they [will] err in many instances because of priestcrafts, all having corrupt minds."[b] Nephi tells us that "because of pride, and wickedness, and abominations, and whoredoms . . . [all have] gone astray save it be a few, who are the humble followers of Christ; nevertheless . . . in many instances they do err because they are taught by the precepts of men."[c] The devil frequently disguises his wickedness in the form of pleasurable and even intellectually stimulating things, and it is often difficult for the righteous to recognize his evil enticements.

In the book of Isaiah, the Lord declared that He would make "the earth empty, and . . . waste, and turneth it upside down, and scattereth abroad the inhabitants thereof."[d] This will involve both the righteous and the wicked, because the Lord "sendeth rain on the just and on the unjust" alike.[e] Isaiah came to the same conclusion years before: "And it shall be, as with the people, so with the priest; as with the servant, so with his master; as with the maid, so with her mistress; as with the buyer, so with the seller; as with the lender, so with the borrower; as with the taker of usury, so with the giver of usury to him."[f] All mankind, both the wicked and the righteous, will be affected by the devastating general signs prior to the Lord's Second Coming.[131] Even the very elect, those elect according to the covenant, need to be cautious.

The Doctrine and Covenants tells us that the prophesied afflictions will devastate mankind in a manner "such as was not from the beginning of the creation," and if the Lord had not told us that He would shorten those days, "no flesh [would] be saved: but for the elect's sake, [those who hear the Savior's voice and 'harden not their hearts'[g]] . . . he hath shortened the days."[h] This does not mean that the Second Coming will occur before its decreed time, for that time is mandated in heaven, as was the time of Christ's birth. What it does mean is that the Lord will come before everyone has been destroyed. It is up to each individual to be prepared if he or she wants to be counted among the "elect" who remain. In the parables of the talents and the pounds, the Savior gave a talent or a pound to each of His servants so that he might make preparation for the master's return. But in both of the parables, even though each individual had the opportunity to be an elect of the master, there was one who would not do what was required. Not knowing when the master would return, this individual was unprepared to receive him when he finally did appear.[132] And thus it will be in the last days.

It is also prophesied that false Christs and false prophets will appear before the Lord comes and they will perform "great signs and wonders, insomuch, that, if possible, they shall deceive the very elect, who are the elect according to the covenant" (those who have been endowed with the promised blessings of Abraham).[a] These signs and wonders will lead some men and women astray, but it is these same signs that will notify them when the Savior "is near, even at the doors," if they are watching for Him.[b] The devil will continue to practice this art of imitation right to the end. Vigilance is constantly required to maintain righteousness.

The Changing of the Times and Seasons

During the Creation, the Lord set in motion the "lights in the firmament" so that we could determine night from day. He also set them for "signs, and for seasons, and for days, and years."[c] Their cycles establish our normal times and seasons. The preacher in Ecclesiastes declared: "To every thing there is a season, and a time to every purpose under the heaven: A time to be born, and a time to die; a time to plant, and a time to pluck up that which is planted." He also said there was a time to kill and a time to heal, a time to laugh and mourn and dance, a time to get, a time to lose, a time to keep, and a time to cast away.[d] The preacher obviously recognized the normal sequences of life that God's plan of salvation set in motion. During His ministry, Jesus used these established sequences when He chastised the people for their failure to recognize the signs of the times. He marveled that they had become so acquainted with the normal order of the times and seasons that they could discern the weather: a red sky in the evening meant "fair weather," or a "red and lowring" sky in the morning indicated "foul weather." "But," He continued, "can ye not discern the signs of the

a. Joseph Smith–
Matthew 1:22.

b. Joseph
Smith–Matthew
1:39.

c. Genesis
1:14.

d. Ecclesiastes
3:1–8.

times?"[a] Their reliance on the normal order of the times, seasons, and elements had clouded their ability to recognize the general signs of His first coming; therefore, the Savior declared that they were hypocrites.

The seasonal cycles: summer, winter, spring, fall, rainy, dry etc., have been relied upon throughout the ages and continue to be relied upon today. But God declared that a general sign of the last days would be a change in this normal pattern: "God hath set his hand and seal to change the times and seasons." Why will He do this? "To blind [the minds of the wicked] that they may not understand his marvelous workings; that he may prove them also and take them in their own craftiness."[b] This brings to mind Paul's warning to Timothy wherein Timothy was told to avoid "profane and vain babblings, and oppositions of science falsely so called."[c] Scientists today feel they can predict much of what will occur in nature and tend to explain away all that does occur. In this manner, devastating floods, severe winters, hurricanes, tornadoes, earthquakes, and the like become explainable normal or extraordinary events. Therefore, when God changes the times and seasons and makes them unreliable, it becomes a proving to the mind and understanding of man's knowledge. In other words, science may have a logical explanation for the changes that will occur and will not acknowledge them as God's marvelous workings. But eventually they will be proven incorrect, and at that time the scriptures state that great "calamity shall cover the mocker, and the scorner shall be consumed" as God's signs of the times are finally recognized.[d]

It is also possible that the cataclysmic changing of the times and seasons may be the means by which the Lord will bring about the "desolating scourge" which will bring devastation and death to many of the earth's inhabitants just prior to His Second Coming. However, that is yet to be determined. And so we wait, straining to recognize and ever watching "for the signs of the coming of the Son of Man."[e]

a. Matthew
   16:2–3.
b. D&C
   121:12.
c. 1 Timothy 6:20.
d. D&C 45:50.
e. D&C 45:39.

Signs: The Earth's Three Phases

Doctrine and Covenants 29:9   For the hour is nigh and the day soon at hand when the earth is ripe.

Doctrine and Covenants 123:7   And the whole earth groans under the weight of its [the inhabitants'] iniquity.

The Earth

"Enoch looked upon the earth; and he heard a voice from [its depths] saying: Wo, wo is me, the mother of men; I am pained, I am weary, because of the wickedness of my children. When shall I rest, and be cleansed from the filthiness which is gone forth out of me? When will my Creator sanctify me, that I may rest?"[a] Whether this scripture is symbolic or literal, it describes the earth as a living entity capable of communicating and feeling both pleasure and pain.

When Adam and Eve were placed on the earth, it was in a state of paradise. But Adam and Eve sinned, and when they fell from the presence of God, the earth also fell. Isaiah described the earth as being "devoured" by this curse and its inhabitants as being desolate because they were no longer in the presence of God.[b] The earth remained defiled because the inhabitants thereof "transgressed the laws, changed the ordinance, [and broke] the everlasting covenant"[c] The earth is not capable of sinning, but under the plan of salvation, its condition is affected by its inhabitants; therefore, "the Lord maketh the earth empty, and maketh it waste, and turneth it upside down, and scattereth abroad the inhabitants thereof."[d]

a. Moses 7:48.
b. Isaiah 24:6.
c. Isaiah 24:5.
d. Isaiah 24:1.

There are at least three phases the earth must go through in the latter days before it will be sanctified, made ready to receive its Creator, and have "righteousness for a season [the millennium] abide upon [its] face."[a]

Phase One—Tumults That Will Occur to the Earth

The earth will remain under the curse brought on by the Fall of Adam until the Lord comes again. Before that time, however, many signs of His coming will affect it. These general signs, while symbolically bringing great tumults to mind, are described in terms that leave almost everything to the imagination. Isaiah said that the very "foundations of the earth" would shake. The earth would be "utterly broken down . . . dissolved . . . moved," and would "reel to and fro" like a drunken man.[b] A like description given in the latter days adds that the earth will "tremble" before it reels to and fro as a drunken man.[c]

Both latter-day revelation and the ancient psalmist declare that the earth will quake or shake at the Lord's Advent.[d] Joel, an Old Testament prophet, describes these quaking disturbances and declares that they will cause the people to "run to and fro."[e] There are many scriptures that predict these shakings and quakings as earthquakes that will occur in diverse places in the latter days.[f] They are to be a testimony to mankind of the Second Coming, and they will be so severe that men and women will "fall upon the ground" and "not be able to stand."[g] The magnitude of these earthquakes will even cause the "waves of the sea" to heave "themselves beyond their bounds,"[h] a description painfully acknowledged by anyone who has been near the ocean after an earthquake and experienced a tsunami.

Due to the many earthquakes that are predicted, the scriptures indicate that mountains will be made low, valleys will disappear, crooked places will be made straight, and rough places will be made plain, or smooth.[i] The scriptures also testify that the mountains will be made to "flow down" at the Lord's presence,[j][133] and in another mind-expanding prediction, Isaiah declares that the Lord will shake the heavens and "remove" the earth "out of her place."[k] Could this mean that the continents will abruptly change their position or that the earth's orbit will change, or is there some other explanation?

Although the general descriptions of these signs leave the individual

a. Moses 7:48.

b. Isaiah 24:14–20.

c. D&C 45:48; 88:87.

d. Psalm 77:18; D&C 29:13; D&C 43:18; D&C 84:118.

e. Joel 2:9–10.

f. Mark 13:8; Luke 21:11; D&C 45:33.

g. D&C 88:89.

h. D&C 88:90.

i. Isaiah 40:4; D&C 49:23; D&C 133:22.

j. Isaiah 64:1; D&C 109:74.

k. Isaiah 13:13.

to determine when and where they will occur, there is evidence of what will *make* them occur. It is the voice of the Lord! Ezekiel heard the Lord's voice coming from the "east," and it sounded "like a noise of many waters."[a] John the Revelator heard the voice and said it was "as the sound of many waters."[b] Joseph Smith also heard it and described it as "the sound of the rushing of great waters" and "as the voice of a great thunder."[c] Are the scriptures saying that the Lord initiates these incidents by the mere *sound* of His voice? Or does He do it by His command? Probably the latter, since the descriptions seem to be symbolic. However, it is the power of His voice that in some way causes the general disasters described,[d] and some of the earth's population will be injured or killed as a result. The primary purpose of these tumultuous general signs, however, is not to kill but to warn the people of the earth that the coming of the Lord is near.

Phase Two—The Physical Cleansing of the Earth

The earth will be cleansed of all wickedness prior to the Second Coming, and while the catastrophes of phase one are designed as a warning and constant reminder of the Lord's pending Advent, the destructions of phase two are specifically intended to destroy the wicked who will not heed the Savior's warnings and repent. The vision of this final cleansing was given to the Apostle John and is recorded in multiple chapters of Revelation.[134]

In Revelation 7:1–3, John introduces us to four destroying angels. These angels are given the power to hurt the earth and the sea. They are ready to begin their cleansing task at once, but are restrained by another of the Lord's angels. This restraint allows time for the final proselyting of the gospel so that all those who are to be converted prior to the Second Coming will have received the symbolic seal of God in their foreheads. Acceptance or rejection of the gospel will give everyone the opportunity to either be saved from or subject to the wrath of the four angels, and by extension, to either be saved in or cast out of the Father's kingdom.[e] John does not tell us how these four angels will function, and he does not refer to them again until Revelation 9:14.

The balance of the 7th chapter (verses 4–17) deals with those who will receive the seal of God during the proselyting that will occur while

a. Ezekiel 43:2.
b. Revelation 1:15; 14:2.
c. D&C 110:3; 133:22.
d. D&C 133:22,
e. D&C 77:8.

the four angels are restrained. These righteous people are symbolically placed into two groups: (1) the 144,000 sealed individuals (12,000 from each of the tribes of Israel) who have received their judgment and had their calling and election made sure,[a] and (2) the multitude of the righteous which John sees as "a great multitude . . . of all nations" who stand before God "clothed with white robes." "These are they," John explains, who "came out of great tribulation, and have washed their robes, and made them white in the blood of the Lamb."[b] These individuals have also made their calling and election sure and will serve God "day and night in his temple," and will "hunger" and "thirst" no more. The Lord will even "wipe away all tears from their eyes."[c] John's descriptive symbolism indicates that they have been relieved of all their earthly problems: their sins have been forgiven and forgotten, and they will be made joint heirs with Christ in His kingdom.

The Opening of the Seventh Seal

When the seventh seal is opened, the tribulation which will culminate with the Lord's Advent will begin.

Revelation 8 And when he had opened the seventh seal, there was silence in heaven about the space of half an hour. And I saw the seven angels which stood before God; and to them were given seven trumpets. And another angel came and stood at the altar, having a golden censer; and there was given unto him much incense, that he should offer it with the prayers of all saints upon the golden altar which was before the throne. And the smoke of the incense, which came with the prayers of the saints, ascended up before God out of the angel's hand. And the angel took the censer, and filled it with fire of the altar, and cast it into the earth: and there were voices, and thunderings, and lightnings, and an earthquake. And the seven angels which had the seven trumpets prepared themselves to sound. The first angel sounded, and there followed hail and fire mingled with blood, and they were cast upon the earth: and the third part of trees was burnt up, and all green grass was burnt up. And the second angel sounded, and as it were a great mountain burning with fire was cast into the sea: and the third part of the sea became blood; and the third part of the creatures which were in the sea, and had life, died; and the third part of the ships were destroyed. And the third angel sounded, and there fell a great star from heaven, burning as it were a lamp, and it fell upon the third part of the rivers, and upon the fountains of waters; and the name of the star is called Wormwood: and the third part of the waters became wormwood; and many men died of the waters, because they were made bitter. And the fourth angel sounded, and the third part of the sun was smitten, and the third part of the moon, and the third part of the stars;

a. Chapter 12 and Chapter 2.

b. Revelation 7:9, 14.

c. Revelation 7:15–17.

so as the third part of them was darkened, and the day shone not for a third part of it, and the night likewise. And I beheld, and heard an angel flying through the midst of heaven, saying with a loud voice, Woe, woe, woe, to the inhabiters of the earth by reason of the other voices of the trumpet of the three angels, which are yet to sound!

The opening of the seventh seal is generally thought of as the beginning of the Millennium, but it is evident from John's vision that this is actually the beginning of the final cleansing of the earth *before* the Lord comes. Immediately after the seal is opened, there is a pause before the great calamities begin. The actual time of this pause is short but undefined (described by John as silence in heaven for one-half hour). John now introduces seven new angels, each bearing a trumpet to announce his cleansing efforts. The devastation wrought by these angels will be symbolically initiated when each angel blows his trumpet. They are waiting for the command to "reap down the earth,"[a] a harvest that will lead to the lifting of the "curtain of heaven" where the face of the Lord will be revealed (a symbolic description of the Second Coming).[b]

Before explaining the cleansing of the earth by these angels, John interjects "another angel" into his text.[c] This unidentified angel has no part in the cleansing process. His actions are symbolically described in terms of the temple ceremony of John's time. He holds a "golden censer" filled with incense, which he offers (along with the prayers of all the saints) upon a "golden altar" situated before the throne of God. The smoke of the incense represents the prayers or pleas of the Saints who seek redress against the wicked who have destroyed them. When the angel fills the censer with fire from the altar and casts it to the earth, it produces "voices, and thunderings, and lightnings, and an earthquake": the Lord's answer to the prayers of the Saints and a summary description of the destructive events that will follow in Revelation 8:7–13 and Revelation 9 and 10. The imagery in these chapters is vivid and the results are devastating, but John is symbolically portraying what will take place rather than describing actual events. Thus begins God's judgment on the wicked and the cleansing of the earth prior to the Second Coming.

The First Angel

The first angel blows his trumpet and something John describes as "hail and fire mingled with blood" falls upon the earth and scorches or destroys a "third part" of the trees and all the "green grass." This symbolism seems to describe an environmental catastrophe of some kind. The earth's ecological cycles are integrally balanced, and if a massive amount of its plant life were suddenly destroyed, it would play havoc with that balance. The animal kingdom would be adversely affected through the loss of a major food supply. There would be a sharp increase in the amount of carbon dioxide in the air, which could affect the earth's ability to sustain animal life as we now know it. Famine, or at least a major impact upon normal agricultural productivity, would also be a predictable result of this type of destruction.

That the "hail and fire" will be "mingled with blood" seems to indicate that many people will be destroyed by this cataclysmic event. It may also indicate that some unusual atmospheric condition could accompany or produce this prophesied *storm* which would cause a third part of all trees and grass to be destroyed. An interesting phenomenon of this type was recorded on September 7, 1841:

> Another shower of flesh and blood is reported in the Boston papers to have fallen in Kensington. 'There had been a drizzling rain during a great part of the day, until about 4 o'clock in the afternoon, when the rain stopped and the dark clouds began gradually to assume a brassy hue, until the whole heavens above seemed a sea of fire. The sky continued to grow more bright until about a quarter past five, when almost instantly it became of burnished red, and in a few moments it rained moderately a thick liquid of the appearance of blood, clothing fields and roads for two miles in circumference in a blood-stained garment. The bloody rain continued for about ten minutes, when it suddenly cleared away, and the atmosphere became so intensely cold that overcoats were needed.[135]

Whether or not this unusual story was factually reported, the cleansing by the first angel in the 8th chapter of Revelation will obviously have a devastating effect upon the earth.

The Second Angel
When this angel sounds his trumpet, something like a "great mountain

burning with fire" will affect the seas. John states that a "third part" of the living creatures therein and a "third part" of the ships thereon will be destroyed. Whether the "third part" is literal or not, we at least know that a large part of the ocean's life forms will be annihilated and that either a significant number of ships will be destroyed or the use of the oceans for transportation will become significantly impeded.

John's description of a "great mountain burning with fire" could be depicting a gigantic volcanic eruption adjacent to (or in) the ocean. A small prototype of this destruction occurred on August 24, A.D. 79 (John may have known about it). On that day, Vesuvius exploded and "hurled dust and rock high into the air amid clouds of smoke and flashes of flame." Within hours, Pompeii and Herculaneum were buried "to a depth of eight or ten feet" as giant walls of ash and molten rock rolled from the mountain's slopes. Many people were also killed as "tidal waves shut off [the] escape by sea."[136] Volcanic activity of the volume that could fulfill John's vision is readily available in the "Ring of Fire," a geological ring of fault systems and volcanoes that surrounds the Pacific Ocean basin.[137] Did John envision this system in a collective explosion? Only time will tell.

John also saw the "sea [become] blood."[a] This symbolic phrase could refer to either the enormous number of people that will be affected by this cleansing or to the change in the sea water brought about by the "mountain of fire" being cast into it—a change that resembles the plague Moses put on the waters of Egypt when Pharaoh refused to let the children of Israel go free.[b] Such a change would certainly bring death to a high percentage of life forms in the ocean, just as it did to the fish in Egypt's rivers.

The Third Angel

This angel causes "a great star" called "Wormwood" to fall from heaven, "burning as it were a lamp." It will affect an enormous quantity of the earth's fresh water supply, and many men and women will die when it pollutes the waters and makes them "bitter." This is another reference by John to future ecological problems of such magnitude that the earth will have difficulty supporting life as we know it. What is the star John refers to, and why is it named Wormwood? John leaves this to our imagination. It is interesting to note, however, that one of the definitions for *wormwood* in *Webster's New World Dictionary* states that it refers to a "bitter, unpleasant, or mortifying experience"; and *The Torah* describes "wormwood" as "a bitter herb, genus *Artemisia.*"[a][138]

The Fourth Angel

When the fourth angel sounds his trumpet, something catastrophic will occur to the heavens. John says "the third part" of the sun, the moon, and the stars will be "darkened," and the day will only shine for a "third part of it, and the night likewise." The result of this catastrophe is that day and night will have one-third of their capability or capacity reduced. Will they be shortened? While scientifically this is an anomaly, the description makes us aware that not only will the earth be affected by these angelic devastations, the heavens also will not escape.

In the above verses, everything John talks about is either reduced or destroyed by one-third. However, this is undoubtedly a symbolic figure used to represent the vastness of the prophesied destructions, and not a precise one-third measurement of everything. All of these *cleansing* destructions are general signs for the people of the earth. They are given not only to cleanse the earth of all wickedness, but also to warn those who remain of how close the coming of the Lord is. The Lord would like us all to be prepared, yet most of mankind refuses to heed His warnings.

In the last verse of Revelation 8, John sees yet another angel flying through "the midst of heaven" ominously crying, "Woe, woe, woe" to mankind below. He has no trumpet and he causes no destruction—he is symbolic. His purpose is to warn the inhabitants of the earth about the remaining three angels which are "yet to sound" their trumpets and bring more destruction upon the earth. The "woes" begin with the fifth angel in Revelation 9.

The Fifth Angel

When this angel sounds his trumpet, a "star" (the devil) falls from heaven to earth and is given the "key of the bottomless pit." This angel's activities represent the first "woe."[†]

---

† The "woes" of Revelation 9:1–12, along with other specific activities of the devil in the latter days, are discussed in Chapter 7.

a. Deuteronomy 29:18.

The Sixth Angel

Revelation 9:13–21   And the sixth angel sounded, and I heard a voice from the four horns of the golden altar which is before God, saying to the sixth angel which had the trumpet, Loose the four angels which are bound in the great river Euphrates. And the four angels were loosed, which were prepared for an hour, and a day, and a month, and a year, for to slay the third part of men. And the number of the army of the horsemen were two hundred thousand thousand: and I heard the number of them. And thus I saw the horses in the vision, and them that sat on them, having breastplates of fire, and of jacinth, and brimstone: and the heads of the horses were as the heads of lions; and out of their mouths issued fire and smoke and brimstone. By these three was the third part of men killed, by the fire, and by the smoke, and by the brimstone, which issued out of their mouths. For their power is in their mouth, and in their tails: for their tails were like unto serpents, and had heads, and with them they do hurt. And the rest of the men which were not killed by these plagues yet repented not of the works of their hands, that they should not worship devils, and idols of gold, and silver, and brass, and stone, and of wood: which neither can see, nor hear, nor walk: neither repented they of their murders, nor of their sorceries, nor of their fornication, nor of their thefts.

This angel represents the second "woe." When he sounds his trumpet, a voice tells him to release four other angels who have been prepared for their purposes for a lengthy period that John describes as "an hour, and a day, and a month, and a year." According to Revelation, they have been prepared since the inception of the plan of salvation.[a] These are the four angels of Revelation 7:1–3 who were previously discussed at the beginning of Phase Two. Their stated purpose is to slay "the third part of men" (again probably meaning a large number and not exactly one-third).[b] The four angels will accomplish their destruction by means of the great war described in the balance of Revelation 9.

This last great war is portrayed symbolically in John's vision; however, it is not initiated by the four angels. How long it will continue is not revealed, but it will be launched by the devil's evil latter-day kingdom and will culminate against Jerusalem and the kingdom of Judah just before the Second Coming. It is evident from John's description of the carnage it will cause that all peoples of the world will be involved in one way or another. Revelation 16:14 states that the devil's latter-day kingdom will send forth emissaries to the kings of the earth to gather armies for the last great battle against Jerusalem. According to Revelation 17:16, it appears that some resistance to this forced participation

a. Revelation 4:1.

b. Revelation 9:15.

will take place, thus causing a worldwide conflict. Nonetheless, the armies that will be arrayed against the Jews will be enormous. They are described by John as numbering 200,000,000 horsemen, and he states that he "heard the number of them"—a comment that fires the imagination.

These horsemen will wear breastplates of fire, jacinth (a dark reddish-purple colored precious stone), and brimstone, and while John states that they will be riding on animals he describes as "horses," the horses' heads will be like the "heads of lions" whose mouths will issue forth "fire and smoke and brimstone," and the horses' tails will be "like unto serpents" whose heads can "hurt." The power of these war machines will be in their "mouth" and in their "tails," and they will be responsible for slaying "the third part of men."

John is obviously seeing implements of war that he does not have the vocabulary to describe, so he compares them to the things he knows. His vivid descriptions leave us with the following specific information about the war and its evil army:

1. The army John describes will be extremely large.

2. The entire destructive force of this army will eventually be directed against Jerusalem.

3. The modern implements of war that John sees will be extremely destructive. He could be describing tanks, artillery, even atomic weapons, but since this war is yet to take place, future weapons may better fit his description than existing ones. Regardless, the weapons are not the important part of John's vision: it is the destructive force of the war and the results of the war that are significant.

4. The war will kill an enormous number of people. John uses the figure of one-third of the earth's population to describe the enormity of the destruction that will occur; however, as in many other verses in Revelation, this is probably representative and not actual. Although this war is eventually focused on Jerusalem, John's description indicates that all mankind will be involved at one time or another.

5. The duration of this war (once it converges on Jerusalem) will cover the same period of time as that described in Revelation 11:1–10 where two special witnesses are called to prophesy in Jerusalem: i.e., for three and one-half years.[a]

6. The information John is giving us is connected with the information he received in Revelation 13:1–5 concerning Satan's kingdom in the latter-days.[b]

Amazingly, after all of this colossal devastation, those wicked men and women yet alive will still not repent! They will continue to worship "the works of their hands," those worldly possessions symbolically identified as "idols of gold, and silver, and brass, and stone, and of wood,"[c] instead of the Savior who can give them a place in His kingdom. As we saw earlier in Chapter 7, worldly possessions—things that can neither "see, nor hear, nor walk"—will be the hallmark of the devil's kingdom in the latter days. John sees that through their earthly possessions, people have substituted all types of false gods for the Lord. Then, as now, the worship of power and economic wealth will supersede the worship of the living God.

At the height of the devastation caused by the massive conflict, John sees the death of the two special prophets who had been raised up to prophesy to the inhabitants of Jerusalem. Then he sees their miraculous resurrection.[d] At this point, he declares that the second woe is past and the third woe will come quickly.

The Seventh Angel

Revelation 11:15–19   And the seventh angel sounded; and there were great voices in heaven, saying, The kingdoms of this world are become the kingdoms of our Lord, and of his Christ; and he shall reign for ever and ever. And the four and twenty elders, which sat before God on their seats, fell upon their faces, and worshipped God, Saying, We give thee thanks, O Lord God Almighty, which art, and wast, and art to come; because thou hast taken to thee thy great power, and hast reigned. And the nations were angry, and thy wrath is come, and the time of the dead, that they should be judged, and that thou shouldest give reward unto thy servants the prophets, and to the saints, and them that fear thy name, small and great; and shouldest destroy them which destroy the earth. And the temple of God was opened in heaven, and there was seen in his temple the ark of his testament: and there were lightnings, and voices, and thunderings, and an earthquake, and great hail.

a. Chapter 5.

b. Chapter 7.

c. Revelation 9:20–21.

d. Revelation 11:11–14; and Chapter 5 herein.

The seventh angel brings the third woe, but John now pauses in the vision (as he often does) and inserts information in summary form that he will subsequently detail. As he envisions the closing of the second *woe,* it is obvious that the actual coming of the Lord is near, and he inserts general information about that coming before he proceeds.

He first prophesies that all nations will become subject to the Lord at His Advent and that He will reign over them "for ever and ever" (circumstances that relate specifically to the Second Coming and the beginning of the Millennium).[a] He next sees the same twenty-four elders that he envisioned at the beginning of his revelation[b] speaking with the Lord. They note the anger of the wicked (due to their great tribulation) and the anticipation the righteous have for their resurrection.[c] He then sees God's final judgments upon the wicked, as represented by the trump of the seventh angel with the third *woe.* He does not indicate at this point how the seventh angel will bring his destructions to pass, but he summarily represents them as "lightnings, and voices, and thunderings, and an earthquake, and great hail" that will occur as the "temple of God" is "opened in the heaven" and "the ark of his testament" is exposed to view.[d] The third *woe* will be accomplished by the seventh angel with a trumpet when he releases the seven angels with vials full of the final plagues found in Revelation 16.

John inserts Chapters 12, 13, and 14 of Revelation before he returns to the plagues of the seven angels with vials. Chapter 12 is a historical flashback that reveals information about the Great Apostasy, the flight of the gospel into the wilderness,[e] and the preexistent activities of the devil.[f] Revelation 13 is John's vision of the devil's great latter-day kingdom.[g] Revelation 14 concerns three subjects: the 144,000 righteous individuals who have the "Father's name written in their foreheads,"[h] the vision of the restoration,[i] and the final judgment of the devil and those who follow him.[j] Finally, in Revelation 14:15–20 John returns to the conclusions he recorded at the close of Chapter 11. He sees angels with sickles ready to execute the earth's final cleansing (as presaged in Revelation 11:19). They first declare that "the harvest of the earth is ripe," and then they state that the earth is "reaped." The reaping will be done by the plagues of the seven angels with vials as final preparation is made for the Lord's Advent.[139]

The fifteenth chapter of Revelation is a transition chapter that

a. Revelation 11:15.

b. Revelation 4:4.

c. Revelation 11:17–18.

d. Revelation 11:19.

e. Chapter 2.

f. Chapter 7.

g. Chapters 7 and 8.

h. Chapter 12.

i. Chapter 4.

j. Chapter 8.

again introduces us to the seven angels with vials who will control the last seven plagues before the Second Coming.[†] However, before John discusses these angels, he again pauses in his narrative (as if he had begun to write and then suddenly remembered something he had forgotten as he closed Chapter 11), and inserts Revelation 15:2–5. These verses record more information about God's heaven and beautifully describe the condition of the righteous who will live there: "And I saw as it were a sea of glass mingled with fire: and them that had gotten the victory over the beast, and over his image, and over his mark, and over the number of his name, stand on the sea of glass, having the harps of God."[a] The righteous individuals John sees are singing and praising God.

After this insert, John finally returns to the seven angels with vials. He explains that the seven angels received their vials from one of the four beasts that were praising God in Revelation 4:7. Revelation 15 then closes (as if it were a continuation of Revelation 11) by providing us with a witness of God couched in terms reminiscent of His appearances in the Old Testament.[b] His heavenly temple is filled with the smoke of His power as the angels pour out His wrath to completely cleanse the earth of all wickedness, for no one will enter God's kingdom until the seven angels have delivered the seven plagues.

Revelation 16 And I heard a great voice out of the temple saying to the seven angels, Go your ways, and pour out the vials of the wrath of God upon the earth. And the first went, and poured out his vial upon the earth; and there fell a noisome and grievous sore upon the men which had the mark of the beast, and upon them which worshipped his image. And the second angel poured out his vial upon the sea; and it became as the blood of a dead man: and every living soul died in the sea. And the third angel poured out his vial upon the rivers and fountains of waters; and they became blood. And I heard the angel of the waters say, Thou art righteous, O Lord, which art, and wast, and shalt be, because thou hast judged thus. For they have shed the blood of saints and prophets, and thou hast given them blood to drink; for they are worthy. And I heard another out of the altar say, Even so, Lord God Almighty, true and righteous are thy judgments. And the fourth angel poured out his vial upon the sun; and power was given unto him to scorch men with fire. And men were scorched with great heat, and blasphemed the name of God, which hath power over

---

a. Revelation 15:2.

b. Exodus 40:34–35.

† There are three sets of seven angels in John's Revelation and four angels of destruction. One: the seven angels with seals. Two: the seven trumpet angels. Three: the seven angels with vials. The seventh seal angel releases the seven trumpet angels and the seventh trumpet angel releases the seven vial angels. The sixth trumpet angel releases the four angels of destruction which give John the vision of the last great war.

these plagues: and they repented not to give him glory. And the fifth angel poured out his vial upon the seat of the beast; and his kingdom was full of darkness; and they gnawed their tongues for pain, And blasphemed the God of heaven because of their pains and their sores, and repented not of their deeds. And the sixth angel poured out his vial upon the great river Euphrates; and the water thereof was dried up, that the way of the kings of the east might be prepared. And I saw three unclean spirits like frogs come out of the mouth of the dragon, and out of the mouth of the beast, and out of the mouth of the false prophet. For they are the spirits of devils, working miracles, which go forth unto the kings of the earth and of the whole world, to gather them to the battle of that great day of God Almighty. Behold, I come as a thief. Blessed is he that watcheth, and keepeth his garments, lest he walk naked, and they see his shame. And he gathered them together into a place called in the Hebrew tongue Armageddon. And the seventh angel poured out his vial into the air; and there came a great voice out of the temple of heaven, from the throne, saying, It is done. And there were voices, and thunders, and lightnings; and there was a great earthquake, such as was not since men were upon the earth, so mighty an earthquake, and so great. And the great city was divided into three parts, and the cities of the nations fell: and great Babylon came in remembrance before God, to give unto her the cup of the wine of the fierceness of his wrath. And every island fled away, and the mountains were not found. And there fell upon men a great hail out of heaven, every stone about the weight of a talent: and men blasphemed God because of the plague of the hail; for the plague thereof was exceeding great.

In Revelation 16, God commands the seven angels to pour out their "vials of the wrath of God upon the earth." These plagues commence the final destruction of the wicked who cannot abide the Lord's presence at His coming.

First Plague
The first angel with a vial will deliver the scourge of a "noisome and grievous sore." Because so much symbolism is used throughout Revelation, we do not know if John is describing an actual "sore" or whether he is just symbolically describing a terrible pestilence of some kind. Three scriptural examples demonstrate God's use of *grievous sores:*

1.	Leprosy is described in the scriptures as a "white reddish sore."[a] Under the law of Moses, this disease symbolized exclusion from God. The leper in Israel represented the very epitome of sin and uncleanliness and was used by God as a living example of sin.[140]

a. Leviticus 13:42.

2.   Job was afflicted with "sore boils from the sole of his foot unto his crown"[a] to test his obedience to God.

3.   In the parable of Lazarus and the rich man, the Lord depicted Lazarus' pitiful condition by describing him as being "full of sores."[b]

This affliction will be widespread and deadly, and it will specifically attack both those who bear the "mark of the beast" and those who worship the beast's image.[c]

This information gives us insight as to when this plague will occur. Each generation looks for the signs of the Lord's coming in the events of its time; thus, in modern times, there is a tendency to assign destructive diseases such as AIDS to the fulfillment of this plague. But the *timing* of the plague preempts any existing or previous "noisome and grievous" sores. This plague will not occur until the devil has established his latter-day kingdom.

Second Plague

The second angel will pour out his vial upon the sea. The scriptures state that the sea will become "as the blood of a dead man." It would be difficult to take this prediction literally since that would mean the seas would become coagulated. If taken symbolically, however, this may refer to the verse where John sees a star named Wormwood which destroys a third part of the waters.[d] The Lord told Joseph Smith in latter-day revelation: "Behold, I, the Lord, in the beginning blessed the waters; but in the last days, by the mouth of my servant John, I cursed the waters. Wherefore, the days will come that no flesh shall be safe upon the waters."[e] The Lord thereafter forbade general travel upon the waters while the Saints were gathering to Missouri, stating that "the destroyer rideth upon the face thereof."[f] The result of this plague on the waters is defined as being so catastrophic that "every living soul" who ventures out upon the sea will die.[g] The seas will no longer function as they have in the past, which will have a devastating effect upon a vast number of the earth's inhabitants.

Third Plague

The third angel will pour his vial into "the rivers and fountains of

a. Job 2:7.

b. Luke 16:20.

c. Chapter 7.

d. Revelation 8:8–11.

e. D&C 61:14–15.

f. D&C 61:18–19.

g. Revelation 16:3.

water" that are found upon the land, and they will also be turned to "blood." In the latter days, the Lord confirms that this plague will occur and gives us the following additional information: "I [will] make the rivers a wilderness; their fish [will] stink, and die for thirst."[a] Neither this latter-day revelation nor John reveal the source of this plague, but their descriptions have some interesting modern-day parallels. Red Tides have caused devastation when their "blooms . . . poisoned the water" and killed fish "by the millions,"[141] and a dinoflagellate organism named *Pfiesteria piscicida* (translated as "fish killer") was implicated in the death of more than a billion fish in 1990.[142] Both of these modern-day plagues are attributed to widespread and increased "eutrophication—the abundant accumulation of nutrients from domestic, agricultural, and industrial effluent . . ." which results in a virtual epidemic of coastal algae blooms.[143]

While these are small examples of John's predicted catastrophic plagues, they readily show how simple it will be for the third angel to "pour out his vial." Something will happen to the earth's fresh water supply—a pollution so severe that the water will no longer be able to sustain life. The angel of the waters in Revelation 16:5 states that the Lord will be justified in destroying the wicked in this manner since "they have shed the blood of saints and prophets." (It is possible that the wicked could literally kill some of the Lord's Saints and His prophets before the Second Coming; however, because of the symbolism found in Revelation, this is probably a metaphoric representation of the devil's evil kingdom leading people astray—thus "killing" God's righteous influence.) If people choose wicked paths, however, they will justify their own eventual destruction.

Fourth Plague

The fourth angel will pour out his vial upon the sun, "and power [will be] given unto him to scorch men with fire" and "great heat." John gives no explanation of what this plague is, but in Revelation 8:12 he states that a "third part of the sun [will be] smitten." These two occurrences are related in that they both contribute to an ecological imbalance that could make many areas of the planet uninhabitable. There is an interesting natural phenomenon that occurs with the sun every eleven years. Scientists call it the *Solar Maximum* event. During this

a. D&C 133:68.

event the sun emits enormous energy that can affect electronic capabilities on earth—electrical transmission lines, satellites, etc. No one is killed from this solar event, but the environment man has developed, and will yet become more dependant upon, may be catastrophically affected by this or a similar event. (While not claiming that this is the potential fulfillment of what John is describing in his vision, it could be a method God might use to fulfill the prophecy.)[144]

Mankind's predictable reaction to both of these phenomena is to blaspheme the name of God and repent not. In other words, men and women still will not acknowledge the fact that God is orchestrating the devastation they are experiencing. Interestingly, no deaths are mentioned in this verse. The people seem to survive, indicating that this is not a plague of death but rather of torment that will come upon earth's inhabitants. Because the people curse God for the plague and refuse to repent of their wickedness, however, they seal their ultimate fate.

Fifth Plague

The fifth angel will pour out his vial upon the "seat of the beast." This plague is unidentified, but in some way it will fall upon the devil's evil kingdom in the latter days and will cause "darkness," "pain," and "sores" to come upon it.[a] The darkness is symbolic.

There are several scriptural references to darkness, both actual and spiritual. But there are three specific instances where the Lord uses actual darkness for symbolic purposes: (1) Moses called down three days of darkness upon the Egyptians as one of the plagues;[b] (2) while the Savior hung on the cross, there was darkness "over all the land" from the "sixth hour" until the "ninth hour";[c] and (3) on the Western Hemisphere, darkness fell upon the land at the Savior's crucifixion.[d] All of these occurrences are similitudes for the death of the "light of the world"— Jesus Christ[e]— a death that left the world in spiritual darkness.[145] Therefore, John's envisioned darkness seems to symbolize the spiritual condition of the wicked as compared to those enlightened by the light or knowledge of Christ—much like the condition of the wicked during the Dark Ages.[f] If spiritual darkness is the interpretation the Lord intended in these verses, this darkness is probably grounded in mankind's desire for earthly power and wealth, certainly not in the wealth of God's kingdom. Perhaps the vial of the

a. Chapter 7.

b. Exodus
   10:22–23.

c. Matthew
   27:45.

d. 3 Nephi
   8:19 ff.

e. John 8:12.

f. Chapter 3.

fifth angel represents an economic collapse where "no man buyeth [the] merchandise [of the wicked] any more."[a] Again, John gives no indication what the source is of the pain or sores to be inflicted upon mankind. Perhaps they are also symbolic, representing the trauma suffered by the loss of worldly wealth and power upon which the wicked will come to rely.

Regardless of the interpretation of this plague, it is clear that the discomfort it inflicts will cause the wicked to gnaw "their tongues for pain"—yet again blaspheme God and "[repent] not of their deeds." Even then, they will value their power and possessions more than they will value their God.

Sixth Plague

The sixth angel will pour out his vial upon the Euphrates River. The results in the vision are amazing: the river dries up to prepare the way for the "kings of the east"—perhaps (whether the river actually dries up or not) symbolically erasing any hindrance in the path of the great evil army that will attack Jerusalem just before the Second Coming. Next, the vision describes three spirits which are like frogs. They will "come out of the mouth of the dragon [the devil], and out of the mouth of the beast [the anti-Christ], and out of the mouth of the false prophet."[b] They are the "spirits of devils, working miracles, which go forth unto the kings of the earth and of the whole world, to gather them to the battle of that great day of God almighty."[c] They appear to be representatives (people or entities) of the devil's kingdom who will go forth to the nations of the earth to gather them for the battle of Armageddon, the last great war against God, Israel, and Jerusalem. The Lord again warns us in Revelation 16 that He comes "as a thief"—emphasizing the fact that the time of His coming is unknown, and mankind must therefore be constantly prepared and vigilant.[d]

Seventh Plague

Finally, the seventh angel will come and pour his vial into the air. A voice will then emanate "out of the temple of heaven, from the throne [of God], saying, It is done."[e] After the heavenly voice speaks there will be "thunders, and lightnings" and a tremendous earthquake will occur, "such as was not since men were upon the earth." It will be so

a. Revelation 18:11.

b. Revelation 13; and Chapter 7 herein.

c. Revelation 16:14.

d. Ezekiel 38:39.

e. Revelation 16:17.

cataclysmic that John identifies it as a singular event in the earth's history. The earth will be transformed: islands will flee, and mountains will not be found in their place. The entire face of the earth will be changed. In 1831, Joseph Smith received additional information on this transformation:

> **D&C 133:22–24**   And it shall be a voice as the voice of many waters, and as the voice of a great thunder, which shall break down the mountains, and the valleys shall not be found. He shall command the great deep, and it shall be driven back into the north countries, and the islands shall become one land; and the land of Jerusalem and the land of Zion shall be turned back into their own place, and the earth shall be like as it was in the days before it was divided.

The face of the land will change. The physical location of the land masses will be as they were when Adam came out of the Garden of Eden. This massive earthquake will also cause the Mount of Olives to split in two at the conclusion of the great war in Jerusalem, and the Lord will appear in the cleft to the tribe of Judah.[a] In addition, at or just before the time this massive earthquake takes place, a great hailstorm will occur "out of heaven, every stone about the weight of a talent [a talent equals about 57 pounds, according to the Bible Dictionary]." John does not mention what destruction these massive hailstones will cause, nor can we determine if he is again speaking symbolically, but the terrible storm will cause men to blaspheme God "because of the plague of the hail; for the plague thereof [will be] exceedingly great." The people will be so wicked at this point that they will be immune to any influence from the Spirit. Again they will not repent, and they will subsequently be destroyed.

By the end of Revelation 16:21, the seven plagues have been fulfilled—the beleaguered earth will soon rest.

Phase Three–The Earth Returns to Its Paradisiacal Glory

The curse that God placed on the earth because of the Fall of Adam and Eve has continued throughout the millennia because mankind has continued to sin. The great destructions described in phases one and two of this chapter are a consequence of that sin. These destructions will be brought down upon the earth as judgments of God upon the

a. Chapter 5.

wicked. The destruction of the wicked (especially that destruction related by John in Revelation) is described elsewhere in the scriptures as a *burning* so intense that few men will be left alive after it occurs.[a] As a result of these destructions, the present configuration of the earth will come to an end. The earth will literally *pass away,* or die, as it were. This process is described in the scriptures as the earth being "consumed" or "dissolved," melting "with fervent heat" and being "wrapt" or "rolled together as a scroll";[b] The Lord declared early in His ministry that the "meek . . . [would] inherit the earth,"[c] and as the Second Coming approaches, it is to this end that these powerful destructive forces will decimate the wicked. Peter said that the day of the Lord would come "as a thief in the night; in the which the heavens shall pass away with a great noise, and the elements shall melt with fervent heat, the earth also and the works that are therein shall be burned up."[d] In subsequent verses he again states that the heavens will be "on fire [and will] be dissolved, and the elements [will] melt with fervent heat."[e] With these terrifying conflagrations in mind, he asks, "Seeing . . . that all these things shall be dissolved, *what manner of persons ought ye to be?*"[f146]

The theme of brilliance or fire associated with paradisiacal glory and other of God's works is common in the scriptures. Joseph Smith saw the gate of the celestial kingdom (which itself may have been a metaphor) and described it as the "gate through which the heirs of that kingdom will enter, which [is] like unto circling flames of fire."[g] He also saw and described the "blazing throne of God."[h] In Helaman 5:23–24, the Lord protected Nephi and Lehi from their enemies by encircling them about with a "pillar of fire," and although they stood "in the midst of the fire," they "were not burned." Shadrach, Meshach, and Abed-nego experienced the same miracle in the "fiery furnace" of Daniel 3:23–25.

The glory of the Lord was first described as a "devouring fire" when the children of Israel gathered at Sinai after their exodus from Egypt.[i] Isaiah records that the name of the Lord will come "from far, burning with his anger . . . his lips . . . full of indignation, and his tongue as a devouring fire."[j] Job used the *fire* and *heat* metaphors quite differently when he said that "leviathan" (a name of the devil or evil) made the "deep to boil like a pot."[k] This heat and fire metaphor,

a. Isaiah 24:6.

b. Isaiah 34:4; Revelation 6:14; 3 Nephi 26:3; Mormon 5:23.

c. Matthew 5:5.

d. 2 Peter 3:10.

e. 2 Peter 3:12.

f. 2 Peter 3:11; emphasis added.

g. D&C 137:2.

h. D&C 137:3.

i. Exodus 24:17.

j. Isaiah 30:27.

k. Job 41:31.

as applied by Job, is also used in a latter-day description of the Lord: "for the presence of the Lord shall be as the melting fire that burneth, and as the fire which causeth the waters to boil."[a] All of these descriptions foretell changes that will occur as the curse of Adam is nullified and a renewed earth is transfigured to receive its paradisiacal glory. At that time the earth will become as it was "before [the land] was divided."[b] In the tenth article of faith, Joseph Smith recorded the following: "We believe . . . that the earth will be renewed and receive its paradisiacal glory." The Lord had told Joseph that this change to the earth would occur "according to the pattern which was shown unto mine apostles upon the mount [of Transfiguration]; of which account the fulness ye have not yet received."[c]

When the Lord was transfigured on the Mount of Transfiguration, a somnolent Peter, James, and John were suddenly awakened by a great brilliance. It was the Messiah, transfigured and appearing in His glorified state: "His face did shine as the sun, and his raiment was white as the light."[d][147] The Apostles had difficulty describing the Lord in His glory, even when He stood directly before them. In like manner, the prophets down through the ages have had difficulty describing the earth in its paradisiacal glory, let alone the means by which that glory was acquired. They therefore relied upon metaphors to describe the glory of the Lord, His exalted creations, and the paradisiacal earth.

The most detailed description of the earth's paradisiacal transformation at the Lord's Advent was given to Joseph Smith in December 1833. In this revelation, Jesus declared that the day would come when "all flesh" would see Him. He then proceeded to give a staccato account of what His Advent would cause:

D&C 101: 24–34 (see also Isaiah 65:17–25; Revelation 21:4)   Every corruptible thing, both of man, or of the beasts of the field, or of the fowls of the heavens, or of the fish of the sea, that [dwell] upon all the face of the earth, shall be consumed; and also that of element shall melt with fervent heat; and all things shall become new, that my knowledge and glory may dwell upon all the earth. The enmity of beasts, yea, the enmity of all flesh, shall cease from before my face. Whatsoever any man shall ask, it shall be given unto him. Satan shall not have power to tempt any man. There shall be no sorrow because there [will be] no death [for the righteous]. [Revelation also states that there shall be no pain.] An infant shall not die until he is old; and his life shall be as the age of a tree [described by Isaiah as 100 years]; and when he dies

a. D&C 133:41.

b. D&C 133:24.

c. D&C 63:21.

d. Matthew 17:2.

> he shall not sleep . . . in the earth, but shall be changed in the twinkling of an eye, and shall be caught up, and his rest shall be glorious. Yea, verily I say unto you, in that day when the Lord shall come, he shall reveal all things— things which have passed, and hidden things which no man knew, things of the earth, by which it was made, and the purpose and the end thereof—things most precious, things that are above, and things that are beneath, things that are in the earth, and upon the earth, and in heaven.

These verses truly reveal a promised paradise for mankind, but what will the physical earth be like after all these changes? The scriptures again give us detailed information. They reveal that the mountains will "flow down" at the Savior's presence,[a] or, according to Isaiah, they will "depart."[b] Every valley will be "exalted," every "mountain and hill" will be made "low," the "crooked" will be made "straight," and the "rough places" will be made smooth.[c] Whether this scripture is describing a relatively flat earth or a reconfigured earth, only time will tell. As for the waters, the great seas will return to the "north countries, and the islands [will] become one land."[d] John confirms this reunification of the land masses by stating that there will be "no more sea."[e] He further states that the islands will be gone,[f] "moved out of their places,"[g] which latter-day revelation defines as becoming "one land."[h] At the time of the Garden of Eden the land was apparently all in one place, and it remained that way until after the flood. The scripture states that in the days of Peleg (which means division) "the earth was divided."[i] Peleg lived after the flood and before the Tower of Babel; therefore, whether this scripture is referring back to the division of the land after the flood or is contemplating the confusion of languages and scattering of nations at the Tower of Babel (which means confusion) is unknown. But with clarity the Lord has declared that before His coming, the land will return to its former place and "be like it was in the days before it was divided."[j] How will this change take place? Some of it will undoubtedly be caused by the great earthquake John describes,[k] but the balance of the changes will be caused by the transfiguration of the earth at the Lord's coming.

The transfiguration descriptions, if taken literally when they speak of "fervent heat," might lead to the conclusion that a great fire will rain down from heaven such as fell upon Sodom and Gomorrah,[l] or that a cataclysmic man-caused infernal heat—perhaps of a nuclear

a. D&C 133:40, 44.

b. Isaiah 54:10.

c. Isaiah 40:4.

d. D&C 133:23.

e. Revelation 21:1.

f. Revelation 16:20.

g. Revelation 6:14.

h. D&C 133:23.

i. Genesis 10:25; 1 Chronicles 1:19.

j. D&C 133:24.

k. Revelation 16:18,

l. Genesis 19:24.

type[148]— might occur. But more likely these descriptions are symbolic because the prophets who saw the glory of the Lord and His cleansing works did not have the vocabulary to describe them; therefore, they had to compare them to the things they knew. It is obvious that if these descriptions of destruction were literal, no man, plant, animal, or element would survive without the direct intervention of the Lord.

The description of the earth's destruction is a recurring theme, both in regards to the cleansing of the earth by the destruction of the wicked, and in regards to the changes the earth will experience in preparation for the Lord's coming.[149] We know with certainty that the coming of the Lord will physically change the earth and restore it to the way it was in the days of Eden, with a twist, for it will also possess the glory of the Messiah. Who will inherit this new earth? The righteous![a] It will be given to those who have been faithful to God's covenants and who have not been deceived by the devil, as represented by the faithful virgins of the parable.[b][150] These will have the Lord in their midst, and their children will be blessed to grow thereafter in righteousness from generation to generation.[c]

a. D&C 59:2.

b. D&C 45:56–
57; 63:20.

c. D&C 45:57–
59; 56:20.

11

Signs: Increased Devastations

Doctrine and Covenants 97:22 For behold, and lo, vengeance cometh speedily upon the ungodly as the whirlwind; and who shall escape it?

One of the most interesting general signs of the Second Coming is described in scripture as a "desolating scourge" that will go forth upon mankind. The scourge is not portrayed as a singular event, nor is it considered a unique event in any given period of time. Indeed, it is just the opposite. It can and does take many forms. The Lord states that it will "go forth among the inhabitants of the earth, and shall continue to be poured out [upon them] *from time to time,* if they repent not, until the earth is empty."[a]

The "desolating scourge" is also defined as a "desolating sickness" which will "cover the land,"[b] and while this may incline us to look for a specific illness to fit this description, it may in fact refer to many different disorders—anything from the "black death" of the 14th century to the influenza, AIDS, or Ebola epidemics of the 20th century. Perhaps it refers to some future scourge—or it could refer to them all! That is what makes this sign so difficult to identify.

The mysterious "desolating scourge" will also adversely affect the heavens. Because of it "the sun shall be darkened, and the moon shall be turned into blood, and the stars shall fall from heaven, and there shall be greater signs in heaven above and in the earth beneath." It causes a great hailstorm that will be "sent forth to destroy the crops of the earth," and it causes flies to come "upon the face of the earth," flies "which shall take hold of the inhabitants thereof, and shall eat

a. D&C 5:19; emphasis added.

b. D&C 45:31

their flesh, and shall cause maggots to come in upon them . . . [until] their flesh shall fall from off their bones, and their eyes from their sockets." As a result, "the beasts of the forest and the fowls of the air shall devour them up."[a]

More devastating scourges are found in Revelation 16 wherein the great plagues of the seven angels are described.[b] These scourges include wars, pestilence, and earthquakes; and their specific purpose is to cleanse the earth for the last time in preparation for the Lord's coming.[c] Another scourge in Revelation is described as a "noisome and grievous" sore which will be inflicted upon those in the latter days who bear the mark of the beast.[d] Other nonspecific scourges recorded in the scriptures are blood and fire, smoke,[151] vapors of smoke, thunder and lightning,[152] and famine.[e] The "desolating scourge" of famine will be the fulfillment of John's vision of a black horseman who holds a "pair of balances in his hand:" balances which signify a famine so devastating that the value of food will be far greater than the value of money.[f] This condition is described by Joseph Smith as having also occurred during the third thousand years of the earth's existence—prior to Christ's birth.[g]

One problem mankind has with these scourges (besides having to live through them) is recognition since the devil uses them to deceive mankind just as the Lord uses them to remind mankind of His coming. The righteous men and women of the latter days will have to rely upon spiritual insight to recognize the difference between the normal occurrences of nature and God's hand moving upon the wicked. Science (or the natural man) is always ready with a plausible explanation for unusual natural occurrences—such as shifts in El Nino's current, unusual sun spots, erosion of the ozone layer, or a new virus—and science may be right. However, scientists may fail to recognize that God also has the power to cause scourges, through natural means or otherwise.

Isaiah perceived the problem of the Lord using scourges as warnings while the devil uses them to deceive (he cannot create or cause them) as a "covenant" with death and hell. While addressing the Jewish leadership, the Lord said through Isaiah, "Ye have said, We have made a covenant with death, and with hell are we at agreement; when the overflowing scourge shall pass through, it shall not come unto us:

a. D&C 29:14–21.

b. Chapter 8.

c. Joseph Smith–Matthew 1:39.

d. Revelation 16:2.

e. D&C 29:16; Joseph Smith–History 1:45.

f. Revelation 6:5–6.

g. D&C 77:7.

for we have made lies our refuge, and under falsehood have we hid ourselves."[a] What he is explaining is that the devil can use our own intelligence and sophistication to deceive us. Many of the "scourges" that befall mankind are just normal life's circumstances and can be explained as such; however, because of their supposed intelligence or sophistication, mankind may also attempt to explain away those scourges that come from God, and that is the key to Isaiah's comment. We can easily be deceived into believing that any or all of the scourges that befall mankind have a natural explanation and have nothing to do with God's condemnation of the wicked. Conversely, we may attribute God's vengeance to a given scourge when in reality it is only one of life's circumstances. This problem can subject us to one of two consequences: *first,* we may rely upon our own knowledge and scientific sophistication to explain away God's signs as natural phenomena, thereby rejecting the possibility of God's involvement and possibly withdrawing ourselves from His kingdom; or *second,* we may justify our own righteousness by citing the destruction of others as a scourge from God upon the wicked, when in fact they may have only fallen subject to a normal occurrence.

An interesting example of not recognizing God's influence in our lives is found in the New Testament. Herod Agrippa had been promoted by Rome for his allegiance to the empire. He was allowed to take the title of king, and following the death of Philip was given Philip's territory as part of his kingdom. Soon thereafter he dressed himself in formal royal attire, sat upon his throne, and delivered an oration to the people. Apparently the Spirit influenced his talk and the people listening recognized it, for his audience declared that the speech had come from God. But Herod did not recognize Deity's hand and failed to give God the glory for the speech. As a result, "the angel of the Lord [immediately] smote him, because he gave not God the glory: and he was eaten of worms, and gave up the ghost."[b]

During the latter days, God will send devastating scourges through what may appear to be normal and natural processes as He changes the times and seasons and puts the general signs of the Second Coming into place. But through the self-serving, obdurate, and dishonest characteristics of humankind (the covenant with death and hell), they will reject the signs of the times and the admonitions of the prophets. Isaiah warned mankind that "your covenant with death shall be disannulled, and your agreement with hell shall not stand; when the overflowing scourge shall pass through, then ye shall be trodden down by it."[a] The scourges which will assail men and women prior to the Second Coming may have the power to destroy them physically, but their disbelief in God will have the power to destroy them spiritually.

Wars and Rumors of War

Wars and rumors of war have always been a part of earth's history. In a double-reference prophecy found in Matthew, the Lord warned His Apostles about the impending destruction of Jerusalem and the great calamities of war in the last days: "And ye shall hear of wars and rumors of wars: see that ye be not troubled . . . For nation shall rise against nation, and kingdom against kingdom . . . [and] all these are [but] the beginning of sorrows."[b]

The last days began with the restoration of the gospel, and it is from that time forward that the double-reference portion of the prophecy applies. On Christmas day in 1832, Joseph Smith, the prophet of the restoration, received the following prophecy concerning war in the latter days:

> **D&C 87:1–4**   Verily, thus saith the Lord concerning the wars that will shortly come to pass, beginning at the rebellion of South Carolina, which will eventually terminate in the death and misery of many souls; and the time will come that war will be poured out upon all nations, beginning at this place. For behold, the Southern States shall be divided against the Northern States, and the Southern States will call on other nations, even the nation of Great Britain, as it is called, and they shall also call upon other nations, in order to defend themselves against other nations; and then war shall be poured out upon all nations. And it shall come to pass, after many days, slaves shall rise up against their masters, who shall be marshaled and disciplined for war.

The Civil War marked the beginning of "wars and rumors of wars" in the latter days. It was the fulfillment of John the Revelator's vision of the red horseman, to whom was given the power to "take peace from the earth" so that mankind would "kill one another."[c] (This is a condition that Joseph Smith described in Doctrine and Covenants 77:7 as having also occurred in the second thousand years of the earth's existence, a pattern of repetition that appears throughout history.) John's

a. Isaiah 28:18.

b. Matthew 24:6–8.

c. Revelation 6:4.

vision of warning was confirmed in 1831 when the Lord stated that His Advent was "nigh at hand," that peace would be "taken from the earth, and [that] the devil [would soon] have power over his own dominion."[a]

In 1839, seven years after he received the revelation on the Civil War, the prophet Joseph Smith declared: "The Saints and the world will have little peace from henceforth . . . [for] wars are at hand."[153] Again referring to the Civil War he said:

> I saw men hunting the lives of their own sons, and brother murdering brother, women killing their own daughters, and daughters seeking the lives of their mothers. I saw armies arrayed against armies. I saw blood, desolation, fires. The Son of Man has said that the mother shall be against the daughter, and the daughter against the mother. These things are at the doors. They will follow the Saints of God from city to city. Satan will rage, and the spirit of the devil is now enraged. I know not how soon these things will take place; but with a view of them, shall I cry peace? No! I will lift up my voice and testify of them.[154]

From the time of the Civil War forward, the Saints were repeatedly warned of wars in other nations and in their own land, and the scriptures tell us that these wars will continue until the whole earth is in commotion.[b]

On April 2, 1843, Joseph Smith gave the following prophecy to the Saints:

> **D&C 130:12–13** I prophesy, in the name of the Lord God, that the commencement of the difficulties which will cause much bloodshed previous to the coming of the Son of Man will be in South Carolina. It may probably arise through the slave question. This a voice declared to me, while I was praying earnestly on the subject, December 25th, 1832.

Doctrine and Covenants 87:1–4 and 130:12–13 are reminiscent of Samuel the Lamanite's prophecy to the Nephites concerning the Savior's coming birth and death.[c] Both prophecies identify very specific information. Why was the Lord so definite about the Civil War being a sign? Because wars and rumors of wars have been so common

a. D&C 1:35.

b. D&C 38:29; 45:26, 63.

c. Helaman 13–15.

throughout the ages that believers and nonbelievers alike may not recognize them in the latter days as a sign of the Second Coming. However, the specific prophecy of the Civil War initiated the fulfillment of this sign in the latter days, and the sign will not be fulfilled until war is poured out upon *all* nations.[a] Nonetheless, in the Gospel of Luke the Lord comforts us by telling us to "be not terrified: for these things must first come to pass; but the end is not by and by."[b]

Although the *general* prophecies concerning wars will be fulfilled, there will still be *one last specific war* before the Savior's coming. It will center around Jerusalem,[c] for the Lord has declared that Jerusalem will become "a burdensome stone for all people" in the last days.[d] Through this war (and all other wars and rumors of wars) "the inhabitants of the earth [will] be made to feel the wrath, and indignation, and chastening hand of an Almighty God, until the consumption decreed hath made a full end of all nations."[e]

The Hailstorm

In Revelation 11:19, John said there would be "lightnings, and voices, and thunderings, and an earthquake, and great hail" just prior to the Second Coming. In Revelation 16:18–21, he again refers to this great hailstorm and states that it will occur in association with a massive earthquake—an earthquake that will change the face of the land.

There are several references to the Lord's use of hailstorms throughout the scriptures. They were used symbolically when the false prophets in Ezekiel's time prescribed a belief in a counterfeit peace (a situation Ezekiel described as a wall created with "untempered mortar"). Ezekiel prophesied that the Lord would send "an overflowing shower in [His] anger, and great hailstones in [His] fury to consume" the symbolic wall and destroy the prophesied peace.[f]

Ezekiel again spoke of a great hailstorm when he had a vision of the same storm John had seen. While prophesying of the terrible latter-day invasion of Israel and Jerusalem by an army he called "Gog," he cited the same great earthquake John had seen and stated that God would send "great hailstones" (among other natural calamities) to afflict the wicked.[g]

When Mosiah recorded God's judgments against the wicked people of King Noah's time, he stated that the Lord would send "hail among

a. Joel 3:9–14.

b. Luke 21:9.

c. Chapter 5.

d. Zechariah
   12:3.

e. D&C 87:6.

f. Ezekiel
   13:13.

g. Ezekiel
   38:19–22.

them" to "smite them."[a] In the dedicatory prayer of the Kirtland Temple, Joseph Smith asked the Lord to send hail as a judgment upon those who were slandering the Saints of his time.[b] In his battle with the five kings at Gibeon, Joshua records that the Lord discomforted the enemies of Israel by casting down "great stones from heaven " upon them. In this storm, there were more soldiers "which died with hailstones than they whom the children of Israel slew with the sword."[c]

However, the hailstorm seen in vision by John and Ezekiel will make all former hailstorms pale in comparison. The severity of this storm will cause men to suffer greatly and to blaspheme God "because of the plague of the hail."[d] This is not an unwarranted assumption since John describes the weight of the hailstones as that of a "talent," and while the weight of a talent has differed historically depending upon how it was used, its minimum weight was approximately 57 pounds.[155]

Whether the weight of these hailstones is symbolic or literal, it is unquestionable that they will be extremely large and destructive. Their purpose will be twofold: to destroy the crops of the earth[e] and to plague the army (Gog) which will assail Judah just prior to the Second Coming.[f]

The Nations

There are many scriptures that describe the suffering that the nations of the earth will experience prior to the Second Coming. The Lord in Luke predicts that nation will "rise against nation and kingdom against kingdom, and there shall be signs in the sun, and in the moon, and in the stars; and upon the earth distress of nations,"[g] The word *distress* is used metaphorically to describe all judgments that will come upon the nations because of their wickedness. In another scripture, the Lord said all nations would "tremble" at His coming[h] and that after the establishment of Zion, they would "tremble because of her" and would "fear because of her terrible ones."[i] Jackson County, Missouri—the City of Zion—is where people will flee for protection from the great conflicts that will occur between the nations because they will be "the only people that shall not be at war one with another"[j] at a time when there will be "wars and rumors of war among all the nations."[k]

Isaiah saw the great destruction that will occur among the nations in the latter days and described it in *historical double-reference*

a. Mosiah 12:6.

b. D&C 109:30.

c. Joshua 10:11.

d. Revelation 16:21.

e. D&C 29:16.

f. Ezekiel 38:19.

g. Luke 21:10, 25.

h. D&C 34:8.

i. D&C 64:43.

j. D&C 45:68–69.

k. 1 Nephi 14:15.

prophecy (prophecy written as if it has already occurred, yet which actually applies to two or more time periods in the future). His vision of the tribulations that will come upon nations is written in Isaiah 13–23. The fulfillment of these prophecies started shortly after Isaiah's prediction, and they will continue to be fulfilled with the distress which the Lord will bring upon all nations prior to His Second Coming.[a]

Through double-reference prophecy, Isaiah described both the destruction which God would bring upon the nations surrounding Israel during Isaiah's time, and the destruction that will occur to those nations and all other nations in the latter days. In his writings, the nation of Israel (meaning the covenant people consisting of the twelve tribes) represents the kingdom of God.[b] The double-reference prophecy in his visions (which he calls "burdens") describes the afflictions which the Lord will place upon *all* nations of the earth that fight against the kingdom of God.[c] John, in Revelation, sees the latter-day distress of the nations in terms of the devil's latter-day kingdom as it opposes the kingdom of God.

When discussing the distress of nations in Isaiah and Revelation, it should be remembered that Israel and the kingdom of God are synonymous and include not only the state of Israel and the tribe of Judah, but also the other eleven tribes of Israel (as well as any entity, including the Church, which represents the gospel or the covenant people in the last days).

Chapters 13 through 23 of Isaiah testify of the following salient points concerning the distress of nations:

1. The Lord sometimes uses outside nations or entities to *punish* the tribes of Israel. A latter-day example of this involves the establishment and abandonment of Zion in Missouri by the early Church. The Lord gave instructions for the establishment of Zion and specified its location,[d] and while the Saints gathered there, they soon found persecution heaped upon them to such a degree that they were forced to abandon the promised city. Why? Because of the transgression of the Saints.[e] And what was the nature of their offense? "They sinned against the Lord, . . . they sinned against each other . . . they failed to live in accordance with the high moral and spiritual law of the

a. Zechariah
9:1–8.

b. Exodus
19:5–6; Ephe-
sians 2:12; 1
Peter 2:9.

c. Isaiah
13–23.

d. D&C
57:2–3.

e. D&C 101:2;
103:4; 105:9.

Gospel; they failed to meet the conditions on which God was pledged to their maintenance upon the land of Zion, and hence were left in the hands of their enemies."[156] And what did the Lord use to evict the Saints from Zion? The state of Missouri and its people, "including the Governor and Lieutenant Governor, and finally . . . the state legislature."[157]

2. As stated, the Lord sometimes uses the nations of the earth to *punish* each other. The Missouri expulsion of the Saints also provides us with an example of this Isaiah principle. While it is true that the Lord used both the state of Missouri and its inhabitants to expel the Mormons and to punish them for their iniquity and disobedience, he also punished Missouri—both the state and the people—for the sins they committed against the Saints. During the Civil War, "all the hardships the Missourians had inflicted upon the Saints were . . . visited upon their heads, only more abundantly."[158] And by whom? The United States of America!

3. While the Lord used the nations surrounding Israel to punish her, He did not accept any of them as her replacement. He rejected them because of their wickedness and idolatry.

4. Double-reference prophecy involves the following aspects of the Lord's relationship to the nations of the earth:

    a. They will again be punished for their wickedness prior to the Second Coming.

    b. They will reject the Lord, even though He has prophesied to them of His coming.

    c. Their Savior is Christ, just as He is the Savior of the covenant people.

    d. As Israel's God, the Messiah is superior to the gods of other nations.

5. The most important aspects of Isaiah's double-reference prophecies are the references to the judgments that will come upon all nations of the earth prior to the Second Coming.

6.	The judgments of the Lord upon the nations of the latter days will occur for the same reasons that they did historically: the nations of the earth will (a) reject God, (b) afflict Israel, (c) worship false gods, and (d) revere material things over spiritual truths.

7.	All material power, political power, false gods of whatever nature, and all nations will fall before the wrath of God; only the blessings of the Lord's covenant people will remain.

Zechariah confirms Isaiah's prophecies regarding the fate of nations, although he couches his prophecies in terms of all those nations that had "vexed" Israel.[a]

Although Isaiah's prophecies involve all nations, it is interesting to note the Lord's particular interest in Egypt. In his visions, Isaiah views Egypt's past, present, and future.[b] He foresaw Israel's reliance upon treaties with Egypt for protection and warned them against such alliances: those that would imminently occur,[c] those that would occur during the Babylonian captivity,[d] and those that would yet occur during the latter days.[e] Isaiah warned Israel against alliances with Egypt—or any worldly nation—as opposed to her alliance with God, and he reiterated the Lord's promise to Israel that He would protect her if she would but rely upon Him.[f] Only God can protect the chosen people—worldly alliances will prove false.[g] Isaiah further notes that in spite of the judgments that will come upon Egypt, the Lord loves the Egyptian people and will yet send the Savior to them after their repentance and punishment.[h]

The judgment of the nations is, in most instances, another general sign of the Second Coming. However, it is not easy to determine whether a nation's particular distress is the result of the Lord's judgment or whether it is based upon natural causes. This determination can only be made through the Spirit.

a. Zechariah 9:1–8.

b. Isaiah 19.

c. Isaiah 30:2–7.

d. Isaiah 30:7; Jeremiah 37:5, 7.

e. Isaiah 19:23–24.

f. Isaiah 31:1–5.

g. Isaiah 31.

h. Isaiah 19:20.

Six Signs: Beginning with the Church 12

12

Ezekiel 33:12   Therefore, thou son of man, say unto the children of thy people, The righteousness of the righteous shall not deliver him in the day of his transgression.

Beginning with the Church

In the early years of the restoration of the gospel, the Lord gave a warning to two eager members of the Church: "Wherefore, be faithful," He said, "praying always, having your lamps trimmed and burning, and oil with you, that you may be ready at the coming of the Bridegroom."[a] The Lord is referring to the parable of the ten virgins in this admonition,[b] and since the bridegroom represents the Savior and the ten virgins represent His followers, this parable applies directly to the status of the members of The Church of Jesus Christ of Latter-day Saints at the time of the Second Coming.[c]

Initially, all of the virgins in the parable are prepared to join the wedding feast as was the custom in Christ's time. But when the bridegroom tarried (the time of the Savior's coming is unknown), their oil (the spiritual preparation required to be members of Christ's church under the covenant) diminishes. The parable tells us that five of the virgins were adequately prepared to wait for the bridegroom—no matter how long it took. They had "received the truth, and [had] taken the Holy Spirit for their guide, and [had] not been deceived"[d]—this was their extra oil. And while the other five virgins had participated in all

a. D&C 33:17.

b. Matthew 25:1–13.

c. D&C 45:56–59.

d. D&C 45:57.

that was required of them to get them to the point where they were *entitled to wait* for the bridegroom, they were not prepared for the duration of the wait—they could not *endure to the end.* Consequently, they would not be able to enter in with the bridegroom when he came (join the Lord in His kingdom).

To be spiritually prepared means that an individual has a personal testimony of Jesus Christ, a thorough knowledge of the gospel, and will constantly and consistently subject his or her own will to God's will. These individuals are "agents unto themselves" with the power to do "much righteousness," and they must not wait to be commanded to do good lest they find themselves damned—shut out from the presence of the Lord at His coming.[a] Five virgins had the depth of spiritual preparedness necessary to gain the kingdom and five did not. Whether or not the split between those prepared and those not prepared is literally fifty-fifty, this figure at least indicates that a substantial number of Church members will not be ready to greet the Savior. They will be destroyed in the cleansing of the earth and will not be allowed to enter His kingdom.[159]

The Lord declared early in the restoration of the gospel that the great calamities which will come upon the earth to judge the inhabitants and destroy those who cannot abide the Second Coming will begin with the Church. "Upon my house shall it begin, and from my house shall it go forth, saith the Lord."[b] This warning applies directly to the members of the Church identified in the parable as the five foolish virgins who "professed to know [His] name," but still "blasphemed against [Him]."[c] How do members of the Church blaspheme against Christ today? By accepting the covenant of Abraham via baptism[d] and then failing to live according to God's commandments. They are like the scribes and Pharisees of Christ's day who were "like unto whited sepulchres, which indeed appear beautiful outward, but are within full of dead men's bones, and of all uncleanness." They are men and women who "outwardly appear righteous unto men, but within . . . are full of hypocrisy and iniquity."[e] These scribes and Pharisees were also like the five foolish virgins. They accepted the covenant and outwardly lived the law to perfection, but their personal reasons for living the law were unacceptable to the Lord. They used their outward perfection to justify their failure in complying with the weightier matters of the

a. D&C 58:26–29.

b. D&C 112:25.

c. D&C 112:26.

d. Chapter 3.

e. Matthew 23:27–28.

law, and the parable of the virgins makes it clear that in like manner, many Latter-day Saints will be judged and found wanting by the Lord in the last days.

The judgment of unfaithful members at the Second Coming will resemble the Lord's judgment of His covenant people at the time of Micah. Through Micah, He declared that He had "a controversy with his people,"[a] because He had required them "to do justly, and to love mercy, and to walk humbly with [their] God,"[b] but they had not kept His commandments. Members of the Church today, as well as all mankind, will not be judged by outward appearances. God sees the heart, and He will judge by the spirit of the law and our reasons for living it. At His coming, He will "recompense unto every man according to his work [how well men and women live the first great commandment], and measure to every man according to the measure which he has measured to his fellow man [how well they live the second great commandment]."[c]

While warning the members of the Church in general of the need for righteousness if they are to survive His destructive judgments in preparation for the Second Coming, the Lord also narrows the warning specifically to Priesthood holders. Prophets have specifically, metaphorically, and symbolically couched this warning to the priesthood using such terms as priest, prophet, rights of the priesthood, and men and watchmen.

Isaiah contended that some of the priesthood of his day had "erred, . . . the priest and the prophet have erred . . . they err in vision, they stumble in judgment."[d] He uses the metaphor of strong drink to represent errors of judgment and the unrighteous use of power, stating that "through strong drink, they are swallowed up of wine, they are out of the way through strong drink . . . For all [their] tables are full of vomit and filthiness, so that there is no place clean."[e] These statements are graphically symbolic. The Lord clarified some of Isaiah's symbolic prophecy in terms of the rights of priesthood in the latter days as follows:

D&C 121:36–39 The rights of the priesthood are inseparably connected with the powers of heaven, and . . . the powers of heaven cannot be con-

a. Micah 6:2.

b. Micah 6:8.

c. D&C 1:10.

d. Isaiah 28:7.

e. Isaiah 28:7–8.

trolled nor handled only upon the principles of righteousness. That they may be conferred upon us, it is true; but when we undertake to cover our sins, or to gratify our pride, our vain ambition, or to exercise control or dominion or compulsion upon the souls of the children of men, in any degree of unrighteousness, behold, the heavens withdraw themselves; the Spirit of the Lord is grieved; and when it is withdrawn, Amen to the priesthood or the authority of that man. Behold, ere he is aware, he is left unto himself, to kick against the pricks, to persecute the saints, and to fight against God. We have learned by sad experience that it is the nature and disposition of almost all men, as soon as they get a little authority, as they suppose, [that] they will immediately begin to exercise unrighteous dominion.

The unrighteous dominion of priesthood holders is the unrighteous use of power, position, and authority—from the least to the greatest in the priesthood. Isaiah again warns priesthood holders (whom he refers to as watchmen):

Isaiah 56:10–11   His watchmen are blind: they are all ignorant, they are all dumb dogs, they cannot bark; sleeping, lying down, loving to slumber. Yea, they are greedy dogs which can never have enough, and they are shepherds that cannot understand: they all look to their own way, every one for his gain, from his quarter.

Priesthood holders have a special calling in the plan of salvation for the human family. They must not only *teach* righteousness, they must also *be* righteous as they receive and accept the requirements of the kingdom. The Lord illustrated this obligation when He instructed His Apostles (and by application all priesthood holders) that they were the "salt of the earth: but if the salt have lost his savour, wherewith shall it be salted? It is henceforth good for nothing, but to be cast out . . . ."[a]

Salt was the great preservative of Christ's day. To the Jews, salt specifically symbolized fidelity and hospitality—it was an evidence of their covenant with the Lord, and it was used in every meat offering under the Law.[b] The "salt" (all priesthood holders, and by application all members) had to be pure. Any object which adulterated it caused it to lose its savor. Therefore, the disciples would lose their savor if they became fainthearted or slothful or if they broke the commandments. By so doing, they would lose their worth to the kingdom of God and thereafter be cast out. In the restored application of this warning in the Doctrine and Covenants, the Lord put it this way:

a. Matthew 5:13.

b. Leviticus 2:13; Numbers 18:19; 2 Chronicles 13:5.

D&C 121:41–45 No power or influence can or ought to be maintained by virtue of the priesthood, only by persuasion, by long-suffering, by gentleness and meekness, and by love unfeigned; by kindness, and pure knowledge, which shall greatly enlarge the soul without hypocrisy, and without guile—reproving betimes with sharpness, when moved upon by the Holy Ghost; and then showing forth afterwards an increase of love toward him whom thou hast reproved, lest he esteem thee to be his enemy; that he may know that thy faithfulness is stronger than the cords of death. Let thy bowels also be full of charity towards all men, and to the household of faith, and let virtue garnish thy thoughts unceasingly; then shall thy confidence wax strong in the presence of God; and the doctrine of the priesthood shall distil upon thy soul as the dews from heaven.

All men and women are subject to God's judgment, from the newest convert to the highest authority. The scriptures teach us that being a member of the Church does not mean that all we do is automatically correct or justified. Isaiah put it simply: "And it shall be, as with the people, so with the priest; as with the servant, so with his master"[a]—all are equally responsible to God under the covenant—but "of him unto whom much is given much is required; and he who sins against the greater light shall receive the greater condemnation."[b]

As members of the Church, we have all been invited to the wedding supper which the Lord of the vineyard has scheduled. Let us look to our preparation that we may be ready to enter in with the Lord at His coming—appropriately dressed[160] and secure in the knowledge that our lamps are sufficiently full of oil.

The 144,000

Revelation 7:4 records that there are 144,000 children of Israel (12,000 from each tribe) who have received the seal of God in their foreheads. This seal of God is mentioned again by John in Revelation 9:4 where it is symbolic of those who have made their calling and election sure and will return to the Father's presence at the final judgment.

When John listed the twelve tribes of Israel (each of which will supply 12,000 men), he listed Manasseh and Joseph as separate tribes and excluded the tribe of Dan. There has been discussion about why he listed the tribes in this manner, but it appears to have been for one of two simple reasons: (1) he may have made an error as he recorded his revelation, or (2) scribes over the centuries may have made an er-

a. Isaiah 24:2.

b. D&C 82:3.

ror while transcribing the text. One of these two reasons seems likely since John notes that the 144,000 are to come from *all* the tribes of Israel. Therefore, it is probable that the listing of the names is nothing more than an inconsequential error. This theory seems to be born out by the revelation Joseph Smith received (as recorded in the 77th Section of the Doctrine and Covenants): "What are we to understand by sealing the one hundred and forty-four thousand, out of *all* the tribes of Israel—twelve thousand out of *every* tribe?"[a] The Lord did not correct the error in John's list nor enumerate the tribes in His answer. But He did direct that the selection would be from *all* of the original twelve tribes, just as John's use of the word *all* indicates.

The answer Joseph records to this question sheds more light on the 144,000:

> **D&C 77:11** We are to understand that those who are sealed are high priests, ordained unto the holy order of God, to administer the everlasting gospel; for they are they who are ordained out of every nation, kindred, tongue, and people, by the angels to whom is given power over the nations of the earth, to bring as many as will come to the church of the Firstborn.

In a revelation given in November 1831, the Lord revealed that the 144,000 would be with Him on Mount Zion[b]—in other words, they will be with Christ at His coming. Although Joseph did not discuss John's revelation often, at a prayer meeting in February of 1844 he "made some remarks respecting the one hundred and forty-four thousand mentioned by John the Revelator, showing that the selection of the persons to form that number had already commenced."[161] No other details are given.

From this limited information concerning the 144,000, we learn the following:

1.   They are high priests.

2.   There are 12,000 from each of the twelve tribes of Israel.

3.   They are "sealed," or have the name of God in their foreheads, meaning that their calling and election is sure.

4.   They are not "defiled with women; for they are virgins"[c] (this may mean that they are pure and holy rather than unmarried).

a. D&C 77:11;
   italics added.

b. D&C 133:18.

c. Revelation 14:4.

5.   They are as Nathaniel, without guile, or perfect.[a]

6.   They are to "administer the everlasting gospel."

7.   They are ordained by angels.

8.   Their work is to bring as many into the "church of the First-born" as will come.

9.   They will be with Christ at His coming.

10. Their selection has already begun.

The Last Laborers

The Lord has given His Church of the latter days the same charge He gave His Apostles before He ascended into heaven: "Go ye therefore, and teach all nations . . . and, lo, I am with you alway, even unto the end of the world."[b] Before the Millennium is ushered in, the Lord has said that the Church must declare "the voice of warning . . . unto all people by the mouths of [His] disciples whom [He has] chosen in [the] last days."[c] They are to go forth to the inhabitants of the earth so that "all that will hear may hear,"[d] for "it is the eleventh hour, and the last time" that the Lord will "call laborers into [His] vineyard."[e] This last great call will prune the vineyard and gather all the righteous out of the wickedness of the world prior to the great judgment that God will pour out upon the wicked before the Second Coming. This gathering of the righteous need not be to a central, geographical location. They will be gathered to the covenant of Abraham, or the Church.

The Lord has always called His children to repentance before cataclysmic judgments came upon them: Noah was sent to warn the people before the Flood;[f] Lot was sent to his unrepentant sons-in-law to warn them of the destruction of Sodom and Gomorrah;[g] Isaiah and Micah were sent to warn the Israelites before the Northern Kingdom of Israel was destroyed; Jeremiah, Lehi, and "many prophets" were sent to call Judah to repentance and to warn her of Jerusalem's destruction before the city was destroyed and her inhabitants carried off into Babylon;[h] and in the latter days, the final pruning and nourishing of the vineyard before the ultimate destruction of the wicked is recounted in Jacob's great vineyard allegory found in the Book of Mormon.[i]

Exactly who are those who are called to labor for the last time? All

a. Revelation 14:5.

b. Matthew 28:19–20.

c. D&C 1:4.

d. D&C 1:11.

e. D&C 33:3.

f. Moses 8:17–30.

g. Genesis 19:12–15.

h. Book of Jeremiah; 1 Nephi 1:4.

i. Jacob 5:71–75.

those who desire to serve![a] Perhaps the 144,000 spoken of by John will be established to assist in this work,[b] or perhaps their number simply represents a righteous multitude of missionaries that will be called to serve in this final gathering. The Lord confirms by revelation that He has "committed the keys of [His] kingdom, and a dispensation of the gospel for the last times."[c] Therefore, the Lord leaves us with this command: "Labor ye in my vineyard for the last time—for the last time call upon the inhabitants of the earth . . . For . . . I come upon the earth in judgment, and my people shall be redeemed . . . For the great Millennium . . . shall come."[d]

The Heavens

While many signs of the Second Coming will occur upon the earth, even greater signs will occur in the heavens. These signs will cause "weeping and wailing among the hosts of men."[e] Many references describe these heavenly occurrences as signs and wonders,[f] or declare that while the earth will "shake," "the starry heavens shall tremble."[g] Occasionally the scriptures reverse the descriptive words or combine them,[h] leaving the exactness of the sign undefined.

Isaiah declares that "all the host of heaven shall be dissolved, and the heavens shall be rolled together as a scroll: and all their host shall fall down, as the leaf falleth off from the vine, and as a falling fig from the fig tree."[i] He further states that the Lord will "rend the heavens" at His coming,[j] and latter-day revelation says that "the curtain of heaven [will be] unfolded, as a scroll is unfolded after it is rolled up."[k] The Lord states that all of these events will occur as the "heavens" pass away[l] to the accompaniment of great "lightnings, and voices, and thunderings, and an earthquake, and great hail."[m] No wonder men will become fearful[n] and have their hearts "fail them;" the "powers of Heaven" will be shaken.[o] These descriptions are very general, however, and just *how* these events will be fulfilled is left up to the imagination. Only one thing is attested to by the prophets over and over again: something devastating is going to happen to the heavenly orbs, and the prophets describe the cataclysmic results of these events with great clarity.

The *sun* will refuse to give its light and hide its face in shame

a. D&C 4:3.

b. D&C 133:18.

c. D&C 27:13.

d. D&C 43:28–30.

e. D&C 29:15.

f. Joel 2:30; Acts 2:19; D&C 45:40.

g. D&C 84:118; Joel 2:10.

h. D&C 43:18; Joel 3:16.

i. Isaiah 34:4.

j. Isaiah 64:1.

k. D&C 88:95; Revelation 6:14.

l. 3 Nephi 26:3.

m. Revelation 11:19; Revelation 16:18; D&C 88:90.

n. Luke 21:11.

o. Luke 21:26.

because of the glory of the Lord. He will become our everlasting light and the days of our mourning will end.[a] The *moon* also will be darkened. It will become a color as blood, reflecting the sacrifice of the Lord and the color of His robes when He shall appear.[b] Finally, the *stars* also shall be darkened, cast down as if in anger, and hurled from their heavenly places.[c]

These signs of heavenly destruction defy description, and perhaps that is why the prophets have given us such generalized reports of their occurrence. All that can be factually determined is that these signs will occur *after* the cleansing of the earth and *before* the Savior's specific sign of the Second Coming.[d]

The Rainbow

After the great flood, wherein all men and women were destroyed because of their wickedness (save eight souls), the Lord spoke with Noah and reestablished His covenant with him. He declared at that time that "neither shall all flesh be cut off any more by the waters of a flood; neither shall there any more be a flood to destroy the earth."[e] The token God gave to Noah of this promise was the rainbow. "This is the token of the covenant . . . I do set my bow in the cloud . . . [as an] everlasting covenant between God and every living creature of all flesh that is upon the earth."[f]

Joseph Smith declared that when the rainbow no longer appears in the heavens, the Second Coming will be imminent. He states:

> I have asked of the Lord concerning His coming; and while asking the Lord, He gave a sign and said, 'In the days of Noah I set a bow in the heavens as a sign and token that in any year that the bow should be seen the Lord would not come; but there should be seed time and harvest during that year: but whenever you see the bow withdrawn, it shall be a token that there shall be famine, pestilence, and great distress among the nations, and that the coming of the Messiah is not far distant.'[162]

Joseph asked the Lord about His coming because a Father Miller had prophesied that the Savior would come in 1844. After he received

a. Isaiah 13:10; Joel 2:10; Joel 3:15; Acts 2:19–20; D&C 29:14; D&C 34:9; D&C 45:42; D&C 88:87; Joseph Smith–Matthew 1:33; Isaiah 24:23; D&C 133:49; Isaiah 60:19–20; Revelation 21:23; 22:5; Isaiah 60:20.

b. Acts 2:19; Revelation 6:12; D&C 29:14; D&C 34:9; D&C 45:42; D&C 88:87; Joel 2:10; Isaiah 13:10; D&C 133:49; Joseph Smith–Matthew 1:33; Isaiah 24:23; Isaiah 60:19.

c. Revelation 6:13; D&C 29:14; D&C 34:9; D&C 45:42; Joseph Smith–Matthew 1:33; Joel 2:10; 3:15; Revelation 8:12; D&C 34:9; D&C 88:87; Isaiah 13:10; D&C 133:49.

d. Joseph Smith–Matthew 1:36; Mark 13:24–26.

e. Genesis 9:11.

f. Genesis 9:12–16.

the above statement, he further stated: "But I will take the responsibility upon myself to prophesy in the name of the Lord, that Christ will not come this year, as Father Miller has prophesied, for we have seen the bow."[163]

The only knowledge we are left with is that the disappearance of the rainbow for one year is a sign of the Savior's coming. No information is given as to whether this disappearance will be local or worldwide, only that it will cause "famine" (since rainbows are created by rain in the atmosphere), "pestilence, and great distress among nations." We can draw the logical conclusion that as long as the rainbow is with us, the Second Coming will be at some future time.

Adam-ondi-Ahman

On May 19, 1838, the Lord designated "Spring Hill, Daviess County, Missouri" as the location of Adam-ondi-Ahman.[a] Joseph received this revelation while in the process of "selecting and laying claim to a city plat" at that location.[164] This is the place where Adam "called together his children and blessed them with a patriarchal blessing" prior to his death.[165] All the righteous of Adam's posterity were gathered there. The Lord Jesus Christ (whose name is also declared to be Son Ahman)[b] appeared to them and blessed Adam, and declared him to be Michael—the prince and archangel. The Lord comforted Adam and set him forever at the head of the human family.[c]

The Old Testament prophet Daniel declared that there would be another great council at Adam-ondi-Ahman prior to the Second Coming. He saw it in a vision wherein he described Adam as the "Ancient of days." He saw Adam dressed in a garment as "white as snow." "The hair of his head [was] like the pure wool: [and] his throne was like the fiery flame." Adam will be at this council to set in order the books of life for the final judgment.[d] Of this great council Joseph Smith declared:

Daniel in his seventh chapter speaks of the Ancient of Days; he means the oldest man, our Father Adam, Michael, he will call his children together and hold a council with them to prepare them for the coming of the Son of Man. He (Adam) is the father of the human family, and presides over the spirits of all men, and

a. D&C 116.

b. D&C 95:17.

c. D&C 107:53–57.

d. Daniel 7:9–14.

all that have had the keys must stand before him in this grand council . . . The Son of Man stands before him, and there is given him glory and dominion. Adam delivers up his stewardship to Christ, that which was delivered to him as holding keys of the universe, but retains his standing as head of the human family.[166]

Who will attend this great council? According to the statements of Daniel and Joseph, a great multitude! It will include all those who have ever held the "keys of the priesthood" plus all of the righteous (presumably either all the righteous then living, or who have ever lived upon the earth). Daniel describes their number as "a thousand thousands . . . and ten thousand times ten thousand."[a] When will this council meeting take place? After the destruction of the devil's earthly kingdom and the cleansing of the earth in the latter days,[b] but before the coming of the Lord.

The Three Cities   13

Revelation 22:14   Blessed are they that do his commandments, that they may have right to the tree of life, and may enter in through the gates into the city.

Three holy cities will play an integral part in the Lord's Second Coming: the translated City of Enoch, the City of Zion on the Western Hemisphere, and Jerusalem on the Eastern Hemisphere. At one time or another, all three of these cities have been referred to by the name *Zion*.[a] In fact, as the following chart shows, at least seventeen different doctrines or entities are referred to as *Zion* in the scriptures.

Zion Used to Represent:	Specific Doctrine or Entity Being Described:	Scriptural Reference:
A Mountain	Mt. Zion (Sion)	Deuteronomy 4:48
A City	The City of David	2 Samuel 5:7
A City	The City of Enoch	Moses 7:19
A Struggle	The Birth of a Nation	Isaiah 66:8
A System	The Gospel of Salvation	1 Nephi 13:36 37
A Sense of Security	"All's Well" Doctrine	2 Nephi 28:21
The Future City of Zion	The New Jerusalem	D&C 84:2
A City	The City of God	D&C 97:19
A People	The Pure in Heart	D&C 97:21
As a Kingdom	The Kingdom of God	D&C 105:32
A Religious Tenet	The Gospel	D&C 133:9
The Lord's People	A United People	Moses 7:18
An Article of Faith	Zion/New Jerusalem	A. of F. 1:10

a. Moses 7:19;
   D&C 57:2; 2
   Samuel 5:7.

Zion Used to Represent:	Specific Doctrine or Entity Being Described:	Scriptural Reference:
A Geographical Description	Land	D&C 64:30
A Synonym	"She" (person/place/city)	D&C 97:25–26
An Entire Country	The United States of America	HC 6:318–319

From the examples listed above, it is obvious that care must be taken to determine what is being referred to when the scriptures reference the name *Zion*. The same care must be exercised with the name *New Jerusalem*. While it can be seen in the table that the term *Zion* is sometimes interchanged with the term *New Jerusalem* when referencing both the City of Zion on the Western Hemisphere and the City of Enoch, there are other scriptural references where the determination of what is being referred to is left up to the reader.[a] For the purposes of discussion in this chapter, the three cities will be identified as follows:

The City of Enoch was established by Enoch during his ministry and was later translated into heaven in anticipation of the great Flood at the time of Noah. This city is prophesied to return at the Second Coming of the Savior, and while its return is probably symbolic in regards to its buildings, streets, and so forth, it is literal in regards to the righteous people who were translated, both at the time of Enoch and thereafter until the time of the Flood.

The City of Zion is the city that will be built on the Western Hemisphere in Jackson County, Missouri. It will be one of the two cities from which the Lord will govern during the Millennium. Zion is the eventual focal point for the gathering of all the tribes of Israel except Judah, and the future center place of the promised land of the restoration.

The City of Jerusalem is the ancient holy city that is located in Israel (the promised land of the Children of Israel in antiquity). It is the other city from which the Lord will govern during the Millennium and is the focal point for the gathering of the tribe of Judah in the last days.

The City of Enoch

Enoch was an ancient prophet, the "seventh from Adam." His father's name was Jared, and his only known son was named Mathusala

a. An example of this is found in Ether 13:3, 10.

(Methuselah).[a] The biblical record concerning Enoch is scanty. In addition to his lineage, however, we know that he was a righteous man since he "walked with God,"[b] and was *taken* by God,[c] which could give rise to much speculation save for Paul's text to the Hebrews wherein he stated: "By faith Enoch was translated that he should not see death; and was not found, because God had translated him."[d] The only other mention of Enoch in the Bible is by Jude, who uses Enoch's teachings as an example of God's future judgments upon the ungodly.[e]

The book of Moses in the Pearl of Great Price and other latter-day revelation gives us more in-depth information about Enoch. They state that he was taught the ways of God by his father, Jared,[f] that he was twenty-five years old when he was ordained by Adam, and that he was sixty-five when Adam blessed him.[g] His son Methuselah was born when Enoch was sixty-five years old; it was at this time that "the Spirit of God descended out of heaven, and abode upon him," thus calling him to be a prophet. Enoch's response to his prophetic call is interesting: "Why is it that I have found favor in thy sight, and am but a lad [he was sixty-five years old], and all the people hate me; for I am slow of speech; wherefore am I thy servant?" But the Lord comforted Enoch with this response: "Go forth and do as I have commanded thee, and no man shall pierce thee. Open thy mouth, and it shall be filled, and I will give thee utterance, for all flesh is in my hands, and I will do as seemeth me good."[h]

Enoch went on to become a powerful prophet. He was given the power to move mountains, to turn rivers from their course, and to cause the "roar of the lions [to be] heard [in] the wilderness."[i] He received tremendous visions wherein he "beheld the spirits that God had created . . . for the space of many generations."[j] He saw Noah and the great Flood and heard the earth lament, "Wo, wo is me, the mother of men;" because of the wickedness of mankind.[k] In anguish of soul, he wept for the earth's sorrows and asked the Lord to never again bring such terrible devastation upon mankind.

Enoch also saw "the Lord . . . before [his] face" and spoke with Him "as a man talketh one with another."[l] He saw the Savior crucified on the cross, and he observed the ensuing Dark Ages give way to the light of the Restoration. He beheld the great tribulations that would precede the Second Coming, and he saw the Millennial reign

a. Luke 3:37.

b. Genesis 5:18–24.

c. Genesis 5:24.

d. Hebrews 11:5.

e. Jude 1:14–15.

f. Moses 6:21.

g. D&C 107:48.

h. Moses 6:25–26, 31, 32.

i. Moses 7:13.

j. Moses 7:4.

k. Moses 7:48.

l. Moses 7:4.

of Christ. He was privileged to see "all things, even unto the end of the world."a

In obedience to God's command, Enoch successfully called his people to repentance, and with his righteous followers he founded a city that was called the "City of Holiness, even Zion."b The Lord blessed Enoch's city—but he cursed the rest of the people. When enemies came against Enoch and his people, he merely spoke "the word of the Lord" and the earth "trembled, and the mountains fled."c "So powerful was the word of Enoch" that he caused land to come up out of the "depth of the sea."d The wicked were astonished and feared him, and "all men were offended because of him."e They declared that a "seer" was among them as a "strange thing in the land," and accused him of being a "wild man."f

The righteous who gathered to Enoch's city were, in the "process of time[,] . . . taken up into heaven."g Thereafter, angels continued to bear testimony "of the Father and Son," and "the Holy Ghost fell on many." These souls were also translated, "caught up by the powers of heaven into Zion"h in anticipation of the Flood that would cleanse the earth of the wicked. The Lord revealed to Joseph Smith that Enoch's city had been translated, thus confirming the fact that He was "the same [God] which [had] taken the Zion of Enoch into [His] own bosom."i

The scriptures tell us that the City of Enoch will eventually return to the earth when "a day of righteousness [the Second Coming] shall come."j Ether prophesied that at His Advent, the Lord would come to Zion on the Western Hemisphere and the City of Enoch would also "come down out of heaven" to Zion on this, the American continent.k

John the Revelator was carried away by God to a "great and high mountain" where he saw Enoch's city descend from heaven.l It came "down from God out of heaven, prepared as a bride adorned for her husband,"m a *metaphoric* description of its great beauty and the happiness of its inhabitants. The city was encompassed with the glory of God, and its light was like a most precious stone, "a jasper stone [diamond], clear as crystal."n Its wall was high, symbolic of the security its people enjoyed. There were twelve gates in the wall representing the twelve tribes of Israel, and "the wall of the city had twelve foundations, and in them the names of the twelve apostles of the Lamb."o This

a. Moses 7:67.

b. Moses 7:19.

c. Moses 7:13.

d. Moses 7:14.

e. Moses 6:37.

f. Moses 6:38.

g. Moses 7:21.

h. Moses 7:27.

i. D&C 38:4.

j. D&C 45:12.

k. Ether 13:3–4.

l. Revelation 21:10.

m. Revelation 21:2.

n. Revelation 21:11.

o. Revelation 21:14.

symbolic description reveals the purity of the city's inhabitants and the fact that they are the covenant people of the Lord (as represented by twelve gates, one for each tribe of Israel). They had fulfilled all of the requirements of the gospel as it was taught by the twelve Apostles after Jesus' death.

John also observed that the city gates were never closed, that "glory and honor" from the nations of the earth were brought to it, and that nothing could defile it. He further records, "For there shall be no night there." The inhabitants will have no need for a "candle, neither light of the sun . . . neither of the moon, to shine in it: for the glory of God [will] lighten it, and the Lamb [will be] the light thereof."[a]

The City of Zion

"We believe in the literal gathering of Israel and in the restoration of the Ten Tribes; *that Zion (the New Jerusalem) will be built upon the American continent;* that Christ will reign personally upon the earth; and, that the earth will be renewed and receive its paradisiacal glory."[b][167] Joseph Smith's astonishing declaration pertaining to the location of the City of Zion represented a radical departure from the apostate belief concerning Zion, for at that time Zion was—and continues to be—interpreted as only a synonym for old Jerusalem and its environs. This is one of the major reasons for the misinterpretation of the scriptures surrounding the latter days involving Zion and Jerusalem.

For the gospel to be true (and not just another reformation of an apostate Christianity), its restoration had to include a promised land— not the *old* promised land, which was reserved for the gathering and restoring of Judah, but a *new* promised land for the establishment of the restored covenant of Abraham and a gathering place for all of the tribes of Israel *except* Judah. Ether saw this land in vision hundreds of years before the time of Christ. He called it a "New Jerusalem" and stated that it would be established "upon this land," meaning the Western Hemisphere.[c]

The location of the New Jerusalem (or the City of Zion—also called Zion) has been specifically defined.[d] But the Lord led His early latter-day followers slowly through the following step-by-step process, building their anticipation before He revealed the city's location to them:

a. Revelation 21:10–14, 23, 25–27; 22:5.

b. Articles of Faith 1:10; emphasis added.

c. Ether 13:4–6.

d. D&C 45:66–67.

1. He first declared its existence in September 1830 when he said, "No man knoweth where the city Zion shall be built, but it shall be given hereafter. Behold, I say unto you that it shall be on the borders by the Lamanites."[a]

2. In February 1831, the Lord commanded the elders of the Church to move westward from Kirtland, Ohio, building "up [his] church in every region" until the time that Zion would be prepared for the gathering, "that ye may be my people and I will be your God."[b] The land for the city was to be purchased[c] so that the people could be gathered and the Lord could come to His temple.[d] But the Savior still did not tell the Saints where the city would be located, only that its exact location would be revealed "in [His] own due time."[e]

    While the Lord designates the city as *Zion*,[f] He also calls it the *New Jerusalem*. It will be "a land of peace," and it will be "a city of refuge, [and] a place of safety for the saints."[g] Both the glory and the terror of the Lord will be there, and the wicked will not "come unto it."[h] Those numbered in it will be from every nation of the earth, and it will be the only city where the people will "not be at war one with another."[i] The righteous who gather to the city will sing "songs of everlasting joy" under the Lord's protection, and the wicked will refuse to go up against it, contending that "the inhabitants of Zion are terrible."[j]

3. In Doctrine and Covenants 48, the Lord was still not ready to reveal Zion's location, but He promised to do so after some of the brethren returned to Kirtland, Ohio, from the east. At that time, "certain men" would be "appointed" to know the place,[k] and the Lord would "hasten the city in its time" since its location was currently in the land of their "enemies."[l]

4. Finally, on July 20, 1831, the Lord revealed to Joseph Smith the exact location of Zion. Pursuant to the Lord's command, the prophet and others had traveled to Missouri in June 1831 to join another company of Saints.[m] Upon their arrival, Joseph pondered the great differences between what he called

a. D&C 28:9.

b. D&C 42:8–9.

c. D&C 42:35.

d. D&C 42:36.

e. D&C 42:62.

f. D&C 45:67.

g. D&C 45:66.

h. D&C 45:67.

i. D&C 45:69.

j. D&C 45:70–71.

k. D&C 48:5.

l. D&C 52:42–43.

m. D&C 52:1–3.

the "highly cultivated state of society in the east" and the "degradation, leanness of intellect, ferocity, and jealousy of the people that were nearly a century behind the times" in Missouri. While under the influence of these opinions, he cried to the Lord saying, "When will Zion be built up in her glory?"[168] In response, the Lord declared:

> **D&C 57:1–3**   Hearken, O ye elders of my church . . . who have assembled yourselves together, according to my commandments, in this land, which is the land of Missouri, which is the land which I have appointed and consecrated for the gathering of the saints. Wherefore, this is the land of promise, and the place for the city of Zion. And thus saith the Lord your God, if you will receive wisdom here is wisdom. Behold, the place which is now called Independence is the center place; and a spot for the temple is lying westward, upon a lot which is not far from the courthouse.

Thereupon, Sidney Rigdon was appointed to "consecrate and dedicate" the land for the establishment of Zion,[a] which he did on August 2, 1831.[169] On August 3, 1831, Joseph Smith dedicated a spot for the temple;[170] however, according to his plat, the completed city would eventually have a total of twenty-four temples within its boundaries to ensure that the Lord's work would go forth.[171] The building up of the city was to begin from the original "temple lot" which, while not being in mountainous country, was designated by the Lord as Mount Zion[b]— a term symbolically referring to the exaltation or lifting up of Christ's gospel upon the earth.

After the dedication of the land, the Saints proceeded to move into Missouri, acquiring territory for the establishment of Zion as they arrived. But Zion was not to be redeemed in their time. Severe persecutions befell them and this oppression culminated when Lilburn W. Boggs, then governor of Missouri, conspired with mobbers and other persecutors of the Church to issue his infamous *Extermination Order.* This order expelled the Saints from the State of Missouri.[172] Still, the Lord recognized the diligence and hard work of those early Saints. He acknowledged the obstacles their enemies had placed in their way when He relieved them of the duty to build Zion at that time, and He severely cursed those who had hindered His work:

a. D&C 58:57.

b. D&C 84:2–4.

> **D&C 124:49–52**   Verily, verily, I say unto you, that when I give a command-

ment to any of the sons of men to do a work unto my name, and those sons of men go with all their might and with all they have to perform that work, and cease not their diligence, and their enemies come upon them and hinder them from performing that work, behold, it behooveth me to require that work no more at the hands of those sons of men, but to accept of their offerings. And the iniquity and transgression of my holy laws and commandments I will visit upon the heads of those who hindered my work, unto the third and fourth generation, so long as they repent not, and hate me, saith the Lord God. Therefore, for this cause have I accepted the offerings of those whom I commanded to build up a city and a house unto my name, in Jackson county, Missouri, and were hindered by their enemies, saith the Lord your God. And I will answer judgment, wrath, and indignation, wailing, and anguish, and gnashing of teeth upon their heads, unto the third and fourth generation, so long as they repent not, and hate me, saith the Lord your God.

God's judgment and wrath befell the people of Missouri because they hindered the establishment of this holy city in the early days of the restoration so severely that "all the hardships the Missourians had inflected upon the Saints were now visited upon their heads, only more abundantly."[173] While discussing his arrest and pending trial during his incarceration in Liberty Jail, Joseph Smith prophesied to A. W. Doniphan (his attorney) that "God's wrath hangs over Jackson County . . . The Lord of Hosts will sweep it with the besom of destruction. The fields and farms and houses will be destroyed, and only the chimneys will be left to mark the desolation."[174] This remarkable prophecy was fulfilled with the destruction that came upon Missouri and its people prior to and during the Civil War. Governor Robert W. Stewart reported that several of Missouri's western counties were made desolate "and almost depopulated, from fear of a bandit horde" which had been and was committing "depredations—arson, theft, and foul murder."[175] General Sterling Price, who had custody of and mistreated Joseph Smith and many other members of the Church,[176] "destroyed upwards of 'ten million dollars worth of property,' a fair share of which belonged to his friends," during his Civil War skirmishes in Missouri.[177] And under Military Order No. 11 issued from Kansas City by General Thomas Ewing, the very people who had expelled the Saints from Missouri by driving them from their homes and confiscating their personal property were themselves driven and expelled from their homes. "Their dwellings [were] burned, their farms laid waste, and the great bulk of their movable property handed over, without let or hindrance, to the Kansas 'jayhawkers.'"[178] During the first nineteen months of the war, between April 20, 1861, and November 20, 1862, "over three hundred battles and skirmishes were fought within the limits of the State . . . [and probably] half as many more" during the last two years[179]— the result of which was to depopulate "a large part of the western border."[180]

Did God smite Missouri because it hindered His work? He most certainly did! The ancient prophet Mormon warned those who would attempt to prevent the progress of God's work: "He that shall breathe out wrath and strifes against the work of the Lord, and against the covenant people of the Lord who are the house of Israel . . . the same is in danger to be hewn down and cast into the fire."[a] Missouri itself, from the governor down to the common citizen, had been "made to feel the wrath, and indignation, and chastening hand of an Almighty God."[b]

While visiting the Western Hemisphere after His resurrection, the Lord prophesied of Zion's future existence. He declared that it would be established "in this land," meaning America,[c] and that both the "remnant of Jacob" and the Gentiles would assist in its construction.[d] Enoch viewed its establishment after his translation into heaven.[e] But it was the Lord's ancient prophets who foresaw and described its glory. Isaiah and Micah saw it as one of the two world capitals from which the Lord would govern during the millennium: "for out of Zion shall go forth the law," they declared, and as Joel metaphorically described it, "the Lord also shall roar out of Zion."[f]

Although the City of Zion is yet to be established, when the time comes it will be located exactly where the Lord said it would be: Jackson County, Missouri! It will be ready for Him when He comes in His glory. It will be ready when "the graves of the saints shall be opened; and they shall come forth and stand on the right hand of the Lamb, when he shall stand upon Mount Zion, and upon the holy city, the New Jerusalem."[g] The righteousness of the Saints will prevail over the wicked and the Lord will cleanse "the daughters of Zion" in preparation for His coming.[h] The City of Zion and ancient Jerusalem will become a haven for the righteous[i] as these two cities regain the paradisiacal glory that was once enjoyed by Adam and Eve and return to the geographical locales they occupied before the earth was

a. Mormon 8:21.

b. D&C 87:6.

c. 3 Nephi 20:22.

d. 3 Nephi 21:22–23.

e. Moses 7:62.

f. Isaiah 2:3; Micah 4:2; Joel 3:16.

g. D&C 133:56.

h. Isaiah 4:1–4.

i. Isaiah 33:20–24.

divided.[a] The Lord will come and "stand in [their] midst," and the lost tribes of Israel will return "unto the children of Ephraim" where they will be "crowned with glory, even in Zion,"[b] and shall receive (along with "as many of the Gentiles as shall comply") all the blessings of the new and everlasting covenant of Abraham.[181]

The Temple in Zion: When the Lord revealed the location for the City of Zion, He also revealed that there would be a temple there. The temple would be "lying westward, upon a lot which is not far from the court-house."[c] On August 3, 1831, shortly after this revelation, Joseph Smith dedicated the "spot for the Temple."[182] In June 1833, Joseph described the plat of the City of Zion which contained not only the temple referenced above, but twenty-three other temples as well. Joseph also *named* these temples and described their construction and use.[183] In August 1835, it was declared that the "Elders [had] failed in the outset to fill their great and important mission" pertaining to the construction of the temple. It was then declared that "Zion could not be redeemed" until the temple was built and endowments were taking place.[184]

While it is evident that the Lord desires both the City of Zion and its temple to be "redeemed," it will not be done until the Lord commands it. Then, and only then, will the way be opened to acquire the latter-day *promised land* of Zion.

The City of Jerusalem

Ancient Jerusalem "has known the hosts of thirty-six wars. She has been reduced to ashes seventeen times. She has risen eighteen."[185] Her beauty has always been renowned. "It is said the world has ten measures of beauty and nine of these belong to Jerusalem."[186] She is loved deeply by three religious cultures—Christian, Jew, and Muslim—but the "Jews have always loved her the most." This love has remained deeply ingrained throughout the centuries, ever since David first made Jerusalem his capital. "It is the longest, deepest love affair in all of history."[187]

We know little about the City of Enoch because of its ancient existence, and the City of Zion (the New Jerusalem) because it was never firmly established, but much is known about ancient Jerusalem. To detail its history would take volumes, but a brief chronology showing its development is interesting.

a. D&C 133:24;
Articles of Faith
1:10.

b. D&C
133:25–32.

c. D&C 57:3.

Antiquity (3000 B.C. - 537 B.C.)

3000   Earliest discovered remains of habitation at Jerusalem discovered on the hill of Ophel.

1850   Jerusalem referred to in Egyptian Execration Texts.

1280   Exodus from Egypt.

1250   Conquest of Canaan under Joshua.

1013–973   King David makes Jerusalem the capital of the united kingdom of Israel.

973–933   King Solomon builds the First Temple.

928   United kingdom splits into Judah and Israel.

715–687   King Hezekiah of Judah builds tunnel from Gihon Spring to Pool of Siloam and strengthens the city walls.

587   Nebuchadnezzar, King of Babylon, conquers Jerusalem, destroys the Temple and exiles Jews to Babylonia.

538   Cyrus, King of Persia, conquers Babylon and allows Jews to return to Jerusalem.

The Persian Period (537 B.C.–332 B.C.)

515   Completion of the Second Temple.

445   Nehemiah, Governor of Judea, rebuilds the walls of Jerusalem.

The Hellenistic Period (332 B.C. –167 B.C.)

331   Alexander the Great passes through Palestine and perhaps visits Jerusalem.

Rule of the Seleucids of Syeria (198 B.C.–128 B.C.)

172   Jerusalem becomes a Hellenistic polis named Antiochia.

169   Antiochus IV Epiphanes, Seleucid king, plunders the Temple. Practice of Judaism forbidden.

The Hasmoneans (Maccabees) (167 B.C.–63 B.C.)

167–141   Maccabean war of liberation.

139   Roman Senate recognizes independence of Judea.

131   Siege of Jerusalem by Antiochus VII.

The Roman Period (63 B.C.–A.D. 324)

63   The Roman General Pompey conquers Jerusalem and destroys the Temple.

40–37	Romans ousted briefly by Zealots.
37–4 B.C.	Reign of Herod the Great, who rebuilds the Temple.
A.D. 26–36	The Christian Era begins. Pontius Pilate procurator.
30	Crucifixion of Jesus.
41–44	Agrippa I, King of Judea, builds new city wall know as the "third wall."
66–70	First great Jewish revolt against the Romans.
67	Vespasian arrives; the Zealots take over in Jerusalem.
70	Destruction of the Second Temple by Titus and fall of Jerusalem.
132–135	Bar Kochba's war of freedom; Jerusalem again Jewish capital; second revolt of the Jews.
135	Emperor Hadrian's total destruction of Jerusalem. Building of new city called Aelia Capitolina. Jews banned from the city.

The Byzantine Period (A.D. 324–A.D. 638)

326	Emperor Constantine declares Christianity the state religion. His mother, Queen Helena, visits Jerusalem and names Christian sites. Building of the Church of the Holy Sepulchre begins.
614	Persian conquest of Jerusalem.

The Muslim Period (A.D. 638–A.D. 1099)

638	Caliph Omar enters Jerusalem; city falls to Arabs.
691	Dome of the Rock completed.
996–1020	Church of the Holy Sepulchre destroyed.
1037	Church of the Holy Sepulchre rebuilt.

The Crusader Kingdom/Ottoman Conquest (A.D. 1099–A.D. 1516)

1099	Crusaders capture Jerusalem; Jews and Muslims banned.
1099–1187	Jerusalem capital of the Latin Kingdom.
1187	Saladin captures Jerusalem from the Crusaders.
1250	The Mamelukes, slave kings of Egypt, seize the city.
1516	Ottoman conquest of Jerusalem.

The Modern World

1838	First consulate (British) opened in Jerusalem.

1841   *October 4, Orson Hyde's dedicatory prayer on the Mount*
               of Olives.

1861   First Jewish settlement outside the city walls.

1898   Visit by Dr. Theodor Herzel, founder of World Zionist
              Organization.

1917   November 2, Balfour Declaration; December 11: British
              conquest; General Allenby enters Jerusalem.

1923   British Mandate confirmed by League of Nations.

1947   United Nations resolution recommending the partition
              of Palestine into Arab and Jewish states.

1948   British Mandate ends and State of Israel proclaimed.

1948–1949   Israel's War of Independence (May 1948–January
              1949), the first Arab-Israeli War, ending with a divided
              city. New City of Jerusalem remains intact but Jewish
              Quarter in Old City falls (May 28, 1948). Signing of Is-
              rael-Transjordan armistice agreement in which Jerusalem
              is divided between the two countries (April 1949). West
              Jerusalem declared the capital of Israel.

1967   Six-Day War in which Israeli troops capture the Old City
              from the Jordanians. Jerusalem liberated and reunited.[188]

This outline of the history of the Lord's holy city was summarized
(with some additional items not significant to this topic excluded) by
Leon Uris in his book, *Jerusalem Song of Songs;* and while totally un-
intentional (after inserting Orson Hyde's dedicatory prayer date), the
outline confirms the following prophetic utterances:

1. Christ's prophecy of the destruction of Jerusalem.[a]

2. Paul's prophecy of the apostasy from the truth of the gospel.[b]

3. Daniel's prophecy of the end of sacrifice.[c]

4. The prophecies of many prophets regarding the scattering of
    both Israel and Judah.[d]

5. The gather of the Jews in the latter days.

The above historical outline clearly shows the establishment of Je-

a. Matthew
   24:1–3.

b. 2 Thessalo-
   nians 2:1–3.

c. Daniel
   11:31.

d. Chapter 2.

rusalem, its adoption by David as the holy city, its place in Israel until the end of sacrifice, the destruction of the temple by the Romans, the end of the kingdom of Judah through the scatterings, the false prophets predicted by Jesus and His Apostles (the most conspicuous being Bar Kochba),[189] and the Jews being prohibited from returning to their holy city until after the dedicatory prayer of Orson Hyde.

Except for brief periods of peace, Jerusalem, since it came into existence, has been a city under siege for thousands of years. The prophecies of the Lord and His prophets have thus far been fulfilled (and will continue to be fulfilled) with the result that Jerusalem will continue to be embroiled in conflict and war until the Second Coming.

Isaiah and Micah declared that Jerusalem will be one of the two cities from which the Lord will govern during the millennium: "The word of the Lord [will go forth] from Jerusalem."[a] The many signs of the Second Coming that are yet to be fulfilled concerning Jerusalem were discussed in Chapter 5 of this text. It is the glory of what the city and its inhabitants will become, however, that now interests us.

Isaiah describes Jerusalem in his historical prophecy of the last days *as if its exaltation had already occurred.* In the 62nd chapter of his text he begins by identifying both Zion and Jerusalem, but in the third verse he shifts to a singular noun and thereafter speaks only of Jerusalem. He describes the scattered and forsaken Jews as becoming "Hephzibah," or *delightful,* and they are "Beulah," or *married*—united with the land. He again uses the analogy of a marriage covenant, with Jesus as the husband and Israel (the Jews in this instance) as the bride, for the Lord will "set watchmen upon [the] walls . . . till he make[s] Jerusalem a praise in the earth."[b] The people shall then be called "the holy people," and Jerusalem will be "sought out, A city not forsaken."[c] Isaiah made this declaration toward the end of his book, but he began his book with a double-reference prophecy that Jerusalem and Zion would be restored "as at the first." In other words, Isaiah's beloved Jerusalem will again be favored of the Lord.[d]

The remnant of the Jews that survive the last great battles around Jerusalem just prior to the Second Coming will be delivered from annihilation by the Lord Himself.[e] Judah will again be cleansed by her Master[f] and be able to produce "excellent and comely" fruit, a reference to not only the product of the land but the righteousness of the

a. Isaiah 2:3;
Micah 4:2.

b. Isaiah
62:1–7.

c. Isaiah
62:12.

d. Isaiah 1:26–
27; 33:20.

e. Joel 2:32.

f. Joel
3:20–21.

people.[a] Jerusalem will finally be restored as a great "city of truth" and peace. Her inhabitants will be the Lord's people, and He "will be their God, in truth and in righteousness."[b] The land Jerusalem occupies will also return to its "own place, and the earth shall be like as it was in the days before it was divided."[c] Isaiah writes an eloquent description of this millennial Jerusalem:

> **Isaiah 60:18–21**   Violence shall no more be heard in thy land, wasting nor destruction within thy borders; but thou shall call thy walls Salvation, and thy gates Praise. The sun shall be no more thy light by day; neither for brightness shall the moon give light unto thee: but the Lord shall be unto thee an everlasting light, and thy God thy glory. Thy sun shall no more go down; neither shall thy moon withdraw itself: for the Lord shall be thine everlasting light, and the days of thy mourning shall be ended. Thy people also shall be all righteous: they shall inherit the land for ever.

Zechariah describes this desirable time in personal terms: "There shall yet old men and old women dwell in the streets of Jerusalem, and every man with his staff in his hand for *a multitude of days*. And the streets of the city shall be full of boys and girls playing in the streets thereof."[d] These are visions of pure joy.

Then, as Ether declares, there will be a "new heaven and a new earth"[e] and the three glorious cities shall be as one. Zion in America will be joined by the City of Enoch from its heavenly abode, "and then also cometh the Jerusalem of old; and the inhabitants thereof, blessed are they, for they have been washed in the blood of the Lamb; and they are they who were scattered and gathered in from the four quarters of the earth, and from the north countries, and are partakers of the fulfilling of the covenant which God made with their father, Abraham."[f]

And then shall the Lord reign forever and ever.

a. Isaiah 4:1–4.

b. Zechariah 8:1–8.

c. D&C 133:24.

d. Zechariah 8:4–5; italics indicates alternative language used.

e. Ether 13:9.

f. Ether 13:11.

The Coming of the Lord 14

Joel 2:1, 11 Blow ye the trumpet in Zion, and sound an alarm in my holy mountain: let all the inhabitants of the land tremble: for the day of the Lord cometh, for it is nigh at hand; . . . for the day of the Lord is great and very terrible; and who can abide it?

The Great and Terrible Day of the Lord

The *great* and *terrible* day of the Lord—seemingly an oxymoron—is a perfect description of the Lord's Advent. For the righteous it will be a *great* day, a day long awaited and eagerly anticipated; for the wicked, however, it will be a *terrible* day of fear and trembling, for *the Atonement will not apply to the unrepentant sinner.*

The catastrophic devastations preceding the Lord's Second Coming will undoubtedly cause some of the righteous pain and even death, but the wicked will be completely annihilated—none will escape—for no unclean thing can enter into the Lord's presence.

Through the prophet Zephaniah, the Lord speaks of His coming as "a day of wrath": a day of "trouble . . . distress . . . wasteness . . . desolation . . . gloominess . . . and thick darkness." He describes the wicked as those who "walk like blind men" and whose "blood shall be poured out as dust." He states that their flesh will be "as the dung," and that "neither their silver nor their gold shall be able to deliver them in the day of the Lord's wrath," for instead of being clothed in garments of righteousness, they will be "clothed with strange apparel."[a]

In the parable of the marriage of the king's son, the Lord confirmed the warning of Zephaniah when He invited all mankind to come into

a. Zephaniah 1:4–18.

His kingdom (represented in the parable as the marriage feast). Those initially invited to attend the feast refused and responded with pathetic excuses for their absence, and they both abused and killed the Lord's servants who had been sent with the invitation. They were unwilling to comply with the requirements of righteousness needed to gain admission to the feast, so the Lord invited others to the celebration. As the new guests came, they were given an appropriate "wedding garment" which indicated that they had clothed themselves in righteousness in compliance with the Savior's commandments. When the guests were seated, however, one of them was found to be clothed in "strange apparel."[a] This guest had attempted to enter the feast without complying with the entrance requirements, even though they had been readily available to him. When questioned, he was speechless; he had no defense. The Lord's kingdom can only be enjoyed by those who comply with its prerequisites. *There are no valid excuses for unrighteous choices!* Therefore, the king bound his errant guest and cast him out of his presence.[b][190]

When Moroni came to Joseph Smith in 1823 to declare the glorious news of the coming forth of the Book of Mormon, he reemphasized the need for spiritual preparation and reinstated the warning of Malachi to the world:

> **Joseph Smith–History 1:37; D&C 29:9** For behold, the day cometh that shall burn as an oven, and all the proud, yea, and all that do wickedly shall burn as stubble; for they that come shall burn them, saith the Lord of Hosts, that it shall leave them neither root nor branch.

The allegory of the wicked being burned is used over and over again in the scriptures.[191] Some have speculated that the *burning* could be literal—the possible result of a nuclear holocaust.[192] But the Lord is probably speaking symbolically. He states in another revelation: "For after today [the latter days] cometh the burning—this is speaking *after the manner of the Lord.*"[c] He also uses the symbolism of burning to describe the state of the wicked after the final judgment[193] and the ultimate fate of the earth itself, descriptions that lend credence to the position that the burning is not literal.[d] However, one of the most interesting and descriptive of these symbolic scriptures is found in Zephaniah. "Wait ye upon me . . . until the day that I rise up to the prey," the Lord declares as He describes (through Zephaniah) what He will do to the evil kingdom prior to His coming; "for my determination is to gather the nations, that I may assemble the kingdoms, to pour upon them mine indignation, even all my fierce anger." He concludes with a warning: *"all the earth shall be devoured with the fire of my jealousy."*[a]

The Savior's Second Coming is almost always couched in terms of fear and devastation in an attempt to warn the wicked[b] because the righteous will *"not* be hewn down and cast into the fire"—they "shall abide the day" of the Savior's Coming, whether in life or in death.[c] In regards to the wicked, however, the scriptures provide the following conclusions:

1. The Lord does not like disobedience.

2. He will punish the world for evil, and the wicked for their iniquity, arrogance, haughtiness,[d] and for other like reasons as detailed in scripture,[194] and He will do it speedily, as the whirlwind,[e] trampling the wicked in His fury and anger.[f195]

The Lord has described the great anger He feels for disobedience in language mankind can easily comprehend. He has expressed this anger in both general and symbolic terms as He warns the wicked that they will be afflicted "with famine, and plague, and earthquake," all of which will issue forth from the "chastening hand of an Almighty God, until the consumption decreed hath made a full end" and men have seen the "salvation of their God."[g] The great consolation for the righteous is that even if they are destroyed physically in these devastations, they will die unto the Lord and their reward will be great.

The Lord Delayeth His Coming

"Fear ye not, stand still, and see the salvation of the Lord, which he will show to you to day."[h] Moses delivered this admonition to the children of Israel as they fearfully stood on the shores of the Red Sea and watched the armies of Pharaoh descend upon them. After 430 years of captivity, Pharaoh had finally been persuaded by the Lord's plagues[196] to let the Israelites leave Egypt; but they had barely departed the city gates before Pharaoh asked himself, "Why have we done this, that we

a. Zephaniah 3:8; emphasis added—this verse also gives us a glimpse into the Lord's personality. See also Isaiah 13:6–9, 11–12.

b. D&C 133:63–74.

c. D&C 45:57; emphasis added.

d. 2 Nephi 23:11.

e. D&C 97:22.

f. D&C 133:51.

g. D&C 87:6; 133:3.

h. Exodus 14:13.

have let Israel go from serving us?"[a] So he pursued them to the shores of the Red Sea. The children of Israel "were sore afraid: and . . . cried out unto the Lord. And they said unto Moses, Because there were no graves in Egypt, hast thou taken us away to die in the wilderness? . . . Is not this the word that we did tell thee in Egypt, saying, Let us alone, that we may serve the Egyptians? For it had been better for us to serve the Egyptians, than that we should die in the wilderness."[b] Thus the faithless Israelites complained against Moses and against the Lord, in spite of the miracles they had witnessed as the Lord delivered them.

There is an interesting parallel in the Book of Mormon to this example of faithlessness. Samuel the Lamanite was sent to call the wicked Nephites to repentance. They initially cast him out, but he ultimately delivered his message by ascending the walls of the city and preaching from their heights. He prophesied to the Nephites that the Savior's birth would take place in exactly five years, and he told them that this miraculous event would be accompanied by a sign: "one day and a night and a day, as if it were one day and there were no night . . . for ye shall know of the rising of the sun and also of its setting . . . nevertheless the night shall not be darkened."[c] He then predicted the Savior's death and its accompanying sign: the "sun shall be darkened and refuse to give his light unto you; and also the moon and the stars; and there shall be no light upon the face of this land . . . for the space of three days."[d]

As the time for the first sign approached, many disbelievers claimed that "the time [appointed for the Savior's birth] was [already] past," and they began to "rejoice over their brethren saying: Behold the time is past, and the words of Samuel are not fulfilled."[e] They decreed a certain date wherein those who believed in Christ's birth would be "put to death except the sign should come to pass."[f]

Of course, the sign occurred and the righteous were spared, but shortly thereafter "the people began to forget those signs and wonders which they had heard, and began to be less and less astonished at a sign."[g] As the time for the sign of the Savior's death approached, there again "began to be great doubtings and disputations among the people, notwithstanding [that] so many signs had been given [to them]."[h] But again the sign was given as prophesied, and with devastating results![i]

Why use these two stories in a book about the Second Coming? Because they exemplify what the mind-set of civilization will be like in the

a. Exodus 14:5.

b. Exodus 14:10–12.

c. Helaman 14:4.

d. Helaman 14:20.

e. 3 Nephi 1:5–6.

f. 3 Nephi 1:9.

g. 3 Nephi 2:1.

h. 3 Nephi 8:4.

i. 3 Nephi 8–10.

days prior to the Lord's final Advent. Like the Israelites and Nephites of old, people will again be faithless and disbelieving. They will be like the people in the days of Noah "before the flood . . . eating and drinking, marrying and giving in marriage," and paying no attention to Noah until he entered the ark and the flood came and destroyed them. "So shall also the coming of the Son of man be."[a]

Belief and faith have always been complicated, and they will continue to be complicated in the latter days. We anticipate the Second Coming, but we don't know when that day will be. The signs we are given are predominately nonspecific, and many of them involve disturbances that have been occurring since the dawn of time. Prophets foresaw this difficulty and prophesied what people's reaction to it would be. Peter declared: "There shall come in the last days scoffers, walking after their own lusts, And saying, Where is the promise of his coming? for since the fathers fell asleep, all things continue as they were from the beginning of the creation."[b]

Peter then recites the evidences of the Lord's presence from the creation of the earth to the final judgment and he warns us that "the Lord is not slack concerning his promise, as some men count slackness; but is longsuffering to us-ward, not willing that any should perish, but that all should come to repentance. But the day of the Lord will come as a thief in the night."[c]

Even after the tribulation when "the whole earth shall be in commotion, and men's hearts shall fail them," there will be disbelievers who will claim that "Christ delayeth his coming."[d] There is no question that recognizing the signs as they occur may be a problem, and there may even be confusion as to which signs have already occurred, *but the real problem mankind will face is a lack of faith that the Savior will come at all!*

Just as the signs of the Messiah's First Coming were fulfilled, so will the signs of His Second Coming be fulfilled. And in spite of all the devastation that will occur, His coming will be as simple as His ascension: "This same Jesus, which is taken up from you into heaven, shall so come in like manner as ye have seen him go into heaven."[e]

When Will the Lord Come?

When will the Lord come? What is the exact date? Almost every bibli-

a. Matthew 24:38–39.

b. 2 Peter 3:3–4.

c. 2 Peter 3:9–10.

d. D&C 45:26; Matthew 24:48.

e. Acts 1:9–11.

cal prophet since Enoch has pondered these questions. Enoch saw a vision of the Lord's coming in Moses 7:65 and John the Revelator closed his book with it in Revelation 19–22, but the Old Testament prophet Daniel appears to have been the first to record the question, "When?"

Daniel was given a great vision showing the destruction of the temple in Jerusalem (which ended daily sacrifice) and the destruction of Jerusalem itself.[a] He described this destruction as the *abomination of desolation* because:

1. It destroyed the Jewish kingdom (which to Daniel represented Israel).

2. It desecrated the holy temple, thereby defiling the God of Israel.

3. It laid waste the holy city.[b]

His vision continued to the "time of the end,"[c] where he saw Michael lead the great battles against evil that resulted in terrible consequences for the wicked. Finally, he saw the resurrection of both the just and the unjust.[d] As these great visions closed, he was commanded to "seal the book even to the time of the end."[e] But in spite of the power of these visions, Daniel was left without definition as to when they would take place, so he asked the angel, "How long shall it be to the end of these wonders?"[f] The angel responded, "It shall be for a time, times, and an half; and when he shall have accomplished to scatter the power of the holy people, all these things shall be finished."[g]

A bewildered Daniel stated, "I heard, but I understood not." He again asked, "O my Lord, what shall be the end of these things"?[h]

But the vision was over. The angel said, "Go thy way, Daniel: for the words are closed up and sealed till the time of the end. Many shall be purified, and made white, and tried; but the wicked shall do wickedly: and none of the wicked shall understand; *but the wise shall understand.*"[i]

Then the angel again expressed the time of the end in terms of the vision: "And from the time that the daily sacrifice shall be taken away, and the abomination that maketh desolate set up, there shall be a thousand two hundred and ninety days."[j]

a. Daniel 11:1–34.

b. Daniel 11:35–45.

c. Daniel 12:4, 9.

d. Daniel 12:1–3.

e. Daniel 12:4.

f. Daniel 12:6.

g. Daniel 12:7.

h. Daniel 12:8.

i. Daniel 12:9–10; emphasis added.

j. Daniel 12:11; Joseph changed "days" to "years".

Although the Savior fulfilled the law of Moses in His final sacrifice upon the cross, the Jews as a whole continued to function under the law's requirements through the Roman conquest in A.D. 70 and on up to the present time, even though they have not been able to perform the ritual of sacrifice since the Romans destroyed the temple. According to Daniel's prophecy, it is the destruction of the temple, of Jerusalem, and of the kingdom of Judah (the "abomination that maketh desolate"), together with the cessation of daily sacrifice, that provides the _key_ to the "time of the end."[a]

The angel in Daniel 12 then added another specific time period to his prophecy: that it would be 1,290 days from the destruction of Jerusalem until the "time of the end." He continued, "Blessed is he that waiteth, and cometh to the _thousand three hundred and five and thirty days_"[b]—a _different_ period of time. Daniel was left with two conflicting time periods which were scheduled to begin after the destruction of Jerusalem (obviously clues to the time of the Second Coming), but the angel gave no further explanation.

Daniel was dismissed from the vision with the promise that he would "rest, and stand in [his] lot at the end of the days."[c] He was not given the "time of the end," but he was told that he would be present when it occurred and that he would be counted among the righteous at that time.

The same curiosity which prompted Daniel to ask "when" was also aroused in the Lord's Apostles shortly after the Savior's scathing comments to the Jewish leadership during His last public discourse.[d] After His discourse, the Lord and His Apostles left Jerusalem, crossed through the valley of Kidron, and climbed the Mount of Olives. The Savior's ministry was coming to a close and as He stood upon the mount, He gazed back at the beauty of Jerusalem and its magnificent temple and prophesied of their future destruction. The Apostles asked the Lord, "When shall these things be? and what shall be the sign of thy coming, and of the end of the world?"[e] This same question had also been asked by the Lord's enemies, the Pharisees, earlier in His ministry.[f] He would not give them a direct answer because they did not believe in Him; however, even though His Apostles did believe in Him, He did not give them a direct answer either. Instead, He gave them the great double-reference sermon recorded in Matthew 24 which

a. This prophecy is reinforced by the Savior as He speaks to His Apostles in the 24th chapter of Matthew.

b. Daniel 12:12; emphasis added.

c. Daniel 12:13.

d. Matthew 23.

e. Matthew 24:3.

f. Luke 17:20.

describes both the destruction of the Jewish kingdom as seen by Daniel and the cleansing of the earth prior to the Second Coming.[197]

After the Savior's resurrection, the Saints at Thessalonica became concerned about the immediacy of the Second Coming. In response to their concern, Paul wrote the following:

> **1 Thessalonians 4:16–18; 5:1–2 (emphasis added)**   For the Lord himself shall descend from heaven with a shout, with the voice of the archangel, and with the trump of God: and the dead in Christ shall rise first: then *we which are alive and remain* shall be caught up together with them in the clouds, to meet the Lord in the air: and so shall we ever be with the Lord. Wherefore comfort one another with these words. But of the times and the seasons, brethren, ye have no need that I write unto you. For yourselves know perfectly that the day of the Lord so cometh as a thief in the night.

Paul wrote as if this occurrence would take place immediately, which caused the Saints in Thessalonica to misunderstand him. They literally anticipated that they would be "caught up together . . . in the clouds, to meet the Lord in the air" during their lifetime. Some of the Saints may have even quit their occupations and sold their possessions in anticipation of this glorious event. They became "busy-bodies"[a] in the church in the sense that they spent much of their time talking about and planning for the Second Coming.[198] As a result of this incorrect belief, Paul again dealt with the subject in a second letter:

> **2 Thessalonians 2:1–3**   Now we beseech you, brethren, by the coming of our Lord Jesus Christ, and by our gathering together unto him, that ye be not soon shaken in mind, or be troubled, neither by spirit, nor by word, nor by letter as from us, as that the day of Christ is at hand. Let no man deceive you by any means: for that day shall not come, except there come a falling away first, and that man of sin be revealed, the son of perdition.

Thus, Paul made it clear that the day of Christ's coming would not be an immediate event but would occur sometime far in the future.

Curiosity concerning the time of the Second Coming has not been limited to the members and prophets of Christ's ancient church. Joseph Smith had a similar interest and asked the same question as that posed by Daniel and the early Apostles:

> **D&C 130:14–17**   I was once praying very earnestly to know the time of the

coming of the Son of Man, when I heard a voice repeat the following: Joseph, my son, if thou livest until thou art eighty-five years old, thou shalt see the face of the Son of Man; therefore let this suffice, and trouble me no more on this matter. I was left thus, without being able to decide whether this coming referred to the beginning of the millennium or to some previous appearing, or whether I should die and thus see his face. I believe the coming of the Son of Man will not be any sooner than that time.

The Lord has made it clear that the time of His coming is known only to the Father, but it still excites such curiosity among individuals both in and out of the Church that many have ventured to speculate on it.

In the early history of the restored Church, a man named William Miller founded a Christian belief known as *Millerism*. It was based on his calculations for the date of the Second Coming, which he derived from the books of Daniel and Revelation. His first proposed date was general—between March 21, 1843, and March 21, 1844,[199]— but he later identified April 3, 1843, as an exact date. However, the day came and went without event, as Joseph Smith noted with some sarcasm.[200] Father Miller, as he was known, then reworked his calculations and derived a new date for the Lord's Advent: October 22, 1844. Anticipation again surged among his followers, only to end in disappointment when the prophecy failed a second time.[201]

In 1949 a small group called the Children of Light left Canada in search of immortality. After sixteen years of wandering from area to area, their preacher declared that Jesus had visited her and that she had seen the name "Agua Caliente" spelled out in the clouds. She proclaimed that this was the place where her followers should settle to await the Apocalypse. So in 1967 the group moved to Agua Caliente, Arizona. At the date of this writing, the apocalypse has not yet arrived, and none of the group remain. Like Father Miller, the prophecy failed and today the property is desolate.[202]

The detail found in the book of Daniel and the book of Revelation, along with the many numerical anomalies of the scriptures (such as the use of the numbers 7 and 12; the cycle of 40 days; the cycles of 40, 70, 430, 490, and 2,520 years; and the fact that many of the major events in Israel occurred on these cycles and correlate with many of their major anniversaries: i.e., the Passover, the Day of Atonement, and the Feast of Tabernacles) has led many to speculate on the date of the Lord's coming. They use these cyclical biblical numbers in an attempt to mathematically calculate and manipulate the Jewish, Roman, and Christian calendars in order to predict the date of Christ's Advent. Most, if not all of the current prognosticators, settled on the fall of the year 2000.[203] Again, nothing happened.

Not all modern predictions of the Lord's Advent come from apostate Christianity. Even the Prophet Joseph Smith could not resist. In February 1835 he declared that it was time for the last pruning of the vineyard, and that the "coming of the Lord . . . was . . . nigh." He stated that "fifty-six years should wind up the scene."[204] On another occasion he said, "There are those of the rising generation who shall not taste death till Christ comes," and "the Son of Man will not come in the clouds of heaven till I am eighty-five years old." Joseph then read Revelation 14:6–7 and the sixth chapter of Hosea and stated that 2,520 years would "bring it to [the year] 1890."[205] The method of his calculation and the means by which he determined his beginning date are left unexplained, but his revelation from the Lord intimated that if Joseph lived until he was eighty-five years of age, he would see the Lord's face.[a] This seems to have had an influence upon his calculations.

Many of the early Brethren believed that the Second Coming would be in the lifetime of those present in their audiences—especially the children. Wilford Woodruff stated this over the pulpit four times between 1871 and 1898,[206] and Lorenzo Snow said it in 1901.[207] In 1873, Charles C. Rich stated:

> I did not expect forty-seven years to pass away before the prophecies would be fulfilled concerning the second coming of the Savior, and the end of the world. I expected the Savior would come . . . before this time . . . We are not accustomed to hear the Lord speak, and when he spoke of a short time, we understood it according to our use of the language.
>
> It takes a long time according to our reckoning to do the work the Lord has decreed concerning the children of men in this last dispensation.[208]

a. D&C 130:15.

With all of the calculations that have been made and the many speculations that have failed in their accuracy, the question still remains: *when* will the Lord come? The answer remains the same: "But of that day and hour knoweth no man, no, not the angels of heaven, but my Father only."[a] This utterance was made at the close of the Lord's ministry almost 2,000 years ago. Without question the time is nearer now than when the statement was made, but the exact date remains unknown.

On November 4, 1830, the Lord revealed to Joseph Smith that "the time is soon at hand that I shall come in a cloud with power and great glory."[b] In February 1831 He continued: "For in mine own due time will I come upon the earth in judgment, and my people shall be redeemed and shall reign with me on earth."[c] But lest anyone anticipates His coming as the Thessalonians did, the Lord gave the following caution in the forty-ninth section of the Doctrine and Covenants: "The hour and the day no man knoweth, neither the angels in heaven, *nor shall they know until he comes.*"[d]

Obviously, the time of His coming will remain a mystery—and there is a purpose for this. The anticipation of Christ's appearance motivates devout men and women to constantly strive for righteousness in thought and action so that they might be found worthy of His presence when the time comes. The Lord explained it this way:

Matthew 24:42–44 Watch therefore: for ye know not what hour your Lord doth come. But know this, that if the goodman of the house had known in what watch the thief would come, he would have watched, and would not have suffered his house to be broken up. Therefore be ye also ready: for in such an hour as ye think not the Son of man cometh.

The righteous will be rewarded at the Lord's coming, but the wicked, thinking that the "Lord delayeth His coming" will procrastinate their repentance and be "cut . . . asunder." Their portion will be with the "hypocrites . . . [where] there shall be weeping and gnashing of teeth."[e]

Blessed is the man or woman who will be caught up to meet the Savior at His Advent, but as the Lord cautioned, our meeting with Him might occur sooner than that since we may die at any time. Therefore, "pray always that you enter not into temptation, that you may abide the

a. Matthew 24:36; Mark 13:32.

b. D&C 34:7.

c. D&C 43:29.

d. D&C 49:7; emphasis added.

e. Matthew 24:48–51.

day of his coming, *whether in life or in death.* Even so. Amen."[a] We would be well advised to heed the advice of Paul to the Thessalonians and let the Lord direct our hearts "into the love of God, and into the patient waiting for Christ."[b]

The Bridegroom Cometh

All of the signs and prophecies of the Second Coming have been given so that man can anticipate and prepare himself for entrance into God's kingdom. The parable of the ten virgins gives us insight into that preparation,[209] and the Lord announced in March 1831 that the parable would be fulfilled when He came in His glory.[c]

As we have previously discussed, the ten virgins (representing the Church) await the bridegroom (the Lord). Half of the virgins are wise and have properly prepared themselves to receive the bridegroom, no matter how long it takes. They have "received the truth, and have taken the Holy Spirit for their guide, and have not been deceived."[d] The other virgins are foolish and unprepared and will remain so right up to the hour of His coming when there will be a "separation of the righteous and the wicked."[e] Recognizing that the Lord is talking directly to the members of the Church today, it becomes especially important that we listen to His counsel: "Wherefore, be faithful, praying always, having your lamps trimmed and burning, and oil with you, that you may be ready at the coming of the Bridegroom."[f]

In December 1832, in a revelation known as the "olive leaf," He reemphasized this admonition: "Prepare ye, prepare ye, O inhabitants of the earth; for the judgment of our God is come. Behold, and lo, the Bridegroom cometh; go ye out to meet him."[g] Nearly 200 years have passed since the Lord gave this warning. Many have already passed on to meet Him, but among those who remain alive, the wise are prepared.

The Sign of the Son of Man

The Lord will come after all the great signs of His Advent have been completed and the wicked have been destroyed[h]—after the sun is darkened and the moon stops giving her light and the stars have fallen from heaven. He will come at a time when all the "powers of the heavens shall be shaken."[i] Only then will the angel of God sound his trump to

a. D&C 61:39; emphasis added.

b. 2 Thessalonians 3:5.

c. D&C 45:56.

d. D&C 45:57.

e. D&C 63:54.

f. D&C 33:17.

g. D&C 88:92.

h. D&C 49:23.

i. Matthew 24:29.

prepare the earth for His arrival.[a] And that is when the "sign of the Son of man" will appear in heaven[b]—"a great sign" that "all people shall see . . . together."[c]

Just as John the Baptist recognized the Savior by the sign of the dove, so shall we recognize the Savior by the "sign of the Son of man."[210] All mankind will recognize it as the veil is lifted from our minds, for it is a sign we all learned in the preexistence. The Savior will appear and His glory "shall be revealed, and all flesh shall see it together."[d] He will come in the clouds of heaven, clothed "with power and great glory,"[e] with "all the holy angels,"[f] and "every eye shall see him."[g] The tribes of the earth will mourn as they see Him appear,[h] for "the nations are as a drop of a bucket, and are counted as the small dust of the balance . . . All nations before him are as nothing; and they are counted to him less than nothing, and vanity."[i]

His glory will be like "a pillar of fire,"[j] and He warns us not to be deceived[k] since He will not come "in the form of a woman, neither of a man traveling on the earth."[l] He will not come in secret; rather, His appearance will be dramatic: "For as the light of the morning cometh out of the east, and shineth even unto the west, and covereth the whole earth, so shall also the coming of the Son of Man be."[m]

Dressed in Red

John the Revelator described the Savior's miraculous Advent symbolically in the 19th chapter of Revelation:

> **Revelation 19:11–16** And I saw heaven opened, and behold a white horse; and he that sat upon him was called Faithful and True, and in righteousness he doth judge and make war. His eyes were as a flame of fire, and on his head were many crowns; and he had a name written, that no man knew, but he himself. And he was clothed with a vesture dipped in blood: and his name is called The Word of God. And the armies which were in heaven followed him upon white horses, clothed in fine linen, white and clean. And out of his mouth goeth a sharp sword, that with it he should smite the nations: and he shall rule them with a rod of iron: and he treadeth the winepress of the fierceness and wrath of Almighty God. And he hath on his vesture and on his thigh a name written, KING OF KINGS, AND LORD OF LORDS.

Isaiah also saw the Lord dressed in red apparel at his coming:

a. D&C 88:92.

b. Matthew 24:30.

c. D&C 88:93.

d. Isaiah 40:5.

e. D&C 34:7.

f. D&C 45:44.

g. Revelation 1:7.

h. Matthew 24:30.

i. Isaiah 40:15–17.

j. D&C 29:12.

k. Matthew 24:4; D&C 49:23.

l. D&C 49:22.

m. Matthew 24:27.

Isaiah 63:1–3   Who is this that cometh from Edom, with dyed garments from Bozrah? this that is glorious in his apparel, travelling in the greatness of his strength? I that speak in righteousness, mighty to save. Wherefore art thou red in thine apparel, and thy garments like him that treadeth in the winefat? I have trodden the winepress alone; and of the people there was none with me: for I will tread them in mine anger, and trample them in my fury; and their blood shall be sprinkled upon my garments, and I will stain all my raiment.

The Lord Himself confirmed his vesture in November 1831:

D&C 133:46–51   And it shall be said: Who is this that cometh down from God in heaven with dyed garments; yea, from the regions which are not known, clothed in his glorious apparel, traveling in the greatness of his strength? And he shall say: I am he who spake in righteousness, mighty to save. And the Lord shall be red in his apparel, and his garments like him that treadeth in the wine-vat. And so great shall be the glory of his presence that the sun shall hide his face in shame, and the moon shall withhold its light, and the stars shall be hurled from their places. And his voice shall be heard: I have trodden the wine-press alone, and have brought judgment upon all people; and none were with me; and I have trampled them in my fury, and I did tread upon them in mine anger, and their blood have I sprinkled upon my garments, and stained all my raiment; for this was the day of vengeance which was in my heart.

The Lord's robes will be red at the Second Coming representing the fact that He has suffered the sins of the world, bled the blood of the Atonement, and with vengeance destroyed the unrepentant sinner. The blood of His (and their) suffering has symbolically stained His garments red.

The Messiah will "reign over all flesh."[a] He will be in the midst of the righteous.[b] "His glory shall be upon them, and he will be their king and their lawgiver."[c] He will strengthen the weak and those that are infirm. He will comfort the fearful, heal the blind, and unstop the ears of the deaf. The lame shall walk and the "tongue of the dumb [shall] sing." Waters shall break forth in the wilderness and streams appear in the desert,[d] and the Dead Sea will be healed.[e][211] In that day the Lord "shall be king over all the earth."[f]

He will appear in the exalted form of a man, with flesh and bones as tangible as a man's;[g] and the righteous who are with Him, and all who know Him, shall sing the song of His coming:

a. D&C 133:25.

b. D&C 29:13.

c. D&C 45:59.

d. Isaiah 35:3–7.

e. Zechariah 14:8.

f. Zechariah 14:9.

g. D&C 130:1, 22.

The Lord hath brought again Zion;
The Lord hath redeemed his people, Israel,
According to the election of grace,
Which was brought to pass by the faith
And covenant of their fathers.
The Lord hath redeemed his people;
And Satan is bound and time is no longer.
The Lord hath gathered all things in one.
The Lord hath brought down Zion from above.
The Lord hath brought up Zion from beneath.
The earth hath travailed and brought forth her strength;
And truth is established in her bowels;
And the heavens have smiled upon her;
And she is clothed with the glory of her God;
For he stands in the midst of his people.
Glory, and honor, and power, and might,
Be ascribed to our God; for he is full of mercy,
Justice, grace and truth, and peace,
Forever and ever, Amen.[a]

a. D&C 84:99–102.

Judgment 15

John 5:22 For the Father judgeth no man, but hath committed all judgment unto the Son.

When God the Father presented the plan of salvation to His spirit children at the great premortal council, He laid out its purpose and the standard by which all mankind would be judged: "And we will prove them herewith," He declared, "to see if they will do all things whatsoever the Lord their God shall command them."[a] This standard of judgment is relatively simple: to regain His presence, we must do everything that our Father in heaven tells us to do!

Judgment in the Preexistence

Our judgment began early. After being educated by our Father in the preexistence, and after having Lucifer's dissent from the Father's plan, we arrived at a point in our progression where we were required to choose whom we would follow: God or Satan. The plan required us to follow God, but we were free to make our own decision. However, once we exercised that choice, a judgment came into play: those who chose to follow God would continue on to a temporal existence under the plan of salvation; those who chose to follow Satan would not because a final judgment was pronounced upon them that prohibited them from coming to the earth to receive a physical body. They were doomed to eventually reside in outer darkness, a kingdom devoid of the Father's glory wherein—because there is no glory—there is "everlasting . . . endless . . . eternal punishment," a place where the "worm dieth

a. Abraham 3:25.

not, and the fire is not quenched." "The end, the width, the height, the depth, and the misery thereof" cannot be understood by any except those who find themselves under this "condemnation."[a]

A degree of judgment also appears to have been exercised upon some of those who accepted God's plan while they were yet in their preexistent state, as evidenced by the experiences of Abraham and Jeremiah. After Abraham came to earth, he received a personal revelation from God wherein he spoke with God "face to face."[b] It was during this revelation that God made a great covenant with him—the Abrahamic covenant. During this vision, God showed Abraham many preexistent spirits and told him that some of those spirits had been chosen to be leaders on the earth because they had been "noble and great" in their premortal existence. God informed Abraham that he was one of these noble and great spirits and that he had been chosen before he was born.[c]

Jeremiah was also told about his preexistent state. The scriptures indicate that the Lord "knew" him before he was born and had "sanctified" and "ordained" him to be a prophet to the nations.[d] It would be reasonable to assume that all of the great ancient prophets were so distinguished. In addition, Joseph Smith declared that all who were called to minister to the people of the world were designated to receive such a call *before the world was.*[212]

This evidence leads us to the conclusion that some type of judgment in the preexistence could have affected our earthly circumstances. However, it should be remembered that we left the extent of this judgment or knowledge behind the veil at our birth. In most instances, we can only speculate as to whether there is a relationship between our mortal circumstances and what we did in the preexistence.

Judgment on Earth

We all make judgments. This is one way we comprehend our relationship with God and our fellowman. Our parents and other adults exercised judgment over us as children regarding our food, our clothing, our friends, our recreation, our early education, and our religion. "Train up a child in the way he should go," the scripture says, "and when he is old, he will not depart from it."[e] As we became adults, we started making our own judgments. However, our judgments are

a. D&C 76:25–39, 43–49; Abraham 3:22–28.

b. Abraham 3:11.

c. Abraham 3:22–23.

d. Jeremiah 1:5.

e. Proverbs 22:6.

not always sound, and the wisdom so simply expressed in Proverbs is often lost in the results of our actions. God will ultimately judge our choices in this life by the same standard that He judged our premortal choices. Whenever He commands, we are expected to obey.

We are all familiar with the *sin-disease-punishment* and *obey-success-blessing* relationships recorded in the scriptures. Mormon records what seems to be a direct relationship between sin and poverty, and righteousness and riches as he records the history of the Book of Mormon cultures,[213] yet the very wealth they considered a blessing of righteousness became a curse to them when they sinned as a result of it.[214]

The Jews at the time of Jesus were trained to regard different types of suffering as necessary or consequential to a corresponding sin.[215] They had even determined that many situations of suffering or apostasy were consequential to undisclosed or known sins. For example, "up to thirteen years of age a child was considered, as it were, part of his father, and as suffering for his guilt. More than that, the thoughts of a mother might affect the moral state of her unborn offspring, and the terrible apostasy of one of the greatest Rabbis, had, in popular belief, been caused by the sinful delight his mother had taken when passing through an idol-grove. Lastly, certain special sins in the parents would result in specific diseases in their offspring, and one is mentioned as causing blindness in the children."[216]

With regard to the relationship between worldly riches and righteousness, the Jews taught the following: "The good man, if prosperous, was so as the son of a righteous man; while the unfortunate good man suffered as the son of a sinful parent. So, also, the wicked man might be prosperous, if the son of a goodly parent; but if unfortunate, it showed that his parents had been sinners."[217] The Savior disavowed this cause and effect theory when He healed a man who had been born blind.[a] On this occasion the Apostles asked, "who did sin, this man, or his parents, that he was born blind?" Jesus answered that in this case, *neither* had sinned. The man had been born blind to manifest the works of God.[b][218]

On another occasion, some people told the Savior about some "Galilaeans" whose blood had been mingled with Pilate's sacrifices. "Jesus answering said unto them, Suppose ye that these Galilaeans

a. John 9.
b. John 9:1–3.

were sinners above all the Galilaeans, because they suffered such things? I tell you, Nay." He also made it clear that the eighteen men who were killed when a tower in Siloam fell on them had not died because of sin. They had simply been in the wrong place at the wrong time.[a] While we should give thanks to God for all of our blessings, material or otherwise, we do not necessarily receive worldly wealth and health because of our righteousness—nor are we necessarily poor, unhealthy, or accident prone because of our unrighteousness. Man developed the *sin-disease-punishment, obey-success-blessing* formulas—not God![219]

The statement, "Go thy way and sin no more," occasionally uttered or inferred by a forgiving Lord to those caught in transgression, makes it clear that he *does* judge us in this life.[220] But these passing judgments are predicated on the repentant state of the individual. The Lord recognizes that even after He has extended forgiveness to those who sin, they can still fall from grace if they make the wrong choices.

There are two judgments potentially given during the earth life of a recipient that *do* have eternal consequences: they involve the *state of our individual righteousness or wickedness* and whether our *calling and election is made sure* for either exaltation or condemnation. Either judgment can take place while we are yet in the flesh. To achieve the blessing of having one's calling and election made sure for exaltation, an individual must become so righteous that the Lord will *advance* his or her day of judgment and "reward" the individual not with earthly wealth, but with the riches of eternal life. According to Peter, this blessing will be received by the "more sure word of prophecy"[b]—in other words, testimony extended and sealed by the Holy Ghost that this judgment has been given. Joseph Smith explained that this is "knowing that [an individual] is sealed up unto eternal life, by revelation and the spirit of prophecy, through the power of the Holy Priesthood."[c] Peter advised each Saint to "give diligence to make your calling and election sure: for if ye do these things, ye shall never fall."[d]

When Joseph Smith was teaching from the text in 2 Peter, he noted that once an individual's calling and election has been made sure, "they [are] sealed in the heavens and [have] the promise of eternal life in the kingdom of God."[221] He explained that *knowledge* is the key to the acquisition of this blessing, for "it is impossible for a man

a. Luke 13:1–5.

b. 2 Peter 1:19.

c. D&C 131:5.

d. 2 Peter 1:10.

to be saved in ignorance."[a] "Knowledge through our Lord and Savior Jesus Christ" and "knowledge of the priesthood," Joseph declared, are the keys that will unlock the "glories and mysteries of the kingdom of heaven." It is clear from the comments of both Peter and Joseph that *knowledge* and *obedience* are the keys to accomplishing this advanced judgment. This is not an ordinance or blessing given by a priesthood holder but the fact that it is through the priesthood that the ordinances and knowledge of the plan of salvation are upon the earth. *We make our calling and election sure by perfecting our obedience to God in the gospel and relying upon His grace,* and Joseph exhorted the Saints to "continue to call upon God" until they all made their calling and election sure.[222] On May 12, 1844, he again advised "all [members of the Church] to go on to perfection, and [to] search deeper and deeper into the mysteries of Godliness. A man can do nothing for himself," he maintained, "unless God direct[s] him in the right way; and the priesthood is for that purpose."[223]

On the other hand, John teaches us in Revelation that individuals can become so wicked that they can *advance* the day of their judgment (a negative calling and election making their condemnation "sure"), thereby sealing themselves to the devil and his kingdom in outer darkness—a condemnation from which they cannot escape![b] In each of these two instances, God makes the determination to advance judgment; however, individual men and women are responsible for bringing that judgment upon themselves.

The problem we all face in this life is knowing when we have received a judgment from God. In all probability, we would not misidentify a witness from the Spirit regarding our "calling and election," yet even here we may be deceived.[c] When speaking of the relationship between reward and punishment as pertaining to righteousness and wickedness, it is difficult to determine if God is giving us a blessing or a punishment, or whether we just made a wise or an unwise decision. After all, it was the widow in her poverty who gave two mites and was judged by the Lord to be righteous, not the wealthy who only gave of their abundance.[d] Isaiah gives us a superb description of our personal relationship with sin: "For the bed [representing sin] is shorter than that a man can stretch himself on it: and the covering narrower than that he can wrap himself in it."[e] We are not always

a. D&C 131:6.

b. Chapter 8; Revelation 13:16–18.

c. Joseph Smith–Matthew 1:22.

d. Mark 12:42–44.

e. Isaiah 28:20.

qualified to determine our own righteousness, let alone the blessings we feel we deserve, or have, or have not received. We are especially unqualified to determine the state of righteousness of others or to ascertain what blessings they should receive. It is sufficient to know that this life is a determining factor in our final judgment and that the judgment we receive will be based on our individual wickedness or righteousness. God, through His Son, will be our ultimate judge.

John the Revelator saw the "small and great" standing before God at the final judgment. He records that the "books were opened," even "the book of life," and that it was from these books that all mankind would be judged.[a] He informs us that God knows what our thoughts and actions are and why we think and act as we do. Malachi used this same image when he said that "a book of remembrance was written before [the Lord]" from which those "that feared the Lord, and that thought upon his name" were remembered.[b] The book motif was carried forward from Adam[c] to the latter days when the Lord declared, "All they who are not found written in the book of remembrance shall find none inheritance in" the day of judgment.[d]

The scriptures tell us that as a person "thinketh in his heart, so is he."[e] God knows what is in our hearts and understands the reasons for our actions; therefore, it behooves us to ask by what standard He will judge us. We are aware of His commandments and we know that those commandments must be obeyed. When we have faith in God, we want to obey Him. However, obedience requires action, and action implies work. James confirms that "faith without works is dead."[f] Why? Because it is by our works that our faith is demonstrated. But *works* alone will not get us to heaven.

Faith is the term used throughout the scriptures to characterize the degree of our commitment and obedience to God. Our *faith* is the *standard* by which the Lord will judge us. However, the evidence of our faith and our obedience is our *works,* works that are performed for the right reasons. Thus, our faith gives rise to action, but we must act for the right reasons if we are to be judged righteous in the Lord's sight.

Early in the restoration of the gospel, the Lord testified that at the day of judgment He would "come to recompense unto every man

a. Revelation 20:12.

b. Malachi 3:16.

c. Moses 6:5–8.

d. D&C 85:9.

e. Proverbs 23:7.

f. James 2:26.

according to his work, and measure to every man according to the measure which he has measured to his fellow man."[a] *Recompense* is an interesting word in this scripture. It means "to give compensation for" or "to repay or reward."[224] Therefore, we are going to receive compensation in kind for our works as a result of two things:

> *One:* our work for God. This work is objective. We know exactly what we have to do to fulfill the commandments. This work measures our absolute obedience to the first great commandment since nothing comes before God and our obedience to His commandments.

> *Two:* how we "measure" or "treat" our fellow man. This work is subjective, undefined, and without limits. This work demonstrates how well we keep the second great commandment. After reciting the parable of the ten virgins[225] and the parable of the talents[226] to His Apostles, the Lord gave this warning and explanation of His future judgment:

Matthew 25:34–46 Then shall the King say unto them on his right hand, Come, ye blessed of my Father, inherit the kingdom prepared for you from the foundation of the world: for I was an hungred, and ye gave me meat: I was thirsty, and ye gave me drink: I was a stranger, and ye took me in: naked, and ye clothed me: I was sick, and ye visited me: I was in prison, and ye came unto me. Then shall the righteous answer him, saying, Lord, when saw we thee an hungred, and fed thee? or thirsty, and gave thee drink? When saw we thee a stranger, and took thee in? or naked, and clothed thee? Or when saw we thee sick, or in prison, and came unto thee? And the King shall answer and say unto them, Verily I say unto you, Inasmuch as ye have done it unto one of the least of these my brethren, ye have done it unto me. Then shall he say also unto them on the left hand, Depart from me, ye cursed, into everlasting fire, prepared for the devil and his angels: for I was an hungred, and ye gave me no meat: I was thirsty, and ye gave me no drink: I was a stranger, and ye took me not in: naked, and ye clothed me not: sick, and in prison, and ye visited me not. Then shall they also answer him, saying, Lord, when saw we thee an hungred, or athirst, or a stranger, or naked, or sick, or in prison, and did not minister unto thee? Then shall he answer them, saying, Verily I say unto you, Inasmuch as ye did it not to one of the least of these, ye did it not to me. And these shall go away into everlasting punishment: but the righteous into life eternal.[227]

a. D&C 1:10.

We are all responsible for our actions: we will reap as we have sown,[a] we will be repaid according to our deeds,[b] and we will reap a reward from our works. "If they have been righteous" works, we will reap exaltation; but "if they have been evil" works, we will reap "the damnation of [our] souls."[c] We will have restored to us exactly what we have done to God and to our fellow man.[d]

Judgment is simple!

Judgment at Death

When we die our spirits move on, either to the paradise of God or to a spirit prison. The judgment as to where we will reside in this phase of our existence will be determined by our earthly righteousness and knowledge.

A notable example of judgment at death is found in the stories of Enoch and Noah. The world was judged by God prior to the Flood and found sorely wanting. As a result, the righteous were taken and translated with Enoch and his city into heaven until only eight righteous people were left on the earth—Noah and his family. Noah had warned the people of God's impending judgment. He had told them about the Flood that would come upon them if they did not repent. But they would not listen. Consequently, Noah built the Ark, the flood came, and only "eight souls were saved" alive.[e] The balance—all the people of the earth—died in the flood.

During the centuries between the time the City of Enoch was taken into heaven and the time Noah built his ark, many righteous people made their calling and election sure and were translated into Enoch's city to await the resurrection. The wicked who lived during the same period, however, including those who died in the flood, went to the spirit prison to await the mercies of God. Missionary work to these imprisoned souls was initiated by the Lord during His stay in the spirit world following His crucifixion.[228] Peter describes this event, indicating that the Savior arranged for the gospel to be preached to those spirits "which sometime were disobedient, when once the long suffering of God waited in the days of Noah." The Doctrine and Covenants gives us further insight into how this missionary work is being carried out and expands this work to include *all* disobedient spirits who reside or will reside in the spirit prison.[f]

a. D&C 6:33.

b. Isaiah 59:18.

c. Alma 9:28.

d. Alma 41:2–5.

e. 1 Peter 3:20.

f. 1 Peter 3:18–20; D&C 138.

Judgment at the Second Coming

The wicked of Noah's time were drowned in a universal flood. The wicked on the Western Hemisphere died in the massive destruction that occurred when the Savior of the world was crucified. And prophecy tells us that *all* the wicked of the earth (those unable to abide the Lord's presence) will again be destroyed in the devastation that will occur prior to the Lord's Second Coming.

The Savior will come "with ten thousands of His saints, to execute judgment upon all . . . that are ungodly."[a] He will purge the earth to gather the righteous and destroy the wicked, as described in the parable of the wheat and tares.[b][229] John's vision of the Second Coming indicates that "one . . . like unto the son of man" will receive this instruction: "Thrust in thy sickle, and reap: for the time is come for thee to reap; for the harvest of the earth is ripe." And the vision indicates that he "thrust in his sickle on the earth; and the earth was reaped."[c]

Judgment at the Second Coming will complete the two great harvests of the righteous. The first harvest occurred at Jesus' resurrection when all the righteous who had previously died were themselves resurrected. This resurrection is *part* of the first resurrection and is the first resurrection Alma looked forward to.[d] All who die after this resurrection (except those few men who had work to do in the restoration) will sleep until the general resurrection at the Lord's Second Coming. This is the resurrection we commonly refer to as the first resurrection. These two resurrections reflect major judgments that have taken place to separate the righteous from the wicked—the wicked being destroyed temporally to await a later resurrection, and the righteous being resurrected when the Lord comes.

In addition to those who are resurrected at His coming, the righteous living upon the earth at His Advent will be caught up to meet Him. But these individuals will not be resurrected at this time, for if they were, there would be no righteous men or women left upon the earth to carry on His work during the Millennium. These righteous disciples, and other worthy people living during the Millennium, will automatically be resurrected when they reach "the age of a tree." They will then be "caught up" to the Lord's kingdom, and their "rest shall be glorious."[e]

At this time, the Lord will "bring to light the hidden things of

a. Jude 1:14–15.

b. Matthew 13:24–30.

c. Revelation 14:13–16.

d. Alma 40:16.

e. D&C 101:30–31.

darkness, and will make manifest the counsels of the hearts."[a] Isaiah describes this condition:

> **Isaiah 32:5–6**   The vile person shall be no more called liberal, nor the churl said to be bountiful. For the vile person will speak villany, and his heart will work iniquity, to practise hypocrisy, and to utter error against the Lord, to make empty the soul of the hungry, and he will cause the drink of the thirsty to fail.

This means that there will be no deception possible at this time. People will actually be what they appear to be.

Delegated Judgment

The Lord is our supreme judge. However, He has delegated some preliminary judgment to others. There are several specific references where He delegates the responsibility of judgment to certain people or groups:

The Original Twelve Apostles: The Lord delegated judgment of the entire twelve tribes of Israel to His original Twelve Apostles:

> **D&C 29:12**   And again, verily, verily, I say unto you, and it hath gone forth in a firm decree, by the will of the Father, that mine apostles, the Twelve which were with me in my ministry at Jerusalem, shall stand at my right hand at the day of my coming in a pillar of fire, being clothed with robes of righteousness, with crowns upon their heads, in glory even as I am, to judge the whole house of Israel, even as many as have loved me and kept my commandments, and none else.

From this scripture it would appear that Judas Iscariot is included in this edict; however, because he fell from his position and became a "son of perdition,"[b] he will not serve as a judge over Israel. After Christ's ascension, the Twelve met in council to choose a new member. They selected "of these men which have companied with us all the time that the Lord Jesus went in and out among us."[c] Two candidates were considered, and their names were presented to the quorum for final selection. They were "Joseph called Barsabas, who was surnamed Justus, and Matthias."[d] Both men were disciples who had traveled with Jesus and the Apostles throughout the Lord's ministry. Because of this, the man selected would be considered as one of the Twelve who were with Jesus "in [His] ministry at Jerusalem."[e] Matthias was

a. 1 Corinthians 4:5.

b. John 17:12.

c. Acts 1:21.

d. Acts 1:23.

e. D&C 29:12.

the disciple subsequently selected to replace Judas Iscariot as one of
the Lord's Apostles.

The Nephite Disciples: The Lord chose these twelve men to minister
to the Nephite people after His visit to the Western Hemisphere. They
were to administer the gospel to their people in a manner similar to
that of the Apostles on the Eastern Hemisphere. Nephi saw these men
in vision during his early ministry:

> **1 Nephi 12:7–10**   And I also saw and bear record that the Holy Ghost fell
> upon twelve others; and they were ordained of God, and chosen. And the
> angel spake unto me, saying: Behold the twelve disciples of the Lamb, who
> are chosen to minister unto thy seed. And he said unto me: Thou remember-
> est the twelve apostles of the Lamb? Behold they are they who shall judge
> the twelve tribes of Israel; wherefore, the twelve ministers of thy seed shall be
> judged of them; for ye are of the house of Israel. And these twelve ministers
> whom thou beholdest shall judge thy seed. And, behold, they are righteous
> forever; for because of their faith in the Lamb of God their garments are made
> white in his blood.

The relationship between these twelve disciples and the Twelve
Apostles on the Eastern Hemisphere seems clear from this scripture,
but to ensure clarity, Mormon added the following: "And I write also
unto the remnant of this people, who shall also be judged by the twelve
whom Jesus chose in this land; and they shall be judged by the other
twelve whom Jesus chose in the land of Jerusalem."[a] Thus, the twelve
disciples and their people will also be judged by the Lord's Apostles on
the Eastern Hemisphere, who will judge all Israel as well.[b]

The Bishop: During the restoration of the gospel in the latter days,
the Lord established the priesthood office of bishop. The individual
holding this office is to "be a judge in Israel, like as it was in ancient
days." Initially, bishops were instructed to oversee the division of lands
under the United Order so that these divisions would be equitable, and
to ensure that each individual who received land would be accountable
for it. He was also authorized to "judge his people by the testimony of
the just, and by the assistance of his counselors, according to the laws
of the kingdom which are given by the prophets of God."[c][230] These
scriptures indicate that a bishop is authorized to judge the temporal
affairs of Church members and to help maintain the integrity of the

a. Mormon 3:19.

b. Matthew
   19:28; Luke
   22:30.

c. D&C
   58:16–18.

Church. The bishop, therefore, can judge whether each member of his congregation is worthy to participate in the blessings the Church has to offer: the priesthood, temple attendance, membership, callings, and similar opportunities. But it is the Lord who judges the intent and honesty of each individual as he deals with the bishop. Thus, no eternal judgments are made by the bishop himself.

The Elders: There is an interesting scripture concerning missionaries pronouncing judgment upon people:

D&C 75:19–22 And in whatsoever house ye enter, and they receive you, leave your blessing upon that house. And in whatsoever house ye enter, and they receive you not, ye shall depart speedily from that house, and shake off the dust of your feet as a testimony against them. And you shall be filled with joy and gladness; and know this, that in the day of judgment you shall be judges of that house, and condemn them; and it shall be more tolerable for the heathen in the day of judgment, than for that house; therefore, gird up your loins and be faithful, and ye shall overcome all things, and be lifted up at the last day. Even so. Amen.

This scripture declares that missionaries can potentially judge the people they proselyte. This judgment is limited, however, by the type of contact the missionaries make at the time of their visit. The following circumstances have to be taken into consideration: (1) Were the missionaries in the proper spirit and did they take ample time to indicate who and what they were representing (as well as bear their testimonies to the truthfulness of their representations)? (2) What was the condition of the contact (represented in the scriptures as the "house") at the time the visit was made? (3) Did the Holy Ghost bear witness to the contact, and did he or she knowingly rejected it? (4) Did the contact continue to reject the gospel, or did he or she later repent and embrace it? It seems obvious that any judgment which affects the eternity of the soul should be used judiciously and should require a confirmation from the Lord. Only God knows the intentions of the heart.

Judgment is always difficult when it concerns the eternal disposition of the soul, but we come from a loving Father who is always willing to forgive those who repent. Through the Atonement of Christ and by His grace, all mankind can be saved. [a] We all have a tendency to be hard on ourselves when we evaluate our lives, but "if our heart condemn us," know that "God is greater than our heart, and knoweth all things."[b] We can place our confidence and trust in the Lord, for all His judgments will be correct and just.

a. Articles of Faith
   1:3; 2 Nephi
   25:23.
b. 1 John 3:20.

Millennial Peace, War, and Resurrection

Doctrine and Covenants 88:110, 116   There shall be time no longer, . . . and they shall not any more see death.

Millennial Judgment

Judgment will continue during the Millennium as the human life cycle continues. Men and women will be born and will live to the "age of a tree" (or as Isaiah notes, "100 years"); then they will die and be caught up and changed in the "twinkling of an eye." The righteous will enjoy instant resurrection and their "rest shall be glorious," but those who are unworthy to be in God's kingdom will be "accursed." They will die and go into the spirit world to await their resurrection at a later time.[a]

Great changes will occur to the earth as the Millennium is ushered in. The world as we know it will no longer exist. The earth will return to its paradisiacal glory and will become a new earth.[b] "Old things shall pass away, and all things [will] become new."[c] "In that day the enmity of man, and the enmity of beasts, yea the enmity of all flesh, shall cease from before [God's] face."[d] "The wolf . . . shall dwell with the lamb, and the leopard shall lie down with the kid; and the calf and the young lion and the fatling [shall live] together; and a little child shall lead them." Wild and domestic animals will be able to live together in peace, and children will be able to play by the "hole of the asp" and the "cocka-trice' den" without being harmed.[e] Man and beast will be in harmony.

There will be an explosion of knowledge during the Millen-

a. Isaiah 65:20; D&C 63:49–51; D&C 101:31.

b. Articles of Faith 1:10.

c. D&C 63:49.

d. D&C 101:26.

e. Isaiah 11:6–9.

nium. When the Lord comes "he shall reveal all things—things which have passed, and hidden things which no man knew, things of the earth, by which it was made, and the purpose and the end thereof—things most precious, things that are above, and things that are beneath, things that are in the earth, and upon the earth, and in heaven."[a] The gospel will continue to be preached until all men "either come into the Church, or kingdom of God, or the wicked die and pass away."[231] Temples will also continue to be built as the ordinances of salvation continue.

During the Millennium, Satan will not have the power to tempt mankind; furthermore, there will be no sorrow because for the righteous there will be no death.[b] God will remove all curses from the earth: the curse of weeds and thistles instituted after the Fall,[c] the curse on Cain and his seed,[d] and the curse on the waters[e]—all curses shall become null and void.[f]

Zephaniah tells us that the Lord will return a "pure language" to the people living during the Millennium so that they can all call upon Him "to serve him with one consent";[g] Ezekiel tells us that the Dead Sea will be "healed" and full of many kinds of edible fish;[h] Isaiah states that the deserts will blossom as a rose;[i] the Doctrine and Covenants describes "pools of living water" that will appear in "barren deserts";[j] Christ will rule the earth in His glory and all people will both see Him and hear His voice;[k] all that the Lord has said and promised will be accomplished, for His words will not pass away unfulfilled;[l] and there will be no king but God,[m] who will resolve all sorrows.[n]

John informs us that everyone who is judged worthy to inherit the celestial kingdom will be given a "white stone" bearing the inscription of a new name. He writes, "To him that overcometh will I give to eat of the hidden manna, and will give him a white stone, and in the stone a new name written, which no man knoweth saving he that receiveth it."[o] Joseph Smith gives the following commentary on this subject:

D&C 130:10–11   Then the white stone mentioned in Revelation 2:17, will become a Urim and Thummim to each individual who receives one, whereby things pertaining to a higher order of kingdoms will be made known; and a white stone is given to each of those who come into the celestial kingdom, whereon is a new name written, which no man knoweth save he that receiveth it. The new name is the key word.

a. D&C 101:32–34.

b. D&C 101:26–30.

c. Genesis 3:18.

d. Genesis 4:11–15.

e. Revelation 16:3–5; D&C 61:14.

f. Revelation 22:3; 2 Nephi 30:17.

g. Zephaniah 3:9.

h. Ezekiel 47:1–12.

i. Isaiah 35:1–2, 7.

j. D&C 133:29.

k. D&C 29:7; 133:21.

l. Matthew 24:35.

m. D&C 38:21.

n. Revelation 21:4.

o. Revelation 2:17.

Two world capitals will be in existence during the Millennium: Zion and Jerusalem.[a] Those inhabiting these cities, as well as all others who inhabit the earth during the Millennium, will enjoy a wonderful quality of life. Anger and pain will be swept away. There will be no more weeping.[b] People will see "eye to eye."[c] They will understand each other, and deception will not be possible. Everyone will be exactly as they *appear* to be.[d] People will build and inhabit their houses and plant, harvest, and eat their food in peace, and no one will be able to take these things away from them.[e] Men and women will be able to perpetrate sin and evil through their agency, but Satan will be bound.[f] He will not have the power to "tempt any man," and only peace will prevail.[g] There will be no more war during the Millennium, and swords will be turned into plowshares.[h] The great prophet-poet Isaiah puts all of this in his own words:

Isaiah 65:17–25   For, behold, I create new heavens and a new earth: and the former shall not be remembered, nor come into mind. But be ye glad and rejoice for ever in that which I create: for, behold, I create Jerusalem a rejoicing, and her people a joy. And I will rejoice in Jerusalem, and joy in my people: and the voice of weeping shall be no more heard in her, nor the voice of crying. There shall be no more thence an infant of days, nor an old man that hath not filled his days: for the child shall die an hundred years old; but the sinner being an hundred years old shall be accursed. And they shall build houses, and inhabit them; and they shall plant vineyards, and eat the fruit of them. They shall not build, and another inhabit; they shall not plant, and another eat: for as the days of a tree are the days of my people, and mine elect shall long enjoy the work of their hands. They shall not labour in vain, nor bring forth for trouble; for they are the seed of the blessed of the Lord, and their offspring with them. And it shall come to pass, that before they call, I will answer; and while they are yet speaking, I will hear. The wolf and the lamb shall feed together, and the lion shall eat straw like the bullock: and dust shall be the serpent's meat. They shall not hurt nor destroy in all my holy mountain, saith the Lord.

The prophet Nephi saw this same vision and described it in similar terms:

2 Nephi 30:12–18   And then shall the wolf dwell with the lamb; and the leopard shall lie down with the kid, and the calf, and the young lion, and the fatling, together; and a little child shall lead them. And the cow and the

a. Isaiah 2:3.

b. Isaiah 65:19.

c. D&C 84:98.

d. Isaiah 32:5–6.

e. Isaiah 65:21–22.

f. Revelation 20:2–3.

g. D&C 101:28.

h. Isaiah 2:4; Joel 3:10; Micah 4:3–5.

bear shall feed; their young ones shall lie down together; and the lion shall eat straw like the ox. And the sucking child shall play on the hole of the asp, and the weaned child shall put his hand on the cockatrice's den. They shall not hurt nor destroy in all my holy mountain; for the earth shall be full of the knowledge of the Lord as the waters cover the sea. Wherefore, the things of all nations shall be made known; yea, all things shall be made known unto the children of men. There is nothing which is secret save it shall be revealed; there is no work of darkness save it shall be made manifest in the light; and there is nothing which is sealed upon the earth save it shall be loosed. Wherefore, all things which have been revealed unto the children of men shall at that day be revealed; and Satan shall have power over the hearts of the children of men no more, for a long time.

Men will act for themselves during the Millennium, without excuse, and will receive in kind according to their actions.

The Little Season of Judgment and War

After the Millennium is over, there will follow what has been described as a "little season." Some have inferred that it will also last for a thousand years,[232] but the scriptures do not specifically define its length. During this time, the righteous and the wicked will become strongly divided; but toward the end of the "season" they will gather to fight the last great battle of Gog and Magog.[a]

The Battles of Gog and Magog: There are two great battles that will occur known as the battles of Gog and Magog. The terms *Gog* and *Magog* are used symbolically in the scriptures to represent the armies and countries that will oppose the forces of good at two climatic points in history.[233] One battle will take place before the Second Coming and will lead to the battle at Armageddon. This will be an actual war conducted between armies and nations. The second battle will take place after the Millennium and at the end of the "little season." It will not involve actual warfare but is merely a symbolic representation of the final conflict between the devil and his followers and Michael (the archangel of God) and the righteous—a final conflict between good and evil.

In Ezekiel's description of the first battle of Gog and Magog, Gog appears to be the prince of a country identified as Magog. Gog and the armies from Magog come from the north,[b] a land located adjacent to that of Togarmah[c] and only a short distance from "the isles."[d] A

a. Revelation
   20:7–10; D&C
   88:111–16.

b. Ezekiel 38:2.

c. known as
   Armenia today;
   Ezekiel 38:6.

d. perhaps the
   maritime re-
   gions of Europe;
   Ezekiel 39:6.

large battle takes place between these armies and the people of Israel—armies that are armed with bows and arrows[a] and that have cavalry.[b] While Ezekiel may initially be speaking of a battle that took place in his own time involving the Scythians,[234] he is also speaking in double reference-prophecy since he declares that this war will take place "in the latter-days."[c]

This latter-day war of Gog and Magog will occur just prior to the Second Coming.[d][235] It will lead to the Second Coming battle at Armageddon where great earthquakes will ravage the land as the Lord destroys the armies of Gog and Magog in His fight for Israel. The battle will climax when the Mount of Olives splits in two and the Lord physically appears to save His people.[e] It is at the conclusion of this devastating battle that the Millennium will be ushered in.

When the Millennium ends, the devil will again be free upon the earth for a "little season." His main objective will be to "gather together his armies" one last time.[f] John the Revelator saw this time and gave a brief description of it:

> **Revelation 20:7–10**   And when the thousand years are expired, Satan shall be loosed out of his prison, and shall go out to deceive the nations which are in the four quarters of the earth, Gog and Magog, to gather them together to battle: the number of whom is as the sand of the sea. And they went up on the breadth of the earth, and compassed the camp of the saints about, and the beloved city: and fire came down from God out of heaven, and devoured them. And the devil that deceived them was cast into the lake of fire and brimstone, where the beast and the false prophet are, and shall be tormented day and night for ever and ever.

From John's description of the second battle of Gog and Magog, it is evident that the devil will be as powerful and persuasive after the Millennium as he was before.[g] His motivation will also remain the same: to deceive men and lead them captive to his will.[h] His success will be great, for John describes those who follow him as being as numerous as the "sand of the sea." He will do all that he can to destroy the souls of men and thwart the Father's plan. To this end, he will gather his evil followers (described as armies) together as he did in the preexistence and do battle against "the great God."[i]

While Satan gathers his forces, the Archangel Michael will also

a. Ezekiel 39:3.

b. Ezekiel 38:15.

c. Ezekiel 38:16.

d. this war is also referred to by other Old Testament prophets besides Ezekiel.

e. Chapter 5.

f. D&C 88:110.

g. Chapters 7 and 8.

h. Moses 4:4.

i. D&C 88:114.

gather his armies together in preparation for battle. But this will not be a *war* in the technical sense—nor are these *armies* as we envision armies. This will not be a physical battle involving a force of arms. John's vision is symbolic. The conflict that will take place will be much like the premortal war in heaven where the angry disobedience of Lucifer and his followers was pitted against God and His plan of salvation.[a] By the end of the little season, however, the plan will have reached its apex: the Saints of God will have been resurrected, and Michael will be gathering the righteous together to witness God's final and eternal expulsion of the wicked.

Both John the Revelator and Joseph Smith describe this climatic battle in abrupt terms. John states: "Fire came down from God out of heaven, and devoured them [the wicked]," and they were "cast into the lake of fire and brimstone . . . for ever and ever."[b] Joseph calls Satan's armies the "hosts of hell"[c] and states: "And then cometh the battle of the great God; and the devil and his armies shall be cast away into their own place, that they shall not have power over the saints any more at all. For Michael shall fight their battles, and shall overcome him who seeketh the throne of him who sitteth upon the throne, even the Lamb."[d]

This final destruction of all wickedness is described by Joseph as "the glory of God, and the sanctified."[e] The devil and his followers will be cast down into a kingdom wherein there is *no* glory. They will live for eternity in this "outer darkness" where they will endure "everlasting punishment, which is eternal punishment," meaning "God's punishment."[f] They can never associate with the Father's glory again. The "end thereof, neither the place thereof, nor their torment, no man knows." And it is not revealed—nor will it ever be to any man— except to them who are made partakers thereof."[g]

The final dismissal of Satan—he who would "ascend into heaven . . . [and] exalt [his] throne above the stars of God"[h]—is succinctly described by Isaiah:

Isaiah 14:16–22 Is this the man that made the earth to tremble, that did shake kingdoms; that made the world as a wilderness, and destroyed the cities thereof; that opened not the house of his prisoners? All the kings of the nations, even all of them, lie in glory, every one in his own house. But thou art cast out of thy grave like an abominable branch, and as the raiment of those

a. Revelation 12:7.

b. Revelation 20:9–10.

c. D&C 88:113.

d. D&C 88:114–115.

e. D&C 88:116.

f. D&C 19:3–12.

g. D&C 76:44–46.

h. Isaiah 14:13.

that are slain, thrust through with a sword, that go down to the stones of the pit; as a carcase trodden under feet. Thou shalt not be joined with them in burial, because thou hast destroyed thy land, and slain thy people: the seed of evildoers shall never be renowned. Prepare slaughter for his children for the iniquity of their fathers; that they do not rise, nor possess the land, nor fill the face of the world with cities. For I will rise up against them, saith the Lord of hosts, and cut off from Babylon the name, and remnant, and son, and nephew, saith the Lord.

The Resurrection

The body and the spirit make up the soul of man.[a] When we are born, the spirit and the body unite; at death, the spirit separates from the body and the body returns to the earth. Resurrection is the re-uniting of body and spirit. With resurrection (the "redemption of the soul"),[b] the reunited body and spirit will be "restored to its perfect frame,"[c] "never to be divided" again.[d] Alma describes this process as the restoration of the body to the spirit. He writes, "Yea, and every limb and joint shall be restored to its body; yea, even a hair of the head shall not be lost; but all things shall be restored to their proper and perfect frame."[e]

Because of the fall of Adam and Eve, all men and women born to this earth will eventually die. But through the death and resurrection of Christ, all mankind will be made alive again.[f] Paul writes:

1 Corinthians 15:20–26, 28 (emphasis added)   But now is Christ risen from the dead, and become the firstfruits of them that slept. For since by man came death, by man came also the resurrection of the dead. For as in Adam all die, even so in Christ shall all be made alive. But every man in his own order: Christ the firstfruits; afterward they that are Christ's at his coming. Then cometh the end, when he shall have delivered up the kingdom to God, even the Father; when he shall have put down all rule and all authority and power. For he must reign, till he hath put all enemies under his feet. *The last enemy that shall be destroyed is death.* . . . And when all things shall be subdued unto him, then shall the Son also himself be subject unto him that put all things under him, that God may be all in all.

Before the final judgment is over, all men and women who have lived upon this earth—be they good or evil—will have been resurrected, and death will be destroyed thereby. Were it not so, the mission of Jesus Christ would be thwarted and the Father's plan of salvation defeated.

a. D&C 88:15.

b. D&C 88:16.

c. Alma 11:44.

d. Alma 11:45.

e. Alma 40:23; D&C 29:25.

f. 1 Corinthians 15:22.

There are three resurrections of the just that are all considered part of the "first" resurrection.

1. The first resurrection began with the resurrection of Jesus Christ and all the righteous who had died from the time of Adam up to the Savior's resurrection. This resurrection also includes certain righteous individuals (i.e., John the Baptist, Peter, James, and Moroni) who died after Christ's resurrection because of the part they would play in the restoration of the gospel.[a]

2. The second part of the first resurrection will occur at the Lord's Second Coming. This resurrection is symbolically described as beginning with the sounding of the "trump of God," which will awaken the Saints from death's slumber.[236] Michael (Adam), along with the angels of God, will gather the elect from the four winds,[b] and it will be Michael who "plays" the trump and sounds the call to resurrection. "Then shall all the dead awake, for their graves shall be opened, and they shall come forth—yea, even all."[c]

3. The third part of the first resurrection will continue intermittently throughout the Millennium (and perhaps the "little season") as the worthy Saints of that period reach the age of a "tree" and are "changed [resurrected] in the twinkling of an eye."[d]

a. Alma 40:16–19.

b. Matthew 24:31.

c. D&C 29:26.

d. D&C 101:31.

e. D&C 29:13; 88:96–98.

f. D&C 133:52.

g. D&C 63:49; 133:53–56.

h. Isaiah 26:19.

Only the righteous, those who have died in Christ, will be blessed to come forth in the first resurrection.[e] They are the "redeemed" of the Lord[f] who will "stand on the right hand of the Lamb" and be partakers of His glory.[g]

Isaiah foresaw the first resurrection and in poetic prophesy he declared: "Thy dead men shall live, together with my dead body shall they arise. Awake and sing, ye that dwell in dust: for thy dew is as the dew of herbs, and the earth shall cast out the dead."[h] The souls he describes are those who will inherit a celestial glory, those who receive the testimony of Jesus Christ and keep His commandments. They are those who have repented of their sins, have been baptized, have received the

Holy Ghost as their personal guide, and have been washed clean by the blood of the Lord's Atonement. They are the men and women who will be "sealed by the Holy Spirit of promise" to receive the fulness of the Father's kingdom, and they will "dwell in the presence of God and his Christ forever and ever."[a] All other men and women born to this earth will inherit a lesser glory—that of the terrestrial or telestial kingdoms—according to the state of their righteousness. And some, who have been wicked beyond redemption, will be cast into "outer darkness" where there is no glory at all.[237]

Thus, our faith, our knowledge, our works, and our repentance from sin will determine our reward.

The Final Judgment

Instead of calling this event the final judgment, it might be more accurate to describe it as the time when all judgment will become final for as has been shown, judgment has been going on in one form or another since the preexistence; and it will continue to go on throughout the Millennium and the "little season." Nevertheless, by the end of the little season, each soul born to this earth will have appeared before the judgment seat of God to receive his or her just reward.[b] Every man and woman will ultimately be judged according to his or her works, "whether they be good or whether they be evil."[c] They will be rewarded for their works—good for good and evil for evil—and both heaven and earth will bear witness to God's just and final judgment.[d]

The final judgment is the time when the devil, his angels, and all who have chosen to follow him in this life will be cast forever into outer darkness.[e] Mosiah states that they will be "consigned to an awful view of their own guilt and abominations, which [will] cause them to shrink from the presence of the Lord into a state of misery and endless torment, from whence they can no more return . . . [because] they have drunk damnation to their own souls." As a result, they will receive no mercy from the Lord.[f]

Even the earth will receive a final judgment. It was initially created as part of the plan to give mankind a home, and when the plan has been completed the earth will receive its second and final transformation. It will "pass away so as by fire."[g] for by the end of the little season it will have fulfilled "the measure of its creation." It will be

a. D&C 76:51–70; 88:17–28.

b. 2 Corinthians 5:10.

c. Mosiah 3:24.

d. Psalm 50:4.

e. Jude 1:6.

f. Mosiah 3:25–27.

g. D&C 43:32.

"crowned with glory, even with the presence of God the Father,"[a] and it will become the celestial kingdom for those who are worthy to reside there. "For this intent was it made and created."[b]

The earth's final, glorified state is described in the Doctrine and Covenants:

D&C 130:9 This earth, in its sanctified and immortal state, will be made like unto crystal and will be a Urim and Thummim to the inhabitants who dwell thereon, whereby all things pertaining to an inferior kingdom, or all kingdoms of a lower order, will be manifest to those who dwell on it; and this earth will be Christ's.[c]

D&C 29:24–25 For all old things shall pass away, and all things shall become new, even the heaven and the earth, and all the fulness thereof, both men and beasts, the fowls of the air, and the fishes of the sea; and not one hair, neither mote, shall be lost, for it is the workmanship of mine hand.[d]

Marvelous things await the faithful followers of Jesus the Messiah.

a. D&C 88:19.

b. D&C 88:20.

c. D&C 130:9.

d. D&C 29:24–25.

Conclusion

Joseph Smith–Matthew 1:26 For as the light of the morning cometh out of the east, and shineth even unto the west, and covereth the whole earth, so shall also the coming of the Son of Man be.

Ever since the Lord first appeared in the flesh, men and women have looked for His Second Coming. In their yearning for the choice lifestyle they believed the Second Coming would provide, the Jews of Christ's time transposed the signs of His first coming with those of His second, and when the blessings they anticipated did not materialize, they rejected their Savior. Even the Lord's Apostles could not forebear asking Him when the Second Coming would be. However, only the Father knows when the Lord will come again—and He is silent on this point. What *has* been given us are the prophesied signs of Christ's Advent to make us vigilant, lest we be caught unawares when He arrives.

The exact *time* of the Savior's coming is not important, but the *words* that prophesy of His coming are, for they will all be fulfilled. "Heaven and earth shall pass away," He said, "but my words shall not pass away."[a] Every Second Coming prophecy recorded in scripture—during Old Testament times, in the New Testament, the Book of Mormon, or in the latter days—will come to pass. It is up to us to recognize them when they occur.

The following eight facts consistently apply to Second Coming prophecies:

1. The general signs that have been prophesied—wars, rumors of

a. Matthew 24:35.

wars, earthquakes in diverse places, unusual weather patterns, etc.— were not given as *specific* indicators of when the Lord would come. Rather, they were given to make the believer constantly aware of the fact that the Savior *will* come. These general signs are timeless—each generation has had them and future generations will receive them. Why? To remind mankind of the need to be prepared to meet the Lord.[a]

2. Specific signs of the Savior's Second Coming identify specific events. The believers who lived in the era following Christ's crucifixion witnessed the fulfillment of some of these specific signs; i.e., the destruction of Jerusalem and the razing of the temple of Herod. These signs would have bolstered their faith. The fulfillment of these specific signs, along with those of the Great Apostasy, the Restoration, and the completion of the times of the Gentiles, bolster our faith and mark the mileposts of His coming. And they will continue until the time of His Advent.

3. The tribe of Judah is part of the Lord's covenant people, and a close observation of its history and its prophesied future will reveal more signs of the Second Coming. Judah is the only known tribe of Israel which has continuously maintained its identity under the covenant of Abraham, and it will continue to retain this unique identity until the Lord comes again. This unique identity, however, has caused confusion when trying to unravel the meaning of the prophecies regarding Judah, the other eleven tribes, and Israel as a whole.[b]

4. The gathering is one of the major signs of the Second Coming. It involves the gathering of the tribe of Judah, the tribe of Joseph (both Ephraim and Manasseh), the ten lost tribes of Israel, the Gentiles as a group, and the non-Gentile and non-Israel groups (generalized as the Arabs and people of African descent). The doctrine of gathering is a major evidence of the truthfulness of the restored gospel.[c]

5. The devil's influence and the establishment of his evil latter-day kingdom are major signs of the Second Coming. These

a. Chapter 9.
b. Chapter 5.
c. Chapter 6.

prophecies, however, are *specifically general.* Why? Because, while many of the prophecies describe specific events and identify specific entities, they are written symbolically. John the Revelator marveled when he witnessed Satan's influence[a] while Isaiah described the devil's intentions with contempt.[b]

6. Three cities play a prominent part in the prophecies of the Second Coming: Jerusalem, Zion, and the City of Enoch.

    Jerusalem will continue to be "a burdensome stone for all people" until the Lord comes, but will play a major role in both the signs of the Second Coming and the rule of Christ during the Millennium.

    Zion, specifically located by the Lord in Jackson County, Missouri, could not be maintained because of severe persecution by the Missourians and disobedience by the Saints. However, Latter-day Saints look forward to the time when the Lord will yet establish this righteous city and allow it to fulfill its prophetic destiny—both at the Second Coming and during Christ's millennial reign.

    The City of Enoch is an example of what can be accomplished by a righteous people. It will return to the earth at Christ's Advent, and its inhabitants will participate in a joyous reunion with the righteous at the Second Coming.[c]

7. Catastrophic devastations, unparalleled in mankind's history, will occur prior to the Second Coming to cleanse the earth of all wickedness. However, most of mankind will not recognize them as signs of the Second Coming, but will consider them abnormalities that occur in an otherwise normal life cycle. As in the days of Noah, people will continue in normal life experiences until it is too late.[d] The wicked will be destroyed and the earth itself will revolt and change its aspect in preparation for the Lord's Advent.[e]

8. The Savior will come again to rule upon the earth, to judge all men, and to destroy evil forever:

    The Millennium: Christ will reign throughout the Millennium, and although He is the ultimate judge of all mankind,

a. Revelation 17:6–7.

b. Isaiah 14:12–16; Chapters 7 and 8.

c. Chapter 13.

d. Matthew 24:38.

e. Chapters 11 and 14.

He will employ others to assist Him in determining the eternal glory that each man and woman born to this earth will receive.[a]

The Little Season: At the beginning of the Millennium, the devil and his angels will be restrained for a thousand years; thereafter, they will be loosed for a "little season" to pursue their evil course and ensnare all who will accept them. He will gather his disciples together to do battle against righteousness. The righteous will also gather—to observe the final destruction and punishment of the wicked.[b]

The wicked: The battles of Armageddon and Gog and Magog prophetically describe the last two conflicts between wickedness and righteousness, with the conclusion that the wicked will be cast out into an eternal kingdom of darkness wherein the glory of the Father and that of the Light of the World, Jesus Christ, will never be seen.[c]

The prophesied signs of the Second Coming have been given so that we might recognize the fact that the Savior *will* come. The signs help us prepare, and remain vigilant. The Savior gave us the parable of the ten virgins so that as members of the Church, we will clearly understand what can happen if our preparation is inadequate.[d][238] Remember, the five unprepared virgins had *some* oil! They were neither totally unprepared nor entirely unknowledgeable, and had the bridegroom come when *they* expected Him, they would have participated in the joy of His kingdom. But the bridegroom tarried, and only half of the virgins had sufficient oil to sustain them through the night.

There are many reasons for unpreparedness. The Lord may come later than many people anticipate, causing them to falter and lose faith. Some may say that there will be no Second Coming, that there are no living prophets, and that the scriptures are not true but are merely babblings of religious fanatics. Some will leave the strait and narrow path and follow after false Christs or false prophets; some will succumb to the ways of the world and allow their spiritual senses to become dulled to the truth; still others will try to force the fulfillment of prophecy and will become disillusioned when the times they live in do not fit the signs of His coming, causing them to become discouraged and fall by the wayside.

a. Chapter 15.

b. Chapter 16.

c. Chapter 16.

d. Matthew 25:1–13.

In these and many other ways, the oil that so many of us have so tediously acquired over the years may be wasted and used up; and when the cry is heard—"Behold, the bridegroom cometh; go ye out to meet him"[a]—we may (or will) have no reserves.

Waiting for the bridegroom requires faith, patience, and work. Recognizing the signs of the Savior's Second Coming can be very difficult. But the rewards are glorious! "The ransomed of the Lord shall return, and come to Zion with songs and everlasting joy upon their heads: they shall obtain joy and gladness, and sorrow and sighing shall flee away."[b] When that day comes we will greet the loved ones who parted the veil before us, we will fall upon each other's neck and weep for happiness, and we will receive a *fullness* of joy, because we will live again, as Christ lives:

> And body and spirit will be restored, made perfect,
> Free of pain,
> Full of light,
> Never to be parted again.[239]

How glorious is the Second Coming of Jesus the Messiah!

a. Matthew 25:6.

b. Isaiah 35:10.

Notes

1.   Life p. 6.
2.   Life p. 396.
3.   Ed 2:28.
4.   Life p. 472.
5.   MM 3:408.
6.   For example, Acts 5:36; 8:9; and 21:38, where individuals claimed authority which they did not have, and Revelation 2:2, 9, in which some claimed to be the Lord's Apostles when they were not, or "representative" Jews when they were not.
7.   Josephus, Wars II:13:4–5; Antiquities XX:5; 8:10.
8.   Jerusalem pp. 128–29.
9.   Josephus, Wars, Preface, Books I–VII.
10.   CC p. 259 et. seq.
11.   Josephus, Wars V:4.
12.   Josephus, Wars VI:3:4.
13.   Ed 1:120.
14.   Sermons p. 214.
15.   Some remnants of the lost tribes are identified in the New Testament: Elizabeth, the mother of John the Baptist, was from the tribe of Levi (Luke 1:5); Anna the prophetess was from the tribe of Asher (Luke 2:36), and Paul declared that he was from the tribe of Benjamin (Philippians 3:5). There were undoubtedly others.
16.   AGQ 1:142.
17.   Miracles p. 131.
18.   CC p. 577.
19.   CHCC p. 27.
20.   CHCC p. 43.
21.   CHCC p. 39.
22.   CHCC p. 40.
23.   CHCC p. 44.
24.   CHCC p. 51.
25.   CHCC p. 50.
26.   CC p. 664; CHCC p. 50.
27.   CC p. 559.
28.   CHCC p. 46.
29.   CHCC p. 11.
30.   CHCC p. 45.
31.   "We believe in one God, the Father almighty, maker of all things visible and invisible; and in one Lord Jesus Christ, the Son of God, begotten from the Father, only-begotten, that is, from the substance of the Father, God from God, light from light, true God from true God, begotten not made, of one substance with the Father, through Whom all things came into being, things in heaven and things on earth, Who because of us men and because of our salvation, came down and became incarnate, becoming man, suffered and rose again on the third day, ascended into heaven, and will come to judge the living and the dead; And in the Holy Spirit. "But as for those who say, there was when He was not, and, before being born He was not, and that He came into existence out of nothing, or, who assert that the Son of God is of a different hypostasis or substance, or is created, or is subject to alteration or change–these the Catholic Church anathematizes" (CE IV, p. 435).
32.   "We believe in one God, the Father almighty, maker of heaven and earth, of all things visible and invisible; and in one Lord Jesus Christ, the only begotten Son of God, begotten from the Father before all ages, light from light, true God from true God, begotten not made, of one substance with the Father, through Whom all things came into existence; Who because of our salvation came down from heaven, and was incarnate from the Holy Spirit and the Virgin Mary and became man, and was crucified for us under Pontius Pilate, and suffered and was buried, and rose again on the third day according to the Scriptures, and ascended to heaven, and sits on the right hand of the Father, and will come again with glory to judge living and dead, of Whose kingdom there will be no end; and in the Holy Spirit, the Lord and life-giver, Who proceeds from the Father, Who with the Father and the Son is together worshipped and together glorified, Who spoke through the prophets; in one holy Catholic and apostolic Church. We confess one baptism to the remission of sins; we look forward to the resurrection of the dead, and the life of the world to come. Amen" (CE IV, p. 435).
33.   CC p. 595.
34.   HC 2:193. For the complete charge to the restored Twelve, HC 2:193–98.
35.   Exodus 29:45; Leviticus 26:12; 2 Samuel 7:24; Ezekiel 14:11; Romans 9:4.
36.   CHCC p. 168.
37.   CHCC p. 168.
38.   CHCC p. 11.
39.   CHCC p. 223.
40.   CHCC pp. 236, 238, 247.
41.   Miracles pp. 45–49.
42.   HC 3:51.
43.   The ten kingdoms and the approximate time of

their organization after the fall of Rome are: Italy (496), France (752), England (830), Belgium (865), Holland (922), Austria (1158), Portugal (1138), Prussia (Germany) (1139), Spain (1471), and Greece (1828).

44. ER p. 197, wherein John A. Widtsoe states that every President of the Church is a seer "like as Moses."

45. Revelation 14:6–7; D&C 20:6–12; D&C 133:36.

46. HC 1:75.

47. Parables p. 30.

48. 2 Nephi 30:8; 3 Nephi 25:5–6; D&C 2:1; D&C 35:4; D&C 113:6; D&C 124:58; D&C 128:17, 19–21; Joseph Smith–History 1.

49. HC 4:456–57.

50. HC 4:459.

51. GM p. 23 (emphasis added).

52. AIC p. 21.

53. GM p. 210; OJ pp. 17–18, 29–39.

54. GM p. 226.

55. Zechariah 10:6, 12; 1 Nephi 19:13–17; 2 Nephi 10:7–8; Ether 13:11–12; D&C 110:11.

56. GM p. 105.

57. HC 4:457.

58. GM p. 23.

59. JD 15:277; WW p. 509.

60. GM p. 214.

61. Jeremiah 31:31–34; 1 Nephi 10:14; 2 Nephi 6:11; 3 Nephi 20:29–31.

62. JD 18:111.

63. Deuteronomy 10:8; Malachi 3:3; 3 Nephi 24:3; D&C 84:31; D&C 124:39; D&C 128:24; HC 4:211.

64. Ezekiel 38:1–7, 9, 13; Joel 3:1–21; Zechariah 14:1–21; Revelation 11:1–13; D&C 45:26–27.

65. IDYK p. 197.

66. DNTC 3:509.

67. Torah p. 593.

68. JD 16:329 (Orson Pratt).

69. Isaiah 54:15–17; Jeremiah 30:3–9; Zechariah 14:3; 3 Nephi 22:12, 15–17; JD 15:277–78.

70. HC 4:457.

71. Torah p. 309.

72. Isaiah 55:3–4; Jeremiah 23:5–8; Ezekiel 37:24–28; Hosea 3:4–5; Zechariah 12:6–9.

73. Joel 3:14; D&C 45:48; D&C 133:20.

74. Zechariah 14:9; 2 Nephi 6:14–15; D&C 133:41–42; Charles W. Penrose, "The Second Advent," MS 21:582–83.

75. Hebrews 12:22; D&C 133:19–24.

76. Torah p. 526.

77. Torah p. 431.

78. An example of this nondefinitive use of both the words Jew and Gentile is in the title page of the Book of Mormon where it states that it came forth "to the convincing of the Jew and Gentile that Jesus is the Christ." There are numerous such uses throughout all the scriptures.

79. HC 1:176 ftnt.

80. Isaiah 43:6; 49:12; Jeremiah 23:8: 31:8: Zechariah 10:10; Ether 13:11.

81. Isaiah 35:8–10; 51:11; Jeremiah 31:10–14; D&C 66:11.

82. Isaiah 35:1–2; 2 Nephi 30:6; 3 Nephi 21:22–25; D&C 3:20; D&C 30:6; D&C 109:65.

83. Isaiah 11:11; 1 Nephi 22:4; 2 Nephi 10:8, 20; 2 Nephi 29:7.

84. HC 2:492.

85. HC 2:XXVII.

86. HC 6:12.

87. HC 2:254.

88. HC 1:315.

89. Isaiah 2:2–3; 10:20–22; 11:11, 13; 13:2–4; 14:1–3; 30:18–25; 33:17–24; 40:27–31; 43:5–7; 49; 52:2–3, 6–7; 62.

90. Jeremiah 3:17–18; 23:3–8; 31; 32:37–44; 50:4–6.

91. Ezekiel 11:16–20; 20:34–38; 34:11–19; 36:16–38; 37:1–14, 16–22.

92. Micah 2:12; 4:6–7; 5:3.

93. Joel 2:32; Zephaniah 3:14–21; Zechariah 8:4–7, 12–13; 10:6–12; 14:10–11.

94. 1 Nephi 15:14; 22:11–12; 3 Nephi 5:24–26; Chapters 20–21.

95. D&C Index, s.v. Gather, Gathering.

96. Moses 4; Genesis 3, while the devil was in the garden of Eden; the temptations of Moses, Moses 1:12–24; the temptations of Jesus, Matthew 4:1–11; Mark 1:12–13; Luke 4:1–13.

97. HC 1:5.

98. HC 1:82–83.

99. HC 1:175 ftnt; 2:352.

100. HC 1:182.

101. HC 3:LIX–LXII.

102. HC 3:68.

103. HC 1:109.

104. HC 2:140.

105. HC 2:139–141.

106. HC 3:178–179.

107. HC 1:203.

108. HC 3:391.

109. HC 3:392.

110. HC 2:352.

111. HC 4:608.

112. HC 1:146.

113. HC 5:36–40.

114. HC 5:24.

115. HC 4:358.

116. Isaiah 24–27; Ezekiel 1; 9–10; 38; 40; Daniel 7–12; Zechariah 9–14.

117. The tefillin are small boxes with leather straps to attach to hand and forehead. The box contains parch-

ments of scripture. They are worn during morning worship, The Torah p. 1367.

118. CC pp. 63–64.

119. CC p. 388.

120. Isaiah 62:5; Hosea; 22:17; Matthew 9:15; 25:1; John 3:29; Revelation 19.

121. Isaiah 5:24–25; Isaiah 13:14–22; Isaiah 14:17–32; Isaiah 18:4–6; Isaiah 24:1–18; Isaiah 65:1–16; Isaiah 66:3–4, 15–18; D&C 112:24–26; Joseph Smith – Matthew 1:31.

122. Deuteronomy 32:21; 2 Nephi 15:25; Moses 6:27.

123. Psalm 72:4; Ezekiel 5:9–12; 38:22; Joel 1:19–20; 2:3; Zephaniah 1:2–3; Malachi 4:1; D&C 45:40–41; D&C 97:25–26; D&C 101:24.

124. Jeremiah 8:13; Zechariah 14:12; Matthew 3:12; 2 Nephi 26:6; D&C 29:3, 9, 21; D&C 45:57; D&C 63:34; D&C 64:24; D&C 88:94; D&C 101:23–25, 66.

125. Torah p. 61 emphasis added.

126. Torah p. 61.

127. Torah pp. 133–34.

128. Torah p. 135.

129. Life p. 777.

130. Such circumstances were prophesied by several other prophets as well with both specific and general reference as to upon whom it would occur. Isaiah 18:6; Jeremiah 15:3; Ezekiel 39:17–20; Revelation 19:17–18.

131. HC 4:11.

132. Life p. 261, 266.

133. Judges 5:1–5 where Deborah and Barak used the phrase in their song of praise to God after their military victories and Moses 6:34 where Enoch was blessed with the power to cause mountains to flee before him.

134. Because many of the visions John saw were also seen in full or in part by other prophets, Revelation 7–22 should be read in conjunction with Isaiah 24–27; Daniel 7–12; and Zechariah 9–14 to get their perspective.

135. HC 4:414–15.

136. CC pp. 457–58.

137. The National Geographic, May 1986; June 1992 (map).

138. Torah p. 1538.

139. Other visions and scriptures also refer to these events. Joel 3:12–14; D&C 76:107; D&C 88:106; D&C 133:46–51.

140. Life p. 140.

141. WTB p. 33.

142. WTB p. 58.

143. WTB p. 105.

144. NBC Evening News 2/27/00.

145. Life p. 658.

146. Isaiah 24:6; Nahum 1:5; 1 Nephi 22:15; D&C 29:9; D&C 63:34; D&C 64:24.

147. Life p. 571.

148. DNTC 3:499.

149. Isaiah 10:16–19; Malachi 3:1–6; Malachi 4:1–6; 2 Thessalonians 1:7–8; D&C 133:41, 64.

150. Life p. 298.

151. Joel 1:19–20; D&C 45:40–41; D&C 97:26.

152. Genesis 19:28; 1 Nephi 19:11; 3 Nephi 10:13; Mormon 8:29; D&C 87:6.

153. HC 3:390.

154. HC 3:391.

155. Bible Dictionary p. 789.

156. HC 3:XLI.

157. HC 3:XVIII.

158. HC 3:LXIII.

159. Life p. 298.

160. Life p. 290.

161. HC 6:196.

162. HC 6:254.

163. HC 6:254.

164. HC 3:35.

165. HC 3:388.

166. HC 3:386–387.

167. HC 4:541.

168. HC 1:189.

169. HC 1:196.

170. HC 1:199.

171. HC 1:358–359.

172. HC 3:175.

173. HC 3:LXIII.

174. Junius F. Wells, Improvement Era, "A Prophecy and Its Fulfillment," November, 1902, p. 9.

175. FM p. 14.

176. HC 3:208.

177. AC p. 360.

178. AC p. 351.

179. AC p. 342.

180. AC p. 348.

181. TPJS p. 17.

182. HC 1:199.

183. HC 1:359 et seq.

184. HC 2:239.

185. Jerusalem p. 9.

186. Jerusalem p. 9.

187. Jerusalem p. 13.

188. Jerusalem p. 320. Orson Hyde's dedicatory prayer date inserted in italics.

189. Jerusalem pp. 128–29.

190. Life p. 290.

191. David uses it when he says the Lord will make His enemies "as a fiery oven" in the time of His anger (Psalm 21:8–10), Nahum says the wicked will be "devoured as stubble" (Nahum 1:10), Nephi uses the descriptive words of Malachi and Nahum (1 Nephi 22:15,23), Isaiah warns earth's inhabitants that the Lord will burn them with "flames of fire" (Isaiah 24:6; 66:15–16), Joseph

Smith recorded that those who tithe "shall not be burned" (D&C 64:23; emphasis added; Malachi 3:10), and the Lord also used the example in the terms of Malachi both to the Book of Mormon people (3 Nephi 25:1) and in the restoration warnings (Malachi 4:1; D&C 64:24; Joseph Smith–History 1:37).

192. Mill M p. 382.

193. Revelation 21:8; D&C 29:28; D&C 43:33; D&C 63:54.

194. Other descriptions of the wicked and warnings of their eventual destruction are couched in terms such as those who "watch for iniquity" and seek "opportunity" to do evil. They will be "brought to naught." "Calamity shall cover the mocker" and the "scorner [will] be consumed." All of these will be "hewn down and cast into the fire." (Isaiah 29:20; D&C 45:50.)

195. That the Lord in His wrath will take vengeance upon and destroy the wicked is found in many scriptures (Revelation 6:16; D&C 1:9; D&C 29:17; D&C 43:26). The Lord spoke through Ezekiel to give a type and warning to future wickedness as He condemned the kingdom of Judah for their refusal to repent, thinking they could hide their evil (Ezekiel 21:31–32). And even the writer of Proverbs, while praising the righteous, warns that mere "riches" will "profit not in the day of wrath" (Proverbs 11:4–8).

196. The plagues of Egypt were: blood (Exodus 7:19); frogs (Exodus 8:2); lice (Exodus 8:16, 18); flies (Exodus 8:21); grievous murrain (Exodus 9:3); boils and blains (Exodus 9:9); hail (Exodus 9:18); fire along the ground (Exodus 9:23); locusts (Exodus 10:14); thick darkness (Exodus 10:22); and death of the firstborn, both of man and of beast (Exodus 11:5).

197. Life p. 478.

198. CL p. 13–14.

199. CL p. 14.

200. HC 5:326.

201. CL p. 14.

202. The Phoenix Gazette, October 30, 1995, Paul Brinkley - Rogers. Page A1, "Children of Light Only 7 Left as Shaker-Like Commune Fades Away."

203. GRF: particularly Chapter 14.

204. HC 2:182.

205. HC 5:336–37.

206. JD 14:5, January 1, 1871; JD 18:37, June 27, 1875; MS 51:595–96, July 29, 1889; CR p. 57, April 1898.

207. Deseret News, June 15, 1901.

208. JD 19:161.

209. Life p. 298.

210. Joseph Smith stated that the "devil knows many signs, but does not know the sign of the Son of Man, or Jesus" (HC 4:608).

211. HC 5:337.

212. TPJS p. 365.

213. Alma 1:29; Helaman 6:17; 12:1–2; 4 Nephi 1:23. Generally assumed and proclaimed throughout the Book of Mormon record.

214. Helaman 13:20–21, 31–33; Mormon 1:18.

215. Farrar 2:80.

216. Ed 2:178–79.

217. Geikie 2:298.

218. Life p. 60.

219. Life p. 63–6.

220. Matthew 7:1–5; Mark 2:1–12; John 5:1–14; 8:4–11.

221. HC 5:388.

222. HC 5:389, 402–3.

223. HC 6:363.

224. The Random House Dictionary (New York: Ballantine Books, 1978).

225. Life p. 298.

226. Life p. 261.

227. Life p. 430.

228. Life p. 640.

229. Life p. 203.

230. D&C 64:40; 107:72, 75.

231. DS 1:86.

232. DS 1:81.

233. The first mention of the name Magog is in Genesis. It is the name of the second son of Japheth (Genesis 10:2). The first mention of Gog is in 1 Chronicles (1Chronicles 5:4). It is the name of the son of Shemaiah from the tribe of Reuben. These referenced names have nothing to do with the battles being described.

234. Smith's Bible Dictionary p. 375.

235. Zephaniah 3:8–20; Zechariah 12–14; Revelation 16:16; D&C 29:21.

236. D&C 43:18; 45:45; 49:23.

237. D&C 76:25–38, 43–49; 88:99–102.

238. Life p. 298.

239. Excerpt from a poem by Gail Braithwaite Howick.

Bibliography

The Holy Bible   containing the Old and New Testaments, (Salt Lake City, Utah: The Church of Jesus Christ of Latter-Day Saints, 1989).

The Book of Mormon, The Doctrine and Covenants of the Church of Jesus Christ of Latter-Day Saints, The Pearl of Great Price   (Published by the Church of Jesus Christ of Latter-Day Saints: Salt Lake City, Utah 1981).

AC   Lucien Carr, *American Commonwealths*, Missouri A Bone of Contention (Boston and New York: Haughton, Mifflin and Company, 1896).

AF   James E. Talmage, *The Articles of Faith* (Salt Lake City, Deseret Book Company, 1955).

AGAGQ   Joseph Fielding Smith, *Answers To Gospel Questions*, Vol. 1 (Salt Lake City: Deseret Book Company, 1979).

AIC   *Arab-Israeli Conflict* (St. Paul, Minnesota: Greenhaven Press, Inc., 1979).

Armstrong   Edward A. Armstrong, *The Gospel parables* (New York: Sheed and Ward, 1967).

Barclay   William Barclay, *And Jesus Said, A Handbook on the Parables of Jesus* (Philadelphia, Pennsylvania: The Westminster Press, 1970).

Barnett   Albert E. Barnett, *Understanding the Parables of Our Lord* (Nashville, Tennessee: Cokesbury Press, 1940).

Bruce   Alexander Balmain Bruce, *The Training of the Twelve*, reprint ed. (Grand Rapids, Michigan: Kregel Publications, 1982).

Buttrick   George A. Buttrick, *The Parables of Jesus* (Grand Rapids, Michigan: Baker Book House, 1981).

Cadman   Samuel Parkes Cadman, D.D., *The Parables of Jesus* (Philadelphia, Pennsylvania: David McKay Company, 1931).

CC   Will Durant, *The Story of Civilization: 3 Caesar & Christ* (New York: MJF Books, npd).

CE   *New Catholic Encyclopedia Vol. IV* (Washington D.C.: The Catholic University of America, 1967).

CHCC   Thomas Bokenkotter, *A Concise History of the Catholic Church*, rev.ed. (Garden City, New York: Image Books, 1979).

CL   Gerald N. Lund, *The Coming of the Lord* (Salt Lake City, Utah: Bookcraft, 1986).

DNTC   Bruce R. McConkie, *Doctrinal New Testament Commentary, Vol. 1, The Gospels* (Salt Lake City: Bookcraft, 1975).

Dodd   C. H. Dodd, *The Parables of the Kingdom* (New York: Charles Scribner's Sons, 1961).

DS   Joseph Fielding Smith, *Doctrines of Salvation* Comp. Bruce R. McConkie, 3 vols. (Salt Lake City, Utah: Bookcraft, 1954).

EB   *Encyclopedia Britannica*, 15th ed. (Chicago: Encyclopedia Brittanica, Inc., 1978).

Ed   Alfred Edersheim, *The Life and Times of Jesus the Messiah*, reprint ed. (Grand Rapids, Michigan: Wm. B. Eerdmans Publishing Company, 1981).

Ed BHOT   Alfred Edersheim, *Bible History — Old Testament*, reprint ed. (Grand Rapids, Michigan: Wm. B. Eerdmans Publishing Company, 1982).

Ed JSL   Alfred Edersheim, *Sketches of Jewish Social Life in the Days of Christ* (Grand Rapids, Michigan: William B. Eerdmans Publishing Company, 1982).

Ed Temple   Alfred Edersheim, *The Temple: Its Ministry and Services As They Were at the Time of Jesus Christ*, reprint ed. (Grand Rapids, Michigan: Wm. B. Eerdmans Publishing Company, 1982).

ER   John A. Widtsoe, *Evidences and Reconciliations* (Salt Lake City: Bookcraft, npd).

Farrar   Frederic W. Farrar, *The Life of Christ*, 2 vols. (New York: E. P. Dutton and Company, 1874).

Filas   Francis L. Filas, *The Parables of Jesus, A Popular Explanation* (New York: The Macmillan Company, 1959).

FM   Thomas L. Snead, *The Fight For Missouri* (New York: Charles Scribner's Sons, 1888).

FPM   Spencer W. Kimball, *Faith Precedes the Miracle* (Salt Lake City: Deseret Book, 1972).

Geikie   Cunningham Geikie, *The Life and Words of Christ*, revised ed., 2 vols. (New York: D. Appleton and Company, 1891, 1894).

GM   Golda Meir, *My Life by Golda Meir*, First American Edition (New York: G.P. Putnam's Sons, 1975).

GRF   Grant R. Jeffrey, *Armageddon Appointment with Destiny* (NY: Bantam Books, July 1990).

HC   Joseph Smith, Jr., *History of The Church of Jesus Christ of Latter-day Saints*, ed. B.H. Roberts, 7 vols. (Salt Lake City: The Church of Jesus Christ of Latter-day Saints, 1955).

IDYK   LeGrand Richards, *Israel! Do You Know?*, (Salt Lake City, Utah: Deseret Book Company, 1982).

JC   James E. Talmage, *Jesus the Christ* (Salt Lake City: Deseret Book Company, 1959).

JD   Brigham Young and others, *Journal of Discourses* (Salt Lake City, Utah: R. James 39 South Castle Street, Liverpool, 1967).

IV   *Inspired Version The Holy Scriptures*, Board of Publication of the Reorganized Church of Jesus Christ of Latter Day Saints (Independence, Missouri, 1966).

JAW   John A. Widtsoe, *Discourses on the Holy Ghost*, compiled by N. B. Lundwall, Bookcraft, Inc., Salt Lake City, Utah 1959, fifth printing 1967

Jeremias   Joachim Jeremias, *The Parables of Jesus*, revised ed. (New York: Charles Scribner's Sons, 1963).

Jerusalem   Jill & Leon Uris, *Jerusalem Song of Songs* (Garden City, New York: Doubleday & Company, Inc., 1981).

JFS   Joseph Fielding Smith, *Doctrines of Salvation*, comp. Bruce R. McConkie, Vol. 1 (Salt Lake City: Bookcraft, 1959).

Josephus   Flavius Josephus, *Josephus: Complete Works*, trans. William Whiston (Grand Rapids, Michigan: Kregel Publications, 1971).

Life   E. Keith Howick, *The Life of Jesus the Messiah* (Silverton, Idaho: WindRiver Publishing, Inc., 2012).

MD   Bruce R. McConkie, *Mormon Doctrine* (Salt Lake City: Bookcraft, 1966).

MF   Spencer W. Kimball, *The Miracle of Forgiveness* (Salt Lake City: Deseret Book, 1979-1981).

Mill M   Bruce R. McConkie, *The Millennial Messiah* (Salt Lake City: Deseret Book Company, 1978).

MM   Bruce R. McConkie, *The Mortal Messiah*, 4 vols. (Salt Lake City: Deseret Book Company, 1979-81).

OJ   Larry Collins & Dominique LaPierre, *O Jerusalem!* (New York: Simon and Schuster, 1972).

PM   Bruce R. McConkie, *The Promised Messiah*, The First Coming of Christ (Salt Lake City: Deseret Book, 1978).

SJSL   Alfred Edersheim, *Sketches of Jewish Social Life in the Days of Christ*, reprint ed. (Grand Rapids, Michigan: Wm. B. Eerdmans Publishing Company, 1982).

Smith   Joseph Fielding Smith, *The Way to Perfection* (Salt Lake City: Deseret Book, 1972).

Smith's   William Smith, LLD, *Smith's Bible Dictionary* Rev. F.N. & M.A. Peloubet (Nashville: Thomas Nelson, 1962).

Strauss   David Friedrich Strauss, *The Life of Jesus*, trans. George Eliot (London: Messrs. George Allen & Company, Ltd., 1906).

Tennyson   Alfred, Lord Tennyson, *Idylls of the King and a Selection of Poems* (New York: A Signet Classic, The New American Library, Inc., 1961).

TG   *Topical Guide* (Salt Lake City: The Church of Jesus Christ of Latter-day Saints, 1979).

Torah   *The Torah A Modern Commentary*, Edited by Gunther Plaut, (New York: Union of American Hebrew Congregations, 1981).

TPJS   Joseph Smith, Jr., *Teachings of the Prophet Joseph Smith*, sel. Joseph Fielding Smith (Salt Lake City: Deseret Book Company, 1958).

Trench   Richard Chenevix Trench, *Notes on the Miracles of Our Lord* (Westwood, New Jersey:

Fleming H. Revell Company, n.d.).

WMC Walter M. Chandler, *The Trial of Jesus from a Lawyer's Standpoint, Vol. 1, The Hebrew Trial* (New York City: The Federal Book Co., 1925).

WW Matthias F. Cowley, *Wilford Woodruff* (Salt Lake City, Utah: Bookcraft, 1986).

WTB Rodney Barker, *And The Waters Turned To Blood* (New York: Simon and Schuster, 1997).

Scripture Index

Genesis

1:10	93
1:14	782
3	29
3:15	528
3:17	201
3:18	201, 872
3:19	201
4:3–4	520
4:11–15	872
5:18–24	830
6:11	775
7:85	732
8:10–12	555
8:20	520
9:11–16	825
10:1	732
10:2	732, 889n233
10:3–6	732
10:25	670, 805
12:3	521
17:8	703
17:17–19	549
17:21	704
17:23	549
18:4	242
18:12, 15	549
18:18	521
19:12–15	823
19:24	755, 805
21:1–14	187
21:15–19	569
22:1	321n179, 579
22:2	520, 579
22:3–12	579
22:13	520, 579
22:14	579
22:18	521
25:32	230
25:33	569
26:4	521
28:9	177n191
28:14	521
31:54	520
32:28	704
35:2	553
36:3	177n191
46:1	520
49:10	521

Exodus

2:15	543
3:1	552
3:2	167, 552
3:3–4	167
3:5	143, 167
3:11	83
3:13	48, 414
3:14	48, 414, 522
4:10–17	83
4:20	579
6:7–8	704
7:10–12	5
7:15–18	790
7:19–21	5, 790
7:22	5
8:5–7, 19	5
9:23	755
10:22–23	800
12:46	638
13:9	759
13:13	535
14:5, 10–12	846
14:13	845
14:21–22	93
15:20–21	531
16:1–13	24
16:14	6, 24
16:15	6, 24, 569
16:16–17	6, 24
16:18–25	24
17:1–7	113
19:5	731, 814
19:6	814
19:10, 14	553
21:32	605
23:1	371, 461
23:2–3	371
23:4	345, 371
24:5–11	371
24:16	175n58
24:17	803
30:13–16	168
34:20	535
38:25–26	168
40:34–35	796

Leviticus

2:13	339, 382, 820

(column 3)

10:6	622
10:9	165
12:1–3	536
12:4	535, 536
12:5–8	536
13:42	797
13:45–46	141
16:29	279, 348, 436
19:18	257, 345
20:10	410
21:10	622
23:42–43	408
27:30	279

Numbers

2	339
5:2–4	141
6:1–3	165
6:8	759
9:12	638
11:4–15	25
11:16–17	25, 371
11:18–20	25
12:1–10	142
15:37	138
15:38	138, 474
15:39–40	138
18:15	535
18:16	535, 538
18:19	339, 820
21:8	505n118
21:9	423
24:17	540
25:7–8	175n50

Deuteronomy

1:16	461
4:20	704
4:27	694
4:29–31	740
6:5	257
6:7	543
7:2	109
8:4	6
9:9	567
11:19	543
11:29	392
14:22	279

6:37–38	831
6:52	521
6:64	171, 562
6:65	562, 563
7	29
7:4	830
7:13	830, 831
7:14	831
7:19	828, 831
7:21, 27	831
7:48	784, 785, 830
7:60–61	682n477
7:62	740, 836
7:63–64	671
7:65	671, 848
7:66	780
7:67	831
8:12	732
8:17–21	822
8:22–30	682n477, 822

Abraham

1:3–4	703
2:11	703, 704
3:11	859
3:22–23	28, 859
3:24	859
3:25	704, 858, 859
3:26	29, 743, 859
3:27–28	34, 517, 859
12:9	29

Joseph Smith Matthew

1	479
1:18	689
1:22	760, 782, 862
1:26	881
1:30	780
1:31	716
1:33	824
1:36	825
1:37	682n477, 740
1:38	682n477
1:39	682n477, 782, 808
1:40–43	682n477
3:22–23	742

Joseph Smith History

1	713
1:10–14	664
1:15–16	664, 744
1:17	206, 664, 744
1:18–29	206
1:30–36	206, 713
1:37	206, 713, 889n191
1:38–39	206, 713
1:40	206, 713, 719
1:41	206, 667, 713
1:42–44	206, 713
1:45	206, 713, 808
1:46–54	206, 713
1:55–67	206
1:68–69	206, 565
1:70–71	206
1:72	206, 565, 716
1:73–74	206

Articles of Faith

1:3	870
1:10	735, 832, 837, 871
1:12	464
2	64

Subject Index

-C-